How does CONTEXT impact our growth and development?
Do the places, sociocultural environments, and ways in which we were raised influence who we will become and how we will grow and change?

Explore development through the theme of CONTEXTS

A thoroughly integrated emphasis on the role of context in the lifespan and the diverse forms that context takes (gender, race, ethnicity, socioeconomic status, etc.) helps readers understand the wide range of dynamic influences that shape human development.

Lives in Context and **Cultural Influences on Development** boxes include compelling examples of contextual and cultural influences on development and highlight issues informed by lifespan research including cyberbullying, cultural differences in childbirth, the gender divide in STEM fields, and more.

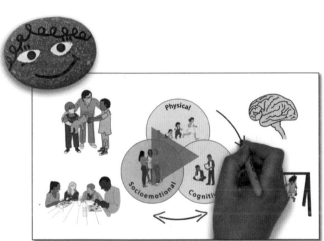

"I was happy to see the special effort by the author to bridge the gap between the theories, research, and applications."
—**Michiko Iwasaki,** *Loyola University Maryland*

Dr. Kuther's Chalk Talks, whiteboard-style animations narrated by the author, provide a foundational overview of basic concepts outside the classroom.

Lives in Context Video Cases with follow-up assessments spotlight individuals in every stage of the lifespan, allowing students to see theories of development through a culturally rich, real-world lens.

Explore development through
APPLICATION

Applying Developmental Science boxes reflect the increasing relevance and influence of developmental science, providing the reader opportunities to explore real-world questions on contemporary issues influencing our lives, such as the effectiveness of the federal Head Start Program, infant sign language, gender disparities in poverty, and the availability of family leave.

APPLYING DEVELOPMENTAL SCIENCE

• • The Importance of Context in Developmental Science

Dutch children raised in Amsterdam are immersed in a different context than that of children reared in North America

In its early years, the study of human development was based in laboratory research devoted to uncovering universal aspects of development by stripping away contextual influences (Wertlieb, 2003). This basic research was designed to examine universal processes that apply to all people, such as perceptual development (e.g., what visual skills are infants born with?).

As developmental scientists began apply their knowledge outside of laboratory settings, however, it became apparent that there are a great many individual differences in development.

Developmental scientists have since realized the importance of context. The field of **applied developmental science** has emerged, studying individuals within the contexts in which they live. This approach promotes the ability to understand the diverse range of patterns development takes throughout the life course (Lerner, 2010; Wertlieb, 2003).

Research in human development is now directed toward understanding a variety of social problems and issues of immediate social relevance, such as the capacities of preterm infants, children's ability to provide eyewitness testimony, adolescent sexual practices, and the impact of disability on the psychological and social adjustment of older adults and their adult children (Fisher, Busch-Rossnagel, Jopp, & Brown, 2013; Lerner, 2012). Applying developmental scientists study and make contributions to social policies on a issues that affect children, adolescents, adults, and their families, including environmental quality, health and health care delivery, violence, hunger and poor nutrition, school failure, and pervasive poverty (Tseng, 2012). Developmental scientists seek to enhance the life chances of diverse groups of individuals, families, and communities. Throughout this book you will be introduced to these and more issues studied by applying developmental scientists.

What Do You Think?

1. Identify three areas that you believe are in need of study or intervention by developmental scientists.

2. What are some challenges faced by children, adolescents, or adults that you believe should be studied and addressed?

LIFESPAN BRAIN DEVELOPMENT

• • Sleep as Brain Cleanser

Sleep may act as a "mental janitor," discarding the biological waste that accumulates with thinking.

Sleep is essential for information processing, including forming and consolidating memories (Stickgold & Walker, 2013). Sleep also plays a role in forming neural connections and pruning existing connections (Tononi & Cirelli, 2014). Recent research suggests that sleep is even more critical to maintaining neurocognitive functioning. Specifically, sleep may act as a "mental janitor" clearing the brain of biological waste that accumulates as a result of daily thinking (Xie et al., 2013). The spaces between neurons are filled with cerebrospinal fluid whose flow washes away the cells' daily waste.

In a groundbreaking study, Maiken Nedergaard and colleagues (2013) demonstrated that sleep influences the flow of cerebrospinal fluid in mice. The researchers injected dye into the cerebrospinal fluid of mice and monitored the animals' brains, tracking the movement of dye. When the mice were awake the dye barely moved, flowing only along the brain's surface. In contrast, when the mice were asleep the dye indicated that the cerebrospinal fluid flowed rapidly and reached further into the brain.

Why does the fluid flow more easily during sleep? The team discovered that the increased flow was possible because when mice went to sleep, their brain cells shrank. The space between brain cells increased during sleep, making it easier for fluid to circulate. When an animal woke up, the brain cells enlarged again and the fluid's movement between cells slowed to a trickle. The sleeping mice processed neural wastes, such as excess beta-amyloid, twice as quickly as the awake mice, suggesting that sleep plays a critical role in the brain's waste management. This brain-cleaning process has been observed in rats and baboons, but it has yet to be studied in humans. Yet these findings might explain why we may not think clearly after a sleepless night. More important, the waste management role of cerebrospinal fluid might offer a new way of understanding and perhaps treating brain diseases that involve the buildup of wastes, such as amyloid plaques in Alzheimer's disease.

What Do You Think?

How does sleep affect your thinking and performance? What do these results mean to you?

Explore development through
THE BRAIN

Lifespan Brain Development boxes discuss cutting-edge studies that apply research to neurological development so students can see the importance of research in understanding human development.

"An inclusive textbook that presents complex research information (current and classic studies) in ways that a general audience not familiarized with the discipline of developmental psychology can understand and relate. Very engaging!"
—**Andrea Garvey,** *American River College*

"The videos cover a variety of important concepts in human development, and they bring the textbook information to life. Human development is a lot of information to learn in a short time span, so these are helpful in making it easier to learn."
—**Lakitta Johnson,** *Jackson State University*

Explore development through
USEFUL LEARNING & STUDYING TOOLS

Concept maps that introduce each part of the text, and learning objectives paired with digital resources anchor student goals while emphasizing key concepts.

Thinking in Context critical-thinking questions at the end of each section encourage students to consider and apply theory and research to solve problems.

What Do You Think? questions at the end of every boxed feature challenge students to assess and evaluate the issues highlighted in that feature.

Chapter-ending **Apply Your Knowledge** case scenarios followed by in-depth questions help students apply their understanding to particular situations or problems.

Visual Reviews provide an opportunity to revisit and reflect on the text's core themes at the chapter level.

"[Kuther has] *structured each chapter with sensitivity to the ways introductory-level students are likely to think about this content. The textbook is more consistent than others available in offering cross-cultural research on each topic, and it provides many compelling conversation starters for class, including special-topic boxes and questions for discussion.*"

—Stacy DeZutter, *Millsaps College*

To Alison Kuther — forever in my heart

LIFESPAN
DEVELOPMENT
IN CONTEXT

A TOPICAL APPROACH

TARA L. KUTHER

Western Connecticut State University

SAGE

Los Angeles | London | New Delhi
Singapore | Washington DC | Melbourne

FOR INFORMATION:

SAGE Publications, Inc.
2455 Teller Road
Thousand Oaks, California 91320
E-mail: order@sagepub.com

SAGE Publications Ltd.
1 Oliver's Yard
55 City Road
London EC1Y 1SP
United Kingdom

SAGE Publications India Pvt. Ltd.
B 1/I 1 Mohan Cooperative Industrial Area
Mathura Road, New Delhi 110 044
India

SAGE Publications Asia-Pacific Pte. Ltd.
3 Church Street
#10-04 Samsung Hub
Singapore 049483

Printed in Canada.

ISBN 978-1-5063-7339-3

Acquisitions Editor: Lara Parra
Development Editor: Lucy Berbeo
Editorial Assistant: Zachary Valladon
Production Editor: Olivia Weber-Stenis
Copy Editor: Diana Breti
Typesetter: C&M Digitals (P) Ltd.
Proofreader: Dennis Webb
Indexer: Sheila Bodell
Cover Designer: Gail Buschman
Marketing Manager: Katherine Hepburn

This book is printed on acid-free paper.

18 19 20 21 22 10 9 8 7 6 5 4 3 2 1

BRIEF CONTENTS

DETAILED CONTENTS

PART I: FOUNDATIONS OF DEVELOPMENT

1

UNDERSTANDING HUMAN DEVELOPMENT: APPROACHES AND THEORIES

PART II: BIOLOGICAL DEVELOPMENT AND HEALTH

2

BIOLOGICAL AND ENVIRONMENTAL FOUNDATIONS AND PRENATAL DEVELOPMENT

PART III: COGNITIVE DEVELOPMENT

6

COGNITIVE CHANGE: COGNITIVE-DEVELOPMENTAL AND SOCIOCULTURAL APPROACHES

7

COGNITIVE CHANGE: INFORMATION PROCESSING APPROACH

15

SCHOOL, ACHIEVEMENT, AND WORK

PART VI: ENDINGS

16

DEATH AND DYING

PREFACE

Lifespan Development in Context: A Topical Approach has its origins in 20-plus years of class discussions about the nature of development. In these discussions, my students have questioned, challenged, and inspired me. My goal in writing this text is to explain, in a way that is comprehensive yet concise, the sophisticated interactions that constitute development.

Lifespan Development in Context: A Topical Approach focuses on two key themes that promote understanding of how humans develop through the lifespan: the centrality of context and the applied value of developmental science. These two themes are highlighted throughout the text as well as in boxed features. This text also emphasizes cutting-edge research and a student-friendly writing style.

CONTEXTUAL PERSPECTIVE

Development does not occur in a vacuum; it is a function of dynamic interactions among individuals, their genetic makeup, and myriad contextual influences. We are all embedded in multiple layers of context, including tangible and intangible circumstances that surround our development, such as family, ethnicity, culture, neighborhood, community, norms, values, and historical events. The contextual approach of *Lifespan Development in Context: A Topical Approach* emphasizes understanding the role of context in diversity and the many forms that diversity takes (gender, race and ethnicity, socioeconomic status, etc.). The text emphasizes how the places, sociocultural environments, and ways in which we are raised influence who we become and how we grow and change throughout the lifespan. This theme is infused throughout the text and highlighted specifically in two types of boxed features: Lives in Context and Cultural Influences on Development.

EMPHASIS ON APPLICATION

The field of lifespan developmental science is unique because so much of its content has immediate relevance to our daily lives. Students come to the field with a variety of questions and interests: Do the first three years shape the brain for a lifetime of experiences? Is learning more than one language beneficial to children? Should teens work? Do people's personalities change over their lifetimes? Do adults go through a midlife crisis? How common is dementia in older adulthood? *Lifespan Development in Context: A Topical Approach* engages students by exploring these and many more real-world questions. The emphasis on application is highlighted specifically in the Applying Developmental Science boxed feature, which examines applied topics such as the implications of poverty for development, Project Head Start, whether video games cause aggression, anti-bullying legislation, and the issue of disclosing dementia diagnoses to patients.

CURRENT RESEARCH

The lifespan course comes with the challenge of covering the growing mass of research findings within the confines of a single semester. In writing *Lifespan Development in*

Context: A Topical Approach, I have sifted through the most current research available, selecting important findings. However, classic theory and research remain important foundations for today's most exciting scholarly work. I integrate cutting-edge and classic research to present a unified story of what is currently known in developmental psychology. One of the most rapidly growing areas of developmental science research is in neuroscience, and this is reflected in the Lifespan Brain Development boxed features, which apply research on neurological development to issues such as videos that claim to promote precocious infant learning, chronic traumatic encephalopathy in athletes, the multidimensional "brain-based education" movement, and the legitimacy of brain-training apps.

ACCESSIBLE WRITING STYLE

Having taught at a regional public university for more than 22 years, I write in a style intended to engage undergraduate readers like my own students. This text is intended to help them understand challenging concepts in language that will not overwhelm: I have avoided jargon but maintained the use of professional and research terms that students need to know in order to comprehend classic and current literature in the lifespan development field. I regularly use my own texts in class, and my writing is guided by my students' responses and learning.

ORGANIZATION

Lifespan Development in Context: A Topical Approach is organized into sixteen topical chapters, within six units, that depict the wide range of developments that occur over the lifespan. Part I, Chapter 1, introduces lifespan theory and research design within a single chapter. I chose this approach because, given limited class time, many instructors do not cover stand-alone research chapters. The streamlined approach combines comprehensive coverage of methods of data collection, research design, developmental designs (such as sequential designs), and ethical issues in research with full coverage of the major theories in developmental psychology.

Part II includes Chapters 2, 3, 4, and 5. Chapter 2 presents the biological foundations of development, prenatal development, and birth, including patterns of genetic inheritance, gene-environment interactions, and epigenetics. Chapters 4 and 5 describe processes of physical development from birth to death and the role of health in development.

Part III covers cognitive processes of development. Chapters 6 and 7 describe findings on lifespan cognitive development from the cognitive-developmental and information processing perspectives. Intelligence and language development are covered in Chapters 8 and 9, respectively.

Part IV organizes findings regarding socioemotional development into Chapters 10, 11, 12, and 13. Emotional development, including attachment across the lifespan, is discussed in Chapter 10. Chapter 11 explores the development of the sense of self, identity, and personality. Moral development, prosocial and antisocial behavior, and spirituality are discussed in Chapter 12. Chapter 13 describes gender across the lifespan and developmental changes in sexuality.

Part V explores the contexts in which development unfolds. Chapter 14 examines the family, including the range of lifestyles adults may choose and parenting, as well as the role of friendships across life. Chapter 16 examines important contexts outside of the family and peer world, such as school and work, including career development in adolescence and emerging adulthood and the transition to retirement in later adulthood.

Finally, Part VI, Chapter 16, presents death and dying, including the process of death, how children and adults understand death, and coping with bereavement.

PEDAGOGY

My day-to-day experiences in the classroom have helped me to keep college students' interests and abilities at the forefront. Unlike many textbook authors, I teach four classes each semester at a comprehensive regional public university (and have done so since 1996). Fifteen years ago I began teaching online and hybrid courses. My daily exposure to multiple classes and many students helps keep me grounded in the ever-changing concerns and interests of college students. I teach a diverse group of students. Some live on campus but most commute. Most of my students are ages 18 to 24, but my classes also include many so-called nontraditional students over the age of 24. A growing number are veterans. I have many opportunities to try new examples and activities. I believe that what works in my classroom will be helpful to readers and instructors. I use the pedagogical elements of *Lifespan Development in Context: A Topical Approach* in my own classes and modify them based on my experiences.

LEARNING OBJECTIVES AND SUMMARIES

Core learning objectives are listed at the beginning of each chapter. The end-of-chapter summary returns to each learning objective, recapping the key concepts presented in the chapter related to that objective.

CRITICAL THINKING

Thinking in Context: At the end of each main section within the chapter, these critical thinking questions encourage readers to compare concepts, apply theoretical perspectives, and consider applications of research findings presented. In addition, each boxed feature concludes with critical thinking questions that challenge students to assess and evaluate the issues highlighted in that feature. The boxed features are as follows:

- Applying Developmental Science
- Cultural Influences on Development
- Lifespan Brain Development
- Lives in Context

APPLICATION

Apply Your Knowledge: Each chapter closes with a case scenario, followed by in-depth questions that require students to apply their understanding to address a particular situation or problem.

SUPPLEMENTS

ORIGINAL VIDEO

Lifespan Development in Context is accompanied by a robust collection of **Lives in Context Video Cases** that demonstrate key concepts through real-life examples, as well as **Dr. Kuther's Chalk Talks**, a series of whiteboard-style videos carefully crafted to engage students with course content. All videos are accessible through the interactive eBook available to pair with the text.

FOR INSTRUCTORS

SAGE edge is a robust online environment featuring an impressive array of free tools and resources. At **edge.sagepub.com/kuthertopical**, instructors using this book can access customizable PowerPoint slides, along with an extensive test bank built on Bloom's taxonomy that features multiple-choice, true/false, essay and short answer questions for each chapter. The instructor's manual is mapped to learning objectives and features lecture notes, discussion questions, chapter exercises, class assignments and more.

FOR STUDENTS

At the outset of every chapter, learning objectives are paired with **Digital Resources** available at **edge.sagepub.com/kuthertopical** and designed to promote mastery of course material. Students are encouraged to access articles from award-winning SAGE journals, listen to podcasts, and watch open-access video resources. The text can also be paired with an **interactive eBook** that offers one-click access to these study tools and to the book's **Original Video** package for a seamless learning experience. Students can then practice with mobile-friendly **eFlashcards** and **eQuizzes** to find out what they've learned.

ACKNOWLEDGMENTS

This book has benefited from the support of many. I have been very fortunate to work with an exceptionally talented and accommodating team at SAGE. I thank Elsa Peterson for feedback and editorial suggestions, Gail Buschman for her creativity and expertise in design and figures, and Nathan Davidson for his keen eye for photos and figures. Sara Harris provided invaluable support in constructing digital resources and videos, for which I am appreciative. Thanks go to Zach Valladon for answering my many questions and going above and beyond to help. I also thank Olivia Weber-Stenis, Katherine Hepburn, and Diana Breti. I am indebted to Lucy Berbeo for her insight and ability to keep the multiple parts of this project consistently moving forward, and especially for keeping me on track, no easy feat. My editor Lara Parra has the ineffable ability to foresee my questions and needs, bring the right people and information together at the right time, and exude a sense of calm that reminds me to breathe. Thank you, Lara!

Thanks go to SAGE family and friends and the faculty and students at California State University, Northridge, who participated in the chapter videos, and to Peck Media for developing the animations.

I thank my students for asking the questions and engaging in the discussions that inform this book. Finally, I thank my family, especially my parents, Phil and Irene, and stepchildren, Freddy and Julia. Most of all, I thank my husband, Fred, for his love, patience, and unwavering optimism. He sees the good in everything and reminds me to don my rosy glasses, much needed to complete a massive project like this (or suffer through a rough Rangers season). Thank you, babe. I love you.

SAGE wishes to thank the following reviewers for their valuable contributions to the development of this manuscript:

Jessamy E. Comer, Rochester Institute of Technology

Roger Copeland, El Centro College

Stacy L. DeZutter, Millsaps College

R. Cole Eidson, Northeastern University

Andrea P.P. Garvey, American River College

Patricia K. Gleich, University of West Florida

Jerry Green, Tarrant County College

Glenna S. Gustafson, Radford University

Jonathan Hart, The College of New Jersey

Micheal Huff, College of the Canyons

Marisha L Humphries, University of Illinois at Chicago

Michiko Iwasaki, Loyola University Maryland

J. Osia Jaoko, Campbellsville University

Lakitta D. Johnson, Jackson State University

Sue A. Kelley, Lycoming College

Melanie E. Keyes, Eastern Connecticut State University

Joseph Lao, Hunter College

Gina J. Mariano, Troy University

Robert J. Martinez, Northwest Vista College

Clark E. McKinney, Southwest Tennessee Community College, Memphis, Tennessee

Jillian Pierucci, St. Mary's University

Colleen J. Sullivan, Worcester State University

Vanessa Volpe, Ursinus College

Erin L. Woodhead, San Jose State University

Larolyn S. Zylicz, Cape Fear Community College

ABOUT THE AUTHOR

Tara L. Kuther is professor of psychology at Western Connecticut State University where she has taught courses in child, adolescent, and adult development since 1996. She earned her BA in psychology from Western Connecticut State University and her MA and PhD in developmental psychology from Fordham University. Dr. Kuther is fellow of the Society for the Teaching of Psychology (American Psychological Association, Division 2), has served in various capacities in the Society for the Teaching of Psychology and the Society for Research on Adolescence, and is the former chair of the Teaching Committee for the Society for Research in Child Development. Her research interests include social cognition and risky activity in adolescence and adulthood. She is also interested in promoting undergraduate and graduate students' professional development and helping them navigate the challenges of pursuing undergraduate and graduate degrees in psychology.

PART I

Foundations of Development

CHAPTER 1
UNDERSTANDING HUMAN DEVELOPMENT: APPROACHES AND THEORIES

Development—the ways in which we grow, change, and stay the same—occurs from conception to death. It is multidimensional, consisting of physical, cognitive, and socioemotional developments that interact over time. For example, a physical change such as brain development permits more sophisticated thinking: cognitive development. This, in turn, can influence how children understand emotions, and how they interact with other people: socioemotional development.

All throughout life we are embedded in multiple contexts that influence us, and are influenced by us. Early in life, the family context is perhaps the most important. But as the child goes off to school, the peer group and the school context become increasingly salient. In adolescence and adulthood, the work context emerges. The contexts in which we are embedded interact with and influence each other. For example, interactions at home with parents and siblings influence interactions within the school context and peer group.

Family, peer, and school are embedded in a larger neighborhood context. A neighborhood has a more distal influence on us, through factors such as the availability of parks and playgrounds, after-school programs, health care services, and feelings of safety. Finally, we and our ever-changing contexts are also embedded in a culture that influences our values, attitudes, and beliefs throughout our lives.

NEIGHBORHOOD

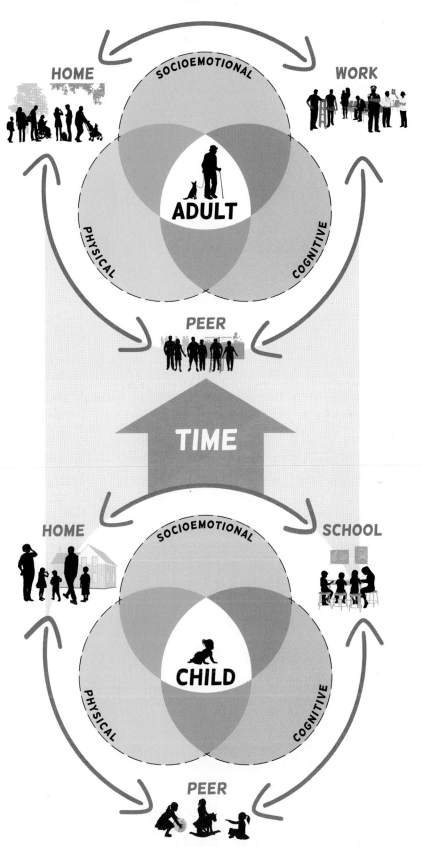

Images: ©iStock.com

Understanding Human Development: Approaches and Theories

Learning Objectives

1.1 Outline five principles of the lifespan developmental perspective.

1.2 Discuss three theoretical controversies about human development.

1.3 Summarize five theoretical perspectives on human development.

1.4 Describe the methods used in studying human development, including types of data and designs.

1.5 Discuss the responsibility of researchers to their participants and how they may protect them.

Digital Resources

- Resilience: It Takes a Village
- Poverty and Brain Development

- Second Couplehood in Late Adulthood
- Nature and Nurture

- Educational Aspirations
- Sociocultural Influences on Development: Desegregation

- Children of Katrina: Longitudinal Research
- Childhood Exposure to Lead

- Voluntary Participation in HIV Research

$SAGE edge™ Master these learning objectives with multimedia resources available at **edge.sagepub.com/kuthertopical** and *Lives in Context* video cases available in the interactive eBook.

Think back over your lifetime. How have you grown and changed through the years? Do your parents describe you as a happy baby? Were you fussy? Do you remember your first day of kindergarten? What are some of your most vivid childhood memories? Did you begin puberty early, late, or was your development similar to others your age? Were your adolescent years a stressful time? What types of changes do you expect to undergo in your adult years? Where will you live? Will you have a spouse? Will you have children? What career will you choose? How might these life choices and circumstances influence how you age and your perspective in older adulthood? Will your personality remain the same or change over time? In short, how will you change over the course of your lifespan?

WHAT IS LIFESPAN HUMAN DEVELOPMENT?

LO 1.1 Outline five principles of the lifespan developmental perspective.

This is a book about **lifespan human development**—the ways in which people grow, change, and stay the same throughout their lives, from conception to death.

When people use the term *development*, they often mean the transformation from infant to adult. However, development does not end with adulthood. We continue to change in predictable ways throughout our lifetime, even into old age. Developmental scientists study human development. They seek to understand lifetime patterns of change.

Table 1.1 illustrates the many phases of life that we progress through from conception to death. Each phase of life may have a different label and set of developmental tasks, but all have value. The changes that we undergo during infancy influence how we experience later changes, such as those during adolescence and beyond. This is true for all ages in life. Each phase of life is important and accompanied by its own demands and opportunities.

Change is the most obvious indicator of development. The muscle strength and coordination needed to play sports increases over childhood and adolescence, peaks in early adulthood, and begins to decline thereafter, declining more rapidly from middle to late adulthood. Similarly, children's capacity to learn and perform cognitive tasks increases as they progress from infancy through adolescence, and adults typically experience a decline in the speed of cognitive processing. However, there also are ways in which we change little over our lifetimes. Some personality traits, for example, are highly stable

lifespan human development
An approach to studying human development that examines ways in which individuals grow, change, and stay the same throughout their lives, from conception to death.

TABLE 1.1 • Ages in Human Development

LIFE STAGE	APPROXIMATE AGE RANGE	DESCRIPTION
Prenatal	Conception to birth	Shortly after conception, a single-celled organism grows and multiplies. This is the most rapid period of physical development in the lifespan as basic body structures and organs form and grow. The fetus hears, responds to sensory stimuli (such as the sound of its mother's voice), learns, remembers, and begins the process of adjusting to life after birth.
Infancy and toddlerhood	Birth to 2 years	The newborn is equipped with senses that help it to learn about the world. Environmental influences stimulate the brain to grow more complex, and the child interacts with her environment, shaping it. Physical growth occurs as well as the development of motor, perceptual, and intellectual skills. Children show advances in language comprehension and use, problem solving, self-awareness, and emotional control. They become more independent and interested in interacting with other children and form bonds with parents and others.
Early childhood	2 to 6 years	Children grow steadily over these years of play prior to beginning elementary school. Children's muscles strengthen, and they become better at controlling and coordinating their bodies. Children's bodies become more slender and adultlike in proportions. Memory, language, and imagination improve. Children become more independent and better able to regulate their emotions as well as develop a sense of right and wrong. Children become more aware of their own characteristics and feelings. Family remains children's primary social tie, but other children become more important and new ties to peers are established.
Middle childhood	6 to 11 years	Growth slows, and health tends to be better in middle childhood than at any other time during the lifespan. Strength and athletic ability increase dramatically. Children show improvements in their ability to reason, remember, read, and use arithmetic. As children advance cognitively and gain social experience, they understand themselves and think about moral issues in more complex ways as compared with younger children. As friendships develop, peers and group memberships become more important
Adolescence	11 to 18 years	Adolescents' bodies grow rapidly. They become physically and sexually mature. Though some immature thinking persists, adolescents can reason in sophisticated and adultlike ways. Adolescents are driven to learn about themselves and begin the process of discovering who they are, apart from their parents. Most adolescents retain good relationships with parents, but peer groups increase in importance. Adolescents and their peers influence each other reciprocally. It is through adolescents' interactions with family and peers that they begin to establish a sense of who they are.
Early adulthood	18 to 40 years	In early adulthood, physical condition peaks and then shows slight declines with time. Lifestyle choices, such as smoking, diet, and physical activity, play a large role in influencing health. As they enter early adulthood, young adults experience

LIFE STAGE	APPROXIMATE AGE RANGE	DESCRIPTION
		a great many changes, such as moving out of the family home, going to college, establishing mature romantic relationships, and beginning careers. Young adults' understanding of themselves is complex and shifts as they experience life changes and take on new responsibilities and new roles. Young adults make and carry out decisions regarding career, lifestyle, and intimate relationships. Most young adults join the workforce, marry or establish a long-term bond with a spouse, and become parents. The timing of these transitions varies, but most fully enter adult roles by the mid-20s. Some developmental scientists define a transitional period between adolescence and early adulthood, referred to as *emerging adulthood*, which represents the period between completing secondary education and adopting adult roles, such as work and family. Emerging adulthood spans ages 18 to 25, or even as late as age 29; however, not all young people experience a period of emerging adulthood as not all are embedded in contexts that permit a gradual transition to adulthood.
Middle adulthood	40 to 65 years	In middle adulthood, people begin to notice changes in their vision, hearing, physical stamina, and sexuality. Basic mental abilities, expertise, and practical problem-solving skills peak. Career changes and family transitions require that adults continue to refine their understandings of themselves. Some adults experience burnout and career changes while others enjoy successful leadership positions and increased earning power at the peak of their careers. Stress stems from assisting children to become independent, adapting to an empty nest, and assisting elderly parents with their health and personal needs.
Late adulthood	65 years and beyond	Most older adults remain healthy and active despite physical declines. Reaction time slows, and most older adults show decline in some aspects of memory and intelligence, but an increase in expertise and wisdom compensates for losses. Most older adult friendships are old friendships, and these tend to be very close and a source of support. At the same time, older adults are less likely to form new friendships than at other times in life. They face adjustments to retirement, confront decreased physical health and strength, cope with personal losses (such as the death of a loved one), think about impending death, and search for meaning in their lives.
Death		Death itself is a process. Regardless of whether it is sudden and unexpected, the result of a lengthy illness, or simply old age, death entails the stopping of heartbeat, circulation, breathing, and brain activity. A person's death causes changes in his or her social context—family members and friends must adjust to and accept the loss.

over the lifespan, so that we remain largely the "same person" into old age (McCrae, 2002; Roberts & Caspi, 2003; Wortman, Lucas, & Donnellan, 2012).

Lifespan human development can be described by several principles. As discussed in the following sections, development is: (1) multidimensional, (2) multidirectional, (3) plastic, (4) influenced by multiple contexts, and (5) multidisciplinary (Baltes & Carstensen, 2003; Baltes, Lindenberger, & Staudinger, 1998; Baltes, 1997).

DEVELOPMENT IS MULTIDIMENSIONAL

Physical changes such as body growth are the most obvious forms of development. Not only do our bodies change, but so do our minds, the ways in which we show emotion, and our social relationships. In this way, development is *multidimensional*: It entails changes in many areas of development, including the physical, the cognitive, and the socioemotional (Baltes et al., 1998; Baltes, 1997; Staudinger & Lindenberger, 2003). **Physical development** refers to body maturation and growth, including body size, proportion, appearance, health, and perceptual abilities. **Cognitive development** refers to the maturation of thought processes and the tools that we use to obtain knowledge, become aware of the world around us, and solve problems. **Socioemotional development** includes changes in personality, emotions, views of oneself, social skills, and interpersonal relationships with family and friends. Each of these areas of development overlap and interact. With advances in

physical development
Body maturation, including body size, proportion, appearance, health, and perceptual abilities.

cognitive development
Maturation of mental processes and tools individuals use to obtain knowledge, think, and solve problems.

socioemotional development
Maturation of social and emotional functioning, which includes changes in personality, emotions, personal perceptions, social skills, and interpersonal relationships.

FIGURE 1.1: Multidimensional Nature of Development

Physical

Cognitive

Socioemotional

Advances in physical, cognitive, and socioemotional development interact, permitting children to play sports, learn more efficiently, and develop close friendships.

cognitive development, for example, a child may become better able to take her best friend's point of view, which in turn influences her socioemotional development as she becomes more empathetic and sensitive to her friend's needs and develops a more mature friendship. Figure 1.1 illustrates these three areas of development and how they interact.

DEVELOPMENT IS MULTIDIRECTIONAL

Development is commonly described as a series of improvements in performance and functioning, but in fact development is *multidirectional*, meaning that it consists of both gains and losses, growth and decline, throughout the lifespan (Baltes et al., 1998; Baltes, 1997; Staudinger & Lindenberger, 2003). For example, we are born with a *stepping reflex,* an innate involuntary response in which infants make step-like movements when held upright over a table, bed, or hard horizontal surface (for more on infant reflexes, see Chapter 4). Over the first year, infants gain new motor skills and the stepping reflex disappears (Thelen, Fisher, & Ridley-Johnson, 2002). As another example of multidirectionality, in older adulthood people's social networks narrow and they have fewer friends; however, their relationships become more significant and meaningful (Carstensen & Mikels, 2005). Throughout life there is a shifting balance between gains and improvements in performance (common early in life) and losses and declines in performance (common late in life; Baltes & Carstensen, 2003). At all ages, however, individuals can compensate for losses by improving existing skills and developing new ones (Boker, 2013; Freund & Baltes, 2007). For example, though the speed at which people think tends to slow in older adulthood, increases in knowledge and experience enable older adults to compensate for the loss of speed, so that they generally retain their ability to complete day-to-day tasks and solve everyday problems (Bluck & Gluck, 2004; Hess, Leclerc, Swaim, & Weatherbee, 2009; Margrett, Allaire, Johnson, Daugherty, & Weatherbee, 2010). Outside of our awareness, the brain naturally adapts to a lifetime of sensory experiences in order to portray the world around us efficiently and accurately as we age well into older adulthood (Moran, Symmonds, Dolan, & Friston, 2014).

DEVELOPMENT IS PLASTIC

Development is characterized by **plasticity**: It is malleable or changeable. Frequently the brain and body can compensate for illness and injury. Children who are injured and experience brain damage may show resilience as other parts of the brain take on new functions. The plastic nature of human development allows people to modify their traits, capacities, and behavior throughout life (Baltes et al., 1998; Baltes, 1997; Staudinger & Lindenberger, 2003). For example, older adults who have experienced a decline in balance and muscle strength can regain and improve these capabilities through exercise (McAuley et al., 2013). Plasticity generally tends to decline as we age, but it does not disappear entirely. Short instruction, for instance, can enhance the memory capacities of very old adults, but less so than younger

plasticity A characteristic of development that refers to malleability, or openness to change in response to experience.

adults (Singer, Lindenberger, & Baltes, 2003). Thus, memory plasticity is preserved, but to a reduced degree, in very old age. Plasticity makes it possible for individuals to adjust to change and to demonstrate **resilience**, which is the capacity to adapt effectively to adverse contexts and circumstances (Luthar et al., 2015; Masten, 2016).

DEVELOPMENT IS INFLUENCED BY MULTIPLE CONTEXTS

In its simplest terms, **context** refers to where and when a person develops. Context includes aspects of the physical and social environment such as family, neighborhood, country, culture, and historical time period. Context also includes intangible factors, characteristics that are not visible to the naked eye, such as values, customs, and ideals. Culture is a particularly important context that influences us, as illustrated in Cultural Influences on Development: Defining Culture.

Some plasticity is retained throughout life. Practicing athletic activities can help older adults rebuild muscle and improve balance.

In order to understand a given individual's development, we must look to his or her context. For example, consider the context in which you were raised. Where did you grow up? City? Suburb? Rural area? What was your neighborhood like? Were you encouraged to be assertive and actively question the adults around you, or were you expected to be quiet and avoid confrontation? How large a part was religion in your family's life? How did religious values shape your parent's child-rearing practices and your own values? How did your family's economic status affect your development?

An important context that influences our development is the time period in which we live. Some contextual influences are tied to particular historical eras and explain why a generation of people born at the same time, called a **cohort**, are similar in ways that people born at other times are different. History-graded influences include wars, epidemics, and economic shifts such as periods of depression or prosperity (Baltes, 1987). These influences shape our development and our views of the world—and set cohorts apart from one another. Adults who came of age during the Great Depression and World War II are similar in some ways that make them different from later cohorts; for example, they tend to have particularly strong views on the importance of the family, civic mindedness, and social connection (Rogler, 2002). Age-graded influences, those tied to chronological age, such as the age at which the average person enters school, reaches puberty, graduates from high school, gets married, or has children, are also shaped by context as the normative age of each of these events has shifted over the last few generations (Baltes, 1987).

What roles have larger historical events played in your development? For example, consider Hurricane Sandy of October 2012, the second costliest hurricane in U.S. history, which affected 24 states, including the entire eastern seaboard, with flooding, downed power lines, and many destroyed homes. Historical events include the terrorist attacks of September 11, 2001; the election of the first African American president of the United States in 2008; and the school shooting in Newtown, Connecticut in 2012. How have historical events influenced you and those around you? Can you identify ways in which your cohort differs from your parents' cohort because of historical events?

DEVELOPMENTAL SCIENCE IS MULTIDISCIPLINARY

To say that people are complex is an understatement. Scientists who study lifespan human development attempt to understand people's bodies, minds, and social worlds. The contributions of many disciplines are needed to understand how people grow, think, and interact with their world. Psychologists, sociologists, anthropologists, biologists, neuroscientists,

resilience The ability to adapt to serious adversity.

context Unique conditions in which a person develops, including aspects of the physical and social environment such as family, neighborhood, culture, and historical time period.

cohort A generation of people born at the same time, influenced by the same historical and cultural conditions.

CULTURAL INFLUENCES ON DEVELOPMENT

• • Defining Culture

Cultural influences on development are illustrated by the many ethnic communities that comprise most U.S. cities. What subcultures and neighborhoods can you identify in your community?

A large and influential part of our context is **culture**, which is the set of customs, knowledge, attitudes, and values that are shared by members of a group and are learned early in life through interactions with group members (Hofstede, 2001). Most classic theories and research on human development are based on Western samples, and developmental researchers once believed that the processes of human development were universal. Early studies of culture and human development took the form of *cross-cultural research*, comparing individuals and groups from different cultures to examine how these universal processes worked in different contexts (Gardiner & Kosmitzki, 2002).

More recently we have learned that the cultural context in which individuals live influences the timing and expression of many aspects of development (Gardiner & Kosmitzki, 2002). For example, the average age that infants begin to walk varies with cultural context. In Uganda, infants begin to walk at about 10 months of age, in France at about 15 months, and the United States at about 12 months. These differences are influenced by parenting practices that vary by culture. African parents tend to handle infants in ways that stimulate walking, by playing games that allow infants to practice jumping and walking skills (Hopkins & Westra, 1989; Super, 1981). Developmental researchers have argued that because much of the research in human development has focused on individuals from Western industrialized societies, there is a danger of defining typical

development in Western samples as the norm, which can lead to narrow views of human development that do not take into account the variety of contexts in which people live. At the extreme, differences in human development within other cultural groups might be viewed as abnormal (Rogoff & Morelli, 1989). Some argue that cross-cultural research that compares the development of people from different cultures in order to understand universals in development is misguided because norms vary by cultural context (Schweder et al., 1998).

There is a growing trend favoring cultural research, which examines *how* culture influences development, over cross-cultural research, which simply examines differences among cultures (Schweder et al., 1998). From a cultural research perspective, culture influences our development because it contributes to the context in which we are embedded, transmitting values, attitudes, and beliefs that shape our thoughts, beliefs, and behaviors (Cole, 1999). The shift toward cultural research permits the examination of the multiple cultures that exist within a society. For example, North American culture is not homogenous; many subcultures exist, defined by factors such as ethnicity (e.g., African American, Asian American), religion (e.g., Christian, Muslim), geography (e.g., southern, Midwestern), and others, as well as combinations of these factors. Instead of looking for universal similarities in development, cultural research in human development aims to document diversity and understand how the historical and cultural context in which we live influences development throughout our lifetime (Schweder et al., 1998).

What Do You Think?

1. **How would you describe North American culture? Can you identify aspects of North American culture that describe most, if not all, people who live there? Are there aspects of culture in which people or subgroups of people differ?**

2. **What subcultures can you identify in your own neighborhood, state, or region of the country? What characterizes each of these subcultures?**

3. **Consider your own experience. With which culture or subculture do you identify? How much of a role do you think your cultural membership has had in your own development?**

---

culture A set of customs, knowledge, attitudes, and values shared by a group of people and learned through interactions with group members.

and medical researchers all conduct research that is relevant to understanding aspects of human development. For example, consider cognitive development. Children's performance on cognitive measures, such as problem solving, are influenced by their physical health and nutrition (Anjos et al., 2013), interactions with peers (Fawcett & Garton, 2005; Holmes, Kim-Spoon, & Deater-Deckard, 2016), and neurological development (Ullman, Almeida, & Klingberg, 2014)—findings from the fields of medicine, psychology, and neuroscience, respectively. In order to understand how people develop at all periods in life, developmental scientists must combine insights from all of these disciplines.

The field of lifespan human development studies the ways in which people grow, change, and stay the same throughout their lives. Human development is complex. We change in multiple ways, show gains and losses over time, and retain the ability to change over our lifespan. The context in which we live influences who we become. Developmental science incorporates research from multiple disciplines.

⚙ Thinking in Context 1.1

1. Describe your own development. In what ways have you changed over your lifetime? What characteristics have remained the same?

2. Lifespan human development is multidimensional, multidirectional, plastic, and influenced by multiple contexts. Consider your own experience and provide examples from your life that illustrate the multidimensional nature of your own development. Can you do the same for multidirectionality and for plasticity? How does the context in which you were raised and live influence your development?

3. Compare the historical context in which you, your parents, and your grandparents were raised. How did historical and societal influences affect your grandparents' development, their world view, and their child-rearing strategies? What about your parents? How might historical influences affect your own development, world view, and perspective on parenting?

BASIC ISSUES IN LIFESPAN HUMAN DEVELOPMENT

LO 1.2 Discuss three theoretical controversies about human development.

Developmental scientists agree that people change throughout life and show increases in some capacities and decreases in others from conception to death. Yet, how development proceeds, the specific changes that occur, and the causes of change are debated. Developmental scientists' explanations of how people grow and change over their lives are influenced by their perspectives on three basic issues, or fundamental questions, about human development:

1. Do people remain largely the same over time, or do they change dramatically?

2. What role do people play in their own development? How much are they influenced by their surroundings, and how much do they influence their surroundings?

3. To what extent is development a function of inborn genetic endowments, as compared with the environment in which individuals live?

The following sections examine each of these questions.

CONTINUITIES AND DISCONTINUITIES IN DEVELOPMENT

Do children slowly grow into adults, steadily gain more knowledge and experience, and become better at reasoning? Or do children grow in spurts, showing sudden and large gains in knowledge and reasoning capacities? In other words, in what ways is developmental change **continuous**, characterized by slow and gradual change, or **discontinuous**, characterized by abrupt change? As shown in Figure 1.2, a discontinuous view of development emphasizes sudden transformation in abilities and capacities whereas a continuous view emphasizes the gradual and steady changes that occur. Scientists who argue that development is continuous in nature point to slow and cumulative changes we experience in the amount or degree of skills, such as a child slowly gaining experience, expanding his or her vocabulary, and becoming quicker at problem solving, or a middle-aged adult experiencing gradual losses of muscle and strength. The discontinuous view of development describes the changes we experience as large and abrupt, with individuals of

continuous development
The view that development consists of gradual cumulative changes in existing skills and capacities.

discontinuous development
The view that growth entails abrupt transformations in abilities and capacities in which new ways of interacting with the world emerge.

FIGURE 1.2: Continuous and Discontinuous Development

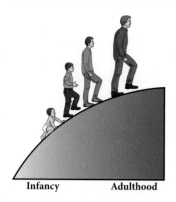

Infancy　　　　　　Adulthood

(a) Continuous Development

Infancy　　　　　　Adulthood

(b) Discontinuous Development

various ages dramatically different from one another. For example, puberty quickly transforms children's bodies into more adult-like adolescent bodies, infants' understanding and capacity for language is fundamentally different from that of school-aged children, and children make leaps in their reasoning abilities over the course of childhood (Piek, Dawson, Smith, & Gasson, 2008). For example, children progress from believing that robotic dogs and other inanimate objects are alive to understanding that life is a biological process (Gelman & Opfer, 2002).

It was once believed that development was either continuous or discontinuous—that changes were either slow and gradual or sudden and dramatic—but not both. Today, developmental scientists agree that development includes both continuity and discontinuity (Kagan, 2008; Lerner, Agans, DeSouza, & Gasca, 2013; Miller, 2016). Whether a particular developmental change appears continuous or discontinuous depends on our point of view. For example, consider human growth. We often think of increases in height as a slow and steady process of simply getting taller with time; each month infants are taller than the prior month, illustrating continuous change. However, as shown in Figure 1.3, when researchers measured infants' height every day they discovered that infants have growth days and non-growth days, days that they show rapid change in height interspersed with days in which there is no change in height, thus illustrating discontinuous change (Lampl, Johnson, Frongillo Jr., & Frongillo, 2001; Lampl, Veldhuis, & Johnson, 1992). In this example, monthly measurements of infant height suggest gradual increases, but daily measurements show spurts of growth, each lasting 24 hours or less. In this way, whether a given phenomenon, such as height, is described as continuous or discontinuous can vary. Most developmental scientists agree that some aspects of lifespan development are best described as continuous and others as discontinuous (Miller, 2016).

FIGURE 1.3: Infant Growth: A Continuous or Discontinuous Process?

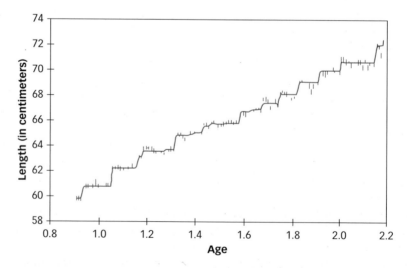

Infants' growth occurs in a random series of roughly 1-centimeter spurts in height that occur in 24 hours or less. The overall pattern of growth entails increases in height, but whether the growth appears to be continuous or discontinuous depends on our point of view.

Source: Figure 1 from Lampl, M., Veldhuis, J. D., & Johnson, M. L. 1992. Saltation and stasis: A model of human growth. *Science, 258*, 801–803. With permission from AAAS.

INDIVIDUALS ARE ACTIVE IN DEVELOPMENT

Do people have a role in influencing how they change over their lifetimes? That is, are people active in influencing their own development? Taking an active role means that they interact with and influence the world around them, create experiences that lead to developmental change, and thereby influence how they themselves change over the lifespan. Alternatively, if individuals take a passive role in their development, they are shaped by, but do not influence, the world around them—including home and relationships with family, school, and neighborhood characteristics, such the availability of playgrounds or health care.

The prevailing view among developmental scientists is that people are active contributors to their own development. People are influenced by the physical and social contexts in which they live, but

Stephanie Rausser/Image Bank/Getty Images

Infants naturally influence people and the world around them. What reactions might these two babies elicit?

they also play a role in influencing their development by interacting with, and changing, those contexts. Even infants influence the world around them and construct their own development through their interactions. Consider an infant who smiles at each adult he sees; he influences his world because adults are likely to smile, use "baby talk," and play with him in response. The infant brings adults into close contact, making one-on-one interactions and creating opportunities for learning. By engaging the world around them, thinking, being curious, and interacting with people, objects, and the world around them, individuals of all ages are "manufacturers of their own development" (Flavell, 1992, p. 998).

NATURE AND NURTURE INFLUENCE DEVELOPMENT

Perhaps the most fundamental question about lifespan human development is: What is its cause? Why do people change in predictable ways over the course of their lifetimes? The answer to this question reflects perhaps the oldest and most heated debate within the field of human development: the **nature-nurture issue**. Is development caused by nature or nurture? Explanations that rely on nature point to inborn genetic endowments or heredity, maturational processes, and evolution as causes of developmental change. For example, most infants take their first steps at roughly the same age as other children, suggesting a maturational trend that supports the role of nature in development. An alternative explanation for developmental change is nurture, the view that individuals are molded by the physical and social environment in which they are raised, including the home, school, workplace, neighborhood, and society. From this perspective, although most begin to walk at about the same time, environmental conditions can speed up or slow down the process. Infants who experience malnutrition may walk later than well-nourished infants, and—as mentioned in Cultural Influences on Development—those who are given practice making stepping or jumping movements may walk earlier (Sigman, 1995; Vereijken & Thelen, 1997; Worobey, 2014).

Although developmental scientists once attempted to determine whether nature *or* nurture influenced development, most now agree that *both* nature and nurture are important contributors (Grigorenko & Sternberg, 2003; Scarr & McCartney, 1983). As in the prior example, walking is heavily influenced by maturation (nature), but experiences and environmental conditions can influence the timing of a child's first steps (nurture). Today developmental scientists attempt to determine *how* nature and nurture work together to influence how people grow and change throughout life (Anastasi, 1958; Crews, Gillette, Miller-Crews, & Gore, 2014; Rutter, 2012).

nature–nurture issue
A debate within the field of human development regarding whether development is caused by nature (genetics or heredity) or nurture (the physical and social environment).

To review, there are three basic questions regarding lifespan human development:

1. Do people remain largely the same over time, showing continuity, or do they change dramatically, illustrating discontinuity?

2. What role do people play in their own development? How much are they influenced by their surroundings, and how much do they influence their surroundings? To what degree are they active or passive participants in their development?

3. To what extent is development a function of inborn genetic endowments, as compared with the environment in which individuals live?

Developmental scientists vary in their responses to these questions, as we will discover throughout this book. Different answers reflect different assumptions about the causes of development and different explanations for human development.

 Thinking in Context 1.2

1. Can you identify ways in which you have changed very gradually over the years? Were there other times in which you showed abrupt change, such as physical growth, strength and coordination, thinking abilities, or social skills? In other words, in what ways is your development characterized by continuity? Discontinuity?

2. Are people active or passive participants in their development? What role did your physical and social environment play in your growth? In what ways, if any, did you take an active role in your own development?

3. How much of who you are today is a function of nature? Nurture?

THEORETICAL PERSPECTIVES ON HUMAN DEVELOPMENT

LO 1.3 Summarize five theoretical perspectives on human development.

Human development researchers offer many theoretical explanations for the changes that occur over the lifetime. Over the past century, developmental scientists have learned much about how individuals progress from infants to children to adolescents, and to adults, as well as how they change throughout adulthood. Scientists explain their observations by constructing theories of human development. A **theory** is a way of organizing a set of observations or facts into a comprehensive explanation of how something works. Theories are important tools for compiling and interpreting the growing body of research in human development as well as determining gaps in our knowledge about a given phenomenon and making predictions about what is not yet known (Crain, 2011; Green & Piel, 2010; Miller, 2016).

Effective theories generate specific **hypotheses**, or proposed explanations for a given phenomenon, that can be tested by research. It is important to note that this testing seeks to find flaws in the hypothesis—not to "prove" that it is flawless. A good theory is one that is *falsifiable*, or capable of generating hypotheses that can be tested and, potentially, refuted. As scientists conduct research and learn more about a topic, they modify their theories. Updated theories often give rise to new questions and new research studies, whose findings may further modify theories.

The great body of research findings in the field of lifespan human development has been organized into several theoretical perspectives to explain how we change throughout our lives. Given the myriad ways in which we develop, theories vary in their explanatory

theory An organized set of observations to describe, explain, and predict a phenomenon.

hypothesis A proposed explanation for a phenomenon that can be tested.

focus and emphasis. For example, some theories examine personality development and others address changes in how individuals reason and solve problems. As the following sections illustrate, these theoretical perspectives vary greatly in how they account for the developmental changes that occur over the lifespan.

PSYCHOANALYTIC THEORIES

Are there powerful forces within us that make us behave as we do? Are we pushed by inner drives? **Psychoanalytic theories** describe development and behavior as a result of the interplay of inner drives, memories, and conflicts we are unaware of and cannot control. These inner forces influence our behavior throughout our lives. Freud and Erikson are two key psychoanalytic theorists whose theories remain influential today.

Sigmund Freud (1856–1939), the father of the psychoanalytic perspective, believed that much of our behavior is driven by unconscious impulses.

Freud's Psychosexual Theory

Sigmund Freud (1856–1939), a Viennese physician, is credited as the father of the psychoanalytic perspective. Freud believed that much of our behavior is driven by

psychoanalytic theory A perspective introduced by Freud that development and behavior is stagelike and influenced by inner drives, memories, and conflicts of which an individual is unaware and cannot control.

TABLE 1.2 • Freud's Psychosexual Stages

STAGE	APPROXIMATE AGE	DESCRIPTION
Oral	0 to 18 months	Basic drives focus on the mouth, tongue, and gums, whereby the infant obtains pleasure by feeding and sucking. Feeding and weaning are particularly important influences on personality development at this time. Failure to meet oral needs can be shown in behaviors that center on the mouth, such as fingernail biting, overeating, smoking, or excessive drinking.
Anal	18 months to 3 years	Basic drives are oriented toward the anus, and the infant obtains pleasure by retaining or passing of bowel and bladder movements. Toilet training is an important influence on personality development. If caregivers are too demanding, pushing the child before he or she is ready, or if caregivers are too lax, children may develop issues of control such as a need to impose extreme order and cleanliness on their environment or extreme messiness and disorder.
Phallic	3 to 6 years	Basic drives shift to the genitals. The child develops a romantic desire for the opposite-sex parent and a sense of hostility and/or fear of the same-sex parent. The conflict between the child's desires and fears arouses anxiety and discomfort. It is resolved by pushing the desires into the unconscious and spending time with the same-sex parent and adopting his or her behaviors and roles. It is through this process that children begin to become members of society by adopting societal expectations and values. Failure to resolve this conflict may result in guilt and a lack of conscience.
Latency	6 years to puberty	This is not a stage but a time of calm between stages when the child develops talents and skills and focuses on school, sports, and friendships.
Genital	Puberty to adulthood	With the physical changes of early adolescence, the basic drives again become oriented toward the genitals. The person becomes concerned with developing mature adult sexual interests and sexual satisfaction in adult relationships throughout life.

unconscious impulses that are outside of our awareness. As shown in Table 1.2, Freud believed we progress through a series of *psychosexual stages*, periods in which unconscious drives are focused on different parts of the body, making stimulation to those parts a source of pleasure. How parents direct and gratify their children's basic drives influences their personality development. Freud explained that the task for parents is to strike a balance between over- and under-gratifying a child's needs at each stage in order to help the child develop a healthy personality with the capacity for mature relationships throughout life.

Freud made many contributions to psychology, psychiatry, and Western thought. Many of his insights have stood up well to the test of time, such as the notion of unconscious processes that we are not aware of (Adolph & Berger, 2005; Bargh, 2013; Fonagy & Target, 2000). The idea that early experiences in the family are important contributors to development is also accepted by the general public, as is the role of emotions in development, both of which Freud espoused. However, Freud did not study children; his theory grew from his work with female psychotherapy patients. Because of its heavy emphasis on infant sexuality, Freud's psychosexual stage framework, especially the phallic stage, is not widely accepted (Westen, 1998).

Freud's theory has declined in popularity, partly because it cannot be directly tested and is therefore not supported by research (Crews, 1996). How are we to study unconscious drives when we are not aware of them? Only about 2% of today's psychotherapists practice traditional Freudian psychoanalysis that emphasizes unconscious motivators of behavior because shorter and more behaviorally focused therapies have been found to be more effective at helping people (Leichsenring & Rabung, 2008; McDonald, 1998).

Erikson's Psychosocial Theory

Jon Erikson/Science Source

Erik Erikson (1902–1994), shown with his wife and collaborator, Joan, posited that, throughout their lives, people progress through eight stages of psychosocial development.

Erik Erikson (1902–1994) was influenced by Freud, but he placed less emphasis on instinctual drives as motivators of development and instead focused on the role of the social world, society, and culture in shaping development. Erikson posed a lifespan theory of development in which individuals progress through eight stages of psychosocial development that include changes in how they understand and interact with others, as well as changes in how they understand themselves and their roles as members of society (Erikson, 1950; see Table 1.3). Each stage presents a unique developmental task, which Erikson referred to as a crisis or conflict that must be resolved. How well individuals address the crisis determines their ability to deal with the demands made by the next stage of development.

Regardless of their success in resolving a crisis of a given stage, individuals are driven by biological maturation and social expectations to the next psychosocial stage. No crisis is ever fully resolved, and unresolved crises are revisited throughout life. Although Erikson believed that it is never too late to resolve a crisis, resolving a crisis from a previous stage may become more challenging over time as people focus on current demands and the crises of their psychosocial stages.

Erikson's psychosocial theory is well regarded as one of the first lifespan views of development. He took a positive view of development and included the role of society and culture by basing his theory on a broad range of cases including larger and more diverse samples than did Freud (Thomas, 2004). Erikson's theory is criticized as difficult to test, but it has nonetheless sparked research on specific stages, most notably on the development of identity during adolescence and the drive to guide youth and contribute to the next generation during middle adulthood (Crain, 2011; Miller, 2016).

TABLE 1.3 • Erikson's Psychosocial Stages of Development

STAGE	APPROXIMATE AGE	DESCRIPTION
Trust vs. mistrust	Birth to 1 year	Infants learn to trust that others will fulfill their basic needs (nourishment, warmth, comfort) or to lack confidence that their needs will be met.
Autonomy vs. shame and doubt	1 to 3 years	Toddlers learn to be self-sufficient and independent through toilet training, feeding, walking, talking, and exploring, or they lack confidence in their own abilities and doubt themselves.
Initiative vs. guilt	3 to 6 years	Young children become inquisitive, ambitious, and eager for responsibility, or they experience overwhelming guilt for their curiosity and overstepping boundaries.
Industry vs. inferiority	6 to 12 years	Children learn to be hard working, competent, and productive by mastering new skills in school, friendships, and home life, or they experience difficulty, leading to feelings of inadequacy and incompetence.
Identity vs. role confusion	Puberty to early adulthood	Adolescents search for a sense of self by experimenting with roles. They also look for answers to the question, "Who am I?" in terms of career, sexual, and political roles, or they remain confused about who they are and their place in the world.
Intimacy vs. isolation	Early adulthood	Young adults seek companionship and close relationship with another person, or they experience isolation and self-absorption due to difficulty developing intimate relationships and sharing with others.
Generativity vs. stagnation	Middle adulthood	Adults contribute to, establish, and guide the next generation through work, creative activities, and parenting, or they stagnate, remaining emotionally impoverished and concerned about themselves.
Integrity vs. despair	Late adulthood	Older adults look back at life to make sense of it, accept mistakes, and view life as meaningful and productive, or they feel despair over goals never reached and fear of death.

Because Erikson's lifespan theory of development holds implications for every period of life, we will revisit his theory throughout this book at each period in the lifespan: infancy, childhood, adolescence, adulthood, and old age.

BEHAVIORIST AND SOCIAL LEARNING THEORIES

In response to psychoanalytic theorists' emphasis on the psyche as an invisible influence on development and behavior, some scientists pointed to the importance of studying observable behavior rather than thoughts and emotion, which cannot be seen or objectively verified. Theorists who study **behaviorism** examine only behavior that can be observed and believe that all behavior is influenced by the physical and social environment. For example, consider this famous quote from John Watson, an early founder of behaviorism:

> Give me a dozen healthy infants, well formed, and my own specified world to bring them up in and I'll guarantee to take any one at random and train him to become any type of specialist I might select—doctor, lawyer, artist, merchant, chief, and yes, even beggar-man and thief, regardless of his talents, penchants, tendencies, abilities, vocations, and race of his ancestors. (Watson, 1925, p. 82)

behaviorism A theoretical approach that studies how observable behavior is controlled by the physical and social environment through conditioning.

Ivan Pavlov (1849–1936) discovered classical conditioning when he noticed that dogs naturally salivate when they taste food, but they also salivate in response to various sights and sounds that they associate with food.

FIGURE 1.4: **Classical Conditioning in a Newborn**

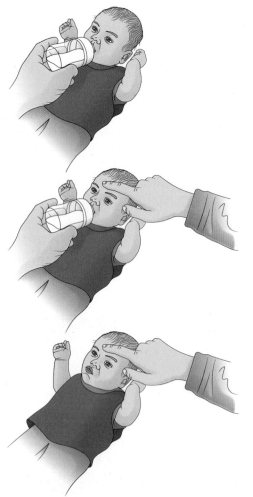

Classical conditioning has been observed in newborns, who naturally make sucking movements (unconditioned response) in response to sugar water (unconditioned stimulus). When stroking the forehead (neutral stimulus) is paired with sugar water, infants come to make sucking movements (conditioned response) in response to forehead strokes (conditioned stimulus).

Source: Lampl et al. (1992).

By controlling an infant's physical and social environment, Watson believed he could control the child's destiny. Behaviorist theory is also known as *learning theory* because it emphasizes how people and animals learn new behaviors as a function of their environment. As discussed in the following sections, classical and operant conditioning are two forms of behaviorist learning; social learning integrates elements of behaviorist theory and information processing theories.

Classical Conditioning

Classical conditioning is a form of learning in which the person or animal comes to associate environmental stimuli with physiological responses. Ivan Pavlov (1849–1936), a Russian physiologist, discovered classical conditioning when he noticed that dogs naturally salivate when they taste food, but they also salivate in response to various sights and sounds that occur before they taste food, such as their bowl clattering or their owner opening the food cupboard. Pavlov tested his observation by pairing the sound of a tone with the dog's food; the dogs heard the tone, then received their food. Soon the tone itself began to elicit the dogs' salivation. Through classical conditioning a neutral stimulus (in this example, the sound of the tone) comes to elicit a response originally produced by another stimulus (food). Many fears as well as emotional associations are the result of classical conditioning. For example, some children may fear a trip to the doctor's office because they associate the doctor's office with the discomfort they felt upon receiving a vaccination shot. Classical conditioning applies to physiological and emotional responses only, yet it is a cornerstone of psychological theory. (See Figure 1.4 for an example of classical conditioning in humans.) A second behaviorist theory accounts for voluntary, nonphysiological responses, as described in the following section.

Operant Conditioning

Perhaps it is human nature to notice that the consequences of our behavior influence our future behavior. A teenager who arrives home after curfew and is greeted with a severe scolding may be less likely to return home late in the future. An employer who brings coffee and muffins to her staff on Monday morning and then notices that her employees are in good spirits and productive may be more likely to bring them snacks in the future. These two examples illustrate the basic tenet of B. F. Skinner's (1905–1990) theory of **operant conditioning**: Behavior becomes more or less probable depending on its consequences. We repeat behaviors that have pleasant outcomes and stop behaviors with unpleasant outcomes. Behaviorist ideas about operant conditioning and the nature of human behavior are woven into the fabric of North American culture and appear often in discussions of parenting (Rutherford, 2000).

According to Skinner, a behavior followed by a rewarding or pleasant outcome, called **reinforcement**, will be more likely to recur, but one followed by an aversive or unpleasant outcome, called **punishment**, will be less likely to recur. Operant conditioning is a very important concept because it explains much of human behavior, including how we learn skills and habits.

Social Learning Theory

A common criticism of behaviorist theory is its overemphasis on the observable and neglect of internal influences on development and behavior (Miller, 2016). Albert Bandura (b. 1925) agreed that the physical and social environments are important, but he also advocated for the role of thought and emotion as contributors to development. According to Bandura's **social learning theory**, people actively process information—they think and they feel emotion—and their thoughts and feelings influence their behavior. The physical and social environment influences our behavior through their influence on our thoughts and emotions. For example, the teenager who breaks his curfew and is met by upset parents may experience remorse, feeling bad about his actions, which may then make him less likely to come home late in the future. In this example, the social environment (a discussion with upset parents) influenced the teen's thoughts and emotions (feeling bad for upsetting his parents), which then influenced the teen's behavior (not breaking curfew in the future). In this way, our thoughts and emotions about the consequences of our behavior influence our future behavior. We do not need to experience punishment or reinforcement in order to change our behavior (Bandura, 2001). We can learn by thinking about the potential consequences of our actions.

One of Bandura's most enduring ideas about development is that people learn through observing and imitating models, which he referred to as **observational learning** (Bandura, Ross, & Ross, 1963; Bandura, 1986). People learn by watching others. This finding suggests that children who observe violence rewarded, such as a child grabbing (and successfully obtaining) another child's toy, may imitate what they see and use aggressive means to take other children's toys. People also learn by observing the consequences of others' actions. A child observer might be less likely to imitate a child who takes another child's toy if the aggressor is scolded by a teacher and placed in time out. Observational learning, learning by watching and imitating others around us, is one of the most powerful ways in which we learn.

Another of Bandura's contributions that has influenced the field of lifespan human development is the concept of **reciprocal determinism**, according to which individuals and the environment interact and influence each other (Bandura, 2011, 2012). In contrast with behaviorist theorists, Bandura viewed individuals as active in their development rather than passively molded by their physical and social environment. Individuals can influence and change their physical and social surroundings. Specifically, development is a result of interactions between the individual's characteristics, his or her behavior, and the physical and social environment (see Figure 1.5).

As an example, let us examine how characteristics of a given person might influence that person's behavior and the surrounding social environment. Suppose Isaac is an excitable person, and his excitability makes him quick to debate with others. This behavioral tendency, in turn, stimulates others around him to engage in debate. In addition to Isaac's characteristics, his behavior (being quick to debate) also is

classical conditioning A form of learning in which an environmental stimulus becomes associated with stimuli that elicit reflex responses.

operant conditioning A form of learning in which behavior increases or decreases based on environmental consequences.

reinforcement In operant conditioning, the process by which a behavior is followed by a desirable outcome increases the likelihood of a response.

punishment In operant conditioning, the process in which a behavior is followed by an aversive or unpleasant outcome that decreases the likelihood of a response.

social learning theory An approach that emphasizes the role of modeling and observational learning over people's behavior in addition to reinforcement and punishment.

observational learning Learning that occurs by watching and imitating models, as posited by social learning theory.

reciprocal determinism A perspective positing that individuals and the environment interact and influence each other.

Albert Bandura

In a classic study conducted by Albert Bandura, children who observed an adult playing with a bobo doll toy roughly imitated those behaviors, suggesting that children learn through observation.

FIGURE 1.5: Bandura's Model of Reciprocal Determinism

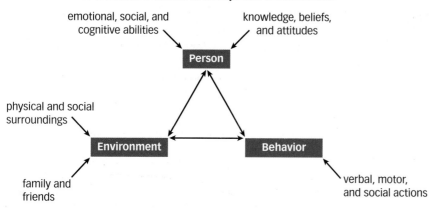

influenced by the environment (e.g., being surrounded by smart people who enjoy debating) and influences the environment (e.g., people who enjoy debating are more likely to talk to Isaac, while people who avoid debating are less likely to talk to him). This is an example of the complex interplay between person, behavior, and physical and social environment that underlies much of what we will discuss throughout this book.

Behaviorist theories make important contributions to understanding lifespan human development. Classical and operant conditioning and social learning are powerful means of explaining human behavior at all ages. Concepts such as observational learning, reinforcement, and punishment hold implications for parents, teachers, and anyone who works with people. Moreover, social learning theory and reciprocal determinism offer a more complex explanation for development and behavior than do behaviorist theories. We will revisit these concepts throughout this book.

COGNITIVE THEORIES

According to the lifespan developmental perspective, there are multiple domains of development. We grow and change in many ways over our lifetime. Whereas psychoanalytic theories examine inner influences on our personality and behavior, and behaviorist and social learning theories look to the environment as an influence on development, cognitive theorists examine the role of thought on behavior. Cognitive-developmental theory and information processing theorists view cognition—thought—as essential in understanding people's functioning across the lifespan.

cognitive-developmental perspective A perspective posited by Piaget that views individuals as active explorers of their world, learning by interacting with the world around them and describes cognitive development as progressing through stages.

schema A mental representation, such as concepts, ideas, and ways of interacting with the world.

Piaget's Cognitive-Developmental Theory

Do infants think? How do children understand physical phenomena, such as whether a ball of modeling clay changes in mass when it is rolled into the shape of a hot dog? As the first scientist to systematically examine children's thinking and reasoning, Swiss scholar Jean Piaget (1896–1980) believed that in order to understand children we must understand how they think because thinking influences all of behavior. Piaget founded the **cognitive-developmental perspective** on child development, which views children and adults as active explorers of their world, learning by interacting with the world around them, and organizing what they learn into cognitive **schemas**, or concepts, ideas, and ways of interacting on the world. In this way people contribute to their own cognitive development because they are biologically driven to interact with others and through these interactions they construct and refine their own cognitive schemas.

Piaget proposed that children's drive to explore and understand the world propels them through four stages of cognitive development. With each advancing stage, people create and use more sophisticated cognitive schemas so that they think, reason, and understand their world in more complex ways. As shown in Table 1.4, individuals move from understanding

Jean Piaget (1896–1980) believed that children's drive to explore and understand the world around them propels them through four stages of cognitive development.

TABLE 1.4 • Piaget's Stages of Cognitive Development

STAGE	APPROXIMATE AGE	DESCRIPTION
Sensorimotor	Birth to 2 years	Infants understand the world and think using only their senses and motor skills, by watching, listening, touching, and tasting.
Preoperational	2 to 6 years	Preschoolers are able to explore the world using their own thoughts as guides and develop the language skills to communicate their thoughts to others. Despite these advances, their thinking is characterized by several errors in logic.
Concrete operational	7 to 11 years	School-aged children become able to solve everyday logic problems. Their thinking is not yet fully mature because they are able to apply their thinking only to problems that are tangible and tied to specific substances.
Formal operational	12 years to adulthood	Adolescents and adults can reason logically and abstractly about possibilities, imagined instances and events, and hypothetical concepts.

the world through their senses and motor skills, to a thought-based understanding, to viewing the world in logical but concrete terms, to viewing it in complex and abstract forms. Each stage corresponds to a different period in life. We will discuss each stage in further detail in Chapter 6.

Piaget's cognitive-developmental theory transformed the field of developmental psychology and remains one of the most widely cited developmental theories (Lourenco & Machado, 1996). It was the first to consider *how* infants and children think and to view people as active contributors to their development. Piaget's concept of cognitive stages and the suggestion that children's reasoning is limited by their stage holds implications for education—specifically the idea that effective instruction must match the child's developmental level.

Some critics of cognitive-developmental theory argue that Piaget focused too heavily on cognition and ignored emotional and social factors in development (Broughton, 1981; Winegar & Valsiner, 1992). Others believe that Piaget neglected the influence of contextual factors by assuming that cognitive-developmental stages are universal, that all individuals everywhere progress through the stages in a sequence that does not vary (Lutz & Sternberg, 1999). Some cognitive theorists disagree with Piaget and argue that cognitive development is not a discontinuous, stage-like process; instead, it is a continuous process, as described in the following section.

Information Processing Theory

A developmental scientist presents a 5-year-old child with a puzzle in which a dog, cat, and mouse must find their way to a bone, piece of fish, and hunk of cheese (Klahr, 1985). To solve the puzzle, the child must move all three animals to the appropriate locations. How will the child approach this task? Which item will she move first? What steps will she take? Will the child keep all three animals in mind? Will she remember the task and show what item goes with each animal? How quickly will the child respond? What strategies will she use? What factors influence whether and how quickly a child completes this task? Finally, how does the 5-year-old child's process and performance differ from that of children older and younger than herself?

The problem described above illustrates the questions studied by developmental scientists who favor **information processing theory**, a perspective that views thinking as information processing and posits that the mind works in ways similar to a computer because information enters, is manipulated, stored, recalled, and used to solve problems

information processing theory A perspective that uses a computer analogy to describe how the mind receives information and manipulates, stores, recalls, and uses it to solve problems.

(Halford & Andrews, 2011; Klahr, 1992). Unlike the theories we have discussed thus far, information processing theory is not one theory that is attributed to an individual theorist. Instead there are many information processing theories, and each emphasizes a different aspect of thinking. Some theories focus on how people perceive, focus on, and take in information. Others examine how people store information, create memories, and how they remember information. Still others examine problem solving—how people approach and solve problems in school, the workplace, and everyday life.

According to information processing theorists, we are born with the ability to process information. Our mind itself and its processes of noticing, taking in, manipulating, storing, and retrieving information does not show the radical changes that are associated with stage theories. Instead, from an information processing perspective, development is continuous and entails changes in the efficiency and speed with which we think. Maturation of the brain and nervous system contributes to changes in our information processing abilities, our tendency to become more efficient at processing information over the childhood years and to slow over the adult years (Kail, 2003; Luna, Garver, Urban, Lazar, & Sweeney, 2004). Experience and interaction with others also contributes by helping us learn new ways of managing and manipulating information. Over the childhood years, we become better able to attend to and store information, and we operate on the information we have stored with a greater repertoire of strategies and greater efficiency.

Information processing theory offers a complex and detailed view of how we think, which permits scientists to make specific predictions about behavior and performance that can be tested in research studies. Information processing theory has generated a great many research studies and has garnered much empirical support (Halford & Andrews, 2011). Critics of the information processing perspective argue that a computer model cannot capture the complexity of the human mind and people's unique cognitive abilities. In addition, findings from laboratory research may not extend to the everyday contexts in which people adapt to changing circumstances in contexts that pose great challenges to attention and require flexibility (Miller, 2009). Because findings from information processing research are fundamental to any discussion of cognitive development, we will explore the research in information processing as we discuss each age period throughout this book.

SOCIOCULTURAL SYSTEMS THEORY

A major tenet of lifespan development is that people play an active role in their development by interacting with the world around them. Sociocultural systems theories emphasize the role of the sociocultural context in development. People of all ages are immersed in their social contexts; they are inseparable from the cultural beliefs and societal, neighborhood, and familial contexts in which they live. The origins of sociocultural systems theory lie with two theorists, Lev Vygotsky and Urie Bronfenbrenner.

Vygotsky's Sociocultural Theory

Writing at the same time as Piaget, Russian scholar Lev Vygotsky (1896–1934) offered a different perspective on development that emphasized the importance of culture. As illustrated in Cultural Influences on Development: Defining Culture, *culture* refers to the beliefs, values, customs and skills of a group. Vygotsky's (1978) **sociocultural theory** examines how culture is transmitted from one generation to the next through social interaction. Children interact with adults and more experienced peers as they talk, play, and work alongside them. It is through these formal and informal social contacts that children learn about their culture and what it means to belong to it. By participating in cooperative dialogues and receiving guidance from adults and more expert peers, children adopt their culture's perspectives and practices, learning to think and behave as members of their society (Rogoff, 2003, 2016). As children acquire their culture's patterns of thought and

sociocultural theory Vygotsky's perspective that individuals acquire culturally relevant ways of thinking through social interactions with members of their culture.

behavior, they are able to apply these skills and ways of thinking to guide their own actions, thus requiring less assistance from adults and peers (Rogoff, Mosier, Mistry, & Göncü, 1993; Winsler, Carlton, & Barry, 2000).

Vygotsky's sociocultural theory holds important implications for understanding cognitive development. Like Piaget, Vygotsky emphasized that children are active in their development by engaging with the world around them. However, Vygotsky also viewed cognitive development as a social process that relies on interactions with adults, more mature peers, and other members of society. Children engage their social world, and the social world shapes development by transmitting culturally relevant ways of thinking and acting. Vygotsky also argued that acquiring language is a particularly important milestone for children because it enables them to think in new ways and have more sophisticated dialogues with others in their culture, advancing their learning about culturally valued perspectives and activities (Vygotsky, 1962). We will revisit Vygotsky's ideas about the roles of culture, language, and thought in Chapter 6.

Vygotsky's sociocultural theory is an important addition to the field of lifespan human development because it is the first theory to emphasize the role of the cultural context in influencing people's development throughout life. Critics argue that sociocultural theory overemphasizes the role of context, minimizes the role of individuals in their own development, and neglects the influence of genetic and biological factors (Wertsch, 1998). Another perspective on cognitive development, described below, refocuses attention on the individual.

SPUTNIK/Alamy

Lev Vygotsky (1896–1934) emphasized the importance of culture in development. Children actively engage their social world, which transmits culturally relevant ways of thinking and acting that influence children's thought and behavior.

Bronfenbrenner's Bioecological Systems Theory

Similar to other developmental theorists, Urie Bronfenbrenner (1917–2005) believed that we are active in our development and interact with the world around us. Specifically, Bronfenbrenner's **bioecological systems theory** poses that development is a result of the ongoing interactions among biological, cognitive, and psychological changes within the person and his or her changing context (Bronfenbrenner & Morris, 2006; Bronfenbrenner, 1979, 2005). Bronfenbrenner proposed that individuals are all embedded in, or surrounded by, a series of contexts: home, school, neighborhood, culture, and society. The bioecological systems theory offers a comprehensive perspective on the role of context as an influence on development. As shown in Figure 1.6, contexts are organized into a series of systems in which individuals are embedded and that interact with one another and the person to influence development.

At the center of the bioecological model is the individual. The developing person's genetic, psychological, socioemotional, and personality traits interact, influencing each other. For example, biological development, such as brain maturation, may influence cognitive development, which in turn might influence social development, such as a child's understanding of friendship. Social development then may influence cognitive development, as children may learn activities or ideas from each other. In this way the various forms of development interact. The individual interacts with the contexts in which he or she is embedded, influencing and being influenced by them (Bronfenbrenner & Ceci, 1994; Bronfenbrenner & Morris, 2006).

The individual is embedded in the innermost level of context, the **microsystem**, which includes the immediate physical and social environment surrounding the person, such as family, peers, and school. The individual interacts with elements of the microsystem by, for example, developing relationships with peers in which peers influence the person and vice versa. Because the microsystem contains the developing person, it has an immediate and direct influence on his or her development. Peer relationships can influence a person's sense of self-esteem, social skills, and emotional development.

bioecological systems theory A theory introduced by Bronfenbrenner that emphasizes the role of context in development, positing that contexts are organized into a series of systems in which individuals are embedded and that interact with one another and the person to influence development.

microsystem In bioecological systems theory, the innermost level of context, which includes an individual's immediate physical and social environment.

FIGURE 1.6: Bronfenbrenner's Bioecological Model

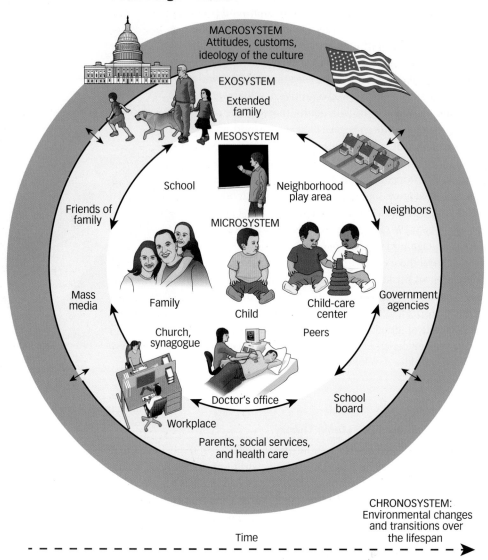

Source: Adapted from Bronfenbrenner and Morris (2006).

Bronfenbrenner's next level, the **mesosystem**, refers to the relations and interactions among microsystems, or connections among contexts. For example, experiences in the home (one microsystem) influence those at school (another microsystem); parents who encourage and provide support for reading will influence the child's experiences in the classroom. Like the microsystem, the mesosystem has a direct influence on the individual because he or she is a participant in it.

An important contribution of bioecological theory is the role of the **exosystem**, which consists of other settings in which the individual is not a participant but that nevertheless influence him or her. For example, a child typically does not participate in a parent's work setting, yet the work setting has an indirect influence on the child because it affects the parent's mood. The availability of funding for schools, another exosystem factor, indirectly affects children by influencing the availability of classroom resources. The exosystem is an important contribution to our understanding of development because the effects of outside factors trickle down and indirectly affect children and adults.

mesosystem In bioecological systems theory, the relations and interactions among microsystems.

exosystem In bioecological systems theory, social settings in which an individual does not participate but has an indirect influence on development.

The **macrosystem** is the greater sociocultural context in which the microsystem, mesosystem and exosystem are embedded. It includes cultural values, legal and political practices, and other elements of the society at large. The macrosystem indirectly influences the child because it affects each of the other contextual levels. For example, cultural beliefs about the value of education (macrosystem) influence funding decisions made at national and local levels (exosystem), as well as what happens in the classroom and in the home (mesosystem and microsystem). Lives in Context: Sociohistorical Influences on Development illustrates how one element of the macrosystem, historical events, may influence development.

A final element of the bioecological system is the **chronosystem**, which refers to how the bioecological system changes over time. As people grow and change, they take on and let go of various roles. For example, graduating from college, getting married, and becoming a parent involve changes in roles and shifts in microsystems. These shifts in contexts, called *ecological transitions,* occur throughout life. The complexity of the bioecological model, the attention to patterns and interrelations among multiple determinants of development, is both a strength and weakness of the theory (Darling, 2007; Dixon & Lerner, 1999). Human development is complex, and only when we consider the multiple interacting influences within the individual and context will we gain insight into the processes and outcomes of developmental change. However, we can never measure and account for all of the potential influences on development at once. Therefore, it is difficult to devise research studies to test the validity of the bioecological model. Despite this, bioecological theory remains an important contribution toward explaining developmental change across the lifespan.

Lives in Context Video 1.1
Sociocultural Influences on Development: Desegregation

ETHOLOGY AND EVOLUTIONARY DEVELOPMENTAL THEORY

Why do infants bond to their parents? Are parents innately attuned to their infants? How might attachments between infants and parents contribute to infants' development? Some theorists argue that parenting is innate and has survival value. In 1859, Charles Darwin proposed his theory of evolution, explaining that all species adapt and evolve over time. Specifically, traits that enable a species to adapt, thrive, and mate tend to be passed to succeeding generations because they improve the likelihood of the individual's and species' survival. **Ethology** is the scientific study of the evolutionary history of behavior and its survival value (Dewsbury, 1992). Konrad Lorenz and Kiko Tinbergen, two European zoologists, observed animal species in their natural environments and noticed patterns of behavior that appeared to be inborn, emerged early in life, and ensured their survival. For example, shortly after birth, goslings imprint on their mothers, meaning that they bond to her and will follow her, thereby ensuring they stay close to the mother, get fed, and remain protected. Imprinting ensures the goslings' survival. In order for imprinting to occur, the mother goose must be present immediately after the goslings hatch; mothers instinctively stay close to the nest so that their young may imprint and enhance their odds of surviving (Lorenz, 1952).

According to Bowlby (1969), humans also display biologically preprogrammed behaviors that have survival value and promote development. For example, caregivers naturally respond to infants' cues. Crying, smiling, and grasping are inborn ways that infants get attention from caregivers, bringing them physical contact and ensuring that the infants will be safe and cared for. Many infant behaviors have adaptive significance because they meet infants' needs and promote the formation of bonds with caregivers, ensuring that the caregivers will feel a strong desire and obligation to care for them (Bowlby, 1973). In this way innate biological drives and behaviors work together with experience to influence adaptation and ultimately an individual's survival.

Are you—your abilities, personality, and competencies—a result of your genes and inborn influences? Or did the physical and social environment in which you were

macrosystem In bioecological systems theory, the sociohistorical context—cultural values, laws, and cultural values—in which the microsystem, mesosystem, and exosystem are embedded, posing indirect influences on individuals.

chronosystem In bioecological systems theory, refers to how the people and contexts change over time.

ethology A perspective that emphasizes the evolutionary basis of behavior and its adaptive value in ensuring survival of a species.

• • Sociohistorical Influences on Development

Sociohistorical influences, such as the Great Depression (1929–1939), contribute to cohort, or generational, differences in development.

Historical events, such as wars, economic and natural disasters, and periods of social unrest, are contextual influences that shape our world and our development. Glen Elder (1999) illustrated the influence of historical events by examining the progress of two generations, or cohorts, of California-born Americans from childhood to adulthood. The Oakland Growth Study consisted of individuals born in 1920–1921 who were adolescents during the Great Depression. The Berkeley Guidance Study consisted of individuals born in 1928–1929 who were young children when their families experienced the economic losses of the Great Depression. The decades-long studies of these two cohorts, who were 8 years apart in age, demonstrated that they had very different experiences during their adolescent and early adult years. Influenced in part by the findings of these studies, Elder (2000) believed that the impact of historical events depends on when they occur in a person's life.

For all participants of both studies, family roles and relationships changed in response to the economic adversity wrought by the Great Depression. As fathers lost jobs and income, more work was required of children, giving them opportunities to participate in helping their families. Mothers took on an increasingly important role in the family as income earners as well as authority figures. This upheaval of traditional gender roles was accompanied by an increase in family discord and conflicts.

The older, Oakland cohort were children during the affluent 1920s, a time of economic growth in California, and they experienced a prosperous and relatively stress-free childhood. But they entered adolescence during the Great Depression, a period of severe economic stress in which unemployment skyrocketed and people's savings were

depleted. As adolescents during the Great Depression, the Oakland cohort tended to behave responsibly and assist their families in coping. The boys often assumed jobs outside the home to aid financially troubled families. Their activities outside the home enhanced their social independence and reduced their exposure to family stress. Girls spent more time at home caring for siblings and completing household chores as many mothers worked outside the home; they were exposed to greater amounts of family stress and showed poorer adjustment than did the boys.

The Berkeley children, the younger cohort, experienced the Great Depression during their vulnerable early childhood years. The children experienced economic scarcity and family discord early in life, at a time when they were very dependent on family. The Berkeley cohort entered adolescence during World War II, a period of additional economic and emotional stress from empty households (as both parents worked to support the war effort) and the military service and war trauma of older brothers. As adolescents, the Berkeley cohort (especially the boys) experienced greater emotional difficulties, more poor attitudes toward school, and less hope, self-direction, and confidence about their future than did the Oakland cohort (who were children during the prosperous 1920s).

However, the Berkeley cohort demonstrated resilience in adulthood, largely because of the influence of military service. Seventy percent of the males in the Berkeley sample served in the military during World War II. Military service appeared to offer the men several opportunities, such as to begin again and reconsider their lives, to travel, and access to the GI Bill of Rights, which enabled them to expand their education and acquire new skills after the war. These two cohorts of young people offer striking examples of how sociohistorical context influences development. Context always plays a role in development—not only in times of social upheaval, but every day and for every generation of people.

What Do You Think?

1. Consider the sociohistorical context in which you were raised. What historical and societal events may have influenced you? What events have shaped your generation's childhood and adolescence?

2. Consider the societal and cultural events that your parents may have experienced in childhood and adolescence. What technology was available? What historical events did they experience? What were the popular fads of their youth? What influence do you think these sociohistorical factors may have had on your parents' development?

3. Compare the sociohistorical context in which you are embedded today with that of your parents and grandparents at your age.

Rolls Press/Popperfoto/Popperfoto/Getty Images

raised, your family, friends, and school make you who you are today? Evolutionary developmental scientists explain that these are the wrong questions to ask. **Evolutionary developmental theory** applies principles of evolution and scientific knowledge about the interactive influence of genetic and environmental mechanisms to understand the changes people undergo throughout their lives. From this perspective, genes and context interact in an ever-changing way so that it is impossible to isolate the contributions of each to development (Gottesman & Hanson, 2005; Gottlieb, 2003; LaFreniere & MacDonald, 2013; Lickliter & Honeycutt, 2003). Although all of our traits and characteristics are influenced by genes, contextual factors influence the expression of genetic instructions, as illustrated by Figure 1.7. Contextual factors such as gravity, light, temperature, and moisture influence how genes are expressed and therefore how individuals develop (Gilbert, 2001; Meaney, 2010; Rutter, 2010). For example, in crocodiles, sex is determined by the temperature in which the organism develops. Eggs incubated at one range of temperatures produce male crocodiles and at another temperature produce female crocodiles (Gans & Crews, 1992).

According to evolutionary developmental theory, genetic programs and biological predispositions interact with the physical and social environment to influence development and Darwinian natural selection determines what genes and traits are passed on to the next generation (Bjorklund & Pellegrini, 2000; Krebs, 2003; Lickliter & Honeycutt, 2003). People are viewed as active in their development, influencing their contexts (through their genetic characteristics and by choosing and interacting within settings), responding to the demands for adaptation posed by their contexts, and constantly interacting with and adapting to the world around them. The relevance of both biological and contextual factors to human development is indisputable and most developmental scientists appreciate the contributions of evolutionary developmental theory (Frankenhuis, Panchanathan, & Clark Barrett, 2013; Gottlieb, Wahlsten, & Lickliter, 1998; Lickliter & Honeycutt, 2013). The ways in which biology and context interact and their influence on development changes over the course of the lifetime, as we will discuss throughout this book.

In summary, there are many theories of human development that offer complementary and contrasting views of how we change throughout our lifetimes. Psychoanalytic theories emphasize personality change—how unconscious forces shape people (Freud) and how sociocultural forces influence ego development (Erikson). Behaviorist and social learning theories point to the physical and social environment as a shaper of development and behavior, as well as the role of observation and imitation in learning. Other theories emphasize cognitive development. Piaget's cognitive-developmental theory explains how individuals construct their own knowledge structures through interaction with the world, whereas Vygotsky emphasizes the role of sociocultural context in influencing thought. Information processing theories examine the ways in which attention, processing speed, and strategy use lead to advances in thinking and problem solving ability. Finally, Bronfenbrenner's bioecological theory takes a comprehensive look at the many contextual systems in which people live and how people and their contexts interact. Table 1.5 provides an at-a-glance comparison of theories of human development.

FIGURE 1.7: Interaction of Genetic and Environmental Factors

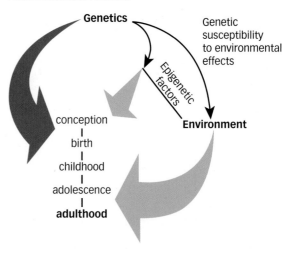

Development is influenced by the dynamic interplay of genetic and environmental factors. Genetic predispositions may influence how we experience environmental factors, and environmental factors may influence how genes are expressed.

Source: Picker (2005).

evolutionary developmental theory A perspective that applies principles of evolution and scientific knowledge about the interactive influence of genetic and environmental mechanisms to understand the adaptive value of developmental changes that are experienced with age.

TABLE 1.5 • Comparing Theories of Human Development

	CONTINUITY VS. DISCONTINUITY	ACTIVE VS. PASSIVE INDIVIDUAL	NATURE VS. NURTURE
Freud's psychosexual theory	Discontinuous stages	Passive individuals are motivated by inborn basic drives.	Greater emphasis on nature: People are driven by inborn drives, but the extent to which the drives are satisfied influences developmental outcomes.
Erikson's psychosocial theory	Discontinuous stages	Active individuals interact with their social world to resolve psychosocial tasks.	Both nature and nurture: Biological and social forces propel people through the stages and social and psychosocial influences determine the outcome of each stage.
Behaviorist theory	Continuous process of learning new behaviors	Passive individuals are shaped by their environment.	Nurture: Environmental influences shape behavior.
Bandura's social learning theory	Continuous process of learning new behaviors	Individuals' characteristics and behavior interact with the environment.	Both nature and nurture: Inborn characteristics and the physical and social environment influence behavior.
Piaget's cognitive-developmental theory	Discontinuous stages, but also continuous process of seeking equilibration	Active individuals interact with the world to create their own schemas.	Both nature and nurture: An innate drive to learn coupled with brain development leads people to interact with the world. Opportunities provided by the physical and social environment influence development.
Vygotsky's sociocultural theory	Continuous interactions with others lead to developing new reasoning capacities and skills.	Active individuals interact with members of their culture.	Both nature and nurture: People learn through interactions with more skilled members of their culture; however, capacities are influenced by genes, brain development, and maturation.
Information processing theory	Continuous increase of skills and capacities	Active individuals attend to, process, and store information.	Both nature and nurture: People are born with processing capacities that develop through maturation and environmental influences.
Bronfenbrenner's bioecological systems theory	Continuous: People constantly change through their interactions with the contexts in which they are embedded.	Active individuals interact with their contexts, being influenced by their contexts but also determining what kinds of physical and social environments are created and how they change.	Both nature and nurture: People's inborn and biological characteristics interact with an ever changing context to influence behavior.
Ethology and evolutionary developmental theory	Both continuous and discontinuous: People gradually grow and change throughout life but there are sensitive periods during which specific experiences and developments must occur.	Active individuals interact with their physical and social environment.	Both nature and nurture: Genetic programs and biological predispositions interact with the physical and social environment to influence development, and Darwinian natural selection determines what genes and traits are passed on to the next generation.

Thinking in Context 1.3

Maria and Fernando have just given birth to their first child, a healthy baby boy. Like most new parents, Maria and Fernando are nervous and overwhelmed with their new responsibilities. Of utmost importance to them is that the baby develop a strong and secure bond to them. They want their baby to feel loved and to love them.

1. What advice would a psychoanalytic theorist give Maria and Fernando? Contrast psychoanalytic with behaviorist perspectives. How might a behaviorist theorist approach this question?

2. How might an evolutionary developmental theorist explain bonding between parents and infants? What advice might an evolutionary developmental theorist give to Maria and Fernando?

3. Considering bioecological systems theory, what microsystem and mesosystem factors influence the parent–child bond? What role might exosystem and macrosystem factors take?

RESEARCH IN HUMAN DEVELOPMENT

LO 1.4 Describe the methods used in studying human development, including types of data and designs.

The many theories of lifespan human development differ in focus and explanation, but they all are the result of scientists' attempts to organize observations of people at all ages. Developmental scientists conduct research studies to gather information and answer questions about how people grow and change over their lives. They devise theories to organize what they learn from research and to suggest new hypotheses to test in research studies. In turn, research findings are used to modify theories. By conducting multiple studies over time, developmental scientists refine their theories about lifespan human development and determine new questions to ask. Developmental science also finds significant influences in contexts, as discussed in Applying Developmental Science.

THE SCIENTIFIC METHOD

Researchers employ the **scientific method**, a process of posing and answering questions by making careful and systematic observations and gathering information. The scientific method provides an organized way of formulating questions, finding answers, and communicating research discoveries. Its basic steps are as follows:

1. Identify the research question or problem to be studied and formulate the hypothesis, or proposed explanation, to be tested.

2. Gather information to address the research question.

3. Summarize the information gathered and determine whether the hypothesis is refuted, or shown to be false.

4. Interpret the summarized information, consider the findings in light of prior research studies, and share findings with the scientific community and world at large.

In practice, the scientific method usually does not proceed in such a straightforward, linear fashion. Frequently research studies raise as many questions as they answer—and sometimes more. Unexpected findings can prompt new studies. For example, researchers

scientific method The process of forming and answering questions using systematic observations and gathering information.

APPLYING DEVELOPMENTAL SCIENCE

• • The Importance of Context in Developmental Science

Dutch children raised in Amsterdam are immersed in a different context than that of children reared in North America

In its early years, the study of human development was based in laboratory research devoted to uncovering universal aspects of development by stripping away contextual influences (Wertlieb, 2003). This basic research was designed to examine universal processes that apply to all people, such as perceptual development (e.g., what visual skills are infants born with?).

As developmental scientists began apply their knowledge outside of laboratory settings, however, it became apparent that there are a great many individual differences in development.

Developmental scientists have since realized the importance of context. The field of **applied developmental science** has emerged, studying individuals within the contexts in which they live. This approach promotes the ability to understand the diverse range of patterns development takes throughout the life course (Lerner, 2010; Wertlieb, 2003).

Research in human development is now directed toward understanding a variety of social problems and issues of immediate social relevance, such as the capacities of preterm infants, children's ability to provide eyewitness testimony, adolescent sexual practices, and the impact of disability on the psychological and social adjustment of older adults and their adult children (Fisher, Busch-Rossnagel, Jopp, & Brown, 2013; Lerner, 2012). Applying developmental scientists study and make contributions to social policies on a issues that affect children, adolescents, adults, and their families, including environmental quality, health and health care delivery, violence, hunger and poor nutrition, school failure, and pervasive poverty (Tseng, 2012). Developmental scientists seek to enhance the life chances of diverse groups of individuals, families, and communities. Throughout this book you will be introduced to these and more issues studied by applying developmental scientists.

What Do You Think?

1. **Identify three areas that you believe are in need of study or intervention by developmental scientists.**

2. **What are some challenges faced by children, adolescents, or adults that you believe should be studied and addressed?**

---

may perform an experiment again (i.e., a replication) to see whether the results are the same as previous ones. Sometimes analyses reveal flaws in data collection methods or research design, prompting a revised study. Experts may also disagree on the interpretation of a study. Researchers may then conduct new studies to test new hypotheses and shed more light on a given topic. For all of these reasons, scientists often say the scientific method is "messy."

METHODS OF DATA COLLECTION

applied developmental science A field that studies lifespan interactions between individuals and the contexts in which they live and applies research findings to real-world settings, such as to influence social policy and create interventions.

The basic challenge that scientists face in conducting research is determining what information is important and how to gather it. Scientists use the term *data* to refer to the information they collect. How can we gather data about children, adolescents, and adults? Should we simply talk with our participants? Watch them as they progress through their days? Hook them up to machines that measure physiological activity such as heart rate or brain waves? Developmental scientists use a variety of different methods, or measures, to collect information.

Self-Report Measures

Interviews and questionnaires are known as self-report measures because the person under study answers questions about his or her experiences, attitudes, opinions, beliefs, and behavior. Interviews can take place in person, over the phone, or over the Internet.

The **open-ended interview** is very flexible because the trained interviewer uses a conversational style that encourages the participant, or the person under study, to expand his or her responses. Interviewers may vary the order of questions, probe, and ask follow up questions based on responses. The scientist begins with a question and then follows up with prompts to obtain a better view of the person's reasoning (Ginsburg, 1997). An example of this is the Piagetian Clinical Interview, which requires specialized training to administer. Consider this dialogue between Piaget and a 5-year-old child:

Where does the dream come from?

I think you sleep so well that you dream.

Does it come from us or from outside?

From outside.

What do we dream with?

I don't know.

With the hands? With nothing?

Yes, with nothing.

When you are in bed and you dream, where is the dream?

In my bed, under the blanket. I don't really know. If it was in my stomach the bones would be in the way and I shouldn't see it.

Is the dream there when you sleep?

Yes, it is in my bed beside me.

Is the dream in your head?

It is I that am in the dream; it isn't in my head. When you dream, you don't know you are in the bed. You know you are walking. You are in the dream. You are in bed, but you don't know you are. (Piaget, 1929, pp. 97–98)

Open-ended interviews permit participants to explain their thoughts thoroughly and in their own way. This method also enables researchers to gather a large amount of information quickly. However, the flexibility of open-ended interviews poses a challenge: When questions are phrased differently for each person, responses may not capture real differences in how people think about a given topic and instead may reflect differences in how the questions were posed and followed up by the interviewer.

A **structured interview** poses the same set of questions to each participant in the same way, and therefore is less flexible than open-ended interviews. Because all participants receive the same set of questions, differences in responses are more likely to reflect true differences among participants and not merely differences in the manner of interviewing. For example Evans, Milanak, Medeiros, and Ross (2002) used a structured interview to examine American children's beliefs about magic. Children between the ages of 3 and 8 were asked the following set of questions:

What is magic? Who can do magic?

Is it possible to have special powers? Who has special powers?

Does someone have to learn to do magic? Where have you seen magic?

What are tricks? Who can do tricks? What is the difference between tricks and magic?

open-ended interview
A research method in which a researcher asks a participant questions using a flexible, conversational style and may vary the order of questions, probe, and ask follow-up questions based on the participant's responses.

structured interview A research method in which each participant is asked the same set of questions in the same way.

How do wishes work? What does it mean to make a wish? Do wishes come true? Who makes wishes come true?

What do you think about Santa Claus/the Tooth Fairy?

What do you think about Monsters? (p. 49)

After compiling and analyzing the children's responses as well as administering several cognitive tasks, Evans and colleagues concluded that even older children, who have the ability to think logically and perform concrete operations, may display magical beliefs.

A **questionnaire**, also called a survey, is a set of questions, typically multiple choice, that scientists compile and use to collect data from large samples of people. Questionnaires can be administered in person, online, or by telephone, e-mail, or postal mail. Questionnaires are popular data collection methods because they are easy to use and enable scientists to collect information from a large number of people quickly and inexpensively. Scientists who conduct research on sensitive topics, such as sexual interest and experience, often use questionnaires because they can easily be administered anonymously, protecting participants' privacy by not including any identifying information on the survey. For example, the Monitoring the Future Study is an annual survey of 50,000 students in Grades 8, 10, and 12 that collects information about their behaviors, attitudes, and values concerning drug and alcohol use (Miech, Johnston, O'Malley, Bachman, & Schulenberg, 2015). In this example, the survey permits scientists to gather an enormous amount of data yet its anonymity protects the adolescents from the consequences of sharing personal information that they may not otherwise reveal.

Despite their ease of use, self-report measures are not without challenges. Sometimes people give socially desirable answers: They respond in ways they would like themselves to be perceived or believe researchers desire. A college student completing a survey about cheating, for example, might choose answers that do not truly reflect her behavior of sometimes looking at nearby students' papers during examinations, but instead match the person she aspires to be or the behaviors she believes the world values—that is, someone who does not cheat on exams. Self-report data may not always reflect people's true attitudes and behavior. Some argue that we are not always fully aware of our feelings and therefore cannot always provide useful insight into our own thoughts and behavior with the use of self-report measures (Westen, 1998). Whereas interviews and questionnaires measure people's self-reports of their attitudes, beliefs, and behaviors, observational measures examine people in action as they go about their daily lives.

Observational Measures

Are you a people watcher? Have you ever sat in a coffee shop or at the student center and observed people interact, rush from place to place, laugh with others, or scowl at their laptops? If so, you have used observational skills that are similar to those used by scientists who conduct research in everyday settings. Observational measures are methods that scientists use to collect and organize information based on watching and monitoring people's behavior. Developmental scientists employ two types of observational measures: naturalistic observation and structured observation.

Scientists who use **naturalistic observation** observe and record behavior in natural, real-world settings. For example Ginsburg, Pappas, and Seo (2001) analyzed videotapes of 4- and 5-year-old children's everyday behavior during free play to determine the extent to which they used mathematical thinking in their play. Naturalistic observation is challenging because one must first decide on an *operational definition* of the behavior of interest. In this case, many operational definitions were required as Ginsburg and colleagues designed an elaborate coding system to categorize children's behaviors in terms of their mathematical content, location, preferred play objects, peer interaction, and play activity.

questionnaire A research method in which researchers use a survey or set of questions to collect data from large samples of people.

naturalistic observation A research method in which a researcher views and records an individual's behavior in natural, real-world settings.

Sometimes the presence of an observer causes the person to behave in unnatural ways or ways that are not typical for him or her. This is known as *participant reactivity,* and it poses a challenge to gathering by naturalistic observation. To minimize the effect that observation might have on the children's behaviors, Ginsburg and colleagues made video recordings and permitted the children to get used to the video recorder by exposing them to it many times before using it to collect observations. The video recorded observations revealed that children spend a surprising amount of play time (almost 50%) spontaneously engaging in mathematical activities like ordering objects, counting, comparing sizes and quantities, and exploring positions, direction, distances, and patterns.

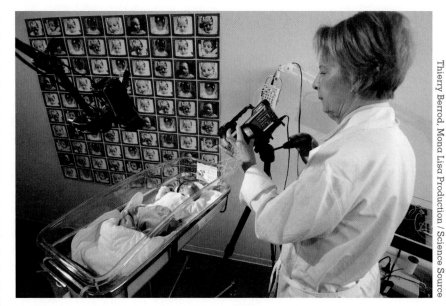

Researchers use video cameras to observe and record the facial expressions a newborn baby makes while it sleeps.

These results suggest that children naturally engage in mathematics-related play and are more competent in mathematics than many adults realize (Ginsburg et al., 2001).

Naturalistic observation permits researchers to observe behaviors in real-world settings and to observe patterns, such as whether a particular event or behavior typically precedes another. Such observations can help researchers determine which behaviors are important to study in the first place. For example, a scientist who studies bullying by observing children's play may notice that some victims act aggressively *before* a bullying encounter. The scientist may then decide to examine aggression in victims not only after a bullying incident, but beforehand. Naturalistic observation is a useful way of studying events and behaviors that are common. Some behaviors and events, however, are uncommon or are difficult to observe, such as physical aggression among adults, requiring a researcher to observe for very long periods of time to obtain data on the behavior of interest. For this reason, many researchers make structured observations.

TABLE 1.6 • Data Collection Methods

	ADVANTAGE	**DISADVANTAGE**
Open-ended interview	Gathers a large amount of information quickly and inexpensively.	Nonstandardized questions. Characteristics of the interviewer may influence participant responses.
Structured interview	Permits gathering a large amount of information quickly and inexpensively.	Characteristics of the interviewer may influence participant responses.
Questionnaire	Permits collecting data from a large sample more quickly and inexpensively than by interview methods.	Some participants may respond in socially desirable or inaccurate ways.
Naturalistic observation	Gathers data on everyday behavior in a natural environment as behaviors occur.	The observer's presence may influence the participants' behavior. No control over the observational environment.
Structured observation	Observation in a controlled setting.	May not reflect real-life reactions and behavior
Physiological measures	Assesses biological indicators and does not rely on participant report	May be difficult to interpret

LIFESPAN BRAIN DEVELOPMENT

• • Methods of Studying the Brain

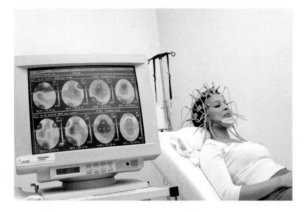

Modern brain imaging techniques enable us to view the active brain as it thinks and solves problems.

What parts of the brain are active when we solve problems or feel emotions? How does the brain change with development? Until recently, the brain was a mystery. Over the last hundred years, researchers have devised several methods of studying brain activity that have increased our understanding of how the brain functions and how it develops.

The earliest instrument created to measure brain activity was the electroencephalogram, first used with humans in the 1920s (Collura, 1993). Electroencephalography (EEG) uses electrodes placed on the scalp to measure electrical activity patterns produced by the brain. Researchers study fluctuations in activity that occur when participants are presented with stimuli or when they sleep. EEG recordings measure electrical activity in the brain, but they do not provide information about the location of activity.

It was not until the invention of positron emission tomography (PET), in the early 1950s, that researchers obtained the first glimpse of the inner workings of the brain (Portnow, Vaillancourt, & Okun, 2013). A small dose of radioactive material is injected into the participant's blood stream and detected by the PET scan. The radioactive material enables researchers to monitor the flow of blood. Blood flows more readily to active areas of the brain, and the resulting images can illustrate what parts of the brain are active as participants view stimuli and solve problems.

Developed in 1971, computerized tomography, known as the CT scan, produces X-ray images of brain structures (Cierniak, 2011). A movable X-ray unit rotates around a person's head and records images of the brain (Herman, 2009). The images are then combined to make a 3-D picture of a person's brain, providing images of bone, brain vasculature, and tissue. CT scans can provide researchers with information about the density of brain structures to illustrate, for example, how the thickness of the cortex changes with development.

Functional magnetic resonance imaging (fMRI) measures brain activity by monitoring changes in blood flow in the brain (Bandettini, 2012). Developed in the 1990s, MRI machines house a powerful magnet that uses radio waves to measure blood oxygen level. Active areas of the brain require more oxygen-rich blood. Like PET scans, fMRI enables researchers to determine what parts of the brain are active as individuals complete cognitive tasks. However, fMRI images are much more detailed than PET scans. An important advantage of fMRI over a PET scan is that it does not rely on radioactive molecules, which can only be administered a few times before becoming unsafe.

Another imaging process, called diffusion tensor imaging (DTI), uses a MRI machine to track how water molecules move in and around the fibers connecting different parts of the brain (Soares, Marques, Alves, & Sousa, 2013). DTI gauges the thickness and density of the brain's connections, permitting researchers to measure the brain's white matter and determine changes that occur with development and with age-related illnesses, such as Alzheimer's disease. Researchers have devised many ways of studying brain activity, an important physiological measure.

What Do You Think?

1. **If you were going to study the brain, which measure would you choose and why? What type of information would you obtain from your chosen measure?**

2. **Identify a research question that your measure might help you answer.**

Structured observation entails observing and recording behaviors displayed in a controlled environment, which is a situation constructed by the experimenter. For example, children might be observed within a laboratory setting as they play with another child or complete a puzzle-solving task. The challenges of identifying and categorizing which behaviors to record are similar to those entailed by naturalistic observation. However, the laboratory environment permits researchers to exert more control on the situation than is possible in natural settings. In addition to cataloguing observable behaviors, some researchers use technology to measure biological functions such as heart rate, brain waves, and blood pressure. One challenge to conducting structured observations is that people do not always behave in laboratory settings as they do in real life.

structured observation
An observational measure in which an individual's behavior is viewed and recorded in a controlled environment; a situation created by the experimenter.

Physiological Measures

Physiological measures are increasingly used in developmental research because cognition, emotion, and behavior have physiological indicators. For example, when speaking in public, such as when you give a class presentation, do you feel your heart beat more rapidly or your palms grow sweaty? An increase in heart rate and perspiration are physiological measures of anxiety. Other researchers might measure cortisol, a hormone triggered by the experience of stress. An advantage of physiological measures is they do not rely on verbal reports and generally cannot be faked. They are also useful for studying infants. A researcher who employs physiological measures might use an infant's heart rate as a measure of interest or may measure the infant's eye movement or pupil dilation. A challenge to physiological measures is that, although physiological responses can be recorded, they may be difficult to interpret. For example, excitement and anger may both cause an increase in heart rate. Physiological measures of brain activity are a particularly promising source of data, as discussed in the Lifespan Brain Development feature. Data collection methods are summarized in Table 1.6.

RESEARCH DESIGNS

There are many steps in conducting research. In addition to determining the research question and deciding what information to collect, scientists must choose a research design—a technique for conducting the research study.

Case Study

A case study is an in-depth examination of a single person (or small group of individuals). It is conducted by gathering information from many sources, such as through observations, interviews, and conversations with family, friends, and others who know the individual. A case study may include samples or interpretations of a person's writing, such as poetry or journal entries, artwork, and other creations. A case study provides a rich description of a person's life and the influences on his or her development. It is often employed to study individuals who have unique and unusual experiences, abilities, or disorders. Conclusions drawn from a case study may shed light on an individual's development, but they may not be generalized or applied to others. Case studies can be a source of hypotheses to examine in large scale research.

Correlational Research

Are children with high self-esteem more likely to excel at school? Are older adults with more friends happier than those with few? Are college students who work part-time less likely to graduate? All of these questions can be studied with **correlational research**, which permits researchers to examine relations among measured characteristics, behaviors, and events. For example, in one study scientists examined the relationship between children's after-school activities and their academic achievement and found that children who reported watching more television on school nights scored lower on achievement tests (Cooper, Valentine, Nye, & Lindsay, 1999). However, this correlation does not tell us *why* television viewing was associated with academic achievement. Correlational research cannot answer this question because it simply describes relationships that exist among variables; it does not enable us to make conclusions about the causes of those relationships. It is likely that other variables influence both a child's television watching and achievement (e.g., motivation), but correlation does not enable us to determine the causes for behavior; for that, we need an experiment.

Experimental Research

Scientists who seek to test hypotheses about *causal* relationships, such as whether media exposure influences behavior or whether hearing particular types of music influences

correlational research
A research design that measures relationships among participants' measured characteristics, behaviors, and development.

mood, employ **experimental research**. An experiment is a procedure that uses control to determine causal relationships among factors, known as variables. Specifically, one or more variables thought to influence a behavior of interest are changed, or manipulated, while other variables are held constant. By doing so, researchers can examine how the changing variable influences the behavior under study. If the behavior changes as the variable changes, this suggests that the variable *caused* the change in the behavior.

For example, suppose a scientist examined the influence of exposure to aggressive media on children's aggressive behavior by choosing two cartoons: one containing many aggressive acts (e.g., hitting or punching) and another depicting few aggressive acts (e.g., including themes of sharing). Each child is asked to play with a set of toys containing cars, dolls, and stuffed animals. Researchers observe and record the number of aggressive acts the child engages in, such as hitting and throwing. Each child is tested in the same room, controlling other sounds, the temperature, and time of day of testing. If researchers' ratings of children's aggression change in response to varying the type of media—showing more or less aggressive behavior—then the results suggest a causal relationship: Media exposure changed behavior.

Let us take a closer look at the components of an experiment. Conducting an experiment requires choosing at least one **dependent variable**, the behavior under study (e.g., hitting and throwing), and one **independent variable**, the factor proposed to change the behavior under study (e.g., type of cartoon). The independent variable is manipulated or varied systematically by the researcher during the experiment (e.g., a child views many aggressive acts or few aggressive acts). The dependent variable is expected to change as a result of varying the independent variable, and how it changes is thought to depend on how the independent variable is manipulated.

In an experiment, the independent variable is administered to one or more *experimental groups,* or test groups whose experiences are manipulated by varying the independent variable. The *control group* is treated just like the experimental group except that it does not receive the independent variable in order to compare the effect of the manipulation. For example, in an experiment investigating whether particular types of music influence mood, the experimental group would experience a change in music (e.g., from "easy listening" to rock), whereas the control would hear only one type of music (e.g., "easy listening"). **Random assignment**, whereby each participant has an equal chance of being assigned to the experimental or control group, is essential for ensuring that the groups are as equal as possible in all preexisting characteristics (e.g., age, ethnicity, and gender). Random assignment makes it less likely that any observed differences in the outcomes of the experimental and control groups are not due to preexisting differences between the groups. After the independent variable is manipulated, if the experimental and control groups differ on the dependent variable, it is concluded that the independent variable *caused* the change in the dependent variable. That is, a cause and effect relationship has been demonstrated.

As another example, consider a study designed to examine whether massage therapy improves weight gain in preterm infants (infants who were born well before their due date; Dieter, Field, Hernandez-Reif, Emory, & Redzepi, 2003). Infants housed in a neonatal unit were randomly assigned either to a massage group (independent variable), who were touched and their arms and legs moved for three 15-minute periods per day, or to a control group, which received no massage. Other than the massage/no massage periods, the two groups of

experimental research A research design that permits inferences about cause and effect by exerting control, systematically manipulating a variable, and studying the effects on measured variables.

dependent variable The behavior under study in an experiment; it is expected to be affected by changes in the independent variable.

independent variable The factor proposed to change the behavior under study in an experiment; it is systematically manipulated during an experiment.

random assignment A method of assigning participants that ensures each participant has an equal chance of being assigned to the experimental group or control group.

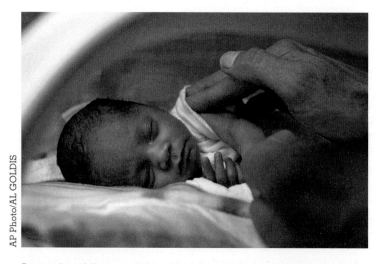

AP Photo/AL GOLDIS

By experimentally manipulating which infants receive massage therapy, researchers determined that massage can help preterm infants gain weight, an important correlate of health.

infants were cared for in the same way. After five days, the preterm infants who received massage therapy gained more weight (dependent variable) than those who did not receive massage therapy. The researchers concluded that massage therapy causes improved weight gain in preterm infants.

Developmental scientists conduct studies that use both correlational and experimental research. Studying development, however, requires that scientists pay close attention to age and how people change over time, which requires the use of specialized research designs, as described in the following sections.

DEVELOPMENTAL RESEARCH DESIGNS

Does personality change over the lifespan? Do children outgrow shyness? Are infants' bonds with their parents associated with their adult relationships? These challenging questions require that developmental scientists examine relationships among variables over time. The following sections discuss the designs that researchers use to learn about human development. As you learn about each design, consider how we might employ it to answer a question about development. For example, how does alcohol use among adolescents change from 6th grade through 12th grade?

Cross-Sectional Research Design

A common way in which developmental scientists examine questions about how variables change with age is to conduct **cross-sectional research**, comparing groups of people of different ages at one time. For example, to examine how alcohol use changes from 6th through 12th grade, a scientist might visit a school system in 2020 and administer a survey about alcohol use to students in 6th, 8th, 10th, and 12th grades. By analyzing the survey results, the scientist can describe grade differences in alcohol use, such as how 6th graders differ from 12th graders. Cross-sectional research permits scientists to draw conclusions about age differences, for example, how the 6th graders differed in alcohol use from the 8th, 10th, and 12th graders. However, it is unknown whether the observed age differences in alcohol use reflect age-related or developmental change. In other words, it is unclear whether 6th graders will show the same pattern of change in alcohol use over the high school years as the 12th graders.

Cross-sectional research gathers information from people of several ages at one time. It permits age comparisons, but because participants differ in terms of age and cohort, it does not permit conclusions about development. Recall that a cohort is a group of people of the same age who are exposed to similar historical events and cultural and societal influences. The 6th-grade students are a different age than the 12th-grade students, but they are also a different cohort in the school, so the two groups may differ in reported alcohol use because of development (age-related changes) or cohort (group-related changes). For example, perhaps the 6th-grade students received a new early prevention program in the school that was not available to the 12th-grade students back when they were in 6th grade. In this example, the difference in alcohol use between 6th graders and 12th graders may be related to the prevention program, not to age. Cross-sectional research is an important source of information about age differences, but it cannot provide information about developmental change.

Longitudinal Research Design

Developmental scientists who study age-related change must examine individuals over time. In **longitudinal research**, one group of participants is studied at many points in time. To examine how alcohol use changes from 6th through 12th grade, a developmental scientist who used longitudinal research might administer a survey on alcohol use to 6th graders and then follow up 2 years later when they enter 8th grade, again when they

cross-sectional research
A developmental research design that compares people of different ages at a single point in time to infer age differences.

longitudinal research
A developmental study in which one group of participants is studied repeatedly to infer age changes.

enter 10th grade, and finally in 12th grade. If a researcher began this study in 2020, the last round of data collection would not occur until 2026. Longitudinal research provides information about age change because it follows people over time, enabling scientists to describe how the 6th graders' alcohol use changed as they progressed through the school years. However, because longitudinal research studies only one cohort or one generation, it is prone to *cohort effects*. Do the findings indicate developmental change, or are they an artifact of the cohort under study? Was the group of 6th graders that the scientist chose to follow through 12th grade somehow different from the cohorts or groups of students who came before or after? Because only one cohort is assessed, it is not possible to determine whether the observed changes are age-related changes or changes that are unique to the cohorts examined.

Sequential Research Designs

Both cross-sectional and longitudinal studies provide useful information but, as we have seen, each has limitations. A **sequential research design** combines the best features of cross-sectional and longitudinal research by assessing multiple cohorts over time, enabling scientists to make comparisons that disentangle the effects of cohort and age (see Table 1.7). Consider the alcohol use study once more. A sequential design would begin in 2020 by administering a survey to students in 6th, 8th, 10th, and 12th grades. Two years later, in 2022, the initial sample is surveyed again; the 6th graders are now 8th graders, 8th graders have become 10th graders, 10th graders have become 12th graders, and the 12th graders have graduated from the school and so are not assessed. Instead, a new group of 6th graders is surveyed. Two years later, in 2024, the participants are surveyed again, and so on.

The sequential design provides information about age, cohort, and age-related change. The cross-sectional data (comparisons of 6th, 8th, 10th, and 12th graders from a given year) permit comparisons among age groups. The longitudinal data (annual follow-up of 6th graders through 12th grade) permit study of age-related change. The sequential component helps scientists separate cohort effects from age-related change. Because several cohorts are studied at once, the effect of the cohort can be studied. The sequential design is complex, but it permits human development researchers to disentangle the effects of age and cohort and answer questions about developmental change.

In summary, scientists use the scientific method to systematically ask and seek answers to questions about human development. Researchers' decisions about measures, such as whether to use self-report or observational measures, influence the information that they collect and the conclusions that they make. Choice of research method also influences conclusions researchers make about development, including statements about age differences, age change, and information about cohort effects. Researchers have responsibilities to conduct sound research and also to adhere to standards of ethical conduct in research, as the next section describes. See Table 1.8 for a comparison of research designs.

TABLE 1.7 • Sequential Research Design

	2020	2022	2024	2026	2028
6th grade	A	E	F		
8th grade	B	A	E	F	
10th grade	C	B	A	E	F
12th grade	D	C	B	A	E

sequential research design
A developmental design in which multiple groups of participants of different ages are followed over time, combining cross-sectional and longitudinal research.

A sequential design combines cross-sectional and longitudinal designs, permitting the researcher to study multiple cohorts over time.

Source: Table 1 from Kim & Böckenholt, *Psychological Methods*, 5(3), Sep 2000, 380–400.

TABLE 1.8 • Comparing Research Designs

DESIGN	STRENGTHS	LIMITATIONS
Research Designs		
Case study	Provides a rich description of an individual.	Conclusions may not be generalized to other individuals.
Correlational	Permits the analysis of relationships among variables as they exist in the real world.	Cannot determine cause and effect relations.
Experimental	Permits a determination of cause-and-effect relations.	Data collected artificial environments may not represent behavior in real-world environments.
Developmental Research Designs		
Longitudinal	Permits the determination of age-related changes in a sample of participants assessed for a period of time.	Requires a great deal of time, resources, and expense. Participant attrition may limit conclusions. Cohort-related changes may limit the generalizability of conclusions.
Cross-sectional	More efficient and less costly than the longitudinal design. Permits the determination of age differences.	Does not permit inferences regarding age change. Confounds age and cohort.
Sequential	More efficient and less costly than the longitudinal model. Allows for both longitudinal and cross-sectional comparisons which reveal age differences and age change, as well as cohort effects.	Time consuming, expensive, and complicated in data collection and analysis.

Thinking in Context 1.4

Dorothy is interested in understanding smoking in middle school students. Specifically, she believes that low self-esteem causes students to smoke.

1. How might Dorothy gather information to address her hypothesis?

2. What kind of research design should Dorothy use? What are the advantages and disadvantages of this design?

3. What are some of the challenges of measuring behaviors such as smoking and internal characteristics such as self-esteem?

4. How can her study be improved to overcome the weaknesses you have identified?

ETHICAL ISSUES IN RESEARCH

LO 1.5 Discuss the responsibility of researchers to their participants and how they may protect them.

Suppose a researcher wanted to determine the effects of an illegal drug on pregnant women, or the effects of malnutrition on kindergarteners. Would it be possible to design a study in which certain pregnant women were assigned to ingest the illegal drug? Or one in which certain kindergarteners were deprived of food? If you answered "no," you are correct, for United States and international laws regulate what kinds of research can be conducted and whether such research can expose participants to any harm, or risk of harm. These kinds of questions, laws, and regulations are in the realm of *ethics*—the determination of right and wrong.

Developmental scientists' work is guided by five ethical principles: (1) beneficence and nonmaleficence; (2) responsibility; (3) integrity; (4) justice; and (5) respect for autonomy (American Psychological Association, 2010). Beneficence and nonmaleficence are the dual responsibilities to do good and not to do harm. Researchers must protect and help the individuals, families, and communities with which they work by maximizing the benefits and minimizing the potential harms of their work. For example, when interviewing survivors of a natural disaster, such as an earthquake or tornado, a scientist pays attention to their participants' demeanor. If a participant shows distress in response to a particular set of questions, the scientist might direct, or even accompany, the participant to a therapist or mental health professional who can help him or her manage the distress.

Scientists act responsibly by adhering to professional standards of conduct, clarifying their obligations and roles to others, and avoiding conflicts of interest. For example, a psychologist who conducts research with children and parents must clarify her role as scientist and not therapist and help her participants understand that she is simply gathering information from them rather than conducting therapy. In this way, scientists recognize that they are *responsible* to people, communities, and society.

The principle of *integrity* requires that scientists be accurate, honest, and truthful in their work and make every effort to keep their promises to the people and communities with which they work.

Scientists have a special obligation to respect participants' *autonomy*, the ability to make and implement decisions. Scientists show respect for the individuals and families they work with by giving them information about the research study, answering questions, helping them to make their own decisions about whether to participate in the study, and accepting their decisions. Respecting people's autonomy also means protecting those who are not capable of making judgments and asserting themselves. For example, some adults, such as those who have suffered traumatic brain injuries, may have cognitive and social deficits that make them unable to make and carry out decisions about whether to participate in research. Scientists who work with patients who may be unable to make such judgments must carefully assess each patient's capacity and devise ways of protecting those who are not competent, such as by approaching the individual who is responsible for making legal decisions on the part of the patient.

Finally, the principle of *justice* means that the benefits and risks of participation in research must be spread equitably across individuals and groups. Scientists must take care to ensure that all people have access to the contributions and benefits of research.

These ethical principles form the basis of professional codes of ethics of the Society for Research in Child Development (2007) and American Psychological Association (2010), which provide guidelines for researchers who work with human participants.

RESPONSIBILITIES TO PARTICIPANTS

Researchers' desire to answer questions, learn, and solve problems by conducting research may sometimes conflict with the need to protect participants. For example, suppose a physician is testing the effectiveness of a drug designed to lower blood pressure.

The decision to participate in research must be reasoned, with an understanding of what is involved and that participation is voluntary.

Robert Kneschke/Shutterstock.com

Over the course of the study, the scientist discovers that a participant has a heart defect that might someday require treatment. If the scientist discloses this information to the participant and encourages him or her to seek treatment, the scientist will have to remove the participant from the study. How should the scientist balance the research needs with the needs of participants? Scientists work to balance the benefits of research against the possible harm that can occur to participants, which includes mental, emotional, and physical risks.

In the United States and most other developed countries, carrying out research is a regulated activity. Each college, university, hospital, and organization that conducts research has an institutional review board (IRB) that examines all plans for conducting a study before it can begin. The IRB examines the proposed study in light of professional ethical codes as well as those articulated by the U. S. Department of Health and Human Services (2009). Do the study's benefits for advancing knowledge and improving conditions of life outweigh the potential costs in terms of time, money, and possible harm on the part of participants? IRBs act to protect participants by ensuring that the study has scientific merit and that risks of participating in research do not outweigh its potential benefits.

Ethical codes of conduct require that researchers obtain **informed consent** from each participant—their informed, rational, and voluntary agreement to participate. Consent must be informed, meaning it is made with knowledge of the scope of the research, the potential for harm (if any), and the possible benefits of participating. Consent must be rational, meaning it must be made by a person capable of making a reasoned decision. Parents provide parental permission for their minor children to participate because researchers (and lawmakers) assume that minors are not able to meet the rational criteria of informed consent. Finally, participation must be voluntary, meaning that the decision to participate must be made freely and without coercion—individuals must understand that they are free to decide not to participate in the research study and that they will not be penalized in any way if they refuse.

Although children cannot provide informed consent, researchers respect their growing capacities for decision making in ways that are appropriate to their age by seeking *assent,* children's agreement to participate. For a young child, obtaining assent may involve simply asking if he or she wants to play with the researcher and answer some questions. With increasing cognitive and social development, children are better able to understand the nature of science and engage meaningfully in decisions about research participation (Thompson, 1990). Researchers should tailor discussions about the nature of research participation to children's capacities, provide more detailed information, and seek more comprehensive assent as children grow older (Kuther, 2003; Roth-Cline & Nelson, 2013). For example, a researcher about to administer early adolescents a questionnaire about their experiences with parental divorce might explain the kinds of questions the adolescents will encounter; explain that in some cases a question might feel personal and might bring up memories; remind the adolescents that they are free to stop or skip any questions they choose; and, finally, remind the adolescents that if they feel uncomfortable or would like to talk to someone about their feelings about the issues examined in the study, a counselor is available or the researcher can help them find someone who can help them. Moreover, seeking assent helps children learn how to make decisions and participate in decision-making as they are able. Assent provides minors with opportunities to gain decision-making experience within safe contexts.

The researcher's ethical responsibilities do not end with obtaining informed consent. Most research studies are routine and uneventful because they are carried out according to plan. Sometimes, however, ethical issues arise during the course of a study. For example, suppose a researcher learns that a participant is in jeopardy, whether engaging in health-compromising behaviors (e.g., cigarette smoking, unsafe driving, or unhealthy behavior), contemplating suicide, or engaging in illegal or harmful activities

informed consent A participant's informed (knowledge of the scope of the research and potential harm and benefits of participating), rational, and voluntary agreement to participate in a study.

(e.g., drug addiction, stealing, or violence). Is a researcher responsible for helping the participant? Although current ethical guidelines address questions of researchers' responsibilities to help participants in such situations, they leave a certain amount of judgment to the researcher.

The Society for Research in Child Development (SRCD) code of ethics (2007) suggests that researchers must help children in jeopardy by discussing the information with parents and guardians or with experts who may offer insight. Moreover, researchers may be faced with a conflict if they believe that helping the participant and dropping him or her from the research study may compromise the scientific integrity of the research, which may be especially likely if many participants are dropped. One study investigated this very issue by asking adolescents for their opinions on what researchers should do if they discover that a minor participant has a problem (Fisher, Higgins-D'Alessandro, Rau, Kuther, 1996). Older adolescents (e.g., age 17) tended to prefer that researchers not tell others about the problems and provide minors with self-referral information, whereas young adolescents (e.g., age 13) tended to prefer that researchers report problems and potential threats to parents or trusted adults (Fisher et al., 1996). In addition, the adolescents' judgments depended on how serious they believed each problem to be. Adolescents favored reporting serious problems like abuse and threats of suicide to a parent or adult who can help. However, they preferred that the researcher not tell anyone about the problem and provide the child with self-referral information in cases of problems they rated as less serious, like smoking and nonviolent delinquent acts. Many questions remain unresolved. For example, does the age of the child matter in determining when to provide help? These are difficult decisions. Fortunately, serious ethical issues do not arise in most studies, but scientists should remain vigilant so that problems can be addressed should they arise. Table 1.9 summarizes the rights of research participants.

TABLE 1.9 • Rights of Research Participants

RIGHT	DESCRIPTION
Protection from harm	Regardless of age, research participants have the right to be protected from physical and psychological harm. Investigators must use the least stressful research procedure in testing hypotheses and when in doubt, consult with others. When harm is possible, researchers must determine another way to study the problem or abandon the research.
Informed consent	Participants have the right to be informed about the purpose of the research, expected duration, procedures, risks and benefits of participation, and any other aspects of the research that may influence their willingness to participate. When children are participants, a parent or guardian must provide informed consent on behalf of the child. The child should be provided information about research participation in terms appropriate to his or her development and the investigator should seek assent from the child as a way of respecting the child's autonomy.
Voluntariness	Participants, regardless of age, have the right to choose not to participate or to discontinue participation in research at any time and without penalty.
Confidentiality	Participants have the right to conceal their identity on all information and reports obtained in the course of research.
Reporting results	Participants have the right to be informed of the results of research in language that is appropriate to their level of understanding.
Right to treatment	If an experimental treatment under investigation is believed to be beneficial, participants in control groups have the right to obtain the beneficial treatment.

Source: APA (2010); SRCD (2007).

RESPONSIBILITIES TO SOCIETY

Researchers are responsible not only to their participants but also to society at large. In reporting results, researchers should be mindful of the social and political implications of their work (SRCD, 2007). Researchers must consider how their findings will be portrayed in the media and attempt to foresee ways in which their results may be misinterpreted. This is a difficult task, but it is very important for researchers to be prepared to address questions raised as well as correct misinterpretations of research (National Academy of Sciences, 1995).

For example, one highly publicized study compiled the existing research literature examining college students who had become sexually involved with an adult prior to reaching the legal age of consent (Rind, Tromovitch, & Bauserman, 1998). After using statistics to summarize the findings of many research studies, the scientists determined that the college students' coping and development varied depending on a number of other factors within the individual, situation, and broader context. Not all appeared to be harmed and many did well. However, some organizations, media outlets, and politicians misinterpreted the researchers' findings as suggesting that sexual involvement with minors was acceptable or even beneficial (Garrison & Kobor, 2002). Instead, the findings suggested that there are a range of outcomes to adult–minor relationships, and that the outcomes varied with the age of the minor and other characteristics of the situation. For example, the participants who seemed to be unharmed were more likely to be older (e.g., age 17) when the relationship began. Researchers must consider the potential social and political implications of their work, attempt to foresee the inferences that people may draw about their findings, and prepare to correct misinterpretations.

Lifespan human development is a broad field of study that integrates theory and research from many disciplines in order to describe, predict, and explain how we grow and change throughout our lifetime. Developmental scientists apply their knowledge to identify, prevent, and solve problems, and improve opportunities for individuals, families, and communities. Throughout this book you will learn the fundamentals of lifespan human development, including physical, cognitive, and socioemotional change, as well the implications development science holds for social issues. We begin our journey by considering the role of genetics and environment in shaping who we become, as described in Chapter 2.

 Thinking in Context 1.5

1. Suppose, as part of your research, you wanted to interview children at school. What ethical principles should you keep in mind? Why? What challenges do you anticipate?

2. Consider collecting observations and interviews of older adults in a nursing home. What ethical issues can you anticipate? What principles are most pertinent?

 Apply Your Knowledge

1. Steven enters the school psychologist's office with a frown, grumbling to himself. His teacher, Ms. Marta, has suggested that he visit the school psychologist for help understanding and treating his academic problems. Steven is a bright fifth grader, but he has great difficulties reading and his mathematics skills lag far behind his peers. Ms. Marta contacts Steven's mother, reassuring her that the school has excellent resources for diagnosing children's learning problems and special education professionals who can intervene and help children overcome learning difficulties.

    The school psychologist interviews Steven's mother in order to compile a history of Steven's development. Through this interview he learns that Steven suffered a great deal of trauma early in life; as an infant he was physically abused by his biological mother, then taken away and placed in foster care. At age 3 he was adopted into a middle-class, suburban family with two older, non-adopted, children.

As we have seen, each developmental theory has a unique emphasis. How might each theory address Steven's academic difficulties?

(a) What factors would psychoanalytic theories point to in order to explain Steven's functioning?

(b) How would cognitively oriented theories, such as Piaget's cognitive-developmental theory and information processing theory, account for and intervene with Steven's difficulties?

(c) Identify contextual factors that may play a role in Steven's academic problems; from Bronfenbrenner's bioecological theory, what factors may be addressed?

2. Suppose you wanted to conduct research on academic achievement during elementary and middle school.

(a) Identify a research question appropriate for a correlational research study.

(b) How would you address that question with a cross-sectional research study? Longitudinal? Sequential?

(c) What are the advantages and disadvantages of each type of study?

Give your students the SAGE edge!

SAGE edge offers a robust online environment featuring an impressive array of free tools and resources for review, study, and further exploration, keeping both instructors and students on the cutting edge of teaching and learning. Learn more at **edge.sagepub.com/kuthertopical.**

CHAPTER 1 IN REVIEW

1.1 Outline five principles of the lifespan developmental perspective.

SUMMARY

Development is a lifelong process. It is multidimensional, multidirectional, plastic, influenced by the multiple contexts in which we are embedded, and multidisciplinary.

KEY TERMS

lifespan human development	resilience
physical development	context
cognitive development	culture
socioemotional development	cohort
plasticity	

REVIEW QUESTION

What are five principles developmental scientists use to explain lifespan development?

1.2 Discuss three theoretical controversies about human development.

SUMMARY

Theories of human development can be compared with respect to their stance on the following questions. First, in what ways is developmental change continuous, characterized by slow and gradual change; or discontinuous, characterized by sudden and abrupt change? Second, to what extent do people play an active role in their own development, interacting with and influencing the world around them? Finally, is development caused by nature or nurture—genetic endowments and heredity or the physical and social environment? Most developmental scientists agree that some aspects of development appear continuous and others discontinuous, individuals are active in influencing their development, and development reflects the interactions of nature and nurture.

KEY TERMS

continuous (development)	nature-nurture issue
discontinuous (development)	

REVIEW QUESTION

What position do most contemporary developmental scientists take on each of the three theoretical controversies about human development?

1.3 Summarize five theoretical perspectives on human development.

SUMMARY

Freud's psychosexual theory explains personality development as progressing through a series of psychosexual stages during childhood. Erikson's psychosocial theory suggests that individuals move through eight stages of psychosocial development across the lifespan, with each stage presenting a unique psychosocial task, or crisis. Behaviorist theory emphasizes environmental influences on behavior, specifically classical conditioning and operant conditioning. In classical conditioning neutral stimuli become associated with stimuli that elicit reflex responses. Operant conditioning emphasizes the role of environmental stimuli in shaping behavior through reinforcement and punishment. Bandura's social learning theory includes cognition, and Bandura suggested that individuals and the environment interact and influence each other through reciprocal determinism. Piaget's cognitive-developmental theory explains that children actively interact with the world around them and their cognition develops through four stages. Information processing theorists study the steps entailed in cognition: perceiving and attending, representing, encoding, retrieving, and problem solving. Sociocultural systems theories look to the importance of context in shaping development. Vygotsky's sociocultural theory emphasizes interactions with members of our culture in influencing development. Bronfenbrenner's bioecological model explains development as a function of the ongoing reciprocal interaction among biological and psychological changes in the person and his or her changing context: the microsystem, mesosystem, exosystem, macrosystem, and chronosystem. Ethology and evolutionary developmental psychology integrate Darwinian principles of evolution and scientific knowledge about the interactive influence of genetic and environmental mechanisms.

KEY TERMS

theory	cognitive schemas
hypotheses	information processing theory
Psychoanalytic theories	sociocultural theory
behaviorism	bioecological systems theory
classical conditioning	microsystem
operant conditioning	mesosystem
reinforcement	exosystem
punishment	macrosystem
social learning theory	chronosystem
observational learning	ethology
reciprocal determinism	evolutionary developmental
cognitive-developmental	theory
perspective	psychosocial development

REVIEW QUESTION

How do five major theoretical perspectives account for human development?

1.4 Describe the methods used in studying human development, including types of data and designs.

SUMMARY

A case study is an in-depth examination of an individual. Interviews and questionnaires are called self-report measures because they ask the persons under study questions about their own experiences, attitudes, opinions, beliefs, and behavior. Observational measures are methods that scientists use to collect and organize information based on watching and monitoring people's behavior. Physiological measures gather the body's physiological responses as data. Scientists use correlational research to describe relations among measured characteristics, behaviors, and events. To test hypotheses about causal relationships among variables, scientists employ experimental research. Developmental designs include cross-sectional research, which compares groups of people at different ages simultaneously, and longitudinal research, which studies one group of participants at many points in time. Sequential designs combine the best features of cross-sectional and longitudinal designs, by assessing assess multiple cohorts over time.

KEY TERMS

applying developmental science	experimental research
scientific method	dependent variable
open-ended interview	independent variable
structured interview	random assignment
questionnaire	cross-sectional research
naturalistic observation	longitudinal research
structured observation	sequential research
correlational research	design

REVIEW QUESTIONS

1. What are methods for collecting data and answering research questions?
2. What designs do researchers use to study development?

1.5 Discuss the responsibility of researchers to their participants and how they may protect them.

SUMMARY

Researchers must maximize the benefits to research participants and minimize the harms, safeguarding participants' welfare. They must be accurate and honest in their work and respect participants' autonomy, including seeking informed consent and child assent. In addition, the benefits and risks of participation in research must be spread equitably across individuals and groups.

KEY TERM

informed consent

REVIEW QUESTION

What ethical responsibilities do researchers have to their participants?

Test your understanding of the content.
Review the flashcards and quizzes at
edge.sagepub.com/kuthertopical

PRACTICE AND APPLY WHAT YOU'VE LEARNED

▶ **edge.sagepub.com/kuthertopical**

PART II

Biological Development and Health

Physical development is perhaps the most easily recognizable developmental change that we experience over our lives. It comprises growth and maturation, and changes in sensory, neurological, and motor abilities.

Physical development begins at conception with the formation of a zygote. Our traits are influenced by complex interactions of genes and contextual factors, such as environmental circumstances, stressors, and opportunities, that determine whether genetic potentials are realized.

Most of us are born with all of our senses—able to see, hear, smell, taste, and touch. Likewise, we are born with billions of brain cells called neurons. As we develop, the number of connections among neurons increases, and neural communication becomes quicker, contributing to more efficient cognition. Brain development continues throughout life. Some neural plasticity, the capacity to change in response to experience, is retained in adulthood.

Like other aspects of physical development, motor development unfolds in a predictable sequence in infancy and childhood and continues to change over the lifespan. In adulthood the rate and extent of change varies. Adults who remain physically active can compensate for age-related declines and may retain their strength, balance, and endurance as well as experience better overall health and well-being, with positive implications for cognitive and socioemotional functioning in the many contexts in which they live.

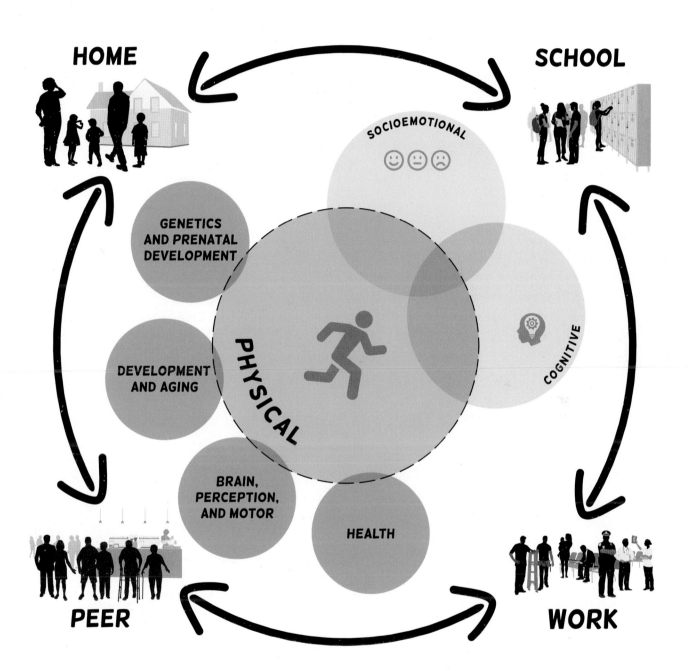

HOME

SCHOOL

SOCIOEMOTIONAL

GENETICS AND PRENATAL DEVELOPMENT

DEVELOPMENT AND AGING

PHYSICAL

COGNITIVE

BRAIN, PERCEPTION, AND MOTOR

HEALTH

PEER

WORK

Biological and Environmental Foundations and Prenatal Development

Learning Objectives

2.1 Describe the process of cell reproduction and patterns of genetic inheritance.

2.2 Define and provide examples of genetic disorders and chromosomal abnormalities.

2.3 Explain how the dynamic interactions of heredity and environment influence development.

2.4 Discuss the stages of prenatal development, stages of childbirth, and challenges for infants at risk.

2.5 Identify the principles of teratology, types of teratogens, and ways that teratogens can be used to predict prenatal outcomes.

Digital Resources

🔊 Sickle Cell Disease

📄 Genomic Imprinting

▶ Iceland's Down Syndrome Dilemma

🔊 Amniocentesis

▶ Twins Separated at Birth

⏏ Holocaust Survivors' Trauma

▶ Ultrasound

▶ The Process of Childbirth

📄 Fetal Alcohol Spectrum Disorders

⏏ Marijuana During Pregnancy

Master these learning objectives with multimedia resources available at **edge.sagepub.com/kuthertopical** and *Lives in Context* video cases available in the interactive eBook.

"Roger and Ricky couldn't be more different," marveled their mother. "People are surprised to find out they are brothers." Roger is tall and athletic, with blond hair and striking blue eyes. He spends most afternoons playing ball with his friends and often invites them home to play in the yard. Ricky, two years older than Roger, is much smaller, thin and wiry. He wears thick glasses over his brown eyes that are nearly as dark as his hair. Unlike his brother, Ricky prefers solitary games and spends most afternoons at home playing video games, building model cars, and reading comic books. How can Roger and Ricky have the same parents and live in the same home yet differ markedly in appearance, personality, and preferences? In this chapter, we discuss the process of genetic inheritance and principles that can help us to understand how members of a family can share a great many similarities—and many differences. We also examine the process by which a single cell containing genes from two biological parents develops over a short period of time into an infant.

GENETIC FOUNDATIONS OF DEVELOPMENT

LO 2.1 Describe the process of cell reproduction and patterns of genetic inheritance.

Although Roger is quite different from his older brother, Ricky, he shares so many of his father's characteristics that most people comment on the strong physical resemblance. In other ways, however, Roger is more like his highly sociable mother. Ricky also shares similarities with each of his parents: In physical appearance, he resembles his mother and her brothers, but his quiet personality is similar to that of his father. Most of us learn early in life, and take it for granted, that children tend to resemble their parents. But to understand just how parents transmit their inborn characteristics and tendencies to their children, we must consider the human body at a cellular level.

GENETICS

The human body is composed of trillions of units called cells. Within each cell is a nucleus that contains 23 matching pairs of rod-shaped structures called **chromosomes** (Plomin, DeFries, Knopik, & Neiderhiser, 2013). Each chromosome holds the basic units of heredity, known as genes, composed of stretches of **deoxyribonucleic acid (DNA)**, a complex molecule shaped like a twisted ladder or staircase. The 20,000 to 25,000 genes that reside within our chromosomes are the blueprint for creating all of the traits that organisms carry (Barlow-Stewart, 2012; Finegold, 2013). People around the world share 99.7% of their genes (Watson, 2008). Although all humans share the same basic genome, or set of genetic instructions, every person has a slightly different code, making him or her genetically distinct from other humans.

chromosome One of 46 rodlike molecules that contain 23 pairs of DNA found in every body cell and collectively contain all of the genes.

DNA Deoxyribonucleic acid; the chemical structure, shaped like a twisted ladder, that contains all of the genes.

FIGURE 2.1: Meiosis and Mitosis

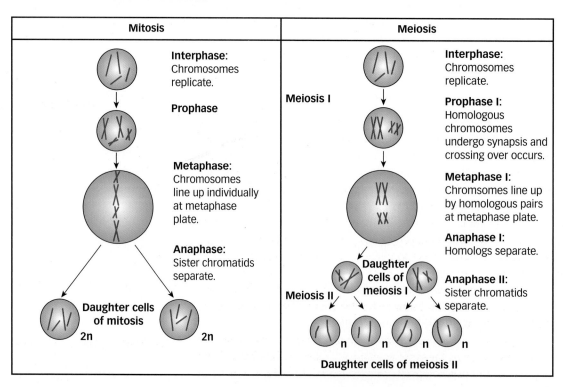

Cell Reproduction

Most cells in the human body reproduce through a process known as **mitosis**, in which DNA replicates itself, permitting the duplication of chromosomes and, ultimately, the formation of new cells with identical genetic material (Sadler, 2015). Sex cells reproduce in a different way, called **meiosis**, which results in gametes (sperm in males and ova in females; see Figure 2.1). Gametes each contain 23 chromosomes (one-half of the 46 chromosomes, or 23 pairs, present in body cells). This permits the joining of sperm and ovum at fertilization to produce a fertilized egg, or **zygote**, with 46 chromosomes forming 23 pairs, half from the biological mother and half from the biological father. Each gamete has a unique genetic profile. It is estimated that individuals can produce millions of versions of their own chromosomes (National Library of Medicine, 2013).

As shown in Figure 2.2, 22 of the 23 pairs of chromosomes are matched; they contain similar genes in almost identical positions and sequence, reflecting the distinct genetic blueprint of the biological mother and father. The 23rd pair are sex chromosomes that specify the biological sex of the individual. In females, sex chromosomes consist of two large X-shaped chromosomes (XX). Males' sex chromosomes consist of one large X-shaped chromosome and one much smaller Y-shaped chromosome (XY; Moore & Persaud, 2016; Plomin et al., 2013).

Because females have two X sex chromosomes, all ova contain one X sex chromosome. Males' sex chromosome pair includes both X and Y chromosomes. Therefore, one half of the sperm males produce contains an X chromosome and one half contains a Y. Whether the fetus develops into a boy or girl is determined by which sperm fertilizes the ovum. If the ovum is fertilized by a Y sperm, a male fetus will develop, and if the ovum is fertilized by an X sperm, a female fetus will form, as shown in Figure 2.3.

FIGURE 2.2: Chromosomes

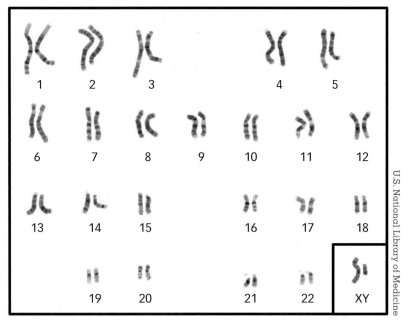

autosomes   sex chromosomes

U.S. National Library of Medicine

mitosis The process of cell duplication in which DNA is replicated and the resulting cell is genetically identical to the original.

meiosis The process by which a gamete is formed, containing one-half of the cell's chromosomes producing creating ova and sperm with 23 single, unpaired chromosomes.

zygote A fertilized ovum.

Genes Shared by Twins

Twins are siblings who share the same womb. Twins occur in about 1 out of every 30 births in the United States (Martin, Hamilton, & Osterman, 2012). About two-thirds of naturally conceived twins are **dizygotic (DZ) twins**, or fraternal twins, conceived when a woman releases more than one ovum and each is fertilized by a different sperm. DZ twins share about one-half of their genes and, like other siblings, most fraternal twins differ in appearance, with different hair color, eye color, and height. In about half of fraternal twin pairs, one twin is a boy and the other a girl. DZ twins tend to run in families, suggesting a genetic component that controls the tendency for a woman to release more than one ovum each month. However, rates of DZ twins also increase with in vitro fertilization, maternal age, and with each subsequent birth (Fletcher, Zach, Pramanik, & Ford, 2012; Martin et al., 2012).

Monozygotic (MZ) twins, or identical twins, originate from the same zygote, sharing the same genotype with identical instructions for all physical and psychological characteristics. MZ twins occur when

FIGURE 2.3: Sex Determination

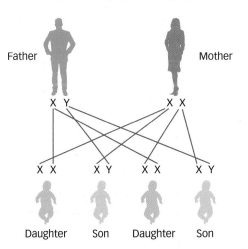

Monozygotic, or identical, twins share 100% of their DNA.

the zygote splits into two separate but identical zygotes that develop into two infants. It is estimated that MZ twins occur in 4 of every 1,000 U.S. births (Fletcher et al., 2012). The causes of MZ twinning are not well understood. Temperature fluctuations are associated with MZ births in animals, but it is unknown whether similar effects occur in humans (Aston, Peterson, & Carrell, 2008). In vitro fertilization and advanced maternal age (35 and older) may increase the occurrence of MZ twins (Aston et al., 2008; Knopman et al., 2014).

PATTERNS OF GENETIC INHERITANCE

Although the differences among various members of a given family may appear haphazard, they are the result of a genetic blueprint unfolding. Researchers are just beginning to uncover the instructions contained in the human genome, but we have learned that traits and characteristics are inherited in predictable ways.

Dominant–Recessive Inheritance

Lynn has red hair while her brother, Jim, does not—and neither do their parents. How did Lynn end up with red hair? These outcomes can be explained by patterns of genetic inheritance, how the sets of genes from each parent interact. As we have discussed, each person has 23 pairs of chromosomes, one pair inherited from the mother and one from the father. The genes within each chromosome can be expressed in different forms, or *alleles*, that influence a variety of physical characteristics. When alleles of the pair of chromosomes are alike with regard to a specific characteristic, such as hair color, the person is said to be **homozygous** for the characteristic and will display the inherited trait. If they are different, the person is **heterozygous**, and the trait expressed will depend on the relations among the genes (Moore & Persaud, 2016; National Center for Biotechnology Information, 2004). Some genes are passed through **dominant–recessive inheritance**, in which some genes are dominant and are always expressed regardless of the gene they are paired with. Other genes are recessive and will be expressed only if paired with another recessive gene (see Table 2.1).

dizygotic (DZ) twin Also known as a fraternal twin; occurs when two ova are released and each is fertilized by a different sperm; the resulting offspring share 50% of the genetic material.

monozygotic (MZ) twin Also known as an identical twin; occurs when the zygote splits apart early in development. The resulting offspring share 100% of their genetic material.

homozygous Refers to a chromosomal pair consisting of two identical alleles.

heterozygous Refers to a chromosomal pair consisting of two different alleles.

dominant–recessive inheritance A form of genetic inheritance in which the phenotype reflects only the dominant allele of a heterozygous pair.

TABLE 2.1 • Dominant and Recessive Characteristics

DOMINANT TRAIT	RECESSIVE TRAIT
Dark hair	Blond hair
Curly hair	Straight hair
Hair	Baldness
Non-red hair	Red hair
Facial dimples	No dimples
Brown eyes	Blue, green, hazel eyes
Second toe longer than big toe	Big toe longer than second toe
Type A blood	Type O blood
Type B blood	Type O blood
Rh-positive blood	Rh-negative blood
Normal color vision	Color blindness

Source: McKusick (1998); McKusick-Nathans Institute of Genetic Medicine (2014).

Lynn and Jim's parents are heterozygous for red hair; both have dark hair, but they each carry a recessive gene for red hair. When an individual is heterozygous for a particular trait, the dominant gene is expressed, and the person becomes a carrier of the recessive gene, as shown in Figure 2.4.

Incomplete Dominance

In most cases, dominant–recessive inheritance is an oversimplified explanation for patterns of genetic inheritance. **Incomplete dominance** is a genetic inheritance pattern in which both genes influence the characteristic (Plomin et al., 2013). For example, consider blood type. Neither the alleles for blood type A and B dominate each other. A heterozygous person with the alleles for blood type A and B will express both A and B alleles and have blood type AB.

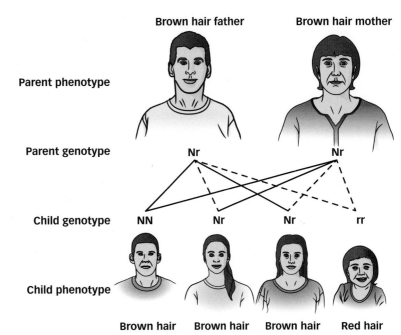

FIGURE 2.4: Dominant–Recessive Inheritance

Brown hair father   Brown hair mother

Parent phenotype

Parent genotype   Nr   Nr

Child genotype   NN   Nr   Nr   rr

Child phenotype

Brown hair   Brown hair   Brown hair   Red hair

A different type of inheritance pattern is seen when a person inherits heterozygous alleles in which one allele is stronger than the other yet does not completely dominate. In this situation, the stronger allele does not mask all of the effects of the weaker allele. Therefore some, but not all, characteristics of the recessive allele appear. For example, the trait for developing normal blood cells does not completely mask the allele for developing sickle-shaped blood cells. About 8% of African Americans (and relatively few Caucasians or Asian Americans) carry the recessive **sickle cell trait** (Ashley-Koch, Yang, & Olney, 2000; Ojodu, Hulihan, Pope, & Grant, 2014). Sickle cell alleles cause red blood cells to become crescent, or sickle, shaped. Cells that are sickle-shaped cannot distribute oxygen effectively throughout the circulatory system (Ware, de Montalembert, Tshilolo, & Abboud, 2017). However, sickle cell carriers do not develop full-blown sickle cell anemia. Carriers of the trait for sickle cell anemia may function normally but may show some symptoms such as reduced oxygen distribution throughout the body and exhaustion after exercise. Only individuals who are homozygous for the recessive sickle cell trait develop sickle cell anemia.

incomplete dominance
A genetic inheritance pattern in which both genes are expressed in the phenotype.

Polygenic Inheritance

Hereditary influences act in complex ways, and researchers cannot trace most characteristics to only one or two genes. Most traits are a function of the interaction of many genes, known as **polygenic inheritance**. Examples of polygenic traits include height, intelligence, temperament, and susceptibility to certain forms of cancer (Bouchard, 2014; Plomin et al., 2013). As the number of genes that contribute to a trait increases, so does the range of possible traits. Genetic propensities interact with environmental influences to produce a wide range of individual differences in human traits.

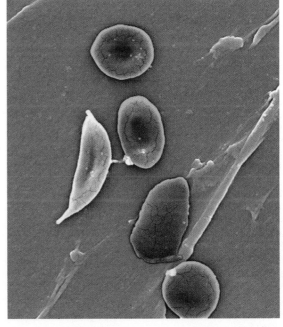

Recessive sickle cell alleles cause red blood cells to become crescent shaped and unable to distribute oxygen effectively throughout the circulatory system. Alleles for normal blood cells do not mask all of the characteristics of recessive sickle cell alleles, illustrating incomplete dominance.

Genomic Imprinting

The principles of dominant–recessive and incomplete dominance inheritance can account for more than 1,000 human traits (McKusick, 2007). However, a few traits are determined by a process known as **genomic imprinting**. Genomic imprinting refers to the instance in which the expression of a gene is determined by whether it is inherited from the mother or the father (Kelly & Spencer, 2017; National Library of Medicine, 2013). For example, consider two conditions that illustrate genomic imprinting: Prader-Willi syndrome and Angelman syndrome. Both syndromes are caused by an abnormality in the 15th chromosome (Kalsner & Chamberlain, 2015). If the abnormality occurs on chromosome 15 acquired by the father, the individual—whether a daughter or son—will develop Prader-Willi syndrome, a set of specific physical and behavioral characteristics including obesity, insatiable hunger, short stature, motor slowness, and mild to moderate intellectual impairment. If the abnormal chromosome 15 arises from the mother, the individual—again, whether it is a daughter or a son—will develop Angelman syndrome, characterized by hyperactivity, thin body frame, seizures, disturbances in gait, and severe learning disabilities including severe problems with speech. Prader-Willi and Angelman syndromes each occur in about 1 in 15,000 persons (Everman & Cassidy, 2000). Patterns of genetic inheritance can be complex, yet they follow predictable principles. For a summary of patterns of genetic inheritance, refer to Table 2.2.

TABLE 2.2 • Summary: Patterns of Genetic Inheritance

INHERITANCE PATTERN	DESCRIPTION
Dominant–recessive inheritance	Genes that are dominant are always expressed, regardless of the gene they are paired with, and recessive genes are expressed only if paired with another recessive gene.
Incomplete dominance	Both genes influence the characteristic, and aspects of both genes appear.
Polygenic inheritance	Polygenic traits are the result of interactions among many genes.
Genomic imprinting	The expression of a gene is determined by whether it is inherited from the mother or the father.

Thinking in Context 2.1

1. Why do twins occur? From an evolutionary developmental perspective, does twinning serve an adaptive purpose for our species? Why or why not?

2. Consider your own physical characteristics, such as hair and eye color. Are they indicative of recessive traits or dominant ones?

3. Do you think that you might be a carrier of recessive traits? Why or why not?

CHROMOSOMAL AND GENETIC PROBLEMS

LO 2.2 Define and provide examples of genetic disorders and chromosomal abnormalities.

Many disorders are caused by inherited genes. Some disorders and abnormalities are the result of dominant–recessive inheritance to which one or both parents contribute. Others are the result of variations in chromosomes.

sickle cell trait A recessive trait, more often affecting African Americans than Caucasians or Asian Americans, that causes red blood cells to become crescent or sickle shaped, resulting in difficulty distributing oxygen throughout the circulatory system.

polygenic inheritance Occurs when a trait is a function of the interaction of many genes, such as with height, intelligence, and temperament.

genomic imprinting The instance when the expression of a gene is determined by whether it is inherited from the mother or father.

GENETIC DISORDERS

Disorders and abnormalities that are inherited through the parents' genes include such well-known conditions as cystic fibrosis and sickle cell anemia, as well as others that are rare and, in some cases, never even noticed throughout the individual's life.

Dominant–Recessive Disorders

Recall that in dominant–recessive inheritance, dominant genes are always expressed, regardless of the gene they are paired with, and recessive genes are expressed only if paired with another recessive gene. Table 2.3 illustrates diseases that are inherited through dominant–recessive inheritance. Few severe disorders are inherited through dominant–recessive inheritance because individuals who inherit the allele often do not survive long enough to reproduce and pass it to the next generation. One exception is Huntington's disease, a fatal disease in which the central nervous system deteriorates (National Library of Medicine, 2013; Sadler, 2015). Individuals with the Huntington's allele develop normally in childhood, adolescence, and young adulthood. Symptoms of Huntington's disease do not appear until age 35 or later. By then, many individuals have already had children, and one half of them, on average, will inherit the dominant Huntington's gene.

Phenylketonuria (PKU) is a common recessive disorder that prevents the body from producing an enzyme that breaks down the amino acid phenylalanine from proteins (Blau, van Spronsen, & Levy, 2010; Romani et al., 2017). Without treatment, the phenylalanine builds up quickly to toxic levels that damage the central nervous system, contributing to intellectual developmental disability, once known as mental retardation. PKU illustrates how genes interact with the environment to produce developmental outcomes because

phenylketonuria (PKU)
A recessive disorder that prevents the body from producing an enzyme that breaks down phenylalanine (an amino acid) from proteins, that, without treatment, leads to buildup that damages the central nervous system.

TABLE 2.3 • Diseases Inherited Through Dominant–Recessive Inheritance

DISEASE	OCCURRENCE	MODE OF INHERITANCE	DESCRIPTION	TREATMENT
Huntington's disease	1 in 20,000	Dominant	Degenerative brain disorder that affects muscular coordination and cognition	No cure; death usually occurs 10 to 20 years after onset
Cystic fibrosis	1 in 2,000–2,500	Recessive	An abnormally thick, sticky mucus clogs the lungs and digestive system, leading to respiratory infections and digestive difficulty	Bronchial drainage, diet, gene replacement therapy
Phenylketonuria (PKU)	1 in 8,000–10,000	Recessive	Inability to digest phenylalanine that, if untreated, results in neurological damage and death	Diet
Sickle cell anemia	1 in 500 African Americans	Recessive	Sickling of red blood cells leads to inefficient distribution of oxygen throughout the body that leads to organ damage and respiratory infections	No cure; blood transfusions, treat infections, bone marrow transplant; death by middle age
Tay-Sachs disease	1 in 3,600 to 4,000 descendants of Central and Eastern European Jews	Recessive	Degenerative brain disease	None; most die by 4 years of age

Source: McKusick-Nathans Institute of Genetic Medicine (2014).

Chris Walker/MCT/Newscom

This young man is diagnosed with fragile X syndrome, a recessive disorder carried on the X chromosome and the most common form of inherited intellectual impairment.

intellectual disability results from the interaction of the genetic predisposition and exposure to phenylalanine from the environment (Blau, 2016a). The United States and Canada require all newborns to be screened for PKU (Blau, Shen, & Carducci, 2014). If the disease is discovered, the infant is placed on a diet low in phenylalanine. Children who maintain a strict diet usually attain average or near-average levels of intelligence (Blau, 2016; Widaman, 2009). Some cognitive and psychological problems may appear in childhood and persist into adulthood, particularly difficulty in attention and planning skills, emotional regulation, depression, and anxiety (Blau et al. 2010; Enns et al., 2010; Huijbregts, Gassió, & Campistol, 2013).

X-Linked Disorders

Some recessive genetic disorders are carried on the X chromosome, like the gene for hemophilia, a condition in which the blood does not clot normally (Barlow-Stewart, 2012). Males are more likely to be affected by X-linked genetic disorders because they have only one X chromosome, and therefore any genetic marks on their X chromosome are displayed. Females (XX) have two X chromosomes; a recessive gene located on one X chromosome will be masked by a dominant gene on the other X chromosome. Females are, therefore, less likely to display X-linked genetic disorders because both of their X-chromosomes must carry the recessive genetic disorder for it to be displayed. In contrast, **fragile X syndrome** is an example of a dominant–recessive disorder carried on the X chromosome (Hagerman, 2011). Because the gene is dominant, it need appear on only one X chromosome to be displayed. That means that fragile X syndrome occurs in both males and females. Table 2.4 illustrates diseases acquired through X-linked inheritance.

TABLE 2.4 • Diseases Acquired Through X-Linked Inheritance

SYNDROME/ DISEASE	OCCURRENCE	DESCRIPTION	TREATMENT
Color blindness	1 in 12 males	Difficulty distinguishing red from green; less common is difficulty distinguishing blue from green	No cure
Duchenne muscular dystrophy	1 in 3,500 males	Weakness and wasting of limb and trunk muscles; progresses slowly but will affect all voluntary muscles	Physical therapy, exercise, body braces; survival rare beyond late 20s
Fragile X syndrome	1 in 2,000 males	Symptoms include cognitive impairment; attention problems; anxiety; unstable mood; long face; large ears; flat feet; and hyperextensible joints, especially fingers	No cure
Hemophilia	1 in 3,000–7,000 males	Blood disorder in which the blood does not clot	Blood transfusions

Source: McKusick-Nathans Institute of Genetic Medicine (2016)

fragile X syndrome An example of a dominant–recessive disorder carried on the X chromosome.

CHROMOSOMAL ABNORMALITIES

Chromosomal abnormalities are the result of errors during cell reproduction, meiosis, or mitosis or damage caused afterward. Occurring in 1 of about every 700 births, the most widely known chromosome disorder is trisomy 21, more commonly called **Down syndrome** (Parker et al., 2010). Down syndrome occurs when a third chromosome appears alongside the 21st pair of chromosomes. Although individuals with Down syndrome vary in the severity of their symptoms, Down syndrome is associated with marked physical, health, and cognitive attributes, including a short, stocky build and striking facial features, such as a round face, almond-shaped eyes, and a flattened nose

Down syndrome Also known as trisomy 21; a condition in which a third, extra chromosome appears at the 21st site. Down syndrome is associated with distinctive physical characteristics accompanied by developmental disability.

TABLE 2.5 • Sex Chromosome Abnormalities

FEMALE GENOTYPE	SYNDROME	DESCRIPTION	PREVALENCE
XO	Turner	As adults, they are short in stature, often have small jaws with extra folds of skin around their necks (webbing), lack prominent female secondary sex characteristics, such as breasts, and show abnormal development of the ovaries. Elevated risk for thyroid disease, vision and hearing problems, heart defects, diabetes, and autoimmune disorders.	1 in 2,500 females
XXX	Triple-X	Grow about an inch or so taller than average, with unusually long legs and slender torsos, and show normal development of sexual characteristics and fertility. Because many cases of triple-X syndrome often go unnoticed, little is known about the syndrome.	Unknown
MALE GENOTYPE	**SYNDROME**	**DESCRIPTION**	**PREVALENCE**
XXY	Klinefelter	Symptoms range in severity from unnoticeable to severe symptoms such as a high-pitched voice, feminine body shape, breast enlargement, and infertility. Many boys and men with Klinefelter syndrome have short stature, a tendency to be overweight, and language and short-term memory impairments that can cause difficulties in learning.	1 in 500 to 1 in 1,000
XYY	XYY, Jacob's Syndrome	Accompanied by high levels of testosterone.	Prevalence of XYY syndrome is uncertain as most men with XYY syndrome are unaware that they have a chromosomal abnormality

Sources: Bardsley et al. (2013); Bird & Hurren (2016); Herlihy & McLachlan (2015); National Library of Medicine (2013); Otter, Schrander-Stumpel, & Curfs (2009); Pinsker (2012); Powell & Schulte (2011).

Down syndrome is the most common cause of intellectual disability. Children with Down syndrome show more positive developmental outcomes when adults are sensitive to their needs. Interventions that encourage children to interact with their environment can promote motor, social, and emotional development.

(Davis & Escobar, 2013; Kruszka et al., 2017). Children with Down syndrome tend to show delays in physical and motor development relative to other children and health problems such as congenital heart defects, vision impairments, poor hearing, and immune system deficiencies (Ram & Chinen, 2011; Zampieri et al., 2014). Down syndrome is the most common genetic cause of intellectual developmental disability (Davis & Escobar, 2013), but children's abilities vary. Children who participate in early intervention and receive sensitive caregiving and encouragement to explore their environment show positive outcomes, especially in the motor, social, and emotional areas of functioning (Hazlett, Hammer, Hooper, & Kamphaus, 2011).

Advances in medicine have addressed many of the physical health problems associated with Down syndrome so that today, many individuals with Down syndrome live well into middle age, with an average life expectancy of 60 (Glasson, Dye, & Bittles, 2014; Torr, Strydom, Patti, & Jokinen, 2010). As more adults age with Down syndrome, we have discovered a link between Down syndrome and Alzheimer's disease, a brain degenerative disease that typically strikes in older adulthood (Hithersay, Hamburg, Knight, & Strydom, 2017; Wiseman et al., 2015). This is an example of how disorders and illnesses can be influenced by multiple genes and complex contextual interactions; in this case, Down syndrome and Alzheimer's disease share genetic markers.

Some of the most common chromosomal abnormalities concern the 23rd pair of chromosomes: the sex chromosomes. Given their different genetic makeup, sex chromosome abnormalities yield different effects in males and females. They are summarized in Table 2.5.

MUTATION

Not all inborn characteristics are inherited. Some result from **mutations**, sudden changes and abnormalities in the structure of genes that occur spontaneously or may be induced by exposure to environmental toxins such as radiation and agricultural chemicals in food (Burns & Bottino, 1989; Lewis, 2006). A mutation may involve only one gene or many. It is estimated that as many as one-half of all conceptions include mutated chromosomes (Plomin et al., 2013). Most mutations are fatal—the developing organism dies very soon after conception, often before the woman knows she is pregnant (Lewis, 2006; Rimoin, Connor, & Pyeritz, 1997).

Sometimes mutations are beneficial. This is especially true if the mutation is induced by stressors in the environment and provides an adaptive advantage to the individual. For example, the sickle cell gene is a mutation that originated in areas where malaria is widespread, such as Africa. Children who inherited a single sickle cell allele were more resistant to malarial infection and more likely to survive and pass it along to their offspring (Allison, 2004; Gong, Parikh, Rosenthal, & Greenhouse, 2013). The sickle cell gene is not helpful in places of the world where malaria is not a risk. The frequency of the gene is decreasing in areas of the world where malaria is uncommon. For example, only 8% of African Americans are carriers, compared with as many as 30% of black Africans in some African countries (Maakaron & Taher, 2017). Therefore, the developmental implications of genotypes—and mutations—are context specific, posing benefits in some contexts and risks in others.

mutation A sudden permanent change in the structure of genes.

PREDICTING AND DETECTING GENETIC DISORDERS

The likelihood of genetic disorders often can be predicted before conception. Moreover, advances in technology permit abnormalities to be detected earlier than ever before.

Genetic Counseling

When considering having children, many couples seek genetic counseling to determine the risk of their children inheriting genetic defects and chromosomal abnormalities (Uhlmann, Schuette, & Yashar, 2009). The genetic counselor constructs a family history of heritable disorders for both prospective parents. If either member of the couple appears to carry a genetic disorder, genetic screening blood tests may be carried out on both parents to detect chromosomal abnormalities and the presence of dominant and recessive genes for various disorders.

Candidates for genetic counseling include those whose relatives have a genetic condition, couples who have had difficulties bearing children, women over the age of 35, and couples from the same ethnic group. Once prospective parents learn about the risk of conceiving a child with a disorder, they can determine how to proceed—whether to conceive a child naturally or through the use of in vitro fertilization—after screening gametes for the disorders of concern. Given advances in our knowledge of genetic disorders and ability to screen for them, some argue that genetic counseling should be available to all prospective parents (Minkoff & Berkowitz, 2014).

Prenatal Diagnosis

Prenatal testing is recommended when genetic counseling has determined a risk for genetic abnormalities, when the woman is older than age 35, when both parents are members of an ethnicity at risk for particular genetic disorders, or when fetal development appears abnormal (Barlow-Stewart & Saleh, 2012). Technology has advanced rapidly, equipping professionals with an array of tools to assess the health of the fetus. Table 2.6 summarizes methods of prenatal diagnosis.

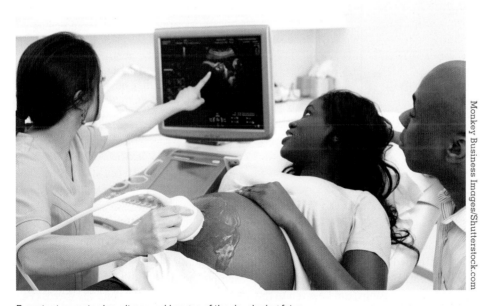

Expectant parents view ultrasound images of the developing fetus.

TABLE 2.6 • Methods of Prenatal Diagnosis

METHOD	EXPLANATION	ADVANTAGES	DISADVANTAGES
Ultrasound	High-frequency sound waves directed at the mother's abdomen provide clear images of the womb projected on to a video monitor.	Ultrasound enables physicians to observe the fetus, measure fetal growth, reveal the sex of the fetus, and to determine physical abnormalities in the fetus.	Many abnormalities and deformities cannot be easily observed.
Amniocentesis	A small sample of the amniotic fluid that surrounds the fetus is extracted from the mother's uterus through a long, hollow needle inserted into the mother's abdomen. The amniotic fluid contains fetal cells. The fetal cells are grown in a laboratory dish in order to create enough cells for genetic analysis.	It permits a thorough analysis of the fetus's genotype. There is 100% diagnostic success rate.	Safe, but poses a greater risk to the fetus than ultrasound. If conducted before the 15th week of pregnancy, it may increase the risk of miscarriage.
Chorionic villus sampling (CVS)	Chorionic villus sampling requires studying a small amount of tissue from the chorion, part of the membrane surrounding the fetus, for the presence of chromosomal abnormalities. The tissue sample is obtained through a long needle inserted either abdominally or vaginally, depending on the location of the fetus.	It permits a thorough analysis of the fetus's genotype. CVS is relatively painless, and there is a 100% diagnostic success rate. Can be conducted earlier than amniocentesis, between 10 and 12 weeks.	It may pose a higher rate of spontaneous abortion and limb defects when conducted prior to 10 weeks' gestation.
Noninvasive prenatal testing (NIPT)	Cell-free fetal DNA is examined by drawing blood from the mother.	There is no risk to the fetus. It can diagnose several chromosomal abnormalities.	It cannot yet detect the full range of abnormalities. It may be less accurate than other methods. Researchers have identified the entire genome sequence using NIPT, suggesting that someday NIPT may be as effective as other, more invasive techniques.

Sources: Akolekar, Beta, Picciarelli, Ogilvie, & D'Antonio (2015); Chan, Kwok, Choy, Leung, & Wang (2013); Fan et al. (2012); Gregg et al. (2013); Odibo (2015); Shahbazian, Barati, Arian, & Saadati (2012); Shim et al. (2014); Tabor & Alfirevic (2010); Theodora et al. (2016).

Prenatal Treatment of Genetic Disorders

What happens when a genetic or chromosomal abnormality is found? Advances in genetics and in medicine have led to therapies that can be administered prenatally to reduce the effects of many genetic abnormalities. For example, hormones and other drugs, as well as blood transfusions, can be given to the fetus by inserting a needle into the uterus (Fox & Saade, 2012; Lindenburg, van Kamp, & Oepkes, 2014). Most strikingly, fetal surgery can repair defects of the heart, lung, urinary tract, and other areas (Danzer & Johnson, 2014; Sala et al., 2014). Researchers believe that one day we may be able to treat many heritable disorders thorough genetic engineering, by synthesizing normal genes to replace defective ones. It may someday be possible to sample cells from an embryo, detect harmful genes and replace them with healthy ones, then return the healthy cells to the embryo, where they will reproduce and correct the genetic defect (Coutelle & Waddington, 2012). This approach has been used to correct certain heritable disorders in animals and holds promise for treating humans.

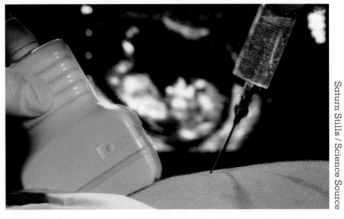

During amniocentesis, ultrasound is used to guide the insertion of a long, hollow needle into the mother's abdomen in order to extract a sample of the amniotic fluid that surrounds the fetus. The amniotic fluid contains fetal cells, which are grown in a laboratory dish and tested for genetic and chromosomal anomalies and defects.

Thinking in Context 2.2

1. Discuss how PKU illustrates the following two themes in human development: (1) the role of nature and nurture in development and (2) interactions among domains of development.

2. Identify risk factors for genetic and chromosomal disorders. What can prospective parents do to minimize the risks? What specific advice do you give?

3. Suppose you are a 36-year-old woman pregnant with your first child. What would be the advantages and disadvantages of the four types of prenatal diagnostic testing described in Table 2.6? What information would your health care provider need in order to recommend testing appropriate for your particular case?

HEREDITY AND ENVIRONMENT

LO 2.3 Explain how the dynamic interactions of heredity and environment influence development.

We have learned a great deal about genetic inheritance. Most human traits, however, are influenced by a combination of genes working in concert with environmental influences. Our genetic makeup, inherited from our biological parents, consists of a complex blend of hereditary characteristics known as genotype. Our **genotype** is a biological influence on all of our traits, from hair and eye color to personality, health, and behavior. However, our **phenotype**, the traits we ultimately show, such as our specific eye or hair color, is not determined by genotypes alone. Phenotypes are influenced by the interaction of genotypes and our experiences.

BEHAVIORAL GENETICS

Behavioral genetics is the field of study that examines how genes and experience combine to influence the diversity of human traits, abilities, and behaviors (Maxson, 2013; Plomin et al., 2013). Genotypes alone do not determine people's traits, characteristics, or personalities; instead, development is the process by which our genetic inheritance (genotype) is expressed in observable characteristics and behaviors (phenotype). Behavioral geneticists recognize that even traits that have a strong genetic component, such as height, are modified by environmental influences (Dubois et al., 2012; Plomin, DeFries, Knopik, & Neiderhiser, 2016). Moreover, most human traits, such as intelligence, are influenced by multiple genes, and there are often multiple variants of each gene (Bouchard, 2014; Chabris, Lee, Cesarini, Benjamin, & Laibson, 2015).

genotype An individual's collection of genes that contain instructions for all physical and psychological characteristics, including hair, eye color, personality, health, and behavior.

phenotype The observable physical or behavioral characteristics of a person, eye, hair color, or height.

behavioral genetics The field of study that examines how genes and environment combine to influence the diversity of human traits, abilities, and behaviors.

Methods of Behavioral Genetics

Behavioral geneticists devise ways of estimating the heritability of specific traits and behaviors. **Heritability** refers to the extent to which variation among people on a given characteristic is due to genetic differences. The remaining variation not due to genetic differences is instead a result of the environment and experiences. Heritability research therefore examines the contributions of the genotype but also provides information on the role of experience in determining phenotypes (Plomin & Daniels, 2011). Behavioral geneticists assess the hereditary contributions to behavior by conducting selective breeding and family studies (Maxson, 2013).

Using selective breeding studies, behavioral geneticists deliberately modify the genetic makeup of animals to examine the influence of heredity on attributes and behavior. For example, in a classic study, behavioral geneticists demonstrated that they can breed mice to be very physically active or sedentary. They selectively breed highly active mice only with each other and, similarly, breed mice with a very low level of activity with each other. Over subsequent generations, mice bred for high levels of activity become many times more active than those bred for low levels of activity (DeFries, Gervais, & Thomas, 1978). Selective breeding in rats, mice, and other animals such as chickens has revealed genetic contributions to many traits and characteristics, such as aggressiveness, emotionality, sex drive, and even maze learning (Plomin et al., 2016).

Behavioral geneticists conduct *family studies* to compare people who live together and share varying degrees of relatedness. Two kinds of family studies are common: twin studies and adoption studies (Koenen, Amstadter, & Nugent, 2012). Twin studies compare identical and fraternal twins to estimate how much of a trait or behavior is attributable to genes. If genes affect the attribute, identical twins should be more similar than fraternal twins because identical twins share 100% of their genes whereas fraternal twins share about only 50%. Adoption studies, on the other hand, compare the degree of similarity between adopted children and their biological parents whose genes they share (50%) and their adoptive parents with whom they share no genes. If the adopted children share similarities with their biological parents, even though they were not raised by them, it suggests that the similarities are genetic.

Adoption studies also shed light on the extent to which attributes and behaviors are influenced by the environment. For example, the degree to which two genetically unrelated adopted children reared together are similar speaks to the role of environment. Comparisons of identical twins reared in the same home with those reared in different environments can also illustrate environmental contributions to phenotypes. If identical twins reared together are more similar than those reared apart, an environmental influence can be inferred.

Genetic Influences on Personal Characteristics

Research examining the contribution of genotype and environment to intellectual abilities has found a moderate role for heredity. Twin studies have shown that identical twins consistently have more highly correlated scores than do fraternal twins. For example, a study of intelligence in over 10,000 twin pairs showed a correlation of .86 for identical and .60 for fraternal twins (Plomin & Spinath, 2004). Table 2.7 summarizes the results of comparisons of intelligence scores from individuals who share different genetic relationships with each other. Note that correlations for all levels of kin are higher when they are reared together, supporting the role of environment. Average correlations also rise with increases in shared genes.

Genes contribute to many other traits, such as sociability, anxiety, temperament, obesity, happiness, and susceptibility to various illnesses such as heart disease and cancer, poor mental health, and a propensity to be physically aggressive (H. Chen et al., 2013; Pemment, 2013; Veroude et al., 2016; Yoon-Mi, 2009). Yet even traits that are thought to be heavily influenced by genetics can be modified by physical and social interventions.

heritability A measure of the extent to which variation of a certain trait can be traced to genes.

TABLE 2.7 • Average Correlation of Intelligence Scores From Family Studies for Related and Unrelated Kin Reared Together or Apart

	REARED TOGETHER	REARED APART
MZ twins (100% shared genes)	.86	.72
DZ twins (50% shared genes)	.60	.52
Siblings (50% shared genes)	.47	.24
Biological parent/child (50% shared genes)	.42	.22
Half-siblings (25% shared genes)	.31	—
Unrelated (adopted) siblings (0% shared genes)*	.34	—
Nonbiological parent/child (0% shared genes)*	.19	—

Notes: * Estimated correlation for individuals sharing neither genes nor environment = .0; MZ = monozygotic; DZ = dizygotic.

Source: Adapted from Bouchard & McGue (1981).

For example, growth, body weight, and body height are largely predicted by genetics, yet environmental circumstances and opportunities influence whether genetic potentials are realized (Dubois et al., 2012). Even identical twins who share 100% of their genes are not 100% alike. Those differences are due to the influence of environmental factors, which interact with genes in a variety of ways.

GENE-ENVIRONMENT INTERACTIONS

"You two are so different. Edward and Evan, are you sure you're twins?" kidded Aunt Joan. As fraternal twins, Edward and Evan share 50% of their genes and are reared in the same home. One might expect them to be quite similar, but their similar genes are not the whole story. Genes do not act alone in shaping our development. Instead, genes and the environment work together in complex way to determine our characteristics; behavior; physical, cognitive, and social development; and health (Chabris et al., 2015; Rutter, 2012). **Gene–environment interactions** refer to the dynamic interplay between our genes and our environment. Several principles illustrate these interactions.

Range of Reaction

Everyone has a different genetic makeup and therefore responds to the environment in a unique way. In addition, any one genotype can be expressed in a variety of phenotypes. There is a **range of reaction** (see Figure 2.5), a wide range of potential expressions of a genetic trait, depending on environmental opportunities and constraints (Gottlieb, 2000). For example, consider height. Height is largely a function of genetics, yet an individual may show a range of sizes depending on environment and behavior. Suppose that a child is born to two very tall parents. She may have the genes to be tall, but unless she has adequate nutrition, she will not fulfill her genetic potential for height. In societies in which nutrition has improved dramatically over a generation, it is common for children to tower over their parents. The enhanced environmental opportunities, in this case nutrition, enabled the children to fulfill their genetic potential for height. Therefore, a genotype sets boundaries on the range of possible phenotypes, but the phenotypes ultimately displayed vary in response to different environments (Manuck & McCaffery, 2014). In this way, genetics

gene–environment interactions Refer to the dynamic interplay between our genes and our environment in determining out characteristics, behavior, physical, cognitive, and social development as well as health.

range of reaction The concept that a genetic trait may be expressed in a wide range of phenotypes dependent on environmental opportunities and constraints.

FIGURE 2.5: Range of Reaction

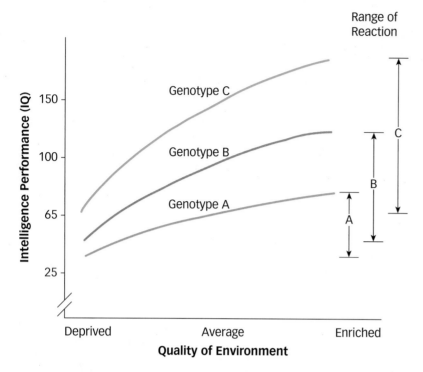

Source: Gottlieb (2007).

sets the range of development outcomes and the environment influences where, within the range, that person will fall.

Canalization

Some traits illustrate a wide reaction range. Others are examples of **canalization**, in which heredity narrows the range of development to only one or a few outcomes. Canalized traits are biologically programmed, and only powerful environmental forces can change their developmental path (Flatt, 2005; Waddington, 1971). For example, infants follow an age-related sequence of motor development, from crawling, to walking, to running. Around the world, most infants walk at about 12 months of age. Generally, only extreme experiences or changes in the environment can prevent this developmental sequence from occurring. For example, children reared in impoverished Romanian and Ethiopian orphanages and exposed to extreme environmental deprivation demonstrated delayed motor development, with some children not walking by 2 years of age (Miller, Tseng, Tirella, Chan, & Feig, 2008; Wilson, 2003). The Lives in Context feature examines gene–environment interactions and responses to child maltreatment.

Motor development is not entirely canalized, however, because some minor changes in the environment can subtly alter its pace and timing. For example, practice facilitates stepping movements in young infants, prevents the disappearance of stepping movements in the early months of life, and leads to an earlier onset of walking (Ulrich, Lloyd, Tiernan, Looper, & Angulo-Barroso, 2008; Zelazo, Zelazo, Cohen, & Zelazo, 1993). These observations demonstrate that even highly canalized traits, such as motor development, which largely unfolds via maturation, can be subtly influenced by contextual factors.

Gene–Environment Correlations

Heredity and environment are each powerful influences on development. Not only do they interact, but heredity and environmental factors are often correlated with each other (Plomin & Asbury, 2001; Scarr & McCartney, 1983). **Gene–environment correlation** refers to the idea that many of our traits are supported by both our genes and environment (Plomin, DeFries, & Loehlin, 1977). Genes give rise to behaviors, which are associated with the environment (Knafo & Jaffee, 2013). There are three types of gene–environment correlations—passive, reactive, and active—as shown in Figure 2.6.

Parents create homes that reflect their own genotypes. Because parents are genetically similar to their children, the homes that they create are not only in line with their own interests and preferences but they also correspond with the child's genotype—an example of a *passive gene–environment correlation* (Wilkinson, Trzaskowski, Haworth, & Eley, 2013). For example, parents might provide genes that predispose a child to develop music ability and also provide a home environment that supports the development of music ability, such as by playing music in the home and owning musical instruments. This type

canalization The tendency for a trait that is biologically programmed to be restricted to only a few outcomes.

gene–environment correlation The idea that many of an individual's traits are supported by his or her genes and environment; there are three types of correlations: passive, reactive, and active.

LIVES IN CONTEXT

• • Gene–Environment Interactions and Responses to Child Maltreatment

The MAOA gene influences adaptation to adversity, such as the trauma of child maltreatment

Children who are maltreated or abused by their parents are at risk for developing many problems, including aggression and violent tendencies. Yet not all children who are maltreated become violent adolescents and adults. Why? A classic study examined this question.

Caspi and colleagues (2002) followed a sample of males from birth until adulthood and observed that not all maltreated boys developed problems with violence. Only boys who carried a certain type of gene were at risk for becoming violent after experiencing maltreatment. Specifically, there are two versions of a gene that controls monoamine oxidase A (MAOA), an enzyme that regulates specific chemicals in the brain; one produces high levels of the enzyme and the other produces low levels. Boys who experienced abuse and other traumatic experiences were about twice as likely to develop problems with aggression, violence, and to even be convicted

of a violent crime—but only if they carried the low-MAOA gene. Maltreated boys who carried the high-MAOA gene were no more likely to become violent than non-maltreated boys. In addition, the presence of the low MAOA gene itself was not associated with violence. The low-MAOA gene predicted violence only for boys who experience abuse early in life. These findings have been replicated in another 30-year longitudinal study of boys (Fergusson, Boden, Horwood, Miller, & Kennedy, 2011) as well as a meta-analysis of 27 studies (Byrd & Manuck, 2014).

Similar findings of a MAOA gene x environment interaction in which low-MAOA, but not high-MAOA, predicts negative outcomes in response to childhood adversity has been extended to include other mental health outcomes such as antisocial personality disorder and depression (Beach et al., 2010; Cicchetti, Rogosch, & Sturge-Apple, 2007; Manuck & McCaffery, 2014; Nikulina, Widom, & Brzustowicz, 2012). Many of these studies have examined only males. Females show a more mixed pattern with some studies showing that girls display the MAOA gene x environment interaction but to a much lesser extent than boys whereas other studies suggest no relationship (Byrd & Manuck, 2014).

Although there is no single gene that will predict general developmental outcomes, these findings suggest that some genes may increase or decrease our risk for problems in the presence of particular contexts (Belsky & Hartman, 2014a; Conradt, 2017).

In addition, some genes might increase our sensitivity to, and the effectiveness of, environmental interventions (Bakermans-Kranenburg & van IJzendoorn, 2015). Just as we may adjust contextual factors to contribute to successful developmental outcomes and resilience, in the future we might learn how to "turn on" protective genes and "turn off" those that contribute to risk.

What Do You Think?

1. In your view, how important are genetic contributors to development?

2. If some genes may be protective in particular contexts, should scientists learn how to turn them on? Why or why not? What about genes that may be harmful in particular contexts?

of gene–environment correlation is seen early in life because children are reared in environments that are created by their parents, who share their genotype.

People naturally evoke responses from others and the environment, just as the environment and the actions of others evoke responses from the individual. In an *evocative gene–environment correlation*, a child's genetic traits (e.g., personality characteristics including openness to experience) influence the social and physical environment, which

FIGURE 2.6: Gene–Environment Correlation

The availability of instruments in the home corresponds to the child's musical abilities and she begins to play guitar (passive gene–environment correlation). As she plays guitar, she evokes positive responses in others, increasing her interest in music (evocative gene–environment correlation). Over time she seeks opportunities to play, such as performing in front of an audience (niche-picking).

shape development in ways that support the genetic trait (Burt, 2009; Klahr, Thomas, Hopwood, Klump, & Burt, 2013). For example, active, happy infants tend to receive more adult attention than do passive or moody infants (Deater-Deckard & O'Connor, 2000), and even among infant twins reared in the same family, the more outgoing and happy twin receives more positive attention than does the more subdued twin (Deater-Deckard, 2001). Why? Babies who are cheerful and smile often influence their social world by evoking smiles from others, which in turn support the genetic tendency to be cheerful. In this way, genotypes influence the physical and social environment to respond in ways that support the genotype. Children who engage in disruptive play tend to later experience problems with peers (Boivin et al., 2013). To return to the music example, a child with a genetic trait for music talent will evoke pleasurable responses (e.g., parental approval) when she plays music; this environmental support, in turn, encourages further development of the child's musical trait. In addition, some individuals may be more affected by environmental stimuli due to their genetic makeup (Belsky & Hartman, 2014).

Children also take a hands-on role in shaping their development. Recall from Chapter 1 that a major theme in understanding human development is the finding that individuals are active in their development; here we have an example of this pattern. As children grow older, they have increasing freedom in choosing their own activities and environments. An *active gene–environment correlation* occurs when the child actively creates experiences and environments that correspond to and influence his genetic predisposition. For example, the child with a genetic trait for interest and ability in music actively seeks experiences and environments that support that trait, such as friends with similar interests and after-school music classes. This tendency to actively seek out experiences and environments compatible and supportive of our genetic tendencies is called **niche-picking** (Scarr & McCartney, 1983).

niche-picking An active gene–environment correlation in which individuals seek out experiences and environments that complement their genetic tendencies.

FIGURE 2.7: Development Stage and Gene–Environment Correlations

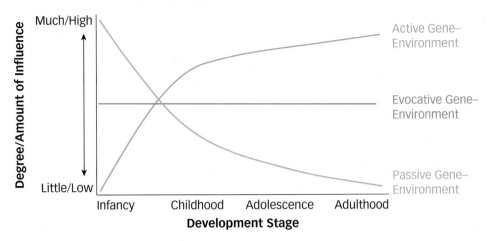

The strength of passive, evocative, and active gene–environment correlations changes with development, as shown in Figure 2.7 (Scarr, 1992). Passive gene–environment correlations are common at birth as caregivers determine infants' experiences. Correlations between their genotype and environment tend to occur because their environments are made by genetically similar parents. Evocative gene–environment correlations also occur from birth, as infants' inborn traits and tendencies influence others, evoking responses that support their own genetic predispositions. In contrast, active gene–environment correlations take place as children grow older and more independent (Scarr & McCartney, 1983). As they become increasingly capable of controlling parts of their environment, they engage in niche-picking by choosing their own interests and activities, actively shaping their own development. Niche-picking contributes to the differences we see in siblings, including fraternal twins, as they grow older. But identical twins tend to become more similar over time, perhaps because they are increasingly able to select the environments that best fit their genetic propensities (Bouchard et al., 2004; Steves, Spector, & Jackson, 2012). As they age, identical twins—even those reared apart—become alike in attitudes, personality, cognitive ability, intelligence, and preferences; as well, they select similar spouses and best friends (Briley & Tucker-Drob, 2013; Plomin & Deary, 2015; Rushton & Bons, 2005).

EPIGENETIC FRAMEWORK

We have seen that every aspect of our development is the result of dynamic interactions of heredity and environment. Without a doubt, genes provide a biological foundation for our development. However, genes never act alone in determining human characteristics. Moreover, genes themselves may show stable changes not due to DNA (Holliday, 2006a; Lux, 2013). The dynamic interplay between heredity and environment is known as the **epigenetic framework** (Gottlieb, 2003, 2007; Lickliter & Honeycutt, 2013). From this perspective, development results from ongoing reciprocal interactions between genetics and environment.

Genes provide a blueprint for development, determining a range of reaction in which characteristics may develop, depending on environmental circumstances. Not all genes are expressed, however. Genetic expression is influenced by epigenetics (Crews, Gillette, Miller-Crews, & Gore, 2014; Holliday, 2006b; Lester, Conradt, & Marsit, 2016). The term *epigenetics* literally means "above the gene." The epigenome is a molecule that stretches along the length of DNA and provides instructions to genes, determining how they are expressed and whether they are turned on or off. Epigenetic mechanisms determine how genetic instructions are carried out to determine the phenotype. At birth, each cell in our body turns on only a fraction of its genes. Genes continue to be turned on and off over

epigenetic framework A perspective stating that development results from reciprocal interactions between genetics and the environment such that the expression of genetic inheritance is influenced by environmental forces.

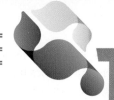

• • Altering the Epigenome

These two mice are genetically identical. Both carry the agouti gene but in the yellow mouse the agouti gene is turned on all the time. In the brown mouse it is turned off.

One of the earliest examples of epigenetics is the case of agouti mice, which carry the agouti gene. Mice that carry the agouti gene have yellow fur, are extremely obese, shaped much like a pincushion, and prone to diabetes and cancer. When agouti mice breed, most of the offspring are identical to the parents—yellow, obese, and susceptible to life shortening disease. However, a groundbreaking study showed that yellow agouti mice can produce offspring that look very different (Waterland & Jirtle, 2003). The mice in the photo above both carry the agouti gene, yet they look very different; the brown mouse is slender, lean, and has a low risk of developing diabetes and cancer, living well into old age.

Why are these mice so different? Epigenetics. The epigenome carries the instructions that determine what each cell in your body will become—a heart cell, muscle cell, or brain cell, for example. Those instructions are carried out by turning genes on and off.

In the case of the yellow and brown mice, the phenotype of the brown mice has been altered, but the DNA remains the same. Both carry the agouti gene, but in the yellow mouse the agouti gene is turned on all the time. In the brown mouse, it is turned off. In 2003, Waterland and Jirtle discovered that the agouti female's diet can determine her offspring's phenotype.

In this study, female mice were fed foods containing chemicals that attach to a gene and turn it off. These chemical clusters are found in many foods such as onions, garlic, beets, soy, and the nutrients in prenatal vitamins. Yellow agouti mothers fed extra nutrients passed along the agouti gene to their offspring, but it was turned off. The mice looked radically different from them (brown) and were healthier (lean, not susceptible to disease) even though they carried the same genes.

Another example supports the finding that the prenatal environment can alter the epigenome and influence the lifelong characteristics of offspring. Pregnant mice were exposed to a chemical (bisphenol-A or BPA, found in certain plastics). When female mice were fed BPA two weeks prior to conception, the number of offspring with the yellow obese coat color signaling an activated agouti gene increased (Dolinoy, 2008). When the pregnant mice were exposed to BPA plus nutritional supplementation (folic acid and an ingredient found in soy products), the offspring tended to be slender and have brown coats, signaling that the agouti gene was turned off. These findings suggest that the prenatal environment can influence the epigenome—and thereby influence how genes are expressed—and that nutrition has the potential to buffer harm.

The most surprising finding emerging from studies of epigenetics, however, is that the epigenome can be influenced by the environment before birth and can be passed by males and females from one generation to the next without changing the DNA itself (Soubry, Hoyo, Jirtle, & Murphy, 2014; Szyf, 2015). This means that what you eat and do today could affect the epigenome—the development, characteristics, and health—of your children, grandchildren, and great grandchildren (Bale, 2015; Vanhees, Vonhögen, van Schooten, & Godschalk, 2014).

What Do You Think?

1. Much of the research on epigenetics examines animals, but there is a growing body of work studying humans. In what ways, if any, might you expect research findings based on people to differ from the findings of animal research, described previously? Explain.

2. What might you do to "care for" your epigenome? Identify activities and behaviors that you think might affect the health of your genome.

the course of development and also in response to the environment (Gottlieb, 2000). In this way, even traits that are highly canalized can be influenced by the environment. Environmental factors such as toxins, injuries, crowding, diet, and responsive parenting can influence the expression of genetic traits.

For example, consider brain development. Providing an infant with a healthy diet and opportunities to explore the world will support the development of brain cells, governed by genes that are switched on or off. Brain development influences motor development, further supporting the infant's exploration of the physical and social world, thereby promoting cognitive and social development. Active engagement with the world encourages connections among brain cells. Exposure to toxins might suppress the activity of some genes, potentially influencing brain development and its cascading effects on motor, cognitive, and social development. In this way, brain development, like all other aspects of development, is influenced by dynamic interactions between biological and environmental factors.

Evocative gene–environmental correlations and niche-picking illustrate the ways in which genetically expressed characteristics can influence the environment. Genes, and the epigenome, influence development and experience, yet gene expression is also influenced by development and experience, as illustrated in Figure 2.8 (Dodge & Rutter, 2011). These complex gene–environment interactions mean that humans are more than their genes. Interactions between heredity and environment change throughout development as does the role we play in constructing environments that support our genotypes, influence our epigenome, and determine who we become. For a striking example of epigenetics, see the Applying Developmental Science feature.

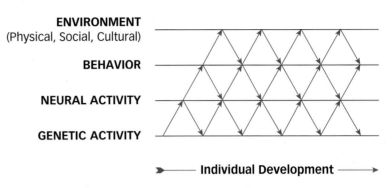

FIGURE 2.8: Epigenetic Framework

BIDIRECTIONAL INFLUENCES

Source: Gottlieb (2007).

 Thinking in Context 2.3

To answer the following questions, begin by thinking about how your own development reflects interactions among your genes and sociocultural context. Then, describe a skill, ability, or hobby in which you excel.

1. How might a passive gene–environment correlation account for this ability? For example, in what ways has the context in which you were raised shaped this ability?

2. In what ways might this ability be influenced by an evocative-genetic-environment correlation?

3. Provide an example of how this ability might reflect an active gene–environment correlation.

4. Which genetic-environment correlation do you think most accurately accounts for your skill, ability, or hobby?

5. How might you apply the epigenetic framework to account for your ability?

PRENATAL DEVELOPMENT

LO 2.4 Discuss the stages of prenatal development, stages of childbirth, and challenges for infants at risk.

Remarkably, a human infant progresses from fertilization to birth in just 166 days or 38 weeks. Conception, the union of **ovum** and sperm, marks the beginning of prenatal development, the transformative process in which the fertilized ovum, or zygote, progresses through several periods of development, finally emerging from the womb as a neonate. Prenatal development takes place over several stages representing shifts in developmental processes.

GERMINAL PERIOD (FIRST 2 WEEKS AFTER CONCEPTION)

During the **germinal period**, also known as the period of the zygote, the newly created zygote begins cell division as it travels down the fallopian tube, where fertilization took place, toward the uterus. About 30 hours after conception, the zygote then splits down

ovum The female reproductive cell or egg cell.

germinal period Also referred to as the period of the zygote, refers to the first two weeks after conception.

FIGURE 2.9: Germinal Period

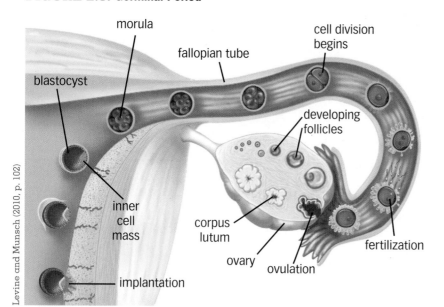

Levine and Munsch (2010, p. 102)

cell differentiation Begins roughly 72 hours after fertilization when the organism consists of about 16 to 32 cells.

blastocyst A thin-walled, fluid-filled sphere containing an inner mass of cells from which the embryo will develop; is implanted into the uterine wall during the germinal period.

embryo Prenatal organism between about 2 and 8 weeks after conception; a period of major structural development.

implantation The process by which the blastocyst becomes attached to the uterine wall, completed by about 10 days after fertilization.

the middle, forming two identical cells (Moore & Persaud, 2016; Sadler, 2015). As shown in Figure 2.9, the two cells each split to form four cells, then eight, and so on. This process of cell division continues at a rapid pace. Any of these cells may become a person (or two, in the case of monozygotic or identical twins).

Cell differentiation begins roughly 72 hours after fertilization when the organism consists of about 16 to 32 cells. Differentiation means that the cells begin to specialize and are no longer identical. At 4 days, the organism consists of about 60 to 70 cells formed into a hollow ball called a **blastocyst**, a fluid-filled sphere with cells forming a protective circle around an inner cluster of cells from which the **embryo** will develop.

Implantation, in which the blastocyst burrows into the wall of the uterus, begins at about day 6 and is complete by about day 11 (Moore & Persaud, 2016; Sadler, 2015). By the end of the second week, when fully implanted into the uterine wall, the outer layer of the blastocyst begins to develop into part of the **placenta**, the principal organ of exchange between the mother and developing organism. The placenta will enable the exchange of nutrients, oxygen, and wastes via the umbilical cord. Also during this stage, the developing organism is encased in amniotic fluid, providing temperature regulation, cushioning, and protection from shocks.

EMBRYONIC PERIOD (3 TO 8 WEEKS AFTER CONCEPTION)

By the third week after conception, the developing organism—now called an embryo—begins a period of structural development during which the most rapid developments of the prenatal period take place. All of the organs and major body systems form during

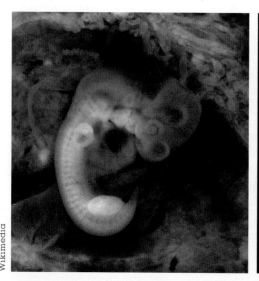

Wikimedia

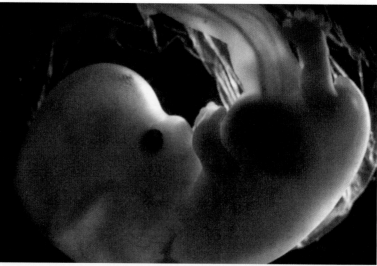

Petit Format / Science Source

Development proceeds very quickly during the embryonic period. Note the dramatic changes from the fifth week (left) to the seventh week (right) of prenatal development.

this **embryonic period**. The mass of cells composing the embryonic disk develops into two layers: The *ectoderm*, the upper layer, will become skin, nails, hair, teeth, sensory organs, and the nervous system; and the *endoderm*, the lower layer, will become the digestive system, liver, lungs, pancreas, salivary glands, and respiratory system. The middle layer, the *mesoderm*, forms later and will become muscles, skeleton, circulatory system, and internal organs.

During the third week, at about 22 days after conception, the endoderm folds to form the **neural tube**, which will develop into the central nervous system (brain and spinal cord; Moore & Persaud, 2016; Stiles & Jernigan, 2010). Now the head can be distinguished. A blood vessel that will become the heart begins to pulse and blood begins to circulate throughout the body (Dye, 2000; Larsen, 2001). During days 26 and 27 arm buds appear, followed by leg buds on days 28 through 30 (Moore & Persaud, 2016; Sadler, 2015). The brain develops rapidly and the head grows faster than the other parts of the body during the fifth week of development. The eyes, ears, nose, and mouth begin to form during the sixth week. Upper arms, forearms, palms, legs, and feet appear. The embryo shows reflex responses to touch.

During the seventh week, webbed fingers and toes are apparent; they separate completely by the end of the eighth week. A ridge called the **indifferent gonad** appears; it will develop into the male or female genitals, depending on the fetus's sex chromosomes (Moore & Persaud, 2016). The Y chromosome of the male embryo instructs it to secrete testosterone, causing the indifferent gonad to create testes. In female embryos, no testosterone is released, and the indifferent gonad produces ovaries. The sex organs take several weeks to develop. The external genital organs are not apparent until about 12 weeks.

At the end of the embryonic period, 8 weeks after conception, the embryo weighs about one-seventh of an ounce and is one inch long. All of the basic organs and body parts have formed in a very rudimentary way. The embryo displays spontaneous reflexive movements, but it is still too small for the movements to be felt by the mother (Hepper, 2015). Serious defects that emerge during the embryonic period often cause a miscarriage, or *spontaneous abortion* (loss of the fetus); indeed, most miscarriages are the result of chromosomal abnormalities (Bainbridge, 2003; Suzumori & Sugiura-Ogasawara, 2010). The most severely defective organisms do not survive beyond the first trimester, or third month of pregnancy. It is estimated that up to 45% of all conceptions abort spontaneously, and most occur before the pregnancy is detected (Larsen, 2001; Moore & Persaud, 2016).

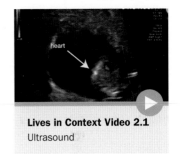

Lives in Context Video 2.1
Ultrasound

FETAL PERIOD (9 WEEKS TO BIRTH)

The fetal period is marked by the appearance of bone—at about the end of the eighth week. From 9 weeks until birth, the fetus grows rapidly, and its organs become more complex and begin to function. The end of the third month marks the close of the first trimester, at which time all parts of the fetus's body can move spontaneously, the legs kick, and the fetus can suck its thumb (an involuntary reflex). By the end of the 12th week, the upper limbs have almost reached their final relative lengths, but the lower limbs are slightly shorter than their final relative lengths (Sadler, 2015).

Second Trimester (14 to 26 Weeks)

By the 14th week, at the start of the second trimester, limb movements are coordinated, but they will be too slight to be felt by the mother until about 17 to 20 weeks. The heartbeat gets stronger. Eyelids, eyebrows, fingernails, toenails, and tooth buds form. The first hair to appear is **lanugo**, a fine down-like hair that covers the fetus's body; it is gradually replaced by human hair (Dye, 2000). The skin is covered with a greasy material called the **vernix caseosa**, which protects the fetal skin from abrasions, chapping, and hardening that can

placenta The principal organ of exchange between the mother and the developing organism, enabling the exchange of nutrients, oxygen, and wastes via the umbilical cord.

embryonic period Occurs about 2 to 8 weeks after pregnancy, in which rapid structural development takes place.

neural tube Forms during the third week after conception and will develop into the central nervous system (brain and spinal cord).

indifferent gonad A gonad in an embryo that has not yet differentiated into testes or ovaries.

lanugo A fine, down-like hair that covers the fetus's body.

vernix caseosa Greasy material that protects the fetal skin from abrasions, chapping, and hardening that can occur from exposure to amniotic fluid.

occur with exposure to amniotic fluid (Moore & Persaud, 2016). At 21 weeks, rapid eye movements begin, signifying an important time of growth and development for the fetal brain. The brain begins to become more responsive. For example, startle responses have been reported at 22 to 23 weeks in response to sudden vibrations and noises (Hepper, 2015; Sadler, 2015). During weeks 21 to 25, the fetus gains substantial weight, and its body proportions become more like those of a newborn infant. Growth of the fetal body begins to catch up to the head, yet the head remains disproportionately larger than the body at birth.

Third Trimester (27 to 40 Weeks)

During the last 3 months of pregnancy, the fetal body grows substantially in weight and length; specifically, it typically gains over 5 pounds and grows 7 inches. At about 28 weeks after conception brain development grows in leaps and bounds. The cerebral cortex develops convolutions and furrows, taking on the brain's characteristic wrinkly appearance (Dye, 2000). The fetal brain wave pattern shifts to include occasional bursts of activity, similar to the sleep-wake cycles of newborns. By 30 weeks, the pupils of the eyes dilate in response to light. At 35 weeks, the fetus has a firm hand grasp and spontaneously orients itself toward light.

During the third trimester, pregnant women and their caregivers are mindful that the baby may be born prematurely. Although the expected date of delivery is 166 days or 38 weeks from conception (40 weeks from the mother's last menstrual period), about one in every eight American births is premature (Centers for Disease Control, 2014a). The age of viability—the age at which advanced medical care permits a preterm newborn to survive outside the womb—begins at about 22 weeks after conception (Sadler, 2015). Infants born before 22 weeks rarely survive more than a few days because their brain and lungs have not begun to function. Although a 22- to 25-week fetus born prematurely may survive in intensive care, it is still at risk because its immature respiratory system may lead to death in early infancy. At about 26 weeks, the lungs become capable of breathing air and the premature infant stands a better chance of surviving if given intensive care. About 80% of infants born at 26 weeks survive and 87% of those born at 27 weeks (Stoll, Hansen, Bell, & Shankaran, 2010; Tucker & McGuire, 2004). Ninety-eight percent of 32-week premature infants survive.

At about the 166th day after conception, the placenta releases a hormone that triggers the onset of labor (Bainbridge, 2003). Hormones cause the mother's uterus to contract and relax at regular intervals, aiding delivery.

CHILDBIRTH

Childbirth, also known as labor, progresses in three stages, as shown in Figure 2.10.

Sometimes a vaginal birth is not possible because of concerns for the health or safety reasons of the mother or fetus. A **cesarean section**, or C-section, is a surgical procedure that removes the fetus from the uterus through the abdomen. About 33% of all single-ton births are cesarean deliveries (Hamilton, Martin, Osterman, Curtin, & Mathews, 2015). Cesarean sections are performed when labor progresses too slowly, the fetus is in breech position (feet first) or transverse position (crosswise in the uterus), the head is too large to pass through the pelvis, or the fetus or mother is in danger (Jha, Baliga, Kumar, Rangnekar, & Baliga, 2015; Visscher & Narendran, 2014). Babies delivered by cesarean are exposed to more maternal medication and secrete lower levels of the stress hormones that occur with vaginal birth that are needed to facilitate respiration, enhance circulation of blood to the brain, and help the infant adapt to the world outside of the womb. Interactions between mothers and infants, however, are similar for infants

Lives in Context Video 2.2
The Process of Childbirth

cesarean section Also known as a C-section; a surgical procedure that removes the fetus from the uterus through the abdomen.

FIGURE 2.10: Stages of Labor

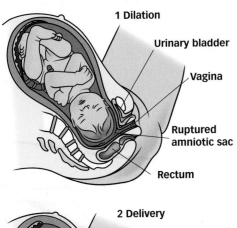

1 Dilation

Urinary bladder

Vagina

Ruptured amniotic sac

Rectum

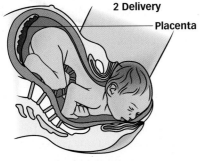

2 Delivery

Placenta

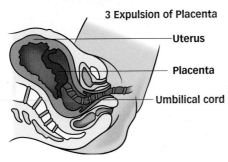

3 Expulsion of Placenta

Uterus

Placenta

Umbilical cord

STAGE	DETAILS	DURATION
Stage 1: Dilation	Labor begins when the mother experiences regular uterine contractions spaced at 10- to 15-minute intervals. The amniotic sac ("water") may rupture at any time during this stage. The contractions, which gradually become stronger and closer together, cause the cervix to dilate so that the fetus's head can pass through.	8 to 14 hours for a woman having her first child; for later-born children, the average is 3 to 8 hours.
Stage 2: Delivery	Begins when the cervix is fully dilated to 10 centimeters and the fetus's head is positioned at the opening of the cervix—known as "crowning." It ends when the baby emerges completely from the mother's body.	30 minutes to an hour and a half.
Stage 3: Delivery of the placenta	The placenta separates from the uterine wall and is expelled by uterine contractions.	Typically happens about 5 to 15 minutes after the baby has emerged, and the process can take up to a half hour.

delivered vaginally and by cesarean section (Durik, Hyde, & Clark, 2000). The Cultural Influences on Development feature examines some cultural differences in childbirth.

The average newborn is about 20 inches long and weighs about 7½ pounds. Boys tend to be slightly longer and heavier than girls. Newborns have distinctive features, including a large head (about ¼ of body length) that is often long and misshapen from passing through the birth canal. The newborn's skull bones are not yet fused—and will not be until about 18 months of age—permitting the bones to move and the head to mold to the birth canal, easing its passage. A healthy newborn is red-skinned and wrinkly at birth; skin that is bluish in color indicates that the newborn has experienced oxygen deprivation. Some babies emerge covered with lanugo, the fuzzy hair that protects the skin in the womb; other babies lose the lanugo prior to birth. The newborn's body is covered with vernix caseosa, a waxy substance that protects against infection; this dries up within the first few days. Although many hospital staff wash the vernix caseosa away, research suggests that it is a naturally occurring barrier to infection and should be retained at birth (Jha et al., 2015).

CULTURAL INFLUENCES ON DEVELOPMENT

• • Cultural Differences in Childbirth

An Uzbekistan midwife prepares to deliver a baby by first listening to its heartbeat.

Societies vary in their customs and perceptions of childbirth, including the privacy afforded to giving birth and how newborns are integrated into the community. In the United States, birth is a private event that usually occurs in a hospital, attended by medical personnel and one or two family members. In most cases, the first-time mother has never witnessed a birth but is well educated and may have well-informed expectations. After birth, the mother and infant are often visited by family during designated hospital visiting hours; the newborn usually rooms with the mother all or part of the day.

In a small village in southern Italy, birth is a community event. It usually takes place in a hospital, attended by a midwife (Fogel, 2007; Schreiber, 1977). Just after birth, the midwife brings the mother's entire family (immediate and extended) to the mother's room and they take turns congratulating the mother and baby, kissing them. The family provides a party including pastry and liqueurs. During labor and afterward the mother is supported and visited by many of her friends and relatives, to recognize the contribution that the mother has made to the community. The mother-in-law is an example of the social support system in place because from a few days before until about 1 month after the birth, she brings and feeds the mother ritual foods of broth, marsala, and fresh cheeses (Fogel, 2007; Schreiber, 1977).

In other cultures, birth is an even more public process. The Jahara of South America give birth under a shelter in full view of everyone in the village (Fogel, 2007). On the Indonesian island of Bali it is assumed that the husband, children, and other family will want to be present. The birth occurs in the home with the aid of a midwife and female relatives. As a result, Balinese women know what to expect in giving birth to their first child because they have been present at many births (Diener, 2000). The baby is immediately integrated into the family and community as he or she is considered a reincarnated soul of an ancestor. Many kin are present to support the mother and baby because the child is considered to be related to many more people than its parents.

Childbirth is tied to social status in the Brong-Ahafo region in Ghana: After a delivery, women achieve a higher social position and can then give advice to other women (Jansen, 2006). Home deliveries are highly valued. The more difficult the delivery and the less skilled assistance she receives, the more respect a woman attains, the higher her position will be, and the more influence she has on the childbirth decisions of other women, such as whether to give birth at home or in a medical setting and how to combine traditional and modern practices (Bazzano, Kirkwood, Tawiah-Agyemang, Owusu-Agyei, & Adongo, 2008).

Many cultures conduct rites that they believe protect newborns from evil spirits. Among the Maya of the Yucatan region of Mexico, there are few changes in the expectant mother's surroundings; the Mayan woman lies in the same hammock in which she sleeps each night. The father-to-be is expected to be present during labor and birth to take an active role but also to witness the suffering that accompanies labor. If the father is not present and the child is stillborn, it is blamed on the father's absence. The pregnant woman's mother is present, often in the company of other females including sisters, sisters-in-law, mothers-in-law, godmothers, and sometimes neighbors and close friends. The mother and child must remain inside the house for one week before returning to normal activity after birth because it is believed that the mother and newborn are susceptible to the influence of evil spirits from the bush (Gardiner & Kosmitzki, 2018).

A neighboring ethnic group, the Zinacanteco, place their newborns naked before a fire. The midwife who assisted the mother says prayers asking the gods to look kindly upon the infant. The infant is dressed in a long skirt made of heavy fabric extending beyond the feet; this garment is to be worn throughout the first year. The newborn is then wrapped in several layers of blankets, even covering the face, to protect against losing parts of the soul. These traditional practices are believed to protect the infant from illnesses as well as evil spirits (Brazelton, 1977; Fogel, 2007).

What Do You Think?

1. Which of these birthing customs most appeals to you? Why?

2. If you, a family member, or friend have given birth, describe the process. Where did the birth occur? Who witnessed it? What happened afterward? When did family and friends meet the baby?

After birth, newborns are routinely screened with the **Apgar scale**, which provides a quick and easy overall assessment of the baby's immediate health. As shown in Table 2.8, the Apgar scale is composed of five subtests: appearance (color), pulse (heart rate), grimace (reflex irritability), activity (muscle tone), and respiration (breathing). The newborn is rated 0, 1, or 2 on each subscale for a maximum total score of 10. A score of 4 or lower means that the newborn is in serious condition and requires immediate medical attention. The rating is conducted twice, 1 minute after delivery and again 5 minutes after birth; this timing ensures that hospital staff will monitor the newborn over several minutes. More than 98% of all newborns in the United States achieve a 5-minute score of 7 to 10, indicating good health (Martin, Hamilton, Osterman, Curtin, & Mathews, 2013).

TABLE 2.8 • Apgar Scale

INDICATOR	RATING (ABSENCE-PRESENCE)		
	0	1	2
Appearance (Color)	Blue	Pink body, blue extremities	Pink
Pulse (Heart rate)	Absent	Slow (below 100)	Rapid (over 100)
Grimace (Reflex irritability)	No response	Grimace	Coughing, crying
Activity (Muscle tone)	Limp	Weak and inactive	Active and strong
Respiration (Breathing)	Absent	Irregular and slow	Crying, good

Source: Apgar (1953).

INFANTS AT RISK: LOW BIRTH WEIGHT AND SMALL-FOR-DATE BABIES

One of the leading causes of infant mortality is low birth weight, accounting for 35% of mortality cases in infancy (Mathews & MacDorman, 2013). There are two types of low birth weight infants: those who are **preterm**, or premature (born before their due date) and those who are **small for date**, who are full term but have experienced slow growth and are smaller than expected for their gestational age. Infants are classified as **low birth weight** when they weigh less than 2,500 grams (5 ½ pounds) at birth; "very low" birth weight refers to a weight less than 1,500 grams (3 ½ pounds), and "extremely low" birth weight refers to a weight less than 750 grams (1 lb. 10 oz.; Alexander & Slay, 2002). Infants who are extremely low birth weight are most at risk for developmental challenges, handicaps, and difficulty surviving (under 1,000 grams; Fogel, 2007).

Low birth weight infants are at a disadvantage when it comes to adapting to the world outside the womb. At birth, they often experience difficulty breathing and are likely to suffer from respiratory distress syndrome, in which the newborn breathes irregularly and, at times, may stop breathing. Their survival depends on care in neonatal hospital units, where they are confined in isolettes that separate them from the world, regulating their body temperature, aiding their breathing with the use of respirators, and protecting them from infection. Many low birth weight infants cannot yet suck from a bottle, so they are fed intravenously.

The deficits that low birth weight infants endure range from mild to severe and correspond closely to the infant's birth weight, with extremely low birth weight infants suffering the greatest deficits (Hutchinson, De Luca, Doyle, Roberts, & Anderson, 2013). Low birth weight infants are at higher risk for poor growth, cerebral palsy, seizure disorders, neurological difficulties, respiratory problems, and illness (Adams-Chapman et al., 2013; Agustines et al., 2000; Aylward, 2005; McGowan, Alderdice, Holmes, & Johnston, 2011; J. E. Miller et al., 2016). Higher rates of sensory, motor, and cognitive problems mean that low birth weight children are more likely to require special education and display poor academic achievement in childhood, adolescence, and even adulthood (Aarnoudse-Moens, Weisglas-Kuperus, van Goudoever, & Oosterlaan, 2009; Eichenwald & Stark, 2009; Hutchinson et al., 2013; MacKay, Smith, Dobbie, & Pell, 2010). Low birth weight children often experience difficulty in self-regulation, poor social competence, and poor peer relationships, including peer rejection and victimization in adolescence (Georgsdottir, Haraldsson, & Dagbjartsson, 2013; Ritchie, Bora, & Woodward, 2015; Yau et al., 2013). As adults, low birth weight individuals tend to be less socially engaged, show poor communication skills, and may score high on measures of anxiety (Eryigit Madzwamuse, Baumann, Jaekel, Bartmann, & Wolke, 2015).

Apgar scale A quick overall assessment of a baby's immediate health at birth, including appearance, pulse, grimace, activity, and respiration.

preterm A birth that occurs 35 or fewer weeks after conception.

small for date Describes an infant who is full term but who has significantly lower weight than expected for the gestational age.

low birthweight Classifies infants who weigh less than 2,500 grams (5.5 pounds) at birth.

Low birthweight infants require extensive care. They are at risk for poor developmental outcomes and even death.

Parenting a low birth weight infant is stressful even in the best of circumstances (Howe, Sheu, Wang, & Hsu, 2014). Such infants tend to be easily overwhelmed by stimulation and difficult to soothe; they smile less and fuss more than their normal-weight counterparts, making caregivers feel unrewarded for their efforts. Often these infants are slow to initiate social interactions and do not attend to caregivers, looking away or otherwise resisting attempts to attract their attention (Eckerman, Hsu, Molitor, Leung, & Goldstein, 1999). Because low birth weight infants often do not respond to attempts to solicit interaction, they can be frustrating to interact with, can be difficult to soothe, and are at risk for less secure attachment to their parents (Jean & Stack, 2012; Mangelsdorf et al., 1996; Wolke, Eryigit Madzwamuse, & Gutbrod, 2014). Research also indicates that they may experience higher rates of child abuse (Bugental & Happaney, 2004; Klein & Stern, 1971).

Parental responses to having a low birth weight infant influence the child's long-term health outcomes, independently of perinatal risk, suggesting that the parenting context is an important influence on infant health (Pierrehumbert, Nicole, Muller-Nix, Forcada-Guex, & Ansermet, 2003). When mothers have knowledge about child development and how to foster healthy development, are involved with their children, and create a stimulating home environment, low birth weight infants tend to have good long-term outcomes (Benasich & Brooks-Gunn, 1996; Jones, Rowe, & Becker, 2009). For example, one study of low birth weight children showed that those who experienced sensitive parenting showed faster improvements in executive function and were indistinguishable from their normal-weight peers by age 5; however, those who experienced below-average levels of sensitive parenting showed lasting deficits (Camerota, Willoughby, Cox, Greenberg, & Investigators, 2015). Likewise, exposure to sensitive, positive, parenting predicted low birth weight children's catching up to their normal birth weight peers at age 8 in academic achievement, but exposure to insensitive parenting predicted much poorer functioning (Jaekel, Pluess, Belsky, & Wolke, 2015). Longitudinal research has found that low birth weight children raised in unstable, economically disadvantaged families tend to remain smaller in stature, experience more emotional problems, and show more long-term deficits in intelligence and academic performance than do those raised in more advantaged homes (Taylor, Klein, Minich, & Hack, 2001).

Interventions to promote the development of low birth weight children often emphasize helping parents learn coping strategies for interacting with their infants and managing stress (Chang et al., 2015; Lau & Morse, 2003). Interventions focused on teaching parents how to massage and touch their infants in therapeutic ways as well as increase skin-to-skin contact with their infants are associated with better cognitive and neuro-developmental outcomes at age 2 (Procianoy, Mendes, & Silveira, 2010). One intervention common in developing countries where mothers may not have access to hospitals is **kangaroo care**, in which the infant is placed vertically against the parent's chest, under the shirt, providing skin-to-skin contact (Charpak et al., 2005). As the parent goes about daily activities, the infant remains warm and close, hears the voice and heartbeat, smells the body, and feels constant skin-to-skin contact. Kangaroo care is so effective that the majority of hospitals in the U.S. offer kangaroo care to preterm infants. Babies who receive early and consistent kangaroo care grow more quickly, sleep better, score higher on measures of health, and show more cognitive gains throughout the first year of life (Boundy et al., 2015; Jefferies, 2012).

 Thinking in Context 2.4

1. Petra noticed that her abdomen has not grown much since she became pregnant 3 months ago. She concluded that the fetus must not undergo significant development early in pregnancy. How would you respond to Petra?

2. Parents' decisions about childbirth reflect their knowledge about birth options as well as cultural values. Referring to Bronfenbrenner's bioecological model (see Chapter 1), identify factors at each bioecological level that may influence childbirth. For example, how might neighborhood factors influence birth options? Culture?

3. Thinking of how society and medical science have changed in recent decades, in what ways might recent cohorts of parents differ from prior cohorts? What implications might these differences hold for prenatal development and childbirth?

ENVIRONMENTAL INFLUENCES ON PRENATAL DEVELOPMENT

LO 2.5 Identify the principles of teratology, types of teratogens, and ways that teratogens can be used to predict prenatal outcomes.

The vast majority of infants are born healthy, but some are exposed before birth to environmental obstacles that hinder their development. A **teratogen** is an agent that causes damage to prenatal development, such as a disease, drug, or other environmental factor, producing a birth defect. The field of *teratology* attempts to find the causes of birth defects so that they may be avoided. Health care providers help pregnant women and those who intend to become pregnant to be aware of teratogens and avoid them, as much as possible, to maximize the likelihood of having a healthy baby.

PRINCIPLES OF TERATOLOGY

There are many ways in which teratogens may affect prenatal development, but it is not always easy to predict the harm caused by teratogens. Generally, the effects of exposure to teratogens on prenatal development vary depending on the following principles (Collins, 2006; Moore & Persaud, 2016; Sadler, 2015).

- *Critical Periods.* There are critical periods during prenatal development in which an embryo is more susceptible to damage from exposure to teratogens. The extent to which exposure to a teratogen disrupts prenatal development depends on the stage of prenatal development when exposure occurs. Generally, sensitivity to teratogens begins at about 3 weeks after conception (Sadler, 2015). Structural defects occur when the embryo is exposed to teratogen while that part

kangaroo care An intervention for low-birthweight babies in which the infant is placed vertically against the parent's chest, under the shirt, providing skin-to-skin contact.

teratogen An environmental factor that causes damage to prenatal development.

of the body is developing. As shown in Figure 2.11, each organ of the body has a sensitive period in development during which it is most susceptible to damage from teratogens. Once a body part is fully formed, it is less likely to be harmed by exposure to teratogens; however, some body parts, like the brain, remain vulnerable throughout pregnancy.

- *Dose.* The amount of exposure (i.e., dosage) to a teratogen influences its effects. Generally, the greater the dose, the more damage to development; however, teratogens also differ in their strength. Some teratogens, like alcohol, display a powerful dose–response relationship so that larger doses—heavier and more frequent drinking—result in greater damage.

- *Individual differences.* Individuals vary in their susceptibility to particular teratogens based on the genetic makeup of both the organism and mother, as well as the quality of the prenatal environment.

- *Teratogens show complicated effects on development.* Different teratogens can cause the same birth defect, and a variety of birth defects can result from the same teratogen. Also, some teratogens have subtle effects that result in developmental delays that are not obvious at birth. For example, infants exposed prenatally to as little as an ounce of alcohol a day usually display no obvious physical deformities, but later, as children, they may demonstrate cognitive delays (Jacobson & Jacobson, 1996). Other teratogens display sleeper effects—effects that are not visible until many years later. For example, infants born to women who consumed diethylstilbestrol (DES), a hormone that was widely prescribed between 1945 and 1970 to prevent miscarriages, were born healthy, but as adults they were more likely to experience problems with their reproductive systems. Daughters born to mothers who took DES were more likely to develop a rare form of cervical cancer, have miscarriages, and give birth to infants who were premature or low birth weight (Barnes et al., 1980; Schrager & Potter, 2004).

FIGURE 2.11: **Sensitive Periods in Prenatal Development**

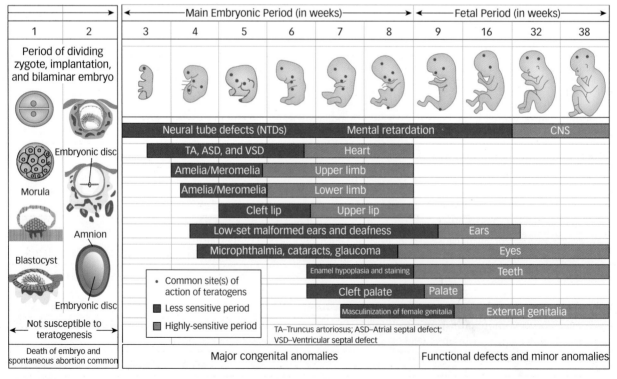

Source: Levine and Munsch (2010, p. 113).

TYPES OF TERATOGENS

Prenatal development can be influenced by many contextual factors, including maternal consumption of over-the-counter (OTC), prescription, and recreational drugs; illness; environmental factors; and more, as shown in Table 2.9. Although the developing organism is vulnerable to many teratogens, the mother's body is designed to protect the growing fetus.

Some teratogens can be avoided by choice; for example, a woman can choose not to drink alcohol or smoke cigarettes during pregnancy. Others, however, may be involuntary, as in the case of maternal illness. Sometimes a pregnant woman and her doctor may have to make a difficult choice between forgoing a needed prescription drug and putting the fetus at risk. And, in any case, a woman may not know she is pregnant until after the first few weeks of the embryonic stage are already past. Thus, in the real world, almost no pregnancy can be entirely free of exposure to teratogens. However, each year about 97% of infants are born without defects (Centers for Disease Control, 2014).

Prescription and Nonprescription Drugs

More than 90% of pregnant women take prescription or over-the-counter (OTC) medications (Servey & Chang, 2014). Prescription drugs that can act as teratogens include antibiotics, certain hormones, anticoagulants, anticonvulsants, and some acne drugs (Collins, 2006; Moore & Persaud, 2016; Sadler, 2015). In several cases physicians have unwittingly prescribed drugs to ease pregnant women's discomfort that caused harm to the fetus. For example, in the late 1950s and early 1960s many pregnant women were prescribed thalidomide to prevent morning sickness. However, it was found that taking thalidomide

TABLE 2.9 • Hazards to Prenatal Development

DRUGS	
Alcohol	Fetal alcohol syndrome, mental retardation; retarded fetal growth; joint abnormalities; ocular abnormalities
Amphetamines	Premature delivery; stillbirth; irritability and poor feeding among newborns
Antibiotics (Tetracycline, Streptomycin, Terramycin)	Premature delivery; restricted skeletal growth; cataracts
Barbiturates	Lethargy in the fetus; large doses cause anoxia (oxygen starvation), restricts fetal growth
Cocaine	Retarded fetal growth; prematurity, microcephaly; neurobehavioral disturbances; genital abnormalities
Heroin	Retarded fetal growth; premature labor; newborns suffer withdrawal
Lithium	Heart and blood vessel abnormalities
Marijuana	Retarded fetal growth
Tobacco	Retarded fetal growth; miscarriage, still birth; infant mortality
MATERNAL ILLNESS	
HIV/AIDS	Retarded fetal growth; microcephaly; mental retardation; mother-to-child transmission
Rubella	During embryonic period, causes blindness and deafness; in first and second trimesters, brain damage
ENVIRONMENTAL POLLUTANTS	
Lead and mercury	Spontaneous miscarriage; preterm labor; brain damage
Radiation	Retarded fetal growth; microcephaly; mental retardation; skeletal anomalies; cataracts

Sources: Moore & Persaud (2016); Sadler (2015); Weinhold (2009).

Betty Udesen/KRT/Newscom

Fetal alcohol syndrome is associated with distinct facial characteristics, growth deficiencies, and deficits in intellectual development, language, motor coordination, and the combined abilities to plan, focus attention, problem solve, and use goal directed behavior that persist throughout childhood and into adulthood.

4 to 6 weeks after conception (in some cases, even just one dose) caused deformities of the child's arms and legs, and, less frequently, damage to the ears, heart, kidneys, and genitals (Laughton, Cornell, Boivin, & Van Rie, 2012; Vargesson, 2009). Nonprescription drugs, such as diet pills and cold medicine, can also cause harm, but research on OTC drugs lags far behind research on prescription drugs, and we know little about the teratogenic effect of many OTC drugs (Cabbage & Neal, 2011).

Alcohol

An estimated 14% to nearly 30% of pregnant women report consuming alcohol during their pregnancies (Arria et al., 2006; Meschke, Holl, & Messelt, 2013; Zhao et al., 2012). Indeed, alcohol abuse during pregnancy has been identified as the leading cause of developmental disabilities (O'Leary et al., 2013; Warren, Hewitt, & Thomas, 2011). **Fetal alcohol spectrum disorders** refer to the continuum of effects of exposure to alcohol, which vary with the timing and amount of exposure (Riley, Infante, & Warren, 2011). At the extreme end of the spectrum is **fetal alcohol syndrome (FAS)**, a cluster of defects appearing after heavy prenatal exposure to alcohol that is detected in 2 to 7 infants per 1,000 births (May et al., 2014; Thomas, Warren, & Hewitt, 2010). FAS is associated with a distinct pattern of facial characteristics (such as small head circumference, short nose, small eye opening, and small midface), pre- and postnatal growth deficiencies, and deficits in motor coordination, language, and cognitive development, including the combined abilities to plan, focus attention, problem solve, and use goal-directed behavior (Jirikowic, Gelo, & Astley, 2010; Mattson, Crocker, & Nguyen, 2011; Thomas et al., 2010). The effects of exposure to alcohol within the womb persist throughout childhood and have been found to be associated with deficits in learning and memory in early adulthood (Coles et al., 2011; McLachlan, Roesch, Viljoen, & Douglas, 2014; Wheeler, Kenney, & Temple, 2013).

Even moderate drinking is harmful as children may be born displaying some, but not all, of the problems of FAS, or *fetal alcohol effects* (Thomas et al., 2010). Consuming 7 to 14 drinks per week during pregnancy is associated with lower birth size; growth deficits through adolescence; and deficits in attention, memory, and cognitive development (Alati et al., 2013; J.-H. Chen, 2012; Lundsberg, Illuzzi, Belanger, Triche, & Bracken, 2015; O'Leary & Bower, 2012). Even less than one drink per day has been associated with negative effects on fetal growth (Day et al., 2002; Day & Richardson, 2004; Mariscal et al., 2006) and with deficits in cognition at 1 year of age (Lu, 2005; Testa, Quigley, & Das Eiden, 2003) and behavior problems through 5 years of age (Flak et al., 2014). Scientists have yet to determine whether there is a safe level of drinking, but the only way to be certain of preventing alcohol-related risks is to avoid alcohol during pregnancy altogether.

fetal alcohol syndrome (FAS) The most severe form of fetal alcohol spectrum disorder accompanying heavy prenatal exposure to alcohol, including a distinct pattern of facial characteristics, growth deficiencies, and deficits in intellectual development.

fetal alcohol spectrum disorders The continuum of physical, mental, and behavioral outcomes caused by prenatal exposure to alcohol.

Cigarette Smoking

Every package of cigarettes sold in the United States includes a warning about the dangers of smoking while pregnant. Fetal deaths, premature births, and low birth weight are up to twice as frequent in mothers who are smokers than in those who do not smoke (Juárez & Merlo, 2013). Infants exposed to smoke while in the womb are prone to congenital heart defects, respiratory problems, and sudden infant death syndrome and, as children, show more behavior problems and attention difficulties and score lower on intelligence and achievement tests (Kiechl-Kohlendorfer et al., 2010; Lee & Lupo, 2013). Moreover, maternal smoking during pregnancy shows epigenetic effects on offspring, influencing how genetic processes and pathways of growth and development unfold in childhood into late adolescence and likely beyond (Han et al., 2015; Knopik, Maccani, Francazio, & McGeary, 2012; Richmond et al., 2015). There is no safe level of smoking during pregnancy.

Marijuana

The effects of marijuana on prenatal development are not well understood. Marijuana use during early pregnancy negatively affects fetal length and birth weight (A. C. Huizink, 2013; Hurd et al., 2005; Moore & Persaud, 2016). Although some studies suggest few consistent findings from infancy through adolescence (Huizink, 2013), others link prenatal exposure to marijuana to impairments in attention, memory and cognitive skills, as well as impulsivity at ages 4 and 10 and poor achievement in adolescence (Goldschmidt, Richardson, Willford, Severtson, & Day, 2012; Gray, Day, Leech, & Richardson, 2005; A. Huizink & Mulder, 2006; Wu, Jew, & Lu, 2011). Some researchers have found that once the effects of exposure to other teratogens is controlled, marijuana does not show a teratogenic effect (Nordstrom-Klee, Delaney-Black, Covington, Ager, & Sokol, 2002; van Gelder et al., 2010). Regardless, the safest course is for pregnant women to avoid marijuana.

Cocaine and Heroin

Infants exposed to cocaine and heroin face special challenges, such as signs of addiction and withdrawal symptoms including tremors, irritability, abnormal crying, disturbed sleep, and impaired motor control. Prenatal exposure to cocaine and heroin is associated with reduced birthweight, shorter length, smaller head circumference, and impaired motor performance at birth (Frank, Augustyn, Knight, Pell, & Zuckerman, 2001). Exposure to these drugs during prenatal development influences brain development, particularly the regions associated with attention, arousal, and regulation (Behnke & Smith, 2013; Coyle, 2013; Lebel et al., 2013; Roussotte et al., 2011). At one month after birth, babies who were exposed to cocaine had difficulty regulating their arousal states and showed poor movement skills, poor reflexes, and greater excitability (Fallone et al., 2014).

Though it was once believed that cocaine- and heroin-exposed infants would suffer life-long cognitive deficits, research suggests more mixed and subtle effects (Bandstra, Morrow, Mansoor, & Accornero, 2010; Behnke & Smith, 2013; Lambert & Bauer, 2012). Prenatal cocaine exposure has a small but lasting effect on attention and behavioral control and language skills through late childhood (Lewis et al., 2011, 2013; Singer, Minnes, Min, Lewis, & Short, 2015), but it is not linked with impairments in overall development, IQ, or school readiness in toddlers, elementary school–aged children, or middle school–aged children (Accornero et al., 2011; Behnke & Smith, 2013; Goldschmidt et al., 2012; Min, Minnes, Yoon, Short, & Singer, 2014). Moreover, quality care can lessen the long-term impact of prenatal exposure to substances (Behnke & Smith, 2013; Lewis et al., 2011).

The challenge of determining the effects of prenatal exposure to drugs is that most infants exposed to illicit drugs, such as cocaine and heroin, are also exposed to other substances, including tobacco, alcohol, and marijuana (Jones, 2006; Passey, Sanson-Fisher, D'Este, & Stirling, 2014), making it difficult to isolate the effect of each drug on prenatal development. We must be cautious in interpreting findings about illicit drug use and the effects on prenatal development because there are many other contextual factors that often co-occur with substance use and also pose risks for development—including poverty, malnutrition, social isolation, stress, and diminished parental responsiveness (Bandstra et al., 2010; Bendersky & Lewis, 1999; Frank et al., 2001). For example, parents who abuse drugs tend to provide poorer quality care, a home environment less conducive to cognitive development, and parent–child interaction that is less sensitive and positive than the environments provided by other parents (Hans, 2002). Children raised by substance-abusing parents are at risk for being subjected to overly harsh discipline and lack of supervision (Burlew et al., 2012) as well as disruptions in care due to factors such as parental incarceration, inability to care for a child, and even death (e.g., from a drug overdose or drug gang violence). Disentangling the long-term effects of prenatal exposure to substances, subsequent parenting, and contextual factors is challenging. Researchers and health care providers who construct interventions must address the contextual and parenting-related risk factors to improve the developmental outlook for children exposed to drugs prenatally (Butz et al., 2001; Calhoun, Conner, Miller, & Messina, 2015; Kilbride, Castor, Hoffman, & Fuger, 2000).

Maternal Illness

Depending on the type and when it occurs, an illness experienced by the mother during pregnancy can have devastating consequences for the developing fetus. For example, rubella (German measles) prior to the 11th week of pregnancy can cause a variety of defects including blindness, deafness, heart defects, and brain damage, but after the first trimester, adverse consequences become less likely (Santis, Cavaliere, Straface, & Caruso, 2006). Some sexually transmitted diseases, such as syphilis, can be transmitted to the fetus during pregnancy (Gomez et al., 2013; Sánchez & Wendel, 1997). Others, such as gonorrhea, genital herpes, and HIV, can be transmitted as the child passes through the birth canal during birth or though bodily fluids after birth (see the Lives in Context feature). Because some diseases, such as rubella, can be prevented with vaccinations, it is important for women who are considering becoming pregnant to discuss their immunization status with their health care provider.

Some illnesses with teratogenic effects, such as the Zika virus, are not well understood. Children born to women infected with the Zika virus are at greater risk of microcephaly (reduced head size). They may also show a pattern of defects now known as *congenital Zika syndrome*, which includes severe microcephaly characterized by partial skull collapse, damage to the back of the eye, and body deformities including joints and muscles with restricted range of motion (Centers for Disease Control and Prevention, 2017a).

Environmental Hazards

Prenatal exposure to chemicals, radiation, air pollution, and extremes of heat and humidity can impair development. Infants prenatally exposed to heavy metals, such as lead and mercury, whether through ingestion or inhalation, score lower on tests of cognitive ability and intelligence and have higher rates of childhood illness (Sadler, 2015; Vigeh, Yokoyama, Matsukawa, Shinohara, & Ohtani, 2014; Xie et al., 2013). Exposure to radiation can cause genetic mutations. Infants born to mothers pregnant during the atomic bomb explosions in Hiroshima and Nagasaki and after the nuclear power accident at Chernobyl displayed many physical deformities, mutations, and intellectual deficits. Prenatal exposure to radiation is associated with Down syndrome, reduced head circumference, intellectual disability, reduced intelligence scores and school performance, and heightened risk of cancer (Chang, Lasley, Das, Mendonca, & Dynlacht, 2014). About 85% of the world's birth defects occur in developing countries, supporting the role of context in influencing prenatal development directly via environmental hazards and also indirectly through the lack of opportunities and resources for education, health, and financial support (Weinhold, 2009).

MATERNAL CHARACTERISTICS AND BEHAVIORS

Teratogens—and the avoidance of them—are, of course, not the only determinants of how healthy a baby will be. A pregnant woman's characteristics, such as her age, and her behaviors during pregnancy, including nutrition and emotional well-being, also influence prenatal outcomes.

Maternal Age

U.S. women are becoming pregnant later in life than ever before. Between 1990 and 2010, the pregnancy rate for women aged 35 to 39 increased from 119 per 1,000 women to

• • HIV Infection in Newborns

David Turnley/Corbis Historical/Getty Images

HIV can be transmitted from mother to infant through breastfeeding.

The rate of mother-to-child transmission of HIV has dropped in recent years as scientists have learned more about HIV. The use of cesarean delivery as well as prescribing anti-HIV drugs to the mother during the second and third trimesters of pregnancy, and to the infant for the first six weeks of life, has reduced mother-to-child HIV transmission from more than 20% to less than 2% in the United States and Europe (Rudin, 2004; Torpey, Kabaso, et al., 2010; Torpey, Kasonde, et al., 2010). Aggressive treatment may further reduce the transmission

of HIV to newborns, and research suggests that it may even induce remission (Rainwater-Lovett, Luzuriaga, & Persaud, 2015; Pollack & McNeil, 2013; National Institute of Allergy and Infectious Diseases, 2014). However, in developing countries such interventions are widely unavailable. Worldwide, mother-to-child HIV transmission remains a serious issue. For example, in Zambia, 40,000 infants acquire HIV each year (Torpey, Kasonde, et al., 2010). Treating newborns is critical, though not always possible. Worldwide, 20% to 30% of neonates with HIV develop AIDS during the first year of life and most die in infancy (United Nations Children's Fund, 2013).

Globally, breastfeeding accounts for 30% to 50% of HIV transmission in newborns (Sullivan, 2003; World Health Organization, 2011). The World Health Organization (2010) recommends providing women who test positive for HIV with information about how HIV may be transmitted to their infants and counseling them not to breast feed. Yet cultural, economic, and hygienic reasons often prevent mothers in developing nations from seeking alternatives to breastfeeding. For example, the widespread lack of clean water in some countries makes the use of powdered formulas dangerous. Also, in some cultures, women who do not breast feed may be ostracized from the community (Sullivan, 2003). Balancing cultural values with medical needs is a challenge.

Children with HIV are at high risk for a range of illnesses and health conditions, including chronic bacterial infections; disorders of the central nervous system, heart, gastrointestinal tract, lungs, kidneys, and skin; growth stunting; neurodevelopmental delays, including brain atrophy, which contribute to cognitive and motor impairment; and delays in reaching developmental milestones (Blanchette, Smith, Fernandes-Penney, King, & Read, 2001; Laughton, Cornell, Boivin, & Van Rie, 2013; Sherr, Mueller, & Varrall, 2009; Palmer, 2003; Venkatesh et al., 2010).

What Do You Think?

Imagine that you work as an HIV educator with women in an underdeveloped country. What challenges might you face in encouraging women to take steps to reduce the potential for HIV transmission to their infants? How might you help them?

137 per 1,000 women. During the same 20-year period, the rate for women aged 40 to 44 increased from 11 to 19 per 1,000 (Curtin, Abma, & Kost, 2015). Women who give birth past the age of 35, and especially past 40, are at greater risk for pregnancy and birth complications, including miscarriage and stillbirth, than are younger women. They are more vulnerable to pregnancy-related illnesses such as hypertension and diabetes, and their pregnancies involve increased risks to the newborn, including low birth weight, preterm birth, respiratory problems, and related conditions requiring intensive neonatal care (Grotegut et al., 2014; Kenny et al., 2013; Khalil, Syngelaki, Maiz, Zinevich, & Nicolaides, 2013). The risk of having a child with Down syndrome also increases sharply with maternal age, especially after age 40 (Hazlett et al., 2011; see Figure 2.12).

FIGURE 2.12: Maternal Age and Risk of Down Syndrome

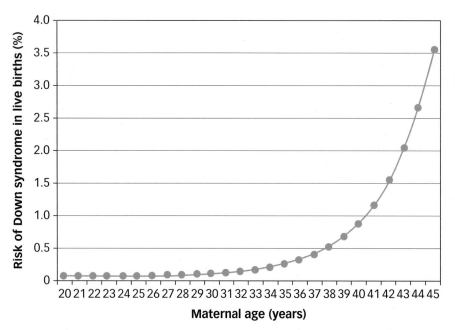

Although the risk for Down Syndrome increases dramatically with maternal age, most infants are born healthy, regardless of maternal age.

Sources: Data from Cuckle, Wald, and Thompson (1987); figure from Newberger (2000).

Although risks for complications rise linearly with each year (Salem Yaniv et al., 2011), it is important to realize that the majority of women older than 35 give birth to healthy infants. Differences in context and behavior may compensate for some of the risks of advanced maternal age. For example, longer use of oral contraceptives is associated with a lower risk of giving birth to a child with Down syndrome (Nagy, Győrffy, Nagy, & Rigó, 2013). Older mothers tend to be healthier and show lower rates of alcohol consumption and cigarette smoking than do younger mothers (Salihu, Shumpert, Slay, Kirby, & Alexander, 2003).

Nutrition

The quality of the father's and mother's diets influences the health of the sperm and egg (Sinclair & Watkins, 2013). Most women need to consume 2,200 to 2,900 calories per day to sustain a pregnancy (Kaiser, Allen, & American Dietetic Association, 2008; Simkin, Whalley, & Keppler, 2001), but over 1 billion people in the world are chronically hungry (Food and Agriculture Organization of the United Nations, 2009) and even more are food insecure. Dietary supplements can reduce many of the problems caused by maternal malnourishment, but adequate caloric intake is crucial for healthy prenatal development (Ortolano, Mahmud, Iqbal Kabir, & Levinson, 2003).

Some deficits resulting from an inadequate diet cannot be remedied. For example, inadequate consumption of folic acid (a B vitamin) very early in pregnancy can result in the formation of neural tube defects stemming from the failure of the neural tube to close. **Spina bifida** occurs when the lower part of the neural tube fails to close and spinal nerves begin to grow outside of the vertebrae, often resulting in paralysis. Surgery must be performed before or shortly after birth, but lost capacities cannot be restored (Scott Adzick, 2013). Another neural tube defect, **anencephaly**, occurs when the top part of the neural tube fails to close and all or part of the brain fails to develop, resulting in death shortly after birth. As researchers have learned and disseminated the knowledge that folic acid helps prevent these defects, the frequency of neural tube defects has declined to about 1 in 1,000 births (Cordero et al., 2010; Williams et al., 2015). However, in a national study of U.S. mothers, only 24% consumed the recommended dose of folic acid during pregnancy (Tinker, Cogswell, Devine, & Berry, 2010).

Mothers who consume nutritious diets tend to have fewer complications during pregnancy and give birth to healthier babies

spina bifida A neural tube that results in spinal nerves growing outside of the vertebrae, often resulting in paralysis and developmental disability.

anencephaly A neural tube defect that results in the failure of all or part of the brain to develop, resulting in death prior to or shortly after birth.

Emotional Well-Being

Although stress is inherently part of almost everyone's life, exposure to chronic and severe stress during pregnancy poses risks including low birth weight, premature birth, and a longer postpartum hospital stay (Dunkel, Schetter, & Tanner, 2012; Field, 2011). Maternal stress influences prenatal development because stress hormones cross the placenta, raising the fetus's heart rate and activity level. Long-term exposure to stress hormones in utero is associated with higher levels of stress hormones in newborns (Kapoor, Lubach, Ziegler, & Coe, 2016). As a result, the newborn may be more irritable and active than a

LIFESPAN BRAIN DEVELOPMENT

• • Pregnancy and the Maternal Brain

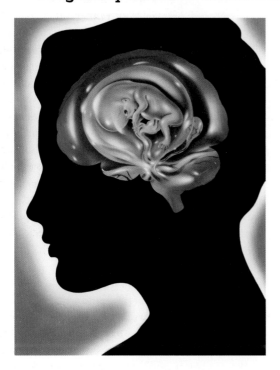

Pregnancy is associated with neurological changes especially in the areas of the brain responsible for social cognition.

How does pregnancy influence mothers? The developing embryo and fetus receive a great deal of research attention, but what does pregnancy mean for mothers' development? Women's bodies undergo a radical transformation during pregnancy. For example, the hormone progesterone increases up to 15-fold and is accompanied by a flood of estrogen that is greater than the lifelong exposure prior to pregnancy. Research has shown that hormonal shifts are associated with brain changes during puberty as well as later in life. Do the hormonal changes with pregnancy influence women's brain structure? Animal research suggests that pregnancy is accompanied by neurological changes, including changes in neural receptors, neuron generation, and gene expression, that are long-lasting (Kinsley & Amory-Meyer, 2011). It is likely that pregnancy is also associated with neural changes in humans, but there is little research to date (Hillerer, Jacobs, Fischer, & Aigner, 2014).

In a recent groundbreaking study, Elseine Hoekzema and colleagues (2017) conducted brain scans of women who were attempting to become pregnant for the first time, as well as their partners. Women who became pregnant were scanned again after giving birth and again at least 2 years later. The fathers and women who had not become pregnant were also assessed. The new mothers experienced reductions in the brain's gray matter, signifying increased neural efficiency in regions of the brain involved in social cognition—specifically, theory of mind, which enables us to sense another person's emotions and perspective (Schurz, Radua, Aichhorn, Richlan, & Perner, 2014). Theory of mind underlies a mother's ability to interpret her infant's mental states and is important for secure parent–infant attachment and for the development of the child's own social cognitive functions (Meins, Fernyhough, Fradley, & Tuckey, 2001). The changes in gray matter volume predicted mothers' attachment to their infants in the postpartum period, as indicated by mothers' increased neural activity in response to viewing photos of their infant as compared with other infants. Other research suggests that pregnancy is associated with the enhanced ability to recognize faces, especially those displaying emotions (Pearson, Lightman, & Evans, 2009). Gestational alterations in the brain structures that are implicated in social processes may offer an adaptive advantage to a mother by facilitating her ability to recognize the needs of her child and to promote mother–infant bonding. Moreover, similar to findings with animals (Kinsley & Amory-Meyer, 2011), the neural changes that accompanied pregnancy were long-lasting and persistent 2 years after giving birth.

The pregnancy-related neurological changes were so marked and predictable that all of the women could be classified as having undergone pregnancy or not on the basis of the volume changes in gray matter. Notably, fathers did not show a change in gray matter volume, suggesting that the neural effects of pregnancy are biological in nature, rather than associated with the contextual changes that occur with the transition to parenthood.

What Do You Think?

What adaptive purpose might pregnancy-related neurological changes serve?

low-stress infant and may have difficulties in sleep, digestion, and self-regulation (Davis, Glynn, Waffarn, & Sandman, 2011; Kingston, Tough, & Whitfield, 2012). Later in childhood, he or she may have symptoms of anxiety, attention-deficit/hyperactivity disorder, and aggression (Glover, 2011). Stress in the home may make it difficult for parents to respond with warmth and sensitivity to an irritable infant (Brockington, 1996; Sameroff & Chandler, 1975). Social support can mitigate the effects of stress on pregnancy and infant care (Feldman, Dunkel-Schetter, Sandman, & Wadhwa, 2000; Ghosh, Wilhelm, Dunkel-Schetter, Lombardi, & Ritz, 2010).

Prenatal Care

Prenatal care, a set of services provided to improve pregnancy outcomes and engage the expectant mother, family members, and friends in health care decisions, is critical for the health of both mother and infant. About 26% of pregnant women in the U.S. do not seek prenatal care until after the first trimester; 6% seek prenatal care at the end of pregnancy or not at all (U.S. Department of Health and Human Services, 2014). Inadequate prenatal care is a risk factor for low birth weight and preterm births as well as infant mortality during the first year (Partridge, Balayla, Holcroft, & Abenhaim, 2012). In addition, use of prenatal care predicts pediatric care throughout childhood, which serves as a foundation for health and development throughout the lifespan (Handler et al., 2003).

Why do women delay or avoid seeking prenatal care? A common reason is the lack of health insurance (Maupin et al., 2004). Although government-sponsored health care is available for the poorest mothers, many low-income mothers do not qualify for care, or lack information on how to take advantage of care that may be available. Other barriers to seeking prenatal care include difficulty in finding a doctor, lack of transportation, demands of caring for young children, ambivalence about the pregnancy, depression, lack of education about the importance of prenatal care, lack of social support, poor prior experiences in the health care system, and family crises (Daniels, Noe, & Mayberry, 2006; Heaman et al., 2015; Mazul, Salm Ward, & Ngui, 2016).

Moreover, there are significant ethnic and socioeconomic disparities in prenatal care. Inadequate prenatal care is most likely among Native American women (23%), followed by African American (19%), Latino (17%), Asian American (14%), and white American women (13%; U.S. Department of Health and Human Services, 2013a). African American women, in particular, are far more likely than all other groups to give birth to low birth weight or preterm infants (U.S. Department of Health and Human Services, 2014). Ethnic differences are thought to be largely influenced by socioeconomic factors, as the ethnic groups least likely to seek early prenatal care are also the most economically disadvantaged members of society.

Although prenatal care predicts better birth outcomes, cultural factors also appear to protect some women and infants from the negative consequences of inadequate prenatal care. In a phenomenon termed the *Latino paradox,* Latino mothers, despite low rates of prenatal care, tend to experience low birth weight and mortality rates below national averages. These favorable birth outcomes are striking because of the strong and consistent association between socioeconomic status and birth outcomes, and because Latinos as a group are among the most socioeconomically disadvantaged ethnic populations in the United States (McGlade, Saha, & Dahlstrom, 2004; Ruiz, Hamann, Mehl, & O'Connor, 2016).

Several factors are thought to account for the Latino paradox, including strong cultural support for maternity, healthy traditional dietary practices, and the norm of selfless devotion to the maternal role (*marianismo;* Fracasso & Busch-Rossnagel, 1992; McGlade et al., 2004). These protective cultural factors interact with strong social support networks and informal systems of health care among Latino women, in which women tend to take responsibility for the health needs of those beyond their nuclear households. Mothers benefit from the support of other family members such as sisters, aunts, and other extended family. In this way, knowledge about health is passed down from generation to generation. There is a strong tradition of women helping other women in the community and warm interpersonal relationships, known as *personalismo,* are highly valued (Fracasso & Busch-Rossnagel, 1992; McGlade et al., 2004).

Although these cultural factors are thought to underlie the positive birth outcomes seen in Latino women, they appear to erode as Latino women acculturate to American society: The birth advantage has been found to decline in subsequent U.S.-born generations. Recent findings have called the existence of the Latino paradox into question, as some samples have illustrated that socioeconomic disadvantage cannot be easily ameliorated by cultural supports (Hoggatt, Flores, Solorio, Wilhelm, & Ritz, 2012; Sanchez-Vaznaugh et al., 2016).

Thinking in Context 2.5

1. Referring to Bronfenbrenner's bioecological model (see Chapter 1), identify factors at each bioecological level that may influence development in the womb.

2. Imagine that you are a health care provider conferring with a woman who is contemplating becoming pregnant. Give some examples of specific advice you would offer to help her promote a healthy pregnancy and baby.

 Apply Your Knowledge

Dr. Preemie is conducting a research study of the prevalence and correlates of drug use in college students. Because of the sensitive nature of the research topic, Dr. Preemie promises her participants confidentiality. Each college student who participates completes a set of surveys and an interview about his or her lifestyle and drug use habits. One participant, Carrie, reveals that she engages in moderate to heavy drug use (i.e., drinks two to four alcoholic beverages each day, and smokes marijuana several times per week). During the interview, Carrie mentions that she's feeling nauseous. Concerned, Dr. Preemie asks, "Do you want to stop the interview and go to the campus medical center?" "No," Carrie replies, "It's just morning sickness. I'm pregnant." "Oh," says Dr. Preemie, who nods, and continues with the interview.

Afterward, in her office, Dr. Preemie is torn and wonders to herself, "I'm worried about Carrie. Drugs and alcohol disrupt prenatal development, but I promised confidentiality. I can't tell anyone about this! Should I say something to Carrie? I'm supposed to be nonjudgmental! Intervening might keep other students from participating in my research, for fear that I'd break my promises. I don't know what to do."

1. What are the effects of teratogens, like drugs and alcohol, on prenatal development?

2. Describe the course of prenatal development. How do the effects of exposure to teratogens change during prenatal development?

3. Consider Dr. Preemie's dueling obligations. As a researcher, is she is responsible to Carrie as a participant in her study? Is Dr. Preemie responsible to the developing fetus? Her institution? Do Dr. Preemie's actions have any ramifications for the other participants in her study? How might these responsibilities conflict?

4. What should Dr. Preemie do?

5. How might your response change if Carrie were smoking cigarettes rather than using alcohol and drugs? What are the effects of smoking on prenatal development?

Give your students the SAGE edge!

SAGE edge offers a robust online environment featuring an impressive array of free tools and resources for review, study, and further exploration, keeping both instructors and students on the cutting edge of teaching and learning. Learn more at **edge.sagepub.com/kuthertopical.**

CHAPTER 2 IN REVIEW

2.1 Describe the process of cell reproduction and patterns of genetic inheritance.

SUMMARY

Most cells in the human body reproduce through mitosis, but sex cells reproduce by meiosis, creating gametes with 23 single, unpaired chromosomes. Some genes are passed through dominant–recessive inheritance, in which some genes are dominant and will always be expressed regardless of the gene it is paired with. Other genes are recessive and will only be expressed if paired with another recessive gene. When a person is heterozygous for a particular trait, the dominant gene is expressed and the person remains a carrier of the recessive gene. Incomplete dominance is a genetic inheritance pattern in which both genes influence the characteristic. Polygenic traits are the result of interactions among many genes. Some traits are determined by genomic imprinting, determined by whether it is inherited by the mother or the father.

KEY TERMS

chromosomes	homozygous
deoxyribonucleic acid (DNA)	heterozygous
mitosis	dominant–recessive inheritance
meiosis	incomplete dominance
zygote	sickle cell trait
dizygotic (DZ) twins	polygenic inheritance
monozygotic (MZ) twins	genomic imprinting

REVIEW QUESTIONS

1. How do cells reproduce?
2. What are four patterns of genetic inheritance?

 2.2 Define and provide examples of genetic disorders and chromosomal abnormalities.

SUMMARY

PKU is a recessive disorder that occurs when both parents carry the allele. Disorders carried by dominant alleles, such as Huntington's disease, are expressed when the individual has a single allele. Some recessive genetic disorders, like the gene for hemophilia, are carried on the X chromosome. Males are more likely to be affected by X-linked genetic disorders, such as hemophilia. Fragile X syndrome is an example of a dominant recessive disorder carried on the X chromosome. Because the gene is dominant, it must appear on only one X chromosome to be displayed. Klinefelter syndrome occurs in males born with an extra X chromosome (XXY) and Jacob's syndrome occurs when males have an extra Y chromosome (XYY). Females are diagnosed with triple X syndrome when they are three X chromosomes and Turner syndrome when they are born with only one X chromosome. The most common chromosome disorder is trisomy 21, known as Down syndrome.

KEY TERMS

phenylketonuria (PKU)	Down syndrome
fragile X syndrome	mutations

REVIEW QUESTIONS

Give an example of:

- a dominant-recessive disorder
- an X-linked disorder
- a chromosomal abnormality

 2.3 Explain how the dynamic interactions of heredity and environment influence development.

SUMMARY

Behavioral genetics is the field of study that examines how genes and experience combine to influence the diversity of human traits, abilities, and behaviors. Heritability research examines the contributions of the genotype in determining phenotypes but also provides information on the role of experience through three types of studies: selective breeding studies, family studies, and adoption studies. Genetics contributes to many traits, such as intellectual ability, sociability, anxiety, agreeableness, activity level, obesity, and susceptibility to various illnesses.

Passive, evocative, and active gene–environment correlations illustrate how traits often are supported by both our genes and environment. Gene-environment interactions illustrate the ways that heredity and environment influence each other. Reaction range refers to the idea that there is a wide range of potential expressions of a genetic trait, depending on environmental opportunities and constraints. Some traits illustrate canalization and require extreme changes in the environment to alter their course. The epigenetic framework is a model for understanding the dynamic ongoing interactions between heredity and environment whereby the epigenome's instructions to turn genes on and off throughout development are influenced by the environment.

KEY TERMS

genotype	range of reaction
phenotype	canalization
behavioral genetics	gene-environment correlation
heritability	niche-picking
gene-environment interactions	epigenetic framework

REVIEW QUESTIONS

1. What is behavioral genetics?
2. What are three types of gene–environment correlations?
3. What is the range of reaction?
4. What is the epigenetic framework?

2.4 Discuss the stages of prenatal development, stages of childbirth, and challenges for infants at risk.

2.5 Identify the principles of teratology, types of teratogens, and ways that teratogens can be used to predict prenatal outcomes.

SUMMARY

The germinal period is a time of rapid cell division. The embryonic period, from weeks 2 to 8, is a period of rapid cell differentiation. From 9 weeks until birth, the fetus grows rapidly, and the organs become more complex and begin to function. At about the 166th day after conception, the placenta releases a hormone that triggers the onset of labor. The first stage of labor begins when the mother experiences regular uterine contractions that cause the cervix to dilate so that the fetus's head can pass through. Delivery occurs during the second stage, and the placenta is expelled during the third stage. At birth, low birth weight infants often experience difficulty breathing and are at high risk for mortality. Low birth weight infants experience higher rates of sensory, motor, and language problems, learning disabilities, behavior problems and deficits in social skills into adolescence. The long-term outcomes of low birth weight vary considerably and depend on the environment in which the children are raised.

KEY TERMS

ovum	indifferent gonad
germinal period	lanugo
cell differentiation	vernix caseosa
blastocyst	cesarean section
embryo	Apgar scale
Implantation	preterm
placenta	small for date
embryonic period	low birth weight
neural tube	kangaroo care

REVIEW QUESTIONS

1. What are the three periods of prenatal development?

2. What are the stages of childbirth?

3. What challenges do at-risk infants face and what outcomes can be expected?

SUMMARY

Teratogens include diseases, drugs, and other agents that influence the prenatal environment to disrupt development. Generally, the effects of exposure to teratogens on prenatal development vary depending on the stage of prenatal development and dose. There are individual differences in effects, different teratogens can cause the same birth defect, a variety of birth defects can result from the same teratogen, and some teratogens have subtle effects that result in developmental delays that are not obvious at birth or not visible until many years later. Prescription and nonprescription drugs, maternal substance use, material illness, and environmental factors can potentially harm the developing fetus.

KEY TERMS

teratogen	fetal alcohol syndrome (FAS)
fetal alcohol	spina bifida
spectrum disorders	anencephaly

REVIEW QUESTIONS

1. Define and provide examples of teratogens.

2. What are four principles that determine the effects of exposure to teratogens during prenatal development?

Test your understanding of the content.
Review the flashcards and quizzes at
edge.sagepub.com/kuthertopical

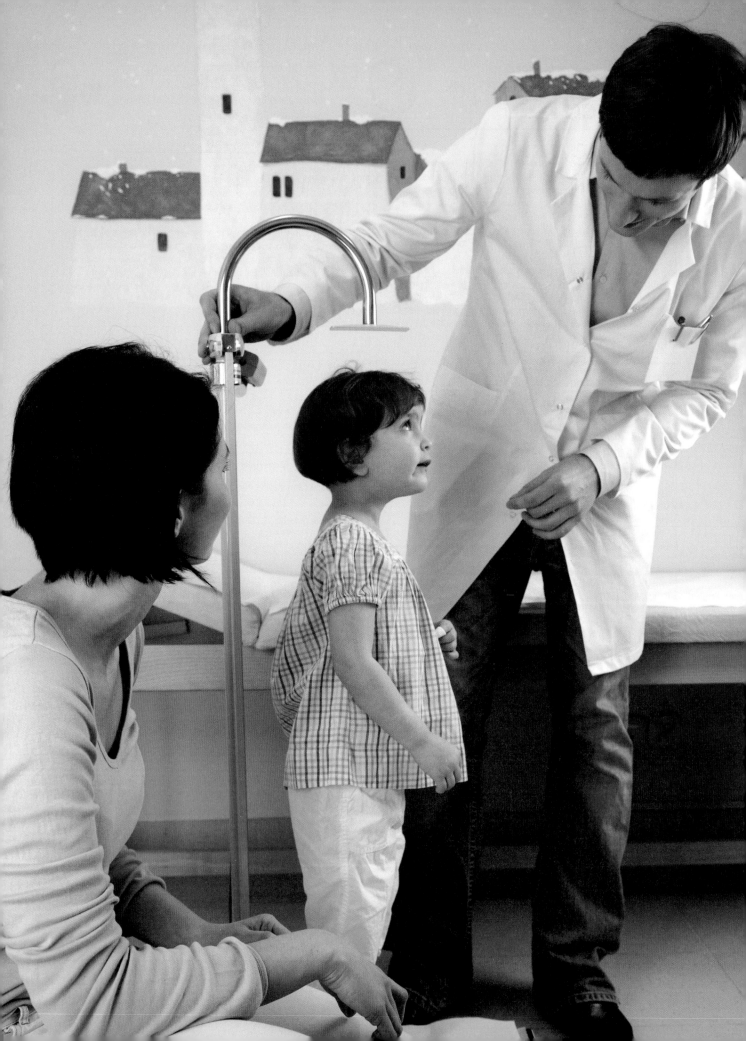

Physical Development and Aging

Learning Objectives

3.1 Summarize patterns of body growth and biological and contextual influences on growth during infancy and childhood.

3.2 Discuss the physical changes that occur with puberty, influences on pubertal timing, and the psychosocial effects of early and late puberty.

3.3 Identify normative patterns of physical and reproductive change as well as explanations for the causes of aging.

3.4 Analyze the influence of eating habits, obesity, and physical activity on physical development and functioning over the lifespan.

Digital Resources

- Body Proportions in Infancy and Early Childhood
- Infant and Preschooler Growth

- Attachment, Stress, and Menarche
- Menarche Timing

- Aging and Physical Development
- Menopause in Killer Whales

- Weight Loss in Teens
- The Fountain of Youth

$SAGE edge™ Master these learning objectives with multimedia resources available at **edge.sagepub.com/kuthertopical** and *Lives in Context* video cases available in the interactive eBook.

"You're such a big girl!" the pediatric nurse exclaimed as she weighed baby Regina. Regina's mother marveled at how much her daughter had grown and changed during the first 6 months of her life. From a newborn unable to raise her head, she was now transformed into a baby who can sit up on her own. Her mother told the nurse, "She seems to like spending time on all fours. Maybe she's practicing and getting ready to crawl." The nurse smiled. "Start thinking about baby-proofing your home because Regina will be crawling before you know it!"

As Regina progressed through childhood, her growth slowed but she became much more coordinated. Her third-grade gym teacher suggested that she join the after-school soccer games. She did and discovered what would become a lifelong hobby. Right before she started middle school, Regina noticed that her athletic shoes didn't fit quite right, and neither did her other clothes. "Another pair of cleats?" asked her mother. "You haven't grown out of clothes like this since you were a baby. But your clothes are way more expensive now!" she teased. In adolescence, Regina became stronger and even better at soccer, earning a college scholarship. After graduating from college, she joined an after-work soccer league, playing each weekend. As a mother, she encouraged her children to play and often practiced with them in the backyard. One day as she read the mail, she discovered an invitation to her 20th high school reunion. "I wonder what everyone is up to—what happened to my old classmates," Regina said to her husband. Weeks later, as they drove home after attending the reunion, Regina marveled at how much some of her classmates had changed and how others seemed much the same. Although we all progress through the same aging process, the rate and extent of change and its effects on our day-to-day function vary. In this chapter, we examine physical development and aging over the lifespan.

PHYSICAL DEVELOPMENT IN INFANCY AND CHILDHOOD

LO 3.1 Summarize patterns of body growth and biological and contextual influences on growth during infancy and childhood.

Perhaps the most obvious change infants undergo during the first year of life is very rapid growth. The first 2 years are collectively called the developmental stage of infancy and toddlerhood; the term *toddler* refers to toddling, the unsteady gait of babies who are just learning to walk. During this stage, infants and toddlers experience advances in growth that are so rapid that they often surprise parents. As children enter early childhood their bodies slim, grow taller, and reshape into proportions similar to those of adults. How do these developments take place? How do children grow and what influences their growth?

PATTERNS OF GROWTH

Growth during the prenatal period and infancy follows two patterns, which are known as **cephalocaudal development** and **proximodistal development**. Cephalocaudal development refers to the principle that growth proceeds from the head downward. The head and upper regions of the body develop before the lower regions. For example, recall the fetus's disproportionately large head. During prenatal development, the head grows before the other body parts. Even at birth, the newborn's head is about one-fourth the total body length, as shown in Figure 3.1. As the lower parts of the body develop, the head becomes more proportionate to the body. By 3 years of age, the child is less top heavy. Proximodistal development refers to the principle that growth and development proceed from the center of the body outward. During prenatal development, the internal organs develop before the arms and legs. After birth, the trunk grows before the limbs and the limbs before the hands and feet.

cephalocaudal development The principle that growth proceeds from the head downward; the head and upper regions of the body develop before the lower regions.

proximodistal development The principle that growth and development proceed from the center of the body outward.

growth norm The expectation for typical gains and variations in height and weight for children based on their chronological age and ethnic background.

GROWTH IN INFANCY

It is easy to observe that infants grow substantially larger and heavier over time—but there are many individual differences in growth. How can parents and caregivers tell if a child's growth is normal? By compiling information about the height and weight of large samples of children from diverse populations, researchers have determined growth norms. **Growth norms** are expectations for typical gains and variations in height and weight for children based on their chronological age and ethnic background.

FIGURE 3.1: Body Proportions Throughout Life

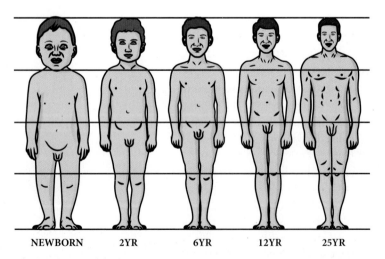

NEWBORN   2YR   6YR   12YR   25YR

Source: Huelke, D. M. (1998).

Genetic and environmental factors can cause some children to grow more quickly than others and fall outside of the norm.

In the first few days after birth, newborns shed excess fluid and typically lose 5% to 10% of their body weight. After this initial loss, however, infants gain weight quickly. Infants typically double their birth weight at about 5 months of age and triple it by 12 months. Most toddlers gain 5 or 6 pounds during the second year of life and another 4 to 5 pounds during the third year so that the average 3-year-old weighs about 31 pounds (Kuczmarski et al., 2000). Gains in height of 10 to 12 inches can be expected over the first year of life, making the average 1-year-old child about 30 inches tall. Most children grow about 5 inches during their second year of life and 3 to 4 inches during their third. To parents, growth may appear slow and steady, but research has shown that it often occurs in spurts in which an infant or toddler can grow up to one quarter of an inch overnight (Lampl, Johnson, Frongillo, & Frongillo, 2001; Lampl, Veldhuis, & Johnson, 1992). At about 2 years of age, both girls and boys have reached one half of their adult height (Huelke, 1998). During their first three years, infants and toddlers grow faster than they ever will again.

Lives in Context Video 3.1
Body Proportions in Infancy and Early Childhood

GROWTH IN EARLY AND MIDDLE CHILDHOOD

As compared with the first 2 years of life, growth slows during early childhood. From ages 2 through 6, the average child grows 2 to 3 inches taller and gains nearly 5 pounds in weight each year. The average 6-year-old child weighs about 45 pounds and is about 46 inches tall. Growth continues to slow in middle childhood, with most children gaining nearly 2 inches and 5 to 8 pounds per year, so that the average 10-year-old child weighs about 70 pounds and is about 4.5 feet tall. Despite a slower rate of growth, gradual day-to-day increases in height and weight add up quickly and can seemingly sneak up on a school-aged child. As children grow taller, their body proportions become more like those of adults, slimmer and with longer limbs. Physical growth is often accompanied by growing pains, which are intermittent aches and stiffness in the legs often experienced at night that are caused by the stretching and molding of the muscles to fit the child's growing skeleton (Pavone et al., 2011). Body growth is an important indicator of health, and body growth within the first 2 years of life is associated with cognitive and motor development, illustrating the interaction among domains of development (Sudfeld et al., 2015).

BIOLOGICAL AND CONTEXTUAL INFLUENCES ON GROWTH

Biological factors play a large role in physical development (Han-Na et al., 2010). Children's height and rate of growth is closely related to that of their parents (Malina & Bouchard, 1991). Genes influence the rate of growth by stipulating the amount of **hormones** to be released. Hormones are chemicals that are produced and secreted into the bloodstream by glands. Hormones influence cells and are a way in which genetic instructions are transformed into physical development. Growth hormone is secreted from birth and influences growth of nearly all parts of the body. Children with growth hormone deficiencies show slowed growth (Mayer et al., 2010), but growth hormone supplements can stimulate growth when needed (Hardin, Kemp, & Allen, 2007).

Ethnic differences in patterns of growth are apparent in England, France, Canada, Australia, and the United States. Generally, children of African descent tend to be tallest, then those of European descent, then Asian, then Latino. In the United States, African American children grow faster and are taller and heavier than white children of the same age. For example, 6-year-old African American girls tend to have greater muscle and bone mass than white non-Hispanic or Mexican American girls their age

hormone A chemical that is produced and secreted into the bloodstream to affect and influence physiological functions

(Ellis, Abrams, & Wong, 1997). However, there are many individual differences. Even within a given culture, some families are much taller than others (Eveleth & Tanner, 1991).

Growth is largely maturational, but it can be influenced by health and environmental factors, especially nutrition. Today's children grow taller and faster than ever before, and the average adult is taller today than a century ago (Cole, 2003). Improved sanitation, nutrition, and access to medical care have contributed to an increase in children's growth over the past century in the United States and other industrialized countries.

Thinking in Context 3.1

1. In your view, are patterns of growth best described as continuous or discontinuous development? Why?

2. How would you explain to parents the influence of nature and nurture on children's growth?

PHYSICAL DEVELOPMENT IN ADOLESCENCE

LO 3.2 Discuss the physical changes that occur with puberty, influences on pubertal timing, and the psychosocial effects of early and late puberty.

Even the most casual observer can't help noticing that adolescents' bodies undergo dramatic changes. **Puberty** is the biological transition to adulthood, in which adolescents mature physically and become capable of reproduction. Although puberty is considered a biological marker of adolescence, the hormonal changes entailed by puberty begin in late childhood, by 8 or 9 years of age (DeRose & Brooks-Gunn, 2006). The hormones that drive puberty, as well as many other functions including growth, appetite, responses to stress, and sexual responses, are regulated by the **hypothalamus-pituitary-gonadal axis** (Figure 3.2). Levels of **testosterone**, a hormone responsible for male sex characteristics, and **estrogen**, responsible for female sex characteristics, increase in both boys and girls. However, testosterone is produced at a much higher rate in boys than girls, and estrogen is produced at a much higher rate in girls than boys, leading to different patterns in reproductive development (Bogin, 2011). Hormonal changes also influence adolescents' growing sexual interests and activities, as well as psychosocial development (Berenbaum & Beltz, 2011).

On average, boys enter puberty at about 12 years of age, but they may begin to show pubertal changes any time between ages 9 and 16 (Tinggaard et al., 2012). Girls display signs of pubertal changes at 8 to 10 years of age, but some may show breast and pubic hair growth as early as 6 or 7 years of age (for African American or European American girls, respectively) or as late as 14 years of age. Generally, African American girls tend to be heavier and enter puberty about a year earlier than European American girls (Herman-Giddens, 2006; Wu, Mendola, & Buck, 2002). Puberty is not an event; rather, it is a process that takes about 4 years for boys and girls to complete, but can range from as little as 1 year up to 7 years in duration (Marceau, Ram, Houts, Grimm, & Susman, 2011; J. Mendle, 2014). Puberty entails the development of reproductive capacity, but that is not the whole story, for puberty influences a great variety of physical changes—not simply those typically associated with sexual maturity.

GROWTH IN ADOLESCENCE

As a child, Sharene was always the same height as most of her classmates and never the tallest child in class. But when the students lined up for their fifth-grade class photograph,

puberty The biological transition to adulthood, in which hormones cause the body to physically mature and permit sexual reproduction.

hypothalamus-pituitary-gonadal axis (HPG) The collective effects of the hypothalamus, pituitary gland, and gonads behaving in cooperation in regulating the hormones that drive puberty.

testosterone The primary male sex hormone responsible for development and regulation of the male reproductive system and secondary sex characteristics.

estrogen The primary female sex hormone responsible for development and regulation of the female reproductive system and secondary sex characteristics.

Sharene found herself in the very center of the portrait, as the tallest child. Surprised, Sharene wondered, "How did everyone get to be so short?" Although the hormonal changes that trigger puberty begin in late childhood, the first outward sign of puberty is the **adolescent growth spurt**, a rapid gain in height and weight that generally begins in girls at about age 10 (as early as 9.5 and as late as 14.5) and in boys at about age 12 (from 10.5 to16; Malina & Bouchard, 2004). By starting their growth spurts two years later than girls, boys begin with an extra two years of prepubertal growth on which the adolescent growth spurt builds, leading boys to end up taller than girls (Tinggaard et al., 2012). On average, the growth spurt lasts about two years, but body growth continues at a more gradual pace. Most girls complete growth in body size by about 16 and most boys by about 18. Adolescents gain a total of about 10 inches in height (Graber, Petersen, & Brooks-Gunn, 1996). Table 3.1 lists the physical changes that boys and girls undergo with puberty.

During the growth spurt, sex differences in body shape emerge. Rapid growth and development of muscle precedes increases in bone density, and is thought to influence bone strength. Although both boys and girls gain fat and muscle, they show different ratios of fat to muscle (DeRose & Brooks-Gunn, 2006). Girls gain more fat overall, particularly on their legs and hips, to comprise one-fourth of their body weight—nearly twice as much as boys. Boys gain more muscle than do girls, especially in their upper bodies, doubling their arm strength between ages 13 and 18 (Seger & Thorstensson, 2000; Welsman et al., 1997).

Sixteen-year-old Juan has always excelled in sports. However, lately he has noticed a substantial improvement in his athletic ability. He can run faster and for longer periods than ever before and he is not easily winded like the younger players on his team. The adolescent growth spurt has caused Juan's lungs to increase in size and capacity, permitting him to breathe more deeply than ever before. His heart has also grown, doubling in size and the total volume of blood in his body has increased.

tom carter/Alamy

Body growth often surpasses muscle strength and coordination, increasing adolescents' risk for athletic injuries.

FIGURE 3.2: Hypothalamus-Pituitary-Gonadal Axis

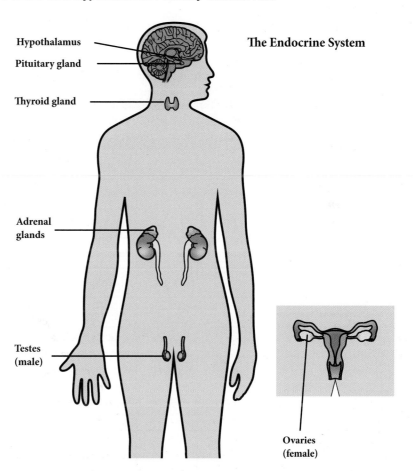

The Endocrine System

Hypothalamus
Pituitary gland
Thyroid gland
Adrenal glands
Testes (male)
Ovaries (female)

Source: Garrett (2017). Copyright SAGE Publishing.

The hypothalamus, a region at the base of the brain that is responsible for maintaining basic body functions such as eating, drinking, temperature, and the production of hormones, signals the pituitary gland, located adjacent to the hypothalamus, to produce hormones that stimulate the adrenal glands. The adrenal glands are located above the kidneys and regulate the body's response to stress via the secretion of epinephrine (adrenaline) and norepinephrine (noradrenaline). The pituitary also releases GnRH (gonadotropin-releasing hormone), which causes the gonads, or sex glands (ovaries in females and testes in males) to mature, enlarge, and in turn to begin producing hormones themselves.

These changes increase the overall amount of oxygen that meets with Juan's muscles, improving his physical performance and endurance.

During the adolescent growth spurt, the cephalocaudal growth trend of infancy and childhood reverses. The extremities grow first, the fingers and toes; then hands and feet; then arms and legs; and finally, the torso (Sheehy, Gasser, & Molinari, 2009). This asynchronous pattern of growth makes adolescents' bodies appear lanky and awkward, contributing to a temporary increase in clumsiness as adolescents attempt to control their quickly changing bodies. In addition, adolescents' bodies become taller and heavier before their muscles grow stronger and their internal organs mature (DeRose & Brooks-Gunn, 2006; Seger & Thorstensson, 2000). Unfortunately, adolescents, coaches, and parents often overestimate young people's capacities for athletic performance as changes in strength and endurance are not as visible as physical growth—and come after physical growth. Consequently, athletic injuries are very common during adolescence (Patel & Luckstead, 2000).

PRIMARY AND SECONDARY SEX CHARACTERISTICS

The most noticeable signs of pubertal maturation are the **secondary sex characteristics**, the body changes that indicate physical maturation but are not directly related to fertility. Examples of changes in secondary sex characteristics include breast development, deepening of the voice, growth of facial and body hair, and, for many, the emergence of acne

adolescent growth spurt The first outward sign of puberty, refers to a rapid gain in height and weight that generally begins in girls at about age 10 and in boys about age 12.

secondary sex characteristics Physical traits that indicate sexual maturity but are not directly related to fertility, such as breast development and the growth of body hair.

TABLE 3.1 • Sequence of Physical Changes During Puberty

GIRLS			BOYS		
CHARACTERISTIC	**MEAN AGE**	**RANGE**	**CHARACTERISTIC**	**MEAN AGE**	**RANGE**
Breast growth begins	10	7–13	Growth spurt begins	12.5	10.5–16
Growth spurt begins	10	8–14	Testes and scrotum grow larger	11	9.5–13.5
Pubic hair appears	10.5	7–14	Pubic hair appears	12	10–15
Peak strength spurt	11.5	9.5–14	Penis growth begins	12	11–14.5
Peak height spurt	11.5	10–13.5	Spermarche	13	12–16
Peak weight spurt	12.5	10–14	Peak height spurt	14	12.5–15.5
Menarche	12.5	10–16	Peak weight spurt	14	12.5–15.5
Adult stature	13	10–16	Voice lowers	14	11.5-15.5
Pubic hair growth completed	14.5	14–15	Facial and underarm hair begins	14	12.5–15.5
Breast growth completed	15	10–18	Penis and testes growth completed	14.5	12.5–16
			Peak strength spurt	15	13–17
			Adult stature	15.5	13.5–18
			Pubic hair growth completed	15.5	14–18

Sources: Bundak et al. (2007); Herman-Giddens (2006); and Wu et al. (2002).

(Hodges-Simeon, Gurven, Cárdenas, & Gaulin, 2013; Cordain et al., 2002).

Maturation of the **primary sex characteristics** is less noticeable, but it is the most important developmental change that accompanies puberty. In girls, maturation of the primary sex characteristics entails growth of the uterus and ovaries. Sexual maturity is marked by the onset of menstruation, the monthly shedding of the uterine lining, which has thickened in preparation for the implantation of a fertilized egg. **Menarche**, the first menstruation, occurs toward the end of puberty, after the peak of the height spurt. First menstruation most commonly occurs between ages 10 and 14, but as late as 16.5 (Brooks-Gunn & Ruble, 2013; Norman, 2008). In North America, the average European American girl experiences menarche shortly before turning 13 and the average African American girl shortly after turning 12 (Al-Sahab, Ardern, Hamadeh, & Tamim, 2010; Herman-Giddens, Kaplowitz, & Wasserman, 2004; Obeidallah, Brennan, Brooks-Gunn, Kindlon, & Earls, 2000). African American girls begin puberty and reach pubertal milestones such as the growth spurt and menarche earlier than do other girls (Kelly et al., 2014). Menarche occurs relatively late in the process of puberty, yet most children and adults view it as a critical marker of puberty because it occurs suddenly and is memorable (Brooks-Gunn & Ruble, 2013).

As part of a menarche ritual, Brahmin Nepali girls spend 7 days in the dark, in isolation without permission to look outside, see any men, pray, or cook.

What does menarche mean to girls? How girls experience menarche is influenced by their knowledge about menstruation as well as their expectations (Brooks-Gunn & Ruble, 2013). Girls who view menstruation negatively are likely to experience menstruation negatively, with more menstrual symptoms and distress (Rembeck, Möller, & Gunnarsson, 2006). Generations ago, as girls received little to no information about menarche, they tended to be surprised by it and often were afraid. For example, about one-half of girls in the 1950s received little information about menarche beforehand, and when information was provided, it portrayed menstruation in a negative light as something to be endured (Costos, Ackerman, & Paradis, 2002). Today, girls are often surprised by menarche, but they are not frightened because they are informed about puberty by health education classes and parents who are more willing to talk about pubertal development than did parents in prior generations (Omar, McElderry, & Zakharia, 2003; Stidham-Hall, Moreau, & Trussell, 2012).

However, the extent to which adolescents discuss menarche and sexuality varies by context and culture. A study of 12- to 16-year-old Bangladeshi girls revealed that they generally were not informed about menarche, and over two-thirds reacted with fear (Bosch, Hutter, & van Ginneken, 2008). Their mothers also tended to lack an adequate understanding of pubertal processes. Other research has suggested that girls in low- and middle-income countries, such as India, Turkey, Pakistan, Nigeria, and Malaysia, often know little about menarche and, for religious and cultural reasons, may feel shame about menstruation. In some cultures girls can be excluded from interaction with others, including attending school, when they are menstruating (Chandra-Mouli & Patel, 2017).

In boys, the first primary sex characteristic to emerge is the growth of the testes, the glands that produce sperm (Tinggaard et al., 2012). About a year later, the penis and scrotum enlarge, and pubic hair, a secondary sex characteristic, appears. As the penis grows, the prostate gland and seminal vesicles begin to produce semen, the fluid that contains sperm. At about age 13, boys demonstrate a principal sign of sexual maturation: the first ejaculation, known as spermarche (Gaddis & Brooks-Gunn, 1985; Tomova, Lalabonova, Robeva, & Kumanov, 2011). The first ejaculations contain few living sperm. Many boys experience their first ejaculations as nocturnal emissions, or wet dreams: involuntary ejaculations that are sometimes accompanied by erotic dreams.

primary sex characteristics
The reproductive organs; in females, this includes the ovaries, fallopian tubes, uterus, and vagina and in males, this includes the penis, testes, scrotum, seminal vesicles, and prostate gland.

menarche A girl's first menstrual period.

We know little about boys' perceptions of spermarche, but some studies of small groups of adolescent boys have suggested that most boys react positively to first ejaculation, although many experience uneasiness and confusion, especially if they are uninformed about this pubertal change (Frankel, 2002; Stein & Reiser, 1994). Data on male puberty are difficult to obtain because of the absence of easily determined markers, such as menarche (Herman-Giddens et al., 2012). Boys who know about ejaculation beforehand are more likely to show positive reactions, such as feeling pleasure, happiness, and pride; unfortunately, however, many boys report that health education classes and parents generally do not discuss ejaculation (Omar et al., 2003; Stein & Reiser, 1994). Parents sometimes report discomfort talking with their sons about reproductive development, particularly ejaculation, because of the close link with sexual desire, sexuality, and masturbation (Frankel, 2002). Perhaps because of its sexual nature, boys are less likely to tell a friend about spermarche than are girls to discuss their own reproductive development (Downs & Fuller, 1991).

BIOLOGICAL AND CONTEXTUAL INFLUENCES ON PUBERTAL TIMING

Although the process of puberty follows certain norms, it is important to remember that adolescents vary in their level of physical maturation. Some 14-year-old adolescents have adult-like bodies. Many girls have fully developed breasts and hips, and many boys have broad shoulders and facial hair. Other 14-year-old adolescents have childlike bodies or are just beginning the pubertal transformation. Why do adolescents' bodies vary so much, and how do such variations influence their day-to-day behavior?

The timing of puberty reflects the interaction of biological, contextual, and emotional influences. Without question, genes play a strong role in pubertal timing (Gajdos, Henderson, Hirschhorn, & Palmert, 2010; Tu et al., 2015; Wohlfahrt-Veje et al., 2016). The age at which mothers and fathers began puberty predicts the onset of puberty in both their sons and daughters (Golub, 1992; Wohlfahrt-Veje et al., 2016). Identical twins experience menarche at roughly the same time, within a month or so of each other; fraternal twins, on the other hand, can vary by a year or more (Kaprio et al., 1995). Puberty is a complex polygenetic trait (recall from Chapter 2 that polygenic inheritance is influenced by many genes; Day et al., 2017).

But puberty is influenced by more than genes. Adequate nutrition is essential to healthy development during adolescence to support the many changes that young people experience (Das et al., 2017). The onset of puberty is triggered by achieving a critical level of body weight, as an accumulation of leptin, a protein found in fat, may stimulate the HPA axis to increase the production and secretion of hormones (Elias, 2012; Maqsood et al., 2007; Sanchez-Garrido & Tena-Sempere, 2013). Leptin receptors have been identified in the hypothalamus, as well as in cells in the ovaries and testicles (Shalitin & Kiess, 2017). Girls with a greater body mass index (discussed later in this chapter), especially those who are obese, mature earlier than do other girls. In contrast, girls who have a low percentage of body fat, whether from athletic training or severe dieting, often experience menarche later than their same-age peers (Al-Sahab et al., 2010; Deardorff et al., 2011; Villamor & Jansen, 2016). Similarly, some research suggests that weight affects the onset and tempo of puberty in boys, with higher BMI associated with earlier puberty (Lee et al., 2016; Song et al., 2016), but less so as compared with girls (Tinggaard et al., 2012), and the mechanism is not well understood (Cousminer et al., 2014).

Adolescents' social contexts also influence pubertal timing. Exposure to stress, such as the experience of sexual abuse, is associated with an earlier onset of menarche (Boynton-Jarrett et al., 2013; Ellis, 2004). Poor family relationships, harsh parenting, family stress and conflict, parents' marital conflict, and anxiety are associated with early menarche in North American and European girls (Graber, Nichols, & Brooks-Gunn, 2010; Rickard, Frankenhuis, & Nettle, 2014). In industrialized countries such as the United States, Canada, and New Zealand, girls who are raised by single mothers begin puberty earlier than those raised in two-parent homes (Mendle et al., 2006; Posner, 2006). In addition, the absence of a biological father and the presence in the home of a biological unrelated male, such as a stepfather or mother's live-in boyfriend, is associated with earlier onset of menarche (Deardorff et al., 2011; Neberich, Penke, Lehnart, & Asendorpf, 2010; Tither & Ellis, 2008). Animal studies show a similar trend: The presence of a biologically related male delays reproductive maturation and functioning while the presence of unrelated males speeds female reproductive maturation (Neberich et al., 2010). Father absence and social stress may hold similar implications for boys' pubertal development, speeding it (Sun, Mensah, Azzopardi, Patton, & Wake, 2017); however, there is much less research on boys' development (Bogaert, 2005; Sheppard & Sear, 2012).

Contextual factors outside the home also influence pubertal timing. Adolescents who live in similar contextual conditions, particularly those of socioeconomic advantage, reach menarche at about the same age, despite having different genetic backgrounds (Obeidallah, Brennan, Brooks-Gunn, & Earls, 2004). Low socioeconomic status (SES) is associated with early pubertal onset in the United States and Canada (Arim, Tramonte, Shapka, Dahinten, & Willms, 2011; Deardorff, Abrams, Ekwaru, & Rehkopf, 2014). For example, African American and Hispanic girls tend to reach menarche earlier than white non-Hispanic girls. However, in some studies ethnic differences in the timing of menarche are reduced or disappear when researchers control for the influence of SES, suggesting that ethnic differences in pubertal timing may be attributable, at least in part, to low SES (Obeidallah et al., 2000). Yet in regions of the world that are impoverished, malnutrition and high rates of infectious disease prevent the accumulation of adequate fat stores needed to support pubertal development so that menarche is delayed. In many parts of Africa, for example, menarche does not occur until ages 14 to 17, several years later than in Western nations (Leenstra et al., 2005; Tunau, Adamu, Hassan, Ahmed, & Ekele, 2012). Swift declines in the age of menarche accompanied the rapid economic growth and advances in the standard of living in South Korea over the last half of the 20th century, illustrating the role of context in biological development (Sohn, 2016).

The influence of contextual conditions and physical health in triggering puberty is thought to underlie the **secular trend**, or the lowering of the average age of puberty with each generation (see Figure 3.3). Through the 18th century in Europe, puberty occurred as late as age 17; between 1860 and 1970, the age of menarche declined by about 3 to 4 months per decade (Tanner, 1990). Boys in the United States and Canada began puberty

FIGURE 3.3: Secular Trend in Girls' Pubertal Development, 1830–2010

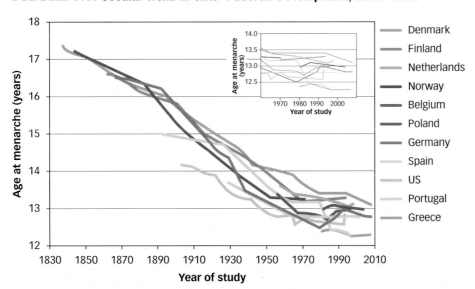

Source: Sørensen et al. (2012).

secular trend The change from one generation to the next in an aspect of development, such as body size or in the timing of puberty.

LIVES IN CONTEXT

• • Puberty and Sleep Patterns

Delayed phase preference leads most adolescents to feel sleepy and groggy in their early morning classes.

Classes begin at 7:35 a.m., way too early for Raul, who yawns and stretches as he sits down at his desk. Raul did not go to bed until about 1:00 a.m. His mother shouted and shouted for him to get up this morning. He had barely enough time to put on clothes and brush his teeth before heading to school. Grumpy, Raul pulls out his notebook and tries to pay attention to his geometry teacher, but it is hard to focus with his headache.

Raul is not alone in feeling tired and grumpy. A less well-known effect of puberty is a change in adolescents' sleep patterns and preferred sleep schedule, known as a *delayed phase preference* (Carskadon, 2009; Crowley, Acebo, & Carskadon, 2007). Delayed phase preference is triggered by a change in the nightly release of a hormone that influences sleep, called melatonin. The rise in melatonin that accompanies the onset of sleep occurs, on average, about 2 hours later among adolescents who have experienced puberty as compared those who have not begun puberty (Carskadon, Acebo, & Jenni, 2004). When adolescents are allowed to regulate their own sleep schedule, they will tend to go to bed at about 1:00 a.m. and sleep until about 10:00 a.m. (Colrain & Baker, 2011). Adolescents naturally feel awake when it is time to go to sleep and groggy when it is time to wake for school in the morning. As a result, adolescents stay up later, miss out on sleep, and report sleepiness (Carskadon et al., 2004; Loessl et al., 2008). This tendency for adolescents to go to bed later is influenced by puberty, but it also has increased over the last three decades, along with the increased

availability of television and other media that compete with sleep for adolescents' time (Bartel, Gradisar, & Williamson, 2014; Carskadon & Tarokh, 2014). Most adolescents have electronic devices such as cell phones and computers in their rooms and many report using electronic devices in bed. The more bedtime devise use reported, the later most adolescents report falling asleep and the later they report waking on weekdays.

From ages 13 to 19, the average hours of sleep reported by adolescents in Western countries, such as the United States and Germany, decrease from about 8 hours to 7 hours, with greater reductions in sleep with each year (Carskadon, 2009; Loessl et al., 2008). Yet researchers estimate that adolescents need about 9 hours of sleep each night to support healthy development. Poor sleep is associated with anxiety, irritability, and depression; increases the probability of obesity, illnesses, and accidents; and is associated with less engagement in extracurricular school activities and declines in academic performance (Darchia & Cervena, 2014; J. A. Mitchell, Rodriguez, Schmitz, & Audrain-McGovern, 2013b; Wong, Robertson, & Dyson, 2015). Sleep problems are also associated with risky behaviors including cigarette smoking and other substance use (McKnight-Eily et al., 2011; Pieters et al., 2015; Telzer, Fuligni, Lieberman, & Galván, 2013).

Most middle and high schools start earlier than elementary school, often to allot time for after school sports and activities. Some districts use earlier start times to save on transportation costs by having the same buses and drivers make multiple runs—first to high schools and then to elementary and middle schools. Adolescents making the transition into middle school and then high school may be faced with not only earlier start times but also increased travel time, significantly decreasing their total sleep time (Adam, Snell, & Pendry, 2007; Wolfson & Carskadon, 1998).

Regardless of what time school begins, adolescents tend to go to bed at approximately the same time. One comparison of middle school students who attended an early-starting school (7:15 a.m.) and a later-starting school (8:37 a.m.) found that students who attended the early-starting school obtained about ¾ of an hour less sleep each night, or about 3.5 hours less each week (Wolfson, Spaulding, Dandrow, & Baroni, 2007). After the students had been on their early or late school schedules for over 6 months, those who attended school early were tardy 4 times more often, and had more absences and worse grades, than the students who attended the school with the later starting time. Similar findings were apparent in another study that examined the effects of starting school 30 minutes later (i.e., from 8:00 a.m. to 8:30 a.m.). In a similar study, after 3 months students reported getting more sleep and the change in school start time was associated with significant improvements in measures of adolescent alertness, mood, and health (Owens, Belon, & Moss, 2010).

Sleep matters, and perhaps some of the moodiness characteristic of the stereotypical adolescent is related to changes in sleep patterns. In 2017, the American Academy of Sleep Medicine (Watson et al., 2017) issued a policy statement calling on communities, school boards, and educational institutions to implement start times of 8:30 a.m. or later for middle schools and high schools to ensure that every student arrives at school healthy, awake, alert, and ready to learn.

What Do You Think?

1. When did your high school start? What were your mornings like? How does your experience compare with the research on delayed phase preference?

2. How might we help adolescents get the sleep that they need? Consider this problem from a bioecological perspective. Provide examples of factors at the microsystem, mesosystem, exosystem, and macrosystem levels that can help adolescents arrive to school well rested.

about a year to a year and one-half earlier in 2000 than did boys in the 1960s (Herman-Giddens, 2006; Herman-Giddens et al., 2012). Likewise, boys reached peak velocity of growth over one month earlier each decade between 1946 and 1991 (Bygdell, Vandenput, Ohlsson, & Kindblom, 2014). The secular trend parallels increases in the standard of living and average BMI among children in Western countries and is especially influenced by the growing problem of childhood obesity (Biro, Khoury, & Morrison, 2006; Himes, 2006; Walvoord, 2010). The secular tend may be slowing but it is unclear when the secular trend will stop (Kleanthous, Dermitzaki, Papadimitriou, Papaevangelou, & Papadimitriou, 2017; Papadimitriou, 2016). Girls have shown precocious puberty as early as age 5 (Scutti, 2015); however, it is unlikely that the average age of puberty will ever drop that low. The secular trend poses challenges for young people and parents because the biological entry to adolescence is lowering at the same time as the passage to adulthood is lengthening, making the period of adolescence longer than ever before.

PSYCHOSOCIAL EFFECTS OF EARLY AND LATE PUBERTY

How do adolescents feel about experiencing puberty much earlier or later than their peers, and what effects does early or late puberty have on adolescents' social relationships? First, we need to define early and late puberty. Children who show signs of physical maturation before age 8 (in girls) or 9 (in boys) are considered early-maturing, whereas girls who begin puberty after age 13 and boys who begin after age 14 are considered late-maturing adolescents (Dorn, Dahl, Woodward, & Biro, 2006). Adolescents who mature early or late look different from their same-age peers, and they often are treated differently by adults and peers, with consequences for their development (Graber et al., 2010). For example, adolescents who look older than their years are more likely to be treated in ways similar to older adolescents, which adolescents may perceive as stressful (Rudolph, Troop-Gordon, Lambert, & Natsuaki, 2014). Longitudinal

Peter Dazeley/Getty

Body image dissatisfaction is often first seen in girls during middle childhood.

research suggests that boys and girls who matured off-time, early or late relative to their peers, were more likely to show anxiety and depressed mood than their on-time peers in late adolescence and early adulthood (Mendle & Ferrero, 2012; Natsuaki, Biehl, Ge, & Xiaojia, 2009; Rudolph et al., 2014). Early maturation, in particular, poses specific challenges for girls' and boys' adaptation.

Girls who mature early relative to peers tend to feel less positive about their bodies, physical appearance, and menstruation itself than do girls who mature on time or late (Cesario & Hughes, 2007; Mendle, Turkheimer, & Emery, 2007). Indeed, several studies found they are at risk for negative psychosocial outcomes such as depression, anxiety, and low self-esteem (Benoit, Lacourse, & Claes, 2013; Stojković, 2013; Wang, Lin, Leung, & Schooling, 2016). One reason may be that, although early-maturing girls are often popular, they are also more likely to be victims of rumor-spreading and sexual harassment, which is associated with feelings of depression, anxiety, and poor self-esteem (Reynolds & Juvonen, 2011; Skoog, Özdemir, & Stattin, 2016).

Girls' perception of their pubertal development, whether they see themselves as maturing much earlier or later than their peers, influences puberty-related outcomes (Carter, Jaccard, Silverman, & Pina, 2009; Mendle, 2014). Interestingly, though, girls' perceptions of their own development often are only loosely related to their actual development (Dorn & Biro, 2011; Rasmussen et al., 2015). That is, girls are likely to hold inaccurate views of their bodies, seeing themselves are more or less developed than they are. Rather than actual pubertal development, girls' own views of their early pubertal timing—whether or not they view themselves as maturing much earlier than their peers—are often a better predictor of their age at first intercourse as well as their engagement in sexual risk taking and substance use, and their likelihood of experiencing depression and anxiety (Mendle, 2014; Moore, Harden, & Mendle, 2014). Early-maturing boys tend to be athletic, popular with peers, school leaders, and confident (Stojković, 2013). But, like early maturing girls, they are more likely to experience depression and anxiety when they judge their peer relationships as stressful (Benoit et al., 2013; Blumenthal, Leen-Feldner, Trainor, Babson, & Bunaciu, 2009).

Contextual factors are thought to amplify the effects of pubertal timing on behavior (Graber et al., 2010; Skoog & Stattin, 2014). Some of the problems that early-maturing boys and girls experience arise because they tend to seek relationships with older peers who are more similar to them in physical maturity than their classmates. Spending time with older peers makes early-maturing adolescents more likely to engage in age-inappropriate behaviors, such as early sexual activity and risky sexual activity (Baams, Dubas, Overbeek, & van Aken, 2015; Moore et al., 2014). Early-maturing boys and girls around the world show higher rates of risky activity, including smoking, abusing substances, and displaying aggressive behavior than do peers their age (Dimler & Natsuaki, 2015; Mrug et al., 2014; Skoog & Stattin, 2014). Early maturers tend to show higher rates of problematic drinking, including consuming alcohol more frequently and in greater quantities, and becoming intoxicated more often than their on-time and late-maturing peers (Biehl, Natsuaki, & Ge, 2007; Schelleman-Offermans, Knibbe, & Kuntsche, 2013). Moreover, these patterns of problematic alcohol use often persist into late adolescence and early adulthood, suggesting that early pubertal maturation may hold long-term implications for young people's health (Biehl et al., 2007).

Developmental scientists also study adolescents who mature later than their peers. The effects of late maturation tend to differ for boys and girls. Late maturation appears to have a protective effect on girls with regard to depression (Negriff & Susman, 2011). Findings regarding the effects of late maturation on boys are mixed and less consistent (Mendle & Ferrero, 2012). Late-maturing boys may experience more social and emotional difficulties. During early adolescence, they may be less well liked by their peers and may be more likely than their peers to experience a poor body image, overall body dissatisfaction, and depression during early adolescence, but these effects tend to decline with physical maturation (Negriff & Susman, 2011). Other research suggests that late-maturing boys do not differ in anxiety or depression from their on-time peers (Crockett, Carlo, Wolff, & Hope, 2013; Marceau et al., 2011) or that it is only late-maturing boys with poor peer relationships who experience depression (Benoit et al., 2013).

Thinking in Context 3.2

1. In what ways might the changing sociocultural context contribute to the secular trend and the collection of psychosocial characteristics that most adults view as "typical" of adolescents?

2. How might the dramatic physical changes that adolescents undergo—and the accompanying reactions from others—influence other aspects of development, such as social or emotional development?

PHYSICAL CHANGES IN ADULTHOOD

LO 3.3 Identify normative patterns of physical and reproductive change as well as explanations for the causes of aging.

All of the organs and body systems, including digestive, respiratory, circulatory, and reproductive systems, reach their peak in functioning in early adulthood. We may not think of people in their 20s as aging, but the biological fact is that once individuals are physically mature, **senescence**—a pattern of gradual age-related declines in physical functioning—begins (Cristofalo, Tresini, & Francis, 1999). Measurable age-related changes in functioning are visible by about age 30, but most people do not notice these until middle adulthood. Aging entails gradual changes in appearance, strength, body proportions, and fertility.

CHANGING APPEARANCE

Karen looked at the pictures of her daughter's wedding. "What a beautiful day. Ouch! Look at this picture of me in the sunlight. When did I get so many lines around my eyes?" Like Karen, many adults find that the age-related changes in the skin seemingly appear overnight. Age-related changes in the skin are gradual, predictable, unavoidable, and begin at about age 20. The connective tissue begins to thin by about 1% per year, resulting in less elastic skin and some visible wrinkles around the eyes by age 30 (Timiras, 2003). The skin becomes more dry as oil glands become less active. Most adults in their 30s notice lines developing on their foreheads, and by the 40s these lines are accompanied by crow's feet around the eyes and lines around the mouth—markers of four decades of smiles, frowns, laughter, and other emotions. During middle adulthood the process continues: Skin becomes less taut as the epidermis, the outer protective layer of the skin that produces new skin cells, loosens its attachment to the thinning dermis, the middle layer of skin consisting of connective tissue that gives skin its flexibility (Quan & Fisher, 2015). The resulting loss in elasticity is accompanied by the loss of fat in the hypodermis, the innermost layer of skin composed of fat, which leads to wrinkling and loosening of the skin (Kohl, Steinbauer, Landthaler, & Szeimies, 2011). In older adulthood, thinning skin and the loss of fat make blood vessels more visible and increase older adults' sensitivity to cold (Farage, Miller, Elsner, & Maibach, 2013). In addition, many older adults develop pigmented marks called age spots on their hands and faces. Some adults seek a more youthful appearance through cosemtic procedures (see Lives in Context: Cosmetic Procedures in Midlife).

Women tend to experience age-related changes sooner and more quickly than do men. Their dermis is thinner, and as they age they experience hormonal changes that exacerbate aging, particularly a reduction in the female hormone estrogen (Castelo-Branco & Davila, 2015; Farage et al., 2013; Firooz et al., 2017). Although age-related changes in the skin are unavoidable, there is great variability in appearance (Miyamoto et al., 2011). For people of all skin types and ethnicities, the rate of skin aging is influenced by exposure to the elements—sun, heat, cold, and pollution—and by lifestyle factors such as smoking

senescence A pattern of gradual age-related declines in physical functioning.

• • Cosmetic Procedures in Midlife

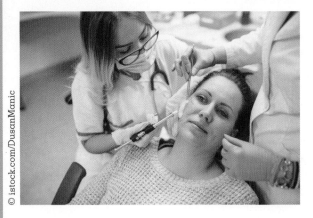

Nonsurgical cosmetic procedures, such as the injection of Botox, are increasingly popular.

The many physical changes that occur in middle adulthood influence adults' views of themselves as well as how they interact with, and are treated by, others. Changes in appearance are hard to deny in midlife. Most midlife adults can list how their appearance has changed, noting, for example, lines that have appeared on their face (Honigman & Castle, 2006). As people age, their concerns about

FIGURE 3.4: **Cosmetic Procedures by Age in the United States, 2014**

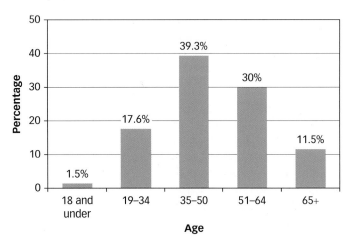

Source: American Society for Aesthetic Plastic Surgery, 2014.

their appearance increasingly focus on the face. It is not uncommon for midlife adults, especially women, to develop concerns and worries about losing their attractiveness, as judged by Western beauty standards that emphasize youth (Barrett & Robbins, 2008).

Many adults seek to improve their appearance through cosmetic procedures, both surgical and nonsurgical. As the name suggests, surgical cosmetic procedures entail surgery. Nearly 1.7 million surgical cosmetic procedures were conducted in 2015 including procedures such as liposuction,

eyelid surgery, tummy tucks, and breast augmentation (American Society of Plastic Surgeons, 2016). Nonsurgical cosmetic procedures are far more common, with 14.2 million conducted in 2015. The most common noninvasive procedures include Botox injections (which paralyze facial muscles, making them unable to contract and "wrinkle"), so-called injectable "fillers" (substances injected into wrinkles, temporarily filling them), and chemical peels and microdermabrasion (chemical and physical means of removing the outermost layers of skin, purporting to reveal smooth new skin).

At all ages, about 90% of cosmetic procedures are conducted on women. Middle-aged adults and those transitioning to midlife (ages 35–64) are most likely to obtain cosmetic procedures, accounting for 69% of the total in 2016, followed by young adults under the age of 35 (18%; American Society of Plastic Surgeons, 2016; see Figure 3.4). Why do women pursue cosmetic procedures? Not surprising, women report undergoing cosmetic procedures in order to improve their appearance (Sobanko et al., 2015), and those who fear negative appearance evaluations tend to have more positive attitudes about cosmetic procedures (Dunaev, Schulz, & Markey, 2016).

There are multiple individual and contextual factors at play when considering how middle-aged women view themselves and their attitudes toward these procedures (Saucier, 2004; Slevec & Tiggemann, 2010). Western cultural norms equate women's aging with a decline in physical attractiveness. Television, magazines, and advertising feature the latest advances in cosmetic surgical procedures as well as prolific discussions of the latest celebrity to "go under the knife" (Sarwer & Crerand, 2004). Cosmetic surgery has also become the focus of a number of popular television programs, such as *Botched* and *Extreme Makeover.* Continued media exposure can shape people's perceptions and normalize values and behaviors, such as those related to cosmetic procedures as a means for addressing body discontent (Slevec & Tiggemann, 2010).

Even in adulthood, peers are an important influence on women's attitude and behaviors. Women who perceive their friends as supportive of the use of cosmetic procedures, and especially those whose friends obtain such procedures, are likely to view cosmetic procedures positively and are more likely to obtain them (Nerini, Matera, & Stefanile, 2014; Sharp, Tiggemann, & Mattiske, 2014).

What Do You Think?

1. In your opinion, why are cosmetic procedures most popular in midlife?

2. What are some of the advantages and disadvantages or risks of such procedures?

3. How might someone make a decision about whether to pursue cosmetic procedures?

(Gragnani et al., 2014; Kohl et al., 2011; Wiegand, Raschke, & Elsner, 2017). The sun is the most dramatic contributor to skin aging, responsible for about 80% of skin changes (Flament, Bazin, & Piot, 2013; Kammeyer & Luiten, 2015; Tobin, 2017). The use of sunscreen has been shown to retard skin aging (Hughes, Williams, Baker, & Green, 2013).

Lives in Context Video 3.2
Aging and Physical Development

BODY SHAPE, MUSCLE, AND BONE

Muscle development increases throughout the 20s and peaks at about age 30 (Masoro & Austad, 2005). Muscle strength, as measured by the maximum force with which one can throw a ball, for example, shows a gradual decline beginning at about age 30 but is generally not noticeable to most people until middle age (Rice & Cunningham, 2002). **Sarcopenia**, the age-related loss of muscle mass and strength, tends to accelerate in the 40s (Keller & Engelhardt, 2013). By age 60, about 10% to 15% of maximum strength is lost and, by age 80, 30% to 50% (Buford et al., 2010). Physical activity, especially resistance exercise, as well as the regular consumption of protein, can strengthen muscles and offset losses into the 90s (Gomes et al., 2017; Naseeb & Volpe, 2017; Peterson, Rhea, Sen, & Gordon, 2010).

Adults' performance on activities that require body coordination and bursts of strength, such as sprinting and playing basketball, tend to peak in the early 20s whereas those that require endurance, such as distance running, peak in the early 30s and show declines after age 40 (Hayslip, Panek, & Patrick, 2007; Schulz & Curnow, 1988). Although physical abilities show a predictable pattern of change, adults vary in the rate of change in their performance. Activity plays a large role in maintaining weight, muscle mass, and endurance throughout adulthood (Aldwin, Spiro, & Park, 2006). Adults who remain active tend to retain their physique and physical competencies (Newell, Vaillancourt, & Sosnoff, 2006). Research with expert athletes illustrates that practice and athletic training maintains strength and motor skills. As compared with nonathlete peers, athletes experience more subtle and gradual declines in physical abilities from the late 30s to the 60s. Their muscles and motor skills age much more slowly than their peers (Faulkner, Larkin, Claflin, & Brooks, 2007). Moreover, some physical abilities, such as isometric muscle strength—the subtle contractions used to hold a hand grip, push off against a wall, stretch, or practice yoga—are maintained throughout adulthood (Lavender & Nosaka, 2007; Mitchell et al., 2012).

Body composition shifts over the course of adulthood as the metabolic rate slows. Both men and women tend to experience weight gain in middle adulthood, with an increase in body fat and loss of muscle and bone. In men, fat accumulates on the back and upper abdomen, while women experience an increase in fat in the upper arms and around the waist. Good nutrition and an active lifestyle can reduce losses and even increase muscular density. When adults gradually reduce their caloric intake to match their reduced need for calories, age-related weight gain is minimized. For example, a 7-year-long study of about 30,000 women aged 50 to 79 showed that a low-fat diet with lots of vegetables, fruits, and grains predicted weight loss and maintenance, regardless of SES and ethnicity (Howard et al., 2006).

Many age-related changes, like those of the skin and body composition, are visible. Others, like skeletal changes, are less obvious. Bone density reaches its height in the mid- to late 30s, after which adults tend to experience gradual bone loss. Bones become thinner, more porous, and more brittle as calcium is absorbed. Bone loss increases in the 50s, especially in women, whose bones have less calcium to begin with and who lose the protective influence of estrogen on bones after menopause (Chan & Duque, 2002). As the bones that make up the vertebrae in the spinal column become thin and more brittle, the disks collapse and adults lose height, about an inch or more by age 60, and more thereafter (Hannan et al., 2012). Loss of bone density causes bones to break more easily and heal more slowly, making a broken bone more serious as we age. The condition of reduced bone density is known as osteopenia, and more severe bone thinning is diagnosed as osteoporosis; calcium supplements and a program of regular

sarcopenia The age-related loss of muscle mass and strength.

weight-bearing exercise are recommended to prevent, and to some extent to treat, both conditions. Like other physical changes, losses in bone density can be slowed by behavior and lifestyle choices, such as avoiding smoking and excess drinking and engaging in weight-bearing exercise (Berg et al., 2008; Bleicher et al., 2011; Gass & Dawson-Hughes, 2006).

REPRODUCTIVE CHANGES IN WOMEN

Martina holds her newborn close to her while chatting with her family who has come to visit her in the maternity ward. At 32 years of age, Martina is older than the average first-time mother; most women are in their 20s they give birth to their first child. However, as shown in Figure 3.5, births to women in their 30s and 40s have increased substantially since the early 1990s (Hamilton, Martin, Osterman, Curtin, & Mathews, 2015). Many young adults wait to have children until they have completed their education and established their careers. The maturity and financial stability that accompany the 30s can make for better parents. However, reproductive capacity declines with age, increasing the risk for women in their mid- to late 30s of experiencing difficulty conceiving (Schmidt, Sobotka, Bentzen, & Nyboe Andersen, 2012; Tatone, 2008). Although women are born with about 400,000 ova (Jadav, 2004), they decay with age, becoming less viable for conception and producing a healthy offspring. In addition, dwindling reserves of ova can prevent conception because it is thought that the body requires a minimum number of ova in order to ovulate (Baird et al., 2005). However, the exact minimum is unknown and, like other aspects of physical development, may vary with genetic and contextual factors (Schuh-Huerta et al., 2012).

With advancing age, ovulation becomes less regular, one of the first signs that **menopause**, the cessation of ovulation and menstruation, is on the horizon. At about 51 years of age on average, but starting as early as age 42 and as late as 58, women experience menopause (Avis & Crawford, 2006; Do et al., 2013). The timing of menopause is influenced by heredity but also by lifestyle choices and contextual influences, such as exposure to pollution (Grindler et al., 2015; Hartge, 2009). Menopause occurs earlier in women who smoke, who are malnourished, who have not given birth, and who are of lower SES (Gold et al., 2013; Saraç, Öztekin, & Çelebi, 2011; Tawfik et al., 2015). Specifically, a woman is said to have reached menopause 1 year after her last menstrual period. *Perimenopause* refers to the transition to menopause, extending approximately 3 years before and after menopause. It is during perimenopause that the production of reproductive hormones declines and symptoms associated with menopause first appear (McNamara, Batur, & DeSapri, 2015).

The first indicator of perimenopause is a shorter menstrual cycle, followed by erratic periods (Burger, Hale, Robertson, & Dennerstein, 2007). Ovulation becomes less predictable, occurring early or late in the cycle; sometimes several ova are released and sometimes none (Nelson, 2008). The most common and long-lasting symptom of perimenopause is hot flashes, in which the expansion and contraction of blood vessels cause sudden sensations of heat throughout the body accompanied by sweating (McNamara et al., 2015; Sussman et al., 2015). One-third to as many as three-quarters of U.S. women experience hot flashes, which may persist for 7 or more years (Avis et al., 2015; Nelson, 2008; Santoro, 2016). Hormone replacement therapy, as discussed in the Applying Developmental Science feature, is designed to address perimenopause symptoms.

menopause The end of menstruation and a woman's reproductive capacity.

FIGURE 3.5: Births to Women Ages 15 to 44 in the United States, 1990 to 2015

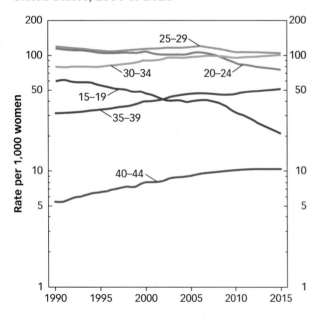

Note: Live births per 1,000 women. This figure illustrates the trend of increasing births among women in their thirties and forties.

Source: NCHS, National Vital Statistics System.

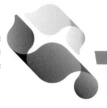

APPLYING DEVELOPMENTAL SCIENCE

• • Hormone Replacement Therapy

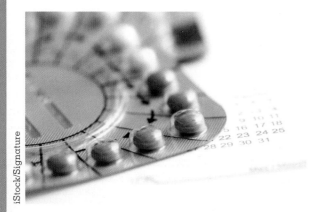

Hormone replacement therapy is commonly prescribed to manage menopausal symptoms. However, the U.S. Food and Drug Administration recommends that physicians prescribe the smallest dose to reduce menopausal symptoms and for the shortest time.

From the 1950s until recently, it was common for women to be prescribed hormones to increase the levels of estrogen and/or progesterone in their bodies. Hormone therapy was considered a "fountain of youth" as well as a way to reduce severe perimenopause symptoms and manage common symptoms such as hot flashes. Many healthcare professionals advised postmenopausal women to use hormone replacement in the belief that it reduced heart disease and improved cognitive function. The results of correlational studies supported the use of hormone therapy and it was widely prescribed (Hersh, Stefanick, & Stafford, 2004).

But in 2002, the results of the Women's Health Initiative Study, a longitudinal study of thousands of perimenopausal women, suggested that although hormone replacement therapy reduces the incidence of hot flashes and decreases the risk of osteoporosis, it does not protect against heart disease. On the contrary, the results suggested that hormone replacement therapy may increase the risk of heart disease, stroke, and breast cancer (Nelson et al., 2002). These findings resulted in a dramatic worldwide decline in the use of hormone replacement therapy (Stevenson, Hodis, Pickar, & Lobo, 2009). Research with international samples indicates that the breast cancer rate declined from 2000 to 2007, as hormone replacement therapy became less common, suggesting its role (Sharpe et al., 2010).

However, like most aspects of development, the relation of hormone replacement therapy and health outcomes is much more complex than the Women's Health Initiative findings, as it is influenced by the dynamic interaction of genetic and contextual factors. In one study, hormone replacement therapy did not lower the overall risk of heart disease across all women, but after the researchers controlled for other risk factors (such as hypertension) the risk for heart disease was lower for women taking hormone supplements (Rossouw et al., 2007). The cardiovascular risks associated with hormone replacement therapy increased with age starting only at age 60 (Stevenson et al., 2009). The breast cancer risks associated with hormone replacement therapy vary by race and ethnicity, body mass index (BMI), and breast density (Hou et al., 2013), with some women experiencing no increased risk (Kotsopoulos et al., 2016). There is no universal relationship; instead, it varies by unique interactions between individuals' biological propensities and the contexts in which they reside.

Other research shows that hormone replacement therapy can help some postmenopausal women with selected comorbid conditions such as osteoporosis, type II diabetes, certain cardiovascular pathologies, rheumatoid arthritis, and colorectal cancer (Britto et al., 2011; Islander, Jochems, Lagerquist, Forsblad-d'Elia, & Carlsten, 2011; Panay, Hamoda, Arya, & Savvas, 2013). Findings such as these may suggest that hormone replacement therapy is a reasonable option to manage menopausal symptoms over the short term (Canderelli, Leccesse, & Miller, 2007; Hickey, Elliott, & Davison, 2012). The U.S. Food and Drug Administration recommends that physicians prescribe the smallest dose needed to reduce menopausal symptoms and for the shortest time (Hannon, 2010). The decision as to who should use any form of hormone replacement therapy needs to be based on the individual woman's needs, quality of life, and potential risks versus benefits (Panay et al., 2013).

What Do You Think?

1. **Why have researchers' conclusions regarding the safety of hormone replacement therapy varied so dramatically across studies and over recent decades?**

2. **What factors do you think are important for women to consider when it comes to hormone replacement therapy? What advice would you give a friend?**

Similar to girls' reactions to menarche, how women experience menopause, whether they report severe mood changes and irritability or few psychological and physical consequences, varies with their attitudes and expectations for menopause, which are influenced by personal characteristics, circumstances, and societal views about women and aging (Ayers, Forshaw, & Hunter, 2010; Delanoë et al., 2012; Lindh-Åstrand, Hoffmann, Hammar, & Kjellgren, 2007; Nosek, Kennedy, & Gudmundsdottir, 2012). Women who have

CULTURAL INFLUENCES ON DEVELOPMENT

• • Cultural Perspectives on Menopause

Ashley Cooper pics/Alamy

Cultural depictions of menopause influence women's experience of menopause.

Societal and cultural views influence how menopause is perceived. In societies that value youth, women may fear the bodily changes of menopause and their perceived loss of sex appeal (Howell & Beth, 2002). On the other hand, in cultures where older women are respected and achieve social or religious power with age (e.g., powerful mother-in-law and grandmother roles), women report few complaints about menopausal symptoms (Delanoë et al., 2012).

In Japan, where women gain power and responsibility (such as monitoring household finances and caring for dependent parents) with age, women rarely report hot flashes or other menopausal symptoms (Huang, Xu, I, & Jaisamrarn, 2010; Lock & Kaufert, 2001). Middle adulthood is seen as a mature and productive time of life; menopause is not viewed as a marker of decline by Japanese women or their physicians. Research has shown that women in Asian cultures, as well as non-industrialized cultures, consistently report fewer and less severe menopausal symptoms (Gupta, Sturdee, & Hunter, 2006; Huang et al., 2010). For example, one study of Chinese women found that only one third

reported experiencing hot flashes and fewer than one third experienced night sweats (Liu & Eden, 2007).

Similarly, Mayan women of the Yucatán achieve increased status with menopause along with freedom from child-rearing (Beyene & Martin, 2001). Mayan women marry as teenagers and by their late 30s typically have given birth to many children. Many Mayan women are eager to escape the burden of child-rearing and describe menopause in positive terms such as providing freedom, being happy, and feeling like a young girl again. Few report menopausal symptoms such as hot flashes (Beyene & Martin, 2001). In fact, there is no word in the Mayan language to describe hot flashes (Beyene, 1986). Women in rural India also report menopause as a welcomed time that is accompanied by enhanced mobility, freedom from unwanted pregnancy, and increased authority (Gupta et al., 2006).

Women in Western industrialized societies tend to have mixed feelings about menopause. They frequently describe the negatives, including a loss of fertility and the physical changes that accompany it, feeling less feminine, and having a clear sign of aging (Chrisler, 2008). At the same time, menopause represents the end of dealing with menstrual periods, the end of contraceptive worries, and a sense of liberation. Post-menopausal women tend to have more positive views of menopause than do younger women and are more likely to report feeling a sense of freedom and confidence (Chrisler, 2008).

What Do You Think?

1. From your perspective, how do adults in the United States view menopause? For example, how does television depict menopause or menopausal women? Identify examples in popular media to support your perspective.

2. How might individuals' perception of developments such as menopause influence what they experience (and the reverse)?

children may view menopause as providing sexual freedom and enjoyment without worry of contraception or pregnancy. In contrast, women who desire a family but who have not given birth may view menopause as the end of fertility and the accompanying possibility of child-rearing, making menopause a difficult time indeed (Howell & Beth, 2002). High levels of education and high SES are both associated with more positive views of menopause and fewer reports of menopausal symptoms (Lawlor, Ebrahim, & Smith, 2003). Ethnicity is also related to views about menopause. African American and Mexican American women tend to hold more favorable views toward menopause than white non-Hispanic American women, often describing it as a normal part of life, one that many women look forward to (Avis et al., 2001; Sampselle, Harris, Harlow, & Sowers, 2002).

Contextual factors influence how women make sense of menopause (Delanoë et al., 2012; Strauss, 2011). When menopause is viewed as a medical event whose symptoms require treatment, women tend to view it more negatively and report more physical and emotional symptoms (Hvas & Dorte Effersøe, 2008). However, recent generations of women have objected to the notion of menopause as a disease and instead view it as a naturally occurring process. Adults of both sexes, as well as their families, tend to view menopause more positively when it is described as a life transition or symbol of aging, as compared with a medical event whose symptoms are problematic and require treatment (Dillaway, 2008; Hvas & Dorte Effersøe, 2008). In the United States, postmenopausal women tend to view menopause more positively than do younger women (Avis, Brockwell, & Colvin, 2005). They tend to report menopause as causing few difficulties and instead view it as a beginning. In one study of over 2,000 postmenopausal women, about two thirds reported feeling relieved over freedom from birth control (Rossi, 2004). This pattern may also be true cross culturally. A study of about 1,400 women aged 40 to 55 years from West Bengal, India, revealed that postmenopausal women had more positive attitudes about menopause and aging than did perimenopausal women (Dasgupta & Ray, 2016) Cultural factors also influence how menopause is experienced, as discussed in Cultural Influences on Development: Cultural Perspectives on Menopause.

REPRODUCTIVE CHANGES IN MEN

Do men experience a sudden drop in reproductive ability similar to women? No. Unlike women, men's reproductive ability declines gradually and steadily over the adult years, with declines in testosterone beginning as early as age 30 in some men and continuing at a pace of about a 1% decrease per year to a total decline in testosterone of about 30% by age 70 (Federman & Walford, 2007). Men's bodies produce less testosterone and they become less fertile, but about 75% of men retain testosterone levels in the normal range with most adult males continuing to produce sperm throughout adulthood; many are able to father children into their 80s and beyond (Ehlert & Fischbacher, 2013). However, the number and quality of sperm produced declines in middle adulthood, beginning at about age 40, and offspring of older men may be at greater risk of congenital abnormalities (Almeida, Rato, Sousa, Alves, & Oliveira, 2017; Johnson, Dunleavy, Gemmell, & Nakagawa, 2015; Khan, 2017).

Although men experience gradual declines in testosterone over their lifetimes, levels can shift dramatically in response to stress and illness, creating the appearance of a "male menopause" (Shores, 2014). Stress from problems such as unemployment, illness, marital problems, children leaving home, or sexual inactivity can cause reductions in testosterone, which decreases sexual desire and responses. Low levels of testosterone may interfere with a man's ability to achieve or maintain an erection, which can influence anxiety about his sexual capacity, which can lead to further declines in testosterone (Seidman & Weiser, 2013). In this way, it might appear as if some men go through a form of menopause, but the sudden declines in testosterone tend to be a correlate of stress and health problems rather than a biological inevitability (Donatelle, 2004). Regardless, media and popular views in the United States and Europe have contributed to the notion of a male menopause and a corresponding medicalization of masculinity in middle and older adulthood though the use of hormone and other treatments (Marshall, 2007; Vainionpää & Topo, 2006). For example, products designed to treat so-called "low T" are commonly advertised on television despite research suggesting that only about 6% to 10% of men experience testosterone deficiency (Araujo et al., 2004; Haring et al., 2010). Similar to the medicalization of menopause, viewing normative hormonal changes experienced by men as a disease contributes to negative views of normal aging.

THEORIES OF AGING

Why do we age? There are many theoretical explanations for aging. According to the wear and tear theory of aging, an early theory, the body wears out from use and thus ages (Bengston, Gans, Pulney, & Silverstein, 2009). On the contrary, research suggests that we must "use it or lose it." That is, regular exercise increases longevity in all people regardless of ethnicity or SES (Sanchis-Gomar, Olaso-Gonzalez, Corella, Gomez-Cabrera, & Vina, 2011; Stessman, Hammerman-Rozenberg, Maaravi, Azoulai, & Cohen, 2005). Activity is a critical component of a long and healthy life.

Several other theories offer additional explanations for aging. A more recent perspective explains it as a function of programmed genetics: DNA and heredity. Recall from Chapter 2 that our genes are composed of DNA and serve as the genetic blueprint, handed down through heredity, for all of our characteristics. Parents' lifespans predict those of their children, and identical twins share more similar lifespans than do fraternal twins, suggesting a role for heredity in aging (Hjelmborg et al., 2006; Montesanto et al., 2011). Yet kin relations for markers of biological age, such as strength, respiratory capacity, blood pressure, and bone density, are relatively small as health is influenced not just by genetics but by context and lifestyle. Lifespans among family members often vary with context and behaviors. Aging therefore reflects the interaction of epigenetic factors (Mitteldorf, 2016; Moskalev, Aliper, Smit-McBride, Buzdin, & Zhavoronkov, 2014). It may be that it is not lifespan that we inherit but a set of genetic factors that may predict lifespan (Walter et al., 2011). Ultimately, it is the contextual factors, such as the availability of health care, and lifestyle factors, such as health-related behaviors, that matter in predicting lifespan.

Whether genetic predispositions for longevity are realized depends on environmental factors such as diet and exercise, behaviors such as alcohol use or smoking, and exposure to environmental toxins (Karasik, Demissie, Cupples, & Kiel, 2005; Tourlouki et al., 2010). Experiments with animals support the role of caloric restriction in longevity (Smith, Nagy, & Allison, 2010; Speakman & Mitchell, 2011). A nutritious diet that is extremely low in calories is associated with a longer lifespan, but the up to 40% caloric deprivation required is uncomfortable and difficult to sustain (Anton & Leeuwenburgh, 2013; C. Lee & Longo, 2016). The immune system plays a role in aging by influencing the body's adjustment to external stressors and pathogens encountered throughout life. From this perspective, an aging immune system is less able to differentiate healthy cells from pathology, may direct the body's defenses against healthy cells, and may ignore harmful cells (Montecino-Rodriguez, Berent-Maoz, & Dorshkind, 2013; Salvioli et al., 2013).

Another account of aging relies on cellular mutation, damage to DNA and chromosomes. Research with animals shows that cell mutations increase exponentially with age (Baines, Turnbull, & Greaves, 2014; Lee, Chang, & Chi, 2010; Milholland, Suh, & Vijg, 2017). Cellular mutations lead to a deterioration in functioning and an increase in age-related diseases and cancers. Some of this damage may be due to **free radicals**, highly reactive and corrosive substances that form when cells are exposed to oxygen. As oxygen decomposes within the cell, changes occur at the level of the atom: An electron is stripped, creating a free radical. Through chemical reactions, free radicals destroy DNA, proteins, and other cellular materials in an attempt to replace the missing electrons. Free radicals are thought to contribute to many age-related diseases such as cancer, cardiovascular disorders, and arthritis (Lagouge & Larsson, 2013; Shringarpure & Davies, 2009; Valko, Jomova, Rhodes, Kuča, & Musílek, 2016) and predict mortality (Schöttker et al., 2015). Environmental factors may work to defend the body from free radicals by producing material that neutralizes free radicals and reduces the harm caused by them (Miura & Endo, 2010). A diet rich in antioxidants, including vitamins C and E and beta carotene, can protect against damage from free radicals (Harman, 2006).

Reductions in the capacity for cell division, specifically the limited capacity for human cells to divide, are the basis for another explanation for aging. Human cells have the capacity to divide about 50 times in their lifespan (Hayflick, 1996). Each time the cell divides, **telomeres**, tiny caps of DNA located at both ends of the chromosomes, become shorter. Shorter telomeres may protect the cell from common mutations that occur with repeated divisions, but they also reduce the cell's capacity to reproduce itself (Sedivy, 2007; Xi, Li, Ren, Zhang, & Zhang, 2013). Telomeres that shorten past

free radical A highly reactive, corrosive substance that forms when a cell is exposed to oxygen. Through chemical reactions, free radicals destroy DNA, proteins, and other cellular materials.

telomere A type of DNA that caps both ends of chromosomes and shortens with each cell division. Eventually telomeres shorten past a critical length and cause the cell to stop duplicating.

TABLE 3.2 • Theories of Aging

THEORY	EXPLANATION
Wear and tear	The body wears out, aging from use.
Programmed genetics	The rate of aging is influenced by DNA and heredity.
Caloric restriction	A nutritious diet that is extremely low in calories is associated with a longer lifespan.
Aging immune system	With age, the immune system is less able to differentiate healthy cells from pathology and may direct the body's defenses against healthy cells instead of harmful cells.
Cellular mutation	Aging results from damage to DNA and chromosomes, leading to an increase in cellular mutations that result in age-related diseases and cancers.
Free radicals	Free radicals, highly reactive and corrosive substances that form when cells are exposed to oxygen, destroy DNA, proteins, and other cellular materials and contribute to age-related diseases and cancers.
Reduced capacity for cell division	Each time human cells divide, telomeres become shorter, protecting the cell from mutations that occur with repeated divisions but also reducing the cell's capacity to reproduce itself. Eventually, telomeres become so short that the cell stops dividing, diseases increase, and cells die.

a critical length cause the cell to stop dividing all together, leading to increases in disease, cell death, and body aging (Andrews, Fujii, Goronzy, & Weyand, 2010; Campisi, 2013; Opresko & Shay, 2017). For example, telomere length is associated with dozens of cancers (Barthel et al., 2017). In this sense, telomere length may serve as a biomarker of aging (Epel, 2009; Mather, Jorm, Parslow, & Christensen, 2011; Xu, Duc, Holcman, & Teixeira, 2013). Stress contributes to the shortening of telomeres, as well as oxidative stress such as that which results from free radicals (Cannon, Einstein, & Tulp, 2017; Shalev et al., 2013). For people of all ages, regular physical activity is associated with a longer telomere length (Arsenis, You, Ogawa, Tinsley, & Zuo, 2015; Roth, 2015; Saßenroth et al., 2015), suggesting that lifestyle factors can attenuate telomere shortening, and thereby aspects of aging (Blackburn et al., 2015).

Each of these theories of aging offers a different perspective on the causes of aging, as shown in Table 3.2. Given the complexities of development, it is likely that one needs to draw from all of these perspectives to arrive at an adequate account of aging.

 Thinking in Context 3.3

1. The physical changes that adults undergo influence how they view themselves as well as how others view and treat them. What are some of the implications of physical aging for adults' sense of self?

2. There are many patterns of physical change in adulthood. Discuss influences on the timing and scope of physical changes throughout adulthood. What are sources of variation? How might contextual factors influence the changes that occur over the adult years?

3. Consider theories of aging. In your view, which theory is the least adequate in accounting for how we change over our lifetimes? Which theory do you think best accounts for how people develop over the lifespan? Why?

EATING AND EXERCISE OVER THE LIFESPAN

LO 3.4 Analyze the influence of eating habits, obesity, and physical activity on physical development and functioning over the lifespan.

An important theme of lifespan development is that individuals are active contributors to their development. That is, we all play a role in our physical, cognitive, and socioemotional development as well as how we age. Through behaviors such as eating and physical activity, we influence our own physical development and functioning.

EATING BEHAVIORS IN INFANCY AND CHILDHOOD

We begin to develop eating habits early in life through interactions with our caregivers and contexts. Breast milk is many infants' first food.

Breastfeeding

One of the best ways of meeting infants' complex nutritional needs is through breastfeeding. Recommended by the U.S. Department of Health and Human Services (2011), breastfeeding has increased in popularity in the United States from about one-half of mothers ever breastfeeding in 1990 to more than three-quarters in 2010 (Child Trends, 2013a; Li, Zhao, Mokdad, & Barker, 2003). About 49% of women continue to breastfeed after 6 months and 27% at 12 months. Breastfeeding practices vary by ethnicity, education, SES, and maternal age (Hauck, Fenwick, Dhaliwal, & Butt, 2011).

Countries where working women are allowed paid maternity leave for part or all of their infant's first year of life, such as Denmark, Norway, Sweden, and Australia, show very high breastfeeding rates of 94% and more (Hauck et al., 2011; Imdad, Yakoob, & Bhutta, 2011; Roelants, Hauspie, & Hoppenbrouwers, 2010). In the United States and the United Kingdom, the lowest rates of breastfeeding are among low-income mothers, mothers who are young, and mothers with low levels of education. In contrast to industrialized countries, in developing countries women with low educational levels and in the poorest social classes are usually more likely to breastfeed their children and educated women of higher income brackets tend to shun breastfeeding, viewing it as option primarily for low-income women who are unable to afford formula (Berra et al., 2003; Imdad et al., 2011; Rasheed, Frongillo, Devine, Alam, & Rasmussen, 2009).

Breastfeeding offers benefits for mothers and infants. Mothers who breastfeed have lower rates of diabetes, cardiovascular disease, and depression, and after they reach menopause they are at lower risk for ovarian and breast cancer and bone fractures (Godfrey & Lawrence, 2010; Islami et al., 2015). A mother's milk is tailored to her infant and has the right amount of fat, sugar, water, and protein needed for the baby's growth and development. Most babies find it easier to digest breast milk than formula. In addition, breast milk contains immunizing agents that protect the infant against infections (Cabinian et al., 2016; Turfkruyer & Verhasselt, 2015) and breastfed infants tend to experience lower rates of allergies and gastrointestinal symptoms as well as with fewer visits to physicians (Schulze & Carlisle, 2010; Stein & Kuhn, 2009).

Breastfeeding for more than 6 months is associated with reduced risk of obesity and childhood cancer, especially lymphomas (Amitay, Dubnov Raz, & Keinan-Boker, 2016; Schulze & Carlisle, 2010; Victora et al., 2016). Recent research suggests that exclusively breastfeeding during the first 4 to 6 weeks of life may be associated with longer telomeres at ages 4 and 5 (Wojcicki et al., 2016).

Breastfeeding is associated with many health benefits for infants and mothers, and provides opportunities for infant–mother bonding.

comstock/lucidwaters

Despite these benefits, many mothers do not breastfeed, either by choice or by necessity. In this case, infant formula is a safe and healthy alternative to breast milk. Formula production is monitored by the U.S. Food and Drug Administration. Most formulas are made from cow's milk, but soy-based alternatives exist for infants with allergies or parents who choose to raise their child vegetarian. Infants subsist on milk or formula alone for the first few months of life, after which other foods begin to be integrated into their diet.

Eating

Somewhere between 4 and 6 months of age, infants eat their first solid food—although "solid food" is actually a misnomer; the first food consumed is usually iron-fortified baby cereal mixed with breast milk or formula to make a very thin gruel. As babies get older, they are introduced to other pureed foods, such as vegetables and fruits, and later, pureed meats. Infants do not necessarily like these new flavors and textures—many foods must be introduced over a dozen times before an infant will accept them.

As infants grow to become toddlers, their appetites decrease. They begin to feed themselves, which means meals may take more time; self-feeding might also reduce toddlers' food consumption. From ages 2 to 6, young children's appetites continue to decline as compared with infants and toddlers. This decline is normal and occurs as growth slows. At around age 3, it is not uncommon for children to go through a fussy eating phase where previously tolerated food is no longer accepted and it is hard to introduce new food (Fildes et al., 2014; Nicklaus, 2009). Some argue that young children's common dislike of new foods may be adaptive from an evolutionary perspective because it encourages them to eat familiar and safe foods rather than novel and potentially dangerous foods (Birch & Fisher, 1995).

The overall incidence of picky eating declines with time, but for many children, it is chronic, lasting for several years. Parents of picky eaters report that their children consume a limited variety of foods, require foods to be prepared in specific ways, express strong likes and dislikes, and throw tantrums over feeding. Children with a difficult temperament at 1.5 years of age are more likely to be picky eaters 2 years later (Hafstad, Abebe, Torgersen, & von Soest, 2013). This example illustrates the dynamic interaction of developmental domains, as an emotional factor—temperament—influences eating habits, which in turn influences physical development. Moreover, fussy eating tends to elicit parental pressure to eat, which tends to precede fussiness, suggesting that fussy eating is sustained through bidirectional parent-child interactions (Jansen et al., 2017; Walton, Kuczynski, Haycraft, Breen, & Haines, 2017). Yet in most cases, picky eating does not show significant effects on growth (Mascola, Bryson, & Agras, 2010). Regardless, picky eating is an important concern for parents and may remain so through much of childhood.

Malnutrition

Consuming adequate calories and nutrition is a challenge for many children, especially those in developing countries where chronic malnutrition is common (Petrou & Kupek, 2010). Malnutrition has devastating effects on physical growth. For example, during a 3-month-long drought that took place in Kenya in 1984 children's intake of food declined dramatically, and they gained only half as much weight as normal (McDonald, Sigman, Espinosa, & Neumann, 1994). About one third of 3- to 5-year-old children in developing countries show growth stunting (de Onis, Blössner, & Borghi, 2012). A diet that is chronically insufficient in protein and calories commonly results in **marasmus**, a wasting disease in which the body's fat and muscle are depleted. Growth stops, the body wastes away, the skin becomes wrinkly and aged looking, the abdomen shrinks, and the body takes on

marasmus A wasting disease in which the body's fat and muscle are depleted; growth stops, the body wastes away, taking on a hollow appearance.

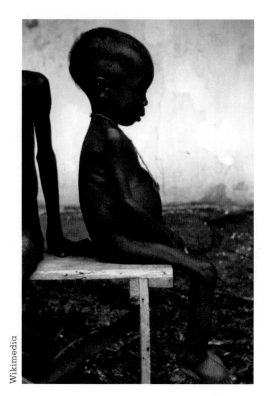

This child suffers from an extreme nutritional deficiency, kwashiorkor. Early treatment can reduce the deficits associated with kwashiorkor, but most children will not reach their full potential for height and growth.

a hollow appearance. Another malnutritive disease is **kwashiorkor**, found in children who experience a sudden deprivation of food and calories. It is characterized by lethargy; wrinkled skin; and a bloating and swelling of the stomach, face, legs and arms. Because the vital organs of the body take all of the available nutrients, the other parts of the body deteriorate and the hair becomes thin, brittle, and colorless.

Malnutrition influences development in multiple ways, not simply growth. Malnourished children show cognitive deficits as well as impairments in motivation, curiosity, language, and the ability to interact with the environment throughout childhood and adolescence (Arija et al., 2006; Smithers, Golley, Brazionis, & Lynch, 2011). For example, during the drought in Kenya, the children became less active during play and less focused in class (McDonald et al., 1994). Deficits from early malnutrition last. For example, among Ghanaian children who survived a severe famine in 1983, those who were youngest at the time of the famine (under age 2) scored lower on cognitive measures throughout childhood and into adulthood than did those who were older (ages 6 to 8; Ampaabeng & Tan, 2013). Malnutrition during the first year of life is associated with depression years later, when those children are 11 to 17 years old (Galler et al., 2010). Some of the damage caused by malnutrition can be reversed, and motor and mental development enhanced, if nutrition is reinstated early, but long-term difficulties in attention, learning, and intelligence often remain, even into young adulthood (Schoenmaker et al., 2015; UNICEF, 2009; Victora, 2009). It is believed that growth stunting is largely irreversible after 2 years of age (UNICEF, 2009).

Though malnutrition is common in developing countries, it is also found in some of the world's wealthiest countries. Because of socioeconomic factors, many children in the United States and other developed countries are deprived of diets that support healthy growth. In 2015, about 13% (or 15.8 million) households were categorized as *food insecure*. That is, they lacked consistent access to food to support a healthy lifestyle for all family at some point during the year (Coleman-Jensen, Rabbitt, Gregory, & Singh, 2016). Low-income families may have difficulty providing children with the range of foods needed for healthy development. In the United States, we have linked inadequate nutrition with stunted growth, health problems, poor school performance, and poor relationships with peers (Abdelhadi et al., 2016; Alaimo, Olson, & Frongillo, 2001; Hampton, 2007).

EATING BEHAVIORS IN ADOLESCENCE

The adolescent growth spurt demands that young people increase their caloric intake to about 2,200 (for girls) and 2,700 (for boys) calories a day (Jahns, Siega-Riz, & Popkin, 2001). Good nutrition is essential to support adolescents' growth, yet young people's diets tend to worsen as they enter adolescence. Adolescents increase their consumption of fast food, soft drinks, and salty snacks at the same time as they drink less milk (Stang & Stotmeister, 2017). Fast food is high in calories, but when adolescents eat a fast-food meal they do not appear to adjust their other meals to make up for the excess calories. On days when adolescents consume high-calorie fast food, which may be as much as one third of the time, they tend to consume more calories overall as compared with days when they do not consume fast food (Bowman, Gortmaker, Ebbeling, Pereira, & Ludwig, 2004; Ebbeling et al., 2004). When a fast-food restaurant is near school, students eat fewer fruits and vegetables, drink more soda, and overeat more often than students who attend schools that are not near fast-food restaurants (Davis & Carpenter, 2009). Longitudinal research shows that young people increase

kwashiorkor A malnutritive disease in children caused by deprivation of protein and calories and characterized by lethargy and the bloating and swelling of the stomach.

their consumption of fast food over time as they progress through adolescence (Bauer, Larson, Nelson, Story, & Neumark-Sztainer, 2009).

Poor diets leave many adolescents in industrialized nations with nutritional deficiencies. In one study of nearly 6,000 U.S. adolescents, less than 1% met the U.S. calorie-specific recommendations for the consumption of fruits and vegetables (Kimmons, Gillespie, Seymour, Serdula, & Blanck, 2008). Only about one-third of adolescents aged 12 to 19 drink the recommended 3 cups of milk a day; about 40% report never drinking milk (Rehm, Drewnowski, Monsivais, 2015; Tabrizi, Segovia-Siapco, Burkholder, & Sabate, 2014). Adolescents who do not consume dairy compromise their intake of calcium, which is particularly important for the growth of bones. Because about one-half of adult bone mass is accumulated during adolescence, reduced milk consumption contributes to insufficient bone mass in adulthood and a higher risk for osteoporosis, especially in women (Kalkwarf, 2007).

Despite consuming many calories, many adolescents have nutritional deficiencies because of poor dietary choices.

Family meals are an important way of establishing healthy eating habits. At home, U.S. children and adolescents who eat an evening meal with parents tend to have more healthy diets that include more fruits and vegetables and less fried foods and soft drinks, and they are less likely to be overweight than other children (Hauser et al., 2014). Young people who participate in preparing and eating family meals tend to have healthier eating habits 5 years later, from early to middle adolescence through young adulthood (Berge et al., 2015; Berge, MacLehose, Larson, Laska, & Neumark-Sztainer, 2016). Research with families in Netherlands, Poland, Portugal, and the United Kingdom suggests that family meals are associated with healthier eating habits and enhanced self-control over eating (de Wit et al., 2015). However, the frequency of family dinnertimes drops sharply between ages 9 and 14, and family dinners have become less common in recent decades (Rollins, Francis, & BeLue, 2007).

EATING BEHAVIORS IN ADULTHOOD

Busy schedules and multiple obligations pose challenges to healthy eating in early and middle adulthood. As adults age, they require fewer calories to maintain their weight, yet many adults fail to reduce their food intake. Healthy eating, such as eating unrefined carbohydrates instead of refined carbohydrates, avoiding trans fats and saturated fats, and monitoring salt intake, can promote wellness throughout adulthood. Consuming foods high in antioxidants, such as strawberries, blueberries, and other colorful fruits and vegetables, reduces the risk of cancer.

Nutritional needs change over the course of adulthood. In middle and older adulthood losses in muscle mass contributes to weight loss and a slowed metabolism. For this reason, older adults require fewer calories than younger adults and their diets must be more nutrient dense to meet their nutritional needs with fewer calories (Baker, 2007). Their changing dietary needs mean that older adults are less likely to get all of their nutritional needs met through their diet and are therefore at risk for a nutritional deficiency. In fact, it is estimated that two thirds of older adults in many developed countries, including the United States, Germany, the Netherlands, Italy, and Japan, are at risk for malnutrition (Kaiser et al., 2010; van Bokhorst-de van der Schueren et al., 2013).

Malnutrition is associated with illness, functional disability, and mortality (Charlton et al., 2013; Payette, 2005). Older adults who live alone may be reluctant to shop, cook, and eat by themselves. Illness, lengthy hospitalizations, bereavement, depression, and social isolation also contribute to malnutrition (Brownie, 2006). Older adults' nutritional needs

Monkey Business Images/Shutterstock.com

Healthy eating is important at all times in life, but busy schedules and multiple obligations pose challenges for adults' diets.

are also influenced by medication. For example, daily use of aspirin, commonly prescribed to adults at risk of heart disease, depletes Vitamin C and antibiotics interfere with the absorption of calcium, iron, and Vitamin K (Meletis & Zabriskie, 2007). To counteract such problems, adults can make an effort to choose nutritious foods, including fruits, whole grains; low-fat dairy products; leafy green vegetables; and healthy sources of protein, such as fish, nuts, beans, and chicken—foods that are nutrient dense—and limit salt, sugar, and fats. However, this is easier said than done given that many older adults have a lifelong pattern of less healthy food preferences, and that healthy food choices are not readily available or affordable in all local areas.

Supplements for vitamins A, B6, B12, C, and E can fill in gaps in adults' diets and boost immunity. Specifically, antioxidant vitamins and trace elements (vitamins C, E, selenium, copper, and zinc) counteract potential damage caused by free radicals and promote an effective immune system response (Wintergerst, Maggini, & Hornig, 2007). Omega-3, an oil found in fish that is high in polyunsaturated fatty acids, promotes vascular health and is associated with reduced inflammation and degenerative diseases such as cardiovascular disease, arthritis, and potentially Alzheimer's disease (Lorente-Cebrián et al., 2013, 2015). Moreover, consumption of Omega-3 appears to have an epigenetic effect on longevity through its action on telomeres, slowing and even reducing telomere shortening over 5- to 8-year periods (Farzaneh-Far et al., 2010; Paul, 2011). Improved nutrition holds the promise of protection against age-related declines, but more research is needed.

OBESITY

Although people of all ages require adequate calories and nutrition to grow and function, some individuals consume many more calories than they need. Obesity is an increasing problem for people of all ages, infants through adults.

Child and Adolescent Obesity

Children today weigh more than ever before. The prevalence of child overweight and obesity has doubled since the 1970s (Lobstein et al., 2015). Health care professionals determine whether someone's weight is in the healthy range by examining **body mass index (BMI)**, calculated as weight in kilograms/height in meters squared (k/m²; World Health Organization, 2009). Obesity is defined as having BMI at or above the 95th percentile for height and age, as indicated by the 2000 Centers for Disease Control and Prevention (CDC) growth charts (Reilly, 2007). More than 17% of American youth are classified as obese (National Survey of Children's Health, 2014b; see Figure 3.6).

Rising rates of overweight and obesity among children and adolescents are a problem in the United States, and all other developed nations, including Australia, Canada, Denmark, Finland, Germany, Great Britain, Ireland, Japan, Hong Kong, and New Zealand (de Onis, Blössner, & Borghi, 2010; Janssen et al., 2005; Lobstein et al., 2015; Wang & Lim, 2012), as shown in Figure 3.7. Obesity is also becoming more common in developing nations, such as India, Pakistan, and China, as they transition to Western-style diets higher in meats, fats, and refined foods as well as show the increased snacking and declines in physical activity linked with watching television (Poskitt, 2009; Wang & Lim, 2012).

body mass index (BMI) A measure of body fat based on weight in kilograms divided by height in meters squared (k/m²).

LIFESPAN BRAIN DEVELOPMENT

• • Chronic Traumatic Encephalopathy in Athletes

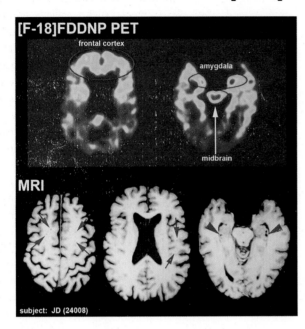

Recent brain scans of NFL hall of famer Joe DeLamielleure illustrate the extensive neurodegeneration that comprises CTE.

Recently, professional sports have come under scrutiny for the dangers posed to athletes. Sports like soccer, hockey, and football involve player-on-player or player–equipment collisions in which injuries, such as concussions, are common. A concussion is a brain injury. Athletes who experience multiple concussions—that is, repeated mild traumatic brain injury—are at risk to develop a progressive form of neurodegeneration known as chronic traumatic encephalopathy (CTE).

First identified in boxers, CTE is associated with symptoms of irritability, impulsivity, aggression, depression, short-term memory loss, and heightened suicidality, which typically appears 8 to 10 years after the disease onset. As CTE advances, dementia appears. Gait and speech abnormalities are common and, in the late stages, CTE may be mistaken for Alzheimer's disease. CTE has been identified in football, hockey, wrestling, and rugby players and may accompany exposure to blast or concussive injury associated with military service.

To date, research on CTE has centered on American football players. In a critical 2013 study, Ann McKee and colleagues conducted post-mortem evaluations of 85 brains from former athletes, and military veterans or civilians with a history of repetitive mild traumatic brain injury, as well as 18 "control" brains from individuals without a history of mild traumatic brain injury. The results were striking: Eighty percent of the individuals with a history of repetitive mild traumatic brain injury showed CTE symptoms (McKee et al., 2013). Thirty-four of the 35 former professional American football players showed CTE symptoms. Among the five hockey players studied, only one showed no disease. Football received a lot of attention as the sample of athletes was mostly football players—and the football players were overwhelmingly diagnosed with CTE.

More recent research has confirmed the link. Ann McKee and colleagues studied a sample of 202 deceased individuals from a brain donation program who played American football at all levels: high school, college, semiprofessional, and professional (Mez, Daneshvar, Kiernan, Abdolmohammadi, Alvarez, Huber, et al., 2017). CTE was diagnosed in 177 of the brains (88%), including 110 of 111 former National Football League (NFL) players (99%). CTE appears to be strongly linked with head trauma experienced by participating in football as 48 of 53 college players, 9 of 14 semiprofessional players, and 7 of 8 Canadian Football League players were diagnosed with CTE. Football poses risks; however, the risk of CTE is not limited to football.

An important caveat to this research is that CTE can be diagnosed definitively only postmortem. In these studies the researchers examined donated brains. Many of the brains were donated by players for testing because they suspected they had the disease. The sample is therefore skewed, but the results clearly indicate an association between the head trauma that often accompanies participating in football and CTE. In 2013, 4,500 retired NFL players filed a lawsuit against the league, claiming that the NFL concealed information about the dangers of head trauma, resulting in a $765 million settlement (Belson, 2013). The National Hockey League (NHL) is facing a similar lawsuit from hockey players (McIndoe, 2017). In 2016, the NFL and NHL issued new protocols for identifying and evaluating concussions, in order to better protect players (Flynn, 2016; NHL Public Relations, 2016).

What Do You Think?

1. To what degree are organizations such as the NFL and NHL responsible for player injuries?

2. What can be done to reduce the risks of CTE?

3. How concerned should parents and coaches be about CTE in children and adolescents?

Obesity in childhood and adolescence is a serious problem because the vast majority of obese youngsters do not outgrow obesity; instead, they become obese adults (Lakshman, Elks, & Ong, 2012). Overweight and obesity in early childhood, as early as age 2, predicts overweight and obesity in early adolescence (Cunningham, Kramer, & Narayan, 2014; Nader et al., 2006). Likewise, about 80% of obese adolescents become obese adults (Simmonds 2016).

FIGURE 3.6: Prevalence of Child and Adolescent Obesity in the United States, 1971–2014

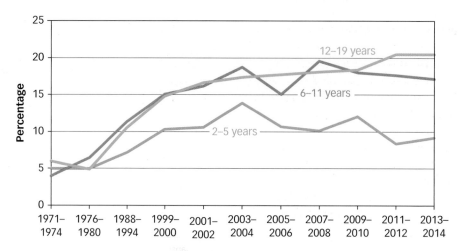

Source: Fryar, Carroll, and Ogden (2014).

Child and adolescent obesity is associated with short- and long-term health problems, including heart disease, high blood pressure, orthopedic problems, and diabetes (Pulgarón, 2013). Obese children and adolescents are at risk for peer rejection, depression, low self-esteem, and body dissatisfaction (Gibson et al., 2008; Harrist et al., 2016; Pulgarón, 2013; Quek, Tam, Zhang, & Ho, 2017). Both children and adults are more likely to report negative perceptions of obese children as sloppy, unattractive, unintelligent, and generally unlikable as compared with other children (Puhl & Heuer, 2009; Puhl & Latner, 2007). The social correlates of overweight and obesity, weight-related teasing, hold long-term implications. Adolescents who are teased about their weight tend to have a higher BMI, are more likely to be obese, and have unhealthy eating habits as adults, 15 years later (Puhl et al., 2017).

Strides in genetic research in recent years have increased our understanding of the strong contribution of genetics to obesity (Drong, Lindgren, & McCarthy, 2012; Herrera, Keildson, & Lindgren, 2011). Contextual factors determine whether genetic predispositions to weight gain are fulfilled. For example, community-level influences on obesity include the lack of safe playgrounds with climbing and play equipment that encourage activity (Black, Menzel, & Bungum, 2015; Fan & Jin, 2014). Rates of child obesity are higher in schools that are located within one mile of a fast food restaurant (Alviola, Nayga, Thomsen, Danforth, & Smartt, 2014).

In the United States, low SES is associated with poor access to health insurance, health care, and transportation as well as unsafe neighborhoods and poor proximity to grocery stores that carry healthy foods (Vieweg, Johnston, Lanier, Fernandez, & Pandurangi, 2007). Children in low-SES homes are at higher risk for obesity as compared with their peers who live in high-SES homes (Chung et al., 2016; Fradkin et al., 2015; Frederick, Snellman, & Putnam, 2014) For example, kindergarten-age children from high-SES families tend to have a lower prevalence of obesity than other children, and the differences increase through to early adolescence (Cunningham, 2014). Research also suggests that the effects of SES may vary with individuals' genetic predispositions. For example, in one study children who were carriers of a particular allele of the OXTR gene had greater BMI when reared in low-SES environments, but they had the lowest BMI as compared with other children when reared in high-SES homes (Bush et al., 2017). Body mass and obesity result from a complex interaction of genetic and environmental factors.

Programs that effectively reduce obesity in children and adolescents target their screen time, increase their physical activity and time spent outdoors, and teach them about nutrition, reducing their consumption of high calorie foods and increasing their consumption of fruits and vegetables (Bleich, Segal, Wu, Wilson, & Wang, 2013; Kumar & Kelly, 2017; Lobstein et al., 2015; Nowicka & Flodmark, 2007). To prevent obesity, parents should monitor their children's activities and engage in physical activities with them such as walking, biking, and swimming. Intervention is important to reduce child and adolescent obesity, but it must be done sensitively, as young people who are pressured to lose weight may become obsessed with body size and develop a poor body image.

Obesity in Adulthood

During his first year of college, Byron welcomed the ability to make choices about food and plan his own meals. Without his health-conscious mother's input, he was able to munch on fried chicken wings whenever he wanted and enjoyed exercising this new freedom. By his senior year of college, Byron was 45 pounds overweight. The absence of parental controls, access to an abundance of food, and busy lives make it difficult for young adults to eat healthily. Eating habits begun in early adulthood often persist for life. Obesity, defined as a body mass index (BMI) of 30 or above, and overweight (BMI greater than 25) have increased substantially in recent decades. Over three-quarters of American adults over the age of 20 are overweight (33%) or obese (45%; Fryar, Carroll, & Ogden, 2016). Young adult women show higher rates of weight gain than women in other age groups, perhaps because of differences in contraception, dietary behavior, physical activity, and stresses associated with life transitions (such as to college; Wane, Van Uffelen, & Brown, 2010).

FIGURE 3.7: Worldwide Prevalence of Overweight Children (ages 5 to 17) in 2010

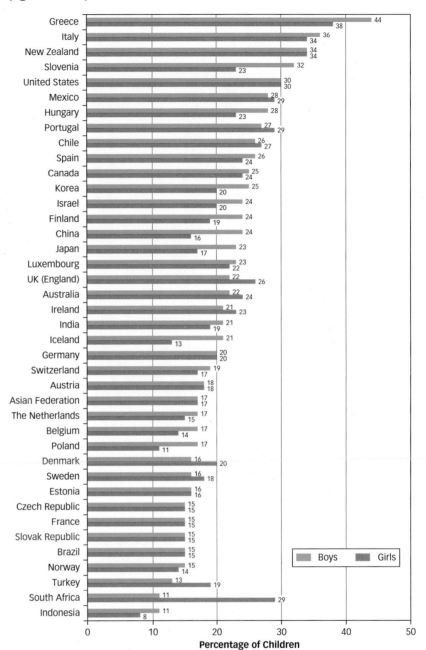

Source: Organization for Economic Co-operation and Development (2014).

Adult obesity is influenced by heredity, but today's obesity epidemic in Western nations has stronger ties to environmental pressures than genetic factors. Physical labor is less a part of the lifestyle in industrialized nations than ever before. Access to safe parks and other green spaces is associated with increased walking and lower rates of overweight and obesity (Pearson et al., 2014). Food has become more abundant at the same time as people have become more sedentary, and this is especially true for sugary, fatty, and fried foods. Sedentary lifestyles, and especially the number of hours spent viewing television, are closely associated with obesity (Heinonen et al., 2013; Pearson & Biddle, 2011). Young adults who are obese are more likely to make fewer healthy food choices and to overeat

FIGURE 3.8: Obesity and Overweight Rates for Adults, 2013–2014

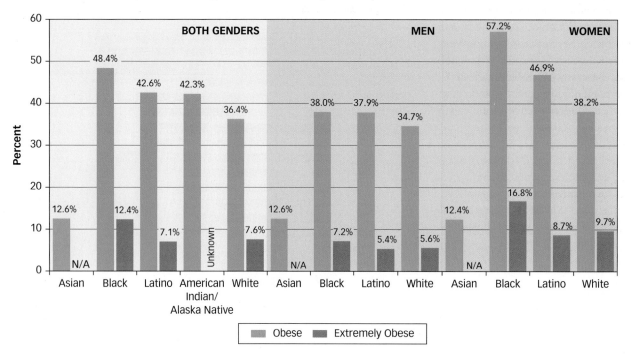

Source: *The State of Obesity 2017: Better Politics for a Healthier America.* August 2017. Reprinted with permission from The Trust for America's Health.

than their non-obese counterparts (Keski-Rahkonen et al., 2007). With age, it becomes more difficult to avoid overeating because caloric needs drop between the ages of 25 and 50, and the metabolic rate, the amount of energy the body uses at rest, gradually falls as muscle cells decline in number and size (Roberts & Rosenberg, 2006). Low SES in early adulthood predicts obesity in young adults, even after controlling for childhood SES (Baum & Ruhm, 2009; Giskes, van Lenthe, Avendano-Pabon, & Brug, 2011).

Obesity is a serious health risk, associated with a range of health problems and illnesses such as high blood pressure stroke circulatory problems diabetes digestive disorders arthritis cancer and, ultimately, early death (Calle, Rodriguez, Walker-Thurmond, & Thun, 2003; Drong et al., 2012; Tchernof & Després, 2013). Consumption of high levels of saturated fat is associated with heightened cardiovascular reactivity (e.g., increases in heart rate), and even a single high-fat meal predicts short-term increases in cardiovascular reactivity (Jakulj et al., 2007). Midlife obesity is also associated with dementia in old age (Loef & Walach, 2013; Pedditizi, Peters, & Beckett, 2016). Obesity also holds risks for mental health and social functioning. Obese adults are more likely to report moderate to severe depression symptoms; report more relationship difficulties with family, peers, and coworkers; and have more difficulty finding mates, rental apartments, and jobs than do non-obese adults (Ambwani, Thomas, Hopwood, Moss, & Grilo, 2014; Carr & Friedman, 2005; Pachucki & Goodman, 2015).

Although adults who have been overweight since childhood may feel it's "hopeless" to seek treatment for obesity, the fact is that health outcomes improve with even moderate weight loss (Orzano & Scott, 2004). Successful long-term weight loss, however, is challenging, as indicated by the vast array of "quick" weight loss programs advertised in the media. Only about 20% of overweight individuals are successful at long-term weight loss, defined as losing at least 10% of initial body weight and maintaining the loss for at least 1 year (Wing & Phelan, 2005). Successful weight loss is most often a result of lifestyle changes, such as regular moderate exercise coupled with a nutritionally balanced diet low in calories and fat (Douketis, Macie, Thabane, & Williamson, 2005; Holt, Warren, & Wallace, 2006; Nicklas, Huskey, Davis, & Wee, 2012; Nurkkala et al., 2015). Effective weight loss interventions emphasize behaviors and encourage individuals to keep accurate records of what they eat and analyze eating patterns in their food choices (LeBlanc, O'Connor, Whitlock, Patnode, & Kapka, 2011; MacLean et al., 2015). Since many people overeat as a reaction to stress, training in problem-solving skills helps participants learn non-food-related ways of managing day-to-day conflicts and difficulties, as well as increasing social support to help individuals attain and sustain weight loss.

PHYSICAL ACTIVITY AND EXERCISE

"You beat me again, Dad!" Anna put her tennis racket down and wiped her forehead. At 30, she wished she could play well enough to win a match against her 57-year-old father, but this rarely happened. Still, the two of them treasured their weekly tennis date. At all ages physical activity—exercise—is associated with physical and mental health and wellness.

Maridav/Shutterstock.com

U.S. national guidelines recommend engaging in at least 150 minutes of moderate activity (such as brisk walking) or 75 minutes of vigorous activity (such as running) each week, plus muscle strengthening exercises at least twice each week.

Physical Activity in Childhood and Adolescence

Health care professionals agree that regular physical activity is essential to achieving optimal health in childhood and adolescence. It is associated with many beneficial correlates, such as bone health, cardiovascular health, muscle strength, motor control, cognitive performance, and mental health (Carson et al., 2013; Janssen et al., 2010; van der Niet et al., 2015). The majority of children and adolescents in the United States do not meet the recommended guidelines of at least 60 minutes of moderate to vigorous physical activity every day. It is estimated that only about one-quarter of children and adolescents age 6 to 15 are at least moderately active for 60 minutes per day on at least 5 days per week, with activity dropping with age such that only 8% of 12- to 15-year-old adolescents meet the guideline (Kann et al., 2014). Children can meet recommended guidelines through physical play involving running, chasing, climbing, and jumping. Playing on a jungle gym, throwing balls, and participating in sports improve children's fitness. Physical activity tends to decline beginning in middle childhood, about age 7 (Farooq et al., 2017). Although some teens engage in competitive sports, levels of physical activity decrease on average throughout adolescence, and many adolescents engage in no regular exercise or activity (Dumith, Gigante, Domingues, & Kohl, 2011; Duncan, Duncan, Strycker, & Chaumeton, 2007). Longitudinal research with U.S. adolescents has shown that the reductions in physical activity during adolescence are consistent across contextual settings, whether rural or urban, and across SES (Metcalf, Hosking, Jeffery, Henley, & Wilkin, 2015). Yet adolescents of low SES are more likely to be sedentary and obese; this holds true for adolescents from a variety of countries, such as Canada, England, Finland, France, and the United States (Frederick, Snellman, & Putnam, 2014; Kantomaa, Tammelin, Näyhä, & Taanila, 2007; Lioret, Maire, Volatier, & Charles, 2007; Wang & Lim, 2012).

Screen time—time spent in front of a television, computer, or electronic device screen watching television or videos, playing video games, engaging with social media—and other sedentary activities are risk factors for a high BMI. Five- to 8-year-old children tend to average about 2.5 hours of screen time each day, about an hour of which is spent watching television (Rideout, 2013). Screen time increases with age, time that is not spent on physical play and other activities (Fakhouri, Hughes, Brody, Kit, & Ogden, 2013; Nader, Bradley, Houts, McRitchie, & O'Brien, 2008). It is estimated that American adolescents spend over 11 hours each day in front of a screen, viewing television and media, playing games, and participating in social media (American Academy of Pediatrics,

2013; Rideout, 2010), and screen time is associated with obesity (Mitchell, Rodriguez, Schmitz, & Audrain-McGovern, 2013).

Schools play a role in promoting physical fitness. Physical education classes can increase activity levels in school-aged children (Lee et al., 2002). But participation in physical education is highest among students in 9th grade, decreases among 10th- and 11th-grade students, and is lowest among 12th-grade students (Kann et al., 2014).

Physical Activity in Adulthood

Exercise offers powerful health benefits to adults. The physical benefits of regular exercise influence increases in strength, balance, posture, and endurance and permit older adults to carry out everyday activities such as grocery shopping, lifting grandchildren, reaching for objects, and opening jars and bottles (Peterson et al., 2010). Throughout the adult years moderate physical activity is associated with improved physiological function, a decreased incidence of disease, and reduced incidence of disability (Chakravarty, Hubert, Lingala, & Fries, 2008; Radak, Chung, Koltai, Taylor, & Goto, 2008). Regular moderate exercise enhances immunity, lowering the risk of, and speeding recovery to, illnesses (Horn et al., 2015). Other benefits of exercise include stress reduction, cardiovascular health, and cancer prevention (Sloan et al., 2009). Exercise reduces risks for obesity-related illnesses such as heart disease, cancer, and diabetes (Bassuk & Manson, 2005; Tardon et al., 2005; Wannamethee, Shaper, & Alberti, 2000). Most important is that it is never too late to begin a program of physical activity. Individuals as old as 80 who begin a program of cardiovascular activity, such as walking, cycling, or aerobic dance, show gains similar to those of much younger adults. Weight-bearing exercise begun as late as 90 years of age can improve blood flow to the muscles and increase muscle size (Rice & Cunningham, 2002).

Exercise is not only good for the body; it is also good for the mind. Exercise offers adults stress relief, protects against depression, and is associated with higher quality of life (Windle, Hughes, Linck, Russell, & Woods, 2010). Mental health benefits of regular physical activity include improved mood, energy, self-esteem, and ability to cope; and reductions in stress, anxiety, and depression (Hogan, Mata, & Carstensen, 2013; Rebar et al., 2015; Stroth, Hille, Spitzer, & Reinhardt, 2009). In addition, fitness is linked to cognitive performance throughout adulthood. Young adults who demonstrate high levels of cardiovascular fitness tend to perform better on measures of basic cognitive abilities, such as attention, reaction time, working memory, and processing speed, than low-fitness young adults (Newson & Kemps, 2008). Exercise is also associated with cognitive vitality in middle and older adulthood (Prakash, Voss, Erickson, & Kramer, 2015).

The increased blood flow to the brain that comes with exercise is protective. Older adults who are physically active show less neural and glial cell losses throughout their cortex and less cognitive decline than do those who are sedentary (Muscari et al., 2010; Nithianantharajah & Hannan, 2009). Perhaps more significant is that exercise in older adults is associated with increased hippocampal volume (recall that new neurons are created there; Niemann, Godde, & Voelcker-Rehage, 2014; Ryan & Nolan, 2016). In addition, adults who get regular cardiovascular exercise, such as brisk walks, show increased brain activity in areas that control attention and perform better on tasks measuring attention than do sedentary adults. They also demonstrate improved performance on tasks examining executive function, processing speed, memory and other cognitive processes (Erickson et al., 2011; Hindin & Zelinski, 2012). Moreover, dementia patients who engage in a program of physical exercise, specifically cardiovascular exercise, show improvements in cognitive function, regardless of the intervention frequency or the specific dementia diagnosis (Groot et al., 2016), suggesting that exercise has powerful benefits for cognitive health.

How much exercise is enough to reap health benefits? To obtain health benefits such as reduced cholesterol levels, decreased body fat, and reduced risk of developing diabetes or heart disease, national guidelines recommend engaging in at least 150 minutes of moderate activity each week (e.g., brisk walking, raking the lawn, or pushing a lawn mower) or 75 minutes of vigorous activity, plus muscle strengthening exercises on at least 2 days each week (U.S. Department of Health and Human Services, 2008). About 300 minutes of moderate or 150 minutes of vigorous exercise may be required each week to lose weight. The activity does not have to be performed in a single block of time but may be accumulated in 10-minute increments throughout the day.

It is estimated that about 31% of the world's population is physically inactive (Hallal et al., 2012). The prevalence of physical activity varies widely around the world, from 2% of women in Saudi Arabia to 81% of women in Denmark engaging in regular physical activity, and 4% of men in Brazil to 77% of men in Sweden (Sisson & Katzmarzyk, 2008). Despite the importance of physical activity in promoting health, less than one half of adults in the United States (47% of men and 43% of women) and about one half of Canadians (55% of men and 50% of women) are moderately active, with at least 30 minutes of moderate activity or its equivalent in vigorous activity daily (Gilmour, 2007; Slack, 2006). Common barriers to physical activity reported by adults include fears of falling, neighborhood safety, bad weather, and chronic conditions (Belza et al., 2004). Many older adults believe that the best way to manage chronic illnesses such as arthritis is to rest, and that exercise will make symptoms worse. Instead, exercise offers physical and mental benefits that slow the negative effects of aging. Older adults who exercise often report feeling more energetic, experience greater life enhancement, and a more positive psychological outlook than sedentary elders (Ruppar & Schneider, 2007). In addition, older adults who identify themselves as physical exercisers and physically fit show greater levels of life satisfaction (Strachan, Brawley, Spink, & Glazebrook, 2010).

 Thinking in Context 3.4

1. Why are marasmus and kwashiorkor uncommon in the United States? What contextual factors place children in developing nations at risk for these impairments? What contextual factors are protective for children in the United States?

2. What aspects of young and middle adulthood increase people's risk for obesity and poor health behaviors, such as engaging in little physical activity?

3. Apply the bioecological framework to explain the myriad factors that influence eating and exercise habits over the lifespan. Identify factors in the microsystem, mesosystem, exosystem, and macrosystem that can act as risk and protective factors to health. How do these shift from childhood into adolescence? Throughout adulthood?

 Apply Your Knowledge

Over coffee, 48-year-old Wendy shares her concerns about her daughter with her closest friend:

> Kayla still hasn't gotten her period. I'm wondering whether to make an appointment with her doctor.

Her friend Latisha replies,

> Not everyone starts the same time. Kayla's 14, right? My Aisha started menstruating at 10. Boy, was that a shock! I think I'd rather that she began a little later than earlier.

Wendy:

> You're probably right. I just don't want her to feel left out. I started at about 12. I wonder why she's late.

Latisha:

> Well, one thing about having teenage girls is they make you feel your age! Or maybe it's the hot flashes.

Wendy chuckles,

I thought that was just me.

1. What do we know about the timing of pubertal development? Are Kayla and Aisha on time?

2. Discuss influences on pubertal timing. Should Wendy expect her daughter to show similar pubertal timing?

3. Why are Latisha and Wendy experiencing hot flashes?

4. What physical changes, such as strength, appearance, and reproductive changes, for example,

can midlife adults expect? How might these physical changes influence their functioning?

5. Do you think that Kayla and Aisha's fathers would have a similar conversation? Do men and women show similar patterns of physical changes and corresponding changes in functioning?

6. What role might SES and contextual factors play in physical change and how adults respond to them during middle adulthood? Is this pattern the same for men as for women?

Give your students the SAGE edge!

SAGE edge offers a robust online environment featuring an impressive array of free tools and resources for review, study, and further exploration, keeping both instructors and students on the cutting edge of teaching and learning. Learn more at **edge.sagepub.com/kuthertopical.**

CHAPTER 3 IN REVIEW

3.1 Summarize patterns of body growth and biological and contextual influences on growth during infancy and childhood.

SUMMARY

During the first year of life infants undergo very rapid growth in both cephalocaudal and proximodistal patterns. Growth slows during early childhood through middle childhood. As children grow taller, their body proportions become more like those of adults. Growth is largely maturational, but it can be influenced by health and environmental factors. Improved sanitation, nutrition, and access to medical care have contributed to an increase in children's growth over the past century in the United States and other industrialized countries. Genetics also play a role in physical development. There are also ethnic differences in patterns of growth in many Western countries.

KEY TERMS

cephalocaudal development	growth norms
proximodistal development	hormones

REVIEW QUESTIONS

1. What are two patterns that describe growth in infancy and childhood?
2. Name two biological and two contextual influences on growth.

3.2 Discuss the physical changes that occur with puberty, influences on pubertal timing, and the psychosocial effects of early and late puberty.

SUMMARY

The most noticeable signs of pubertal maturation are the growth spurt and secondary sex characteristics. As the primary sex characteristics, mature adolescents become capable of reproduction. Pubertal timing is influenced by genetic and contextual factors including physical health, nutrition, body fat, exposure to stress, socioeconomic status (SES), and the secular trend. The consequences of early and late maturation differ dramatically for girls and boys. Girls who mature early are at risk for problems with depression, anxiety, and poor body image. Both boys and girls who mature early are more likely to engage in risk behaviors and age-inappropriate behaviors such as sexual activity. Late maturation appears to have a protective effect on girls, but findings regarding the effects of late maturation on boys are mixed and less consistent.

KEY TERMS

puberty	adolescent growth spurt
hypothalamus-pituitary-gonadal axis	secondary sex characteristics
	primary sex characteristics
testosterone	menarche
estrogen	secular trend

REVIEW QUESTIONS

1. List pubertal changes for boys and girls.
2. What influences pubertal timing?
3. What are the effects of experiencing puberty early or late relative to peers?

3.3 Identify normative patterns of physical and reproductive change as well as explanations for the causes of aging.

SUMMARY

Age-related physical changes are gradual and, at first, unnoticed. Declines in strength and endurance become noticeable in middle adulthood but the rate and extent of change varies. In women, ovulation becomes less regular with age and is impaired by a variety of behavioral and environmental factors. Women experience menopause in midlife. The loss of estrogen increases some health risks, such as cardiovascular disease and osteoporosis. The timing of menopause is influenced by heredity but also by lifestyle choices and contextual factors. Men's reproductive ability declines gradually and steadily over the adult years, but most men continue to produce sperm throughout adulthood. Explanations of aging include theories that emphasize programmed genetics, telomere shortening, immune system function, collagen, and increases in cellular mutations and free radicals.

KEY TERMS

senescence	free radicals
sarcopenia	telomeres
menopause	

REVIEW QUESTIONS

1. How does physical functioning change in adulthood?
2. What reproductive changes do men and women experience?
3. What are some ways that scientists explain why we age?

3.4 Analyze the influence of eating habits, obesity, and physical activity on physical development and functioning over the lifespan.

KEY TERMS

marasmus

kwashiorkor

body mass index (BMI)

SUMMARY

Nutrition influences growth, learning, concentration, and language skills throughout childhood and adolescence. Yet young people's diets tend to worsen with time. As adults age, they require fewer calories to maintain their weight, yet many adults fail to reduce their food intake. Obesity is associated with short- and long-term health problems in childhood, adolescence, and adulthood. Genetic factors contribute to obesity, but contextual factors determine whether genetic predispositions to weight gain are fulfilled. Programs that effectively reduce obesity couple lifestyle changes such as reduced screen time and increased physical activity with a healthy diet. Regular physical activity is associated with many benefits and, in adulthood, is an important influence on physical and cognitive longevity.

REVIEW QUESTIONS

1. How do eating habits and caloric needs change over the lifespan?

2. What are some influences on obesity and how does obesity affect health?

3. Explain the role of physical activity in a healthy lifestyle.

Test your understanding of the content.
Review the flashcards and quizzes at
edge.sagepub.com/kuthertopical

PRACTICE AND APPLY WHAT YOU'VE LEARNED

▶ **edge.sagepub.com/kuthertopical**

Brain, Perception, and Motor Development

Learning Objectives

4.1 Discuss neural development from infancy through older adulthood, including the role of experience.

4.2 Summarize patterns of gross and fine motor development and influences on motor development.

4.3 Describe age-related changes in vision, hearing, and other senses.

Digital Resources

⏵ Infants, Young Children, and Technology
◉ Play and Brain Development

⏵ Motor Development in Infancy
▤ Health in Older Adults

▣ Neonatal Sense of Touch
▤ Puberty and Personal Odors

 **$SAGE edge™** Master these learning objectives with multimedia resources available at **edge.sagepub.com/kuthertopical** and *Lives in Context* video cases available in the interactive eBook.

One-year-old Sophia grunted and stared at her mother as she let go of the sofa and made her first independent steps toward her. A child's first steps are a watershed moment for parents—and often the cause of waterworks on their part. But those first steps are the culmination of a year-long process that began with newborn Sophia struggling to control her flailing arms and legs. Learning to walk is a developmental milestone influenced by our sensory abilities and, especially, neurological development. In this chapter, we examine biological development, specifically brain and motor development and sensation and perception.

BRAIN DEVELOPMENT

LO 4.1 Discuss neural development from infancy through older adulthood, including the role of experience.

The brain is made up of billions of cells called **neurons**. Like other cells in your body, neurons contain a cell body and nucleus, but they also have other structures that enable them to communicate with other cells. Neuronal communication makes it possible for people to sense the world, think, move their body, and carry out their lives.

David Bagnall/Alamy

THE NEURON

Neurons are specialized to process information and communicate with other neurons, sensory cells (including those responsible for vision and hearing), and motor cells (responsible for movement). As shown in Figure 4.1, neurons have distinct structures that set them apart from other cells and enable their communicative functions. *Dendrites* are branching receptors that receive chemical messages from other neurons that are translated into an electrical signal (Markant & Thomas, 2013). The *axon* is a long tube-like structure that extends from the neuron and carries electrical signals to other neurons. Neurons do not touch. Instead, there are gaps between neurons called *synapses.* Once the electrical signal reaches the end of the axon, it is translated to chemical messenger, called a *neurotransmitter,* and crosses the synapse to communicate with the dendrites of another neuron (Carson, 2014). This process of neural transmission is how neurons communicate with other neurons. Neurons also communicate with sensory and motor cells. Some axons synapse with muscle cells and are responsible for movement. The dendrites of some neurons synapse with sensory cells, such as those in the eyes or ears, to transfer sensory information, such as vision and hearing (Kolb, 2015). Finally, axons are often coated with a fatty substance called myelin, which speeds the transmission of electrical impulses and neurological function.

neuron A nerve cell that stores and transmits information; billions of neurons comprise the brain.

neurogenesis The production of new neurons.

glial cell A type of brain cell that nourishes neurons and provides structure to the brain.

FIGURE 4.1: Neurons and Neural Transmission

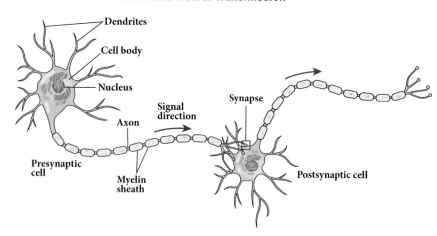

The first neurons form early in prenatal development, in the embryo's neural tube, through a process called **neurogenesis**. We are born with more than 100 billion neurons, more than we will ever need—and more than we will ever have at any other time in our lives (Kolb, 2015). Over time, some of our neurons die, and new ones are formed. Neurogenesis continues throughout life, though at a much slower pace than during prenatal development (Stiles & Jernigan, 2010). As the brain develops, new neurons migrate along a network of **glial cells**, a second type of brain cell that outnumbers neurons 10 to 1 (Jessen, 2004; Nelson & Bloom, 1997). Glial cells nourish neurons and move throughout the brain to provide a physical structure to the brain (Klämbt, 2009). As shown in Figure 4.2, neurons travel along glial cells to the location of the brain

FIGURE 4.2: Glial Cell–Neuron Relationship

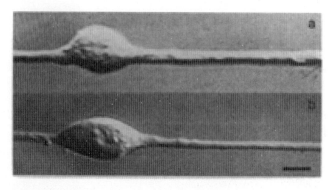
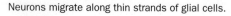
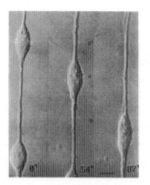

Neurons migrate along thin strands of glial cells.

Source: Gasser and Hatten (1990).

where they will function (Nelson & Bloom, 1997; Zhang et al., 2010), such as the outer layer of the brain, known as the cortex, and glial cells instruct neurons to form synapses with other neurons (Ullian, Sapperstein, Christopherson, & Barres, 2001).

EXPERIENCE AND BRAIN DEVELOPMENT

Brain development is a multifaceted process that is not a result of maturational or environmental input alone. Much of what we know about brain development comes from studying animals. Animals raised in stimulating environments with many toys and companions to play with develop brains that are heavier and have more synapses than do those who grow up in standard laboratory conditions (Greenough & Black, 1992; Grossman, Churchill, McKinney, Kodish, & Otte, 2003; Rosenzweig, 1984). Likewise, when animals raised in stimulating environments are moved to unstimulating standard laboratory conditions, their brains lose neural connections (Grossman, Churchill, McKinney, Kodish, & Otte, 2003; Thompson, 1993).

This is true for humans, too. Infants who are understimulated, including those who experience child maltreatment or who are reared in deprivation, such as in poor understaffed orphanages, also show cognitive and perceptual deficits (Twardosz & Lutzker, 2009; Wilson, 2003). Experience influences the physical structure of our brains throughout life. Though infancy is a particularly important time for the formation and strengthening of synapses, experience shapes brain structure at all ages of life, even into adulthood (Rosenzweig, 2002; Zeanah, 2009).

The powerful role that experience plays in brain development can be categorized into two types. First, the brain depends on experiencing certain basic events and stimuli at key points in time in order to develop normally (Fox, Levitt, & Nelson, 2010); this is referred to as **experience–expectant brain development**. Experience–expectant brain development is demonstrated in sensory deprivation research with animals. If animals are blindfolded and prevented from using their visual system for the first several weeks after birth, they never acquire normal vision because the connections among the neurons that transmit sensory information from the eyes to the visual cortex fail to develop; instead, they decay (DiPietro, 2000; Neville & Bavelier, 2001). If only one eye is prevented from seeing, the animal will be able to see well with one eye but will not develop *binocular vision*, the ability to focus two eyes together on a single object. Similarly, human infants born with a congenital cataract in one eye (an opaque clouding that blocks light from reaching the retina) will lose the capacity to process visual stimuli in the affected eye if they do not receive treatment. Even with treatment, subtle defects in facial processing may remain (Fox et al., 2010; Maurer, 2017). Brain organization depends on experiencing certain ordinary events early in life, such as opportunities to hear language, see the world, touch objects, and explore the environment (Kolb, Mychasiuk, & Gibb, 2014; Maurer & Lewis, 2013). All infants around the world need these basic experiences in order to develop normally.

A second type of development, **experience–dependent brain development**, refers to the growth that occurs in response to learning experiences (Greenough & Black, 1992). For example, experiences such as learning to stack blocks or crawl on a slippery wood floor are unique to individual infants, and they influence what particular brain areas and functions are developed and reinforced. Experience–dependent development is the result of lifelong experiences that vary by individual based on contextual and cultural circumstances (Nelson & Luciana, 2008; Stiles & Jernigan, 2010; Kolb et al., 2014). Exposure to enriching experiences, such as interactive play with toy cars and other objects that move; hands-on play with blocks, balls, and cups; and stimulating face-to-face play, can all enhance children's development (Fox et al., 2010). For example, a longitudinal study that followed more than 350 infants from 5 to 24 months of age found that the quality of mother–infant interactions at 5 months predicted greater brain activity in the prefrontal cortex at 10 and 24 months of age, suggesting that parenting quality may contribute to brain development in infancy (Bernier, Calkins, & Bell, 2016).

experience–expectant brain development Brain growth and development that is dependent on basic environmental experiences, such as visual and auditory stimulation, in order to develop normally.

experience–dependent brain development Brain growth and development in response to specific learning experiences.

Lives in Context Video 4.1
Infants, Young Children, and Technology

BRAIN DEVELOPMENT IN INFANCY

The newborn's brain is about 25% of its adult weight, and it grows rapidly throughout infancy, reaching 80% of its adult weight by 2 years of age (Nelson & Luciana, 2008). At birth, the neural networks of axons and dendrites are simple, with few synapses (DiPietro, 2000). Early in infancy, major growth takes place. Neurons and glial cells enlarge. As the dendrites grow and branch out, neurons form synapses and thereby increase connections with others (Kolb, 2015; Markant & Thomas, 2013). Synaptogenesis, the formation of new synapses, peaks in different brain regions at different ages (Price, Jarman, Mason, & Kind, 2011). The most active areas of synaptogenesis during the first 5 weeks of life are in the sensorimotor cortex and subcortical parts of the brain, which are responsible for respiration and other essential survival processes. The visual cortex develops very rapidly between 3 and 4 months and reaches peak density by 12 months of age. The prefrontal cortex—responsible for planning and higher thinking—develops more slowly from infancy through early adulthood (Nelson & Luciana, 2008).

Throughout the lifespan, stimulation and experience are key components needed to maximize neural connections and brain development. In response to exposure to stimulation from the outside world, the number of synapses initially rises meteorically in the first year of life and the dendrites increase 500% by age 2 (Monk, Webb, & Nelson, 2001). By age 3, children have more synapses than at any other point in life, with at least 50% more synapses than in the adult brain (DiPietro, 2000; Monk et al., 2001). This explosion in connections in the early years of life has been called *transient exuberance* because the brain makes more connections than it needs, in preparation to receive any and all conceivable kinds of stimulation (Nowakowski, 1987). Those connections that are used become stronger and more efficient, while unused ones eventually shrink, atrophy, and disappear. This loss of unused neural connections is a process called **synaptic pruning**. The first 3 years of life have been identified as a particularly important time for neural development because stimulation during infancy and early childhood influences the number of connections among neurons and, by extension, the child's cognitive potential (DiPietro, 2000).

BRAIN DEVELOPMENT IN CHILDHOOD

An increase in synapses and connections among brain regions causes the brain to reach 90% of its adult weight by age 5 (Dubois et al., 2013). Children's brains tend to grow in spurts, with very rapid periods of growth followed by little growth or even reductions in volume with pruning (Gogtay & Thompson, 2010). Little-used synapses are pruned in response to experience, an important part of neurological development that leads to more efficient thought (Brown & Jernigan, 2012; Stiles & Jernigan, 2010). In addition, a process called **myelination** contributes to many of the changes that we see in children's capacities. Myelination refers to the process by which glial cells produce and coat the axons of neurons with fatty myelin, which speeds the transmission of neural impulses (Markant & Thomas, 2013). Myelination predicts general cognitive function (Deoni et al., 2011). That is, with myelination, children's thought and behavior becomes faster, more coordinated, and complex (Chevalier et al., 2015; Dubois et al., 2013; Mabbott, Noseworthy, Bouffet, Laughlin, & Rockel, 2006). Myelination proceeds most rapidly from birth to age 4, first in the sensory and motor cortex in infancy, and continues through childhood into adolescence and early adulthood (Jessen, 2004; Qiu, Mori, & Miller, 2015).

In addition to the changes just described, parts of the brain become specialized for different functions. The two halves of the brain, known as hemispheres, may look alike but are not identical. Each hemisphere of the brain (and the parts of the brain that comprise each hemisphere) is specialized for particular functions and become more specialized with experience. This process of the hemispheres becoming specialized to carry out different functions is called **lateralization** (Duboc, Dufourcq, Blader, & Roussigné, 2015). Lateralization (from the Latin *lateralis,* meaning "belonging to the side") begins before

synaptic pruning The process by which neural connections that are seldom used disappear.

myelination The process in which neurons are coated in a fatty substance, myelin, which contributes to faster neural communication.

lateralization The process by which the two hemispheres of the brain become specialized to carry out different functions.

birth and is influenced both by genes and by early experiences (Friederici, 2006; Goymer, 2007). For example, in the womb, most fetuses face toward the left, freeing the right side of the body, which permits more movement on that side and the development of greater control over the right side of the body (Previc, 1991). In newborns, the left hemisphere tends to have greater structural connectivity and efficiency—more connections and pathways—than the right, suggesting that newborns are better able to control the right side of their bodies (Ratnarajah et al., 2013). Children display a preference for the right or left hand, and their subsequent activity makes the hand more dominant because experience strengthens the hand and neural connections and improves agility. In this way, one hemisphere becomes stronger and more adept, a process known as **hemispheric dominance**. Most people experience hemispheric dominance, usually with the left hemisphere dominating over the right (Duboc et al., 2015), so that about 90% of people in Western countries are right-handed.

As children's brains mature they become capable of playing games that involve reasoning and planning, such as chess.

Among right-handed people, the left hemisphere plays an important role in language and the right hemisphere influences spatial skills. In left-handed people, the right hemisphere is dominant, and language is influenced by both hemispheres (Szaflarski et al., 2002). In some cultures, left-handedness is discouraged. For example, less than 1% of adults in Tanzania are left-handed because left-handed children often are physically restrained and punished for using their left hand (Provins, 1997). When left-handed children are forced to use their right hands, they typically learn to write with their right hand but carry out most other activities with their left, and brain scans reveal that their brains remain right-dominant (Klöppel, Vongerichten, van Eimeren, Frackowiak, & Siebner, 2007).

Although the left and right hemispheres are implicated for different functions, some researchers note that a strict right/spatial and left/language dichotomy is overly simplistic (Vilasboas, Herbet, & Duffau, 2017). Despite lateralization, the two hemispheres interact in a great many complex ways to enable us to think, move, create, and exercise our senses (Efron, 1990; Richmond, Johnson, Seal, Allen, & Whittle, 2016; Springer & Deutsch, 1998). Complex activities such as thinking and problem solving involve communication between both hemispheres of the brain (Turner, Marinsek, Ryhal, & Miller, 2015). The **corpus callosum**, a collection of 250 to 800 million neural fibers, connects the left and right hemispheres of the brain, permitting them to communicate and coordinate processing (Banich & Heller, 1998). During early childhood, the corpus callosum grows and begins to myelinate, permitting the two halves of the brain to communicate in more sophisticated and efficient ways and to act as one, enabling the child to execute large and fine motor activities such as catching and throwing a ball or tying shoelaces (Banich, 1998; Brown & Jernigan, 2012).

At all ages, the human brain has a capacity to change its organization and function in response to experience; this is known as **plasticity** (Kolb, Gibb, & Robinson, 2003). The brain is most plastic during the first few years of life (Nelson, Thomas, & de Haan, 2006; Stiles & Jernigan, 2010). The young child's brain can reorganize itself in response to injury in ways that the adult's brain cannot. Adults who suffered brain injuries during infancy or early childhood often have fewer cognitive difficulties than do adults who were injured later in life. The immature young brain, although offering opportunities for plasticity, is also uniquely sensitive to injury (Johnston et al., 2009; Uylings, 2006). If a part of the brain is damaged at a critical point in development, functions linked to that region will be irreversibly impaired (Luciana, 2003). How well a young child's brain compensates for an

hemispheric dominance A process in which one hemisphere becomes stronger and more adept than the other.

corpus callosum A thick band of nerve fibers that connects the left and right hemispheres of the brain, allowing communication.

plasticity A characteristic of development that refers to malleability, or openness to change in response to experience.

injury depends on the age at the time of injury, site of injury, and brain areas and capacities compromised. Generally speaking, plasticity is greatest when neurons are forming many synapses, and it declines with pruning (Kolb et al., 2003; Nelson, 2011). However, brain injuries sustained before age 2, and in some cases 3, can result in more global, severe, and long-lasting deficits than do those sustained later in childhood (Anderson et al., 2014; Anderson et al., 2010), suggesting that a reserve of neurons is needed for the brain to show plasticity. Overall, the degree to which individuals recover from an injury depends on the injury, its nature and severity, age, experiences after the injury, and contextual factors supporting recovery, such as interventions (Anderson, Spencer-Smith, & Wood, 2011; Bryck & Fisher, 2012).

BRAIN DEVELOPMENT IN ADOLESCENCE

In early adolescence, the increase in sex hormones with puberty triggers a variety of neurological developments, including a second burst of synaptogenesis, resulting in a rapid increase of connections among neurons (Goddings, 2015; Vigil et al., 2011). Connections between the prefrontal cortex and various brain regions strengthen, permitting rapid communication, enhanced cognitive functioning, and greater behavioral control (Jolles, van Buchem, Crone, & Rombouts, 2011; Spear, 2013). Connections strengthen especially among areas associated with higher cognitive and emotional functions. These rapid changes and the corresponding shaping of the cortex make it likely that adolescence is a sensitive period for brain development (Fuhrmann, Knoll, & Blakemore, 2015); only in the first years of life are there as many rapid and significant changes.

The volume of the cerebral cortex increases, peaking at about 10.5 years of age in girls and 14.5 in boys, although this age difference provides no functional advantage to girls or boys (Giedd et al., 2009). Synaptic pruning in response to experience occurs at an accelerated rate during adolescence as compared with childhood and adulthood (Zhou, Lebel, Treit, Evans, & Beaulieu, 2015). Synaptic pruning decreases the volume of gray matter, thins and molds the prefrontal cortex, which is responsible for rational thought and executive function, and results in markedly more efficient cognition and neural functioning (Blakemore, 2012; Mills, Goddings, Clasen, Giedd, & Blakemore, 2014).

As shown in Figure 4.3, myelination continues throughout adolescence and leads to steady increases in the brain's white matter, especially in the prefrontal cortex and the corpus callosum, which increases up to 20% in size, speeding communication between the right and left hemispheres (Barnea-Goraly et al., 2005; Luders, Thompson, & Toga, 2010). Increases in white matter are linked with improved performance on measures of working memory, executive functioning, and learning (Blakemore & Choudhury, 2006). Over the course of adolescence, adolescents' brains become larger, faster, and more efficient (Richmond et al., 2016). However, different parts of the brain develop at different times, leaving adolescents with somewhat lopsided functioning for a time. The prefrontal cortex requires the most time to develop, continuing maturation into the 20s.

Pubertal hormones cause the **limbic system**, responsible for emotion, to undergo a burst of development in early adolescence, well ahead of the prefrontal cortex, responsible for judgment (Goddings et al., 2014; Strang, Chein, & Steinberg, 2013). According to the **dual process model**, the lag in development between

limbic system A collection of brain structures responsible for emotion.

dual process model A model of the brain consisting of two systems, one emotional and the other rational, that develop on different timeframes, accounting for typical adolescent behavior.

FIGURE 4.3: **Developmental Changes in Gray and White Matter Across Adolescence**

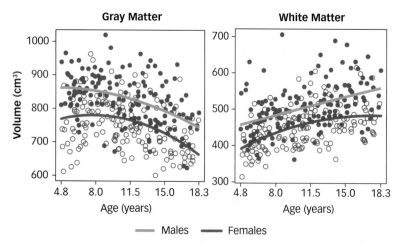

Source: Brain Development Cooperative Group (2012).

the limbic system and prefrontal cortex is difference can account for many "typical" adolescent behaviors (Mills et al., 2014; Shulman et al., 2016). Full development entails the prefrontal cortex catching up. These changes influence adolescents' thought and behavior in a myriad of ways. For example, parents often wonder whether they are speaking in a foreign language when their teens unexpectedly break off a conversation and storm away or when conflict arises over seemingly innocuous events. However, in a way, parents *are* speaking in a foreign language because adolescents' brains do not always lead them to accurately assess situations. Adolescents have difficulty identifying emotions depicted in facial expressions. Performance on tasks measuring sensitivity to facial expressions improves steadily during the first decade of life but dips in early adolescence, increasing in late adolescence into young adulthood (Motta-Mena & Scherf, 2017; Thomas, De Bellis, Graham, & LaBar, 2007). Why? Blame the brain.

In studies in which both adults and adolescents are shown photographs of people's faces depicting fear, adults correctly identify the emotion shown in the photograph, but many adolescents incorrectly identify the emotion as anger (Monk et al., 2003; Yurgelun-Todd, 2007). Moreover, fMRI scans indicate that when adults view facial expressions indicating fear, both their limbic system and prefrontal cortex are active. Scans of adolescents' brains, however, reveal a highly active limbic system but relatively inactive prefrontal cortex relative to adults, suggesting that adolescents experience emotional activation with relatively little executive processing in response to facial stimuli indicating fear (Monk et al., 2003; Yurgelun-Todd, 2007). This often results in adolescents incorrectly labeling emotions, such as mistaking fear for anger. Research with people aged 7 to 37 reveals developmental changes in facial processing; activity in parts of the frontal cortex increases during childhood, dips in early adolescence, then increases in late adolescence into adulthood (Cohen Kadosh, Johnson, Dick, Cohen Kadosh, & Blakemore, 2013). In another study, older children and adolescents viewed images of fearful and happy faces while undergoing fMRI. As shown in Figure 4.4, in response to fearful stimuli, girls showed increases in bilateral prefrontal activity through mid-adolescence but in males, age-related increase in brain activity were

FIGURE 4.4: Sex Differences in Face Processing During Adolescence

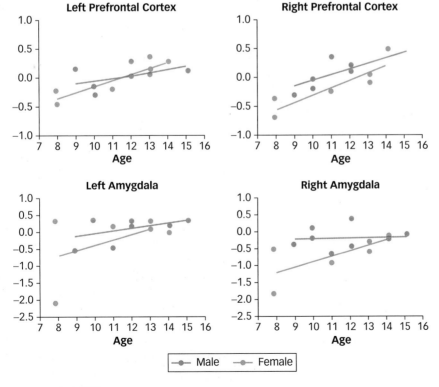

Source: Yurgelun-Todd (2007).

limited to the right prefrontal cortex (Yurgelun-Todd & Kilgore, 2006). Given that girls begin puberty two years before boys, a lag in prefrontal maturation is expected.

Brain structure influences affective responses and interactions with others. For example, one part of the limbic system, the **amygdala**, is implicated in aggression. When faced with emotionally arousing contexts and stimuli, adolescents tend to show exaggerated amygdala activity relative to adults and fewer functional connections between the prefrontal cortex and amygdala, suggesting that adolescents experience more emotional arousal yet less cortical processing and control than adults (Blakemore & Mills, 2014; Hare et al., 2008). Generally, amygdala volume increases more in adolescent males than females (Blakemore, 2012; Giedd et al., 2009). It seems that adolescents are wired to experience strong emotional reactions and to misidentify emotions in others' facial expressions, which can make communication and social interactions difficult.

Most adults look back upon their own adolescence and recall engaging in activities that included an element of risk or were even outright dangerous, such as racing bikes off ramps to soar through the air or driving at fast speeds. Risk taking and adolescence go hand in hand, and the brain plays a large part in such behavior. In early adolescence, the balance of neurotransmitters shifts. At 9 to 10 years of age, the prefrontal cortex and limbic system experience a marked shift in levels of serotonin and dopamine, neurotransmitters that are associated with impulsivity, novelty seeking, and reward salience (Padmanabhan & Luna, 2014; Smith, Chein, & Steinberg, 2013; Van Leijenhorst et al., 2010). Sensitivity to rewards peaks at the same time as adolescents experience difficulty with response inhibition, the ability to control a response (Geier, 2013; Spear, 2013). A heightened response to motivational cues coupled with immature behavioral control results in adolescents being biased toward immediate goals instead of long-term consequences (Casey, Jones, & Somerville, 2011). The shift is larger for boys than girls and is thought to make potentially rewarding stimuli even more rewarding for teens (Steinberg, 2008). As a result, risky situations, those that entail an element of danger, become enticing. Risks become experienced as thrills (Spielberg, Olino, Forbes, & Dahl, 2014). Adolescents may find themselves drawn to extreme sports, for example, enjoying the high and element of the unknown when they direct their skateboard into the air for a daring turn.

Yet not all adolescents engage in the same risks. Contextual factors, such as adult supervision, exposure to stressors, and impoverished communities, for example, influence the direction that adolescents' propensities for risk taking (Smith et al., 2013). One study examined adolescents in 11 countries in Africa, Asia, Europe, and the Americas and found that sensation seeking increased in preadolescence, peaked at around age 19, and declined thereafter (Steinberg et al., 2017). Risky activity is thought to decline in late adolescence in part because of increases in adolescents' self-regulatory capacities and their capacities for long-term planning that accompany maturation of the frontal cortex (Albert, Chein, & Steinberg, 2013; Casey, 2015).

BRAIN DEVELOPMENT IN ADULTHOOD

Brain development continues into emerging adulthood, maturing roughly in the mid-twenties (Dumontheil, 2016; Taber-Thomas & Perez-Edgar, 2015). As we age, the nervous system changes in predictable ways. Many neural fibers lose their coating of myelin, and communication among neurons slows accordingly. Declines are especially marked in the prefrontal cortex, responsible for executive functioning and judgment (Lu et al., 2013). Myelin losses contribute to cognitive declines with aging (Kohama, Rosene, & Sherman, 2012; Peters & Kemper, 2012). The last areas of the brain to myelinate are also the first to show reductions in myelin, a pattern some experts call the "last-in first-out" hypothesis of brain aging (Bender, Völkle, & Raz, 2016). The sensory regions of the brain, including the areas responsible for vision and hearing, and the motor cortex are the

amygdala A brain structure that is part of the limbic system and plays a role in emotion, especially fear and anger.

LIFESPAN BRAIN DEVELOPMENT

• • Brain Growth in Older Adulthood

The brain remains plastic throughout life. Aerobic exercise can reverse volume loss in the hippocampus, responsible for memory.

One of the most important findings in recent years about neurological development is that the brain retains some plasticity throughout life. The adult brain holds the potential to grow and change in response to experience. For example, older adults who are taught multiple cognitive strategies and problem-solving approaches show widespread positive effects on cognition that generalize to everyday tasks and last over time, often for years (Dunlosky, Kubat-Silman, & Hertzog, 2003; Schaie & Willis, 1986). Cognitive training does not simply influence older adults' skills—it changes their brains. Cognitive training has consistently been associated with increases in volume in the brain structures thought to be critical to the trained task (Lustig et al., 2009). Moreover, expertise is associated with brain growth and changes in connectivity (Strenziok et al., 2014). Experts tend to have enlarged brain structures related to their type of expertise (Maguire et al., 2003).

Physical health is associated with neurological health and plasticity throughout adulthood and well into older adulthood. Recent research suggests that caloric restriction may hold potential for improving memory, improving connectivity among neurons, and increasing gray matter volume in parts of the brain implicated in memory (Lin, Parikh, Hoffman, & Ma, 2017; Prehn et al., 2016). Many cross-sectional and longitudinal studies have shown that aerobic exercise training in older adulthood is associated with increases in brain volume and cognitive function, especially

executive function (Lang, Featherman, & Nesselroade, 1997; Stillman, Weinstein, Marsland, Gianaros, & Erickson, 2017). Aerobic exercise and activities that improve coordination are associated with increases in volume and connectivity in the frontal cortex, temporal lobe, and the hippocampus, areas responsible for memory, planning, and problem solving and prone to age-related deterioration (Erickson et al., 2011; Niemann, Godde, & Voelcker-Rehage, 2014; ten Brinke et al., 2015; Voss et al., 2013).

In one study (shown in Figure 4.5), greater amounts of physical activity were associated with greater gray matter volume in several areas of the brain, including the prefrontal cortex and hippocampus, over a 9-year period and a reduced risk for cognitive impairment (Erickson et al., 2010). Moreover, even sedentary older adults introduced to a long-term program of moderate physical activity showed increases in hippocampal volume over a 2-year period, suggesting that it is never too late to improve physical and neurological function (Rosano et al., 2017). These exercise experiments demonstrate that the brain remains modifiable throughout adulthood and that aerobic exercise offers important opportunities for neural plasticity (Hötting & Röder, 2013).

Although the phrase "use it or lose it" is often used in reference to cognitive function, recent research suggest that the aging brain can do more than just retain its functions; plasticity means that it can also grow. Perhaps the phrase should be changed to "use it to improve it."

FIGURE 4.5: Change in Hippocampal Volume With Aerobic Exercise

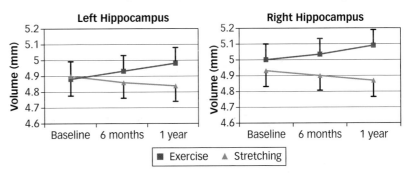

Source: Erickson et al. (2011).

What Do You Think?

Identify three things that an adult of any age can do to promote positive brain development and functioning in older adulthood.

FIGURE 4.6: Age Differences in Neural Activity During a Memory Task

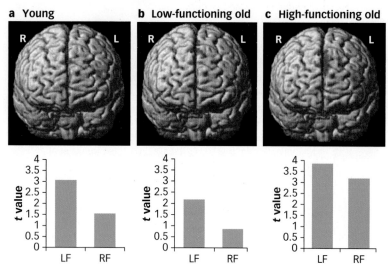

a Young

b Low-functioning old

c High-functioning old

Source: Hedden and Gabrieli (2004).

first brain areas to myelinate in infancy; they are also the last areas to show loss with age (Wu, Kumar, & Yang, 2016). Finally, some myelination continues throughout adulthood, but at a slower rate, permitting plasticity (Wang & Young, 2014).

Brain volume shrinks as dendrites contract and are lost, accompanied by a decrease in synapses and a loss of glial cells (Schuff et al., 2012). However, the reduction is, on average, less than half of 1% each year (Salthouse, 2011). For example, one study of men and women followed up from the early thirties to early forties found a 3% to 4% change in volume in men and women, respectively (Guo et al., 2016). Also, estimates of age-related changes in brain volume vary with measurement and across research studies. For example, some cross-sectional samples that compare adults of different ages at one time show greater age differences in brain volume than do longitudinal samples, which tend to show more continuous and gradual changes in brain volume that are less tied to age (Salthouse, 2011). A program of aerobic exercise has been shown to restore brain volume, especially in the hippocampus, a brain region closely involved with memory, supporting the role individuals have in their own development (see the Applying Developmental Science feature).

The brain retains plasticity and compensates for structural changes throughout older adulthood. Older adults' brains compensate for cognitive declines by showing more brain activity and using different brain areas in solving problems than do younger adults (Turner & Spreng, 2012). Older adults often show brain activity that is spread out over a larger area, including both hemispheres, compensating for neural losses, as shown in Figure 4.6 (Daselaar & Cabeza, 2005; Reuter-Lorenz & Cappell, 2008). For example, in one study older adults compensated for lower levels of parietal and occipital activity with greater activity in the frontal lobes and performed better on a working memory task than did younger adults (Osorio, Fay, Pouthas, & Ballesteros, 2010).

Age-related brain changes are not always apparent in adults' functioning. Adults' brains naturally compensate for losses through **cognitive reserve**, the ability to make flexible and efficient use of available brain resources that permits cognitive efficiency, flexibility, and adaptability (Barulli & Stern, 2013; Nair, Sabbagh, Tucker, & Stern, 2014). Cognitive reserve is a type of plasticity cultivated throughout life from experience and environmental factors. Educational and occupational attainment and engagement in leisure activities allows some adults to cope with age-related changes better than others and show more successful aging (Barulli & Stern, 2013; Scarmeas & Stern, 2003). For example, bilingualism is associated with cognitive benefits throughout life. Adults who have daily experiences in using two languages, such as determining when to use one and inhibit another, show enhanced cognitive control abilities, more mental flexibility as well as being better able to handle tasks involving switching, inhibition, and conflict monitoring (Barac & Bialystok, 2012; Grant, Dennis, & Li, 2014). In addition, bilingual older adults show preserved white matter integrity, especially in the frontal lobe, as compared with their monolingual peers (Olsen et al., 2015; Pliatsikas, Moschopoulou, & Saddy, 2015).

A particularly exciting finding is that neurogenesis, the creation of new neurons, continues throughout life. New neurons are created in the hippocampus and striatum (a subcortical part of the brain responsible for coordinating motivation with body movement)

cognitive reserve The ability to make flexible and efficient use of available brain resources that permits cognitive efficiency, flexibility, and adaptability; it is cultivated throughout life from experience and environmental factors.

and the olfactory bulb throughout life but at a much slower rate than prenatally (Ernst et al., 2014; Gonçalves, Schafer, & Gage, 2016; Sailor, Schinder, & Lledo, 2017). Most of these neurons die off, but some survive, especially if exposed to experiences that require learning (Shores, 2014). As with neurogenesis early in life, surviving neurons migrate to the parts of the brain where they will function and create synapses with other neurons (Braun & Jessberger, 2014), permitting lifelong plasticity (Obernier, Tong, & Alvarez-Buylla, 2014). It is estimated that about 2% of neurons are renewed each year (Spalding et al., 2013). The corresponding synaptogenesis is associated with learning and plays a role in cognition and in stress and emotional responses, contributing to plasticity and the maintenance of cognitive abilities and advances in psychosocial maturing in the adult years (Cameron & Glover, 2015; Gonçalves et al., 2016; Nelson & Alkon, 2015; Sailor et al., 2017).

 Thinking in Context 4.1

1. What do parents need to know about their children's brain development? What advice might you give to parents of infants, children, and adolescents on how to promote brain development? Would you give similar advice at all ages? Why or why not?

2. Children who suffer brain injuries often regain some, and sometimes all, of their capacities. Adults sometimes, but not always, show this resilience as well. How might you explain this, given what you have learned about brain development?

3. Most adults blame puberty for much of adolescent behavior. Researchers, however, point to the dual process model's role in influencing adolescent behavior. Explain.

4. How are cultural, contextual, and lifestyle factors, such as neighborhood, socioeconomic status, ethnicity, and interactions with family and peers, reflected in brain development and change from infancy through older adulthood?

MOTOR DEVELOPMENT

LO 4.2 Summarize patterns of gross and fine motor development and influences on motor development.

Newborns are equipped to respond to the stimulation they encounter in the world. The earliest ways in which infants adapt are through the use of their **reflexes**, involuntary and automatic responses to stimuli such as touch, light, and sound. Each reflex has its own developmental course (Payne & Isaacs, 2016). Some disappear early in life, and others persist throughout life, as shown in Table 4.1. Infants show individual differences in how reflexes are displayed, specifically the intensity of the response. Preterm newborns, for example, show reflexes suggesting a more immature neurological system than full-term newborns (Barros, Mitsuhiro, Chalem, Laranjeira, & Guinsburg, 2011). The absence of reflexes, however, may signal neurological deficits (Gabbard, 2012).

reflex An involuntary and automatic response to stimuli.

gross motor development Development of the ability to control large movements of the body, such as walking and jumping.

GROSS MOTOR DEVELOPMENT

Gross motor development refers to the ability to control the large movements of the body, which are the actions that help us move around in our environment. Like physical development, motor skills evolve in a predictable sequence. By the end of the first month of life, most infants can reach the first milestone, or achievement, in motor development: lifting their heads while lying on their stomachs. After lifting the head, infants progress through an orderly series of motor milestones: lifting the chest, reaching for objects, rolling over, and sitting up with support (see Table 4.2). Notice that these motor achievements reflect a cephalocaudal progression of motor control, proceeding from the head downward (Payne & Isaacs, 2016). Success at initiating forward motion, or crawling (6–10 months), is particularly significant for both infants and parents. Infants vary in how they crawl. Some use

Lives in Context Video 4.2
Motor Development in Infancy

TABLE 4.1 • Newborn Reflexes

NAME OF REFLEX	RESPONSE	DEVELOPMENTAL COURSE
Palmar grasp	Curling fingers around objects that touch the palm	Birth to about 4 months, when it is replaced by voluntary grasp
Rooting	Turning head and tongue toward stimulus when cheek is touched	Disappears over first few weeks of life and is replaced by voluntary head movement
Sucking	Sucking on objects placed into the mouth	Birth to about 6 months
Moro	Giving a startle response in reaction to loud noise or sudden change in the position of the head, resulting in throwing out arms, arching the back, and bringing the arms together as if to grasp something	Birth to about 5 to 7 months
Babinski	Fanning and curling the toes in response to stroking the bottom of the foot	Birth to about 8 to 12 months
Stepping	Making stepping movements as if to walk when held upright with feet touching a flat surface	Birth to about 2 to 3 months
Swimming	Holding breath and moving arms and legs, as if to swim, when placed in water	Birth to about 4 to 6 months

TABLE 4.2 • Early Gross Motor Milestones

AVERAGE AGE ACHIEVED	MOTOR SKILL
2 months	Lifts head Holds head steady when held upright
3 months	Pushes head and chest up with arms Rolls from stomach to back
4 months	Grasps cube
6 months	Sits without support
7 months	Rolls from back to stomach Attempts crawling Uses opposable thumb to grasp objects
8 months	Achieves sitting position alone Pulls to a stand
9 months	"Cruises" by holding on to furniture
10 months	Plays patty-cake
11 months	Stands alone
12 months	Walks alone
14 months	Builds tower of two cubes Scribbles
17 months	Walks up steps
18 months	Runs

their arms to pull and legs to push, some use only their arms or only their legs, and others scoot on their bottoms. Once infants can pull themselves upright while holding on to a chair or table, they begin "cruising," moving by holding on to furniture to maintain their balance while stepping sideways. In most Western industrialized countries, most infants walk alone by about 1 year of age.

Once babies can walk, their entire visual field changes. Whereas crawling babies are more likely to look at the floor as they move, walking babies gaze straight ahead at caregivers, walls, and toys (Kretch, Franchak, & Adolph, 2014). Independent walking holds implications for cognitive, social, and emotional development, as it is associated not only with more attention and manipulation of objects but also with more sophisticated social interactions with caregivers, such as directing mothers' attention to particular objects and sharing. These behaviors, in turn, are associated with advanced language development relative to nonwalkers in both U.S. and Chinese infants (Clearfield, 2011; Ghassabian et al., 2016; He, Walle, & Campos, 2015; Karasik, Tamis-LeMonda, & Adolph, 2011).

Between the ages of 3 and 6, children become physically stronger, with increases in bone and muscle strength as well as lung capacity. Children make gains in coordination as the parts of the brain responsible for sensory and motor skills develop, permitting them to play harder and engage in more complicated play activities that include running, jumping, and climbing (see Table 4.3). Young children practice using their large motor skills to jump, run, and ride tricycles, pedal cars, and other riding toys. Coordinating complex movements, like those entailed in riding a bicycle, is challenging for young children as it requires controlling multiple limbs, balancing, and more. As they grow and gain competence in their motor skills, young children become even more coordinated and begin to show interest in skipping, balancing, and playing games that involve feats of coordination, such as throwing and catching a ball. By age 5, most North American children can throw, catch, and kick a ball; climb a ladder; and ride a tricycle. Some 5-year-olds can even skate or ride a bicycle (Gabbard, 2012).

Like growth, children's motor development proceeds continuously, advancing gradually throughout childhood (Kit, Akinbami, Isfahani, & Ulrich, 2017), so that motor skills from birth to age 4 predict children's motor abilities later, when children enter school (Piek, Dawson, Smith, & Gasson, 2008). During the school-age years, the gross motor skills developed in early childhood refine and combine into more complex abilities, such as running and turning to dodge a ball, walking heel to toe down the length of a balance beam and turning around, or creating elaborate jump rope routines that include twisting, turning, and hopping by quickly alternating their feet (Gallahue & Ozmun, 2006). Increases in body size and strength contribute to advances in motor skills, which are accompanied by advances in flexibility, balance, agility, and strength (Broude, 1995; Gabbard, 2012). Now children can bend their bodies to more easily kick a ball, do a somersault, or carry out a dance routine; balance to jump rope or throw a ball; demonstrate agility to run and change speed and direction rapidly; and have the strength to jump higher and throw a ball farther than ever before (Gallahue & Ozmun, 2006; Haywood & Getchell, 2005).

FINE MOTOR DEVELOPMENT

Fine motor development refers to the ability to control small movements of the fingers such as reaching and grasping. Voluntary reaching plays an important role in cognitive development because it provides new opportunities for interacting with the world. Like other motor skills, reaching and grasping begin as gross activity and are refined with time. Newborns begin by engaging in *prereaching*, swinging their arms and extending them toward nearby objects (Ennouri & Bloch, 1996; von Hofsten & Rönnqvist, 1993). Newborns use both arms equally and cannot control their arms and hands, so they rarely succeed in making contact with objects of interest (Lynch, Lee, Bhat, & Galloway, 2008). Prereaching stops at about 7 weeks of age.

Stacking small blocks such as these tests children's fine motor skills.

zlikovec/Shutterstock.com

Voluntary reaching appears at about 3 months of age and slowly improves in accuracy. At 5 months, infants can successfully reach for moving objects. By 7 months, the arms can reach independently, and infants are able to reach for an object with one arm rather than both (Spencer, Vereijken, Diedrich, & Thelen, 2000). By 10 months, infants can reach for moving objects that change direction (Fagard, Spelke, & von Hofsten, 2009). As they gain experience with reaching and acquiring objects, infants develop cognitively because they learn by exploring and playing with objects—and object preferences change with experience. In one study 4- to 6-month-old infants with less reaching experience spent more time looking at and exploring larger objects, whereas 5- to 6-month-old infants with more reaching experience spent more time looking at and touching smaller objects. The older infants did this despite first looking at and touching the largest object (Libertus et al., 2013). With experience, infants' attention moves away from the motor skill (like the ability to coordinate their movement to hit a mobile), to

fine motor development
Development of the ability to control small movements of the fingers such as reaching and grasping.

TABLE 4.3 • Gross and Fine Motor Skill Development in Childhood

AGE	GROSS MOTOR SKILL	FINE MOTOR SKILL
2–3 years	Walks more smoothly, runs but cannot turn or stop suddenly, jumps, throws a ball with a rigid body and catches by trapping ball against chest, rides push toys using feet	Unzips large zippers, puts on and removes some clothing, uses a spoon
3–4 years	Runs, ascends stairs alternating feet, jumps 15 to 24 inches, hops, pedals and steers a tricycle	Serves food, can work large buttons, copies vertical line and circle, uses scissors
4–5 years	Runs more smoothly with control over stopping and turning, descends stairs alternating feet, jumps 24 to 33 inches, skips, throws ball by rotating the body and transferring weight to one foot, catches ball with hands, rides tricycle and steers effectively	Uses scissors to cut along a line, uses fork effectively, copies simple shapes and some letters
5–6 years	Runs more quickly, skips more effectively, throws and catches a ball like older children, makes a running jump of 28 to 36 inches, rides bicycle with training wheels	Ties shoes, uses knife to cut soft food, copies numbers and simple words

the object (the mobile), as well as to the events that occur before and after acquiring the object (how the mobile swings and how grabbing it stops the swinging or how batting at it makes it swing faster). In this way, infants learn about causality and how to solve simple problems.

As children grow older their fine motor skills improve. The ability to button a shirt, pour milk into a glass, assemble puzzles, and draw pictures all involve eye–hand and small muscle coordination. As children get better at these skills, they are able to become more independent and do more for themselves. Young children become better at grasping eating utensils and become more self-sufficient at feeding. Many fine motor skills are very difficult for young children because they involve both hands and both sides of the brain. With short, stubby fingers that have not yet grown and a cerebral cortex that is not yet myelinated, a challenging task such as tying a shoelace is frustrating for young children. Tying a shoelace is a complex act requiring attention, memory for an intricate series of hand movements, and the dexterity to perform them. Though preschoolers struggle with this task, by 5 to 6 years of age most children can tie their shoes (Payne & Isaacs, 2016). During the school years, children become adept at using pencils to write words and sentences. They become able to control their hands independently and many subsequently learn to play musical instruments. Many children now show interest in activities that require fine motor coordination, such as drawing, building model cars, and sewing. By 12 years of age children show fine motor skills comparable to those of adults.

Not only are older children better at running, jumping, and other physical activities than young children, but they also show advances in fine motor control that allow them to develop new interests. School-age children build model cars, play with yo-yos, braid friendship bracelets, weave potholders, and learn to play musical instruments—all tasks that depend on fine motor control. Fine motor development is particularly important for children's school performance, specifically penmanship. Most 6-year-old children can write the alphabet, their names, and numbers in large print, making strokes with their entire arm. With development, children learn to use their wrists and fingers to write. Uppercase letters are usually mastered first; the lowercase alphabet requires smaller movements of the hand that require much practice. By third grade, most children can write in script, or cursive writing. Girls tend to outperform boys in fine motor skills (Junaid & Fellowes, 2006; Nyiti, 1982). Success in fine motor skills, particularly writing skills, may influence academic skills as children who write with ease may be better able to express themselves in writing, for example.

BIOLOGICAL AND CONTEXTUAL DETERMINANTS OF MOTOR DEVELOPMENT

Motor development illustrates the complex interactions that take place between maturation and contextual factors. Maturation plays a very strong role in motor development. Preterm infants reach motor milestones later than do full-term infants (Gabriel et al., 2009). Cross-cultural research also supports the role of maturation because around the world, infants display roughly the same sequence of motor milestones. Among some Native Americans and other ethnic groups around the world, it is common to follow the tradition of tightly swaddling infants to cradleboards and strapping the board to the mother's back during nearly all waking hours for the first 6 to 12 months of the child's life. Although this might lead one to expect that swaddled babies will not learn to walk as early as babies whose movements are unrestricted, studies of Hopi Indian infants have shown that swaddling has little impact on when Hopi infants initiate walking (Dennis & Dennis, 1991; Harriman & Lukosius, 1982). Such research suggests that walking is very much maturationally programmed. Other evidence for the maturational basis of motor development comes from twin studies. Identical twins, who share the same genes, share more similarities in the timing and pace of motor development than do fraternal twins, who share half of their genes (Fogel, 2007; Wilson & Harpring, 1972). Samples of young children in the United States show no ethnic or socioeconomic status differences in gross motor skill such as running, hopping, kicking, and catching (Kit et al., 2017).

Advancements in motor skill are influenced by body maturation and especially brain development. The pruning of unused synapses contributes to increases in motor speed and reaction time so that 11-year-old children tend to respond twice as quickly as 5-year-olds (Kail, 2003). Growth of the cerebellum (responsible for balance, coordination, and some aspects of emotion and reasoning) and myelination of its connections to the cortex contribute to advances in gross and fine motor skills and speed (Baillieux, De Smet, Paquier, De Deyn, & Mariën, 2008; Diamond, 2000; Tiemeier et al., 2010). Brain development improves children's ability to inhibit actions, which enables children to carry out more sophisticated motor activities that require the use of one hand while controlling the other, such as throwing a ball, or that require both hands to do different things, such as playing a musical instrument (Diamond, 2013). As infants and children gain experience coordinating their motor skills, activity in the areas of the brain responsible for motor skills becomes less diffuse and more focused, consistent with the lifespan principle that domains of development interact (Nishiyori, Bisconti, Meehan, & Ulrich, 2016).

Much of motor development is driven by maturation, yet opportunities to practice motor skills are also important. In a classic naturalistic study of institutionalized orphans in Iran who had spent their first two years of life lying on their backs in their cribs and were never placed in sitting positions or played with, none of the 1- to 2-year-old infants could walk, and fewer than half of them could sit up; the researchers also found that most of the 3- to 4-year-olds could not walk well alone (Dennis, 1960). Recent research suggests that infants raised in orphanages score lower on measures of gross motor milestones at 4, 6, and 8 months of age and walk later as compared with home-reared infants (Chaibal, Bennett, Rattanathanthong, & Siritaratiwat, 2016). While maturation is necessary for motor development, it is not sufficient; we must also have opportunities to practice our motor skills.

In fact, practice can enhance motor development (Lobo & Galloway, 2012). For example, when infants from 1 to 7 weeks of age practice stepping reflexes each day, they retain the movements and walk earlier than

Jeremy van Riemsdyke/Alamy

Babies walk at about a year of age, but cultural and contextual circumstances can speed or delay motor development.

infants who receive no practice (Vereijken & Thelen, 1997; Zelazo, 1983). Even newborns show improvement in stepping when given treadmill practice (Siekerman et al., 2015). Practice in sitting has a similar effect (Zelazo, Zelazo, Cohen, & Zelazo, 1993). Even 1-month-old infants given postural training showed more advanced control of their heads and necks than other infants (Lee & Galloway, 2012). Similarly, infants who spend supervised playtime prone on their stomachs each day reach many motor milestones, including rolling over and crawling, earlier than do infants who spend little time on their stomachs (Fetters & Hsiang-han, 2007; Kuo, Liao, Chen, Hsieh, & Hwang, 2008). In one study, over a two-week period, young infants received daily play experience with "sticky mittens"—Velcro-covered mitts that enabled them to independently pick up objects. These infants showed advances in their reaching behavior and greater visual exploration of objects, while a comparison group of young infants who passively watched an adult's actions on the objects showed no change (Libertus & Needham, 2010). Sticky mittens training in reaching at 3 months of age predicts object exploration at 15 months of age (Libertus, Joh, & Needham, 2016).

Practice contributes to cross-cultural differences in infant motor development. Different cultures provide infants with different experiences and opportunities for development. For example, in many cultures, including several in sub-Saharan Africa and in the West Indies, infants attain motor goals like sitting up and walking much earlier than do North American infants. Among the Kipsigi of Kenya, parents seat babies in holes dug in the ground and use rolled blankets to keep babies upright in the sitting position (Keller, 2003). The Kipsigis help their babies practice walking at 2 to 3 months of age by holding their hands, putting them on the floor, and moving them slowly forward. Notably, Kipsigi mothers do not encourage their infants to crawl; crawling is seen as dangerous as it exposes the child to dirt, insects, and the dangers of fire pits and roaming animals. Crawling is therefore virtually nonexistent in Kipsigi infants (Super & Harkness, 2015). Infants of many sub-Saharan villages, such as the !Kung San, Gusii, and Wolof, are also trained to sit using holes or containers for support and are often held upright and bounced up and down, a social interaction practice that contributes to earlier walking (Lohaus et al., 2011). Caregivers in some of these cultures further encourage walking by setting up two parallel bamboo poles that infants can hold onto with both hands, learning balance and stepping skills (Keller, 2003). Similarly, mothers in Jamaica and other parts of the West Indies use a formal handling routine to exercise their babies' muscles and help them to grow up strong and healthy (Dziewolska & Cautilli, 2006; Hopkins, 1991; Hopkins & Westra, 1989, 1990).

Although practice can speed development and caregivers in many cultures provide their infants with opportunities for early practice of motor skills, sometimes survival and success requires continued dependence on caregivers and delaying motor milestones. For example, crawling may not be encouraged in potentially dangerous environments, such as those with many insects, rodents, and/or reptiles on the ground. For example, the nomadic Ache of eastern Paraguay discourage their infants from crawling or moving independently. Ache infants walk at 18 to 20 months, as compared with the 12-month average of North American infants (Kaplan & Dove, 1987).

Even simple aspects of the child-rearing context, such as choice of clothing, can influence motor development. In the 19th century, 40% of American infants skipped crawling, possibly because the long, flowing gowns they wore impeded movement on hands and knees (Trettien, 1990). One study of 13- and 19-month-old infants compared their gait while wearing a disposable diaper, a thicker cloth diaper, and no diaper (Cole, Lingeman, & Adolph, 2012). When naked, infants demonstrated the most sophisticated walking with fewer missteps and falls. While wearing a diaper, infants walked as poorly as they would have done several weeks earlier had they been walking naked. In sum, motor development is largely maturational, but subtle differences in context and cultural emphasis play a role in its timing.

MOTOR DEVELOPMENT AS A DYNAMIC SYSTEM

Motor milestones, such as the ability to crawl, might look like isolated achievements, but they actually develop systematically and build on each other, with each new skill preparing an infant to tackle the next (Thelen, 1995, 2000). As shown in Figure 4.7, motor development reflects an interaction among developmental domains, maturation, and environment in which we acquire increasingly complex **dynamic systems** of action (Thelen, 1995, 2000). Simple motor skills are combined in increasingly complex ways, permitting advances in movement including a wider range and more precise movements that enable babies to more effectively explore and control their environments. Separate abilities are blended together to provide more complex and effective ways of exploring and controlling the environment. For example, the abilities to sit upright, hold the head upright, match motor movements to vision, reach out an arm, and grasp are all combined into coordinated reaching movements to obtain a desired object (Corbetta & Snapp-Childs, 2009; Spencer et al., 2000).

Motor skills also reflect the interaction of multiple domains of development. All movement relies on the coordination of our senses and cognitive abilities to plan and predict actions. Social and cultural influences provide context to our movements. Motor behavior influences what we sense and our opportunities to engage our world, advance cognition, and interact with others. Motor skills do not develop in isolation; rather, they are influenced by the physical and social context in which they occur (Adolph & Franchak, 2017). Motor skills become more specialized, coordinated, and precise with practice, permitting infants to reach for an object with one hand without needlessly

FIGURE 4.7: Dynamic Systems Theory

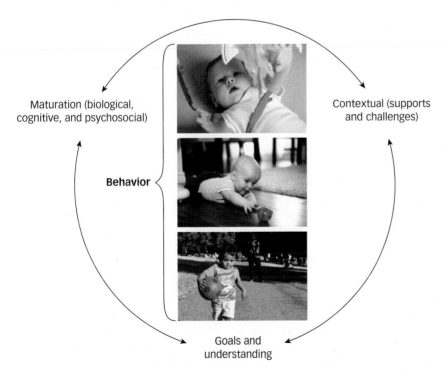

Maturation (biological, cognitive, and psychosocial)

Contextual (supports and challenges)

Behavior

Goals and understanding

The infant's abilities to reach out an arm, stretch, and grasp combine into coordinated reaching movements to obtain desired objects. Motor development progresses to sitting, crawling, walking, and eventually running, all reflections of infants' blending and coordinating abilities to achieve self-chosen goals, such as obtaining toys, and all tailored by environmental supports and challenges. (photos: istock and canstock/harishmarnad.)

dynamic systems A framework describing motor skills as resulting from ongoing interactions among physical, cognitive, and socioemotional influences and environmental supports in which previously mastered skills are combined to provide more complex and effective ways of exploring and controlling the environment

flailing the other, for example (D'Souza, Cowie, Karmiloff-Smith, & Bremner, 2016). With experience in a given task, infants' brain activity shifts from diffuse activity spread through large regions of the brain to functioning that is more refined and localized to the motor cortex (Nishiyori et al., 2016).

Motor development reflects goal-oriented behavior because it is initiated by the infant's or child's desire to accomplish something, such as picking up a toy or moving to the other side of the room. Infants' abilities and their immediate environments (e.g., whether they are being held, lying in a crib, or lying freely on the floor) determine whether and how the goal can be achieved (Spencer et al., 2000). The infant tries out behaviors and persists at those that enable him or her to move closer to the goal, practicing and refining the behavior. For example, infants learn to walk by taking many steps and making many falls, but they persist even though, at the time, crawling is a much faster and more efficient means of transportation (Adolph et al., 2012). Why? Perhaps because upright posture leads to many more interesting sights, objects, and interactions. The upright infant can see more and do more, with two hands free to grasp objects, making walking a very desirable goal (Adolph & Tamis-LeMonda, 2014). New motor skills provide new possibilities for exploration of the environment and new interactions with caregivers that influence opportunities. Differences in caregiver interactions and caregiving environments affect children's motor skills, the form they take, the ages of onset, and the overall developmental trend (Adolph & Franchak, 2017).

Therefore, from a dynamic systems perspective, motor development is the result of several processes: central nervous system maturation, the infant's physical capacities, environmental supports, and the infant's desire to explore the world (see Figure 4.7). It is learned by revising and combining abilities and skills to fit the infant's goals. In this way, motor development is highly individualized as each infant has goals that are particular to his or her specific environment. For example, an infant might respond to slippery hardwood floors by crawling on her stomach rather than all fours or by shuffling her feet and hands rather than raising each. Infants attain the same motor tasks, such as climbing down stairs, at about the same age, yet differ in how they approach the task. Some, for example, might turn around and back down, others descend on their bottoms, and others slide down face first (Berger, Theuring, & Adolph, 2007). By viewing motor development as dynamic systems of action produced by an infant's abilities, goal-directed behavior, and environmental supports and opportunities, we can account for the individual differences that we see in motor development.

MOTOR DEVELOPMENT AND AGING

Motor skills change in predictable ways over the lifespan. One study of fine and gross motor performance found that performance showed a pattern of improvement with age up until early adulthood and a decline with age thereafter. Specifically, performance improved from 7- to 9-year-old children through 19- to 25-year-old young adults and then declined from young adulthood into older adulthood, in 66- to 80-year-old adults (Leversen, Haga, Sigmundsson, Rebollo, & Colom, 2012). We have seen that physical activity can compensate for age-related declines in muscle and strength. A lifetime of regular physical activity is associated with greater mobility in older adulthood (Boyer et al., 2012).

Changes in *balance*, the ability to control the body's position in space, is a particularly important influence on older adults' mobility (Payne & Isaacs, 2016). Balance involves integrating sensory information with awareness of the position of one's body in space and in the surrounding environment (Payne & Isaacs, 2016). As we will see later in this chapter, sensory abilities tend to decline in function, and these declines make balance more difficult to achieve and sustain. However, just as muscle strength can be improved, so can balance. Interventions that encourage exercise and promote strength and balance, such as tai chi, can increase balance and strength and offset loss

(Granacher, Muehlbauer, & Gruber, 2012; Lesinski, Hortobágyi, Muehlbauer, Gollhofer, & Granacher, 2015; Peterson, Rhea, Sen, & Gordon, 2010). With age, balance requires more attention and taps more cognitive resources. In one study, researchers administered four challenging balance tasks to a large sample of healthy 50- to 64- and 65- to 75-year-old participants (Aslan et al., 2008). Balance tasks included a forward reach that required participants to stand with their feet together and reach forward as far as they could without losing balance; a timed task that recorded how quickly the adults could stand from a chair, walk 10 feet, return, and sit back down; standing from a seated position in a chair five times, fully straightening the legs each time before sitting back down; and a timed task in which participants stepped up on a 4-inch step five times. Balance performance declined with age. Tasks that ask

Practicing tai chi can strengthen muscles and improve balance in adults of all ages.

older adults to multitask and perform cognitive tasks (such as counting backwards by threes) show even greater decrements, suggesting that age-related changes are influenced by the ability to allocate attention, and that neurological change plays a role in motor performance (Granacher et al., 2012).

Walking is the result of many integrated functions, including neurological, muscular, and sensory systems (Holtzer, Epstein, Mahoney, Izzetoglu, & Blumen, 2014; Sorond et al., 2015). As muscle strength, bone density, and flexibility declines, people walk more slowly (Shumway-Cook et al., 2007), yet many adults compensate by taking longer steps (Jerome et al., 2015).

Gait (the manner in which people walk) speed naturally declines with age (Payne & Isaacs, 2016). However, rapid or steep decline in gait speed may indicate overall physiological declines that predict mortality because motor function, specifically gait speed, is a marker of overall health and is used in geriatric assessment in addition to measures of blood pressure, respiration, temperature, and pulse (Kuys, Peel, Klein, Slater, & Hubbard, 2014; Studenski, 2011).

 Thinking in Context 4.2

1. Carmen is concerned because her 14-month-old baby is not yet walking. All of the other babies she knows walked by 12 months of age. What would you tell Carmen?

2. How might a fine motor skill, such as learning to use a spoon, reflect the interaction of maturation and sociocultural context? How might contextual factors such as neighborhood, family, school, and culture influence the development of motor skills? Do these factors become more influential over the childhood years? Why or why not?

3. Consider your own development. What do you recall about the development of your motor skills? For example, when did you learn to tie your shoelaces or ride a bike? How did your motor skills influence other aspects of development, such as your relationships with others or your cognitive skills?

4. How do motor skills illustrate the interaction of domains of development in infancy? Adulthood?

SENSATION AND PERCEPTION

LO 4.3 Describe age-related changes in vision, hearing, and other senses.

We have seen that individuals are embedded in and interact dynamically with their context. James and Eleanor Gibson studied perceptual development from an ecological perspective, emphasizing that perception arises through interactions with the environment. Rather than collecting small pieces of sensory information and building a representation of the world, the Gibsons argued that the environment itself provides all the information needed and we perceive the environment directly, without constructing or manipulating sensory information.

Perception arises from action. Infants actively explore their environment with their eyes by moving their heads and, later, reaching with their hands and, eventually, crawling. Through these activities infants perceive **affordances**—the nature, opportunities, and limits of objects (Gibson & Pick, 2000). The features of objects tell infants about possible actions, such as whether an object is squeezable, mouthable, catchable, or reachable. Infants explore their environment systematically, searching to discover the properties of the things around them (Savelsbergh, van der Kamp, & van Wermeskerken, 2013). From this perspective, perception arises from action, just as it influences action (Gibson, 1979). Exploration and discovery of affordances depends on the infant's capacities for action, which is influenced by their development, genetics, and motivation (Miller, 2016). For example, a large pot might offer a 10-year-old the possibility of cooking because the child has developed this capacity and can perceive this affordance of the pot. An 18-month-old infant may perceive very different affordances from the pot based on her capacities, such as a drum to bang or a bucket to fill. We naturally perceive affordances, such as knowing when a surface is safe for walking, by sensing information from the environment and coordinating it with our body sensations, such as our sense of balance, for example (Kretch et al., 2014).

SENSORY AND PERCEPTUAL DEVELOPMENT

Visiting the doctor's office for the first time in her young life, Kerry followed the doctor's finger with her eyes as he passed it over her face. "I think she sees it!" says her surprised mother. "She most certainly does," said the doctor. "Even as a newborn, your Kerry can sense the world. She can see, hear, and smell better than you know." Developmental researchers draw a distinction between sensation and perception. Sensation occurs when our senses detect a stimulus. Perception refers to the sense our brain makes of the stimulus and our awareness of it. Newborns can both detect and perceive stimuli, but many of their abilities are immature relative to those of adults. Yet infants' sensory abilities develop rapidly, achieving adult levels within the first year of life (Courage & Adams, 1990; Northern, 2014). The Applying Developmental Science feature describes some of the methods researchers use to study sensation and perception in infants.

Vision

At birth, vision is the least developed sense, but it improves rapidly. Newborn visual acuity, or sharpness of vision, is approximately 20/400 (Farroni & Menon, 2008). Studies of infants' looking preferences—what the infant looks at and for how long (see Chapter 6)—show that infants reach adult levels of visual acuity between 6 months and 1 year of age (Courage & Adams, 1990; Gwiazda & Birch, 2001; Mercuri, Baranello, Romeo, Cesarini, & Ricci, 2007). Improvement in vision is due to the increasing maturation of the structures of the eye and the visual cortex, the part of the brain that processes visual stimuli.

Newborns are born with preferences for particular visual stimuli. Newborns prefer to look at patterns, such as a few large squares, rather than a plain stimulus such as a black or white oval shape (Fantz, 1961). Newborns also prefer to look at faces, and the preference for faces increases with age (Frank, Vul, & Johnson, 2009; Gliga, Elsabbagh, Andravizou, & Johnson, 2009). How infants explore visual stimuli changes with age (Colombo, Brez, & Curtindale, 2015). Until about 1 month of age, infants tend to scan along the outer perimeter of stimuli. For example, when presented with a face, the infant's gaze will scan along the hairline and not move to the eyes and mouth. By 6 to 7 weeks of age, infants

affordances Refers to the actional properties of objects—their nature, opportunities, and limits.

APPLYING DEVELOPMENTAL SCIENCE

• • Methods of Studying Infant Perception

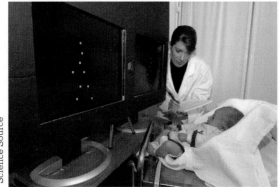

Which display is the baby looking at? Preferential looking tasks tell us about infants' perceptual abilities and preferences.

How do researchers study infant perception? The simplest method is through *preferential looking tasks*, which are experiments designed to determine whether infants prefer to look at one stimulus or another. For example, consider an array of black and white stripes. As shown in Figure 4.8, an array with more stripes (and therefore, many more narrow stripes) tends to appear gray rather than black and white because the pattern becomes more difficult to see as the stripes become more narrow. Researchers determine infants' visual acuity by comparing infants' responses to stimuli with

FIGURE 4.8: Dynamic Systems Theory

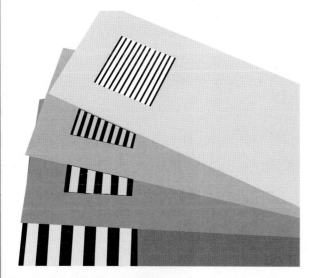

Researchers and pediatricians use stimuli such as the Teller Acuity Cards illustrated here to determine what infants can see. Young infants attend to stimuli with wider lines and stop attending as the lines become smaller.

Source: Leat, Yadev, and Irving (2009).

different frequencies of stripes because infants who are unable to detect the stripes lose interest in the stimulus and look away from it.

Another method of studying infant perception relies on infants' capacity for habituation, which is a gradual decline in the intensity, frequency, or duration of a response to an unchanging stimulus. For example, to examine whether an infant can discriminate between two stimuli, a researcher presents one until the infant habituates to it. Then a second stimulus is presented. If dishabituation, or the recovery of attention, occurs, it indicates that the infant detects that the second stimulus is different from the first. If the infant does not react to the new stimulus by showing dishabituation, it is assumed that the infant does not perceive the difference between the two stimuli. The habituation method is very useful in studying infant perception and cognition, and underlies many of the findings discussed in this chapter.

Operant conditioning is the basis for a third method researchers use to study perception in infants. Recall from Chapter 1 that operant conditioning entails learning behaviors based on their consequences—whether they are followed by reinforcement or punishment. Behaviors increase when they are followed by reinforcement and decrease when they are followed by punishment. Research employing this method has shown that newborns will change their rate of sucking on a pacifier, increasing or decreasing the rate of sucking, in order to hear a tape recording of their mother's voice, a reinforcer (Moon, Cooper, & Fifer, 1993). Other research shows that newborns will change their rate of sucking to see visual designs or hear human voices that they find pleasing (Floccia, Christophe, & Bertoncini, 1997). Researchers have found that premature infants and even third-trimester fetuses can be operantly conditioned (Dziewolska & Cautilli, 2006; Thoman & Ingersoll, 1993). For example, a 35-week-old fetus will change its rate of kicking in response to hearing the father talk against the mother's abdomen, suggesting that hearing begins in the womb (Dziewolska & Cautilli, 2006).

What Do You Think?

Provide examples of how parents and caregivers can apply habituation and operant conditioning to promote infants' development.

study the eyes and mouth, which hold more information than the hairline (Hunnius & Geuze, 2004). Similarly, the ability to follow an object's movement with the eyes, known as visual tracking, is very limited at birth but improves quickly. By 2 months of age, infants can follow a slow-moving object smoothly, and by 3 to 5 months, their eyes can dart ahead to keep pace with a fast-moving object (Agyei, van der Weel, & van der Meer, 2016; Richards & Holley, 1999; Teller, 1997). The parts of the brain that process motion in adults are operative in infants by 7 months of age (Weaver, Crespi, Tosetti, & Morrone, 2015).

Like other aspects of vision, color vision improves with age. Newborns see color, but they have trouble distinguishing between colors. That is, although they can see both red and green, they do not perceive red as different from green. Early visual experience with color is necessary for normal color perception to develop (Colombo et al., 2015; Sugita, 2004). Habituation studies show that by 1 month of age, infants can distinguish among red, green, and white (Teller, 1997). By 2 to 3 months of age, infants are as accurate as adults in discriminating the basic colors of red, yellow, and blue (Matlin & Foley, 1997; Teller, 1998). By 3 to 4 months of age, infants can distinguish many more colors as well as distinctions among closely related colors (Bornstein & Lamb, 1992; Haith, 1993). Seven-month-old infants detect color categories similar to those of adults; they can group slightly different shades (e.g., various shades of blue) into the same basic color categories as adults do (Clifford, Franklin, Davies, & Holmes, 2009).

Depth perception is the ability to perceive the distance of objects from each other and from ourselves. Depth perception is what permits infants to successfully reach for objects and, later, to crawl without bumping into furniture. By observing that newborns prefer to look at three-dimensional objects rather than two-dimensional figures, researchers have found that infants can perceive depth at birth (Slater, Rose, & Morison, 1984). Three- to 4-week-old infants blink their eyes when an object is moved toward their face, as if to hit them, suggesting that they are sensitive to depth cues (Kayed, Farstad, & van der Meer, 2008; Náñez & Yonas, 1994). Infants learn about depth by observing and experiencing motion.

FIGURE 4.9: Visual Cliff

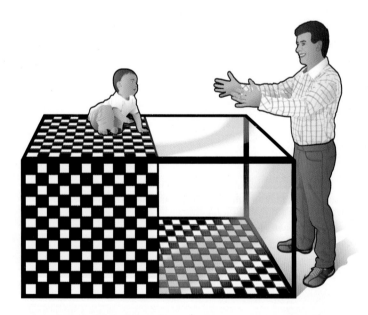

Three month old infants show a change in heart rate when placed face down on the glass surface of the deep side of the visual cliff, suggesting that they perceive depth, but do not fear it. Crawling babies, however, show a different response. In a classic study of visual perception, crawling babies moved to the shallow side of the visual cliff, even if called by their mothers. The more crawling experience infants had, the more likely they were to refuse to cross the deep side of the visual cliff.

Source: Levine and Munsch (2010).

A classic series of studies using an apparatus called the *visual cliff* demonstrated that crawling influences how infants perceive depth. The visual cliff, as shown in Figure 4.9, is a Plexiglas-covered table bisected by a plank so that one side is shallow, with a checkerboard pattern right under the glass, and the other side is deep, with the checkerboard pattern a few feet below the glass (Gibson & Walk, 1960). In this classic study, crawling babies readily moved from the plank to the shallow side, but not to the deep side, even if coaxed by their mothers, suggesting that they perceive the difference in depth (Walk, 1968). The more crawling experience infants have, the more likely they are to refuse to cross the deep side of the visual cliff (Bertenthal, Campos, & Barrett, 1984).

Does this mean that babies cannot distinguish the shallow and deep sides of the visual cliff until they crawl? No, because even 3-month-old infants who are too young to crawl distinguish shallow from deep drops. When placed face down on the glass surface of the deep side of the visual cliff, 3-month-old infants became quieter and showed a decrease in heart rate as compared with when they were placed on the shallow side of the cliff (Campos, Langer, & Krowitz, 1970; Dahl et al., 2013). The young infants can distinguish the difference between shallow and deep drops but do not yet associate fear with deep drops.

As infants gain experience crawling, their perception of depth, the meaning they associate with it, changes. Newly walking infants avoid the cliff's deep side even more consistently than do crawling infants (Dahl et al., 2013; Witherington, Campos, Anderson, Lejeune, & Seah, 2005). A new perspective on the visual cliff studies argues that infants avoid the deep side of the cliff not out of fear but simply because they perceive that they are unable to successfully navigate the drop; fear might be conditioned through later experiences, but infants are not naturally fearful of heights (Adolph, Kretch, & LoBue, 2014).

Hearing

The capacity to hear develops in the womb; in fact, hearing is the most well-developed sense at birth. Newborns are able to hear about as well as adults (Northern, 2014). Shortly after birth, neonates can discriminate among sounds, such as tones (Hernandez-Pavon, Sosa, Lutter, Maier, & Wakai, 2008). By 3 days of age, infants will turn their head and eyes in the general direction of a sound, and this ability to localize sound improves over the first 6 months (Clifton, Rochat, Robin, & Berthier, 1994; Litovsky & Ashmead, 1997).

The process of learning language begins at birth, through listening. Newborns are attentive to voices and can detect their mothers' voices. Newborns only 1 day old prefer to hear speech sounds over acoustically comparable nonspeech sounds. Newborns can perceive and discriminate nearly all sounds in human languages, but from birth, they prefer to hear their native language (Moon et al., 1993). Brain activity in the temporal and left frontal cortex in response to auditory stimuli indicates that newborns can discriminate speech patterns, such as differences in cadence among languages (Gervain, Macagno, Cogoi, Peña, & Mehler, 2008; Gervain & Mehler, 2010). In one study, 4-month-old Japanese infants showed increased brain activity in the left hemisphere of the brain, responsible for language in adults, in response to hearing their native language as compared with nonnative speech, emotional voices (human vocalizations with no linguistic content), monkey calls, and scrambled versions of each vocalization (Minagawa-Kawai et al., 2011). Infants show not only the ability to hear sounds, but clear preferences for their native language, suggesting an early developing neurological specialization for language.

Touch

As compared with vision and hearing, we know much less about the sense of touch in infants. In early infancy, touch, especially with the mouth, is a critical means of learning about the world (Piaget, 1936/1952). The mouth is the first part of the body to show sensitivity to touch prenatally and remains one of the most sensitive areas to touch after birth.

• • Neonatal Circumcision

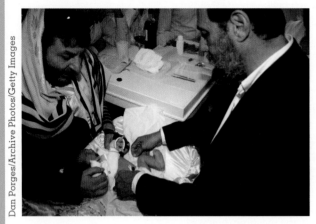

An eight-day-old Jewish boy is circumcised as part of a religious ceremony called a bris.

Neonatal circumcision, removal of the foreskin of the penis, is the oldest known planned surgery (Alanis & Lucidi, 2004). Although it is uncommon throughout much of the world, the United States leads Western nations in rates of infant circumcision (Elder, 2007). As shown in Figure 4.10, circumcision rates declined from 65% of male newborns in 1979 to 57% in 2010, but there are regional differences, with nearly twice as many infant circumcisions in the Midwest as in the West (Owings, Uddin, & Williams, 2013). In recent years circumcision has come under increasing scrutiny within the United States as some charge that it places the newborn under great distress and confers few medical benefits.

For decades many scientists and physicians believed that newborns did not feel pain, leading many to perform

FIGURE 4.10: **Rates of Circumcision Performed, 1979–2010**

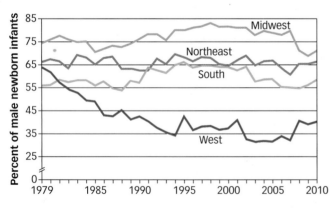

Notes: Rates represent circumcisions performed during the birth hospitalization. Circumcision is identified by International Classification of Diseases, Ninth Revision, Clinical Modification (ICD-9-CM) procedure code 64.0.

Source: Owings et al. (2013).

circumcision without pain management techniques such as anesthesia or analgesia (Alanis & Lucidi, 2004). We now know that even the fetus feels pain (Benatar & Benatar, 2003). Newborns show many indicators of distress during circumcision, such as a high-pitched wail, flailing, grimacing, and dramatic rises in heart rate, blood pressure, palm sweating, pupil dilation, muscle tension, and cortisol levels (Paix & Peterson, 2012; Razmus, Dalton, & Wilson, 2004). According to the American Academy of Pediatrics (1999), analgesia (pain relief in which the newborn remains conscious) is safe and effective in reducing the pain associated with circumcision. The American Society for Pain Management Nursing has issued a position statement that when circumcision is chosen, it must be accompanied by pain management before, during, and after the procedure (O'Conner-Von & Turner, 2013).

The medical benefits of circumcision are debated (Freedman, 2016; Frisch & Earp, 2016). Benefits include reduced risk of urinary tract infections, developing penile cancer, and acquiring HIV (American Academy of Pediatrics Task Force on Circumcision Policy, 1999; American Medical Association, 1999; Morris et al., 2017). Yet urinary tract infections and penile cancer are relatively rare even among men who are uncircumcised. Evidence regarding HIV transmission comes from research with adult males in Africa; whether the same effects apply to infants in Western industrialized countries is uncertain (Alanis & Lucidi, 2004; Benatar & Benatar, 2003). Moreover, behavior is a more important factor in preventing HIV infection than is circumcision.

In 1999, both the American Medical Association and American Academy of Pediatrics joined medical associations in Canada, Europe, and Australia in concluding that the benefits of circumcision are not large enough to recommend routine circumcision; instead it is a parental decision. However, in 2012 the American Academy of Pediatrics modified its view to note that although it is a parental decision, the benefits of circumcision justify providing access to the procedure (by insurance companies) to families who choose it. A critical commentary by physicians and representatives of medical associations and societies in countries in Europe, Canada, and Australia countered that the revised recommendation was not based on medical evidence but instead reflected cultural bias on the part of the AAP to support social practices common in the United States (Frisch et al., 2013).

Regardless, formal recommendations by medical associations may ultimately have little sway on parents (Freedman, 2016). Education about the risks and benefits of circumcision, especially the controversy over the medical necessity of circumcision, generally does not influence parental decisions regarding circumcision (Binner, Mastrobattista, Day, Swaim, & Monga,

2003). Instead it is tradition and culture, especially social factors such as religion, which influence parental decisions about circumcision. For example, in Jewish cultures, a boy is circumcised on the eighth day after birth in a ritual celebration known as a bris, in which the boy is welcomed as a member of the community. Parents' decisions are also influenced by social factors such as whether the father is circumcised and the desire that the child resemble his peers (Bo & Goldman, 2008; Waldeck, 2003). The decision is complicated, as parents weigh health risks and benefits with contextual factors such as religious and cultural beliefs as well as personal desires, in order to determine what is best for their child.

What Do You Think?

1. In your view, what are the most important considerations in making a decision about whether to circumcise a newborn boy?

2. Imagine that you had a newborn boy. Would you choose to circumcise your son? Why or why not?

A stroke to the newborn's cheek elicits the rooting reflex (see Table 4.1 above), which acts as a powerful survival mechanism by enabling the infant to reflexively attach to the mother's breast.

Touch, specifically a caregiver's massage, can reduce stress responses in preterm and full-term neonates and is associated with weight gain in newborns (Diego et al., 2007; Hernandez-Reif, Diego, & Field, 2007). Skin-to-skin contact with a caregiver, as in kangaroo care (see Chapter 2), has an analgesic effect, reducing infants' pain response to being stuck with a needle for blood testing (de Sousa Freire, Santos Garcia, & Carvalho Lamy, 2008; Ferber & Makhoul, 2008). Although it was once believed that newborns were too immature to feel pain, we now know that the capacity to feel pain develops even before birth; by at least the 30th week of gestation a fetus responds to a pain stimulus (Benatar & Benatar, 2003). The neonate's capacity to feel pain has influenced debates about infant circumcision, as discussed in the Lives in Context feature.

Smell and Taste

Smell and taste are well developed at birth. Classic experiments demonstrate that newborns can discriminate between smells (Goubet et al., 2002). Just hours after birth, newborns display facial expressions signifying disgust in response to odors of ammonia, fish, and other scents that adults find offensive (Steiner, 1979). Within the first days of life, newborns detect and recognize their mother's odor (Macfarlane, 1975; Porter, Varendi, Christensson, Porter, & Winberg, 1998; Schaal et al., 1980). Infants are calmed by their mother's scent. Newborns who smelled their mother's odor displayed less agitation during a heel-stick test and cried less afterward than infants presented with unfamiliar odors (Rattaz, Goubet, & Bullinger, 2005). Familiar scents are reinforcing and can reduce stress responses in infants (Goubet, Strasbaugh, & Chesney, 2007; Nishitani et al., 2009; Schaal, 2017).

Infants show innate preferences for some tastes (Beauchamp & Mennella, 2011; Ross, 2017). For example, both bottle- and breast-fed newborns prefer human milk—even milk from strangers—to formula (Marlier & Schaal, 2005). Newborns prefer sugar to other substances, and a small dose of sugar can serve as an anesthetic, distracting newborns from pain (Gradin, Eriksson, Schollin, Holmqvist, & Holstein, 2002). Experience can modify taste preferences, beginning before birth: Fetuses are exposed to flavors in amniotic fluid that influence their preferences after birth (Beauchamp & Mennella, 2011; Forestell, 2016). In one study, the type of formula fed to infants influenced their taste preferences at 4 to 5 years of age (Mennella & Beauchamp, 2002). Infants who were fed milk-based formulas and protein-based formulas were more likely to prefer sour flavors at 4 to 5 years of age as compared with infants who were fed soy-based formulas, who, in turn, were more likely to prefer bitter flavors. In addition, mothers reported that the infants fed protein- or soy-based formulas were more likely to prefer broccoli than those fed milk-based formulas. Touch, taste, and smell further illustrate infants' amazing capacities to sense and respond to the world around them.

Intermodal Perception

Though we have discussed the senses separately in this chapter, in everyday life when people attend to the environment they combine information from our various sensory systems to understand the world. This process is called **intermodal perception**. Not only are infants able to sense in multiple modalities; they are able to coordinate their senses. Most of the stimuli we experience are intermodal because they provide more than one type of sensory information (Slater, Quinn, Brown, & Hayes, 1999). Research on intermodal perception supports the finding that infants expect vision, auditory, and tactile information to occur together (Hyde, Flom, & Porter, 2016; Sai, 2005). For example, newborns coordinate visual and auditory senses, turning their heads and eyes in the direction of a sound source, suggesting that they intuitively recognize that knowledge about spatial location is provided by both visual and auditory information (Clifton, Morrongiello, Kulig, & Dowd, 1981; Muir & Clifton, 1985; Newell, 2004; Wertheimer, 1961). By 6 months of age, infants who explore an object with their hands alone can recognize it by sight alone and vice versa, a finding that supports the integration of vision and touch (Pineau & Streri, 1990; Rose, Gottfried, & Bridger, 1981; Ruff & Kohler, 1978). Intermodal matching of visual and auditory stimuli shows similar patterns as visual and tactile. By 4 months of age, infants coordinate visual stimuli with expectations about auditory stimuli (Spelke, 1976).

Sensitivity to intermodal relations among stimuli is critical to perceptual development and learning—and this sensitivity emerges early in life (Bahrick, 2002; Gibson & Pick, 2000; Lewkowicz, 2000; Lewkowicz & Lickliter, 1994; Newell, 2004). But just how early? Newborns show a preference for viewing their mother's face at 78, 72, 12, and even just 4 hours after birth (Bushnell, Sai, & Mullin, 1989; Field, Cohen, Garcia, & Greenberg, 1984; Pascalis, Dechonen, Morton, Duruelle, & Grenet, 1995). Because 4-hour-old neonates prefer their mother's face, it was once believed that infants' preference for their mother's face was innate. However, infants are not born knowing their mother's face. Instead, they quickly learn to identify their mother. How? In one study, neonates were able to visually recognize their mother's face only if the face was paired with their mother's voice at least once after birth (Sai, 2005). Thus, intermodal perception is evident at birth because neonates can coordinate auditory and visual stimuli in order to associate their mother's face with her voice. They quickly remember the association and demonstrate a preference for her face even when it is not paired with her voice.

Newborns are equipped with remarkable capacities for sensing and perceiving stimuli. Their senses, although well developed at birth, improve rapidly over the first year of life. Moreover, capacities for intermodal perception mean that infants can combine information from various sensory modalities to construct a sophisticated and accurate picture of the world around them.

SENSORY CHANGES IN ADULTHOOD

Suddenly aware that he holds the newspaper at arm's length and still squints to read, 45-year-old Dominic wonders to himself, "When did this happen? I can't see like I used to." Like much of physical development, the changes that take place in our senses represent continuous change. Over the adult years, vision and hearing capacities gradually decline. Like Dominic, most adults notice changes in vision during their 40s and changes in hearing at around age 50. The use of corrective lenses aids vision problems, and hearing aids amplify sounds, permitting better hearing.

intermodal perception The process of combining information from more than one sensory system such as visual and auditory senses.

Vision Changes in Adulthood

Dominic's need to hold the newspaper at a distance in order to read is not unusual and is related to changes in the eye that occur throughout the adult years. The cornea flattens; the lens loses flexibility; and the muscle that permits the lens to change shape, or accommodate, weakens. The result is that most adults in their 40s develop **presbyopia**, also known as farsightedness—the inability to focus the lens on close objects, such as in reading small print (Hermans, Dubbelman, van der Heijde, & Heethaar, 2008; Strenk, Strenk, & Koretz, 2005). Presbyopia is largely caused by the stiffening of the lens in the eye, related to the loss of collagen that contributes to stiffening of tissues throughout the body (Laughton, Sheppard, & Davies, 2016). By age 50, virtually all adults are presbyopic and require reading glasses or other corrective options (Gil-Cazorla, Shah, & Naroo, 2015; Truscott, 2009). Most also require corrective lenses for distance. Bifocals that combine lenses for nearsightedness and farsightedness are helpful.

Joan experiences presbyopia, as signified by her need to hold her magazine at a distance to read.

In addition to changes in the accommodative ability of the lens, the ability to see in dim light declines because, with age, the lens yellows, and the size of the pupil shrinks. In addition, by middle age most adults have lost about one half of the rods (light receptor cells) in the retina, which reduces their ability to see in dim light and makes adults' night vision decline twice as fast as their day vision (Jackson & Owsley, 2003; Lin, Tsubota, & Apte, 2016; Owsley, 2016). As rods are lost, so too are cones (color receptive cells) because rods secrete substances that permit cones to survive (Bonnel, Mohand-Said, & Sahel, 2003). Color discrimination, thus, becomes limited with gradual declines beginning in the 30s (Kraft & Werner, 1999; Paramei & Oakley, 2014). Night vision is further reduced because the vitreous (transparent gel that fills the eyeball) becomes more opaque with age, scattering light that enters the eye (creating glare) and permitting less light to reach the retina (Owsley, 2011). In middle adulthood, about one third more light is needed to compensate for these changes that reduce vision (Owsley, McGwin, Jackson, Kallies, & Clark, 2007). All of these changes in vision make driving at night more challenging as headlights from other cars become blinding (Gruber, Mosimann, Müri, & Nef, 2013; Owsley, 2016).

Many adults develop **cataracts**, a clouding of the lens resulting in blurred, foggy vision that makes driving hazardous and, if untreated, can lead to blindness (Kline & Li., 2005). Cataracts are the result of a combination of hereditary and environmental factors associated with oxidative damage, including illnesses such as **diabetes** and behaviors such as smoking (David, Nancy, & Ying-Bo, 2010; Lin et al., 2016; Tan et al., 2008). By age 80, more than half of adults have cataracts (American Academy of Ophthalmology, 2011). Cataracts are commonly corrected through a surgical procedure in which the lens is replaced with an artificial lens.

In addition to the lens, other parts of the eye show structural changes (see Figure 4.11). Cells in the retina and optical nerve are lost with aging (Owsley, 2011). Some older adults experience **macular degeneration**, a substantial loss of cells in the center area of the retina, the macula, causing blurring and eventual loss of central vision (Chakravarthy, Evans, & Rosenfeld, 2010; Owsley, 2016). Hereditary and environmental factors, such as smoking and atherosclerosis, influence the onset of macular degeneration (Myers et al., 2014). A healthy diet, including green leafy vegetables high in vitamins A, C, and E; as well as vegetables rich in carotenoids, such as carrots; may protect the retina and offset damage caused by free radicals (Rhone & Basu, 2008; Sin, Liu, & Lam, 2013). Laser surgery, medication, and corrective eyewear can sometimes restore some vision and treat the early stages of macular degeneration. However, macular degeneration is the leading cause of blindness (Chakravarthy et al., 2010; Jager, Mieler, & Miller, 2008).

presbyopia An age-related condition in which the lens becomes less able to adjust its focus on objects at a close range.

cataract A clouding of the lens of the eye, resulting in blurred, foggy vision; can lead to blindness.

diabetes A disease marked by high levels of blood glucose that occurs when the body is unable to regulate the amount of glucose in the bloodstream because there is not enough insulin produced (type 1 diabetes) or the body shows insulin resistance and becomes less sensitive to it, failing to respond to it (type 2 diabetes). Symptoms include fatigue, great thirst, blurred vision, frequent infections, and slow healing.

macular degeneration A substantial loss of cells in the center area of the retina (the macula), causing blurring and eventual loss of central vision; its onset is influenced by heredity and environmental factors.

FIGURE 4.11: Age-Related Changes in the Eye

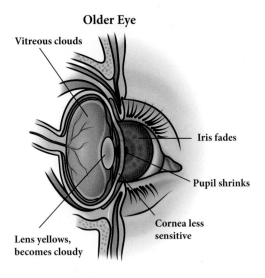

Older Eye

Vitreous clouds

Iris fades

Pupil shrinks

Cornea less sensitive

Lens yellows, becomes cloudy

Most of these changes in vision are so gradual that they may go unnoticed in people who do not receive regular opththalmalogical examinations (Owsley, 2011). Substantial vision loss, however, can have a serious effect on adults' daily lives as it interferes not only with driving but also with reading, watching television, and doing a variety of daily activities from cooking to banking. Not surprisingly, older adults with vision loss participate less than their peers in recreational and sports activities (Alma et al., 2011) and are likely to be depressed (Tabrett & Latham, 2010), especially when vision loss interferes with their day-to-day functioning and independence (van Nispen, Vreeken, Comijs, Deeg, & van Rens, 2016). In a sample of adults from 10 European countries, vision loss was associated with concentration difficulty; losing interest and enjoyment in activities; feeling fatigued, irritable, and tearful; having less hope for the future; and even wishing for death (Mojon-Azzi, Sousa-Poza, & Mojon, 2008).

As with all of our senses, our ability to see depends on not just our sensory organs (in this case, our eyes) but also our brain. We might assume that everyone processes visual stimuli the same way, but the emerging field of cultural neuroscience shows how different the visual experience can be from one person or cultural group to another (see the Cultural Influences on Development feature).

Hearing

In addition to vision changes, 45-year-old Dominic also noticed that he has difficulty hearing, at least in some situations. When he plays with his 4-year-old nephew, Dominic finds that he has to lean in close to hear the boy's speech. Sometimes he finds himself watching his teenage daughter's lips while she speaks, especially when they are having dinner in a crowded restaurant. Age-related hearing loss, **presbycusis** ("old hearing"), becomes apparent in the 50s and is caused by natural cell death that results in the deterioration of the ear structures that convert sound into neural impulses (Quaranta et al., 2015). The loss is first limited to high-pitched sounds, which enable us to distinguish between consonants such as *f* versus *s* and *p* versus *t*; as a result, the person often can hear most of a message but may misinterpret parts of it, such as names. Middle-aged adults tend to experience more difficulty hearing in settings with background noise, such as at a dinner party or restaurant, and perform more poorly under that condition than do young adults (Leigh-Paffenroth & Elangovan, 2011). Presbycusis increases in older adulthood, with cell losses in the inner ear and cortex (Gates & Mills, 2005). Older adults experience difficulty distinguishing high-frequency sounds, soft sounds of all frequencies, and complex tone patterns (Gordon-Salant, 2005) and show less activation of the auditory cortex in response to speech as compared with younger adults (Hwang, Li, Wu, Chen, & Liu, 2007).

About two-thirds of older adults experience hearing loss (Lin, Thorpe, Gordon-Salant, & Ferrucci, 2011), which can greatly diminish quality of life and poses health risks. The inability to hear car horns and other street sounds or to hear the telephone or doorbell is a risk not only to safety but also to self-esteem. Turning up the volume to hear a television or radio program and then being asked by others to turn it down can be frustrating to older adults and their loved ones. Difficulty hearing others' speech can socially isolate older adults, reducing their social network, increasing feelings of loneliness and depression, and reducing life satisfaction (Gordon-Salant, 2005).

Much hearing loss is preventable, the result of exposure to noise in the workplace, at concerts, and through the use of headphones (Tremblay & Ross, 2007). Generally, men's hearing declines occur earlier and more rapidly than women's, perhaps up to twice as quickly (Cruickshanks et al., 2010; Helzner et al., 2005). Men's rapid hearing decline can be traced to exposure to intense noise (e.g., headphones and concerts);

presbycusis Age-related hearing loss, first to the high frequency sounds, gradually spreading.

CULTURAL INFLUENCES ON DEVELOPMENT

● ● Cultural Neuroscience

Do people of Eastern and Western cultures process this image differently?

A critical theme in lifespan developmental science is the central relevance of cultural context in influencing development. Our interactions with our culture influence not simply social development, such as our ways of interacting with others, but our neurological development as well, including patterns of brain activity (Chiao & Immordino-Yang, 2013; Kitayama & Uskul, 2011). Cultural neuroscience is an emerging field that studies how cultural values, practices, and beliefs influence and are influenced by neurological processes and translate to behavior (Han et al., 2013; Sasaki & Kim, 2017).

For example, collectivism, the East Asian cultural valuing of the community over the individual, and individualism, the Western cultural value emphasizing individualism and independence, influence how cultural group members view their worlds, including visual perception itself. People from East Asian and Western cultures show reliable differences in aspects of visual perception and processing. East Asians tend to process visual information in a more holistic manner, attending to and recalling the salient object and surroundings, whereas Westerners tend to process visual information in an

analytic manner, paying attention and recalling the salient object independent of the scene in which it is embedded, a context-independent mode of perception (Nisbett & Miyamoto, 2005; Nisbett, Peng, Choi, & Norenzayan, 2001). These differences in object-context attention and recall are supported by different patterns of brain activation across cultural groups. In one study, U.S. and Chinese participants viewed pictures consisting of a focal object (e.g., a deer, a television) superimposed upon a background scene that was congruent (e.g., a deer in the woods) or incongruent (e.g., a television in the desert) with the target object (Jenkins, Yang, Goh, Hong, & Park, 2010). The Chinese but not the U.S. participants showed greater neural activity in both the right and left lateral visual cortex in response to incongruent scenes as compared with congruent scenes, suggesting greater cortical sensitivity and adaptation to incongruence, likely reflecting more holistic processing among Chinese participants.

Other research examining face processing supports a similar cultural difference in holistic processing. When viewing faces, Westerners show greater activity in the left visual cortex, as compared with Easterners, which is involved in analytic processing of facial features, such as the eyes and lips, perhaps reflecting the cultural value of individualism that tends to emphasize differences between individual identities (Jenkins et al., 2010). East Asians show greater activity in the right visual cortex, as compared with the left, which is implicated in holistic processing of faces where the facial components and their spatial configuration are processed as a whole.

Although visual processing itself is universal, socially transmitted cultural traits, such as an emphasis on analytic versus holistic processing, influence how visual stimuli are perceived, recognized, and interpreted (Chiao & Immordino-Yang, 2013; Han et al., 2013). Culture thereby influences how we view the world, not just metaphorically but also neurologically (Sasaki & Kim, 2017).

loud work environments (e.g., construction, military, and transportation work); and, in later adulthood, illnesses such as cerebrovascular disease (a disease of the blood vessels that supply the brain, often caused by atherosclerosis), which can lead to a stroke that damages the auditory cortex (Ecob et al., 2008; Helzner et al., 2005). Hearing declines are evident in some men as early as 30 years of age and these may also entail a genetic component (Gordon-Salant, 2005; Wingfield, Tun, & McCoy, 2005). Hearing loss can be prevented by wearing protective equipment, such as earplugs, and by lowering the volume on music players and other audio equipment. It is recommended that adults have periodic screening to identify risk for hearing loss and early signs of hearing loss, as early diagnosis can help in preventing or delaying further loss (Chou, Dana, Bougatsos, Fleming, & Beil, 2011).

Many older adults compensate for their hearing loss by reducing background noise, when possible, and paying attention to nonverbal cues such as lip movements, facial expressions, and body language to optimize their ability to hear and participate in conversations. Hearing aids are widely available, but research suggests they are underused for several reasons: social attitudes that undervalue the importance of hearing; stigma associated with being seen wearing hearing aids; and their cost, which is typically not covered by health insurance (Laplante-Lévesque, Hickson, & Worrall, 2010). Quality of life for older adults can be improved with successful hearing loss management, which may include education about communication effectiveness, hearing aids, assistive listening devices, and cochlear implants for severe hearing loss. When hearing aids no longer provide benefit, cochlear implantation is the treatment of choice with excellent results even in octogenarians (Quaranta et al., 2015).

Smell and Taste

Sensitivity to smell declines throughout adulthood beginning as early as the twenties (Margran & Boulton, 2005), but is usually not noticeable until late in midlife (Finkelstein & Schiffman, 1999; Hawkes, 2006). By the sixties olfaction tends to decline markedly (Wang, Sun, & Yang, 2016). About one third of adults experience disruptions in their ability to smell (Shu et al., 2009) and more than two thirds of adults experience significant olfactory dysfunction by age 80 (Attems, Walker, & Jellinger, 2015). In a classic study, young, middle, and older adults were asked to identify 40 different smells, such as peanut butter and gas (Doty et al., 1984). Young and middle adults performed at similar levels but performance declined rapidly at age 60, more rapidly for men than women (Morgan, Covington, Geisler, Polich, & Murphy, 1997). However, individuals vary. Some show marked declines and others more gradual change. The odor itself might matter in determining adults' performance on olfactory tasks. Research suggests that older adults are as able as younger adults to identify and remember unpleasant odors, but they show decline in their abilities to identify and remember pleasant odors (Larsson, Oberg-Blåvarg, & Jönsson, 2009).

Recent research with over 1,100 Swedish adults age 40 to 90 has suggested that poor olfactory performance predicts mortality over a 10-year period (Ekström et al., 2017). Similar findings occurred with a U.S. sample of 2,400 adults age 53–97 followed for 17 years (Schubert et al., 2016), suggesting that olfactory loss might indicate deteriorating health.

Smell and taste are linked such that declines in olfactory abilities hold implications for their abilities to taste. Older adults are generally less sensitive to taste as compared with young and middle-aged adults (Schubert et al., 2012). They also produce less saliva with age, resulting in a dry mouth that interferes with taste (Abrams, 2014).There are also large individual differences, similar to other aspects of development. Some individuals show marked declines while others retain ability. Most older adults report that food seems more bland, and they tend to prefer more intense flavors, especially sweetness (de Graaf, Polet, & van Staveren, 1994). They may lose interest in eating or, alternatively, may overuse salt and spicy seasonings with poor health consequences. A poor sense of taste can even be a health hazard by making it more difficult for an older adult to detect spoiled food.

Developmental changes in both smell and taste are influenced by many factors, such as general health, chronic disease, medications, and smoking (Imoscopi, Inelmen, Sergi, Miotto, & Manzato, 2012; Roberts & Rosenberg, 2006; Schiffman, 2009). Most men show greater deficits with age than do women. This is likely the result of different work environments, since men are more likely to work in factories and other environments that expose them to chemicals that can damage sensory abilities (Corwin, Loury, & Gilbert, 1995; Schiffman, 2009; Ship & Weiffenbach, 1993). Changes in smell and taste, like other physical capacities, are influenced by our lifelong interactions within our contexts.

Thinking in Context 4.3

1. How might parents and caregivers design caregiving environments that stimulate infants' early sensory capacities and development? What advice would you give on how to design such an environment for a newborn? For a 6-month-old infant? For a 3-year-old child?

2. How might the age-related changes that adults experience in vision and hearing influence their day-to-day functioning and interactions with others? Consider adults' roles in the workplace and at home, as employees, parents, spouses, and friends. What are the practical implications of these developmental changes?

3. Contextual factors, such as socioeconomic status, influence all aspects of physical aging, including the rate and form that aging takes. How might contextual factors influence the sensory changes that occur over the adult years?

 Apply Your Knowledge

"Some of the fine details seem so muddy!" 65-year-old artist Lupita thought to herself as she turned on the light and stood back from her artwork. "Once I loved to work in a studio with nothing more than sunlight to brighten the room, but no longer." As a student Lupita used to paint live theater performances, sketching and coloring images of ballerinas as she sat in the dark theater. Now she watches theater intently, etching images into her mind to paint later.

As an art student, Lupita created many detailed pieces of art with little effort. After retiring from a career in nursing, Lupita rediscovered her love of painting. Recently she decided to repaint one of her favorite pieces of art to create "then vs. now" comparison artwork. Lupita was surprised to find herself struggling to recreate her work. Controlling the paintbrush seemed much more difficult than it did in college. As Lupita finished a simpler version of the painting, her son, Jesse, arrived and commented that a green does not match. "It's much more yellow," he said. Lupita protested, "It looks identical; I don't see it." "Mom, it's not the same

color at all," replied Jesse, "and anyway, I'm here to ask your advice about Nico." "What about my favorite 11th grader?" asked Lupita. "Your grandson is grounded for driving recklessly. Nico was caught racing cars around the high school parking lot. No one was hurt, fortunately, but Nico doesn't understand why I'm upset. Sometimes it's like I'm speaking a different language." Lupita smiles, "You were the same way, son."

1. Discuss normative changes in vision over the adult years. What might Lupita expect regarding her artistic talents and how can she compensate for these changes?

2. What other sensory changes might Lupita expect over time?

3. How might neurological development account for adolescent behavior, such as Nico's?

4. What neurological changes can Nico expect as he becomes an adult? As he progresses through adulthood?

 **⑤SAGE** edge™

Give your students the SAGE edge!

SAGE edge offers a robust online environment featuring an impressive array of free tools and resources for review, study, and further exploration, keeping both instructors and students on the cutting edge of teaching and learning. Learn more at **edge.sagepub.com/kuthertopical.**

CHAPTER 4 IN REVIEW

4.1 Discuss the process of neural development over the lifespan, including the role of experience.

SUMMARY

The brain develops through several processes: neurogenesis, synaptogenesis, pruning, and myelination, and both expects and depends on environmental input at different points in time. Increases in the volume of the cortex, interconnections among neurons, and myelination influence the speed, efficiency of thought, and capacity for executive function. Different parts of the brain develop at different times, as illustrated by the dual process model, which can account for many typical adolescent behaviors. The brain is most malleable during the first few years of life but retains some plasticity through adulthood. The loss of neurons and brain volume over the course of adulthood leads to slower communication among neurons. Adults' brains naturally compensate for losses through cognitive reserve and more diffuse activation.

KEY TERMS

neurons	lateralization
neurogenesis	hemispheric dominance
glial cells	corpus callosum
experience–expectant brain development	plasticity
	dual process model
experience–dependent brain development	limbic system
	amygdala
synaptic pruning	cognitive reserve
myelination	

REVIEW QUESTIONS

1. What are 4 processes of neural development?
2. How can brain development explain adolescent behavior?
3. How does the brain change over adulthood?
4. How do adults compensate for neurological change?

4.2 Summarize patterns of gross and fine motor development and influences on motor development.

SUMMARY

Infants are born with reflexes, each with their developmental course. Infant and children progress through an orderly series of motor milestones. Motor development illustrates the complex interactions that take place between developmental domains, maturation, and contextual supports. Motor skills change in predictable ways over the lifespan, with changes in muscle strength, bone density, and flexibility. Physical activity can compensate for age-related declines in muscle and strength.

KEY TERMS

reflexes	fine motor development
gross motor development	dynamic systems

REVIEW QUESTIONS

1. What are some milestones in gross and fine motor development?
2. Identify biological and contextual influences on motor development?
3. What motor changes can adults expect and how can they influence motor change?

4.3 Describe age-related changes in vision, hearing, and other senses.

SUMMARY

Neonates are born with all senses. Vision is most poor but improves rapidly over the first year of life. Newborns show adult-like hearing and perceive and discriminate nearly all sounds in human languages. Smell and taste are also well developed at birth. Intermodal perception, the ability to coordinate sensory stimuli, is evident at birth and develops quickly. Vision declines over adulthood with most midlife adults experiencing presbyopia and changes in night vision. Presbycusis becomes more common over midlife into older adulthood and most adults experience reductions in sensitivity to taste and smell.

KEY TERMS

affordances	diabetes
intermodal perception	macular degeneration
presbyopia	presbycusis
cataracts	

REVIEW QUESTIONS

1. What senses are we born with?
2. How do vision and hearing develop in infancy?
3. What sensory changes can adults expect?
4. What are some ways adults compensate for sensory changes?

Test your understanding of the content.
Review the flashcards and quizzes at
edge.sagepub.com/kuthertopical

PRACTICE AND APPLY WHAT YOU'VE LEARNED

▶ **edge.sagepub.com/kuthertopical**

HEAD TO THE STUDY SITE WHERE YOU'LL FIND

- **eFlashcards to strengthen your understanding of key terms**

- **Practice quizzes to test your comprehension of key concepts**

- **Videos and multimedia content to enhance your exploration of key topics**

Health

Learning Objectives

5.1 Analyze health issues in childhood, including risks and protective factors for healthy development.

5.2 Discuss the prevalence, effects, and treatment of eating disorders and substance use in adolescents and emerging adults.

5.3 Identify common chronic diseases and sources of injury in adulthood, their risk factors, effects, and treatment.

5.4 Distinguish among common dementias, their risk factors, effects, and treatment.

Digital Resources

📄 Children with Autism: Injury-prone?

📑 Child Maltreatment

🔊 Eating Disorders in Boys

▶ College Binge Drinkers

▶ Obesity Becomes a Disease

▶ Managing a Chronic Illness

📄 Preventing Dementia

📑 Parkinson's Disease: Locus of Control

Master these learning objectives with multimedia resources available at **edge.sagepub.com/kuthertopical** and *Lives in Context* video cases available in the interactive eBook.

Alejandro has successfully traversed infancy, the most challenging time of life for mortality, and now at age 8 he has achieved the milestones of physical development for his age. Yet he is sometimes unable to run and play as hard as he would like because chronic asthma makes him wheeze and cough.

The doctor warns 14-year-old Zoe that, although her development is in the normal range, her weight is very low for her age and body size. Zoe looks into the mirror and instead sees an excess of "baby fat" she must lose.

Fifty-five-year-old Matthew is frustrated that knee pain from arthritis has forced him to cut back on his long runs.

These individuals are each experiencing health issues that may influence their development and functioning. Everyone experiences health issues throughout life, from the colds and flu that are common to all of us, to chronic conditions and diseases experienced by many people, to serious diseases that are experienced by relatively few people. Different health issues come into play at different ages. In this chapter, we examine common health issues throughout the lifespan, including risk and protective factors for common conditions.

COMMON HEALTH ISSUES IN INFANCY AND CHILDHOOD

LO 5.1 Analyze health issues in childhood, including risks and protective factors for healthy development.

The phrase *childhood diseases* often brings to mind infectious diseases like measles, mumps, whooping cough, and chicken pox. As we will see in this section, there is much more to health care for infants and children.

INFECTIOUS DISEASE AND IMMUNIZATION

Vaccines are a quick, easy, and vital way of preventing the spread of dangerous, often fatal, diseases.

Over the past 50 years, serious and sometimes fatal childhood diseases such as measles, mumps, and whooping cough have declined dramatically because of the development of vaccines. A **vaccine** is a small dose of inactive virus that is injected into the body to stimulate the production of antibodies to guard against the disease. Because immunization of infants and young children is now widespread, vaccines control infectious diseases that once spread quickly and killed thousands of people. Vaccines are administered early in life because many preventable diseases are more common in infants and young children. Vaccinations protect the child as well as those in the child's community because an immunized person is less susceptible to a disease, and therefore also less likely to transmit it to others. Most public schools require that children be fully immunized before enrollment, a requirement that has increased vaccination rates and prevented many diseases (Salmon et al., 2005).

The Centers for Disease Control and Prevention (CDC) recommends that children be vaccinated against most vaccine-preventable disease by the time they are 2 years of age. Vaccination rates increased markedly between the mid-1990s and the mid-2000s: The proportion of children ages 19 to 35 months receiving the recommended series of vaccines increased from 69% to 83% between 1994 and 2004. However, the rate has stalled since, standing at 82% in 2013 (Child Trends, 2015). Why are not all children vaccinated? Throughout the world, poverty is associated with inadequate vaccination (Bustreo, Okwo-Bele, & Kamara, 2015). Although there are no ethnic differences in childhood vaccination rates in the United States, children in families with incomes below the poverty level are less likely to receive the recommended schedule of vaccination than their peers who reside in homes with incomes at or above the poverty level (Hill, Elam-Evans, Yankey, Singleton, & Kolasa, 2015). Many parents are unaware that children from low-income families who do not have medical insurance can receive vaccinations through the federal Vaccines for Children Program, begun in 1994 (CDC, 1994).

Another, more troubling reason for the stalled vaccination rate is particularly common in children from high-SES homes (Yang, Delamater, Leslie, & Mello, 2016) and based on the common misconception that vaccines are linked with autism (Gust et al., 2004). Extensive research indicates that there is no association between vaccination and autism (Gerber & Offit, 2009; Taylor, Swerdfeger, & Eslick, 2014). One reason for the misconception is that children tend to receive vaccines at the age when some chronic illnesses and developmental disorders—such as autism—tend to emerge, but this correlation is not indicative of a cause-and-effect relationship. (Recall from Chapter 1 that correlational research documents phenomena that occur together, but cannot demonstrate causation.) While specific causes of autism spectrum disorders have yet to be fully identified, we do know that autism has a strong genetic component and is also associated with both maternal and paternal age (Grether, Anderson, Croen, Smith, & Windham, 2009; Idring et al., 2014; Waltes et al., 2014).

Lack of vaccination poses serious risks to the child and also to the community. For example, in January 2015, the California Department of Health was notified of a suspected measles case in an unvaccinated 11-year-old child. The child had visited a popular theme park just prior to showing symptoms. Within weeks, 125 other cases were identified in 7 adjacent states as well as Mexico and Canada, with many of the patients having recently visited the same theme park (Zipprich et al., 2015). Most of the patients were unvaccinated (Gostin et al., 2015).

Even when children receive the full schedule of vaccinations, many do not receive them on the timetable recommended by the National Vaccine Advisory Committee (Luman, Barker, McCauley, & Drews-Botsch, 2005). Vaccine timeliness is important because the efficacy of early and late vaccination is not always known and may vary by disease (Luman et al., 2005). *When* a child receives a vaccination may be just as important as *whether* the child receives it in promoting disease resistance. Finally, several vaccinations are required or recommended for older children and adolescents, such as vaccines to protect against meningitis (a swelling of the membranes covering the brain and spinal cord) and the

vaccine A small dose of inactive virus that is injected into the body to stimulate the production of antibodies to guard against a disease.

human papillomavirus (HPV, an infection transmitted by sexual activity that is linked with several types of cancer; Committee on Infectious Diseases & American Academy of Pediatrics, 2015). Adults should receive booster shots for measles, mumps, and rubella as well as chicken pox and, with age, shingles (a painful skin rash caused by the virus that causes chicken pox) and the pneumococcal virus, which causes many kinds of infections, such as pneumonia, ear infections, and meningitis (Kim, Bridges, & Harriman, 2016).

CHILDHOOD INJURIES

Unintentional injuries from accidents are the most common cause of death in children and adolescents in the United States, causing about one in five deaths (Dellinger & Gilchrist, 2017; Xu, Murphy, Kochanek, & Bastian, 2016). Motor vehicle accidents are the most common cause of fatal injuries in children aged 5 to 19, and drowning is the most common cause of death among children aged 1 to 4 (Safe Kids Worldwide, 2015). Many more children incur nonfatal injuries. As shown by Figure 5.1, rates for nonfatal injuries vary dramatically with age, reaching heights in infancy and adolescence (ages 15 to 19; Child Trends Data Bank, 2014a). At all ages, males experience more injuries than females, likely due to their higher levels of activity and risk taking. The most common types of injuries also vary with age: Falls are the most common source of injuries in children under age 9, whereas adolescents are more often injured by being struck by an object or person (Child Trends Data Bank, 2014b).

A variety of individual and contextual influences place children at risk of injury. Poor parental and adult supervision is closely associated with childhood injury (Ablewhite et al., 2015; Morrongiello, Corbett, McCourt, & Johnston, 2006). Children's risk for injury rises when their parents feel they have little control over them. Moreover, some parents hold the belief that injuries are an inevitable part of child development (Ablewhite et al., 2015) and may, therefore, provide less supervision and intervention. Children who are impulsive, overactive, and difficult, as well as those diagnosed with attention-deficit/hyperactivity disorder (ADHD), experience higher rates of unintentional injuries (Acar et al., 2015;

FIGURE 5.1: Nonfatal Injury Among Children Ages 0–19 in the United States, 2012

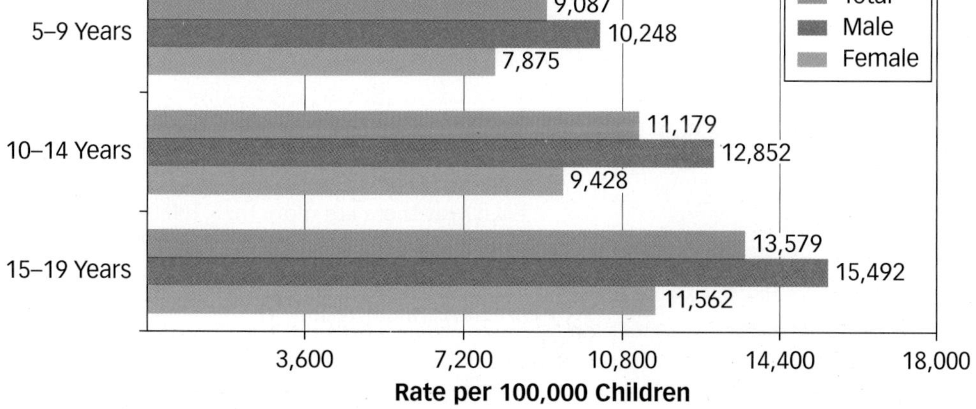

Source: U.S. Department of Health and Human Services, Centers for Disease Control and Prevention, National Center for Injury Prevention & Control. National Electronic Injury Surveillance System—All Injury Program.

https://mchb.hrsa.gov/chusa14/special-features/nonfatal-injury.html

Lange et al., 2016; Morrongiello et al., 2006). Parents of these children are sometimes less likely to intervene and prevent dangerous behavior. Children's risk of injury rises when their parents report feeling little control over their behavior (Acar et al., 2015). Childhood injury is also associated with parental distraction, such as talking to another parent or using the phone (Huynh, Demeter, Burke, & Upperman, 2017). Parents who work long hours or multiple jobs and who live in challenging environments may find it difficult to keep tabs on their children or may feel overwhelmed.

Neighborhood disadvantage, specifically low SES and lack of resources, is associated with higher rates of injuries and bone fractures in children in the United States, Canada, and the UK (Lyons et al., 2000; McClure, Kegler, Davey, & Clay, 2015; Stark, Bennet, Stone, & Chishti, 2002). Disadvantaged neighborhoods may also contribute to children's injuries due to factors that increase overall injury risk, such as poor surface maintenance of streets and sidewalks and poor design or maintenance of housing and playgrounds. In addition to having few opportunities to be active, children in unsafe disadvantaged neighborhoods often have inadequate access to sources of healthy nutrition; this combination of circumstances can interfere with children developing healthy strong bodies.

Just as there are multiple contextual factors that place children at risk of injury, there are many opportunities for preventing and reducing childhood injuries. Parenting interventions that improve supervision and monitoring, teach parents about risks to safety, and model safe practices can help parents reduce injuries in their children (Kendrick, Barlow, Hampshire, Stewart-Brown, & Polnay, 2008). School programs can help students learn and practice safety skills. At the community level, installing and maintaining safe playground equipment and protected floor surfaces can reduce the injuries that accompany falls. Disadvantaged communities, however, may lack the funding to provide safe play spaces, placing residing children at risk.

CHILD MALTREATMENT

According to the Child Abuse Prevention and Treatment Act, a U.S. federal law, **child abuse** is any intentional harm to a minor, an individual under 18 years of age, including actions that harm the child physically, emotionally, sexually, and through neglect (U.S. Department of Health and Human Services, 2016). Many children experience more than one form of abuse.

child abuse Any intentional harm to a minor (under the age of 18), including actions that harm the child physically, emotionally, sexually, or through neglect.

- *Physical abuse* refers to any intentional physical injury to the child, and can include striking, kicking, burning, or biting the child, or any action that results in a physical impairment of the child.

- *Sexual abuse*, more common among older children, refers to inappropriate touching, comments, or engaging in any sexual activity, coerced or persuaded, with a child.

- *Neglect* occurs when a child is deprived of adequate food, clothing, shelter, or medical care.

Each year there are more than 700,000 confirmed cases of abuse or neglect in the United States (U.S. Department of Health and Human Services, 2016). Child maltreatment results in more than 1,500 fatalities per year, about three quarters in children younger than 3 years. Parents are the most common perpetrators (in more than 80% of cases, on average), with relatives other than parents and unmarried partners of parents constituting an additional 10% of perpetrators

Child maltreatment has wideranging effects on children's physical, cognitive, and socioemotional development.

© istock.com/BrianAJackson

(U.S. Department of Health and Human Services, 2016). It is estimated that about 27% of children under the age of 17 have experienced sexual abuse (Finkelhor, Shattuck, Turner, & Hamby, 2014; Kim, Wildeman, Jonson-Reid, & Drake, 2017). Sexual abuse may occur at any time during infancy, childhood, or adolescence, but it is most often reported in middle childhood, with about half of cases occurring between ages 4 and 12 (U.S. Department of Health and Human Services, 2013b). Although these statistics are alarming, they underestimate the incidence of abuse because many more children experience maltreatment that is not reported. Moreover, abuse often is not a one-time event; some children experience maltreatment that persists for years (U.S. Department of Health and Human Services, 2013b).

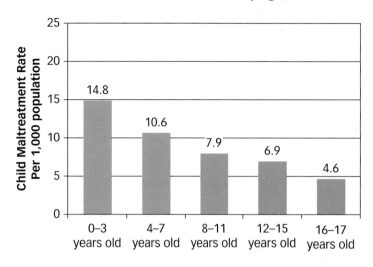

FIGURE 5.2: Child Maltreatment Rate by Age, 2014

Source: Child Trends Databank (2015).

Effects of Child Maltreatment

The effects of physical maltreatment are immediate, ranging from bruises to broken bones to internal bleeding and more. Some physical effects are long lasting. Child abuse can impair brain development and functioning through physical damage, such as that caused by shaking an infant, which damages the brain (Twardosz & Lutzker, 2009). Physical harm and prolonged stress can alter the course of brain development, increasing the child's risk for post-traumatic stress disorder (PTSD), ADHD, conduct disorder, and various learning and memory difficulties (de Bellis, Hooper, Spratt, & Woolley, 2009). Children who are abused score lower on measures of problem solving, experience difficulty understanding and completing day-to-day schoolwork, and sometimes demonstrate learning difficulties serious enough to result in academic failure (Font & Berger, 2014; Widom, 2014).

The socioemotional effects of child maltreatment are especially daunting and long lasting. Young children who are abused tend to have poor coping skills, low self-esteem, difficulty regulating their emotions and impulses, and show more negative affect, such as anger and frustration, and less positive affect than other children (Barth et al., 2007). They tend to have difficulty understanding their own and other people's emotions and often have difficulty making and maintaining friendships (Cicchetti & Banny, 2014). The quality of relationships with peers is closely associated with abuse, such that the younger the child was when the abuse began and the longer it continued, the worse the relationships with peers (Bolger, Patterson, & Kupersmidt, 1998; Font & Berger, 2014). Moreover, children and adolescents who are abused are at risk for a range of psychological disorders, including anxiety, eating, and depressive disorders as well as behavioral problems, delinquency, teen pregnancy, illicit drug use, mental health problems, and risk behavior into young adulthood (Carlson, Oshri, & Kwon, 2015; Cecil, Viding, Fearon, Glaser, & McCrory, 2017; Cicchetti & Banny, 2014; Jones et al., 2013). Children who are sexually abused often are more knowledgeable about sex than is appropriate for their age and engage in age-inappropriate sexual activity such as masturbation, placing objects in their genital areas, or behaving seductively (Kenny et al., 2008). During adolescence they are more likely than same-age peers to engage in risky sexual activity (Abajobir, Kisely, Maravilla, Williams, & Najman, 2017). Many children who are sexually abused display symptoms of PTSD, an anxiety disorder that occurs after experiencing a traumatic event and includes flashbacks, nightmares, and feelings of helplessness (Maniglio, 2013; Putman, 2009).

Risk Factors for Child Maltreatment

Risk factors for child abuse exist at all ecological levels: the child, parent, community, and society (McCoy & Keen, 2009). Certain child characteristics have been found to increase the risk or potential for maltreatment. Children with special needs, such as those with physical and mental disabilities, preterm birth status, or serious illness, require a great deal of care that can overwhelm or frustrate caregivers, placing such children at risk of maltreatment (Bugental, 2009). Similarly, children who are temperamentally difficult, inattentive, overactive, or have other developmental problems are also at risk because they are especially taxing for parents (Crosse, Kaye, & Ratnofsky, 1993; Font & Berger, 2014).

Parents who engage in child maltreatment tend to perceive their child as stubborn and noncompliant and tend to evaluate the child's misdeeds as worse than they are, leading them to use strict and physical methods of discipline (Casanueva et al., 2010). Parents who maltreat their children often lack knowledge about child development and have unrealistic expectations for their children. They may be less skilled in recognizing emotions displayed on their children's faces; find it difficult to recognize, manage, and express their own feelings appropriately; and have poor impulse control, coping, and problem-solving skills (McCoy & Keen, 2009; Wagner et al., 2015). Abuse is more common in homes characterized by poverty, marital instability, and drug and alcohol abuse (Hilarski, 2008; Terry & Talon, 2004). Children who are raised in homes in which adults come and go—repeated marriages, separations, and revolving romantic partners—are at higher risk of sexual abuse. However, sexual abuse also occurs in intact middle-class families. In these families, children's victimization often remains undetected and unreported (Hinkelman & Bruno, 2008).

Community factors, such as inadequate housing, community violence, and poverty place children at risk for abuse (Dodge & Coleman, 2009; Widom, 2014). Neighborhoods with few community level support resources, such as parks, child care centers, preschool programs, recreation centers and churches, increase the likelihood of child maltreatment (Coulton, Korbin, & Su, 1999; Molnar et al., 2016).In contrast, neighborhoods with a low turnover of residents, a sense of community, and connections among neighbors support parents and protect against child maltreatment (McCoy & Keen, 2009; van Dijken, Stams, & de Winter, 2016).

At the societal level, several factors contribute to the problem of child abuse. Legal definitions of violence and abuse and political or religious views that value independence, privacy, and noninterference in families may influence the prevalence of child abuse within a given society (Tzeng, Jackson, & Karlson, 1991). Social acceptance of violence— for example as expressed in video games, music lyrics, and television and films—can send the message that violence is an acceptable method of managing conflict. Overall, there are many complex influences on child maltreatment.

Along with recognizing risk factors, it is important to be aware of signs that abuse may be taking place. Table 5.1 provides a non-exhaustive list of signs of abuse. Not all children who display one or more of the signs on this list experience maltreatment, but each sign is significant enough to merit attention and treatment. All U.S. states and the District of Columbia identify **mandated reporters**, individuals who are legally obligated to report suspected child maltreatment to the appropriate agency, such as child protective services, a law enforcement agency, or a state's child abuse reporting hotline (Child Welfare Information Gateway, 2013). Individuals designated as mandatory reporters typically have frequent contact with children: teachers, principals, and other school personnel; child care providers; physicians, nurses, and other health-care workers; counselors, therapists, and other mental health professionals; and law enforcement officers. Of course, anyone can, and is encouraged to, report suspected maltreatment of a child.

MORTALITY IN INFANCY AND CHILDHOOD

mandated reporter
A professional who is legally obligated to report suspected child maltreatment to law enforcement.

Rates of child mortality are highest among infants today, just as they have been throughout history. Children are much more likely to die during the first year of life than they are at older ages. As shown in Figure 5.3, childhood mortality declines after infancy and has

TABLE 5.1 • Signs of Child Abuse and Neglect

THE CHILD	THE PARENT
• Exhibits extremes in behavior, such as overly compliant or demanding behavior, extreme passivity, withdrawal, or aggression • Has not received help for physical or medical problems (e.g., dental care, eyeglasses, immunizations) brought to the parents' attention • Has difficulty concentrating or learning problems that appear to be without cause • Is very watchful, as if waiting for something bad to happen • Frequently lacks adult supervision • Has unexplained burns, bruises, broken bones, or black eyes • Is absent from school often, especially with fading bruises upon return • Is reluctant to be around a particular person, or shrinks at the approach of a parent or adult • Reports injury by a parent or another adult caregiver • Lacks sufficient clothing for the weather • Is delayed in physical or emotional development • States that there is no one at home to provide care	• Shows indifference and little concern for the child • Denies problems at home • Blames problems on the child • Refers to the child as bad or worthless or berates the child • Has demands that are too high for the child to achieve • Offers conflicting, unconvincing, or no explanation for the child's injury • Uses harsh physical discipline with the child, or suggests that caregivers use harsh physical discipline if the child misbehaves • Is abusing alcohol or other drugs

Source: Adapted from Child Welfare Information Gateway (2013).

FIGURE 5.3: Death Rates for Children Ages 1 to 19 in the United States, 1980–2014

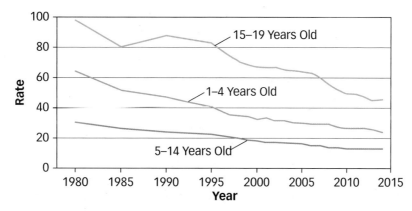

Sources: Data for ages 0 to 14, 1980–1999: Pastor, P. N., Makuc, D. M., Reuben, C., Xia, H. (2002). Health: United States: Chartbook on trends in the health of Americans. Hyattsville, Maryland: National Center for Health Statistics. Available at: http://www.cdc.gov/nchs/data/hus/hus02.pdf. Data for ages 15 to 19, 1980–1998: Federal Interagency Forum on Child and Family Statistics. (2002) America's Children: Key National Indicators of Well-Being, 2002. Federal Interagency Forum on Child and Family Statistics, Washington DC: U.S. Government Printing Office. Tables Health 6.A., Health 6.B. and Health 7. Available at: http://www.childstats.gov/pdf/ac2002/ac_02.pdf. Data for 1999–2013 Centers for Disease Control and Prevention, National Center for Health Statistics. Underlying Cause of Death 1999–2013 on CDC WONDER Online Database. Available at: http:// wonder.cdc.gov/ucd-icd10.html. Data for 2014: Kochanek, K. D., Murphy, S. L., Xu, J., & Tejada-Vera, B. (2016). Deaths: Final data for 2014. National Vital Statistics Reports, 65(4). Hyattsville, Maryland: National Center for Health Statistics. Tables 3–4. Available at: http://www.cdc.gov/nchs/data/nvsr/nvsr65/nvsr65_04.pdf

https://public.tableau.com/profile/childtrends#!/vizhome/Book1_15740/Dashboard1

declined over the last four decades in the United States (Child Trends, 2013). As shown in Figure 5.4, similar patterns of declining childhood mortality appear throughout the world; however, developing regions and those plagued by poverty and violence, such as some countries in sub-Saharan Africa and South Asia, experience rates of childhood mortality 10 times the rate in North America (Roser, 2016).

Low socioeconomic status, poor access to nutrition and medical care, and stressful home and community environments are associated with higher rates of childhood mortality (Singh & Kogan, 2007). Advances in public health, such as increasing access to health care, prenatal care, and availability of vaccinations for potentially fatal illnesses, are effective in reducing child mortality (Soares, 2007).

FIGURE 5.4: Child Mortality by World Region, 1960–2012

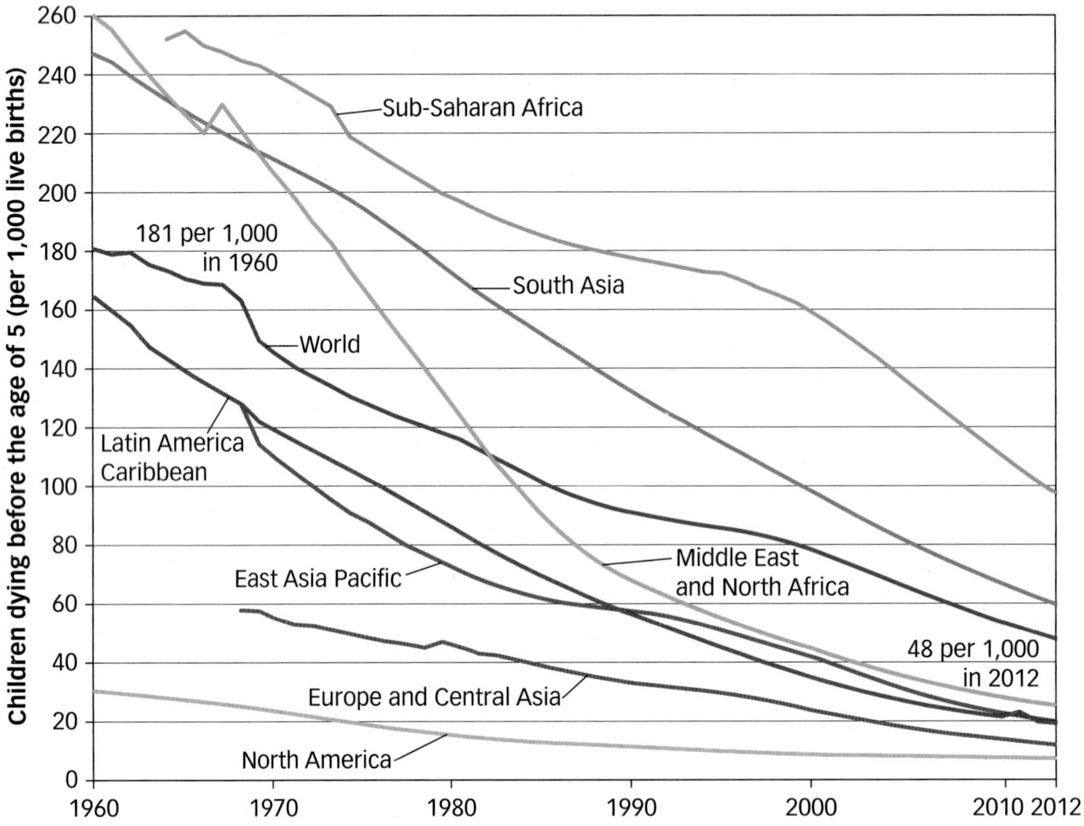

From Rosner 2016 – https://ourworldindata.org/wp-content/uploads/2013/05/ourworldindata_child-mortality-since-1960.png

Thinking in Context 5.1

1. What kinds of accidents do you think are most likely in childhood? How might the nature of injuries change with age? What can parents, schools, and communities do to prevent injuries to children?

2. Child abuse is a problem with a complex set of influences at multiple bioecological levels. The most effective prevention and intervention programs target multiple levels of context. Referring to Bronfenbrenner's model (see Chapter 1), discuss factors at each bioecological level that might be incorporated into prevention and intervention programs to prevent child abuse and promote positive outcomes.

COMMON HEALTH ISSUES IN ADOLESCENCE AND EMERGING ADULTHOOD

LO 5.2 Discuss the prevalence, effects, and treatment of eating disorders and substance use in adolescents and emerging adults.

Adolescence and emerging adulthood are generally healthy periods for most young people. The largest risks that adolescents and emerging adults face to their health stem from their own (and others') behavior. For example, many adolescents engage in unhealthy weight loss behaviors that can escalate into eating disorders.

EATING DISORDERS

Adolescents' rapidly changing physique, coupled with media portrayals of the ideal woman as thin with few curves, leads many to become dissatisfied with their body image, and the dissatisfaction often persists into emerging adulthood (Benowitz-Fredericks, Garcia, Massey, Vasagar, & Borzekowski, 2012). In some girls, body image dissatisfaction may begin much earlier, in childhood, as discussed in the Lives in Context feature. Girls who have a negative body image are at risk of developing eating disorders, characterized by an obsession with weight control, extreme over- or under-control of eating, and extreme behavior patterns designed to control weight such as compulsive exercise, dieting, or purging (American Psychiatric Association, 2013). Two eating disorders, **anorexia nervosa** and **bulimia nervosa**, pose serious challenges to health.

Although both anorexia nervosa and bulimia nervosa entail excessive concern about body weight and attempts to lose weight, they differ in how this concern is manifested. Those who suffer from anorexia nervosa starve themselves and sometimes engage in extreme exercise in order to achieve thinness and maintain a weight that is substantially lower than expected for height and age (American Psychiatric Association, 2013). A distorted body image leads youth with anorexia to perceive themselves as "fat" despite their emaciated appearance, and they continue to lose weight (Gila, Castro, Cesena, & Toro, 2005; Hagman et al., 2015). Anorexia affects about 2% of girls 19 and under; however, many more girls show similar poor eating behaviors (Smink, van Hoeken, & Hoek, 2013; Smink, van Hoeken, Oldehinkel, & Hoek, 2014).

Bulimia nervosa is characterized by recurrent episodes of *binge eating*—consuming an abnormally large amount of food (thousands of calories) in a single sitting coupled with a feeling of being out of control—followed by *purging*, inappropriate behavior designed to compensate for the binge, such as vomiting, excessive exercise, or use of laxatives (American Psychiatric Association, 2013). Like individuals with anorexia, those with bulimia nervosa experience extreme dissatisfaction with body image and attempt to lose weight, but they tend to have a body weight that is normal or high-normal (Golden et al., 2015). Bulimia is more common than anorexia, affecting between 1% and 5% of females across Western Europe and the United States (Kessler et al., 2013; Smink et al., 2014) and many more young people show symptoms of bulimia but remain undiagnosed (Keel, 2014).

Both anorexia and bulimia pose serious health risks. Girls with anorexia may lose 25% to 50% of their body weight (Berkman, Lohr, & Bulik, 2007). They may not experience menarche or may stop menstruating because menstruation is dependent on maintaining at least 15% to 18% body fat (Golden et al., 2015). Starvation and malnutrition not only contribute to extreme sensitivity to cold, pale skin, and growth of fine hairs all over the body; they can also have serious health consequences such as bone loss, kidney failure, shrinkage of the heart, brain damage, and even death in as many as 16% of cases (Golden et al., 2015; Reel, 2012). Side effects of bulimia nervosa include nutritional deficiencies; bad

anorexia nervosa An eating disorder characterized by compulsive starvation and extreme weight loss and accompanied by a distorted body image.

bulimia nervosa An eating disorder characterized by recurrent episodes of binge eating and subsequent purging usually by induced vomiting and the use of laxatives.

LIVES IN CONTEXT

• • Body Image Dissatisfaction

Richard Levine/Alamy

Media depictions of unattainable body ideals influence body dissatisfaction.

"See how my stomach sticks out?" asked Amanda. "Sometimes it sticks out even worse, and I have to wear baggy tops. I hate that. I want to wear cropped tops like that one," Amanda said, pointing to a page in a magazine. "But I'm too fat." "Me too," said her best friend, Betsy. At 9 years of age, Amanda and Betsy display signs of body image dissatisfaction—dissatisfaction with one's physical appearance as shown by a discrepancy between one's ideal body figure and actual body figure.

As early as age 4, children rate thin bodies as more attractive than the average-shaped bodies they report as normal and commonly seen (Brown & Slaughter, 2011). Body image dissatisfaction can be seen as early as the preschool years and rises quickly over the course of childhood (Tremblay & Limbos, 2009). For example, studies of 3- to 6-year-old children have shown that as many as 70% of girls of normal weight report dissatisfaction with their bodies (Tatangelo, McCabe, Mellor, & Mealey, 2016; L. Tremblay, Lovsin, Zecevic, & Larivière, 2011) and up to one-half of elementary school children (6–12 years) are dissatisfied with some aspect of their body and shape (Coughlin, Heinberg, Marinilli, & Guarda, 2003; Littleton & Ollendick, 2003; Smolak, 2011).

Body image dissatisfaction is associated with poor self-esteem, depression, unhealthy eating and exercise behaviors, and inadequate weight gain in childhood (Duchin et al., 2015; Poudevigne et al., 2003; Tiggeman & Wilson-Barrett, 1998). Dieting behaviors often begin in childhood, with about half of 8- to 10-year-old children reporting they have been on a weight-loss

diet at least some of the time (Dohnt & Tiggemann, 2005; Littleton & Ollendick, 2003; McVey, Tweed, & Blackmore, 2004).

Although less well researched, body dissatisfaction also occurs in boys. Studies of United States, British, and Australian boys have shown that between one third and two thirds of boys between the ages of 5 and 10 report body dissatisfaction, desiring a thinner, larger, or broader frame (Cohane & Pope, 2001; Dion et al., 2016; Gustafson-Larson & Terry, 1992; Maloney, McGuire, Daniels, & Specker, 1989). Overall, body image dissatisfaction and body distortion increases with age in both boys and girls from early adolescence into young adulthood, especially with increases in BMI (Bucchianeri, Arikian, Hannan, Eisenberg, & Neumark-Sztainer, 2013; Calzo et al., 2012).

Parents' direct comments about their child's weight, particularly mothers' comments, are most consistently associated with children's reported body concerns and behaviors (Gattario, Frisén, & Anderson-Fye, 2014; McCabe et al., 2007). Peers, however, are also important. Girls and women often bond over "fat talk," criticizing their own bodies (Corning & Gondoli, 2012; McVey, Levine, Piran, & Ferguson, 2013). Negative body talk is related to poor body image, body-related cognitive distortions, disordered eating, and psychological maladjustment in college women (Rudiger & Winstead, 2013). Many school-age girls believe that being thin would make them more likable by their peers and less likely to be teased (Dohnt & Tiggemann, 2005; McCabe, Riccardelli, & Finemore, 2002).

Finally, greater exposure to teen media and images of thin models is associated with dieting awareness, weight concerns, and body dissatisfaction in girls and women (Benowitz-Fredericks et al., 2012; Evans, Tovée, Boothroyd, & Drewett, 2013; Gattario et al., 2014). The influence of the media is perhaps best illustrated by longitudinal studies of teenagers in the Pacific island nation of Fiji before and after television became widely available in the islands. Disordered eating attitudes and behaviors rose after the introduction of television (Dasen, 1994). With the emergence of U.S. television programming, girls from rural Fiji reported comparing their bodies to the program characters and wanting to look like them (Becker, Keel, Anderson-Fye, & Thomas, 2004). Individuals' perceptions of body ideals and their own bodies are influenced by multiple contextual factors.

Improving *media literacy* by teaching children about advertising is an important focus of many school-based intervention programs (McLean, Paxton, & Wertheim, 2016; Richardson, Paxton, & Thomson, 2009; Yager, Diedrichs, Ricciardelli, & Halliwell, 2013). Lessons might include information about the homogeneity of body shapes shown on television and magazines, airbrushing of photos, and why advertisers might want us to be unhappy with the way we look (i.e., to get us to buy the product; Neumark-Sztainer, Sherwood, Coller, & Hannan, 2000). For example, as part of a 2011 governmental initiative in British schools, Britney Spears allowed pre-airbrushed images of herself in a bikini to be shown alongside the airbrushed ones for children aged 10 to 11, to show how media might try to alter and improve images (Gattario et al., 2014). Effective programs emphasize providing children with alternative ways of thinking about beauty and body ideals (Gattario et al., 2014).

breath and tooth damage; and sores, ulcers, and even holes in the mouth and esophagus—as well as increased risk of cancers of the throat and esophagus—caused by repeated exposure to stomach acids (Katzman, 2005).

What causes eating disorders? Both anorexia and bulimia occur more often in both members of identical twins than fraternal twins, indicating a genetic connection (Bulik, Kleiman, & Yilmaz, 2016; Strober, Freeman, Lampert, Diamond, & Kaye, 2014). Eating disorders are more prevalent in females than males, with about 1% of males diagnosed with an eating disorder as compared with about 6% of females (Raevuori, Keski-Rahkonen, & Hoek, 2014). Anorexia is associated with perfectionism and strict regulation of eating, thus it may be viewed as a way to exert control and reduce negative mood states (Kaye, Wierenga, Bailer, Simmons, & Bischoff-Grethe, 2013; Tyrka, Graber, & Brooks-Gunn, 2000). Eating disorders are associated with altered neural activity in several limbic system structures and parts of the prefrontal cortex responsible for aspects of emotion, rewards, and decision making (Fuglset, Landrø, Reas, & Rø, 2016).

Eating disorders occur in all ethnic and socioeconomic groups in Western countries and are increasingly common in Asian and Arab cultures (Isomaa, Isomaa, Marttunen, Kaltiala-Heino, & Björkqvist, 2009; Keski-Rahkonen & Mustelin, 2016; Pike, Hoek, & Dunne, 2014; Thomas et al., 2015). Girls who compete in sports and activities that idealize lean figures, such as ballet, figure skating, gymnastics, and long distance running, are at higher risk for developing eating disorders than are other girls (Nordin, Harris, & Cumming, 2003; Voelker, Gould, & Reel, 2014). In the United States, white and Latina girls, especially those of higher socioeconomic status, are at higher risk for low body image and eating disorders than are black girls, who may be protected by cultural and media portrayals of African American women that value voluptuous figures (Smink et al., 2013). Some researchers suggest, however, that ethnic differences in eating disorders are not as large as they appear. Instead, eating disorders may exist in black girls but remain undetected and undiagnosed because of barriers to diagnosis and treatment (Wilson, Grilo, & Vitousek, 2007).

Eating disorders are difficult to treat. In one study of more than 2,500 adolescents, 82% of those diagnosed with an eating disorder continued to show symptoms 5 years later (Ackard, Fulkerson, & Neumark-Sztainer, 2011). Anorexia nervosa and bulimia nervosa are treated in similar ways but show different success rates. Standard treatment for anorexia includes hospitalization to remedy malnutrition and ensure weight gain, antianxiety or antidepressant medications, and individual and family therapy (Lock, 2011; Wilson et al., 2007). Therapy is designed to enhance girls' motivation to change and engage them as collaborators in treatment, providing them with a sense of control. However, the success of therapy depends on the patients' attitudes about their symptoms and illness (Bulik et al., 2007; Lock, Le Grange, & Forsberg, 2007; Lock, 2011). Unfortunately, girls with anorexia tend to deny that there is a problem as they are unable to objectively perceive their bodies and value thinness and restraint, making anorexia very resistant to treatment (Berkman et al., 2007). As a result, only about 50% of girls with anorexia make a full recovery and anorexia nervosa has the highest mortality rate of all mental disorders (Smink et al., 2013).

Bulimia tends to be more amenable to treatment because girls with bulimia often acknowledge that their behavior is not healthy. Girls with bulimia tend to feel guilty about binging and purging and are more likely than those with anorexia to seek help. Individual therapy, support groups, nutritional education, and antianxiety or antidepressant medications are the treatments of choice for bulimia nervosa (Hay & Bacaltchuk, 2007; le Grange & Schmidt, 2005). Individual and family-based therapy helps girls become aware of the thoughts and behaviors that cause and maintain their binging and purging behaviors, which decreases binge eating and vomiting and reduces the risk of relapse (Lock, 2011; Smink et al., 2013). Another risk to development in adolescence and emerging adulthood lies in experimentation with risky activities such as alcohol and substance use and abuse.

TABLE 5.2 • Substance Use by U.S. Adolescents, 2016

	LIFETIME PREVALENCE (%)	30-DAY PREVALENCE (%)
Cigarettes		
8th grade	9.8	2.6
10th grade	17.5	4.9
12th grade	28.3	10.5
E-Cigarettes		
8th grade	—*	6.2
10th grade	—	11.0
12th grade	—	12.5
Alcohol		
8th grade	22.8	7.3
10th grade	43.4	19.9
12th grade	61.2	33.2
Been Drunk		
8th grade	8.6	1.8
10th grade	26.0	9.0
12th grade	46.3	20.4
Marijuana		
8th grade	13	5.4
10th grade	30	14.0
12th grade	45	22.5
Other Illicit Drugs		
8th grade	9	2.7
10th grade	14	4.4
12th grade	21	6.9

*E-cigarettes is a new addition to survey; lifetime prevalence was not assessed

Source: Miech et al. (2017).

ALCOHOL AND SUBSTANCE USE AND ABUSE

Nearly half of U.S. teens have tried an illicit drug and two-thirds have tried alcohol by the time they leave high school, as shown in Table 5.2. Experimentation with alcohol, tobacco, and marijuana use, that is, "trying out" these substances, is so common that it may be considered somewhat normative for North American adolescents. Rates of experimentation rise during the adolescent years into young adulthood (Miech, Johnston, O'Malley, Bachman, Schulenberg, & Patrick, 2017). Perhaps surprising to some adults is that a limited amount of experimentation with drugs and alcohol is common in well-adjusted middle and older adolescents and associated with psychosocial health and well-being (Mason & Spoth, 2011; Shelder & Block, 1990; Windle et al., 2008). Why? Alcohol and substance use may serve a developmental function in middle and late adolescence, such as a way of asserting independence and autonomy from parents, taking risks, forming social relationships, and learning about oneself (Englund et al., 2013).

Substance use often increases during the transition to adulthood, when emerging adults usually live away from their parents for the first time in their lives and experience the drive to explore the world at the same time as they feel pressure to complete their education, establish a career, and find a mate. These circumstances, coupled with easy access to drugs and alcohol, increase the risk of using and abusing marijuana, alcohol, and other drugs in early adulthood. Substance abuse is most prevalent among people in their twenties, often with dangerous consequences such as overdose, injury, accidents, and even death (Chen & Jacobson, 2012). Substance use tends to decline as emerging adults transition into adult roles, such as becoming parents; however, substance use remains prevalent in adulthood, with about 6% of middle-aged adults reporting use within the past month (Substance Abuse and Mental Health Services Administration, 2014). The following sections examine three commonly used substances: alcohol, tobacco, and marijuana.

Alcohol Use and Abuse

Adolescents are particularly vulnerable to alcohol abuse because they show reduced sensitivity to the effects of alcohol that serve as cues in adults to limit their intake, such as motor impairment, sedation, social impairment, and quietness or distress (Spear, 2011). Adolescents develop a tolerance to the impairing effects of alcohol and have reduced sensitivity to the aversive effects, such as nausea or hangover. They are at risk for developing dependence on alcohol more quickly than do adults (Schepis, Adinoff, & Rao, 2008; Simons, Wills, & Neal, 2014). Adolescents are also more sensitive to neurological damage and show more cognitive impairment in response to alcohol use as compared with adults. Alcohol use in adolescence, even moderate use, is associated with damage to the brain, particularly the prefrontal cortex and hippocampus (Bava & Tapert, 2010; Silveri, Dager, Cohen-Gilbert, & Sneider, 2016; Squeglia et al., 2015). Heavy drinking is associated with reduced frontal cortex response during working memory tasks; slower information processing; and reductions in attention, visiospatial functioning, and problem solving (Carbia et al., 2017; Feldstein Ewing, Sakhardande, & Blakemore, 2014). At the same time, some research suggests that preexisting individual differences, such as poor functioning in tests of inhibition and working memory, smaller gray and white matter volume, and altered brain activation, are not only influenced by substance use, but place adolescents at risk for heavy substance use (Brumback et al., 2016; Squeglia & Gray, 2016).

Of particular concern are rates of **binge drinking**, defined for men as consuming five or more drinks in one sitting and for women, four drinks in one sitting. Heavy drinking is defined as two or more instances of binge drinking within the past 30 days (Kanny, Liu, Brewer, & Lu, 2013). As shown in Figure 5.5, binge drinking and heavy drinking peak in young adulthood, with about one-third of adults aged 18 to 24 and 25 to 34, as well as one in five adults aged 35 to 44, reporting binge drinking within the past 30 days (Kanny et al., 2013). Binge drinking is associated with negative short- and long-term consequences for physical and psychological well-being, including academic problems, fatal and nonfatal injuries, violence and crime, unintended pregnancies, sexually transmitted diseases, and impaired driving (S. A. Brown et al., 2008; Cleveland, Mallett, White, Turrisi, & Favero, 2013; Mallett et al., 2013; Marshall, 2014). For example, as shown in Figure 5.6, in 2013, about 20% of 21- to 25-year-olds and 26- to 29-year-olds and about 18% of 30- to 34-year-olds reported driving under the influence of alcohol within the past year (U.S. Department of Health and Human Services, 2014). Each year alcohol is implicated in one-third of traffic fatalities (National Highway Traffic Safety Administration, 2016) and implicated in 40% of all crimes (National Council on Alcoholism and Drug Dependence, 2015).

Research with college students has suggested that binge and heavy drinking may be part of a "stage of life phenomenon" for which the transition out of high school increases the risk (Jackson, Sher, & Park, 2005). As they enter college, young people experience greater

Experimentation with alcohol is common in adolescence and often signals normative adjustment.

binge drinking Heavy episodic drinking; consuming five or more alcoholic beverages in one sitting for men and four drinks in one sitting for women.

FIGURE 5.5: Current, Binge, and Heavy Alcohol Use Among Persons Ages 12 and Older, by Age, 2014

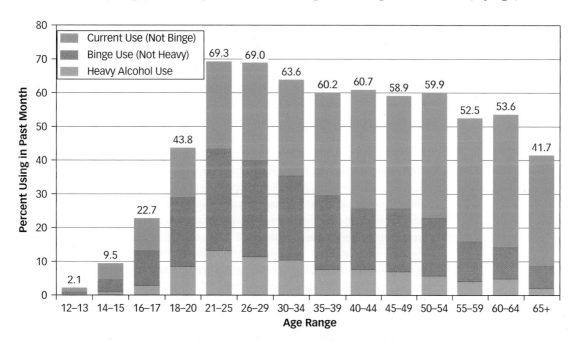

Source: Substance Abuse and Mental Health Services Administration (2014).

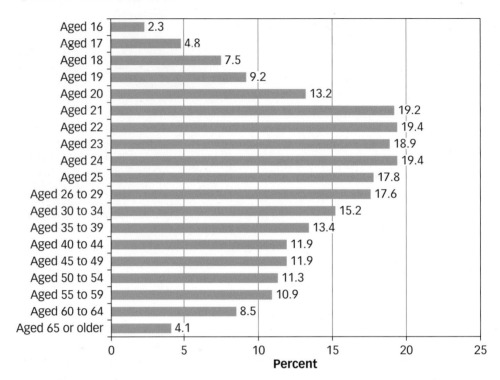

FIGURE 5.6: Driving Under the Influence of Alcohol in the Past Year Among People Aged 16 or Older, by Age: 2014

Source: SAMHSA, Center for Behavioral Health Statistics and Quality, National Survey on Drug Use and Health (NSDUH), 2014.

https://www.samhsa.gov/data/sites/default/files/report_2688/ShortReport-2688.pdf

exposure to drinking and encounter greater amounts of peer drinking and positive peer attitudes toward alcohol (White & Jackson, 2005), and alcohol use tends to increase (Simons-Morton et al., 2016). Most college students report experiencing more positive consequences of drinking (such as feeling social) than negative consequences (such as cognitive impairment), which contributes to high rates of binge and heavy drinking in this age group (Lee, Maggs, Neighbors, & Patrick, 2011). Research is mixed as to whether young adults who attend college drink more than their peers who do not attend college (Carter, Brandon, & Goldman, 2010; Goldman, Greenbaum, Darkes, Brandon, & Del Boca, 2011; Reckdenwald, Ford, & Murray, 2016; Vergés et al., 2011), but heavy drinking and alcohol-related problems are more common among young adults regardless of college enrollment (Barnes, Welte, Hoffman, & Tidwell, 2010; Lanza & Collins, 2006; Vergés et al., 2011).

Most young people show a spontaneous decline in drinking over the course of early adulthood. The transition to adult responsibilities such as career, marriage, and parenthood typically predicts declines in binge drinking and alcohol-related problems (Misch, 2007; Vergés et al., 2011). Most young people "mature out" of drinking, moving from heavy drinking to more moderate drinking (Lee, Chassin, & Villalta, 2013). Yet recent research suggests that although the frequency of drinking declines, for many young people, the amount consumed may remain unchanged (Arria et al., 2016; Reich, Cummings, Greenbaum, Moltisanti, & Goldman, 2015). Heavy drinking and binge drinking remains prevalent in adulthood, with 14% of middle-aged adults reporting binge drinking within the last month (Kanny et al., 2013).

Tobacco Use and Abuse

Nearly 90% of smokers have their first cigarette before age 18, but regular or daily smoking often does not begin until about age 20, and the overall risk of initiating smoking plateaus

• • Substance Use and the Brain

The adolescent brain is particularly vulnerable to negative effects of alcohol and substance use.

AP Photo/David Jones

Experimentation with alcohol and marijuana is normative during adolescence. However, many young people transition to regular use, to the concern of parents, educators, and developmental scientists. We know little about how drinking affects the developing brain, and even less is known about the effects of marijuana use.

Research to date suggests that alcohol use is associated with changes in the structure and function of the adolescent brain. Compared with those who do not use alcohol, adolescents who drink alcohol show smaller brain volumes and grey matter density in areas responsible for executive control, including parts of the temporal and parietal lobes and, especially, the frontal cortex (Feldstein Ewing, Sakhardande, & Blakemore, 2014; Whelan et al., 2014). Executive control is responsible for response inhibition, which is the ability to resist temptation, such as the rewards that come with risky but exciting activities, including drinking. Most worrisome is the inverse relationship between the quantity of alcohol consumed and brain volume, such that greater consumption of alcohol predicts decreased brain volume and less white matter

integrity (Silveri, Dager, Cohen-Gilbert, & Sneider, 2016). Yet there is room for optimism because some research has shown that the adolescent brain can return to typical patterns of functioning when alcohol use is discontinued (Lisdahl, Gilbart, Wright, & Shollenbarger, 2013).

Much less is known about the effects of marijuana use on the adolescent brain. Research to date suggests that regular marijuana use is associated with neurocognitive deficits in attention, learning and memory, and executive function (Lisdahl et al., 2013; Lubman, Cheetham, & Yücel, 2015). Like alcohol use, regular marijuana use is associated primarily with alterations in the frontal lobe, followed by the parietal and temporal lobes, including reduce brain and grey matter volumes (Lopez-Larson et al., 2012; Takagi, Youssef, & Lorenzetti, 2016). Moreover, early onset of marijuana use— before age 18 and especially prior to age 16—is associated with more severe consequences for attention, verbal intelligence, learning and memory, and executive function (Lubman et al., 2015; Silveri et al., 2016). It is unknown whether abstinence over a long period is associated with a rebound in function.

Overall, research suggests that alcohol and marijuana have similar consequences for neurological development in adolescence. A challenge to this research is that alcohol and marijuana use tend to co-occur, making it difficult to disentangle the independent effects of each. Regardless, the literature to date suggests that, although normative, alcohol and marijuana use pose serious risks to neurological development in adolescence.

What Do You Think?

How might findings about the effects of alcohol and marijuana on brain development be applied to prevent or change adolescent behavior? Identify challenges that might arise in applying these findings as well as ways of countering challenges.

---

at about age 22 and is rare after 24 (U.S. Department of Health and Human Services, 2014; Edwards, Carter, Peace, & Blakely, 2013). Each month, more than one-third of 18- to 39-year-olds in the United States report smoking tobacco cigarettes (U.S. Department of Health and Human Services, 2014). Many smokers do not consider themselves smokers because they only engage in occasional social smoking, "bumming" cigarettes rather than buying them, and smoking in social groups rather than as a daily habit (Brown, Carpenter, & Sutfin, 2011; Song & Ling, 2011).

Cigarette smoking is responsible for about one of every five deaths in the United States each year, including a third of all cancer deaths and about 90% of all cases of lung cancer, the top cancer killer of both men and women (U.S. Department of Health and Human Services, 2014). In addition, smoking substantially increases the risk of coronary heart disease, stroke, heart attack, vascular disease, and aneurysm (National Institute on Drug Abuse, 2009). When nonsmokers are exposed to secondhand smoke, they too experience negative health consequences, particularly increased risk of lung cancer and cardiovascular disease (U.S. Department of Health and Human Services, 2014).

Why is smoking such a tenacious habit? With each cigarette, a smoker consumes one to two milligrams of nicotine in about a five-minute period, which enters the blood and reaches the brain quickly and stimulates reward pathways, making it highly addictive. Withdrawal symptoms of nicotine begin quickly, within a few hours after the last cigarette; these include irritability, craving, anxiety, and attention deficits, which often send the smoker in search of another cigarette. Other withdrawal symptoms include depression, sleep problems, and increased appetite. When a smoker quits, withdrawal symptoms often peak within the first few days of smoking cessation and usually subside within a few weeks, but some people continue to experience symptoms for months. Nearly 35 million people in the United States wish to quit smoking each year, but more than 85% of those who try to quit relapse, often within a week (National Institute on Drug Abuse, 2009).

Some smokers turn to e-cigarettes as an alternative to tobacco cigarettes, viewing e-cigarettes as safer than conventional cigarettes (Goniewicz, Lingas, & Hajek, 2013; Huerta, Walker, Mullen, Johnson, & Ford, 2017). E-cigarettes are the most commonly used tobacco product among youth, with 16% of high school and 5% of middle school students reporting regular use (Singh et al., 2016), and their use is also increasing rapidly among adults (Miech, Johnston, O'Malley, Bachman, & Schulenberg, 2015). E-cigarettes aerosolize nicotine and produce a vapor that emulates the smoke of conventional cigarettes (Yamin, Bitton, & Bates, 2010). Although some posit that e-cigarettes may be a less harmful alternative to smoking (Farsalinos & Polosa, 2014), there is little research on their safety (Tremblay et al., 2015). What we do know is that nicotine and the aerosol created by e-cigarettes can include ingredients that are harmful, such as flavorings (e.g., diacetyl, a chemical linked to serious lung disease), heavy metals, and ultrafine particles that reach the lungs (Murthy, 2017; Office of the Surgeon General, 2016). One recent study found that adolescent e-cigarette users showed increased rates of chronic bronchitis symptoms (McConnell et al., 2017). In 2016, the federal government extended restrictions on tobacco production, advertising, and sale to include e-cigarettes; minors can no longer purchase e-cigarettes (U.S. Food and Drug Administration, 2016). Restricting minors' access to e-cigarettes may extend to other beneficial effects, as most adolescents who report e-cigarette use have used other tobacco products (Collins et al., 2017); therefore, adolescents who use e-cigarettes may be at risk for cigarette smoking (Barrington-Trimis et al., 2016; McCabe, West, Veliz, & Boyd, 2017).

Marijuana Use and Abuse

A particularly common substance used by young adults in the United States is marijuana, with 14% of 10th-grade and 23% of 12th-grade students, 20% of 18- to 25-year-old emerging adults, and 13% of 26- to 34-year-old young adults reporting use in the last month (Azofeifa et al., 2016; Miech et al., 2017). Young people consume marijuana for different reasons; those who cite experimentation as their primary reason tend to report fewer marijuana-related problems than do those who list coping, relaxation, and enjoyment (Lee, Neighbors, & Woods, 2007; Patrick, Bray, & Berglund, 2016). For most young people, marijuana use is sporadic and limited in duration, but regular sustained use is associated with current and future dependence and adverse health and social outcomes, including the use of other substances (Griffin, Bang, & Botvin, 2010; Palamar, Griffin-Tomas, & Kamboukos, 2015; Swift, Coffey, Carlin, Degenhardt, & Patton, 2008). In addition, marijuana smokers experience many of the same respiratory problems common to tobacco smokers, such as cough, more frequent chest illnesses, and cancers. Marijuana smoke contains irritants and carcinogens and appears to have 50% to 79% more carcinogens than tobacco smoke (Tashkin, 2013).

Sustained marijuana use is associated with self-reported cognitive difficulties and a variety of personal problems during the middle to late twenties, including lower levels

LIVES IN CONTEXT

• • Marijuana Legalization

Although many states have legalized marijuana, it remains illegal under federal law.

In response to anecdotal reports and some research suggesting that marijuana may be useful for easing symptoms of serious illnesses, such as cancer and AIDS, California passed Proposition 215 in 1996, legalizing marijuana sale and use for medical purposes. Yet despite Proposition 215, marijuana sale and possession remain federal offenses. The U.S. federal government does not distinguish medical marijuana from illicit marijuana. Although federal statutes have not changed, as of this writing, 29 states have legalized medical marijuana (National Conference of State Legislatures, 2017). Critics of medical marijuana argue that it has not been subjected to the careful scientific study and medical trials that other drugs are subjected to, and there are no reliable guidelines on use or implications of prolonged use (Martin, 2016; Monte, Zane, & Heard, 2015). In addition, since a common mode of ingesting marijuana remains smoking, users may be exposed to a variety of health threats common to cigarette smoke.

In 2012, Colorado and Washington became the first U.S. states to legalize the sale and possession of marijuana for recreational use, followed by Alaska, Oregon, and Washington, DC in 2014 and California, Maine, Massachusetts, and Nevada in 2016 (Steinmetz, 2016). Each regulates marijuana in a way similar to alcohol, allowing possession of a small quantity by adults aged 21 and older, with provisions against operating motor vehicles while under the influence. The laws allow for commercial cultivation and sale subject to state regulation and taxation. However, despite state legislation, marijuana remains illegal under federal statute. Yet in 2009, the Justice Department announced that the federal government would not prosecute medical marijuana

providers and consumers who were in compliance with state laws, and in 2013, the Justice Department announced that it would not interfere with the legalization laws in Washington and Colorado (Ammerman et al., 2015).

Supporters of legalized marijuana contend that taxes on the sale of marijuana can produce significant tax revenue. For example, Colorado's legal marijuana sales generated more than $135 million in revenue from taxes and fees that the state used for public projects such as school construction and renovation (Huddleston, 2016). At the same time, marijuana-related emergency room visits and hospitalizations, as well as poison center calls, increased about 1% per month over the first year of legalization (Davis et al., 2016). The number of children evaluated in the emergency department for unintentional marijuana ingestion has also increased substantially (Monte et al., 2015; Wang et al., 2016). Some experts expect heavy use to increase after recreational legalization (Hall & Lynskey, 2016).

One concern of marijuana legalization is the effect on children and adolescents. Although this area of research is somewhat new, some studies have suggested that medical marijuana laws are not associated with increases in recreational use by adolescents in states where medical marijuana is legal (Hasin et al., 2015; Pacula, Powell, Heaton, & Sevigny, 2015). A study of high school students in 14 states where medical marijuana is legal showed no increases in adolescent recreational marijuana use in all of the states but Delaware, and marijuana use declined in two states (Alaska and Montana; Ammerman et al., 2015). Comparisons of 10th-grade students in Washington from 2000 to 2014 found that the prevalence of adolescent use remained stable before and after the legalization of recreational marijuana (Fleming et al., 2016). However, across time, young people showed more risks for marijuana use and abuse, including more favorable attitudes about use, less perceived harm of use, and perceived community attitudes favorable to use. Likewise, Washington parents of adolescents reported increased parental use of marijuana and approval of adult use, as well as reductions in perceived harm after legalization of recreational use (Kosterman et al., 2016). Yet parents also showed wide opposition to marijuana use by adolescents and were opposed to allowing its use in the presence of children. Overall, high school students and their parents generally believe that their marijuana-related attitudes and behaviors changed little as a result of the law (Mason, Hanson, Fleming, Ringle, & Haggerty, 2015). The long-term effects of marijuana legislation, particularly for recreational use, have yet to be determined.

of academic attainment, lower income, greater unemployment, poor relationship satisfaction, conflict with partners, and poor life satisfaction (Conroy, Kurth, Brower, Strong, & Stein, 2015; Fergusson & Boden, 2008; Hall, 2014; Silins et al., 2014; Zhang, Brook, Leukefeld, & Brook, 2016). Regular marijuana use can interfere with completing developmental tasks of young adulthood, such as reaching education and career goals, forming intimate relationships and marriage, and taking on adult roles (Blair, 2010). Marijuana users tend to be less responsive to negative consequences in making decisions (Wesley, Hanlon, & Porrino, 2011). Heavy use of marijuana interferes with thinking, impairing a person's ability to shift attention from one item to another and to learn, form memories, and recall material (Bartholomew, Holroyd, & Heffernan, 2010; Crean, Crane, & Mason, 2011). Heavy marijuana use interferes with executive functioning (problem solving, abstract reasoning, and judgment), and the earlier the age of onset, the greater the negative effects (Crean et al., 2011; Gruber, Sagar, Dahlgren, Racine, & Lukas, 2011). Marijuana use in young adulthood may predict cognitive functioning later in life. One 25-year longitudinal study of more than 5,100 black and white U.S. adults found that current use of marijuana in middle age was associated with worse verbal memory and processing speed; cumulative lifetime exposure was associated with worse verbal memory, with differences for each 5 years of exposure (Auer et al., 2016).

Marijuana is addictive because when it is inhaled, the active ingredient, THC, passes from the lungs to the bloodstream to the brain and activates the brain's reward system. Marijuana is neurologically reinforcing, making the user crave the drug and have a hard time stopping. The usual effects of marijuana include euphoria, a feeling of well-being or elation. Time may seem to pass more slowly and sensations such as color and sound may seem more intense. Sometimes, however, a user may feel anxious, fearful, or distrustful instead of euphoric. THC binds to receptors in the cerebellum, which is responsible for balance, coordination of movement, and integration of thought, critical to executive functioning (Skosnik et al., 2008).

People who try to quit marijuana use report irritability, difficulty sleeping, and anxiety, similar to withdrawal from other substances such as tobacco. In psychological tests, people trying to quit show increased aggression, which peaks about a week after stopping the drug (National Institute on Drug Abuse, 2005). There has been little study of treatments for marijuana dependence because habitual marijuana abuse is very often accompanied by the abuse of alcohol and other drugs.

Although U.S. federal laws prohibit the sale and possession of marijuana, a growing number of countries, including Germany, the Netherlands, Australia, Spain, India, and Canada, have authorized its sale for medical and, increasingly, recreational purposes (Kalvapallé, 2017; Rodriguez, 2017). The issue of marijuana legalization in the United States is examined in the Lives in Context feature.

 Thinking in Context 5.2

1. How might adolescents' physical, cognitive, and social characteristics interact with their context to influence their likelihood of developing an eating disorder such as anorexia nervosa or bulimia nervosa? What roles can various contexts, such as home, peers, and school, play in influencing treatment options?

2. Are there dangers in taking the perspective that some alcohol and substance use is common and simply a part of growing up? How should parents, teachers, and professionals respond to adolescent alcohol and substance use?

3. Explain some of the reasons why substance use is highest in young adulthood. What contributes to its decline as adults grow older?

COMMON HEALTH ISSUES IN ADULTHOOD

LO 5.3 Identify common chronic diseases and sources of injury in adulthood, their risk factors, effects, and treatment.

Over the course of adulthood, the rate of chronic illnesses increases, as do doctor visits and hospital stays. Most adults view themselves as healthy (CDC, 2016; Federal Interagency Forum on Aging-Related Statistics, 2016); however, self-reports of health vary by contextual condition. For example, in nearly all countries of the world, self-reports of health and death rates vary by socioeconomic status. People of high socioeconomic status report better health than those of low socioeconomic status (Chen & Miller, 2013; Mackenbach et al., 2008; Mielck et al., 2014). Education is also positively associated with perceived health (CDC, 2016). The following sections highlight the leading health concerns of middle-aged and older adults. Note that, until recently, nearly all studies of health in adulthood were conducted on men, particularly Caucasian men. Women and minorities are underrepresented in research on prevention and treatment of illness. Researchers have only recently begun to address this deficit in our understanding of illness. The following sections describe what we know about common illnesses in adulthood, discussing sex and ethnic differences when possible.

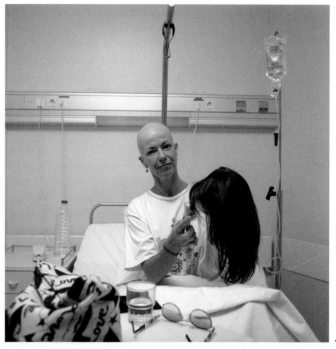

Cancer rates have declined over the last two decades and survival rates have risen to nearly three-quarters of diagnoses, but it remains the leading cause of mortality in middle age.

CANCER

Overall, cancer-related mortality has declined 25% since 1991, yet cancer remains the leading cause of death in adulthood (CDC, 2017; Siegel, Ma, Zou, & Jemal, 2014). The probability of invasive cancer increases with age: 1 in 5 for people aged 50 to 59; 1 in 7 for ages 60 to 69; and 1 in 3 at age 70 and older (Siegel, Miller, & Jemal, 2016). Overall, men tend to be diagnosed with cancer at a higher rate than women (Siegel et al., 2014). Sex differences in cancer are influenced by genetics and lifestyle factors such as workplace exposure to toxins, health-related behaviors such as smoking, and making fewer visits to the doctor. People of low SES tend to experience cancer at higher rates than do other adults, a difference attributable to a range of causes including inadequate access to medical care, poor diet, high levels of stress, and occupations that may place them in contact with toxins (Jemal et al., 2008; Kish, Yu, Percy-Laurry, & Altekruse, 2014; Vona-Davis & Rose, 2009).

What is cancer? Cancerous cells are abnormal cells. Everyone has some of these abnormal cells. Cancer occurs when the genetic program that controls cell growth is disrupted. As a result, abnormal cells reproduce rapidly and spread to normal tissues and organs and the person is diagnosed with cancer (Lin et al., 2007; Vogelstein & Kinzler, 2004). Whether an individual develops cancer is affected by a complex web of genetic and environmental influences.

Scientific breakthroughs have increased our knowledge of genetic risk factors for cancer. For example, women now can be tested for mutations in the genes responsible for suppressing the proliferation of breast cancer cells. Genetics, however, is not destiny. Only about 35% to 50% of women who test positive for the genetic mutation actually develop breast cancer. Those who do show more genetic mutations and tend to develop breast cancer especially early in life, often before age 30 (Stephens et al., 2012). Whether a genetic risk factor for breast cancer leads to developing breast cancer is influenced by the presence of environmental risk factors, such as heavy alcohol use, overweight, use of oral contraceptives, exposure to toxins, and low socioeconomic status (Khan, Afaq, & Mukhtar, 2010; Nickels et al., 2013). The biology of breast cancer is age dependent: early-onset breast cancer is qualitatively different than late-onset breast cancer. While early-onset breast cancers are largely inherited and are often invasive, spreading quickly, late-onset breast cancers tend to grow more slowly, are less biologically aggressive, and likely follow extended exposures to environmental stimuli as well as disruptions in cell division that occur with aging (Anderson, Rosenberg, Prat,

Perou, & Sherman, 2014; Benz, 2008). Although many people persist in the centuries-old belief that a diagnosis of cancer is a death sentence, today's medical advances permit more people to survive cancer than ever before. The survival rate for adults diagnosed with cancer, defined as surviving at least 5 years, and remission ("beating" cancer) varies by type of cancer.

DIABETES

After each meal we eat, the body digests and breaks down food, releasing glucose into the blood. Insulin, a hormone released by the pancreas, maintains a steady concentration of glucose in the blood and excess glucose is absorbed by muscle and fat. **Diabetes** is a disease marked by high levels of blood glucose. Diabetes occurs when the body is unable to regulate the amount of glucose in the bloodstream because there either is not enough insulin produced (Diabetes 1) or the body shows insulin resistance and becomes less sensitive to it, failing to respond to it (Diabetes 2; American Diabetes Association, 2014). Symptoms of diabetes include fatigue, great thirst, blurred vision, frequent infections and slow healing. When glucose levels become too low, hypoglycemia occurs with symptoms of confusion, nervousness, and fainting. Hyperglycemia is characterized by overly high glucose levels, also resulting in serious illness. Managing diabetes entails careful monitoring of the diet and often self-injection of insulin, which permits the body to process glucose, critical to body functioning.

About 16% of adults aged 45 to 64 have diabetes, rising to more than one-quarter of older adults over the age of 65 (CDC, 2014). Diabetes is the fifth leading cause of death among people aged 55 to 64 and sixth leading cause of death among people aged 45 to 54 and 65 and older (CDC, 2017; National Center for Health Statistics, 2015). African American, Mexican American, and Canadian Aboriginal people are diagnosed with diabetes at higher rates than European Americans because of genetic as well as contextual factors, such as the higher rates of obesity, poor health, and a sedentary lifestyle that accompanies poverty (American Diabetes Association, 2014; Best, Hayward, & Hidajat, 2005; Jeffreys et al., 2006). Being overweight at any point during life is associated with an increased risk of diabetes (Djoussé, Driver, Gaziano, Buring, & Lee, 2013; Jeffreys et al., 2006). Diabetes has a genetic component (Patel et al., 2016), but lifestyle choices such as diet and exercise are important risk factors that interact with genetic propensities to influence diabetes risk (Leong, Porneala, Dupuis, Florez, & Meigs, 2016; Scott et al., 2013); hence, many researchers emphasize the role of epigenetics in diabetes (Franks & Pare, 2016; Keating, Plutzky, & El-Osta, 2016).

People with diabetes are at risk for a variety of health problems. A high level of glucose in the bloodstream raises the risk of heart attack, stroke, circulation problems in the legs, blindness, and reduced kidney functions (DeFronzo & Abdul-Ghani, 2011). Although women are about as likely as men to be diagnosed with diabetes, for largely unknown reasons, women with diabetes experience a much larger risk of heart attack and stroke than men (Peters, Huxley, & Woodward, 2014). Diabetes has serious cognitive effects including declines in executive function, processing speed, memory, and motor function (Palta, Schneider, Biessels, Touradji, & Hill-Briggs, 2014). Over time, diabetes is associated with accelerated brain aging, including losses of gray matter, abnormalities in white matter, and a heightened risk of dementia and Alzheimer's disease in older adults (Espeland et al., 2013; R. O. Roberts et al., 2014; Vagelatos & Eslick, 2013).

Diabetes also influences psychosocial functioning. Depression is two to three times more common among people with diabetes compared to their peers and they are more likely to experience chronic depression with up to 80% of those treated for depression experiencing a relapse of depressive symptoms within a 5-year period (Park, Katon, & Wolf, 2013; Roy & Lloyd, 2012). Adults with depression are less likely to follow dietary restrictions, comply with medication, and monitor blood glucose—behaviors

diabetes A disease marked by high levels of blood glucose that occurs when the body is unable to regulate the amount of glucose in the bloodstream because there is not enough insulin produced (type 1 diabetes) or the body shows insulin resistance and becomes less sensitive to it, failing to respond to it (type 2 diabetes). Symptoms include fatigue, great thirst, blurred vision, frequent infections, and slow healing.

Lives in Context Video 5.1
Obesity Becomes a Disease

associated with worse outcomes, including increased risk of mortality (Park et al., 2013; van Dooren et al., 2013).

Maintaining a healthy weight through diet and exercise is a powerful way of preventing diabetes. Individuals can successfully manage the disease by adopting a diet that carefully controls the amount of sugar entering the bloodstream as well as engaging in regular exercise (American Diabetes Association, 2014; Jannasch, Kroger, & Schulze, 2017; Mavros et al., 2013). Frequent blood testing permits the individual to monitor his or her glucose levels and take insulin when needed to lower levels of glucose in the blood. Coping with diabetes requires a great deal of self-monitoring and self-care, but appropriate self-treatment enables adults to manage this chronic illness and live an active life.

CARDIOVASCULAR DISEASE

Cardiovascular disease, commonly referred to as **heart disease**, is responsible for more than one-quarter of all deaths of middle-aged Americans each year (National Center for Health Statistics, 2015). Markers of cardiovascular disease include high blood pressure, high blood cholesterol, plaque buildup in the arteries (atherosclerosis), irregular heartbeat, and, particularly serious, heart attack (blockage of blood flow to the heart caused by a blood clot occurring within a plaque-clogged coronary artery; Koh, Han, Oh, Shin, & Quon, 2010). Cardiovascular disease can also cause a stroke—a blockage of blood flow to brain cells, which can result in neurological damage, paralysis, and death. A stroke occurs when a blood clot, often originating in the coronary arteries, travels to the brain or when a clot forms in the brain itself.

Awareness of the symptoms of heart attack is critical to surviving it. About half of heart attack victims die before being admitted to a hospital (American Heart Association, 2008a). The most common symptom of heart attack is chest pain, uncomfortable pressure, squeezing, fullness, or pain in the chest that may come and go or last. Other symptoms include discomfort or pain in other areas of the upper body, especially the left arm, but also the back, neck, jaw, or stomach. Shortness of breath, nausea, or light-headedness can also occur. Cardiovascular disease has been traditionally viewed as an illness affecting men, as men are more likely to be diagnosed with cardiovascular disease.

However, women are more likely than men to die from cardiovascular disease, especially heart attack (Flink, Sciacca, Bier, Rodriguez, & Giardina, 2013). Many people are unaware that women tend to show different symptoms of heart attack (Kirchberger, Heier, Kuch, Wende, & Meisinger, 2011). The most common symptom experienced by women is shortness of breath and only about one-third report chest pain, the hallmark symptom in men (McSweeney Cody, O'Sullivan, Elberson, Moser, & Garvin, 2003). When they do, women are more likely to describe it as pressure or tightness than pain. Women are more likely than men to report pain in the left shoulder or arm, pain in the throat or jaw, pain in the upper abdomen, pain between the shoulder blades, nausea, dizziness, and vomiting (Kirchberger, Heier, Kuch, Wende, & Meisinger, 2011). Because of these differences, many women do not recognize their symptoms as severe and life threatening (Madsen & Birkelund, 2016).

Risk factors for cardiovascular disease include heredity, age, a diet heavy in saturated fats and trans fatty acids, and smoking (Go et al., 2013). One important risk factor, hypertension, has increased rapidly in the last two decades to account for more than one-third of cardiovascular disease in U.S. adults aged 45 to 59 (Egan, Zhao, & Axon, 2010). By 2030, 41% of the U.S. population is projected to have some form of cardiovascular disease (Heidenreich et al., 2011). Hypertension is a global problem responsible for about 13% of all deaths in the world each year (World Health Organization, 2015). Anxiety, psychological stress, and a poor diet have negative effects on the heart and contribute to

canstock/Farina5000

About one quarter of older adults suffer from diabetes with increased risks for health and cognitive problems. Managing diabetes entails careful monitoring of the diet and often self-injection of insulin to regulate levels of glucose in the body.

cardiovascular disease (heart disease) A disease marked by high blood pressure, high blood cholesterol, plaque buildup in the arteries, irregular heartbeat, and possible heart attack.

hypertension and cardiovascular disease (Backé, Seidler, Latza, Rossnagel, & Schumann, 2012; Holt et al., 2013).

Treatment for cardiovascular disease varies depending on the severity. Medication and behavioral changes, such as increasing physical activity, changing diet, and consuming more fish oil, may reduce hypertension and cholesterol levels (Harris et al., 2008; Koh et al., 2010). In serious cases, a health care provider may recommend coronary bypass surgery, in which damaged coronary blood vessels are replaced with those from the leg, and angioplasty, in which a needle is threaded through the arteries and a tiny balloon is inflated to flatten plaque deposits against the arterial walls and enable blood to flow unobstructed. During angioplasty, a coronary stent is often inserted to help keep the artery open.

OSTEOPOROSIS

In middle adulthood, women undergo hormonal changes accompanying menopause. These changes are associated with bone loss, increasing women's risk for **osteoporosis**, a disorder characterized by severe bone loss resulting in brittle and easily fractured bones (Siris et al., 2014; Walker, 2008). We tend to think of our bones as static and unchanging—almost like sticks of concrete—but the skeleton is actually a dynamic organ made of living cells that continually dissolve and regenerate. In the first 10 years after menopause, women typically lose about 25% of their bone mass, largely due to menopausal declines in estrogen; this loss increases to about 50% by late adulthood (Avis, Brockwell, & Colvin, 2005; Vondracek, 2010). Men experience a more gradual and less extreme loss of bone because age-related decreases in testosterone, which their bodies convert to estrogen, occur slowly, and therefore the loss of bone mass that occurs with declines in estrogen occurs gradually over the adult years (Avis & Crawford, 2006; Walker, 2008). About half of U.S. adults are affected by osteoporosis (10 million people) or low bone mass (Wright et al., 2014); these conditions can be identified through a routine, noninvasive bone scan. Most people—men and women—are diagnosed with osteoporosis only after experiencing bone fractures, but one out of every two women and one in four men over 50 will have an osteoporosis-related fracture in their lifetime (NIH Osteoporosis and Related Bone Diseases National Resource Center, 2007). Men at risk for osteoporosis are those with low body mass and the very old. Because women are more widely known to be at risk, however, men often go undiagnosed and untreated (Liu et al., 2008).

osteoporosis A condition characterized by severe loss of bone mass, leading to increased risk of fractures.

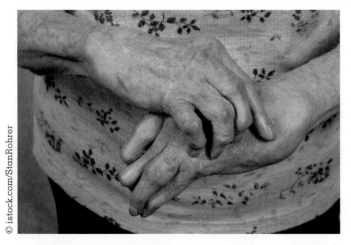

Osteoarthritis, a degenerative joint disease, often occurs in the hands, knees, and hips.

Heredity and lifestyle contribute to the risk of osteoporosis. For example, at least 15 genes contribute to osteoporosis susceptibility (Li et al., 2010). Identical twins are more likely to share a diagnosis of osteoporosis than are fraternal twins (Andersen, 2007). Thin, small-framed women tend to attain a lower peak bone mass than do other women, and are at relatively higher risk of osteoporosis. Other risk factors include a sedentary lifestyle, calcium deficiency, cigarette smoking and heavy alcohol consumption (Bleicher et al., 2011; Nachtigall, Nazem, Nachtigall, & Goldstein, 2013).

The risk of osteoporosis can be reduced by encouraging individuals to maximize their bone density by consuming a diet rich in calcium and vitamin D and engaging in regular exercise from childhood into emerging adulthood, when bone reaches its peak density (Nachtigall et al., 2013; Weaver et al., 2016).

These same guidelines, specifically having a bone-healthy lifestyle by consuming a diet rich in calcium and vitamin D, avoiding smoking and heavy drinking, and engaging in moderate alcohol consumption and weight-bearing exercise, can offset bone loss in post-menopausal women (Bleicher et al., 2011; Cosman et al., 2014). Medication can increase the absorption of calcium and slow the bone loss associated with osteoporosis in middle and late adulthood (Vondracek, 2010).

Lives in Context Video 5.2
Managing a Chronic Illness

ARTHRITIS

One illness that goes hand in hand with aging is arthritis, a degenerative joint disease. There are more than 100 different types of arthritis; the most common is **osteoarthritis**, which affects joints that are injured by overuse, most commonly the hips, knees, lower back, and hands. The cartilage that protects the ends of bones where they meet at joints wears away and joints become less flexible and swell. Those who suffer from osteoarthritis experience a loss of movement and a great deal of pain. Aging is the most prominent risk factor for osteoarthritis; it often first appears in middle adulthood, occurring in about one-third of adults ages 45 to 64, but becomes more common and worsens in severity during older adulthood (Aigner, Haag, Martin, & Buckwalter, 2007; Cooper, Javaid, & Arden, 2014). About half of adults aged 65 or older report a diagnosis of arthritis, and it is likely that many more cases remain undiagnosed (National Center for Chronic Disease Prevention and Health Promotion, 2010). Nearly all older adults show at least some signs of osteoarthritis, but there are great individual differences. People whose job or leisure activities rely on repetitive movements are most likely to experience osteoarthritis. Office workers who type every day, for example, might experience osteoarthritis in their hands. Runners might experience it in their knees. Obesity can also be a cause as it places abnormal pressure on joints.

A second common type of arthritis, rheumatoid arthritis, is not age- or use-related. Rheumatoid arthritis is an autoimmune illness in which the connective tissues, the membranes that line the joints, become inflamed and stiff. They thicken and release enzymes that digest bone and cartilage, often causing the affected joint to lose its shape and alignment. Most people are diagnosed with rheumatoid arthritis between ages 20 and 50 and the prevalence increases with age (Lindstrom & Robinson, 2010). Older adults with rheumatoid arthritis often have lived with a painful chronic illness for many years and likely experience multiple physical disabilities.

Arthritis is a chronic disease because it is managed, not cured. When inflammation flares, more rest is needed as well as pain relief. However, instead of uninterrupted rest, it is best to deal with an arthritis flare-up with some activities or exercises to help the muscles maintain flexibility, known as range of motion. People whose osteoarthritis is related to obesity may experience some relief with weight loss. In some cases, a synthetic material can be injected into a joint to provide more cushioning and improve movement; or a severely affected joint, such as the hip or knee, can be surgically replaced. Joint replacement surgery has become increasingly common in recent decades.

Because adults with arthritis live with chronic pain and reduced ability to engage in activities, they are often at risk for depression (Lin, 2008; Margaretten, Katz, Schmajuk, & Yelin, 2013). In one study, more than one-third of a sample of Latino adults with arthritis experienced depression (Withers, Moran, Nicassio, Weisman, & Karpouzas, 2015). Although arthritis-related stressors are the predominant factors affecting well-being for European American women with arthritis, well-being in African Americans with arthritis is also closely tied to broader life contextual stressors (McIlvane, Baker, & Mingo, 2008). African American patients with rheumatoid arthritis are less likely to receive medication and seek care from a specialist (Solomon et al., 2012). Low SES is associated with a delay in seeking care, greater arthritis-related symptoms, poorer well-being and greater use of maladaptive coping strategies among African Americans,

osteoarthritis The most common type of arthritis; it affects joints that are injured by overuse, most commonly the hips, knees, lower back, and hands, in which the cartilage protecting the ends of the bones where they meet at the joints wears away, and joints become less flexible and swell.

yet socioeconomic status does not predict depressive symptoms and coping among European Americans diagnosed with arthritis (McIlvane, 2007; Molina, del Rincon, Restrepo, Battafarano, & Escalante, 2015).

INJURIES

Although injury-related fatalities are high in adolescence and emerging adulthood (58.6 deaths per 100,000), deaths from unintentional injuries are even more common in later adulthood. They account for 61.5 deaths per 100,000 in 65-year-old adults and a striking 361.9 deaths per 100,000 in adults age 85 and older—about six times the rate in emerging adulthood (see Figure 5.7; U.S. Department of Health and Human Services, 2015). Such injuries arise from a variety of causes, including motor vehicle accidents and falls.

Motor Vehicle Accidents

Driving a car represents autonomy. Many older adults continue to drive as long as they are able to because driving provides a sense of control and freedom. As the Baby Boom generation ages, older adults are more likely to keep their driver's licenses, make up a larger proportion of the driving population, and drive more miles than ever before. The proportion of the 70-and-older drivers increased by one third between 1997 and 2012, as have the typical miles traveled (Insurance Institute for Highway Safety, 2015). Accidents involving older drivers, both nonfatal and fatal, have declined over the last two decades, but there remain predictable age-related increases in accidents in older adulthood. Per mile traveled, crash rates and fatal crash rates also start increasing when the driver reaches age 70 (see Figure 5.8).

Compared with younger drivers, senior drivers are more likely to be involved in collisions in intersections, when merging into traffic, and switching lanes (Cicchino & McCartt, 2015). Although they drive more slowly and carefully than young adults, older adults are more likely to miss traffic signs, make inappropriate turns, fail to yield the right of way, and show slower reaction time—all risks to safe driving. Declines in vision account for much of the decline in older adults' driving performance (Owsley, McGwin, Jackson, Kallies, & Clark, 2007). They are likely to have difficulty with night vision and reading the dashboard. Changes in working memory and attention also account for some of the problems in older adults' driving competence. Many older adults appear to adapt to these changes, naturally reducing their driving as they notice that their vision and reaction time are less acute (see Figure 5.9). In this way they may, at least partially, compensate for

FIGURE 5.7: Fatal Injury Rate by Age in the United States, 2013

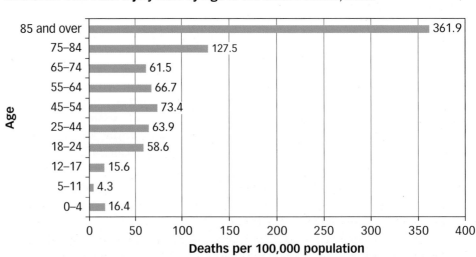

Source: Data from Healthy People 2020.

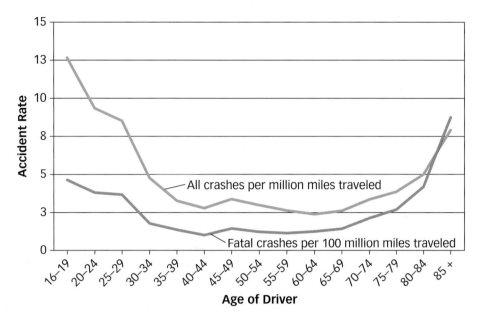

Source: Insurance Institute for Highway Safety (2015).

their higher risk for motor vehicle accidents (Festa, Ott, Manning, Davis, & Heindel, 2013; Sandlin, McGwin, & Owsley, 2014).

Falls

More than one-quarter of U.S. adults over the age of 65 fall each year (Crews, Chou, Stevens, & Saaddine, 2016) including about half of those over the age of 80 (Hosseini & Hosseini, 2008). Many aspects of aging increase the risk of falls, including changes in vision, hearing, motor skills and neuromuscular control, and cognition (Dhital, Pey, & Stanford, 2010). Older adults are less able than their younger counterparts to balance and regulate body sway (Johansson, Nordstrom, Gustafson, Westling, & Nordstrom, 2017; Lee & Chou, 2007), have reduced muscular density (i.e., strength; Frank-Wilson et al., 2016), and are less adept at navigating and avoiding obstacles (Weerdesteyn, Nienhuis, Geurts, & Duysens, 2007). Declines in cognition, particularly in executive functioning and processing speed, also increase the risk of falls (Mirelman et al., 2012; Welmer, Rizzuto, Laukka, Johnell, & Fratiglioni, 2016).

FIGURE 5.9: Older Adult Drivers Who Tend to Avoid Driving Under Specific Conditions by Gender, 2015

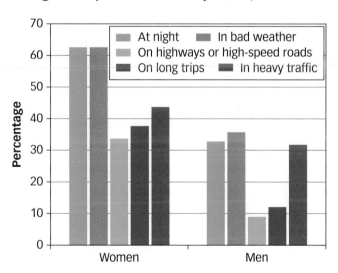

Source: CDC (2015).

Falls are a serious hazard for older adults because the natural loss of bone and high prevalence of osteoporosis increase the risk of bone fractures, especially a fractured hip. Hip fractures are particularly dangerous as they immobilize an older adult, are painful, and take a great deal of time to heal. Following hip fracture, many elderly adults lose the capacity for independent living, and up to 25% die as a result of complications, such as infection, within a year after the fall (Panula et al., 2011).

After experiencing a fall, at least half of older adults report fear of falling (Visschedijk, Achterberg, van Balen, & Hertogh, 2010). Adults who fear falling tend to become more cautious, avoiding activities that pose a risk of falling, but also limiting opportunities for physical activities that support physical health, retention of mobility, psychological well-being, and social connections (Visschedijk et al., 2010). There are a variety of ways to prevent falls and help older adults become more confident about their mobility. Exercise programs such as Tai Chi and strength and agility training can improve older adults' strength, balance, and confidence (Kaniewski, Stevens, Parker, & Lee, 2015). Environmental modifications such as addressing slippery floors, installing handrails on steps, and equipping shower/bath facilities with grip bars can also help to prevent falls.

 Thinking in Context 5.3

Recall from Chapter 1 that development is multidimensional; we develop in many different ways. In addition, changes in one area of development hold implications for other areas of functioning. Consider this principle with regard to health issues and disease in adulthood. How might chronic illnesses in adulthood, such diabetes or arthritis, influence cognitive and socioemotional development? How might these changes influence individuals' interactions in all of the contexts in which they are embedded?

DEMENTIA IN OLDER ADULTHOOD

LO 5.4 Distinguish among common dementias, their risk factors, effects, and treatment.

We saw in Chapter 4 that some loss of neural connections is part of normal aging and does not prevent older adults from engaging in everyday activities. Some older adults, however, experience the high rates of cell death and severe brain deterioration that characterize dementia. **Dementia** refers to a progressive deterioration in mental abilities due to changes in the brain that influence higher cortical functions such as thinking, memory, comprehension, and emotional control, and are reflected in impaired thought and behavior, interfering with the older adult's capacity to engage in everyday activities (McKhann et al., 2011; World Health Organization, 2012). Given that dementia can take many forms, with similar and different neurological features, the most recent version of the *Diagnostic and Statistical Manual of Mental Disorders* (DSM-5) has replaced the term *dementia* with *neurocognitive disorder* (American Psychiatric Association, 2013). Throughout our discussion we will use the more commonly used term, *dementia*.

In 2013, there were 44.4 million people with dementia worldwide. This number is predicted to increase to an estimated 75.6 million in 2030, and 135.5 million in 2050 (Alzheimer's Disease International, 2015). Much of the increase will be in developing countries, as shown in Figure 5.10. Worldwide, currently 62% of people with dementia live in developing countries; by 2050 this will rise to 71%. The fastest growth in the elderly population is taking place in China, India, and their south Asian and western Pacific neighbors (Alzheimer's Disease International, 2015).

The most common cause of dementia is Alzheimer's disease, followed by vascular dementia. Dementia, even in its very early stages, is associated with higher rates of mortality (Andersen, Lolk, Martinussen, & Kragh-Sørensen, 2010). Frequently these forms of dementia co-occur; adults may suffer from more than one form of dementia (Corriveau et al., 2016; Iadecola, 2013). The most common forms of dementia are discussed in the following sections.

ALZHEIMER'S DISEASE

Alzheimer's disease is a neurodegenerative disorder that progresses from general cognitive decline to include personality and behavior changes, motor complications, severe dementia, and death (Bradley-Whitman & Lovell, 2013; Finder, 2011). The risk of

dementia A progressive deterioration in mental abilities due to changes in the brain that influence higher cortical functions such as thinking, memory, comprehension, and emotional control and are reflected in impaired thought and behavior, interfering with the adult's ability to engage in everyday activities.

Alzheimer's disease A neurodegenerative disorder characterized by dementia, the deterioration of memory and personality, and marked by the presence of amyloid plaques and neurofibrillary tangles in the cerebral cortex.

Alzheimer's disease grows exponentially with age, doubling approximately every 5 to 6 years in most Western countries (see Figure 5.10; Ziegler-Graham, Brookmeyer, Johnson, & Arrighi, 2008). Currently 5.5 million Americans, including 1 in 9 people over the age of 65, have Alzheimer's disease (Alzheimer's Association, 2017). Of those with Alzheimer's disease, an estimated 4% are under age 65, 16% are 65 to 74, 44% are 75 to 84, and 38% are 85 or older.

Alzheimer's disease is characterized by widespread brain deterioration associated with inflammation and accumulations of *beta-amyloid*, a protein present in the tissue that surrounds neurons in the healthy brain (Vinters, 2015). Alzheimer's patients experience inflammation that causes the beta-amyloid to accumulate and join with clumps of dead neurons and glial cells, forming large masses called **amyloid plaques** (Finder, 2011; Perl, 2010). It is thought that amyloid plaques disrupt the structure and function of cell membranes (Yang, Askarova, & Lee, 2010), and contribute to the formation of **neurofibrillary tangles**, twisted bundles of threads of a protein called *tau* that occur when neurons collapse (Blurton-Jones & LaFerla, 2006; Takahashi, Nagao, & Gouras, 2017). Even healthy brains have some tangles, but in cases of Alzheimer's there is inflammation and a proliferation of plaques and tangles, as well as a progressive loss of neurons that interfere with brain functioning (Vasto et al., 2008). As neurons die, brain functioning declines. Alzheimer's disease is associated with altered neurogenesis in the hippocampus, impairing the generation and development of new neurons (Grote & Hannan, 2007; Mu & Gage, 2011).

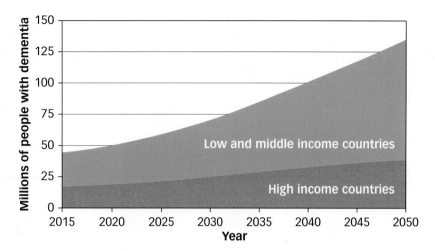

FIGURE 5.10: Projected Growth in Dementia Prevalence: Low-Income vs. High Income Countries, 2015–2050 (Projected)

https://www.alz.co.uk/research/statistics

Source: World Alzheimer Report 2015

Diagnosis of Alzheimer's Disease

Because the characteristic beta-amyloid plaques can only be assessed in a postmortem examination of brain tissue, Alzheimer's disease is generally diagnosed in living patients through exclusion: by ruling out all other causes of dementia (Rektorova, Rusina, Hort, & Matej, 2009). Symptoms, a medical history, comprehensive set of neurological and cognitive tests, and conversations with the adult and family members can provide useful information about a person's level of functioning (Guarch, Marcos, Salamero, Gastó, & Blesa, 2008). Brain imaging can help physicians rule out other, potentially treatable, causes of dementia, such as a tumor or stroke (Hort, O'Brien, et al., 2010).

Advances in brain imaging techniques offer opportunities to diagnose Alzheimer's by studying changes in brain volume and activity. Research with animals has suggested that modified MRI scans can capture images of plaques and tangles (Marcus, 2008). Other research points to the search for biomarkers, genetic or biological traces, of the disease (Castro-Chavira, Fernandez, Nicolini, Diaz-Cintra, & Prado-Alcala, 2015; Fletcher et al., 2013). For example, cerebrospinal fluid concentrations of beta-amyloid appear to serve as biomarkers for Alzheimer's (Kang et al., 2015; Olsson et al., 2016; Smach et al., 2009). These biomarkers are used in clinical diagnosing Alzheimer's disease in Europe; however, countries vary in the cut-off values used to diagnose Alzheimer's (Hort, Bartos, Pirttilä, & Scheltens, 2010). Searching for biomarkers is not part of a routine diagnosis in North America, researchers have concluded that such markers have promise but have not

amyloid plaque Found in the brains of patients with Alzheimer's disease, deposits of beta-amyloid accumulate along with clumps of dead neurons and glial cells.

neurofibrillary tangle A twisted bundle of threads of a protein called tau that occur in the brain when neurons collapse; found in individuals with Alzheimer's disease.

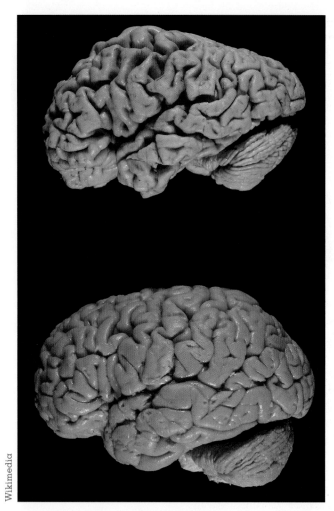

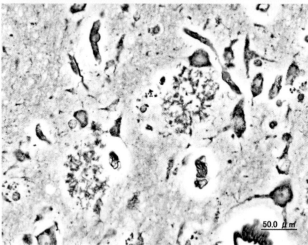

Alzheimer's disease entails a wasting of the brain, as illustrated by the decreased size in the diseased brain (top) as compared with the healthy brain (middle). Alzheimer's disease is characterized by the presence of plaques (bottom) that damage neurons and disrupt functioning.

yet determined how to use them to diagnose individuals (Blennow, Mattsson, Schöll, Hansson, & Zetterberg, 2015; Rosén, Hansson, Blennow, & Zetterberg, 2013).

Progression of Alzheimer's Disease

Alzheimer's disease progresses through several predictable steps, including specific patterns of cognitive and memory loss. The earliest symptoms of Alzheimer's disease are memory problems, likely because the neurological disruptions that comprise Alzheimer's disease usually begin in the hippocampus, which is influential in memory (Grote & Hannan, 2007). First, the older adult experiences impairments in memory that are usually attributed to absentmindedness (Bäckman, 2008). The person may forget the names of new people, recent events, appointments, and tasks such as taking a tea kettle off of the stove or turning off the iron. Memory deficits are soon accompanied by impaired attentional control, which, to an outside observer, may appear as further absentmindedness and inattention, being "lost" in one's own world (Storandt, 2008). Early Alzheimer's disease can be hard to distinguish from normal aging—or at least popular views and stereotypes of aging.

Over time, the cognitive impairments broaden to include severe problems with concentration coupled with more severe memory problems. Older adults may set the TV remote control down and, a moment later, be unable to find it. The person may ask the same question repeatedly, forgetting that an answer has just been given moments earlier. As memory problems increase, the Alzheimer's patient is frequently confused (Carson, Vanderhorst, & Koenig, 2015). The older adult's vocabulary becomes more limited as he or she is likely to forget or mix up words. Speech becomes more long-winded and tangential. Communication skills deteriorate and the person sometimes becomes unpredictably angry or paranoid (Carson et al., 2015). Some adults may show unpredictable aggressive outbursts (Agronin, 2014). Others may become more withdrawn. Personality changes are common. People who are naturally suspicious may become more so, deciding that they are not simply forgetting the location of items but that others are deceiving them (Verkaik, Nuyen, Schellevis, & Francke, 2007).

Up to 50% of Alzheimer's patients experience depression or depressive symptoms (Chi, Yu, Tan, & Tan, 2014; Starkstein, Jorge, Mizrahi, & Robinson, 2005). Some researchers believe that depression may occur prior to and increase risk for Alzheimer's disease, but the mechanism is not clear (Herbert & Lucassen, 2016). Depression is particularly harmful to Alzheimer's patients as it is associated with greater cognitive and behavioral impairment, disability in activities of daily living, and a faster cognitive decline (Spalletta et al., 2012; Starkstein, Mizrahi, & Power, 2008; Van der Mussele et al., 2013). A predictable routine filled with activities that are enjoyed can provide structure to aid adults who are sometimes confused about their surroundings. In addition to antidepressants, some patients' depressive symptoms improve with the use of anti-dementia medication, commonly prescribed drugs that improve memory by increasing the chemical activity in various parts of the brain (Chi et al., 2014).

As the disease progresses patients become unable to care for themselves. They may forget to eat, to dress themselves properly for the weather, or how to get back inside their home after they step outside—for example, to bring in the mail or daily newspaper. Eventually, the

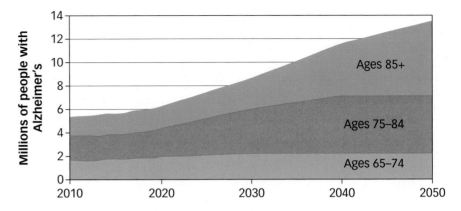

FIGURE 5.11: Projected Prevalence of Alzheimer's Disease in the U.S. Population, 2010–2050 (Projected)

Source: Alzheimer's Association (2015).

brain will fail to process information, no longer recognizing objects and familiar people. A woman may insist on seeing her daughter and not realize that the woman in front of her is her daughter. In the final stages of the disease, Alzheimer's patients lose the ability to comprehend and produce speech, to control bodily functions, and to respond to stimuli (Carson et al., 2015). They show heightened vulnerability to infections and illnesses that often lead to death. Eventually, brain functions deteriorate to the point where organs fail and life cannot be sustained. The average patient progresses to the final stage of Alzheimer's disease over the course of about 10 years, with a typical range of 7 to 15 years (Rektorova et al., 2009).

Risk Factors for Alzheimer's Disease

A person's risk for developing Alzheimer's disease varies with gender, age, and ethnicity. Women are at greater risk than men, perhaps because of their longer lifespans (Kirbach & Mintzer, 2008). In the United States, African Americans and Hispanic older adults are disproportionately more likely to have Alzheimer's disease and other dementias than their European American counterparts (Alzheimer's Association, 2015). The Cultural Influences on Development feature explores this question.

Alzheimer's disease has genetic influences and often runs in families (Bettens, Sleegers, & Van Broeckhoven, 2013; Lambert et al., 2011). Several chromosomes are implicated, including the 21st chromosome. Individuals with Down syndrome are at high risk to develop Alzheimer's disease as many show plaques and tangles in their brains as early as age 40 (Lemere, 2013; Wiseman et al., 2015). Contextual and lifestyle factors also matter. Research suggests that the same factors that contribute to cardiovascular risk, such as high blood pressure and obesity, also heighten the risk for Alzheimer's disease (Knopman & Roberts, 2010; J.-Q. Li et al., 2016; Tosto et al., 2016). Although vitamins such as Vitamin B and E and folate were once thought to reduce the incidence of Alzheimer's, research is mixed (Daviglus et al., 2010; Douaud et al., 2013) and some researchers caution that there are no known nutritional recommendations for preventing Alzheimer's disease (von Arnim, Gola, & Biesalski, 2010).

Education acts as an important protective factor against Alzheimer's disease. The process of learning that accompanies higher education and occupational complexity promotes neural activity and increases connections among neurons, thickening the cortex and boosting cognitive reserve (Boots et al., 2015; Liu et al., 2012; Sattler, Toro, Schönknecht, & Schröder, 2012). Cognitive reserves can protect patients from the handicapping effects of brain atrophy and synaptic loss (Stern, 2012; Xu, Yu, Tan, & Tan, 2015). One recent study

• • Ethnicity and Alzheimer's Disease

Trust in one's medical doctor often determines whether an adult will report symptoms of dementia.

Alzheimer's disease knows no bounds. It is diagnosed in adults around the world, but ethnic differences appear in rates of diagnoses. For example, African Americans are twice as likely, and Hispanic populations 1.5 times as likely, to be diagnosed with Alzheimer's as non-Hispanic whites (Mayeda, Glymour, Quesenberry, & Whitmer, 2016; Mehta & Yeo, 2017).

There is a genetic component to Alzheimer's, but genetics is not thought to influence ethnic differences in rates of diagnoses (Raj et al., 2017). Instead, social and cultural factors are found to play a large role in ethnic differences in Alzheimer's and other dementias. High blood pressure, diabetes, and cardiovascular disease—risk factors for many dementias—are more common among African American and Hispanic groups. These chronic diseases have a large lifestyle component and are influenced by diet, which often varies dramatically across cultural groups. Differences in educational attainment may also influence risk for Alzheimer's. One study of African American, Latino, and non-Latino white adults found that level of education

was strongly associated with rates of dementia and, when age and education were taken into account, ethnic differences in rates of Alzheimer's were no longer consistent (Gurland et al., 1999). Differences in education and socioeconomic status, important contextual factors that influence access to opportunities, may account for some of the ethnic differences in susceptibility to Alzheimer's (Manly, 2006).

Other contextual factors that contribute to Alzheimer's include cultural beliefs about aging, spirituality, and views of the medical profession. African Americans are more likely than white adults to express beliefs that Alzheimer's symptoms, such as substantial memory loss, are just a normal part of aging (Connell, Scott Roberts, McLaughlin, & Akinleye, 2009; J. S. Roberts et al., 2003). Differences in knowledge about normative aging and Alzheimer's may partially explain why African Americans often receive delayed care for dementia (Chin, Negash, & Hamilton, 2011). Religious and spiritual beliefs may also influence views of Alzheimer's. One study found that a larger proportion of African Americans indicated that they believed "God's will" determined who developed Alzheimer's (Connell et al., 2009). Patients may question the efficacy of medicines in treating a disease that stems from a spiritual cause or may resist acting in opposition to a divine plan. In this way, religion and spirituality may play a strong role in the health of African Americans (Chin et al., 2011).

Finally, individuals from minority communities may be distrustful of the medical establishment. Discrimination, including historic events in which minority groups have been denied equal medical treatment, influences individuals' views of the health care system and doctors. Whether or not a patient trusts his or her doctor may determine whether or not he or she will report symptoms of dementia. An understanding of these cultural and contextual influences can help those who work with older adults to be more effective in identifying symptoms of Alzheimer's disease.

showed that patients with higher levels of education showed similar cognitive functioning to those with lower levels of education despite demonstrating more severe neurofibrillary tangles, suggesting that their greater cognitive reserve buffered against losses (Hoenig et al., 2017). Conversely, low socioeconomic status predicts mortality in adults diagnosed with dementia, likely due to the limited access to health care and social resources that promote cognitive reserve (van de Vorst, Koek, Stein, Bots, & Vaartjes, 2016).

It is not simply education that buffers against losses. People who remain socially and physically active show a lower risk of Alzheimer's as well because such activities stimulate and improve blood flow to the brain and increase synaptic connections (Gallaway et al., 2017; Tan et al., 2016). One recent study showed that mice who voluntarily engage in regular running showed reductions in the neurological hallmarks of Alzheimer's, as well as reduced neuronal loss, increased hippocampal neurogenesis, and reduced spatial memory loss (Tapia-Rojas, Aranguiz, Varela-Nallar, & Inestrosa, 2016). Regular physical exercise may not only prevent but reverse neural damage.

VASCULAR DEMENTIA

Vascular dementia, also known as *multi-infarct dementia,* is the second most common form of dementia and loss of mental ability in older adulthood, worldwide (Jiwa, Garrard, & Hainsworth, 2010). Vascular dementia is caused by strokes, or blockages of blood vessels in the brain (Iadecola, 2013). Typically these strokes are very small and unnoticeable to the victim and those around him or her. With each small stroke, brain cells die and an immediate loss of mental functioning occurs. For example, over the last few months Joan had been feeling more scattered. Her daughter noticed that she had some memory lapses such as failing to pay bills and leaving the stove on. One day Joan woke from her nap to find that her arm felt heavy and weak. She called to her daughter, who noticed that Joan's speech was slurred and she seemed especially confused. A visit to the hospital confirmed that Joan had suffered a small stroke. The doctor noted that Joan likely suffered several small strokes over the last few months and that the deficits slowly accumulated. It was only after the most recent stroke that Joan noticed the changes.

Whereas individuals with Alzheimer's disease show slow and steady decrements in mental abilities, those with vascular dementia, like Joan, tend to show sudden, but often mild, losses with each stroke (Kalaria, 2016; Korczyn, Vakhapova, & Grinberg, 2012; Raz, Rodrigue, Kennedy, & Acker, 2007). As time passes, individuals tend to show improvement because the brain's plasticity leads other neurons to take on functions of those that were lost. Additional strokes usually follow, however, and with each stroke brain matter is lost and it becomes harder for the remaining neurons to compensate for losses (Troncoso et al., 2008). As vascular dementia worsens, the symptoms are similar to those of Alzheimer's disease (Korczyn et al., 2012; O'Brien & Thomas, 2015). However, vascular dementia is neurologically different from Alzheimer's disease. Postmortem analyses of the brains of people with vascular dementia show substantial deterioration of areas of the brain and disruptions in white matter (Iadecola, 2013), but not the widespread abundance of plaques and tangles that accompany Alzheimer's disease (Salmon & Bondi, 2009).

Like many disorders, vascular dementia is influenced by both genetic and environmental factors (Schmidt, Freudenberger, Seiler, & Schmidt, 2012; Srinivasan, Braidy, Chan, Xu, & Chan, 2016; Sun et al., 2015). Genetics may influence factors that are known to be linked with vascular dementia, such as obesity, diabetes, and cardiovascular disease. Cardiovascular disease significantly increases the risk of vascular dementia (Lee et al., 2002; Sharp, Aarsland, Day, Sønnesyn, & Ballard, 2011). Men are more likely to suffer early vascular dementia in their 60s than are women because of their heightened vulnerability to cardiovascular disease. Behavioral influences on vascular dementia, such as heavy alcohol use, smoking, inactivity, stress, and poor diet, are more prevalent in men (Andel et al., 2012; Seshadri & Wolf, 2007).

There are also cross-cultural differences in the prevalence of vascular dementia, likely influenced by cultural and socioeconomic factors such as diet and activity patterns. In Europe and North America, vascular dementia constitutes only about 20% of dementia cases (Kalaria et al., 2008; Plassman et al., 2007), but it is the most common form of dementia in Asia (Jhoo et al., 2008; Kalaria et al., 2008). In recent decades, however, the prevalence of vascular dementia in Japan has shifted to the second most common cause of dementia, behind Alzheimer's (Catindig, Venketasubramanian, Ikram, & Chen, 2012). The shift may be attributable to changes in lifestyle, such as diet and accompanying declines in hypertension, that reduce the risk of vascular dementia. Alternatively, increased life expectancy and Westernization of lifestyle, including diet, might have contributed the increased prevalence of Alzheimer's disease, thereby making vascular dementia the second most common form of dementia (Rizzi, Rosset, & Roriz-Cruz, 2014).

Factors that prevent cardiovascular disease, such as physical activity, can also prevent or slow the progression of vascular dementia (Aarsland, Sardahaee, Anderssen, & Ballard, 2010; Gallaway et al., 2017; Verdelho et al., 2012). Thus, prevention and management

vascular dementia
Neurocognitive disorder in which sporadic and progressive losses occur, caused by small blockages of blood vessels in the brain.

of vascular risks may be the best weapon in a fight against age-related cognitive decline (Chertkow, 2008; Corriveau et al., 2016; Raz et al., 2007). In addition, when symptoms of stroke arise such as sudden vision loss, weakening or numbness in part of the body, or problems producing or understanding speech, anti-clotting drugs can prevent the blood from clotting and forming additional strokes.

PARKINSON'S DISEASE

Some dementias first damage the subcortical parts of the brain, areas below the cortex. These dementias are characterized by a progressive loss of motor control. Because the damage occurs first in the subcortical areas of the brain, mental abilities that are controlled by the cortex are not initially affected. As the disease progresses and brain deterioration spreads to include the cortex, thought and memory deficits appear (Toulouse & Sullivan, 2008). The most common cause of subcortical dementia is Parkinson's disease.

Parkinson's disease is a brain disorder that occurs when neurons in a part of the brain called the *substantia nigra* die or become impaired. Neurons in this part of the brain produce the neurotransmitter dopamine, which enables coordinated function of the body's muscles and smooth movement. Parkinson's symptoms appear when at least 50% of the nerve cells in the substantia nigra are damaged (National Parkinson Foundation, 2008). Parkinson's disease includes motor and cognitive symptoms. Motor symptoms occur first and include tremors, slowness of movement, difficulty initiating movement, rigidity, difficulty with balance, and a shuffling walk (Maetzler, Liepelt, & Berg, 2009). Typically these symptoms occur in one part of the body and slowly spread to the extremities on the same side of the body before appearing on the opposite side of the body (Truong & Wolters, 2009). Because the stiffness and rigidity are first located in one part of the body, individuals may assume that it is ordinary stiffness, perhaps the result of too much activity or simply because of aging. As the disease progresses, individuals have difficulties with balance and controlling their body movements. Neurons continue to degenerate, brain functioning declines, cognitive and speech abilities deteriorate, dementia and, finally, death occurs (Maetzler et al., 2009).

Similar to Alzheimer's patients, Parkinson's patients with larger cognitive reserves and more synaptic connections among neurons have a slower progression of neurological changes before dementia appears. The prevalence of Parkinson's disease increases with age, and Parkinson's is found throughout the world, with similar rates occurring in Asia, Africa, South America, Europe, North America, and Australia (Pringsheim, Jette, Frolkis, & Steeves, 2014). People diagnosed with Parkinson's disease at advanced ages tend to develop dementia earlier into their disease than do younger people, likely because of age-related differences in cognitive capacities and neural reserves (Grossman, Bergmann, & Parker, 2006). Multiple studies support a genetic component to Parkinson's (Nalls et al., 2014; Wirdefeldt, Adami, Cole, Trichopoulos, & Mandel, 2011). However, there are few consistent findings regarding environmental and lifestyle influences (Wirdefeldt et al., 2011), suggesting that Parkinson's might be influenced by the complex gene–environment interactions

Parkinson's disease A chronic progressive brain disorder caused by deterioration of neurons in the substantia nigra; characterized by muscle rigidity, tremors, and sometimes dementia.

Mark Wilson/Getty

Boxer Muhammad Ali and actor Michael J. Fox, both diagnosed with Parkinson's disease, pretend to spar before giving their testimony before the U.S. Senate Appropriations Subcommittee on Health and Human Services advocating that more funding be directed to finding a cure for the disease.

characteristic of epigenetics (Cannon & Greenamyre, 2013; Feng, Jankovic, & Wu, 2014). Physical activity may act as a protective factor in developing Parkinson's disease, slowing its progression, and improving motor control (Bellou, Belbasis, Tzoulaki, Evangelou, & Ioannidis, 2016; Paillard et al., 2015). Parkinson's disease shows no gender, ethnic, social, economic or geographic boundaries (National Parkinson Foundation, 2008). In the United States, it is estimated that 60,000 new cases are diagnosed each year, joining the 1.5 million Americans who currently have Parkinson's disease. While the condition usually develops after the age of 65, 15% of those diagnosed are under 50 (National Parkinson Foundation, 2008).

Diagnosing Parkinson's disease is difficult because, like Alzheimer's disease, there is no test that confirms the presence of the disease. Incorrect diagnoses are common, potentially delaying treatment to Parkinson's patients (Rizzo et al., 2015). It is diagnosed by exclusion, by a thorough examination to rule out other possible causes. As is being done with Alzheimer's disease, researchers are searching for biomarkers that may be used to diagnose Parkinson's disease, but the work is still in its early stages (Miller & O'Callaghan, 2015; Parnetti, Cicognola, Eusebi, & Chiasserini, 2016). Parkinson's symptoms can be treated. Some research has suggested that deep brain stimulation, stimulating specific parts of the brain with electricity, as well as resistance training can improve some of the motor symptoms, such as poor gait and posture (Lamotte et al., 2015; Roper et al., 2016). Most medications either replace or mimic dopamine, which temporarily improves the motor symptoms of the disease; anti-inflammatory medications may also help reduce neurodegeneration (Brichta, Greengard, & Flajolet, 2013; Emre, Ford, Bilgiç, & Uç, 2014; Phani, Loike, & Przedborski, 2012). Medication can temporarily reduce symptoms and perhaps slow its path, but Parkinson's disease is not curable.

REVERSIBLE DEMENTIA

Not all dementias represent progressive and irreversible brain damage. Symptoms of dementia sometimes are caused by psychological and behavioral factors that can be reversed. For example, older adults who are socially isolated and lonely can show declines in mental functioning that reverse with the provision of social support (Fisher, Yury, & Buchanan, 2006). The challenge is that reversible dementias are often unrecognized and untreated. Reviews of medical records have suggested that 7% to 18% of the dementia cases had reversible causes (Djukic, Wedekind, Franz, Gremke, & Nau, 2015; Muangpaisan, Petcharat, & Srinonprasert, 2012). Another review of more than 340 medical records over a 10-year period revealed that of the 193 patients with dementia, 37 (19%) were reversible (Bello & Schultz, 2011).

Other common causes of reversible dementia are poor nutrition and dehydration (Gupta, Chari, & Ali, 2015; Muangpaisan et al., 2012; Panza, Solfrizzi, & Capurso, 2004; Srikanth & Nagaraja, 2005). As we have discussed, older adults require fewer calories than do younger adults, but nutritional demands remain or increase with age. In addition, older adults may eat less than younger adults because of depression or a loss of appetite that occurs with some medications. As a result, older adults are at risk for malnutrition and vitamin deficiencies, which are associated with declines in mental abilities and increases in psychological distress including depression and anxiety (Baker, 2007). Specifically, vitamin B12 deficiencies can mirror dementia symptoms, yet correcting for this deficiency restores older adults' functioning (Ringman & Varpetian, 2009).

Prescription and nonprescription drugs and drug interactions can also contribute to symptoms of dementia. Many medications impair nutrition by reducing the body's ability to absorb vitamins. Some pain killers, corticosteroid drugs, and other medications can cause confusion and erratic behavior similar to dementia (Bansal & Parle, 2014; Fisher et al., 2006). Older adults may be more easily overmedicated than younger adults because of their slower metabolism. Physical illnesses themselves can sometimes cause dementia symptoms such as memory loss and agitation which go away as the illness is treated.

• • Disclosing a Dementia Diagnosis

Most adults prefer to be informed of a dementia diagnosis.

The recognition of patients' autonomy, their right to understand and make decisions about their treatment, is a cornerstone of modern physician-patient relations. There is wide agreement that offering clear, honest information about diagnosis can improve psychological adjustment and reduce distress, providing it is done appropriately (Keightley & Mitchell, 2004). For these reasons, most ethical guidelines strongly promote disclosure of a diagnosis of dementia to the affected individual (Fisk, Beattie, Donnelly, Byszewski, & Molnar, 2007). However, the practice of nondisclosure persists in the field of dementia. It is estimated that 50% of Alzheimer's patients are not told about their diagnosis (Alzheimer's Association, 2015). People with dementia are given euphemisms ("memory loss") more often by family members (Woods & Pratt, 2005). Family members often prefer the person not to be told, despite agreeing they would want to know if they were in that situation (Monaghan & Begley, 2004). The defense for withholding information is based on the duty of doctors to do no harm because the lack of certainty about the diagnosis, lack of treatment or cure, cognitive decline leading to poor retention of diagnostic information, and the possibility that receiving such a diagnosis may cause or worsen an existing depression.

However, the majority of people without cognitive impairment as well as those referred to memory clinics say that they wish to know of a diagnosis of dementia

(Hort, O'Brien, et al., 2010; Iliffe et al., 2009; van den Dungen et al., 2014). Learning of a diagnosis of dementia may give people with dementia and their families time to adjust and, for people with dementia, to discuss their management and care preferences and engage in advanced decision-making regarding care. Disclosure has actually been found to decrease anxiety and depression in patients and caregivers (Hort, O'Brien, et al., 2010).

It is often assumed that cognitive decline is accompanied by increasing unawareness (Woods & Pratt, 2005). However, it is becoming increasingly clear that making assessments of awareness may not be at all straightforward. For example, some people with dementia who are described as unaware by those around them may demonstrate greater levels of awareness in different contexts. In recognition of this, it may be helpful to consider disclosure of a dementia diagnosis as a process and modify disclosure practices and descriptions to the patients' level of understanding, adopting an individualized patient-centered approach that maintains the individual's personal integrity (Fisk et al., 2007).

The process of disclosure begins when cognitive impairment is first suspected, and it evolves over time as information is obtained. Whenever possible and appropriate, this process should involve not only the affected individual but also their family and/or other current or potential future care providers (Mastwyk, Ames, Ellis, Chiu, & Dow, 2014). Some recommend that additional time and follow-ups in order to employ a progressive disclosure process to address issues including: discussions of diagnostic uncertainty, treatment options, future plans, financial planning, assigning power of attorney, wills and "living wills," driving privileges and the need to eventually stop driving, available support services, and potential research participation.

What do you think?

1. In your view, should older adults diagnosed with dementia be informed of their diagnosis?

2. Discuss the characteristics and qualities of dementia that influence your decision of whether to inform a patient.

Symptoms of depression and anxiety in older adults, such as forgetfulness, disorientation, and other cognitive difficulties, are often mistaken for dementia (de la Torre, 2016; Engmann, 2011). If anxiety or depressive symptoms are misdiagnosed as dementia, the older adult may be prescribed medications that can increase dementia-like symptoms such as fatigue and slowed mental reactions to stimuli and events. Treating anxiety and depression with combinations of antianxiety and antidepressant medications as well as therapy reduces the cognitive symptoms commonly mistaken for dementia (Davies & Thorn, 2002).

The question of whether or not a patient diagnosed with dementia should be informed of the diagnosis is a sensitive one, carrying implications for not only the patient but also family, other loved ones, and caregivers. The issue is discussed in the Applying Developmental Science feature.

Most individuals of all ages are well, although many experience health issues at various times in life. Although some health problems are influenced by genetics, many are also influenced by contextual factors, including lifestyle. Moreover, people play a large role in their own health through their choices, such as food, and behavior, such as engaging in physical activity and seeking routine health care. Individuals' understanding of their options and their changing capacity to reason, both cognitive factors, also hold implications for their health. In the next chapter, we examine cognitive development and its implications for how individuals function in their world.

 Thinking in Context 5.4

1. Describe some of the differences between the various forms of dementia. What behaviors characterize each? Identify currently known causes of each.

2. What would you suggest to someone who wishes to reduce his or her risk for dementia? What lifestyle factors would you suggest? How might someone take advantage of contextual factors in order to reduce the risk of dementia or show better adjustment in the face of dementia?

 Apply Your Knowledge

At 14, Kendra had her very first alcoholic drink when her friends took her to a party hosted by Dylan, a high school senior. Soon Kendra and Dylan began dating. Kendra had always felt especially self-conscious about her body, as she had started needing a bra at age 10, and by age 13 she had sometimes been mistaken for an adult. She thought of herself as "too big," but Dylan insisted her body was "smokin'." With Dylan, Kendra began drinking regularly at parties as she found it eased her nerves and helped her feel more comfortable interacting with the older kids. After a few drinks she would feel comfortable enough to take off her sweatshirt and show off her tank top. Dylan also introduced Kendra to marijuana, which she preferred over alcohol because it made it easy to forget her self-consciousness. Being high on marijuana made goofing around like her friends much more fun. One

night they climbed the fence surrounding the high school and spray-painted the windows black. Another time they sneaked onto a local golf course and went skinny-dipping in the pond. However, a neighbor called the police and Kendra, Dylan, and their friends were arrested for trespassing and possession of alcohol and drugs.

- What might you discern about Kendra's physical development, relative to her peers? What role might physical development play in Kendra's behavior?

- How might neurological development account for some of Kendra's behavior?

- What role might cognitive factors play?

- What are some of the outcomes that accompany risky activity?

CHAPTER 5 IN REVIEW

5.1 Analyze health issues in childhood, including risks and protective factors for healthy development.

SUMMARY

Declining rates of child mortality are associated with advances in public health, such as increasing access to health care, prenatal care, and availability of vaccinations for diseases that are serous and sometimes fatal. Unintentional injuries are the most common cause of death in children and adolescents in the United States. Children's risk for injury is influenced by their own characteristics, poor parental and adult supervision, neighborhood disadvantage, and low socioeconomic status. Children who are abused are at risk for psychological, cognitive, and social problems. Risk factors for child abuse exist at all ecological levels. Both child and parent characteristics and community factors increase the risk or potential for maltreatment.

KEY TERMS

vaccine   mandated reporters
child abuse

REVIEW QUESTIONS

1. What are common heath issues in childhood?

2. What are risk factors for childhood injury?

3. What are risk factors for child maltreatment?

4. What preventative measures can be taken to reduce risk?

5.2 Discuss the prevalence, effects, and treatment of eating disorders and substance use in adolescents and emerging adults.

SUMMARY

Individuals who suffer from eating disorders often experience a distorted body image. Both anorexia and bulimia are influenced by genetic and contextual factors and occur in all ethnic and socioeconomic groups in Western countries and are becoming increasingly common in some non-Western countries and Arab cultures. Treatment is challenging and often includes medication, therapy, support groups, nutritional education, and sometimes hospitalization to remedy malnutrition. Alcohol and substance use tend to begin during adolescence and peak during young adulthood. They may serve developmental functions but are associated with short- and long-term effects such as accidents, academic problems, risks for dependence and abuse, and impaired neurological development. Alcohol and substance abuse is influenced by genetics as well as contextual factors. Effective prevention and intervention programs provide adolescents with education; teach them skills to resist pressure, refuse offers, and cope; and increase parental awareness of risks and appropriate behavior. Binge drinking and heavy drinking

generally peak in young adulthood and decline by the end of early adulthood with the transition to adult responsibilities; however, alcohol use remains prevalent in adulthood.

KEY TERMS

anorexia nervosa   binge drinking
bulimia nervosa

REVIEW QUESTIONS

1. What are eating disorders? What are their effects? How are they treated?

2. What are typical patterns and influences on alcohol and substance use during adolescence and emerging adulthood? How is alcohol and substance abuse treated?

5.3 Identify common chronic diseases and sources of injury in adulthood, their risk factors, effects, and treatments.

SUMMARY

Cancer and chronic health conditions are the result of a complex web of genetic and environmental influences. Advances in medicine have changed the nature of disease. More people survive cancer than ever before. Risk factors for cardiovascular disease include heredity, high blood pressure, poor diet, diabetes, smoking, and psychological stress. Medication and behavioral changes, such as changes in diet and physical activity, may reduce hypertension and risk of diabetes as well as cardiovascular disease. Declines in estrogen place postmenopausal women at risk for osteoporosis. Intervention in the form of weight-bearing exercise, diet, and medication can prevent and slow its course. Likewise, nearly all adults will show some signs of osteoarthritis and continuing physical activity can help in managing symptoms. Injury-related fatalities are high in adolescence and emerging adulthood, decline in adulthood, and rise in late adulthood. Motor vehicle accidents and falls are major sources of injuries among older adults. Declines in vision and changes in working memory, attention, and neuromuscular control account for the increased risk.

KEY TERMS

diabetes   osteoporosis
cardiovascular disease   osteoarthritis
heart disease

REVIEW QUESTIONS

1. What are some common chronic diseases in adulthood?

2. Give examples of two chronic diseases, listing risk factors, common effects, and treatment options.

3. What injuries are common in adulthood? Why? How might injuries be prevented?

5.4 Distinguish among common dementias, their risk factors, effects, and treatment.

SUMMARY

The risk for dementia increases with age. Alzheimer's disease is characterized by the presence of beta-amyloid plaques and neurofibrillary tangles in the cerebral cortex. Alzheimer's disease progresses through several predictable steps, beginning with memory loss. Vascular dementia is caused by a series of strokes. Parkinson's disease includes motor and muscle symptoms, and dementia often emerges in the late stages. Genetic factors influence susceptibility to dementia, and education and social and physical activity are associated with a lower risk. Symptoms of dementia sometimes are caused by psychological and behavioral factors that can be reversed, such as medication, poor nutrition, or depression.

KEY TERMS

dementia
Alzheimer's disease
amyloid plaques
neurofibrillary tangles
vascular dementia
Parkinson's disease

REVIEW QUESTIONS

1. What is dementia?

2. What are four types of dementia?

3. How do the four types of dementia differ with regard to risk factors, effects, and treatment options?

Test your understanding of the content.
Review the flashcards and quizzes at
edge.sagepub.com/kuthertopical

PART III

Cognitive Development

The cognitive domain of development includes thinking, language, cognitive processing, and intelligence.

Infants grasp basic physical properties of objects. Thinking advances, becoming more complex, throughout childhood. Yet it is not until adolescence that individuals display abstract thinking, which allows them to plan and make inferences, consider ways of solving potential problems, and engage in hypothetical-deductive reasoning. Language development also unfolds in a predictable way, from coos and babbles, to first words, to sentences and more complex constructions. Language influences how individuals communicate, as well as how they think. Cognitive development continues in adulthood as people advance in their reasoning and get better at solving everyday problems and coordinating emotions with thoughts.

Changes in reasoning are possible because of underlying shifts in information processing abilities, including attention, memory, and processing speed. As executive function develops, children become better able to monitor, evaluate, and adjust their thinking to solve problems. Metacognition improves during adolescence, and the reflection that accompanies it plays an important role in the development of scientific reasoning.

Information processing abilities influence the patterns of change we see in intellectual functioning during adulthood. Adults experience a decline in fluid intelligence, which affects their ability to coordinate cognitively demanding tasks. Yet crystallized intelligence, an expanding knowledge base, and growing expertise help most adults compensate for declines. Adults remain adaptive problem solvers, especially in response to everyday problems relevant to the contexts they experience in their daily lives.

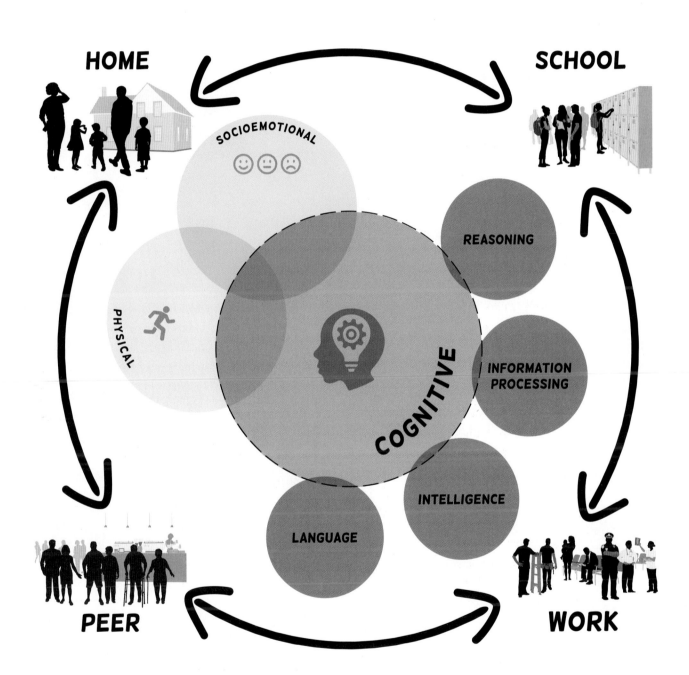

HOME

SCHOOL

PEER

WORK

SOCIOEMOTIONAL

PHYSICAL

COGNITIVE

REASONING

INFORMATION PROCESSING

INTELLIGENCE

LANGUAGE

Images: ©iStock.com

Cognitive Change: Cognitive–Developmental and Sociocultural Approaches

Learning Objectives

6.1 Identify Piaget's six substages of sensorimotor reasoning and summarize criticism of this perspective on infant and early childhood cognitive development.

6.2 Contrast the advances of concrete operational versus those of formal operational reasoning, and summarize common criticisms of Piaget's perspective on these stages.

6.3 Summarize Vygotsky's sociocultural perspective and how it is manifested in scaffolding, the zone of proximal development, and cultural tools.

6.4 Explain postformal reasoning and how it compares with cognitive–affective complexity.

Digital Resources

▶ Object Permanence
📄 Object Permanence in Dogs

▶ Formal Operations
📄 Improving Students' Lives

🔊 Vygotsky's Social Learning Theory
📄 Teachers' Use of Scaffolding

▶ Postformal Thought
📄 Integrative Thinking in Adulthood

Master these learning objectives with multimedia resources available at **edge.sagepub.com/kuthertopical** and *Lives in Context* video cases available in the interactive eBook.

"There you go, little guy," Mateo's uncle says, placing a rattle in the infant's grasp. Six-month-old Mateo shakes the toy and puts it in his mouth, sucking on it. He then removes the rattle from his mouth and gives it a vigorous shake, dropping it to the ground. "Mateo! Where's your rattle?" asks his mother. "Whenever he drops his toy, he never looks for it," she explains to his uncle, "not even when it's his favorite toy." As Mateo grows older, he will soon begin to show an interest in objects that disappear, like his rattle, and his thinking will become more complex as he progresses through toddlerhood and learns language. These are just the first in a lifetime of changes that will transform how Mateo views his world. How do we explain these cognitive changes? Three major perspectives on cognition address this question in different ways. *Cognitive–developmental theories* emphasize the structural changes that underlie development and how the content and organization of thinking changes. *Sociocultural theories* point to the roles of context and our need to communicate in influencing thought. *Information processing theories* (discussed in Chapter 7) emphasize changes in physical capacities and strategy use as contributors to cognitive change. In this chapter, we examine the cognitive–developmental and sociocultural approaches to cognitive change throughout life.

PIAGET'S COGNITIVE-DEVELOPMENTAL PERSPECTIVE: COGNITION IN INFANCY AND EARLY CHILDHOOD

LO 6.1 Identify Piaget's six substages of sensorimotor reasoning and summarize criticism of this perspective on infant and early childhood cognitive development.

The first scientist to systematically examine children's thinking and reasoning, Swiss scholar Jean Piaget (1896–1980), believed that to understand children we must understand how they think because thinking influences all of behavior. Piaget formulated the cognitive developmental perspective, which views children and adults as active explorers who learn by interacting with the world, building their own understanding of everyday phenomena, and applying it to adapt to the world around them.

PROCESSES OF DEVELOPMENT

According to Piaget (1952), children are active in their own development not simply because they engage other people, but because they engage the world, adapting their ways of thinking in response to their experiences. Through these interactions they organize what they learn to construct and refine their own **schemas**, or concepts, ideas, and ways of interacting on the world. Our earliest schemas are inborn motor responses, such as the reflex response that causes infants to close their fingers around an object when it touches their palm. As the infant grows and develops, these early motor schemas are transformed into cognitive schemas, or thought. At all ages we rely on our schemas to make sense of the world, but our schemas are constantly adapting and developing in response to our experiences. According to Piaget, cognitive development is the result of two developmental processes: assimilation and accommodation.

Assimilation involves integrating a new experience into a preexisting schema. For example, suppose that 1-year-old Kelly uses the schema of "grab and shove into the mouth" to learn. He grabs and shoves his rattle into his mouth, learning about the rattle by using his preexisting schema. When Kelly comes across another object, such as Mommy's wristwatch, he transfers the schema to it—and assimilates the wristwatch by grabbing it and shoving it into his mouth. He develops an understanding of the new objects through assimilation, by fitting them into his preexisting schema.

Sometimes we encounter experiences or information that do not fit within an existing schema, so we must change the schema, adapting and modifying it in light of the new information. This process is called **accommodation**. For example, suppose Kelly encounters another object, a beach ball. He tries his schema of grab and shove, but the beach ball won't fit into his mouth; perhaps he cannot even grab it. He must adapt his schema or create a new one in order to incorporate the new information—to learn about the beach ball. Kelly may squeeze and mouth the ball instead, accommodating or changing his schema to interact with the new object.

The processes of assimilation and accommodation are continually occurring and are ways that people adapt to their environment, absorbing the constant flux of information they encounter daily (see Figure 6.1). People—infants, children, and adults—constantly integrate new information into their schemas and continually encounter new information that requires them to modify their schemas. Piaget proposed that people naturally strive for *cognitive equilibrium,* a balance between the processes of assimilation and accommodation. When assimilation and accommodation are balanced, individuals are neither incorporating new information into their schemas nor changing their schemas in light of new information; instead, our schemas match the outside world and represent it clearly. But a state of cognitive equilibrium is rare and fleeting. More frequently, people experience a mismatch or *disequilibrium* between their schemas and the world. For example, when Kelly picks up his mother's wristwatch and tries to learn about it by

schema A mental representation, such as concepts, ideas, and ways of interacting with the world.

assimilation In Piaget's theory, the process by which new experiences are interpreted and integrated into preexisting schemas.

accommodation In Piaget's theory, the process by which schemas are modified or created to include new experiences.

applying his grab-and-shove schema, he displays cognitive disequilibrium because he has discovered information that is new to him and therefore must be assimilated. Likewise, Kelly also displays cognitive disequilibrium when he must accommodate his schema to learn from a new experience, such as an encounter with a beach ball.

Disequilibrium leads to cognitive growth because of the mismatch between children's schemas and reality. This mismatch leads to confusion and discomfort, which in turn motivate children to modify their cognitive schemas so that their view of the world matches reality. It is through assimilation and accommodation that this modification takes place so that cognitive equilibrium is restored. Children's drive for cognitive equilibrium is the basis for cognitive change, propelling them through the four stages of cognitive development proposed by Piaget (see Table 1.4 in Chapter 1). With each advancing stage, children create and use more sophisticated cognitive schemas, enabling them to think, reason, and understand their world in more complex ways. The earliest schemas emerge during the first stage of cognitive development: the sensorimotor stage.

Assimilation   **Accommodation**

Bobby sees a cat that fits his schema for kitty (left). He has never seen a cat like this before (right). He must accommodate his schema for kitty to include a hairless cat.

INFANCY: SENSORIMOTOR REASONING

"Be gentle with Baby Emily," Lila cautions her 22-month-old son, Gabriel. "She's just one week old and very little. You were once little like her." "No," Gabriel giggles: "Big boy!" Gabriel picks up his teddy bear, cradles it like a baby, then holds it to his chest, rubbing its back to imitate what he sees Mommy do with Baby Emily. In less than 2 years, Gabriel has transformed from a tiny infant, like Baby Emily, to a toddler who can imitate what he sees and verbally express his ideas. Like all newborns, Baby Emily is equipped with inborn sensory capacities and preferences that enable her to tune in to the world around her. Baby Emily's abilities to think, reason, problem solve, and interact with objects and people will change dramatically over the next 2 years.

Sensorimotor Substages

During the sensorimotor stage, from birth to about 2 years, infants learn about the world through their senses and motor skills. To think about an object they must act on it by viewing it, listening to it, touching it, smelling it, and tasting it. Piaget (1952) believed that infants are not capable of **mental representation**—thinking about an object using mental pictures. They also lack the ability to remember and think about objects that are not present. Instead, in order to think about an object, an infant must experience it through both the visual and tactile senses. The sensorimotor period of reasoning, as Piaget conceived of it, progresses through six substages in which cognition develops from reflexes to intentional action, to symbolic representation.

Substage 1: Reflexes (birth to 1 month). In the first substage, newborns use their reflexes, such as the sucking and palmar grasp reflexes, to react to stimuli they experience. During the first month of life, infants use these reflexes to learn about their world, through the process of assimilation; they apply their sucking schema to assimilate information and learn about their environment. At about 1 month of age, newborns begin to accommodate, or modify, their sucking behaviors to specific objects, sucking differently in response to a bottle verses a pacifier. For example, they may modify their sucking schema when they encounter a pacifier, perhaps sucking less vigorously and without swallowing.

mental representation An internal depiction of an object; thinking of an object using mental pictures.

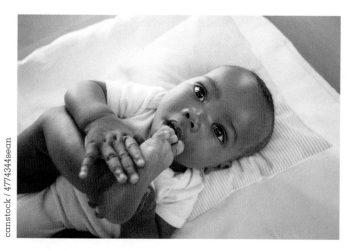

Primary circular reactions are babies' first discoveries.

During the first month of life, newborns strengthen and modify their original reflexive schemas to explore the world around them.

Substage 2: Primary Circular Reactions (1 to 4 months). During the second substage, infants begin to make accidental discoveries. Early cognitive growth in the sensorimotor period comes through engaging in **circular reactions**, the repetition of an action and its response. Infants learn to repeat pleasurable or interesting events that originally occurred by chance. Between 1 and 4 months infants engage in behaviors called **primary circular reactions**, which consist of repeating actions involving the parts of the body that produce pleasurable or interesting results. A primary circular reaction begins by chance or by accident, as the infant produces a pleasurable sensation and learns to repeat the behavior to make the event happen again and experience the pleasurable effect again. For example, an infant flails her arms and accidentally puts her hand in her mouth. She is surprised at the outcome (her hand in her mouth) and tries to make it happen again. Therefore the infant repeats the behavior to experience and explore her body.

Substage 3: Secondary Circular Reactions (4 to 8 months). During the third sensorimotor substage, as infants' awareness extends further, they engage in **secondary circular reactions**, which are repetitions of actions that trigger responses in the external environment, outside of the baby's body. Now the patterns of repetition are oriented toward making interesting events occur in the infant's environment. For example, the infant shakes a rattle to hear its noise or kicks his or her legs to move a mobile hanging over the crib. Secondary circular reactions indicate that infants' attention has expanded to include the environment outside their bodies and that they are beginning to understand that their actions cause results in the external environment. In this way, infants discover new ways of interacting with their environments to continue experiencing sensations and events that they find pleasing.

Substage 4: Coordination of Secondary Circular Reactions (8 to 12 months). Unlike primary and secondary circular reactions, which are behaviors that are discovered by accident, the coordination of secondary circular reactions substage represents true means–end behavior and signifies the beginning of intentional behavior. During this substage, infants purposefully coordinate two secondary circular reactions and apply them in new situations to achieve a goal. For example, Piaget described how his son, Laurent, combined the two activities of knocking a barrier out of his way and grasping an object. When Piaget put a pillow in front of a matchbox that Laurent desired, the boy pushed the pillow aside and grabbed the box. In this way, Laurent integrated two secondary circular reactions to achieve a goal. Now planning and goal-directed behavior have emerged.

One of the most important advances during the coordination of secondary circular reactions stage is **object permanence**, the understanding that objects continue to exist outside of sensory awareness (e.g., are no longer visible). According to Piaget, infants younger than 8 months of age do not yet have object permanence—out of sight is literally out of mind. An infant loses interest and stops reaching for or looking at a small toy after it is covered by a cloth. It is not until 8 to 12 months, during the coordination of secondary circular reactions stage, that object permanence emerges and infants will search for hidden objects. Displaying object permanence is an important cognitive advance because it signifies a capacity for mental representation, or internal thought. The ability to think about an object internally is an important step toward learning language because language

circular reaction In Piaget's theory, the repetition of an action and its response in which infants try to repeat a newly discovered event caused by their own motor activity.

primary circular reaction In Piaget's theory, repeating an action that produced a chance event involving the infant's body.

secondary circular reaction In Piaget's theory, repeating an action that produced a chance event that triggers a response in the external environment.

object permanence The understanding that objects continue to exist outside of sight.

uses symbols: Sounds symbolize and stand for objects (e.g., infants must understand that the sound "ball" represents an object, a ball).

Stage 5: Tertiary Circular Reactions (12 to 18 months). During the fifth substage, infants begin to experiment with new behaviors to see the results. Piaget described infants as "little scientists" during this period because they move from intentional behavior to systematic exploration. In what Piaget referred to as **tertiary circular reactions**, infants now engage in mini-experiments: active, purposeful, trial-and-error exploration to search for new discoveries. They vary their actions to see how the changes affect the outcomes. For example, many infants

This infant is showing object permanence by reaching over to uncover the toy. What does object permanence signify?

begin to experiment with gravity by dropping objects to the floor while sitting in a high chair. First an infant throws a ball and watches it bounce. Next a piece of paper floats slowly down. Then mommy's keys clatter down. And so on. This purposeful exploration is how infants search for new discoveries and learn about the world. When presented with a problem, babies in the tertiary circular reactions substage engage in trial-and-error analyses, trying out behaviors until they find the best one to attain their goal.

Substage 6: Mental Representation (18 to 24 months). The sixth sensorimotor substage marks a transition between the sensorimotor and preoperational reasoning stages. Between 18 and 24 months of age, infants develop *representational thought*, the ability to use symbols such as words and mental pictures to represent objects and actions in memory. In developing this ability, infants are freed from immediate experience: They can think about objects that they no longer see directly in front of them and can engage in deferred imitation, imitating actions of an absent model. Now, external physical exploration of the world gives way to internal mental exploration. Children can think through potential solutions and create new solutions to problems without engaging in physical trial and error, but by simply considering the potential solutions and their consequences. Table 6.1 summarizes the substages of sensorimotor reasoning.

Lives in Context Video 6.1
Object Permanence

Evaluating Sensorimotor Reasoning

Piaget's contributions to our understanding of cognitive development are vast and invaluable. He was the first to ask what develops during childhood and how it occurs. Piaget recognized that motor action and cognition are inextricably linked, a view still accepted by today's developmental scientists (Adolph & Berger, 2005; Beilin & Fireman, 2000; Woods & Wilcox, 2013).

Piaget's work has stimulated a great deal of research as developmental scientists have tested his theory. However, measuring the cognitive capabilities of infants and toddlers is very challenging because, unlike older children and adults, babies cannot fill out questionnaires or answer questions orally. Researchers have had to devise methods of measuring observable behavior that can provide clues to what an infant is thinking. For example, researchers measure infants' looking behavior: What does the infant look at, and for how long? Using such methods, they have found support for some of

tertiary circular reaction
In Piaget's theory, repeating an action to explore and experiment in order to see the results and learn about the world.

TABLE 6.1 • Substages of Sensorimotor Reasoning

SUBSTAGE	MAJOR FEATURES	EXAMPLE
Reflexive activity (0–1 month)	Newborn strengthens and adapts reflexes	Newborn shows a different sucking response to a nipple versus a pacifier
Primary circular reactions (1–4 months)	Repeats motor actions that produce interesting outcomes that are centered on the body	Infant pats hand against the floor to feel sensation on palm
Secondary circular reactions (4–8 months)	Repeats motor actions that produce interesting outcomes that are directed toward the environment	Infant bats mobile with his arm and watches the mobile move
Coordination of secondary circular reactions (8–12 months)	Combines secondary circular reactions to achieve goals and solve problems; the beginnings of intentional behavior	Infant uses one hand to lift a bucket covering a ball and the other to grasp the ball. Infant uses both hands to pull a string attached to a ball and eventually reach the ball
Tertiary circular reactions (12–18 months)	Experiments with different actions to achieve the same goal or observe the outcome and make new discoveries	Infant hits a pot with a wooden spoon and listens to the sound, then hits other objects in the kitchen, such as the refrigerator, stove, plates, to hear the sound that the spoon makes against the objects
Mental representation (18–24 months)	Internal mental representation of objects and events; thinking to solve problems rather than relying on trial and error	When confronted with a problem, like a toy that is out of reach on the counter, the infant can consider possible solutions to a problem in his mind, decide on a solution, and implement it

Piaget's claims and evidence that challenges others. One of the most contested aspects of Piaget's theory concerns his assumption that infants are not capable of mental representation until late in the sensorimotor period. A growing body of research conducted with object permanence and imitation tasks suggests otherwise, as described in the following sections.

Violation-of-Expectation Tasks. Piaget's method of determining whether an infant understood object permanence relied on the infant's ability to demonstrate it by uncovering a hidden object. Critics argue that many infants may understand that the object is hidden but lack the motor ability to coordinate their hands to physically demonstrate their understanding. Studying infants' looking behavior enables researchers to study object permanence in younger infants with undeveloped motor skills because it eliminates the need for infants to use motor activity to demonstrate their cognitive competence.

violation-of-expectation task A method in which infants are shown events that appear to violate physical laws. Increased attention to the unexpected event suggests that the infant is surprised and therefore has an understanding and expectations of the physical world.

One such research design uses a **violation-of-expectation task**, in which a stimulus appears to violate physical laws (Baillargeon, 1994). Specifically, in a violation-of-expectation task an infant is shown two events: one that is labeled *expected* because it follows physical laws and a second that is called *unexpected* because it violates physical laws. If the infant looks longer at the unexpected event it suggests that he or she is surprised by it, is aware of physical properties of objects, and can mentally represent them.

FIGURE 6.2: Object Permanence in Young Infants: Baillargeon's Drawbridge Study

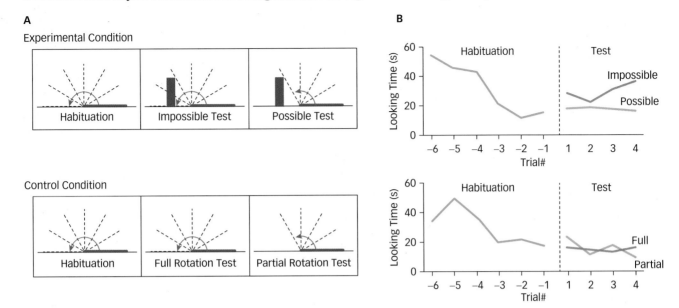

(A) Side view of habituation and test displays. Infants were habituated to a 180-degree drawbridge-like motion. (B) In the Experimental Condition, infants completed two types of test trials with a new object, a box. The Impossible Test involved the same full 180° rotation from habituation, but now the screen surprisingly passed through the box as it completed its rotation (with the box disappearing as it became obscured). The Possible Test involved a novel shorter rotation of screen up to the point where it would contact the box, where it stopped; this motion was "possible" in terms of solidity and object permanence. In the Control Condition, the screen rotations were identical, but no box was presented (such that both motions were equally possible). The results from the test phase are depicted in the right panels of (B). In the Experimental Condition, infants looked longer at the Impossible Test but not the Possible Test. However, in the Control Condition no preference was observed. They looked equally at the full and partial rotation. These results suggest a violation of infants' expectations regarding object permanence.

Sources: Baillargeon (1987). http://www.ncbi.nlm.nih.gov/pmc/articles/PMC2605404

In a classic study, developmental researcher Renée Baillargeon (1987) utilized the violation-of-expectation method to study the mental representation capacities of very young infants. Infants were shown a drawbridge that rotated 180 degrees. Then the infants watched as a box was placed behind the drawbridge to impede its movement. Infants watched as either the drawbridge rotated and stopped upon hitting the box or did not stop and appeared to move through the box (an "impossible" event). As shown in Figure 6.2, 4.5-month-old infants looked longer when the drawbridge appeared to move through the box (the "impossible" unexpected event), rather than when it stopped upon hitting the box. Baillargeon and colleagues interpreted infants' looking longer at the unexpected event as suggesting that they maintained a mental representation of the box, even though they could not see it, and therefore understood that the drawbridge could not move through the entire box.

Other researchers counter that these results do not demonstrate object permanence in young infants, but rather illustrate infants' preference for novelty or for greater movement (Bogartz, Shinskey, & Schilling, 2000). For example, when the study was replicated without the box, 5-month-old infants looked longer at the full rotation, suggesting that infants looked at the unexpected event not because it violated physical laws, but because it represented greater movement (Rivera, Wakely, & Langer, 1999). However, studies that use simpler tasks have shown support for young infants' competence. At 4 and 5 months, infants will watch a ball roll behind a barrier, gazing to where they expect it to reappear (Bertenthal, Longo, & Kenny, 2007; von Hofsten, Kochukhova, & Rosander, 2007).

When 6-month-old infants are shown an object and the lights are then turned off, they will reach in the dark for the object (Goubet & Clifton, 1998; Shinskey & Munakata, 2003). They will also reach for an object hidden by being immersed in liquid (Shinskey, 2012), suggesting that they maintain a mental representation of the object and therefore have object permanence earlier than Piaget believed.

A-Not-B Tasks. Other critics of Piaget's views of infants' capacities for object permanence focus on an error that 8- to 12-month-old infants make, known as the *A-not-B error*. The A-not-B error occurs when infants are able to uncover a toy hidden behind a barrier, yet when they observe the toy moved from behind one barrier (Place A) to another (Place B), they look for the toy in the first place it was hidden, Place A, even after watching the toy be moved to Place B (see Figure 6.3). Piaget believed that the infant incorrectly, but persistently, searches for the object in Place A because he or she lacks object permanence. More recent research shows that infants look at Place B, the correct location, at the same time as they mistakenly reach for Place A (Diamond, 1985), suggesting that they understand the correct location of the object (Place B), but cannot keep themselves from reaching for Place A because of neural and motor immaturity (Diamond, 1991).

Other researchers propose that infants cannot restrain the impulse to repeat a behavior that was previously rewarded (Zelazo, Reznick, & Spinazzola, 1998). When looking time procedures are used to study the A-not-B error (Ahmed & Ruffman, 1998), infants look longer when the impossible illusory event occurs (when the toy is moved from Place A to Place B but is then found at Place A) than when the expected, possible event occurs (when the toy is moved from Place A to Place B and is found at Place B). This suggests that infants have object permanence but their motor skills prohibit them from demonstrating it in A-not-B tasks. One longitudinal study followed infants from 5 to 10 months of age and found that between 5 and 8 months infants showed better performance on an A-not-B looking task rather than a reaching task. Nine- and 10-month old infants performed equally well on A-not-B looking and reaching tasks (Cuevas & Bell, 2010). Age-related changes in performance on A-not-B and other object permanence tasks may be due to maturation of brain circuitry controlling motor skills and inhibition as well as advances in the ability to control attention (Cuevas & Bell, 2010; Marcovitch, Clearfield, Swingler, Calkins, & Bell, 2016; Watanabe, Forssman, Green, Bohlin, & von Hofsten, 2012).

FIGURE 6.3: A-Not-B Error

The infant continues to look for the ball under place A despite having seen the ball moved to place B.

Deferred-Imitation Tasks. Another method of studying infants' capacities for mental representation relies on **deferred imitation**, the ability to repeat an act performed some time ago. Piaget (1962) believed that infants under 18 months cannot engage in deferred imitation because they lack mental representation abilities. Yet laboratory research on infant facial imitation has found that 6-week-old infants who watch an unfamiliar adult's facial expression will imitate it when they see the same adult the next day (Meltzoff & Moore, 1994). Six- and 9-month-old infants also display deferred imitation of unique actions performed with toys, such as taking a puppet's glove off, shaking it to ring a bell inside, and replacing it, over a 24-hour delay (Barr, Marrott, & Rovee-Collier, 2003).

When infants engage in deferred imitation, they act on the basis of stored representations of actions—memories—that counter Piaget's beliefs about infants' capabilities (Jones & Herbert, 2006). Many researchers now suggest that deferred imitation, along with object permanence itself, is better viewed as a continuously developing ability, rather than the stage-like shift in representational capacities that Piaget proposed (Hayne, 2004; Rovee-Collier, Hayne, & Colombo, 2002). For example, a 3-year longitudinal study of infants 12, 18, and 24 months old showed that performance on deferred imitation tasks improved throughout the second year of life (Kolling, Goertz, Stefanie, & Knopf, 2010). Between 12 and 18 months, infants remember modeled behaviors for several months and imitate peers as well as adults (Hayne, Boniface, & Barr, 2000; Klein & Meltzoff, 1999). Increases in imitative capacity are observed with development up to 30 months of age as well as when shorter sequences of action are used, such as a sequence of fewer than eight unique actions (Barr, Dowden, & Hayne, 1996; Herbert & Hayne, 2000; Kressley-Mba, Lurg, & Knopf, 2005). In addition, research following infants from 9 months to 14 months of age suggests that individual differences in imitation are stable; children who show lower levels of imitation at 9 months of age continue to score lower on imitation at 14 months (Heimann & Meltzoff, 1996). These gradual changes suggest that infants and toddlers increase their representational capacities in a continuous developmental progression.

Core Knowledge Perspective as an Alternative Theory

Developmental psychologists generally agree with Piaget's description of infants as interacting with the world, actively taking in information, and constructing their own thinking. However, most researchers no longer agree with Piaget's belief that all knowledge begins with sensorimotor activity. Instead, infants are thought to have some innate, or inborn, cognitive capacities. Conservative theorists believe that infants are born with limited learning capacities such as a set of biases that cause them to attend to features of the environment that will help them to learn quickly (Kagan, 2008). Alternatively, the **core knowledge perspective** explains that infants are born with several innate knowledge systems or core domains of thought that enable early rapid learning and adaptation (Spelke, Lee, & Izard, 2010; Spelke & Kinzler, 2007).

According to core knowledge theorists, infants learn so quickly and encounter such a great amount of sensory information that some prewired evolutionary understanding, including the early ability to learn rules, must be at work (Spelke, 2016; Wang, Zhang, & Baillargeon, 2016). Using the violation-of-expectation method, core knowledge researchers have found that young infants have a grasp of the physical properties of objects, including the knowledge that objects do not disappear out of existence (permanence), they cannot pass through another (solidity), and they will fall without support (gravity; Baillargeon, Li, Gertner, & Wu, 2011). Newborns are sensitive to the physical properties of objects and show preferences for causality, looking longer at stimuli that illustrate physical causality (e.g., Ball A rolling and hitting Ball B and Ball B rolling) than those that do not (e.g., Ball A rolling and Ball B rolling after a delay; Mascalzoni, Regolin, Vallortigara, & Simion, 2013). Infants are also thought to have early knowledge of numbers.

deferred imitation Imitating the behavior of an absent model.

core knowledge perspective A framework explaining that infants are born with several innate knowledge systems or core domains of thought that enable early rapid learning and adaptation.

Five-month-old infants can discriminate between small and large numbers of items (Cordes & Brannon, 2009; Libertus & Brannon, 2009). Even newborns are sensitive to large differences in number, distinguishing nine items from three, for example, but newborns show difficulty distinguishing small numbers from each other (two vs. three items; Coubart, Izard, Spelke, Marie, & Streri, 2014). Comparative research has shown that animals display these systems of knowledge early in life and without much experience (Vallortigara, 2012), suggesting that it is possible—and perhaps evolutionarily adaptive—for infants to quickly yet naturally construct an understanding of the world (Xu & Kushnir, 2013).

Much core knowledge research employs the same looking paradigms described earlier, in which infants' visual preferences are measured as indicators of what they know. Critics argue that it is unclear whether we can interpret infants' looking in the same way as adults (Kagan, 2008). Such measures demonstrate discrimination—that young infants can tell the difference between stimuli—yet perceiving the difference between two stimuli does not necessarily mean that an infant understands *how* the two stimuli differ (Bremner, Slater, & Johnson, 2015). Others have suggested that infants are not detecting differences in number, but rather differences in area (Mix, Huttenlocher, & Levine, 2002). For example, it may be that the infant differentiates nine items from three not because of the change in number, but simply because nine items take up more space than three. More recent research has shown that 7-month-old infants can differentiate changes in number and area, are more sensitive to changes in number than area, and prefer to look at number changes over area changes (Libertus, Starr, & Brannon, 2014). Infants apply basic inferential mechanisms to quickly yet naturally construct an understanding of the world (Xu & Kushnir, 2013). Research with toddlers has suggested that they can understand, learn, and use causal principles to guide their actions (Walker & Gopnik, 2013).

Overall, Piaget's theory has had a profound influence on how we view cognitive development. However, infants and toddlers are more cognitively competent than Piaget imagined, showing signs of representational ability and conceptual thought that he believed were not possible (Flavell, 1993). Developmental scientists agree with Piaget that immature forms of cognition give way to more mature forms, that the individual is active in development, and that interaction with the environment is critical for cognitive growth. Electronic media are an important part of children's, adolescents', and adults' environments. Do infants interact with electronic media? The Applying Developmental Science feature examines whether infants can learn from electronic media.

EARLY CHILDHOOD: PREOPERATIONAL REASONING

Four-year-old Timothy stands up on his toes and releases his parachute toy, letting the action figure dangling from a parachute drift a few feet from him and collapse on the floor. "I'm going to go up high and make it faster," he says, imagining standing on the sofa and making the toy sail far into the clouds. He stands on the sofa and releases the toy, which sails a bit farther this time. "Next time he'll jump out of the plane even higher!" Timothy thinks, excitedly. His friend Isaiah calls out, "Let's make him land on the moon! He can meet space people!"

Timothy and Isaiah can plan, think of solutions to problems, and use language to communicate their ideas. They learn through play and by interacting with people and objects around them. From the cognitive-developmental perspective, young children's thought progresses from the sensory and motor schemes of infancy to more sophisticated representational thought. **Preoperational reasoning** appears in young children from about ages 2 to 6 and is characterized by a dramatic leap in the use of symbolic thinking that permits young children to use language, interact with others, and play using their own thoughts and imaginations to guide their behavior. It is symbolic thought that enables Timothy and Martin to use language to communicate their thoughts and

preoperational reasoning
Piaget's second stage of cognitive development, between about age 2 and 6, characterized by advances in symbolic thought, but thought is not yet logical.

LIVES IN CONTEXT

• • The Media and Baby Geniuses

Pictorium/Alamy

Most babies watch at least some television or play with electronic devices, such as their parents' mobile phones and tablets. How might viewing media influence infants' development?

Nine-month-old Derek sat in his high chair, munching cereal and watching the flickering television screen in front of him. In fact, 90% of parents report that their infants under the age of 2 years watch some form of electronic media, and the programming they watch is often specifically tailored to infants (Brown, 2011).

Infant-directed videos are often advertised as a way to enhance babies' brain development, intelligence, and early learning as they offer educational content embedded in an engaging video format and focused on themes such as language and general knowledge, including, shape, color, reading, and numbers (Fenstermacher et al., 2010). Most parents believe that age-appropriate videos can have an important positive impact on early child development, providing good entertainment for babies and convenience for parents (Robb, Richert, & Wartella, 2009).

But do baby videos really aid development? Brain-building claims made by baby media manufacturers are not supported by the research literature (Christakis, 2009), and longitudinal studies suggest no evidence of long-term benefits of media use in early childhood (American Academy of Pediatrics Council on Communications and Media, 2016; Courage & Howe, 2010; Ferguson & Donnellan, 2014). One study tested a popular DVD program that claims to help young infants learn to read. Ten- to 18-month-old infants who regularly watched the program for 7 months did not differ from other infants in intelligence, cognitive skills, reading skill, or word knowledge (Neuman, Kaefer, Pinkham, & Strouse, 2014). Other research has demonstrated that infants learn more readily from people than from TV, a finding known as the *video deficit effect* (Anderson & Pempek, 2005). For example, when 12- to 18-month-old infants watched a bestselling DVD that labels household objects, the infants learned very little from it as compared with what

they learned though interaction with parents (DeLoache et al., 2010). Yet the video deficit is reduced when infants' memory capacities are taken into account, such as by repeating content and adding visual and auditory cues (Barr, 2013). Infants and toddlers may be capable of learning from screen media, depending on the degree to which the media content resembles infants' and toddlers' real-life experiences, including the use of simple stories and familiar objects or routines (Linebarger & Vaala, 2010).

Are baby videos harmful? Some studies suggest that exposure to baby media may be associated with deficits and delays in language development (Chonchaiya & Pruksananonda, 2008; Zimmerman, Christakis, & Meltzoff, 2007). The effects of media use vary with its content, quality, and context. For example, one study showed that Hispanic infants and toddlers who viewed more than two hours of television per day showed poor scores on a language measure—but the relationship was true only for infant media; those who viewed adult media showed no difference in language scores (uch, Fisher, Ensari, & Harrington, 2013). It may not be the quantity of television viewing that is related with language outcomes but the quality. Poor quality viewing (e.g., background television, solitary viewing, and earlier age of viewing) is associated with lower vocabulary scores (Hudon, Fennell, & Hoftyzer, 2013). Age certainly matters. For example, one study showed that infants who are 17 months old and older were able to learn words from infant DVDs, as evidenced by looking measures, whereas younger infants did not display this learning (Krcmar, 2014).

Although infant media will not transform ordinary infants into brilliant geniuses, in limited doses it does not seem to cause harm (Neuman et al., 2014). Parents play a role in influencing the effects of educational and interactive baby media on their infants. (American Academy of Pediatrics Council on Communications and Media, 2016). When parents watch videos along with their infants and talk to them about the content, infants spend more time looking at the screen, learn more from the media, and show greater knowledge of language as toddlers (Linebarger & Vaala, 2010). In today's electronically connected world, it is impossible for most families to prevent infants from coming into contact with screens, whether television, tablet, or mobile phone. Considering that nearly 40% of infants under the age of 2 have viewed a mobile device, it appears that a developmental task for today's infants and toddlers is to learn *how* to learn from screens (Wartella & Lauricella, 2012).

What Do You Think?

1. **How might you teach infants and toddlers how to learn from screens, such as from televisions, cell phones, and tablets?**

2. **Imagine that you are a parent. Why might you allow your young child to play with your mobile phone or tablet? In your view, what are some disadvantages of screen use by infants and toddlers?**

desires—and it is also what allows them to send their toy on a mission to the moon to visit with pretend space people.

Characteristics of Preoperational Reasoning

Young children in the preoperational stage show impressive advances in representational thinking, but they are unable to grasp logic and cannot understand complex relationships. For example, a child may not understand that her father was once her grandmother's little boy. Alternatively, a child may not understand that his brother is also his sister's brother. Understanding each of these complex relationships requires the use of cognitive operations that are beyond the preoperational child's capacities. Children who show preoperational reasoning tend to make several common errors, including egocentrism, animism, centration, and irreversibility.

Egocentrism. "See my picture?" Ricardo asks as he holds up a blank sheet of paper. Mr. Seris answers, "You can see your picture, but I can't. Turn your page around so that I can see your picture. There it is! It's beautiful," he proclaims after Ricardo flips the piece of paper, permitting him to see his drawing. Ricardo did not realize that even though he could see his drawing, Mr. Seris could not. Ricardo displays **egocentrism**, the inability to take another person's point of view or perspective. The egocentric child views the world from his or her own perspective, assuming that other people share her feelings, knowledge, and even physical view of the world. For example, the egocentric child may present Mommy with her teddy bear when Mommy looks sad, not realizing that although the teddy bear may make *her* feel better, Mommy has different needs and preferences.

A classic task used to illustrate preoperational children's egocentrism is the **three mountains task**. As shown in Figure 6.4, the child sits at a table facing three large mountains. A doll is placed in a chair across the table from the child. The child is asked how the mountains look to the doll. Piaget found that young children in the preoperational stage described the scene from their own perspective rather than the doll's. They could not complete the task correctly because they could not imagine that someone else could see the world differently. The children exhibited egocentrism; they were not able to take another point of view (the doll's; Piaget & Inhelder, 1967).

FIGURE 6.4: The Three Mountains Task

egocentrism Piaget's term for children's inability to take another person's point of view or perspective and to assume that others share the same feelings, knowledge, and physical view of the world.

three mountains task A classic Piagetian task used to illustrate preoperational children's egocentrism.

Children who display preoperational reasoning cannot describe the scene depicted in the three mountains task from the point of view of the teddy bear.

Animism. Egocentric thinking can also take the form of **animism**, the belief that inanimate objects are alive and have feelings and intentions. "It's raining because the sun is sad and it is crying," 3-year-old Melinda explains. Children accept their own explanations for phenomena as they are unable to consider another viewpoint or alternative reason. The 4-year-old child who cries after bumping her head on a table may feel better after her mother smacks the table, saying, "Bad table!" In the child's eyes, the table got what it deserved—payback!

Centration. Preoperational children exhibit **centration**, the tendency to focus on one part of a stimulus or situation and exclude all others. For example, a boy may believe that if he wears a dress he will become a girl. He focuses entirely on the appearance (the dress) rather than the other characteristics that make him a boy. Consider a group of children who are lined up according to height. If one child is asked, "Who is the tallest?" he or she will correctly point to the tallest child. Then, if the child is asked, "Who is the oldest?" he or she may point to the tallest child. "Who is the smartest?" Again the child points to the tallest child of the group, demonstrating centration: the child focuses on height to the exclusion of the other attributes.

Centration is illustrated by a classic task that requires the preoperational child to distinguish what something appears to be from what it really is, the **appearance–reality distinction**. In a classic study illustrating this effect, DeVries (1969) presented 3- to 6-year-old children with a cat named Maynard (see Figure 6.5). The children were permitted to pet Maynard. Then, while his head and shoulders were hidden behind a screen (and his back and tail were still visible), a dog mask was placed onto Maynard's head. The children were then asked, "What kind of animal is it now?" "Does it bark or meow?" Three-year-old children, despite Maynard's body and tail being visible during the transformation, replied that he was now a dog. Six-year-old children were able to distinguish Maynard's appearance from reality and explained that he only *looked* like a dog.

One reason that 3-year-old children fail appearance–reality tasks is because they are not yet capable of effective *dual encoding*, the ability to mentally represent an object in more than one way at a time (Flavell, Green, & Flavell, 1986). For example, young children are not able to understand that a scale model (like a doll house) can be both an object (something to play with) and a symbol (of an actual house; DeLoache, 2000; MacConnell & Daehler, 2004).

Irreversibility. "You ruined it!" cried Johnson after his older sister, Monique, placed a triangular block atop the tower of blocks he had just built. "No, I just put a triangle there to show it was the top and finish it," she explains. "No!" insists Johnson. "OK, I'll take it off," says Monique. "See? Now it's just how you left it." "No. It's ruined," Johnson sighs. Johnson continued to be upset after his sister removed the triangular block, not realizing that by removing the block she has restored the block structure to its original state. Young children's thinking is characterized by **irreversibility**, meaning that they do not understand that reversing a process can often undo it and restore the original state.

Preoperational children's irreversible thinking is illustrated by **conservation** tasks that require them to understand that the quantity of a substance is not transformed by changes in its appearance;

animism The belief that inanimate objects are alive and have feelings and intentions.

centration The tendency to focus on one part of a stimulus, situation, or idea and exclude all others; a characteristic of preoperational thought.

appearance–reality distinction The ability to distinguish between what something appears to be from what it really is.

irreversibility A characteristic of preoperational thought in which a child does not understand that an action can be reversed and a thing restored to its original state.

conservation The principle that a physical quantity, such as number, mass, or volume, remains the same even when its appearance changes.

FIGURE 6.5: Appearance vs. Reality: Is It a Cat or Dog?

Wiley/DeVries

Young children did not understand that Maynard the cat remained a cat despite wearing a dog mask and looking like a dog.

Source: DeVries (1969).

FIGURE 6.6: Additional Conservation Problems

Conservation Task	Original Presentation	Transformation
Number	Are there the same number of pennies in each row?	Now are there the same number of pennies in each row, or does one row have more?
Mass	Is there the same amount of clay in each ball?	Now does each piece have the same amount of clay, or does one have more?
Liquid	Is there the same amount of water in each glass?	Now does each glass have the same amount of water, or does one have more?

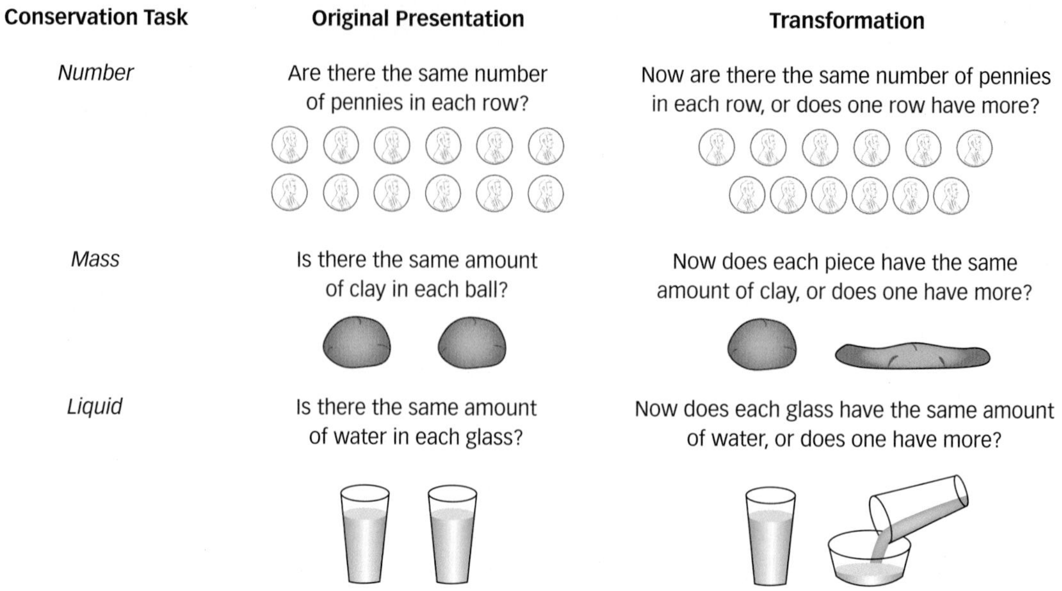

TABLE 6.2 • Characteristics of Preoperational Children's Reasoning

Egocentrism	The inability to take another person's point of view or perspective
Animism	The belief that inanimate objects are alive and have feelings and intentions
Irreversibility	Failure to understand that reversing a process can often undo a process and restore the original state
Centration	Tendency to focus attention on one part of a stimulus or situation and exclude all others

that a change in appearance can be reversed. For example, a child is shown two identical glasses. The same amount of liquid is poured into each glass. After the child agrees that the two glasses contain the same amount of water, the liquid from one glass is poured into a taller, narrower glass and the child is asked whether one glass contains more liquid than the other. Young children in the preoperational stage reply that the taller narrower glass contains more liquid. Why? It has a higher liquid level than the shorter, wider glass has. They center on the appearance of the liquid without realizing that the process can be reversed by pouring the liquid back into the shorter, wider glass. They focus on the height of the water, ignoring other aspects such as the change in width, not understanding that it is still the same water.

Figure 6.6 displays additional conservation problems. Characteristics of preoperational children's reasoning are summarized in Table 6.2.

Evaluating Preoperational Reasoning

Similar to findings that infants are more capable than Piaget envisioned, research with young children has contravened some of Piaget's conclusions. Just as Piaget's sensorimotor tasks underestimated infants' cognitive abilities, his tests of preoperational thinking underestimated young children. Success on Piaget's tasks appears to depend more on the child's language abilities than his or her actions. To be successful at the three mountain task, for example, the child must not only understand how the mounds look from the other side of the table, but must be able to communicate that understanding. Appearance–reality tasks require not simply an understanding of dual representation, but the ability to express it. However, if the task is nonverbal, such as requiring reaching for an object rather than talking about it, even 3-year-old children can distinguish appearance from reality, as we will discuss in the following sections (Sapp, Lee, & Muir, 2000).

Research Findings on Egocentrism and Animism. Simple tasks demonstrate that young children are less egocentric than Piaget posited. When a 3-year-old child is shown a card that depicts a dog on one side and a cat on another, and the card is held up between the researcher who can see the cat and the child who can see the dog, the child correctly responds that the researcher can see the cat (Flavell, Everett, Croft, & Flavell, 1981). In a variation of the three mountain task, called the doll and police officer task, the child sits in front of a square board that is divided into four sections (Hughes, 1975). A toy police officer is placed at the edge of the board. A doll is placed in one section, moved to another section, and so on. With each move the child is asked whether the police officer can see the doll. Finally another police officer is placed on the board and the child is asked to hide the doll from both police officers. In this task, nearly all children ages 3 ½ to 5 were able to take the police officers' perspectives and successfully complete the task. By making the task more relevant to children's everyday lives (i.e., hiding), and less difficult, it became clear that young children are less egocentric than Piaget theorized (M. Hughes, 1975; Newcombe & Huttenlocher, 1992).

Likewise, although young children sometimes provide animistic answers to questions, they do not display animism as often as Piaget believed. Three-year-old children do not tend to describe inanimate objects with lifelike qualities, even when the object is a robot that can move (Gelman & Gottfried, 1996; Jipson, Gülgöz, & Gelman, 2016). Three- and 4-year-old children recognize that living things are regulated by their own internal energy but inanimate objects are not (Gottfried & Gelman, 2005). Most 4-year-old children understand that animals grow, and even plants grow, but objects do not (Backschneider, Shatz, & Gelman, 1993). Sometimes, however, young children provide animistic responses. For example, Dolgin and Behrend (1984) found that animistic statements are not due to a belief that all objects are alive but rather that novel objects that seem to move independently are alive. Three-year-old children may display animism when considering trains and airplanes, believing that they are alive because these objects appear to move on their own, like other living things (Gjersoe, Hall, & Hood, 2015; Massey & Gelman, 1988; Poulin-Dublis & Héroux, 1994). Gjersoe et al. (2015) suggest an emotional component to animistic beliefs. They found that 3-year-olds attribute mental stages to toys to which they are emotionally attached, but not to other favorite toys, even those with which they frequently engage in imaginary play. Finally, children show individual differences in their expressions of animism and reasoning about living things and these differences are linked with aspects of cognitive development such as memory, working memory, and inhibition (Zaitchik, Iqbal, & Carey, 2014).

Research Findings on Reversibility and the Appearance–Reality Distinction. Piaget (1970) posited that young children cannot solve or be taught to solve conservation problems because they lack the cognitive operations needed to understand reversibility and that transformations in appearance do not change a given substance. However, research has shown that 4-year-old children can be taught to conserve (Gelman, 1969; Hendler & Weisberg, 1992), suggesting that children's difficulties with reversibility and conservation tasks can be overcome (Gallagher, 2008). In addition, when a conservation of numbers task is scaled down to include only three objects instead of six, even 3-year-olds perform well without training (Gelman, 1972).

In the classic appearance–reality task, when 3-year-old children are shown a sponge that looks like a rock, they tend to say that it "really and truly is" a rock (Flavell, Flavell, & Green, 1987; Flavell, Green, & Flavell, 1989). They focus on the most salient feature, its rock-like appearance, displaying centration. However, if the children are told to play a trick on someone (i.e., "let's pretend that this sponge is a rock and tell Anne that it is a rock when it really is a sponge") or are asked to choose an object that can be used to clean spilled water, many choose the sponge, illustrating that they can form a dual representation of the sponge as an object that looks like a rock (Rice, Koinis, Sullivan, Tager-Flusberg, & Winner, 1997; Sapp et al., 2000). Research suggests that 3-year-old children can shift between describing the real and fake or imagined aspects of an object or situation, and can flexibly describe misleading appearances and functions of objects in response to natural conversational prompts, as compared with the more formal language in the typical prompts used in traditional appearance–reality tasks (e.g., "What is it really and truly?"; Deák, 2006; Hansen & Markman, 2005).

Some responses to appearance–reality tasks may reflect how children respond to sequences of questions rather than confusing appearance and reality (Deák, 2006). Some preschoolers will repeat their first answer to every successive question about a topic, making it hard to determine what they understand. These types of errors are related to age: 3-year-old children are especially likely to make such errors, 5-year-olds make few repetitive errors, and 4-year-old children tend to make intermediate errors. This suggests a clear developmental trend in language ability that appears on appearance–reality tests as well as other tests of cognitive ability (Deák, 2006). In sum, preschoolers show an understanding of the appearance–reality distinction and it develops throughout childhood (Woolley & Ghossainy, 2013).

Researchers generally conclude that typical Piagetian tasks emphasize what young children *cannot* understand more than what they *can* understand (Beilin, 1992). Traditional appearance–reality tasks require that young children articulate their understanding rather than demonstrate it nonverbally. Often asking different, simplified, questions enables children to demonstrate their understanding (Bullock, 1985; Deák, 2006; Hansen & Markman, 2005; Waxman & Hatch, 1992). Certainly young children are more egocentric and illogical than older, school-aged children, but they are able to demonstrate logical reasoning about simple problems in familiar contexts. Young children can adapt their speech to their listeners: For example, they use simpler language when talking to younger siblings (Gelman & Shatz, 1978), suggesting understanding that their sibling has a different perspective and capacity for language than they do. Young children also quickly develop increasingly sophisticated representational abilities through their symbolic play activities. Pretending that objects and people are something other than what they really are helps young children to develop capacities for dual representation, and they slowly begin to differentiate misleading appearances from reality (Golomb & Galasso, 1995).

Children can also imagine what something looks like and draw a picture to represent that vision. Drawing requires dual representation: the ability for the child to understand that her scratches and squiggles on the page are a picture as well as represent something else—an object, person, or scene. Drawing may seem simple, but it illustrates complex thinking skills.

Thinking in Context 6.1

1. Toys offer infants important opportunities to practice and hone their development. Infants play with toys in different ways at different ages. Identify a toy appropriate for an infant in the secondary circular reactions substage (e.g., a loud rattle or jingling set of toy keys). Compare and contrast how infants in the secondary circular reactions substage and infants in the coordination of secondary circular reactions substage might play with the toy. How might infants in the tertiary reactions substage play with it? How might infants' play align with their developing schemas?

2. Infants around the world delight in playing peekaboo. Compare and contrast how Piaget and core knowledge theorists might account for infants' attention and interest in the caregiver's disappearing and reappearing face.

3. Might parent–infant interactions, the home environment, and sociocultural context influence cognitive development? For example, does such influence occur when infants

develop object permanence or young children overcome egocentrism? Why or why not?

4. Do you think that young children can be taught to respond correctly to conservation problems? Why or why not? If so, what sort of training might children need?

PIAGET'S COGNITIVE-DEVELOPMENTAL PERSPECTIVE: COGNITION IN MIDDLE CHILDHOOD AND ADOLESCENCE

LO 6.2 Contrast the advances of concrete operational versus those of formal operational reasoning, and summarize common criticisms of Piaget's perspective on these stages.

Infants and young children experience cognitive transformations that change their understanding of the world. Their earliest thinking, limited to the here and now, is transformed by the emergence of mental representation and the corresponding ability to learn language. Similarly, older children and adolescents undergo radical changes in their ability to think and solve problems. These changes are marked by the emergence of logical thinking in middle childhood and abstract reasoning in adolescence.

MIDDLE CHILDHOOD: CONCRETE OPERATIONAL REASONING

When children enter the **concrete operational stage of reasoning**, at about age 6 or 7, they gain the capacity to use logic to solve problems. School-age children demonstrate a more sophisticated understanding of the physical world around them.

Characteristics of Concrete Operational Reasoning

Older children's newly developed ability for logical thinking enables them to reason about physical quantities and is evident in their skills for conservation and classification. These cognitive capacities, in turn, influence their interests, interactions with others, and how they spend their time.

Conservation. As we saw earlier in this chapter, young children typically lack understanding of conservation, as demonstrated in the classic experiment with liquid and two containers of different shapes (see Figure 6.6). In another classic conservation problem, a child is shown two identical balls of clay and watches while the experimenter rolls one ball into a long hotdog shape. When asked which piece contains more clay, a child who reasons at the preoperational stage will say that the hotdog shape contains more clay because it is longer. Eight-year-old Julio, on the other hand, knows that the two shapes contain the same amount of clay. At the concrete operational stage of reasoning, Julio grasps the principle of **object identity**: the understanding that certain characteristics of an object do not change despite superficial changes to the object's appearance. Julio notices that the ball shape is shorter than the hotdog shape, but it is also thicker. An understanding of **reversibility**—that an object can be returned to its original state, undoing the superficial physical alterations by which it was changed—means Julio realizes that the hotdog-shaped clay can be reformed into its original ball shape.

Most children solve this conservation problem of substance by age 7 or 8. At about age 9 or 10, children also correctly solve conservation of weight tasks ("Which is heavier, the hotdog or the ball?"). Conservation of volume tasks (after placing the hotdog and ball-shaped clay in glasses of liquid: "Which displaces more liquid?") are solved last, at about age 12. The ability to conserve develops slowly, and children show inconsistencies in their ability to solve different types of conservation problems.

concrete operational stage of reasoning Piaget's third stage of reasoning, from about 6 to 11, in which thought becomes logical and is applied to direct tangible experiences but not to abstract problems.

object identity The understanding that certain characteristics of an object do not change despite superficial changes in the object's appearance.

reversibility The understanding that an object that has been physically altered can be returned to its original state or a process can be done and undone.

LIFESPAN BRAIN DEVELOPMENT

• • Brain-Based Education

Educational practices that emphasize active learning foster development through creative play, artwork, physical activity, and social play.

Children play an active role in their own cognitive development by interacting with the world. Some educators advocate for brain-based education that capitalizes on children's natural inclinations toward active learning. Brain-based education views learning as multidimensional, including more than academics. In its simplest sense, brain-based education encourages children to develop all aspects of their brains, tapping physical, musical, creative, cognitive, and other abilities. Given that the brain changes with experience, enriched everyday experiences such as learning a musical instrument, role playing, and expanding vocabulary may alter children's brains.

Neurological researchers, however, are critical of some popular brain-based educational approaches, such as those that emphasize teaching different parts of the brain separately (Howard-Jones, 2014). For example, a common brain-based education instructional strategy is to teach for the left or right lateralized brain. The "left brain" is said to be the "logical" hemisphere, concerned with language and analysis, while the "right brain" is said to be the "intuitive" hemisphere, concerned with spatial patterns and creativity (Sousa, 2001). Brain-based learning theorists may then encourage teachers to teach specific hemispheres during adapted lessons. To teach to the left hemisphere, teachers have students engage in reading and writing, while right hemisphere–oriented lessons have students create visual representations of

concepts (Sousa, 2001). Brain researchers, however, are sharply critical of left/right brain teaching because, although the brain is lateralized, it functions as a whole (Howard-Jones, 2014). Language and spatial information—and, for that matter, most other abilities—are processed differently but simultaneously by the two hemispheres (Corballis, Lalueza-Fox, Orlando, Enard, & Green, 2014). It is highly improbable, then, that any given lesson, regardless of analytic or spatial type, can stimulate activation of only one hemisphere.

For this reason, some experts argue that the leap from neurological research to the classroom is large and not supported (Alferink & Farmer-Dougan, 2010). For many researchers, the problem of brain-based education is its reliance on the brain itself and its oversimplification of complex theories and research (Alferink & Farmer-Dougan, 2010; Busso & Pollack, 2014). Although we have learned much, brain research is in its infancy. Researchers do not know enough about how the brain functions and learns to draw direct inferences about teaching (Bruer, 2008). For example, MRI research illuminates patterns of brain activity, but researchers do not yet conclusively know what those patterns mean or whether those patterns of brain activity have implications for behavior (Willis, 2007). Applying these findings to inform education is premature. Many researchers, therefore, find it problematic to state that teaching strategies should be derived from brain research.

On the positive side, however, brain-based education emphasizes active learning. Teachers who foster active learning encourage students to become engaged and participate in their own learning, such as being creative in artwork, physical activity, and story making (Bruer, 2008). Active learning is an important educational strategy. Although many developmental researchers argue that the neurological science behind brain-based education is questionable, the active learning practices that comprise many brain-based learning activities do advance children's learning.

What Do You Think?

Identify an advantage and a disadvantage to brain-based education. In your view, should preschools emphasize teaching specifically to a specific part of the brain, such as the left or right hemisphere?

Piaget posited that young school-age children's thinking is so concrete that principles often seem to be tied to particular situations. In his view, they cannot yet apply their understanding of one type of conservation to another problem, even though the principles underlying all conservation problems are the same. Alternatively, some theorists argue that children's capacities to solve conservation problems correspond to brain development and advances in information processing abilities (Morra, Gobbo, Marini, & Sheese, 2008). The earliest type of conservation, numerical conservation, is associated with development of information processing capacities, such as working memory and the ability to control impulses, which permit children to manipulate numerical information to solve problems (Borst, Poirel, Pineau, Cassotti, & Houdé, 2013). As compared with 5-year-olds, 9-year-olds show more activity in parts of the temporal and prefrontal cortex as well as other parts of the brain associated with working memory, inhibitory control, and executive control (Houdé et al., 2011; Poirel et al., 2012). With practice, the cognitive abilities tested in Piagetian tasks become automatic and require less attention and fewer processing resources, enabling children to think in more complex ways (Case, 1998, 1999; Pascual-Leone, 2000). For example, once a child realizes that the hotdog-shaped clay was once in the shape of a ball, and thereby demonstrates an understanding of conservation of substance, the scheme becomes routine and requires less attention and mental resources than before (Siegler & Richards, 1982). Now the child can consider more challenging conservation problems. Children must practice one form of conservation in order for it to become automatic and free cognitive resources to apply that scheme to other conservation problems.

Stamp collecting is a hobby that relies on cognitive skills such as categorization.

Classification. What hobbies did you enjoy as a child? Did you build model cars or airplanes? Collect and trade coins, stamps, rocks, or baseball cards? School-age children develop interests and hobbies that require advanced thinking skills, such as the ability to compare multiple items across several dimensions. **Classification** is the ability to understand hierarchies and to simultaneously consider relations between a general category and more specific subcategories. The classification skills that accompany concrete operational reasoning permit school-age children to categorize or organize objects based on physical dimensions. Several types of classification skills emerge during the concrete operational stage: seriation, transitive influence, and class inclusion. For example, in one classification experiment, a child is shown a bunch of flowers (seven daisies and two roses) and is told that there are nine flowers: seven are called daisies and two are called roses. The child is then asked, "Are there more daisies or flowers?" Preoperational children will answer that there are more daisies, as they do not understand that daisies are a subclass of flowers (Inhelder & Piaget, 1964). By age 5, children have some knowledge of classification hierarchies and may grasp that daisies are flowers, but they still may not fully understand and apply classification hierarchies (Deneault & Ricard, 2006). By about age 8, children can not only classify objects, in this case flowers, but make quantitative judgments and respond that there are more flowers than daisies (Borst et al., 2013).

Children's ability to perform and interest in hierarchical classification becomes apparent in middle childhood when they begin to collect items and spend hours sorting their collections along various dimensions. For example, one day Susan sorts her rock collection by geographic location (e.g., part of the world in which it is most commonly found), with subcategories based on hardness and color. At other times, Susan organizes her rocks based on other characteristics, such as age, composition, and more.

Seriation is the ability to order objects in a series according to a physical dimension, such as height, weight, or color. For example, ask a child to arrange a handful of sticks in order by length, from shortest to longest. Four- to 5-year-old children can pick out the smallest and largest stick, but they will arrange the others haphazardly. Six- to 7-year-old children, on the other hand, arrange the sticks by picking out the smallest, and next smallest, and so on (Inhelder & Piaget, 1964).

The ability to infer the relationship between two objects by understanding each object's relationship to a third is called **transitive inference**. For example, present a child with three sticks: A, B, and C. She is shown that stick A is longer than stick B and stick B is longer than stick C. The concrete operational child does not need to physically compare sticks A and C to know that stick A is longer than the stick C. She uses the information given about the two sticks to infer their relative lengths (Ameel, Verschueren, & Schaeken, 2007; Wright & Smailes, 2015). Transitive inference emerges earlier than other concrete operational skills. By about 5 years of age, children are able to infer that A is longer than C (Goodwin & Johnson-Laird, 2008).

classification The ability to organize things into groups based on similar characteristics.

seriation A type of classification that involves ordering objects in a series according to a physical dimension such as height, weight, or color.

transitive inference A classification skill in which a child can infer the relationship between two objects by understanding each object's relationship to a third object.

Evaluating Concrete Operational Reasoning

According to Piaget, the cognitive stages of development are universal: All children around the world progress through stages that determine their reasoning and their perspective on the world. Piaget emphasized the universal nature of development and placed less attention on culture and context as influences on development. Today's researchers, however, find that the cultural context in which children are immersed plays a critical role in development (Goodnow & Lawrence, 2015). Although it is generally accepted that the features and correlates of Piaget's conception of concrete operational reasoning are universal, cultural factors play a role in the rate of cognitive development (Siegler, 1998). Studies of children in non-Western cultures suggest that they achieve conservation and other concrete operational tasks later than children from Western cultures. When 10- and 11-year-old Canadian Micmac Indian children were tested in English on conservation problems (substance, weight, and volume), they performed worse than 10- to 11-year-old white English-speaking children. But when tested in their native language, by researchers from their own culture, the children performed as well as the English-speaking children (Collette & Van der Linden, 2002). Cultural differences in children's performance on tasks that measure concrete operational reasoning may be more a result of methodology and how questions are asked rather than children's abilities (D'Esposito et al., 1995).

Children around the world demonstrate concrete operational reasoning, but experience, specific cultural practices, and education play a role in how it is displayed (Manoach et al., 1997). Children are more likely to display logical reasoning when considering substances with which they are familiar. Mexican children who make pottery understand at an early age that clay remains the same when its shape is changed. They demonstrate conservation of substance earlier than other forms of conservation (Fry & Hale, 1996) and earlier than children who do not make pottery (Hitch, Towse, & Hutton, 2001; Leather & Henry, 1994).

Despite having never attended school and scoring low on measures of mathematics achievement, many 6- to 15-year-old children living in the streets of Brazil demonstrate sophisticated logical and computational reasoning. Why? These children sell items such as fruit and candy to earn their living. In addition to pricing their products competitively, collecting money, making change, and giving discounts, the children must adjust prices daily to account for changes in demand, overhead, and the rate of inflation (Gathercole, Pickering, Ambridge, & Wearing, 2004). Researchers found that the children's competence in mathematics was influenced by experience, situational demands, and learning from others. Despite this, schooling also matters in promoting cognitive development because children with some schooling were more adept at these tasks than were unschooled children (Siegel, 1994).

Schooling influences the rate at which principles are understood. For example, children who have been in school longer tend to do better on transitive inference tasks than same-age children with less schooling (Artman & Cahan, 1993). Likewise, Zimbabwean children's understanding of conservation is influenced by academic

This child in Brazil shows advanced computational skills because she sells candy and other items to earn a living. Experience and situational demands influence cultural differences in cognitive skills.

REUTERS/Ricardo Moraes

CULTURAL INFLUENCES ON DEVELOPMENT

•• Children's Understanding of Illness

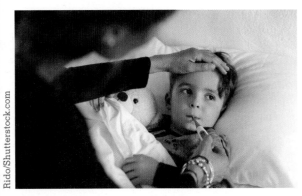

Cultural and contextual factors influence children's reasoning about illness.

School-age children's emerging capacities for reasoning influence their understanding of a variety of phenomena, including their conceptions of illness (Brodie, 1974). Experts formerly thought that children's understanding of illness was unsophisticated; for example, they were thought to view illness as being caused by misdeeds, a view referred to as *immanent justice* (Kister & Patterson, 1980; Myant & Williams, 2005).

As children advance in cognitive maturity from older childhood into adolescence, they develop more advanced conceptions of illness and distinguish specific symptoms and diseases, appreciate psychological, emotional, and social aspects of physical illness, associate illness with germs and infection, and demonstrate an understanding of contagiousness (Brewster, 1982; Kister & Patterson, 1980; Mouratidi, Bonoti, & Leondari, 2016). Older children tend to refer to germs in their explanations of illness, but they tend to view germs as operating in an all-or-nothing fashion such that the presence of germs alone is seen as enough to make a child sick (Raman & Gelman, 2005). It is not until early adolescence or later that they understand the complexity of causal influences and interactions.

Children in Western cultures and adults in non-Western cultures tend to rely on immanent justice and other nonbiological explanations (e.g., magic or fate) for contagious illnesses such as colds, coughs, and stomachaches (Raman & Winer, 2002). However, open-ended interviews require that

the child not only understand the phenomenon, but be able to explain it. When researchers use less demanding tasks, such as forced choice (multiple choice) tasks, they find that Chinese and U.S. children as young as 3 years of age have an understanding that illness is not intentional, that some behaviors can prevent illness and others can make it more likely, and that germs or contamination are responsible for the transmission of contagious illnesses (Legare, Wellman, & Gelman, 2009; Raman & Gelman, 2008; Zhu & Liu, 2007).

Overall, school-aged children tend to prefer biological explanations of illness and use immanent justice reasoning only as a fallback position to explain an illness that is not within the range of their personal experience. Cultural influences also shape children's understanding of illness. For example, one study of 5- to 15-year-old children and adults from Sesotho-speaking South African communities showed that the participants, who were exposed to Western medicine, endorsed biological explanations for illness at high levels, but also often endorsed witchcraft (Legare & Gelman, 2008). Bewitchment explanations were neither the result of ignorance nor replaced by biological explanations. Instead, both natural and supernatural explanations were used to explain the same phenomena and were viewed as complementary. Although specific explanations may vary by culture, the coexistence of biological and supernatural reasoning about causes of illness is not confined to specific cultures. U.S. children and adults retain some supernatural explanations in addition to developing biological explanations (Legare, Evans, Rosengren, & Harris, 2012). Diverse, culturally constructed belief systems about illness co-exist with factual understanding and explanations of illness change with development.

What Do You Think?

1. Does Piaget's theory adequately explain the changes that occur in children's understanding of illness? Why or why not?

2. Consider your own views and experience. Do you remember "catching a cold" when you were a child? What did that mean to you?

experience, age, and family socioeconomic status (Mpofu & Vijver, 2000). Japanese children's understanding of mathematical concepts tends to follow a path consistent with Piaget's maturational view, but other mathematical concepts are understood because of formal instruction, supportive of Vygotsky's principle of scaffolding (discussed later in this chapter) as an influence on cognitive development (Case, Kurland, & Goldberg, 1982; Dempster, 1985). The Cultural Influences on Development feature below explores the development of children's capacities to understand illness.

ADOLESCENCE: FORMAL OPERATIONAL REASONING

Fourteen-year-old Eric spends much of his time learning about astronomy. He wonders about the existence of dark matter—cosmological matter that cannot be observed but is inferred by its gravitational pull on objects like planets and even galaxies. Eric reads blogs written by astronomers and has started his own blog where he comments on the best websites for teenagers who are interested in learning about the galaxy. Eric's newfound ability and interest in considering complex, abstract phenomena illustrates the ways in which adolescents' thinking departs from children's.

As compared with childhood, cognitive development during the adolescent period receives much less attention from theorists and researchers, but adolescents show significant advances in their reasoning capacities (Kuhn, 2008). Similar to earlier periods in life, the cognitive–developmental perspective on cognition describes adolescence as a time of transformation in thought.

Characteristics of Formal Operational Reasoning

In early adolescence, at about 11 years of age, individuals enter the final stage of Piaget's scheme of cognitive development: formal operations. **Formal operational reasoning** entails the ability to think abstractly, logically, and systematically (Inhelder & Piaget, 1958; Piaget, 1972). Children in the concrete operational stage reason about *things*—concepts that exist in reality, such as the problem of how to divide a bowl of pudding into five equal servings. Adolescents in the formal operational stage, however, reason about *ideas*—possibilities that do not exist in reality and that may have no tangible substance, such as whether it is possible to distribute love equally among several targets (Inhelder & Piaget, 1958; Piaget, 1972). The ability to think about possibilities beyond the here and now permits adolescents to plan for the future, make inferences from available information, and consider ways of solving potential, but not yet real, problems.

Formal operational thought enables adolescents to engage in **hypothetical–deductive reasoning**, or the ability to consider problems, generate and systematically test hypotheses, and draw conclusions. Piaget's pendulum task (Figure 6.7) tests children's and adolescents' abilities to use scientific reasoning to solve a problem with multiple possible solutions (Inhelder & Piaget, 1958). Adolescents display formal operational reasoning when they develop hypotheses and systematically test them. For example, in the pendulum task they change one variable while holding the others constant (e.g., trying each of the lengths of string while keeping the weight, height, and force the same). Concrete operational children, on the other hand, fail to disentangle the variables and do not take into account nontangible variables such as height and force. They do not proceed systematically in a way that permits them to solve the pendulum problem; for example, they might test a short string with a heavy weight, then try a long string with a short weight. Solving the pendulum problem requires the scientific reasoning capacities that come with formal operational reasoning.

Adolescents soon learn that hypothetical thought makes for a much more interesting, but complicated, world. Now they are primed to think about possibility and the possible becomes a reality of its own (Inhelder & Piaget, 1958). However, adolescents can get carried away with their consideration of the possible. When Nadia tries to solve the problem of how to organize her room, she might become paralyzed by all the possibilities—myriad ways of arranging furniture, organizing books, and classifying all the things she owns—rather than simply beginning the task.

formal operational reasoning Piaget's fourth stage of cognitive development, characterized by abstract, logical, and systematic thinking.

hypothetical–deductive reasoning The ability to consider propositions, probabilities, generate and systematically test hypotheses, and draw conclusions.

adolescent egocentrism A characteristic of adolescents thinking in which adolescents show preoccupation with themselves and have difficulty separating others' perspectives from their own.

FIGURE 6.7: Measuring Formal Operations: The Pendulum Task

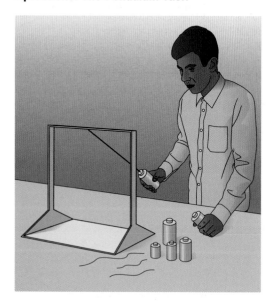

Children and adolescents are presented with a pendulum and are asked what determines the speed with which the pendulum swings. They are given materials and told that there are four variables to consider: (1) length of string (short, medium, long); (2) weight (light, medium, heavy); (3) height at which the weight is dropped; and (4) force with which the weight is dropped.

APPLYING DEVELOPMENTAL SCIENCE

• • Implications of Adolescent Thinking: Adolescent Egocentrism

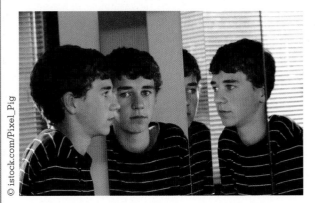

Adolescents' self-preoccupation is influenced by egocentrism.

Adolescents' emerging abilities to reason influence how they view the world and themselves. However, abstract thought develops gradually. Teenagers are prone to errors in reasoning and lapses in judgment, as evidenced by the emergence of adolescent egocentrism.

Adolescents' new cognitive abilities draw them to consider the intangible, such as ideas and possibilities. At the same time, they undergo physical changes and psychological changes that lead them to direct their new abstract abilities toward themselves. Adolescents are naturally self-conscious. As 14-year-old Mayla's mother explains, "She's always in her head but also outside, paying attention to her clothes and the smallest details of her appearance, as if anyone would notice anyway." Adolescents are egocentric. They have difficulty with perspective-taking, specifically with separating their own and others' perspectives (Inhelder & Piaget, 1958). Researcher David Elkind proposed that **adolescent egocentrism** is manifested in two phenomena: the imaginary audience and the personal fable (Elkind & Bowen, 1979).

The **imaginary audience** is just that: Adolescents project their own preoccupation about themselves onto others and assume that they are the focus of others' attention (Elkind & Bowen, 1979). In this way, they are unable to accurately take other people's perspectives. The imaginary audience fuels adolescents' concerns with their appearance, and can make the slightest criticism made in public sting painfully, as teens are convinced that all eyes are on them. The imaginary audience contributes to the heightened self-consciousness characteristic of adolescence (Alberts, Elkind, & Ginsberg, 2007).

Adolescents' preoccupation with themselves also leads them to believe that they are special, unique, and invulnerable—a perspective known as the **personal fable** (Elkind & Bowen, 1979). A sense of self-importance underlies the personal fable belief that they will be admired, achieve fame, and be remembered. Many adolescents perceive their own experiences as unique. They believe that their emotions, the highs of happiness and depths of despair that they feel, are different and more intense than other people's emotions and that others simply do not understand. The invulnerability aspect of the personal fable, coupled with brain development that predisposes adolescents to seek risks, makes adolescents more likely to engage in risky activities, such as drug use, delinquency, and unsafe sex; they believe that they, unlike other teens, are invulnerable to the negative consequences of such behaviors (Alberts et al., 2007; Greene & Krcmar, 2000). Specifically, research with 6th-through 12th-graders suggests that the invulnerability aspect of the personal fable is associated with engaging in risky activities while the sense of personal uniqueness is associated with depression and suicidal ideation (Aalsma, Lapsley, & Flannery, 2006).

Both the imaginary audience and personal fable are thought to increase in early adolescence, peak in middle adolescence, and decline in late adolescence (Alberts et al., 2007; Elkind & Bowen, 1979; Lapsley, Jackson, Rice, & Shadid, 1988), but some research suggests that adolescent egocentrism may persist into late adolescence and beyond (Schwartz, Maynard, & Uzelac, 2008). Even adults are susceptible to these lapses in perspective. in studies many instances adolescents may be *less* likely to see themselves as invincible than are adults. Studies in which adolescents and adults evaluate the possible consequences of various behaviors, adolescents perceive more risks inherent to health behaviors and activities, such as substance use and risky driving, for example, than do adults (Fischhoff, 2008; Millstein & Halpern-Felsher, 2002). Perhaps adolescent egocentrism, specifically the personal fable, may not be a feature unique to adolescence.

What Do You Think?

1. **Do you remember experiencing the imaginary audience or personal fable? Provide an example of the imaginary audience and personal fable from your own experience or create hypothetical examples.**

2. **Do you think adolescent egocentrism disappears? If so, what factors might contribute to the fall of adolescent egocentrism? If not, why?**

© istock.com/Pixel_Pig

Lives in Context Video 6.2
Formal Operations

Evaluating Formal Operational Reasoning

An assumption of Piaget's cognitive–developmental theory is that development is a universal process, yet the reality is that people vary in their cognitive development. Although adults are presumably capable of abstract reasoning, many of them fail hypothetical-deductive tasks (Kuhn, Langer, Kohlberg, & Haan, 1977). Does this mean they cannot think abstractly? In response to research findings suggesting variability in formal operational reasoning, Piaget (1972) explained that opportunities to use formal operational reasoning influence its development. In contrast to his position on earlier stage structures, Piaget argued that formal operations structures may vary by content area. Individuals reason at the most advanced levels when considering material with which they have the greatest experience. For example, completing college courses in math and science is associated with gains in propositional thought, while courses in social science are associated with advances in statistical reasoning skills (Lehman & Nisbett, 1990; Lehman, Lempert, & Nisbett, 1988). In one study in the early 1990s, adolescents from 10 to 15 years of age performed better on Piagetian tasks, such as the pendulum task, than adolescents had done more than two decades before. The researchers attributed the difference to the fact that (in France, where the studies were done) secondary education was less common in the earlier decades, therefore adolescents had fewer opportunities to practice the reasoning measured by Piagetian tasks (Flieller, 1999).

The appearance of formal operational reasoning is not consistent across people or across intellectual domains, but instead varies with situation, task, experience, context, and motivation (Kuhn, 2008; Labouvie-Vief, 2015a; Piaget, 1972). Moreover, many theorists explain that formal operational reasoning does not suddenly appear in early adolescence. Instead, cognitive change occurs gradually from childhood on, with gains in knowledge, experience, and information processing capacity (Keating, 2004; Kuhn & Franklin, 2006; Moshman, 2005). Finally, many developmental scientists believe that cognitive development continues throughout adulthood, as we discuss later in this chapter.

 Thinking in Context 6.2

1. Cognitive changes influence children's interests and how they spend their time. Consider your own childhood interests. How did they change in late childhood and into adolescence? How might your shifting and intensifying interests reflect cognitive development?

2. Do you think that most young adolescents show formal operational reasoning? Give examples to support your answer.

3. The cognitive developmental perspective has been criticized for downplaying the role of context in cognitive development. Identify contextual factors that might influence the path of cognitive development. Consider it from a bioecological perspective. What factors at the micro, meso, exo, and macrosystem levels might influence cognitive change in childhood and adolescence?

VYGOTSKY'S SOCIOCULTURAL PERSPECTIVE

LO 6.3 Summarize Vygotsky's sociocultural perspective and how it is manifested in scaffolding, the zone of proximal development, and cultural tools.

While Piaget searched for universal patterns, Russian psychologist Lev Vygotsky emphasized the influence of culture on children's thinking. Specifically, he proposed that cognitive development is influenced by differences in the ways particular cultures and societies approach problems. Although Vygotsky wrote at the same time as Piaget, his writings remained relatively unknown for decades. For political reasons his work was banned in his

imaginary audience
A manifestation of adolescent egocentrism in which they assume that they are the focus of others' attention.

personal fable A manifestation of adolescent egocentrism in which adolescents believe their thoughts, feelings, and experiences are more special and unique than anyone else's, as well as the sense that they are invulnerable.

country, the Soviet Union, and English translations of his writing did not become available until the 1980s. Vygotsky's sociocultural perspective asserts that we are embedded in a context that shapes how we think and who we become. Much of children's learning comes not from working alone, but from collaborating with others.

SCAFFOLDING AND GUIDED PARTICIPATION

According to the sociocultural perspective, children's social experiences teach them how to think. Children interact with more skilled partners who serve as models and provide instruction. Over time, children internalize the instruction, making it part of their skill set, and they thereby master tasks. For example, children of the Zinacantec Maya of Chiapas, Mexico, learn by actively participating in informal tasks such as making tortillas and weaving (Maynard, 2002, 2004). Children learn by working alongside more experienced partners who provide assistance when needed (Rogoff, 1998; Rogoff, Mosier, Mistry, & Göncü, 1993). Older and more skilled members of society stimulate children's cognitive development by presenting new challenges and guiding or assisting them with particularly difficult tasks. Parents and child care providers often provide this informal instruction, but anyone who is more skilled at a given task, including older siblings and peers, can promote children's cognitive development (Maynard, 2002; Rogoff, 1990).

In this way, children learn through **guided participation** (also known as an *apprenticeship in thinking*), a form of sensitive teaching in which the partner is attuned to the needs of the child and helps him or her to accomplish more than the child could do alone (Rogoff, 1990). As novices, children learn from more skilled, or expert, partners by observing them and asking questions. In this way children are apprentices, learning how others approach problems. The expert partner provides **scaffolding** that permits the child to bridge the gap between his or her current competence level and the task at hand. For example, consider a child working on a jigsaw puzzle. She is stumped, unable to complete it on her own. Suppose a more skilled partner, such as an adult, sibling, or another child who has more experience with puzzles, provides a little bit of assistance, a scaffold. The expert partner might point to an empty space on the puzzle and encourage the child to find a piece that fits that spot. If the child remains stumped, the partner might point out a piece or rotate it to help the child see the relationship. The partner acts to motivate the child and provide support to help the child finish the puzzle, emphasizing that they are working together. The child novice and expert partner interact to accomplish the goal and the expert adjusts his or her responses to meet the needs of the child.

guided participation Also known as apprenticeship in thinking; the process by which people learn from others who guide them, providing a scaffold to help them accomplish more than the child could do alone.

scaffolding Temporary support that permits a child to bridge the gap between his or her current competence level and the task at hand.

With time, the child internalizes the scaffolding lesson and learns to accomplish the task on her own. In this way cognitive development and learning occurs as the child actively internalizes elements of context, such as interactions with more skilled people (Fernyhough, 2008). Scaffolding occurs in formal educational settings, but also informally, any time a partner adjusts his or her interactional style to fit the needs of a child and guide the child to complete a task that he or she could not complete alone.

The quality of scaffolding influences children's development. In one study of preschool teachers and children, the degree to which the adult matched the child's needs for help in playing predicted more autonomous play on the part of children over a 6-month period (Trawick-Smith & Dziurgot, 2011). Adults may intentionally encourage and support children's

Pura learns the tools of her culture through guided particpation.

learning (Zuckerman, 2007). For example, one study of parents and young children visiting a science museum found that when parents provided specific guidance in considering a conservation of volume problem, such as discussing the size of the containers, asking "how" and "why" questions, and talking about simple math, children were more likely to give correct responses to scientific reasoning problems, including those involving conservation (Vandermaas-Peeler, Massey, & Kendall, 2016).

Scaffolding also occurs informally. Mothers vary their scaffolding behaviors in response to children's attempts at tasks. For example, they spontaneously use different behaviors depending on the child's attention skills, using more verbal engagement, strategic questions, verbal hints, and verbal prompts when children show difficulty paying attention during a task (Robinson, Burns, & Davis, 2009). Moreover, maternal reading, scaffolding, and verbal guidance are associated with 2- to 4-year-olds' capacities for cognitive control and planning (Bibok, Carpendale, & Müller, 2009; Hughes & Ensor, 2009; Moriguchi, 2014). In this way, learning is a social activity, and children can learn from many social partners, including peers. Collaboration with more skilled peers improves performance on cognitive tasks such as card sorting tasks, Piagetian tasks, planning, and academic tasks (Ellis & Gauvain, 1992; Sills, Rowse, & Emerson, 2016). Social interaction may have varying effects on learning depending on social factors. For example, in a problem-solving task, child dyads who were not friends spent more time determining the division of labor and angling for control than completing the task (Azmitia & Perlmutter, 1989). Children's ability to learn from peer interactions may, therefore, depend on their peer relationships.

ZONE OF PROXIMAL DEVELOPMENT

As Vygotsky explained, "What the child can do in cooperation today, he can do alone tomorrow" (1962, p. 104). Effective scaffolding works within the **zone of proximal development**, the gap between the child's competence level—what he can do alone—and what he can do with assistance. The upper limit of this zone is what the child can accomplish with a skilled partner. Over time, the child internalizes the scaffolding, the skill becomes within his range of competence, and his zone of proximal development shifts. Adults tend to naturally provide children with instruction within the zone of proximal development (Conner, Knight, & Cross, 1997; Rogoff, 1998). For example, adults reading a book to a child tend to point to items, label and describe characters' emotional states, explain, ask questions, listen, and respond sensitively, helping the child understand challenging material that is just beyond what the child can understand on his or her own (Adrián, Clemente, & Villanueva, 2007; Danis, Bernard, & Leproux, 2000; Silva, Strasser, & Cain, 2014). Adults learn as they participate in the child's zone of proximal development and they modify their behaviors (Ferholt & Lecusay, 2010). For example, mothers may observe that the timing of their suggestions and feedback helps children attend and switch tasks appropriately (Bibok et al., 2009).

Effective teachers take advantage of the social nature of learning by assigning children tasks that they can accomplish with some assistance, providing just enough help so that students learn to complete the tasks independently, and creating learning environments that stimulate children to complete more challenging tasks on their own (Wass & Golding, 2014).

CULTURAL TOOLS

zone of proximal development Vygotsky's term for the tasks that children cannot do alone but can exercise with the aid of more skilled partners.

Mental activity is influenced by cultural tools that are passed on to members of the culture (Robbins, 2005; Vygotsky, 1978). Cultural tools include physical items such as computers, pencils, and paper, but also ways of thinking about phenomena, including how to approach math and scientific problems. Children learn how to use the tools of their culture by interacting with skilled partners who provide scaffolding within the zone of proximal development. For example, suppose a child wanted to bake cookies for the first time. Rather than send the child into the kitchen alone, we would probably accompany the child and provide the tools needed to accomplish the task, such as the ingredients, a rolling pin to roll the dough, cookie cutters, and a baking sheet. We would probably show the child how to use each tool, such as how to roll out the dough, and watch as he or she does it, scaffolding his or her learning. With interaction and experience, the child adopts and internalizes the tools and knowledge, becoming able to use them independently.

Vygotsky argued that in this way, culturally valued ways of thinking and problem solving get passed on to children. Spoken language is an important tool of thought, as we will discuss in Chapter 7, as are writing, numeracy, and problem-solving techniques.

The contextual nature of learning is illustrated by a study of two generations of Zinacantec Mayan children, one generation studied in 1969 and 1970, and a second generation in 1991 and 1993 (Greenfield, Maynard, & Childs, 2003). In the intervening two decades, the community, located in Chiapas, Mexico, was involved in a transition from an economy based primarily on subsistence and agriculture to an economy based primarily on money and commerce. Researchers examined the number and quality of weaving apprenticeships as well as visual representation ability. They concluded that the processes of learning and cognition changed over this period, trending toward greater emphasis on independent cultural learning, abstract thinking, and creativity, and away from scaffolding, simple representation of tasks, and imitation strategies

This mother is providing a scaffold to help her daughter learn how to complete a puzzle. Effective scaffolding occurs within the zone of proximal development, the gap between what the child can do on her own and what she can accomplish with a little bit of help.

(Greenfield et al., 2003). Changes in cultural apprenticeships were associated with shifts in the process of child cognition. The contexts in which we are embedded are always changing and evolving, as are our ways of thinking.

EVALUATING VYGOTSKY'S SOCIOCULTURAL PERSPECTIVE

Although relatively unknown until recent decades, Vygotsky's ideas about the sociocultural nature of cognitive development have influenced prominent theories of development, such as Bronfenbrenner's (1979) bioecological theory. They have been applied in educational settings, supporting the use of assisted discovery, guiding children's learning, and cooperative learning with peers.

Similar to Piaget's theory, Vygotsky's theory has been criticized for a lack of precision. The mechanisms or processes underlying the social transmission of thought are not described (Ellis & Gauvain, 1992; Göncü & Gauvain, 2012). Moreover, constructs such as the zone of proximal development are not easily testable (Wertsch, 1998). In addition, underlying cognitive capacities, such as attention and memory, are not addressed. It is understandable, however, that Vygotsky's theory is incomplete, as he died of tuberculosis at the age of 37. We can only speculate about how his ideas might have evolved over a longer lifetime. Nevertheless, Vygotsky provided a new framework for understanding development as a process of transmitting culturally valued tools that influence how we look at the world, think, and approach problems.

Thinking in Context 6.3

1. Contrast Vygotsky and Piaget's perspectives on cognitive development.

2. What cultural tools have you adopted? How have interactions with others influenced your cognitive development?

3. How might Vygotsky's ideas be applied to children's learning at home and in the classroom? Give some examples.

COGNITIVE DEVELOPMENT IN ADULTHOOD

LO 6.4 Explain postformal reasoning and how it compares with cognitive affective complexity.

For Alexander, a college junior majoring in biology, weighing hypotheses on evolutionary theory is easy. As he sees it, there is one account that is clearly more rational and supported by data than the others. However, like most young adults, Alexander finds personal decisions much more difficult because many are vague and have multiple options with both costs and benefits. As teenagers mature into adults, their thinking becomes increasingly flexible and practical. Adults come to expect uncertainty and ambiguity, and to recognize that everyday problems are influenced by emotion and experience rather than pure reasoning. Researchers who study adult cognition often focus on **epistemic cognition**— the ways in which individuals understand the nature of knowledge and how they arrive at ideas, beliefs, and conclusions.

POSTFORMAL REASONING AND REFLECTIVE JUDGMENT

Many researchers who adopt Piaget's perspective on cognitive development agree that formal operations, Piaget's final stage of cognitive development, does not adequately describe adult cognition. Instead, adults develop a more advanced form of thinking known as **postformal reasoning**, which integrates abstract reasoning with practical considerations (Sinnott, 1998). Young adults who demonstrate postformal reasoning recognize that most problems have multiple causes and solutions, that some solutions are better choices than others, and that all problems involve uncertainty.

With maturation, young people become more likely to compare their reasoning process and justifications with others'. When their justifications fall short, adults seek a more adequate explanation and adjust their thinking accordingly. People's understanding of the nature of knowledge advances along a predictable path in young adulthood, especially among college students (King & Kitchener, 1994; Magolda, 2002; Perry, 1970).

When they enter college, young people tend to view knowledge as a set of facts that hold true across people and contexts (King & Kitchener, 2004; Perry, 1970). They view learning as a matter of acquiring and assessing facts. Beginning college students tend to display **dualistic thinking**: polar reasoning in which knowledge and accounts of phenomena are viewed as either right or wrong, with no in between. They tend to have difficulty grasping that several contradictory arguments can each have supporting evidence. The entering college student may sit through class lectures, wondering, "Which theory is right?" and become frustrated when the professor explains that multiple theories each have various strengths and weaknesses.

With experience in college, such as exposure to multiple viewpoints, multiple arguments, and their inherent contradictions, students become aware of the diversity of viewpoints that exist in every area study. Their thinking becomes more flexible and they relinquish the belief in absolute knowledge that characterizes dualistic thinking (Baxter Magolda, 2004). Instead they move toward **relativistic thinking**, in which

epistemic cognition The ways in which an individual understands how he or she arrived at ideas, beliefs, and conclusions.

postformal reasoning A stage of cognitive development proposed to follow Piaget's formal operational stage. Thinking and problem solving is restructured in adulthood to integrate abstract reasoning with practical considerations, recognizing that most problems have multiple causes and solutions, some solutions are better than others, and all problems involve uncertainty.

dualistic thinking Polar reasoning in which knowledge and accounts of phenomena are viewed as absolute facts, either right or wrong with no in-between.

relativistic thinking Type of reasoning in which knowledge is viewed as subjective and dependent on the situation.

most knowledge is viewed as relative, dependent on the situation and thinker (King & Kitchener, 2004; Perry, 1970). Relativistic thinkers recognize that beliefs are subjective, that there are multiple perspectives on a given issue, and that all perspectives are defensible (Magolda, 2002; Sinnott, 1998). Often students become overwhelmed by relativism and conclude that most topics are simply a matter of opinion and perspective and all views are valid. For example, they may conclude that all solutions to a problem are correct as it all depends on a person's perspective. A more mature thinker, however, begins to acknowledge the multiple options yet carefully evaluate them to choose the most adequate solution.

As shown in Table 6.3, the most mature type of reasoning entails **reflective judgment**: reasoning that synthesizes contradictions among perspectives (King & Kitchener, 2004; Perry, 1970). While a relativistic thinker may approach a problem such as deciding which theory is most adequate or which short story is best by explaining that it is simply a matter of opinion and it "depends on the person," the individual who displays reflective judgment recognizes that options and opinions can be evaluated—and generates criteria to do so (Sinnott, 2003). Although reasoning tends to advance throughout the college years, ultimately few adults demonstrate reflective judgment (Perry, 1970).

Development beyond formal operations is dependent on experience and the ability to reflect one one's thought process (known as metacognition, discussed in Chapter 7). Exposure to situations and reasoning that challenges students' knowledge and belief systems, coupled with more explicit, powerful, and effective cognitive abilities, permits individuals to consider the adequacy of their own thought and reasoning processes and modify them as needed (Kuhn, 2000). Advancement to postformal reasoning is associated with contextual factors; specifically, it is associated with exposure to realistic but ambiguous problems and supportive guidance, such as that which is often a part of college education in Western cultures (King & Kitchener, 2002; Zeidler, Sadler, Applebaum, & Callahan, 2009).

reflective judgment Mature type of reasoning that synthesizes contradictions among perspectives.

TABLE 6.3 • Postformal Reasoning

	UNDERSTANDING OF KNOWLEDGE	EXAMPLES FROM INTERVIEWS WITH YOUNG ADULTS
Dualistic thinking	Knowledge is a collection of facts, and a given idea is either right or wrong.	". . . . theory might be convenient . . . , but. . . . The facts are what's there . . . and . . . should be the main thing." (Perry, 1970/1998)
Relativistic thinking	Knowledge is relative, dependent on the situation and thinker, and a matter of opinion and perspective.	"I really can't [choose a point of view] on this issue. It depends on your beliefs since there is no way of proving either one. . . . I believe they're both the same as far as accuracy." (King & Kitchener, 2004, p. 6) "People think differently and so they attack the problem differently. Other theories could be as true as my own but based on different evidence." (King & Kitchener, 2004, p. 7)
Reflective judgment	Knowledge is a synthesis of contradictory information and perspectives whose evidence can be evaluated according to certain criteria.	"[when approaching a problem] there are probably several ways to do it. What are they? Which one's most efficient? Which one will give us the most accurate results?" (Marra & Palmer, 2004, p. 117) "One can judge an argument by how well thought-out the positions are, what kinds of reasoning and evidence are used to support it, and how consistent the way one argues on this topic is, as compared with how one argues on other topics." (King & Kitchener, 2004, p. 7) "It is very difficult in this life to be sure. There are degrees of sureness. You come to a point at which you are sure enough for a personal stance on the issue." (King & Kitchener, 2004, p. 7)

Yet postformal reasoning is not universal across cultures. For example, Chinese college students generally do not display the typical advancement from dualism to relativism to reflective judgment (Zhang, 2004; Zhang & Watkins, 2001). When compared with their U.S. counterparts, Chinese students tend to lack opportunities for making their own choices and decisions in many areas such as curricula, career choices, academic majors, and residential arrangements (Zhang, 1999). Experience in decision making matters. Some theorists argue that even in Western cultures, the most advanced level of postformal reasoning (commitment within relativism) may come only with graduate study and wrestling with challenging philosophical and practical problems (King & Kitchener, 2004).

Regardless of education, culture, or age, social interaction is a critical influence on the development of postformal cognition (Kuhn, 2008). Social interaction entails discussing multiple perspectives and solutions to a problem as well as encouraging individuals to consider others' perspectives, evaluate their own reasoning, and perhaps advance to more sophisticated forms of reasoning. People's reasoning advances throughout adulthood; however, reasoning and decision-making are not simply cognitive endeavors but are influenced by emotion.

PRAGMATIC THOUGHT AND COGNITIVE-EMOTIONAL COMPLEXITY

Development in adulthood entails changes in abstract reasoning and also an extension of reflective judgment, which permits the acceptance of inconsistency and ambiguity, to **pragmatic thought** emphasizing the use of logic to address everyday problems (Labouvie-Vief, 1980, 2006, 2015b). Managing various roles and tackling the problems of everyday life requires thinking that is adaptive and accepting of contradiction. For example, adults must come to terms with their relative power across various contexts: At home they have autonomy and are able to carve out their own niche, whereas at work they must follow the directions of their employer. Coordinating dynamic roles as spouse, parent, friend, employee, and manager requires flexibility.

However, reasoning in everyday situations is not simply a matter of logic; it is fused with emotion. Over the course of adulthood, individuals become better at understanding and regulating their emotions, which influences their reasoning in everyday situations (Blanchard-Fields, 2007; Mather, 2012; Watson & Blanchard-Fields, 1998). In turn, advancing cognitive capacities transform how adults experience and understand emotion, so that it becomes integrated with cognition. For example, in dealing with complex hypothetical interpersonal problems, young and middle-aged adults prefer problem-focused strategies that directly address the problem, whereas older adults prefer to combine problem-focused with emotion-focused strategies that emphasize regulating their affective reactions (Watson & Blanchard-Fields 1998).

Successfully coordinating emotion and cognition improves people's capacity to adapt to the complexities of adult life and the inherent balancing of many roles and obligations (Labouvie-Vief, 2006). This capacity to be aware of emotions, integrate positive and negative feelings about an issue, and regulate intense emotions to make logical decisions about complicated issues is known as **cognitive–affective complexity** (Labouvie-Vief, 2003, 2015a; Mikels et al., 2010). Cognitive–affective complexity increases from early adulthood through late middle adulthood (Labouvie-Vief et al., 2010). With gains in cognitive–affective complexity, adults better understand others, including their perspectives, feelings, and motivations. This, in turn, helps them to participate in social interactions, become more tolerant of other viewpoints, and solve day-to-day problems. As adults progress through older adulthood, however, cognitive–affective complexity declines, and they tend to prefer solutions that emphasize emotional regulation over problem-focused solutions. Some researchers attribute this shift toward maintaining positive emotions over affective complexity to neurological and cognitive changes (Labouvie-Vief et al., 2010), yet others argue that it serves a coping function to

pragmatic thought In Labouvie-Vief's theory, a type of thinking where logic is used as a tool to address everyday problems and contradictions are viewed as part of life.

cognitive-affective complexity A form of mature thinking that involves emotional awareness, the ability to integrate and regulate intense emotions, and the recognition and appreciation of individual experience.

preserve a positive sense of self and relationships (Carstensen & Mikels, 2005; Reed & Carstensen, 2012; see Chapter 10).

EVALUATING COGNITIVE-DEVELOPMENTAL APPROACHES TO ADULT DEVELOPMENT

Similar to research on the development of formal operations, advances in postformal reasoning and cognitive–affective complexity vary among individuals. Adults are more likely than adolescents to demonstrate postformal reasoning, but not all adults reach the most advanced levels of reasoning (Commons & Richards, 2002; Sinnott, 2003). In fact, most do not. People seem to show more mature reasoning when considering material and problems with which they have the greatest experience.

As with findings with younger ages, the ways in which researchers ask questions influences individuals' responses and, ultimately, what is concluded about cognition (Ojalehto & Medin, 2015). For example, researchers have learned that more complex responses are yielded when they ask participants to consider systems of causation using prompts such as "how are x and y related to each other and to the larger system?" as compared with prompts that encourage reasoning about individual causal links ("does x cause y?"). This work has shown that there is cultural variation in reasoning about causal events (Ojalehto & Medin, 2015). Westerners tend to explain events using a single or a few direct causes. In contrast, people from East Asian cultures tend to explain events as caused by multiple factors that interact, creating a ripple effect whereby one event holds many complex consequences that may not be easily anticipated (Maddux & Yuki, 2006). This reasoning is conceptually similar to the interacting systems posited by Bronfenbrenner (see Chapter 1). Other research has shown that a multifactor interactive view of causality is present among people of many non-Western cultural communities. For example, Indigenous Itza' Maya and Native American Menominee people tend to emphasize complex interactions across many entities, such as animal and spiritual entities; contexts, such as habitats; and time frames (Atran & Medin, 2008; Unsworth et al., 2012).

Likewise, cognitive–affective complexity relies on advances in emotional awareness and regulation (Labouvie-Vief, 2003). The ability to coordinate sophisticated emotions and cognitions varies with situations, tasks, contexts, and motivations (Kuhn, 2008; Labouvie-Vief, 2015a; Piaget, 1972). Furthermore, advanced forms of pragmatic reasoning likely do not suddenly appear; rather, they emerge with gains in knowledge, experience, and information-processing capacity (Keating, 2004; Kuhn & Franklin, 2006; Moshman, 2005).

Although cognitive development perspectives offer rich descriptions of how people of various ages think, especially describing what reasoning looks like across development, critics have argued that they provide little explanation of just how these changes occur (Brainerd et al., 1978; Halford, 1989). That is, what causes cognitive change? Most current research on cognitive change across the lifespan examines the changes that occur in information processing capacities, such as advances in attention, memory, and problem solving—topics we discuss in Chapter 7.

 Thinking in Context 6.4

1. What evidence, if any, do you see that most young adolescents show formal operational reasoning? Give examples to support your answer.

2. Can you identify examples of postformal reasoning in your own thinking? What are some challenges of evaluating one's own thinking?

3. What kinds of experiences foster the development of postformal reasoning? In your view, is higher education necessary to develop the capacity for postformal reasoning? Why or why not?

Apply Your Knowledge

Seven-year old Megan sets the large pitcher of lemonade on the table, the essential component to her lemonade stand. Her father explains, "To make money you need to make sure that you spend less on lemonade and cups than you earn." Showing Megan the price of the lemonade mix and cups and the number of servings each jar of lemonade mix makes, he explains that she will make enough money to stay in business if she sells each cup of lemonade for 50 cents. "Don't overfill each cup. See this line?" Megan's father asks, pointing to a line near the top of the cup. "Pour lemonade up to this line." Nodding, Megan excitedly answers, "OK!"

Megan is pleasantly surprised to see that her lemonade stand is popular with the neighborhood kids and adults. So much so that she runs out of cups. Racing into her house, Megan asks her mother for more cups. "These are all we have left," she answers, handing Megan a package of cups. Megan notices that the new cups are a little bit larger than her first set of cups. As she pours lemonade into the new cups, Megan remembers her father's warning that if she wants to make enough money to stay in business she shouldn't overfill cups. She carefully adjusts the amounts, pouring a little bit less into each cup.

At the end of the week Megan happily counts her earnings. Her father reminds her to put aside money to buy more supplies. "How much money do you think we need to buy more lemonade and cups?" he asks. "I don't know," Megan answers. "Well let's see," he responds. "The lemonade powder cost $2 and you needed two jars. How much is that?" "Four!" "How much were the cups? Look at the price sticker." "One dollar, but we need two, right?" "Yes, so how much are the cups?" "Two dollars."

"So how much will our supplies cost?" Megan looks unsure. "How much is the lemonade? How much are the cups? Put those numbers together." "Six!" "Exactly. Now, how much money did you make?" "Thirteen dollars." "And how much will you have left after buying supplies? It's how much money you made, take away what you spend on supplies" "Seven?" "Yes, you earned seven dollars!"

Now 20 years old, Megan fondly looks back on her lemonade-selling days. "I wish everything were that easy. Simple problems and simple answers. It's not like that anymore." Megan sometimes finds her college classes challenging: "There are so many theories and every theory sounds good and makes sense. I think it's just a matter of opinion because every theory explains stuff just as well as the others." Megan's older sister responds, "Not so fast. Not all theories are equally good. It might look that way at first, but if you look a little deeper you'll see that some have more support to back them up than others. Which theory to choose is not really an opinion; it's a judgment based on weighing the evidence." Megan retorts, "You just overthink everything because you're in graduate school!"

1. At what Piagetian stage does 7-year-old Megan reason? Explain the evidence for your answer.

2. What role does Megan's father play in her cognitive advances? Describe his actions from Vygotsky's perspective.

3. What advances in reasoning do 20-year-old Megan and her older sister demonstrate? How do you know? Cite some examples from their conversation.

Give your students the SAGE edge!

SAGE edge offers a robust online environment featuring an impressive array of free tools and resources for review, study, and further exploration, keeping both instructors and students on the cutting edge of teaching and learning. Learn more at **edge.sagepub.com/kuthertopical.**

CHAPTER 6 IN REVIEW

6.1 Identify Piaget's six substages of sensorimotor reasoning and summarize criticism of this perspective on infant and early childhood cognitive development.

SUMMARY

According to Piaget, children construct and refine schemas in response to experience via assimilation and accommodation. Piaget proposed that people naturally strive for cognitive equilibrium, and the confusion that accompanies disequilibrium leads to cognitive growth. During the sensorimotor period, infants move through six substages, from acting on the world with reflexes (Substage 1) to demonstrating representational thought (Stage 6). Research using simpler tasks has shown that very young infants' mental representation abilities may be more advanced than Piaget believed. Core knowledge researchers have shown that young infants have a grasp of the physical properties of objects, such as object permanence, solidity, gravity, number, and language. Preoperational reasoning appears in young children from about ages 2 to 6 and is characterized by advances in representational thinking but also the inability to grasp logic and understand complex relationships. Recent research with simple tasks suggest that young children may be less egocentric than Piaget posited and can solve more advanced tasks than he theorized.

KEY TERMS

schemas	deferred imitation
assimilation	core knowledge perspective
accommodation	preoperational reasoning
mental representation	egocentrism
circular reactions	three mountain task
primary circular reactions	animism
secondary circular reactions	centration
object permanence	appearance–reality distinction
tertiary circular reactions	conservation
violation-of-expectation task	irreversibility

REVIEW QUESTIONS

1. According to Piaget, how does cognition change over infancy?
2. How do contemporary research findings compare with Piaget's theory?

6.2 Contrast the advances of concrete operational versus those of formal operational reasoning, and summarize common criticisms of Piaget's perspective on these stages.

SUMMARY

School-age children demonstrate concrete operational reasoning. They are able to use logic to solve problems but still are unable to apply it to abstract and hypothetical situations. In early adolescence, at about 11 years of age, individuals enter the formal operations stage and become able to think abstractly, logically, and systematically. The ability to think about possibilities beyond the here and now permits adolescents to plan for the future, make inferences from available information, and consider ways of solving potential, but not yet real, problems as well as engage in hypothetical-deductive reasoning. Some theorists argue that children's capacities to solve conservation problems correspond to brain development and advances in information-processing abilities. Although Piaget proposed that the cognitive stages of development are universal, we now know that the cultural context in which we are immersed plays an important role in our development.

KEY TERMS

concrete operational stage of reasoning	transitive inference
object identity	formal operational reasoning
reversibility	hypothetical–deductive reasoning
classification	adolescent egocentrism
seriation	imaginary audience
	personal fable

REVIEW QUESTIONS

1. What are similarities and differences in the thinking of concrete operational children and formal operational adolescents?
2. What are two criticisms of Piaget's explanation of thinking in childhood and adolescence?

6.3 Summarize Vygotsky's sociocultural perspective and how it is manifested in scaffolding, the zone of proximal development, and cultural tools.

SUMMARY

Vygotsky posited that differences in the ways particular cultures and societies approach problems influence cognitive development. According to Vygotsky's sociocultural theory, we are embedded in a context that shapes how we think and who we become, and learning occurs through collaborating with others. Children learn through guided participation *and* scaffolding. Over time, children internalize the instruction, making it part of their skill set, and they thereby master tasks. Effective scaffolding works within the zone of proximal development. Vygotsky posed that mental activity is influenced by cultural tools that are passed on to its members.

KEY TERMS

guided participation	zone of proximal development
scaffolding	

REVIEW QUESTIONS

1. For Vygotsky, what is the most important influence on thinking?

2. Give an example of the zone of proximal development and scaffolding.

3. What is a criticism of Vygotsky's theory?

KEY TERMS

epistemic cognition
postformal reasoning
dualistic thinking
relativistic thinking

reflective judgment
pragmatic thought
cognitive–affective complexity

 6.4 Explain postformal reasoning and how it compares with cognitive–affective complexity.

REVIEW QUESTIONS

1. What are three types of postformal reasoning?

2. What influences the development of postformal reasoning?

3. What is pragmatic thought?

4. What are the qualities of cognitive affective complexity?

SUMMARY

People's understanding of the nature of knowledge advances along a predictable path in adulthood, from dualistic thinking to relativistic thinking, to reflective judgment. Development beyond formal operations is dependent on metacognition and experience. The ability to accept inconsistency and ambiguity, characteristic of reflective judgment, permits advances in pragmatic thought. Successfully coordinating emotion and cognition improves people's capacity to adapt to the complexities adult life. Advances in reasoning during the adult years entails making gains in cognitive–affective complexity.

Test your understanding of the content.
Review the flashcards and quizzes at
edge.sagepub.com/kuthertopical

Cognitive Change: Information Processing Approach

Learning Objectives

7.1 Identify the parts of the information processing system and its function over the lifespan.

7.2 Describe developmental changes in infants' capacities for attention, memory, and thought.

7.3 Describe developmental changes in children's capacities for attention, memory, and thought.

7.4 Explain how advances in brain development during adolescence influence memory, metacognition, and scientific reasoning.

7.5 Compare patterns of change in working memory, long-term memory, problem-solving capacities, and wisdom in adulthood.

Digital Resources

▶ Executive Function
▶ The Central Executive

▶ Infant Habituation
📄 Infant Information Processing

🔊 Brain Injury and Theory of Mind
▶ A Structure for Thinking

▶ Thinking and Decision Making in Adolescence
📄 Risk-Taking or Exploration?

📄 The Reminiscence Bump
📄 With Age Comes Wisdom

Master these learning objectives with multimedia resources available at **edge.sagepub.com/kuthertopical** and *Lives in Context* video cases available in the interactive eBook.

"Say, 'RED!' whenever you see a red car," instructed Dad as he drove Tyler and Shana to school. "Red!" Dad called out as they passed a red minivan. A few minutes later, 3-year-old Tyler shouted, "Red!" "I don't see a red car. Tyler, you have to wait until you see a red car; then you can say, 'Red,'" instructed his older sister. After carefully scanning the roadway, Shana spotted a red car. "Red!" she shouted and turned to Tyler, "See?" This silly game can make a car trip pass more quickly, but it also tells us about people's cognitive development. Advances in information processing skills, such as attention and working memory, contribute to success in this game.

Whereas the cognitive developmental approaches presented in Chapter 6 describe cognitive changes as discontinuous in nature, information processing theorists argue that people's thinking undergoes more gradual and continuous change. From this perspective, our judgment becomes more complex and our reasoning faster and more efficient because of improvements in information processing. In this chapter, we examine the information processing system over the lifespan.

THE INFORMATION PROCESSING SYSTEM

Lives in Context Video 7.1
Executive Function

LO 7.1 Identify the parts of the information processing system and its function over the lifespan.

From an information processing perspective, the mind is composed of three mental stores: sensory memory, working memory, and long-term memory. From early infancy to mature adulthood, information moves through these stores, and we use these three stores to manipulate and store it.

Sensory memory, sometimes called the *sensory register*, is the first step in getting information into the mind; it holds incoming sensory information in its original form. For example, look at this page, then close your eyes. Did you "see" the page for a fraction of a second after you closed your eyes? That image, or icon, represents your sensory memory. Information fades from sensory memory quickly if it is not processed, even as quickly as fractions of a second. Newborn infants display sensory memory, although it is much shorter in duration than adults' memory (Cheour et al., 2002). As a great deal of information is taken in and rapidly moves through sensory memory, much of it is discarded—but when we direct our **attention** or awareness to information, it passes to the next part of the information processing system, working memory.

Working memory, sometimes called short-term memory, holds and processes information that is being "worked on" in some way: manipulated (considered, comprehended), encoded (transformed into a memory), or retrieved (recalled). Working memory is responsible for maintaining and processing information used in many complex cognitive tasks (Gathercole, 1998). All of your thoughts—that is, all conscious mental activity—occur within working memory. For example, reading this paragraph, remembering assignments, and considering how this material applies to your own experience taps your working memory. Just as your thoughts are constantly changing, so are the contents of working memory. A core assumption of the information processing approach is the idea of limited capacity. We can only hold on to so much information in mind, or in working memory, for long. With development, we get better at retaining information in working memory and use it in more efficient ways.

An important part of working memory is the **central executive**, a control processor that directs the flow of information and regulates cognitive activities such as attention, action, and problem solving (Daneman & Carpenter, 1980; Just & Carpenter, 1992). The central executive determines what is important to attend to, combines new information with information already in working memory, and selects and applies strategies for manipulating the information in order to understand it, make decisions, and solve problems (Andersson, 2008; Baddeley, 1986, 1996). Collectively, these cognitive activities are known as **executive function**.

As information is manipulated in working memory it becomes more likely that it will enter long-term memory, the third mental store. **Long-term memory** is an unlimited store that holds information indefinitely. Information is not manipulated or processed in long-term memory; it is simply stored until it is retrieved to manipulate in working memory (e.g., remembering events and thinking about them). With development we amass a great deal of information, organize it in increasingly sophisticated ways, and encode and retrieve it more efficiently and with less effort.

We are born with the ability to take in, store, and manipulate information through our sensory, working, and long-term memory. The structure of the information processing system remains the same throughout the lifespan (see Figure 7.1). With development, we get better at moving information through our cognitive system in ways that allow us to adapt to our world. We can process more

sensory memory The first step in the information processing system in which stimuli are stored for a brief moment in its original form to enable it to be processed.

attention The ability to direct one's awareness.

working memory The component of the information processing system that holds and processes information that is being manipulated, encoded, or retrieved and is responsible for maintaining and processing information used in cognitive tasks.

central executive In information processing, the part of our mental system that directs the flow of information and regulates cognitive activities such as attention, action, and problem solving.

executive function The set of cognitive operations that support planning, decision-making, and goal setting abilities, such as the ability to control attention, coordinate information in working memory, and inhibit impulses.

long-term memory The component of the information processing system that is an unlimited store that holds information indefinitely, until it is retrieved to manipulate working memory.

FIGURE 7.1: Information Processing System

CENTRAL EXECUTIVE

Incoming Information → Sensory Memory → Working Memory ⇄ (Encoding / Retrieval) Long-term Memory

Working Memory → Response

information, retain more information, and do so more quickly and efficiently. We are born with a functioning information processing system, and it develops rapidly and very early in life.

 Thinking in Context 7.1

Compare the information processing model with Piaget's cognitive developmental perspective. How are the perspectives similar and different?

INFORMATION PROCESSING IN INFANCY

LO 7.2 Describe developmental changes in infants' capacities for attention, memory, and thought.

Information processing theorists describe cognition as a set of interrelated components that enable people to process information—to notice, take in, manipulate, store, and retrieve it. Newborns are ready to learn and adapt to their world because, like children and adults, they are born information processors.

ATTENTION IN INFANTS

Attention refers to the ability to direct one's awareness. Infant attention is often studied using the same methods used to learn about their visual perception (see Chapter 4). Preferential looking procedures (measuring and comparing the length of time infants look at two stimuli) and habituation procedures (measuring the length of time it takes infants to habituate or show a reduction in looking time to nonchanging stimulus) are used to study infants' attention to visual stimuli such as geometric patterns (Oakes, 2010; Richards, 2010, 2011). Infants show more attentiveness to dynamic stimuli—stimuli that change over time—than to static, unchanging stimuli (Reynolds, Zhang, & Guy, 2013; Richards, 2010).

By around 10 weeks of age infants show gains in attention. As infants' capacities for attention increase, so do their preferences for complex stimuli. For example, in one experiment, 3- to 13-month-old infants were shown displays that included a range of static and moving stimuli (Courage, Reynolds, & Richards, 2006). From about 6 ½ months of age, infants' looking time varied with stimulus complexity, decreasing for simple stimuli such as dot patterns, increasing slightly for complex stimuli such as faces, and increasing more for very complex stimuli such as video clips (Courage et al., 2006).

Recently, researchers have begun using brain imaging techniques to measure infants' brain activity because the development of infant attention is thought to be closely related to neurological development in the areas underlying attentional control (Reynolds, 2015). In response to tasks that challenge attention, infants show activity in the frontal cortex (used for thinking and planning) that is diffuse (widely spread) at 5.5 months of age, but more specific or localized by 7.5 months of age (Richards, 2010). The ability to focus and switch attention is critical for selecting information to process in working memory and is influenced by neurological development, including advances in myelination (Qiu, Mori, & Miller, 2015). Important developments in attention occur over the course of infancy and continue throughout childhood.

The toy keys have captured this infant's attention. How long will it take for the baby to habituate to this interesting stimulus?

Burger/Phanie/Science Source

MEMORY IN INFANTS

Habituation studies measuring looking time and brain activity demonstrate that neonates can recall visual and auditory stimuli (Muenssinger et al., 2013; Streri, Hevia, Izard, & Coubart, 2013). When infants habituate to a

Photo permission from MaryAnn Vail

Young infants were taught to kick their foot to make an attached mobile move. When tested one week later the infants remembered and kicked their legs vigorously to make the mobile move.

Source: Levine and Munsch (2010).

stimulus and are shown it again after a delay, more rapid habituation on the second exposure indicates that they remember the stimulus (Oakes, 2010). Classic habituation studies have shown that by 3 months of age, infants can remember a visual stimulus for 24 hours, and by the time they are 1 year old, they can retain such memories for several days or even weeks (Fagan., 1973; Martin, 1975).

Infants can also remember motor activities. In one study, 2- to 3-month-old infants were taught to kick their foot, which was tied to a mobile with a ribbon, to make the mobile move (see Figure 7.2). One week later, when the infants were reattached to the mobile they kicked vigorously, indicating their memory of the first occasion. The infants would kick even 4 weeks later if the experimenter gave the mobile a shake to remind them of its movement (Rovee-Collier & Bhatt, 1993; Rovee-Collier, 1999). Infants have basic memory capacities common to children and adults (Rose, Feldman, Jankowski, & Van Rossem, 2011), but they are most likely to remember events when they take place in familiar contexts and when the infants are actively engaged (Learmonth, Lamberth, & Rovee-Collier, 2004).

Emotional engagement also enhances infants' memory. Infants are more likely to remember events that are associated with emotions. For example, the still-face interaction paradigm is an experimental task in which an infant interacts with an adult who first engages in normal social interaction and then suddenly lets his or her face become still and expressionless, not responsive to the infant's actions (Tronick, Als, Adamson, Wise, & Brazelton, 1978). Infants usually respond to the adult's still face with brief smiles followed by negative facial expressions, crying, looking away, thumb sucking, and other indications of emotional distress (Shapiro, Fagen, Prigot, Carroll, & Shalan, 1998; Weinberg & Tronick, 1994, 1996). In one study, 5-month-old infants who were exposed to the still face demonstrated recall over a year later, at 20 months of age, by looking less at the woman who appeared in the still-face paradigm than at two other women whom the infants had never previously seen (Bornstein, Arterberry, & Mash, 2004). These lines of research suggest that memory improves over the course of infancy, but even young infants are likely to recall events in which they are actively engaged, that take place in familiar surroundings, and that are emotionally salient (Courage & Cowan, 2009; Learmonth et al., 2004).

INFANTS' THINKING

In infants' eyes, all of the world is new—"one great blooming, buzzing confusion," in the famous phrase of 19th-century psychologist William James (1890). How do infants think about and make sense of the world? As infants are bombarded with a multitude of stimuli, encountering countless new objects, people, and events, they form concepts by naturally grouping stimuli into classes or categories. **Categorization**, grouping different stimuli from a common class, is an adaptive mental process that allows for organized storage of information in memory, efficient retrieval of that information, and the capacity to respond with familiarity to new stimuli from a common class (Bruner, Goodnow, & Austin, 1956; Murphy, 2002). Infants naturally categorize or organize information, just as older children and adults do, for without the ability to categorize, we would have to respond anew to each novel stimulus we experience (Bornstein & Arterberry, 2010; Rosenberg & Feigenson, 2013).

categorization An adaptive mental process in which objects are grouped into conceptual categories, allowing for organized storage of information in memory, efficient retrieval of that information, and the capacity to respond with familiarity to new stimuli from a common class.

Just as in studying perception and attention, developmental researchers must rely on basic learning capacities, such as habituation, to study how infants categorize objects. For example, infants are shown a series of stimuli belonging to one category (e.g., fruit: apples and oranges), and then are presented with a new stimulus of the same category (e.g., a pear or a lemon) and a stimulus of a different category (e.g., a cat or a horse). If an infant dishabituates, or shows renewed interest by looking longer at the new stimulus (e.g., cat), it suggests that he or she perceives it as belonging to a different category from that of previously encountered stimuli (Cohen & Cashon, 2006). Using this method, researchers have learned that 3-month-old infants categorize pictures of dogs as different from cats based on perceived differences in facial features (Quinn, Eimas, & Rosenkrantz, 1993).

Infants' earliest categories are based on the perceived similarity of objects (Rakison & Butterworth, 1998). By 4 months, infants can form categories based on perceptual properties, grouping objects that are similar in appearance including shape, size, and color (Colombo et al., 1990; Quinn & Eimas, 1996; Rakison & Butterworth, 1998). As early as 7 months of age, infants use conceptual categories based on perceived function and behavior (Mandler, 2000, 2004). Moreover, patterns in 6- to 7-month-old infants' brain waves correspond to their identification of novel and familiar categories (Quinn, Doran, Reiss, & Hoffman, 2010). Seven- to 12-month-old infants use many categories to organize objects, such as food, furniture, birds, animals, vehicles, kitchen utensils, and more, based on perceptual similarity and perceived function and behavior (Mandler & McDonough, 1993, 1998; Oakes, Coppage, & Dingel, 1997).

Researchers also use sequential touching tasks to study the conceptual categories that older infants create (Mandler, Fivush, & Reznick, 1987). Infants are presented with a collection of objects from two categories (e.g., four animals and four vehicles) and their patterns of touching are recorded. If the infants recognize a categorical distinction among the objects, they touch those from within a category in succession more than would be

TABLE 7.1 • Changes in Information Processing Skills During Infancy

Attention	• Increases steadily over infancy
	• From birth infants attend more to dynamic than static stimuli
	• During the second half of their first year infants attend more to complex stimuli such as faces and video clips
	• Linked with diffuse frontal lobe activity in young infants and localized frontal lobe activity by 7.5 months of age
	• Individual differences appear at all ages and are stable over time
	• Associated with performance on visual recognition memory tasks
Memory	• Improves with age
	• 3-month-old infants can remember a visual stimulus for 24 hours
	• By the end of the first year infants can remember a visual stimulus for several days or even weeks
	• Infants are most likely to remember events in familiar, engaging, and emotionally salient contexts
Thinking	• Infants' first concepts are based on perceived similarity
	• By 4 months infants can form categories based on perceptual properties such as shape, size, and color
	• By 6 to 7 months infants' brain waves correspond to their identification of novel and familiar categories
	• 7- to 12-month-old infants can organize objects such as food, furniture, animals, and kitchen utensils, based on perceived function and behavior
	• 12- to 30-month-old infants categorize objects first at a global level and then at more specific levels
	• Infants categorize objects at more global and inclusive levels (such as motor vehicles) before more specific and less inclusive levels (such as cars, trucks, construction equipment)
	• The use of categories improves memory efficiency

expected by chance (Bornstein & Arterberry, 2010). Research using sequential touching procedures has shown that 12- to 30-month-old toddlers organize objects first at a global level and then at more specific levels. They categorize at more inclusive levels (e.g., animals or vehicles) before less inclusive levels (e.g., types of animals or vehicles) and before even less inclusive levels (e.g., specific animals or vehicles; Bornstein & Arterberry, 2010). Infants' and toddlers' everyday experiences and exploration contribute to their growing capacity to recognize commonalities among objects, group them in meaningful ways, and use these concepts to think and solve problems (Mandler, 2004; Oakes & Madole, 2003). Recognizing categories is a way of organizing information that allows for more efficient thinking, including storage and retrieval of information in memory. Therefore, advances in categorization are critical to cognitive development.

As shown in Table 7.1, information processing capacities, such as attention, memory, and categorization skill, show continuous change over the first three years of life (Rose, Feldman, & Jankowski, 2009). Infants get better at attending to the world around them, remembering what they encounter, and organizing and making sense of what they learn. Infants' emerging cognitive capacities influence all aspects of their development and functioning.

 Thinking in Context 7.2

1. What are some of the challenges in studying how infants think and what they know? How do researchers address these issues? Can you identify challenges to information processing researchers' methods, findings, or conclusions?

2. Given what we know about infants' capacities for attention, memory, and thinking, what kinds of toys and activities would you recommend to caregivers who want to entertain infants while promoting their development?

INFORMATION PROCESSING IN CHILDHOOD

LO 7.3 Describe developmental changes in children's capacities for attention, memory, and thought.

"If you're finished, put your head down on your desk and rest for a moment," Mrs. McCalvert advised. She was surprised to see that three-quarters of her students immediately put their heads down. "They are getting quicker and quicker! I guess next time I'll assign more challenging problems," she thought to herself. Information processing theorists would agree with Mrs. McCalvert's observation because the information processing perspective describes development as entailing changes in the efficiency of cognition rather than qualitative changes in reasoning. It is easy to observe that school-age children can take in more information, process it more accurately and quickly, and retain it more effectively than younger children. But what are the changes that enable them to do this? They are better able to determine what information is important, attend to it, and use their understanding of how memory works to choose among strategies to retain information more effectively. Sensory memory does not appear to change much with development: Five-year-old children demonstrate similar capacities and performance as adults (Cowan, Nugent, Elliott, Ponomarev, & Saults, 1999; Kail & Reese, 2002). Yet other information processing abilities, such as attention, advance steadily throughout childhood.

ATTENTION IN CHILDREN

The ability to sustain one's attention improves from early childhood through the early childhood years, but young children often struggle with selective attention. **Selective attention**

selective attention The ability to focus on relevant stimuli and ignore others.

refers to the ability to systematically deploy one's attention, focusing on relevant information and ignoring distractors. Young children do not search thoroughly when asked to compare detailed pictures and explain what's missing from one. They have trouble focusing on one stimulus and switching their attention to compare it with other stimuli (Hanania & Smith, 2010). For example, young children who sort cards according to one dimension, such as color, may later be unable to successfully switch to a different sorting criteria (Honomichl & Zhe, 2011). Young children become better at planning, considering the steps needed to complete a particular act, and focusing their attention (Rueda, 2013). Preschoolers can create and abide by a plan to complete tasks that are familiar and not too complex, such as systematically searching for a lost object in a yard (Wellman, Somerville, & Haake, 1979). But they have difficulty with more complex tasks. Young children

Completing this exercise requires selective attention, the ability to focus on the task at hand and ignore distractors, such as noisy classmates.

have difficulty deciding where to begin and how to proceed to complete a task in an orderly way. When they plan, young children often skip important steps (Friedman & Scholnick, 1987; Ruff & Rothbart, 1996).

Researchers study selective attention using tasks that require children to ignore distractors. For example, children might be asked to watch a computer screen while random numbers flash on and off and then press a button whenever a particular sequence of numbers (such as 7 and then 2) appear. Between ages 6 and 10, children show rapid gains in their ability to control their attention and deploy selective attention, focusing on relevant information and ignoring what is irrelevant (Gómez-Pérez & Ostrosky-Solís, 2006). Selective attention continues to improve in adolescence. Children's success in tasks measuring the ability to direct and control attention are influenced by developments in working memory, and attention, in turn, exerts an influence on working memory (Bertrand & Camos, 2015; Baddeley, 2012; Nelson Cowan, Ricker, Clark, Hinrichs, & Glass, 2015).

WORKING MEMORY AND EXECUTIVE FUNCTION IN CHILDREN

An important part of working memory is the central executive, which regulates cognitive activities that comprise executive function, such as attention, action, and problem solving. Specifically, the central executive is responsible for (1) coordinating performance on two separate tasks or operations, such as both storing and processing information at the same time; (2) quickly switching between tasks, such as manipulating and storing information; (3) selectively attending to specific information and ignoring irrelevant information; and (4) retrieving information from long-term memory (Baddeley, 1996, 2012). Central executive function is thought to have a biological basis because the cognitive activities controlled by the central executive are associated with certain regions of the cortex, specifically several areas of the frontal lobe and part of the parietal lobe (Collette & Van der Linden, 2002; Petersen & Posner, 2012).

Steady increases in executive function and working memory occur throughout childhood, from 3 years of age through adolescence, and are responsible for the cognitive developmental changes seen during childhood (Brocki & Bohlin, 2004; Freier, Cooper, & Mareschal, 2015). For example, during the elementary school years working memory capacity—how much material can be held—improves substantially (Kail & Park, 1994; Schneider & Pressley, 2013). One study demonstrated that between ages 6 and 7 children begin to use strategies to complete memory tasks, permitting the 7-year-old children to show greater recall than the 6-year-old children (Camos & Barrouillet, 2011). Yet even at age 8, children are able to retain only about half the number of items that adults can (Kharitonova, Winter, & Sheridan, 2015). However, changes in performance on working memory tasks are influenced by context. Research with Australian children suggests that the amount of schooling is a better predictor of improvements in working memory than is chronological age (Roberts et al., 2015). High-quality relations with teachers are associated with higher scores on working memory tasks during elementary school (de Wilde, Koot, & van Lier, 2016).

Memory Strategies

One reason why young children perform poorly in recall tasks is that they are not very effective at using **memory strategies**, which are cognitive activities that make us more likely to remember. Common memory strategies are rehearsal, organization, and elaboration. *Rehearsal* refers to systematically repeating information in order to retain it in working memory. A child may say a phone number over and over to not forget it before writing it down. *Organization* refers to categorizing or chunking items to remember by grouping it by theme or type, such as animals, flowers, and furniture. When memorizing a list of words, a child might organize them into meaningful groups or *chunks*—foods, animals, objects, and so forth. Growth in working memory is partially attributed to an increase in the number of chunks children can retain with age (Cowan et al., 2010). Children start to use organization soon after they begin using rehearsal. A third strategy, *elaboration,* entails creating an imagined scene or story to link the material to be remembered. To remember to buy bread, milk, and butter, for example, a child might imagine a slice of buttered bread balancing on a glass of milk. It is not until the later school years that children use elaboration without prompting and apply it to a variety of tasks (Camos & Barrouillet, 2011). As children make use of memory strategies, their recall improves dramatically.

Preschool-age children can be taught strategies, but they generally do not transfer their learning and apply it to new tasks (Titz & Karbach, 2014; Gathercole, Adams, & Hitch, 1994; Miller & Seier, 1994). This utilization deficiency seems to occur because of their limited working memories. They cannot apply the strategy at the same time as they have to retain both the material to be learned and the strategy to be used. Instead, new information competes with the information the child is attempting to recall. Unlike older children and adults, preschoolers are often are unable to inhibit the new information to successfully recall older information (Aslan & Bäuml, 2010). Children do not spontaneously and reliably apply rehearsal until after the first grade (Bjorklund & Douglas, 1997; Schneider & Bjorklund, 1992), and they do not start to apply strategies consistently and effectively until middle childhood (Kron-Sperl, Schneider, & Hasselhorn, 2008). Advances in executive function, working memory, and attention predict strategy use (Stone, Blumberg, Blair, & Cancelli, 2016). Effective strategy use requires that children attend to a problem, keep it in mind, choose among strategies, and devise and implement a plan—a complex set of cognitive activities.

Throughout middle childhood, children learn more strategies and get better at selecting them, modifying them to suit the task at hand, and using them more effectively. All of these memory skills contribute to advances in cognitive performance (Bjorklund, 2013; Imbo & Vandierendonck, 2007). For example, 5th-grade students who use more complex memory strategies are more successful in delayed recall tasks in which they are asked to read a passage and then recall it after a delay (Jonsson, Wiklund-Hörnqvist, Nyroos, & Börjesson, 2014). With development children's strategy use becomes more efficient. They use more than one strategy during a given task and choose different strategies for different tasks (Justice, Baker-Ward, Gupta, & Jannings, 1997; Lehmann & Hasselhorn, 2007).

Knowledge

Throughout childhood, children acquire increasing amounts of information, which they naturally organize in meaningful ways. As children learn more about a topic, their knowledge structures become more elaborate and organized, while the information

memory strategy Deliberate cognitive activities that make an individual more likely to remember information.

becomes more familiar and meaningful and easier to store and recall. It is easier to recall new information about topics with which we are already familiar, and existing knowledge about a topic makes it easier to learn more about that topic (Ericsson & Moxley, 2013). During middle childhood, children develop vast knowledge bases and organize information into elaborate hierarchical networks that enable them to apply strategies in more complex ways and remember more material than ever before—and more easily than ever before (Schneider & Pressley, 2013). For example, 4th-grade students who are experts at soccer show better recall of a list of soccer-related items than do students who are soccer novices, but the groups of children do not differ on the non-soccer-related items (Schneider & Bjorklund, 1992). The soccer experts tended to organize the lists of soccer items into categories; their knowledge helped them to organize the soccer-related information with little effort, using fewer resources on organization and permitting the use of more working memory for problem solving and reasoning. Novices, in contrast, lacked a knowledge base to aid their attempts at organization.

School-age children demonstrate increasingly sophisticated performance in a range of skills such as language comprehension, reading, and mathematics ability (Mazzocco & Kover, 2007). Improvements in memory, attention, and processing speed are possible because of brain development, particularly myelination and pruning. Neural systems for visuospatial working memory, auditory working memory, and response inhibition differentiate, dividing into separate parts to enable faster and more efficient processing of these critical cognitive functions (Tsujimoto, Kuwajima, & Sawaguchi, 2007). Children become quicker at matching pictures and recalling spatial information, among other tasks (Gathercole & Hitch, 1993).

As children gain knowledge and expertise in a topic, they become better at learning and recalling related information.

Between ages 3 and 7, children show increasing prefrontal cortex engagement while completing tasks that measure working memory (Perlman, Huppert, & Luna, 2016). Areas of the prefrontal cortex become more specialized in late childhood (Farber & Beteleva, 2011). Development of the prefrontal cortex leads to advances in response inhibition, the ability to withhold a behavioral response inappropriate in the current context, and this increases children's capacity for self-regulation—controlling their thought and behavior—which, in turn, contributes to advances in metacognition (Tsujimoto et al., 2007).

Over the course of childhood children get better at using strategies in their daily life. However, the strategies that children use to tackle cognitive tasks vary with culture. In fact, daily tasks themselves vary with our cultural context. Children in Western cultures receive lots of experience with tasks that require them to recall bits of information and thereby develop considerable expertise in the use of memory strategies such as rehearsal, organization, and elaboration. On the other hand, research shows that people in nonwestern cultures with no formal schooling do not use or benefit from instruction in memory strategies such as rehearsal (Rogoff & Chavajay, 1995). Instead, they refine memory skills that are adaptive to their way of life. For example, they may rely on spatial cues for memory, such as when recalling items within a three-dimensional miniature scene. Australian aboriginal and Guatemalan Mayan children perform better at these tasks than do children from Western cultures (Rogoff & Waddell, 1982). Culture and contextual demands influence the cognitive strategies that we learn and prefer, as well as how we use our information processing system to gather, manipulate, and store knowledge. Children of all cultures amass a great deal of information and as they get older, they organize it in more sophisticated ways, and encode and retrieve it more efficiently and with less effort.

LONG-TERM MEMORY IN CHILDREN

Unlike infants, young children can speak and follow directions, and these abilities make it easier to study their memory skills. **Episodic memory** refers to memory for events and information acquired during those events (Roediger & Marsh, 2003; Tulving, 2002). For example, a researcher might study episodic memory by asking a child, "Where did you go on vacation?" or "Remember the pictures I showed you yesterday?" Most laboratory studies of memory examine episodic memory, such as memory for specific information, for scripts, and for personal experiences.

Memory for Information

Shana turns over one card and exclaims, "I've seen this one before. I know where it is!" She quickly selects its duplicate by turning over a second card from an array of cards. Shana recognizes a card she has seen before and recalls its location. Children's memory for specific information, such as the location of items, lists of words or numbers, and directions, can be studied using tasks that examine recognition memory and recall memory. **Recognition memory**, the ability to recognize a stimulus one has encountered before, is nearly perfect in 4- and 5-year-old children, but they are much less proficient in **recall memory**, the ability to generate a memory of a stimulus encountered before without seeing it again (Myers & Perlmutter, 2014). Two-year-olds can typically recall just one or two items, whereas 4-year-olds can recall three or four items (Perlmutter, 1984).

episodic memory Memory for everyday experiences.

recognition memory The ability to identify a previously encountered stimulus.

recall memory Remembering a stimulus that is not present.

script Description of what occurs in a certain situation and used as a guide to understand and organize daily experiences.

autobiographical memory The recollection of a personal event that occurred at a specific time and place in one's past.

infantile amnesia A phenomenon in which most children and adults are unable to recall events that happened before age 3.

Memory for Scripts

Young children remember familiar repeated everyday experiences, like the process of eating dinner, taking a bath, or going to nursery school or preschool, as **scripts**, or descriptions of what occurs in a particular situation. When young children begin to use scripts, they remember only the main details. A 3-year-old might describe a trip to a restaurant as follows: "You go in, eat, then pay." These early scripts include only a few acts but usually are recalled in the correct order (Bauer, 1996). As children grow older and gain cognitive competence, scripts become more elaborate. Consider a 5-year-old child's explanation of a trip to a restaurant: "You go in, you can sit at a booth or a table, then you tell the waitress what you want, you eat, if you want dessert, you can have some, then you go pay, and go home" (Hudson, Fivush, & Kuebli, 1992). Scripts help children understand repeated events, serve as an organization tool, and help children predict what to expect in the future. However, scripts may inhibit memory for new details. For example, in one laboratory study children were presented with a script of the same series of events repeated in order multiple times as well as a single alternative event. Preschoolers were less likely than older children to spontaneously recall and provide a detailed account of the event (Brubacher, Glisic, Roberts, & Powell, 2011).

Aurum/Alamy

What script might this child use to explain toothbrushing?

Autobiographical Memory

Autobiographical memory refers to memory of personally meaningful events that took place at a specific time and place in one's past (Nelson & Fivush, 2004). Most people have no memories prior to age 3, a phenomenon known as **infantile amnesia** (Howe & Courage, 1993). Yet, as discussed earlier in this chapter, infants

APPLYING DEVELOPMENTAL SCIENCE

• • Children's Suggestibility

How can we help children to accurately recall their experiences?

The accuracy of children's memory, especially their vulnerability to suggestion, is an important topic because children as young as 3 years of age have been called upon to relate their memories of events that they have experienced or witnessed, including abuse, maltreatment, and domestic violence (Flavell, Friedrich, & Hoyt, 1970; Kail & Park, 1992; Nelson, 1993). How suggestible are young children? Can we trust their memories?

Research suggests that repeated questioning may increase suggestibility in children (La Rooy, Lamb, & Pipe, 2011). For example, in one study, preschoolers were questioned every week about events that had either happened or not happened to them; by the 11th week, nearly two-thirds of the children falsely reported having experienced an event (Ceci et al., 1994). Preschool-age children may be more vulnerable to suggestion about many topics, including those containing sexual themes, than either school-age children or adults (Gordon, Baker-Ward, & Ornstein, 2001; Principe, Ornstein, Baker-Ward, & Gordon, 2000; Rocha, 2013). When children were asked if they could remember several events, including a fictitious instance of getting their finger caught in a mousetrap, almost none of

them initially recalled these events. However, after repeated suggestive questioning, more than half of 3- and 4-year-olds and two-fifths of 5- and 6-year-olds said they recalled these events—often vividly (Poole & White, 1991, 1993).

Young children's natural trust in others may enhance their suggestibility (Jaswal, 2010). In one study, 3-year-olds who received misleading verbal and visual information from an experimenter about a sticker's location continued to search in the wrong, suggested, location despite no success (Jaswal, 2010). In another study, 3- to 5-year-old children watched as an adult hid a toy in one location, then told the children that the toy was in a different location. When retrieving the toy, 4- and 5-year-olds relied on what they had seen and disregarded the adult's false statements, but 3-year-olds deferred to what the adult had said, despite what they had directly observed (Ma & Ganea, 2010).

In some cases children can resist suggestion. For example, in one study, 4- and 7-year-old children either played games with an adult confederate (e.g., dressing up in costumes, playing tickle, being photographed) or merely watched the games (Ceci & Bruck, 1998). Eleven days later, each child was interviewed by an adult who included misleading questions that were often followed up with suggestions relevant to child abuse. Even the 4-year-olds resisted the false suggestions about child abuse.

Children are more vulnerable than adults, but adults are not entirely resistant to suggestion. Like children, adults who are exposed to information that is misleading or inconsistent with their experiences are more likely to perform poorly during memory interviews—and repeated questioning has a similar effect on performance (Ceci & Friedman, 2000; Fivush, 1993; Wysman, Scoboria, Gawrylowicz, & Memon, 2014).

What Do You Think?

Suppose you need to question a preschool child about an event. How would you maximize the likelihood of the child's giving an accurate account of what occurred?

demonstrate recall. Why, then, do we not retain memories from infancy? Just as language development helps us learn more complicated ways of thinking and communicating, it also helps us learn how to use our memory (Fivush & Nelson, 2004). Autobiographical memory is thought to serve a social function, as children learn to remember through interactions with adults and they construct autobiographical memories to share with others (Nelson & Fivush, 2004).

Autobiographical memory develops steadily from the preschool years through adolescence, and it is accompanied by increases in the length, richness, and complexity of recall memory (Fivush, 2011; Pipe, Lamb, Orbach, & Esplin, 2004). Young children report fewer memories for specific events than do older children and adults (Baker-Ward, Gordon, Ornstein, Larus, & Clubb, 1993). But by age 3, they are able to retrieve and report specific memories, especially those that have personal significance, are repeated, or are highly stressful (Fivush, 1993; Nuttall, 2014). For example, in one study, children who were at least 26 months old at the time of an accidental injury and visit to the emergency room accurately recalled the details of these experiences even after a 2-year delay (Goodman, Rudy, Bottoms, & Aman, 1990). Eight-year-old children have been found to accurately remember events that occurred when they were as young as 3½ years of age (Goodman & Aman, 1990).

Events that are unique or new, such as a trip to the circus, are better recalled; 3-year-old children will recall them for a year or longer (Fivush, Hudson, & Nelson, 1983). Frequent events, however, tend to blur together. Young children are better at remembering things they did than things they simply watched. For example, one study examined 5-year-old children's recall of an event they either observed, were told about, or experienced. A few days later the children who actually experienced the event were more likely to recall details in a more accurate and organized way, and to require fewer prompts (Murachver, Pipe, Gordon, Owens, & Fivush, 1996).

The way adults talk with the child about a shared experience can influence how well the child will remember it (Haden & Fivush, 1996; Reese & Fivush, 1993). Parents with an elaborative conversational style discuss new aspects of an experience, provide more information to guide a child through a mutually rewarding conversation, and affirm the child's responses. Three-year-olds of parents who use an elaborative style engage in longer conversations about events, remember more details, and tend to remember the events better at age 5 and 6 (Boland, Haden, & Ornstein, 2003; Fivush, 2011; Reese, Haden, & Fivush, 1993).

Overall, memory improves steadily between ages 4 and 10, with accelerated rates between 5 and 7 (Myers & Perlmutter, 2014; Riggins, 2014). Young children lack knowledge about how to conduct memory searches, determine what is important to recall, and structure narrative accounts of events (Leichtman & Ceci, 1995). They tend to forget information more quickly than older children, rely more on verbatim memory, and confuse different sources of event information (Ackil & Zaragoza, 1995; Levine, Stein, & Liwag, 1999; Warren & Lane, 1995). Young children can have largely accurate memories, but they can also tell tall tales, make errors, and succumb to misleading questions. Their ability to remember events can be influenced by information and experiences that may interfere with accurate recall: conversations with parents and adults, exposure to media, and sometimes intentional suggestions. Children's vulnerability to suggestion is discussed in the Applying Developmental Science feature. Between ages 5 and 7, children get better at linking memory and source and contextual details (Riggins, 2014). Older children can conduct internal memory searches, easily recreate images in their heads, think of information similar to the to-be-remembered event, and organize and present the recalled information in a systematic manner (Ceci, Huffman, Smith, & Loftus, 1994). During the school years, children become more capable of providing detailed and spontaneous memory descriptions; their use of mnemonic strategies increases and they become aware of the needs of listeners.

CHILDREN'S THINKING AND METACOGNITION

Over the childhood years thinking becomes more complex. In particular, children become increasingly aware of the process of thinking and of their own thoughts. **Theory of mind** refers to children's awareness of their own and other people's mental processes. This awareness of the mind can be considered under the broader concept of **metacognition** or knowledge of how the mind works and the ability to control the mind (Lockl & Schneider, 2007). Let's explore these concepts.

Theory of Mind

Young children's understanding of the mind grows and changes between the ages of 2 and 5 (Bower, 1993; Flavell, Green, & Flavell, 1995). For example, 3-year-old children

theory of mind Children's awareness of their own and other people's mental processes and realization that other people do not share their thoughts.

metacognition The ability to think about thinking; knowledge of how the mind works.

understand the difference between thinking about a cookie and having a cookie. They know that having a cookie means that one can touch, eat, or share it, but thinking about a cookie does not permit such actions (Astington, 1993). Young children also understand that a child who wants a cookie will be happy upon receiving one and sad upon not having one (Moses, Coon, & Wusinich, 2000; Wellman, Phillips, & Rodriguez, 2000). Similarly, they understand that a child who believes he is having hot oatmeal for breakfast will be surprised upon receiving cold spaghetti (Wellman & Banerjee, 1991). Theory of mind is commonly assessed by examining children's abilities to understand that people can hold different beliefs about an object or event.

Three-year-old children tend to perform poorly on **false-belief tasks**, which are tasks that require them to understand that someone does not share their knowledge. In a classic false-belief task, children who are presented with a Band-Aid box that contains pencils rather than Band-Aids will show surprise, but they tend to believe that other children will share their knowledge and expect the Band-Aid box to hold pencils (see Figure 7.3; Flavell, 1993; Flavell et al., 1995; Jenkins & Astington, 1996). The children do not yet understand that the other children hold different beliefs. In addition, the children will claim that they knew all along that the Band-Aid box contained pencils (Birch, 2005). They confuse their present knowledge with their memories for prior knowledge and have difficulty remembering ever having believed something that contradicts their current view (Bernstein, Atance, Meltzoff, & Loftus, 2007; Mitchell & Kikuno, 2000).

Three-year-old children show a pattern of false-belief errors that are robust across procedures and cultures (Wellman, Cross, & Watson, 2001; Wellman & Liu, 2004). However, some researchers assert that young children are much more competent than they appear because research using preferential looking and habituation tasks has suggested an understanding of false belief as early as 15 months of age (Buttelmann, Over, Carpenter, & Tomasello, 2014; Onishi & Baillargeon, 2005). Similar to arguments regarding object permanence in infancy and egocentrism in early childhood (see Chapter 6), it may be that children understand the concept (the Band-Aid box contains pencils, not bandages) but may have difficulty communicating their understanding to the researcher (Helming, Strickland, & Jacob, 2014). Yet other researchers counter that false-belief findings with infants reflect perceptual preferences, that is, a desire to look at one object over another, not theory of mind (Heyes, 2014). Indeed, the research to date suggests that theory of mind as evidenced by false-belief tasks emerges at about 3 years of age and shifts reliably between 3 and 4 years of age (Apperly, Samson, Humphreys, & Humphreys, 2009). By age 3, children can understand that two people can believe different things (Rakoczy, Warneken, & Tomasello, 2007). Four-year-old children understand that people who are presented with different versions of the same event develop different beliefs (Eisbach, 2004; Pillow & Henrichon, 1996), and by age 4 or 5, children become aware that they and other people can hold false beliefs (Moses et al., 2000).

Advanced cognition is needed for children to learn abstract concepts such as belief (Carlson, Moses, & Claxton, 2004; Moses, Carlson, & Sabbagh, 2005). Performance on false-belief tasks, such as the Band-Aid task, is associated with measures of executive function—the abilities that enable complex cognitive functions such as planning, decision making, and goal setting (Hughes & Devine, 2015; Sabbagh, Xu, Carlson, Moses, & Lee, 2006). Advances in executive functioning facilitate children's abilities to reflect on and learn from experience and promote development of theory of mind (Benson, Sabbagh, Carlson, & Zelazo, 2013). For example, one longitudinal study following children from ages 2 to 4 found that advances in executive functioning predicted children's performance on false-belief tasks (Hughes & Ensor, 2007).

Children's performance on false-belief tasks is closely related with language development and competence in sustaining conversations (Bernard & Deleau, 2007; Milligan,

FIGURE 7.3: False Belief

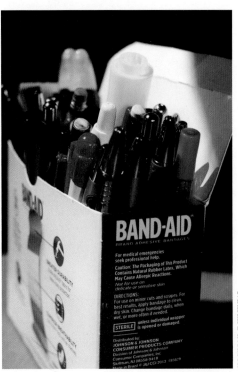

Nathan Davidson

false-belief task A task that requires children to understand that someone does not share their knowledge.

CULTURAL INFLUENCES ON DEVELOPMENT

• • Culture and Theory of Mind

Samoan culture influences theory of mind development in children.

As children develop theory of mind, they become able to read other people's minds; that is, they understand other people's perspectives and can communicate effectively with them. Cultural differences in social norms might influence children's emerging understanding of the mind. Collectivist cultures emphasize the community, whereas individualist cultures focus on the needs of the individual. These differing perspectives may influence how children come to understand mental states as well as their ability to perspective-take (Taumoepeau, 2015). For example, children from Japan tend to show delayed development on false belief tasks as compared with Western children. (Wellman, Cross, & Watson, 2001). When researchers probed children's understanding of the false-belief task by asking them to explain why the actor searched in the wrong location for his chocolate, Japanese children failed to use "thoughts" as an explanation (Naito & Koyama, 2006). Instead of giving explanations associated with mental states, such as, "He didn't know it was moved," Japanese children provided justifications that referenced the physical situation (e.g., "The chocolate is now in a different place") or interpersonal factors (e.g., "He promised to do so"). The findings suggest a cultural difference in mind reading, whereby Japanese children who are raised with collectivist values focus less on an actor's mental state and more on his physical and social situation when answering questions about his behavior.

Other research with Samoan children has supported the influence of culture on theory of mind. For example, research with 3- to 14-year-old Samoan children showed delayed development in theory of mind relative to German children (Mayer & Träuble, 2015, 2013). The Samoan children did not reliably succeed until age 8, and one-third of the 10- to 13-year-old children failed the false belief task. Moreover, the transition from failing the task to passing it took longer for Samoan children as compared with German children.

Samoan children's slow progression on theory of mind tasks is consistent with the Pacific Island doctrine of opacity of mind (Slaughter & Perez-Zapata, 2014). Mindreading or perspective taking is not encouraged. Samoan culture deemphasizes internal mental states as explanations for behavior. Samoan children, therefore, are not exposed to discussions about the mind. They get little experience considering other people's thoughts. Research with English-speaking Western samples has shown that conversations about people's thoughts predicts children's understanding of false beliefs (Slaughter, Peterson, & Mackintosh, 2007). Therefore, Samoan children's delayed success on false-belief tasks is likely a result of their culture's views. In support of this idea is a study of Pacific families living in New Zealand, in which mothers with a stronger Pacific cultural identity referred to beliefs less often when talking to their children than mothers whose Pacific identities were weaker (Slaughter & Perez-Zapata, 2014; Taumoepeau, 2015). Samoan children may be relatively slow to attribute false beliefs because they take longer to recognize that such beliefs exist, when compared to cultures in which minds are less opaque. The culture in which we are immersed influences how we think and how we view the people around us—and even the degree to which we read minds.

What Do You Think?

Is the development of theory of mind universally important? That is, is theory of mind important in all cultures? How might context determine the relevance of theory of mind?

Astington, & Dack, 2007). Everyday conversations aid children in developing a theory of mind because such conversations tend to center on and provide examples of mental states and their relation to behavior (Ruffman, Slade, & Crowe, 2002). When parents and other adults speak with children about mental states and emotions, connect them to behaviors and experiences, and discuss causes and consequences, children develop a more sophisticated understanding of other people's perspectives (Pavarini, Hollanda Souza, & Hawk, 2012;; Slaughter, Peterson, & Mackintosh, 2007). In addition, siblings provide young children with opportunities for social interaction, pretend play, and practice with deception; children with siblings perform better on false-belief tests than do only children (Jenkins & Astington, 1996; McAlister & Peterson, 2007; McAlister & Peterson, 2013). Success in false-belief attribution tasks is most frequent in children who are the most active in shared pretend play (Schwebel, Rosen, & Singer, 1999). Elementary school students' success on false-belief tasks predicts their competence at understanding other people's perspectives in everyday conversations and interactions (De Rosnay et al., 2014). Theory of mind is influenced by interactions with others but also influences interactions with others. Throughout childhood, from ages 2 through 12, theory of mind predicts measures of prosocial behavior, such as helping others (Imuta, Henry, Slaughter, Selcuk, & Ruffman, 2016).

The contexts in which children are embedded contribute to their developing understanding of the mind. Children in many countries, including Canada, India, Thailand, Norway, China, and the United States, show similarity in the onset and development of theory of mind between the ages of 3 and 5 (Callaghan et al., 2005; Melinder et al., 2006; Wellman, Fang, & Peterson, 2011; Sabbagh et al., 2006). Children reared in some contexts, however, show a very different pattern in understanding theory of mind (Lillard, 1998; Vinden, 1996). A study of 8-year-old children from Peru used a culturally appropriate version of the Band-Aid box task in which a sugar bowl contained tiny potatoes (Vinden, 1996). At first the children believed the bowl contained sugar. After learning that it contained potatoes, they answered typical false-belief questions incorrectly, predicting that others would respond that the bowl contained potatoes. Even at age 8, well after Western children succeed on similar tasks, the Peruvian children responded incorrectly, unable to explain why others might initially believe that the bowl contained sugar and be surprised to learn otherwise. One explanation is that the children in this study were raised in an isolated farming village where farmers worked from dawn to dusk, and there was no reason nor time for deception (Vinden, 1996). The Peruvian children's culture did not include ideas such as false belief, or deceiving others, as their day-to-day world was concerned more with tangible activities and things rather than considerations of people's thoughts. The culture in which we are immersed influences how we understand the nature of people's thoughts.

Metacognition

Theory of mind is a precursor to the development of metacognition (Lecce, Demicheli, Zocchi, & Palladino, 2015). Between the ages of 2 and 5, children's understanding of the mind grows; they become aware that the mind is where thinking takes place. Between 3 and 5, children come to understand that they can know something that others do not (essential for success on false-belief tasks), that their thoughts cannot be observed, and that there are individual differences in mental states (Flavell, Flavell, & Green, 1983; Pillow, 2008). They begin to understand that someone can think of one thing while doing something else, that a person whose eyes and ears are covered can think, and that thinking is different from talking, touching, and knowing (Flavell et al., 1995). However, young children's understanding of the mind is not complete. Three- and 4-year-old children do not understand that we think even when we are inactive. They look for visible indicators of thinking—perhaps one reason why teachers of young children refer to "putting on your thinking cap"—and assume their absence indicates the absence of thought. It is not until middle childhood that children understand that the mind is always active (Flavell, 1999; Flavell et al., 1983, 1995). Likewise, preschoolers tend to think of the mind as simply a container for items, but older children tend to see the mind as an active constructor of knowledge that receives, processes, and transforms information (Chandler & Carpendale, 1998; Flavell, 1999).

Young children show limited knowledge of memory functions. Four-year-olds recognize that increasing the number of items on a list makes recall more difficult and that longer retention intervals increase the likelihood of forgetting (Lyon & Flavell, 1993; Pillow, 2008; Wellman, 1977). But they know little about the effectiveness of deliberate memory strategies. In one study, when 4-year-olds were asked to compare the effectiveness of strategies for free recall, they judged looking at the items to be recalled as more effective than naming, rehearsing, or categorizing them (Justice, 1986). Children in kindergarten showed no preference among the four strategies, but second graders judged rehearsal and categorization as more effective than naming or looking. However, one recent study suggests that preschoolers' poor memory performance may result more from over-optimism than from metacognitive deficits (Lipowski, Merriman, & Dunlosky, 2013). As we will discuss in Chapter 11, young children have a strong sense of self-confidence and tend to believe that they will be successful in all endeavors. This overconfidence may overshadow their understanding of how their minds work, leading to biased estimates of their abilities (Lipowski et al., 2013).

Whereas young children tend to see the mind as static container for information, older children view it as an active manipulator of information (Flavell, 2004). Advances in metacognition accompany precortical development and enable school-age children to become mindful of their thinking and better able to consider the requirements of a task, determine how to tackle it, and monitor, evaluate, and adjust their activity to complete the task (Ardila, 2013; Kuhn, 2000).

Metamemory, an aspect of metacognition, refers to the understanding of one's memory and the ability to use strategies to enhance it; metamemory improves steadily throughout the elementary school years (Cavanaugh & Perlmutter, 1982; Flavell, 2004; Lecce et al., 2015). Older preschool children have an understanding that one needs to do "something" to prepare for a memory assessment, but they often do not know what to do (Ornstein, Light, Ornstein, & Light, 2010). Kindergarten and first-grade children understand that forgetting occurs with time and studying improves memory, but by age 8 or 9, metamemory permits children to accurately evaluate what they know, such as vocabulary words, and learn more effectively. Older children perform better on cognitive tasks because metacognition permits them to plan. They can evaluate the task; determine how they will approach it given their cognitive resources, attention span, motivation, and knowledge; and deploy metamemory to choose and monitor the use of memory strategies that will permit them to successfully store and retrieve needed information (Camos & Barrouillet, 2011; Kuhn, 2000; Schneider & Pressley, 2013). These abilities improve with experience, neural maturation, and advances in executive functioning (Roebers & Feurer, 2016).

 Thinking in Context 7.3

1. Identify some personal examples of attention, working memory, and long-term memory from your own childhood. What is your earliest memory of this nature? How have your information processing capacities changed as you have grown older?

2. Physical and motor development have clear implications for cognitive development during infancy. Is the same true in childhood? In what ways might physical and motor development influence cognition in school-age children?

3. Recall from Chapter 1 that development is influenced by multiple contexts. How might contextual influences—family, neighborhood, sociocultural context, and even cohort or generation—influence aspects of cognitive development, such as theory of mind?

INFORMATION PROCESSING IN ADOLESCENCE

LO 7.4 Explain how advances in brain development during adolescence influence memory, metacognition, and scientific reasoning.

Adolescents' advances in the ability to think abstractly and demonstrate hypothetical-deductive reasoning are also the result of improvements in information processing capacities that take place from childhood through adolescence. These improvements affect many

metamemory An aspect of metacognition that refers to the understanding of memory and how to use strategies to enhance memory.

aspects of information processing, such as attention, memory, knowledge base, and speed (Kail, 2008; Luna, Garver, Urban, Lazar, & Sweeney, 2004).

ATTENTION, MEMORY, AND EXECUTIVE FUNCTION IN ADOLESCENTS

Greater control over attention enables adolescents to deploy it selectively, focusing on stimuli deemed important while tuning out others and remaining focused even as task demands change. With increases in attention, adolescents are better able to hold material in working memory while taking in and processing new material (Barrouillet, Gavens, Vergauwe, Gaillard, & Camos, 2009). For example, at age 13, Julia is able to tune out the background noise in class to listen to her teacher, determine what is important, take notes, and remember what she's writing while listening to her teacher. She can shift her attention to take notes from movies shown in class and remain focused when the class format changes to discussion.

As we gain increasing control over our cognitive system we also become better at response inhibition, that is, not responding or not activating cognitive operations in response to a stimulus. Advances in response inhibition enable adolescents to adapt their responses to the situation by inhibiting well-learned responses when they are inappropriate to the situation and thereby speeding cognitive processing (Luna, Paulsen, Padmanabhan, & Geier, 2013; Luna et al., 2004). For example, Hiro is now able to keep himself from raising his hand in response to the teacher's question, telling himself, "I need to give other students a chance, too." The ability to control and inhibit responses emerges first in infancy and advances through childhood, with substantial gains in adolescence (Geier, Terwilliger, Teslovich, Velanova, & Luna, 2010; Zhai et al., 2014). However, the neurological changes that underlie response inhibition continue to develop into the 20s and influence many aspects of adolescent development, including their propensity for risk-taking behavior, as discussed later in this chapter (Albert, Chein, & Steinberg, 2013; Luna et al., 2013).

Working memory reaches adult-like levels by about age 19 and continues to improve into the 20s alongside neurological maturation (Isbell, Fukuda, Neville, & Vogel, 2015; Murty, Calabro, & Luna, 2016; Simmonds & Luna, 2015). Combined with a growing knowledge base and increased strategy use, advances in working memory result in more sophisticated, efficient, and quick thinking and learning. Now adolescents can retain more information at once, better integrate prior experiences and knowledge with new information, and combine information in more complex ways (Cowan et al., 2010; Gaillard, Barrouillet, Jarrold, & Camos, 2011). These advances support adolescents' abilities to solve geometry problems, employ the scientific method, and solve other complex problems. Increased capacities for working memory mean that adolescents can hold more ideas in mind and manipulate them to reason about problems and about ideas and the nature of thinking itself (i.e., metacognition; Cowan et al., 2010; Gaillard et al., 2011; Murty et al., 2016).

THINKING AND METACOGNITION IN ADOLESCENCE

As metacognition develops through middle adolescence, teenagers are better able to plan how they take in, manipulate, and store information (Ardila, 2013; van der Stel & Veenman, 2013). They are better able to understand how they learn and remember and to choose and deploy strategies that enhance the representation, storage, and retrieval of information. As an 11th grader, Travis, explains, "Studying for a biology exam is really different than studying for a history exam. In biology, I visualize the material, but when I study for history, I make up stories to help me remember it all." Travis illustrates the metacognitive skills that emerge in adolescence because he is able to evaluate his understanding and adjust his strategies to the content. Adolescents' abilities to apply metacognition in real-world settings continue to develop into late adolescence and early adulthood.

• • Legal Implications of Adolescent Decision Making

Developmental science has offered important insights into policy questions such as how to treat juvenile offenders.

Developmental scientists' work is often called upon to inform legal issues and influence social policy, as illustrated by a series of Supreme Court cases (Bonnie & Scott, 2013; Cohen & Casey, 2014).

Can adolescents who have been convicted of serious crimes face the death penalty? In *Roper v. Simmons*, the Supreme Court considered whether the death penalty is constitutional as applied to minors. Should minors be subject to the same punishments as adults? At the time, 21 states in the United States permitted the death penalty for adolescents under the age of 18, and most of them permitted it at the age of 16 (Steinberg & Scott, 2003). As the case moved to the Supreme Court, developmental scientists collaborated with the American Psychological Association to submit an *amicus curiae* ("friend of the court") brief to inform the justices about the developmental research relevant to the case, specifically research on adolescent judgment and decision making. The brief explained that adolescents' developmental immaturity makes them less culpable for crimes and justifies a more lenient punishment than that given to adults, but adolescents are actors who retain responsibility for the crime (Cauffman & Steinberg, 2012; Steinberg & Scott, 2003).

Recall that the lag between the development of the emotional part of the brain and the prefrontal cortex, responsible for executive functioning and decision making, contributes to adolescents' tendency to feel strong emotions and impulses that they may have difficulty controlling (Casey & Caudle, 2013). Research suggests that adolescents, especially males, react impulsively to threat cues more so than do adults or children, even when the adolescent is instructed not to respond. This response is associated with enhanced activity in the limbic regions of the brain responsible for detecting and assigning value to emotion (Dreyfuss et al., 2014).

In addition to neurological development, psychosocial development, specifically susceptibility to peer influence and future orientation, plays a prominent role in adolescent decision making and behavior (Albert et al., 2013). When adolescents make decisions in response to hypothetical dilemmas in which they must choose between engaging in an antisocial behavior suggested by friends and a prosocial one, their choices suggest that susceptibility to peer influence increases between childhood and early adolescence, peaking around age 14 and declining slowly during high school (Allen & Antonishak, 2008; Steinberg & Monahan, 2007). Not only are adolescents' decisions more likely to be influenced by peers, but simply thinking about peer evaluation increases risky behavior. Moreover, the presence of peers can increase risky behavior even when the probability of a negative outcome is high (Centifanti, Modecki, MacLellan, & Gowling, 2014; Smith et al., 2014).

Similarly, adults demonstrate a greater ability to envision themselves in the future than do adolescents (Nurmi, 1991; Steinberg et al., 2009). A poor sense of future orientation is associated with participation in risky activities (Chen & Vazsonyi, 2011, 2013). Difficulty envisioning the future combined with the influence of strong emotions, susceptibility to peers, and poor self-control can compromise adolescents' decisions despite their neurological and cognitive advances. In all of these ways, psychosocial factors influence how adolescents weigh the costs and benefits in making decisions: To the extent that teens are less psychosocially mature than adults, their decisions are likely to be inferior to those of adults, even if they score similarly to adults on cognitive measures (Cauffman & Steinberg, 2000, 2012; Modecki, 2014).

In the case of *Roper v. Simmons,* in 2005 the Supreme Court ruled against capital punishment for minors on the basis of their lack of maturity and susceptibility to peer influence (Greenhouse, 2005; Steinberg, 2013). In 2010 and 2012, under a similar rationale, in *Florida v. Graham, Miller v. Alabama,* and *Jackson v. Hobbs,* the Supreme Court ruled that minors cannot be sentenced to life in prison without parole (American Psychological Association, 2012).

What Do You Think?

1. To what degree do you think adolescents should be culpable for criminal offenses they commit? Do you agree with the Supreme Court decisions against the death penalty or life in prison without parole for adolescents? Why or why not?

2. Do you advocate using developmental science research to make policy decisions such as this? Why or why not?

Metacognition improves during adolescence and plays an important role in the development of scientific reasoning because it is by experimenting with and reflecting on cognitive strategies that adolescents learn about and come to appreciate logic, which they increasingly apply to situations (Kuhn, 2000; van der Stel & Veenman, 2013; Weil et al., 2013). Improvements in information processing capacities and metacognition enable adolescents to engage in the more sophisticated, reasoned, and efficient problem solving that underlies capacities for manipulating abstract mental representations and engaging in the hypothetical-deductive thinking that is characteristic of scientific reasoning (Bullock, Sodian, & Koerber, 2009; Demetriou, Christou, Spanoudis, & Platsidou, 2002; Kuhn, 2012). Although adolescents show advances in scientific reasoning, their reasoning tends to emphasize single solutions to problems.

In one study, 6th-grade students were presented with detailed pictorial and written information about variables that were explained to have either a causal or noncausal influence on a hypothetical problem, such as the likelihood of an avalanche occurring. The task was to apply the information in predicting outcomes. Although given information about five different variables, the students consistently chose only one factor as influential, although they chose different variables across trials. For example, a pair of students chose snow pollution as a cause of an avalanche, referring to the written materials, "Because it shows the snow pollution is high; snow is what causes an avalanche." Yet for a second prediction, the student pair turned to another single variable, slope angle, explaining that "slope angle is an important part of how snow falls." In a third prediction, they turned to still another, different, single factor, wind speed: "We chose the wind speed because it affects how fast the snow falls" (Kuhn, Pease, & Wirkala, 2009, p. 439). Although adolescents can demonstrate scientific thinking, they tend to consistently prefer single-factor solutions as they are not yet able to coordinate the effects of multiple casual influences on outcomes (Kuhn, Iordanou, Pease, & Wirkala, 2008; Kuhn et al., 2009). For many young people, the more complex reasoning required to consider multiple influences at once, as well as a more sophisticated understanding of the nature of knowledge and scientific phenomena, emerges in early adulthood.

BRAIN DEVELOPMENT
AND ADOLESCENT COGNITION

Changes in the brain, especially the prefrontal cortex, underlie many improvements in information processing capacities. As the structure of the prefrontal cortex changes, with decreases in gray matter and increases in white matter, cognition becomes markedly more efficient (Asato, Terwilliger, Woo, & Luna, 2010). Myelination underlies improvements in processing speed during childhood and adolescence, permitting quicker physical and cognitive responses (Silveri, Tzilos, & Yurgelun-Todd, 2008). Compared to children, not only do adolescents show faster reaction speed in gym class, but they are quicker at connecting ideas, making arguments, and drawing conclusions. Processing speed increases and reaches adult levels at about age 15 and is associated with advances in working memory and cognition (Coyle, Pillow, Snyder, & Kochunov, 2011).

Development of the prefrontal cortex as well as the cerebellum leads to enhanced executive function, capacities that allow us to control and coordinate our thoughts and behavior, including attention, planning, evaluating, judging, goal-directed behavior, and response inhibition (Ardila, 2013; Tiemeier et al., 2010). Connections between the prefrontal cortex and various brain regions strengthen, improving working memory and permitting rapid communication and enhanced cognitive and behavioral functioning (Tamnes et al., 2013; van den Bosch et al., 2014). With these advances in brain development, routine decisions become automatic, requiring fewer cognitive resources and therefore enabling adolescents to redirect their thinking toward more complicated problems.

Decision Making

Adolescents are faced with a variety of decisions each day, ranging from the mundane, such as when to clean their rooms and how to spend an afternoon, to decisions that are important to their health, well-being, and future, such as which friendships to foster, whether to drink or smoke, what classes to take in school, and whether and where to go to college. With age and experience, adolescents take on increasing decision-making responsibility. Cognitive advances permit adolescents to engage in more sophisticated thinking than ever before and to participate meaningfully in decision making.

Researchers who study decision making from a cognitive perspective explain decision making as a rational process in which, when faced with a decision, people follow several steps. They first identify decision options, then identify the potential positive and negative consequences for each option (i.e., the pros and cons). They estimate how likely each potential outcome is, rate how desirable each outcome is, and finally combine all of this information to make a decision (Furby & Beyth-Marom, 1992). Research from this perspective has shown that adolescents often are capable of demonstrating rational decision making that is in line with their goals and is comparable to that of adults (Reyna & Farley, 2006; Reyna & Rivers, 2008). For example, comparisons of adolescents and adults' decisions on hypothetical dilemmas—such as whether to engage in substance use, have surgery, have sex, or drink and drive—show that adults spontaneously generate more consequences to each decision option and are more likely to spontaneously mention risks and benefits of each option (Furby & Beyth-Marom, 1992; Halpern-Felsher & Cauffman, 2001). However, both adolescents and adults show an optimistic bias wherein they view their own risks as lower than those of peers (Halpern-Felsher & Cauffman, 2001). Moreover, adolescents and adults generally do not differ in their ratings of the perceived harmfulness of risks; in fact, in many cases adolescents perceive greater risks than do adults (Reyna & Farley, 2006).

If adolescents are aware of the risks entailed in decisions, perhaps more so than adults, why do they often make poor decisions and engage in risk taking? Although adolescents' abstract reasoning abilities permit them to consider possibilities, they often do not consider practicalities associated with each option. Adolescents are more approach oriented in response to positive feedback and less responsive to negative feedback than are adults (Cauffman et al., 2010; Javadi, Schmidt, & Smolka, 2014). Adolescents tend to place more importance on the potential benefits of decisions (e.g., social status, pleasure) than their estimation of the potential costs or risks (e.g., physical harm, short- and long-term health; Rivers, Reyna, & Mills, 2008; Shulman & Cauffman, 2013).

Neurological research supports these findings. For example, in the presence of rewards, adolescents show heightened activity in the brain systems that support reward processing and reduced activity in the areas responsible for inhibitory control, as compared with adults (Paulsen, Hallquist, Geier, & Luna, 2014; Smith, Steinberg, Strang, & Chein, 2015). Similarly, adolescents who engage in high-risk behavior more often show less activation of the parts of the prefrontal cortex that are associated with decision making (Luna et al., 2013; Shad et al., 2011).

Recall from Chapter 4 that maturation of the prefrontal cortex, which is associated with executive functions including decision making, lags behind the development of the limbic system, which is responsible for emotional arousal (Mills, Goddings, Clasen, Giedd, & Blakemore, 2014). This difference in maturational timing means that, until maturation of the prefrontal cortex catches up to the limbic system, adolescents feel emotionally charged before they have corresponding self-regulation and decision-making abilities (Albert et al., 2013; Van Leijenhorst et al., 2010). Adolescents show greater activity of the reward parts of the brain than adults and are assumed to be susceptible to risk taking in situations of heightened emotional arousal (Figner, Mackinlay, Wilkening, & Weber, 2009; Mills et al., 2014). Their decisions about risk taking are swayed by so-called hot processes, the emotional arousal-driven thinking that tends to interfere with "cold" rational processes of cost–benefit weighing (van Duijvenvoorde, Jansen, Visser, & Huizenga, 2010; Zelazo & Carlson, 2012). In other words, adolescents often act impulsively, seemingly without thought, and their decisions often are influenced by affective motivators such as the desire for pleasure, relaxation, or excitement (Mills et al., 2014; van Duijvenvoorde et al., 2015).

Adolescents are capable of demonstrating rational decision making that is in line with their goals and is comparable to that of adults, but these results are seen under ideal laboratory conditions (Reyna & Rivers, 2008). In practice, decision making is more complex and influenced by situational, emotional, and individual difference characteristics, such as the presence of peers, temptation of high rewards, excitement, impulsivity, and sensation seeking (Smith, Chein, & Steinberg, 2013). Laboratory studies of decision making usually present adolescents with hypothetical dilemmas which are very different from the everyday decisions they face. Everyday decisions have personal relevance, require quick thinking, are emotional, and often are made in the presence and influence of others. Adolescents often feel strong emotions and impulses that they may be unable to regulate, due to the still-immature condition of their prefrontal cortex (Casey & Caudle, 2013). Therefore laboratory studies of decision making are less useful in understanding how young people compare with adults when they must make choices that are important or occur in stressful situations in which they must rely on experience, knowledge, and intuition (Steinberg, 2013). When faced with unfamiliar emotionally charged situations, spur-of-the-moment decisions, pressures to conform to peers, poor self-control, and risk and benefit estimates that favor good short-term and bad long-term outcomes, adolescents tend to reason more poorly than adults (Albert et al., 2013; Defoe, Dubas, Figner, & Aken, 2012). Figure 7.4 illustrates the many influences on adolescent decision making.

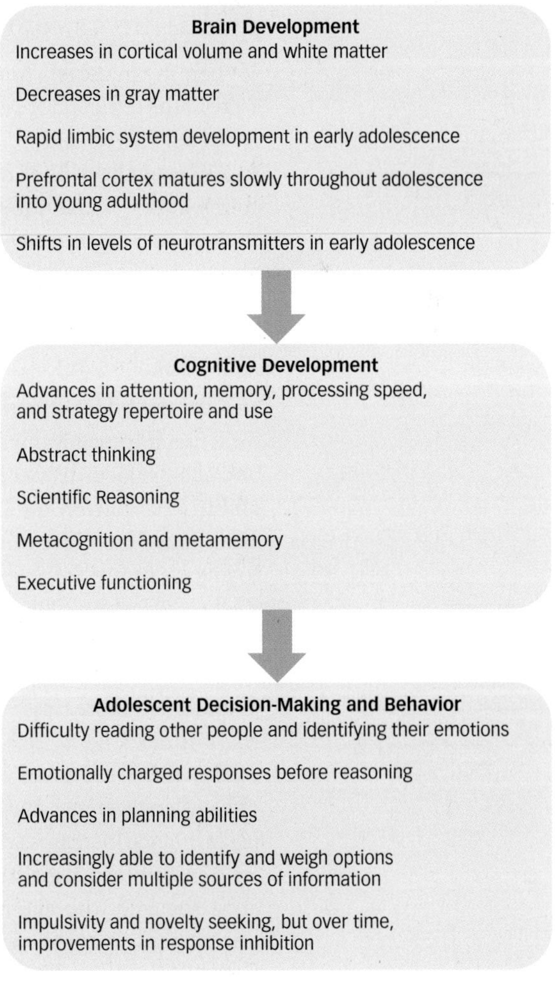

When is adolescents' thinking adult-like enough that they can be treated as adults? The answer to this question holds implications for a variety of contexts. For example, when is an adolescent able to make medical decisions, such as for elective surgery? In academic contexts, when is an adolescent able to drop out of school without parental permission? Perhaps the most controversial question pertains to legal contexts: When should an adolescent offender be tried or sentenced as an adult? At what age can an offender be given the death penalty or sentenced to life in prison without parole? This policy issue is discussed in the Lives in Context feature.

Although many adults display faulty decision making, it is adolescents who are in need of protection from their poor decisions because the consequences of their bad decisions—such as accepting a ride from a friend who has been drinking—are potentially more serious and long lasting. Adult guidance aids adolescents in learning how to make good decisions. Such guidance can include helping adolescents consider options, the pros and cons of each, the likelihood of each, and how to weigh information to come to a decision. Experience making decisions, learning from successes and failures, coupled with developments in cognition, self-control, and emotional regulation, leads to adolescent decision making that is more reflective, confident, and successful.

FIGURE 7.4: Influences on Adolescent Decisions

Brain Development
Increases in cortical volume and white matter

Decreases in gray matter

Rapid limbic system development in early adolescence

Prefrontal cortex matures slowly throughout adolescence into young adulthood

Shifts in levels of neurotransmitters in early adolescence

Cognitive Development
Advances in attention, memory, processing speed, and strategy repertoire and use

Abstract thinking

Scientific Reasoning

Metacognition and metamemory

Executive functioning

Adolescent Decision-Making and Behavior
Difficulty reading other people and identifying their emotions

Emotionally charged responses before reasoning

Advances in planning abilities

Increasingly able to identify and weigh options and consider multiple sources of information

Impulsivity and novelty seeking, but over time, improvements in response inhibition

Lives in Context Video 7.2
Thinking and Decision
Making in Adolescence

⚙️ Thinking in Context 7.4

1. Some might argue that advances in metacognition are the most important aspect of cognitive development during adolescence. Why might metacognition be particularly important? Do you think that it is the most important advance? Why or why not?

2. Considering the biological developments of adolescence described in Chapter 3, describe some ways in which adolescent decision making is a product of interactions among puberty, brain development, cognitive growth, and contextual influences such as parents, peers, and community.

INFORMATION PROCESSING IN ADULTHOOD

LO 7.5 Compare patterns of change in working memory, long-term memory, problem-solving capacities, and wisdom in adulthood.

Changes in thinking and problem solving during adulthood are influenced by adults' capacities for information processing. Changes in attention, working memory, and processing speed influence how adults interact with their world, the development of expertise, and problem-solving skills. Older adults are often described as wise. What is wisdom? How do information processing abilities change during the adult years?

ATTENTION, MEMORY, AND PROCESSING SPEED IN ADULTS

"Where are my keys?" Martinique asked for what felt like the 100th time this week. "They were in the refrigerator last time you lost them. Have you checked under your sandwich?" asked her 15-year-old son, Ramon. "Ok wise guy, I'll look in the fridge." "Um Mom? You're holding your keys. They're in your hand." "Yikes! I'd forget my head if it weren't connected to my neck!" Martinique exclaimed. Are middle-aged adults like Martinique doomed to declining cognitive abilities? How do information processing capacities change over adulthood?

Attention

In what ways does attention change with age? Researchers who study attention examine how much information a person can attend to at once, the ability to divide attention and change focus from one task to another in response to situational demands, and the ability to selectively attend and ignore distracters and irrelevant stimuli. From middle adulthood into older adulthood it becomes more difficult to divide attention, that is, to engage in two complex tasks at once and focus on relevant information (Radvansky, Zacks, & Hasher, 2005). As with other capacities, age-related declines in attention are not uniform across adults, and these differences predict variations in cognitive performance. In one study, those who performed better on cognitive tasks were more attracted to and spent more time viewing novel stimuli than those who performed at average levels (Daffner, Chong, & Riis, 2007). Moreover, the magnitude of the difference between adults with exceptional versus average performance grew from middle adulthood into old age; engagement and a preference for novelty become better predictors of cognitive performance increases with age.

Sensory capacities, such as vision and hearing, decline with age (see Chapter 4) and are associated with age-related declines in cognition (Baldwin & Ash, 2010). Sensory impairments prevent some information from getting into the cognitive system in the first place, so that older adults may never be aware that they have missed it. Reductions in sensory capacities are associated with impaired attention and slower cognition (Anstey, Hofer, & Luszcz, 2003; Wingfield, Tun, & McCoy, 2005). In one study of adults of different ages, 11% of the individual differences in young adults' scores on cognitive measures were associated with sensory impairment, whereas sensory impairment among older adults accounted for 31% of the individual differences in cognitive scores (Lindenberger & Baltes, 1997). Sensory impairments may prevent individuals from attending to stimuli; however, research suggests that neurological changes are the cause of deficits in both attention and sensory capacities (Lindenberger, Scherer, & Baltes, 2001).

Response inhibition becomes more challenging with age, and adults find it increasingly difficult to resist interference from irrelevant information to stay focused on the task at hand (Sylvain-Roy, Lungu, & Belleville, 2014). Researchers have assessed attention with laboratory tasks in which participants are presented with a series of letter combinations and told to press the space bar only when they see a particular combination (such as T-L); they are to ignore all other combinations. In such tasks, adults' performance declines steadily from the 30s on. Older adults make more errors of commission—pressing the space bar after incorrect letter combinations—suggesting that they are less able to inhibit responding to extraneous information (Mani, Bedwell, & Miller, 2005). Older adults also make more errors of omission—not pressing the space bar in response to the correct sequence—when the task was accompanied by extraneous noise. In everyday life, these changes in attention might make older adults appear more easily distracted, less able to attend, and less able to take in information.

In everyday life, however, changes in attention are not always evident (Kramer & Madden, 2008). Experience and practice can make a big difference in adults' information processing capacities (Glisky, 2007). People in occupations that require detecting critical stimuli and engaging in multiple complex tasks, such air traffic controllers, develop expertise in focusing and maintaining attention and show smaller declines with age (Kennedy, Taylor, Reade, & Yesavage, 2010; Morrow et al., 2003). Practice also improves performance and reduces age-related decline. For example, training in how to divide attention between two tasks by using selective attention—switching back and forth between mental operations—improves the performance of older adults as much as that of younger adults, although age differences in performance remain (Kramer & Madden, 2008).

Older adults are less likely to inhibit irrelevant items, are slower at inhibiting a response, and are more likely to retrieve irrelevant items, especially in tasks that require a high memory load and include the presence of distracters (Bloemendaal et al., 2016; Gazzaley, Sheridan, Cooney, & D'Esposito, 2007; Rowe et al., 2010).

Working Memory

Working memory changes substantially over the adult years. Working memory is essential to cognitive competence as it underlies performance on a range of tasks, including problem solving, decision making, language comprehension, abstract reasoning, and complex learning (Darowski, Helder, Zacks, Hasher, & Hambrick, 2008; McCabe, Roediger, McDaniel, Balota, & Hambrick, 2010). Age-related declines in working memory span from the 20s through the 60s and are supported by cross-sectional and longitudinal research (Emery, Hale, & Myerson, 2008).

Changes in attention influence declines in working memory (Rowe, Hasher, & Turcotte, 2010; Sylvain-Roy et al., 2014). With age, older adults become more susceptible to distraction and are less likely to discard distracting information from working memory, which then leaves less space in working memory for completing a given task (Radvansky, Zacks, & Hasher, 2005; Van Gerven, Van Boxtel, Meijer, Willems, & Jolles, 2007). However, once material is encoded in working memory, healthy adults of all ages retain the ability to exert control over working memory—they are able to orient their attention within working memory (and stay on task; Mok, Myers, Wallis, & Nobre, 2016). Problems with working memory vary with the number of tasks and task demands: The greater the number of tasks and demands, the worse the performance (Kessels, Meulenbroek, Fernandez, & Olde Rikkert, 2010; Voelcker-Rehage, Stronge, & Alberts, 2006).

Consider an experiment that requires adults to attend and respond to two tasks at once, such as tapping a computer screen on two alternating targets whose sizes vary systematically at the same time as generating a list of random numbers, spoken at 2-second intervals. With age, most adults find it is more difficult to simultaneously perform a motor and cognitive task such as this than it is to perform either task alone. However, practice in the motor task makes it more automatic, reducing the demands on working memory. In this way, practice can reduce (but not eliminate) age-related deficits in cognitive performance (Voelcker-Rehage & Alberts, 2007).

Age-related decline is less apparent in cognitive tasks that are more passive and less attentionally demanding, such as digit recall and visual pattern recall tasks (Bisiacchi et al., 2008). When working memory maintenance systems are taxed, as in the case of interference, older adults do not perform as well as young and middle-aged adults. **Proactive interference** occurs when information that has previously been remembered interferes with memory for new information (Bowles & Salthouse, 2003). Students may experience proactive interference if they have studied a foreign language for a couple of years and then switch to beginner-level classes in another foreign language: The language they have already learned can interfere with ability to learn and use the new language. Older adults are more susceptible to interference effects than are younger adults, even when they have learned the material equally well (Jacoby, Wahlheim, Rhodes, Daniels, & Rogers, 2010). Researchers study this with working memory span tasks, in which participants are presented with repeated trials of material that they are asked to remember, recall, and then forget. Frequently the old, supposedly forgotten material interferes with older adults' ability to store new material.

With age, adults are less likely to apply the memory strategies of organization and elaboration (Braver & West, 2008; Craik & Rose, 2012). In both of these strategies, the person must link new information with existing knowledge. From middle adulthood into old age, adults begin to have more difficulty retrieving information from long-term memory, which makes them less likely to spontaneously use organization and elaboration as memory strategies (Glisky, 2007).

Context, Task Demands, and Memory Performance. Many laboratory tests of working memory entail tasks that are similar to those encountered in school settings. Middle-aged and older adults may be less motivated by such tasks than younger adults, who likely have more recent experience in school contexts. Laboratory findings, therefore, may not accurately illustrate the everyday memory capacity of middle-aged and older adults (Salthouse, 2012). For example, when the pace of a memory task is slowed, or participants are reminded to use organization or elaboration strategies, middle-aged and older adults show better performance (Braver & West, 2008). In addition, the type of task influences performance. In one study, adults aged 19 to 68 completed memory tests under two conditions: a pressured classroom-like condition and a self-paced condition. When participants were shown a video and tested immediately (classroom-like condition), younger adults showed better recall than did the middle-aged adults. However, when participants were given a packet of information and a video to study on their own (self-paced condition), midlife adults performed just as well as young adults on recall three days later (Ackerman & Beier, 2006; Beier & Ackerman, 2005). This suggests that the ways in which we learn and remember change with age and experience.

The declines in memory evident in laboratory research are less apparent in everyday settings (Salthouse, 2012). Knowledge of facts (e.g., scientific facts), procedures (e.g., how to drive a car), and information related to one's vocation either remain the same or increase over the adult years (Schaie, 2013), and adults' experience and knowledge of their cognitive system (metacognition) enable them to use their memory more effectively. For example, they use external supports and strategies to maximize their memory, such as by organizing their notes or placing their car keys in a designated spot where they can reliably be found (Schwartz & Frazier, 2005). As with attention, memory declines vary with the individual and task. Most adults compensate for declines and show little to no differences in everyday

proactive interference A phenomenon that occurs when information that has previously been remembered interferes with memory for new information.

settings; however, chronic stress impairs working memory (Lee & Goto, 2015). Midlife adults who feel overwhelmed in daily life, such as those faced with many conflicting responsibilities and stressors that demand a great deal of multitasking, are more likely to rate their memory competence as poor (Vestergren & Nilsson, 2011). Multitasking is difficult for all adults, but it becomes more challenging in older adulthood. Managing and coordinating multiple tasks by switching attention among two sets of stimuli is associated with greater disruptions in working memory in older adults as compared with younger adults (Clapp et al., 2011). If, however, older adults have the opportunity to slow down to a pace with which they feel comfortable, they can show performance on working memory tasks similar to that of younger adults (Verhaeghen et al., 2003).

Emotion and Working Memory. Age differences in working memory are usually assessed by tasks that require older and younger adults to complete various tasks in a laboratory setting. Although standard lab tasks often show age-related declines in working memory, there are instances in which older adults show capacities similar to those of younger adults. Older adults score better on measures of complex thinking when the task evokes positive feelings than when the task is designed to evoke neutral or negative feelings (Carpenter, Peters, Västfjäll, & Isen, 2013). For example, one study examined age differences in working memory for emotional versus visual information. Findings demonstrate that, despite an age-related deficit for visual information, working memory for emotion was unimpaired (Mikels, Larkin, Reuter-Lorenz, & Cartensen, 2005). Positive mood enhances working memory capacity so that adults are better able to hold onto information while processing task-irrelevant information when in a positive mood. However, a negative mood is not related to either an increase or decrease in working memory (Storbeck & Maswood, 2016). In another study, although young adults were better able to recall neutral words than were older adults, there were no age differences in recall of emotional words such as "peace," "joy," "love," or "smile" (Mammarella, Borella, Carretti, Leonardi, & Fairfield, 2013). A meta-analysis of the positivity effect of 100 studies shows that older adults are naturally biased toward recalling positive over negative information, although younger adults show the reverse, with more attention on the negative (Reed, Chan, & Mikels, 2014).

What are the reasons for this positivity effect in older adults' memories? It may be due to their greater focus on managing their emotions. That is, older adults may use cognitive control mechanisms that enhance positive and diminish negative information in order to feel good (Mather & Carstensen, 2005). This finding has appeared in research with Chinese and Korean adults, suggesting that the positivity bias with age may appear cross-culturally (Gutchess & Boduroglu, 2015). Although they are often studied separately, emotion and cognition are intertwined (Reed & Carstensen, 2012). Emotion characterizes most real-life decisions, suggesting that older adults are likely able to focus their attention and cognitive capacities on the task at hand, if it has real-world emotional relevance, such as decisions about health care, financial, and living situations (Samanez-Larkin, Robertson, Mikels, Carstensen, & Gotlib, 2009).

Long-Term Memory

Age-related changes in working memory also contribute to changes in long-term memory. As cognitive processing slows, most adults show difficulties with recall. For example, while watching a television show, an older adult may retain fewer details than a young adult. However, the various types of long-term memory show different patterns of change. Semantic memory (memory for factual material) shows little age-related decline, but episodic memory (memory for experiences) tends to deteriorate with age (St-Laurent, Abdi, Burianová, & Grady, 2011).

Episodic memory shows increases from adolescence to about 25 or 30, then begins a steady decline (Bialystok, Craik, Bialystok, & Craik, 2010). Autobiographical memory shows predictable patterns of deterioration. When older adults are asked to discuss a

LIFESPAN BRAIN DEVELOPMENT

• • Sleep as Brain Cleanser

Sleep may act as a "mental janitor," discarding the biological waste that accumulates with thinking.

Sleep is essential for information processing, including forming and consolidating memories (Stickgold & Walker, 2013). Sleep also plays a role in forming neural connections and pruning existing connections (Tononi & Cirelli, 2014). Recent research suggests that sleep is even more critical to maintaining neurocognitive functioning. Specifically, sleep may act as a "mental janitor" clearing the brain of biological waste that accumulates as a result of daily thinking (Xie et al., 2013). The spaces between neurons are filled with cerebrospinal fluid whose flow washes away the cells' daily waste.

In a groundbreaking study, Maiken Nedergaard and colleagues (2013) demonstrated that sleep influences the flow of cerebrospinal fluid in mice. The researchers injected dye into the cerebrospinal fluid of mice and monitored the animals' brains, tracking the movement of dye. When the mice were awake the dye barely moved, flowing only along the brain's surface. In contrast, when the mice were asleep the dye indicated that the cerebrospinal fluid flowed rapidly and reached further into the brain.

Why does the fluid flow more easily during sleep? The team discovered that the increased flow was possible because when mice went to sleep, their brain cells shrank. The space between brain cells increased during sleep, making it easier for fluid to circulate. When an animal woke up, the brain cells enlarged again and the fluid's movement between cells slowed to a trickle. The sleeping mice processed neural wastes, such as excess beta-amyloid, twice as quickly as the awake mice, suggesting that sleep plays a critical role in the brain's waste management. This brain-cleaning process has been observed in rats and baboons, but it has yet to be studied in humans. Yet these findings might explain why we may not think clearly after a sleepless night. More important, the waste management role of cerebrospinal fluid might offer a new way of understanding and perhaps treating brain diseases that involve the buildup of wastes, such as amyloid plaques in Alzheimer's disease.

What Do You Think?

How does sleep affect your thinking and performance? What do these results mean to you?

FIGURE 7.5: Processing Speed Across the Lifespan

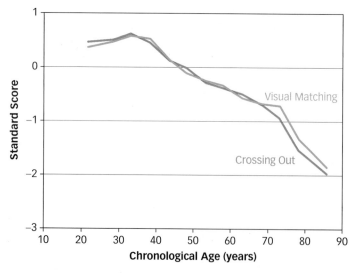

Source: Salthouse (2000).

personal memory or experience that comes to mind in response to cue words, such as the words *surprise* or *song*, they commonly recall experiences they had during adolescence and early adulthood. Similarly, when asked to create a timeline of memorable events in their lives, older adults tend to remember events from adolescence through early adulthood; they also remember recent events better than midlife events (Rubin, 2000; Schroots, van Dijkum, & Assink, 2004). In addition, they are more likely to remember happy events that occurred between ages 10 and 30 than those that occurred any other time in life (Berntsen & Rubin, 2002).

Why does long-term memory follow this pattern? Perhaps we process events differently during our adolescent and early adult years, a time when we are constructing our identities. And perhaps we are less adept at recalling events from middle adulthood because of interference, as new memories interfere with our recall of older memories. Similarities among events may make it difficult to distinguish them. Throughout

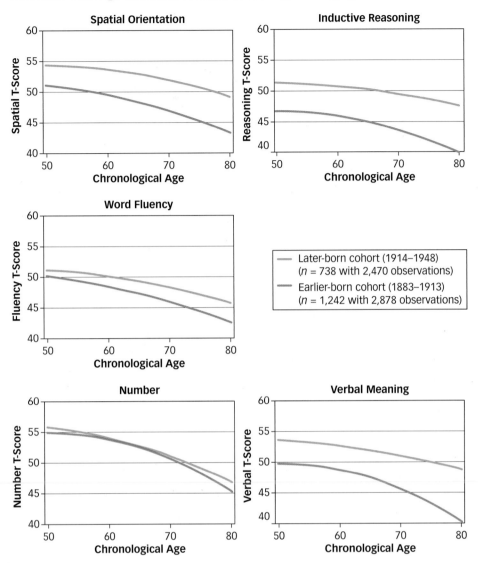

FIGURE 7.6: Age and Cohort Differences in Cognitive Aging

Source: Gerstorf et al. (2011).

life, memory is malleable and we often revise our memories in light of new experiences. However, it also appears that older adults recall fewer details from recent events (within the past 5 years), and different types of details, than do younger adults. This suggests that older and younger adults differ in what stimuli they attend to and select for processing (Gaesser, Sacchetti, Addis, & Schacter, 2010; Piolino et al., 2006; Piolino et al., 2010).

Contextual factors play a role in the rate of cognitive change. Similar to findings of cohort differences in intelligence scores, there are generational differences in overall cognitive performance that are maintained throughout life. Specifically, younger cohorts show better performance on a range of cognitive measures and less steep age-related declines (Gerstorf, Ram, Hoppmann, Willis, & Schaie, 2011; see Figure 7.6). Possible factors underlying cohort differences include secular trends in educational systems, disease prevalence, years of education, and quality of education.

Processing Speed

The greatest change in information processing capacity with age is a reduction in the speed of processing. Simple reaction time tasks, such as pushing a button in response to a light, reveal a steady slowing of responses from the 20s into the 90s (see Figure 7.5; Rozas et al., 2008; Salthouse, 1993). The more complex the task, the greater the age-related decline in reaction time. However, when reaction time tasks require a vocal response rather than a motor response, age-related declines are less dramatic (Johnson & Rybash, 1993).

In addition, adults' performance on standard tasks measuring processing speed is influenced by their capacities for attention. Adults who are highly distractible show slowed responding on standard tasks measuring processing speed, but their performance improves when tasks are designed to reduce distractions (e.g., by listing fewer items on a page). Reducing distractions improves performance, and the magnitude of improvement as a result of reducing distractions on tests of processing speed increases with age (Lustig, Hasher, & Tonev, 2006).

Declines in processing speed with age predict age-related declines in memory, reasoning, and problem-solving tasks (Levitt et al., 2006; Meijer, de Groot, van Gerven, van Boxtel, & Jolles, 2009). Moreover, the relationship between processing speed and performance on cognitive tasks becomes stronger with age (Chen & Li, 2007; Deming, Chang, Tianyong, & Guiyun, 2003; Salthouse & Pink, 2008). Changes in processing speed likely influence many of the cognitive declines associated with aging.

Why does cognitive processing slow with age? Changes in the brain underlie reductions in processing speed. The loss of white matter and myelinated connections reduces processing speed (Bennett & Madden, 2014; Nilsson, Thomas, O'Brien, & Gallagher, 2014). In addition, the loss of neurons forces the remaining neurons to reorganize and form new, often less efficient, connections (Johnson & Rybash, 1993). Another explanation posits a loss of information with each step in cognitive processing. With age, cognitive resources decline and adults show more information loss with each step in cognitive processing; as a result, when attempting a complex task, they perform more poorly than do young adults (Deming et al., 2003; Salthouse & Madden, 2013).

Although clearly apparent in laboratory tasks and highly reliable, the decline in the speed of processing is not as apparent in everyday situations. Middle-aged and older adults proficiently engage in complex tasks every day, showing performance similar to, or better than, that of younger adults. For example, one study tested 19- to 72-year-olds on two tasks: a reaction time task and a typing task. Both tasks measured their speed and accuracy. Although the middle-aged and older adults displayed slower reaction time as compared with young adults, their typing speed and accuracy was no different (Salthouse, 1984). With age, adults compensated for their slower reaction time by looking further ahead in the material to be typed, thereby anticipating keystrokes (Bosman, 1993; Salthouse, 1984). As they age, adults compensate for limitations in processing speed by modifying their activities to emphasize skills that rely on accumulated knowledge and thereby honing their crystallized intelligence (Bugg, Zook, DeLosh, Davalos, & Davis, 2006; Salthouse, 1996).

EXPERTISE, PROBLEM SOLVING, AND WISDOM

Over the course of midlife into old age, adults gain experience and knowledge. As a result, they demonstrate advances in practical problem solving in which they apply their experience and expertise to achieve goals and solve problems in the real world. Adults also gain emotional maturity as they become better able to regulate their emotions and focus on what is appropriate in a given context. These abilities are related to what is often called wisdom, a practical sense of insight or understanding how life can be most meaningful. Let's examine these qualities.

Expertise

expertise An elaborate and integrated knowledge base that underlies extraordinary proficiency in given area.

With age, most adults develop and expand their **expertise**, an elaborate and integrated knowledge base that underlies extraordinary proficiency in a given task and supports gains in practical problem solving. The development of expertise peaks in middle adulthood, when experts are able to solve problems efficiently by using abstract reasoning and making intuitive judgments. Experts are not distinguished by extraordinary intellect but by knowledge and experience (Ericsson, 2014).

It is expertise that enables middle-aged and older adults to compensate for declines in processing speed and memory (Ericsson & Moxley, 2013), like the typists who compensated for declines in reaction time by looking further ahead in the material to be typed (Salthouse, 1984). One study of food service workers found that gains in expertise compensated for declines in physical performance. In this study, 20- to 60-year-old food service workers were compared on several aspects of expert performance: strength and dexterity, technical knowledge (e.g., of the menu), organizational skills (e.g., setting priorities), and social skills (e.g., providing professional service). Although middle-aged workers showed declines in physical abilities, they performed more efficiently and competently than did young adults, suggesting that expertise in other areas compensated for losses in strength and dexterity (Perlmutter, Kaplan, & Nyquest, 1990).

Expert knowledge is transformative in that it permits a more sophisticated approach to problem solving than that used by nonexperts. Expert thought is intuitive, automatic, strategic, and flexible (Ericsson, 2014). Experts rely on their past experience and evaluation of the context in determining their approach. With experience, experts' responses become automatic—well rehearsed, seemingly without thought. They operate on hunches—intuitive judgments of how to approach a problem based on experience. This automaticity enables them to process information more quickly and efficiently, and it makes complex tasks routine (Herzmann & Curran, 2011). As expertise grows, experts find that their responses become so autonomic that it is hard for them to consciously explain what they do. For example, adults are better than children at tying shoelaces, yet children are far better than adults at explaining how to tie shoelaces (McLeod, Sommerville, & Reed, 2005).

In addition to operating more intuitively and automatically, expert behavior is strategic. Experts have a broader range of strategies and have better strategies than novices and can better apply them in response to unanticipated problems (Ericsson & Moxley, 2013). Despite showing slower working memory, experts maintain their performance in their areas of expertise, often by relying on external supports, such as notes (Morrow & Schriver, 2007). For example, one study presented airplane pilots with a flight simulation. They were given directions from air traffic controllers and allowed to take notes. The experienced pilots were more likely to take notes than the nonexpert pilots, and their notes tended to be more accurate and complete (Morrow et al., 2003). In actual flights comparing pilots ages 22 to 76, older pilots take more notes than do younger pilots but do not differ in their ability to repeat complex instructions regarding flight plans and conditions (Morrow et al., 2003). Similarly, expert golfers show fewer declines in performance with age as they compensate for their changing capacities (Logan & Baker, 2007). Longitudinal research with expert chess players showed few age effects in chess skill (Moxley & Charness, 2013); players with greater expertise and participation in tournaments showed fewer age-related declines in chess performance but performed similarly in other measures of cognition (Roring & Charness, 2007).

Finally, intuitive and automatic application of a broad range of strategies permits experts to be more flexible than nonexperts. Experts are more open to deviating from formal procedures when they encounter problems. Experts often approach cases in an individualized way, varying their approach with contextual factors, and are sensitive to exceptions (Ormerod, 2005).

Expertise permits **selective optimization with compensation**, the ability to adapt to changes over time, optimize current functioning, and compensate for losses in order to preserve performance despite declines in fluid abilities (Baltes & Carstensen, 2003; Baltes & Baltes, 1990). As people age, they select aspects of functioning to optimize and improve their proficiency. Typically these are areas in which they excel. People spend effort increasing their expertise in their chosen areas, thereby optimizing their strengths (Bugg et al., 2006; Salthouse, 1984). In addition to emphasizing their strengths, people

selective optimization with compensation An approach by which people maintain high levels of functioning by narrowing their goals, selecting personally valued attributes to optimize, and compensating for losses.

naturally devise ways of compensating for declines in physical functioning and fluid ability. Selective optimization with compensation occurs naturally, often without individuals' awareness as their expertise permits them to adapt to developmental changes. Older typists who look further ahead in their typing and experienced pilots who take more detailed notes are examples of expertise compensating for declines in working memory and processing speed. Successful aging entails selective optimization with compensation (Freund & Baltes, 2007).

Problem Solving and Wisdom

Cognitive changes in older adulthood are also reflected in problem-solving skills. As we have seen in the preceding sections, cognitive functioning—including processing speed, episodic memory, executive functioning, and verbal ability—typically declines in older adulthood, and this trend is closely related to problem-solving ability (Burton, Strauss, Hultsch, & Hunter, 2006). Laboratory studies of problem solving that rely on traditional hypothetical problems show declines with age, likely because of memory changes that make it difficult for older adults to retain and manipulate the information needed to solve the problem (Sinnott, 2003). Yet when decisions tap into relevant experience or knowledge, older adults tend to be as effective at making decisions as younger adults (Denney, Pearce, & Palmer, 1982).

Moreover, examinations of problem-solving skills in everyday settings show that people remain efficient decision makers throughout adulthood. For example, older adults tend to show adaptive problem solving in response to health-related decisions; they are actually better than younger adults at making decisions about whether they require medical attention and seeking medical care (Artistico, Orom, Cervone, Krauss, & Houston, 2010; Löckenhoff & Carstensen, 2007; Thornton & Dumke, 2005). In one study, the quality of reasoning behind decisions of 60- to 74-year-olds and 75- to 85-year-olds did not differ from that of college students, but older adults processed the problems more slowly (Ratcliff, Thapar, & McKoon, 2006).

Generally speaking, adults perform better on everyday problems that are relevant to the contexts they experience in their daily lives (Artistico et al., 2010). Specifically, older adults outperformed young and middle-aged adults on problems set in older adult contexts, such as medical care, suggesting that age-related declines observed in laboratory settings may not be observed in everyday life. In addition, older adults are more likely to act efficiently and decisively in solving problems that they feel are under their control (Thornton & Dumke, 2005). Research suggests that older adults are better at matching their strategies to their goals than are young adults, perhaps because past experience and crystallized knowledge provide an extensive base for making real-life decisions and aligning goals with decisions (Hoppmann & Blanchard-Fields, 2010). Finally, older adults are more likely than younger people to report that they turn to spouses, children, and friends for input in making decisions (Strough, Patrick, & Swenson, 2003).

Related to everyday problem solving, it is commonly thought that older adults become wiser with age. **Wisdom** refers to "expertise in the conduct and meanings of life," characterized by emotional maturity and the ability to show insight and apply it to problems (Baltes & Kunzmann, 2003; Staudinger, Kessler, & Dörner, 2006). It requires knowledge, not in the "book smarts" sense, but the ability to analyze real-world dilemmas in which clean and neat abstractions often give way to messy, disorderly, conflicting concrete interests (Birney & Sternberg, 2011). Wisdom requires metacognition, being aware of one's thought process, creativity, and insightfulness.

The belief that age brings wisdom is reflected in many societies' respect for older adults as society elders and leaders. Research, on the other hand, shows variability in the extent to which older adults actually display wisdom (Karelitz et al., 2010). In typical studies examining wisdom, adults aged 20 to 89 respond to hypothetical situations reflecting uncertain events, such as what to do if a friend is contemplating suicide (Staudinger, Dörner, & Mickler, 2005). Researchers rate each response for the degree

wisdom Expertise in the conduct and meanings of life, characterized by emotional maturity and the ability to show insight and apply it to problems.

• • Informed Consent in Older Adulthood

iStockPhoto.com/AlexRaths

A cornerstone of modern medicine is the recognition of patients' rights to provide informed consent to participate in research or treatment. Informed consent requires that the patient have knowledge and the ability to understand information about any proposed procedures, understand that participation is voluntary, and be able to make a reasoned decision of whether to engage. Many conditions common to older adults, such as dementia, slowly rob older adults of their capacities to engage in the reasoning and decision making that is essential to providing informed consent.

To assess basic cognitive capacities, a caregiver may ask the patient questions about the date, year, and surroundings. A respondent who demonstrates a lack of awareness of such basic matters would likely be considered unable to engage in medical decision making (Purohit & Kalairajah, 2010). In one sample of older adults in residential living facilities, the best predictors of the incapacity to provide informed consent were

cognitive impairments, impairments in activities of daily living, and dementia diagnosis. Only about one-third of those studied were able to meet requirements to provide informed consent (Black et al., 2008). Those who live in residential facilities, however, are more likely to be ill or suffer from dementia than older adults who live independently in the community.

A study of older adults' abilities to consent to medical procedures showed that cognitive scores were positively related to the length of physicians' visits and length of consent discussions: Physicians spent less time discussing procedures with patients who had lower cognitive scores, presumably because these patients had less involvement in decision making (Sugarman et al., 2007). As cognitive impairment increased, patients engaged less in conversations between the physician and the patient's companion, from whom the physician was soliciting consent. When patients spoke, they primarily agreed with and approved of what was said. Although at first this might seem to signal consent, for persons with dementia, such an interpretation should be made with caution. Because affirming statements may simply be a means of engagement rather than a deliberate cognitive act, it is difficult to assess the patient's actual preference. Multiple exposures to information are helpful in enabling ill older adults to comprehend and reason with it. Thus, communicating with patients and soliciting consent is best practiced as a process rather than a one-time event (Purohit & Kalairajah, 2010).

An important alternative to consent is soliciting geriatric assent, which balances the process of engaging patients in decision making with protecting them from harm. Geriatric assent takes into account older adults' remaining capacity for autonomous decision making. Physicians identify the patient's longstanding values and preferences, assess plans of care accordingly, and protect patients' remaining autonomy. Many patients with dementia can still express their values and preferences, even when they remain irreversibly below thresholds of decision-making autonomy. Geriatric assent does not encourage incompetent persons to make decisions that are beyond their capacity, thereby placing them in harm's way, but instead permits older adults to have a say in their care for as long as they are able (Molinari, McCullough, Coverdale, & Workman, 2006).

What do you think?

What factors (cognitive or otherwise) do you think are most important contributors to older adults' capacities to make medical decisions? Under what conditions should an older adults' competence be evaluated?

to which it illustrates several components of wisdom: knowledge about fundamental concerns of life such as human nature, strategies for applying that knowledge to making life decisions, ability to consider multiple contextual demands, and awareness and management of ambiguity, in that many problems have no perfect solutions. A small number of adults at all ages scored high in wisdom; they had experience in dealing with human problems, such as that which is obtained in human service careers or in leadership roles (Staudinger & Baltes, 1996; Staudinger et al., 2006). When both age and experience were taken into account, older adults were, indeed, more likely to show wisdom than were younger adults. In another study, however, only college-educated older adults scored higher on measures of wisdom than did college students, suggesting that wisdom does not necessarily come with age, but rather with the opportunity and motivation to pursue its development (Ardelt, 2010).

Wisdom is especially likely to be shown when considering problems that are most relevant to individuals. For example, in one study younger and older adults completed traditional measures of wisdom (hypothetical dilemmas), and they were asked to discuss problems relevant to young adults, specifically, marital conflict. Marital conflict problems were presented in written vignettes and in video clips. There were no age differences in the traditional wisdom task, but in the marital conflict tasks the young adults gave responses more indicative of wisdom than did the older adults. It appears that relevance matters—age differences in wise reasoning about fundamental life issues depend on relevance of problems (Thomas & Kunzmann, 2014).

Life experience, particularly facing and managing adversity, contributes to the development of wisdom. One study of people who came of age during the Great Depression of the 1930s found that, 40 years later, older adults who had experienced and overcome economic adversity demonstrated higher levels of wisdom than their peers (Ardelt, 1998). Experience, particularly expertise in solving the problems of everyday life, is associated with wisdom (Baltes & Staudinger, 2000). Those who are wise are reflective; they show advanced cognition and emotional regulation skills. These qualities contribute to the development of wisdom, but they also are associated with better physical health, higher levels of education, openness to experience, positive social relationships, and overall psychological well-being, all of which aid adults in tackling the problems of everyday life (Kramer, 2003).

What can we conclude about wisdom? Perhaps that it is a rare quality, one that can be found at all ages but that typically improves with age. And, older adults are more likely to be among the very wise.

INFLUENCES ON COGNITIVE CHANGE IN ADULTHOOD

We have seen that cognition changes in several ways with development. Aspects of cognition that rely on fluid intelligence decline in older adulthood, but those that rely on crystallized intelligence, accumulated knowledge, and experience remain the same or improve. A decline in processing speed, influenced by neurological changes, also influences fluid intelligence and older adults' ability to take in, process, and retain information (Finkel, Reynolds, McArdle, & Pedersen, 2007; Fry & Hale, 1996). Therefore, aspects of cognition that rely on fluid intelligence decline in older adulthood, but those that rely on crystallized intelligence, accumulated knowledge, and experience remain the same or improve. Cognitive abilities tend to remain stable, relative to peers, over the lifespan. For example, high intelligence early in life (e.g., at age 11) is predictive of intelligence in old age (through age 87; Gow, Corley, Starr, & Deary, 2012). However, with advancing age comes greater diversity in cognitive ability. Centenarians (people aged 100 or older) show greater variations in cognitive performance than do older adults aged 85 to 90 (Miller et al., 2010; Paúl, Ribeiro, & Santos, 2010). Differences in experience and lifestyle can account for many differences in cognitive change over adulthood.

Cross-sectional research shows that education, measured by years of formal schooling or by literacy levels on reading tests, is a strong and consistent predictor of cognitive performance and problem-solving tasks in old age (Kavé, Eyal, Shorek, & Cohen-Mansfield, 2008). In fact, findings from the Georgia Centenarian Study suggest that education accounted for the largest proportion of cognitive differences among the centenarians studied (Davey et al., 2010). Recall from Chapter 1 that cross-sectional and longitudinal studies often yield different results. Similar to research on cognitive change in older adulthood, the influence of education on cognitive change varies depending on whether the study is cross-sectional or longitudinal (Van Dijk, Van Gerven, Van Boxtel, Van Der Elst, & Jolles, 2008). Longitudinal research studies with older adults from Germany, Australia, and the United States, spanning 7 to 13 years in length with testing occurring at 3 to 6 time points, do not find a relationship between education and cognitive decline at older age (Anstey et al., 2003; Van Dijk et al., 2008). The effects of education are debated, but it is generally recognized that throughout life, cognitive engagement—through mentally stimulating career, educational, and leisure activities—predicts the maintenance of mental abilities (Bielak, 2010; Schaie, 2013).

Another predictor of cognitive performance and impairment across the lifespan is physical health (Blondell, Hammersley-Mather, & Veerman, 2014; S. Wang, Luo, Barnes, Sano, & Yaffe, 2014). Health conditions such as cardiovascular disease, osteoporosis, and arthritis are associated with cognitive declines (Baltes & Carstensen, 2003; Okonkwo et al., 2010). Longitudinal studies also suggest that poor mental health, such as depression and anxiety, is associated with declines in processing speed, long-term memory and problem solving (Lönnqvist, 2010; Margrett et al., 2010). It is difficult to disentangle the directional effects of health and cognitive decline, however, because people who score higher on cognitive measures are more likely to engage in health-promoting behaviors. Physical health and cognitive functioning intersect when it comes to the question of obtaining informed consent from elderly patients requiring various medical treatments, as discussed in the Lives in Context: Informed Consent in Older Adulthood feature.

Interventions that train older adults and encourage them to use cognitive skills can preserve and even reverse some age-related cognitive declines. One study of participants in the Seattle Longitudinal Study examined the effects of cognitive training on cognitive development in older adulthood (Schaie, 2013). Older adults were administered 51 hours' worth of guided practice completing test items similar to those on a mental ability test and then were tested on two mental ability tests. Two-thirds of adults showed gains in performance, and 40% of those who showed cognitive decline prior to the study returned to their level of functioning 14 years earlier. Training improved strategy use and performance on verbal memory, working memory, and short-term memory tasks. Most promising is that 7 years later, older adults who had received training scored higher on mental ability tests than their peers. In other research, training improved measures of processing speed and fluid intelligence and these improvements were retained over an 8-month period (Borella, Carretti, Riboldi, & De Beni, 2010). Older adults' improvement with intervention is often similar in magnitude to that of younger adults, including gains in working memory, sustained attention, and fewer complaints about memory (Brehmer, Westerberg, & Bäckman, 2012). Other research suggests that gains from working memory interventions generalize to other measures of fluid intelligence (Stepankova et al., 2014). One meta-analysis concluded that working memory and executive functioning training leads to large gains in the trained tasks and large transfer effects to similar tasks measuring the same construct as the trained tasks. There were also clear but smaller transfer effects for different cognitive abilities than those tested. Overall, it seems that generalization takes place in people of all ages who receive cognitive training (Karbach & Verhaeghen, 2014).

However, this should be taken with caution. One meta-analysis of 87 studies of working memory training found immediate transfer right after training on measured tasks—but these improvements were short term and specific. They did not transfer to other cognitive skills, nor did they generalize to real-world cognitive skills (Melby-Lervåg, Redick, & Hulme, 2016)

Although older adults experience cognitive declines, there is a great deal of variability in everyday functioning. It is possible to retain and improve cognitive skills in older adulthood. The challenge is to encourage older adults to seek the experiences that will help them retain their mental abilities. Older adults who maintain a high cognitive functioning tend to engage in selective optimization with compensation: They compensate for declines in cognitive reserve or energy by narrowing their goals and selecting activities that will permit them to maximize their strengths and existing capacities. In all, healthy older adults retain the capacity to engage in efficient controlled processing of information.

Thinking in Context 7.5

1. Consider the cognitive changes that occur over the lifespan. In your view, are cognitive development, reasoning, and decision making best described as developing continuously or discontinuously? (Recall these concepts from Chapter 1.) Why?

2. An important theme of lifespan development is that development is characterized by gains and losses. How might the cognitive changes that adults experience illustrate this?

3. What factors might make older adults better decision makers than young adults? Worse?

4. Consider the lifespan development principle that domains of development interact. How might cognitive changes influence other areas of development in adulthood, such as emotional and social development? How might the reverse be true?

 Apply Your Knowledge

Professor Martell was interested in fostering cognitive ability in children, adolescents, and adults. He began by consulting with a local elementary school.

1. What information would he need to know about the children? What should he measure?

2. What aspects of cognition are the most important to target? Why?

3. How might he intervene? What kinds of activities or assignments might help?

4. How will he know if the intervention worked?

When considering adolescents, Professor Martell decided that he was most interested in helping them to make good choices and behave responsibly.

5. What aspects of cognitive development should he measure? Why?

6. What kinds of activities might he suggest to teachers? How should he intervene to help adolescents?

7. How will he know if the intervention worked?

Professor Martell decided that adults need access to accurate information about cognitive aging.

8. What do adults need to know about cognitive change?

9. What would you tell adults about the aging process, influences on cognitive aging, and the effects of cognitive aging on everyday functioning?

10. What sort of activities or interventions might Professor Martell suggest to adults?

Give your students the SAGE edge!

SAGE edge offers a robust online environment featuring an impressive array of free tools and resources for review, study, and further exploration, keeping both instructors and students on the cutting edge of teaching and learning. Learn more at **edge.sagepub.com/kuthertopical.**

CHAPTER 7 IN REVIEW

7.1 Identify the parts of the information processing system and its function over the lifespan.

SUMMARY

The information processing perspective views the mind as composed of three mental stores: sensory register, working memory, and long-term memory. From infancy to late adulthood, information moves through these stores and we use these three stores to manipulate and store it. With development we get better at moving information through our cognitive system in ways that allow us to adapt to our world.

KEY TERMS

sensory memory
attention
working memory

central executive
long-term memory
executive function

REVIEW QUESTIONS

1. What are the three parts of the information processing system?

2. How does each part function?

3. How does the information processing system change with age?

7.2 Describe developmental changes in infants' capacities for attention, memory, and thought.

SUMMARY

Infants display attention and memory at birth. They show more attentiveness to dynamic than static stimuli and their attention and memory develop over time. Infants are most likely to remember events when they are actively engaged and in familiar contexts, as well as when the events are emotionally arousing. Infants naturally categorize objects, permitting them to store and retrieve memory and respond with familiarity to new stimuli from a common class. As early as 7 months of age, infants use conceptual categories based on perceived function and behavior.

KEY TERM

categorization

REVIEW QUESTIONS

1. How do infants' attention and memory change? Give examples.

2. What is classification and how does it change over infancy?

7.3 Describe developmental changes in children's capacities for attention, memory, and thought.

SUMMARY

Steady increases in central executive function and working memory occur throughout childhood, One reason why young children perform poorly in recall tasks is that they are not very effective at using memory strategies. Episodic memory develops steadily from 3 to 6 years of age, through adolescence, and is accompanied by increases in the length, richness and complexity of recall. The way adults talk with the child about a shared experience can influence how well the child will remember it. Between the ages of 2 and 5, children's understanding of the mind grows. In early childhood children become capable of understanding that people can believe different things, that beliefs can be inaccurate, and that sometimes people act on the basis of false beliefs. Children thereby become able to lie or use deception in play. Children's performance on false-belief tasks is closely related with language development, interaction with others, and measures of executive function. Advances in metacognition accompany precortical development and enable school children to view the mind as an active manipulator of information, become mindful of their thinking and better able to consider the requirements of a task, determine how to tackle it, and monitor, evaluate, and adjust their activity to complete tasks.

KEY TERMS

selective attention
memory strategies
episodic memory
recognition memory
recall memory
scripts

autobiographical memory
infantile amnesia
theory of mind
metacognition
false-belief task
metamemory

REVIEW QUESTIONS

1. How does attention improve during childhood?

2. What are some reasons why working memory improves?

3. What are three examples of gains in long-term memory?

4. When does metacognition develop? What is its role in thinking?

7.4 Explain how advances in brain development during adolescence influence memory, metacognition, and scientific reasoning.

SUMMARY

Connections between the prefrontal cortex and various brain regions strengthen, improving attention and working memory and permitting rapid communication and enhanced cognitive and behavioral functioning. With these advances in brain development, routine decisions become automatic, enabling adolescents to redirect their thinking toward more complicated problems. Advances in response inhibition enable adolescents to adapt their responses to the situation. Working memory reaches adult-like levels by about age 19 and continues to improve into the 20s. Metacognition improves during adolescence and the reflection that accompanies it plays an important role in the development of scientific reasoning. Although adolescents show advances in scientific reasoning, their reasoning tends to emphasize single solutions to problems. The difference in maturational timing between the limbic system and prefrontal cortex means that adolescents feel emotionally charged before they have corresponding self-regulation and decision-making abilities, often leading to poor decisions.

REVIEW QUESTIONS

1. What key changes occur in attention, working memory, and thinking during adolescence?

2. What is the role of brain development in these cognitive advances?

7.5 Compare patterns of change in working memory, long-term memory, problem-solving capacities, and wisdom in adulthood.

SUMMARY

With age, it becomes more difficult to divide attention to engage in two complex tasks at once and focus on relevant information as well as to inhibit irrelevant information. The capacity of working memory declines over the adult years because of a decline in sensory capacity, attention, and the use of memory strategies. Speed declines from early adulthood through the middle to late adult years. An expanding knowledge base and growing expertise permits most adults to show few changes in cognitive capacity within everyday contexts and compensate for declines in processing speed. People remain adaptive problem solvers throughout adulthood. Adults perform best on everyday problems that are relevant to the contexts they experience in their daily lives. With age adults are more likely to report turning to spouses, children, and friends for input in making decisions. Wisdom does not necessarily come with age, but rather with the opportunity and motivation to pursue its development. Experience, particularly expertise in solving the problems of everyday life, is associated with wisdom.

Older adults who maintain a high cognitive functioning tend to engage in selective optimization with compensation. They compensate for declines in cognitive reserve or energy by narrowing their goals and selecting activities that will permit them to maximize their strengths and existing capacities.

KEY TERMS

expertise

proactive interference

selective optimization with compensation

wisdom

REVIEW QUESTIONS

1. How do attention and working memory typically change over adulthood?

2. What cognitive advances compensate for information processing declines?

3. What age-related changes can the typical adult expect in terms of problem solving?

Test your understanding of the content.
Review the flashcards and quizzes at
edge.sagepub.com/kuthertopical

PRACTICE AND APPLY WHAT YOU'VE LEARNED

▶ **edge.sagepub.com/kuthertopical**

Intelligence

Learning Objectives

8.1 Discuss the psychometric approach to intelligence, ways of measuring IQ, and the predictive value of IQ.

8.2 Compare information-processing, neurological, and componential approaches to intelligence.

8.3 Describe how intelligence develops over the lifespan.

8.4 Analyze biological and contextual influences on group differences in IQ.

8.5 Discuss how giftedness, intellectual disability, and special needs are identified and healthy development promoted in such individuals.

Digital Resources

🖥 Try the Weschler!

📄 Working Memory and Intelligence

▶ A Multiple-Intelligences School

▶ Defying Aging Stereotypes

🔊 The Bayley Scales

📄 A Child's Brain on Poverty

📄 Age-based Stereotype Threat

▶ Inclusive Classrooms

🔊 A Minute on Dyscalculia

Master these learning objectives with multimedia resources available at **edge.sagepub.com/kuthertopical** and *Lives in Context* video cases available in the interactive eBook.

By his second birthday, Gregory Smith, born in 1990, could read. He progressed through most of elementary school in a single year and began high school at age 7. Gregory entered college at the age of 10 and graduated with a degree in mathematics at age 13. As an adolescent, Gregory advocated for peace and organized humanitarian aid projects for orphans in East Timor and youth in Sao Paulo, Brazil, and helped Rwanda build its first public library. He has met with world leaders such as former President of the United States Bill Clinton and former President of the Soviet Union Mikhail Gorbachev, and has spoken at the United Nations. In 2004, at the age of 14, Gregory received the first of five nominations for the Nobel Peace Prize (Clynes, 2015). By 25 years of age, Gregory had earned two master's degrees in mathematics and computational biology as well as a doctoral degree in biology. Gregory went on to pursue a career as a researcher, studying gene expression with the hope of creating drugs to treat cancer.

At age 28, Aiden lives with his parents and sleeps in his childhood bedroom. With an IQ score of 35, Aiden can understand what others say, but he has a hard time stringing together words to express his needs and desires. Aiden takes pride in keeping his room clean and completing his daily chores, such as setting the dinner

AP Photo/WAYNE SCARBERRY

Gregory Smith graduated college with a degree in mathematics at the age of 13.

table and taking out the garbage. Each day Aiden rides the school bus that takes him to a center where he learns from teachers, socializes with his friends, and plays games. He likes to color in his coloring books, but the pictures have to be just right—not too detailed because he finds it difficult to manipulate his large crayons and color within the lines.

Gregory and Aiden represent two extremes of ability. Most individuals fall somewhere between the two, more able and independent than Aiden, but less gifted than Gregory. In this chapter, we explore intelligence: approaches toward defining and understanding intelligence, ways of measuring intelligence, influences on intelligence, and extremes of intelligence.

PSYCHOMETRIC APPROACH TO INTELLIGENCE

LO 8.1 Discuss the psychometric approach to intelligence, ways of measuring IQ, and the predictive value of IQ.

At its simplest, **intelligence** refers to one's ability to adapt to the world in which one lives (Sternberg, 2014). As Gregory and Aiden demonstrate, people differ in intelligence, an example of the lifespan concept of individual differences, or variation from person to person. There are many ways of defining intelligence. The earliest conceptions of intelligence, some of which remain popular today, stemmed from attempts to quantify and measure it.

COMPONENTS OF INTELLIGENCE

Some of the earliest views of intelligence come from the psychometric tradition, which proposes that intelligence is composed of a set of psychological traits or characteristics that can be measured and that vary among people, accounting for differences in performance or ability (Nunnally, 1975). One of the first definitions of intelligence referred to it as a single general ability known as *g* (Spearman, 1904). According to Charles Spearman, *g* underlies our performance on all mental tasks and accounts for individual differences in performance in all intellectual skills ranging from visual-spatial skills to verbal reasoning. Most people's performance, however, varies across tasks, suggesting that *g* may oversimplify intelligence. In 1938, after analyzing mental tests administered to eighth graders and college students, L. L. Thurstone proposed that intelligence is composed of several abilities that are independent of one another, which he referred to as **primary mental abilities**, as shown in Table 8.1. Individuals vary in their pattern of strengths and weaknesses. Some people show exceptional skills in word comprehension and are able to comprehend difficult texts. Others are skilled in mathematics and are able to compute complex strings of numbers quickly and easily. Individuals also vary in their capacities for memory, reasoning, and processing speed (see Chapter 7). When we think of intelligence as a collection of primary abilities, we account for the unique pattern of skills that individuals show.

According to Horn and Cattell, the many primary mental abilities can be organized into clusters representing two types of intelligence (Cattell, 1963; Horn & Cattell, 1966): crystallized and fluid intelligence. **Crystallized intelligence** refers to one's knowledge base, acquired through experience, education, and living in a particular culture (Cattell, 1963; Horn & Cattell, 1966). Examples of crystallized intelligence include memory of facts, spelling, vocabulary, formulas, and dates in history. Although critics argue that crystallized intelligence measures examine an individual's accumulated knowledge rather than intelligence itself, people who score high on measures of crystallized intelligence not only know more, but they learn more easily and remember more information than do people with lower levels of crystallized intelligence (Horn & Noll, 1997).

intelligence An individual's ability to adapt to the world.

primary mental abilities A concept proposed by L.L Thurston, intelligence is comprised of several abilities that are independent of one another.

crystallized intelligence Intellectual ability that reflects accumulated knowledge acquired through experience and learning.

TABLE 8.1 • Primary Mental Abilities

VERBAL COMPREHENSION	VOCABULARY AND READING COMPREHENSION
Word fluency	Ability to generate a number of words in a short period of time (e.g., words that begin with *L*)
Number facility	Ability to solve arithmetic problems
Spatial visualization	Ability to mentally manipulate geometric forms or symbols
Memory	Ability to recall lists of words, sentences, or pictures
Reasoning	Ability to solve analogies or other problems involving formal relations
Perceptual speed	Ability to recognize symbols quickly

Source: Thurstone (1938).

Fluid intelligence, in contrast, refers to a person's underlying capacity to make connections among ideas and draw inferences. Information processing abilities, such as the capacity of working memory, attention, and speed of analyzing information, influence fluid intelligence (Salthouse & Pink, 2008). Fluid intelligence permits flexible, creative, and quick thought which enables people to solve problems quickly and adapt to complex and rapidly changing situations. Fluid and crystallized intelligence are distinct components of intelligence (Nisbett et al., 2013), but they interact in the sense that the basic information processing capacities that embody fluid intelligence make it easier for a person to acquire knowledge and develop crystallized intelligence. Horn and Cattell proposed that fluid and crystallized intelligence show different developmental paths. Fluid intelligence was thought to be influenced by biological maturation, increasing through adolescence, leveling off in adulthood, and declining in older adulthood (Horn & Cattell, 1967). Crystallized intelligence, on the other hand, was thought to increase over the lifespan as individuals acquire knowledge and experience. As we will see later in this chapter, many aspects of Horn and Cattell's predictions have since been supported by research (Kaufman, Kaufman, & Plucker, 2013; McArdle, Ferrer-Caja, Hamagami, & Woodcock, 2002).

fluid intelligence Intellectual ability that reflects basic information processing skills, including working memory, processing speed, and the ability to detect relations among stimuli and draw inferences. Underlies learning, is not influenced by culture, and reflects brain functioning.

MEASURING INTELLIGENCE

The first intelligence test was created in 1905 by Alfred Binet and Theodore Simon. They were commissioned by the French government to devise a method of identifying children whose low mental abilities hindered their success in school, marking them as in need of remediation (Boake, 2002). The Binet-Simon test assessed children's ability to reason verbally and numerically, solve problems, and think logically. Shortly after its creation, Binet and Simon age-graded the items on the intelligence test, recording the level of performance that is typical for each age. For example, items graded for 7-year-olds could be passed by most 7-year-olds but few 6-year-olds; items for older children, 12 years of age, could not be correctly

There are many ways of defining intelligence, such as success in games that involve reasoning.

Intelligence tests often involve puzzles, mazes, and analyzing patterns.

intelligence test (IQ test) A test designed to measure the aptitude to learn at school, intellectual aptitude.

answered by younger children. The highest level of age-graded problems that the child could complete is described as the child's mental age (Boake, 2002).

In 1917, Lewis Terman at Stanford University adapted the Binet-Simon test for use with English-speaking children, creating the Stanford-Binet Intelligence Scale, still in use today. Terman developed a procedure for computing an **intelligence quotient** (IQ), defined as mental age (MA) divided by chronological age (CA) and multiplied by 100 (IQ = MA/CA × 100). An IQ score of 100 indicates average intelligence, regardless of a child's age, because it indicates that the child is able to correctly answer the items that same-age peers can. Today's Stanford-Binet Intelligence Scales (5th edition) no longer use the concept of mental age. Instead, they rely on test norms—standards of performance based on average scores and the range of scores around the average. These scores were obtained from testing a large representative sample of people (2 years of age through adults) from many socioeconomic and racial backgrounds (Roid, 2003). The resulting IQ scores reflect how well or poorly individuals do in comparison with same-age peers. Overall, the Stanford-Binet assesses general intelligence as characterized by five intellectual factors that are assessed both verbally and nonverbally: knowledge, quantitative reasoning, visual-spatial processing, working memory, and fluid reasoning (which measures speed of processing).

The most widely used, individually administered measures of intelligence today are a set of tests constructed by David Wechsler, who viewed intelligence as "the global capacity of a person to act purposefully, to think rationally, and to deal effectively with his environment" (Wechsler, 1944, p. 3). The Wechsler Adult Intelligence Scale (WAIS), developed in 1939, measures intelligence as a set of specific cognitive abilities. The current version of the test, the WAIS-IV, yields a general IQ score and scores measuring four broad intellectual factors that include verbal comprehension, and three nonverbal scales: working memory, processing speed, and perceptual reasoning (Wechsler, 2008). Items measure verbal abilities, such as vocabulary and general knowledge, and nonverbal skills such as the ability to assemble puzzles, solve mazes, reproduce geometric designs with colored blocks, and rearrange pictures to tell a meaningful story. The Wechsler Intelligence Scale for Children (WISC-V), suitable for schoolchildren ages 6–16, and the Wechsler Preschool and Primary Scale of Intelligence (WPPSI-III), for children ages 3–8, include five component scores (verbal comprehension, working memory, processing speed, visual spatial ability, and fluid reasoning; Wechsler, 2012, 2014).

Table 8.2 presents the subtests that comprise the WAIS-IV, as well as sample items from the WAIS-IV. As with the Stanford-Binet, a score of 100 is defined as average performance for a person's age. A person's full-scale IQ is a combination of the verbal and performance scores.

Like many human characteristics, IQ scores represent a normal distribution, meaning that most people score close to the mean score and a few people score extremely high or extremely low. Because of the statistical qualities of the normal curve, knowing a person's IQ score tells you where that person stands with respect to IQ relative to other people his or her age (Bjorklund & Myers, 2015). Normal distributions are symmetrical, bell-shaped around the mean value, and most scores fall relatively close to it; the farther a score from the mean, the fewer people obtain it. As shown in Figure 8.1, a person with an IQ of 115 has a score equal to or greater than about 84% of the population, whereas someone with an IQ of 85 has a score equal to or greater than about 16% of the population (or less than or equal to 84% of the population).

Intelligence tests can be useful tools for describing distinct patterns of abilities among individuals. It is important to remember that IQ scores are one indicator of cognitive ability but not the only indicator. As we will discuss later in this chapter, creativity is

TABLE 8.2 • Sample Items Measuring the Four WAIS-IV Indices

WAIS-V SCALE	SAMPLE ITEM
Verbal Comprehension Index (VCI)	Vocabulary: What does *amphibian* mean?
Perceptual Reasoning Index (PRI)	Block Design: In this timed task, adults are shown a design composed of red and white bocks, are given a set of blocks, and are asked to put together the blocks in order to copy the design.
Working Memory Index (WMI)	Digit Span: Adults are read lists of numbers and asked to repeat them as heard or in reverse order.
Processing Speed Index (PSI)	Coding: In this timed task, adults are shown a code that converts numbers into symbols and are asked to transcribe lists of numbers into code.

FIGURE 8.1: Distribution of IQ Scores in the General Population

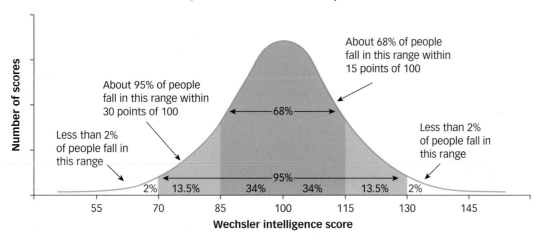

essential for exceptional performance. Finally, the inventors of IQ tests tended to view them as rough gauges rather than precise indicators of intelligence, as they viewed intelligence as a broad ability (Sternberg, 2014).

WHAT DOES IQ PREDICT?

Children with high IQs tend to earn higher than average grades at school (Alloway & Alloway, 2010). As mentioned in earlier in this chapter, IQ tests were first designed to distinguish children who could benefit from standard school instruction from those who required remedial attention. Given this, it should not be surprising that IQ scores predict academic achievement with relatively high correlations of about .50 (recall from Chapter 1 that correlations range from 0 to 1 and can be positive or negative; Mackintosh, 2011). Basically, IQ scores and academic achievement measure the same abilities in different ways—IQ tests were created by considering the kinds of knowledge and reasoning taught to, and required from, children in schools, and attempting to match the cognitive processes required in schools (Richardson & Norgate, 2015). Therefore, a correlation between IQ and school achievement may emerge because answering the test items demand the very kinds of learned abilities and ways of thinking that are also the currency of schooling. In this way, IQ and academic achievement are not independent because schooling influences IQ. Same-age children with more years of schooling tend to have higher IQs than their less educated peers (Cliffordson & Gustafsson, 2008), and correlations between IQ and school achievement tests tend to increase with age (Sternberg, Grigorenko, & Bundy, 2001).

In adulthood, IQ predicts occupational success. People in more prestigious and higher-paying jobs tend to have higher IQ scores than people in less prestigious jobs (Brody & Nathan, 1997; Neisser et al., 1996). IQ also is associated with job performance for people within specific professions. IQ–job performance correlations tend to be smaller for occupations that require little judgment and reasoning, such as assembly-line work (about 0.20) than for more intellectually demanding jobs, such as scientist, accountant, or shop manager (about 0.5; Schmidt & Hunter, 2004).

Similar to the IQ–school performance relationship, academic achievement (itself highly correlated with IQ) is associated with occupational choice, occupational level, and income (Neisser et al., 1996). A recent analysis of the literature examining IQ and job performance concluded that, after considering the role of academic achievement, the correlation between IQ and job performance is low and perhaps may be nonexistent (Richardson & Norgate, 2015). In contrast, a longitudinal study in the 1970s of a cohort of young adolescents in Warsaw, Poland—where, for political reasons, there were no differences in access to education, health, and community services—suggested a strong relationship between IQ in early adolescence and success at age 36, defined as attained education, occupational status, and material well-being (Firkowska-Mankiewicz, 2011). This study, however, found that the effect of IQ on life success varied with individual characteristics. Among individuals with high IQ, personality variables such as self-esteem emerged as important predictors of life success. In addition, IQ did not remain stable over the life course. In this sample of young people, IQ scores measured at 13 and 36 were only moderately correlated, suggesting that experience and contextual factors also influence life success (Firkowska-Mankiewicz, 2011). It is difficult to disentangle the effects of IQ, achievement, and individual characteristics on job performance.

Finally, IQ has been shown to predict health and longevity (Batty, Deary, & Macintyre, 2006; Deary, Batty, Pattie, & Gale, 2008). In one recent study on IQ in early childhood, lower intelligence predicted more advanced biological age at midlife as captured by perceived facial age, heart age, and health and nutrition biomarkers (Schaefer et al., 2016). The differences were not explained by childhood health or parental socioeconomic status (SES). Likewise, a study following youth from ages 14–21 through adulthood found that higher IQ in youth was linked with better physical health at age 50 and a lower risk for a number of chronic health conditions (Wraw, Deary, Gale, & Der, 2015). Measures of SES in adulthood, such as income, education, and occupation status, were not consistently mediators of the IQ–heath relationship, suggesting that socioeconomic factors might account for some, but not all, of the relationship between IQ and health. If intelligence truly taps adaptability, these findings suggest that individuals with high IQ are better able to adapt to their environments.

 Thinking in Context 8.1

1. How do you define intelligence? Is it composed of one factor? Contrast your view with the psychometric approach.

2. Why might IQ be associated with health and longevity? Identify biological and contextual factors that might co-occur with IQ and health and might influence the IQ–health relationship.

NEW APPROACHES TO INTELLIGENCE

LO 8.2 Compare information-processing, neurological, and componential approaches to intelligence.

Most measures of intelligence are based on the psychometric approach and account for intelligence as a collection of abilities. More recent approaches to intelligence underscore the importance of verbal and performance abilities but specify additional capacities that underlie intelligence. Some theorists emphasize the information processing abilities that comprise intelligence, while others study brain development and its contribution to intelligence. Yet other theorists propose additional components to intelligence beyond those articulated by the psychometric approach. Each of the following perspectives poses that intelligence entails the ability to adapt, but each specifies different means.

INTELLIGENCE AS INFORMATION PROCESSING

If you believe that intelligent people are quicker, more efficient thinkers, then you probably agree with the information processing approach to intelligence. The information processing abilities we discussed in Chapter 7, such as attention, working memory, and processing speed, underlie performance in all cognitive tasks, including intelligence tests, and are therefore important indicators of intellectual ability (Kail, 2000). The information processing approach to intelligence relies on the assumption that individuals who process information efficiently should acquire knowledge and thereby adapt to the world quickly, and it applies to infants, children, and adults. Information processing capacities in infancy, such as attention, memory, and processing speed, have been shown to predict cognitive ability and intelligence through late adolescence (Cuevas & Bell, 2013; Luttikhuizen dos Santos, de Kieviet, Königs, van Elburg, & Oosterlaan, 2013; Rose, Feldman, Jankowski, & Van Rossem, 2012).

Information processing abilities can be assessed in simple ways that allow us to study intelligence in infants who are too young to tell us what they think and understand. For example, infants' visual reaction time (how quickly infants look when shown a stimulus) and preference for novelty (the degree to which they prefer new stimuli over familiar ones) are indicators of attention, memory, and processing speed and have been shown to predict intelligence in childhood and adolescence (Fagan, 2011; Kavšek, 2004, 2013; McCall & Carrigher, 1993). Habituation tasks also provide information about the efficiency of information processing because they indicate how quickly an infant learns: Infants who learn quickly look away from an unchanging stimulus (or habituate) rapidly. Longitudinal studies suggest that infants who are fast habituators score higher on measures of intelligence in childhood and adolescence than do those who are slower habituators (Kavšek, 2004, 2013; Rose, Feldman, & Jankowski, 2012). One study demonstrated that, as compared with average and slow habituators, infants who were fast habituators had higher IQs and higher educational achievement when they were followed up 20 years later, in emerging adulthood (Fagan et al., 2007).

Information processing abilities are associated with measures of intelligence throughout life. For example, working memory and visuospatial short-term memory are associated with IQ in 4th- and 5th-grade children (Giofrè, Mammarella, & Cornoldi, 2013). Working memory and processing speed are also associated with intelligence in children and adults (Kail, 2000; Nussbaumer, Grabner, & Stern, 2015; Redick, Unsworth, Kelly, & Engle, 2012; Sheppard, 2008).

NEUROLOGICAL APPROACH TO INTELLIGENCE

Information processing skills such as attention, working memory, and processing speed are essential components of intelligence, but brain development is a fundamental influence on all cognitive abilities, including intelligence. Children's growth in perceptual skills, motor competence, and cognition is accompanied by advances in brain maturation. Neurological change also underlies intelligence. One line of research in this area examines brain size as a predictor of intelligence. Brain volume and cortical thickness are positively associated with IQ in children and adults (Pietschnig, Penke, Wicherts, Zeiler, & Voracek, 2015; Ritchie et al., 2015). Likewise, meta-analyses have suggested that intelligence is positively associated with increased gray matter in the parts of the brain responsible for the processing of sensory experiences (occipital and temporal cortex) and abstract cognitive processing (frontal cortex; Basten, Hilger, & Fiebach, 2015). Research also has linked white, myelinated matter with measures of general intelligence (Ritchie et al., 2015), largely through white matter's influence on processing speed (Penke et al., 2012) and working memory (Privado et al., 2014).

Other researchers examine brain activity to determine what regions of the brain are responsible for intelligence. Intelligence is thought to arise from the interaction of brain regions in the frontal—particularly prefrontal—and partial cortices (Deary, Penke, & Johnson, 2010; Margolis et al., 2013). Brain scans show greater activity in the frontal and parietal brain regions during the performance of cognitive tasks, including those commonly used in intelligence tests (Basten et al., 2015). Other brain regions, including parts of the temporal and occipital lobes and the cerebellum, are also thought to play a role in intelligence (Luders, Narr, Thompson, & Toga, 2009). Individual differences in the structure, function, and connectivity of brain regions associated with intelligence may influence neural activity during cognitive tasks, perhaps accounting for differences in general cognitive ability or intelligence (Khundrakpam et al., 2016).

Another approach to examining the intersection of brain development and intelligence focuses on neurological efficiency. According to the neural efficiency hypothesis of intelligence, people with higher intelligence may exert less neural effort, or show smaller changes in brain activation, during performance of a given cognitive task, and therefore are more neurally efficient than the average person (Haier et al., 1988; Neubauer & Fink, 2009). Research, however, has shown varying support for the neural efficiency hypothesis: Some studies have reported weak, and others strong, brain activation in bright individuals (Basten, Stelzel, & Fiebach, 2013; Ebisch et al., 2012; Neubauer, Fink, & Schrausser, 2002). A recent meta-analysis suggested that the link between behavioral performance and brain activation varies and is influenced by task difficulty as well as by individual differences in task engagement, motivation, and employment of cognitive strategies (Basten et al., 2015).

Overall, neurological research has shown that there are regions of the brain in which people differ in structure or function, depending on intelligence. The challenge is how to explain these associations. Because these measures are correlations, we cannot determine whether the observed differences in the brain are causes of differences in intelligence or consequences of such differences—or perhaps caused by some third factor. Determining how smart brains differ and in what patterns and regions of activity is only a first step in understanding how intelligence evolves from the brain. A complete explanation of intelligence requires accounting for intelligent, adaptive behavior.

TRIARCHIC THEORY OF INTELLIGENCE

Jason Bourne, hero of the popular spy-action novels and movies, is highly adaptive. He can quickly gather information, such as a villain's plot, process it, and devise a plan. He adapts his plan on the fly as the situation changes and thinks creatively in order to escape seemingly impossible situations—traps, car chases, and other dangerous scenarios. Certainly Jason Bourne is a fictional character, but he illustrates another view of intelligence, articulated by Robert Sternberg. According to Sternberg (1985), intelligence is a set of mental abilities that permits individuals to adapt to any context and to select and modify the sociocultural contexts in which they live and behave. Sternberg's **triarchic theory of intelligence** posits three forms of intelligence: analytical, creative, and practical (Sternberg, 2005, 2011; see Figure 8.2). Individuals may have strengths in any or all of them.

triarchic theory of intelligence Sternberg's theory positing three independent forms of intelligence: analytical, creative, and applied.

LIFESPAN BRAIN DEVELOPMENT

• • Can You Boost Your IQ With Brain-Training?

Can you exercise your brain—train it—to improve your thinking? A television advertisement for a popular "brain-training" computer app claims that "it's like a personal trainer for your brain, improving your performance with the science of neuroplasticity but in a way that just feels like games" (Entis, 2016). National surveys reveal that most adults are aware of brain-training and most view it as an exercise or activity that does one or all of the following: improves memory and prevents memory loss, sharpens cognition, improves attention, speeds thinking, and increases IQ (Skufca, 2015). Are the claims of brain-training apps true? Can you improve your IQ with practice?

Brain-training apps and programs consist of simple cognitive games, such as requiring the player to remember briefly presented pictures, keep track of multiple moving objects, or recognize complex patterns. With practice, players become faster and more accurate at performing these tasks (Boot & Kramer, 2014). The rationale behind brain-training, also known as cognitive training, is that if IQ predicts performance and success, then practicing the cognitive abilities that are tested by IQ should improve overall cognitive outcomes (Simons et al., 2016). Does improvement on a brain-training game result in cognitive improvements that influence performance on real-life tasks such as driving or remembering names? Does training on one task, such as a computerized memory game, improve performance on untrained, everyday tasks?

In a classic series of studies, learning theorist Edward Thorndike (1874–1949) demonstrated that extended practice and improvement on one cognitive task (e.g., estimating the area of a rectangle) did not transfer to a different cognitive task (e.g., estimating the area of a triangle). Thorndike concluded that transfer of training occurred only if the practiced task and the transfer task were similar (Thorndike, 1906). Modern research agrees that practice results in cognitive adaptation that is specific to the task, resulting in performance gains that apply to the trained task but do not transfer to other cognitive tasks (Taatgen, 2013). For example, in one study more than 2,800 older adults were randomly assigned to one of four conditions: memory training, reasoning training, speed-of-processing training, or a no-contact control group (Tennstedt & Unverzagt, 2013). After ten 60- or 75-minute training sessions, the adults showed improvements specific for each type of training but the improvements did not generalize across tasks. For example, speed training improved

speed of processing but not memory, memory training improved memory performance but not reasoning, and so on. Cognitive training did not appear to transfer to other cognitive tasks and it was not associated with improvements in everyday functioning.

Brain-training apps often include memory games. Can training in working memory enhance intelligence? Findings are mixed. Some studies have shown that training in working memory tasks that involve juggling multiple pieces of information is associated with improvements in fluid intelligence (Nisbett et al., 2013), whereas others have shown no differences (Harrison et al., 2013; Thompson et al., 2013). A recent meta-analysis examining 20 studies concluded that working memory training has a small positive effect on fluid intelligence, especially among individuals with the poorest performance at baseline. However, most studies of working memory training, even those that entail computerized tasks, are conducted one-on-one in a laboratory setting. It is not clear whether these findings can be generalized to brain-training games played at home, without guidance, on a phone or tablet.

Research examining brain-training games has suggested that they may have more entertainment than cognitive value. In fact, in 2016 the U.S. Federal Trade Commission charged Lumos Labs, maker of the popular game Luminosity, with deceptive advertising, suggesting that the company claimed that its games could "stave off memory loss, dementia, and even Alzheimer's disease . . . but Luminosity simply did not have the science to back up its ads" (U.S. Federal Trade Commission, 2016). In addition to a $2 million fine, the court order stipulated that Lumos Labs have competent and reliable scientific evidence before making claims about benefits of brain-training games for everyday performance, age-related decline, or health conditions (U.S. Federal Trade Commission, 2016).

In sum, brain-training games may be fun, and practice can boost your game performance, but there is little evidence that training enhances performance on distantly related tasks or that training improves everyday cognitive performance. Practicing working memory tasks might influence fluid intelligence, but it is not clear that brain-training games offer effective practice.

What Do You Think?

Your aunt asks you for advice. She is thinking of subscribing to a brain-training app and wants your opinion. What advice do you give her, and why?

Analytical intelligence refers to information processing capacities, such as how efficiently people acquire knowledge, process information, engage in metacognition, and generate and apply strategies to solve problems—much like Bourne's ability to process information quickly and consider different solutions. *Creative intelligence* taps insight and the ability to deal with novelty. People who are high in creative intelligence, like Bourne, respond to new tasks quickly and efficiently. They learn easily, compare information with what is already known, come up with new ways of organizing information, and display original thinking. *Applied intelligence* influences how people deal with their surroundings:

In The Bourne Trilogy, Jason Bourne (played by Matt Damon) illustrates analytical, creative, and applied intelligence, the three forms of intelligence that comprise the triarchic theory of intelligence.

how well they evaluate their environment, selecting and modifying it and adapting it to fit their own needs and external demands—similar to Bourne's ability to modify his plans on the fly, using whatever resources are available. Intelligent people apply their analytical, creative, and applied abilities to suit the setting and problems at hand (Sternberg, 2011). Some situations require careful analysis, others the ability to think creatively, and yet others the ability to solve problems quickly in everyday settings. Many situations tap more than one form of intelligence.

Traditional IQ tests measure analytical ability, which is thought to be associated with school success. However, IQ tests do not measure creative and practical intelligence, which predict success outside of school. Some people are successful in everyday settings but less so in school settings, and therefore they may obtain low scores on traditional IQ tests despite being successful in their careers and personal lives. In this way, traditional IQ tests can underestimate the intellectual strengths of some children.

The triarchic theory facilitates defining intelligent behavior by culture and context. That is, the theory views intelligence as a socially and culturally defined construct that is understood differently in different cultures (Sternberg, 2014). Some actions are more effective, and thereby qualify as more "intelligent," in certain contexts than others. People who are intelligent are able to adapt and succeed in all of the contexts in which they live. In one study, researchers created a test that measures informal knowledge of an important aspect of adaptation to the environment in rural Kenya: knowledge of the identities and uses of natural herbal medicines used to combat illnesses. This information was a routine part of Kenyan children's lives, who used this informal knowledge (not taught in school) on average once a week in treating themselves or suggesting treatments to other children. Children who knew what these medicines were, as well as their use and dosage, were in a better position to adapt to their environment and, therefore, were considered more intelligent (Sternberg & Grigorenko, 2008). As individuals adapt to different contexts, their responses become more automatic, freeing cognitive resources and permitting better functioning and adaptation. Intelligent people intuitively recognize their strengths and weaknesses, finding ways to capitalize on their strengths and compensating or correcting for their weaknesses (Sternberg, 2015).

Cultures vary in the specific skills thought to constitute intelligence, but the three mental abilities that underlie intelligent behavior—analytic, creative, and applied intelligence—are recognized across cultures. Still, the relative importance ascribed to each may differ (Sternberg & Grigorenko, 2008; Sternberg, 2007). In Western cultures, the intelligent person is one who invests a great deal of effort into learning, enjoys it, and enthusiastically seeks opportunities for lifelong learning. In contrast, other cultures emphasize applied intelligence. For example, the Chinese Taoist tradition emphasizes the importance of humility, freedom from conventional standards of judgment, and awareness of the self and the outside world (Yang & Sternberg, 1997). In many African cultures, conceptions of intelligence revolve around the skills that maintain harmonious interpersonal relations (Ruzgis & Grigorenko, 1994). Chewa adults in Zambia emphasize social responsibilities, cooperativeness, obedience, and respectfulness as being important to intelligence and, likewise,

FIGURE 8.2: Sternberg's Triarchic Theory of Intelligence

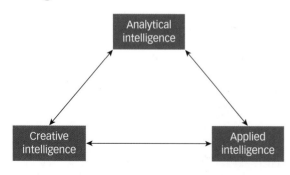

Kenyan parents emphasize responsible participation in family and social life (Serpell, 1974; Serpell & Jere-Folotiya, 2008; Super & Harkness, 1982).

Views of intelligence even vary within a given context (Sternberg, 2014). For example, when parents were asked of the characteristics of an intelligent child in the first grade of elementary school, white American parents emphasized cognitive capacities. Parents who were immigrants from Cambodia, the Philippines, Vietnam, and Mexico, on the other hand, pointed to motivation, self-management, and social skills (Okagaki & Sternberg, 1993), suggesting that characteristics valued as intelligent vary across cultures, and children within the same context may be immersed in different cultures (Sternberg, 2014). Once again, we see the complexity of context and culture as influences on development.

Cultures vary in the skills thought to constitute inteligence, such as the ability to maintain harmonious interpersonal relations.

MULTIPLE INTELLIGENCES

A skilled dancer, a champion athlete, an award-winning musician, and an excellent communicator all have talents that are not measured by traditional IQ tests. According to Howard Gardner (Gardner, 1993, 1995; Gardner & Moran, 2006), intelligence is the ability to solve problems or create culturally valued products. Specifically, Gardner's **multiple intelligence theory** proposes at least eight independent kinds of intelligence, shown in Table 8.3. Multiple intelligence theory expands the use of the term *intelligence* to refer to skills not usually considered by experts as intelligence, and it has led to a great deal of debate among intelligence theorists and researchers (Barnett, Ceci, & Williams, 2006; Kaufman, Kaufman, & Plucker, 2013; Waterhouse, 2006).

According to multiple intelligence theory, each person has a unique pattern of intellectual strengths and weaknesses. A person may be gifted in dance (bodily-kinesthetic intelligence), communication (verbal-linguistic intelligence), or music (musical intelligence), yet score low on traditional measures of IQ. Each form of intelligence is thought to be biologically based and each develops on a different timetable (Gardner, 1999). Assessing multiple intelligences requires observing the products of each form of intelligence (e.g., how well a child can learn a tune, navigate an unfamiliar area, or learn dance steps), which at best is a lengthy proposition and at worst nearly impossible (Barnett et al., 2006). However, through extended observations of individuals, an examiner can identify patterns of strengths and weaknesses and help individuals understand and achieve their potential (Gardner, 1995; Scherer, 1985).

Educators, parents, and students tend to find the idea of multiple intelligences intuitively appealing because it is an optimistic perspective that allows everyone to be intelligent in his or her own way, viewing intelligence as broader than book-learning and academic skills (Halpern, 2005). Currently schools tend to emphasize intelligence as defined by standardized IQ tests (i.e., verbal and logical-mathematic skills). Some educational theorists argue that if intelligence is multidimensional, as Gardner suggests, then school curricula should target the many forms that intelligence may take and help students to develop a range of talents (Eisner, 2004; Gardner, 2013). Although Gardner's theory of multiple intelligences has gained a following, it is not yet grounded in research (Waterhouse, 2006). Despite criticisms, the theory of multiple intelligences draws attention to the fact that IQ tests measure a specific set of mental abilities and ignore others. Another form of intelligence, emotional intelligence, is discussed in the Lives in Context feature. Multiple intelligence theory has helped educators and parents view children's abilities in a new light.

multiple intelligence theory
Gardner's proposition that human intelligence is composed of a varied set of abilities.

● ● Emotional Intelligence

Bob Kreisel/Alamy

Emotional intelligence, the ability to understand, manage, and respond appropriately to others' and our own emotions, enables us to form and sustain successful relationships.

"Four-eyes!" the boys yelled at Stacey, who began to cry. Lisa takes Stacey's hand, saying, "Come with me; don't listen to them!" and she calls out to the boys, "Leave us alone or I'm telling the teacher." Then she told Stacey, "Stay here and play with me, Stacey, ok? Those boys don't know what they're talking about." Stacey nods, sniffing, "OK, thanks." Lisa reacted quickly when her friend was picked on by other children. She knew what to say to make it stop and how to make her friend feel better. Lisa shows the ability to quickly adapt to a changing social situation.

Theories of intelligence tend to emphasize adaptation. One theory of intelligence applies these ideas beyond purely intellectual contexts to include interpersonal and intrapersonal contexts, that is, our interactions with people and ourselves. Emotional intelligence includes the ability to perceive, understand, manage, and respond appropriately to others' emotions as well as our own (Salovey & Mayer, 1989). Popularized by Daniel Goleman (1995), emotional intelligence is a crucial component of so-called "people skills." It underlies our ability to form and sustain successful relationships, including friendships and marriages.

In support of the adaptive advantage posed by emotional intelligence, research has shown that individuals who score high in measures of emotional intelligence tend to release less cortisol, a stress hormone, during stressful situations (Laborde, Lautenbach, Allen, Herbert, & Achtzehn, 2014). In other words, emotional intelligence is associated with lower levels of physiological stress. It may not be surprising, then, that emotional intelligence is associated with well-being and mental health (Davis & Humphrey, 2012; Mavroveli, Petrides, Rieffe, & Bakker, 2007; Zeidner, Matthews, & Roberts, 2012). Emotional intelligence is linked with prosocial behavior and high-quality social relationships characterized by constructive communication and mutual satisfaction (Frederickson, Petrides, & Simmonds, 2012; Malouff, Schutte, & Thorsteinsson, 2014). It is also associated with academic achievement in children, adolescents, and college students, and with job performance in adults (Joseph, Jin, Newman, & O'Boyle, 2015; Mavroveli & Sánchez-Ruiz, 2011; Sanchez-Ruiz, Mavroveli, & Poullis, 2013).

Unlike traditional IQ, emotional intelligence skills are malleable. Although there are individual differences in emotional intelligence, interventions that offer practice in perceiving, interpreting, understanding, and managing emotions have shown that emotional intelligence skills can be taught (Dacre Pool & Qualter, 2012; Schutte, Malouff, & Thorsteinsson, 2013). So far, at least 50 studies have examined the degree to which emotional intelligence skills can be taught, and the vast majority (90%) have shown that training can improve emotional intelligence, at least modestly (Petrides et al., 2016).

What Do You Think?

To what extent do you think emotional intelligence should be measured in children? For example, should tests of emotional intelligence become common assessments alongside intellectual assessments, such as IQ tests? Provide reasons for your response.

TABLE 8.3 • Howard Gardner's Multiple Intelligences

INTELLIGENCE	DESCRIPTION
Verbal-linguistic intelligence	Ability to understand and use the meanings and subtleties of words ("word smarts"). People high in verbal-linguistic intelligence tend to be good at reading, writing, and explaining and often learn second languages with ease.
Logical-mathematical intelligence	Ability to manipulate logic and numbers to solve problems ("number smarts"). People high in logical-mathematic intelligence excel at mathematics, complex calculations, and scientific thinking.
Spatial intelligence	Ability to perceive the visual-spatial world accurately, navigate an environment, and judge spatial relationships ("spatial smarts"). People high in spatial intelligence tend to be good at solving puzzles, have a keen sense of direction, and are often good at drawing.
Bodily-kinesthetic intelligence	Ability to move the body skillfully ("body smarts"). People high in bodily-kinesthetic intelligence excel at physical activities such as sports or dance and often are good at building and making things.
Musical intelligence	Ability to perceive and create patterns of pitch and melody ("music smarts"). People high in musical intelligence are sensitive to sounds, rhythms, music, and pitch and usually are able to sing, play musical instruments, and compose music.
Interpersonal intelligence	Ability to understand and communicate with others ("people smarts"). People high in interpersonal intelligence are socially skilled, sensitive to others' moods, able communicate and work effectively with others, and enjoy discussion and debate.
Intrapersonal intelligence	Ability to understand the self and regulate emotions ("self-smarts"). People high in intrapersonal intelligence are highly self-aware, in control of their own emotions and experience, are often introverts, and enjoy working alone.
Naturalist intelligence	Ability to distinguish and classify elements of nature: animals, minerals and plants ("nature smarts"). People high in naturalist intelligence are sensitive to nature and are able nurture and care for plants, animals, and the natural world around them.

Thinking in Context 8.2

1. Compare the information processing and neurological approaches. How compatible are these approaches?

2. How might contextual factors influence the degree to which a person can demonstrate analytical, creative, and practical intelligence?

3. Identity ways of measuring the multiple intelligences. Which two intelligences are the most challenging to measure? Explain your reasoning.

DEVELOPMENT OF INTELLIGENCE

LO 8.3 Describe how intelligence develops over the lifespan.

To this point in the chapter, we have discussed theories of intelligence and ways of measuring it in childhood and adulthood. We now turn to the question of how intelligence develops over the lifespan, from infancy through old age. We begin with intelligence in infancy—but studying infants is a challenge because infants cannot answer questions. Instead, researchers who study infant intelligence rely on an assortment of nonverbal tasks and standardized tests that compare infants with age-based norms, as we now explore.

INFANT INTELLIGENCE

At 3 months of age, Baby Lourdes can lift and support her upper body with her arms when on her stomach. She grabs and shakes toys with her hands and enjoys playing with other people. Lourdes's pediatrician tells her parents that her development is right on track for babies her age and that she shows typical levels of infant intelligence. Standardized tests permit the pediatrician to determine Lourdes' development relative to other infants her age.

The most often-used standardized measure of infant intelligence is the Bayley Scales of Infant Development III (BSID-III), commonly called "Bayley-III" (see Figure 8.3). This test is appropriate for infants from 1 month through 42 months of age (Bayley, 1969, 2005). The Bayley-III consists of five scales: three measure infant responses and two measure parent responses. The Motor Scale measures gross and fine motor skills, such as grasping objects, drinking from a cup, sitting, and climbing stairs. The Cognitive Scale includes items such as attending to a stimulus or searching for a hidden toy. The Language Scale examines comprehension and production of language, such as following directions and naming objects. The Social-Emotional Scale is derived from parental reports regarding behavior, such as the infant's responsiveness and play activity. Finally, the Adaptive Behavior Scale is based on parental reports of the infant's ability to adapt in everyday situations, including the infant's ability to communicate, regulate his or her emotions, and display certain behavior.

The Bayley-III provides a comprehensive profile of an infant's current functioning, but the performance of infants often varies considerably from one testing session to another (Bornstein, Slater, Brown, Roberts, & Barrett, 1997). Scores vary with infants' states of arousal and motivation. This suggests that pediatricians and parents must exert great care in interpreting scores—particularly poor scores—because an infant's performance may be influenced by factors other than developmental functioning. Alternatively, some researchers have argued that perhaps the variability in Bayley-III scores from one occasion to another suggests that intelligence itself is variable in infancy (Bornstein et al., 1997). Regardless, the low test-retest reliability (see Chapter 1) means that infants who perform poorly on the Bayley-III should be tested more than once.

Although Bayley-III scores offer a comprehensive profile of an infant's abilities, scores do not predict performance on intelligence tests in childhood (Honzik, 1983; Luttikhuizen dos Santos et al., 2013; Rose & Feldman, 1995). Even Nancy Bayley, who invented the Bayley Scales, noted in a longitudinal study (1949) that infant performance was not related to intelligence scores at age 18. Why is infant intelligence relatively unrelated to later intelligence? Consider what is measured by infant tests: perception and motor skills, responsiveness, and language skills. The ability to grasp an object, crawl up stairs, or search for a hidden toy—items that appear on the Bayley-III—are not measured by childhood intelligence tests (Bornstein et al., 1997). Instead, intelligence tests administered in childhood examine more complex and abstract abilities such as verbal reasoning, verbal comprehension, and problem solving.

If the Bayley-III does not predict later intelligence, why administer it? Infants whose performance is poor relative to age norms may suffer from serious developmental problems that can be addressed. The intellectual abilities measured by the Bayley-III are critical indicators of neurological health and are useful for charting

FIGURE 8.3: Bayley-III Scales (BSID-III)

Cliff Moore / Science Source

Infant assessment tests, such as the BSID-III, examine cognitive, language, social-emotional, and motor abilities, such as infants' skill in manipulating objects.

developmental paths, diagnosing neurological disorders, and detecting intellectual disabilities in infants and toddlers. As such, the Bayley-III is primarily used as a screening tool to identify infants who can benefit from medical and developmental intervention.

STABILITY AND CHANGE IN INTELLIGENCE IN CHILDHOOD AND ADOLESCENCE

We have seen that measures of intelligence in infancy are not good predictors of IQ later in life. What about childhood measures of intelligence? IQ shows increasing stability starting at about age 4 (Sameroff, Seifer, Baldwin, & Baldwin, 1993). The correlation between IQ measured at age 5 and again in young adulthood ranges between 0.40 and 0.50 (Bjorklund & Myers, 2015). The correlation between child and adult IQ scores continues to increase to between .70 and .80 by 8 or 9 years of age, and to about 0.80 by 10 years of age (Bayley, 1949; Honzik, Macfarlane, & Allen, 1948). Research studies that examine group changes in intelligence, therefore, conclude that intelligence scores are stable from childhood through adolescence. However, research examining individuals over time suggests that there are also large individual differences (McCall, Appelbaum, & Hogarty, 1973).

In one recent study, elementary school students were evaluated twice over a period of approximately 3 years (Watkins & Smith, 2013). On average children's scores differed by 1 point or less. But about one-quarter of the children's scores differed by 10 or more points up to, for one child, 29 points. There are not many studies examining long-term stability in children's IQ scores, but the results of this study suggest that intelligence is stable for most children but shows substantial change and variation among others. Moreover, children with high IQ scores tend to show more variation over time than children with average to low IQ scores (McCall et al., 1973). Similar to other domains of development, intellectual development is characterized by both stability and change and is influenced by dynamic interactions among the individual and context, as will be explored later in this chapter.

INTELLECTUAL CHANGE IN ADULTHOOD

How does intelligence change over the adult years? There is no simple answer to this question. Researchers using different methods have drawn varying conclusions about adult intelligence. Recall from Chapter 1 that researchers learn about how people differ by age and how they change over time with the use of cross-sectional, longitudinal, and cross-sequential research designs. The conclusions that researchers draw regarding intellectual change in adulthood varies with each research design.

Until recently, most researchers believed that intelligence declined with age. Early cross-sectional studies, comparing adults of various ages at once, showed clear age differences in IQ scores whereby intelligence peaked in early adulthood, declined through middle adulthood, and dropped steeply in late adulthood (Salthouse, 2014). Longitudinal studies, however, show a different picture of intellectual development in adulthood (Horn & Donaldson, 1976; Schaie, 2013). Research following people who were evaluated from childhood through middle age (up to age 50) demonstrated that, contrary to prior findings from cross-sectional research, intelligence scores increased into middle adulthood, especially on tests that reflected accumulated knowledge or expertise (Bayley, 1955; Deary, 2014).

Advances in technology, such as the personal computer, influence cohort trends in intelligence.

Why are the findings of cross-sectional studies very different from those of longitudinal studies? K. Warner Schaie examined this question in his groundbreaking study of intellectual change in adulthood—the Seattle Longitudinal Study. Because cross-sectional and longitudinal studies offer contradictory pictures of intellectual change in adulthood, Schaie employed a cross-sequential design that combined both research methodologies to disentangle the effects of age (change over time) and cohort (change over generations; Schaie, 1993, 2013). During the first wave of data collection, in 1956, adults aged 22 to 70 were tested. These individuals were followed up with at regular intervals and new samples of adults were added. To date, the Seattle Longitudinal Study has examined more than 5,000 men and women and has yielded five cross-sectional comparisons and more than 60 years of longitudinal data.

The findings of the Seattle Longitudinal Study show a drop in intelligence scores after the mid-30s, but they also reflect the typical longitudinal finding that there are modest gains through middle age that are sustained into the 60s, followed by gradual declines thereafter (Schaie, 2013; Schaie & Zanjani, 2006). As shown in Figure 8.4, crystallized and fluid intelligence show different patterns of change over the adult years. The components of crystallized intelligence, such as verbal ability and inductive reasoning, remain stable and even increase into middle adulthood, suggesting that individuals expand and retain their wealth of knowledge over their lifetimes. On the other hand, fluid intelligence, such as perceptual speed and spatial orientation, decreases beginning in the twenties, suggesting that cognitive processing slows, somewhat, with age (Horn & Masunaga, 2000; McArdle et al., 2002; Schaie, 2013). Other samples of adults have supported these findings of gains in crystallized intelligence through middle adulthood coupled with gradual declines in fluid intelligence (Dellenbach & Zimprich, 2008; Kaufman, 2001; Singer, Verhaeghen, Ghisletta, Lindenberger, & Baltes, 2003). In late adulthood both types of intelligence decline (Schaie, 2013).

FIGURE 8.4: Longitudinal Changes in Crystallized and Fluid Intelligence Over the Adult Years

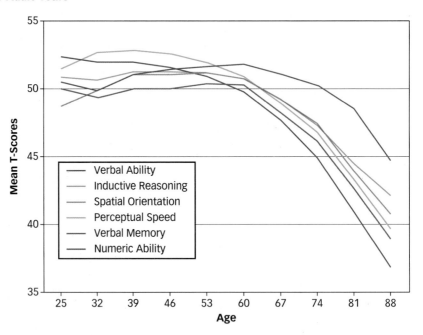

Longitudinal research shows stability over the adult years in most intellectual competencies, especially crystallized abilities, with declines occurring in late adulthood. In contrast, fluid abilities, such as perceptual speed, show steady decline throughout the adult years.

Source: Schaie (2005).

Why does fluid intelligence decline over the adult years? Declines in performance on tasks measuring fluid intelligence may be due to the biological slowing of the central nervous system, as evident in declines in processing speed (Kaufman, 2001; Salthouse & Pink, 2008). Other research points to declines in frontal lobe functioning and reductions in neural interconnectivity in explaining declines in fluid intelligence (Bugg, Zook, DeLosh, Davalos, & Davis, 2006; Geerligs, Maurits, Renken, & Lorist, 2014). The ability to quickly update one's working memory is closely related to measures of fluid intelligence and some research suggests that it is the decline in working memory updating rather than speed that causes age-related changes in fluid intelligence (Unsworth, Fukuda, Awh, & Vogel, 2014). Most notably, training in tasks that tap working memory are associated with improvements in fluid intelligence tasks (Au et al., 2015)

An important finding of the Seattle Longitudinal Study is that there are large cohort effects in intelligence. Each cohort of adults has experiences unique to their generation that influence their intellectual development. From 1889 to 1973, each cohort of adults has scored higher in verbal memory and inductive reasoning, and lower in numeric ability, than previous generations (Schaie & Zanjani, 2006). IQ gains from one generation to another have been found in many countries, typically coinciding with the advent of modernization (Nisbett et al., 2013b; Williams, 2013). This widespread increase in IQ scores, known as the Flynn effect, is explored in the Lives in Context feature. In addition, the drop in intelligence scores that appears after midlife happens later in more recent cohorts (Schaie, 2013). These effects can be at least partially explained by generational changes in educational attainment. With each generation, young people complete more years of education, and have more exposure to testing. In addition, advanced levels of education tend to emphasize logic and self-expression, which are among the skills measured by intelligence tests (Baker et al., 2015; Williams, 2013). Declines in numeric ability with each cohort may reflect each generation's increasing reliance on equipment such as abacuses, calculators, and computers for mathematical computation.

Overall, intellectual ability increases over the adult years, especially when individuals are engaged in complex occupational and leisure activities—which are more common among recent cohorts (Schaie, 2013). Research suggests that the tendency to engage in mentally simulating activities, such as reading, is influenced by crystallized intelligence; however, engaging in stimulating activities can enhance functional intelligence in all adults (Dellenbach & Zimprich, 2008). One study of middle-aged to older adults had an experimental group engage in diverse, novel, and mentally stimulating activities for 10 to 12 weeks and compared them to a control group. The experimental group showed gains in fluid intelligence—gains suggesting that even brief periods of cognitive stimulation can improve problem solving and promote flexible thinking (Tranter & Koutstaal, 2008). In addition, training and practice in attention and working memory skills improve performance on tasks targeting executive control processes (Au et al., 2015; Nisbett et al., 2013b).

Intellectual capacity seems to follow the "use it or lose it" principle. Adults who use their intellectual skills tend to maintain them longer than do those who are less cognitively active. Individuals who have completed higher education, held intellectually challenging occupations, and pursued intellectual leisure activities show a later decline in intellectual ability as compared with adults who are less engaged (Schaie, 2013). Contextual factors also influence intellectual decline (Nisbett et al., 2013). Whereas midlife is typically a time of intellectual growth, individuals who live in unfavorable environments such as those of pervasive poverty, or who have experienced serious illness, may experience intellectual declines far earlier than the average adult (Schaie, 2013).

Lives in Context Video 8.1
Defying Aging Stereotypes

• • The Flynn Effect—Context and IQ

Kenyan children show an especially pronounced Flynn effect, influenced by contextual changes in education, health, and nutrition.

Are people getting smarter? Perhaps, as IQ scores tend to increase with each generation (Lynn, 2013). Documented by Flynn (1984) and known as the **Flynn effect**, scores on IQ measures such as the Stanford-Binet and Weschler tests have increased continuously over many years and with each generation (Flynn, 2012). For example, Flynn (1984) discovered a 13.8-point increase in IQ scores between the years 1932 and 1978, amounting to a rise of about 3 points per decade. More recently, a meta-analysis of 271 samples including nearly 4 million participants from 31 countries confirmed a global increase of about 3 IQ points per decade from 1909 to 2013 (Pietschnig & Voracek, 2015). The Flynn effect means that an individual in the most recent cohort will attain a higher IQ score when set against the norms of an earlier cohort than he will when set against his own (Dutton, van der Linden, & Lynn, 2016). In other words, people score higher than they would today when tested on older tests.

The Flynn effect occurs in developed countries, but the gains are especially pronounced in developing countries, such as Kenya, Sudan, China, Brazil, Argentina, and many Caribbean nations (Colom, Flores-Mendoza, & Abad, 2007; Flynn, 2012; Flynn & Rossi-Casé, 2012; Nisbett et al., 2013). The generational increase in IQ is thought to be a function of contextual factors, such as changes in education, combined with environmental stimulation, that improve children's reasoning and problem-solving skills (Flynn & Weiss, 2007; Richard Lynn, 2009). As Flynn (2012) explains, in modern society we increasingly look at the world through "scientific spectacles" and examine it analytically, boosting IQ. Each generation of children is exposed to more

information and ideas than the generation before, and this exposure likely influences thinking itself (te Nijenhuis, 2013). However, contextual factors also influence the Flynn effect, such as health and nutrition. For example, measures of intelligence in infants mirror the IQ gains of preschool children, school-aged children, and adults, suggesting that the factors influencing the Flynn effect must emerge early in life (Richard Lynn, 2009). Improvements in pre- and postnatal nutrition may influence the Flynn effect, as the generational rise in IQs parallels increases in other nutrition-related characteristics of infants, including height, weight, and head circumference (Lynn, 2009; Trahan, Stuebing, Fletcher, & Hiscock, 2014). In addition, meta-analyses have shown that patterns of IQ gains are closely associated with historical events. Gains were strong between World Wars I and II but showed a marked decrease during the World War II years and a rise following the 1940s, perhaps reflecting the influences of poor nutrition and marked environmental stress experienced by the general population in regions that were most affected by the world wars (Pietschnig & Voracek, 2015).

More recent research suggests that the generational gains are leveling off in industrialized countries and already have flattened in Norway, Sweden, and Denmark (Flynn & Weiss, 2007; Pietschnig & Voracek, 2015; Sundet, Barlaug, & Torjussen, 2004; Teasdale & Owen, 2000). Neisser (1998) suggested that increasing IQ scores have mirrored socioenvironmental changes in developing countries. If IQ test score changes are a product of socioenvironmental

FIGURE 8.5: Change Trajectories

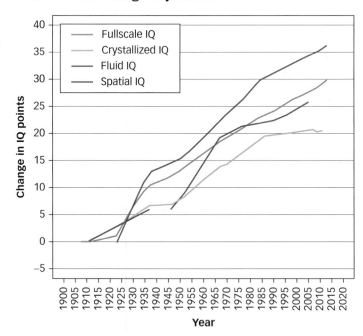

Source: *Perspectives on Psychological Science 2015*, Vol. 10(3) 282–306 © The Author(s) 2015.

improvements, then as living conditions optimize, IQ scores should plateau (Ulric Neisser, 1998; Trahan et al., 2014). Although one recent meta-analysis of studies in six European countries (Norway, Denmark, Britain, the Netherlands, Finland, and France) suggests a "negative Flynn effect," with IQ scores decreasing on average about 2.0 points each decade (Dutton et al., 2016). Another very large meta-analysis of 285 studies, involving more than 14,000 participants since 1951, suggests that the Flynn effect is still at work, yielding an increase of about 2.3 IQ points each decade (Trahan et al., 2014; see Figure 8.5).

What Do You Think?

Why do we typically find large cohort differences in intellectual abilities? Consider the contextual changes that have occurred in recent generations. For example, compare your own experiences with those of your parents, grandparents, and even great-grandparents. How were your worlds different and how might this contribute to differences on intelligence measures?

 Thinking in Context 8.3

1. Describe the progression of intelligence from infancy through older adulthood. Under what conditions would you expect intelligence to change over time?

2. Do you think that your intelligence has changed in your lifetime? Why or why not?

GROUP DIFFERENCES IN IQ

LO 8.4 Analyze biological and contextual influences on group differences in IQ.

A consistent and controversial finding in the intelligence literature is that African Americans tend to score 10 to 15 points below non-Hispanic white Americans on standardized IQ tests (Brooks-Gunn, Klebanov, & Duncan, 1996; Flynn, 2008; Ford, 2008; Rindermann & Thompson, 2013). The IQ scores of Hispanic children tend to fall between those of children of African American and non-Hispanic white descent, and the scores of Asian American children tend to fall at the same level or slightly higher than non-Hispanic white children (Neisser et al., 1996; Nisbett et al., 2013). What do these differences mean? First, it is important to recognize that these findings reflect group averages. Individuals of all races and ethnicities show a wide range of functioning, from severely disabled to exceptionally gifted. An emphasis on differences in group means—how the average scores of African American and non-Hispanic white students differ—overlooks the finding that the overall distribution of scores for African American and non-Hispanic white children overlaps. In other words, despite differences in group averages, the IQ scores of children of all races and ethnicities overlap. For example, at least 20% of African American children score higher on IQ than all other children, whether African American or non-Hispanic white (Flynn, 2008; Phillips, Crouse, & Ralph, 1998; Rindermann & Thompson, 2013). Because there are more differences among African American and non-Hispanic white children than between the two groups, many researchers conclude that group comparisons are meaningless (Daley & Onwuegbuzie, 2011). Like all facets of development, intelligence is influenced by dynamic interactions among genetic or biological factors and context.

GENETICS AND IQ

Genetics is thought to play a role in intelligence, but the degree to which this might be a factor has been hotly debated. To date, researchers have not identified any specific genes that are responsible for IQ (Franić, Dolan, et al., 2015). Intelligence is assumed to

Flynn effect The rise in IQ scores over generations in many nations.

be a polygenic trait, influenced by multiple genes (Franić, Groen-Blokhuis, et al., 2015). Although we have not identified specific genes, heritability estimates point to a role for biology. Recall from Chapter 2 that heritability refers to the extent to which variation among people on a given characteristic is due to genetic differences. Most studies estimate that the heritability of IQ is somewhere between .4 and .8 (Nisbett et al., 2013b). Many researchers, however, argue that it makes no sense to talk about a single variable, such as genes or environment, as causing intelligence because genes and environment never exist in isolation (Dubois et al., 2012; Plomin, DeFries, Knopik, & Neiderhiser, 2016). We cannot disentangle the independent effects of each. A high heritability score does not mean that the environment has no impact or that learning is not involved. Individuals play a role in their own development by creating or selecting their own environment (active gene-environment correlation) and by evoking reactions (reactive gene-environment correlation) due to gene-based traits (Plomin & Asbury, 2001; Scarr & McCartney, 1983).

Perhaps most telling is that the heritability of IQ tends to vary with context. For example, heritability estimates are higher for children of high-SES than low-SES homes. Genes appear to play a large role in determining IQ scores of children from high-SES homes but play less of a role in determining IQ scores for children in low-SES homes (Nisbett et al., 2013). High-SES homes may provide more contextual supports for children's intellectual development, such as opportunities for cognitive stimulation and education. Because high-SES homes tend to provide consistent support to help children achieve their genetic potential, differences in IQ among children reared in high-SES homes are more likely due to genetics as their environments tend to be similarly supportive. Children from impoverished homes, however, often lack consistent access to the basic support needed for intellectual development such as nutrition, health care, and stimulating environments and activities. In other words, their environments do not offer the support needed to help them reach their genetic potential. In these cases, IQ scores are often heavily influenced by the context and opportunities that children have experienced (Nisbett et al., 2013). African American children are disproportionately likely to live in poverty, and impoverished children's IQ scores tend to be more influenced by the disadvantaged contexts in which they are immersed than by the genes with which they are born.

Intelligence is positively associated with educational and career outcomes, but what about social outcomes? Are intelligent people happier? Research has shown inconsistent findings, often showing no relation between IQ and measures of happiness and individuals' life satisfaction (Ali et al., 2013; Veenhoven & Choi, 2012). Some researchers have approached this question from a macrosystem perspective and have examined mean levels of happiness across nations. That is, are "smarter" countries happier? The Cultural Influences on Development feature investigates this research question.

CONTEXT AND IQ

SES is an important contextual factor associated with intelligence scores. As mentioned earlier in the chapter, African American and Hispanic individuals tend to have lower intelligence scores than white non-Hispanic American individuals, but it is important to note that such ethnic differences are reduced and often disappear when socioeconomic differences are taken into account (Brooks-Gunn et al., 1996; Flynn, 2008; Ford, 2008; Rindermann & Thompson, 2013). Children who are adopted from low-SES homes into higher-SES homes typically score 12 points or higher on IQ tests than siblings who are raised by birth parents or adopted into lower-SES homes (Duyme, Dumaret, & Tomkiewicz, 1999; Locurto, 1990). African American children from low-income environments adopted into middle-SES families tend to show IQ scores similar to national averages for middle-SES children (Scarr & Weinberg, 1983). Children from similar middle-class backgrounds tend to have similar IQ scores regardless of their race or ethnicity (Brooks-Gunn et al., 1996).

CULTURAL INFLUENCES ON DEVELOPMENT

• • Are Smart Nations Happy? IQ and Happiness

Intelligence influences the realization of educational goals, such as graduating high school and college, determinants of happiness in individualistic countries.

Like individuals, countries vary in the degree to which IQ and happiness are correlated (Lynn & Vanhanen, 2012). Early comparisons of up to 63 countries yielded small correlations, at most, between IQ and happiness (Lynn, Meisenberg, Mikk, & Williams, 2007). More recent comparisons with as many as 143 nations, however, have yielded more robust correlations between IQ and happiness (Richard Lynn & Vanhanen, 2012; Veenhoven & Choi, 2012). These inconsistent findings, with IQ predicting happiness in some countries but not others, might suggest a role for culture in understanding the IQ–happiness relationship.

One recent study examined IQ and happiness in countries that differed in individualism and collectivism (Stolarski, Jasielska, & Zajenkowski, 2015). Individualistic cultures, such as the United States, Canada, and the majority of Western European countries, tend to focus on the individual. People are expected to take care of themselves and members of their immediate families only and self-serving motives tend to be prioritized (Markus & Kitayama, 1991). In individualistic countries, happiness is often derived from positive emotions related to the self, such as pride, joy, and feeling exceptional (Triandis, 2000). In contrast, in collectivist cultures (such as many Asian, African, and Latin American countries), people are deeply connected to their relatives and in-group members and evaluate themselves in terms of fulfilling their social roles and responsibilities rather than in terms of their personal qualities. The self is interdependent and is defined using the label "we" rather than "I," and well-being tends to be the result of emotions related to others (affiliation; being a part of a

close-knit group) and feeling accepted by people with whom there are relationship bonds.

Stolarski and colleagues (2015) compared 89 countries and found that intelligence was more closely predictive of happiness in individualistic countries, as shown in Figure 8.6. People in individualistic societies seek life satisfaction in self-realization, development of personal qualities, and achievement of individual goals. Intelligence might be an undeniably useful resource in such efforts, as it determines many outcomes associated with life success, such as wealth, longevity, health, and educational achievement, both at the individual and national levels. In collectivistic cultures, satisfaction results from social affiliation and being part of a community remains the main point of reference. Elevating the dignity and raising the status of the family or in-group matters more than the achievement of individual goals. The degree to which IQ is associated with happiness appears to vary with a society's cultural orientation.

FIGURE 8.6: Relationship Between Country-Level IQ and Happiness, as Moderated by Individualism-Collectivism

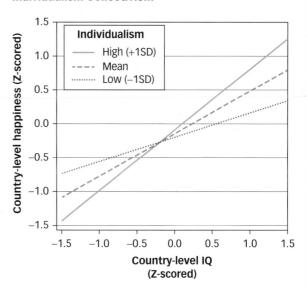

What Do You Think?

What could be done to improve happiness in members of a collectivist culture? How might strategies vary based on whether the culture is collectivist or individualist?

Interestingly, infants do not show SES differences on habituation and other information-processing measures that predict intelligence (McCall & Carriger, 1993), suggesting that SES differences are not inborn but emerge over time. SES contributes to IQ through differences in culture, nutrition, living conditions, school resources, intellectual stimulation, and life circumstances such as the experience of discrimination. Any or all of these factors can influence cognitive and psychosocial factors related to IQ, such as motivation, self-concept, and academic achievement (Plomin & Deary, 2015; Turkheimer, Haley, Waldron, D'Onofrio, & Gottesman, 2003). This view is supported by the finding that the gap between African American and white IQ scores grows smaller with each cohort.

An important contextual factor linked with SES is education. Intelligence scores have been shown in many studies to be closely linked with education. IQ rises with each year spent in school, improves during the school year—which runs from October to April in the United States—and drops over the summer vacation (Ceci, 1991, 1999; Huttenlocher, Levine, & Vevea, 1998). The seasonal drop in IQ scores each summer is larger for children from low-SES homes (Nisbett et al., 2013). Likewise, research has suggested that the knowledge and skills of children in the upper fifth in family SES increase over the summer, likely due to advantaged children's tendency to be enrolled in enrichment activities, such as camps and stimulating extracurricular activities (Burkam, Ready, Lee, & LoGerfo, 2004; Harris, Kelly, Valentine, & Muhlenbruck, 2000). By late elementary school, much of the difference in academic skills between lower- and higher-SES children may be due to the loss of skills over the summer for the low-SES children versus the gains for high-SES children (Alexander, Entwisle, & Kabbani, 2001). School itself provides children with opportunities to be exposed to information and ways of thinking that are valued by the majority culture and reflected in IQ tests. At the same time, the results of children's IQ tests influence the schooling that they receive because IQ tests serve as gatekeepers to gifted programs (Ford, 2008). An intervention designed to boost low-SES children's educational opportunities is Project Head Start, discussed in the Applied Developmental Science feature.

Some researchers point to motivation as a factor in explaining ethnic differences in performance on IQ tests. Specifically, some individuals may not perform at their best in testing situations because of anxiety or fear of being judged, especially by an adult who is of a different ethnic background (Huang, 2009). This is often referred to as **stereotype threat**—the fear that one will be judged to have the qualities associated with negative stereotypes about one's ethnic group (e.g., being less intelligent; Steele, 1997). In one study, students were administered difficult test items. Some were told that they were taking a test of verbal intelligence and that they would get feedback, while others were told that their performance would not be evaluated (Steele & Aronson, 1995). As shown in Figure 8.7, African American students performed worse when they were told that their intellectual ability would be evaluated (the race prime condition), but they performed at levels similar to white students when they didn't think they would be judged (the no race prime condition). It is thought that stereotype threat influenced their performance, perhaps inducing anxiety and concerns about confirming stereotypes.

FIGURE 8.7: Stereotype Threat

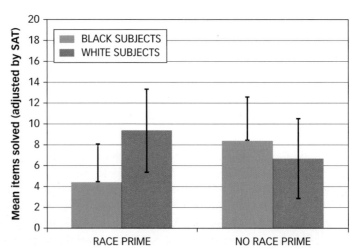

stereotype threat The fear that one will be judged to have the qualities associated with negative stereotypes about one's ethnic group.

● ● Project Head Start

Head Start programs promote children's physical, cognitive, and socioemotional development and also support parents.

Although intelligence tends to be stable, it is malleable. The rationale for Project Head Start, an early intervention program begun in 1965, is that addressing factors that may inhibit children's health and learning will prepare them for school and help them get a "head start" on their education. Children served by Head Start are ethnically diverse and tend to come from families with income below the poverty line.

Intellectual functioning is influenced by overall health. Most Head Start programs include one to two years of preschool as well as nutrition and health services. Parents also receive assistance, such as education about child development, vocational services, and programs addressing their emotional and social needs. Parents are encouraged to be active in Head Start; they serve on committees, contribute to program planning, and act as parent aides in the classroom. Parents must occupy at least one-half of the seats of each Head Start program's Policy Council (Zigler & Styfco, 2004). A large part of Head Start's success is that it reaches parents and gets them involved in their children's education. The more involved parents are, the more they learn about child development, which translates into creating a more stimulating learning environment and overall better parenting.

Over the past four decades, a great deal of research has been conducted on the effectiveness of Head Start. The most common finding is that Head Start improves cognitive performance, as illustrated in a study of young children in 18 U.S. cities (Zhai, Brooks-Gunn, & Waldfogel, 2011). The first year or two after Head Start children begin elementary school, they perform well and show gains in IQ and achievement scores. However, over time the cognitive effects of Head Start fade such that participants' performance on cognitive measures later in childhood is similar to those who have not participated in Head Start (Duncan et al., 2007; McKey et al., 1985; McLloyd, 1998). Why? Early intervention may not compensate for the pervasive and long-lasting effects of poverty-stricken neighborhoods and inadequate public schools (Schnur & Belanger, 2000).

However, there are some lasting benefits. Children who participate in Head Start are less likely to be held back a grade, less likely to be assigned to special education classes, more likely to graduate from high school, and have greater parental involvement in school (Duncan et al., 2007; Joo, 2010; Zigler & Styfco, 1993). Head Start is also associated with other long-lasting effects such as gains in social competence and health-related outcomes including immunizations (Abbott-Shim, Lambert, & McCarty, 2003; Huston, 2008). At the same time, the home environment is often a better and more consistent predictor of long-term outcomes than participation in Head Start (Joo, 2010).

Effective intervention and education programs target young children very early in life to help reduce the negative effects of economic and environmental disadvantage (Ramey & Ramey, 1998). In order to be successful, research has shown that programs must treat the whole child by providing a variety of services to promote development, including health and social services, as well as transportation to ensure that children can attend. Programs should encourage parents to provide a broad range of learning experiences for their children outside of school and become involved in their children's education. In addition, intervention beyond the preschool years have been shown to mitigate the ravaging effects of economic and neighborhood disadvantage.

What Do You Think?

1. **Why do you think the gains in cognitive and achievement scores shown by children in Head Start fade over time? From your perspective, what can be done to improve such outcomes?**

2. **Consider early childhood interventions such as Head Start from the perspective of bioecological theory. Identify factors in the microsystem, mesosystem, and exosystem that programs may address to promote children's development.**

Over the past three decades, research has supported the concept of stereotype threat. Meta-analyses of studies with thousands of students found effects on SAT scores, accounting for 40 points of the score gap between majority (white) and nonmajority (black and Hispanic) test takers, suggesting that minority student performance is underestimated as a result of pervasive negative stereotypes (Walton & Spencer, 2009). The presence of stereotype threat indicates that the degree to which IQ tests capture intelligence may vary with individuals' perceptions of cultural stereotypes. Individual and group performance on IQ tests may also be influenced by subtle biases in the nature of IQ tests.

REDUCING CULTURAL BIAS IN IQ TESTS

Some experts argue that IQ tests tap the thinking style and language of the majority culture, placing individuals of minority groups at disadvantage (Heath, 1989; Helms, 1992), and that examples might be more familiar to children of some backgrounds than others. Items that refer to snow may be biased against children who live in places where it is warm year round. Some children may be more familiar answering word problems about cows than about subways, for example. One way to reduce cultural bias in IQ tests is to include questions that are culture-fair and are familiar to people from all SES and ethnic backgrounds. An item might include explaining how a bird and a fish are different, assuming that all children have experience with bird and fish. It is difficult to eliminate bias, as individuals of varying backgrounds tend to have different experiences. Moreover, the reliance on verbal tasks may place some children at a disadvantage.

IQ tests that rely heavily on verbal tasks are more likely to show ethnic, racial, and SES differences. For example, much of the research that examines group differences in children's IQ used an older WISC measure, the WISC-III, which included many verbal subtests which are thought to be more heavily influenced by culture (Kaufman et al., 2006). Ethnic differences between whites and African Americans tend to be smaller on the newer versions of the WISC as compared with the older WISC-III, suggesting that the structure of the test, specifically the degree to which it relies on spoken language, influences the results (Prifitera & Saklofske, 1998; Prifitera, Saklofske, & Weiss, 2005).

In support of the effect of language on group differences, Latino and Native American children tend to do better on nonverbal tasks than on those that require the use of language (Neisser et al., 1996). However, even nonverbal sorting tasks can be influenced by culture. When presented with a series of cards depicting objects and activities and told to sort the cards into meaningful categories, children from Western cultures tend to sort the cards by category, putting bird and dog in the same category of animal. Children of the Kpelle tribe in Nigeria instead sort the cards by function and activity, placing bird with fly, for example, because birds fly (Sternberg, 1985). Learning experiences and opportunities might also influence children's scores on nonverbal tasks. For example, performance on spatial reasoning tasks is associated with experience with spatially oriented video games (Dirks, 1982; Subrahmanyam & Greenfield, 1996). Likewise, familiarity with test materials influences performance. For example, when Zambian and English children were asked to reproduce patterns in three different media (wire, pencil and paper, or clay), the Zambian children excelled in the wire medium to which they were most accustomed, while the English children were best with pencil and paper. Both groups performed equally well with clay. As this example shows, differences in familiarity with test materials can produce marked differences in test results (Neisser et al., 1996; Serpell, 1974). To truly understand individuals' intelligence, we must use measures that are responsive to contextual differences and variations in socialization and enculturation that influence responses—and corresponding IQ scores.

Thinking in Context 8.4

1. How might the bioecological perspective account for group differences in intelligence scores? Identify macrosystem factors that might contribute to intelligence.

2. Consider exosystem, mesosystem, and microsystem factors. Explain how variations in these bioecological factors might account for group differences in intelligence.

GIFTEDNESS, INTELLECTUAL DISABILITY, AND SPECIAL NEEDS

LO 8.5 Discuss how giftedness, intellectual disability, and special needs are identified and healthy development promoted in such individuals.

Like most human characteristics, some research has shown that people vary in intelligence in predictable ways. Within any given culture, IQ scores tend to represent a normal distribution, with most individuals scoring close to the mean and only a very small minority of individuals have IQ scores that are extremely high or extremely low. Children with extreme intellectual gifts or disabilities, like Gregory and Aiden, whom we met at the beginning of this chapter, are very rare. The following sections examine the extremes of intelligence as well as several types of disabilities that may interfere with learning.

GIFTEDNESS

Traditionally, giftedness has been defined by IQ scores, specifically scores of 130 or greater (Horowitz & O'Brien, 1986); therefore, it is associated primarily with academic skill. Recent definitions of giftedness are broader and include a wide range of human abilities, talents, and accomplishments, including talents in areas such as art, music, creative writing, dance, and sports (Mcclain & Pfeiffer, 2012). Exceptionally talented children share several characteristics. Not only are they smart, but their ability, whether in music, math, or other areas, is substantially above average (Subotnik, Olszewski-Kubilius, & Worrell, 2011). Moreover, gifted children translate their intellectual abilities and talents into outstanding performance and innovation in areas in which they are passionate. Finally, perhaps most essential to exceptional performance is creativity. Gifted persons are creative, meaning that they are able to come up with new thoughts and actions leading them to produce work that is original—that is, something that others have not thought of and that is useful (Kaufman, Plucker, & Russell, 2012).

Creativity is an essential component of giftedness because exceptional individuals apply their talents in unique ways. Creativity can be tested with measures that examine divergent thinking, which is the ability to generate multiple unusual possibilities when confronted with a problem whose purpose is to not identify a single correct answer but rather fresh and unusual lines of thought (Runco & Acar, 2012). An example of a task that taps divergent thinking might be to name uses for common objects (how many things can you do with a newspaper?). Yet divergent thinking, although necessary for creativity, is only one component of creative activity. To demonstrate exceptional talents, gifted individuals must also show creativity in identifying problems, generating ideas, choosing the most promising ideas, and applying their knowledge to understand and solve problems (Guignard & Lubart, 2006). Individuals may have extraordinary mental abilities, but creativity is needed to direct one's talent in novel ways.

Giftedness entails more than intellectual ability; it is a talent that must be developed and nurtured (Pfeiffer 2012). Without encouragement, support, and stimulation, talent may deteriorate. Talented children require home and school environments that are challenging and supportive, with stimulating peers (Subotnik et al., 2011). There are two general approaches toward educating gifted children: enrichment and acceleration. The enrichment approach covers the same curriculum as a typical class, but in greater depth, breadth, or complexity. Students may share the classroom with their average-ability peers and receive enriched content after school, on Saturday, during the summer, or through more challenging assignments (Kim, 2016). In contrast, an accelerated program covers the curriculum at a more advanced pace, in conjunction with student mastery. A student might skip grade levels in particular subjects, such as mathematics, or may skip a grade entirely.

Interventions targeted to the needs of children with intellectual disability can help them develop academic and applied skills to become independent adults.

Some parents and teachers fear that students who accelerate their education may not be emotionally or socially ready to enter college at a young age, but research suggests that gifted children in accelerated programs generally do not report feeling isolated from their peers and do not show negative social or emotional outcomes (Boazman & Sayler, 2011). In fact, some research suggests that they experience fewer emotional problems than their peers and display more emotional maturity (Simonton & Song, 2009; Subotnik et al., 2011). One study of first- through sixth-grade students found that the gifted students scored higher on measures of theory of mind, suggesting that they have greater social understanding than their average-ability peers (Boor-Klip, Cillessen, & van Hell, 2014). As adults, gifted children who accelerated their education report satisfaction with their career, relationships, and life (Lubinski, Benbow, Webb, & Bleske-Rechek, 2006). Longitudinal research following gifted young adolescents through adulthood found that they tend to be, as adults, extraordinarily successful in school and in their careers For example, more than 15% had been awarded patents and more than one-third earned doctorates by age 40 (Kell, Lubinski, Benbow, & Steiger, 2013; Makel, Kell, Lubinski, Putallaz, & Benbow, 2016). Like all children, however, individuals with extraordinary intellectual ability require supportive environments to help them reach their intellectual potential.

INTELLECTUAL DISABILITY

intellectual disability characterized by deficits in cognitive functioning and age-appropriate adaptive behavior, such as social, communication, and self-care skills that begin before 18 years of age; formerly known as mental retardation.

Formerly known as *mental retardation*, **intellectual disability** is a condition in which a child or teenager (under age 18) shows significant deficits in cognition (as defined by an IQ below 70) and in age-appropriate adaptive skills to such a degree that they require ongoing support to adapt to everyday living (American Psychiatric Association, 2013). In recent years the term *mental retardation* has fallen out of favor by professionals because it is stigmatizing and potentially offensive to those with the diagnosis (American Association on Intellectual and Developmental Disabilities [AAIDD], 2009). The new terminology of *intellectual disability* is used in the *Diagnostic and Statistical Manual of Mental Disorders,* 5th edition (DSM-V), which is the manual of diagnoses used by physicians and mental health professionals (American Psychiatric Association, 2013), is exemplified by organization names (e.g., American Association on Intellectual and Developmental Disabilities), and is used by the U.S. federal government agencies such as the Centers for Disease Control. About 1% to 2% of people in the U.S. are diagnosed with intellectual disability (Brown et al., 2008).

Difficulty in adaptation—the inability to appropriately modify one's behavior in light of situational demands—is essential to a diagnosis of intellectual disability. The current definition of intellectual disability emphasizes the degree of support that individuals require in engaging in three categories of adaptive skills, as shown in Table 8.4: conceptual, social, and practical (AAIDD, 2010). Support includes the broad array of assistance that an individual may need to function in society. Support may include formal assistance provided by health care providers, mental health professionals, teachers, and professional caregivers or human service agencies. It may also include informal support from family, friends, and community members. Whereas the DSM-V categorizes intellectual disability as mild, moderate, severe, or profound based on IQ score, the AAIDD does not use these categories. Instead, the AAIDD cautions against extensive use of IQ scores because it is adaptive behavior that determines the ability to function in society. The AAIDD recommends that professionals describe individuals' needs for supports across various domains of functioning. For example, an individual may require extensive support when completing academic tasks but only intermittent support in the social domain, such as one-time training in self-control.

TABLE 8.4 • Severity of Intellectual Disability

SEVERITY	CONCEPTUAL DOMAIN	SOCIAL DOMAIN	PRACTICAL DOMAIN	TYPICAL SUPPORT REQUIRED IN ADULTHOOD
Mild	Preschoolers may show no obvious conceptual differences. School-aged children show difficulties in acquiring academic skills (e.g., reading, writing, arithmetic, telling time, using money). Abstract thinking and planning may be impaired; thinking tends to be concrete.	Communication, conversation, and language are more concrete or immature than the skills of peers. The child may have difficulty accurately understanding the social cues of others. There may be difficulties regulating emotion and behavior compared to peers.	The child may function in an age-expected manner with regard to personal care. In adolescence, assistance may be needed to perform more complex daily living tasks like shopping, cooking, and managing money.	Needs guidance and assistance in complex tasks (such as health care and legal decisions) and during times of unusual social or economic stress. Can usually achieve enough social and vocational skills for self-support.
Moderate	Preschoolers' language and preacademic skills develop slowly. School-aged children show slow progress in academic skills. Academic skill development is usually at the elementary school level.	The child shows marked differences in social and communicative skills compared to peers. Spoken language is simplistic and concrete. Social judgment and decision making are limited. Friendships with peers are often affected by social or communicative deficits.	The child needs more time and practice learning self-care skills, such as eating, dressing, toileting, and hygiene, than peers. Household skills can be acquired by adolescent with ample practice.	Cares for simple personal and household needs after extended guidance. Needs supervision and guidance with managing money, scheduling, and all but simplest daily tasks. May achieve self-support by doing unskilled or semiskilled work in a supportive environment.
Severe	The child generally has little understanding of written language or numbers. Caretakers must provide extensive support for problem solving throughout life.	There are limited spoken language skills with simplistic vocabulary and grammar. Speech may be single words/phrases. The child understands simple speech and gestures. Relationships are with family members and other familiar people.	The child needs ongoing support for all activities of daily living: eating, dressing, bathing, elimination. Caregivers must supervise at all times. Some youths show challenging behaviors, such as self-injury.	Can develop some useful self-protection skills in controlled environment. Requires support for all daily tasks although may contribute partially to self-care under complete supervision.
Profound	Conceptual skills generally involve the physical world rather than symbols (e.g., letters, numbers). Some visuospatial skills, such as matching and sorting, may be acquired with practice. Co-occurring physical problems may greatly limit functioning.	The child has limited understanding of symbolic communication. The child may understand some simple instructions and gestures. Communication is usually through nonverbal, non-symbolic means. Relationships are usually with family members and other familiar people. Co-occurring physical problems may greatly limit functioning. The child is dependent on others for all aspects of physical care, health, and safety, although he or she may participate in some aspects of self-care. Some youths show challenging behaviors, such as self-injury. Co-occurring physical problems may greatly limit functioning.	The child is dependent on others for all aspects of physical care, health, and safety, although he or she may participate in some aspects of self-care. Some youths show challenging behaviors, such as self-injury. Co-occurring physical problems may greatly limit functioning.	Often needs nursing care. May have very limited participation in self-care.

Sources: Shea (2012); Weis (2013).

An individual with intellectual disability shows delayed development—that is, the pattern and sequence follow a typical order but at a slower rate and with limitations with respect to the final level of achievement. Children who show symptoms early, such as the failure to meet gross motor milestones in the first year of life, tend to be more severely affected (Shea, 2012). Most children's intellectual disability is not noticeable until the preschool years when their language skills are markedly behind their peers. They are usually slower to use words and speak in complete sentences; their social development is sometimes delayed; they may be slow to learn to dress and feed themselves. Children with intellectual disability tend to experience more behavioral problems such as explosive outbursts, temper tantrums, and physically aggressive or self-injurious behavior because their ability to communicate, understand, and control their emotional impulses and frustrations is impaired (Shea, 2012).

There are many causes of intellectual disability. Biological influences include genetic disorders such as Down syndrome, metabolic disorders such as phenylketonuria, and mutation (Ellison, Rosenfeld, & Shaffer, 2013; Vissers, Gilissen, & Veltman, 2015; Vorstman & Ophoff, 2013). Contextual factors include neglect, childbirth trauma, and factors associated with poverty such as lack of access to health care and poor nutrition (Heikura et al., 2008; Schalock, 2015). An important principle of development, however, is that biological and contextual factors interact. Prenatal exposure to teratogens, such as maternal use of alcohol or drugs, malnutrition, or poor prenatal care, influences biological development, which in turn influences the child's ability to adapt to stimuli, which may place the child at risk for experiences that may increase the likelihood of intellectual disability.

It is estimated that genetic causes may be responsible for approximately one-fourth to one-half of identified intellectual disability cases (Srour & Shevell, 2014). Genetic counseling, prenatal care, and health care for pregnant women and infants can prevent many cases. Still other causes of intellectual disability occur later in childhood; these include serious head injury, stroke, and certain infections such as meningitis (Centers for Disease Control, 2005). Furthermore, many cases of intellectual disability have no identifiable cause.

A supportive and engaging environment with toys, books, and warm and intellectually stimulating interactions with caregivers during infancy and early childhood coupled with help and guidance through the school years can enhance the outcomes of children with intellectual disabilities (Gorter et al., 2014; Guralnick, 2017). Interventions targeted to the needs of children with mild or moderate disability can help them to become independent and, as adults, live autonomously in the community (Brown et al., 2008b). Children who are profoundly intellectually disabled require greater levels of assistance and more consistent care. As adults, people with profound intellectual disabilities often reside in institutional settings that are able to meet their many needs. However, centers that provide care during the day as well as in-home assistance services are important alternatives to institutional care, as they are less costly and allow individuals with profound intellectual disabilities to remain with their families, in their homes and communities.

LEARNING DISABILITIES

Mr. Bains sits across from his son's teacher and the school psychologist. Ms. Milkauken explains, "Stanton is very bright. He excels at math and is a pleasure to have in class, but he seems to have difficulty reading. He can read sentences out loud but is often unable to explain what he has read." Dr. Roig, the school psychologist, asks permission

Games such as this can help children with dyslexia draw connections between letters and sounds.

AP Photo/Kristin Streff

to test Stanton. "We know that Stanton is a smart boy, but we don't know why he's having such trouble reading. I suspect that he may have a learning disability that affects his reading skills." "What does that mean for Stanton?" asks his father. "If he has a learning disability we can ensure that he receives the educational opportunities he needs to succeed." Mr. Bains nods and agrees to testing.

Learning disabilities are diagnosed in children who demonstrate a measurable discrepancy between aptitude and achievement in a particular academic area given their age, intelligence, and amount of schooling (American Psychiatric Association, 2013). Children with learning disabilities have difficulty with academic achievement despite having normal intelligence and sensory function. Sometimes intelligence test scores of children with learning disabilities show scattered performance, with some subtest scores high and others low (Fletcher, 2012). Although children with learning disabilities tend to have normal vision and hearing, yet often exhibit difficulty managing sensory information and tend to be more easily distracted, less organized, and less likely to use memory strategies than other children (Loomis, 2006). Learning disabilities place children at risk for poor school performance and low self-esteem. There are several types of learning disabilities that affect children's skills in reading and mathematics.

Developmental dyslexia is the most commonly diagnosed learning disability. Children with dyslexia tend to be bright children yet they have difficulty reading, with reading achievement below that predicted by age or IQ. Specifically, children with dyslexia demonstrate age-inappropriate difficulty in matching letters to sounds and difficulty with word recognition and spelling despite adequate instruction and intelligence and intact sensory abilities (Peterson & Pennington, 2012; Ramus, 2014). Dyslexia is estimated to affect 5% to nearly 18% of the school population, boys and girls equally.

Dyslexia is influenced by genetics (Carrion-Castillo, Franke, & Fisher, 2013; Peterson & Pennington, 2012). Children with dyslexia have a neurologically based difficulty in processing speech sounds. They use different regions of the brain during speech tasks and are unable to recognize that words consist of small units of sound, strung together and represented visually by letters (Rosen, 2006; Schurz et al., 2014; Shaywitz et al., 1998). In one study, for example, boys with dyslexia used five times as much area in their brains to perform oral language tasks as compared with boys without dyslexia (Richards et al., 1999). Abnormalities in the brain areas responsible for reading can be seen in 11-year-olds with dyslexia, but not in young children who have not been exposed to reading, suggesting that the brain abnormalities associated with dyslexia occur after reading commences (Clark et al., 2014).

Brain differences and processing defects make it difficult for children with dyslexia to decode or read words, but they do not affect the children's comprehension (Duff & Clarke, 2011). However, reading interventions can improve reading performance and can change the biological structure of the brain. Phonics instruction has been shown to help children with dyslexia learn to read (Shaywitz et al., 1998b). In one study, children who were trained for 8 weeks on phonics and tracing of letters, groups of letters, and words showed improvement in reading and an increase in gray matter volume in the brain areas associated with word and number recognition, memory, and integration of sensory information (Krafnick, Flowers, Napoliello, & Eden, 2011). Successful interventions include training in phonics and supporting emerging skills by linking letters, sounds, and words through writing and reading from developmentally appropriate texts (Snowling, 2013).

Another common learning disability is **dyscalculia**, or mathematics disability. Children with dyscalculia are slow in learning and have a poor understanding of mathematical concepts, such as counting, addition, and subtraction (Gilmore, McCarthy, & Spelke, 2010; Kucian & von Aster, 2015). In early elementary school they may use relatively ineffective strategies for solving math problems, such as using their fingers to add large sums. Like dyslexia, dyscalculia is thought to affect about 5% of students, but it is not well understood (Kaufmann et al., 2013; Rapin et al., 2016). Research

learning disability A diagnosis for a child who demonstrates great difficulty in aspects of learning such as reading or mathematics, and shows achievement behind that expected given the child's IQ.

developmental dyslexia The most commonly diagnosed learning disability in which children tend to be bright yet they have difficulty with reading, with reading achievement below that predicted by age or IQ.

dyscalculia Refers to a mathematics disability.

suggests that it is influenced by brain functioning and difficulty with working memory and executive function, specifically visuospatial short term memory and inhibitory function (Butterworth, 2010; Menon, 2016; Watson & Gable, 2013). Children with dyscalculia are usually given intensive practice to help them understand numbers, but there is much to learn about this disorder (Bryant et al., 2016; Fuchs, Malone, Schumacher, Namkung, & Wang, 2016).

AUTISM SPECTRUM DISORDERS

Autism spectrum disorders (ASD) are a family of disorders that range in severity and are marked by social and communication deficits, often accompanied by restrictive and repetitive behaviors (Tchaconas & Adesman, 2013). Children with ASD show limited engagement in social chat, have difficulty engaging in conversation, often give little eye contact, use few hand gestures, and demonstrate little variation in facial expressions (Kim, Hus, & Lord, 2013). As they grow older they tend to show continued difficulties in initiating and maintaining meaningful conversations, may interact minimally with others, and rarely form close relationships. The second core feature of ASD is restricted and repetitive behaviors and interests (Tchaconas & Adesman, 2013). Children may show intense preoccupations and interests, such as having very specialized knowledge about trains, for example. They may adhere to specific routines like taking a certain route to school or getting dressed in a particular order. Some children with autism show repetitive motor behaviors, such as flapping their hands, and preoccupations with parts of objects, such as focusing on the wheels of toy cars while spinning them.

ASD is heritable (Tick, Bolton, Happé, Rutter, & Rijsdijk, 2016), but the effects are likely epigenetic in nature. Early environmental influences, such as prenatal exposure to a virus or chemical, could interact with a genetic disposition to cause autism. Some of the genes associated with ASD influence the availability of proteins that affect synaptic strength or number and neural connectivity in the brain (Bourgeron, 2015). ASD is associated with atypical brain connectivity (Hahamy, Behrmann, & Malach, 2015). The areas of the brain implicated for facial expression involved in social behavior, emotion, social communication, and theory of mind show reduced and less efficient connectivity within and between each area (Cheng, Rolls, Gu, Zhang, & Feng, 2015a, 2015b; Dajani & Uddin, 2016; Doyle-Thomas et al., 2015). These neurological deficits mean that children with ASD lack a theory of mind (Kana et al., 2015; Senju, 2012). That is, they are unable to consider mental states, which is essential to communication.

Although children are typically not diagnosed until age 3, some ASD symptoms are apparent in infancy. As infants they may demonstrate delays in milestones such as following another person's gaze, smiling at others, and vocalizing back at others (Tchaconas & Adesman, 2013). In one study, researchers found that infants who were later diagnosed with ASD began showing less attention to other people's eyes by 2 months of age (Jones & Klin, 2013). Likewise, brain scans show that infants' brains differentiate people's faces from objects, but infants with ASD show similar brain activity in response to faces and objects, suggesting that they view faces and objects similarly (McCleery, Akshoomoff, Dobkins, & Carver, 2009). Early recognition that faces are special stimuli that are linked with social stimulation is important for developing communication skills, emotional attachments, and theory of mind.

ASD cannot be cured, but a sensitive and supportive environment can help children adapt and function well within the contexts in which they are immersed. Therapists and special education teachers can help children to improve their language and social skills. Medication can help in cases when behavioral symptoms, such as repetitive hand flapping, interfere with or hinder children's progress. Early screening and identification of children with ASD can ensure that they receive behavioral treatment and enriched learning opportunities to optimize their development (Warren et al., 2011).

autism spectrum disorders (ASD) Refer to a family of disorders that range in severity and are marked by social and communication deficits, often accompanied by restrictive and repetitive behaviors.

SPECIAL EDUCATION

In the United States and Canada, legislation mandates that children with learning disabilities are to be placed in the "least restrictive" environment, or classrooms that are as similar as possible to classrooms for children without learning disabilities. Whenever possible, children are to be educated in the general classroom, with their peers, for all or part of the day. This is known as **mainstreaming**. Classes that practice mainstreaming have teachers who are sensitive to the special needs of students with learning disabilities, and provide additional instruction and extra time for them to complete assignments. The assumption is that when children are placed in regular classrooms with peers of all abilities, they are better prepared to function in society. Some mainstreamed children benefit academically

Children with intellectual and learning disabilities in mainstreamed classrooms learn alongside nondisabled peers.

and socially, but others do not. Children's responses to mainstreaming vary with the severity of their disabilities as well as the quality and quantity of support provided in the classroom (Klingner, Vaughn, Hughes, Schumm, & Elbaum, 1998; Waldron & McLeskey, 1998).

Mainstreaming works best when children receive instruction in a resource room that meets their specialized needs for part of the school day and the regular classroom for rest of the school day (Vaughn & Klingner, 1998). Children with learning disabilities report preferring combining time in the regular classroom with time in a resource room that is equipped with a teacher who is trained to meet their special learning needs. Mainstreaming may help children with learning disabilities to overcome difficulties with social awareness and skills that arise from their attention and processing deficits (Gresham & MacMillan, 1997; Sridhar & Vaughn, 2001). Interaction with peers and cooperative learning assignments that require children to work together to achieve academic goals help students with learning disabilities learn social skills and form friendships with peers.

A more recent approach to special education is **inclusion**, which refers to including children with learning disabilities in the regular classroom but providing them with a teacher or paraprofessional specially trained to meet their needs. Inclusion is different from mainstreaming because it entails additional educational support tailored to the learning disabled students' special needs. With an inclusion arrangement, students with learning disabilities have been found to learn more and demonstrate more social advancement than when they are removed from the regular classroom for part of the day and taught separately in a resource room (Swenson, 2000; Waldron & McLeskey, 1998). Around the world, children learn strategies to succeed despite their limitations, but the disabilities themselves and the academic and social challenges posed by them do not disappear. Parents and teachers are most helpful when they understand the learning disabilities are not a matter of intelligence or laziness but rather a function of brain differences, and when they help children to learn to monitor their behavior.

Overall, we have seen in this chapter that intelligence can be defined in many ways, including a pattern of intellectual, social, athletic, artistic, and problem solving abilities. Intelligence taps our capacities for adaptation, and represents the dynamic interplay between biology and context. We are born with genetic propensities that have been shaped by prenatal experiences and we are immersed in a system of contexts that influences the degree to which we fulfill our genetic potential. Finally, while IQ tests may underrepresent intellectual functioning in some individuals, they can identify disabilities and signal the need for intervention, affording individuals the help needed to achieve their potential.

mainstreaming The approach in which children with disabilities are educated in the regular classroom with their nondisabled peers.

inclusion The approach in which children with learning disabilities learn alongside other children in the regular classroom for all or part of the day, accompanied by additional educational support of a teacher or paraprofessional who is specially trained to meet their needs.

Lives in Context Video 8.2
Inclusive Classrooms

Thinking in Context 8.5

1. Suppose you were tasked with creating a class environment that would address the needs of children with intellectual disabilities and learning disabilities as well as children without disabilities. What would your environment include? What are some of the challenges in creating such an environment?

2. Consider intellectual disability from a bioecological perspective. Identify one variable at each contextual level (macrosystem, exosystem, mesosystem, and microsystem) that might serve as a risk factor, posing challenges to children with intellectual disabilities. Also identify a protective factor at each level that might promote adaptive functioning.

 Apply Your Knowledge

Dashawn sighs as he reads the next question. "Hmmm, which one of the following words best match the word 'cup'," he reads to himself, "'wall,' 'table,' 'saucer,' or 'window?'" Dashawn isn't sure what a saucer is. He concludes, "It must be 'table—you put a cup on a table." Dashawn finds that there are a lot of words he doesn't know on this test, like regatta, and situations that didn't make a lot of sense to him, like examples that refer to gardening and playing tennis. "Boy, this is a long test," he mutters to himself.

The next day, Dashawn takes a deep breath and begins his tumbling routine, hurtling his way down the mat, completing a series of forward flips and finishing with a back flip. "Fantastic!" shouts Coach Dawkins, "We should work on your timing, but you are on your way to winning the championship."

Later that week, Coach Dawkins arrives at the high school's conference room to meet with the school's student troubleshooting team. The principal, school psychologist, and several of Dashawn's teachers are in attendance. The school psychologist, Dr. Martinez, begins, "I've brought us together to talk about Dashawn. I'm concerned that he may have special learning needs. His intelligence test scores show a large discrepancy in his performance on verbal and nonverbal test items. I'd like to learn more about your experiences with Dashawn." As the teachers talk, Dr. Martinez takes

notes and creates a profile of Dashawn. Coach Dawkins explains that Dashawn is the most talented gymnast he's coached in his entire career. Dashawn's teachers agree that he's a hard worker, sociable, and well-liked by his classmates. His math teacher explains that Dashawn's performance is in line with his classmates and his English teacher agrees: Dashawn is not the most talented student in class, but his work is on par with his peers and he seems to be a quick learner. Dr Martinez concludes that Dashawn's IQ test scores may not indicate serious cognitive and academic problems, but he decides to monitor Dashawn's progress and discuss his concerns with his mother.

1. Identify reasons why Dashawn might be unfamiliar with some words and terms used in the intelligence test. How might tests be modified to be fair to children of all backgrounds? What do you recommend?

2. Why might have Dashawn scored higher on the performance scale than the verbal scale? Discuss developmental reasons that might underlie his performance. Are there other possible reasons?

3. How might Dashawn's performance be explained using multiple intelligence theory? The triarchic theory of intelligence?

Give your students the SAGE edge!

SAGE edge offers a robust online environment featuring an impressive array of free tools and resources for review, study, and further exploration, keeping both instructors and students on the cutting edge of teaching and learning. Learn more at **edge.sagepub.com/kuthertopical.**

CHAPTER 8 IN REVIEW

8.1 Explain the psychometric approach to intelligence, various ways of measuring IQ, and the predictive value of IQ.

SUMMARY

According to the psychometric approach, intelligence is composed of a set of psychological traits that can be measured and that vary among people. Horn and Cattell organized primary mental abilities into clusters representing fluid intelligence (ability to draw inferences) and crystalized intelligence (knowledge base). Intelligence tests describe patterns of abilities among individuals. The Wechsler intelligence scales (WAIS for adults, WISC for older children and adolescents, and WPPSI for young children) measure intelligence as a set of verbal and nonverbal abilities. Intelligence scores predict academic achievement, occupational success, health, and longevity.

KEY TERMS

intelligence
primary mental abilities
crystallized intelligence

fluid intelligence
intelligence quotient (IQ)

REVIEW QUESTIONS

1. What is intelligence?
2. Compare Spearman's *g* with Thurstone's primary abilities.
3. What are fluid and crystalized intelligence?
4. What is the most common IQ test and how does it define intelligence?
5. What does IQ predict? Why?

8.2 Compare information-processing, neurological, and componential approaches to intelligence.

SUMMARY

According to the information-processing approach, individuals who process information efficiently should acquire knowledge and thereby adapt to the world quickly. Information-processing abilities are associated with measures of intelligence throughout life. Neurological perspectives on intelligence associate brain volume, cortical thickness, myelinated matter, and brain activity with measures of general intelligence. The triarchic theory of intelligence poses three forms of intelligence: Analytical, creative, and practical). Individuals may have strengths in any or all of them. Multiple intelligence theory proposes at least eight independent kinds of intelligence.

KEY TERMS

multiple intelligence theory

triarchic theory of intelligence

REVIEW QUESTIONS

1. What information processing abilities contribute to intelligence?
2. How do neurological researchers account for intelligence?
3. Compare two componential approaches to intelligence.

8.3 Examine the patterns of intelligence across the lifespan.

SUMMARY

IQ shows increasing stability starting at about age 4. Studies that examine group changes in intelligence conclude that intelligence scores are stable from childhood through adolescence, but there are also large individual differences. Cross sectional studies tend to show IQ declines with age, but longitudinal research suggests increases in IQ into midlife followed by slow declines. Schaie's cross-sequential research shows that crystallized and fluid intelligence show different patterns of change over the adult years, with crystallized intelligence remaining stable or increasing, and fluid intelligence declining. There are large cohort effects in intelligence. Intellectual capacity seems to follow the "use it or lose it" principle.

KEY TERM

Flynn effect

REVIEW QUESTIONS

1. To what degree is IQ stable from infancy through adolescence?
2. How do fluid and crystallized intelligence change over adulthood?
3. What skills remain relatively intact adulthood and what skills are likely to decline with age?

8.4 Analyze biological and contextual influences on group differences in IQ.

SUMMARY

Genetics is thought to play a role in intelligence but to date researchers have not identified any specific genes that are responsible for IQ. Intelligence is assumed to be a polygenic trait. The heritability of IQ tends to vary with context. SES contributes to IQ through differences in culture, nutrition, living conditions, school resources, intellectual stimulation, and life circumstances such as the experience of discrimination. IQ tests that rely heavily on verbal tasks are more likely to show ethnic, racial, and SES differences. One way to reduce cultural bias in IQ tests is to include questions that are culture-fair and rely less on verbal measures.

REVIEW QUESTIONS

1. What evidence do researchers who emphasize the role of biology in intelligence cite?

2. What are contextual influences on intelligence scores?

3. Give an example that illustrates the interaction of genetic and contextual factors in intelligence.

8.5 Discuss how giftedness, intellectual disability, and special needs are identified and healthy development promoted in such individuals.

SUMMARY

Gifted children are exceptionally talented and show above average ability, outstanding performance and innovation, and creativity in a specific area such as art, music, writing, and dance. Giftedness is a talent that must be developed and nurtured. Intellectual disability is a condition in which a child or teenager shows significant deficits in cognition (as defined by an IQ below 70) and in age-appropriate adaptive skills to such a degree that they require ongoing support to adapt to everyday living. Learning disabilities, such as developmental dyslexia and dyscalculia, are diagnosed in children who demonstrate a measurable discrepancy between aptitude and achievement in a particular academic area given their age, intelligence, and amount of schooling. Autism spectrum disorders are a family of disorders that range in severity and are marked by social and communication deficits. Children with ASD have difficulty engaging in conversation, often give little eye contact, use few hand gestures, and demonstrate little variation in facial expressions. As they grow older they tend to show continued difficulties in initiating and maintaining social interactions and relationships. In the United States and Canada, legislation mandates that children with learning disabilities are to be placed in the "least restrictive" environment, or classrooms that are as similar as possible to classrooms for children without learning disabilities via mainstreaming and inclusion.

KEY TERMS

intellectual disability
learning disabilities
developmental dyslexia
dyscalculia

autism spectrum disorders
mainstreaming
inclusion

REVIEW QUESTIONS

1. Compare characteristics of students with intellectual disability, learning disabilities, and autistic spectrum disorders. What similarities and differences do they share?

2. How can special education facilitate the learning of children with diverse needs?

Test your understanding of the content.
Review the flashcards and quizzes at
edge.sagepub.com/kuthertopical

PRACTICE AND APPLY WHAT YOU'VE LEARNED

▶ **edge.sagepub.com/kuthertopical**

Language Development

CHAPTER 9

Learning Objectives

9.1 Describe the five basic components of language.

9.2 Explain the process by which infants develop the ability to understand and use language.

9.3 Describe patterns of language development from early childhood through adulthood.

9.4 Distinguish among learning, nativist, and interactionist perspectives on language.

9.5 Discuss cultural and contextual influences on language development.

Digital Resources

- Social Communication Disorder
- From First Sounds to First Words
- Speaking Volumes
- Children's Understanding of Language
- Getting Wasted
- Real-life Broca's Aphasia
- Bilingual Education
- The Word Gap

Master these learning objectives with multimedia resources available at **edge.sagepub.com/kuthertopical** and *Lives in Context* video cases available in the interactive eBook.

Eleven-month-old William is wide-eyed as his father rolls a ball to him and says, "Ball!" "Ba!" says William. Unlike the random cooing and babbling sounds he made a few months ago, William is now beginning to show evidence of understanding words and trying to utter them. By 26 months of age, William can express his desires with simple phrases like, "Want milk!" and "Cracker, please." Soon after, his expressions become more complex, and 3-year-old William can hold conversations with his preschool playmates about toys, play, and pretend characters and activities.

Language development has important implications for children's cognitive, social, and emotional development. Gaining the ability to use words to represent objects, experiences, thoughts, and feelings permits children to think and to communicate with others in increasingly flexible and adaptive ways. In this chapter, we examine the dramatic changes in language that occur in infancy and early childhood and the subtle shifts that occur later in the lifespan.

FOUNDATIONS OF LANGUAGE

LO 9.1 Describe the five basic components of language.

Language is a complex system of associations between sounds and meaning. Specifically, language entails combining a limited number of sounds (or gestures,

Carmo Correia/Alamy

Learning to communicate effectively entails developing competence in the pragmatics of language.

in the case of sign language) according to rules specific to that language. As children learn language, they gain the ability to distinguish its component sounds, combine sounds to form words, combine words to create sentences, and use language to communicate with others. To master language, children must learn to use the five basic components that underlie all languages: phonology, morphology, semantics, syntax, and pragmatics.

Phonology refers to knowledge of the sounds used in a given language (Hoff, 2013). Humans are capable of generating many more sounds than any one language uses, and languages tend to have different phonologies. About 200 different sounds are used in all known spoken languages; about 45 sounds comprise the English language (Owens, 2015). Infants must learn how to detect, discriminate, and later, produce speech sounds. Learning the phonology of language entails learning to discriminate speech sounds, such as the differences among "*b*," "*d*," and "*p*" sounds. Nonnative languages often sound strange because they use phonologies (speech sounds and combinations thereof) that are unfamiliar to us.

As infants attend to and discriminate sounds, they learn that sounds can be combined in meaningful ways. This understanding of the ways that sounds can be combined to form words is known as **morphology** (Hoff, 2015). **Semantics** refers to the meaning or content of words and sentences. Infants' first words and their growing vocabularies illustrate development in their understanding of semantics. Learning language is more than acquiring vocabulary—it also involves learning rules for constructing sentences. **Syntax** refers to knowledge of the structure of sentences; that is, the rules by which words are to be combined to form sentences (Hoff, 2013). For example, consider the following sentences:

(a) Dozer Freddy bit.

(b) Dozer bit Freddy.

(c) Freddy bit Dozer.

A child who understands basic rules of syntax grasps that sentences (b) and (c) have different meanings and that sentence (a) is nonsensical. Our understanding of grammar, or the combination of morphology and syntax, develops throughout childhood and adolescence.

The final component of language is **pragmatics**—understanding how to use language to communicate effectively (Owens, 2015). Five-year-old Destiny knows, for example, that she must speak differently, using different words and structure, when talking to her 2-year-old sister and when talking to her older brother. She learns to tailor and edit her speech in light of her audience. Eleven-year-old Marques asks to share a cookie with his friend ("Yo! Gimme a cookie!") using very different language and intonation than he does when asking his grandmother for a cookie ("May I please have a cookie?"). Although we begin to show some competence in pragmatics in infancy, our grasp of pragmatics develops well into adolescence and is refined during adulthood.

Learning to speak a language entails developing each of these aspects of speech. Infants learn to discriminate, understand, and form sounds for words. They learn the meanings of words and sentences and how to put words together in meaningful ways. Children also learn how to tailor their speech for their audience and acquire the cultural nuances reflected in their language. Children accomplish this in just a few years.

phonology Refers to the knowledge of sounds used in a given language.

morphology The understanding of the way that sounds combine to form words.

semantics Refers to the meaning or content of words and sentences.

syntax Refers to the knowledge of the structure of sentences; that is, the rules by which words are to be combined to form sentences.

pragmatics The practical application of language for everyday communication.

Thinking in Context 9.1

1. Suppose you were having a conversation with a friend and wanted to express disagreement with your friend on some issue. Now imagine the same situation with a parent, teacher, or employer. How might pragmatics influence your message in each of these conversations?

FROM SOUNDS TO SYMBOLS: LANGUAGE DEVELOPMENT IN INFANCY

LO 9.2 Explain the process by which infants develop the ability to understand and use language.

"You just love to hear Mommy talk, don't you?" Velma asked, as newborn Jayson stared up at her. Can Jayson attend to his mother? Is Jayson interested in his mother's speech? As described in Chapter 4, hearing emerges well before birth, and evidence suggests that newborns can recall sounds heard in the womb (Dirix, Nijhuis, Jongsma, & Hornstra, 2009). The process by which infants develop the ability to understand and use language is fascinating and has many facets, as we will explore in this section.

EARLY PREFERENCES FOR SPEECH SOUNDS

We know from experiments with newborns that infants are primed to learn language from birth. Newborns naturally attend to speech. Two-day-old neonates prefer to hear speech sounds over acoustically comparable nonspeech sounds (Vouloumanos, Hauser, Werker, & Martin, 2010).

Research evidence suggests that phonological development may begin before birth. In a series of studies, fetuses as young as 33 weeks of gestational age were familiarized to a tape recording of either their mother or a female stranger reading the same passage in the fetuses' native language (English). Subsequently, they were then presented with one of several speakers: their father or a novel speaker reading the same passage, or a novel speaker using a nonnative language (i.e., Mandarin; Kisilevsky et al., 2009). As evidenced by changes in heart rate, the fetuses showed general preferences for their mothers' voices; they also showed preference for the nonnative speaker, suggesting an early ability to discriminate speech sounds. Once they are born, neonates show a preference for listening to their native language, as well as for stories that they have heard prenatally. This suggests that they are sensitive to the sound of words and the pattern of speech from birth.

Infants naturally notice the complex patterns of sounds around them and organize sounds into meaningful units. They recognize frequently heard words, such as their names (Aslin, Clayards, & Bardhan, 2008). By 4½ months of age, infants will turn their heads to hear their own names but not to hear other names, even when the other names have a similar sound pattern (e.g., Annie vs. Johnny; Aslin et al., 2008; Mandel, Jusczyk, & Pisoni, 1995).

Newborns can perceive and discriminate sounds that comprise all human languages, but their developing capacities and preferences are influenced by context. For example, the Japanese language does not discriminate between the consonant sounds of "r" in *rip* and "l" in *lip*. Japanese adults who are learning English find it very difficult to discriminate between the English pronunciations of these "r" and "l" sounds, yet until about 6 to 8 months of age, Japanese-speaking infants in Japan and English-speaking infants

Communication begins well before infants can speak.

in the U.S. are equally able to distinguish these sounds. By 10 to 12 months, however, discrimination of "r" and "l" improves for U.S. infants and declines for Japanese infants. This likely occurs because U.S. infants hear these sounds often, whereas Japanese infants do not because the Japanese language does not contrast those sounds (Kuhl et al., 2006). Although babies are born with the ability to perceive the full range of human speech sounds, they prefer to hear their native languages, suggesting an early developing neurological specialization for language (Moon, Cooper, & Fifer, 1993). As they are exposed to their native language, they become more attuned to the sounds (and distinctions between sounds) that are meaningful in their own language and become less able to distinguish speech sounds that are not used in their native language (Werker, Yeung, & Yoshida, 2012).

At the same time, infants' speech discrimination abilities remain malleable in response to the social context. In one study, Kuhl and her colleagues exposed 9-month-old English-learning American infants to 12 live interaction sessions with an adult speaker of Mandarin Chinese over the course of 4–5 weeks (Kuhl, Tsao, & Liu, 2003). After the sessions, the infants were tested on a Mandarin phonetic contrast that does not occur in English. The infants discriminated the contrast as well as same-aged Mandarin-learning infants and retained the contrast for several days. But the 9-month-old English-learning infants did not learn the Mandarin phonetic contrast when they were exposed to it only by audio or video. Live interaction may have increased infants' motivation to learn by increasing their attention and arousal. Or perhaps live interaction provides specific information that fosters learning, like the speaker's eye gaze and pointing coupled with interactive contingency (Kuhl et al., 2003). The relevance of context is also illustrated by the infants' loss of the ability to discriminate the Mandarin contrast several days after training and, presumably, the absence of ongoing exposure to the Mandarin language (Fitneva & Matsui, 2015).

Social input, such as the quality of mother–infant interactions, plays a role in determining the timing of infants' narrowing of speech sound discrimination. Specifically, infants who experience high-quality interactions with their mothers, characterized by frequent speech, show a narrowing as early as 6 months of age (Elsabbagh et al., 2013).

PRELINGUISTIC COMMUNICATION

At birth, crying is the infant's only means of communication. Infants soon learn to make many more sounds like gurgles, grunts, squeals, and more. Between 2 and 3 months of age, infants begin **cooing**, making deliberate vowel sounds like "ahhhh," "ohhhh," and "eeeee." The first coos infants make sound like one long vowel (Hoff, 2013). These vocal sounds are a form of vocal play; they are likely to be heard when babies are awake, alert, and contented. At the cooing stage, infants already use pauses that are consistent with the turn-taking pattern of spoken conversations. With age, the quality of coos changes to include different vowel-like sounds and combinations of vowel-like sounds (Hoff, 2013). **Babbling**, repeating strings of consonants and vowels such as "ba-ba-ba" and "ma-ma-ma," begins to appear at about 6 months of age.

At first, babbling is universal. All babies do it, and the sounds they make are similar no matter what language their parents speak or in what part of the world they are raised. However, as mentioned earlier, infants soon become sensitive to the ambient language around them, and it influences their vocalizations (Chen & Kent, 2010). With development and exposure to speech, babbling becomes more word-like and sounds more like

cooing An infant's repetition of vowel sounds, such as "ahhhh," "ohhh," and "eeee" that begins between 2 and 3 months of age.

babbling An infant's repetition of syllables such as "ba-ba-ba-ba" and "ma-ma-ma," which begins at about 6 months of age.

the infant's native language (Goldstein & Schwade, 2008). In one study, French adults listened to the babbling of a French 8-month-old and a second 8-month-old from either an Arabic- or Cantonese-speaking family. Nearly three-quarters of the time, the adults correctly indicated which baby in the pair was French (Boysson-Bardies et al., 1984). By the end of the first year, infants' babbling sounds more like real speech as infants begin to vary the pitch of their speech in ways that reflect the inflections of their native languages (Andruski, Casielles, & Nathan, 2013; Rothgänger, 2003). For example, in spoken English, declarative sentences are characterized by pitch that falls toward the end of the sentence whereas in questions, the pitch rises at the end of the sentence. Older babies' babbling mirrors these patterns when they are raised by English-speaking parents, but babies reared with Japanese or French as their native languages show intonation patterns similar to those of the respective languages (Levitt et al., 1992). Longitudinal observations of infants raised in Catalan-speaking environments likewise show that their babbling shifts to mirror intonations in native speech (Esteve-Gilbert et al., 2013).

Language acquisition is a socially interactive process: Babies learn by hearing others speak and by noticing the reactions that their vocalizations evoke in caregivers. Social interaction elicits cooing (Owens, 2015), and infants modify their babbling in response to caregiver interactions (Tamis-LeMonda, Kuchirko, & Song, 2014). For example, when mothers of 9½-month-old infants speak in response to their infants' babbling, infants restructure their babbling, changing the phonological pattern of sounds in response to their mothers' speech (Goldstein & Schwade, 2008). Babbling repertoires reflect infants' developing morphology and are a foundation for word learning (Ramsdell, Oller, Buder, Ethington, & Chorna, 2012).

FIRST WORDS

At about 1 year of age, the average infant speaks his or her first word. At first, infants use one-word expressions, called **holophrases**, to express complete thoughts. A first word might be a complete word or a syllable. Usually the word has more than one meaning, depending on the context in which it is used. For example, "Da" might mean, "I want that," "There's Daddy!" or "What's that?" Caregivers usually hear and understand first words before other adults do. The first words that infants use are those that they hear often or are meaningful for them, such as their own name, the word *no*, or the word for their caregiver. Infants reared in English-speaking homes tend to use nouns first as they are most concrete and easily understood (Waxman et al., 2013). For example, the word *dog* refers to a concrete thing and is easier to understand than a verb such as *goes*. In contrast, infants reared in homes in which Mandarin Chinese, Korean, or Japanese is spoken tend to learn verbs very early in their development, in response to the greater emphasis on verbs in their native languages (Waxman et al., 2013).

Regardless of what language a child speaks, early words tend to be used in the following ways (MacWhinney, MacWhinney, & Brian, 2015; Owens, 2015):

- Request or state the existence or location of an object or person by naming it (car, dog, outside)
- Request or describe the recurrence of an event or receipt of an object (again, more)
- Describe actions (eat, fall, ride)
- Ask questions (What? That?)
- Attribute a property to an object (hot, big)
- Mark social situations, events, and actions (no, bye)

Throughout language development, babies' *receptive language* (what they can understand) exceeds their *productive language* (what they can produce themselves; Hoff, 2014).

holophrase A one-word expression used to convey a complete thought.

That is, infants understand more words than they can use. Research suggests that infants may understand some commonly spoken words as early as 6 to 9 months of age, long before they are able to speak (Bergelson & Swingley, 2012; Dehaene-Lambertz & Spelke, 2015). In the Applying Developmental Science feature, we examine the practice of teaching infants to use hand signals ("baby signing") to communicate with their caregivers.

LEARNING WORDS: SEMANTIC GROWTH

"I can't believe how quickly Matthew picks up new words. It's time for us to be more careful about what we say around him," warned Elana. Her husband agreed, "He's only 2 years old and he has quite a vocabulary. Who would think that he'd learn so many words so quickly?" By 13 months of age, children begin to quickly learn the meaning of new words and understand that words correspond to particular things or events, but they tend to learn the names of objects more readily than the names of actions (Woodward, Markman, & Fitzsimmons, 1994). Most infants of Matthew's age rapidly expand their vocabularies, often to the surprise of their parents. Infants learn new words through **fast mapping**, a process of quickly acquiring and retaining a word after hearing it applied a few times (Kan & Kohnert, 2008; Marinellie et al., 2012). Two-year-olds have been shown to be able to learn a word even after a single brief exposure under ambiguous conditions (Spiegel & Halberda, 2011). Fast mapping improves with age and accounts for the **naming explosion**, or **vocabulary spurt**—a period of rapid vocabulary learning that occurs between 16 and 24 months of age (Dapretto & Bjork, 2000). During this period, infants simultaneously learn multiple words of varying difficulty. Within weeks, a toddler may increase her vocabulary from 50 words to more than 400 (Bates, Bretherton, & Snyder, 1988).

Recent research has suggested that an explosive growth in vocabulary is not universal. Infants vary in the speed of word acquisition, which occurs gradually for many children, rather than through a sudden spurt (Ganger & Brent, 2004; Parladé & Iverson, 2011). At 18 months, infants are more likely to learn a new word if both they and the speaker are attending to the new object when the speaker introduces the new word (Baldwin et al., 1996). Yet by 24 to 30 months of age, toddlers can often determine the meaning of words even if they simply overhear a speaker talking to someone else (Akhtar, Jipson, & Callanan, 2001),

fast mapping A process by which children learn new words after only a brief encounter, connecting it with their own mental categories.

naming explosion (vocabulary spurt) A period of rapid vocabulary learning that begins about 16 to 18 months of age.

FIGURE 9.1: Number of Words Known as a Function of Time for Individual Children

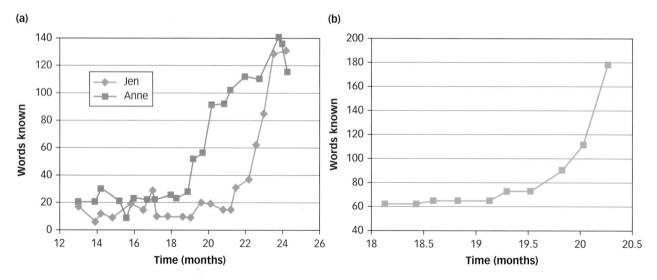

APPLYING DEVELOPMENTAL SCIENCE

• • Baby Signing

AP Photo/JUSTIN HAYWORTH

Although signing may not accelerate language development, it offers opportunities for parent-infant interaction and play.

Few things are as frustrating for a parent as trying to decipher their baby's cry. What does she need? Is she hungry? Cold? Does she have a wet diaper? Is she hurt? Imagine how nice it would be if infants could communicate their needs!

The baby signing movement promotes early communication between infants and parents by teaching infants to communicate with symbolic gestures. The assumption behind baby signing is that the gross motor skills needed for signing develop before the relatively fine motor control of the mouth, tongue, and breath needed to articulate speech (Goodwyn & Acredolo, 1998). Parents who read about the benefits of teaching signs to their infants often embrace the practice. Numerous companies have been created to promote and sell baby signing materials. Most advertise benefits such as facilitating spoken language, reducing tantrums, and increasing IQ.

The roots of baby signing lie in research conducted by Linda Acredolo and Susan Goodwyn. Their research has shown that babies readily acquire symbolic gestures when exposed to the enhanced gestural training that they refer to as "baby signs" (Acredolo, Goodwyn, & Abrams, 2009). They propose that the rewards of baby signing include larger and more expressive vocabulary, advanced mental development, improved parent–child relationships, and fewer tantrums and behavior problems (Acredolo & Goodwyn, 1988; Goodwyn & Acredolo, 1998). Based on their findings, Acredolo and Goodwyn created a signing program for infants with videos, classes, books, and cue cards (Acredolo et al., 2009).

It is generally recognized that gesture and language are linked and that babies naturally make early gestures that precede their use of language (Iverson & Goldin-Meadow, 2005). But is baby signing effective in accelerating language and other aspects of development? One review of 33 websites associated with various baby signing products revealed that all promoters claimed benefits such as faster language development, and many claimed to foster higher IQs, improvements in parent-child interactions, and fewer child tantrums. Yet almost none provided evidence to support these claims. Those that did referred to case studies (such as Acredolo & Goodwyn, 1985) and opinion articles, rather than experiments (Nelson, White, & Grewe, 2012). A review of research studies examining the outcomes of baby signing programs found that although some of the studies suggested some benefits, nearly all contained methodological weaknesses such as a lack of control groups or no random assignment. It was concluded that evidence to support these claims was insufficient (Johnston, 2005).

More recently, a longitudinal study tested the effects of baby signing products. Infants were followed from 8 months of age until 20 months of age (Kirk, Howlett, Pine, & Fletcher, 2013). Babies were randomly assigned to one of three conditions: baby sign training, verbal training (i.e., mothers modeled words without signs), and nonintervention. At 20 months of age, the language development was similar for all babies, regardless of intervention. Encouraging gestures did not result in higher scores on language measures, providing no support for the claims of baby signing proponents.

Nevertheless, many parents report that baby signing has improved their child's ability to communicate and overall parent–infant interactions (Doherty-Sneddon, 2008; Mueller & Sepulveda, 2014). Although baby signing may not have research support for accelerating language development, it has not been shown to be harmful. If the use of baby signing promotes frequent parent–infant interaction, does not rush or pressure infants, and is helpful in parents' estimation, there is no reason to discourage its use.

What Do You Think?

Should we encourage parents to teach their babies how to sign? Why or why not?

and they can learn new words even when their attention is distracted by other objects or events (Moore, Angelopoulos, & Bennett, 1999). Fast mapping helps young children learn many new words, but their own speech lags behind what they can understand because young children, like second-language learners, have difficulty retrieving words from memory (Dapretto & Bjork, 2000). In addition, the speed at which young children acquire words during the vocabulary spurt predicts the size of their vocabulary as preschoolers at

54 months of age (Rowe, 2012). That is, children who rapidly expand their knowledge of words during the vocabulary spurt tend to have larger vocabularies in preschool than their peers who acquire new words at a slower pace.

As children learn words, we see two interesting kinds of mistakes that tell us about how words are acquired (Gershkoff-Stowe, 2002). **Underextension** refers to applying a word more narrowly than it is usually applied so that the word's use is restricted to a single object. For example, *cup* might refer to Daddy's cup but not to the general class of cups. Later, the opposite tendency appears. **Overextension** refers to applying a word too broadly. *Cow* might refer to cows, sheep, horses, and all farm animals. Overextension suggests that the child has learned that a word can signify a whole class of objects. As children develop a larger vocabulary and get feedback on their speech, they demonstrate fewer errors of overextension and underextension.

TWO-WORD UTTERANCES: EMERGING SYNTAX AND PRAGMATICS

At about 21 months of age, or usually about 8 to 12 months after they say their first word, most children compose their first simple two-word sentences, such as "Kitty come," or "Mommy milk." **Telegraphic speech**, like a telegram, includes only a few essential words. Like other milestones in language development, telegraphic speech is universal among toddlers. Children around the world use two-word phrases to express themselves.

Language development follows a predictable path, as shown in Table 9.1. By 2½ years of age, children demonstrate an awareness of the communicative purpose of speech and the importance of being understood, which are developments in pragmatics (Owens, 2015). In one experiment, 2½-year-old children asked an adult to hand them a toy. The child was more likely to repeat and clarify the request for the toy when the adult's verbal response indicated misunderstanding of the child's request ("Did you say to put the toy on the shelf?") than when the adult appeared to understand the request, regardless of whether the adult gave the child the toy (Shwe & Markman, 1997).

It is not until between 20 and 30 months of age that children show competence in using syntax, the rules for forming sentences in a given language. Soon they become more comfortable with using plurals, past tense, articles (such as *a* and *the*), prepositions (such as *in* and *on*), and conjunctions (such as *and* and *but*).

TABLE 9.1 • Language Milestones

AGE	LANGUAGE SKILL
2–3 months	Cooing
6 months	Babbling
1 year	First word Holophrases
16–24 months	Vocabulary spurt Learn new words by fast mapping Underextension Overextension
21 months	Telegraphic speech
21–30 months	Syntax

underextension A vocabulary error in which the infant applies a word too narrowly to a single object rather than the more appropriate, wider class of objects.

overextension A vocabulary error in which the infant applies a word too broadly to a wider class of objects than appropriate.

telegraphic speech Two-word utterances produced by toddlers that communicate only the essential words.

 Thinking in Context 9.2

1. What role do other domains of development hold in influencing infants' language development? Consider motor development, perception, and cognition. How might advances in these domains influence infants' emerging language abilities?

2. Language unfolds in a similar pattern for infants around the world. Yet, is there a role for context in shaping language? Why or why not?

3. Suppose a close friend or family member has a newborn infant. What would you include in an explanation of language development? In your opinion, what does a parent need to know about language development? Why?

LANGUAGE DEVELOPMENT OVER THE LIFESPAN

LO 9.3 Describe patterns of language development from early childhood through adulthood.

Language emerges in infancy, but is refined throughout childhood, matures in adolescence, and continues to change in subtle ways throughout adulthood. Early childhood, however, is a particularly important time for language development.

ADVANCES IN LANGUAGE DURING EARLY CHILDHOOD

Toddlers transitioning from infancy to early childhood tend to use telegraphic speech. They learn to use multiple elements of speech, such as plurals, adjectives, and the past tense. Children's vocabulary and grammar become dramatically more complex during early childhood. If you have ever tried learning a new language and struggled to hear the unique sounds and learn the morphology and syntax of the language well enough to construct meaningful phrases and sentences, you can likely appreciate the dramatic advances that occur in language development during early childhood. Young children's speech reflects gains in semantics and syntax that allow them to not only communicate, but also think, in new ways. In addition, they begin to learn about the pragmatics of language: For example, they realize that speech must be tailored to the audience and that one speaks differently to siblings than to parents.

Vocabulary

At 2 years of age, the average child knows about 500 words; vocabulary acquisition continues at a rapid pace. The average 3-year-old child has a vocabulary of 900 to 1,000 words. By 6 years of age, most children have a vocabulary of about 14,000 words, which means that the average child learns a new word every 1 to 2 hours, every day (Owens, 2015). How is language learned so quickly? Children continue to use fast mapping as a strategy to enable them to learn the meaning of a new word after hearing it once or twice (Brady et al., 2014; Marinellie et al., 2012), based on contextual association and understanding (Kucker, McMurray, & Samuelson, 2015). As mentioned previously, in many languages, children fast map words for objects more easily than words for actions. However, children under 3 years of age, when learning most languages, have been shown to fast map new verbs and apply them to other situations in which the same action occurs (Gershkoff-Stowe & Hahn, 2007; Golinkoff, Jacquet, Hirsh-Pasek, & Nandakumar, 1996). With age, children get better at using fast mapping (Brady & Goodman, 2014).

In order to fast map a word, the child must hear it. Young children can learn words simply by overhearing them in conversation or by watching videos (O'Doherty et al., 2011). Preschoolers can learn words from watching videos with both human and robot speakers, but they learn more quickly in response to human speakers (Moriguchi, Kanda, Ishiguro, Shimada, & Itakura, 2011). Children learn best in interactive contexts that entail turn-taking, joint attention, and scaffolding experiences (recall the sociocultural perspective in Chapter 6; Harris, Golinkoff, & Hirsh-Pasek, 2011; Roseberry, Hirsh-Pasek, & Golinkoff, 2014). Parents who wish to foster language development should have frequent conversations with their children in which they use a wide vocabulary (Hoff & Naigles, 2002) and explain new words, providing hints to meaning and checking for children's understanding (Harris et al., 2011; Roseberry et al., 2014). Children learn words they hear often, that label things and events that interest them, and that they encounter in contexts that are meaningful to them (Harris et al., 2011; Roseberry et al., 2014). Children's vocabulary improves when storybooks are read to them (Leung, 2008). One study examined the effects of adult–child interaction on 3-year-olds' vocabulary acquisition during

Language skills open the door to new opportunities, such as reading, which in turn is associated with advances in cognitive and language development.

storybook reading (Walsh & Blewitt, 2006). All children were read three storybooks repeatedly over four reading sessions. Children who were asked questions about the reading and were encouraged to talk about it showed greater vocabulary and more novel word knowledge after the fourth session than did children who were not engaged in discussion.

Another strategy that children use to increase their vocabulary is **logical extension**. When learning a word, children extend it to other objects in the same category. For example, when learning that a dog with spots is called a Dalmatian, a child may refer to a Dalmatian bunny (a white bunny with black spots) or a Dalmatian horse. Children tend to make words their own and apply them to all situations they want to talk about (Behrend, Scofield, & Kleinknecht, 2001). At about age 3, children demonstrate the **mutual exclusivity assumption** in learning new words: They assume that objects have only one label or name. According to mutual exclusivity, a new word is assumed to be a label for an unfamiliar object, not a synonym or second label for a familiar object (Littschwager & Markman, 1994; Markman, 1987, 1990). In one study, young children were shown one familiar object and one unfamiliar object. They were told, "Show me the X" where X is a nonsense syllable. The children reached for the unfamiliar object, suggesting that they expect new words to label new objects rather than acting as synonyms (Markman & Wachtel, 1988). Similarly, young children use the mutual exclusivity assumption to learn the names of parts of objects, such as the brim of a hat, the cab of a truck, or a bird's beak (Hansen & Markman, 2009).

By 5 years of age, many children can quickly understand and apply most words that they hear. If a word is used in context or explained with examples, most 5-year-olds can learn it. Preschoolers learn words by making inferences given the context—and inferential learning is associated with better retention than learning by direct instruction (Zosh, Brinster, & Halberda, 2013).

Certain classes of words are challenging for young children. For example, they have difficulty understanding that words that express comparisons—tall and short, or high and low—are relative in nature and are used in comparing one object to another. Thus, the context defines their meaning, such that calling an object tall is often meant in relation to another object that is short. Children may erroneously interpret *tall* as referring to all tall things, and therefore they miss the relative nature of the term (Ryalls, 2000). Children also have difficulty with words that express relative place and time, such as *here, there, now, yesterday,* and *tomorrow.* Despite these errors, children make great advances in vocabulary, learning thousands of words each year.

Interestingly, bilingual children use these same strategies in learning words (Van Horn & Kan, 2015). They also show similar rates of word learning for words learned in their first and second languages (Kan & Kohnert, 2008, 2011). Learning a second language is discussed later in this chapter.

logical extension A strategy children use to increase their vocabulary in which they extend a new word to other objects in the same category.

mutual exclusivity assumption When learning new words, young children assume that objects have only one label or name.

Syntax

Day by day, young children learn to combine words into sentences in increasingly sophisticated ways and show growth in morphology and syntax (MacWhinney et al., 2015). Three-year-old children tend to use plurals, possessives, and past tense (Park, Yelland, Taffe, & Gray, 2012). They also tend to understand the use of pronouns such as *I, you,* and *we.*

Similar to telegraphic speech, their sentences are short, leaving out words like *a* and *the*. However, their speech is more sophisticated than telegraphic speech because some pronouns, adjectives, and prepositions are included.

Four- and 5-year-olds use four- to five-word sentences and can express declarative, interrogative, and imperative sentences (Turnbull & Justice, 2016). Context influences the acquisition of syntax. Four-year-old children will use more complex sentences with multiple clauses, such as "I'm resting because I'm tired," if their parents use such sentences (Huttenlocher, Vasilyeva, Cymerman, & Levine, 2002). Parental conversations and support for language learning are associated with faster and more correct language use (Barrett, 1999). Children often use run-on sentences, in which ideas and sentences are strung together.

"See? I goed on the slide!" called out Leona. **Overregularization errors** such as Leona's are very common in young children. They occur because young children are still learning exceptions to grammatical rules. Overregularization errors are grammatical mistakes that young children make because they are applying grammatical rules too stringently. For example, to create a plural noun, the rule is to add *s* to the word. However, there are many exceptions to this rule. Overregularization is expressed when children refer to *foots, gooses, tooths,* and *mouses,* which illustrates that the child understands and is applying the rules. Adult speakers find this usage awkward, but it is actually a sign of the child's increasing grammatical sophistication. And despite all of the common errors young children make, one study of 3-year-olds showed that nearly three-quarters of their utterances were grammatically correct. The most common error was in making tenses (e.g., eat/eated, fall/falled; Eisenberg, Guo, & Germezia, 2012). By the end of the preschool years, most children use grammar rules appropriately and confidently (Tager-Flusberg, 2001).

Private Speech

As Leroy played alone in the corner of the living room, he pretended to drive his toy car up a mountain and said to himself, "It's a high mountain. Got to push it all the way up. Oh no! Out of gas. Now they will have to stay here." Young children like Leroy often talk aloud to themselves, with no apparent intent to communicate with others. This self-talk, called **private speech**, accounts for 20% to 50% of the utterances of children ages 4 to 10 (Berk, 1986).

Piaget and Vygostky offer different views on the significance of private speech in relation to language development. According to Piaget, private speech is a result of cognitive development and is indicative of cognitive immaturity. He posited that children's self-talk, which he called *egocentric speech*, is meaningless, not addressed to anyone, not modified so that a listener can understand it, and simply reflects the egocentrism of the preoperational stage. More recent research, however, suggests that although children's speech is sometimes egocentric, often it is not. Two-year-old children can generate speech relevant to what someone else has said, but they have difficulty remaining on one conversational topic (Owens, 2015). By 3 years of age, most children pay attention to how their speech affects others. If they are not understood, they attempt to explain themselves more clearly. Four-year-old children, especially girls, will use simpler language when speaking to 2-year-old children, suggesting that they can take others' perspectives (Gelman & Shatz, 1978). By 5 years of age, about half of children can stick to a conversational topic for a dozen turns. Thus, research suggests that children's speech is less egocentric that Piaget posited.

Instead, it appears that private speech serves developmental functions. Private speech is thinking; it is personal speech that guides behavior and fosters new ideas (Vygotsky & Minick, 1987). It may be useful to think of private speech is a type of scaffold that children provide for themselves by talking out loud (Mercer, 2008). Children plan, explain events and activities, and review their knowledge by themselves. As children grow older their

overregularization errors Grammatical mistakes that children make because they apply grammatical rules too stringently to words that are exceptions.

private speech Self-directed speech that children use to guide their behavior.

private speech becomes a whisper or a silent moving of the lips (Manfra & Winsler, 2006). Private speech is the child's thinking and eventually becomes internalized as *inner speech*, or word-based internal thought, representing the child's transition to verbal reasoning.

Private speech plays a role in **self-regulation**, which refers to the ability to control one's impulses and appropriately direct behavior; this increases during the preschool years (Berk & Garvin, 1984). Children are more likely to use private speech while working on challenging tasks and attempting to solve problems, especially when they encounter obstacles or do not have adult supervision (Berk, 1992; Berk & Garvin, 1984; Winsler, Fernyhough, & Montero, 2009). In other words, children use private speech to plan strategies, solve problems, and regulate themselves so that they can achieve goals. Children who use private speech during a challenging activity are more attentive and involved and show better performance than children who do not (Alarcón-Rubio, Sánchez-Medina, & Prieto-García, 2014; Behrend, Rosengren, & Perlmetter, 1989; Berk & Spuhl, 1995; Winsler, Diaz, & Montero, 1997). Preschoolers who are aware of their own private speech are better at using language to communicate their needs, use more private speech, and display more understanding of deception than those who are less aware of their use of private speech (Manfra & Winsler, 2006).

As children grow older, they use private speech more effectively to accomplish tasks. Gradually its occurrence declines, becoming a whisper and eventually an entirely internal dialogue not audible or visible to others (Duncan & Pratt, 1997; Patrick & Abravanel, 2000; Winsler, Carlton, & Barry, 2000). Thus, in actuality, private speech never completely disappears. It becomes internalized as inner speech, a silent internal dialogue that individuals use every day to regulate and organize behavior (Al-Namlah, Meins, & Fernyhough, 2012; Berk, 1986; Fernyhough, 2008).

However, there is some evidence that private speech may not be as private as suggested. That is, private speech often occurs in the presence of others. When children ages 2½ to 5 years completed a challenging task either in the presence of an experimenter who sat a few feet behind the child, not interacting, or alone, the children engaged in more private speech in the presence of a listener than they did when alone (McGonigle-Chalmers, Slater, & Smith, 2014). This suggests that private speech may have social value and may not be simply a tool for self-regulation.

Though Vygotsky considered the use of private speech a universal developmental milestone, further research suggests that there are individual differences, with some children using private speech little or not at all (Berk, 1992). Preschool girls tend to use more mature forms of private speech than boys; the same is true of middle-income children as compared with low-income children (Berk, 1986). This pattern corresponds to the children's relative abilities in language use. Talkative children use more private speech than do quiet children (McGonigle-Chalmers et al., 2014). Bright children tend to use private speech earlier, and children with learning disabilities tend to continue its use later in development (Berk, 1992). One of the educational implications of private speech is that parents and teachers must understand that talking to oneself or inaudible muttering is not misbehavior but, rather, indicates an effort to complete a difficult task or self-regulate behavior.

Finally, young children's transition from audible private speech to internalization accompanies advances in theory of mind. As mentioned in Chapter 7, theory of mind means that young children have developed an awareness of how the mind works and are better able to consider other people's perspectives, which helps them become more effective in communicating their ideas (de Villiers & de Villiers, 2014). They also show advances in pragmatics—understanding of the social rules of language. Young children become better at conversation, with improvements in listening, turn-taking, explaining thoughts, and sticking to a topic. They learn social rules such as when to say "please" and "thank you," and they become aware that they must adapt their speech in light of their audience and the situation. Examples include 4-year-old children modifying their speech and using shorter sentences when speaking with 2-year-olds and using more

self-regulation The ability to control one's impulses and appropriately direct behavior.

formal and polite language with adults as compared with same-aged peers (Shatz & Gelman, 1973). These subtleties of language continue to improve throughout middle and late childhood.

LANGUAGE DEVELOPMENT IN SCHOOL-AGE CHILDREN AND ADOLESCENTS

Older children become increasingly aware of and knowledgeable about the nature and qualities of language, known as *metalinguistic awareness* (Gombert, 1992). Language arts classes in elementary school teach children about the parts of language and the syntax of sentences, aiding children as they further develop their ability to think about their use of language. At this point, children can analyze the grammatical acceptability of their utter-

Advances in metalinguistic awareness enable children to judge and correct their own language skills.

ances rather than simply viewing language as a means for communication. By 8 years of age, children make fewer semantic errors and spontaneously self-correct many of their errors (Hanley, Cortis, Budd, & Nozari, 2016). At about age 7 or 8, as children become able to consider multiple aspects of a situation, they are able to consider the grammatical correctness of a sentence apart from the semantics (Owens, 2015). Before this, preschoolers tend to make judgments of an utterance's acceptability based on semantics rather than grammatical structure.

Although school-age children's increases in vocabulary are not as noticeable to parents as compared with the changes that occurred in infancy and early childhood, 6-year-old children have large vocabularies that expand to four times their size by the end of the elementary school years (about 40,000 words) and six times by the end of formal schooling (Bloom, 2000). Older children learn words using the same strategies as younger children, such as by using contextual cues (Nagy & Scott, 2000). They also learn new words by comparing complex words with simpler words. For example, they understand the meaning of the word *sadness* by considering the root word, *sad* (Anglin, 1993).

Children learn that there are many words that can describe a given action, but the words often differ slightly in meaning (e.g., *walk, stride, hike, march, tread, strut,* and *meander*; Hoff, 2014). They become more selective in their use of words, choosing the right word to meet their needs. As their vocabularies grow, children learn that some words can have more than one meaning, such as *run* ("The jogger runs down the street," "The clock runs fast," and so on). They begin to appreciate that some words have psychological meanings as well as physical ones (e.g., a person can be smooth and a surface may be smooth). This understanding that words can be used in more than one way leads 8- to 10-year-old children to understand similes and metaphors (e.g., a person can be described as "cold as ice" or "sharp as a tack"; Nippold, Taylor, & Baker, 1996; Winner, 1988).

Everyday experiences shape our vocabulary, how we think, and how we speak. Words are often acquired incidentally from uses in writing and verbal contexts rather than through explicit vocabulary instruction (Best, Dockrell, & Braisby, 2006). Some words, such as scientific terms, are conceptually complex and require acquisition of deep conceptual knowledge, such as an understanding of physical processes, over repeated exposure in different contexts. One study examined 4- to 10-year-old children's knowledge of two scientific terms, *eclipse* and *comet*, before and after the natural occurrence of a solar eclipse. Two weeks after the solar eclipse and without additional instruction, the children showed improvement in their knowledge of eclipses but not comets; older and younger children did not differ in their knowledge (Best et al., 2006).

In middle childhood, children become better able to understand complex grammatical structures. They begin to use the passive voice ("The dog is being fed"), complex constructions such as the use of the auxiliary *have* ("I have already fed the dog"), and conditional sentences ("If I had been home earlier I would have fed the dog"; Chomsky, 1969; Horgan, 1978; Pinker, Lebeaux, & Frost, 1987). Despite these advances, school-age children often have difficulty understanding spoken sentences whose meaning depends on subtle shifts in intonation (Turnbull & Justice, 2016). An example can be found in the sentence, "John gave a lollipop to David and he gave one to Bob." With the emphasis placed on "and," the sentence means that John gave a lollipop to both David and Bob, whereas if the emphasis is on "he," the sentence means that John gave a lollipop to David and David gave a lollipop to Bob.

Experience with language and exposure to complex constructions influence grammatical development. For example, most English-speaking children find passive voice sentences (such as *The boy was struck by the car*) difficult to understand and therefore master passive voice sentences much later than other structures. (Horgan, 1978; Owens, 2015). In contrast, the Inuit children of Arctic Canada hear and speak the Inuktitut language, which emphasizes full passives; they produce passive voice sentences in their language sooner than do children from other cultures (Allen & Crago, 1996). The culture and language systems in which children are immersed influence their use of language and, ultimately, the ways in which they communicate. Throughout middle childhood, sentence structure and use of grammar becomes more sophisticated, children become better at communicating their ideas, and they their understanding of pragmatics improves.

Recall from earlier in this chapter, pragmatics refers to the practical application of language to communicate. With age and advances in perspective-taking skills that come with cognitive development, children are more likely to change their speech in response to the needs of listeners. They are also able to succeed at challenging tasks such as precisely describing differences within a group of similar objects, and to modify their communication in light of the audience to achieve their goals (Deutsch & Pechmann, 1982). For example, when faced with an adult who will not give the child a desired toy, 9-year-old children are more polite in restating their request than are 5-year-old children (Axia & Baroni, 1985). Children speak to adults differently than to other children, and they speak differently on the playground than in class or at home. In addition, older children begin to understand that there is often a distinction between what people say and what they mean.

One example of pragmatics that develops is the use of irony. Many contextual, linguistic, and developmental factors influence the processing and comprehension of irony, such as the ability to interpret intonation and facial expressions as well as the capacity to evaluate how well a statement matches the situation (Colston, 2002; Pexman, Glenwright, Hala, Kowbel, & Jungen, 2006). Children at the ages of 5 to 6 become capable of recognizing irony when they are able to understand that a speaker might believe something different from what has been said. Yet most tend to interpret irony as sincere, relying on the person's statement and disregarding other cues in the story, such as intonation and gestures (Creusere, 2000; Demorest, Meyer, Phelps, Gardner, & Winner, 1984; Harris & Pexman, 2003). Cognitive development permits children to detect the discrepancy between what the speaker says and what he or she believes, and their ability to understand ironic remarks continues to develop through middle childhood, improving rapidly between ages 5 and 8 (Hancock, Dunham, & Purdy, 2000). By 9 years of age children are able to identify and interpret inconsistencies between ironic utterances and contextual facts but are not fully aware of the intentional use of irony (Demorest et al., 1984). However, even in adolescence the understanding of irony is still developing; children as old as 13 do not reliably distinguish irony from deception (Filippova & Astington, 2008).

Adolescents continue to learn new words and become increasingly sophisticated in their use. Advances in abstract reasoning, as discussed in Chapter 6, mean that adolescents become better able to understand and use metaphor, sarcasm, and irony.

Lives in Context Video 9.1
Children's Understanding of Language

CULTURAL INFLUENCES ON DEVELOPMENT

•• Dialects

So called "Yoopers," inhabitants of the Upper Peninsula of Michigan, are known for a distinct dialect that includes replacing the "-ing" at the end of certain words with "-een" (doing becomes "do-een", happening becomes "happen-een", something becomes "some-theen").

Is there a standard American English dialect? The form of American English used on network newscasts and in newspapers and textbooks is an idealized version of English that occurs rarely in conversation. Some people refer to General American English as lacking any distinctly regional, ethnic, or socioeconomic characteristics (Kövecses, 2000), yet given that we are all immersed in context, we all naturally speak a dialect of some kind.

As shown in Figure 9.2, there are at least 10 regional dialects in the United States, each with distinct phonologies and speech patterns. Generally there are more dialect variations in the eastern part of the country, decreasing to the west, mirroring the settlement of the United States (Owens, 2015). The western United States was settled more recently than other regions of the country; thus, the western dialect area remains relatively undefined (Turnbull & Justice, 2016).

Although each geographic area in the United States is marked by a dominant dialect, there

FIGURE 9.2: Major American Geographic Dialects

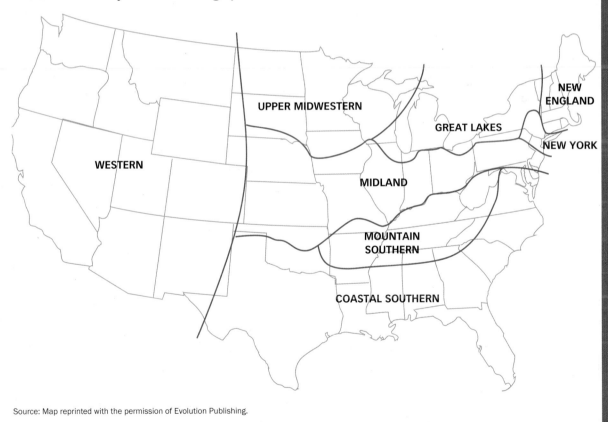

Source: Map reprinted with the permission of Evolution Publishing.

(Continued)

(Continued)

are also variations within each region that are influenced by contextual factors such as ethnicity, geography, and socioeconomic status (SES). Children raised by parents who have attained relatively high levels of education and live in high-SES homes tend to adopt more mainstream styles of speaking as compared with regional dialects. The major ethnic dialects in the United States are Asian English, African American English, and Spanish-influenced or Latino English (Owens, 2015).

There are also differences within these dialects, often influenced by geography. For example, subtle variations in Spanish-influenced dialects may differ depending on the speakers' countries of origin—whether they are from Argentina or Puerto Rico, for example. The Spanish-influenced dialect spoken in Southern California may show subtle differences from those spoken in New York or South Florida. From this you can see that, whether you live in the United States or elsewhere, your geographic and cultural

context influences your speech. The dialect we each speak is reflected in the sound patterns we use, word choices, and sayings. For example, what do you call a soft drink? Your response will likely vary with your geographic location and dialect. Most people from the Northeast U.S. refer to sweetened carbonated beverages as *soda* whereas *pop* is more common in the Midwest and *coke* is popular in many Southern states (Hamblin, 2013).

What Do You Think?

1. **What dialects are most often depicted in television shows and movies? How might dialects by writers and directors to portray a character's context and background?**

2. **Does your speech reflect a dialect? Why or why not?**

They understand that words can have multiple meanings, depending on context: For example, *wired* can refer to technology that uses wires, to the figurative connection between entities (e.g., we say our brains are wired for language, but we don't literally have wires inside our brains), or to a state of nervousness or edginess due to overcaffeination. Adolescents also they become adept at using slang.

Perhaps one of the most obvious indicators of the influence of context in our language development is the presence of *dialects*, subtle geographical variations in vocabulary, grammar, and language use. An *accent* refers to the pronunciation, or phonology, aspect of a dialect. Everyone speaks a dialect, whether we realize it or not. Dialects are discussed in the Cultural Influences on Development feature.

LANGUAGE DEVELOPMENT DURING ADULTHOOD

Language development continues from adolescence into adulthood, but the changes are subtle and often go unnoticed. Throughout life, healthy adults continue to add new words to their vocabulary, an example of the increases in crystallized intelligence that occur into older adulthood. Researchers generally agree that the average healthy older adult does not suffer significant losses in the ability to use language effectively (Hoyte, Brownell, & Wingfield, 2009).

The basic ability to carry on a conversation remains intact throughout later life. Changes in sensory and cognitive processing, however, can affect language comprehension and production. Hearing loss can make it more difficult to hear all of the words spoken in a conversation, so that listeners must work hard to make sense of what other people are saying (Janse, 2009). Hearing deficits may lead older adults to miss critical pieces of information, such that they have difficulty effectively participating in conversations. Yet older adults also have a rich backlog of experiences from which to draw when they listen, enabling them to compensate for impaired hearing. Even if they are unable to hear each word, they are often able to derive the meaning of the collective words used in a straightforward conversation (Stewart & Wingfield, 2009). In addition, experience can compensate for reductions in processing speed. For example, after watching a particular soap opera for many years, an adult can often anticipate and understand what the characters are saying as well as the content of interactions even without hearing every spoken word (Stine-Morrow, Soederberg Miller, Gagne, & Hertzog, 2008).

Most older adults experience some deficits, primarily in the accuracy and speed of word retrieval and naming (Owens, 2015). The most common language-related deficit older adults report is difficulty recalling specific words while in conversation (Ossher, Flegal, & Lustig, 2013). For example, older adults are more prone to the *"tip-of-the-tongue" phenomenon*, in which one temporarily cannot recall a specific word but can recall words with similar meaning (Brown, 1991; Brown & McNeill, 1966). Older adults are, therefore, more likely than younger adults to use indefinite words, such as *thing*, in place of specific names. This is likely due to deficits in working memory and slower processing speed (Burke & Shafto, 2004; Mortensen, Meyer, & Humphreys, 2006; Salthouse & Madden, 2013).

Thinking in Context 9.3

1. Recall from Chapter 1 that lifespan development is characterized by continuities (slow, gradual changes) and discontinuities (sudden or abrupt changes). In what way might language exemplify continuous development? Can you identify an example in which an aspect of language development might be considered discontinuous?

2. Suppose that you are a first-grade teacher. How might you apply what we know about private speech to your students?

3. In your opinion, are the changes that occur with adult language development continuous with development in childhood and adolescence? Provide reasons to support your position.

PERSPECTIVES ON LANGUAGE DEVELOPMENT

LO 9.4 Distinguish among learning, nativist, and interactionist perspectives on language.

During the first 2 years of life, children transform from wailing newborns who communicate their needs through cries to toddlers who can use words to articulate their needs, desires, and thoughts. Developmental scientists have offered several explanations for infants' rapid acquisition of language. Some explanations emphasize the role of the environment in accounting for language, whereas others emphasize biological factors.

LEARNING THEORY AND LANGUAGE DEVELOPMENT

Baby Howie gurgles, "Babababa!" His parents encourage him excitedly, "Say bottle; ba-ba!" Howie squeals, "Babababa!" Parents play an important role in language development. They provide specific instruction and communicate excitement about their infants' developing competence, encouraging infants to practice new language skills. Learning theorist B. F. Skinner (1957) proposed that language, just like all other behaviors, is learned through operant conditioning: reinforcement and punishment.

From birth, infants make sounds at random. Caregivers respond to infants' early utterances with interest and attention, imitating and reinforcing their verbal behavior (Gratier & Devouche, 2011; Pelaez, Virues-Ortega, & Gewirtz, 2011). Infants repeat the sounds. Caregivers then reward sounds that resemble adult speech with attention, smiles, and affection. Infants imitate sounds that adults make and repeat sounds that are reinforced. From this perspective, imitation and reinforcement shape children's language development. The quantity and quality of the parents' verbal interactions with the child and responses to the child's communication attempts influence the child's rate of language development.

Infants and children learn by observing the world around them. Parents and caregivers offer important encouragement and reinforcement of infants' language learning. However, critics point out that learning theory cannot account for all of language development because it cannot account for the unique utterances and errors that young children make (Epstein, 1991). Word combinations are complex and varied—they cannot be acquired solely by imitation and reinforcement. Toddlers often put words together in ways that they likely have never heard (e.g., "Mommy milk"). Young children make grammatical errors, such as "mouses" instead of "mice" or "goed" instead of "went," that cannot be the result of imitation. If language is learned through imitation, how do young children make grammatical errors that they have never heard spoken? Young children repeat things that they hear (sometimes to parents' chagrin!), but they also construct new phrases and utterances that are unique. Reinforcement from parents and caregivers is powerful encouragement for children, but language development cannot be completely explained by learning theory alone. Despite wide variations in circumstances, living situations, and contexts, infants around the world achieve language milestones at about the same ages, suggesting a biological component to language development.

NATIVIST THEORY AND LANGUAGE DEVELOPMENT

Nativist theorist Noam Chomsky (1959, 1965) argued that language use comprises behavior that is too complex to be learned so early and quickly via conditioning alone. Chomsky noted that all young children grasp the essentials of **grammar**, the rules of language, at an early age, and that the languages of the world have many similarities. The human brain thus has an innate capacity to learn language. Specifically, Chomsky believed that infants are born with a **language acquisition device (LAD)**, an innate facilitator of language that permits infants to quickly and efficiently analyze everyday speech and determine its rules, regardless of whether their native language is English, German, Chinese, or Urdu. The LAD has an innate storehouse of rules that apply to all human languages that Chomsky (1965) referred to as **universal grammar**. When infants hear language spoken, they naturally notice its linguistic properties and they acquire the language.

The nativist perspective can account for children's unique utterances and the unusual grammatical mistakes they make in speaking because children are biologically primed to learn language and do not rely on learning. However, like learning theory, the nativist perspective offers an incomplete account of language development. Specifically, Chomsky's nativist perspective does not explain the process of language development and how it occurs (Miller, 2016). Researchers have not identified the language acquisition device or universal grammar that Chomsky thought underlies all languages (Tomasello, 2009). Moreover, language does not emerge in a finished form. Instead, children learn to string words together over time based on their experiences as well as trial and error (Tomasello, 2012). Language learning does not occur as quickly and requires more effort on the part of children than Chomsky described. Instead, language development is influenced by both nature and nurture—biology and learning. An interactionist perspective offers the most comprehensive perspective of language development by encompassing both biology and social interaction. Because of this, as described in the Lives in Context feature below,

Noam Chomsky (1928–) theorized that we are born with a language acquisition device with an innate storehouse of rules known as universal grammar.

grammar The rules of language.

language acquisition device (LAD) In Chomsky's theory, an innate facilitator of language that allows infants to quickly and efficiently analyze everyday speech and determine its rules, regardless of their native language.

universal grammar In Chomsky's theory, rules that apply to all human languages.

many children who are adopted from other countries experience particular challenges in learning language.

INTERACTIONIST PERSPECTIVE ON LANGUAGE DEVELOPMENT

Language development is a complex process that is influenced by both maturation and context. A newborn's ability to discriminate a wide variety of speech sounds and to prefer human speech over recorded sounds—as well as to prefer their native-language sounds and patterns over those of other languages—suggests an inborn sensitivity to language (Posner, 2001). Yet the language that an infant learns and the pace of learning is influenced by environmental factors. From an interactionist perspective, language development occurs through the interaction of two factors: children's biological capacities and the social context in which children are reared. Let's explore each of these factors.

Biological Contributions to Language Development

From an evolutionary perspective, language evolved as a function of natural selection as it gave some of our early human ancestors an advantage in survival and reproduction over those who did not have language (Hauser et al., 2014; Pinker & Bloom, 1990). Specifically, language evolved as an adaptation that fulfilled early humans' needs to communicate information that was more complex than could be conveyed by simple calls and hoots (Hoff, 2015). Language may have emerged with increases in the size of human communities and the corresponding complexity of social dynamics, and increasingly large, more sophisticated brains (Aiello & Dunbar, 1993; Turnbull & Justice, 2016).

The brain, specifically the left hemisphere, is wired for language at birth. Speech sounds produce more electrical activity in the left hemisphere of newborns' brains, while nonspeech sounds elicit more activity in the right hemisphere (Ghislaine Dehaene-Lambertz et al., 2006; Molfese, 1977). Adult language, too, is largely governed by the left hemisphere, but adults show greater left hemispheric specificity than infants. That is, studies of brain activation by speech show that lateralization for speech becomes stronger as children's language skills develop (Ghislaine Dehaene-Lambertz et al., 2006). By studying individuals who have suffered brain damage, scientists have learned about two areas in the left hemisphere of the brain that are vital for language: Broca's and Wernicke's areas (Price, Jarman, Mason, & Kind, 2011). **Broca's area** controls the ability to use language for expression. Damage to this area inhibits the ability to speak fluently, leading to errors in the production of language. **Wernicke's area** is responsible for language comprehension. Damage to Wernicke's area impairs the ability to understand the speech of others and sometimes affects the ability to speak coherently.

The brain plays a crucial role in language capacities throughout life. However, biological factors, though powerful, cannot completely account for language development. For example, infants' abilities to detect sounds not used in their native language decline throughout the first year of life, suggesting that contextual factors, specifically exposure to the native language, influences older infants' sensitivity to speech sounds (Posner, 2001; Sansavini, Bertoncini, & Giovanelli, 1997). At the same time, information-processing factors largely enhanced by neurological development, such as attention and memory, affect how infants comprehend and respond to social interaction and other contextual influences on language development.

Contextual Contributions to Language Development

Language development occurs in a social context. When babies begin to engage in **canonical babbling**, a type of babbling with well-formed syllables that sounds remarkably like language, parents, regardless of SES, ethnicity, and home environment, tune in and treat the vocalizations in a new way (Oller, Eilers, & Basinger, 2001). Because the utterances sound like words, parents help infants to associate the word-like utterances with objects and

Broca's area The region in the brain that controls the ability to use language for expression; damage to the area inhibits fluent speech.

Wernicke's area The region of the brain that is responsible for language comprehension; damage to this area impairs the ability to understand others' speech and sometimes the ability to speak coherently.

canonical babbling A type of babbling with well-formed syllables that sounds like language.

events, encouraging vocabulary development. In this way, infants are predisposed to learn language and reside in a social context that fosters language learning (Oller et al., 2001).

Parental responsiveness to infants' vocalizations predicts the size of infants' vocabularies, the diversity of infants' communications, and the timing of language milestones (Tamis-LeMonda et al., 2014). One study showed that infants of highly responsive mothers achieved language milestones such as first words, vocabulary spurt, and telegraphic speech at 9 to 13 months of age, which was 4 to 6 months earlier than infants of low-responsive mothers (Tamis-LeMonda, Bornstein, & Baumwell, 2001). Interactions with fathers are also important contributors to language development. Fathers' responsiveness to their 2- and 3-year-olds predicted toddlers' cognitive and language abilities (Tamis-LeMonda, Shannon, Cabrera, & Lamb, 2004). Parental responsiveness is also associated with the language skills of adopted children, supporting the contextual influence of parents (Stams, Juffer, & van IJzendoorn, 2002).

Though parents do not reliably reinforce correct grammar, they tend to communicate in ways that tell young children when they have made errors and show how to correct them (Saxton, 1997). Adults often respond to children's utterances with **expansions**, which are enriched versions of the children's statements. For example, if a child says, "bottle fall," the parent might respond "Yes, the bottle fell off the table." Adults also tend to **recast** children's sentences into new grammatical forms. For example, "Kitty go," might be recast into, "Where is the kitty going?" When children use grammatically correct statements, parents maintain and extend the conversation (Bohannon & Stanowicz, 1988). When adults recast and expand young children's speech, the children tend to acquire grammatical rules more quickly and score higher on tests of expressive language ability than when parents rely less on these conversational techniques (Abraham, Crais, & Vernon-Feagans, 2013; Bohannon, Padgett, Nelson, & Mark, 1996).

The interactionist perspective on language development points to the dynamic and reciprocal influence of biology and context. Infants are equipped with biological propensities and information processing capacities that permit them to perceive and analyze speech and learn to speak. Infants are motivated to communicate with others and language is a tool for communication. Interactions with others provide important learning experiences which help infants expand their language capacities and learn to think in ways similar to members of their culture (Fitneva & Matsui, 2015).

Theories of language development are summarized in Table 9.2.

expansion Adult response to children's speech that elaborates and enriches its complexity.

recast When an adult repeats a child's sentence back to him or her in a new grammatical form, helping the child to acquire grammatical rules more quickly.

TABLE 9.2 • Theories of Language Development

Learning Theory	• Language is learned through reinforcement, punishment, and imitation.
	• Caregivers reward sounds that resemble adult speech with attention, smiles, and affection. Infants imitate sounds that adults make and repeat sounds that are reinforced.
	• The quantity and quality of the parents' verbal interactions with the child and responses to the child's communication attempts influence the child's rate of language development.
	• Learning theory cannot account for the unique utterances and errors that young children make. Young children put words together in ways that they likely have never heard and make grammatical errors that cannot be the result of imitation and reinforcement.
Nativist Theory	• Despite wide variations in circumstances, living situations, and contexts, infants around the world achieve language milestones at similar ages.
	• Children are biologically primed to learn language and do not rely on learning.
	• An inborn "language acquisition device," equipped with universal grammar, permits infants to quickly and efficiently analyze everyday speech and determine its rules. When infants hear language spoken, they naturally notice its linguistic properties and acquire the language.
	• Researchers have not identified the "language acquisition device," or universal grammar, thought to underlie all languages.
	• Language does not emerge in a finished form. Instead, children learn to string words together over time based on their experiences plus trial and error.

Interactionist Theory	• Language development is a complex process influenced by both maturation and context.
	• Infants have an inborn sensitivity to language and discriminate a wide variety of speech sounds including those that adults can no longer distinguish.
	• The left hemisphere of the brain, including the Broca's and Wernicke's areas, is wired for language at birth.
	• Exposure to language influences infants' sensitivity to speech sounds; the ability to detect sounds not used in their native languages declines throughout the first year of life.
	• Language development occurs in a social context. Babies learn language by interacting with more mature, expert speakers who can speak at their developmental level.
	• Parents respond to children's utterances with expansions and recasting children's sentences into new grammatical forms.

Thinking in Context 9.4

1. Consider the language development of a child—your own child, a sibling or other family member, or a friend's child. What aspects of language seem to be maturational or biologically influenced? For example, what aspects seem to unfold naturally? What, in contrast, reflects learning through interactions with others? Consider the interactionist perspective and provide one or two additional examples that might illustrate this perspective.

2. Apply the interactionist perspective to describe language development after infancy. What factors promote language development in childhood and adolescence?

3. In your opinion, what value do these theories have in explaining language development in adulthood? Provide reasons to support your response.

CONTEXTUAL INFLUENCES ON LANGUAGE DEVELOPMENT

LO 9.5 Discuss cultural and contextual influences on language development.

As with all domains of development, the contexts in which infants and children are immersed influence their developing capacities for language. Interactions with adults, particularly parents, are a primary influence on language development and there are individual differences in the quality of parent-child interactions.

INFANT-DIRECTED SPEECH

Most adults naturally speak to infants in a sing-song way that attracts their attention. **Infant-directed speech,** or "**motherese**," uses repetition, short words and sentences, high and varied pitch, and long pauses (Thiessen, Hill, & Saffran, 2005). Despite these variations, infant-directed speech itself is not necessarily slower than adult-directed speech (Martin, Igarashi, Jincho, & Mazuka, 2016). In one study, it was shown that pre-verbal infants prefer listening to infant-directed speech compared to typical adult speech (Fernald & McRoberts, 1996). Another demonstrated that infant-directed speech influences social preferences: Infants prefer adults who use it (Schachner & Hannon, 2011). Infant-directed speech appears to facilitate language development by making sounds more exaggerated, helping infants hear and distinguish the different sounds, as well as enabling them to map sounds to meanings (Burnham, Kitamura, & Vollmer-Conna, 2002; Estes, 2013; Kitamura & Burnham, 2003; Thiessen et al., 2005). It also exaggerates lip movements, helping infants to distinguish such movements relevant to speech (Green, Nip, Wilson, Mefferd, & Yunusova, 2010). EEG recordings show that babies demonstrate more neural activity in response to infant-directed speech than adult speech, suggesting

infant-directed speech (motherese) Uses shorter words and sentences, higher and more varied pitch, repetitions, a slower rate, and longer pauses.

that they are better able to attend to it and distinguish the sounds (Peter, Kalashnikova, Santos, & Burnham, 2016). It teaches babies how to take turns talking, models how to carry on a conversation, and helps babies learn to respond to emotional cues and link word meanings with familiar things. In one study, 7- and 8-month-old infants were more likely to learn words presented by infant-directed speech than those presented through adult-directed speech (Fernald, Marchman, & Weisleder, 2013; Singh, Nestor, Parikh, & Yull, 2009). Even as infants learn speech, they continue to display preference for some features of infant-directed speech. A study of 12- and 16-month-old infants indicated that they preferred the high pitch and pitch variability of infant-directed speech, but not the shorter utterances or simplified syntax (Segal & Newman, 2015).

Babies learn language by interacting with more mature, expert speakers who can speak at their developmental level. Parents often adjust their infant-directed speech to match infants' linguistic needs. For example, parents use longer and more complicated words and sentences as infants' comprehension increases (Englund & Behne, 2006; Sundberg, 1998). In this way, parents naturally scaffold children's language development (recall Vygotsky's sociocultural perspective, described in Chapter 6). The quality of language input from parents and the number of words children hear is related to their vocabulary size at age 2 (Hoff & Naigles, 2002). Children whose mothers address a great deal of speech to them develop vocabulary more rapidly, are faster at processing words they know, and faster at producing speech than children whose mothers speak to them less often (Hurtado, Marchman, & Fernald, 2008; Weisleder & Fernald, 2013). The number of words and different grammatical structures used in maternal speech, as well as grammatical complexity, predict the size of children's vocabulary and understanding of grammar (Hadley, Rispoli, Fitzgerald, & Bahnsen, 2011; Huttenlocher, Waterfall, Vasilyeva, Vevea, & Hedges, 2010).

Infant-directed speech has been documented in many languages and cultures (Bryant, 2012; Kuhl et al., 1997). Comparisons of mothers from Fiji, Kenya, and the United States show the use of high-pitched speech, which is characteristic of infant-directed speech, with infants (Broesch & Bryant, 2015). The pattern of infant-directed speech is similar across cultures such that adults can discriminate it from adult-directed speech even while listening to a language they do not speak. For example, when adults in the Turkana region of northwestern Kenya listened to speech produced in English by American mothers, they were able to discriminate between infant-directed and adult-directed speech, suggesting that infant-directed speech is recognizable to adults of many cultures (Bryant, 2012). Despite this, adults of different cultures vary in their interactions with infants.

Language development poses a special challenge for children who are adopted internationally and raised in a country where a language other than their native language is spoken. Lives in Context examines this challenge for internationally adopted children who were housed in substandard orphanages before being adopted.

CULTURE AND LANGUAGE DEVELOPMENT

Culture also shapes language development. Parents from different cultures vary in how often they respond to their infants; however, parental response patterns that are warm, consistent, and contingent on infant actions are associated with positive language development in infants across cultures (Tamis-LeMonda et al., 2014). For example, in a study of six cultural communities, mothers from Berlin and Los Angeles were more likely to respond to infant nondistress vocalizations and gazes than were mothers from Beijing and Delhi, as well as Nso mothers from various cities in Cameroon (Kärtner et al., 2008). In contrast, Nso mothers responded more often to infant touch than did mothers from other cultures. Although parental responsiveness may look different and take different forms across cultures, its benefits generalize across families from varying cultural communities and socioeconomic strata (Rodriguez & Tamis-LeMonda, 2011).

Cultures differ in the use of infant-directed speech. For example, in Samoa, infants are not addressed directly by caregivers until they begin to crawl. Parents tend to interpret their

• • Development in Internationally Adopted Children

Many internationally adopted children experience speech and language delays. Younger children tend to adapt to a new language more quickly but over time most children reach age-expected language levels.

In the three decades since the mid-1980s, international adoption has become commonplace. After the dissolution of the Soviet Union in 1990, the media drew attention to the large number of children who lived in orphanages in substandard conditions—without adequate food, clothing, or shelter and with poorly trained caregivers. Such orphanages have been found in a number of countries, including China, Ethiopia, Ukraine, Congo, and Haiti, accounting for more than two-thirds of internationally adopted children (U.S. Department of State, 2014).

Underfunded and understaffed orphanages often provide poor, nonnurturing care for children, increasing the risks for malnutrition, infections, and physical and mental handicaps and delays. With infant-to-caregiver ratios ranging from 10 to 60 infants per adult (Mason & Narad, 2005), children available for adoption often spend a significant amount of time deprived of consistent human contact. Observations of infants and toddlers in a Russian orphanage revealed that they experienced few opportunities for interacting with caregivers. Most conversations tended to be caregiver to caregiver, even while feeding infants (Glennen, 2002). Toddlers were expected to feed themselves at the table without interaction from adults. Even when being held, children were faced outward, reducing opportunities for interaction with adults.

Few internationally adopted children from such orphanages enter the United States healthy and having reached age-appropriate developmental norms. Not surprisingly, the longer the children have been institutionalized, the more developmental challenges they face (Jacobs, Miller, & Tirella, 2010). Physical growth stunting is directly associated with the length of institutionalization, but catch-up growth is commonly seen after adoption (Wilson & Weaver, 2009). As with growth, the time spent in an orphanage predicts the degree of developmental delay. Longer institutionalization is associated with delays in development of language, fine motor skills, social skills, and attention and other cognitive skills (Mason & Narad, 2005; Wiik et al., 2011).

Speech and language delays are the most consistent deficiencies among internationally adopted children (Johnson, 2000). In one study, 60% of 2½-year-old children in a Russian orphanage lacked the ability to use language to express themselves (Glennen, 2002; Miller, 2000). One year later, only 14% used two-word utterances; at the ages of 3 to 4 the children had limited vocabulary, receptive language delays, and unintelligible speech phrases (Glennen, 2002). Other studies have demonstrated that 40% to 60% of children evaluated who were adopted from Eastern Europe and China showed language delays (Albers et al., 1997; Miller & Hendrie, 2000). More than half of internationally adopted children need the help of speech language pathologists (Pollack & Bechner, 2000).

The few available studies of the long-term prognosis for language development in internationally adopted children suggest that children can catch up from language delays if they are adopted at a young age (Frank, Vul, & Johnson, 2009; Mason & Narad, 2005). For example, Glennen and Masters (2002) noted an improvement in speech delay by 36 to 40 months of age; however, children adopted at older ages lagged in their language improvement. Generally, the younger a child is at adoption, the more quickly he or she will adapt to a new language and close any gaps in language delays (Glennen & Masters, 2002; Mason & Narad, 2005). More recent research suggests that in the presence of a high quality parent–child relationship, the age of adoption does not influence language, speech, or academic outcomes, and most children reach age-expected language levels (Glennen, 2014; Harwood, Feng, & Yu, 2013). Despite this, surveys of adoptive parents have revealed that one year following adoption, speech and language development is their top concern (Clauss & Baxter, 1997). Although there are individual differences in the degree of resilience and functioning across developmental domains, adopted children overall show great developmental gains and resilience in physical, cognitive, and emotional development (Misca, 2014; Palacios, Román, Moreno, León, & Peñarrubia, 2014; Wilson & Weaver, 2009).

What Do You Think?

1. How might learning theory, nativist theory, and interactionist theory account for the findings about children who lived in poor-quality orphanages before being adopted?

2. In your view, what are the most important challenges faced by internationally adopted children and their families? Identify sources and forms of support that might help such children and their parents.

Children reared in poverty experience contextual disadvantages that place them at risk for cognitive, academic, and social problems.

vocalizations as indicators of physiological state rather than as attempts to communicate. Because of the status hierarchy in Samoa, child-directed speech is uncommon in adults because it would reflect someone of higher status (i.e., an adult) adjusting their speech to someone of lower status (Ochs & Schieffein, 1984). Instead, older children are tasked with responding to infants' utterances, and it is largely older children who talk with infants (Lieven & Stoll, 2010). Similarly, the Kaluli of Papua New Guinea do not engage in infant-directed speech (Fitneva & Matsui, 2015). Infants are held oriented outward rather than toward the mother. When infants are addressed by others, the mother speaks for the infant in a high-pitched voice, but she does not use simplified language. Only when children themselves begin to talk do parents start talking to them, and then they focus on teaching them what to say (Ochs & Schieffein, 1984).

Culture even shapes the types of words that infants learn. In Asian cultures, such as those of Japan, China, and Korea that stress interpersonal harmony, children tend to acquire verbs and social words much more quickly than do North American toddlers (Gopnik & Choi, 1995; Tardif et al., 2008). In another study, U.S. mothers responded to infant object play more than social play, whereas Japanese mothers responded more to social play (Tamis-LeMonda, Bornstein, Cyphers, Toda, & Ogino, 1992). For example, North American infants' first words tend to include more referential language, or naming words such as "ball," "dog," "cup," and the like, while Japanese infants tend to use more expressive language, or words that are used mainly in social interaction, such as "please" and "want" (Fernald & Morikawa, 1993). Italian-, Spanish-, French-, Dutch-, Hebrew-, and English-speaking infants tend to display a preference for using more nouns than verbs (Bassano, 2000; Bornstein et al., 2004; de Houwer & Gillis, 1998; Maital, Dromi, Sagi, & Bornstein, 2000; Tardif, Shatz, & Naigles, 1997). Different cultures have different views of infants and communication, and sometimes provide strikingly different kinds of interactions and contexts for language learning; yet all infants learn language.

POVERTY AND LANGUAGE DEVELOPMENT

We have seen that individual and cultural differences in environmental support can influence children's outcomes in language development. SES is another factor that is associated with dramatic differences in language development. Young children living in the United States are disproportionately likely to live in poverty, with 25% of all children under the age of 6 residing in poverty and an additional 23% raised in near poverty (defined as having a household income at or beneath 200% of the federal poverty level; Jiang, Ekono, & Skinner, 2015). Children from persistently poor families are at risk of malnutrition, growth stunting, and deficits in cognitive and language development (Hanson et al., 2013; Votruba-Drzal, Miller, & Coley, 2016). Children raised in poor and low-SES households tend to know fewer words, use a smaller variety of words, produce shorter utterances, and demonstrate less developed syntax than their peers raised in more advantaged homes (Fernald et al., 2013; Hoff, 2015). Family income levels within the first 4 to 5 years of life predict verbal and achievement outcomes in elementary school and beyond (Klebanov, Brooks-Gunn, McCarton, & McCormick, 1998; Ryan, Fauth, & Brooks-Gunn, 2006).

Poverty is thought to influence language development in several ways. The first is through exposure to speech. In a classic study, Hart and Risley (1995) followed the children of 42 families of varying SES for 2½ years (from ages 7–9 months to 36 months). They observed the families at home each month for one hour. By age 3, the children from high-SES families had about twice the vocabulary as those from low-SES families. Hart and Risley attributed the difference in vocabulary to the number of words that the children had been exposed to in the home. The authors concluded that over the course of a year, the high-SES children would have been exposed to about 11 million words and the low-SES children to about 3.2 million words. By age 4, the average lower-SES child would have been exposed to about 30 million fewer words than the upper-SES child. Particularly striking is that by age 9 to 10, the differences in language development among children raised in high- and low-SES homes was even larger, suggesting that early experiences with language can serve as a foundation for later word learning, making early deficits challenging to fix. A more recent study followed infants from higher- and lower-SES families from age 18 to 24 months (Fernald et al., 2013). As shown in Figure 9.3, significant disparities in vocabulary and language-processing efficiency were already evident at 18 months between infants from higher- and lower-SES families, and by 24 months there was a 6-month gap between the SES groups in processing skills crucial to language development.

The quality of parent–child interactions also influences children's language development. Children in higher-SES homes are talked to more and the speech they hear is often more complicated and supportive of language development than is the case in lower-SES homes (Fernald & Marchman, 2012; Hoff, 2003). Parent–child interaction is influenced by parents' emotional resources, which are often compromised by poverty (Conger & Donnellan, 2007). For example, economic insecurity is associated with maternal depression (Casey et al., 2004). Compared with higher-income parents, parents in low-SES households and with lower levels of education have been shown to be less responsive to their children's language, as well as less sensitive, engaged, and verbally stimulating in interactions with their infants and young children—and, in turn, tend to have children with poorer language skills (Hart & Risley, 1995; Hoff, 2003, 2015; Raviv, Kessenich, & Morrison, 2004). It is important to note, however, that there is variability within each SES group. That is, just as there are differences among low-SES families in the extent of parent–child interaction and the support that parents provide for language development, there is similar variability among parents in high-SES households (Hoff, 2015; Huttenlocher et al., 2010).

Poverty is also thought to affect children's outcomes indirectly by contributing to household chaos, which refers to a combination of household instability and disorder (Bronfenbrenner & Evans, 2000). Children reared in economic uncertainty are more likely to experience disruptions in relationships and home settings, caused by household moves, adults moving in and out of the home, and changes in authority figures (Pascoe, Wood, Duffee, & Kuo, 2016), as well as disorder, such as household crowding, lack of structure, and excessive ambient noise in the home or neighborhood (Evans & Kim, 2013; Sameroff, 2010). Such chaos may influence children's cognitive and language development by overwhelming them with too much stimulation (Matheny, Wachs, Ludwig, & Phillips, 1995). Children may cope with overstimulation by withdrawing. For example, in a home with excessive background noise and many people going in and out of the house, a young child may find it difficult to process language because of the many distractions. Rather than try to persist and concentrate on the language directed toward the child, the child might turn away and avert their eyes from the overstimulation, perhaps playing alone or engaging in an activity that blocks out the stimulation, such as pounding a hammer or singing. The child's withdrawal, an adaptation to a challenging environment, prohibits engaging in parent–child interactions that promote language development. Research has shown that exposure to chronic noise in the neighborhood and residential crowding are negatively related to preschool children's language development, even after controlling for SES and other influences such as maternal education and depression (Evans, 2006; Maxwell & Evans, 2000; Vernon-Feagans, Garrett-Peters, Willoughby, & Mills-Koonce, 2012).

FIGURE 9.3: Mean Number of Spoken Words Reported on the MacArthur/Bates CDI by Age and SES (HI)

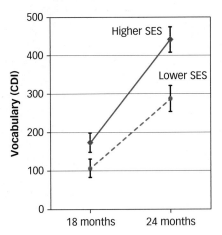

Source: Fernald, Marchman & Weisleder (2013).

Children learn second languages through formal education as well as mere exposure.

The Washington Post/The Washington Post/Getty Images

BILINGUALISM AND LEARNING A SECOND LANGUAGE

It is estimated that more than 50% of the world's children are exposed to more than one language (Grosjean, 2010). Researchers have explored many questions related to what transpires when a child learns two or more languages, whether at the same time or one after another.

Simultaneous Bilingualism

Infants can simultaneously learn two languages. Children who are exposed to two languages from birth are referred to as *simultaneous bilinguals,* or *bilingual first-language learners* (Genesee, 2006). Although early research suggested that children exposed to two languages experienced confusion and only gradually realized that they were hearing and using two different languages (Volterra & Taeschner, 1978), current research instead suggests that infants who are exposed to two languages build distinct language systems from birth (MacWhinney et al., 2015).

Sometimes it takes infants longer to learn the different phonics of two languages than it would to learn just one, but by the time they are 1 year old, bilingual babies show understanding of the phonetic categories for both languages (Hoff, 2015). The speed of this process is influenced by the degree to which the two languages differ, how often the child hears each language, and how clearly the speakers enunciate speech sounds (Petitto et al., 2012; Werker, 2012). As bilingual infants begin to speak, they use different phonological sounds for each language and generally use accurate speech sounds for each language (Fabiano-Smith & Goldstein, 2010; Lin & Johnson, 2010).

Typically, bilingual children have words in both languages for the same thing; for example, they might say "all done" in English and "*pau*" in Hawaiian. In contrast, monolingual children tend to avoid learning synonyms for words (Littschwager & Markman, 1994). This difference suggests that bilingual children are aware that the words are part of two separate language systems (Hoff 2015). Bilingual children do not appear to mix the grammatical rules for the two languages. For example, bilingual children learning French and German do not incorrectly use German words with French syntax or vice versa (Meisel, 1989). Moreover, bilingual children tend to select the appropriate language to use with other speakers, suggesting that they are aware that they know two languages (Genesee & Nicoladis, 2007).

The course of language development is similar for each language the bilingual child learns. The pattern of vocabulary and grammatical development in each language tends to follow the developmental course for each language (Conboy & Thal, 2006; Parra, Hoff, & Core, 2011). The pace of simultaneous language learning, however, is not the same as learning one language. Similar to acquiring one language, the rate of acquisition for two languages depends on the quantity and quality of the input in each language (Hoff & Core, 2015). Frequently bilingual children hear one language spoken more than another; in their dominant language they may seem similar to monolingual children in terms of development. But because children who hear two languages will tend to hear less of either language than their monolingual peers, their rate of growth in each language tends to be slower than those who hear and acquire a single language. That is, a bilingual child may hear Spanish two-thirds of the time and English one-third of the time, whereas a child learning English hears English 100% of the time. Bilingual children, therefore, hear less of each language than monolingual children and tend to lag behind monolingual children in vocabulary and grammar in each language, when measured separately

(Hindman & Wasik, 2015; Hoff, Core, Place, & Rumiche, 2012). The gap in vocabulary between monolingual and bilingual children persists but narrows with age (Hoff, Rumiche, Burridge, Ribot, & Welsh, 2014). Likewise, a lag in grammatical development can be observed throughout the school years, but with continued and consistent exposure to two languages, bilingual children may catch up to monolingual peers by the age of 10 years (Gathercole & Thomas, 2009). It is important to note, however, that bilingual children acquire language at a similar rate as monolingual peers. As shown in Figure 9.4, the combined vocabularies for both languages are similar in size to the vocabulary of monolingual children; some research suggests that the total vocabulary growth in bilingual children may be greater than that of monolinguals (Bosch & Ramon-Casas, 2014; Hoff et al., 2014).

Advantages of Bilingualism

The ability to speak more than one language is associated with many cognitive skills. Individuals who have mastered two or more languages have higher scores on measures of memory, selective attention, analytical reasoning, concept formation, and cognitive flexibility (Bialystok, 2011, 2015; Kormi-Nouri et al., 2008). The process of learning two languages encourages a more complex understanding of language and an ability to reflect on it. Other research shows that bilingual children score higher on measures of executive function, particularly the ability to control attention and ignore misleading information, suggesting that the brains of bilingual children are different than those of monolingual children (Barac & Bialystok, 2012; Barac, Bialystok, Castro, & Sanchez, 2014; Bialystok, 2015). These effects emerge slowly over the course of several years; one study of 2nd- and 5th-grade students showed improvements over a 5-year span in tasks such as verbal fluency and executive control (Bialystok, Peets, & Moreno, 2014).

Moreover, when children are able to speak, read, and write in two languages, they are more cognitively and socially flexible and can participate in both cultures (Huang, 1995). At the same time, children who are bilingual show greater achievement in their native language than monolingual children; in one study, this was shown to be true whether the children's native languages were Spanish or English (Sheng, Bedore, Peña, & Fiestas, 2011).

Second Language Learning

More than 6,900 languages are spoken in the world (Simons & Fennig, 2017), but most are not used in school settings; (Tucker, 1998). In attending school, most of the world's children must learn in a foreign language. An estimated 350 languages, including 150 native North American languages, are spoken in U.S. homes (U.S. Bureau of the Census, 2015). About 22% of school-age children in the United States speak a language other than English at home; of these, about one-fourth struggle with English at school (Federal Interagency Forum on Child and Family Statistics, 2014). Although it was once thought that there was a critical period for learning a second language, we now know that people retain the capacity to acquire language throughout life (Hakuta, Bialystok, & Wiley, 2003). School-age children are especially well equipped to learn a second language because they have developed the necessary reasoning and communication skills, yet their brains are more plastic than those of adults.

An issue that is discussed in many countries is how best to teach second languages. In the United States, English as a Second Language (ESL) is most often taught to children

FIGURE 9.4: English Vocabulary Scores for Monolingually Developing Children and Total Vocabulary Scores (English+Spanish) for Bilingually Developing Children at 1;10, 2;1 and 2;6

Source: Hoff et al. (2012).

Lives in Context Video 9.2
Bilingual Education

• • Brain Lateralization and Language Development

© iStockPhoto.com/Skodadad

Are you a righty or a lefty? People usually show a strong preference for one hand over the other. The right hand is dominant for most infants and adults, suggesting that handedness is lateralized to the left hemisphere (Annett, 2002). Language is also processed asymmetrically in the brain. Infants and adults tend to show activity in their left hemisphere in response to language (Dehaene-Lambertz, 2017), especially in response to their native language as compared with nonnative language (Vannasing et al., 2016). Given that hand preference has been observed prenatally (Hepper, 2013), some researchers have begun to examine whether hand preference is an early indicator of hemispheric specialization and, thereby, language development. What is the relationship between handedness and language development? Does hand preference predict language development in infancy?

Although hand preferences have been observed in the womb, infants show individual differences. Some infants show consistent hand preferences across motor tasks and others show a more unstable pattern, switching hands often (Cochet, 2012; Kotwica, Ferre, & Michel, 2008). Infants who consistently prefer the right hand demonstrate greater left hemispheric specialization than those without a consistent hand preference (Nelson, Campbell, & Michel, 2015). One longitudinal study followed infants at monthly intervals from 6 to 14 months and again from 18 to 24 months, to examine the relationship of handedness and language development (Nelson, Campbell, & Michel, 2013). Although the infants did not differ on measures of cognition or general motor skills, infants who showed early preferences for their right hand also showed advanced language abilities at 2 months of age. A consistent right-hand preference during infancy suggests greater lateralization and activity in the left hemisphere, in regions long associated with language. It is important to note, however, that an early hand preference predicted *advanced* language skill, but children without a stable hand preference showed normative language development.

Why is having a consistent hand preference associated with advanced language acquisition? Perhaps infants who show a consistent hand preference are better at manipulating objects than those without a stable preference (Kotwica et al., 2008). Infants' skill in object manipulation is associated with cognition because it permits infants to examine objects in greater detail (Bruner, 1973). Fine motor skills enable infants to play in sophisticated ways, such as stacking blocks, picking up small objects, and filling cups and other containers—and then dumping out the contents. Infants with a dominant hand are likely to show greater skill in manipulating objects to carry out these tasks, and each of these activities promotes cognitive development, a contributor to language development.

What Do You Think?

What might be the long-term implications for a consistent hand preference early in infancy? For language? Cognition? Motor skill?

---

immersion A strategy in which all instruction occurs in the majority language; children learn a second language, such as English, and course content simultaneously.

dual language learning Also known as two-way immersion; an approach in which children are taught and develop skills in two languages.

by English **immersion**, which places foreign-language-speaking children into English-speaking classes, requiring them to learn English and course content at the same time. Another approach is **dual language learning** (also called *two-way immersion*), in which English-speaking and non-English-speaking students learn together in both languages and both languages are valued equally. Advocates argue that bringing a child's native language into the classroom sends children the message that their cultural heritage is respected and strengthens their cultural identity and self-esteem. Some studies suggest that immersion brings a loss in native language (Baus, Costa, & Carreiras, 2013), but others find that dual-language immersion retains the native language while enhancing the new language (Castro, Páez, Dickinson, & Frede, 2011).

Many proponents of immersion point to its effectiveness in Canada, where both English and French are official languages. About 10% of Canadian students are enrolled in immersion programs in which English-speaking children are enrolled in French classes, learning the entire curriculum in French. Canadian children in French immersion programs become proficient in both languages with no decline in their skills in English or in reading or academic achievement (Harley & Jean, 1999; Hermanto, Moreno, & Bialystok, 2012; Lipka & Siegel, 2007). However, because both English and French are official languages, Canadian children and adults are exposed to both languages in a great many contexts, not just in school. Researchers argue that immersion is not as effective for U.S. non-English speaking children because the children's native languages are not official languages in the United States. English is thus seen as a replacement for the children's native languages, which may contribute to children's feelings of isolation, anxiety, and frustration (Crawford, 1997; Midobuche, 2001). Perhaps it is for this reason that longitudinal research with U.S. samples suggests that dual-language immersion approaches, which encourage students to retain their native language while learning English, are more effective than immersion approaches at promoting successful learning of English and as well as overall academic achievement (Relji, Ferring, & Martin, 2014; Rolstad, 2005). Nevertheless, other research suggests that no one approach is best for all children in all contexts (Bialystok, 2001).

Learning a second language during childhood often affects proficiency in the first or native language. Sometimes the first language is lost (Fillmore, 1991) or the second language becomes dominant—the language that the child uses more often. In one study of Chinese immigrant children in New York City, children who were under the age of 9 when they immigrated reported preferring English to Mandarin one year later. They were more proficient in English than children who were older than 9 at the time of immigration, as measured by tests of grammar knowledge and translation three years later (Jia & Aaronson, 2003). Children older than 9 at the time of immigration retained a preference for Mandarin and remained more proficient in Mandarin over the 3-year span. Why the difference? The younger children reported becoming friends with children who spoke English and spent more time interacting with peers who spoke English than the older children. Peers and the surrounding community influence bilingual children's language acquisition and use, and the language that is used most becomes dominant.

A similar switch in language preference and dominance has been shown in a study of children in Southern California who first learned Spanish at home and then began to learn English at school at 5 years of age (Kohnert et al., 2002). The children improved their proficiency in both Spanish and English but made faster progress in English, so that by middle childhood they were more proficient in English. Children who are living in the United States or another English-speaking country and are Spanish-English bilingual at 2 years of age often become English dominant by age 4, and many adults who grew up in Spanish-speaking homes retain little ability to speak Spanish (Hoff, 2015; Hoff et al., 2014).

 Thinking in Context 9.5

Referring to Bronfenbrenner's bioecological model (see Figure 1.7 in Chapter 1), identify contextual factors that influence language development. What factors at the level of Bronfenbrenner's microsystem and mesosystem play a role in language? How might the exosystem influence language development? Macrosystem? Provide examples.

Eleven-month old Alvaro exclaimed, "Che!" "Oh, you want leche, milk?" beamed his mother, Lucia. Alvaro reached his hands out to grasp his bottle.

As Lucia's mother watched the two she suggested, in Spanish, "Maybe Alvaro should learn to speak in English. You should speak English at home."

"Mama, then you won't understand us!" Lucia replied.

"I'll understand what you say, but speaking English is too hard for me."

"No. I want Alvaro to know his culture. He learns English at the child care center. Besides, everyone around here speaks Spanish." Lucia gestured, referring to their neighbors.

Two years later, Lucia enrolled Alvaro in a preschool near her workplace. In a parent-teacher conference, his teacher explained to Lucia, "Alvaro's mathematics skills are exceptional. He's way ahead of his peers in counting and understanding math concepts. But he lags behind his peers in vocabulary and syntax. I think he needs some extra practice speaking English to help to catch up and start first grade with his peers. Does he speak English at home?"

"A little, but we speak mostly Spanish. My mother only speaks Spanish. She lives with us and cares for Alvaro outside of preschool hours. And everyone in our neighborhood speaks Spanish," replied Lucia.

"Do you read stories to Alvaro?"

"Sometimes. I work at night and go to school. I'm thankful for my mother's help or I'd never be able to keep up. I try to read to Alvaro a couple of times a week."

1. What challenges do bilingual children commonly face in learning language?

2. What benefits might we expect of bilingualism for a student like Alvaro?

3. How might contextual factors might influence Alvaro's language development?

4. Alvaro appears to be better at speaking Spanish than English. How might this be explained by a learning theorist? Nativist? Interactionist?

Give your students the SAGE edge!

SAGE edge offers a robust online environment featuring an impressive array of free tools and resources for review, study, and further exploration, keeping both instructors and students on the cutting edge of teaching and learning. Learn more at **edge.sagepub.com/kuthertopical.**

CHAPTER 9 IN REVIEW

9.1 Describe the five basic components of language.

SUMMARY

To master language, children must learn to use the five basic components that underlie all languages: phonology, morphology, semantics, syntax, and pragmatics. Phonology refers knowledge of the sounds used in a given language. The understanding of the ways that sounds can be combined to form words is known as morphology. Semantics refers to the meaning or content of words and sentences. Syntax refers to the rules by which words are to be combined to form sentences. Pragmatics refers to understanding how to use language to communicate effectively.

KEY TERMS

phonology
semantics
morphology

syntax
pragmatics

REVIEW QUESTION

Define the five components of language.

9.2 Explain the process by which infants develop the ability to understand and use language.

SUMMARY

Newborns can perceive and discriminate sounds that comprise all human languages, but their developing capacities and preferences are influenced by their contexts. Between 2 and 3 months, infants begin cooing. Babbling follows at about 6 months of age. At first, babbling is universal; later it becomes more word-like and sounds more like the infant's native language. At about a year of age, the average infant speaks his or her first word. Throughout language development, babies' receptive language exceeds their productive language. Infants learn new words through fast mapping, which improves with age and accounts for the vocabulary spurt. As children develop a larger vocabulary and get feedback on their speech, they demonstrate fewer errors of overextension and underextension. At about 21 months of age, or usually about 8 to 12 months after they say their first word, most children use telegraphic speech.

KEY TERMS

cooing
babbling
holophrases
fast mapping

naming explosion (vocabulary
   spurt)
overextension
underextension
telegraphic speech

REVIEW QUESTIONS

1. What evidence suggests that newborns and young infants are prepared to learn language?

2. Describe milestones in language development that parents of children under the age of 2 can expect.

3. How do infants learn words?

9.3 Describe patterns of language development from early childhood through adulthood.

SUMMARY

Young children continue to use fast mapping as a word-learning strategy as well as logical extension and the mutual exclusivity assumption. Parental conversations and support for language learning are associated with faster and more correct language use. At the end of the preschool years, overregularization errors decline. By 8 years of age children make fewer semantic errors and spontaneously self-correct many of their errors. During middle childhood, pragmatics grows and becomes more sophisticated, and children become more likely to change their speech in response to the needs of listeners. Advances in abstract reasoning make adolescents better able to understand and use metaphor, sarcasm, and irony. Throughout life healthy adults continue to add new words to their vocabulary and the average healthy older adult does not suffer significant losses in the ability to use language effectively. Changes in sensory and cognitive processing, such as hearing deficits and changes in working memory, can affect language comprehension and production. Yet older adults can compensate for such losses by drawing from their rich backlog of experiences when they listen.

KEY TERMS

logical extension
mutual exclusivity assumption
overregularization errors

private speech
self-regulation

REVIEW QUESTIONS

1. Give examples of how children learn vocabulary and syntax.

2. What is the role of private speech in communication and development?

3. How do children's grammar skills develop?

4. How does their understanding of pragmatics improve into adolescence?

9.4 Distinguish among learning, nativist, and interactionist perspectives on language.

9.5 Discuss cultural and contextual influences on language development.

SUMMARY

Learning theory poses that language is learned through operant conditioning: Imitation and reinforcement shape children's language development. Nativist theorists pose that the human brain has an innate capacity to learn language, called a language acquisition device. An interactionist perspective integrates nature and nurture, noting that we have innate perceptual biases for discriminating and listening to language, and the brain is wired for language at birth. At the same time, language development occurs in a social context in which adults facilitate language development by responding in ways that foster language learning, such as by using expansions and recasts.

KEY TERMS

grammar
language acquisition device (LAD)
universal grammar
Broca's area

Wernicke's area
canonical babbling
expansions
recast

REVIEW QUESTIONS

1. How is the learning approach applied to language development?

2. What is the nativist approach to language?

3. Give examples of how the interactionist perspective accounts for language learning.

SUMMARY

Interactions with adults are a primary influence on language development. Babies learn language by interacting with more mature, expert speakers who can speak at their developmental level. The quality of language input from parents and the number of words a child hears is related to children's vocabulary size at age 2. Infant-directed speech has been documented in many languages and cultures. Parental response patterns that are warm, contingent on infant responses, and consistent are associated with positive language development in infants across cultures. Poverty influences language development through exposure to speech and the quality of parent–child interactions as well as the potential for household chaos. Children who are exposed to two languages build distinct language systems from birth. The pattern of vocabulary and grammatical development in each language tends to follow the developmental course for each language and is influenced by the quality of input in each language. The ability to speak more than one language is associated with many cognitive skills and higher scores on measures of executive function. Non-English-speaking students often learn English as a second language in school using the immersion approach. The dual-language learning approach fosters and values both languages.

KEY TERMS

infant-directed speech ("motherese")
immersion

dual language learning (two-way immersion)

REVIEW QUESTIONS

1. How do contextual factors within the home and caregiving settings influence language? Provide examples.

2. How do children learn a second language and what are the developmental effects of bilingualism?

Test your understanding of the content.
Review the flashcards and quizzes at
edge.sagepub.com/kuthertopical

PRACTICE AND APPLY WHAT YOU'VE LEARNED

► **edge.sagepub.com/kuthertopical**

PART IV

Socioemotional Development

Socioemotional development describes the shifts in how we experience our emotions, our sense of self, moral issues, and gender roles.

Our earliest emotions emerge in infancy. More sophisticated emotions that rely on cognitive development develop in early childhood. With age, children and adolescents get better at managing and controlling how they display their emotions. Adults can connect their emotions with cognition, integrate positive and negative feelings, and regulate intense emotions, which contributes to well-being.

Young children tend to understand themselves in concrete and unrealistically positive ways. With time, children's views of themselves become increasingly accurate and better reflect their skills and accomplishments. Adolescents describe themselves in ways that are abstract and often contradictory, reflecting their drive to discover and understand themselves. The developmental task of forming an identity is first encountered during adolescence, but identity is revised all throughout life.

Cognition influences how children think about morality. As thinking advances, children's views of right and wrong tend to shift from an emphasis on self-interest, to a concern with maintaining social norms, to—in adolescence and adulthood—autonomous decision-making that respects individuals and human rights.

Views of gender also shift. Young children tend to have rigid beliefs about gender that influence their preferences and behavior. As cognitive advances influence how we express emotions, experience our sense of self, and view moral issues, we develop more flexible views about gender into adulthood.

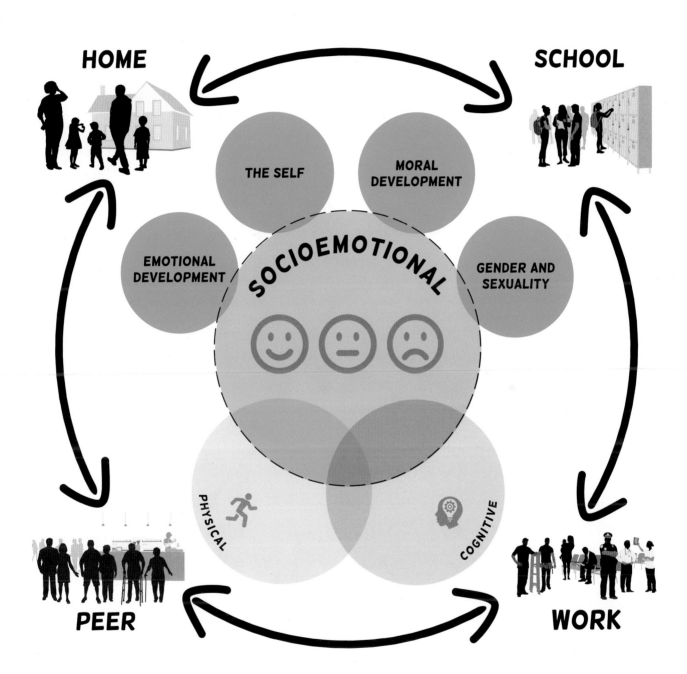

HOME

SCHOOL

THE SELF

MORAL DEVELOPMENT

EMOTIONAL DEVELOPMENT

SOCIOEMOTIONAL

GENDER AND SEXUALITY

PHYSICAL

COGNITIVE

PEER

WORK

Images: ©iStock.com

Emotional Development

Learning Objectives

10.1 Examine infants' developing capacities for basic and self-conscious emotions and emotion regulation.

10.2 Describe the progression of children's understanding and regulation of emotion.

10.3 Contrast the emotional experiences and coping skills of adolescents and adults.

10.4 Compare attachment styles in infancy and adulthood.

10.5 Discuss the lifespan stability of temperament and the role of goodness of fit in adjustment.

Digital Resources

▶ An Emotional Robot

◀)) Emotional Regulation in Children

▤ Resilience Worldwide

▶ Resilience and Hardiness in Adulthood

▶ Parent and Infant Psychotherapy

▶ The Strange Situation

◀)) Temperament

▤ Infant Temperament Across Cultures

Master these learning objectives with multimedia resources available at edge.sagepub.com/kuthertopical and *Lives in Context* video cases available in the interactive eBook.

As a newborn, Terrence expressed distress by spreading his arms, kicking his legs, and crying. When he did this, his mother or father would scoop him up and hold him, trying to comfort him. Terrence quickly began to prefer interacting with attentive adults who cared for him. Soon baby Terrence began to smile and gurgle when held. In turn, Terrence's parents played with him and were delighted to see his animated, excited responses. As a toddler, his emerging language skills enabled Terrence to express his needs in words. He quickly learned that words are powerful tools that can convey emotions ("I love you, Mommy"). Without realizing it, Terrence used words to help him manage strong emotions and difficult situations. For example, he distracted himself from stressful stimuli, like the neighbor's scary dog, by singing to himself. Terrence could express his ideas and feelings to everyone around him, making for new and more complex relationships with his parents and siblings. Terrence also learned that it is sometimes best to hold in emotions that might hurt other people's feelings—instead of telling Grandma that he had really wanted a video game for his birthday, he thanked her for the superhero toy she gave him. In adulthood, Terrence's skill in emotional management has helped him cope with stressful situations, get along with colleagues, and become a leader in his company.

As Terrence illustrates, from birth we learn new ways of expressing our emotions. As we develop, we become capable of new and more complex emotions and relationships with others and develop a greater sense of self-understanding, social awareness, and self-management. These processes collectively are referred to as **emotional competence**. In this chapter, we examine emotional development from infancy through adulthood.

EMOTIONAL DEVELOPMENT IN INFANCY

LO 10.1 Examine infants' developing capacities for basic and self-conscious emotions and emotion regulation.

What emotions do infants feel? Infants cannot describe their experiences and feelings, which makes studying infants' emotional development quite challenging. How do you determine what another person is feeling? Most people show their emotions on their faces, such as by smiling or frowning. If we use facial expressions as a guide to what emotions infants might feel, the first and most reliable emotion that newborns show is distress. They cry, wail, and flail their arms and bodies, alerting caregivers to their need for attention. Newborns also show interest with wide-eyed gazes when something catches their attention, and they smile when they are happy.

INFANTS' EMOTIONAL EXPERIENCE

Are we born with the ability to feel emotions? No one knows for sure, but observation of newborn facial expressions suggests that newborns experience interest, distress, disgust, and contentment (Campos et al., 2000; Izard et al., 1995). Between 2 and 7 months of age, infants begin to display additional expressions including anger, sadness, joy, surprise, and fear (Bennett, Bendersky, & Lewis, 2005). Of course, we do not know whether internal emotional states accompany these facial expressions, but infants' facial expressions are remarkably similar to those of adults (Sullivan & Lewis, 2003). These discrete emotional expressions, known as **basic emotions** or primary emotions, appear so early in life that researchers generally agree that they are biologically predetermined (Izard, 2007). The basic emotions of anger, sadness, joy, surprise, and fear emerge in all infants at about the same ages and are seen and interpreted similarly in all cultures that have been studied, suggesting that they are inborn (Camras, Oster, Campos, Miyake, & Bradshaw, 1992; Izard, 2007).

Emotions arise from interactions of richly connected, largely subcortical (below the cortex) brain structures, including the brainstem (the lower part of the brain located between the cortex and spine) and the limbic system (Phelps & LeDoux, 2005). These structures develop prenatally and are present in animals, suggesting that emotions serve a biological purpose and are crucial to survival (LeDoux & Phelps, 2008).

emotional competence The combination of processes we develop as we become capable of new and more complex emotions and relationships with others and develop a greater sense of self-understanding, social awareness, and self-management.

basic emotions Emotions that are universal in humans, appear early in life, and are thought to have a long evolutionary history, such as happiness, interest, surprise, fear, anger, sadness, and disgust.

ROMEO GACAD/AFP/Getty Images

What emotion is this baby displaying?

During the first few months of life, the form of basic emotions as well as the conditions that elicit them change. For example, consider smiling, which typically indicates happiness and is one of the most important emotional expressions in infancy. Newborns smile. Newborn smiles are reflexive, involuntary, linked with shifts in arousal state (e.g., going from being asleep to drowsy wakefulness), and occur frequently during periods of REM sleep (Kawakami et al., 2008; Korner, 1969). At about 3 weeks, infants smile while awake and alert and in response to familiarity—familiar sounds, voices, and tastes (Sroufe & Waters, 1976). During the second month of life, babies smile more in response to visual stimuli (Sroufe, 1997). The **social smile**, in response to seeing familiar people, emerges between 6 and 10 weeks of age (Lewis, Hitchcock, & Sullivan, 2004). The social smile is an important milestone in infant development because it is indicative of social engagement (Messinger & Fogel, 2007) and plays a large role in initiating and maintaining social interactions between infants and adults, especially by enhancing caregiver–child bonding. Parents are enthralled when their baby shows delight in seeing them.

As infants grow, laughs begin to accompany their smiles and they laugh more often and at more things. For example, at 6 months of age, an infant might laugh at unusual sounds or sights, such as when Mommy makes a face or hides her head under a blanket. Laughing at unusual events illustrates the baby's increasing cognitive competence as he or she knows what to expect and is surprised when something unexpected occurs. Infants may show clear expressions of joy as early as 2½ months of age while playing with a parent and at 3 to 4 months of age when they laugh at stimuli that they find intensely arousing (Bornstein & Lamb, 2011).

Anger appears at about 6 months of age and develops rapidly, becoming more complex in terms of elicitors and responses (Lemerise & Dodge, 2008). Initially, physical restrictions can elicit anger, such as being restrained in a high chair or when being dressed. The inability to carry out a desired act, such as unsuccessfully reaching to obtain a desired toy, can also provoke frustration and anger (Sullivan & Lewis, 2003, 2012). Between 8 and 20 months of age, infants gradually become more reactive and anger is more easily elicited (Braungart-Rieker, Hill-Soderlund, & Karrass, 2010). They become aware of the actions of others, so that anger can be elicited by others' behavior. For example, an infant may become upset when Mommy goes to the door to leave, or when Grandma takes out the towels in preparation for bath time. During the second year of life, temper tantrums become common when the toddler's attempts at autonomy are thwarted and he or she experiences frustration or stress. The anger escalates with the child's stress level (Potegal, Robison, Anderson, Jordan, & Shapiro, 2007). Some toddlers show extreme tantrums, lie on the floor, scream, and jerk their arms and legs. Other children's tantrums are more subtle. They may whine, mope, and stick out their lower lip.

The development of **self-conscious emotions**, or secondary emotions—such as empathy, pride, embarrassment, shame, and guilt—depends on cognitive development, as well as an awareness of self. Self-conscious emotions do not begin to emerge until about 15 to 18 months (Lewis, 2008, 2011), and they largely develop during the second and third years of life (Goodvin, Thompson, & Winer, 2015; Lagattuta & Thompson, 2007). In order to experience self-conscious emotions, the toddler must be able to observe himself and others, be aware of standards and rules, and compare his behavior with those standards (Lagattuta & Thompson, 2007). Feelings of pride, for example, arise from accomplishing a personally meaningful goal, whereas guilt derives from realizing that one has violated a standard of conduct. Parental evaluations are the initial basis for many secondary emotions (Stipek, 1995).

social smile A smile that emerges between 6 and 10 weeks in response to seeing familiar people.

self-conscious emotions Emotions that requires cognitive development and an awareness of self, such as empathy, embarrassment, shame, and guilt.

What cognitive and social capacities are needed to display embarrassment?

EMOTION REGULATION

As children become aware of social standards and rules, **emotion regulation**—the ability to control their emotions—becomes important. How do infants regulate emotions? Very young infants have been observed to manage negative emotions by sucking vigorously on objects or turning their bodies away from distressing stimuli (Mangelsdorf, Shapiro, & Marzolf, 1995). Smiling is also thought to serve a purpose in regulating emotions, as it allows the infant to control aspects of a situation without losing touch with it. When an infant gets excited and smiles, she looks away briefly. This may be a way of breaking herself away from the stimulus and allowing her to regroup, preventing overstimulation. Smiling is associated with a decline in heart rate, suggesting that it is a relaxation response to decrease an infant's level of arousal.

Whereas 6-month-old infants are more likely to use gaze aversion and fussing as primary emotion regulatory strategies, 12-month-old infants are more likely to use self-soothing (e.g., thumb sucking, rocking themselves) and distraction (chewing on objects, playing with toys), and 18-month-old toddlers use distraction and active attempts to change the situation, such as moving away from upsetting stimuli (Crockenberg & Leerkes, 2004; Mangelsdorf et al., 1995). By 18 to 24 months of age, toddlers try to adjust their emotional reactions to a comfortable level of intensity by distracting themselves when they are distressed, such as by playing with toys or talking (Cole, Martin, & Dennis, 2004; Feldman, Dollberg, & Nadam, 2011; Grolnick, Bridges, & Connell, 1996). Researchers have found that infants' abilities to self-regulate at 15 months predict executive functioning at 4 years (Ursache, Blair, Stifter, & Voegtline, 2013).

Emotion regulation is also related to children's increasing ability to use language. After 18 months of age, toddlers' vocabulary for talking about feelings develops rapidly, presenting new opportunities for emotion regulation because toddlers can tell caregivers how they feel (Bretherton, Fritz, Zahn-Waxler, & Ridgeway, 1986). Vocabulary has been found to predict self-regulation abilities in 24-month-old infants (Vallotton & Ayoub, 2011).

emotional regulation The ability to adjust and control our emotional state to influence how and when emotions are expressed.

SOCIAL INTERACTION AND EMOTIONAL DEVELOPMENT

Social engagement increases rapidly during the first year of life (Feldman et al., 2009). The parent–child relationship is an important context for developing emotion regulation skills. Warm and supportive interactions with parents and other caregivers can help infants understand their emotions and learn how to manage them. Responsive parenting that is attuned to infants' needs helps infants develop skills in emotion regulation, especially in managing negative emotions like anxiety, as well as their physiological correlates, such as accelerated heart rate (Feldman et al., 2011; Haley & Stansbury, 2003). For example, when mothers responded promptly to their 2-month-old infants' cries, these same infants, at 4 months of age, cried for shorter durations, were better able to manage their emotions, and stopped crying more quickly than other infants (Jahromi & Stifter, 2007). Infants and young children often need outside assistance in regulating their emotions.

Parental Interaction

Parents can help their infants learn to manage emotions with the use of many techniques, including direct intervention, modeling, selective reinforcement, control of the environment, verbal instruction, and touch (Crockenberg & Leerkes, 2004; Meléndez, 2005; Wolfe & Bell, 2007). The techniques parents use to soothe infants change as their infants grow older. Touching becomes a less common regulatory strategy with age, whereas vocalizing and distracting techniques increase (Jahromi & Stifter, 2007). At 7½ months of age, infants tend to change their patterns of expression to show more positive and less

Responsive parenting helps infants learn to manage their emotions and self-regulate.

© istock.com/photog1

negative emotions, at least partly in response to their mothers' behavior—which tends to be increasingly responsive to expressions of interest and decreasingly responsive to expressions of discomfort (Malatesta & Haviland, 1982). When mothers provide guidance in helping infants regulate their emotions, infants tend to engage in distraction and mother-oriented strategies, such as seeking help, during frustrating events (Calkins & Johnson, 1998).

Some caregivers, however, interpret certain emotional displays as attempts at manipulation ("He's just trying to get attention") rather than as valid expressions of feeling, which may result in insensitive responses to children's emotional displays ("That's enough, stop it!") and interfere with children's emotional development. In one study, fathers' negativity was associated with higher levels of stress hormones in infants at 7 and 24 months of age (Mills-Koonce et al., 2011).

Maladaptive social contexts, such as parental stress, depression, and conflict, pose risks to infants' emotional development. Mothers who are depressed tend to be less responsive to their babies, show less affection, use more negative forms of touch, and show more negative emotions and behaviors such as withdrawal, intrusiveness, hostility, coerciveness, and insensitivity (Jennings et al., 2008; Zajicek-Farber, 2009). Mothers who are depressed not only interact with their babies differently, but they perceive them differently—they rate their infant's behavior more negatively than do nondepressed mothers and independent observers (Field et al., 1996; Hart, Field, & Roitfarb, 1999).

Not surprising, given the poor parent-child interaction styles that accompany maternal depression, infants of depressed mothers show a variety of negative outcomes, including overall distress, withdrawn behavior, poor social engagement, and difficulty regulating emotions (Feldman et al., 2009; Leventon & Bauer, 2013; Muscat, Obst, Cockshaw, & Thorpe, 2014). They often show poor attentiveness, limited capacity to interact with objects and people, and difficulty reading and understanding others' emotions (Field, 2011; Lyubchik & Schlosser, 2010). The ongoing reciprocal interactions between mothers and infants account for the long-term effects of maternal depression. In one study, maternal depressive symptoms 9 months after giving birth predicted infants' negative reactions to maternal behavior at 18 months of age and, in turn, higher levels of depressive symptoms on the part of mothers when the children reached 27 months of age (Roben et al., 2015). Similarly, in a sample of infants studied from 4 to 18 months of age, family factors such as maternal depression and the mother's experience of relationship stress were associated with the infants' developing strong negative emotions early in infancy, which compromised their emotion regulation capacities (Bridgett et al., 2009). Declines in infants' regulatory control were in turn associated with negative parenting in toddlerhood because parents and children interact and influence each other reciprocally.

Changes in emotional expression and regulation are dynamic because the changing child influences the changing parent. In particular, mothers and infants systematically influence and regulate each other's emotions and behaviors. Mothers regulate infant emotional states by interpreting their emotional signals, providing appropriate arousal, and reciprocating and reinforcing infant reactions. Infants regulate their mother's emotions through their receptivity to her initiations and stimulation, and by responding to her emotions (Cole et al., 2004). By experiencing a range of emotional interactions—times when their emotions mirror those of their caregivers and times when their emotions are different from those of their caregivers—infants learn how to transform negative emotions into neutral or positive emotions and regulate their own emotional states (Cole et al., 2004; Lyons-Ruth, Bronfman, & Parsons, 1999).

Interactive Play and Test of Wills

Face-to-face social play is an important way in which infants learn how to manage their emotions. Face-to-face play involves short but intense episodes of focused interaction in which an infant and adult entertain each other with smiling, vocalizing, and animated facial expressions. The goal of these interactions is to establish and maintain synchronous, or coordinated, exchanges that are pleasurable for both infant and adult.

However, synchronous exchanges occur only about one third of the time that mothers and infants interact with each other (Tronick & Cohn, 1989; Tronick, 1989). Instead, the typical mother–infant interaction is one that cycles from coordinated synchrony to nonmatching states and back again. Successfully regaining synchrony and experiencing coordinated mother–infant states are associated with positive affect on the part of infants. Thus infants' affective experience is influenced by this dyadic regulatory process.

At 6 or 7 months of age, face-to-face play transforms into more active kinds of play that correspond to the baby's developing motor skills (Tronick & Cohn, 1989). In addition, crawling and walking introduce new challenges to parent–infant interaction and socioemotional growth (Bertenthal & Campos, 1990; Campos et al., 2000; Campos, Kermoian, & Zumbahlen, 1992). Motor development thereby holds important implications for socioemotional development. As crawling begins, parents and caregivers respond with happiness and pride, providing the infant with an increase in emotional communication (Bertenthal, Campos, & Barrett, 1984). Crawling increases a toddler's capability to attain goals—a capability that, while often satisfying to the toddler, involves hazards such as wandering away from parents and encountering hazards.

As infants become more mobile, the emotional outbursts become more common. Parents report that advances in locomotion are accompanied by increased frustration as toddlers attempt to move in ways that often exceed their abilities or are not permitted by parents (Clearfield, 2011; Karasik, Tamis-LeMonda, & Adolph, 2011; Pemberton Roben et al., 2012)

When mothers recognize the dangers posed to toddlers by objects such as houseplants, vases, and electrical appliances, they sharply increase their expressions of anger and fear, often leading to fear and frustration in their toddlers. At this stage, parents must actively monitor toddlers' whereabouts, protect them from dangerous situations, and expect toddlers to comply—a dynamic that is often a struggle, amounting to a test of wills. At the same time, these struggles help the child to begin to develop a grasp of mental states in others that are different from his or her own (Thompson, 2004).

Social Referencing

Early in life, the ability emerges to discriminate facial expressions that indicate emotion; even newborns are able to discriminate happy faces from fearful ones (Farroni, Menon, Rigato, & Johnson, 2007). Between 2 and 4 months of age, infants can distinguish emotional expressions including happiness as opposed to anger, surprise, and sadness (Bornstein, Arterberry, & Lamb, 2013). It is thought that infants are innately prepared to attend to facial displays of emotion as such displays are biologically significant and the ability to recognize them is important for human survival (Leppanen, 2011).

Beyond recognizing the emotional expressions of others, infants also respond to them. Between 6 and 10 months of age, infants begin to use **social referencing**, the tendency to look to caregivers' or other adults' emotional expressions to find clues for how to interpret ambiguous events (Boccia & Campos, 1989; Slaughter & McConnell, 2003; Striano, Vaish, & Benigno, 2006). The use of social referencing is one way that infants demonstrate their understanding that others experience their own emotions and thoughts. For example, when a toddler grabs the sofa to pull herself up, turns, and tumbles over as she takes a step, she will look to her caregiver to determine how to interpret her fall. If the caregiver has a fearful facial expression, the infant is likely to be fearful also, but if the caregiver smiles, the infant will probably remain calm and return to attempts at walking.

Social referencing occurs in ambiguous situations, provides infants and toddlers with guidance in how to interpret events, and influences their emotional responses and subsequent actions (Striano et al., 2006). The caregiver's emotional expression, whether happy, sad, or fearful, influences whether a 1-year-old will play with a new toy, be wary of strangers, or cross to the deep side of a visual cliff (see Chapter 4; Mumme, Fernald, & Herrera, 1996; Rosen, Adamson, & Bakeman, 1992).Older infants tend to show a negativity bias when it comes to social referencing: The effect of social referencing cues is stronger for negative cues than positive. Infants generally attend

social referencing Seeking information from caregivers about how to interpret unfamiliar or ambiguous events by observing their emotional expressions and reactions.

and follow social referencing cues more closely when they indicate negative attitudes toward an object, as compared with neutral or happy (Leventon & Bauer, 2013; Vaish, Grossmann, & Woodward, 2008). In addition, infants may be more influenced by the vocal information conveyed in emotional messages than the facial expressions themselves, especially within the context of fearful messages (Biro, Alink, van IJzendoorn, & Bakermans-Kranenburg, 2014; Kim, Walden, & Knieps, 2010).

How infants employ social referencing changes with development. Ten-month-old infants show selective social referencing. They monitor the caregiver's attention and do not engage in social referencing when the adult is not attending or engaged (Striano & Rochat, 2000). At 12 months, infants use referential cues such as the caregiver's body posture, gaze, and voice direction to determine to what objects caregivers' emotional responses refer (Brooks & Meltzoff, 2008; Moses, Baldwin, Rosicky, & Tidball, 2001). Twelve-month-old infants are more likely to use a caregiver's cues as guides in ambivalent situations when the caregiver has shown responses contingent on the infants' behavior. In sum, social referencing reflects infants' growing understanding of the emotional states of others; it signifies that infants can observe, interpret, and use emotional information from others to form their own interpretation and response to events.

CONTEXTUAL INFLUENCES ON EMOTIONAL DEVELOPMENT

Emotional development does not occur in a vacuum. Contextual factors, such as culture, influence how infants interpret and express emotions, as well as what emotions they feel. In this section, we explore the role of context in shaping children's knowledge about the appropriate display of emotions as well as the degree to children experience a fear common in infancy: stranger wariness.

Emotional Display Rules

Every society has a set of **emotional display rules** that specify the circumstances under which various emotions should or should not be expressed (Gross & Ballif, 1991; LeVine et al., 1994; Safdar et al., 2009). We learn these emotional display rules very early in life, as every interaction between parent and infant is shaped by the culture in which they live, which influences the emotional behavior of mothers, the smiles of infants, and other emotional expressions (Bornstein, Arterberry, & Lamb, 2013). When North American mothers play with their 7-month-old babies, they tend to model positive emotions, restricting their own emotional displays to show joy, interest, and surprise (Malatesta & Haviland, 1982). They also are more attentive to infants' expression of positive emotions, such as interest or surprise, and respond less to negative emotions (Malatesta, Grigoryev, Lamb, Albin, & Culver, 1986). Thus babies are socialized to respond and display their emotions in socially acceptable ways. The emotions that are considered acceptable, as well as ways of expressing them, differ by culture and context. North American parents tickle and stimulate their babies, encouraging squeals of pleasure. The Gusii and Aka people of Central Africa prefer to keep babies calm and quiet; they engage in little face-to-face play (Hewlett, Lamb, Shannon, Leyendecker, & Scholmerich, 1998; LeVine et al., 1994). These differences in caregiving styles communicate cultural expectations about emotions. North American infants learn to express positive emotions and Central African babies learn to restrain strong emotions.

Similarly, cultures often have particular beliefs about how much responsiveness is appropriate when babies cry and fuss (Garcia Coll, 1990; Keller, 2003; Meléndez, 2005). The !Kung hunter-gatherers of Botswana, Africa,

emotional display rules Unstated cultural guidelines for acceptable emotions and emotional expression that are communicated to children via parents' emotional behavior, expressions, and socialization.

John S Lander/LightRocket/Getty Images

In some cultures infants cry very little, perhaps because they are in constant contact with their mothers.

respond to babies' cries nearly immediately (within 10 seconds), whereas Western mothers tend to wait a considerably longer period of time before responding to infants' cries (e.g., 10 minutes; Barr, Konner, Bakeman, & Adamson, 1991). Gusii mothers believe that constant holding, feeding, and physical care are essential for keeping an infant calm, which in turn protects the infant from harm and disease; therefore, like !Kung mothers, Gusii mothers respond immediately to their babies' cries (LeVine et al., 1994). Non-Western infants are thought to cry very little because they are carried often (Bleah & Ellett, 2010). In one study, infants born to parents who were recent immigrants from Africa cried less than U.S. infants, illustrating the role of culture in influencing infant cries (Bleah & Ellett, 2010). Caregivers' responses to infant cries influence infants' capacities for self-regulation and responses to stress (Barr & Gunnar, 2000). Babies who receive more responsive and immediate caregiving when distressed show lower rates of persistent crying, spend more time in happy and calm states, and cry less overall as they approach their first birthday (Axia & Weisner, 2002; Feng, Harwood, Leyendecker, & Miller, 2001; Papoušek & Papoušek, 1990).

Stranger Wariness

Many infants around the world display **stranger wariness** (also known as *stranger anxiety*), a fear of unfamiliar people. Whether infants show stranger wariness depends on the infants' overall temperament, past experience, and the situation in which they meet a stranger (Thompson & Limber, 1991). In many, but not all cultures, stranger wariness emerges at about 6 months and increases throughout the first year of life, beginning to decrease after about 15 months of age (Bornstein et al., 2013; Sroufe, 1977; Waters, Matas, & Sroufe, 1975).

Recent research has suggested that the pattern of stranger wariness varies among infants, as some show rapid increases and others show slow increases in stranger wariness; once wariness has been established, some infants show steady decline and others show more rapid changes. Twin studies suggest that these patterns are influenced by genetics because the patterns of change are more similar among monozygotic twins (who are identical and share 100% of their genes) than dizygotic twins (fraternal twins who share 50% of their genes) twins (Brooker et al., 2013). Recall from Chapter 2 that monozygotic twins come from the same zygote and therefore share 100% of their genes whereas dizygotic twins arise from two zygotes, sharing 50% of their genes.

Among North American infants, stranger wariness is so common that parents and caregivers generally expect it. However, infants of the Efe people of Zaire, Africa, show little stranger wariness; this is likely related to the Efe collective caregiving system in which Efe babies are passed from one adult to another, relatives and nonrelatives alike (Tronick, Morelli, & Ivey, 1992), and the infants form relationships with the many people who care for them (Meehan & Hawks, 2013). In contrast, babies reared in Israeli kibbutzim (cooperative agricultural settlements that tend to be isolated and have been subjected to terrorist attacks) tend to demonstrate widespread wariness of strangers. By the end of the first year, when infants look to others for cues about how to respond emotionally, kibbutz babies display far greater anxiety than babies reared in Israeli cities (Saarni, Mumme, & Campos, 1998). In this way, stranger wariness may be adaptive, modifying infants' drive to explore in light of contextual circumstances (Easterbrooks, Bartlett, Beeghly, & Thompson, 2012; Thompson & Limber, 1990).

Stranger wariness illustrates the dynamic interactions among the individual and context. The infant's tendencies toward social interaction and past experience with strangers are important, of course but so is the mother's anxiety (Brooker et al., 2013; Greenberg, Hillman, & Grice, 1973; Thompson & Limber, 1991; Waters, West, & Mendes, 2014). Infants whose mothers report greater stress reactivity, who experience more anxiety and negative affect in response to stress, show higher rates of stranger wariness (Brooker et al., 2013; Waters et al., 2014). Characteristics of the stranger (e.g., his or her height), the familiarity of the setting, and how quickly the stranger approaches all influence how the infant appraises

stranger wariness Also known as stranger anxiety; an infant's expression of fear of unfamiliar people.

the situation. Infants are more open when the stranger is sensitive to the infant's signals and approaches at the infant's pace (Mangelsdorf, 1992; Thompson & Limber, 1991).

During the first few months of life, infants display the full range of basic emotions. As their cognitive and social capabilities develop, they are able to experience complex social emotions, such as embarrassment. The social world plays a role in emotional development. Adults interact with infants, provide opportunities to observe and practice emotional expressions, and assist in regulating emotions. Much of emotional development is the result of the interplay of infants' emerging capacities and the contexts in which they are raised. Culture influences what emotions infants experience and how they are displayed.

 Thinking in Context 10.1

1. Identify examples of how infants' emotional development is influenced by their interactions with elements of their physical, social, and cultural context. In your view, what aspects of each of these can foster healthy emotional development? What might hinder emotional development? Explain your choices.

2. In what ways might emotional display rules, such as those regarding the display of positive and negative emotions, illustrate adaptive responses to a particular context? Consider the context in which you were raised: What emotional displays do you think are most adaptive for infants?

EMOTIONAL DEVELOPMENT IN CHILDHOOD

LO 10.2 Describe the progression of children's understanding and regulation of emotion.

Children's advances in cognitive development, language, and their growing sense of self influence the emotions they show and the contexts in which they are displayed. In early childhood, children show gains in emotional competence—abilities that permit them to recognize, understand, and talk about their emotions in increasingly complex ways (Denham, Bassett, & Wyatt, 2007; Halberstadt, Denham, & Dunsmore, 2001; Saarni & Carolyn, 2000). As children develop emotional competence they are better able to appraise others' emotions and influences on emotions, are increasingly aware of social rules and conventions, and become better at self-regulation, controlling their emotional reactions (Goodvin et al., 2015).

EMOTIONAL UNDERSTANDING

Donald begins to cry as his mother leaves, dropping him off at preschool. Watching Donald, Amber explains to her mother, "Donald is sad because he misses his mommy," and she brings Donald a toy. "Don't be sad," she says. By 3 to 4 years of age, children recognize and name emotions based on their expressive cues (Levine, Stein, & Liwag, 1999). By age 4, children begin to understand that external factors (such as losing a toy) can affect emotion and can predict a peer's emotion and behavior (e.g., feeling sad and crying or feeling angry and hitting things; Gross & Ballif, 1991; Hughes & Dunn, 1998). Young children's explanations for emotion emphasize external causes (Levine, 1995). The emergence of theory of mind has profound implications for emotional development. As children begin to take other people's perspectives, they are able to apply their understanding of emotions to help others, such as recognizing that a sibling is sad and offering a hug (Fabes, Eisenberg, McCormick, & Wilson, 1988). Children's growing understanding of the mind leads them to appreciate the role of internal factors, such as desires, on emotion and behavior (Lagattuta & Thompson, 2007; Wellman, Phillips, & Rodriguez, 2000). By age 5, most children understand that desire can motivate emotion, and many understand that people's emotional reactions to an event can vary based on their desires (Harris, Johnson, Hutton, Andrews, & Cooke, 1989; Wellman et al., 2000).

Elementary school children are more likely to refer to internal causes, such as thoughts or desires, as motivations for emotions rather than external causes, such as breaking a toy (Flavell, Flavell, & Green, 2001). At about age 6 to 7, children incorporate their growing understanding of beliefs into their attributions for emotion; they begin to appreciate that a person's belief will determine his or her emotional reaction to a situation (Bradmetz & Schneider, 1999; Lagattuta et al., 2015; Pons, Harris, & de Rosnay, 2004). In one study, 4-, 5-, and 7-year-old children listened to scenarios depicting a child alone or accompanied by another person (mother; father; friend) who encounters a scary creature. With age, children were more likely to realize that different people will experience different intensities of fear in the same situation. They also demonstrated an increasing understanding that people's beliefs can increase or reduce fear, depending on the use of strategies (e.g., reminding oneself that the creature is not real; Sayfan & Lagattuta, 2009). Older children's understanding of emotion expands to include a temporal element—for example, that emotional intensity tends to gradually dissipate over time; that emotions can be triggered by thinking about past events; and that personal background, experiences, and personality influence emotional reactions (Goodvin et al., 2015; Lagattuta et al., 2015).

Although a basic understanding of emotion emerges early, it is not until late childhood that children are able to appreciate that people can have mixed or conflicting emotions; that they can feel both happy and sad or fearful (De Rosnay et al., 2014; Pons et al., 2004). In one study, 4- to 11-year-old children listened to a story about a child who got a new kitten to replace one that ran away. Most 5-year-old children believed that the child would feel happy about the new kitten and rejected the idea that child might feel both happy about the new kitten and sad about the lost kitten. Yet most 7- to 8-year-olds and nearly all 10- to 11-year-olds thought that the child would feel mixed emotions (Donaldson & Westerman, 1986). Other research supports the finding that by age 8, most children can recognize that a person can have mixed emotions and that when presented with emotional stimuli, such as a movie with a bittersweet ending, children themselves can report experiencing both happy and sad emotions (Larsen, To, & Fireman, 2007).

Interactions with others play an important role in advancing children's understanding of emotions. When parents talk about emotions and explain their own and their child's emotions, preschoolers are better able to evaluate and label others' emotions (Denham et al., 2007; Denham & Kochanoff, 2002). Young children often discuss emotional experiences with parents and peers and enact emotions in pretend sociodramatic play, providing experience and practice in understanding emotions and their influence on social interactions (Goodvin et al., 2015). Pretend play with siblings and peers gives children practice in acting out feelings, considering others' perspectives, and implementing self-control, improving children's understanding of emotion (Hoffmann & Russ, 2012; Youngblade & Dunn, 1995). One study showed that preschoolers' sociodramatic play predicted their expressiveness, knowledge, and regulation of emotion one year later (Lindsey et al., 2013). Children's interactions with siblings offer important opportunities to practice identifying emotions, decoding the causes of emotions, anticipating the emotional responses of others, and using their emotional understanding to influence their relationships and affect the behavior of others (Kramer, 2014). Parent–child interactions remain important influences on emotional development throughout the elementary-school years (Castro, Halberstadt, Lozada, & Craig, 2015).

David Grossman/Alamy

Children learn about emotions through interactions with other children, teachers, and family members.

EMOTION REGULATION

During the course of childhood, children make great strides in emotion regulation and become better able to manage their emotional experience and how emotions are displayed. Children's capacities for emotion regulation are influenced by advances in cognitive development, theory of mind, and language development. With age, children invoke different strategies for emotional control. By age 4, children can explain simple strategies for reducing emotional arousal, such as limiting sensory input (covering their eyes), talking to themselves ("It's not scary."), or changing their goals ("I want to play blocks," after having been excluded by children who were playing another game; Thompson & Goodvin, 2007). Six- and seven-year-old children continue to prefer behavioral strategies, such as fleeing a distressful situation, whereas by around 8 years of age children start to report that psychological strategies, such as using distracting thoughts, can be more effective (Pons et al., 2004; Terwogt & Stegge, 1995). Now children become more reflective and strategic in managing their emotions. School-age children learn how to redirect their attention, reconceptualize the situation ("It's not so bad"), and use cognitive strategies to manage emotions (Saarni et al., 1998).

Emotion regulation strategies are a response to emotions but also influence emotional experience—how emotions are felt (Cole et al., 2004; Thompson, 1994). Self-regulation helps us manage difficult circumstances, but the specific mechanisms we use vary with context. For example, a child who assertively responds to a bully by protesting loudly when a teacher is nearby but quietly tolerates it when adults are absent may be showing two forms of competent emotion regulation, adaptive to each specific context (Thompson, 2011). Learning to cope with and change intense emotions is adaptive.

Parents remain important resources for emotional management in childhood. Parents who are responsive when children are distressed, who frame experiences for children (e.g., acting cheery during a trip to the doctor), and who explain expectations and strategies for emotional management, are both modeling and fostering emotion regulation (McDowell, Kim, O'Neil, & Parke, 2002; Morris et al., 2011; Sala, Pons, & Molina, 2014). On the other hand, dismissive or hostile reactions to children's emotions prevent them from learning how to manage and not be overwhelmed by their emotions and interferes with children's functioning with peers and at school (Zeman, Cassano, & Adrian, 2012). When children develop skills in emotion regulation, they begin to feel a sense of control over their emotional experience (McClelland et al., 2015; Saarni & Carolyn, 2000). Children who are able to direct their attention and distract themselves when distressed or frustrated become well-behaved students and are well liked by peers (McClelland & Cameron, 2011). Emotion regulation skill, therefore, is associated with both social competence and overall adjustment (Deneault & Ricard, 2013).

CONTEXTUAL INFLUENCES ON CHILDREN'S EMOTIONAL DEVELOPMENT

The contexts in which children are raised influence their understanding and expression of emotion. Children more easily acquire their culture's display rules, as compared with infants. The neighborhoods and communities in which children live play a complex role in their emotional development, varying with children's capacity for resilience.

Culture and Emotional Display Rules

As described earlier in this chapter, infants learn that some displays of emotion are more acceptable than others. However, it is not until middle childhood that children understand that emotions can be intentionally hidden through the use of display rules (Jones, Abbey, & Cumberland, 1998; Misailidi, 2006). Emotional display rules are used to mask the expression of socially undesirable true feelings with a more socially appropriate

Children learn cultural display rules about emotions by interacting with their parents.

emotional expression that will avoid hurting others' feelings, preserve relationships, and protect self-esteem (Goodvin et al., 2015). Awareness and application of display rules emerges during the childhood years. For example, young children often reject undesirable gifts ("I don't want this!") as they are unaware of the social implications of expressing displeasure with a gift. In middle childhood, however, children begin to understand the meaning of display rules and become able to apply them to manage their emotional behavior. Unlike younger children, they will politely express thanks for an undesirable gift, providing "fake" smiles and keeping their feelings private (Kromm, Färber, & Holodynski, 2015; Thompson, Winer, & Goodvin, 2013).

As in infancy, the development of emotional understanding and display rules about what emotions are appropriate to show under what circumstances emerges from parent–child interactions (Malatesta & Haviland, 1982). Parents react to and socialize their children's emotional expressions—and the means and goals of socialization vary with cultural beliefs about emotion (Friedlmeier, Corapci, & Cole, 2011). Parents of preschool- and school-age children tend to comfort and distract their children during challenging situations, as well as encouraging emotional expression and scaffolding the child to manage distress (Eisenberg, Cumberland, & Spinrad, 1998).

In Western parent–child dyads, the encouragement of emotional expression and provision of instrumental support (scaffolding) is viewed as supportive and thought to be associated with children's emotion knowledge and social competence. In contrast, punitive, harsh responses that minimize children's emotions are labeled as nonsupportive and are associated with poor emotional competence in children. U.S. parents tend to endorse supportive socialization responses more than those that are unsupportive (Cassano, Perry-Parrish, & Zeman, 2007). However, parents offer more support in helping children manage some emotions than others. For example, parents of school-age children in the United States tend to be more understanding and provide more emotional and instrumental support in response to children's sadness than anger, similar to parents in India who also are more responsive to sadness than anger (Shipman & Zeman, 2001; Zeman & Garber, 1996).

In the South Asian country of Nepal, naturalistic observation of Tamang (indigenous inhabitants) and Brahman (Hindu upper caste) families illustrate cultural differences in emotional socialization of intense emotions, such as anger. One study showed that Tamang mothers discouraged children's anger by scolding and teasing, perhaps reflecting the Tamang culture's Buddhist values of minimizing emotion, as well as their low social status relative to Brahmans (Cole 2006). Brahman parents, on the other hand, responded to children's anger with reasoning; not encouragement or punishment. Tamang and Brahman parents also differed in responses to shame. Tamang parents responded to children's shame with a combination of ignoring, reasoning, and nurturing. Brahman parents ignored shame, perhaps because shame is inconsistent with the Brahman high social caste. Among school-age children, Brahman children showed a greater awareness of the need to conceal anger as compared with Tamang or U.S. children (Cole, Tamang, & Shrestha, 2006). These findings suggest that emotional socialization varies even within collectivist societies, perhaps reflecting the myriad contexts that can coexist within a society (Friedlmeier et al., 2011).

Contextual Risks to Emotional Development: Neighborhood and Community Violence

The neighborhoods and communities where children reside offer risks and opportunities for development. Pervasive violence is a critical risk in many communities as more than one-third of U.S. children and adolescents witness violence within their communities (Kennedy & Ceballo, 2014), and the proportion is much higher in some inner-city neighborhoods. One study of inner-city mothers of young children enrolled in Head Start programs revealed that nearly three-quarters reported witnessing drug transactions and violence in their neighborhood, such as people being physically assaulted, threatened with a weapon, or robbed, and more than two-thirds of the women reported experiencing violence and threats of violence themselves (Farver, Xu, Eppe, Fernandez, & Schwartz, 2005).

Exposure to community violence shares similarities with experiencing the violence of war (see Lives in Context: Exposure to War and Terrorism and Children's Development) and is particularly damaging to development because it is inescapable, infiltrating all ecological levels—school, playground, neighborhood, and home. The chronic and random nature of community violence presents a constant threat to children's and parents' sense of safety. In such environments, children learn that the world is a dangerous and unpredictable place and that parents are unable to offer protection (Farver et al., 2005). Feeling unsafe may affect children's natural curiosity and their desire to learn by exploring the world (Balter & Tamis-LeMonda, 2006).

Exposure to community violence poses risks not only to children's safety but to their emotional health, cognitive and social development, and well-being.

Children exposed to chronic community violence display anxiety and symptoms of post-traumatic stress disorder (PTSD), which is commonly seen in individuals exposed to the extreme trauma of war and natural disasters. Symptoms of PTSD include exaggerated startle responses, difficulty eating and sleeping, and academic, cognitive, and health problems (Fowler, Tompsett, Braciszewski, Jacques-Tiura, & Baltes, 2009; Kennedy & Ceballo, 2014; Wright, Austin, Booth, & Kliewer, 2016). The periodic and unpredictable experience of intense emotions may interfere with children's emotional development, including the ability to identify and regulate their emotions, and can disrupt the development of empathy and prosocial responses. Children who are exposed to community violence tend to be less socially aware, less skilled, and display more aggressive and disruptive behavior than other children (McMahon et al., 2013; Mohammad, Shapiro, Wainwright, & Carter, 2015). Children who experience prolonged exposure to high levels of violence are at risk to become desensitized to it (Gaylord-Harden, Dickson, & Pierre, 2016).

Community violence targets parents as well as children. The parental distress, frustration, and sense of helplessness that accompany community violence compromise parenting (Vincent, 2009). When dealing with their own grief, fear, anxiety, and depression, parents may be less available for physical and emotional caregiving, which in turn predicts poor child adjustment (Farver et al., 2005). Children who are exposed to violence in their communities and the violence of war are at particular risk for poor adjustment, as discussed in the Lives in Context feature.

Community violence is unquestionably detrimental to developmental outcomes. However, some children display more resilience to its negative effects than others. Three factors appear to protect children from the most negative effects of exposure to community violence: (1) having a supportive person in the environment; (2) having a protected place in the neighborhood that provides a safe haven from violence exposure; and (3) having personal resources such as adaptable temperament, intelligence, or coping capacities (Jain & Cohen, 2013). Unfortunately, the fear that accompanies community violence influences all members of the community, reducing supports and safe havens. Effective interventions to combat the effects of community violence include after-school community centers that allow children to interact with each other and caring adults in a safe context, permitting them to develop skills in coping, conflict resolution, and emotion regulation.

LIVES IN CONTEXT

• • Exposure to War and Terrorism and Children's Development

Children exposed to war and terrorism experience multiple devastating losses of life, homes, and even entire communities.

Acts of war and terror affect the child, family, and community—and hold dire consequences for children's development (Catani et al., 2010). Living through chronic unexpected bouts of terror and trauma, such as responding to air raids, listening to bomb blasts, fleeing a home and community in search of safety, and sudden losses of loved ones to military service, confinement, or death, evokes trauma that disrupts the contextual and social fabric of children and families' lives (Sagi-Schwartz, 2008; Werner, 2012; Williams, 2007). Children require stability—especially in times of trauma. Many children experience not only the loss of a sense of safety, but the loss of the familiar environment and routines of school, social networks, and patterns of family life (Cummings, Goeke-Morey, Merrilees, Taylor, & Shirlow, 2014; Morgos, Worden, & Gupta, 2007).

Preschool children under the age of 6 often respond with anxiety, behavior problems sleep problems and symptoms of PTSD (Slone & Mann, 2016). School-age children are at particular risk for negative outcomes in response to exposure to the trauma of war and terrorism because they are old enough to understand the gravity of the situation but have not yet developed the emotion regulation, abstract reasoning, and psychosocial maturity to process such events (Saraiya, Garakani, & Billick, 2013). Children exposed to acts of terror may show a prolonged fear of being alone,

safety concerns, and preoccupations with danger, but also aggression (Huesmann et al., 2016). They may lose interest in their favorite activities and may engage in repetitive traumatic play and retelling of trauma. Yet many children are naturally resilient. For example, one study of Palestine children exposed to the 2008–2009 War on Gaza found that about three-quarters of the children showed some recovery from PTSD symptoms (Punamäki, Palosaari, Diab, Peltonen, & Qouta, 2014). Likewise, most child survivors of war who participated in long-term follow-up studies showed no enduring patterns of emotional distress or poor psychosocial outcomes (Werner, 2012).

Intervening to assist children exposed to war and terrorism is difficult because typically the trauma is ongoing and unpredictable. Interventions to assist children promote children's attachment with parents and caregivers by ensuring that children stay physically and emotionally close to their parents. Parents who are able to instill a sense of warmth and security are best able to support their children's needs and promote resilience (Saraiya et al., 2013). Children's physical needs must be met through adequate nutrition, health care, and opportunities to engage in physical activity. Children must also have opportunities to express ideas and feelings directly and through play, such as drawing, storytelling, drama, and games. School-based interventions can help children adjust (Asarnow, 2011). However children in war zones often are displaced and lose the daily school routine. Interventions should help restore children's educational routines. When schools are closed, locally trained paraprofessionals can help families establish educational resources until children can return to their usual schools. No intervention can erase the effects of exposure to the trauma of war and terror, but interventions can help to bolster the factors that promote resilience to adversity.

What Do You Think?

Consider the problem of war or terrorism from the standpoint of Bronfenbrenner's bioecological theory. Identify factors within the microsystem that may help children adjust to experiencing terror. What factors might make it more challenging for children to adjust? What about mesosystem factors? Exosystem? Macrosystem?

Fostering Resilience in Children

Best friends Jane and Margarita walk to school together every day, partly because they live next door to each other and enjoy each other's company, but also because their mothers don't allow them to walk around their neighborhood alone. One day while Jane and Margarita played in the living room at Margarita's home, they heard an argument outside and suddenly a bullet crashed through the window, hitting the wall across the room. Since then, they are forbidden to play outside their homes and instead have to play in the kitchen, far away from the living room windows that look out on the street.

Clearly Jane and Margarita live in a community that poses risks to their safety. They also both live with single mothers who often leave their daughters alone at night as they work their part-time second jobs.

Many children like Jane and Margarita are faced with **risk factors**—individual or contextual challenges that tax their coping capacities and can evoke psychological stress, such as the experience of divorce, bullying, sexual abuse, low socioeconomic status, and exposure to poverty-stricken and dangerous neighborhoods, as well as social and emotional predispositions, including anxiety (Luthar, 2006; Masten, Best, & Garmezy, 1990). The more risks that children face, the more difficult it is for them to adjust and the more likely they are to have psychological and behavioral problems such as anxiety, depression, poor academic achievement, and delinquent activity.

Jane and Margarita attend a school with limited resources, overcrowded classrooms, outdated books, and teachers who feel overwhelmed by the large number of students with special needs. Like many of her classmates, Jane finds it hard to stop worrying and concentrate in class, and she performs poorly in reading and math. Margarita, on the other hand, manages to earn A's on many of her assignments. Although Margarita worries about her family and her own safety, she can put aside her worries when she concentrates on her studies. Despite experiencing a variety of intense stressors, some children, like Margarita, display little trauma and are able to manage their anxiety and succeed at home and school, showing high self-esteem, low levels of depression, few behavioral problems, and positive academic achievement (Cicchetti, 2010; Kim-Cohen, 2007).

Margarita displays **resilience**, the ability to respond or perform positively in the face of adversity, to achieve despite the presence of disadvantages, or to significantly exceed expectations given poor home, school, and community circumstances (Masten, 2014).

risk factors Individual or contextual challenges that tax an individual's coping capacities and can evoke psychological stress.

resilience The ability to adapt to serious adversity.

FIGURE 10.1: Characteristics of Resilient Children, as Reported by Their Parents

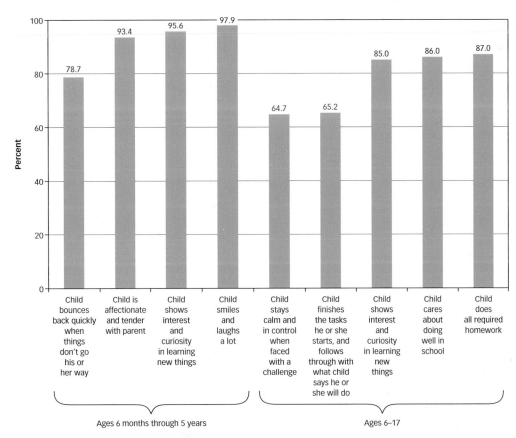

Source: Child Trends (2013).

TABLE 10.1 • Characteristics Associated With Resilience

Individual Competencies

- Coping skills
- Easy temperament
- Emotion regulation abilities
- Good cognitive abilities
- Intelligence
- Positive outlook
- Positive self-concept
- Religiosity
- Self- efficacy (feeling of control over one's destiny)
- Talents valued by others

Family Competencies and Characteristics

- Close relationships with parents and caregivers
- Organized home
- Parental involvement in children's education
- Positive family climate
- Postsecondary education of parents
- Provision of support
- Religiosity and engagement with the church
- Socioeconomic advantage
- Warm but assertive parenting

School and Community Characteristics

- Access to local churches
- After school programs
- Availability of emergency services
- Mentoring programs and opportunities to form relationships with adults
- Health care availability
- Instruction in conflict management
- Opportunity to develop and practice leadership skills
- Peer programs, such as big bother/sister programs
- Programs to assist developing self-management skills
- Public safety
- Support networks outside of the family, such as supportive adults and peers
- Ties to prosocial organizations
- Well-funded schools with highly qualified teachers
- Youth programs

Adaptation to adversity is a dynamic process involving interactions among the child's developmental capacities and his or her changing context, including relationships with other people (Goldman, Stamler, Kleinman, Kerner, & Lewis, 2016; Masten, 2016). It is influenced by prior development, competence, risk factors, and the nature of the current challenges faced, as well as the child's adaptive capacity and strengths, known as protective factors (Cicchetti, 2010; Masten & Narayan, 2012). **Protective factors** are influences that promote positive outcomes reduce the poor outcomes associated with adverse circumstances (Kim-Cohen, 2007; Werner, 1995).

Resilient children have strengths and powerful capacities for coping and adjustment. They benefit from multiple protective influences that help them to maintain a positive developmental trajectory despite adverse circumstances (Domhardt, Münzer, Fegert, & Goldbeck, 2014; Vanderbilt-Adriance & Shaw, 2008). For example, Margarita regularly attends an after-school program where she learns to play basketball and use a computer. Her uncle, Pedro, visits every Wednesday and Sunday and she feels she can talk to him about whatever is happening in her life. Each week, Margarita attends church with her mother and Pedro, and her mother makes a big dinner. Each of these factors—routines, attending church, school and community connections, and positive and close relationships with adults—promotes children's adjustment and protects them against the negative outcomes associated with adversity (Masten & Monn, 2015).

Resilience is not an all-or-nothing attribute that children either have or do not have (Rutter et al., 2015). Instead, children vary in the degree to which they are resilient based on their unique contexts, and children's capacity for resilience can vary over time (Masten, 2014, 2016). Protective factors arise from within the child, from the family or extended family, and from the community (Luthar et al., 2015; Torrey & Haub, 2004; Werner, 2012). Resilient children tend to have personal characteristics that protect them from adversity, such as friendliness, self-control, an easy temperament, a sense of competence, good information processing and problem solving skills, and sensitivity to others, all of which aid them in managing adversity and learning from their experiences (Afifi & MacMillan, 2011; Marriott, Hamilton-Giachritsis, & Harrop, 2014; Masten, 2011). Resilient children are successful in regulating their emotions and behavior (Luthar, 2006; Luthar et al., 2015; Masten, 2014). In addition, resilient individuals have a proactive orientation. They take initiative in their lives, believe in their own effectiveness, and have a positive sense of self (Alvord & Grados, 2005; Lee, Kwong, Cheung, Ungar, & Cheung, 2010). Children who are resilient tend to have strong and supportive relationships with at least one parent, caregiver, or adult who provides guidance and support (Afifi & MacMillan, 2011; Domhardt et al., 2014). It is noteworthy, however, that some

protective factor Variable that is thought to reduce the poor outcomes associated with adverse circumstances.

children who appear resilient may suffer from internalizing problems that are not always readily apparent, such as anxiety, depression, or low self-worth, which may have long-term negative consequences for their development and adjustment (Masten & Coatsworth, 1998). Resilient children illustrate an important finding: Exposure to adversity in childhood does not necessarily lead to maladjustment; many children thrive despite challenging experiences. Table 10.1 illustrates characteristics that promote resilience in children.

 Thinking in Context 10.2

Risk and protective factors illustrate the dynamic interactions among individuals and their contexts.

1. What factors within children might influence their capacity to adjust to adversity? Identify individual characteristics within each domain of development (physical, cognitive, and socioemotional—see Chapter 1) that may act as risk and protective factors.

2. Identify contextual factors that might influence children's capacity to adjust to adversity. That is, identify risk and protective factors within the contexts in which children are raised.

EMOTIONAL DEVELOPMENT IN ADOLESCENCE AND ADULTHOOD

LO 10.3 Contrast the emotional experiences and coping skills of adolescents and adults.

Fourteen-year-old Marissa raced into the house, threw her books on the table and stormed off to her room, calling out, "Leave me alone!" and slamming the door. A moment later the sounds of her stereo blasted and filled the house with a pulsing beat. Most adults are quick to dismiss Marissa's behavior as typical of moody adolescents, consistent with the common belief that the hormones of puberty affect adolescents' moods, leading them to experience unexpected, intense, and volatile shifts. Yet, as we will see in this section, there is more to the story of adolescent emotions—and the issue of emotions and coping skills continues to be of interest throughout adulthood.

ADOLESCENT MOODS

Are adolescents naturally moody? Are moods simply to be expected? The popular view that adolescence is a troubling time for teens and parents to endure originates with the work of G. Stanley Hall, known as the father of adolescence, as he defined the field in his 1904 volume *Adolescence*. Hall theorized that adolescence is a period of "storm and stress;" a universal and inevitable upheaval triggered by puberty, comprising ages 14 to 24. He believed that adolescents' extreme volatility reenacted a tumultuous time in human history, the birth of civilization. Therefore, manifestations of storm and stress and extreme volatility, such as depression, severe troubles with parents, and delinquent activity, was to be expected and was a sign of normal healthy development.

We now know that Hall's beliefs about the nature of adolescence and the source of adolescent moodiness are not accurate. The contemporary perspective is that although adolescence may be stormy and/or stressful for some, it is not typically a developmental problem, nor is it inevitable or universal (Arnett, 1999; Hollenstein & Lougheed, 2013; Larson & Ham, 1993). For example, in interviews with adolescents from 10 countries (United States, Australia, Germany, Italy, Israel, Hungary, Turkey, Japan, Taiwan, and Bangladesh), most reported that they were usually happy, felt that they got along with their parents, and felt good about their progress toward adulthood (Offer, Ostrov, Howard, & Atkinson, 1988).

Although every adolescent experiences puberty, and biological changes undoubtedly influence behavior, it is only early in puberty that hormones rapidly increase and fluctuate enough to cause erratic and powerful shifts in adolescents' emotions and behavior (Reiter & Lee, 2001). Researchers have found that the relationship between pubertal hormones and adolescent mood is weak and inconsistent (Balzer, Duke, Hawke, & Steinbeck, 2015; Buchanan, Eccles, & Becker, 1992; Duke, Balzer, & Steinbeck, 2014). Moreover, there are dramatic individual differences in the effects of pubertal change depending on the age of onset, the duration and intensity of changes, adolescents' temperament- and emotional-regulation skills, and environmental supports (Hollenstein & Lougheed, 2013). Instead, we know that contextual influences also play an important role in adolescent behavior.

A unique research method offers an important perspective on adolescents' experience in relation to contextual influences. In a series of studies, adolescents and adults carried pagers, were beeped randomly throughout the day, and were asked to report what they were doing, who they were with, and how they felt (Larson & Csikszentmihalyi, 2014; Richards & Larson, 1993). This method, known as the **experience sampling method**, permits researchers a window into people's days. Similar to common belief, adolescents' moods overall were less stable than those of adults. They experienced wider and quicker mood changes. Contrary to popular belief, however, adolescents' mood swings varied with context, and adolescents reported moving from one context to another—such as from school to work to family to peers—more often than did adults (Larson & Richards, 1998; Larson & Seepersad, 2003). Rather than representing turmoil, wide mood swings appear to occur naturally with the many situational changes and shifts in peer settings that occur throughout adolescents' days and weeks (Larson et al., 2014). In other words, adolescents' mood shifts are influenced by changes in psychological and social factors that accompany situational changes; mood changes do not occur in a vacuum, but are influenced by adolescents' interactions with their contexts and their own perceptions.

Ultimately, developmental scientists today reject the notion that adolescence is a period extreme storm and stress, replacing it with a more nuanced view that adolescence is a time of change characterized by individual differences in how those changes are experienced. Some adolescents encounter extreme turmoil, but great trauma is not the norm. Most adolescents experience some ups and downs but emerge from adolescence unscathed. The danger of viewing adolescence as an inevitable period of storm and stress lies in that it may influence expectations for adolescent behavior, creating self-fulfilling prophecies that subtly influence how they are treated. For example, believing that adolescents are moody and prone to problems can lead a parent to unwittingly become more easily angered, reduce attempts to interact with the teen, or become overly restrictive or permissive, perhaps increasing the likelihood of problems. Mothers' expectations for underage drinking have been shown to predict their teen's future underage drinking (Madon, Guyll, Spoth, & Willard, 2004). Likewise, a study of 6th- and 7th-graders and their mothers revealed that the students whose mothers expected high risk taking and rebelliousness during adolescence reported engaging in more problem behavior 1 year later (Buchanan & Hughes, 2009). The beliefs we hold about adolescence and what we view as normal can have a profound effect on adolescents' emotional development and their behavior.

ADULTS' EMOTIONAL EXPERIENCE

Similar to the findings regarding the "storm and stress" view of adolescents, the emotional lives of adults—especially older adults—are often mischaracterized. Although popular stereotypes of aging depict loss, sadness, and regret (Reed & Carstensen, 2015), research instead shows that people tend to experience their greatest unhappiness and anxiety in early adulthood when they are faced with many choices and uncertainty

experience sampling method
A technique that gives researchers a window into people's days.

(Fingerman, Turiano, Davis, & Charles, 2013). In addition, well-being tends to increase with age, and older adults' emotional experience has been found to be positive, rich, and complex (Charles & Leger, 2016). Positive emotions, such as feeling active, confident, or in good spirits, tend to increase during adulthood up until 70 to 80 years of age, when they tend to level off and stabilize (Carstensen et al., 2011; Mroczek & Kolarz, 1998).

Positive emotions not only characterize older adults' daily experience, but also their memories. As mentioned in Chapter 7, older adults show an information processing bias toward positive versus negative information, whereas younger adults tend to show the opposite pattern (Reed & Carstensen, 2012; Reed, Chan, & Mikels, 2014). In other words, younger adults tend to focus on and recall negative aspects of their environment and negative experiences more so than older adults. For example, when young, middle-aged, and older adults were asked to recall images viewed on a computer screen, with increasing age adults recalled fewer negative and a greater proportion of positive images (Charles, Mather, & Carstensen, 2003). In addition, there are age differences in brain activation in response to positive and negative images. In one study, when young and older adults viewed upsetting and uplifting images, the young adults (18–29 years of age) tended to show activation in the amygdala for both sets of images, whereas the older adults (70–90 years old) showed amygdala activation for the positive but not the disturbing images (Mather & Carstensen, 2005; Recall that the amygdala is responsible for strong emotional reactions, especially aggression). Beginning in midlife, adults become less sensitive to negative stimuli (Carstensen & Mikels, 2005; Samanez-Larkin, Robertson, Mikels, Carstensen, & Gotlib, 2009).

Not only do adults experience more positive emotions, they also become less negative than their younger counterparts. Longitudinal research shows declines in negative emotions from early adulthood into late adulthood and then stability throughout late adulthood (Charles, Mogle, & Urban, 2016; Mroczek & Kolarz, 1998). For example, 70- to 103-year-old participants in the Berlin Study of Aging did not differ in reports of negative affect, such as feeling upset, angry, sad, or lonely (Kunzmann, Little, & Smith, 2000).

With age, adults experience emotion in more complex ways. For example, older adults are more likely to report the simultaneous experience of both positive and negative emotions (Charles & Carstensen, 2010; Fingerman et al., 2013). An elderly woman may experience the birth of a grandchild with joy but also some sadness, with the realization that she may not live to see her grandchild grow to adulthood. Advances in cognitive affective complexity (see Chapter 6), which refers to the ability to fuse emotion with cognition, improve adults' awareness of emotions and their capacity to integrate positive and negative feelings as well as to regulate intense emotions (Labouvie-Vief, 2003, 2015; Mikels et al., 2010). Perhaps as a consequence of this ability, coping styles and mechanisms for dealing with emotionally conflicted situations become more mature and differentiated, responses become less reactive or impulsive, and adults are less likely to ruminate (Consedine & Magai, 2006). For example, in situations that evoke anxiety and sadness, older adults are more likely to report using the emotional management strategy of acceptance whereas young adults are more likely to report using maladaptive strategies such as worry and rumination (Schirda, Valentine, Aldao, & Prakash, 2016). With advancing age, adults experience emotions in increasingly multi-faceted, conscious, and reflective ways, and develop emotion regulation skills that contribute to advances in well-being.

STRESS, COPING, AND HARDINESS

Caught in a traffic jam, Natasha uses her mobile phone to call her husband. "Hi, Honey, I'm running late. Can you start cooking dinner? He

Blend/Alamy

Middle-aged adults experience more daily hassles than adults of other ages, which pose risks to health and well-being.

replies, "Sorry, I'm not home yet. I've got a late meeting," Natasha sighs, "OK. I'll call the babysitter and ask her to stay late. I still have to stop at Mom's house to drop off her medicine and this traffic doesn't look like it will ease up any time soon. I didn't expect Mom's giving up driving to take up so much of my time." Like Natasha, most adults cannot avoid experiencing the stresses of daily life, such as juggling the demands of traffic, child care difficulties, work deadlines, and conflict with family and friends. Known as **daily hassles**, these small stresses quickly accumulate to influence adults' mood and ability to cope (McIntyre, Korn, & Matsuo, 2008). An overload of daily hassles, negative life events (e.g., divorce, unemployment, death of a loved one, or a serious illness in the family), and unfavorable social conditions (e.g., poverty, lack of resources, and unsafe communities) contribute to poor physical and mental health (Almeida, Neupert, Banks, & Serido, 2005; Lantz, House, Mero, & Williams, 2005), especially when perceived as out of control (Hay & Diehl, 2010).

Is there a time of life that is most stressful? The many choices available and decisions to be made make early adulthood a challenging time; young adults are more likely to report depressive feelings than are middle-aged adults, who tend to show more career and financial stability and better coping skills (Ajdacic-Gross et al., 2006; Schiefman, Van Gundy, & Taylor, 2001). Yet middle-aged adults experience more daily stresses than adults of any other age (Holliday, 2007), yet they tend to show a relatively happy outlook on life. Colloquially referred to as the "sandwich generation," middle-aged adults are pressed to meet not only the multiple demands of career and family, but often the demands of caring for two generations: their children and their elderly parents. Midlife adults' increasing capacities for self-regulation and their focus on the positive influence their ability to cope with the many stresses they experience. They tend to feel competent, in control, and flexible—characteristics that are adaptive for everyday problem solving.

Yet, as with all periods in life, adults show individual differences in their coping skills and adjustment. Some adults are better able than others to adapt as they display the personal characteristic that researchers refer to as hardiness (Maddi, 2007). Individuals who display **hardiness** tend to have a high sense of self-efficacy, feeling a sense of control over their lives and experiences. They also view challenges as opportunities for personal growth, and feel a sense of commitment to their life choices. That is, hardiness is a protective factor that contributes to resilience (Maddi, 2016).

Hardy individuals tend to appraise stressful situations positively, viewing them as manageable; they approach problems with an active coping style, and show relatively few negative reactions to stressful situations (Bartone, 2006; Maddi, 2016; Vogt, Rizvi, & Shipherd, 2008). The positive appraisals and sense of control that come with hardiness serve a protective function as they are negatively associated with emotional reactivity, average blood pressure, and rate of progression of cardiovascular disease, and positively associated with self-ratings of physical and mental health (Maddi, 2013; Sandvik et al., 2013). Conversely, people who score low in hardiness, as compared with their higher scoring peers, tend to feel less control, experience more negative reactions to stressful situations, and are more likely to use an emotion-focused style of coping, such as avoidance or denial, which is maladaptive to health and functioning and is associated with higher stress in response to stimuli (Dolbier, Smith, & Steinhardt, 2007).

Research on hardiness indicates that it is not just an innate trait of certain lucky people; instead, it can be learned (Maddi, 2013; 2016). Training in hardiness skills and attitudes, such as coping, relaxation, and stress reduction, along with adequate social support, good nutrition, and physical activity, can increase feelings

daily hassles Small stresses that quickly accumulate to influence adults' mood and ability to cope.

hardiness Personal qualities, including a sense of control, orientation towards personal growth, and commitment to life choices, that influences adults' ability to adapt to changes and life circumstances.

Jewel Samad/AFP/Getty

Individuals' sense of hardiness can be enhanced by learning stress management and coping techniques, such as meditation.

of control, challenge, and commitment which are central to hardiness (Maddi, 2007a). There is some evidence that hardy individuals in leadership positions can, indeed, increase hardy cognition and behavior in their followers. In the groups they lead, they may influence the meaning-making process so that adverse situations are interpreted as interesting, controllable, and challenging opportunities to grow (Bartone, 2006; Bartone, Roland, & Picano, 2008).

Fortunately, most people tend to show increasingly adaptive responses to stress as they progress through middle adulthood. They learn to anticipate stressful events, take steps to avoid them, and approach stressful situations with more realistic attitudes about their ability to change them (Aldwin & Levenson, 2001).

Lives in Context Video 10.1
Resilience and Hardiness in Adulthood

 Thinking in Context 10.3

1. Consider your emotional experience during adolescence. Do you recall experiencing strong emotions or rapid shifts in mood? If so, what do you think may have contributed these shifts? What aspects of your context may have influenced your emotional experience as an adolescent, whether it was intense and unstable or more mellow and stable?

2. What daily stressors do you face? What changes do you expect in the coming years? What steps can you take to enhance your hardiness and improve your ability to manage multiple stressors?

ATTACHMENT

LO 10.4 Compare attachment styles in infancy and adulthood.

Raj gurgles and cries out while lying in his crib. As his mother enters the room he squeals excitedly. Raj's mother smiles as she reaches into the crib, and Raj giggles with delight as she picks him up. Raj and his mother have formed an important emotional bond called attachment. **Attachment** refers to a lasting emotional tie between two people who each strive to maintain closeness to the other and act to ensure that the relationship continues. It is a strong emotional bond that endures over time. Two theorists have made particularly important contributions to our understanding about infant attachment: John Bowlby and Mary Ainsworth.

BOWLBY'S ETHOLOGICAL PERSPECTIVE ON ATTACHMENT

Bowlby, a British psychiatrist who became one of the first developmental psychologists, volunteered at a school for troubled children after he completed college in 1928. His experiences with two students changed his career: an affectionless, isolated teenager who had been expelled from his previous school for theft and who had no mother figure, and an 8-year-old boy who was anxious and closely followed Bowlby as if he were his shadow (Ainsworth, 1974; Bretherton, 1992). These experiences led Bowlby to wonder about the effects of early family relationships, specifically mother–child relationships, on personality development (Bretherton, 1992). Inspired by ethology, particularly by Lorenz's work on the imprinting of geese (see Chapter 1) and by observations of interactions of monkeys, Bowlby was one of the first theorists to believe that early family experiences influence emotional disturbances rather than aggressive and libidinal drives, as the psychoanalytic theorists had argued (see Chapter 1). Specifically, Bowlby (1969) developed an ethological theory of attachment which characterizes it as an adaptive behavior that evolved because it contributed to the survival of the human species. An attachment bond between caregivers and infants ensures that the two will remain in close proximity, thereby aiding the survival of the infant and, ultimately, the species. From this perspective, caregiving responses are

attachment A lasting emotional tie between two individuals who strive to maintain closeness and act to ensure that the relationship continues.

inherited and are triggered by the presence of infants and young children. Infants are innately drawn to particular aspects of the caregiver. Infants use **signaling behaviors**, such as crying and smiling, to bring the caregiver into contact.

A newborn's cry is an example of a signaling behavior designed to ensure that caregivers remain near him and that he is cared for. Babies develop a repertoire of signals, such as smiling, cooing, and clinging, but crying is a particularly effective signal because it conveys negative emotion that adults can judge reliably, and it motivates adults to relieve the infant's distress (Leger, Thompson, Merritt, & Benz, 1996). During the first months of life, infants rely on caregivers to regulate their states and emotions—to soothe them when they are distressed and help them establish and maintain an alert state. Attachment behaviors provide comfort and security to infants because they bring babies close to adults who can protect them. Infants become attached to those who respond consistently and appropriately to their signaling behavior.

Magnetic resonance imaging (MRI) scans suggest that first-time mothers are innately disposed to respond to infants' signaling behaviors. Mothers' brains light up with activity when they see their own infants' faces, and areas of the brain that are associated with rewards are activated specifically in response to happy, but not sad, infant faces (Strathearn, Jian, Fonagy, & Montague, 2008). Bowlby proposed that attachment formation progresses through several developmental phases during infancy. With each phase, infants' behavior becomes increasingly organized, adaptable, and intentional.

Stage 1: Indiscriminate Social Responsiveness (birth to 2 months): When caregivers are sensitive and consistent in responding to babies' signals, babies learn to associate their caregivers with the relief of distress, forming the basis for an initial bond. Infants respond to any caregiver who reacts to their signals, whether parent, grandparent, child-care provider, or sibling.

Stage 2: Discriminating Sociability (2 through 6–7 months): Babies begin to discriminate among adults and prefer familiar people. Attachment responses are directed toward a particular adult or adults who are best able to soothe the baby.

Stage 3: Attachments (7 to 24 months): Infants develop attachments to specific caregivers who attend, accurately interpret, and consistently respond to their signals. Infants can gain proximity to caregivers through their own motor efforts, such as crawling.

Stage 4: Reciprocal Relationships (24–30 months and onward): With advances in cognitive and language development, children can engage in interactions with their primary caregiver as partners, taking turns and initiating interactions within the attachment relationship. They begin to understand others' emotions and goals and apply this understanding though strategies such as social referencing.

The formation of an attachment bond is crucial for infants' development because infants begin to explore the world, using their attachment figure as a **secure base**, or foundation to return to when frightened. When infants are securely attached to their caregivers, they feel confident to explore the world and to learn by doing so. As attachments are first forming, infants are likely to experience **separation protest** (sometimes called **separation anxiety**), which is a reaction to separations from an attachment figure characterized by fear, distress, crying, and whining (Lamb & Lewis, 2011). Separation protest tends to increase between 8 and 13 to15 months of age and then declines (Kagan, 1983). This pattern appears across many cultures and environments as varied as those of the United States, Israeli kibbutzim, and !Kung hunter-gatherer groups in Africa (Kagan et al., 1994). It is the formation of the attachment bond that makes separation anxiety possible because infants must feel connected to their caregiver in order to feel distress in his or her absence. Separation protest declines during the final stage of attachment as infants develop reciprocal relationships with caregivers and can understand and predict parents' patterns of separation and return, reducing their confusion and distress.

signaling behaviors Behaviors that infants use, including crying and smiling, to bring the caregiver into contact.

secure base The use of a caregiver as a foundation from which to explore and return to for emotional support.

separation protest (separation anxiety) Occurs when infants respond to the departure of a caregiver with fear, distress, and crying.

The attachment bond developed during infancy and toddlerhood influences personality development because it becomes represented as an **internal working model**, or a set of expectations about one's worthiness of love, the availability of attachment figures during times of distress, and how one will be treated. The internal working model influences the development of self-concept, or sense of self, in infancy and becomes a guide to later relationships throughout life (Bretherton, 1992; Johnson, Dweck, & Chen, 2007; Lamb & Lewis, 2011).

AINSWORTH'S STRANGE SITUATION

Mary Salter Ainsworth, a Canadian psychologist, posited that infants must develop a dependence on parents in order to feel comfortable exploring the world (Salter, 1940). In the early 1950s, she began a collaboration with John Bowlby on a project examining the effects of separation from the mother on personality development. Ainsworth's observations of children during this project formed the basis of her theory of attachment (Bretherton, 1992).

Virtually all infants are attached to their parents, but they differ in security of attachment—the extent to which the infant feels that he or she can count on the parent to be there to meet his or her needs. Mary Ainsworth developed the **Strange Situation**, a structured observational procedure that reveals the security of attachment when the infant is placed under stress. As shown in Table 10.2, the Strange Situation is a heavily structured observation task consisting of eight 3-minute episodes. In each segment, the infant is with the parent (typically the mother), with a stranger, with both, or alone. The observation begins with the infant and mother together in an observation room equipped with many toys and a video camera to record the observations. Every 3 minutes the stranger or mother enters or leaves the room. Researchers attend to several aspects of the situation:

- *Exploration of the toys and room.* Does the infant explore and play with the toys? A secure infant happily explores the room when the mother is present.
- *Reaction during separations.* How does the infant react to the mother's departure? Securely attached infants notice the mother's departure and may or may not cry.
- *Reaction during reunions.* How does the infant react to the mother's return? Secure infants welcome the mother's return, seek comfort, and then return to play and exploration.

internal working model A set of expectations about one's worthiness of love and the availability of attachment figures during times of distress.

Strange Situation A structured laboratory procedure that measures the security of attachment by observing infants' reactions to being separated from the caregiver in an unfamiliar environment.

TABLE 10.2 • The Strange Situation

EPISODE	EVENT	ATTACHMENT BEHAVIOR OBSERVED
1	Experimenter introduces mother and infant to playroom and leaves	
2	Infant plays with toys and parent is seated	Mother as secure base
3	Stranger enters, talks with caregiver, and approaches infant	Reaction to unfamiliar adult
4	Mother leaves room; stranger responds to baby if upset	Reaction to separation from mother
5	Mother returns and greets infant	Reaction to reunion
6	Mother leaves room	Reaction to separation from mother
7	Stranger enters room and offers comfort to infant	Reaction to stranger and ability to be soothed by stranger
8	Mother returns and greets infant. Tries to interest the infant in toys	Reaction to reunion

On the basis of responses to the Strange Situation, infants are classified into one of several attachment types (Ainsworth, Blehar, Waters, & Wall, 1978).

- **Secure Attachment:** About two-thirds of infants in middle-class samples display a **secure attachment** in the Strange Situation (Thompson, 1998). Infants who are securely attached display stranger anxiety and separation protest. The infant greets the mother enthusiastically and seeks comfort during reunion sessions. Once comforted, he or she returns to individual play. The infant uses the mother as a secure base as he or she plays and explores but returns regularly to check in with the mother (e.g., brings her a toy). About 60% to 65% of North American infants are classified as securely attached (Ahnert, Pinquart, & Lamb, 2006; Lamb & Lewis, 2015).
- **Insecure Avoidant Attachment:** Infants who display an insecure avoidant attachment show little interest in the mother and busily explore the room during the Strange Situation. The infant is not distressed during the Strange Situation and is not enthusiastic upon reuniting with the mother. The infant ignores or avoids the mother on return or shows subtle signs of avoidance, such as failing to greet her. Infants with avoidant attachment resist attempts to be comforted by turning away. About 20% of samples of North American infants reflect this style of attachment (Lamb & Lewis, 2015).
- **Insecure Resistant Attachment:** Infants with an insecure resistant attachment show a mixed pattern of responses to the mother. The infant remains preoccupied with the mother throughout the procedure, seeking proximity and contact, but the infant's behavior during reunions suggest resistance as well as signs of anger and distress. The child experiences difficulty settling down and simultaneously seeks proximity and pushes away or hits. They may show anger or be passive. About 15% of infants fall into this category (Lamb & Lewis, 2015).
- **Insecure Disorganized Attachment:** The insecure disorganized attachment was identified by Mary Main and Judith Solomon in 1986 to account for the small set of infants who show inconsistent, contradictory behavior. The infant with insecure disorganized attachment shows a conflict between the approaching and fleeing the caregiver, suggesting fear. Frightening parental behavior (at the extreme, child abuse) is thought to play a role in insecure disorganized attachment (Duschinsky, 2015). Disorganized-disoriented attachment is a reliable predictor of social and emotional maladjustment from childhood into adulthood (Bernier & Meins, 2008; Wolke, Eryigit-Madzwamuse, & Gutbrod, 2014).

Attachment has lifelong consequences because it is manifested in the infant's internal working model of self and his or her feelings of worthiness of love. Early interactions with parents also influence infants' mental representations of people and relationships and create a foundation for future interactions with others (Ranson & Urichuk, 2008). Representations of self and other act as filters to social perception, expectations, and memory that influence how children approach new social partners (Raikes & Thompson, 2008).

Security of attachment is not static, however. It varies with the mother's behavior, such that if the mother's behavior changes over time, the infant's security of attachment and internal working model of self can change as well. As discussed in the Applying Developmental Science feature, the issue of attachment is more complex for infants and children who spend many hours in child care.

PROMOTING SECURE ATTACHMENT IN INFANCY

Attachment relationships serve as an important backdrop for emotional and social development. Our earliest attachments are with our primary caregivers, most often

secure attachment The attachment pattern in which an infant uses the caregiver as a secure base from which to explore, seeks contact during reunions, and is easily comforted by the caregiver.

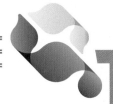

• • Infant Child Care

Gaetano/Corbis

High-quality child care that fosters close connections with caregivers and includes stimulating activities is associated with gains in cognitive and language development and can even compensate for lower-quality home environments.

In the United States, more than half of all mothers of infants under 1 year old, and more than two-thirds of mothers of children under 6, are employed (U.S. Bureau of Labor Statistics, 2016). The infants and young children of working mothers are cared for in a variety of settings: in center-based care; in the home of someone other than a relative; or with a relative such as a father, grandparent, or older sibling (Federal Interagency Forum on Child and Family Statistics, 2014). What are the effects of nonparental care? Early research suggested that infants in child care are at risk for insecure attachment; however, this is not supported in more recent studies conducted with large samples of children in infancy through preschool (Belsky, 2005; Erel, Oberman, & Yirmiya, 2000).

One of the best sources of information about the effects of nonparental care is a longitudinal study of more than 1,300 children, begun in 1991 and conducted by the National Institute of Child Health and Development (NICHD). This study found, perhaps surprisingly, that infants' developmental outcomes are influenced more by characteristics of the family, such as parenting, maternal education, and maternal sensitivity, than by the type of child care (Axe, 2007; Dehaan, 2006). Maternal employment has been shown to be either unrelated to mother-infant attachment or predictive of a positive attachment bond (Barglow, Vaughn, & Molitor, 1987; Harrison & Ungerer, 2002; Hoffman, 1974).

A second critical finding of the NICHD study was not as surprising: Quality of child care matters. Infants and young children exposed to poor-quality child care score lower on measures of cognitive and social competence, regardless of demographic variables such as parental education and socioeconomic status (NICHD Early Child Care Research Network, 2005). On the other hand, high-quality child care that includes specific efforts to stimulate children is associated with gains in cognitive and language development during the first 3 years of life and can even compensate for lower-quality home environments (Albers, Riksen-Walraven, & de Weerth, 2010; Watamura, Phillips, Morrissey, McCartney, & Bub, 2011).

Child care quality has long-term effects as well. Longitudinal research in Sweden showed that older children and adolescents who had received high-quality care as infants and toddlers scored higher on measures of cognitive, emotional, and social competence (Andersson, 1989; Andersson, Duvander, & Hank, 2004; Broberg, Wessels, Lamb, & Hwang, 1997). Other research shows that quality of child care from birth through age 4½ predicted higher cognitive functioning and academic achievement and less problem behavior at age 15, with greater advances accompanying higher-quality care (Vandell, Belsky, Burchinal, Steinberg, & Vandergrift, 2010). A longitudinal analysis of more than 1,200 children from the NICHD study revealed that the quality of care predicted academic grades and behavioral adjustment at the end of high school, at age 18, as well as admission to more selective colleges (Vandell, Burchinal, & Pierce, 2016).

The challenge is that high-quality child care is expensive. In 2015, the annual cost of infant care in the United States ranged from about $4,800 to $17,000, and in some cities, such as Washington, DC, it was nearly $23,000 (Child Care Aware of America, 2016). In some countries, such as Sweden, Denmark, and Japan, child care is heavily subsidized by the government (Allen, 2003; Waldfogel, 2006). In the United States, however, it remains a private responsibility. The few public subsidies for child care available in the United States are tied to economic need and are mainly targeted at low-income families who receive other forms of public assistance.

What Do You Think?

1. Consider your own experience with child care, either as a child or parent. Can you identify examples of high-quality care? Can you identify ways to improve the quality of care?

2. Assume that you are a parent seeking a child care for your own child or that you are providing advice to a parent. What are indicators of quality care? What would you look for?

our mothers. It was once thought that feeding determined patterns of attachment. The psychoanalytic perspective, for example, emphasized feeding as a critical context for infants and caregivers to interact, and for infants to have their needs met and thereby develop a sense of trust. Behaviorist theorists, on the other hand, explain attachment as a function of associating close contact with mothers with feeding, satisfying a biological need. Certainly, feeding brings infants and caregivers into close contact and offers opportunities to develop attachment bonds, but feeding itself does not determine attachment. In one famous study, baby rhesus monkeys were reared with two inanimate surrogate "mothers": one made of wire mesh and a second covered with terrycloth (see Figure 10.2). The baby monkeys clung to the terrycloth mother despite being fed only by the wire mother, suggesting that attachment bonds are not based on feeding but rather on contact comfort (Harlow & Zimmerman, 1959).

The most important determinant of infant attachment is the caregiver's ability to consistently and sensitively respond to the child's signals (Ainsworth et al., 1978; Behrens, Parker, & Haltigan, 2011). Infants become securely attached to mothers who are sensitive and responsive to their signals, who accept their role as caregiver, are accessible and cooperative with infants, are not distracted by their own thoughts and needs, and feel a sense of efficacy (Belsky & Fearon, 2002; DeWolff & van Ijzendoorn, 1997; Gartstein, Iverson, 2014; McElwain & Booth-LaForce, 2006; van den Boom, 1997). Mothers of securely attached infants provide stimulation, warmth, and consistently synchronize or match their interactions with their infants' needs (Beebe et al., 2010; Higley & Dozier, 2009).

Infants who are insecurely attached have mothers who tend to be more rigid, unresponsive, inconsistent, and demanding (Gartstein & Iverson, 2014). The insecure-avoidant attachment pattern is associated with parental rejection. Insecure-resistant attachment is

FIGURE 10.2: Harlow's Study: Contact Comfort and the Attachment Bond

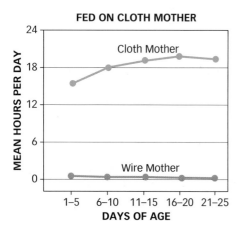

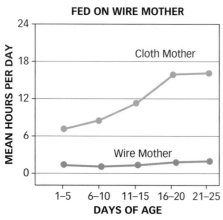

This infant monkey preferred to cling to the cloth-covered mother even if fed by the wire mother. Harlow concluded that attachment is based on contact comfort rather than feeding.

LIVES IN CONTEXT

• • Attachment to Fathers

Infants become attached to their fathers, although fathers tend to have different interaction styles than mothers. Father–infant interaction tends to be play-oriented, with high intensity stimulation and excitement, such as tickling, providing opportunities for babies to practice arousal management.

We know a great deal about the influence of mother–infant relationships on infant attachment and adjustment, but infants also develop attachments to their fathers (Grossmann et al., 2002; van Ijzendoorn & De Wolff, 1997). What do we know about infant–father attachment? At birth, fathers interact with their newborns much like mothers do. They provide similar levels of care by cradling the newborn and performing tasks like diaper changing, bathing, and feeding the newborn (Combs-Orme & Renkert, 2009; Lewis & Lamb, 2003). This is true of fathers in Western contexts as well as those in non-Western contexts, such as the Kadazan of Malaysia and Aka and Bofi of Central Africa (Fouts, 2008; Ziarat Hossain, Roopnarine, Ismail, Hashmi, & Sombuling, 2007; Tamis-LeMonda, Kahana-Kalman, & Yoshikawa, 2009).

Early in an infant's life, fathers and mothers develop different play and communicative styles. Fathers tend to be more stimulating while mothers are more soothing (Feldman, 2003; Grossmann et al., 2002). Father–infant play is more physical in nature as compared with the social exchanges centered on mutual gaze and vocalization that is characteristic of mother–infant play (Feldman, 2003). Fathers tend to engage in more unpredictable rough-and-tumble play throughout infancy and childhood, though it becomes less prevalent as children grow older (Lewis & Lamb, 2003). Paternal play styles are met with more positive reactions and arousal from infants; when young children have a choice of adult play partner, they tend to choose their fathers (Feldman, 2003; Lewis & Lamb, 2003). Overall, interactions with fathers tend to be more play oriented than

care oriented (Lamb, 1997). Fathers provide opportunities for babies to practice arousal management by providing high intensity stimulation and excitement, like tickling, chasing, and laughing (Feldman, 2003).

Differences in mothers and fathers' interaction styles appear in many cultures, including France, Switzerland, Italy, India, and among white non-Hispanic, African American, and Hispanic American families in the United States (Best, House, Barnard, & Spicker, 1994; Zirat Hossain, Field, Pickens, Malphurs, & Del Valle, 1997; Roopnarine, Talukder, Jain, Joshi, & Srivastav, 1992). However, parent–infant interaction styles also vary by culture: German, Swedish, and Israeli kibbutzim fathers, and fathers in the Aka ethnic group of Africa's western Congo basin, are not more playful than mothers (Frodi, Lamb, Hwang, & Frodi, 1983; Hewlett, 2008; Hewlett et al., 1998; Sagi et al., 1985). Despite these findings, overall and across cultures, most of the differences between mothers and fathers are not large (Lewis & Lamb, 2003).

Father–child interaction is an important contributor to children's development and is associated with social competence, independence, and cognitive development in children (Caldera, 2004; Frascarolo, 2004; Sethna et al., 2016). Fathers' play styles influence attachment relationships with infants. Fathers who are sensitive, supportive, and appropriately challenging during play promote father–infant attachment relationships (Grossmann et al., 2002). Rough-and-tumble play contributes to advancements in emotional and behavioral regulation in children (Flanders, Leo, Paquette, Pihl, & Séguin, 2009). When fathers are involved in the caregiving of their infants, their children are more likely to enjoy a warm relationship with their father as they grow older, carry out responsibilities, follow parents' directions, and be well adjusted (Amato, 1987; Caldera, 2004). Similar to findings with mothers, sensitive parenting on the part of fathers predicts secure attachments with their children through age 3 (Brown, Mangelsdorf, & Neff, 2012; Lucassen et al., 2011). The positive social, emotional, and cognitive effects of father–child interaction continue from infancy into childhood and adolescence (Sarkadi, Kristiansson, Oberklaid, & Bremberg, 2008). Simply put, fathers serve a very important role in children's development.

What Do You Think?

1. What are some of the challenges of studying father–child relationships? How might researchers address these challenges?

2. Why do you think fathers are more likely to be "playmates" than mothers?

Gerard Fritz / Science Source

associated with inconsistent and unresponsive parenting. Disorganized attachment is more common among infants who have been abused or raised in particularly poor caregiving environments and is associated with infant fear (Lamb & Lewis, 2011). Although insecure attachment responses may seem suboptimal, they may represent adaptive responses to poor caregiving environments (Weinfield, Sroufe, Egeland, & Carlson, 2008). For example, not relying on an unsupportive parent (such as developing an insecure-avoidant attachment) may represent a good strategy for infants.

Attachment patterns tend to be stable. Securely attached infants are likely to remain secure throughout development (Becker-Stoll, Fremmer-Bombik, Wartner, Zimmermann, & Grossmann, 2008; Ranson & Urichuk, 2008; E. Waters, Merrick, Treboux, Crowell, & Albersheim, 2000). However, negative experience can disrupt attachment. For example, the loss of a parent, parental divorce, a parent's psychiatric disorder, and physical abuse, as well as changes in family stressors, adaptive processes and living conditions, can transform a secure attachment into an insecure attachment pattern later in childhood or adolescence (Hamilton, 2000; Lieberman & Van Horn, 2008; Thompson, 2000; Weinfield et al., 2000). Conversely, it is also the case that quality parent–child interactions can at least partially make up for poor interactions early in life. Children with insecure attachments in infancy who experience subsequent sensitive parenting show more positive social and behavioral outcomes at 54 months of age than do those who receive continuous care of poor quality (Dehaan, 2006). An insecure attachment between child and parent can be overcome by changing maladaptive interaction patterns, increasing sensitivity on the part of the parent, and fostering consistent and developmentally appropriate responses to children's behaviors. Pediatricians, counselors, and social workers can help parents identify and change ineffective parenting behaviors to improve parent–child interaction patterns.

Although most research on attachment has focused on the mother–infant bond, we know that infants form multiple attachments: They also become attached to fathers (see the Lives in Context feature) and other caregivers. An infant's secure attachment relationship with a father, for example, can compensate for the negative effects of an insecure attachment to a mother (Boldt, Kochanska, Yoon, & Koenig Nordling, 2014; Engle & Breaux, 1998; Kochanska & Kim, 2013). It is important that infants develop attachments with some caregivers—but which caregivers, whether mothers, fathers, or other responsive adults, matters less than the bond itself.

CULTURAL VARIATIONS IN ATTACHMENT CLASSIFICATIONS

MENAHEM KAHANA/AFP/Getty Images

Children reared in tight-knit but isolated Israeli kibbutz communities spend much of their time with community members and do not encounter strangers in their day-to-day lives. They tend to form bonds with other community members and experience strangers as threatening.

Whether the Strange Situation is applicable across cultural contexts is a matter of debate. However, research has shown that infants in many countries, including Germany, Holland, Japan, and the United States, approach the Strange Situation in similar ways (Sagi, Van IJzendoorn, & Koren-Karie, 1991). The patterns of attachment identified by Ainsworth occur in a wide variety of cultures in North America, Europe, Asia, Africa, and the Middle East (Bornstein et al., 2013; Cassibba, 2013; Gardiner & Kosmitzki, 2010; Huang, Lewin, Mitchell, & Zhang, 2012; Jin, Jacobvitz, Hazen, & Jung, 2012). Insecure-avoidant attachments are more common in Western European countries, and insecure-resistant attachments are more prevalent in Japan and Israel (Van Ijzendoorn & Kroonenberg, 1988). There are different cultural interpretations of infant behaviors shown in the Strange Situation. For example, although Western parents might interpret insecure-resistant behavior as clingy, Asian parents might interpret it as successful bonding (Gardiner & Kosmitzki, 2018).

Western cultures tend to emphasize individuality and independence, whereas Eastern cultures are more likely to emphasize the importance of relationships and connections with others. Individualist and collectivist cultural perspectives interpret children's development in different ways. Many Japanese and Israeli infants become highly distressed during the Strange Situation and show high rates of insecure resistance. Resistance in Japanese samples of infants can be attributed to cultural child-rearing practices that foster mother–infant closeness and physical intimacy that leaves infants unprepared for the separation episodes; the Strange Situation may be so stressful for them that they resist comforting (Takahashi, 1990). Similarly, infants who are raised in small, close-knit Israeli kibbutz communities do not encounter strangers in their day-to-day lives, so the introduction of a stranger in the Strange Situation procedure can be overly challenging for them. At the same time, kibbutz-reared infants spend much of their time with their peers and caregivers and see their parents infrequently, and therefore may prefer to be comforted by people other than their parents (Sagi et al., 1985).

Dogon infants from Mali, West Africa show rates of secure attachment that are similar to those of Western infants, but the avoidant attachment style is not observed in samples of Dogon infants (McMahan True, Pisani, & Oumar, 2001). Dogon infant care practices diminish the likelihood of avoidant attachment because the infant is in constant proximity to the mother, nurses in response to hunger and distress signals, and receives prompt responsiveness. Infant distress is answered with feeding and infants feed on demand, so mothers cannot behave in ways that would foster avoidant attachment.

As shown in Figure 10.3, although secure attachment is most common, the prevalence of other attachment styles varies internationally. The behaviors that characterize sensitive caregiving vary with culturally specific socialization goals, values, and beliefs of the parents, family, and community (Rothbaum, Weisz, Pott, Miyake, & Morelli, 2000). For example, Puerto Rican mothers often use more physical control in interactions with infants, such as picking up crawling infants and placing them in desired locations, during the first year of life than do European-American mothers. They actively structure interactions in ways consistent with long-term socialization goals oriented

FIGURE 10.3: Cross-Cultural Variations in Attachment

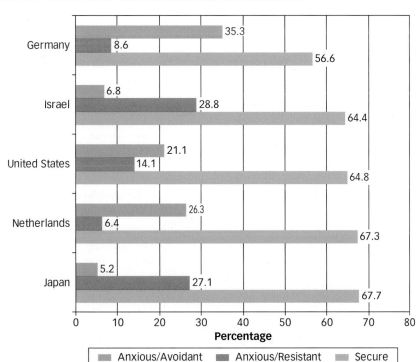

CULTURAL INFLUENCES ON DEVELOPMENT

• • Co-Sleeping

While sharing a bedroom can enhance the infant–parent bond and make nighttime feedings easier, infants are safest in their own bassinets, such as this one, which is adapted to promote safe parent–infant contact.

The practice of *co-sleeping*, which refers to the infant sharing a bed with the mother or with both parents, is common in many countries, yet controversial in others. In Japan, China, Kenya, Bangladesh, and the Mayan peninsula of Mexico, co-sleeping in infancy and early childhood is the norm and is believed to enhance the child's sense of security and attachment to the mother (Morelli, Rogoff, Oppenheim, & Goldsmith, 1992; Super & Harkness, 1982; Xiao-na, Hui-shan, Li-jin, & Xi-cheng, 2010). In Latin America and Asia, infants are not usually expected to go to bed and sleep alone at a regular time each night; instead, they are held until they fall asleep and then are placed in the parental bed (Lozoff, Wolf, & Davis, 1984). In contrast, in many industrialized countries, such as the United States and the United Kingdom, newborns are placed to sleep in their own bassinets, whether in their parents' room or in a separate nursery; learning to sleep by oneself is viewed as fostering independence and the ability to self-regulate (Ball, Hooker, & Kelly, 1999; McKenna & Volpe, 2007). Parents' decisions of whether to co-sleep are influenced by their own values and beliefs, which are often shaped by the context in which they live.

Pediatricians in Western nations tend to advise separate sleeping arrangements for parents and infants. The American Academy of Pediatrics and the United Kingdom Department of Health have declared sharing a bed with an infant to be an unsafe practice; instead, they advise having infants sleep in a crib in the parents' room (American Academy of Pediatrics, 2005; UK Department of Health, 2005). Despite these warnings, co-sleeping has become more common among Western families. When co-sleeping occurs it is usually initiated by the mother, especially if she breast feeds (Ball, Hooker, & Kelly, 2000; McCoy et al., 2004).

Proponents of co-sleeping argue that it best meets the developmental needs of human newborns and aids in forming the attachment bond (McKenna, 2001; McKenna & Mosko, 1993; Trevathan & McKenna, 1994; Willinger, Ko, Hoffman, Kessler, & Corwin, 2003). Infants who sleep with their mothers synchronize their sleep patterns with hers, permitting more awakenings for breast feeding, yet lengthening the total time that infants sleep (Gettler & McKenna, 2011; Goldberg & Keller, 2007; Mosko, Richard, & McKenna, 1997). Both mothers and babies benefit from skin-to-skin contact, as it enhances breast-milk production, stabilizes infants' heart rate, reduces apnea (gaps in the infant's breathing), increases the prevalence and duration of breast feeding, reduces crying, and is associated with more positive mother–infant interactions (McKenna & Volpe, 2007; Taylor, Donovan, & Leavitt, 2008). Fathers report that they find co-sleeping rewarding rather than an intrusion on the marital bed (Ball et al., 2000; McCoy et al., 2004).

In addition to the cautions mentioned earlier, opponents of co-sleeping point to increased risk of accidental suffocation and an increased risk of SIDS (sudden infant death syndrome), especially among mothers who smoke (Brenner et al., 2003; Mitchell, 2009). Yet other studies suggest that co-sleeping is a protective factor against SIDS (McKenna, 2001). Many experts believe that even though the use of comforters and pillows is hazardous, co-sleeping can be safe if appropriate precautions are taken, such as using light bed coverings and a firm mattress (McKenna, 2001). Others argue that bed-sharing should be abandoned in favor of room-sharing, to provide the developmental advantages of co-sleeping and minimize the dangers.

What Do You Think?

1. Should infants and parents co-sleep? Why or why not?

2. How might safety concerns be addressed?

3. In what ways might parent–child sleeping arrangements influence emotional development?

toward calm, attentive, and well-behaved children. Typically, attachment theory conceptualizes this type of control as insensitive, yet physical control is associated with secure attachment status at 12 months in Puerto Rican infants (but not white non-Hispanic infants; Carlson & Harwood, 2003; Harwood, Scholmerich, Schulze, & Gonzalez, 1999). Similarly, German mothers operate according to the shared cultural belief that infants should become independent at an early age and should learn that they cannot rely on the mother's comfort at all times. German mothers may seem unresponsive to their children's crying, yet they are demonstrating sensitive childrearing within their context (Grossmann, Spangler, Suess, & Unzner, 1985). Therefore, the behaviors that reflect sensitive caregiving vary with culture because they are adaptations to different circumstances (Rothbaum et al., 2000).

In some cultures, infants traditionally sleep in the same bed with their parents, and advocates argue that co-sleeping promotes secure infant attachment. The Cultural Influences on Development feature examines this practice.

ATTACHMENT-RELATED OUTCOMES IN CHILDHOOD AND ADOLESCENCE

Secure parent–child attachments are associated with a host of positive developmental outcomes. Infants who are securely attached tend to be more sociable with peers and unfamiliar adults than are those who are insecurely attached (Elicker, Englund, & Sroufe, 1992; Crugnola et al., 2011). They have more positive interactions with peers and their attempts at friendly interactions with peers are more likely to be successful (Fagot, 1997). Secure attachment in infancy predicts social competence and expressive language at 3 years of age, attention at 4.5 years of age, and autonomy in adolescence (Becker-Stoll et al., 2008; Fearon & Belsky, 2004). As preschoolers, securely attached children are better able to read others' emotions and have a more positive self-concept as compared with children with insecure attachments (Goodvin, Meyer, Thompson, & Hayes, 2008; Steele, Steele, & Croft, 2008). Likewise, preschool- and school-age children who were securely attached as infants tend to be more curious, empathetic, self-confident, socially competent, have more positive interactions with peers and have more close friendships than their peers who lacked secure attachment in infancy (Goodvin et al., 2008; Groh, Fearon, van IJzendoorn, Bakermans-Kranenburg, & Roisman, 2016; McElwain & Volling, 2004).

Attachment continues to be associated with positive development and functioning through middle childhood and adolescence (Groh et al., 2016). Children with secure attachments in infancy and early childhood are more socially competent, tend to be better at making and keeping friends and functioning in a social group, and demonstrate greater emotion regulation skills, self-esteem, ego resiliency, and peer competence in adolescence (Boldt et al., 2014; Brumariu, 2015; Jaffari-Bimmel, Juffer, van Ijzendoorn, Bakermans-Kranenburg, & Mooijaart, 2006; Moss & Lecompte, 2015). In contrast, insecure attachment, particularly disorganized attachment, is associated with higher rates of antisocial behavior, depression, and anxiety in later childhood and adolescence (Boldt et al., 2014; Groh, Roisman, van Ijzendoorn, Bakermans-Kranenburg, & Fearon, 2012; Kerns & Brumariu, 2014; Madigan, Atkinson, Laurin, & Benoit, 2013). For example, insecure attachment to mother and father at 12 months of age predicts teacher-rated behavior problems at 6½ years of age (Kochanska & Kim, 2013). In one study, older children (aged 8 to 12) with insecure attachments waited longer to call for help when carrying out a stressful task than did securely attached children, and waiting longer to seek help was associated with depressive symptoms one year later (Dujardin et al., 2016). In addition to fostering healthy development in all children, a secure attachment bond may protect children from the negative effects of being raised in disadvantaged environments (Lamb & Lewis, 2015).

During adolescence, a secure attachment to parents is positively associated with self-esteem, emotional adjustment, reduced engagement in delinquent activity, and healthy adaptation to stress (Cameron et al., 2016; de Vries, Hoeve, Stams, & Asscher, 2016; Hoeve et al., 2012). Adolescents with secure attachment tend to have

Close friendships and peer acceptance are important influences on self-esteem.

Jonathan Selig/The Image Bank/Getty Images

good peer relations and emotion regulation skills, and show positive identity development (Allen & Miga, 2010; Meeus, Oosterwegel, & Vollerbergh, 2002). Secure attachment relationships during adolescence predict satisfying adult relationships and positive adjustment in emerging adulthood (Agerup, Lydersen, Wallander, & Sund, 2015; Dawson, Allen, Marston, Hafen, & Schad, 2014; Kretschmer et al., 2016).

ADULT ATTACHMENT

Early relationships with parents continue to have implications for functioning when we reach adulthood. Maternal sensitivity, specifically, has been found to influence attachment and relationship quality in adults (Fraley, Roisman, Booth-LaForce, Owen, & Holland, 2013; Schoenmaker et al., 2015). Longitudinal studies of up to 23 years in duration suggest that childhood attachment predicts internal working models and relationship quality in early adulthood (Allen, Hauser, & Borman-Spurrell, 1996; Grossmann & Waters, 2005; Waters et al., 2000).

Perhaps the most typical attachments seen in adults are those they develop with their romantic partners (Mikulincer & Shaver, 2012; Shaver & Mikulincer, 2014). Adult attachments—in romantic relationships and in friendships—can be described in terms of four styles, representing combinations of attachment anxiety (the degree of concern about whether partners will be responsive) and avoidance (the degree of discomfort in being dependent on a partner; Hazan & Shaver, 1987). *Securely* attached adults seek to bond with their partners, desire closeness, and are comforted by their partners. They have a secure internal working model of self, they like themselves and tend to feel that they are lovable, and they have the ability to get close to others to establish an intimate relationship. Adults displaying the *anxious* attachment style likely have not developed a secure internal working model of self. They tend to fear abandonment, feel unworthy of love, and become overly dependent on their partners, showing possessiveness and jealousy, as well as feeling less trusting (Hazan & Shaver, 1987). The *avoidantly* attached adult tends to have a secure internal working model of self and feels worthy of love, but may not trust or depend on others, feeling that their partners want more intimacy than they do. They may avoid relationships, finding it difficult to get close to others and instead distance themselves from their partner. Similar to infant attachment classifications, the final adult attachment reflects a *disorganized* attachment style. The disorganized style combines a poor internal working model with a distrust of others, which manifests in a confusing, unpredictable mix of neediness and fear of closeness (fearful or disorganized attachment). However, similar to infants, most adults display a secure attachment style (Bakermans-Kranenburg & van IJzendoorn, 2009; Mickelson, Kessler, & Shaver, 1997).

Not surprisingly, secure attachment predicts positive romantic relationships; securely attached individuals tend to have better relationships with their partners and report greater sexual satisfaction than do individuals with avoidant or anxious attachment styles (Brassard, Péloquin, Dupuy, Wright, & Shaver, 2012; Shaver & Mikulincer, 2014; Stefanou & McCabe, 2012). Securely attached adults also display socioemotional advantages such as optimism, resilience, and emotional control; have a sense of self-esteem and efficacy; and use effective coping strategies (Mikulincer & Shaver, 2008, 2013, 2015). The positive effects of secure attachment on well-being continue into late adulthood (Van Assche et al., 2013).

Just as the internal working models formed through attachment in infancy influence attachment relationships in adulthood, adult attachment style influences parenting behaviors, and the subsequent infant-parent attachment bond. Adults who are classified as securely attached tend to be more sensitive and responsive parents and are more likely to have a child who is categorized as securely attached as compared with adults who are insecure (Jones, Cassidy, & Shaver, 2015). Difficulties with emotion regulation and empathy, common to insecure attachment styles (Britton & Fuendeling, 2005; Mikulincer & Shaver, 2008; Shaver & Mikulincer, 2007), interfere with parenting. Parents with an insecure attachment tend to be less consistent, involved, and accepting (Coyl, Newland, & Freeman, 2010;

Jones et al., 2015; Kilmann, Vendemia, Parnell, & Urbaniak, 2009). Parental sensitivity and responsiveness are at the core of attachment theory and are thought to be among the most important predictors of child attachment security (Ainsworth et al., 1978). Parents with an insecure attachment style have difficulty showing the consistent responsiveness needed for their infants to form secure attachments.

Yet, attachment is not static and unchangeable. Attachment has been found to shift in subtle ways during the adult years (van Assche et al., 2013). Generally, the number of attachments declines with age so that older adults have fewer attachment relationships than younger adults (Cicirelli, 2010). At the same time, the quality of attachment may change, often improving. For example, in one sample of people 18 to 70 years of age, attachment anxiety steadily declined from a high in the early adulthood, when many bonds are first formed, through late adulthood (Chopik, Edelstein, & Fraley, 2013).

In summary, attachment is an adaptive process in which infants and caregivers become attuned to each other and develop an enduring bond. Infants become attached to caregivers—mothers, fathers, and other adults—who are sensitive to their needs. Secure attachment in infancy is associated with emotional and social competence in infancy, early childhood, and even later childhood and adolescence. The attachment bond formed in infancy can also influence the relationships formed in adulthood.

 Thinking in Context 10.4

1. Children reared in impoverished orphanages are at risk of receiving little attention from adults and experiencing few meaningful interactions with caregivers. What might this experience mean for the development of attachment? What behaviors and outcomes might you expect from children reared under such conditions? In your view, what can be done to help such children?

2. The first internal working model of self is composed via the earliest attachments to caregivers. Consider the internal working models that adolescents and adults construct. What kinds of interactions and experiences might determine the internal working models that individuals construct in adolescence and adulthood?

TEMPERAMENT

LO 10.5 Discuss the lifespan stability of temperament and the role of goodness of fit in adjustment.

"Joshua is such an easygoing baby!" gushed his babysitter. "He eats everything, barely cries, and falls asleep without a fuss. I wish all my babies were like him." The babysitter is referring to Joshua's temperament. **Temperament**, the characteristic way in which an individual approaches and reacts to people and situations, is thought to be one of the basic building blocks of emotion and personality. Temperament has strong biological determinants; behavior genetics research has shown genetic bases for temperament (Saudino & Micalizzi, 2015). Yet the expression of temperament reflects reciprocal interactions among genetic predispositions, maturation, and experience (Gagne, Vendlinski, & Goldsmith, 2009; Rothbart, 2011; Thompson, 1998; Thompson, Winer, & Goodvin, 2013). Every infant behaves in a characteristic, predictable style that is influenced by his or her inborn tendencies toward arousal and stimulation as well as by experiences with adults and contexts. In other words, every infant displays a particular temperament style.

STYLES OF TEMPERAMENT

The New York Longitudinal Study (NYLS), begun in 1956, is a pioneering study of temperament that has followed 133 infants into adulthood. Early in life, the infants in

temperament Characteristic differences among individuals in emotional reactivity, self-regulation, and activity that influences reactions to the environment and are stable, and appear early in life.

the study demonstrated differences in nine characteristics that are thought to capture the essence of temperament (Buss & Plomin, 1984; Chess & Thomas, 1991; Goldsmith et al., 1987).

- *Activity level.* Some babies wriggle, kick their legs, wave their arms, and move around a great deal, whereas other babies tend to be more still and stay in one place.
- *Rhythmicity.* Some infants are predictable in their patterns of eating, sleeping, and defecating; other babies are not predictable.
- *Approach-withdrawal.* Some babies tend to approach new situations, people, and objects, whereas others withdraw from novelty.
- *Adaptability.* Some babies get used to new experiences and situations quickly; others do not.
- *Intensity of reaction.* Some babies have very extreme reactions, giggling exuberantly and crying with piercing wails. Other babies show more subdued reactions, such as simple smiles and soft, whimpering cries.
- *Threshold of responsiveness.* Some babies notice many types of stimuli—sights, sounds, and touch sensations—and react to them. Other infants notice few types of stimuli and seem oblivious to changes.
- *Quality of mood.* Some babies tend toward near-constant happiness while others tend toward irritability.
- *Distractibility.* Some babies can be easily distracted from objects or situations while others cannot.
- *Attention span.* Some babies play with one toy for a long time without becoming bored, whereas others get bored easily and change toys often.

Some aspects of infant temperament, particularly activity level, irritability, attention, and sociability or approach-withdrawal, show stability for months and years at a time, and in some cases even into adulthood (Kochanska & Knaack, 2003; Lemery, Goldsmith, Klinnert, & Mrazel, 1999; Pedlow, Sanson, Prior, & Oberklaid, 1993; Salekin & Averett, 2008; van Aken, 2009). Infants' growing ability to regulate their attention and emotions holds implications for some components of temperament, such as rhythmicity, distractibility, and intensity of reaction. The components of infant temperament cluster into three profiles, as summarized in Table 10.3 (Thomas & Chess, 1977; Thomas, Chess, & Birch, 1970).

- **Easy temperament:** Easy babies are often in a positive mood, even-tempered, open, adaptable, regular, and predictable in biological functioning. They establish regular feeding and sleeping schedules easily. About 40% of the NYSL sample fell into this category.
- **Difficult temperament:** Difficult babies are active, irritable, and irregular in biological rhythms. They are slow to adapt to changes in routine or new situations, react vigorously to change, and have trouble adjusting to new routines. About 10% of the NYSL sample fell into this category.
- **Slow-to-warm-up temperament:** Just as it sounds, slow-to-warm-up babies tend to be inactive, moody, and slow to adapt to new situations and people. They react to new situations with mild irritability but adjust more quickly than do infants with difficult temperaments. About 15% of the NYSL sample fell into this category.

Although it may seem as if all babies were easily classifiable, about 35% of the NYSL sample did not fit squarely into any of the three categories but displayed a mix of characteristics, such as eating and sleeping regularly but being slow to warm up to new situations.

easy temperament
A temperament characterized by regularity in biological rhythms, the tendency to adapt easily to new experiences, and a general cheerfulness.

difficult temperament
A temperament characterized by irregularity in biological rhythms, slow adaptation to change, and a tendency for intense negative reactions.

slow-to-warm-up
temperament A temperament characterized by mild irregularity in biological rhythms, slow adaptation to change, mildly negative mood.

TABLE 10.3 • Temperament

EASY CHILD	DIFFICULT CHILD	SLOW-TO-WARM-UP CHILD
Usually positive mood, unpleasant moods are mild	Intense and frequent unpleasant moods, cries often	Positive and unpleasant moods
Responds well to novelty in food, situations, routines, and strangers	Responds poorly to novelty in food, situations, routines, and strangers	Responds slowly to novelty in food, situations, routines, and strangers
Regular in sleep and feeding schedules	Irregular in sleep and feeding schedules	Moderately regular in sleep and feeding schedules
Accepts frustration with little fuss	Reacts to frustration with crying and tantrums	Slow to accept frustrations

STABILITY OF TEMPERAMENT

Temperament is relatively stable during infancy. For example, Rothbart (1986) examined infant temperament at 3, 6, and 9 months of age and reported stability of positive reactivity across both 3- and 6-month intervals and stability of negative and overall reactivity across 3-month intervals. Other researchers have found evidence of stability through the first year of life (Bornstein et al., 2015). In infancy, however, temperament is especially open to environmental influences, such as interactions with others (Gartstein, Putnam, Aron, & Rothbart, 2016). Young infants' temperament can change with experience, neural development, and sensitive caregiving (e.g., helping babies regulate their negative emotions; Jonas et al., 2015; Thompson et al., 2013). As infants gain experience and learn how to regulate their states and emotions, those who are cranky and difficult may become less so. By the second year of life, styles of responding to situations and people are better established and temperament becomes more stable. Temperament at age 3 remains stable, predicting temperament at age 6 (Dyson et al., 2015).

In early childhood, temperament is more consistent than in infancy and predictive of later behavior, even into adulthood (Caspi, 1998; Roberts & DelVecchio, 2000; Shiner, Masten, & Tellegen, 2002; Thompson et al., 2013). In one study, more than 1,000 children in New Zealand were assessed every two years from early childhood to early adulthood (Caspi et al., 2003). Temperament qualities at age 3 were associated with personality traits at age 26. Young children who were temperamentally under-controlled, similar to the difficult-temperament classification (e.g., impulsive, irritable, distractible, moody) were, at age 26, more likely than other children to score high on measures of negative emotionality; they were easily upset, likely to overreact to minor events, and reported feeling mistreated, deceived, and betrayed by others. Childhood temperament can have implications for later personality growth, but there are also individual differences throughout life: Some children's temperament remains the same and that of others changes (Rothbart & Bates, 1998; Salekin & Averett, 2008; van Aken, 2009).

CONTEXT AND GOODNESS OF FIT

Temperament is part of the social exchanges that we all encounter, influenced by reciprocal reactions as one person influences the other and vice versa. An infant's temperament may be continuous over time because certain temperamental qualities evoke certain reactions from others. Easy babies usually get the most positive reactions from others, whereas babies with a difficult

This infant is making her mother smile—and the infant's mother is making her smile. Parents and infants influence each other.

Teodor Lazarev/Shutterstock.com

temperament receive mixed reactions (Chess & Thomas, 1991). For example, an "easy" baby tends to smile often, eliciting smiles and positive interactions from others, which in turn reinforce the baby's "easy" temperamental qualities. Conversely, a "difficult" baby may evoke more frustration and negativity from caregivers as they try unsuccessfully to soothe the baby's fussing. Researchers found that mothers who view their 6-month-old infants as difficult may be less emotionally available to them (Kim & Teti, 2014). Babies' emotionality and negative emotions predict maternal perceptions of parenting stress and poor parenting (Kiang, Moreno, & Robinson, 2004; Oddi, Murdock, Vadnais, Bridgett, & Gartstein, 2013; Paulussen-Hoogeboom, Stams, Hermanns, & Peetsma, 2007). Research with young children (aged 2 and 3) showed reciprocal links between difficult temperament and negative parenting. Specifically, difficult temperament at age 2 predicted negative parenting at age 3 and vice versa (Micalizzi, Wang, & Saudino, 2015).

Temperament can also be related to mothers' expectations about their infants and their ability to parent. In one study, mothers who, *prior to giving birth*, considered themselves less well equipped to care for their infant were found to be more likely to have infants who showed negative aspects of temperament, such as fussiness, irritability, and difficulty being soothed. This suggests that perceptions of parenting may shape views of infant temperament—and thereby shape temperament itself (Verhage, Oosterman, & Schuengel, 2013). In other research, 3 months after giving birth, new mothers' feelings of competence were positively associated with infant temperament. Mothers' beliefs about their ability to nurture are shaped by the interaction between their infants' traits and their own parenting self-efficacy, as well as their opportunities for developing successful caregiving routines (Porter & Hsu, 2003; Verhage et al., 2013). This contextual dynamic has been found to hold true across cultures as well. Both British and Pakistani mothers in the UK reported fewer problems with their infants' temperaments at 6 months of age when the mothers had a greater sense of parenting efficacy and displayed more warm and less hostile parenting styles (Prady, Kiernan, Fairley, Wilson, & Wright, 2014).

However, the most adaptive matches between infant temperament and context can sometimes be surprising. Consider the Maasai, an African semi-nomadic ethnic group. In times of drought, when the environment becomes extremely hostile, herds of cattle and goats die, and infant mortality rises substantially. Under these challenging conditions, infants with difficult temperaments tend to survive at higher rates than do those with easy temperaments. Infants who cry and are demanding are attended to, fed more, and are in better physical condition than easy babies who tend to cry less and therefore are assumed to be content (Gardiner & Kosmitzki, 2018). Thus, the Maasai infants with difficult temperaments demonstrate higher rates of survival because their temperaments better fit the demands of the hostile context in which they are raised.

An important influence on socioemotional development is the **goodness of fit** between the child's temperament and the environment around him or her, especially the parents' temperaments and child-rearing methods (Chess & Thomas, 1991). Infants with difficult temperament are more likely than others to later experience difficulties with externalizing behaviors, such as aggression and conduct problems, and internalizing behaviors, such as anxiety and depression (Rothbart & Bates, 1998; Thomas et al., 1970).

Infants are at particular risk for poor outcomes when their temperaments show poor goodness of fit to the settings in which they live (Rothbart & Bates, 1998; Thomas et al., 1970). For example, if an infant who is fussy, difficult, and slow to adapt to new situations is raised by a patient and sensitive caregiver who requires that the infant comply with rules but provides time for him or her to adapt to new routines, the infant may become less cranky and more flexible over time. The infant may adapt her temperament style to match her context so that later in childhood she may no longer be classified as difficult and no longer display behavioral problems (Bates, Pettit, Dodge, & Ridge, 1998; Chess & Thomas, 1984). If, on the other hand, a child with a difficult temperament is reared by a parent who is insensitive, coercive, and difficult in temperament, the child may not learn how to regulate her emotions and may have behavioral problems and adjustment difficulties that worsen with age, even into early adolescence (Pluess & Birkbeck, 2010; Thompson, 1998).

goodness of fit The compatibility between a child's temperament and his or her environment, especially the parent's temperament and child-rearing methods; the greater the degree of match, the more favorable the child's adjustment.

Likewise, when children are placed in low-quality care-giving environments, those with difficult temperaments respond more negatively and show more behavior problems than do those with easy temperaments (Pluess & Belsky, 2009; Pluess & Birkbeck, 2010; Poehlmann et al., 2011). In preschool, a good fit between the teacher–child relationship and the child's temperament predicts prosocial behavior (Hipson & Séguin, 2016).

However, a child's environment changes over time in ways that can also influence goodness of fit. As children mature, parents, teachers, and other adults increasingly expect more competent, self-controlled behavior; the school setting requires compliance, initiative, and cooperation; and children increasingly participate with adults in circumstances (like church or concerts) in which they must understand and enact socially appropriate behavior. A particular temperamental profile may fit well with environmental demands and opportunities at one age (e.g., low persistence or attention span in infancy) but may be a poor fit later (e.g., the same characteristics in the school years). In this way, the temperament–

Culture plays a role in emotional development. Japanese mothers tend to encourage their infants to develop close ties and depend on their assistance whereas North American mothers tend to emphasize autonomy.

environment fit is developmentally dynamic, and this is likely to influence the stability of temperamental attributes over time as well as relations to later personality (Goodvin et al., 2015).

As mentioned earlier, socioemotional development is a dynamic process in which infants' behavior and temperament styles influence the family processes that shape their development. Sensitive and patient caregiving is not always easy with a challenging child, and adults' own temperamental styles influence their caregiving. A poor fit between the caregiver and infant's temperament can make an infant more fussy and cranky. When a difficult infant is paired with a parent with a similar temperament—one who is impatient, irritable, and forceful—behavioral problems in childhood and adolescence are likely (Chess & Thomas, 1984; Rubin, Hastings, Chen, Stewart, & McNichol, 1998).

Experience can also influence biological functioning in ways that influence temperament. Exposure to extreme adversity, especially early in life, can exacerbate young children's reactivity to stress, heightening biological reactions to stress such as the release of stress hormones. As a result, such children can become more temperamentally wary and irritable (Ashman & Dawson, 2002; Wiik & Gunnar, 2009). Supportive relationships can buffer stress reactivity. For example, children who are temperamentally reactive are able to respond to stress adaptively in the presence of a sensitive caregiver (Nachmias, Gunnar, Mangelsdorf, Parritz, & Buss, 1996).

CULTURAL DIFFERENCES IN TEMPERAMENT

Researchers have observed consistent cultural differences in temperament that are rooted in cultural norms for how individuals are perceived. Japanese mothers, for example, view their infants as independent beings who must learn the importance of relationships and connections with others (Rothbaum et al., 2000). Infants maintain close physical contact with their mothers, who encourage them to develop close ties and depend on their assistance. North American mothers, on the other hand, view their task as shaping babies into autonomous beings (Kojima, 1986). Whereas Japanese mothers tend to interact with their babies in soothing ways, discouraging strong emotions, North American mothers are active and stimulating (Rothbaum et al., 2000). Differences in temperament result, such that Japanese infants tend to be more passive, less irritable and vocal, and more easily soothed when upset as compared with North American infants (Kojima, 1986; Lewis, Ramsay, & Kawakami, 1993; Rothbaum et al., 2000). Culture influences the behaviors that parents view as desirable

LIFESPAN BRAIN DEVELOPMENT

• • Attachment and the Brain

Parents, especially mothers, are biologically wired to form emotional attachments to their infants.

In all contexts and cultures, infants and parents form a powerful bond that is the basis for a lifelong relationship. From an evolutionary perspective, a strong attachment bond is essential to infants' survival and ensures that parents' genetic material is passed to the next generation. Parents' responses to infants may have a biological basis, influenced by neural pathways that motivate responsive parenting (Swain et al., 2014). Specifically, responses to infants are influenced by dopamine, a neurotransmitter associated with rewards, and oxytocin, a hormone that is often referred to as the "love hormone" because it plays a role in social bonding (Berridge & Kringelbach, 2008).

Neuroimaging studies have shown that adults' brain circuits that respond to images and sounds of infants are rich in oxytocin pathways, with the potential to trigger feelings of affection and connection (Galbally, Lewis, van IJzendoorn, & Permezel, 2011). Oxytocin level increases dramatically during labor because it plays a role in triggering and sustaining uterine contractions during childbirth (Fuchs et al., 1991). Oxytocin levels tend to be greater during vaginal births as compared with cesarean births, and the differences in oxytocin levels may persist

after birth. In one study, mothers experiencing vaginal delivery showed greater brain activity in response to their own baby's cry, compared with other babies, at 2–4 weeks postpartum in brain regions responsible for the experience and regulation of emotions (Swain et al., 2008). Oxytocin levels rise with breastfeeding. Mothers who breastfeed showed greater activation in brain areas responsible for emotion regulation in response to their own baby's cries vs. other babies' cries than those who feed by formula (Kim et al., 2011). Note, however, that mothers who deliver by cesarean also experience a rise in oxytocin in the presence of their infants and are just as capable of sensitive parenting as mothers who experience vaginal birth.

Over the first few months of life, infants become more socially engaged and interact reciprocally with parents in ways that strengthen the mothers' attachment and positive feelings toward the infant. Positive interactions with infants increase parental dopamine and oxytocin and make attentive, sensitive parenting more likely (Macdonald & Feifel, 2013; Swain et al., 2014). Specifically, research has shown that mothers who experience a secure attachment bond, as measured by an attachment interview and heightened levels of oxytocin in response to infant play, show greater MRI activation in areas of brain reward regions, including areas that are rich in oxytocin receptors (Strathearn, Fonagy, Amico, & Montague, 2009). Parents and infants interact reciprocally. Infants' oxytocin levels rise when parents are administered oxytocin, likely because parents may become more affectionate; affectionate touch increases oxytocin levels in infants (Feldman, 2015). It appears that parents and infants are neurologically suited to each other and primed for a bond that supports healthy development.

What Do You Think?

More than one-third of infants are delivered by caesarian section each year. Do these findings have long-term implications for infants delivered by caesarian? Why or why not?

and the means that parents use to socialize their infants. Culture, therefore, plays a role in how emotional development—in this case, temperament—unfolds.

Asian cultures often prioritize low arousal and emotionality and thereby socialize infants in line with these values. Chinese American, Japanese American, and Hmong children tend to display lower levels of irritability, less physical activity, and engage in more self-quieting than do European American children (Friedlmeier, Çorapçi, & Benga, 2015; Super & Harkness, 2010). Similarly, a recent comparison of toddlers from Chile, South Korea, Poland, and the United States showed that the South Korean toddlers scored highest on measures of control (Krassner et al., 2016).

Does this mean that infants from Asian cultures are more temperamentally resistant to stress? One study examined the hormone cortisol, which is released as part of the fight-or-flight response, as a marker of stress during an inoculation (Lewis et al., 1993). Four-month-old Japanese infants showed a pronounced cortisol response, suggesting that they were experiencing great stress, coupled with little crying. The U.S. infants, on the other hand, displayed intense behavioral reactions to the pain and took longer to calm down, yet they displayed a lower cortisol response. Thus, although the Japanese babies appeared quiet and calm, they were more physiologically stressed than the U.S. infants.

In summary, we have seen that the cultures in which we are immersed influence how we interpret stimuli and respond to the world, including how we manifest stress.

 ## Thinking in Context 10.5

1. Contrast the inborn nature of temperament with contextual factors that may promote changes in temperament style. What role does goodness of fit play in determining temperament?

2. In your view, is it possible for an infant with a difficult temperament to grow into a young adult with an easy temperament? Why or why not?

3. Under what conditions might a child with an easy temperament become difficult?

 ## Apply Your Knowledge

A friendly lab assistant escorted 12-month-old Cassie and her mother into a research playroom containing special mirrors and hidden equipment to videotape their interactions. After providing instructions, the lab assistant left the mother and Cassie alone, beginning a short procedure to study their interactions. Soon a female stranger entered the room and began playing with Cassie. After a few minutes, the mother left the room and Cassie was alone with the stranger. The mother returned briefly, then left again; finally, the stranger left the room and Cassie was alone. The lab assistant decided to stop the procedure at this point; she ushered the mother back into the room to pick up Cassie.

During each short separation from her mother, Cassie cried and wailed. The first time Cassie cried, her mother responded with surprise and concern, returning almost immediately. She was not able to soothe Cassie, who alternated between clinging to her mother and pushing her away angrily, crying all the while. "It's all right, baby doll, I love you love you love you. If you don't cry I'll give you a big hug when I come back," promised her mother before leaving the room for a second time. After the second separation Cassie continued to cry as her mother, clearly annoyed, waited for her to stop. "See? I came back. Learn to be a big girl."

"Is Cassie upset today?" asked the lab assistant when she ended the procedure. "No, she's always like this," her mother answered. "My Cassie is quite a handful. She's what my mother calls 'spirited.' She's unpredictable and strong willed. She'll eat when she's ready and she'll nap when she's ready—and that changes all the time. My mother says I was the same way. I love my little girl, but sometimes I just need space. She's very clingy. It will be better when she grows up a bit."

1. What was this procedure intended to study? How? Why? Why do you think the lab assistant decided to stop the procedure after the second separation?

2. What might Cassie's behavior indicate about her security of attachment relationship to her mother and her emotional development? Why?

3. What do we know about the stability of infant attachment? What is the likelihood that these observations will influence Cassie's attachment in childhood? In adulthood?

4. What do you observe about the goodness of fit between Cassie's temperament and the parenting she receives from her mother?

Give your students the SAGE edge!

SAGE edge offers a robust online environment featuring an impressive array of free tools and resources for review, study, and further exploration, keeping both instructors and students on the cutting edge of teaching and learning. Learn more at **edge.sagepub.com/kuthertopical.**

CHAPTER 10 IN REVIEW

10.1 Examine infants' developing capacities for basic and self-conscious emotions and emotion regulation.

SUMMARY

Basic emotions emerge in all infants at about the same ages and are seen and interpreted similarly across cultures. The development of self-conscious emotions depends on cognitive development and self-awareness, and begins to emerge between 15 to 18 months, but largely develops during the second and third year of life. Infants use a variety of strategies for emotion regulation and they change with age. Responsive parenting that is attuned to infants' needs helps infants develop skills in emotional regulation. Maladaptive social contexts, such as parental stress and family conflict, pose a risk to infants' development of emotion regulation. Between 6 and 10 months, infants begin to use social referencing, which signifies infants' growing understanding of others' emotional states. Infants naturally pick up emotional display rules, which often vary among cultures. Likewise, whether infants show stranger wariness depends on the infant's overall temperament, past experience, the situation in which the infant meets a stranger, but also his or her culture.

KEY TERMS

emotional competence	social referencing
basic emotions	emotional display rules
social smile	stranger wariness
self-conscious emotions	(stranger anxiety)
emotion regulation	

REVIEW QUESTIONS

1. When do basic and self-conscious emotions appear?
2. How do emotions change over infancy?
3. How do infants regulate their emotions?
4. Describe contextual influences on infants' understand and display of emotions

10.2 Describe the progression of children's understanding and regulation of emotion.

SUMMARY

During childhood children make great strides in emotion regulation and become better able to manage their emotional experience and how emotions are displayed. Children's capacities for emotion regulation are influenced by advances in cognitive development, theory of mind, and language development. With age, children invoke different strategies for emotional control. Emotion regulation strategies are a response to emotions but also influence emotional experience, social competence

and overall adjustment. Neighborhood and community contexts often hold implications for emotional development via associated risk and protective factors. Adaptation to adversity is a dynamic process involving interactions among the child's developmental capacities and his or her changing context, including relationships with other people and is influenced by prior development, competence, risk factors and the nature of the current challenges faced, and the child's adaptive capacity and strengths, especially skills in emotion regulation.

KEY TERMS

risk factors	protective factors
resilience	

REVIEW QUESTIONS

1. How does children's ability to understand and regulate emotion change over childhood?
2. How do interactions with parents and caregivers contribute to emotional development?
3. What is resilience and how can it be fostered?

10.3 Contrast the emotional experiences and coping skills of adolescents and adults.

SUMMARY

Adolescents' mood swings tend to be influenced more by context than biology as they occur naturally with the many situational changes and shifts in peer settings that occur throughout adolescents' days and weeks. Although popular stereotypes of aging emphasize loss, sadness, and regret, well-being tends to increase with age and older adults' emotional experience is positive, rich, and complex. Not only do adults experience more positive emotions and recall more positive memories, they also become less negative. Advances in cognitive affective complexity, the ability to fuse emotion with cognition, improves adults' awareness of emotions, capacity to integrate positive and negative feelings, and regulate intense emotions. With advancing age adults experience emotions in increasingly multifaceted, conscious, and reflective ways and develop emotion regulation skills that contribute to advances in well-being. In addition, some adults display hardiness; they appraise stressful situations more positively, viewing them as manageable, approach problems with an active problem-focused coping style, and show fewer negative reactions to stressful situations.

KEY TERMS

experience sampling method	hardiness
daily hassles	

REVIEW QUESTIONS

1. To what degree is adolescence characterized by moodiness?

2. How do positive and negative emotions change throughout adulthood?

3. How does emotional experience influence coping?

10.4 Compare attachment styles in infancy and adulthood.

SUMMARY

Ainsworth explained that virtually all infants are attached to their parents, but they differ in security of attachment, which she measured via the Strange Situation. Securely attached infants use their mothers' as a secure base during ambiguous situation. There are three types of insecure attachment: Insecure-avoidant attachment, insecure-resistant attachment, and insecure disorganized attachment. The most important determinant of infant attachment is the caregiver's ability to consistently and sensitively respond to the child's signals. The attachment bond developed during infancy and toddlerhood becomes internally represented as an internal working model of self. Children with secure attachments in infancy and early childhood are more socially and emotionally competent in childhood and adolescence. Adult attachments can be described in terms of four styles similar to infant attachment. Securely attached adults have a secure internal working model of self, tend to view themselves as lovable, and are able to form intimate relationships. There are three insecure types of attachment: Anxious attachment, avoidant attachment, and disorganized attachment. Securely attached individuals tend to have satisfactory relationships with their partners and display socioemotional advantages, including resilience. The positive effects of secure attachment on wellbeing continue into late adulthood, but attachment shifts in subtle ways during the adult years.

KEY TERMS

attachment
signaling behaviors
secure base
separation protest
  (separation anxiety)

internal working model
security of attachment
Strange Situation

REVIEW QUESTIONS

1. What is attachment?

2. How do researchers measure infant attachment?

3. Describe four patterns of infant attachment.

4. What are ways of promoting a secure parent-child attachment bond?

5. Compare patterns of infant and adult attachment

10.5 Discuss temperament styles, stability of temperament, and the role of goodness of fit in adjustment.

SUMMARY

Temperament is the characteristic way in which an individual approaches and reacts to people and situations. The components of infant temperament cluster into three profiles. Babies with an easy temperament are often in a positive mood, even-tempered, open, adaptable, regular, and predictable in biological functioning. Difficult temperament is characterized by irritability, irregularity in biological rhythms, and reluctance to adapt to changes in routine or new situations. Slow-to-warm-up babies tend to be inactive, moody, and slow to adapt to new situations and people, but adjust more quickly than do infants with difficult temperaments. Temperament is relatively stable during infancy but can change with sensitive caregiving, experience, and neural development. In early childhood temperament is more consistent and predictive of later behavior even into adulthood. An important influence on socioemotional development is the goodness of fit between the child's temperament and the environment around him or her, especially the parent's temperament and child rearing methods. In addition, there are cultural differences in temperament that are rooted in cultural differences in the behaviors that parents view as desirable and the means that parents use to socialize their infants.

KEY TERMS

goodness of fit
temperament

self-harm

REVIEW QUESTIONS

1. What is temperament?

2. What are three temperament styles?

3. How stable is temperament?

4. What is goodness of fit?

Test your understanding of the content.
Review the flashcards and quizzes at
edge.sagepub.com/kuthertopical

Self, Identity, and Personality

Learning Objectives

11.1 Summarize developmental trends in self-concept from infancy through adulthood.

11.2 Analyze patterns of change and correlates of self-esteem over the lifespan.

11.3 Describe influences and outcomes associated with identity development, including ethnic identity.

11.4 Compare and contrast the trait and stage approaches to personality.

Digital Resources

▶ Subjective Age

📄 Early Dementia

◀)) Self-Esteem in Children and Teens

🖥 Self-Esteem in Adults

▶ Emerging Adulthood

📄 Ethnic Identity

📄 Personality Development

◀)) Erikson's 8 Stages

⑤SAGE edge™   Master these learning objectives with multimedia resources available at **edge.sagepub.com/kuthertopical** and *Lives in Context* video cases available in the interactive eBook.

"I'm a walking contradiction," muses 15-year-old Laqueta as she looks in the mirror. "I'm shy but also outgoing, kind but sometimes I want to be mean—especially when Josie tells me off," she says, thinking about her testy relationship with her "frenemy." "Sometimes I just want to get out of here and can't wait to go away to college. But then I get nervous about leaving my parents and friends. What would I major in, anyway? I think protecting the environment is important and I want to make a difference in the world. But how do I do that? What does that mean for a major? How will I know? Dad says I'll just be able to tell. I hope he's right. I guess I'm still figuring myself out. Will I ever really know myself?"

Laqueta is like most girls and boys her age, managing perhaps the most pressing task of adolescence: Figuring oneself out. How do we become self-aware enough to ask ourselves who we are? Do babies have a sense of self? Do we ever figure ourselves out? How do adults understand themselves? Are we still the same person in older adulthood? In this chapter we consider these questions about the self: When does it develop? What does it mean for our interactions with other people? And how does it change over the lifespan?

SELF-CONCEPT

LO 11.1 Summarize developmental trends in self-concept from infancy through adulthood.

Who are you? List seven words or phrases that describe you. Your response is an example of self-concept. **Self-concept** refers to our beliefs about ourselves; our

David Grossman/Alamy

assessment of our abilities, traits, and characteristics; our knowledge about ourselves; and the ways in which we describe ourselves. Self-concept is an ever-changing process, becoming more complex over our lifespan.

SELF-CONCEPT IN INFANCY

What do babies know about themselves? When do they begin to know that they have a "self"—that they are separate from the people and things that surround them? Infants cannot tell us what they perceive, think, or feel. Instead, researchers must devise ways of inferring infants' states, feelings, and thoughts. As you might imagine, this makes it very challenging to study infants' conceptions of self, as well as their awareness and understanding of themselves.

Infant Self-Awareness

Maya, 4 months of age, delights in seeing that she can make the mobile above her crib move by kicking her feet. Her understanding that she can influence her world suggests that she has a sense of herself as different from her environment (Rochat, 1998). Before infants can take responsibility for their own actions, they must begin to see themselves as physically separate from the world around them and understand that their behavior can be described and evaluated.

Some developmental researchers believe that infants are born with a capacity to distinguish the self from the surrounding environment (Meltzoff, 1990). Newborns show distress at hearing a recording of another infant's cries, but do not show distress at hearing their own cries, suggesting that they can distinguish other infants' cries from their own and thereby have a primitive notion of self (Dondi, Simion, & Caltran, 1999). Newborn facial imitation, their ability to view another person's facial expression and produce it (see Chapter 6), may also suggest a primitive awareness of self and others (Meltzoff, 2007). It is unclear, however, whether these findings suggest that newborns have self-awareness because infants cannot tell us what they know.

Others argue that an awareness of oneself is not innate but emerges by 3 months of age (Lewis & Brooks-Gunn, 1979; Neisser, 1993). Some research suggests that it is indicated by infants' awareness of the consequences of their own actions on others (Langfur, 2013). As infants interact with people and objects, they learn that their behaviors have effects. With this awareness, they begin to experiment to see how their behaviors influence the world around them, begin to differentiate themselves from their environments, and develop a sense of self (Bigelow, 2001; Rochat & Striano, 1999).

Infant Self-Recognition

How do we know whether self-awareness is innate or develops in the early months of life? One way of studying self-awareness in infants is to examine infants' reactions to viewing themselves in a mirror. **Self-recognition**, the ability to recognize or identify the self, is assessed by the "rouge test." In this experiment, a dab of rouge or lipstick is applied to an infant's nose without the infant's awareness—for example, under the pretext of wiping his or her face. The infant is then placed in front of a mirror (Bard, Todd, Bernier, Love, & Leavens, 2006). Whether the infant recognizes himself or herself in the mirror is dependent on cognitive development, especially the ability to engage in mental representation and hold images in one's mind. Infants must be able to retain a memory of their own image in order to display self-recognition in the mirror task. If the infant has an internal representation of her face

self-concept The set of attributes, abilities, and characteristics that a person uses to describe and define him- or herself.

self-recognition The ability to identify the self, typically measured as mirror recognition.

This toddler recognizes herself in the mirror, as shown by her touching the rouge mark on her face.

and recognizes the infant in the mirror as herself, she will notice the dab of rouge and reach for her own nose.

Mirror-recognition develops gradually and systematically (Brandl, 2016; Courage, Edison, & Howe, 2004). From 3 months of age, infants pay attention and react positively to their mirror image, and by 8 to 9 months of age they show awareness of the tandem movement of the mirror image with themselves and play with the image, treating it as if it is another baby (Bullock & Lutkenhaus, 1990; Lewis & Brooks-Gunn, 1979). Some 15- to 17-month-old infants show signs of self-recognition, but it is not until 18 to 24 months that most infants demonstrate self-recognition by touching their nose when they notice the rouge mark in the mirror (Cicchetti, Rogosch, Toth, & Spagnola, 1997; Lewis & Brooks-Gunn, 1979).

Does experience with mirrors influence how infants respond to the rouge test? Interestingly, infants from nomadic tribes with no experience with mirrors demonstrate self-recognition at the same ages as infants reared in surroundings with mirrors (Priel & deSchonen, 1986). This suggests that extensive experience with a mirror is not needed to demonstrate self-recognition in the mirror task. In addition, research with Canadian toddlers shows that their performance on the mirror task is unrelated to their experience with mirrors in the home (Courage et al., 2004). Some primates, specifically chimpanzees and orangutans, have shown the ability to pass the rouge test (Gallup, 1977). Does this mean that they have a sense of self? Many researchers say yes (Hecht, Mahovetz, Preuss, & Hopkins, 2016; Suddendorf & Butler, 2013), although the topic is hotly debated. For example, one recent review argues that prior studies were methodologically flawed and that primates do not spontaneously examine their reflection in the mirror in ways that suggest self-recognition (Anderson & Gallup, 2015).

Mirror recognition is not the only indicator of a sense of self—and may not be the earliest indicator. A recent study suggests that self-recognition may develop before infants can succeed on the mirror task (Stapel, van Wijk, Bekkering, & Hunnius, 2016). Eighteen-month-old infants viewed photographs of their own face, the face of an unfamiliar infant, the face of their caregiver, and the face of an unfamiliar caregiver, while their brain activity was registered via electroencephalography (EEG). The infants showed more brain activity in response to their own face, suggesting self-recognition, yet only one-half of these infants succeeded on the mirror task. By 18 to 24 months of age, children begin to recognize themselves in pictures and refer to themselves in the pictures as "me" or by their first names (Lewis & Brooks-Gunn, 1979). One study of 20- to 25-month-old toddlers showed that 63% could pick themselves out when they were presented with pictures of themselves and two similar children (Bullock & Lutkenhaus, 1990). By 30 months of age, nearly all of the children could pick out their own picture.

With advances in self-awareness, toddlers begin to experience more complex emotions, including secondary, or self-conscious, emotions (Lewis & Carmody, 2008). Self-conscious emotions—which, as mentioned in Chapter 10, include embarrassment, shame, guilt, jealousy, and pride—emerge around the second birthday; they require having an understanding of self and others (Fogel, 2007). An understanding of self is needed before children can be aware of being the focus of attention and feel embarrassment, identify with others' concerns and feel shame, or desire what someone else has and feel jealousy toward them. In a study of 15- to 24-month-old infants, only those who recognized themselves in the mirror looked embarrassed when an adult gave them overwhelming praise. They smiled, looked away, and covered their faces with their hands. The infants who did not recognize themselves in the mirror did not show embarrassment (Lewis, 2011). A developing sense of self and the self-conscious emotions that accompany it lead toddlers to have more complex social interactions with caregivers and others; all of which contribute to the development of self-concept.

Emerging Self-Concept

In toddlerhood, between 18 and 30 months of age, children's sense of self-awareness expands beyond self-recognition to include a **categorical self**, which is a self-description

categorical self A classification of the self based on broad ways in which people differ, such as sex, age, and physical characteristics, which children use to guide their behavior.

How might this boy's categorical self guide his play?

based on broad categories such as sex, age, and physical characteristics (Stipek, Gralinski, & Kopp, 1990). Toddlers describe themselves as "big," "strong," "girl/boy," and "baby/big kid." Children use their categorical self as a guide to behavior. For example, once toddlers label themselves by gender, they spend more time playing with toys stereotyped for their own gender. Applying the categorical self as a guide to behavior illustrates toddlers' advancing capacities for self-control.

At about the same time as toddlers display the categorical self, they begin to show another indicator of their growing self-understanding. As toddlers become proficient with language and their vocabulary expands, they begin to use many personal pronouns and adjectives, such as "I," "me," and "mine," suggesting a sense of self in relation to others (Bates, 1990). Claims of possession emerge by about 21 months and illustrate children's clear representation of "I" versus other (Levine, 1983), a milestone in self-definition and the beginnings of self-concept (Rochat, 2010).

CHILDREN'S SELF-CONCEPT

Children first understand themselves in concrete terms, as illustrated by Wanda: "I'm 4 years old. I have black hair. I'm happy, my doggie is white, and I have a television in my room. I can run really fast. Watch me!" Wanda's self-description, her self-concept, is typical of children her age. Three- and 4-year-old children tend to understand and describe themselves concretely, using observable descriptors including appearance, general abilities, favorite activities, possessions, and simple psychological traits (Harter, 2012). Preschoolers often mention specific possessions when they describe themselves—they often assert their ownership and rights to toys and other objects. This is not selfishness. Rather, young children use objects as a way to set boundaries between themselves and others (Fasig, 2000). In other words, this possessiveness often indicates a strong sense of self-concept. By 3½ years of age, children include emotions and attitudes in their self-descriptions, suggesting an emerging awareness of their own psychological characteristics, such as "I'm sad when my friends can't play" or "I like playing with doggies" (Eder, 1989). A test-retest study found that young children's self-descriptions were fairly stable over time (Marsh, Craven, & Debus, 1998).

When 3-year-olds describe themselves, they often focus on their abilities ("I can jump really high"), offer to demonstrate them ("Want to see?"), and tend to be unrealistically positive about them ("I couldn't land on the chair in one jump, but I'll do it next time!"; Harter, 1999). With age, self-concept becomes correlated with skills, accomplishments, evaluations by others, and other external indicators of competence (Diehl, Youngblade, Hay, Chui, 2011). As children move from early childhood to middle childhood, by around age 7, self-concept shifts from concrete descriptions of behavior to trait-like psychological constructs (e.g., popular, smart, good looking; Harter, 2006). Children's developing cognitive capacities enable them to think about themselves in new, more complex ways and develop more sophisticated and comprehensive self-concepts (Harter, 2012). For example, consider this school-age child's self-description: "I'm pretty popular . . . . That's because I'm nice to people and helpful and can keep secrets. Mostly I am nice to my friends" (Harter, 2012, p. 59). Like most older children, this child's self-concept focuses on competencies and personality traits rather than specific behaviors (Damon & Hart, 1988).

Older children include both positive and negative traits, unlike younger children who tend to describe themselves in all-or-none terms. Through interactions with parents, teachers, and peers, children learn more about themselves (Harter & Bukowski, 2015; Pesu, Viljaranta, & Aunola, 2016). For example, older children understand that their traits can vary with the context—for example, that a person can be nice or mean, depending on the situation (Heyman & Gelman, 2000). As self-concept differentiates, children develop a physical self-concept (referring to physical attributes or what they look like), an academic self-concept (school performance), and a social self-concept (social relationships with peers and others; Dusek & McIntyre, 2003; Harter, 2006).

SELF-CONCEPT IN ADOLESCENCE

Throughout development, the construction of self is a social process. Adolescents' attempts at self-definition and discovery are influenced by their relationships with parents and peers—relationships that become more complex during the adolescent years. Adolescents spend a great deal of time reflecting on themselves and engaging in introspective activities: writing in journals; composing poetry; and posting messages, photos, and videos about their lives on social media. Although adults

Adolescent introspection often takes the form of writing in diaries and journals.

often view these activities as self-indulgent and egotistical, they help adolescents work through the important developmental task of constructing a more complex, differentiated, and organized self-concept. Adolescents move beyond the broad characteristics that older children use to describe their personalities (e.g., funny, smart). Cognitive advances enable adolescents to use more labels to describe themselves and the labels they choose become more abstract and complex (e.g., witty, intelligent). Adolescents learn that they can describe themselves in multiple ways that often are contradictory, such as being both silly and serious, and that they show different aspects of themselves to different people (e.g., parents, teachers, friends; Harter, 2006, 2012). Adolescents' views of themselves influence their behavior. For example, adolescents' views of their academic competencies in early adolescence predict their academic achievement in middle adolescence (Preckel, Niepel, Schneider, & Brunner, 2013).

In middle adolescence, as young people recognize that their feelings, attitudes, and behaviors may change with the situation, they begin to use qualifiers in their self-descriptions (e.g., "I'm sort of shy"). Adolescents' awareness of the situational variability in their psychological and behavioral qualities is evident in statements such as, "I'm assertive in class, speaking out and debating my classmates, but I'm quieter with my friends. I don't want to stir up problems." Many young adolescents find these inconsistencies confusing and wonder who they really are, contributing to their challenge of forming a balanced and consistent sense of self.

Adolescents identify a self that they aspire to be, the **ideal self**, which is characterized by traits that they value. Adjustment is influenced by the match between the **real self**—the adolescents' personal characteristics—and their aspirational, ideal self. Mismatches between ideal and real selves are associated with depression symptoms, low self-esteem, and poor school grades (Ferguson, Hafen, & Laursen, 2010; Stevens, Lovejoy, & Pittman, 2014). Adolescents who show poor self-concept clarity, or poor stability or consistency in their self-descriptions, tend to experience higher rates of depressive and anxiety symptoms throughout adolescence (van Dijk et al., 2014). As adolescents become increasingly concerned with how others view them, positive social characteristics such as being helpful, friendly, and kind become more important (Damon & Hart, 1988).

Self-concept is influenced by experiences in the home, school, and community. At home, an authoritative parenting style can provide support, acceptance, and give-and-take to promote the development of adolescent self-concept (Lee, Daniels, & Kissinger, 2006; van Dijk et al., 2014). At school, particularly among high school students, perceived teacher support predicts positive academic and behavioral self-concept (Dudovitz, Chung, & Wong, 2017). Participation in youth organizations, such as the Boys' and Girls' Clubs of America, has positive effects on the self-concept of young people, especially those reared in impoverished

ideal self A sense of self that is characterized by traits that one values.

real self Who an individual is, his or her personal characteristics. The match between the real self and aspirational, ideal self influences well-being.

neighborhoods, because such organizations foster competence, positive socialization, and connections with the community (Quane & Rankin, 2006). Adolescents' evaluations of their self-concepts are the basis for self-esteem, as discussed later in this chapter (Harter, 2006; Marsh, Trautwein, Lüdtke, Köller, & Baumert, 2006).

ADULT SELF-CONCEPT

By adolescence, self-concept is refined and differentiated into an organized and comprehensive collection of traits, characteristics, and self-descriptors. The process of development continues throughout adulthood as self-concept becomes more complex and integrated (Labouvie-Vief, 2003; Lodi-Smith & Roberts, 2010). In addition to offering more complex self-descriptions, adults are increasingly likely to integrate autobiographical information and experiences into their self-descriptions as they grow older (Pasupathi & Mansour, 2006). With life experience, older adults' self-conceptions become more complex than at other periods of life (Labouvie-Vief & Diehl, 1999).

Subjective Age

Throughout life, subjective evaluations of age are important parts of the sense of self (Barrett & Montepare, 2015). Children, adolescents, and emerging adults tend to perceive themselves as older than their chronological age, but, as shown in Figure 11.1, adults older than 25 tend to have younger subjective ages, and the discrepancy between subjective and chronological age increases during the adult years (Bergland, Nicolaisen, & Thorsen, 2014; Rubin & Berntsen, 2006). Adults tend to consistently identify with their younger selves, perhaps as a compensatory strategy to counteract the negative cultural messages associated with aging and to maximize their happiness. Longitudinal samples suggest that older adults feel about 13 years younger, on average, than their chronological age (Kleinspehn-Ammerlahn, Kotter-Gruhn, & Smith, 2008). Cross-cultural research found this difference between subjective and chronological age among adults in 18 countries (Barak, 2009). As compared with men, women tend to hold more youthful self-concepts, perhaps because Western cultures tend to define aging as a more negative experience for women than men (Izard, 2007). Women with younger age identities tend to be more optimistic than men about their cognitive competencies, their ability to maintain memory, and other aspects of cognitive abilities regardless of their actual age, although this effect is also seen in men to some degree (Schafer & Shippee, 2010).

Why do older adults feel younger than their years? One reason may have to do with self-categorization of being old (Kornadt & Rothermund, 2012); categorizing oneself as a member of one's age group influences how individuals think about themselves, their competencies, and their future (Weiss & Lang, 2012). Given the negative stereotypes associated with aging, adults may employ strategies to avoid the negative consequences of identification with their age group such as denying or hiding their age by excluding themselves from the "old age" category; at the same time, they may actually endorse negative stereotypes about their own age group (Heckhausen & Brim, 1997). In contrast, individuals in challenging contexts, such as those experiencing financial distress, tend to report older subjective ages (Agrigoroaei, Lee-Attardo, & Lachman, 2016).

Midlife adults who view themselves as younger than their chronological age (e.g., those who feel 35 years old when in fact they are 45 years old) tend to score high on

FIGURE 11.1: Subjective Age Across the Lifespan

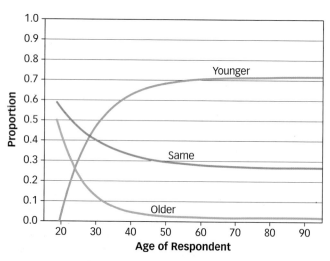

Source: Rubin and Berntsen (2006).

measures of well-being, mental health, and life satisfaction (Keyes & Westerhof, 2012; Ryff, 2014). Subjective age is associated with performance on memory tasks (Stephan, Sutin, Caudroit, & Terracciano, 2015). In one longitudinal study, adults who reported feeling younger relative to their peers tended to show better performance and slower declines in recall tasks over a 10-year period than same-age peers (Stephan, Caudroit, Jaconelli, & Terracciano, 2014). Another longitudinal study showed that, among 50- to 75-year-old adults, a lower subjective age was associated with higher scores on measures of episodic memory and executive function 10 years later (Stephan et al., 2014). Other research, however, suggests that older subjective age predicts poor life satisfaction only when adults have negative attitudes about aging, but not when aging attitudes are more favorable (Mock & Eibach, 2011). Ultimately, the midlife adults with the greatest well-being are those who recognize their age but remain active, engage in preventive health habits, and do not become distressed by age-related physical changes (Ryff, 2014; Vandewater & Stewart, 2006).

Subjective age is malleable. For example, one study found that older adults reported feeling older after taking a memory test but not after a vocabulary test (Hughes, Geraci, & De Forrest, 2013). Recall from Chapter 7 that age-related declines are seen in tasks tapping fluid intelligence, such as a working memory test, but not tasks tapping crystallized intelligence, such as vocabulary. More importantly, simply *expecting* to take a memory test was associated with feeling subjectively older, suggesting that perception of abilities in various domains can influence perceived age (Hughes et al., 2013). Age stereotypes influence health and well-being, including the risk for cardiovascular disease, engagement in health behaviors, life satisfaction, and longevity (Kornadt & Rothermund, 2012; Mock & Eibach, 2011). Collectively, these findings suggest that the old adage, "You're only as old as you feel," is partially true as one's perception of one's own age is dynamically associated with health, well-being, and cognitive performance.

Possible Selves

Possible selves—individuals' conceptions of who they might become in the future—are self-orientations that guide and motivate choices and future-oriented behaviors (Cross & Markus, 1991). The possible self is a motivator of behavior from early adulthood into older adulthood (Smith & Freund, 2002). People are motivated to try to become the hoped-for ideal self and avoid becoming the *feared self*—the self that they hope never to become. As they approach middle adulthood, people compare their real self and the lives they have achieved with their hoped-for ideal self; the degree of match between the two influences life satisfaction. Failure to achieve the hoped-for self, or failure to avoid the feared self, results in negative self-evaluations and affect. However, people often protect themselves from failure by revising their possible selves to be more consistent with their actual experience, thereby avoiding disappointment and frustration.

Possible selves shift throughout adulthood. Many young adults in their 20s describe the aspirations of their possible selves as idealistic and grand—visions of fame, wealth, exceptional health, and athletic prowess. By middle adulthood, most people realize that their time and life opportunities are limited and they become motivated to balance images of their possible selves with their experiences in order to find meaning and happiness in their lives. Thus, midlife is an important time of self-growth (Lilgendahl, Helson, & John, 2013). During their lifetimes, adults revise their possible selves to be more practical and realistic (Lapp & Spaniol, 2016), typically aspiring to competently perform the roles of worker, spouse, and parent, and to be wealthy enough to live comfortably and meet the needs of children and aging parents (Bybee & Wells, 2003).

Reminiscence and Life Review

Self-concept remains stable over the lifespan. Adults who have lived a relatively long life tend to reminisce and review their past experiences and achievements, reaffirming their

Lives in Context Video 11.1
Subjective Age

possible self Future-oriented representations of self-concept into the future; who an individual might become, both hoped for and feared, that guides and motivates choices and behaviors.

sense of self (Prebble, Addis, & Tippett, 2013). They often tell stories and discuss their thoughts about people and events they have experienced. **Reminiscence**, the vocal or silent recall of events in a person's life, serves a variety of functions (Bohlmeijer, Roemer, Cuijpers, & Smit, 2007). Older adults who engage in knowledge-based reminiscence recall problems that they have encountered and problem-solving strategies they have used. Recalling past experience and acquired knowledge and sharing it with young people is rewarding, life enriching, and positively associated with well-being (O'Rourke, Cappeliez, & Claxton, 2011; Westerhof, Bohlmeijer, & Webster, 2010). Reminiscence can also help adults in managing life transitions, such as retirement or widowhood, and provide a sense of personal continuity, preserving a sense of self despite these changes (Fry, 1995; Parker, 1995). The tendency to reminisce and the positive or negative content of shared memories tends to remain stable over time. For example, in one study of adults over the age of 50, people who reminisced about positive experiences continued to do so 16 months later (O'Rourke, King, & Cappeliez, 2016). Unfortunately, ruminating over negative events was also stable. When adults focus on and ruminate bitterly over difficult events, they sustain and even increase negative emotions and show poor adjustment (Cully, LaVoie, & Gfeller, 2001).

Related to reminiscence, but more comprehensive, is **life review**: reflecting on past experiences and contemplating the meaning of those experiences and their role in shaping one's life (Butler, 1963). Life review permits self-understanding and helps older adults assign meaning to their lives (Butler, 1974; Erikson, 1982). Specifically, life review can help elders adapt to and accept the triumphs and disappointments of their lives, become more tolerant and accepting of others, become free of the feeling that time is running out, and enhance emotional integration, life satisfaction, and well-being.

Individual and group interventions can encourage and aid older adults in reminiscence and life review (Davis & Degges-White, 2008). Reminiscence is fostered by encouraging autobiographical story telling in order to teach others, remember positive events, and enhance positive feelings. Life-review interventions, often conducted by therapists and case workers at community mental health centers and senior centers, tend to focus on helping older adults to evaluate and integrate positive and negative life events into a coherent life story (Webster, Bohlmeijer, & Westerhof, 2010; Westerhof, 2015). Social support may facilitate the life review process in elders, as interaction with others can help to point out blind spots and self-serving biases that arise in the process of autobiographical reconstruction (Korte, Drossaert, Westerhof, & Bohlmeijer, 2014). Close family members and friends can provide feedback and guidance that enhance the life review process (Krause, 2007). Encouraging adults to engage in reminiscence and life review is associated with increases in a sense of mastery, well-being, purpose in life, positive mental health (including the reduction of depressive symptoms), and social integration (Pinquart & Forstmeier, 2012; Westerhof & Bohlmeijer, 2014).

 Thinking in Context 11.1

1. Suppose you wanted to examine self-awareness in your 18-month-old nephew or niece. How might you assess or determine whether he or she has developed a sense of self-concept?

2. In what ways does developing self-concept influence school children's and adolescents' relationships with peers? In turn, how do peer interactions and relationships influence children's and adolescents' development of self-concept?

3. Consider your own self-concept. What characteristics might comprise your ideal self? Your feared self? In what ways do you think these have changed since your adolescent years? Consider the life tasks that you expect to engage in 15 years from now. What might your possible and feared selves look like in the future?

reminiscence The process of telling stories from one's past, to oneself or others.

life review The reflection on past experiences and one's life, permitting greater self-understanding and the assignment of meaning to their lives.

SELF-ESTEEM

LO 11.2 Analyze patterns of change and correlates of self-esteem over the lifespan.

If self-concept is based on description ("What am I like?"), **self-esteem** is based on evaluation ("How well do I like myself?"). Three-year-old Dorian exclaims, "I'm the smartest! I know all my ABCs! Listen! A, B, C, D, F, G, H! L, K, O, M, P, Q, V!" Like Dorian, young children tend to be excited, and often unrealistically positive, about their abilities. Self-esteem involves feelings of self-worth, self-acceptance, and self-respect, qualities that rely on the cognitive development and a sense of self that emerge over the course of childhood (Donnellan, Trzesniewski, & Robins, 2011; Harter, 2006).

CHILDREN'S SELF-ESTEEM

The preschool child typically has a very positive sense of self. Any goal is seen as achievable and they tend to view their performance favorably, even when it is not up to par (Boseovski, 2010). Young children tend to believe they will be successful at any time, underestimating the difficulty of tasks and often failing to recognize deficits in their abilities (Harter, 1990, 1998). Even after failing at a task several times, they often continue to believe that the next try will bring success (Ruble, Grosovsky, Frey, & Cohen, 1992). Young children's overly optimistic perspective on their skills can be attributed to their cognitive development, secure attachment with caregivers, and the overwhelmingly positive feedback they usually receive when they attempt a task (Goodvin, Meyer, Thompson, & Hayes, 2008). These unrealistically positive expectations serve a developmental purpose: They contribute to young children's developing sense of initiative as well as aiding them in learning new skills. As children gain life experience and develop cognitively, they begin to learn their relative strengths and weaknesses, thus their self-evaluations become more realistic (Marsh, Craven, & Debus, 1998).

Advances in cognitive development, including perspective taking and social comparison, lead children to make more complex descriptions and evaluations of themselves as they grow older. School-age children can organize their observations of their behavior, abilities, and experiences in more complex ways than younger children, yielding more accurate and comprehensive descriptions of themselves that recognize temporal and contextual fluctuations, such as being shy in one situation and not another (Harter, 2012). Whereas preschoolers tend to have unrealistically positive self-evaluations, school-age children's sense of self-esteem becomes more realistic and connected to their abilities (Boseovski, 2010; Jacobs, Lanza, Osgood, Eccles, & Wigfield, 2002; Robins & Trzesniewski, 2005). From late childhood into adolescence, beliefs about the self become more closely related to behavior (Davis-Kean, Jager, & Andrew Collins, 2009). **Social comparison**, a process by which children compare their abilities and skills with other children, permits children to evaluate their own performance in relation to their peers and influences children's views of their ability and overall sense of competence (Butler, 1998). Children receive feedback about their abilities from parents, teachers, and peers, and this contributes to their growing sense of self-esteem (Hart, Atkins, & Tursi, 2006). Perceived disapproval by peers, for example, is associated with concurrent declines in self-esteem (Thomaes et al., 2010).

self-esteem The general emotional evaluation of one's own worth.

social comparison The tendency to compare and judge one's abilities, achievements, and behaviors in relation to others.

Close friendships and peer acceptance are important influences on self-esteem.

Digital Light Source/Universal Images Group/Getty Images

Self-esteem is influenced by children's self-conceptions as well as by the importance they assign to the particular ability (Hart et al., 2006; Harter, 2006), as illustrated by a child's comment, "Even though I'm not doing well in those subjects, I still like myself as a person because Math and Science just aren't that important to me. How I look and how popular I am are more important" (Harter, 2012, p. 95). Children tend to report feeling most interested in activities in which they perform well and areas that they view as their strengths (Denissen, Zarrett, & Eccles, 2007).

Children's ratings of self-esteem vary with ethnic, contextual, and cultural factors. For example, adverse contextual conditions such as poverty, unsafe neighborhoods, ongoing stressors, and the experience of racism and discrimination contributes to low scores on measures of self-esteem on the part of African American children relative to those of white and Hispanic children (Kenny & McEachern, 2009). Despite their higher academic achievement than North American children, Chinese and Japanese children tend to score lower in self-esteem, perhaps because competition is high and Asian children experience great pressure to achieve (Chiu, 1992; Hawkins, 1994; Stevenson, Lee, & Mu, 2000). At the same time, Asian cultures emphasize collectivism, social harmony, and modesty, and do not encourage children to use social comparison to enhance their self-esteem (Toyama, 2001). Instead, children are encouraged to praise others, including their peers, while minimizing attention to themselves, in order to foster and maintain relationships (Falbo, Poston, Triscari, & Zhang, 1997; Heine & Lehman, 1995).

Self-Esteem in Adolescence

As self-conceptions become more differentiated, so do self-evaluations. Adolescents describe and evaluate themselves overall as well as in specific areas, such as academics, athletic ability, and social competence (Harter, 2012). **Global self-esteem**, an overall evaluation of self-worth, tends to decline at about 11 years of age, reaching its lowest point at about 12 or 13, and then rises (Harter, 2006; Orth & Robins, 2014). This pattern is true for both boys and girls, with girls tending to show lower self-esteem (von Soest, Wichstrøm, & Kvalem, 2016). Declines in global self-esteem are likely due to the multiple transitions that young adolescents undergo, such as body changes and the emotions that accompany those changes, as well as adolescents' self-comparisons to their peers. Although school transitions (to be discussed in Chapter 16) are often associated with temporary declines in self-esteem, most adolescents view themselves more positively as they progress from early adolescence through the high school years (von Soest et al., 2016; Zeiders, Umaña-Taylor, & Derlan, 2013). For example, comparisons of adolescents in grades 8, 10, and 12 reveal higher ratings of self-esteem with age for European American, African American, Asian American, and Latino youth (Bachman, O'Malley, Freedman-Doan, Trzesniewski, & Donnellan, 2011).

global self-esteem An overall evaluation of self-worth.

Global evaluations of self-worth give way to more complex views. Adolescents evaluate themselves with respect to multiple dimensions and relationships, such as within the context of friendships, academics, and athletic abilities (Harter, 2012). Adolescents describe and evaluate their capacities in many areas, and view their abilities more positively in some and more negatively in others. Adolescents develop a positive sense of self-esteem when they evaluate themselves favorably in the areas that they view as important. For example, sports accomplishments are more closely associated with physical self-esteem in adolescent athletes, who tend to highly value physical athleticism, than nonathletes, who tend to place less importance on athleticism (Findlay & Bowker, 2009; Wagnsson, Lindwall, & Gustafsson, 2014). Similarly, adolescents with high academic self-esteem

Adolescents benefit from friendships with peers of different ethnicities. Cross-ethnic friendships are associated with self-esteem, well-being, and less victimization. Why are friendships with diverse peers so beneficial?

Ryuhei Shindo/Taxi/Getty Images

tend to spend more time and effort on schoolwork, view academics as more important, and demonstrate high academic achievement (Preckel et al., 2013; Valentine, DuBois, & Cooper, 2004). There is also spillover: Exemplary performance and self-esteem in one area, such as athletics, often is associated with positive self-evaluations in other areas, such as social, physical, and appearance (Marsh, Trautwein, Lüdtke, Gerlach, & Brettschneider, 2007; Stein, Fisher, Berkey, & Colditz, 2007).

Whereas favorable self-evaluations are associated with positive adjustment and sociability in adolescents of all socioeconomic status and ethnic groups, low self-esteem is associated with adjustment difficulties (Burwell & Shirk, 2006; McCarty, Stoep, & McCauley, 2007). For example, low self-esteem is associated with depression during adolescence and adulthood (Orth & Robins, 2014). One longitudinal study assessed self-esteem annually in more than 1,500 12- to 16-year-old adolescents and found that both level and change in self-esteem predicted depression at ages 16 and 35 (Steiger, Allemand, Robins, & Fend, 2014). Those who entered adolescence with low self-esteem and whose self-esteem declined further during the adolescent years were more likely to show depression two decades later; this pattern held for both global and domain-specific self-esteem (physical appearance and academic competence).

High-quality relationships with peers, parents, and other adults (relationships characterized by many positive and few negative features) are associated with higher estimates of self-worth and better adjustment. Adolescents who feel supported and well-liked by peers tend to show high self-esteem (Litwack, Aikins, & Cillessen, 2010; Vanhalst, Luyckx, Scholte, Engels, & Goossens, 2013). Relationships with peers may have long-lasting effects on self-evaluations. For example, a longitudinal study that spanned 2 decades showed that peer approval during ages 12–16 predicted self-esteem in adolescence as well as at age 35 (Gruenenfelder-Steiger, Harris, & Fend, 2016). However, it is important to note that these are correlational data. The direction of the relationship cannot conclusively be determined. For example, other data collected over a 5-year period, beginning at about age 13, suggested that self-esteem predicted social support quality increasingly over time (Marshall, Parker, Ciarrochi, & Heaven, 2014). The direction of influence is difficult to interpret and complicated; it is likely a two-way relationship in which self-esteem influences and is influenced by social support.

Relationships with parents play an important role in influencing adolescents' self-evaluations. A study of Dutch, Moroccan, Turkish, and Surinamese adolescents living in the Netherlands as well as adolescents from China, Australia, Germany, and the United States confirmed that the overall quality of the parent–adolescent relationship predicted self-esteem (Harris et al., 2015; Wang & Sheikh-Khalil; Wissink, Dekovic, & Meijer, 2006). Parents who adopt a warm, encouraging, but firm style of parenting are more likely to raise adolescents who display high self-esteem (Milevsky, Schlechter, Netter, & Keehn, 2007; Steinberg, 2001; Wouters, Doumen, Germeijs, Colpin, & Verschueren, 2013). Among Latino adolescents in the United States, high self-esteem is predicted by authoritative parenting coupled with **biculturalism**, adopting values and practices of two cultures, and **familism**, valuing the family over the individual and community (Bámaca, Umaña-Taylor, Shin, & Alfaro, 2005; Smokowski, Rose, & Bacallao, 2010; Telzer, Tsai, Gonzales, & Fuligni, 2015). In contrast, if parental feedback is critical, insulting, inconsistent, and not contingent on behavior, and parent–adolescent conflict is high, adolescents tend to develop poor self-esteem, are at risk to turn to peers for self-affirmation, and show adjustment difficulties (Milevsky et al., 2007; Wang et al., 2014). Peer acceptance appears to have a protective effect on self-esteem and can buffer the negative effects of a distant relationship with parents (Birkeland, Breivik, & Wold, 2014).

ADULT SELF-ESTEEM

Generally speaking, our self-evaluations become more positive during the course of our lifespan. Cross-sectional and longitudinal research suggest that self-esteem increases

biculturalism The practice of adopting values and practices from two cultures.

familism The cultural belief that family members should support one another; that the family should take precedence over individuals and the community.

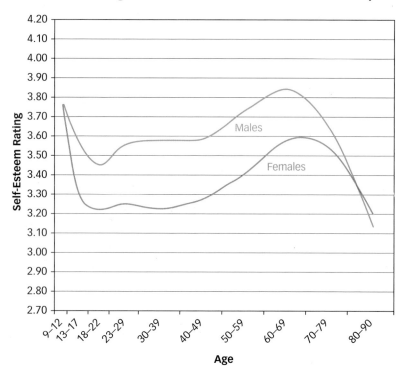

Source: Robins et al. (2002).

during adolescence, young adulthood, and middle adulthood, peaking in the mid-60s and then declining in late adulthood (Ulrich Orth, Maes, & Schmitt, 2015; Robins, Trzesniewski, Tracy, Gosling, & Potter, 2002), as shown in Figure 11.2.

During young adulthood people establish many new social roles—for example, by entering into working life, marrying or cohabiting with a relationship partner, or having a baby (Hutteman, Hennecke, Orth, Reitz, & Specht, 2014). As young adults become competent in these roles, their confidence in themselves rises. During middle adulthood, people further invest in their social roles by maintaining a satisfying relationship with their spouse, helping children to become responsible and well-functioning adults, improving their professional competencies, and perhaps taking on more managerial functions at work (Marks, Bumpass, & Jun, 2004). Increases in adults' self-esteem are the result of their successful investments in social roles and, in turn, these increases contribute to adults' performance in their social roles (Orth et al., 2015).

As adults progress through middle age they become more autonomous, less concerned with the evaluations and expectations of others, and more concerned with living up to self-chosen ideals and standards than younger adults do (Ryff, 1991). With advances in cognitive affective complexity (see Chapter 6), middle-aged adults are more likely than young adults to acknowledge and accept both their good and bad qualities and feel positively about themselves (Ryff, 1995). Revised, more modest possible selves influence adults' sense of well-being, permitting middle-aged and older adults to show higher self-esteem than young adults (Orth, Trzesniewski, & Robins, 2010). But as adults progress through older adulthood, many of these roles decline or even disappear through retirement, the empty nest, or widowhood. Role changes also change relationships, potentially reducing social contact, and by extension, social support. For example, retirement reduces or ends contact with coworkers, and widowhood entails more than the loss of a partner as it often changes one's relationships with family and friends. Given that roles and relationships are important aspects of the self-concept, the loss of valued social roles can contribute to declines in self-esteem very late in life (Orth et al., 2015).

Although global self-esteem tends to decline in late life, elders often come to view themselves in complex ways and show positive evaluations in specific areas. Life experience and advances in cognitive affective complexity underlie older adults' multifaceted self-conceptions and evaluations (Labouvie-Vief & Diehl, 1999). The positivity effect extends to adults' views of themselves, as older adults tend to express more positive than negative self-evaluations well into old age (Meier, Orth, Denissen, & Kühnel, 2011; Rice & Pasupathi, 2010). In one study, both old (70 to 84) and very old (85 to 103) adults rated themselves more positively than negatively with regard to a variety of domains including hobbies, interests, family, health, and personality, and these positive self-evaluations predicted psychological well-being (Freund & Smith, 1999). Older adults tend to compartmentalize their self-concept more so than younger and middle-aged adults by categorizing the positive and negative aspects of self as separate roles, whereas younger and middle-aged adults tend to integrate them into one (Ready, Carvalho, & Åkerstedt, 2012). The developmental task for older adults is to accept their weaknesses and compensate by

• • Are There Generational Shifts in Self-Esteem?

Does taking selfies signal narcissism?

"I feel pretty confident in my ability to do well in school," explained Madison, "in fact, I feel pretty good about myself, in general. I like being me." Madison has succeed in an important developmental task: She views herself in a positive light. Self-esteem is an important contributor to well-being. But, can one have self-esteem that is too high? According to some theorists, the answer is, "Perhaps."

Since the 1980s there has been an increasing emphasis on promoting self-esteem to aid children's development (Twenge & Campbell, 2009). Many schools have incorporated self-esteem-promoting strategies into their curricula, stemming from the belief that boosting self-esteem would help solve societal problems. We now know, however, that it is difficult to determine a causal relationship between self-esteem with academic and social outcomes.

Some researchers argue that promoting self-esteem in children has resulted in generational increases in self-esteem, such that the measures we use to assess self-esteem must be recalibrated (Gentile, Twenge, & Campbell, 2010). One of the most frequently used measures of self-esteem is the Rosenberg Self-Esteem Scale (Rosenberg, 1965). In a recent study employing the Rosenberg Scale, the most common score was the highest score possible, with 18% of middle school, high school, and college students earning a perfect score (Gentile et al., 2010). Scores on self-esteem measures are often so high that even those who score low in self-esteem, relative to others, actually have moderate scores as compared with prior generations (Baumeister, Tice, & Hutton, 1989; Schmitt & Allik, 2005).

An excessively high sense of self-esteem, when it reaches grandiose proportions, becomes *narcissism*, a pathological, grandiose view of one's abilities and a craving for admiration (Morf & Rhodewalt, 2001). Have increases in narcissism mirrored those of self-esteem? Meta-analyses that synthesize the results of many research studies suggest so. College students' scores on a popular measure of narcissism have increased from 1982 to 2008, the most recent date of measurement (Twenge & Foster, 2010; Twenge, Konrath, Foster, Campbell, & Bushman, 2008). More recently, studies

of college students have linked Twitter and Instagram usage with narcissism (Davenport, Bergman, Bergman, & Fearrington, 2014; Sheldon & Bryant, 2016). Research with Norwegian adolescents and adults ages 16 to 88 supports a link between Facebook usage and narcissism (Andreassen, Pallesen, & Griffiths, 2017). These findings are supported by a recent meta-analysis of 62 studies that found that narcissism was positively related to "selfies" (photos of oneself), time spent on social media, frequency of status updates/tweets, and the number of followers or friends (McCain & Campbell, 2017).

Many of these studies, however, examined adults of all ages, suggesting that narcissism is not just for the young. Moreover, as these findings are based on correlations, they do not allow us to determine causality: Narcissist individuals may be more active on social media, or social media may promote narcissism. A recent study of Chilean adults aged 18–34 may shed light on this question (Halpern, Valenzuela, & Katz, 2016). The researchers measured narcissism and the number and frequency of "selfies" posted on social media at two time points, 1 year apart. The results suggested that individuals high in narcissism posted more selfies, but also that selfie posting was associated with higher levels of narcissism over time.

Other researchers counter that today's young people are no more narcissistic than prior generations. For example, Trzesniewski and colleagues examined samples of nearly 27,000 college students' scores on a measure of narcissism from the 1980s through 2007 and found little evidence for an increase in narcissism (Trzesniewski, Donnellan, & Robins, 2008). They also examined more than 410,000 high school students' level of self-enhancement, defined by the discrepancy between their perceived intelligence and their actual academic achievements, and found no change from 1976 to 2006. Similar comparisons of narcissism scores in nearly 2,700 adolescents sampled between 2005 and 2014 revealed no differences (Barry & Lee-Rowland, 2015). Likewise, other research using cohort sequential designs suggests no generational changes in self-esteem over the past century (Orth & Robins, 2014; Orth, Maes, & Schmitt, 2015). These results cast doubt on the belief that young people today have increasingly inflated impressions of themselves as compared with previous generations.

What Do You Think?

1. Why do you think people use social media sites like Instagram, Facebook, and Twitter?

2. Based on the information in this discussion, how would you decide when self-esteem becomes narcissism?

3. What contextual factors might contribute to changing scores on measures of self-esteem and narcissism over the past few decades? Can you identify factors that might contribute to stability, or few-to-no changes in levels of self-esteem and narcissism?

focusing on their strengths. Over time, adults reframe their sense of self by revising their possible selves in light of experience and emphasizing goals related to the sense of self, relationships, and health (Smith & Freund, 2002).

Individual differences in self-esteem tend to be stable over the lifetime, meaning that individuals with high self-esteem relative to peers in early adulthood will mostly retain this outlook, showing high self-esteem relative to peers throughout adulthood (Kuster & Orth, 2013). Although gender differences in self-esteem are apparent in adolescence, males and females in adulthood show no differences (Erol & Orth, 2017) or only small differences (Wagner, Lüdtke, Jonkmann, & Trautwein, 2013). Cross-sectional and longitudinal research suggests that Black adults show higher self-esteem and a more positive trajectory than white, Hispanic, and Asian adults (Sprecher, Brooks, & Avogo, 2013). However, although black adults showed a more positive trajectory during early adulthood, their self-esteem declined much more sharply in older adulthood (Ruth Yasemin Erol & Orth, 2011; Ulrich Orth et al., 2010).

Self-esteem is associated with positive emotional, social, and career outcomes throughout life, from adolescence through older adulthood (Orth, Robins, & Widaman, 2012). Longitudinal research indicates that self-esteem predicts many indicators of success, such as social support, satisfaction in marriage and close relationships, well-being in working life, and mental and physical health (Erol & Orth, 2017; Kuster, Orth, & Meier, 2013; Marshall et al., 2014; Orth et al., 2012). In turn, employment status, household income, and satisfaction in the domains of work, relationships, and health contribute to a positive lifespan trajectory of self-esteem (Ulrich Orth et al., 2015). Finally, negative changes in health and socioeconomic status are associated with a decline in self-esteem in old age (Orth et al., 2010). Shifts in self-esteem illustrate the complex bidirectional relationships between gains and losses experienced by the individual in context. Some researchers point to sociohistorical context as an influence on self-esteem, noting that self-esteem has been increasing since the 1980s. The implications of such a trend are discussed in the Applying Developmental Science feature.

 Thinking in Context 11.2

1. What role do interactions and relationships with others have in influencing self-esteem in early childhood? How does this change in middle childhood and, later, in adolescence? From adolescence to adulthood? Throughout adulthood?

2. How might cognitive abilities influence how individuals experience self-esteem over the lifespan? Consider cognitive changes from the cognitive developmental and information processing perspectives (Chapters 6 and 7). What role might cognition play in our self-evaluations from early childhood through late adulthood?

IDENTITY

LO 11.3 Describe influences and outcomes associated with identity development, including ethnic identity.

As children enter adolescence, their ability to think abstractly leads them to consider themselves in new ways. Adolescents' self-concept and self-esteem become more descriptive, comprehensive, and organized and they begin to form an **identity**, that is, a coherent sense of self. Recall from Chapter 1 that Erik Erikson posited that each age in life has its own developmental task. In adolescence, during the identity versus identity-confusion stage, we face the crisis of determining who we are and who we would like to become. In devising an identity, young people integrate all that they know about themselves—their self-conceptions—along with their evaluations of themselves, to construct a self that is coherent and consistent over time (Erikson, 1950). **Identity achievement** represents the

identity A coherent organized sense of self that includes values, attitudes, and goals to which one is committed.

identity achievement The identity state in which after undergoing a period of exploration a person commits to self-chosen values and goals.

LIVES IN CONTEXT

• • Emerging Adulthood

As young people develop a sense of identity they increasingly perceive themselves as adults.

Emerging adulthood is a time of instability and exploration, as young people examine various life options and meet the developmental challenge of devising a sense of self. Emerging adults explore alternatives and make frequent changes in educational paths, romantic partners, and jobs. No longer under parental restrictions yet without the full range of adult responsibilities, emerging adults are able to fully engage in identity development processes, such as sampling opportunities and possible selves (Schwartz, Zamboanga, Luyckx, Meca, & Ritchie, 2013). As young people make progress toward resolving their identity they are more likely to perceive themselves as adults (Fadjukoff, Kokko, & Pulkkinen, 2007; Nelson & Barry, 2005).

Some theorists argue that emerging adulthood is not a life stage—it does not exist everywhere and for everyone—but is simply an indicator of medium to high socioeconomic status and the educational and career opportunities that accompany such status (Côté, 2006, 2014; Molgat, 2007). Young people in Western industrialized nations who drop out of high school, experience early parenthood, begin working at a job immediately after high school, or who reside in low-SES homes and communities may experience only a limited period of emerging adulthood or may not experience emerging adulthood at all (Hendry & Kloep, 2010; Maggs, Jager, Patrick, & Schulenberg, 2012). In contrast, emerging adulthood may be extended into the late twenties for young people who obtain advanced training, such as attending medical school or law school, thus delaying their entry into career, other adult roles, and financial independence.

Although emerging adulthood is not universal, it has been observed among young people in many cultures, including North American, German, Israeli, Chinese, Czech, Romanian, Austrian, Mexican, Spanish, and Argentinean (Arias & Hernández, 2007; Facio & Micocci, 2003; Macek, Bejček, & Vaníčková, 2007; Mayseless & Scharf, 2003; Nelson, Badger, & Wu, 2004; Nelson, 2009; Sirsch, Dreher, Mayr, & Willinger, 2009). Each of these cultures endorses similar criteria for adulthood as well as criteria that are unique to their own culture. Specifically, each culture rates accepting responsibility for the consequences of one's actions as the most important criterion for adulthood, but other important criteria vary by culture. North American emerging adults also rate making independent decisions and becoming financially independent as criteria for adulthood (Arnett, 1997, 2003; Sharon, 2015). Argentinians rate the capacity to care for young children as an important criterion for women (Facio & Micocci, 2003). Israeli young adults list being able to withstand pressure as a required attribute (Mayseless & Scharf, 2003), yet Romanians rate norm compliance as important (Nelson, 2009). Chinese emerging adults rate learning to have good control of emotions as being necessary for adulthood (Nelson et al., 2004). Although emerging adulthood is common among Western industrialized cultures, the specific features and characteristics with which young people define adulthood vary.

What Do You Think?

1. **What are some advantages and disadvantages encountered by people as they go through the emerging adulthood stage?**

2. **How does the concept of emerging adulthood relate to the experiences of people in the 18–25 age range who do not attend college or undergo other lengthy career preparation?**

3. **What effects on society as a whole are likely to result from the emerging adulthood phenomenon?**

4. **To what extent can people in the 18–25 age range fulfill the criteria for adulthood even if they are not financially independent? Explain how the answers will vary from one culture to another.**

successful resolution of this process, establishing a coherent sense of self after exploring a range of possibilities. In establishing a sense of identity, individuals must consider their past and future, and come to a sense of their values, beliefs, and goals with regard to vocation, politics, religion, and sexuality.

Crucial to a successful identity search is having the time and space to do the hard work of figuring oneself out. Adolescents are best positioned to construct an identity when they experience what Erikson referred to as a **psychosocial moratorium**: a time-out

psychosocial moratorium In Erikson's theory, a period in which the individual is free to explore identity possibilities before committing to an identity.

Lives in Context Video 11.2
Emerging Adulthood

period that provides more freedom and autonomy than childhood but is without the full autonomy and responsibilities of adulthood. This period allows adolescents the opportunity to explore possibilities of whom they might become. They might sample careers, considering becoming an actor one week and a lawyer the next. Adolescents explore personalities and desires, trying out different personas and styles. Some adolescents examine their religion more closely and consider their own beliefs, perhaps learning about other religions. Young people who successfully engage in this process emerge with a sense of identity—an understanding of who they are and where they are going. The unsuccessful resolution of the identity search is confusion, in which one withdraws from the world, isolating oneself from loved ones, parents, and peers. Alternatively, confusion may take the form of immersing oneself in the peer world, losing the self. Erikson's ideas about identity have influenced thinking in this area for the past half century and researchers have devised ways of measuring identity, permitting his ideas to be tested.

The developmental tasks of early adulthood include making decisions, transitioning, and committing to relationships, family, career, and lifestyles. Some young people transition to adult roles very quickly, while others take a lengthy path. With more high-school graduates entering college than ever before, the traditional markers of adulthood are delayed relative to prior generations. Increasingly, young people have extended educational experiences prior to career entry, take longer to commit to a career and settle into occupational tracks, and become financially independent more gradually and at later ages than ever before and, by extension, get married and form families later than previous generations (Shanahan, 2000; Tanner, 2014; Cohen, Kasen, Chen, Hartmark, & Gordon, 2003). Many young people, therefore, tend to report feeling a subjective sense of being in-between; they are not adolescents but they have not yet assumed the roles that comprise adulthood (Arnett, 1997, 2003). This extended transition to adulthood, known as **emerging adulthood**, takes place roughly from ages 18 to 25 or even into the late twenties (Arnett, 2000, 2004). Emerging adulthood is examined in the Lives in Context feature.

IDENTITY STATUS

"Wearing black again?" Rose sighs, "Your closet looks like someone spilled black dye all over the place." Her daughter, Stephanie, retorts, "How can anyone wear too much black?" Rose wonders where last year's preppy girl went and hopes that Stephanie will lose interest in wearing goth attire. "Maybe next year she'll try a new style and stop wearing so much black." Stephanie's changing styles of dress reflect her struggle with figuring out who she is—her identity. Researchers classify individuals' progress in identity development into four categories known as **identity status**, the degree to which individuals have explored possible selves and whether they have committed to specific beliefs and goals (Marcia, 1966).

Identity statuses reflect different ways of viewing and responding to the world. Table 11.1 summarizes four identity statuses, or categories, describing a person's identity development. The least mature status is **identity diffusion** (not having explored or committed to a sense of self), characterized by pervasive uncertainty with little motive for resolution (Berzonsky & Kuk, 2000; Boyes & Chandler, 1992). Individuals who are in the **identity foreclosed** status have prematurely chosen an identity without having engaged in exploration; they tend to be inflexible and view the world in black and white, right and wrong, terms. The moratorium status involves an active exploration of ideas and a sense of openness to possibilities, coupled with some uncertainty. As the uncertainty is experienced as discomfort, young people are highly motivated to seek resolution and reduce the discomfort. The fourth category, identity achievement status, requires that individuals construct a sense of self through reflection, critical examination, and exploring or trying out new ideas and belief systems; and that they have formed a commitment to a particular set of ideas, values, and beliefs. Identity diffusion and foreclosure become less common in late adolescence, when moratorium and identity achievement are more prevalent.

emerging adulthood An extended transition to adulthood that takes place from ages 18 to 25, in which a young person is no longer an adolescent yet has not assumed the roles that comprise adulthood.

identity status The degree to which individuals have explored possible selves and whether they have committed to specific beliefs and goals, assessed by administering interview and survey measures, and categorized into four identity statuses.

identity diffusion The identity state in which an individual has not undergone exploration nor committed to self-chosen values and goals.

identity foreclosure The identity state in which an individual has not undergone exploration but has committed to values and goals chosen by an authority figure.

TABLE 11.1 • Identity Status

		COMMITMENT	
		PRESENT	**ABSENT**
EXPLORATION	**PRESENT**	**Identity Achievement** **Description:** Has committed to an identity after exploring multiple possibilities **Characteristics:** Active problem solving style, high self-esteem, feelings of control, high moral reasoning, and positive views of work and school	**Moratorium** **Description:** Has not committed to an identity, but is exploring alternatives **Characteristics:** Information seeking, active problem solving style, open to experience, anxiety, experimentation with alcohol or substance use
	ABSENT	**Identity Foreclosure** **Description:** Has committed to an identity without having explored multiple possibilities **Characteristics:** Avoidance of reflecting on identity choice; not open to new information, especially if it contradicts their position; rigid and inflexible	**Identity Diffusion** **Description:** Has neither committed to an identity nor explored alternatives **Characteristics:** Avoidance, tending to not solve personal problems in favor of letting issues decide themselves, academic difficulties, apathy, alcohol and substance use

Source: Based on Marcia (1966).

INFLUENCES ON IDENTITY DEVELOPMENT

Relationships with parents are renegotiated during adolescence and emerging adulthood as young people claim more and more autonomy, gaining space to develop their own sense of identity (Meeus & de Wied, 2007). When parents provide a sense of security along with autonomy, adolescents tend to explore, much as toddlers do, by using their parents as a secure base (Schwartz, Zamboanga, Luyckx, Meca, & Ritchie, 2013; Schwartz, Luyckx, & Crocetti, 2015). Young people who feel connected to their parents, supported and accepted by them, but also feel encouraged to develop and voice their own views, are more likely to engage in the exploration necessary to advance to the moratorium and achieved statuses. As young people become individuated from parents, they begin to make identity commitments and move toward identity achievement (Meeus, Iedema, Maassen, & Engels, 2005). Adolescents who are not encouraged or permitted to explore, such as those raised in authoritarian homes, are more likely to show the foreclosed status. For example, a 14-year-old in a family of doctors who has not considered any careers and comes to the decision, after prodding by her parents and grandparents, that she wants to be a doctor may be in the identity foreclosed status. The degree of freedom adolescents are afforded for exploration varies with family and community contextual factors, such as socioeconomic status. Adolescents from high socioeconomic status homes may have fewer responsibilities to work outside the home, may reside in communities with more extracurricular opportunities, and may be more likely to attend postsecondary education than their peers from low socioeconomic homes—all factors that support the exploration needed for identity achievement (Kroger, 2015; Spencer, Swanson, & Harpalani, 2015). Adolescents who do not receive support and encouragement to develop and express ideas are likely to experience identity diffusion, as they lack opportunities to seek out and make commitments to possible selves (Hall & Brassard, 2008; Reis & Youniss, 2004; Zimmermann & Becker-Stoll, 2002).

Attachment to peers is also associated with identity exploration (Harter, 2006; Meeus, Oosterwegel, & Vollerbergh, 2002). Peers serve as a mirror in which adolescents view their emerging identities, an audience to which they relay their self-narratives (McLean, 2005). When adolescents feel supported and respected by peers, they feel more comfortable exploring identity alternatives (Ragelienė, 2016). As with parents, conflict with peers harms identity development as adolescents often feel less free to explore identity alternatives and lack a supportive peer group to offer input on identity alternatives, which holds negative implications for identity development, such as identity foreclosure or diffusion (Hall & Brassard, 2008). In emerging adulthood, romantic relationships are an important context for identity development as the attachment to partners provides security for exploration, similar to infants' secure base (Pittman, Keiley, Kerpelman, & Vaughn, 2011). Romantic partners influence each other reciprocally, illustrating some of the many interactions that occur between individuals and the people in their immediate contexts (Wängqvist, Carlsson, van der Lee, & Frisén, 2016).

DEVELOPMENTAL SHIFTS IN IDENTITY

Researchers assess identity status by administering interview and survey measures (Årseth, Kroger, Martinussen, & Marcia, 2009; Jones, Akers, & White, 1994; Schwartz, 2004). Young people typically shift among identity statuses during the adolescent years, but the specific pattern of identity development varies among adolescents (Meeus, 2011). Some adolescents remain in one identity status, such as identity moratorium, for the bulk of adolescence; while others experience multiple transitions in identity status. The most common shifts in identity status are from the least mature statuses, identity diffusion and identity foreclosure, to moratorium and the most mature status, achievement, in middle and late adolescence (Al-Owidha, Green, & Kroger, 2009; Meeus, 1996; Yip, 2014). The overall proportion of young people in the moratorium status tends to increase during adolescence, peaking at about age 19 and declining thereafter (Kroger, Martinussen, & Marcia, 2010). Many adolescents experience daily shifts in identity certainty that accompany shifts in circumstances and moods (Becht et al., 2016). Although some adolescents attain a sense of certainty in their commitments that persists through adolescence, variability is the norm (Becht et al., 2016).

Identity is not an all-or-nothing concept. People form a sense of identity in many different realms within both the ideological (i.e., occupation, religion, and politics) and interpersonal domains (i.e., friendships and dating; Grotevant, Thorbecke, & Meyer, 1982). Patterns of development vary across identity domains and adolescents with a strong sense of identity in one domain do not necessarily have a strong sense of identity in other domains (Goossens, 2001; Klimstra et al., 2016). For example, having chosen a career, an adolescent may demonstrate identity achievement with

FIGURE 11.3: Identity Status Frequencies for Women and Men at Ages 27, 36, 42, and 50

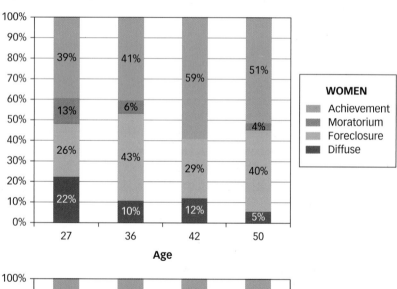

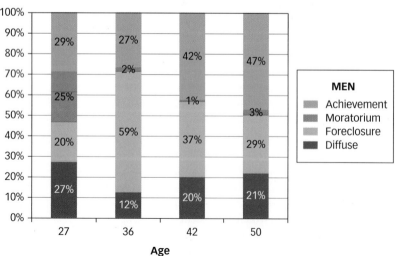

regard to vocation yet remain diffused with regard to political ideology, never having considered political affiliations.

Although the task of forming an identity is first encountered during adolescence, it is often not resolved in adolescence and the resulting identity is still not final thereafter (Kroger, 2015; Marcia, 2002). For example, one longitudinal study examined change in identity status at ages 18, 22, and 35. Although the overall sample demonstrated a shift toward identity achieved, there was substantial variability among participants in the degree to which they had changed (Cramer, 2017). In agreement, a meta-analysis covering 124 identity studies, Kroger, Martinussen, and Marcia (2010) concluded that it was not until age 36 that almost half of participants (47%) had reached overall identity achievement. Other research suggests that identity development continues through early adulthood even after achievement has been reached (Carlsson, Wängqvist, & Frisén, 2015). Changing life circumstances, contexts, and developmental needs spur identity development during adulthood. Adults often move in and out of identity statuses. For example, in one study of young adults, nearly half shifted identity statuses between ages 25 and 29, and all four statuses were represented at both ages (Carlsson, Wängqvist, & Frisén, 2016).

Identity commitments continue to change and evolve in content and in certainty (Bosma & Kunnen, 2001; Luyckx, Goossens, & Soenens, 2006; Marcia, 2002). This process proceeds well into middle adulthood. For example, one longitudinal study followed a sample of Finnish adults, born in 1959, across ages 27, 36, 42, and 50 (Fadjukoff & Kroger, 2016). All four identity statuses were observed at all ages across five identity domains: religious beliefs, political identity, occupational career, intimate relationships, and lifestyle. From age 27 to 50, participants showed a trend toward achievement of overall identity as well as achievement within each domain. Although women tended to outnumber men in terms of having reached achievement status early in life, there were no gender differences at age 50. Figure 11.3 illustrates the pattern of change across domains (Fadjukoff & Kroger, 2016).

OUTCOMES ASSOCIATED WITH IDENTITY DEVELOPMENT

Identity development is associated with well-being and positive functioning (Spencer et al., 2015). Specifically, the more advanced statuses—identity achievement and identity moratorium—are both associated with positive functioning, prosocial behavior, the capacity for romantic attachments, and an adaptive, mature sense of self (Berman, Weems, Rodriguez, & Zamora, 2006). Identity achievement is also associated with high self-esteem, feelings of control, high moral reasoning, and positive views of work and school (Adams & Marshall, 1996; Kroger, 2000). In contrast, identity moratorium is associated with anxiety (Lillevoll, Kroger, & Martinussen, 2013). Young people in the moratorium status often feel puzzled by the multiple choices before them and are driven to make decisions and solve problems by using an active information-gathering style characterized by seeking, evaluating, and reflecting on information to determine their views and make decisions (Luyckx et al., 2008). Sorting through and determining commitments in the educational and relationship domains is stressful and is associated with negative mood (Klimstra et al., 2016). Some adolescents experience moratorium as extremely overwhelming and they become anxious, which may be paralyzing and prevent identity exploration (Crocetti, Klimstra, Keijsers, Hale Iii, & Meeus, 2009).

Identity foreclosure and diffusion are associated with passivity and, from late adolescence on, maladaptive long-term outcomes (Archer & Waterman, 1990; Berzonsky & Kuk, 2000). Young people who show identity foreclosure tend to take a rigid and inflexible stance, avoid reflecting on their identity choice, and reject information that may contradict their position (Kroger, 2007). They are not open to new experiences or considering new ways of thinking.

The identity-diffused status is the least mature form of identity. While it is developmentally appropriate for early adolescents to have neither explored nor committed to a sense of identity, by late adolescence identity diffusion is uncommon and has been considered indicative of maladjustment (Kroger et al., 2010). Young people who show identity diffusion tend to use a cognitive style that is characterized by avoidance; rather than dealing with personal problems and making decisions, their choices are dictated by situational pressures instead of reflection. Identity-diffused individuals tend not to make independent decisions; they call upon fate, follow others, or let issues decide themselves. Academic difficulties, general apathy, organization and time management problems, and alcohol and substance abuse are associated with identity diffusion (Laghi, Baiocco, Lonigro, & Baumgartner, 2013). "Bryan's on academic probation again and it looks like he'll be expelled from the dormitory because the resident assistant found drugs in his room. And he doesn't seem to care. I just don't get it!" exclaims Bryan's academic advisor. Behavior problems both precede and accompany identity diffusion. Longitudinal research suggests that behavior problems in early adolescence predict identity diffusion in late adolescence (Crocetti, Klimstra, Hale, Koot, & Meeus, 2013). Young people in identity diffusion keep life on hold; they don't seek the meaning-making experiences needed to form a sense of identity (Carlsson et al., 2016).

ETHNIC IDENTITY

An important aspect of identity, especially for ethnic minority adolescents, is **ethnic identity**, or a sense of membership to an ethnic group including the attitudes, values, and culture associated with that group (whether Latino, Asian American, African American, white, etc.; (Phinney, 2000; Phinney & Ong, 2007; Rivas-Drake et al., 2014; Umaña-Taylor et al., 2014). Some researchers instead refer to *ethnic-racial identity*, which includes both the aspect of identity that is based on one's ethnic heritage and the aspect based on one's racial group in a specific sociohistorical context (Umaña-Taylor, 2016; Umaña-Taylor et al., 2014). This type of identity emerges when children begin to identify and categorize themselves and others according to ethnic and racial labels.

During adolescence, the process of ethnic identity development involves exploring one's ethnicity and internalizing values from one's ethnic group (Quintana, 2007). Like other components of a sense of self, ethnic identity develops and changes over time as individuals explore, gain experience, and make choices in various contexts. Adolescents explore their ethnic identity by learning about the cultural practices associated with their ethnicity by reading, attending cultural events, and talking to members of their culture (Quintana, 2007; Romero, Edwards, Fryberg, & Orduña, 2014; Wakefield & Hudley, 2007). After developing a sense of belonging, young people may become committed to an ethnic identity. A strong sense of ethnic identity helps young people to reject negative views of their culture that are based on stereotypes (Rivas-Drake et al., 2014). One study found that feelings of affirmation and belonging to ethnic heritage predicted positive psychological adjustment in Navajo youth (Jones & Galliher, 2007).

Ethnic minority adolescents often face challenges to the development of identity. With cognitive advances, adolescents are able to consider themselves and their worlds in more complicated ways—and become better at taking other people's perspectives. Many ethnic minority adolescents also become sensitive to negative feedback, discrimination, and inequality from the majority group. Many adolescents find it difficult to develop a feeling of cultural belonging and personal goals, especially when the standards of the larger society are different from those of the culture of origin, such as the differing emphases of collectivism and individualism. Collectivist cultures stress commitment to family, although the emphasis on family obligations

ethnic identity A sense of membership to an ethnic group and viewing the attitudes and practicesassociated with that group as an enduring part of the self.

Steve Granitz/WireImage/Getty Images

Adolescents explore their ethnic identity by learning about their culture, including its literature, music, dance, and customs. A strong sense of ethnic identity predicts healthy adjustment.

often lessens the longer the family has been living in an emigrant country that emphasizes individualism (Phinney, 2000). Sometimes adolescents are restricted from participating in the larger culture out of parental fear that assimilation will undermine cultural values.

One study of Vietnamese American adolescents living in an ethnic enclave in southern California provides an example. Most of the adolescents felt that their parents encouraged them to embrace their heritage, and make friends and engage in activities within the Vietnamese community, rather than become involved with the larger community of school and neighborhood (Vo-Jutabha, Dinh, McHale, & Valsiner, 2009). As one boy explained, "My parents expect me to speak Vietnamese consistently. Every now and then they just say that I forgot it and that I don't know how to speak it anymore. . . . Of course, I understand it and my parents expect me to be in a Viet Club or something. But I mean c'mon, really c'mon" (pp. 683–684). Another girl adds, "I think living in the Asian community kinda stops me from branching out. I live in this area and all of my friends are mostly Asian and I want to have other friends" (p. 680).

Adolescents are more likely to construct a favorable ethnic identity when they learn about their culture's values, language, and history, and celebrate cultural traditions, and regularly interact with parents and peers within their culture.

Discrimination against particular ethnic groups can make it difficult for youth to form a positive sense of identity. Adolescents from a variety of racial and ethnic groups, both native born and immigrant, report experiences of discrimination which are associated with low self-esteem, depression, low social competence, behavior problems, and distress (Mrick & Mrtorell, 2011; Rivas-Drake et al., 2014; Wakefield & Hudley, 2007). For example, Mexican American youth who perceive and experience discrimination are less likely than other Mexican American youth to explore their ethnicity, feel positive feelings about their ethnicity, and incorporate a sense of ethnic identity (Romero & Roberts, 2003). Some ethnic minority adolescents perceive discrimination in the classroom, such as feeling that their teachers call on them less, grade them more harshly, or discipline them more harshly than other students. African American adolescents who face racial discrimination from teachers and peers at school tend to show declines in their sense of ethnic identity. They also show declines in grades, academic self-concept, and school engagement, as well as poor mental health (anger, depression, self-esteem, and psychological resilience) and reduced sense of ethnic identity (Dotterer, McHale, & Crouter, 2009; Wong, Eccles, & Sameroff, 2003). Likewise, in a study of Navajo 9th- and 10th-grade adolescents, those who perceived discrimination showed poorer psychosocial adjustment and higher levels of substance use over a 1-year period (Galliher, Jones, & Dahl, 2011). Minority adolescents often must manage confusing messages to embrace their heritage while confronting discrimination, making the path to exploring and achieving ethnic identity challenging and painful, and leading many to remain diffused or foreclosed (Markstrom-Adams & Adams, 1995).

A strong positive sense of ethnic identity can reduce the magnitude of the negative effects of racial discrimination on self-concept, academic achievement, and problem behaviors among African American adolescents, as well as acting as a buffer to stress, including discrimination stress (Douglass & Umaña-Taylor, 2016; Kiang, Gonzales-Backen, Yip, Witkow, & Fuligni, 2006; Romero et al., 2014; Williams, Aiyer, Durkee, & Tolan, 2014). Adolescents who have achieved a strong sense of ethnic identity tend to have high self-esteem, optimism, effective coping strategies, and a view their ethnicity positively (Umaña-Taylor, 2016; Galliher et al., 2011; Gonzales-Backen, Bámaca-Colbert, & Allen, 2016). Ethnic identity is an important contributor to well-being and is associated with school achievement in adolescents from diverse ethnicities, such as those of Mexican, Chinese, Latino, African American, and European backgrounds (Adelabu, 2008; Fuligni, Witkow, & Garcia, 2005; Miller-Cotto & Byrnes, 2016). Adolescents with a strong sense of ethnic identity tend to show better adjustment and coping skills as well as fewer emotional and behavior problems than do those who do not or only weakly identify with ethnicity (Chavous et al., 2003; Kerpelman, Eryigit, & Stephens, 2008; Mrick & Mrtorell, 2011).

What fosters ethnic identity development? The exploration and commitment process that is key to identity achievement also underlies establishment of a sense of ethnic identity (Yip, 2014). The family is a particularly important context for ethnic identity formation, as close and warm relationships with parents are associated with more well-developed ethnic identities (Umaña-Taylor et al., 2014). Parents who provide positive ethnic socialization messages promote ethnic identity (Douglass & Umaña-Taylor, 2016). In contrast, adolescents who perceive excessive parental pressure and restrictions might respond with rebellion and rejection of ethnic heritage. Parents can help adolescents withstand discrimination and contradictory messages and develop a positive ethnic identity by encouraging them to act prosocially and to disprove stereotypes of low academic achievement or problem behavior (Phinney & Chavira, 1995; Rivas-Drake et al., 2014; Umaña-Taylor, Alfaro, Bámaca, & Guimond, 2009). Adolescents who learn about their culture, such as values, attitudes, language, and traditions, and regularly interact with parents and peers within their culture are more likely to construct a favorable ethnic identity (Phinney, Romero, Nava, & Huang, 2001; Romero et al., 2014; Umaña-Taylor, Bhanot, & Shin, 2006). For example, ethnic identity is positively associated with an adolescent's proficiency in speaking his or her heritage language (Oh & Fuligni, 2010).

Similar to other aspects of development, perception matters. Adolescents' perception of their ethnic socialization—their view of the degree to which they adopt the customs and values of their culture—predicts ethnic identity rather than simply following their parents' views (Hughes, Hagelskamp, Way, & Foust, 2009). Likewise, among African American adolescents, high levels of peer acceptance and popularity among African American peers is associated with a strong sense of ethnic identity (Rivas-Drake et al., 2014; Rock, Cole, Houshyar, Lythcott, & Prinstein, 2011). Adolescents' perceptions of their ethnicity and ethnic groups are influenced by multiple layers of a dynamic ecological system, including families, schools, and peers, as well as the political social and economic climate (Way, Santos, Niwa, & Kim-Gervey, 2008).

Ethnic identity continues to influence adjustment in adulthood (Syed et al., 2013). Whereas ethnic identity development in adolescence involves deriving personal meaning from one's ethnicity, in adulthood the process expands to include multiple life domains. Ethnic identity becomes integrated with and interacts with other domains of identity, such as gender, career, and relationship, to create a coherent overall identity (Umaña-Taylor et al., 2014).

 Thinking in Context 11.3

1. Identify contextual influences on the development of a sense of self and identity. In what ways do interactions with contextual influences such as parents, peers, school, community, and societal forces shape adolescents' emerging sense of self?

2. Consider your own sense of ethnic identity. Is ethnicity an important part of your sense of self? Why or why not? Have you experienced shifts in your experience of ethnicity from childhood to adulthood?

PERSONALITY

LO 11.4 Compare and contrast the trait and stage approaches to personality.

"Clearly you're extroverted!" laughed Carlos. "You're way more social than I am. You always were the social one, even back in high school," he recalled. "Yeah, but that's not saying much, as you're the complete opposite—so introverted that you might even be antisocial," retorted David to his childhood friend. As Carlos and David agree, we all have a personality, particular dispositions, and ways of interaction that persist over time. How stable is personality? Do people typically change little, like Carlos and David have observed? There are several ways of considering personality development. The most popular approach considers personality as a set of traits.

TRAIT APPROACH TO PERSONALITY

Extensive research on the nature of personality, conducted with multiple samples over several decades, has resulted in an empirically based theory that has collapsed the many characteristics on which people differ into five clusters of personality traits, collectively known as the **Big 5 personality traits**, shown in Table 11.2 (McCrae & Costa, 2008). The Big 5 personality factors are thought to reflect inherited predispositions that persist throughout life, and a growing body of evidence supports their genetic origins (Penke, Denissen, & Miller, 2007; Power & Pluess, 2015).

Is personality stable? Do extroverted, outgoing children and adolescents become extroverted adults?

Personality Development

From a trait perspective, personality begins at birth and first manifests as temperament, a collection of individual traits and behavioral tendencies constructed of inborn biological tendencies in areas such as mood, distractibility, and regularity (see Chapter 10). Temperament evolves into recognizable personality traits by early childhood that influence how emotions are experienced and expressed and how the child acts (Chen, Schmidt, Chen, & Schmidt, 2015). Although the traits tend to be less distinctive in early childhood than they are later in life (Wilson, Schalet, Hicks, & Zucker, 2013), there is consensus among experts that the five-factor model applies to children and there are reliable age differences in traits (Shiner & DeYoung, 2013; Wängqvist, Lamb, Frisén, & Hwang, 2015). Cross-sectional and longitudinal research has shown that mean levels of agreeableness, conscientiousness, openness to experience, and extroversion tend to decline from late childhood into early adolescence (Denissen, van Aken, Penke, & Wood,

Big 5 personality traits Five clusters of personality traits that reflect an inborn predisposition that is stable throughout life. The five traits are: openness, conscientiousness, extroversion, agreeableness, and neuroticism.

TABLE 11.2 • Big 5 Personality Traits

Openness	The degree to which one is open to experience, ranging from curious, explorative, and creative to disinterested, uncreative, and not open to new experiences.
Conscientiousness	The tendency to be responsible, disciplined, task oriented, and planful. This trait relates to effortful self-regulation. Individuals low in this trait tend to be irresponsible, impulsive, and inattentive.
Extroversion	Includes social outgoingness, high activity, enthusiastic interest, and assertive tendencies. This trait is related to positive emotionality. On the opposite pole, descriptors include social withdrawal and constrictedness.
Agreeableness	This trait includes descriptors such as trusting, cooperative, helpful, caring behaviors and attitudes toward others. Individuals low in agreeableness are seen as difficult, unhelpful, oppositional, and stingy.
Neuroticism	This trait relates to negative emotionality. Descriptors include moodiness, fear, worry, insecurity, and irritability. The opposite pole includes traits such as self-confidence.

FIGURE 11.4: Change in Three Big 5 Personality-Trait Domains

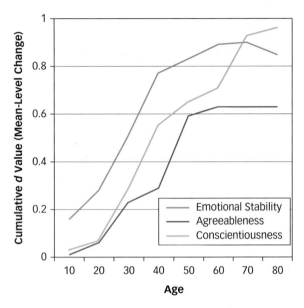

Cumulative mean-level change in three Big Five personality-trait domains, based on data from a meta-analysis of 92 longitudinal studies by Roberts, Walton, and Viechtbauer (2006). Mean-level change reflects the degree to which a population decreases or increases in specific traits over a specific period of time. These graphs were created by adding average amounts of standardized mean-level change (d scores) from separate decades of the life course together, under the assumption that personality-trait change may be cumulative.

Source: Adapted from "Patterns of Mean-Level Change in Personality Traits Across the Life Course: A Meta-Analysis of Longitudinal Studies," by B. W. Roberts, K. E. Walton, and W. Viechtbauer, 2006, Psychological Bulletin, 132(1), p. 15. Copyright 2006 by the American Psychological Association. Adapted with permission.

2013; Soto & Tackett, 2015; Van den Akker, Deković, Asscher, & Prinzie, 2014). In addition, neuroticism tends to increase, leveling off in adolescence (Wängqvist et al., 2015). The biological, social, and psychological transitions from childhood to adolescence appear to be accompanied by temporary dips in some aspects of personality maturity, lending credence to the stereotype of adolescent moodiness (Soto, John, Gosling, & Potter, 2011). In sum, children become more challenging and set in their ways and less sociable as they enter adolescence.

It is in early adulthood, between ages 18 and 40, that we see the most pronounced changes in personality traits (Roberts, Walton, & Viechtbauer, 2006). For example, personality traits may change in response to new roles and demands (Leszko, Elleman, Bastarache, Graham, & Mroczek, 2016). The average young adult experiences increases in emotional stability (the reverse of neuroticism), conscientiousness, and, to a lesser degree, agreeableness (Soto & Tackett, 2015). These substantial mean-level shifts in these three Big 5 personality traits is a pattern that has often been referred to as the *maturity principle* of personality development (see Figure 11.4; Bleidorn, 2015; Roberts & Mroczek, 2008). With gains in social maturity, people increase their capacity to be productive contributors to society. This pattern of increasing maturity in early adulthood appears in young people around the world, likely because the majority of people in a majority of cultures go through similar life transitions at approximately the same ages (Bleidorn, 2015; Bleidorn et al., 2013).

Personality traits shift subtly during adulthood. Cross-sectional studies of adults in 26 countries, including Canada, Germany, Italy, Japan, Russia, South Korea, and the United States, have found that agreeableness and conscientiousness increase and neuroticism, extroversion, and openness decline into middle adulthood, suggesting that adults mellow with age (Löckenhoff et al., 2009; McCrae & Costa, 2006; McCrae, Terracciano, & The Personality Profiles of Cultures Project, 2005; Soto et al., 2011). These patterns continue into older adulthood. Extroversion and openness to experience decline with age from 30 to 90, with the most pronounced drops after the mid-50s (Lucas & Donnellan, 2011; Mroczek, Spiro, & Griffin, 2006; Srivastava, John, Gosling, & Potter, 2003). Conscientiousness increases from emerging adulthood to mid-adulthood, peaks between 50 and 70, and then declines; agreeableness tends to increase with age (Leszko et al., 2016; McCrae, 2002; McCrae & Costa, 2006). Thus cross-cultural similarities in patterns of change support arguments that personality itself and age-related changes have biological origins; however, cultures often share some contextual similarities (see Figure 11.5).

How might context influence group patterns of personality change? Recall from Chapter 1 that individuals are active in influencing their own development. On the one hand, people's behaviors and choices shape their contexts and their personalities, while on the other hand people often experience predictable changes in context. These include age-graded events, such as graduating from college or experiencing menopause, as well as normative role transitions, such as getting married or becoming a parent. Such experiences, which are experienced around the same time by most people in a given culture, have the potential to influence personality change (Bleidorn et al., 2013; Mroczek et al., 2006). In addition, normative history-graded influences, or cohort differences, contribute to personality change across generations. Exposure to events and experiences unique to a given historical period may cause some cohorts to show a greater range of personality change during their lifetime than others.

FIGURE 11.5: Age Differences in Big 5 Personality Traits

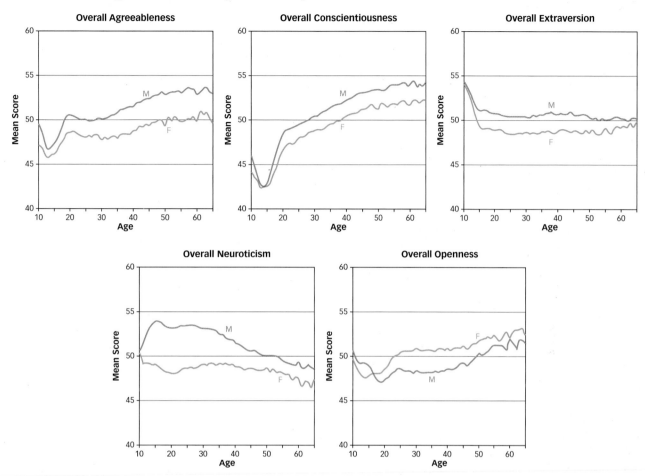

Source: Soto et al. (2011).

Personality Stability

Although there are predictable age-related shifts in Big 5 traits, there are also individual differences in the pattern and magnitude of change (Graham & Lachman, 2012). Not all individuals follow the normative increase in conscientiousness scores during adulthood, for example. Some people change more than others, and some change in ways that are contrary to general population trends (McAdams & Olson, 2010). In addition, individuals' relative position with regard to traits does not change (Deary, Pattie, & Starr, 2013; Roberts & Mroczek, 2008). In other words, someone who is high in openness relative to age peers is likely to remain high in openness over time, even though, as a group, the adults may show a decline during the adult years. Adults who scored high in extroversion relative to their peers at age 30 tend to continue to score high relative to their peers in older adulthood (Graham & Lachman, 2012). Individual differences in personality traits are highly stable over periods of time ranging from 3 to 30 years (McAdams & Olson, 2010; Wängqvist et al., 2015). For example, childhood personality ratings by teachers predict personality ratings in middle adulthood (Edmonds, Goldberg, Hampson, & Barckley, 2013; Hampson & Goldberg, 2006), as do personality ratings collected during adolescence (Morizot & Le Blanc, 2003).

Continuity in personality traits increases with age, from early adulthood, peaking in the late 30s into middle adulthood, with some decline in late adulthood (Lucas & Donnellan, 2011; McAdams & Olson, 2010). Rank order stability increases throughout adulthood; adults retain their position relative to peers throughout adulthood (Roberts & DelVecchio, 2000; Soto et al., 2011). Why does an individual's personality remain largely the same during a lifetime? Personality influences a person's life choices and experiences, yet folk wisdom usually adheres to the opposite: that a personality in adulthood is influenced by

• • Sense of Self

During adolescence mPFC activity increases in response to self-knowledge and evaluation tasks.

A critical task of adolescence is to construct a sense of self. What role does the brain play in this process? Neuroimaging studies have shown developmental changes in regions of the brain thought to be important for the sense of self, specifically the medial prefrontal cortex (mPFC; Mills, Lalonde, Clasen, Giedd, & Blakemore, 2014; Pfeifer & Peake, 2012). For example, in a longitudinal study of young adolescents engaged in a self-evaluation task at ages 10 and 13, in which they judged their own social skills and those of a familiar fictional character (e.g., Harry Potter), the adolescents showed more activity in the mPFC during self-evaluations than evaluations of the fictional character, and mPFC activity increased from age 10 to 13 (Pfeifer et al., 2013). The mPFC is associated with processing information about the self (Northoff & Hayes, 2011) and also plays a role in reward and evaluation processes (Rangel, Camerer, & Montague, 2008), suggesting that self-evaluation may be experienced as more rewarding with age.

The mPFC undergoes significant development in adolescence and is one of the last parts of the brain to develop (Mills, Goddings, Clasen, Giedd, & Blakemore, 2014). Overall, mPFC activity increases between childhood and adolescence in response to self-knowledge and evaluation tasks and is followed by a decrease from adolescence to adulthood (Blakemore, 2012).

In one study, 10-year-olds and adults completed a task examining their ability to retrieve information about the self (Pfeifer, Lieberman, & Dapretto, 2007). Participants judged whether phrases such as "I like to read just for fun," described either themselves or a familiar fictional character. The young adolescents showed more activity in the mPFC when retrieving information about themselves than did adults, and the adults showed more activity in the lateral temporal cortex (LTC), which is associated with semantic memory (Cabeza & Nyberg, 2000). Adolescents and adults may approach self-knowledge tasks differently (Pfeifer et al., 2007). The adolescents' increased mPFC activity suggests that they were actively processing the task, engaging in self-reflection. The increased activity of the LTC and decreased mPFC activity in adults suggests that the adults engaged in less active processing and, instead, relied on memory to complete the task, perhaps because they have more extensive knowledge about themselves. In the young adolescents, however, greater involvement of the mPFC and relatively less activation of semantic knowledge stores in the LTC imply active construction of self-descriptive attributes in response to the task at hand.

Developing a sense of self requires exploration and learning about oneself. The process of self-examination and processing information about the self has neural correlates, corresponding to activity in areas of the brain linked with the sense of self and with rewards. The critical—but often uncomfortable—developmental task of self-exploration may be experienced as rewarding for adolescents. As they learn more about themselves, individuals rely on their stored memories, and brain activity in response to self-knowledge tasks shifts from the mPFC to the LTC, as reflected in the adults' performance of self-knowledge tasks.

What Do You Think?

How might these findings of neurological correlates of self-understanding correspond to Erikson's description of the challenge of devising a sense of identity and the features of the psychosocial moratorium?

events and experience during a lifetime. The logic goes that after a humiliating experience at a party, a person becomes more introverted and anxious about social gatherings. However, research suggests that experience rarely causes dramatic changes in personality and that instead, it is our personalities that influence our choices and experiences (McCrae, 2002; McCrae & Costa, 2006). That is, introverted and socially anxious people may be prone to find parties and social gatherings challenging—and in their distress they may behave in ways that increase the likelihood of humiliating experiences (e.g., grasping a cup too tightly and inadvertently spilling its contents). People choose behaviors, lifestyles, mates, and contexts based on their personalities, and then the outcomes of these choices and life experiences may strengthen and stabilize personality traits (Soto, 2015; Wrzus,

Wagner, & Riediger, 2016). In one study conducted over a 9-year period, social well-being correlated positively with extroversion, agreeableness, conscientiousness, emotional stability, and openness; and changes in social well-being coincided with changes in these traits (Hill, Turiano, Mroczek, & Roberts, 2012). In this sense, stability of personality is influenced by individuals' behaviors and choice of environments as well as by environmental factors themselves (Kandler et al., 2010).

Contextual factors play a role in stabilizing personality throughout adulthood as social, living, and working contexts and social roles, such as spouse or parent, become established and, for most people, are largely stable during adulthood contributing to continuity in personality and individual differences in personality (Kandler, Kornadt, Hagemeyer, & Neyer, 2015; Roberts, Walton, & Viechtbauer, 2006). Dramatic life changes, such as divorce, serious illness, or widowhood may bring about new behaviors and patterns of traits, but more commonly such events evoke and strengthen existing patterns of traits (Mroczek et al., 2006; Roberts & Caspi, 2003). Personality traits can be expressed in many ways, depending on the situation and on the individual's personality makeup. Most people are motivated to maintain a stable sense of personality as part of developing and maintaining a consistent sense of self (Kandler et al., 2010).

Correlates of Personality

Children's personality traits influence their relationships with peers (Soto & Tackett, 2015). For example, children higher in neuroticism and lower in agreeableness and conscientiousness are more likely to engage in relational aggression, hurting peers through gossip and verbal bullying (Tackett et al., 2014). In adolescence, personality scores predict a wide range of variables, including academic engagement, externalizing behavior, and substance use (Clark, Durbin, Hicks, Iacono, & McGue, 2016; Wilson et al., 2013). For example, youths low in agreeableness, low in conscientiousness, and high in neuroticism show higher rates of externalizing, or rule-breaking behaviors, whereas youths low in extroversion and high in neuroticism show higher rates of internalizing psychopathology, such as anxiety and depression (Caspi & Shiner, 2008; Tackett, 2006).

Big 5 personality traits predict career, family, and personal choices in adulthood. People who are high in conscientiousness are more likely than others to complete college, those high in extroversion are more likely to marry, and those high in neuroticism are more likely to divorce (Hill et al., 2012; Shiota & Levenson, 2007). Individuals' patterns of Big 5 personality traits are associated with cognitive functioning. For example, high scores on measures of conscientiousness predict better performance on cognitive tasks and slower rates of cognitive decline (Bogg & Roberts, 2013; Curtis, Windsor, & Soubelet, 2015; Luchetti, Terracciano, Stephan, & Sutin, 2016). High scores on neuroticism scales, on the other hand, are associated with worse average cognitive functioning, steeper rate of cognitive decline, and higher risk for dementia (Chapman et al., 2012; Leszko et al., 2016; Luchetti, Terracciano, Stephan, & Sutin, 2015).

Big 5 traits even predict mortality. For example, increased mortality risk is associated with each of the following: low conscientiousness, low extroversion, and high neuroticism, as well as long-term increases in neuroticism (Mroczek & Spiro, 2007). Conscientiousness has an especially close association with health as it influences the behaviors persons engage in—exercise, eating habits, and risky behaviors such as smoking—and these behaviors affect the likelihood of good or poor health outcomes (Friedman & Kern, 2014; Turiano, Chapman, Gruenewald, & Mroczek, 2015). In fact, conscientiousness measured in childhood predicts health in midlife (Hampson et al., 2016).

Big 5 personality traits show complex associations with well-being. Specifically, well-being correlates with higher levels of extroversion, agreeableness, and conscientiousness, and with lower levels of neuroticism (Cox, Wilt, Olson, & McAdams, 2010). Moreover, this relationship may be bidirectional. A study of 16,000 Australian adults revealed that their personality traits predicted changes in well-being, yet changes in well-being in turn influenced their traits (Soto, 2015). Individuals who were initially extroverted, agreeable, conscientious, and emotionally stable subsequently increased in well-being and in turn became even more agreeable, conscientious, emotionally stable, and extroverted. We have seen that well-being tends to increase during the adult years. Research from the Big 5 trait approach to personality supports this, as people in their later years tend to become happier (more agreeable and less neurotic), more self-contented and self-centered (less extroverted and open), more laid back and satisfied with what they have, and less preoccupied with productivity (less conscientious) (Kandler et al., 2015; Marsh, Nagengast, & Morin, 2012). This mellowing of personality aids older adults in developing a sense of acceptance, which they view as important to their well-being (Ryff, 1991).

PERSONALITY AS PSYCHOSOCIAL STAGES

While the trait approach views personality as a system of internal dispositions that are largely inborn and subtly shift as they influence and are influenced by people's contexts, the stage approach to personality views change as inherent to personality growth. From this perspective, people progress through a series of qualitative stages that shape who they become. At each stage individuals face specific developmental tasks and questions.

Erikson's Psychosocial Stages

According to Erik Erikson, throughout the lifespan we all proceed through a series of psychosocial crises or developmental tasks. As discussed in Chapter 1, how well each crisis is resolved, or the extent to which each developmental task is completed, influences psychological development and how the individual approaches the next crisis or developmental task.

Trust versus mistrust. From the day she was born, each time Elysia cried her mother or father would come to her bassinet and hold her, check her diaper, and feed her if necessary. Soon Elysia developed the basic expectation that her parents would meet her needs. According to Erikson (1950), developing a sense of *trust versus mistrust* (birth to 1 year of age) is the first developmental task of life: Infants must develop a view of the world as a safe place where their basic needs will be met. Throughout the first year of life, infants depend on their caregivers for food, warmth and affection. If parents and caregivers attend to the infant's physical and emotional needs and consistently fulfill them, the infant will develop a basic sense of trust in his or her caregivers and, by extension, in the world in general.

However, if caregivers are neglectful or inconsistent in meeting an infant's needs, he will develop a sense of mistrust toward the world and interpersonal relationships, feeling that he cannot count on others for love, affection, or the fulfillment of other basic human needs. The sense of trust or mistrust developed in infancy influences how people approach the subsequent stages of development. Specifically, when interaction with adults around them inspires trust and security, babies are more likely to feel comfortable exploring the world, which enhances their learning, social development, and emotional development.

Autonomy versus shame and doubt. Toddlers walk on their own, talk and express their own ideas and needs and become more independent. The developmental task for toddlers is to learn to do things for themselves and feel confident in their ability to maneuver themselves in their environment—to progress through the second stage in Erikson's scheme of psychosocial development, *autonomy versus shame and doubt* (1 to 3 years of age). If parents encourage the toddler's initiative and allow her to explore, experiment, make mistakes, and test limits, the toddler will develop autonomy, self-reliance, self-control, and confidence. If parents are overprotective or disapprove of her struggle for independence, the child may begin to doubt her abilities to do things by herself, feel ashamed of her desire for autonomy, passively observe, and not develop a sense of independence and self-reliance.

Initiative versus guilt. The task is for young children in the *initiative versus guilt* stage, ages 3 to 6 years, is to develop a sense of purposefulness and take pride in their accomplishments. In developing a sense of initiative, young children make plans, tackle new tasks, set goals (e.g., climbing a tree, writing their name, counting to ten), and work to achieve them. They persist enthusiastically in tasks, whether physical or social, even when frustrated. If parents are controlling—not permitting children to carry out their sense of purpose—or are highly punitive, critical, or threatening, then children may not develop high standards and the initiative to meet them. Instead, children will be paralyzed by guilt and worry about their inability to measure up to parental expectations. The negative outcome of this stage of Erikson's (1950) scheme is that children will develop an

Success influences children's sense of competence.

overly critical conscience and be enveloped in guilt, reducing their motivation to exert the effort to master new tasks. Children who develop a sense of initiative develop social skills, a confident self-image, control over their emotions, and a sense of conscience. Their success in taking initiative and the feeling of competence and self-esteem that accompanies it is an important basis for developing a sense of self.

Industry over inferiority. Middle childhood, ages 6 to 11, represents an important transition in children's conceptions of themselves and their abilities. According to Erik Erikson, school-age children face the task of developing a sense of *industry over inferiority*, feeling more competent than inadequate. Children must learn and master skills that are valued in their society, such as reading, mathematics, writing, and using computers. Six year-old Kia ties her shoelace and smiles to herself, "I did it again. I'm really good at tying my shoelaces, much better than my little brother." Success at culturally valued tasks as simple as shoelace tying influences children's feelings of competence and curiosity as well as their motivation to persist and succeed in all of the contexts in which they are embedded (Kowaz & Marcia, 1991). When children are unable to succeed or receive consistently negative feedback from parents or teachers, they may lose confidence in their ability to succeed and be productive at culturally valued tasks. Children's sense of industry influences their self-concept, self-esteem, and their readiness to face the physical, cognitive, and social challenges of middle childhood.

Identity versus role confusion. Perhaps the most commonly known stage in Erikson's theory examines identity development. As mentioned earlier in this chapter, young people struggle with figuring out who they are; their sense of self. Erikson theorized that the *identity versus role confusion* task runs throughout adolescence, beginning with puberty and extending to early adulthood. Adolescents must experience a period of exploration, a psychosocial moratorium, and must commit to resolutions in order to reach identity achievement. Maladaptive outcomes of the identity search process include identity foreclosure and identity diffusion. The sense of identity established in adolescence forms an important base for the task of early adulthood.

Intimacy versus isolation. The crisis of early adulthood, *intimacy versus isolation*, entails developing the capacity for intimacy and making a permanent commitment to a romantic partner. Establishing an intimate relationship that is mutual and satisfying is a challenge for emerging and young adults who often continue to struggle with identity issues and are just gaining social and financial independence. Commitment to an identity, including a sense of self, values, and goals, prepares young people for establishing intimate relationships (Kroger, 2007a; Zimmer-Gembeck & Petherick, 2006) and is associated with establishing intimate relationships in early adulthood (Beyers & Seiffge-Krenke, 2010). Yet, as young adults form intimate relationships, they must reshape their identity to include their role as partner and the goals, plans, and interests shared with their partner. Thus, they must resolve identity and intimacy demands that may conflict. For example, as they engage in continued identity development, they must do the work of establishing an intimate relationship—making sacrifices and compromises which may involve a temporary loss of self—before expanding the sense of self to include a partner. The formation of intimate relationships is associated with well-being in young adults (Busch & Hofer, 2012). The flip side—not attaining a sense of intimacy and not making personal commitments to others—is the negative psychosocial outcome of isolation, entailing a sense of loneliness and self-absorption.

Generativity versus stagnation. For Erikson (1959), the developmental task of middle adulthood entails cultivating a sense of *generativity,* which is a concern and sense of responsibility for future generations and society as a whole and "giving back" to others. The alternative to generativity, *stagnation,* refers to apathy and disengagement from younger generations and from society.

In early midlife, generativity is often expressed through child rearing. During the middle adult years, generativity expands to include a commitment to community and society at large. Personal goals become framed within the context of contributing to the social world beyond oneself and one's immediate family to future generations and even the species itself (McAdams, 2014; McAdams & Logan, 2004). Adults fulfill generative needs through volunteering, engaging in creative work, and teaching and mentoring others in the workplace and community. Generativity fulfills adults' needs to feel needed and to make contributions that will last beyond their lifetimes, achieving a sense of immortality (Kotre, 1999). For the active and generative, middle adulthood is the prime of life even as they experience multiple conflicting demands. In Erikson's view, adults who fail to develop a sense of generativity experience stagnation, a lack of growth, as well as self-absorption that interferes with personal developent, preventing them from contributing to the welfare of others (Erikson, 1959).

Generativity is associated with life satisfaction, self-acceptance, low rates of anxiety and depression, and overall well-being (An & Cooney, 2006; Cox et al., 2010). Generativity increases from the 30s through the 60s in adults of all ethnicities and socioeconomic backgrounds (Ackerman, Zuroff, & Moskowitz, 2000; Newton & Stewart, 2010). However, it is characterized by a gender difference: Men who have children tend to score higher in measures of generativity than do childless men, although having children is not related to generativity in women (Marks et al., 2004). Likewise, engaging in child-care activities is associated with increases in generativity in men, but not women (McKeering & Pakenham, 2000). Having children may draw men's attention to need to the care for the next generation, while women may already be socialized to nurture their children. That said, generativity is a stronger influence on well-being in women than men (An & Cooney, 2006). For both men and women, however, generativity is influenced by psychosocial issues addressed earlier in life, such as developing a sense of trust (Wilt, Cox, & McAdams, 2010). Developing generativity in middle adulthood relies on a lifetime of psychosocial development including the ability to trust others and oneself, understand ones' self, and sustain meaningful relationships.

Ego integrity. Life review, or reflecting on the cumulative choices that compose the story of the individual's life, is integral to developing a sense of *ego integrity*—the last stage in Erikson's (1950, 1982) psychosocial theory. Older adults who are successful in establishing a sense of ego integrity are able to find a sense of coherence in life experiences, and ultimately conclude that their lives are meaningful and valuable (Whiting & Bradley, 2007). Adults who achieve ego integrity are able to see their lives within a larger global and historical context, and recognize that their own experiences, while important, are only a very small part of the big picture. Viewing one's life within the context of humanity can make death less fearsome, more a part of life, and simply the next step in one's path (Vaillant, 1994, 2004).

According to Erikson, the alternative to developing a sense of integrity is despair, the tragedy experienced if the retrospective look at one's life is evaluated as meaningless and disappointing, emphasizing faults, mistakes, and what could have been (Whiting & Bradley, 2007). The despairing older adult may ruminate over lost chances and feel overwhelmed with bitterness and defeat, becoming contemptuous toward others in order to mask self-contempt. As might be expected, older adults who do not develop a sense of ego integrity are more likely to experience a poor sense of well-being and depression (Dezutter, Toussaint, & Leijssen, 2014). Similar to the development of identity and generativity, ego integrity is influenced by interactions with others. When older adults share their experiences, tell family stories from their lives, and provide advice, they have opportunities to engage in the self-evaluation that can lead to ego integrity.

Levinson's Seasons of Life

Similar to Erikson, Daniel Levinson (1978, 1996) viewed development as consisting of qualitative shifts in challenges that result from the interplay of intrapersonal and social forces. Based on interviews with 40 men aged 35 to 45 and, later, 45 women aged 35 to 45—both the men and the women were workers in a wide variety of occupations—Levinson concluded that adults progress through a common set of phases that he called *seasons of life.*

The key element of Levinson's psychosocial theory is the **life structure**, which refers to the overall organization of a person's life: relationships with significant others as well as institutions such as marriage, family, and vocation. In Levinson's model, individuals progress through several seasons over the lifespan in which their life structures are constructed, then tested and modified. Each season begins with a transition period, lasting about five years, when individuals conclude tasks of the prior stage and prepare for the next set of challenges. After individuals transition to the new stage, they must create and refine a life structure by integrating intrapersonal and social demands. Once adults master the developmental task of a given stage, they begin to question the resulting life structure and are spurred to progress to the next stage.

During the transition to early adulthood (ages 17 to 22), according to Levinson, we construct our life structure by creating a dream, an image of what we are to be in the adult world, which then guides our life choices. Young adults then work to realize their dreams and construct the resulting life structure (ages 22 to 28). Men tend to emphasize the occupational role and construct images of themselves as independent and successful in career settings. For example, Ben aspired to be a manager at his firm. He considered the skills he needed to develop, such as communication, leadership, and presentation skills, and focused his energy on making progress toward his goal. Women often create dual images that emphasize both marriage and career. Like Ben, Martha aspired to become a manager, but she also wanted to be home early enough each day to spend time with her children and participate in their lives. Although Martha worked to develop her career skills, she chose not to spend the necessary hours at the office until the children were in elementary school. Levinson found that men who were career oriented spent their 20s working toward their goals by gaining professional experience and credentials. And among women and men who took on primary caregiving roles, career development tended to show a slower path and extended into middle age (Kogan & Vacha-Haase, 2002; Levinson, 1996).

During what Levinson calls the age 30 transition (28 to 33), adults reconsider their life structure. Some adults who emphasized career over family may change their focus toward finding a partner or having children. Women who emphasized caregiver roles may become more individualistic, developing interests outside of the home, as their children grow older. Adults who do not have satisfying accomplishments at work or at home may

life structure In Levenson's theory, a person's overall organization of his or her life, particularly dreams, goals, and relationships with significant others as well as institutions, such as marriage, family, and vocation.

LIVES IN CONTEXT

• • Midlife Crisis

The midlife crisis is a popular stereotype with little research support.

The 45-year-old who purchases a red convertible sports car. The middle-aged husband or wife who suddenly leaves the marriage and moves out of the home, beginning a new life in a new city. The midlifer who is suddenly gripped with anxiety that half of life is over and despair that life has not turned out as planned. Each of these people embodies aspects of the most popular stereotype about middle age, depicted in television dramas and self-help magazine articles: the **midlife crisis**, a stressful time in the early to middle 40s when adults are thought to re-evaluate their lives.

Although the existence of a midlife crisis is widely accepted among laypersons (Wethington, 2000), research is at odds with this popular view. Surveys of adults over age 40 have revealed that only about 10% to 20% report having experienced a midlife crisis (Wethington, et al., 2004). Research consistently suggests that a period of crisis or psychological disturbance is not universal among middle-aged adults but instead exhibits significant individual differences, occurring at various periods of life (Brim, Ryff, & Kessler, 2004; McCrae & Costa, 2006; Rosenberg, Rosenberg, & Farrell, 1999).

Those who experience a crisis in midlife are usually those who have had upheavals at other times in their lives, and these experiences seem to be driven by personal style more than by advancing age (Freund & Ritter, 2009). Personal characteristics may determine whether a person experiences midlife, or any other point in life, as a crisis. For example, men who scored higher on measures of psychological problems earlier in adulthood were more likely to report experiencing a

midlife crisis ten years later than did men who scored lower on psychological problems (Costa et al., 1986; McCrae & Costa, 2006). Outside events that can occur at any time in adulthood, such as job loss, financial problems, or illness, may trigger responses that adults and their families may interpret as midlife crises (Beutel, Glaesmer, Wiltink, Marian, & Brähler, 2010; Wethington, Kessler, & Pixley, 2004).

Most developmental scientists adopt the perspective that midlife represents a transition similar to the transition to adulthood; it entails creating, clarifying, and evaluating values, goals, and priorities (Lachman et al., 2015). A close examination of this kind can lead to insights about oneself and decisions to revise life plans in light of conclusions (Vandewater & Stewart, 2006). Although first addressed in adolescence, identity development is a lifelong process. Life experiences, achievement of personal milestones, and movement through life transitions often spur adults to revisit the identity development process and reassess their sense of self (Erikson, 1959). Life evaluation is common in midlife but most people respond by making minor adjustments, creating turning points in their lives rather than dramatic changes. If they cannot revise their life paths, they try to develop a positive outlook (Wethington et al., 2004). Moreover, goals are not set in stone; they are dynamic and change over time. Adults assess and adjust goals throughout life, often without awareness.

Midlife is unquestionably a transition, given changes in middle-aged adults' bodies, families, careers, and contexts. Whether this transition takes the form of a crisis depends on individual factors and circumstances rather than age (Freund & Ritter, 2009). Despite this, the concept of a midlife

FIGURE 11.6: Views of Midlife, by Age

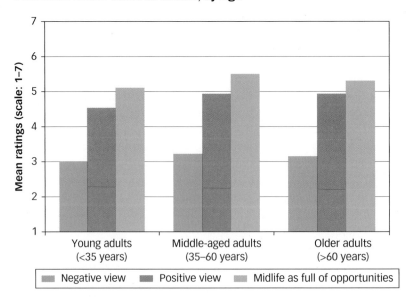

Source: Freund, A. M., & Ritter, J. O. 2009. Midlife Crisis: A Debate. *Gerontology, 55*(5), 582–591. With permission from Karger Publishers.

crisis remains popular in our culture, perhaps because it describes exciting possibilities for making major life changes, or perhaps because it is a simple explanation for the many changes that occur.

Paradoxically, though, most adults of all ages tend to view middle adulthood as a positive time in life, as shown in Figure 11.6 (Freund & Ritter, 2009). In addition, research suggests that midlife is a time of increasing life satisfaction, self-esteem, and well-being (Lachman et al., 2015; Ulrich Orth et al., 2010). Moreover, longitudinal studies show that personality remains stable from young adulthood through middle adulthood to older adulthood, suggesting that a period of upheaval and turmoil does not exist in midlife, or at least is not evidenced in personality change (McCrae & Costa, 2006).

What Do You Think?

1. Do you think the midlife crisis is a normal part of aging? Why or why not?

2. Considering what we know about lifetime changes in self-concept, self-esteem, and identity, how might this knowledge inform the question of how prevalent a midlife crisis is?

wonder if they can create and sustain a meaningful life structure; for them the age 30 transition is particularly challenging; perhaps constituting a crisis. Men tend to experience the mid- to late 30s (34 to 40) as a period of settling down, focusing on some goals and relationships and giving up others based on their overall values. Women at this stage are more likely to remain unsettled as they take on new career or family commitments and balance multiple roles and aspirations; they generally do not achieve a similar level of stability until middle age (Levinson, 1996).

Levinson observed that as adults transition to middle adulthood (40 to 45), they reexamine their dream established in early adulthood and evaluate their success in achieving it. This process of entering middle adulthood is often tumultuous. The crisis is one of identity and it arises because of the awareness of time passing: half of life is spent. Midlife adults look back at their dreams of adolescence and early adulthood and evaluate their progress, coming to terms with the fact that they will not realize many of them. In areas where they have achieved hoped-for success, they must reconcile reality with their dream and perhaps wonder whether the experience was "worth it," or whether they are missing out on some other aspects of life. Given a limited amount of time left in life, many adults reexamine the goals and values underlying their life structure. Some middle-aged adults make substantial changes by changing careers, divorcing, or beginning a new project such as writing a book. Others make smaller changes while remaining in the same context, such as devoting more time to the family.

The seasons of life are influenced by context because the process of evaluating and revising the life structure is influenced by the social opportunities and situations around us. Contexts of disadvantage—poverty, discrimination, or limited opportunities—deplete individuals of the energy needed to examine and revise the life structure. Opportunities to advance in one's career provide avenues of growth as individuals develop satisfying life structures, achieve their modified dreams, and become able to focus on the tasks of middle adulthood, such as accepting aging and becoming generative. Although the seasons of life conceptualization may be intuitively pleasing, critics note that Levinson's conclusions are based on a very small sample that overrepresents highly educated professional people of high socioeconomic status (Dare, 2011). Nevertheless, Levinson's ideas have shaped popular views of adulthood, most notably the concept of a midlife crisis, as discussed in the Lives in Context feature.

Overall, our sense of self emerges early in life as a simple awareness of self and then of simple descriptors such as *boy* or *girl*. Temperament is evident at birth and aspects of personality emerge soon after. As we progress from childhood into adolescence, we think about ourselves in more complex ways, and we begin to construct an identity, a critical psychosocial task. Both identity and personality continue to shift during our lives. These changes hold implications for how we feel about ourselves, our abilities, and our relationships, and influence how we interact with the world around us.

midlife crisis A period of self-doubt and stress attributed to entering midlife once thought to contribute to a major reorganization of personality in midlife. Now thought to occur in a small minority of adults and to be related to history more than age.

Thinking in Context 11.4

1.   In what ways has your personality changed during your lifetime? What do you think has contributed to those changes—and if you have not changed, why not?

2.   An important theme of lifespan development is that individuals and contexts interact and influence each other dynamically over time. What aspects of your personality influence the contexts in which you are embedded? In what ways might aspects of your context have influenced your personality?

3.   To what extent do you subscribe to stage views of personality change? To trait views? In your own life, do you feel that you have experienced qualitative shifts in your psychosocial functioning?

 # Apply Your Knowledge

Sixty-year-old Duane congratulated himself on a powerful finish to a long swim as he dried himself off at poolside. "Sixty years old? More like 45, my friend," he smiled to himself.

Later that day, over lunch, Duane's grandson told him of an opportunity to enroll in a hotel management training program. But, he said, "I don't see myself as a manager. I don't think that program is for me."

"Lashawn, this is a great opportunity," argued Duane. "Do well and they'll offer you a job with benefits. You can work your way up and maybe someday be the manager of a high-class hotel."

Over the next half hour, Lashawn described his long-held goal of becoming a professional musician. "Gramps, I'm not a clean-cut business person. I'm creative. Besides, the band is doing really well. We have a weekly gig lined up and we're talking about going on tour. That's who I am—a musician."

Duane continued to encourage Lashawn to register for the training program. "You can play with your band on weekends and go to the training during the week," he advised. Then he confided, "You know, when I was your age I planned on being a musician. I wanted to be famous and have a glamourous life."

This caught Lashawn by surprise. "What happened, Gramps?"

"Life," answered Duane. "I met your grandmother and settled down. I started to want different things, like being a good father. I realized I wasn't a very good guitar player—at least not as good as I thought when I was a

kid. Looking back, I am proud of the life I built with your grandmother, and it's OK that I'm not a great musician or famous. I'll admit, though, that I don't love my job."

"See? I want to love what I do!" Lashawn interjected.

Duane nodded. "But I didn't have the same opportunities as you. I started working at the factory because I was 18 and I needed to support myself. Now I have children and grandchildren I'm proud of, and, heck, I look pretty good too! Yes, work days are long but I manage the floor now so it's easier on my bones. Just a little while longer and I'll retire."

"Gramps, I don't want to wake up and see I've spent 40 years in a job I don't love."

"Lashawn, it takes time to figure yourself out and that's something that only you can do. I can only say I wish I'd had this opportunity when I was 18. Everything might have been very different. I hope you'll think about it some more."

1.   Describe Duane's sense of self, including his self-concept, self-esteem, and identity. How does he view his own age and capacities? How has his sense of self shifted during his lifetime?

2.   In what ways do Lashawn's concerns reflect his developing sense of self?

3.   Compare Lashawn and Duane's progression on Erikson's psychosocial stage model.

4.   What do you expect for Lashawn and Duane in the coming years?

Give your students the SAGE edge!

SAGE edge offers a robust online environment featuring an impressive array of free tools and resources for review, study, and further exploration, keeping both instructors and students on the cutting edge of teaching and learning. Learn more at **edge.sagepub.com/kuthertopical.**

CHAPTER 11 IN REVIEW

11.1 Summarize developmental trends in self-concept from infancy through adulthood.

SUMMARY

Self-awareness emerges in early infancy. In toddlerhood the sense of self-awareness expands beyond self-recognition to include a categorical self which guides behavior. Children first understand themselves in concrete and unrealistically positive terms, but with age self-concept becomes correlated with skills, accomplishments, and external indicators of competence. As children move from early childhood to middle childhood, self-concept includes trait-like psychological constructs. Older children include both positive and negative traits to describe themselves and differentiate among multiple types of self-concept. Cognitive advances enable adolescents to use more labels to describe themselves and the labels they choose become more abstract, complex, situational, and often contradictory. They begin to identify an ideal verses actual self whose match influences well-being. This pattern of increasing complexity and integration of self concept continues in adulthood, including changes in subjective age and possible selves.

KEY TERMS

self-concept
self-recognition
categorical self
possible selves

ideal self
real self
reminiscence
life review

REVIEW QUESTIONS

1. What is self-concept?
2. How do infants understand themselves?
3. Give examples of how self-concept develops during childhood.
4. Compare adolescents and adults' self-concept. Give examples.

11.2 Analyze patterns of change and correlates of self-esteem over the lifespan.

SUMMARY

Young children's self-evaluations are very positive. They often overestimate their abilities and underestimate the difficulty of tasks. School-age children's sense of self-esteem is influenced by social comparison and becomes more realistic, connected to their abilities, and more comprehensive. Adolescents evaluate themselves with respect to multiple dimensions and relationships. They develop a positive sense of self-esteem when they evaluate themselves favorably in the areas that they view as important. Overall, global self-esteem tends to decline in early adolescence and then rise during adolescence, young adulthood, and middle adulthood, peaking in the mid-60s and then declining in late adulthood. In adulthood, self-esteem is influenced by cognitive affective complexity, and changes in possible selves as well as roles.

KEY TERMS

self-esteem
social comparison
global self-esteem

biculturalism
familism

REVIEW QUESTIONS

1. How does self-esteem change from early childhood into adolescence?
2. What factors are associated with high self-esteem in childhood and adolescence?
3. How does self-esteem shift over adulthood?

11.3 Discuss influences and outcomes associated with identity development, including ethnic identity.

SUMMARY

Developing an identity entails integrating self-conceptions and self-evaluations to construct a self that is coherent and consistent over time. Identity achievement represents the successful resolution of this process, the culmination of a successful psychosocial moratorium. Researchers classify individuals' progress in identity development into four categories known as identity status. A lack of exploration and commitment, identity diffusion, is the least mature status. Having not engaged in any exploration, individuals who are in the identity foreclosed status have prematurely chosen an identity. An active exploration of ideas and a sense of openness to possibilities, coupled with some uncertainty, characterizes the moratorium status. The identity achieved status requires that individuals construct a sense of self through exploring and committing to a particular set of ideas, values, and beliefs. Although the task of forming an identity is first encountered during adolescence, adults often move in and out of identity statuses. Ethnic identity involves exploring one's ethnicity and internalizing values from one's ethnic group. Ethnic identity develops and changes over time as individuals explore, gain experience, and make choices in various contexts. A strong sense of ethnic identity helps young people to reject negative views of their culture that are based on stereotypes. Ethnic identity continues to develop during adulthood, representing a continuation of the processes that were salient during adolescence.

KEY TERMS

identity
identity achievement
psychosocial moratorium
identity status

identity diffusion
identity foreclosed
ethnic identity
emerging adulthood

REVIEW QUESTIONS

1. What is identity and what are Marcia's four identity statuses?

2. What outcomes are associated with identity status?

3. What is ethnic identity and what are some of the effects of a positive sense of ethnic identity?

11.4 Compare and contrast the trait and stage approaches to personality.

SUMMARY

From the trait perspective, the many characteristics on which people differ can be categorized into five clusters of personality traits, collectively known as the Big 5 personality traits. The Big 5 personal factors are thought to reflect inherited predispositions that first manifest as temperament, evolving into recognizable personality traits by early childhood that persist throughout life and predict career, family, and personal choices in adulthood. People show unique patterns of traits and patterns and individual differences in personality traits are highly stable with continuity in personality traits increasing from early adulthood, peaking in the late 30s into middle adulthood, with some decline in late adulthood. There are also reliable age shifts in traits.

Young adults, as a group, tend to experience increases in emotional stability, conscientiousness, and agreeableness, a pattern referred to as the maturity principle of personality development. Additional subtle changes occur in traits during adulthood, suggesting that adults mellow with age. The stage approach to personality, such as Erikson's theory, proposes that people progress through a series of qualitative stages that shape who they become. At each stage individuals face specific developmental tasks and questions. According to Levinson, adults progress through a common set of phases that he called seasons of life in which the life structure is created, tested, and modified.

KEY TERMS

life structure
midlife crisis

Big 5 personality traits

REVIEW QUESTIONS

1. What are the Big 5 personality traits?

2. How do personality traits change over time?

3. Compare two stage theories of personality. How does each theory explain personality change over the lifespan?

Test your understanding of the content.
Review the flashcards and quizzes at
edge.sagepub.com/kuthertopical

PRACTICE AND APPLY WHAT YOU'VE LEARNED

▶ **edge.sagepub.com/kuthertopical**

HEAD TO THE STUDY SITE WHERE YOU'LL FIND

- **eFlashcards to strengthen your understanding of key terms**

- **Practice quizzes to test your comprehension of key concepts**

- **Videos and multimedia content to enhance your exploration of key topics**

Moral Development

Learning Objectives

12.1 Discuss the development of moral reasoning from childhood through adulthood.

12.2 Describe the progression of prosocial behavior, including biological and contextual influences.

12.3 Explain how children learn to engage in acceptable behavior.

12.4 Identify normative patterns of aggressive behavior and influences on atypical aggression during childhood and adolescence.

12.5 Describe the typical progression of religiosity or spirituality over the lifespan.

Digital Resources

▶ Moral Development During Adolescence

▶ Can Babies Tell Right from Wrong?

▶ The Marshmallow Test

📄 Physical Discipline and Adjustment

🔊 Social Bullying

📄 Conduct Disorder

▶ Religion in Adulthood

📄 Religion and Health

$SAGE edge™

Master these learning objectives with multimedia resources available at **edge.sagepub.com/kuthertopical** and *Lives in Context* video cases available in the interactive eBook.

"Just do the right thing," Vidal advised his son. "But how do I know what's right?" asked Romeo. "You'll know. Think about other people—try to take their point of view. Think about what's fair to everyone." "But, Pop, sometimes that's not so easy," Romeo replied. "I never said it would be," said Vidal. The exchange between Vidal and Romeo calls attention to the role of morality in development. How do children come to understand "right" and "wrong?" In this chapter, we examine how people reason about fairness and learn to engage in moral behavior, including helping others and controlling aggression.

MORAL REASONING

LO 12.1 Discuss the development of moral reasoning from childhood through adulthood.

We encounter the need to make moral decisions every day. Is it ever acceptable to cut the line at the grocery store? Park in a fire lane? Tell a white lie? Our capacity to think about everyday moral dilemmas, and issues of rights and justice, emerges early in life (Skitka, Bauman, & Mullen, 2016). Specifically, young children's moral reasoning—how they view and make judgments in their social world—develops and grows rapidly according to their cognitive capacities and skills in theory of mind. Two-year-old children classify behavior as good or bad. They respond with distress

Piaget began studying morality by asking children about their understanding of the rules of marbles. Fewer children play marbles today. If you were to study children's understanding of rules today, what game would you choose?

when viewing or experiencing aggressive or potentially harmful actions (Kochanska, Casey, & Fukumoto, 1995). By age 3, children judge a child who knocks another child off a swing intentionally as worse than one who does so accidentally (Yuill & Perner, 1988). Four-year-old children can understand the difference between truth and lies (Bussey, 1992). By age 5, children are aware of many moral rules, such as those regarding lying and stealing. They also demonstrate conceptions of justice or fairness (e.g., "It's my turn," "Hers is bigger," "It's not fair!"). How do these capacities develop?

CHILDREN'S UNDERSTANDING OF RULES: PIAGET'S PERSPECTIVE

Cognitive-developmental theorist Jean Piaget (1932) studied children's moral development—specifically, how children understand rules—by applying the methods he used to study cognitive development: observation and the Piagetian clinical interview. Piaget observed children playing marbles, a common game played in every schoolyard during Piaget's time, and asked them questions about the rules. What are the rules to the game? Where do the rules come from? Have they always been the same? Can they be changed? Piaget found that preschool-age children's play was not guided by rules. The young children engaged in solitary play without regard for rules, tossing the marbles about in random ways. Piaget posited that moral thinking develops in stages similar to those in his theory of cognition.

By 6 years of age, children enter the first stage of Piaget's theory of morality, **heteronomous morality** (also known as the *morality of constraint*). In this stage, as children first become aware of rules, they view them as sacred and unalterable. For example, the children interviewed by Piaget believed that people have always played marbles in the same way and that the rules cannot be changed. At this stage, moral behavior is behavior that is consistent with the rules set by authority figures. Young children see rules, even those created in play, as sacred, absolute, and unchangeable; they see behavior as either right or wrong; and they view the violation of rules as meriting punishment regardless of intent (DeVries & Zan, 2003; Nobes & Pawson, 2003). Young children may proclaim, without question, that there is only one way to play softball: As their coach advocates, the youngest children must be first to bat. Preschoolers will hold to this rule, explaining that it is simply the "right way" to play.

In middle childhood, at about age 7, children enter the second stage of Piaget's scheme, **autonomous morality** (also known as the *morality of cooperation*). This stage corresponds to the advancement to the Piagetian cognitive stage of concrete operational reasoning; it refers to a more flexible view of rules as self-chosen rather than simply imposed on children. As children spend more time with peers and become better at taking their friends' perspectives, their understanding of rules becomes more flexible. They begin to value fairness and equality and see rules as products of group agreement and instruments of cooperative purposes. For example, older children are likely to recognize their coach's rule of softball batting order as a way to help the youngest children. Some children might agree that the rule promotes fairness, while others might argue to abandon the rule as it gives younger children an unfair advantage. At this stage children see a need for agreement on rules and consequences for violations, Piaget's theory of moral reasoning inspired Lawrence Kohlberg, who created perhaps the most well-known theory of moral reasoning.

heteronomous morality Piaget's first stage of morality when children become aware of rules and view them as sacred and unalterable.

autonomous morality Piaget's second stage of morality in which children have a more flexible view of rules, believing that rules are self-chosen rather than simply imposed upon them.

CHILDREN'S CONCEPTIONS OF JUSTICE: KOHLBERG'S COGNITIVE DEVELOPMENTAL PERSPECTIVE

Is stealing ever acceptable? Would stealing be justified if it helped another person? Lawrence Kohlberg (1969, 1976) studied how people think about moral issues involving justice, fairness, and rights. Much of Kohlberg's theory was based on longitudinal research with a group of boys, beginning at ages 10, 13, and 16 (Kohlberg, 1969). Over the next three decades, Kohlberg periodically interviewed these participants and discovered that their reasoning progressed through sequential stages and in a predictable order (Colby, Kohlberg, Gibbs, & Lieberman, 1983; Kohlberg, 1981). Kohlberg measured moral reasoning by presenting individuals with hypothetical dilemmas such as the following, known as the Heinz dilemma:

> Near death, a woman with cancer learns of a drug that may save her. The woman's husband, Heinz, approaches the druggist who created the drug, but the druggist refuses to sell the drug for anything less than $2,000. After borrowing from everyone he knows, Heinz has only scraped together $1,000. Heinz asks the druggist to let him have the drug for $1,000 and he will pay him the rest later. The druggist says that it is his right to make money from the drug he developed and refuses to sell it to Heinz. Desperate for the drug, Heinz breaks into the druggist's store and steals the drug. Should Heinz have done that? Why or why not? (Kohlberg, 1969)

The Heinz dilemma is the most popular example of the hypothetical conflicts that Kohlberg used to study moral development. These problems examine how people make decisions when fairness and people's rights are pitted against obedience to authority and law. Participants' explanations of how they arrived at their decisions undergo predictable changes that correspond to developments in cognition and perspective taking. Reasoning progresses through six universal stages that are organized into three broad levels that represent qualitative changes in conceptions of justice (Kohlberg, 1969, 1981).

Beginning in early childhood and persisting until about age 9, children demonstrate what Kohlberg called **preconventional reasoning**. Similar to Piaget, Kohlberg argued that young children's behavior is governed by *self-interest*, the desire to gain rewards and avoid punishments ("Don't steal because you don't want to go to jail"). Moral behavior is a response to external pressure. Young children have not yet internalized societal norms and their behavior is motivated by desires rather than internalized principles. The preconventional level comprises two stages, in which children move from concern with punishment as a motivator of moral judgments (Stage 1) to self-interest and concern about what others can do for them (Stage 2). Responses to the Heinz dilemma tend to emphasize self-interest. For example, "Heinz should not steal the drug because he'll be punished and go to jail" (Stage 1) or "Heinz should steal the drug because his wife will be happy and be very good to him" (Stage 2). Note that a person's level of moral reasoning is indicated by the *reasoning* behind the decision, not the decision itself (i.e., whether Heinz should steal the drug or not).

At about age 9 or 10, children's advances in cognitive development and perspective-taking ability enable them to demonstrate reasoning at the second level of Kohlberg's scheme, **conventional moral reasoning**. At this stage, children's moral decisions tend to be socially driven. Conventional moral reasoning entails internalizing the norms and standards of authority figures, seeking to be accepted and avoid disapproval. Like the preconventional level, the conventional level comprises two stages. At Stage 3, children uphold rules in order to please others and gain affection and sympathy: "Heinz should steal the drug because people will think he's an awful husband if he doesn't." At Stage 4, individuals buy into the rules and standards because they are concerned with maintaining

preconventional reasoning
Kohlberg's first level of reasoning in which young children's behavior is governed by punishment and gaining rewards.

conventional moral reasoning
The second level of Kohlberg's theory in which moral decisions are based on conforming to social rules.

social order. Rules are seen as reflecting rights and duties assigned by authorities for the good of everyone. People who reason at Stage 4 seek approval and are bothered only by disapproval if it is expressed by legitimate authorities: "Heinz should not steal the drug because stealing is against the law. It's his duty to obey the law. What would happen if everyone disobeyed?"

It is not until adolescence, according to Kohlberg, that people become capable of demonstrating the most advanced moral thinking, **post-conventional moral reasoning**, which entails autonomous decision making based on moral principles that value respect for individual rights above all else. Although post-conventional reasoning becomes possible in adolescence, many people do not attain this level of reasoning until later in life, if at all. Post-conventional moral thinkers recognize that their self-chosen principles of fairness and justice may sometimes conflict with the law, such that when laws are unjust, they may be broken.

The first of the two stages of post-conventional moral reasoning is Stage 5, in which individuals view laws and rules as flexible and part of the social contract or agreement meant to further human interests. Laws and rules are to be followed as they bring good to people, but can be changed if they are inconsistent with the needs and rights of the majority. Sometimes, if laws are unjust—if they harm more people than they protect—they can be broken. At Stage 5, individuals uphold individual rights over the law: "Sure it's against the law, but the law wasn't intended for situations like this. Heinz should steal the drug."

Kohlberg's ultimate stage, Stage 6, is defined by abstract ethical principles that are universal and valid for all people regardless of law, such as equality and respect for human dignity. In this stage, concerns about human rights take precedence over laws and social rules, so Heinz must steal the drug because his wife's right to life trumps the druggists' rights for profit as well as laws against stealing: "Life is more important than laws. Heinz should steal the drug to save his wife's life."

A great deal of research has confirmed that individuals proceed through the first four stages of moral reasoning (i.e., Kohlberg's first two levels) in a slow, gradual, and predictable fashion (Colby et al., 1983; Dawson, 2002; Walker, 1989). Specifically, reasoning at the preconventional level (Stages 1 and 2) decreases by early adolescence; Stage 3 conventional reasoning increases through middle adolescence; and Stage 4 reasoning increases in middle to late adolescence and becomes typical of most individuals by early adulthood. Few people, however, advance beyond Stage 4 moral reasoning. Post-conventional reasoning is rare and, when it occurs, appears as Stage 5 reasoning (Kohlberg, 1981; Kohlberg, Levine, & Hewer, 1983). The existence of Stage 6, the hypothesized most advanced type of moral reasoning, is supported only by case-based anecdotal evidence. Kohlberg himself questioned the validity of Stage 6 and dropped it from the stage scheme, but later added it again because it represented an end goal state to which human development strives (Kohlberg & Ryncarz, 1990).

CONTEXTUAL INFLUENCES ON MORAL REASONING

Moral reasoning is influenced by cognitive and social development, and especially, social interaction. Contextual factors—such as family and peers, gender, and culture—are particularly important influences on moral development. Let's explore these.

Family and Peer Contexts and Moral Reasoning

Children develop and hone their understanding of morality through social interactions within the home. Disputes with siblings over toys, for example, help young children develop conceptions about justice and fairness (Killen & Nucci, 1995). How parents and caregivers discuss moral issues, such as truth-telling, harm, and property rights, influences how children come to understand these issues. When adults discuss moral issues in ways that are sensitive to children's developmental needs, children develop more sophisticated conceptions of morality (Janssens & Dekovic, 1997; Walker & Taylor, 1991).

post-conventional moral reasoning Kohlberg's third level of moral reasoning emphasizing autonomous decision-making based on principles such as valuing human dignity.

Children's reasoning advances when parents engage their children in discussion about personal, local, and media events and encourage their children to take different points of view. Presenting alternative points of view and asking questions to help adolescents take multiple perspectives advances reasoning. For example, "Why do you think he did that? Was there something else he could have done? How do you think other people might interpret his actions?" Reasoning advances when children have opportunities to engage in discussions that are characterized by mutual perspective taking and opportunities to discuss different points of view. When children engage in issue-focused discussions involving reasoning that is slightly more advanced than their own, it may prompt them to reconsider their own thinking. As a result, they often internalize the new reasoning, advancing their moral thinking to a new level.

High quality parent–child relationships predict advanced moral reasoning (Malti & Latzko, 2010). Parents who engage their children in discussion, listen with sensitivity, ask for children's input, praise them, engage them with questioning, and use humor promote the development of moral reasoning (Carlo, Mestre, Samper, Tur, & Armenta, 2011; Walker & Taylor, 1991; Wyatt & Carlo, 2002). Likewise, interactions in which peers offer one another differing perspectives and engage each other with in-depth discussions promote the development of moral reasoning (Power, Higgins, & Kohlberg, 1989). Adolescents who report having more close friendships in which they engage in deep conversations tend to show more advanced moral reasoning than do teens who have little social contact (Schonert-Reichl, 1999). They also report feeling positive emotions when they make unselfish moral decisions (Malti, Keller, & Buchmann, 2013).

Gender Differences in Moral Reasoning

Some have argued that the social basis of morality means that men and women should reason in very different ways. A popular criticism of Kohlberg's theory of moral reasoning arises because his initial research was conducted with all-male samples. Early research that studied both males and females suggested gender differences in moral reasoning, with males typically showing Stage 4 reasoning, characterized by concerns about law and order, and females showing Stage 3 reasoning, characterized by concerns about maintaining relationships (Fishkin, Keniston, & McKinnon, 1973; Kohlberg & Kramer, 1969; Poppen, 1974).

Carol Gilligan (1982) argued that Kohlberg's theory neglected a distinctively female mode of moral reasoning, a **care orientation**, which is characterized by a desire to maintain relationships and a responsibility not to cause hurt. As Gilligan explains, the care orientation contrasts with the distinctively male mode of moral reasoning, a **justice orientation**, which is based on the abstract principles of fairness and individualism captured by Kohlberg. Care and justice represent frameworks modified by experience that influence how people interpret and resolve moral problems.

Although most people are capable of raising both justice and care concerns in describing moral dilemmas, Gilligan argued that they tend to predominantly focus on one or the other. Males and females could use either a justice or a care perspective, but care reasoning was thought to be used predominantly by females and justice reasoning by males (Gilligan, 1982; Gilligan & Attanucci, 1988). In agreement with Gilligan, most researchers acknowledge that more than one mode of moral reasoning exists (Kohlberg et al., 1983), but there is considerable controversy as to whether those moral orientations are linked with gender. Early research suggested that males and females differ in moral orientation (Gilligan & Attanucci, 1988), but other studies have shown no gender differences in moral orientation (Knox, Fagley, & Miller, 2004). Male and female adolescents and adults display similar reasoning that combines concerns of justice (e.g., being fair) with those of care (e.g., being supportive and helpful), and when there are sex differences, they are very small (Jaffee & Hyde, 2000; Wark & Krebs, 1996; Weisz & Black, 2002). The most mature forms of moral reasoning incorporate both justice and care concerns.

care orientation Gilligan's feminine mode of moral reasoning, characterized by a desire to maintain relationships and a responsibility to avoid hurting others.

justice orientation A male mode of moral reasoning proposed by Gilligan that emphasizes the abstract principles of fairness and individualism.

Children in collectivisit cultures, such these Japanese children, learn to define moral dilemmas from the perspective of the community rather than the individual.

Culture and Moral Reasoning

A cornerstone of Kohlberg's theory is that children are active in constructing their own moral understanding through social experiences with adults and peers (Smetana, 1995; Smetana & Braeges, 1990). Kohlberg viewed the process of moral development as universal, occurring in all cultures around the world. Cross-cultural studies of Kohlberg's theory show that the sequence appears in all cultures, but that people in non-Western cultures rarely score above Stage 3 (Gibbs, Basinger, Grime, & Snarey, 2007; Nisan & Kohlberg, 1982; Snarey, 1985). Similar to our discussion of cross-cultural differences in cognitive development (Chapter 6), morality and appropriate responses to ethical dilemmas are defined by each society and its cultural perspectives. Whereas Western cultures tend to emphasize the rights of the individual (justice-based reasoning), non-Western cultures tend to value collectivism, focusing on human interdependence (care-based reasoning; Miller, 1997). For example, observations of 4-year-old Chinese children and their mothers showed that the mothers consistently drew children's attention to transgressions and emphasized the consequences for others. The children learned quickly and were able to spontaneously discuss their mothers' examples and strategies and reenact them in their own interactions. Moreover, the children's explanations reflected their understanding of rules and expectations in their own terms, rather than reflecting simple memorization (Wang et al., 2008). In this way, individuals in collectivist cultures learn to define moral dilemmas in terms of the responsibility to the entire community rather than simply to the individual (Miller & Bersoff, 1995). Such emphasis on the needs of others is characteristic of Stage 3 in Kohlberg's scheme, which emphasizes the cultural value of individualism. However, in collectivist cultures, interdependence and relationships are highly valued; therefore, reasoning characterized as Stage 3 in Kohlberg's scheme represents advanced reasoning within collectivist cultures.

Despite these cross-cultural differences, individuals in many cultures show similarities in reasoning. For example, one study examined Chinese and Canadian 12- to 19-year-old adolescents' views of the fairness of various forms of democratic and nondemocratic government (Helwig, Arnold, Tan, & Boyd, 2007). Adolescents from both China and Canada preferred democratic forms of government and appealed to fundamental democratic justice principles such as representation, voice, and majority rule to support their judgments, suggesting that adolescents in collectivist cultures are able to reason with justice principles in particular contexts. In addition, similar age-related patterns in judgments and reasoning were found across cultures and across diverse regions within China. It appears that the development of moral reasoning progresses in a similar pattern across cultures. People of different cultures are able to reason using both care and justice orientations even though cultures tend to vary in the weight they assign each moral orientation.

Intuition and Moral Reasoning

According to Jonathan Haidt (2008, 2013) cross-cultural similarities in moral development have little to do with reasoning. Although Kohlberg's perspective emphasizes the role of cognition in moral reasoning, individuals often make decisions off the cuff rather than through careful contemplation. Moral issues tend to evoke intuitive reactions, and individuals report implicit knowledge—they simply *know* how to respond. Individuals' gut reactions to moral issues determines their responses. Haidt explains that the cognitive component, moral reasoning, occurs after the fact, to justify the decision. Therefore, moral behavior is the result of intuitive gut reactions rather than reasoning.

LIFESPAN BRAIN DEVELOPMENT

• • Moral Brain

RGR Collection / Alamy Stock Photo

Viewers of the television show *Dexter* tend to offer complex opinions about the lead character, Dexter Morgan, who is a respected forensic expert but also a serial killer who assassinates murderers. How does the brain represent moral dilemmas, such as Dexter's behavior?

In the popular television series *Dexter,* the main character, Dexter Morgan, was a family man and respected forensic expert employed by a police department. However, in his free time Dexter was a serial killer who applied his own moral code to assassinate murderers who had fallen through the cracks in the legal system. Dexter's behavior was immoral, yet he acted in the pursuit of justice. Many viewers judged Dexter's behavior to be wrong, yet they felt a sense of emotional satisfaction that his prey "got what they deserved." Morality is multidimensional, consisting of cognitive and emotional processes that include deliberate reasoning and quick, intuitive emotional responses (De Neys & Glumicic, 2008; Greene et al., 2002; Haidt, 2008). How is morality represented in the brain?

Several regions of the brain are implicated in morality, most notably the frontal cortex, responsible for reasoning and executive function. The ventromedial prefrontal cortex plays a role in planning, responding to decision uncertainty, and response inhibition, mediating the emotions engaged while solving moral problems (Prehn et al., 2008; Young & Koenigs, 2008). People with lesions to this area tend to have trouble thinking about the abstract consequences of their decisions, adhering to social norms, and understanding others' intensions (Cooper, Kreps, Wiebe, Pirkl, & Knutson, 2010; Moll, Zahn, Oliveira-Souza, & Krueger, 2005).

Another part of the frontal lobe, the orbitofrontal cortex, represents and links emotion with reward in decision making and making judgments of wrongdoing (Horne et al., 2016; Shenhav & Greene, 2010). It is activated when viewing moral stimuli compared with nonmoral stimuli and processing emotionally salient statements with moral value (Harenski & Hamann, 2006).

The amygdala, a subcortical structure involved in experiencing emotions, interacts with the ventromedial and orbitofrontal cortices (Schoenbaum & Roesch, 2005). The amygdala triggers implicit and automatic moral attitudes and responses. The amygdala is responsible for drawing connections between stimuli and reinforcement and provides the ventromedial and orbitofrontal cortices with expectations about reinforcement contingencies (Everitt, Cardinal, Parkinson, & Robbins, 2003). The ventromedial prefrontal cortex then represents this information to determine the outcomes of actions (Knutson & Cooper, 2005; Schoenbaum & Roesch, 2005). Increased amygdala and ventromedial prefrontal activity is observed in response to considering more severe, relative to less severe, moral transgressions (Luo et al., 2006). Similarly, individuals who score high on moral reasoning tasks tend to show greater functional connectivity between the amygdala and ventromedial prefrontal cortex, as compared with individuals with low scores on moral reasoning tasks (Jung et al., 2016). Some researchers have suggested that it is the amygdala that enables the individual to learn, and then label, the goodness and badness of objects and actions, indicating that emotion plays a large role in morality (Blair, 2007).

In addition to the amygdala and prefrontal and orbitofrontal cortices, the complex emotional and cognitive processes that comprise morality are influenced by many other brain regions that interact. All in all, morality is supported not by a single brain circuitry or structure but by a multiplicity of circuits that overlap with other general complex processes (Decety, Michalska, & Kinzler, 2012).

What Do You Think?

1. **What might the neurological basis of morality mean for the nature–nurture question?**

2. **What role do you think context plays in moral development?**

3. **How do you reconcile findings supporting biological and contextual influences on moral development?**

UNDERSTANDING SOCIAL CONVENTIONS

Moral reasoning is inherently social. We face social dilemmas each day, and some of these dilemmas concern issues of fairness or morality. As early as 3 years of age, children can differentiate between moral imperatives, which concern people's rights and welfare, and social conventions, or social customs (Smetana & Braeges, 1990; Smetana, Jambon, & Ball, 2013). For example, they judge stealing an apple, a moral violation, more harshly than violating a social convention, such as eating with one's fingers (Nucci & Turiel, 1978; Smetana & Braeges, 1990; Smetana, 1995; Turiel, 1998). Children judge conventional rules created by adults as more legitimate than those created by children and they view transgressions and alterations of rules by adults as more acceptable than those by children (Nobes & Pawson, 2003). Recent research suggests that even young children can consider intention in judging violations of conventional or moral rules. Three-year-old children watched a puppet announce that it would either take part in or opt out of an activity, then the puppet acted in accordance with or against a conventional or moral rule. The children judged moral rule violations as wrong regardless of the puppet's announcement, but violations of conventions were judged less wrong when the puppet announced intentions to opt out (Josephs & Rakoczy, 2016).

Like younger children, school-age children distinguish between moral and conventional rules, judging moral rules as more absolute than conventional rules (Turiel, 2008). Moral rules are seen as less violable, contingent on authority or rules, or alterable than social conventions (Smetana et al., 2013). They anticipate feeling positive emotions after following moral rules and are likely to label violations of moral rules as disgusting (Danovitch & Bloom, 2009). With advances in cognitive development, children can consider multiple perspectives and become better able to consider the situation and weigh a variety of variables in making decisions. They discriminate social conventions that have a purpose from those with no obvious purpose. Social conventions that serve a purpose, such as preventing injuries (not running indoors), are evaluated as more important and more similar to moral issues than social conventions with no obvious purpose (avoiding a section of the school-yard despite no apparent danger; Buchanan-Barrow & Barrett, 1998). School-age children also consider intent and the context. For example, Canadian 8- to 10-year-old children understood that a flag serves as a powerful symbol of a country and its values—and that burning it purposefully is worse than accidentally burning it. The 10-year-old children also understood that flag burning is an example of freedom of expression and can be used to express disapproval of a country or its activities. They agreed that if one were in a country that is unjust, burning its flag would be acceptable (Helwig & Prencipe, 1999).

School-age children also distinguish among moral issues. For example, although 4th- and 5th-grade students tended to adopt a moral orientation about both physical and relational aggression, they saw physical aggression as more wrong and harmful than relational aggression (Murray-Close, Crick, & Galotti, 2006). Girls, however, rated both types of aggression as more wrong, and relational aggression (which they are more likely to experience) as more harmful, than did boys. As children grow older, they become better able to consider complex moral dilemmas and demonstrate more nuanced judgments. For example, 5- to 11-year-old children become increasingly tolerant of necessary harm; that is, violating moral rules in order to prevent injury to others (Jambon & Smetana, 2014).

In addition to moral and conventional issues, between ages 3 and 5 children come to differentiate *personal issues*—matters of personal choice that do not violate rights—across home and school settings (Killen & Smetana, 2015; Nucci, 1996; Yau & Smetana, 2003). Like older children, adolescents, and adults, preschoolers believe they have control over matters of personal choice. In early childhood personal issues might include favorite playmates, play-styles, and neatness. In late childhood through adolescence the contents of a diary, media preferences, hairstyles and fashion, and friendships fall under the realm of personal issues.

Cross-cultural research suggests that children in diverse cultures in Europe, Africa, Asia, Southeast Asia, and North and South America differentiate moral, social-conventional, and personal issues (Killen, McGlothlin, & Lee-Kim, 2002; Nucci, 2001; Smetana, 1995; Turiel, 1998; Yau & Smetana, 2003). However, cultural differences in socialization contribute to children's conceptions. For example, a study of Chinese children ages 3 to 4 and 5 to 6 showed that, similar to Western samples, the children overwhelmingly considered personal issues as permissible and up to the child, rather than the adults. However, the Chinese children's justifications for moral transgressions focused overwhelmingly on the intrinsic consequences of the acts in terms of fairness and effects on the welfare of others, as compared with the emphasis on avoiding punishment common in Western samples of preschoolers (Yau & Smetana, 2003). These differences are consistent with cultural preferences for collectivism and individualism.

People's reasoning about moral issues undergoes systematic change with development. With advances in moral reasoning, people often begin to behave in ways that are in line with their beliefs (Brugman, 2010; Gibbs, 2003). For example, adolescents who demonstrate higher levels of moral reasoning are more likely to share with and help others (Carlo & Eisenberg, 1996; Comunian & Gielen, 2000) and are less likely to engage in antisocial behaviors such as cheating, aggression, or delinquency (Gregg, Gibbs, & Basinger, 1994; Taylor & Walker, 1997). Yet, generally speaking, moral reasoning is only moderately correlated with behavior (Colby & Damon, 1992; Kupfersmid & Wonderly, 1980). People often behave in ways that they know they should not. For example, an adolescent who explains that stealing and cheating are wrong may slip a pack of gum into her pocket and leave a store without paying or may peek at a classmate's paper during an exam. Like other situations that require decisions, ethical conflicts experienced in real life are complex, and are accompanied by intense emotions, social obligations, and practical considerations which lead people to act in ways that contradict their judgments (Walker, 2004). Another perspective on moral development focuses on the drive to help others and engage in prosocial behavior, which we discuss next.

Lives in Context Video 12.1
Moral Development During Adolescence

⚙ Thinking in Context 12.1

1. In what ways do people's decisions about right and wrong reflect maturation, cognitive change, and contextual influences such as interactions with family, friends, school, and neighborhood factors?

2. To what extent are distinctions among moral, conventional, and personal issues universal? Do all people progress through the same developmental processes in thinking about these issues? Why or why not?

3. Do you think morality can be taught? If so, how? If not, why not?

PROSOCIAL BEHAVIOR

LO 12.2 Describe the progression of prosocial behavior, including biological and contextual influences.

Eighteen-month-old Lionel placed the block in the lap of his baby brother, who was seated in an infant chair, and exclaimed, "Dat!" "You want your brother to have the block, Lionel? Good job sharing your block, Lionel!" said his babysitter. Like Lionel, infants and toddlers have been shown to behave prosocially toward others, including sharing resources (Paulus, 2014; Svetlova, Nichols, & Brownell, 2010). **Prosocial behavior** is voluntary behavior intended to benefit another (Eisenberg, Spinrad, & Knafo-Noam, 2015). Prosocial behavior usually is motivated by **empathy**, the capacity to understand someone's feelings (Taylor, Eisenberg, Spinrad, Eggum, & Sulik, 2013).

prosocial behavior Actions that are oriented toward others for the pure sake of helping, without a reward.

empathy The capacity to understand another person's emotions and concerns.

DEVELOPMENT OF EMPATHY AND PROSOCIAL BEHAVIOR

When does prosocial behavior emerge? For toddlers as young as 18 months, prosocial behavior includes the ability to help adults, even unfamiliar experimenters, instrumentally. For example, the toddler will aid in achieving a simple action-based goal such as picking up markers that have fallen or getting something that is out of reach (Thompson & Newton, 2013; Warneken & Tomasello, 2006). Demonstrating instrumental prosocial

Young children show prosocial behaviors, such as sharing.

Darren Baker/Shutterstock.com

behavior in such a situation relies on motor development. Recall from Chapter 6 that infants' understanding of a concept (e.g., object permanence) often precedes their ability to demonstrate that understanding with their motor skills (e.g., to uncover a hidden object). Do infants have a prosocial drive before they can demonstrate it? When do young infants feel the urge to help others?

A series of research studies using the violation-of-expectation method (recall from Chapter 6) have shown that infants change their pattern of looking and demonstrate preferences that suggest that they possess simple conceptions of prosocial behavior; a moral intuition (van de Vondervoort & Hamlin, 2016). In one scenario, a character is shown pushing a ball up a hill. A second character either helps push the ball or hinders the first character's effort by pushing the ball back down the hill. Four- to six-month-old babies prefer the helper over the hinderer, and prefer viewing helpers get rewarded and hinderers punished (Hamlin, 2013; Hamlin, 2014), suggesting a sensitivity to intent (van de Vondervoort & Hamlin, 2016). Infants may have a basic sense of empathy, the capacity to understand another person's emotions, well before they have the capacity to demonstrate it.

Between 18 and 24 months of age, toddlers show increasingly prosocial responses to others' emotional and physical distress, respond with expressions of concern and comfort, and even show nervous system activation suggesting that they themselves have become distressed (Hepach, Vaish, & Tomasello, 2012; Hoffman, 2007). Toddlers' prosocial behavior is limited to their own perspective; they tend to offer the aid that they themselves would prefer, such as bringing their own mother to help a distressed peer (Hoffman, 2000). Although toddlers show increases in prosocial behavior, it should be noted that spontaneous prosocial behavior toward distressed others is rare in toddlerhood (Eisenberg et al., 2015). Other behaviors, such as sharing, are more common, although sharing behaviors change over time in predictable ways.

Between 3 and 5 years of age, young children show selectivity in sharing. They share more with children and adults who show prosocial behaviors such as sharing and helping others (Kuhlmeier, Dunfield, & O'Neill, 2014). Children also progress from self-serving reasons for sharing, expressed in early childhood (e.g., "I get more candy because I want it" or "I share candy so that Mikey will play with me") to more sophisticated and mature conceptions of fairness as they approach middle childhood (Damon, 1977, 1988). Using nonverbal measures, researchers have shown that 3-year-old children identify and react negatively to unfair distributions of stickers, especially if they receive fewer than another child (LoBue, Nishida, Chiong, DeLoache, & Haidt, 2011). Yet after working together actively to obtain rewards in a collaboration task, most 3-year-old children share equally with a peer, even if they could easily monopolize those rewards (Warneken, Lohse, Melis, & Tomasello, 2011). Four- and five-year-olds believe in an obligation to share, but they often allocate rewards based on observable characteristics, such as age, size, or other obvious physical characteristics (e.g., "The oldest should get more candy"). Often these decisions are based on personal desires and characteristics that adults would deem irrelevant, such as proclaiming, "Girls should get more because they're girls!" Many 5- and 6-year-old children conceptualize fair sharing as strict equality—for example, that each child should get the same amount of candy, no matter what (Damon, 1977; Enright et al., 1984). Yet, when told that they must make an unequal distribution, 5-year-olds tend to share more with others whom they expect will reciprocate and more with friends than with peers they dislike (Paulus & Moore, 2014).

At about 7 years of age, children begin taking merit into account, believing that extra candy should be shared with a child who has excelled or worked especially hard. By around 8 years of age children's sharing is influenced by empathy, as they can act on the basis of benevolence, believing that others who are at a disadvantage should get special consideration. For example, they think extra candy should go to the child who does not get chosen to play on a sports team or a child who is excluded from an activity. Children are also sensitive to social disadvantage. For example, 5- and 8-year-old children are more likely to give stickers to needy children than are 3- and 4-year-olds (Ongley, Nola, & Malti, 2014; Paulus, 2014).

Helping, sharing, and other prosocial behaviors increase from school age into adolescence (Eisenberg & Fabes, 1998; Knafo, Zahn-Waxler, Van Hulle, Robinson, & Rhee, 2008). By the preadolescent and early adolescent years, young people try to coordinate claims of merit, need, and equality; they often give sophisticated explanations that cannot be expressed in a single sentence (Damon, 1980). Yet, in early to mid-adolescence (about ages 13 to 15), empathy and prosocial behavior often plateau or even decline (Luengo Kanacri, Pastorelli, Eisenberg, Zuffianò, & Caprara, 2013; Nantel-Vivier et al., 2009). As we saw in the discussion of personality (see Chapter 11), the biological, social, and psychological transitions from childhood to adolescence appear to be accompanied by temporary dips in psychosocial maturity (Soto, John, Gosling, & Potter, 2011). With advances in perspective taking, emotional control, and cognitive capacities, prosocial behavior rebounds in late adolescence and increases into early adulthood (Eisenberg, Cumberland, Guthrie, Murphy, & Shepard, 2005; Luengo Kanacri et al., 2013; Nantel-Vivier et al., 2009).

In childhood and adolescence, prosocial behavior is associated with social competence, positive social interactions with peers, and having friends, as well as low levels of aggressive behavior and externalizing problem behaviors (Carlo, 2013; Carlo et al., 2014). Prosocial children tend to be successful in school, likely because they are cooperative, socially competent, and show appropriate school behavior. Prosocial children tend to score high on measures of vocabulary, reading, and language—perhaps because prosocial children are friendly and engage in interaction with teacher and peers (Eisenberg et al., 2015).

Prosocial behavior, such as volunteering, continues through adulthood (Dulin, 2015). We know less about empathy development in adulthood as compared with childhood and adolescence. Emotion regulation tends to improve with age (see Chapter 10), and empathetic understanding should also increase during the adult years (Birditt & Fingerman, 2005; Carstensen, Pasupathi, Mayr, & Nesselroade, 2000). However, cross-sectional studies tend to indicate either no age differences or negative age trends in empathy (Diehl, Coyle, & Labouvie-Vief, 1996; O'Brien, Konrath, Grühn, & Hagen, 2013; Phillips, MacLean, & Allen, 2002). As noted in discussions of other topics (e.g., intelligence), cross-sectional and longitudinal studies sometimes yield conflicting conclusions. This may be true for empathy as well. For example, Grühn and colleagues examined 400 people, aged 10 to 87, at four different times over a 12-year period and analyzed the results according to both cross-sectional and longitudinal criteria (Grühn, Rebucal, Diehl, Lumley, & Labouvie-Vief, 2008). The cross-sectional age comparisons indicated a negative trend such that older adults were less empathetic than younger adults, yet the longitudinal analyses suggested stability within individuals.

INFLUENCES ON PROSOCIAL BEHAVIOR

Prosocial behavior, of course, does not develop in a vacuum. Instead, it is promoted or inhibited by a wide variety of factors, including biology and genes, family contexts, the larger social context, and the development of reasoning skills. Let's explore these influences.

Biological Influences

Like other kinds of behavior, prosocial behavior reflects interactions between biology and context. Genetic factors are thought to contribute to individual differences in prosocial behavior (Waldman et al., 2011) Twin studies, for example, have revealed that adult identical twins show more similar reports of prosocial behavior than do their fraternal twin peers (Gregory, Light-Häusermann, Rijsdijk, & Eley, 2009; Knafo-Noam, Uzefovsky, Israel, Davidov, & Zahn-Waxler, 2015). Several genes have been

• • Volunteer Work and Social Responsibility

For many adolescents prosocial behavior takes the form of a sense of social responsibility, a personal commitment to contribute to the community and society.

Prosocial behavior takes many forms and changes with development from sharing a toy or a cookie to working to help others, known and unknown, and near and far away. It is in adolescence that a prosocial orientation often grows to include a sense of social responsibility, a personal commitment to contribute to community and society (Wray-Lake & Syvertsen, 2011). Social responsibility values predict a variety of prosocial civic behaviors such as volunteering, voting, political activism, and environmental conservation (Caprara, Schwartz, Capanna, Vecchione, & Barbaranelli, 2006; Hart, Donnelly, Youniss, & Atkins, 2007; Pratt, Hunsberger, Pancer, & Alisat, 2003).

How does social responsibility develop? Surprisingly, prosocial behavior tends to plateau or even dip in middle adolescence (Eisenberg et al., 2005; Smetana et al., 2009). Early and middle adolescents experience many transitions, often view schools as an unfriendly place, and tend to prioritize personal issues over social and moral concerns (Wang & Dishion, 2012). A 3-year study following elementary, middle, and high school students ages 9 to 18 found that social responsibility values significantly decreased from age 9 to 16 before leveling off in later adolescence (Wray-Lake, Syvertsen, & Flanagan, 2016). Advances in social responsibility were associated with feelings of school solidarity, having trusted friendships, and a sense of compassion and democratic climate within the family. Connections to

family, peers, school, and community contribute dynamically to a sense of social responsibility. Parents often model volunteering, and their behavior influences children and adolescents. Adolescents who participate in community service tend to have parents who volunteer and talk about volunteering and giving (Ottoni-Wilhelm, Estell, & Perdue, 2014). When parents recruit their children into community service, it transmits prosocial values, including the meaning of service and its effect on others (White & Mistry, 2016). Parental encouragement and modeling of volunteer work predicts *sympathy*, feeling compassion for another person, and helping and predicts adolescents' volunteer work (McGinley, Lipperman-Kreda, Byrnes, & Carlo, 2010; van Goethem, van Hoof, van Aken, Orobio de Castro, & Raaijmakers, 2014).

Volunteerism itself predicts social responsibility. When youth volunteer and engage in service learning, they demonstrate increases in prosocial attitudes toward others, as well as social responsibility and civic values (Conway, Amel, & Gerwien, 2009; van Goethem et al., 2014). Community service offers adolescents opportunities to explore their identity as they interact with a heterogeneous group of people in their community who likely differ from them in age, ethnicity, religion, or social class (Flanagan, Kim, Collura, & Kopish, 2015; Yates & Youniss, 1996). Community service holds the potential to enhance sensitivity toward others. Compared to their nonvolunteer peers, early adolescents who do community volunteer work are more likely to see similarities between themselves and disadvantaged groups, less likely to stereotype out-groups, and more likely to believe that people are capable of change (Flanagan et al., 2015; Karafantis & Levy, 2004). In addition, volunteering during adolescence predicts voting, volunteering, and joining community organizations in adulthood (Hart, Donnelly, Youniss, & Atkins, 2007; McFarland & Thomas, 2006).

What Do You Think?

1. What are some of the potential barriers to engaging in volunteer work during adolescence? How can adolescents overcome those barriers?

2. Do you engage in volunteer work? What does it mean to you?

implicated in prosocial tendencies, including one that influences the hormone oxytocin, which is associated with attachment and other socioemotional behaviors (Carter, 2014; Striepens, Kendrick, Maier, & Hurlemann, 2011). A child's inborn temperament influences how the child regulates emotion, which is related to feelings of empathy for a distressed child or adult, and, in turn, whether empathetic feelings result in personal distress or prosocial behavior (Eisenberg et al., 2015). Empathy and prosocial responses such as sympathetic concern, helping, sharing, and comforting others are more likely in children who are sociable and successful in regulating their emotions (Eisenberg et al., 1998). Children who are unable to successfully regulate their emotions and are unable to display appropriately sympathetic and other-oriented responses tend to react to distressed others with evidence of their own physiological and emotional distress—such as frowning, lip-biting, and increases in heart rate and brain activity in regions known to process negative emotions—which suggest a feeling of being overwhelmed (Pickens, Field, & Nawrocki, 2001).

Family Influences

Children's biological tendencies play out within the sociocultural context in which they are immersed, especially through their interactions with parents. Newborns' neural and perceptual capacities predispose them to learn from physical, social, and emotional experiences (Karmiloff-Smith, 2009). Prosocial behavior is socialized continuously from birth via active social engagement in which rich interactions with parents engage the emotions, cognitions, and behaviors critical to prosocial responding, gradually giving rise to the infant's own prosocial motives and behavior (Brownell, 2016). Prosocial behavior develops progressively from immature precursor forms such as showing, giving, and taking turns during social play with caregivers. These basic forms of prosocial behavior, often initially conducted without prosocial intent, become integrated into routine interactions with caregivers, altering the infant's social environment, producing new social experiences and demands.

Parents also actively encourage prosocial behavior by including toddlers in their household and caregiving activities. In one recent study, 93% of mothers reported that they encouraged their 13- to 24-month-olds to help in household routines and praised them for their efforts (Dahl, 2015). Toddlers whose parents more often encouraged and praised helpfulness became more spontaneously helpful 6 months later. Parents' encouragement of toddlers' participation in a household cleanup routines predict children's willingness to help another adult in a new context (Hammond & Carpendale, 2015; Pettygrove, Hammond, Karahuta, Waugh, & Brownell, 2013). Children's prosocial behavior emerges out of shared prosocial activity shared with adults, and parental encouragement promotes its development (Brownell, 2016).

When parents describe feelings and model the use of language to discuss feelings, toddlers are more likely to use words to describe their thoughts and emotions and attempt to understand others' emotional states (Garner, 2003). Parents who are warm and encouraging, and who model sympathetic concern, give rise to preschoolers who are more likely to display concern in response to others' distress (Taylor et al., 2013). Parents of prosocial children draw attention to models of prosocial behavior in peers and in media, such as in storybooks, movies, and television programs. They point out characters who display sharing, empathy, and cooperation, thereby modeling and encouraging prosocial behavior in children (Singer & Singer, 1998). Some parents point out similarities among people with different backgrounds (Eisenberg et al., 2015). Other caregivers and early childhood teachers play similar roles in emotional socialization, helping children learn how to understand their own and others' emotions, express their emotions appropriately, and help others (Denham, Bassett, & Zinsser, 2012).

At the same time as parents influence children, children play a role in their own development by influencing their parents. One study that followed children from 4½ years of age through sixth grade found that although maternal sensitivity influenced children's prosocial behavior as rated by both mothers and teachers when the children were in third and fifth grade; prosocial behavior, in turn, predicted mothers' subsequent sensitivity, suggesting that mothers and children influence each other (Newton, Laible, Carlo, Steele, & McGinley, 2014). Children who are kind, compassionate, and helpful earlier in childhood may be more likely to elicit responsive and warm parenting from their mothers later in childhood.

CULTURAL INFLUENCES ON DEVELOPMENT

• • Children's Participation in Household Work

Jake Lyell/Alamy

Often assigned chores and responsibilites at an early age and expected to contribute to the family's well-being, Kenyan children tend to show pronounced levels of prosocial behavior.

Societies differ along many dimensions that have implications for prosocial behavior. Children in collectivist societies that foster group orientation tend to show more other-oriented prosocial behavior than do children in more individualist societies. For example, Israeli children from kibbutz communities, which typically emphasize communal living and high cooperation to meet shared goals, have been shown to display more prosocial, cooperative, and otherwise other-oriented behaviors compared with their urban-dwelling peers.

In a groundbreaking study of children in six cultures, Whiting and Whiting (1975) observed that children's prosocial behavior varied with culture. Children in Mexico and the Philippines were more often observed offering help and support (e.g., by offering food, toys, and information) than were children in Okinawa, India, and the United States. Children in rural Kenya, the most traditional society of

those studied, demonstrated the most pronounced levels of prosocial behavior. The differences in prosocial behavior are influenced by cultural and contextual differences, such as the tendency for people to live together in extended families. The most prosocial children lived in cultures where the female role was important to the family's economic well-being, and children were assigned chores and responsibilities at an early age and were expected to contribute to the family's well-being.

Cultures vary widely in the degree to which children are expected to aid the family by participating in household and economic work—activities that offer opportunities for prosocial development (Lancy, 2008; Ochs & Izquierdo, 2009). Although Western industrialized societies tend to conceptualize childhood as an innocent, playful period free from labor, children in many societies participate extensively in household and economic labor. In these societies adults naturally scale down responsibilities to match children's developmental stage and capabilities (Lancy, 2008). Participation in work often begins by children's simply being present and watching adults' activities (Paradise & Rogoff, 2009). Young children and toddlers might perform simple tasks in close proximity to adults and later on their own (Ochs & Izquierdo, 2009). For example, Tarong parents express strong expectations for prosocial behavior and expect children as young as 3 or 4 years of age to contribute to household and wage labor by performing simple tasks such as pushing a baby's hammock or helping string tobacco leaves (Guzman, Do, & Kok, 2014). Alternatively, children might engage in work alongside adults but be expected to produce less, as in the case of Mikea children in Madagascar who forage for edibles as part of adult groups but are not expected to accomplish the same level of success (Tucker & Young, 2005). Compared with able-bodied adults, children might gather younger tubers that are easier to dig for or gather and carry fewer nuts and fruits. Older Tarong children, at 6 or 7 years of age, are expected to participate in more sophisticated ways, such as tending to animals or helping to gather weeds, prepare food, or clean the home (Guzman et al., 2014). From these examples, we can see that cultures and economic environments vary dramatically in their expectations for children's behavior, with implications for their development.

What Do You Think?

1. In your view, what role does participation in household work or responsibility play in prosocial development?

2. To what extent and in what ways should parents and other adults require children to participate in household work? What expectations are appropriate, in your view?

Siblings offer opportunities to learn and practice helping and other prosocial behavior. Older siblings who display positive emotional responsiveness promote preschoolers' emotional and social competence (Sawyer et al., 2002). Researchers have observed that children with siblings tend to develop a theory of mind earlier than those without siblings. Recall from Chapter 7 that theory of mind helps children learn how to take another person's perspective and is associated with empathetic and prosocial behavior (Walker, 2005). Children who are unable to demonstrate the perspective-taking and cognitive skills that contribute to theory of mind will find it difficult to understand how others feel and help them.

Another way in which family context affects children's prosocial development is their participation in household work. This influence is explored in the Cultural Influences on Development feature.

The Broader Social World

The broader social world also influences the development of prosocial behavior. Collectivist cultures, in which people live with extended families, work is shared, and the maintenance of positive relationships with others is emphasized, tend to promote prosocial values and behavior more so than do cultures that emphasize the individual, as is common in most Western cultures (Eisenberg et al., 1998). One study of mother–child dyads in Japan and the United States found that the Japanese mothers of 4-year-old children tended to emphasize mutuality in their interactions, stressing the relationship (e.g., "This puzzle is difficult for us. Let's see if we can solve it."), while the U.S. mothers tended to emphasize individuality (e.g., "This puzzle is hard for you, isn't it? Let's see you try again"; Dennis, Cole, Zahn-Waxler, & Mizuta, 2002). These different styles influence how children display empathy, whether as sharing another's emotion or simply understanding another's emotion. These cultural differences also extend to children's reasons for sharing. When Filipino and American fifth graders were presented with hypothetical scenarios that required that they determine how resources should be shared, both the Filipino and American children preferred equal division of the resources regardless of merit or need (Carson & Banuazizi, 2008). However, the children offered different explanations of their choices. U.S. children emphasized that the characters in the scenario preformed equally and therefore deserved equal amounts of the resources, reflecting U.S. culture's emphasis on individuality and merit. Filipino children, on the other hand, tended to be more concerned with the interpersonal and emotional consequences of an unequal distribution, in line with their culture's emphasis on the collective and the importance of interpersonal relationships (Carson & Banuazizi, 2008).

Cognitive Influences

Prosocial behavior is influenced by emotion, but also by reasoning; it is associated with measures of cognitive maturation, self-regulation and perspective taking (Eisenberg et al., 2015). Although moral reasoning and empathy-based prosocial behavior have been discussed separately, they interact and influence each other. Prosocial emotions such as empathy reflect an orientation toward others' welfare and influence how children think about moral issues and ultimately how they behave (Eisenberg, Fabes, & Spinrad, 2006; Malti & Latzko, 2010). In one study of 3- and 4-year-olds, children who scored higher on empathy tended to rate moral transgressions more severely and viewed punishment for infractions as more deserved (Ball, Smetana, & Sturge-Apple, 2016). Prosocial behavior, however, can be influenced by multiple factors beyond moral thoughts and emotions, such as socialization attempts by parents and caregivers and the ability to resist temptation, which we will discuss in the next section.

Thinking in Context 12.2

1. How can we determine whether infants are born with a basic prosocial intuition or drive? Why might they have such an innate drive? If it is not innate, when do prosocial tendencies emerge?

2. What can parents and teachers do to encourage children's prosocial tendencies? What about those of adolescents?

MORAL SOCIALIZATION

LO 12.3 Explain how children learn to engage in acceptable behavior.

Children naturally construct their conceptions of right and wrong and what it means to help others. Parents play an important role in socializing children's prosocial behavior by exposing them to rules and models that children then internalize. Children's ability to abide by rules and display prosocial behavior, such as helping and sharing, is augmented by their growing capacities for self-control.

SELF-CONTROL

The degree to which children's actions match their prosocial beliefs varies with their will-power or self-control, the ability to manage their behavior. How do children learn to resist urges to violate moral standards? How do children avoid temptation?

The roots of self-control lie in infancy and toddlerhood, with self-awareness, and the emergence of a sense self. With motor development comes opportunities for exercising self-control. The onset of crawling increases infants' risk of injury and is accompanied by parental warnings and directives that increase as infants become increasingly mobile. Toddling infants are warned to avoid touching specific objects ("Don't touch the TV remote!"), to avoid dangerous situations ("The stove is hot!") and to not hurt others ("Don't hit; pet nicely."). Fourteen-month-old infants can recall instructions, but show very rudimentary efforts to inhibit their behavior. For example, an infant may look at the kitchen stove, approach it and even reach out to it, saying "no" or "hot."

Young children eventually learn to meet socialization demands such as sitting still, assisting in household management (e.g., helping to set the table; putting away their toys), and engaging in self-care activities (e.g., brushing their teeth; Kuczynski & Kochanska, 1995). Each of these tasks requires that children motivate their own behavior and resist impulsive activities, such as playing with the toys they were instructed to put away. Between 2 and 3 years of age, children's ability to resist impulses improves (Vaughn, Kopp, & Krakow, 1984). Self-control is initially motivated by external demands from parents and caregivers, but it develops rapidly to self-guidance.

Researchers study the development of self-control by administering tasks that require **delay of gratification**—that children wait a period of time to achieve a reward, such as a tempting object or treat. In a typical delay-of-gratification task, children are given two choices: a small reward immediately or a much larger reward if they wait. The ability to resist temptation tends to increase with age (Walter Mischel & Ebbesen, 1970). In one study that required children to wait 4 minutes for a cookie, nearly all 4-year-olds succeeded, but very few 2-year-olds did (Steelandt, Thierry, Broihanne, & Dufour, 2012). Preschool children show an emerging ability to resist impulses and self-control continues to develop during childhood, especially during the elementary school years (Vazsonyi & Huang, 2010). For example, children and adolescents were given the choice of eating a small piece of candy immediately or, if they waited one day, being given an entire bag of chips. About one third of 6- to 8-year-old children waited for the chips, as compared with half of the 9- to 11-year-olds and nearly all of the 12- to 15-year-olds (Rotenberg & Mayer, 1990).

delay of gratification A measure of self-control in which researchers administer tasks in which children have to wait a period of time to achieve a reward.

What strategies do children use to regulate their behavior? How children think about the rewards affects their ability to delay gratification (Atance & Jackson, 2009; Mischel, Shoda, & Rodriguez, 1989). Preschoolers were better able to delay gratification when they were instructed to focus on the abstract qualities of the reward ("Imagine the marshmallow is a big white fluffy cloud") rather than emphasizing the consumable qualities ("It is sweet and tasty"; Mischel & Baker, 1975). Preschool and elementary school children waited longer when instructed to focus on the task ("I am waiting for . . .") and less when they made reward-oriented statements ("The reward is yummy"; Miller, Weinstein, & Karniol, 1978; Toner & Smith, 1977). What strategies do children use in the absence of instruction?

Children show developmental changes in their knowledge and understanding of effective delay strategies. Preschoolers often show awareness that distraction can aid them in waiting for a reward ("I don't look at it"), yet most tend to prefer to keep the reward in view, suggesting that they fail to anticipate the difficulty of resisting the reward (Mischel & Mischel, 1983). By third grade, children know that not attending to the reward and keeping it out of sight will help them resist temptation. Although they know that focusing on the overall goal rather than the consumable properties of the reward is most effective, they do not put this preference into practice when they are given an actual task. By the time they reach sixth grade, children emphasize the goal; they also report efforts to change how they think about rewards. For example, they suggest thinking about the rewards and their own desires in unattractive ways, such as "The marshmallows are filled with an evil spell," or "I hate marshmallows; I can't stand them. But when the grown-up gets back, I'll say to myself, 'I love marshmallows' and eat it" (Mischel & Mischel, 1983, p. 609). Children's understanding of strategies for delaying gratification is influenced by cognitive development, especially metacognition, and maturation of the prefrontal cortex (Duckworth & Gross, 2014; Gagne, 2017). Children's awareness of how their mind works is essential for understanding how they can direct their thinking about a desired object.

Individual differences in self-control during childhood have implications for later functioning. Longitudinal research has suggested that self-control in preschool, as measured by delay-of-gratification tasks, predicts behavior in adolescence and early adulthood. For example, preschoolers with low self-control relative to their peers engaged in greater risky behavior such as smoking, alcohol, and substance use, and were more likely to be overweight and show poor school performance as adolescents (Mischel et al., 2011; Moffitt, Poulton, & Caspi, 2013; Schlam, Wilson, Shoda, Mischel, & Ayduk, 2013). As adults, children with low self-control were disproportionately likely to engage in criminal activity, have poor health, and have poor employment outcomes, lower income, and lower savings than children with higher self-control (Fergusson, Boden, & Horwood, 2013; Moffitt et al., 2013; Wolfe, Reisig, & Holtfreter, 2016).

Self-control continues to develop in adolescence, influenced largely by cognitive and neurological development. As discussed in Chapter 7, maturation and improved connectivity of the prefrontal cortex and cerebellum is associated with advances in many aspects of executive function—the ability to control and coordinate our thoughts and behavior. These aspects include attention, planning ahead, weighing risks and rewards, simultaneously considering multiple sources of information, and goal-directed behavior (Ardila, 2013; Tiemeier et al., 2010).

Advances in response inhibition enable adolescents to adapt their responses to the situation by restraining well-learned responses when they are inappropriate to the situation (Luna, Paulsen, Padmanabhan, & Geier, 2013; Luna et al., 2004). For example, Robin is now able to keep herself from raising her hand in response to the teacher's question, telling herself, "I need to give other students a chance, too." The ability to control and inhibit responses emerges first in infancy and advances through childhood, with substantial gains in adolescence (Geier, Terwilliger, Teslovich, Velanova, & Luna, 2010; Zhai et al., 2014). However, the neurological changes that underlie response inhibition continue to develop into the 20s. In adolescence, the still-immature capacities for response inhibition are thought to underlie the risk-taking behaviors that teenagers often exhibit (Albert, Chein, & Steinberg, 2013; Casey, 2015; Luna et al., 2013).

SOCIAL LEARNING

Children naturally attend to other people and often mimic what they see. According to social learning theory (see Chapter 1), moral behavior can be acquired through modeling and shaped through reinforcement and punishment (Bandura, 1977; Grusec, 1992). Attention from others, as well as the withdrawal of attention, are examples of the subtle ways that behavior is reinforced and punished. Adults and other children model behavior that the child might acquire. When children observe a model touching a forbidden toy, they are more likely to touch the toy. Some research suggests that children who observe a model resisting temptation are more likely to resist temptation themselves (Rosenkoetter, 1973). However, models are more effective at encouraging rather than inhibiting behavior that violates a rule or expectation. Children are more likely to follow a model's transgressions rather than appropriate behavior (Hoffman, 1970).

In order to learn by modeling, children must pay attention to the events that are modeled. Attention is influenced by many factors. Children are more likely to imitate behavior when the model is competent and powerful (Bandura, 1977). They are also more likely to imitate a model that is perceived as warm and responsive rather than cold and distant (Yarrow, Scott, & Waxler, 1973). Over the course of early childhood, children develop internalized standards of conduct based on reinforcements and punishments, and observing others and considering their explanations for behavior (Bandura, 1986; Mussen & Eisenberg-Berg, 1977). Those adopted standards are then used by children as guides for behavior. Children attempt to behave in ways that are consistent with their internalizations (Grusec & Goodnow, 1994). In this way, moral values and actions are learned and internalized, similar to other behavior. Children's behavior is shaped to conform with the rules of society. Modeling continues to influence behavior in adolescence. For example, adolescents whose parents model prosocial behavior, such as volunteering, are more likely to engage in prosocial behavior themselves (Ottoni-Wilhelm et al., 2014). Refer back to the Lives in Context feature for a discussion of community service work by adolescents.

When fathers participate in household chores children show less gender-stereotyped beliefs about the division of labor in the home.

DISCIPLINE

Parents serve as models of moral behavior, but they also influence their children's moral development directly through their interactions and their disciplinary strategies. **Discipline** refers to the methods a parent uses to teach and socialize children toward acceptable behavior. What discipline strategies are most effective? How can parents teach children appropriate behavior? In a classic comprehensive review of the parenting literature, Hoffman (1970) examined the disciplinary methods parents used and their children's moral development. He compared three approaches to discipline:

Love withdrawal: withholding attention, affection, or approval when a child misbehaves

Power assertion: controlling the child's behavior through the use of power, such as spankings, commands, and physical restraint

Induction: explaining why a behavior is wrong, emphasizing how it affects other people, and often providing a better option or suggestions on how the child can undo any damage

discipline The methods a parent uses to teach and socialize children.

Four-year-old Andre angrily yelled, "That's mine!" He hit his 2-year-old cousin as he pushed him away. A parent who relies on love withdrawal might say, "That's not nice! I don't want to look at you. Go away until you can be nice." A parent who uses power assertion might announce, "Enough! I'm taking your toy," or might spank Andre. Instead, a parent who uses induction explains the problem and how the child's behavior affects those around him or her. For example, "Look at how your cousin is crying. Pushing and hitting hurts. See how sad he is?"

Research has suggested that love withdrawal and power assertion are not effective in promoting prosocial development and can even hinder the development of prosocial behavior (Krevans & Gibbs, 1996). In both types of discipline, children are motivated to obey parents out of fear—fear of losing a parent's love, fear of losing privileges, or fear of being spanked (Hoffman, 2000). Children who are disciplined with threats of love withdrawal and power assertion are at risk to show internalizing problems, such as anxiety and depression, more externalizing behavior, including conduct problems, and little prosocial behavior (Barber, 2002). Love withdrawal and power assertion are discipline styles that emphasize punishment.

Punishment

Five-year-old Jayden throws blocks at his brother, Harlan. When Harlan cries out to their mother, Sheila, she yells at Jayden and tells him to sit down at the kitchen table while she cooks. Each day, Jayden throws blocks or hits Harlan and then is told to sit at the kitchen table. Sometimes he plays nicely with his brother, but soon he returns to his usual behavior of throwing blocks. Sheila becomes frustrated because Jayden continues to torment his brother despite being punished for his misbehavior each day. What is happening here? Frequently parents ignore good behavior but scold bad behavior, drawing attention to it and inadvertently reinforcing it. Jayden's good behavior goes unnoticed; Sheila does not reinforce it by complimenting his attempts to play nicely with Harlan. But Jayden gets attention when he misbehaves, not only by having Sheila notice his behavior, but also by being seated in the kitchen close to her. Sheila believes she is punishing his misbehavior, but requiring him to sit at the table while she cooks may be making Jayden more likely to misbehave.

One form of punishment, *physical punishment*, can be particularly damaging to children. The use of physical or corporal punishment, often referred to as spanking, is hotly contested around the world despite considerable research demonstrating its harm to children's development. Spanking is against the law in Sweden, yet parents in most countries of Asia, Africa, the Middle East, and both North and South America report that spanking is acceptable, appropriate, and sometimes necessary (Hicks-Pass, 2009; Oveisi et al., 2010). In the United States, the majority of adults report that they were spanked as children without harm. Why the controversy on spanking if it occurs in most cultures?

Children who are punished harshly show higher rates of emotional and social problems than other children (Mulvaney & Mebert, 2007). They may have difficulty accurately interpreting others' actions and words and are more likely to attribute hostile intentions and assume that others are "out to get them" (Weiss, Dodge, Bates, & Pettit, 1992). Corporal punishment is damaging to the parent–child relationship. When parents lose their self-control and yell, scream, or hit the child, the child may feel helpless, become fearful of the parent, avoid him or her, and become passive (Grusec & Goodnow, 1994). Moreover, physical punishment can foster the very behavior that parents seek to stop. Parents often punish children for aggressive behavior, yet physical punishment models the use of aggression as an effective way of resolving conflict and other problems, teaching children that might makes right (Hicks-Pass, 2009).

Physical punishment tends to increase compliance only temporarily. Physical punishment is associated with behavior problems at age 3 and continued behavior problems

Time out removes the child from overstimulating situations and stops inappropriate behaviors without humiliating him or her. Time out is effective when it is accompanied by explanation and a warm parent-child relationship.

at age 5 (Choe, Olson, & Sameroff, 2013; Mendez, Durtschi, Neppl, & Stith, 2016), poor adjustment in childhood and adolescence (Balan, Dobrean, Roman, & Balazsi, 2017; Coley, Kull, & Carrano, 2014; Wang & Kenny, 2014), and health problems in adulthood (Afifi, Mota, MacMillan, & Sareen, 2013). For example, in one study of nearly 5,000 teenagers and adults of Ontario, Canada, those who recalled being spanked or slapped sometimes or often as children were more likely to report having problems with anxiety, alcohol use, and antisocial behavior than those who reported never having been spanked (MacMillan et al., 1999). Some parents assert that spanking and physical punishment within the context of a warm parenting relationship reduces the negative effects of physical punishment. However, a study that followed children from ages 1 to 5 found that beginning as early as age 1, maternal spanking was predictive of child behavior problems, and maternal warmth did not counteract the negative consequences of the use of spanking (Lee, Altschul, & Gershoff, 2013). Corporal punishment tends to become less effective at controlling children's behavior with repeated use and as children grow older (AAP Committee on Psychosocial Aspects of Child and Family Health, 1998). For example, the use of spanking is impractical with teenagers.

What can parents do about their children's undesirable behavior? Is it ever permissible—and effective—to use punishment? Certainly, in small doses and specific contexts. Running into the street or touching a hot stove, for example, are behaviors that are dangerous to children or to others. These behaviors must be stopped immediately to prevent injury. To be effective, punishment should occur immediately after the dangerous behavior, be applied consistently, and be clearly connected to the behavior. The purpose of such punishment is to keep the child from engaging in the dangerous behavior, to make him or her comply, but not to feel guilt. **Time out**, which entails removing a child from the situation and from social contact for a short period of time, is often effective in reducing inappropriate behavior (Morawska & Sanders, 2011). Effective punishment, such as time out, does not humiliate the child. It is administered calmly, privately, within the context of a warm parent–child relationship, and is accompanied by an explanation so that the child understands the reason for the punishment (AAP Committee on Psychosocial Aspects of Child and Family Health, 1998; Baumrind, 1996).

Children learn best when they are reinforced for good behavior. Recall from social learning theory that the child must view a reinforcement as rewarding in order for it to be effective in encouraging his or her behavior. Reinforcement can be tangible, such as money or candy; or intangible, such as attention or a smile. Effective reinforcement is administered consistently when the desired behavior occurs. Eventually the reinforcement becomes internalized by the child and the behavior itself becomes reinforcing. The child comes to associate the behavior with pleasurable feelings and the behavior itself eventually produces a positive feeling; a sense of accomplishment.

Induction

Inductive discipline, or methods that use reasoning, are effective alternatives to spanking in changing a child's behavior (AAP Committee on Psychosocial Aspects of Child and Family Health, 1998). Examples of inductive methods include helping children find and use words to express their feelings. Another inductive method is to provide children with choices (e.g., peas or carrots), permitting them to feel some control over the situation and be empowered. Parents who use inductive techniques model effective conflict resolution and help children to become aware of the consequences of their actions. Inductive methods are very effective in helping children to internalize rules and standards (Choe et al., 2013). One study of 54 African American kindergarten-age children from an inner city found that those whose mothers used inductive reasoning were more likely to see that hurting other people is not just a question of breaking rules, but is wrong, as compared with children whose mothers reported taking away privileges (Jagers, Bingham, & Hans, 1996).

time out A discipline technique in which a child is removed from a situation for a period of time.
inductive discipline Strategy to control children's behavior that relies on reasoning and discussion.

The American Association of Pediatrics recommends that parents positively reinforce good behavior and, when necessary, discourage inappropriate behavior with the use of time out, removal of privileges, and verbal reprimands aimed at the behavior rather than the child (AAP Committee on Psychosocial Aspects of Child and Family Health, 1998). Researchers advise that punishment be used sparingly, as it often directs children's attention to themselves and their own feelings rather than to how their behavior affects others, increasing children's emphasis on themselves rather than empathetic and prosocial motives (McCord, 1996). Overall, developmental professionals agree that discipline that relies on a warm parent–child relationship, clear expectations, communication, and limit setting is most effective in modifying children's behavior.

Culture and Discipline

The strategies parents use to control children's behavior vary according to many factors, including the parent and child's personalities, the age of the child, the parent–child relationship, and cultural customs and expectations (Grusec & Goodnow, 1994). One concern that researchers have regarding discussions of discipline is that there is not just one effective way to parent. Instead, there are many cultural variations in parenting, and the effectiveness of disciplinary techniques may differ by cultural context (Cauce, 2008).

Expectations for behavior as well as methods of discipline vary with culture. North American parents permit and encourage children to express emotions, including anger, while Japanese parents encourage children to refrain from displaying strong emotions. In one cross-cultural experiment, U.S. preschoolers exposed to situations designed to elicit stress and anger demonstrated more aggressive behaviors than did Japanese children (Zahn-Waxler, Friedman, Cole, Mizuta, & Hiruma, 1996). In comparison with North American mothers, Japanese mothers are more likely to use reasoning, empathy, and disapproval to discipline their children. Such techniques are effective for Japanese mothers because of the strong mother–child relationship and collectivist values that are prevalent in Japan, illustrating the importance of relationships in that culture (Rothbaum, Pott, Azuma, Miyake, & Weisz, 2000).

Chinese parents tend to describe their parenting as relatively controlling without emphasizing individuality and choice (Chao, 2001). They are directive and view exerting control as a way of teaching children self-control and encouraging high achievement (Huntsinger, Jose, & Larson, 1998). Yet most Chinese parents couple the emphasis on control with warmth (Xu et al., 2005). The combination of warmth and control is linked with cognitive and social competence, but, similar to findings with American samples, excessive control without warmth is associated with depression, social difficulties, and poor academic achievement in Chinese children (Cheah, Leung, Tahseen, & Schultz, 2009).

Is strict control always harmful? Researchers have identified a disciplinary style common in African American families that combines strict parental control with affection (Tamis-LeMonda, Briggs, McClowry, & Snow, 2009). In this style, mothers often stress obedience and view strict control as important in helping children develop self-control and attentiveness. African American parents who use such controlling strategies tend to raise children who are more cognitively mature and socially competent than their peers whose parents do not use this style. This difference is particularly apparent in children reared in low-income homes and communities where vigilant, strict parenting enhances children's safety (Weis & Toolis, 2010). Whereas physical discipline is associated with behavioral problems in European American children, it appears to protect some African American children from conduct problems in adolescence (Lansford, Deater-Deckard, Dodge, Bates, & Pettit, 2004). The warmth and affection buffers some of the negative consequences of strictness (McLoyd & Smith, 2002; Stacks, Oshio, Gerard, & Roe, 2009). The child's perception of parental discipline and intention is important in determining its effect. Children evaluate parental behavior in light of their culture and the emotional tone of the relationship. African American children reared in homes with strict but warm parents often see this style of discipline as indicative of concern about their well-being (Brody & Flor, 1998).

In the United States, it is often difficult to disentangle the effects of culture and neighborhood context on parenting behaviors because African American families are disproportionately represented in disadvantaged neighborhoods. Does strict discipline embody cultural beliefs about parenting? Or is it a response to raising children in a disadvantaged environment (Murry, Brody, Simons, Cutrona, & Gibbons, 2008)? Parental perceptions of danger and their own distress influences how they parent (Cuellar, Jones, & Sterrett, 2013). Parenting behaviors, including discipline, must be considered within their cultural and environmental context, as parenting is not one size fits all (Sorkhabi, 2005).

Thinking in Context 12.3

1. How do children learn strategies for self-control? What role might peers and siblings play in helping children learn to manage their impulses?

2. What factors might influence how parents discipline their children, such as the methods they choose, for example? Consider the parents, family, community, and society.

AGGRESSION AND ANTISOCIAL BEHAVIOR

LO 12.4 Identify normative patterns of aggressive behavior and influences on atypical aggression during childhood and adolescence.

So far in this chapter, the term *aggression* has been used but not defined. The term *prosocial behavior*, defined in the preceding section, is an antonym for **antisocial behavior**—behavior that harms others, is disruptive or hostile, or that transgresses social norms. **Aggression** is a main component of antisocial behavior, consisting of behavior that harms or violates the rights of others, whether overtly or covertly.

DEVELOPMENT OF AGGRESSION AND ANTISOCIAL BEHAVIOR

Although infants and young children display increasing capacities for empathy and prosocial responses as they develop, they also commonly show aggressive behavior. More than half of a sample of children, followed from the age of 5 months through 42 months of age, showed some aggressive behaviors—hitting, biting, or kicking—suggesting that aggression is a part of human nature (Tremblay et al., 2004). At 14 or 15 months, physical aggression against peers or siblings (e.g., pushing, hitting, pulling hair, or biting) is evident, and by 17 months almost 80% of children show some physical aggression: taking things or pushing to get what they want (Eisenberg et al., 2015). Infants' aggression is usually not intended to harm; rather, it represents **instrumental aggression**, which is aggression that is oriented toward achieving a goal (e.g., to get a toy) and typically appears at about 1 year of age (Hay, Hurst, Waters, & Chadwick, 2011). It increases from toddlerhood into early childhood, to around 4 or 5 years of age, as children begin to play with other children and act in their own interests. All children will sometimes hit, fight, kick, and take other children's toys. In addition to toys, young children often battle over space ("I was sitting there!"). Instrumental aggression usually occurs during play and is an important step in development, as it is often displayed by sociable and confident children.

By age 4 to 5, most children have developed the self-control to express their desires and to wait for what they want, at least for a little while, moving from expressing aggression through physical means to using words (Coie & Dodge, 1998). As children's language skills improve, they become able to express their needs orally; at this stage physical

antisocial behavior Behavior that harms others, is disruptive or hostile, or that transgresses social norms.

aggression Behavior that harms or violates the rights of others, whether overtly or covertly.

instrumental aggression Behavior that hurts someone else in order to achieve a goal such as gaining a possession.

aggression declines, but verbal aggression becomes more frequent (Mesman et al., 2009; Miner & Clarke-Stewart, 2008). Verbal aggression is a form of **relational aggression**, intended to harm others' social relationships (Ostrov & Godleski, 2010). In preschool and elementary school, relational aggression often takes the form of name calling and excluding peers from play (Pellegrini & Roseth, 2006).

Physical aggression declines throughout elementary school and high school (Eisner, Malti, Eisner, & Malti, 2015). However, there are individual differences in aggression. Individual differences in expressing anger are apparent by 6 months of age and persist through early childhood. Excessive rage and using physical force in infancy predict problematic levels of aggressiveness in later childhood (Hay, 2016). A small minority of children show high levels of aggression (e.g., repeated hitting, kicking, or biting) that increase during childhood, placing them at risk for long-term problems with aggression and antisocial behavior (Kjeldsen, Janson, Stoolmiller, Torgersen, & Mathiesen, 2014; Tremblay, 2009). Aggression is associated with poor school performance. Children who show high levels of aggression often direct it toward their peers, as bullies.

Children who show physical forms of bullying, such as hair pulling, are often reared in homes with poor supervision, coercive control, and physical discipline.

AGGRESSION AND PEER VICTIMIZATION

Bullying, also known as **peer victimization**, refers to an ongoing interaction in which a child repeatedly attempts to inflict physical, verbal, or social harm on another child by, for example, hitting, kicking, name calling, teasing, shunning, or humiliating them (Olweus, 1995). Bullying is a problem for school-age children in many countries. Estimated rates of bullying and victimization range from 15% to 25% of children in Australia, Austria, England, Finland, Germany, Norway and the United States (Analitis et al., 2009; Cook, Williams, Guerra, & Kim, 2010). Physical bullying is most common in childhood; verbal forms of bullying, including bullying on social media, increase during childhood and remain common in adolescence (Finkelhor, Ormrod, & Turner, 2009).

Boys who bully tend to be above average in size, use physical aggression, and target both boys and girls. Girls who bully tend to be verbally assertive, target other girls, and use relational aggression, such as ridiculing, embarrassing, or spreading rumors (Veenstra et al., 2005). Boys and girls who bully tend to be impulsive, domineering, and show little anxiety or insecurity in peer contexts (Kumpulainen & Räsänen, 2000; Menesini & Salmivalli, 2017). Bullying can be motivated by the pursuit of high status and a powerful dominant position in the peer group (Rodkin, Espelage, & Hanish, 2015; Salmivalli, 2014). Indeed, bullying can be helpful in maintaining prestige: Relationally aggressive children, including bullies, are frequently perceived by peers as cool, powerful, and popular (Salmivalli, 2010). Indirect forms of bullying, such as relational bullying, require social skills, such as the ability to persuade others, which contribute to bullies' high social status among peers (Juvonen & Graham, 2014). In support of this, many bullies report making friends easily and are seen to receive similar levels of support from their classmates as other children (Demaray, Malecki, & DeLong, 2006).

Children who show physically aggressive forms of bullying often display a range of problems, including hyperactive behavior and poor school achievement. They perceive less support from teachers than do other children and may show higher rates of depression than other children (Turcotte Benedict, Vivier, & Gjelsvik, 2014). Parents of bullies are more likely to provide poor supervision, prefer coercive control and physical discipline, and tend to be permissive toward aggressive behavior, even teaching their children

peer victimization Also known as bullying; an ongoing interaction in which a child becomes a frequent target of physical, verbal, or social harm by another child or children.

relational aggression Harming someone through nonphysical acts aimed at harming a person's connections with others, such as by exclusion and rumor spreading.

to strike back at perceived provocation (Holt, Kaufman Kantor, & Finkelhor, 2009; Rodkin et al., 2015; Shetgiri, Lin, & Flores, 2013). Inconsistent, hostile, and rejecting parenting place children at risk to bully throughout childhood and adolescence (Gómez-Ortiz, Romera, & Ortega-Ruiz, 2016).

Characteristics of Victims

"I don't know why Victor hates me. He just won't leave me alone," cries Tyler to his teacher, Mr. Johnson, after being knocked onto the ground again. Mr. Johnson thinks to himself, "Tyler is the smallest kid in class, keeps to himself, and is sensitive. He cries easily. Maybe that's why he's a target." Victims of bullying, like Tyler, are more likely to be inhibited, frail in appearance, and younger than their peers (Olweus, 1995). Bullies report choosing their victims because they do not like them, often because victims are particularly weak or stand out in some way (Juvonen & Graham, 2014). Children who are bullied are often perceived by their peers as "different," or as more quiet and cautious than other children (DeRosier & Mercer, 2009). They often experience intrusive parenting, overprotectiveness, and parental criticism that increases their vulnerability to bullying. Perhaps not surprisingly, children who are bullied often report feeling lonely, being less happy at school, and having fewer good friends than their classmates (Reavis, Keane, & Calkins, 2010).

Many victim characteristics, such as shyness, passivity, social withdrawal, and nonassertive styles of interacting with peers—as well as anxiety, depression and poor emotional control—are present before the child becomes a target of peer victimization. They are then amplified by victimization (Gini & Pozzoli, 2009; Jenkins, Demaray, & Tennant, 2017; Perren, Ettekal, & Ladd, 2013). Much of the long-term stability of peer victimization and its negative effects can be explained by the dynamic interactions between risk factors for victimization and the effects of victimization (Shetgiri et al., 2013). Although children respond in various ways to bullying, avoidance behaviors (e.g., avoiding school and refusing to go to play dates, parties, and sport activities) are common (Waasdorp & Bradshaw, 2011). Victims of bullying, such as Tyler, tend to respond to victimization in ways that reinforce bullies, by becoming defensive, crying, and giving in to bullies' demands (Champion & Clay, 2007). Not all victims of bullying are passive and withdrawn, however. Older children who experience frequent victimization may respond with more intense feelings of anger and greater desires to retaliate, making them more likely to show **reactive aggression**, an aggressive response provoked by an insult, confrontation, or frustration (Waasdorp & Bradshaw, 2011).

Bullies Who Are Also Victims

Not all victims of bullying are shy and withdrawn. Some children become targets of bullying because they are aggressive and have difficulty controlling their emotions. About half of children who bully report also being victims of bullying (Champion & Clay, 2007). Provocative victims or **bully/victims** share characteristics of both bullies and victims but function more poorly than either (Veenstra et al., 2005). For example, bully/victims tend to show high levels of anxiety and depression and low rates of social acceptance and self-esteem common to victims, but they also show levels of aggression, impulsivity, and poor self-control similar to bullies (Simon, Nail, Swindle, Bihm, & Joshi, 2016; Swearer & Hymel, 2015). Children who are bully/victims have difficulty managing emotions, increasing their risk for reactive aggression and acting out behaviors that invite aggressive exchanges with others (O'Brennan, Bradshaw, & Sawyer, 2009). These characteristics lead children who are both bullies and victims to have problems in peer relationships. Bully/victims often are among the most disliked members of a classroom (Dill, Vernberg, Fonagy, Twemlow, & Gamm, 2004).

Physical and relational bullying have negative emotional and academic consequences that appear as early as in kindergarten and persist during the childhood

reactive aggression An impulsive, hostile response to provocation or a blocked goal.

bully/victim A child who attacks or inflicts harm on others and who is also attacked or harmed by others; the child is both bully and victim.

and adolescent years, often well after the bullying ends (Juvonen & Graham, 2014). For example, children who were bully/victims were more likely to experience anxiety and depression in late adolescence and in early adulthood—and even into middle adulthood (Copeland, Wolke, Angold, & Costello, 2013; Klomek et al., 2008; McDougall & Vaillancourt, 2015; Zwierzynska, Wolke, & Lereya, 2013). Furthermore, the meaning and implications of bullying may vary with context. For example, relational bullying may be more emotionally damaging to children reared in collectivist cultures that heavily value relationships. One comparison of Japanese and U.S. fourth graders showed more depression in Japanese victims (Kawabata, Crick, & Hamaguchi, 2010).

Intervening in Bullying

How can adults and peers reduce the incidence of bullying? Research suggests that patterns of bullying can be broken by changing victims' negative perceptions of themselves, helping them to acquire the skills needed to maintain relationships with peers, and teaching them to respond to bullying in ways that do not reinforce their attackers (Olweus & Limber, 2010). Although victims' submissive behavior is reinforcing to bullies, interventions must stress that victimized children are not to blame for the abuse. Targeting victims of bullying is not enough—perpetrators of bullying also need help. Parents and teachers should help bullies learn to identify, understand, and manage their and other people's emotions, as well as to direct anger in safe and appropriate ways.

Teacher awareness of bullying and willingness to intervene make a difference (Espelage, Low, & Jimerson, 2014). There is a higher victimization rate in classrooms of teachers who attribute bullying to external factors outside of their control; the teacher's own perceived ability to handle bullying and the teacher's own bullying history are positively associated with classroom victimization rate (Oldenburg et al., 2014). Many teachers are unaware of how serious and extensive the bullying is within their schools, and are often ineffective in being able to identify bullying incidents (Espelage et al., 2014). In addition, bystanders—children who watch episodes of bullying but do not act—reinforce bullies' behaviors and increase bullying (Kärnä, Voeten, Poskiparta, & Salmivalli, 2010; Salmivalli, 2014). Class norms can influence whether bystanders intervene (Pozzoli, Gini, & Vieno, 2012). Classmates can be encouraged to support one another when bullying events occur: rather than being bystanders or egging on the bully, children should tell a teacher, refuse to watch, and even, if safe, encourage bullies to stop.

Bullying is not simply a child-to-child problem, therefore it requires more than a child-centered solution. Stopping bullying requires awareness and change within the school by reviewing and modifying practices with an eye toward identifying how school procedures, such as grouping students by characteristics such as height, maintain and increase bullying (Nese et al., 2014). In recognition of the pervasiveness and severity of bullying, specific bullying-related policies are included in public school laws in most states. Addressing the problem of bullying requires that children, teachers, and parents voice concerns about bullying, schools develop policies against bullying, teachers supervise and monitor children during lunch and recess times, and parents learn how to identify and change victims' and bullies' behaviors.

Table 12.1 summarizes interventions to combat bullying; such interventions address victims, bullies, and schools (Nese, Horner, Dickey, Stiller, & Tomlanovich, 2014; Olweus & Limber, 2010; Slee & Mohyla, 2007). The Applying Developmental Science feature discusses anti-bullying legislation.

ANTISOCIAL AND DELINQUENT BEHAVIOR

"Have you got it?" asked Corey. "Here it is—right from Ms. Scarcela's mailbox!" Adam announced as he dropped the stolen item on the floor in front of his friends. During adolescence young people experiment with new ideas, activities, and limits. For many

TABLE 12.1 • Tips for Intervening in Bullying

Child	Victim	• Teach assertiveness skills • Teach alternative responses to bullying • Teach anxiety management, social and coping skills.
	Bully	• Teach alternatives to violence. • Help children develop empathy • Teach coping skills to reduce impulsive behavior
Parent	Victim	• Teach authoritative parenting skills • Encourage parents to aid children in being independent and developing coping skills
	Bully	• Teach authoritative parenting skills • Parent with sensitivity and consistency • Model nonaggressive behavior, interpersonal interactions, and conflict management strategies • Provide positive feedback to children for appropriate social behavior • Use alternatives to physical punishment
School		• Avoid grouping students by physical characteristics such as height • Stress that victims are not to blame • Teach social skills and conflict management • Promote a positive school climate that encourages students to feel good about themselves • Encourage fair discipline that is non-punitive • Train teachers to identify and respond to potentially damaging victimization • Teachers use positive feedback and modeling to address appropriate social interactions • School personnel never ignore bullying behaviors • Encourage classmates to support one another and, rather than simply watch bullying events occur, tell a teacher, and refuse to watch or encourage the bully • Review and modifying school practices with an eye toward identifying how school procedures may contribute to bullying

adolescents, like Adam, experimentation takes the form of delinquent activity. Nearly all young people engage in at least one *delinquent* or illegal act, such as stealing, during the adolescent years, without coming into police contact (Flannery, Hussey, & Jefferis, 2005). In one study, boys admitted to engaging in, on average, three serious delinquent acts and girls reported one serious delinquent act between ages 10 and 20, yet nearly none of the adolescents had been arrested (Fergusson & Horwood, 2002). Adolescents account for 8% of police arrests in the United States (Federal Bureau of Investigation, 2015). Males are about four times as likely to be arrested as females. African American youth are disproportionately likely to be arrested as compared with European American and Latino youth, who are similar in their likelihood of arrest; Asian American youth are least likely to be arrested (Andersen, 2015; Federal Bureau of Investigation, 2015). Adolescents' own reports, however, tend to suggest few to no gender or ethnic differences in delinquent activity (Rutter, Giller, & Hagell, 1998). Differences in arrest rates may be influenced by the tendency for police to arrest and charge ethnic minority youths in low-SES communities more often than European American and Asian American youths in higher-SES communities (Rutter, et al., 1998).

Most adolescents tend to show an increase in delinquent activity in early adolescence that continues into middle adolescence and then declines in late adolescence into early adulthood (Farrington, 2004). Although mild delinquency is common and not

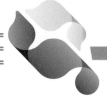

• • Anti-Bullying Legislation

School policies that emphasize community, such as proclaiming school as a no-bullying zone and encouraging bystanders to intervene, are effective in reducing peer victimization.

Schools are responsible for children's physical well-being, but how far does that responsibility extend? What is the role of schools in addressing peer victimization? In a landmark case, the mother of fifth grader LaShonda Davis filed suit against the Monroe County [Georgia] Board after the school failed to intervene during the months in which her daughter was the victim of severe harassment, often sexual, by a fellow student. The 1999 decision in *Davis v. Monroe County Board of Education* ruled that sexual harassment by peers violates Title IX of the Equal Opportunity in Education Act of 1972, which stipulates that "No person in the United States shall, on the basis of sex, be excluded from participation in, be denied the benefits of, or be subjected to discrimination under any education program or activity receiving Federal financial assistance." The court deemed that sexual harassment in the school setting violates students' rights to education. *Davis v. Monroe* applies specifically to peer-to-peer sexual harassment, but researchers and legislators look to this ruling as an important precedent

for anti-bullying legislation because bullying violates students' rights.

In recognition of the pervasiveness and severity of bullying, 49 states in the United States include specific bullying-related policies into their public school laws (Hinduja & Patchin, 2015). Anti-bullying laws do not criminalize bullying itself but stipulate that school districts must take action to prevent or intervene when bullying occurs (Stuart-Cassel, Bell, & Springer, 2011). State anti-bullying laws vary enormously, but nearly all require or strongly encourage school districts to establish anti-bullying policies and usually place the responsibility for policy development on school boards (Cornell & Limber, 2015).

Most developmental researchers agree that a model bullying law should include, at minimum, the following: a clear definition of bullying, explicit articulation of a bullying prohibition, implementation of prevention and treatment programs, and acknowledgment of the association between bullying and public health risks (Limber & Small, 2003; Srabstein et al., 2008). The Safe Schools Improvement Act, proposed in 2013, is an example of legislation that would require states to collect and report information on the incidence of bullying and harassment. It would also permit schools to use federal grants to prevent and respond to incidents of bullying and harassment, require schools to provide annual reports of bullying prevalence and policies, and establish grievance procedures for students and parents to register complaints regarding such conduct. Although not passed by Congress, the Safe Schools Improvement Act sets an important precedent by acknowledging the relevance of peer victimization to children's everyday lives.

What Do You Think?

1. **What role should schools take in addressing bullying? Give reasons for your answer.**

2. **Think about the schools you attended. Did your schools draw attention to bullying and have rules or policies about bullying?**

necessarily cause for concern, about one-quarter of violent offenses in the United States, including murder, rape, robbery, and aggravated assault, are conducted by adolescents (Office of Juvenile Justice and Delinquency Prevention, 2014). Adolescents who engage in serious crime are at risk to become repeat offenders who continue criminal activity into adulthood. Yet most young people whose delinquent activity persists and evolves into a life of crime show multiple problem behaviors that began in childhood, not in adolescence (Farrington & Loeber, 2000). Chronic offenders and those who commit more serious crimes are more likely to have their first contacts with the criminal justice system by age 12 or earlier and likely fit the profile for conduct disorder (Baglivio, Jackowski, Greenwald, & Howell, 2014).

Conduct disorder is a psychiatric diagnosis that refers to a severe form of antisocial behavior, characterized by aggressive behaviors that involve destruction of property, stealing or robbing others, or causing pain to others (e.g., harming others, animal cruelty; American Psychiatric Association, 2013). Other signs of conduct disorder include frequently running away from home, frequently staying out all night, and frequent school truancy prior to age 13. Although nearly all adolescents engage in some mild antisocial behaviors at some point, adolescents with conduct disorder tend to show more serious behavioral problems beginning at a younger age (Evans, Simons, & Simons, 2014; Farrington, 2004). Adolescents with conduct disorder are more likely to show deficits in executive function and commit serious violent offenses that are not normative for adolescence (Fanti, Kimonis, Hadjicharalambous, & Steinberg, 2016; Johnson, Kemp, Heard, Lennings, & Hickie, 2015).

Fortunately, most delinquent acts are limited to the adolescent years and do not continue into adulthood (Piquero & Moffitt, 2013). Antisocial behavior tends to increase during puberty and is sustained by affiliation with similar peers. With advances in cognition, moral reasoning, emotional regulation, social skills, and empathy, antisocial activity declines (Monahan, Steinberg, Cauffman, & Mulvey, 2013). Preventing and intervening in delinquency requires examining individual, family, and community factors. Training parents in discipline, communication, and monitoring fosters healthy parent–child relationships, which buffers young people who are at risk for delinquency (Bowman, Prelow, & Weaver, 2007). High-quality teachers, teacher support, resources, and economic aid foster an educational environment that protects young people from risks for antisocial behavior. A 3-year longitudinal study following adolescents of low-income single mothers transitioning off welfare showed that involvement in school activities protects adolescents from some of the negative effects of low-income contexts and is associated with lower levels of delinquency over time (Mahatmya & Lohman, 2011). Economic, social, and employment resources empower communities to create environments that reduce criminal activity by all age groups and promote the development of children and adolescents.

INFLUENCES ON AGGRESSION

As other behaviors, aggression is influenced by both biological and contextual factors. Individuals vary in genetic predispositions toward traits and tendencies that contribute to aggression, such as temperament, personality, and response tendencies (Eisner et al., 2015; Veroude et al., 2016). Several genes have been associated with antisocial behavior, and early experiences are thought to play an epigenetic effect on the expression of genes (Barker et al., 2009; Tremblay, 2009). For example, the MAO-A gene influences our response to stress and feeling threatened. Individuals with genotypes for low MAO-A activity are at risk for aggression, impulsivity, and antisocial behavior from childhood through adulthood—if they are abused or experience severe stress (Byrd & Manuck, 2014). The maladaptive MAO-A response is an example of an epigenetic effect because it is more likely when the individual experiences extreme stress, but aggression is *not* more likely if the individual does not experience extreme stress.

Brain development—specifically, immaturity or impairments in parts of the prefrontal cortex—is associated with poor planning, reduced ability to sustain attention, poor ability to evaluate emotions, and reduced ability to process rewards and punishments, all of which may increase the risk of aggressive, impulsive responses (Bannon, Salis, & Daniel O'Leary, 2015; Geier et al., 2010). The amygdala is involved in forming links between conditioned stimuli and emotional responses (recall classical conditioning from Chapter 1), enabling people to associate emotions with behaviors and label them as good or bad (Phelps & LeDoux, 2005). An individual with an immature or underactive amygdala may fail to signal and grasp the value of aversive stimuli, such

conduct disorder A psychiatric diagnosis that refers to a severe form of antisocial behavior, characterized by aggressive behaviors that involve the destruction of property, stealing, or robbing others, or causing pain to others.

as facial expressions indicating distress, which might otherwise act to inhibit their behavior (Jones, Laurens, Herba, Barker, & Viding, 2009; Monk et al., 2003).

When biological and individual risk factors are coupled with challenging home and community environments, the risk for childhood onset of serious antisocial behavior that persists into adulthood increases (Dishion & Patterson, 2016; Granic & Patterson, 2006). Parenting that is inconsistent, highly controlling and/or negligent, accompanied by harsh punishment, and/or low in monitoring can worsen impulsive, defiant, and aggressive tendencies in children and adolescents (Bowman et al., 2007; Chen, Voisin, & Jacobson, 2013; Harris-McKoy & Cui, 2012; Lahey, Hulle, D'Onofrio, Rodgers, & Waldman, 2008). Young children who show high levels of aggression are more likely to have experienced coercive parenting, family dysfunction, or low income; and to be parented by mothers with a history of antisocial behavior and early childbearing (Tremblay, 2014; Wang, Christ, Mills-Koonce, Garrett-Peters, & Cox, 2013). Children who do not develop the impulse control and self-management skills to inhibit their aggressive responses are at risk of continuing and escalating aggressive behavior during the childhood years and showing poor social and academic outcomes during the school-age years and beyond (Gower, Lingras, Mathieson, Kawabata, & Crick, 2014; Wang et al., 2013).

We have discussed the power of social learning in Chapter 1. Exposure to aggressive models also influences children's behavior. In a famous experiment, Bandura and colleagues demonstrated how models can influence aggression (Bandura, Ross, & Ross, 1961). In this study, one group of preschool-age children watched a film of an adult playing violently with a Bobo doll (a child-size inflated plastic clown, weighted at the bottom so that it always returns upright when knocked down). Other children watched an adult ignore the Bobo doll and instead calmly play with Tinkertoys, a set of building toys. A third group of children was not exposed to any model. All of the children were then exposed to a situation designed to elicit frustration. They were taken to a room with attractive toys but were not allowed to play with them. Finally the children were brought to another room filled with aggressive toys (such as the Bobo doll, dart guns, and a mallet) and nonaggressive toys (Tinker toys, crayons, and plastic farm animals). The children exposed to the aggressive model made more aggressive responses than the other children, including imitating specific behaviors. This study showed that exposure to aggressive models can increase aggression on the part of observers. Later research showed that watching an aggressive model get reinforced or punished influenced children's behavior. They were more likely to imitate a model whose behavior is reinforced and avoid engaging in behaviors that they observed punished (Bandura & Albert, 1965). The Bobo doll research indicates that children who observe aggressive models are more likely to behave aggressively. Does observing virtual aggression through violent media, such as video games, influence children's behavior? The Applying Developmental Science feature examines this question.

Contextual factors in the community also matter. Communities of pervasive poverty are characterized by limited educational, recreational, and employment activities, coupled with access to drugs and firearms, opportunities to witness and be victimized by violence, and offers of protection and companionship by gangs that engage in criminal acts—all of which contribute to the onset of antisocial behavior (Chen et al., 2013; Chung & Steinberg, 2006; C. Hay, Fortson, Hollist, Altheimer, & Schaible, 2007). Exposure to high levels of community violence predicts delinquent activity (Jain & Cohen, 2013; Mrug, Loosier, & Windle, 2008). Low-income communities tend to have schools that struggle to meet students' educational and developmental needs, with crowding, limited resources, and overtaxed teachers (Flannery et al., 2005). Young people who experience individual, home, community, and school risk factors for antisocial behavior tend to associate with similarly troubled peers, a pattern that tends to increase delinquent activity as well as chronic delinquency (Evans et al., 2014; Lacourse, Nagin, & Tremblay, 2003). However, one powerful protective factor for development across the lifespan is a sense of a higher power or religiosity, which we discuss in the next section.

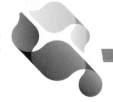

● ● Video Games and Aggression

Does playing violent video games influence children's aggression?

More than 90% of U.S. children play video games, including 97% of adolescents aged 12 to 17 (Lenhart et al., 2008; NPD Group, 2011). It is estimated that more than 85% of video games on the market contain some form of violence (Rideout, 2013). Some of the most popular video games enable users to play roles as car thieves, soldiers in combat, and even criminals who attempt to kill innocent bystanders and thwart police officers with guns, bombs, and flamethrowers. It is no surprise that parents, researchers, and policy makers have concerns about the effects on children of playing violent video games. Does violent video game play increase aggression in children?

Over the past two decades, research has linked violent video game use with parent, teacher, peer, and self-reports of aggressive behavior, as well as observed aggression in children, adolescents, and young adults (Anderson et al., 2010; Ferguson, 2007; Saleem, Anderson, & Gentile, 2012). Use of violent video games is also associated with aggressive emotional responses, such as decreased empathy and higher levels of hostility and desensitization to others' distress (Arriaga, Montiero, & Esteves, 2011; Happ, Melzer, & Steffgen, 2013; Saleem et al., 2012).

One way in which exposure to video game violence may influence aggression is through its influence on cognition. Children and adolescents who play violent video games are more likely to demonstrate hostile expectations and attributions, naturally assuming that others intend to harm them (Hasan, Bègue, Scharkow, & Bushman, 2013). One 3-year study of more than 3,300 children and adolescents (ages 8-17) from Singapore found that violent game play was associated with increases in aggressive cognition in boys and girls, including hostile attribution biases and the belief that aggressive behavior is an appropriate response to provocation (Gentile, Li, Khoo, Prot, & Anderson, 2014). In this study,

playing violent video games predicted aggressive cognition and behavior in children of all ages, regardless of their initial aggressiveness or reports of parental involvement.

Excessive use of violent video games is especially troublesome. For example, a survey of nearly 3,400 Flemish adolescents ages 12 to 18 found that violent video games contributed to delinquent behavior over and beyond multiple known risk variables (e.g., peer delinquency, sensation seeking, prior victimization, and alienation; Exelmans, Custers, & Van den Bulck, 2015). Moreover, the effects were cumulative, with exponential increases (i.e., the negative effects accumulated more rapidly over time).

Although violent video game use has been consistently associated with aggression, some researchers argue that the magnitude of the relation is small and other factors play a larger role in influencing aggressive behavior (Ferguson, 2015; Furuya-Kanamori & Doi, 2016). For example, a study of more than 9,000 8th- and 11th-grade students found an effect of video game use on aggressive behavior, but social and familial background played a larger role in determining risk of violent behavior. Specifically, youth who witnessed actual violence in their homes were at greater risk for engaging in violence (DeCamp & Ferguson, 2017).

Although all behavior is multifaceted and influenced by many factors, exposure to violent video games has consistently been shown to be a factor in predicting aggression in young people. The American Academy of Pediatrics and American Psychological Association have therefore concluded that children must be protected from the negative effects of exposure to violent video games (AAP Council on Communications and Media, 2016; APA Task Force on Violent Media, 2015). The AAP and APA propose that policy makers promote legislation that provides parents with specific information about the content of media, including a parent-centric rating system, and enact laws that prohibit easy access to violent media for minors. Moreover, the AAP and APA advise that media avoid the glamorization of weapon carrying and the normalization of violence as an acceptable means of resolving conflict. Most important, the AAP advises, "video games should not use human or other living targets or award points for killing because this teaches children to associate pleasure and success with their ability to cause pain and suffering to others."

What Do You Think?

1. **What sorts of limits might be placed on children's video game use? Should any games be off limits to children younger than a certain age?**

2. **What advice about video games do you have for parents?**

1. Children's aggressive behavior occurs in context. Identify influences on children's behavior at each of the bioecological levels: microsystem, mesosystem, exosystem, and macrosystem.

2. As a parent, what might you to do lessen the likelihood of your child becoming a bully or a victim of bullying?

3. How might adults distinguish normative from atypical delinquent activity in adolescents?

RELIGION AND SPIRITUALITY

LO 12.5 Describe the typical progression of religiosity or spirituality over the lifespan.

When people define their values and their beliefs about moral and prosocial behavior, they often refer to religion. **Religiosity**, or religiousness, refers to religious involvement, sharing the attitudes and beliefs of a religion, and participating in its practices (e.g., attending religious services or engaging in prayer; George, Ellison, & Larson, 2002). Many people use the terms *religion* and *spirituality* interchangeably, but **spirituality** is a more general term that denotes a search for meaning beyond the self; it may refer to a higher being, such as God, or some other entity, such as nature, or the search for ways to benefit others and society (King & Boyatzis, 2015). Religiosity and spirituality may co-occur, as some individuals seek meaning through religious involvement, but some are spiritual without being religious and others are religious without being spiritual.

RELIGION AND SPIRITUALITY IN CHILDHOOD

Most people have their first experiences with religion in childhood. Children learn about religion through formal education, such as by attending Sunday school and parochial schools. Parents play an important role in religious socialization and encourage their children to adopt the parents' religious beliefs (Power & McKinney, 2013). Most people do grow up to practice the religion of their youth, yet religious development is not simply a matter of passive socialization (Emmons & Paloutzian, 2003). In one study, parents, mainly mothers, of children aged 3 to 12 completed a daily diary chronicling their conversations about religion for 2 weeks (Boyatzis & Janicki, 2003). Parents reported discussing religious and spiritual issues about three times each week, on average. Frequent topics were God, Jesus, and prayer. Similar to findings of cognitive and language development, children were active participants, speaking as often as parents and beginning and concluding about half of the conversations. Children shared their views and asked questions, suggesting that learning about religion is an active process in which children construct meaning (Boyatzis & Janicki, 2003).

ADOLESCENT RELIGION AND SPIRITUALITY

Adolescence has been recognized as a critical phase for religious and spiritual development (King et al., 2015). Many adolescents around the world endorse strong religious beliefs (King & Roeser, 2009; Lippman & Keith, 2006). The marked biological, cognitive, and social changes that adolescents experience prime them to undergo transformations in their religious experience as well as their understanding of religious beliefs, rituals, and community (King, Ramos, & Clardy, 2013).

religiosity Refers to religious involvement, sharing the attitudes and beliefs of a religion, and participating in its practices.

spirituality A more general term than religiosity and denotes a search for meaning beyond the self.

Adolescents often develop strong religious beliefs and interests, such as these boys who are learning about the Koran.

As in childhood, cognitive development fuels changes in religiosity and spirituality. As discussed in Chapter 6, advances in cognitive development lead adolescents to think about the world in new, more complex ways. Adolescents apply abstract reasoning to consider religious concepts and question their beliefs. They may consider spiritual questions, such as the presence of an afterlife, and construct hypotheses that they systematically examine (Good & Willoughby, 2008). Adolescents' ability to consider multiple perspectives on a problem may lead them to realize that there are multiple perspectives on religious and spiritual questions and cause them to consider alternative views.

The questioning that becomes possible with adolescents' new, more sophisticated, cognitive abilities leads adolescents to consider their place in the world, who they are, and who they would like to become. Identity development, a central task for adolescents (Erikson, 1959; Kroger, 2015), often includes questions about the role of religion in their lives (Alisat & Pratt, 2012; Good & Willoughby, 2008). Adolescents consider a variety of beliefs, values, and roles along with existential questions that include a search for meaning or purpose (Damon, Menon, & Cotton Bronk, 2003; King et al., 2013). Now they engage in spiritual endeavors as they attempt to make sense of the world and wrestle with doubt. Just as adolescents raise questions and explore possible identities in other aspects of their lives, many will question their religious traditions and beliefs and explore alternatives to the religious tradition in which they were raised. Yet, the family context is an important factor, as socialization comes from family rituals and conversations about religion. Adolescents are most likely to adopt their parents' views of religion, and are less likely to rebel, when their relationships with parents are warm, close, and marked by trust and acceptance (Hardy, Pratt, Pancer, Olsen, & Lawford, 2011).

Religious commitment during adolescence is associated with a variety of positive outcomes, including prosocial behavior, self-esteem, and well-being (King et al., 2015; Yonker, Schnabelrauch, & DeHaan, 2012). The personality traits of conscientiousness, openness, and agreeableness are positively associated with religiosity (Yonker et al., 2012). Compared with their less religious peers, adolescents who are more religious engage in less risky or problem behaviors, including smoking, truancy, delinquency, and alcohol and substance use (Hardy, Walker, Rackham, & Olsen, 2012; King et al., 2013; Sinha, Cnaan, & Gelles, 2007).

Many people, however, do not commit to religious or spiritual identities during adolescence. Recall that many young people engage in identity development during emerging adulthood. In one national study of nearly 5,500 U.S. students from 39 colleges and universities, Johnson and Hayes (2003) found that more than one-quarter of the students reported experiencing considerable distress as a result of religious or spiritual problems. One-fifth of the students sought help at university counseling centers for managing self-reported moderate distress due to religious and spiritual issues, including confusion about beliefs and values (Johnson & Hayes, 2003). In another study, more than 800 students attending a Christian college showed several patterns of change in religiosity and spirituality over a 4-year period (Hall, Edwards, & Wang, 2016). Some showed rapid declines in religious commitment and acceptance; others showed a steady decline or an initial decline followed by a rebound back toward original or higher levels, and some showed curvilinear patterns of increase and decreases over the college years. Religious and spiritual development is a complex process characterized by individual differences through emerging adulthood and into the adult years.

RELIGION AND SPIRITUALITY IN ADULTHOOD

Nearly three-quarters of U.S. adults report being "absolutely certain" of the existence of God or a similar spiritual entity (Pew Forum on Religious and Public Life, 2008). British samples suggest that over a 20-year period, most older adults show stability in their views of the importance of religion, with nearly all indicating that religion is very important to them (Coleman, Ivani-Chalian, & Robinson, 2004). Adults in the United States were shown to maintain consistent levels of religiosity and spirituality over a 40-year span, from the 1930s to the 1970s (Wink & Dillon, 2002). Other research suggests that, with age, adults experience an increase in religious intensity and strength of beliefs, supporting the role of individual differences in religiosity (Bengtson, Silverstein, Putney, & Harris, 2015). People tend to consider participation in personal religious activity such as prayer more important as they age (see Figure 12.1; Argue, Johnson, & White, 1999; Wink & Dillon, 2002). Adults are also more likely to attend religious services with age, from middle adulthood into late adulthood. Although religious attendance declines in late adulthood, this is likely due to changes in health, mobility, and transportation (Hayward & Krause, 2013).

In North America, low-SES ethnic minority groups, such as African American, Hispanic, Native American, and Canadian Aboriginal elders, show the highest rates of religious participation. For example, African American older adults tend to report higher levels of private religious practice and daily spiritual experiences, as well as perceptions of God as holding a great deal of control over the world, than do their European American counterparts (Krause, 2005;. Lee & Sharpe, 2007). Among U.S. residents, 79% report that religion is very important in their lives, as compared with 56% of the U.S. population overall (Pew Research Center, 2009). For many older adults, the church is a place of worship that enables them to find meaning in their lives. For African American older adults, the church often provides tangible support in the form of social connections, health interventions, and activities that improve welfare. In one study, African American respondents identified God as both their primary source of social support and their personal consultant for health-related matters, whereas European American respondents identified a variety of secular sources of help from family, friends, professionals, and clergy (Lee & Sharpe, 2007). Throughout adulthood, women show higher rates of religiosity and religious participation than men (Levin & Taylor, 1994; Pew Research Center, 2016; Simpson, Cloud, Newman, & Fuqua, 2008). This may be because women find religion helpful in buffering the stresses that accompany juggling multiple roles such as parent, employee, and caregiver. Although adults generally show increases in religiosity and spirituality with age, women tend to show greater increases than men (Wink & Dillon, 2002).

Religiosity in adulthood is positively associated with physical health, including more time exercising, reductions in hypertension, and increased longevity (Boswell, Kahana, & Dilworth-Anderson, 2006; Homan & Boyatzis, 2010; Lee, 2007; Wink, Dillon, & Prettyman, 2007; Ysseldyk, Haslam, & Haslam, 2013). Religiosity and spirituality are also associated with well-being throughout adulthood and especially in older adulthood (Abu-Raiya, Pargament, Krause, & Ironson, 2015; Galek, Flannelly, Ellison, Silton, & Jankowski,

FIGURE 12.1: Importance of Religion in the United States, by Age Group

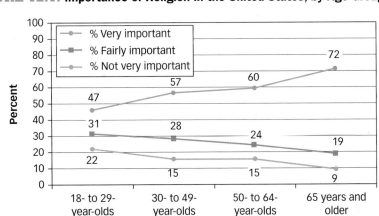

Lives in Context Video 12.2
Religion in Adulthood

2015; Green & Elliott, 2010). A strong sense of religiosity can buffer stress in the face of disadvantages and stressful life events and help older adults to find meaning in life. It is also associated with optimism, a sense of self-worth, life satisfaction, and low rates of depression (Keyes & Reitzes, 2007; Reed & Neville, 2014; Ronneberg, Miller, Dugan, & Porell, 2014; Ysseldyk et al., 2013).

Religious attendance may facilitate mental health through social means by increasing an older adult's connections with other people in the community, both in giving and in receiving support. Church attendance is positively associated with social network size, frequency of social contact, and perceived support (Keyes & Reitzes, 2007; Lee & Sharpe, 2007). One study of nearly 1,200 older adults who attended church regularly found that most—and especially African Americans—perceived increases in the amount of emotional support they gave and received over a 7-year period and were more satisfied with the support they received (Hayward & Krause, 2013). Social engagement and feeling part of a community are important benefits of religious service attendance.

 Thinking in Context 12.5

Recall from Chapter 1 that an important principle of lifespan development is the interaction among multiple domains of development. How might the development of religiosity illustrate the interaction of multiple domains (physical, cognitive, and socioemotional development) over the lifespan?

Apply Your Knowledge

Nikola, a preschool teacher, watches as a toy block whizzes across the room, hitting Lorissa in the side of the head. As another teacher tends to Lorissa, Nikola approaches the culprit, Christopher. Before she can kneel to his level, Christopher exclaims, "I'm sorry! I'm sorry!"

"What are you sorry for?" Nikola asks.

"I don't know."

"Hmm . . . Why is Lorissa crying?"

"I don't know."

"Was she hit with a block?"

"Yes."

"Who threw that block?"

"I don't know."

"Are you sure that you don't know? Did you throw it?"

"Yes. I'm sorry!"

"Why don't we throw blocks, Christopher?"

"We'll go to time out."

"Is there another reason?"

Christopher nods his head. "It's bad."

"Throwing blocks can hurt other children. See how Lorissa is rubbing her head? That block hurt her. See how she's crying?"

"Yes."

"Throwing blocks can hurt our friends."

"Okay."

That afternoon Nikola hears a screech. Christopher has just snatched a toy from Jorge, pushing him.

"Christopher?"

"I'm sorry!"

"Why don't we push other children?"

"Time out. I don't want time out."

"Is there another reason why we don't push?"

Christopher nods his head, "Because the teacher says no."

"All right, but there's another reason why we don't push—a very important reason. Do you know what that is?"

"Hurting?"

"Yes! Exactly. Pushing hurts other children and makes them sad. Do you like being pushed?"

1. How would you characterize Christopher's level of moral reasoning? What stage and level of reasoning does he display?

2. Do you think Christopher's prosocial development is similar to other preschoolers his age?

3. What form of aggression is common to preschoolers? If Christopher is like most preschoolers, how would you expect his aggressive behavior to change as he develops and grows older?

4. How can Christopher's parents and teachers foster prosocial behavior and sophisticated moral reasoning while deterring aggressive behavior? What suggestions can you offer?

Give your students the SAGE edge!

SAGE edge offers a robust online environment featuring an impressive array of free tools and resources for review, study, and further exploration, keeping both instructors and students on the cutting edge of teaching and learning. Learn more at **edge.sagepub.com/kuthertopical.**

CHAPTER 12 IN REVIEW

12.1 Discuss the development of moral reasoning from childhood through adulthood.

SUMMARY

Piaget posed that children's moral reasoning develops in stages, from the morality of constraint in early childhood to the morality of cooperation in middle childhood. Kohlberg proposed that moral reasoning progresses through universal stages that are organized into three broad levels that represent qualitative changes in conceptions of justice. Children first display preconventional reasoning (self-interest). At about age 9 or 10, children demonstrate conventional moral reasoning (internalizing the norms and standards of authority figures). In adolescence, people become capable of demonstrating post-conventional moral reasoning (autonomous decision making from moral principles that value respect for individual and human rights). Research has confirmed that individuals proceed through the first four stages of moral reasoning in a slow, gradual, and predictable fashion. Few people, however, advance beyond Stage 4 moral reasoning.

KEY TERMS

heteronomous morality	post-conventional moral
autonomous morality	reasoning
preconventional reasoning	care orientation
conventional moral reasoning	justice orientation

REVIEW QUESTIONS

1. What is moral reasoning?
2. What are Kohlberg's three stages of moral reasoning?
3. Give examples of how children, adolescents, and adults reason.
4. What are contextual influences on the development of moral reasoning?

12.2 Describe the progression of prosocial behavior, including biological and contextual influences.

SUMMARY

Infants may have a basic sense of empathy well before they have the capacity to demonstrate it. Toddlers as young as 18 months offer instrumental help to others, and show increasingly prosocial responses. Sharing changes in predictable ways, as young children prefer equal distributions of rewards, but school-age children take merit into account and are influenced by empathy, sharing more with needy children. Prosocial behavior tends to increase from school age into adolescence, plateau in early to middle adolescence, and then rise in late adolescence. Prosocial behavior continues through adulthood. Several genes have been implicated in prosocial tendencies. Parents who describe feelings, model the use of language to discuss feelings, and draw attention to models of prosocial behavior foster prosocial behavior in children. Prosocial behavior is also influenced by culture.

KEY TERMS

prosocial behavior	empathy

REVIEW QUESTIONS

1. What is prosocial behavior?
2. When does prosocial behavior emerge?
3. How does it change from childhood into adulthood?
4. What roles do biology and context play in prosocial development?

12.3 Explain how children learn to engage in acceptable behavior.

SUMMARY

Children learn to regulate their behavior through the use of strategies that are aided by advances in neurological and cognitive development. Moral behavior can be acquired in childhood and adolescence through modeling and shaped through reinforcement and punishment. Parents serve as models of moral behavior, but they also influence their children's moral development directly through interactions and disciplinary styles. Children who are punished harshly show higher rates of emotional and social problems than other children. Children learn best when they are reinforced for good behavior. Inductive discipline, methods that use reasoning, are effective alternatives to spanking. The effectiveness of disciplinary techniques may differ by cultural context.

KEY TERMS

discipline	time out
inductive discipline	delay of gratification

REVIEW QUESTIONS

1. How do children learn to regulate their behavior?
2. What is the role of cognitive development, parent-child interactions, and socialization in influencing children's behavior?

12.4 Identify normative patterns of aggressive behavior and influences on atypical aggression during childhood and adolescence.

12.5 Describe the typical progression of religiosity or spirituality over the lifespan.

SUMMARY

Instrumental aggression appears in infancy and increases to around ages 4 or 5. All children will sometimes hit, fight, kick, and take other children's toys. By age 4 to 5 children's language skills improve and physical aggression declines, but verbal aggression becomes more frequent. Adolescents tend to show an increase in delinquent activity in early adolescence that continues into middle adolescence and then declines in late adolescence into early adulthood. Aggression is influenced by both biological (e.g., genetic, brain development) and contextual (e.g., parenting) factors. Exposure to aggressive models also influences children's behavior.

KEY TERMS

antisocial behavior
aggression
instrumental aggression
relational aggression

peer victimization
reactive aggression
bully/victims
conduct disorder

REVIEW QUESTIONS

1. How does aggression shift from infancy and early childhood to later childhood and adolescence?

2. What are some causes of peer victimization and consequences for victims and bullies?

3. What are ways of intervening in bullying?

SUMMARY

Children generally learn about religion through formal education and from their parents. Children often adopt their parents' religious beliefs. Adolescents undergo transformations in their religious experience and understanding of religion and spirituality prompted by their increased cognitive and social abilities. Adults in the United States maintain consistent levels of religiosity and spirituality over the lifespan and attend religious services increasingly with age. Religiosity in adulthood is positively associated with physical health and well-being. Religious attendance may facilitate mental health by increasing an older adults' connections to the community.

KEY TERMS

religiosity

spirituality

REVIEW QUESTIONS

1. What is the difference between religiosity and spirituality?

2. How do religiosity and spirituality change from childhood to adulthood?

3. What are some influences on religious and spiritual development?

Test your understanding of the content.
Review the flashcards and quizzes at
edge.sagepub.com/kuthertopical

Gender and Sexuality

Learning Objectives

13.1 Describe the progression of gender development from infancy through late adulthood, including common stereotypes and sex differences.

13.2 Compare and contrast biological, cognitive, and contextual accounts of gender role development.

13.3 Discuss the development of sexuality and sexual orientation.

13.4 Identify the forms that sexuality and sexual activity take from adolescence through late adulthood, as well as associated health issues.

Digital Resources

▶ Gender Schemas and Play Preferences

◀ Regendering Toys

▶ Transgender Youth

📄 Gender Cognition in Transgender Children

📖 Gaydar

📱 Hook-up Culture

◀ Older Adults and Sex

 **$SAGE edge**™

Master these learning objectives with multimedia resources available at **edge.sagepub.com/kuthertopical** and *Lives in Context* video cases available in the interactive eBook.

When a baby is born, the first question people typically ask is about its biological sex: "Is it a girl or boy?" Why is knowing the baby's sex so important? For friends and relatives who plan to give gifts, the baby's sex may indicate what colors to choose in clothing and other layette items and what kinds of toys they want to encourage the child to play with. In a wide variety of ways, biological sex has an influence on infants' experiences from the moment they are born. A child's biological sex usually also determines his or her gender. Throughout the lifespan, we tend to make generalizations about the gender-typical "masculine" and "feminine" behaviors and traits we expect to see in girls and boys, women and men. In this chapter, we explore developmental changes in how sex and gender are experienced across the lifespan.

GENDER STEREOTYPES, GENDER DIFFERENCES, AND GENDER DEVELOPMENT

LO 13.1 Describe the progression of gender development from infancy through late adulthood, including common stereotypes and sex differences.

What is gender and how it different from sex? Many people use the terms interchangeably, but to developmental scientists, sex and gender have distinct meanings. **Sex** is biological and determined by genetics—specifically, by the presence of a

Y chromosome in the 23rd pair of chromosomes that determine sex—and is indicated by the infants' genitals. **Gender**, on the other hand, is social: It is determined by socialization and the roles that the individual adopts. Most people naturally expect that men and women will behave differently according to their society's gender roles. These expectations sometimes reflect **gender stereotypes**, which are broad generalized judgments of the activities, attitudes, skills, and characteristics deemed appropriate for males or females in a given culture. Gender stereotypes are exaggerated beliefs about what males and females should and should not do. One way to think about it—perhaps an irreverent way—is that sex refers to what is "between one's legs" whereas gender refers to what is "between one's ears."

GENDER STEREOTYPES AND GENDER ROLE NORMS

Most societies have **gender role norms**, normative expectations for males and females that are applied to individuals' everyday behavior. Many such norms derive from women's traditional role as child bearer and caregiver (Best & Williams, 2001). Nurturing the young and forming close family bonds requires emotional regulation skills and sensitivity to others. Expressive traits such as kindness, creativity, gentleness, and cooperation are key characteristics of the feminine gender role, as are physical traits such as being soft, small, and graceful (Bem, 1974). In contrast, the traditional masculine gender role entails instrumental agency—acting on the world to fulfill the role of provider and protector of the family—as well as physical characteristics such as being strong, powerful, and large. Instrumental traits include dominance, independence, and competitiveness. Gender role norms are seen in most cultures. For example, adults in 30 countries generally agree on the instrumental and expressive traits thought to characterize males and females, respectively (Best & Williams, 2001; Guimond, Chatard, & Lorenzi-Cioldi, 2013; Lockenhoff et al., 2014).

Since the 1980s, the roles and activities of women have shifted. In 2016, women represented 47% of the U.S. workforce, compared to 38% in the mid-1980s (U.S. Department of Labor, 2017). Girls' participation in organized sports, traditionally the purview of males, has increased radically. For example, girls accounted for only 7% of high school athletes in 1971–1972; that number is now more than 40% (National Coalition for Women and Girls in Education, 2017). Women earned 40% of bachelor's degrees in the early 1980s as compared with 57% today (National Center for Education Statistics, 2016). Despite these changes, gender stereotypes in the United States have changed little over the past three decades. A recent study compared adults surveyed in the early 1980s with those in the early 2010s and found no change in beliefs about expressive and instrumental traits (Haines, Deaux, & Lofaro, 2016) Across both time periods, women were rated as more communal than men and men as more instrumental than women. Adults in both samples reported similar judgments about male and female stereotyped occupations. Likewise, college students agreed that women should be cheerful, friendly, patient, and emotionally expressive but not stubborn, intimidating, or arrogant, whereas men were expected to be ambitious, assertive, and have strong personalities but not be emotional or approval seeking (Prentice & Carranza, 2002).

Perhaps there is a cultural lag between societal changes, such as women's increasing levels of education, and gender beliefs (Diekman, Brown, Johnston, & Clark, 2010). The depth and durability of gender stereotypes means that even people who explicitly describe themselves as free of gender stereotypes may be implicitly influenced by them (Rudman & Glick, 2001). Gender stereotypes are seen in children as early as 2 years of age and increase during the preschool years as children acquire gender role norms, a process called **gender typing** (Liben, Bigler, & Hilliard, 2013; Carol Lynn Martin & Ruble, 2010). For example, young children attribute characteristics such as "strong" to boys and "helpless" to girls. Children's knowledge of their own gender influences how they see themselves and others. Children tend to describe their own sex in positive terms and the

sex Is biological and determined by genetics.

gender Is determined by socialization and the roles that the individual adopts.

gender stereotypes Refer to broad generalized judgments of the activities, attitudes, skills, and characteristics deemed appropriate for males or females in a given culture.

gender typing The process in which young children acquire the characteristics and attitudes that are considered appropriate for males or females.

other sex in more negative terms. As early as age 2, and consistently from age 3, young children tend to choose same-sex playmates, as well as toys and activities associated with their sex (Jadva, Hines, & Golombok, 2010). From birth, children are immersed in a gendered world that influences how they understand themselves, others, and their world.

Lives in Context Video 13.1
Gender Schemas and Play Preferences

SEX DIFFERENCES

Is there any truth to gender stereotypes? Certainly, males and females after puberty differ in physical attributes such as height, strength, and speed, but thousands of studies have shown that average sex differences in cognitive abilities and social behaviors are small or negligible at all ages (Hyde, 2014; Liben et al., 2013). Moreover, there is much overlap between the sexes and a great deal of variability within each sex, more so than between the sexes (Blakemore, Berenbaum, & Liben, 2009; Hyde, 2016; Miller & Halpern, 2014). In other words, there is a greater number and variety of differences among boys and among girls than there is between boys and girls. Thus, generalizations about males and females should be understood as referring to the average, but not necessarily to any particular individual boy or girl.

Physical Differences

Girls and boys are similar in weight and height and show similar rates of growth in childhood. Yet, at all ages, even before birth, boys tend to be more physically active than girls, and this difference increases during childhood (Alexander & Wilcox, 2012; C. Leaper, 2013). Boys engage in more physical, active play, including rough-and-tumble interactions that involve playful aggression and overall body contact (Scott & Panksepp, 2003). Puberty triggers many sex differences in physical attributes and abilities. After puberty, males tend to be bigger, stronger, and faster than females (Malina, Bouchard, & Bar-Or, 2004). Males continue to show more physical activity than females in adolescence and adulthood (Belcher et al., 2010; Colley et al., 2011).

Cognitive Differences

Many studies have shown no sex differences in intelligence test scores (Halpern & LaMay, 2000). Despite similarities in intelligence scores, decades of research have shown that males and females show subtle differences in several aspects of cognition—specifically, certain aspects of verbal, mathematic, and spatial ability (Ardila, Rosselli, Matute, & Inozemtseva, 2011; Miller & Halpern, 2014).

Sex differences in verbal ability emerge in infancy, as girls begin to talk earlier than boys and have a larger vocabulary than boys through age 5 (Bornstein et al., 2004). In all industrialized countries, girls show a small advantage on reading comprehension and verbal fluency tasks through adolescence (Ardila, Rosselli, Matute, & Inozemtseva, 2011; Miller & Halpern, 2014). Yet these differences disappear as children grow up. Most tests of vocabulary and other verbal abilities show negligible or no sex difference in adults (Hines, 2013; Hyde, 2016).

One consistent difference between males and females lies in a specific type of spatial reasoning task—*mental rotation,* or the ability to recognize a stimulus that is rotated in space (Hines, 2015). As infants, boys are more likely than girls to recognize stimuli that have been rotated (Alexander & Wilcox, 2012; Quinn & Liben, 2014). Males' advantage in mental rotation ability persists across the lifespan (Choi & Silverman, 2003; Roberts & Bell, 2002). Yet sex differences are not apparent on other spatial tasks (Hyde, 2016; Miller & Halpern, 2014).

Boys show higher rates of physical aggression than girls, including play fighting.

Sex differences in math abilities are more complicated. Girls tend to do better at tests of computational mathematics skills through adolescence (Hyde, 2014; Wei et al., 2012). However, in adolescence boys tend to perform better at tasks measuring mathematical reasoning (Byrnes & Takahira, 1993; Leahey & Guo, 2001). Yet boys and girls do not differ in their understanding of math concepts (Hines, 2015). Some sex differences have become smaller in recent decades. For example, boys used to earn much higher scores on standardized math tests such as the Scholastic Aptitude Test (SAT), which is commonly administered in U.S. high schools. The sex difference has markedly reduced over the past three decades such that boys show a negligible advantage (Hyde, 2016; Lindberg, Hyde, Petersen, & Linn, 2010). This shift in mathematics performance accompanies the increasing emphasis by educational institutions, government, and industry on encouraging females to enter careers in the sciences (Ceci, Ginther, Kahn, & Williams, 2014; Dasgupta & Stout, 2014).

Socioemotional Differences

From an early age, girls are better able to manage and express their emotions than boys. For example, at 6 months of age, males have more difficulty than girls at regulating their emotions in frustrating or ambiguous situations (Weinberg, Tronick, Cohn, & Olson, 1999). In infancy, childhood, and adolescence, girls are more accurate at identifying facial expressions, such as happy or sad, than are boys (Alexander & Wilcox, 2012; Thompson & Voyer, 2014). Although girls tend to express happiness and sadness more often than boys, boys express more anger (Chaplin & Aldao, 2013). Girls also express shame and guilt, complex emotions that rely on cognitive and social development (see Chapter 10), more often than boys (Else-Quest, Higgins, Allison, & Morton, 2012). Throughout adulthood, females tend to express a greater range of emotions more intensely than do males (Birditt & Fingerman, 2003; Chaplin, 2015; Zimmermann & Iwanski, 2014).

Beginning at preschool age, boys tend to exhibit more physical and verbal aggression whereas girls tend to demonstrate more relational aggression—excluding a peer from social activities, withdrawing friendship, spreading rumors, or humiliating the person—than do boys (Card, Stucky, Sawalani, & Little, 2008; Ostrov & Godleski, 2010). Gender differences in aggression have been observed as early as 17 months of age (Hyde, 2014). Boys and girls also differ in inhibitory control, from as early as 3 months of age (Else-Quest, Hyde, Goldsmith, & Van Hulle, 2006). Differences in activity and the ability to restrain impulses likely play a role in sex differences in terms of aggression. Throughout childhood, adolescence, and adulthood, males tend to demonstrate higher rates of impulsivity (Cross, Copping, & Campbell, 2011).

Among adults, gender differences in socioemotional development vary somewhat with culture. Costa, Terracciano, and McCrae (2001) examined sex differences in five broad personality factors (recall the Big 5 theory of personality discussed in Chapter 11). Results with more than 23,000 adults revealed that sex differences are relatively small overall, but quite consistent across nations: Women were generally higher in self-reported neuroticism, agreeableness, and warmth, whereas men were higher in assertiveness and dominance, and such differences did not vary with age. However, there were some important variations across cultures. Gender differences were greatest in highly individualistic cultures that emphasize autonomy and equality, such as European and American cultures, and weakest among collectivistic cultures that emphasize interdependence, such as African and Asian cultures. Similarly, Fischer and Manstead (2000) studied people from 37 countries and found larger gender differences in the expression of emotions in individualistic than in collectivistic cultures, with women in individualistic, but not collectivistic, cultures expressing more stereotyped emotions (joy, sadness, guilt) than men. One interpretation of these findings is that men in individualistic cultures may be especially likely to minimize emotional expressions because expressing emotions might threaten the control that is critical to their status. Overall, the greatest gender differences between males and females lie in socioemotional functioning; however, even in this domain they are more alike than different.

GENDER DEVELOPMENT IN INFANCY

From birth, infants observe their world and actively process their observations. Studies using habituation and preferential looking (see Chapter 4) demonstrate that infants as early as 3 months of age distinguish male and female faces (Quinn, Yahr, Kuhn, Slater, & Pascalis, 2002). By about 6 months of age, infants can discriminate voices by sex and show intermodal matching, associating male voices with male faces and female voices with female faces (Patterson & Werker, 2002). By 10 months, infants associate faces of men and women with gender-typed objects (e.g., hammer and frying pan; Levy & Haaf, 1994), suggesting early gender stereotypes. In one study, about half of 18-month-old girls showed knowledge of gender labels ("man" and "lady"), looking longer at corresponding photographs of males or females, but boys did not (Poulin-Dubois, Serbin, & Derbyshire, 1998). In addition, about half of 18- and 24-month-old boys and girls looked longer at a photograph of a boy after hearing "boy" but did not show recognition of the verbal label "girl." Most 24- and 28-month-old children select the correct picture in response to gender labels provided by an experimenter (Campbell, Shirley, & Caygill, 2002; Levy, 1999).

Young infants may not understand gender, but they show more interest in toys that match their biological sex. In one study of 3- to 8-month-old infants, boys looked longer at a toy truck than a doll, whereas girls looked longer at the doll (Alexander, Wilcox, & Woods, 2009). Three-month-old babies are too young to understand what gender means, but these findings suggest early preferences.

When do infants recognize their own sex? Infants develop a basic awareness of their own "self" at roughly 18 months, including whether they are male or female (Martin, Ruble, & Szkrybalo, 2002). By around 2 to 2½ years, children label their own sex, referring to themselves as "boy" or "girl" (Campbell, Shirley, & Candy, 2004). As children develop a sense of gender, they actively seek information about gender, expand their knowledge of gender stereotypes, and demonstrate more stereotyping (Martin & Ruble, 2010). Sex differences in toy preferences increase (Jadva et al., 2010). By 18 to 24 months of age, many toddlers will not play with toys associated with the opposite sex even when there are no other toys available (Caldera, Huston, & O'Brien, 1989). Boys show gender-stereotyped behavior at an earlier age than do girls (Servin, Bohlin, & Berlin, 1999), even though their gender stereotypic knowledge lags behind that of girls (Bussey, 2013).

GENDER DEVELOPMENT IN CHILDHOOD

Twenty-eight-month-old Conrad lunged for the toy truck while his twin sister, Candee, clutched her baby doll. From 2 years of age, young children show rigid beliefs about how boys and girls should act and what they should play with (Freeman, 2007; Halim, Ruble, Tamis-LeMonda, & Shrout, 2013; Poulin-Dubois, Serbin, Eichstedt, Sen, & Beissel, 2002). Their knowledge of gender stereotypes expands during early childhood. By 5 or 6 years of age, children have extensive knowledge of the activities and interests stereotyped for males and females (Blakemore et al., 2009) that are expressed as rigid rules about the behavior appropriate for boys and girls (Baker, Tisak, & Tisak, 2016). Preschoolers expect males to be independent, forceful, and competitive and females to be warm, nurturing, and expressive (Martin et al., 2013; Miller, Trautner, & Ruble, 2006; Tisak, Holub, & Tisak, 2007). Gender stereotypes appear in many countries, but they vary in intensity. For example, in one study of children in 25 countries, high rates of gender stereotyping and stereotyped beliefs were observed in Pakistan, New Zealand, and England, whereas stereotypes were very low in Brazil, Taiwan, Germany, and France (Williams & Best, 1982). Preschoolers often apply gender stereotypes as rigid rules, with more than half of 3- and 4-year-old children agreeing that gender stereotypes for clothing (wearing a dress), hairstyle (long hair), and toys (Barbie doll and GI Joe) cannot be violated (Blakemore, 2003). It would not be surprising, then, if the 4-year-old twins Conrad and Candee agreed that doctors are always boys and nurses must be girls.

Similar to infancy, young children's knowledge of their own gender influences their preferences for toys, activities, and playmates (Hines, 2015). Boys tend to prefer toys such as vehicles and weapons and prefer rough-and-tumble games, whereas girls prefer dolls, tea sets, and organized games (Campbell et al., 2002; Maccoby & Jacklin, 1974). Children prefer same-sex peers. At 4½ years of age, children spend about three times as much time with same-sex peers as with opposite-sex peers, and this difference increases to 10 times by 6.5 years of age (Hines, 2013; Maccoby & Jacklin, 1987). The tendency of children to play with others of the same sex is seen in a range of cultures (Whiting & Whiting, 1975). Children also expect gender-stereotypical play from their peers. In one study, most of the 3- to 6-year-old children surveyed reported not wanting to be friends with nonconforming children, such as boys who wear nail polish or girls who play with trucks (Ruble et al., 2007). Older children broaden their gender-stereotypic knowledge beyond activities and physical appearance to include personality traits and characteristics (Heyman & Legare, 2004).

There is continuity in gender beliefs—that is, children's preferences remain stable over time (Dunham, Baron, & Banaji, 2016). Children with more gender-stereotypical play and activity preferences than peers at 2½ years remained the most gender stereotypical at age 5 (Golombok et al., 2008). Children tend to be most rigid about adhering to gender-stereotypic beliefs at about age 5 or 6, as they enter elementary school. In middle childhood, knowledge of stereotypes expands to include beliefs about personality and achievement (Bussey, 2013; Serbin, Powlishta, & Gulko, 1993). As with toys, stereotypes influence children's preferences and views of their own abilities. For example, by age 6 girls are less likely than boys to believe that members of their gender are "really, really smart." Also at age 6, girls begin to avoid activities said to be for children who are "really, really smart," lump more boys into the "really, really smart" category, and steer themselves away from games intended for the "really, really smart." (Bian, Leslie, & Cimpian, 2017). Elementary school children describe reading, spelling, art, and music as appropriate subjects for girls and mathematics and athletics as for boys (Cvencek, Meltzoff, & Greenwald, 2011; Kurtz-Costes, Copping, Rowley, & Kinlaw, 2014; Passolunghi, Rueda Ferreira, & Tomasetto, 2014).

As shown in Figure 13.1, gender rigidity tends to peak and decline in middle to late childhood (Ruble et al., 2007; Trautner et al., 2005). However, becoming more open-minded

FIGURE 13.1: Developmental Changes in Gender Constancy and Rigidity

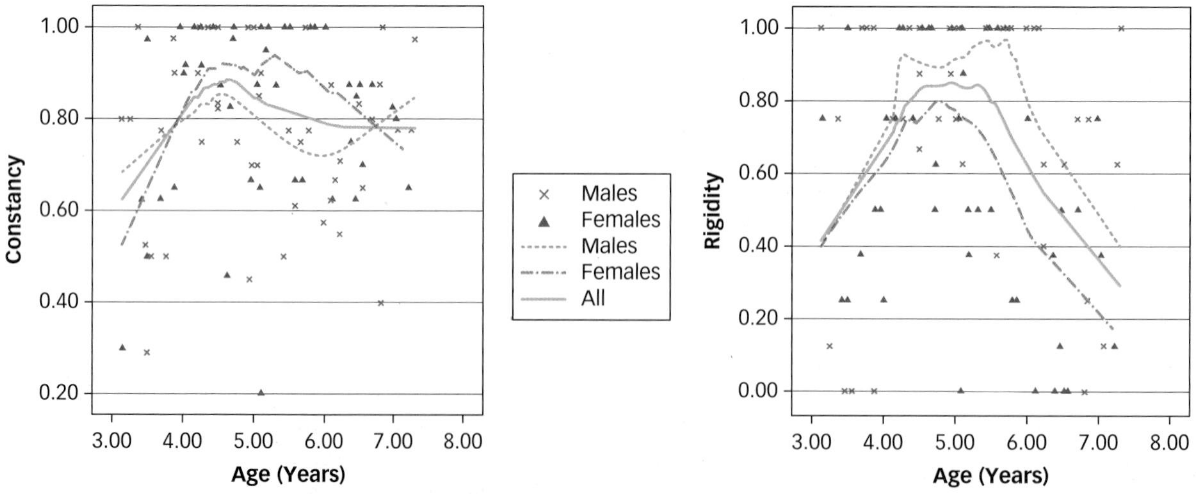

From (Ruble et al., 2007) [left is constancy; right is rigidity]

about boys' and girls' gendered behavior does not mean that school-age children approve of violating gender stereotypes. School-age children remain intolerant to certain violations, especially boys playing with dolls or wearing dresses and girls playing noisily and roughly, which they rate as severely as moral violations (Blakemore, 2003; Levy, Taylor, & Gelman, 1995). Yet advances in cognitive development enable older children to understand that gender-stereotyped traits are associated with gender, not defined by gender (Banse, Gawronski, Rebetez, Gutt, & Bruce Morton, 2010; Martin et al., 2002). This trend toward flexibility in views of what males and females can do increases with age, with girls showing more flexible gender-stereotype beliefs than boys (Blakemore et al., 2009).

GENDER DEVELOPMENT IN ADOLESCENCE

In early adolescence, boys and girls experience dramatic physical, cognitive, and social changes. Physical development takes center stage and adolescents think about themselves in new ways, are treated differently by others, and often become acutely aware of their appearance as their bodies become adult-like. The onset of puberty often heightens boys' and girls' awareness of sex differences and gender becomes a more relevant label. Young adolescents become increasingly sensitive to gender stereotypes and their behavior is likely to adhere to gender stereotypes, a phenomenon referred to as the gender intensification hypothesis (Galambos, Berenbaum, & McHale, 2009; Priess & Lindberg, 2016). Although adolescents' thinking becomes more flexible and abstract, their views about gender roles become more rigid and their thinking adheres to strict gender stereotypes. Similar to young children, adolescents tend to negatively evaluate peers who violate expectations for gendered behavior by, for example, engaging in behaviors or expressing interests stereotyped for the other sex (Alfieri, Ruble, & Higgins, 1996; Sigelman, Carr, & Begley, 1986; Toomey, Card, & Casper, 2014).

Social pressures may also drive adolescents toward more gender-stereotypic behavior (Galambos et al., 2009). As they begin to date, many adolescents feel it is important to act in gender-consistent ways that are approved of by peers. Boys who are perceived as less masculine and girls as less feminine than peers may feel less accepted, be less popular, and experience higher rates of victimization (Smith & Leaper, 2006; Toomey et al., 2014). Some researchers, however, question whether all adolescents experience gender intensification (Priess & Lindberg, 2016). Research findings examining the gender intensity hypothesis are mixed. For example, Galambos, Almeida, and Petersen (1990) found that sex differences in instrumental (masculine) qualities, such as independence and leadership, increased in early adolescence, but sex differences in expressive (stereotypically feminine) qualities, such as sensitivity and kindness, did not. Similarly, a longitudinal study found that adolescents did not become more stereotypical in their gender role identity during adolescence, suggesting that patterns of gender socialization may have shifted in recent decades, perhaps voiding the gender intensification hypothesis (Priess, Lindberg, & Hyde, 2009). In present-day society, boys are free to be more expressive and girls are encouraged to be more independent than they were in the past (Steensma, Kreukels, de Vries, & Cohen-Kettenis, 2013). By late adolescence, even young people who earlier displayed gender intensification tend to become more flexible in their thinking and adoption of gender roles.

GENDER ROLES IN ADULTHOOD

Adults' views of gender and the roles they adopt tend to shift over the lifespan. Some theorists argue that adult gender roles are shaped by the *parental imperative*, the need for mothers and fathers to adopt different roles in order to successfully raise children (Gutmann, 1985). In many cultures, young and middle-aged men emphasize their ability to feed and protect families, characteristics that rely on traditionally masculine traits, while young and middle-aged women emphasize their potential to nurture the young and care for families, traditional female traits.

Although today most men and women in developed nations express more flexible views of gender than traditional roles dictate (Brooks & Bolzendahl, 2004; Twenge, 1997), parenthood often signals a shift in couples' behavior and division of labor. Most couples adopt traditional roles after the birth of a child (Schober, 2013; Yavorsky, Dush, & Schoppe-Sullivan, 2015); for example, couples tend to agree that mothers do more of the housework and the fathers do less (Goldberg & Perry-Jenkins, 2004; Katz-Wise, Priess, & Hyde, 2010). In one study that followed 205 first-time and 198 experienced mothers and fathers from 5 months pregnant to 12 months postpartum, parents became more traditional in their gender role attitudes and behavior following the child's birth; for example, mothers did more of the housework than fathers (Katz-Wise et al., 2010; see Figure 13.2). Overall, women showed greater changes in gender role attitudes and behavior than did men, and first-time parents changed more than experienced parents. Gender differences in couples' division of labor continue throughout childhood. For example, the American Time Use Survey found that in most couples the mother typically spends about twice as much time as the father on both housework and childcare, whereas fathers spend more time working outside the home (37 hours as compared with 21 hours for mothers; Parker & Wang, 2013). However, it should be noted that fathers today spend twice as much time doing household chores than in 1965 (from an average of about 4 hours per week in 1965 to about 10 hours per week today), suggesting a shift in perceived responsibility (Parker & Wang, 2013).

As children grow up and leave the nest, adults' activities shift away from parenting. Some theorists argue that as adults are freed of the parental imperative they become less tied to traditional gender roles (Gutmann, 1985). During the middle adult years, **gender identity**, individuals' identification with the masculine or feminine gender role, tends to become more fluid and integrated. Many middle-aged adults begin to integrate masculine and feminine aspects of themselves, becoming more similar and more androgynous (James & Lewkowicz, 1995). That is, men begin to adopt more traditionally feminine characteristics, such as being sensitive, considerate, and dependent; and women adopt more traditionally masculine characteristics, such as confidence, self-reliance, and assertiveness (Huyck, 1996). In one study that followed a representative sample of third-grade Finnish children for 30 years (Pulkkinen, Feldt, & Kokko, 2005), boys and girls adopted traditional gender characteristics in adolescence, but by age 40 the men had become less

FIGURE 13.2: Changes in Gender Role Attitudes Among Mothers and Fathers, Before Birth to 1 Year Postpartum

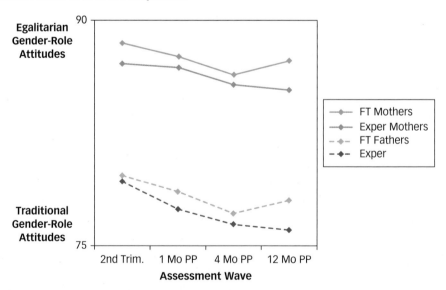

From Katz-Wise 2010: Katz Caption: Changes in gender role attitudes, for first-time (FT) and experienced (Exper) mothers and fathers across four assessment waves from pre-birth to one year postpartum: second trimester (2nd Tri), one month postpartum (1 Mo PP), four months postpartum (4 Mo PP), and 12 months postpartum (12 Mo PP).

gender identity One's image of oneself as masculine or feminine, embodying the roles and behaviors that society associates with males and females.

aggressive and more conforming in contrast to the women, who showed a reverse pattern of becoming more assertive. Longitudinal research following adults from their 30s to 80s mirrors this finding: Although there are individual differences, the average man, initially low in femininity, becomes significantly higher in femininity across the lifespan; the average woman, initially high in femininity, becomes significantly lower in femininity across the lifespan (Jones, Peskin, & Livson, 2011). This pattern of gender convergence increases in middle adulthood in Western nations as well as in nonwestern cultures, such as the Mayan people of Guatemala and the Druze of the Middle East (Fry, 1985).

Androgyny, integrating masculine and feminine characteristics, provides adults with a greater repertoire of skills for meeting the demands of middle and late adulthood. Middle-aged women who may be newly independent after experiencing divorce, death of a partner, or the end of childrearing may enter the workplace, seek advancement in current careers, or enroll in college. Successfully meeting these new challenges requires self-reliance, assertiveness, and confidence. Men, on the other hand, may become more sensitive and self-reflective as they complete generative tasks of mentoring and caring for the next generation. A great deal of research has shown that androgyny predicts positive adjustment and is associated with high self-esteem, advanced moral reasoning, psycho-social maturity, and life satisfaction in later years (Bem, 1985; Lefkowitz & Zeldow, 2006; Pilar Matud, Bethencourt, & Ibáñez, 2014). Men and women with androgynous gender roles have a greater repertoire of skills, both instrumental and expressive, which permits them to adapt to a variety of situations with greater ease than do those who adopt either a masculine or feminine gender role.

 Thinking in Context 13.1

1. How might contextual factors contribute to the sex differences that we see in cognitive and socioemotional development? How might parents, teachers, peers, and environments influence sex differences?

2. Why do rigid views of gender roles increase and peak in childhood, declining thereafter? Why do children view gender in extremely strict terms and why do their views change?

3. Adult gender development is linked with roles and contexts. Agree or disagree? Explain your reasoning given the discussion thus far.

INFLUENCES ON GENDER DEVELOPMENT

LO 13.2 Compare and contrast biological, cognitive, and contextual accounts of gender role development.

Three year-old Camila calls out, "I want the pink dress, just like a princess." Demarco pushes his truck and proclaims, "This monster truck is going to drive over the battlefield." Ask any adult and they will likely tell you that boys and girls are very different. Yet we have seen that boys and girls show reliable differences in only a few domains of development. However, boys and girls do, on average, adopt different gender roles. How do we explain the acquisition of gender roles? Several theoretical perspectives offer explanations of gender typing. Some lean more toward nature-oriented or biological explanations. Others use cognitive explanations, and still others turn to contextual explanations. A sufficient explanation of gender development integrates aspects of each theory.

BIOLOGICAL EXPLANATIONS

Because most cultures have similar gender roles, sex differences may be a function of biology (Whiting & Edwards, 1988). Biological explanations point to the role of evolution

androgyny The gender identity of those who score high on both masculine and feminine characteristics.

and look to differences in biological structures, especially the brain, as well as hormones as contributors to sex differences in psychological and behavioral functioning (Hines, 2015).

From an evolutionary perspective, males adapted to become aggressive and competitive because these traits were advantageous in securing a mate and thereby passing along their genetic inheritance (Côté, 2009). Females became more nurturing as it was adaptive to care for the young to ensure that their genes survived to be passed along to the next generation. In support of this evolutionary perspective, most mammalian species demonstrate a preference for same-sex playmates, males are more active and aggressive, and females are more nurturing (Beatty, 1992; de Waal, 1993). These behaviors suggest that such gender differences in behavior are adaptive across species, including our own.

Gender differences begin at conception with the union of sex chromosomes, either XX (female) or XY (male). Genetic information on the Y chromosome leads to the formation of testes, and the subsequent production of testosterone results in the formation of the male genitals and reproductive system. Estrogens in the absence of testosterone lead to the formation of the female reproductive system (Sadler, 2015). In animals, testosterone produced prenatally influences neural survival and neural connectivity, leading to subtle sex differences in brain structure and function (Nugent & McCarthy, 2011).

Boys' and girls' behavior may also be explained by hormonal differences. Animal and human studies have demonstrated that exposure to relatively high levels of testosterone promotes male-typical behavior development. When females are exposed to male sex hormones prenatally (e.g., in the case of congenital adrenal hyperplasia, a genetic disorder that causes excess androgen production beginning prenatally) they show more active play and fewer caregiving activities in early childhood, as compared with their female peers (Auyeung et al., 2009; Hines et al., 2016). Testosterone is linked with aggression. Higher levels of testosterone, prenatally and after birth, can account for boys' tendency to be more aggressive than girls. Hormonally influenced differences in behavioral styles then influence play styles; children choose to play with children who have similar styles, resulting in a preference for same-sex playmates (Berenbaum, Blakemore, & Beltz, 2011). In this way, biological factors influence the behaviors that are associated with gender roles. Other explanations for gender role development rely on understanding children's thinking, as described in the next section.

COGNITIVE-DEVELOPMENTAL EXPLANATIONS

From the cognitive-developmental perspective, children's understanding of gender is constructed in the same manner as their understanding of the world: by interacting with people and things and thinking about their experiences. As mentioned previously in this chapter, infants as young as 3 to 4 months of age distinguish between female and male faces (Quinn et al., 2002). Most children develop the ability to label gender groups and to use gender labels in their speech between 18 and 24 months of age (Martin & Ruble, 2010).

Gender identity, awareness of whether one is a boy or a girl, occurs at about age 2 (Bussey, 2013). Once children label themselves as male or female, they classify the world around them, as well as their own behaviors, according to those labels (e.g., like me, not like me; Kohlberg, 1966). In this way, children construct their own understandings of what it means to be a boy or a girl and thereby begin to acquire gender roles (Levy & Carter, 1989). By 2 to 2½ years of age, once children have established gender identity, they show more interest in gender-appropriate toys (e.g., dolls for girls, cars for boys) and they show a preference for playing with children of their own sex (Zosuls et al., 2009).

Recently, increased attention has been drawn to **transgender** children—those who do not identify with their biological sex but instead adopt an opposite-sex identity. Although there is much to learn, a recent study compared transgender and gender-conforming children on cognitive measures of gender preferences (Olson, Key, & Eaton, 2015). Transgender children showed a clear preference for peers and objects endorsed by peers who shared their expressed gender and an explicit and implicit identity that aligned with

transgender Refers to those who do not identify with their biological sex but instead adopt an opposite-sex identity.

their expressed gender. Their implicit preference responses were indistinguishable from those of other children, when matched by gender identity. Although transgender issues have received a great deal of attention in the media and courts, a transgender identity is rare. About .5% to 1% of the population of adults identify themselves as transgender (Conron, Scott, Stowell, & Landers, 2012; Gates, 2011), although the true figure may be higher. One nationally representative survey of adolescents in New Zealand (nearly 8,200 individuals) found that 1.2% of participants identified themselves as transgender and 2.5% reported not being sure about their gender (Clark et al., 2014). Although the prevalence of transgender identity is still not well documented, the vast majority of children adopt a gender identity that is congruent with their biological sex. The Lives in Context feature provides additional information about transgender children and adolescents.

By about age 3, children acquire **gender stability**, the understanding that gender does not change over time. However, they do not yet understand gender as a biological construct; instead, their conceptions of gender are based on external behaviors and traits. Therefore, children think it is possible for gender to change with a change in hairstyle or dress. Recall from Chapter 6 that young children's thinking is often limited by centration, the tendency to focus on only one aspect of a stimulus. For example, children who watched as a dog mask was placed on a cat believed that the animal now looked like and in fact was a dog. They focused on only one aspect of the stimulus: the animal's head. Likewise, children who have acquired gender stability focus on appearance and therefore tend to believe that wearing a dress, for example, can change a child from boy to girl.

Between ages 3 and 5, after acquiring gender stability, children show an increase in stereotype knowledge, evaluate their own gender more positively, and tend to show more rigidly sex-typed behaviors (Halim et al., 2013). In one study of diverse children from Mexican, Chinese, Dominican, and African American ethnic backgrounds, gender stereotypes held at age 4 predicted positive same-gender attitudes and gender-stereotyped behavior at age 5 (Halim, Ruble, Tamis-LeMonda, Shrout, & Amodio, 2017). The more positively children view their own gender and the more they understand that gender categories remain stable over time, the more likely girls are to insist on wearing dresses, and the more likely boys are to refuse to wear anything with a hint of femininity (Halim et al., 2014). In contrast, positive other-gender attitudes are associated with flexible thoughts about gender appropriateness and gender-related cognition and nongender biased behavior (Halim, Ruble, Tamis-LeMonda, Shrout, & Amodio, 2017).

Only toward the end of the preschool years, when children come to understand Piagetian conservation tasks, do children come to realize that a boy will always be a boy, even if he grows long hair and wears a skirt; and a girl will remain a girl no matter what she wears or which activities she chooses. **Gender constancy** refers to the child's understanding that gender does not change; that he or she will always be the same regardless of appearance, activities, or attitudes (Kohlberg, 1966). Gender constancy may further gender typing as children become more aware of and pay more attention to gender norms (Arthur, Bigler, & Ruble, 2009). For example, preschool-age boys who have achieved gender constancy or are close to achieving it tend to focus on male characters, as well as watching more sports programs on television than preschool-age boys who have not achieved gender constancy (Luecke-Aleksa, Anderson, Collins, & Schmitt, 1995). Awareness that a person's sex is a biological characteristic occurs around 8 years of age (Ruble et al., 2007).

Once children develop the ability to label their sex, they begin to form a **gender schema**, which is a concept or a mental structure that organizes gender-related information and embodies their understanding of what it means to be a male or female. Researchers have proposed **gender schema theory**, a cognitive explanation of gender role development, similar to Piaget's concept of schemes, which emphasizes information processing and environmental influences (Martin, Ruble, & Szkrybalo, 2002). A child's gender schema becomes an organizing principle and children notice more and more differences between males and females, such as preferred clothes, toys, and activities. Children also notice that their culture classifies males and females as different and encompassing different roles.

gender stability In Kohlberg's view, young children's recognition that gender does not change over time, though it is not yet understood as a biological construct but rather based on external traits and behaviors.

gender constancy A child's understanding of the biological permanence of gender and that it does not change regardless of appearance, activities, or attitudes.

gender schema A concept or a mental structure that organizes gender-related information and embodies their understanding of what it means to be a male or female.

gender schema theory An approach to gender typing that emphasizes information processing and environmental influences that influence the development of gender-related beliefs, which then guide children's behaviors and attitudes.

© iStockPhoto.com/f8grapher

Lives in Context Video 13.2
Transgender Youth

• • Transgender Children and Adolescents

Josie Romero is a transgender child who was born a boy called Joey Romero.

By 2 years of age, most children begin to identify with gender, labeling themselves as "boy" or "girl." This early sense of gender identity tends to intensify with development. However, a small minority of children experience incongruence between their gender identity and their genital anatomy, their biological sex. That is, some boys feel that they are really girls and some girls feel that they are really boys. Transgender individuals have a gender identity that does not fully correspond with their biological sex.

We have seen that parents, peers, and teachers generally discourage gender nonconformity in children, especially boys who show interest in girls' activities and toys. Transgender children resist such pressure, insisting on their true gender identity. While in the past parents may have ignored children's wishes or outright prohibited them from adopting a transgender identity, some parents today adopt a different approach, permitting their children to "socially transition" to the gender identity that feels right to them. This type of social transitioning is reversible and nonmedical. It entails changing the pronouns used to describe a child, changes in appearance, including hair and clothing, and often changing the child's name. In this way, children appear to be and are raised as their gender identity rather than their biological sex.

Whether or not parents should support children's desire to live presenting as their gender identity is hotly debated (Steensma & Cohen-Kettenis, 2011; Zucker, Wood, Singh, & Bradley, 2012). The few studies that have examined transgender children have found that children who have not socially transitioned reported increased rates of anxiety and depression, with more than 50% of older children in some samples falling in the clinical range of internalizing symptoms (Ryan, Russell, Huebner, Diaz, & Sanchez, 2010; Simons, Schrager, Clark, Belzer, & Olson, 2013). Yet studies of transitioned transgender children suggest levels of depression and anxiety comparable to gender-matched controls and overall norms (Olson, Durwood, DeMeules, & McLaughlin, 2016). There is growing evidence that social support is linked to better mental health outcomes among transgender adolescents and adults (Durwood, McLaughlin, & Olson, 2017). These findings suggest the possibility that social transitions in children, a form of affirmation and support by a prepubescent child's parents, could be associated with good mental health outcomes in transgender children (Fuss, Auer, & Briken, 2015; Ryan et al., 2010). A sense of acceptance and the ability to live as one's perceived gender may buffer stresses that tend to accompany gender nonconformity.

In contrast to social transition, biological transition is a medical process. It typically involves both developmental changes, induced by means of hormone therapy, and permanent changes to the external genitals, accomplished by means of gender-reassignment surgery.

Children who identify as transgender, in consultation with their parents and pediatrician, may take medication to delay the onset of puberty and the reproductive maturation that goes with it. Postponing puberty provides the child with additional time to socially transition, decide whether biological transition is the right decision for them, and to make a mature, informed choice.

What Do You Think?

What is entailed in a child's transition to a transgender identity? What changes must take place for a child to socially transition? What challenges might transgender children face along the way?

Children then use their gender schemas as guides for their behavior and attitudes, and gender typing occurs. For example, when given gender-neutral toys, children first try to figure out whether they were boys or girls' toys and then decide whether they would play with them (Martin, Eisenbud, & Rose, 1995; Martin et al., 2002). When told that an attractive toy is for the opposite sex, children will avoid playing with it and expect same-sex peers to avoid it as well (Miller et al., 2006; Weisgram, 2016). Young children play with

Barcroft/Barcroft Media/Getty Images

peers who engage in similar levels of gender-typed activities (e.g., playing dress up, playing with tools) and, over time, engage in increasingly similar levels of gender-typed activities, contributing to sex segregation in children's play groups (Martin et al., 2013).

Gender schemas are such an important organizing principle that they can influence children's memory. For example, preschool children tend to notice and recall information that is consistent with their gender schemas (Liben et al., 2013). Children who see others behaving in gender inconsistent ways, such as a boy baking cookies or a girl playing with toy trucks, often will misrecall the event, distorting it in ways that are gender consistent, or they may not even recall gender-inconsistent information (Signorella & Liben, 1984). It is not until around age 8 that children notice and recall information that contradicts their gender schemas. Yet even elementary school children have been shown to misrecall gender-inconsistent story information (Frawley, 2008). Clearly, children's knowledge and beliefs about gender and gender roles influence their own gender role and behavior. However, the world around the child also holds implications for gender role development. Terms that pertain to gender role development are summarized in Table 13.1.

TABLE 13.1 • Gender Role Development: Terms

TERM	DEFINITION
Gender differences	Psychological or behavioral differences between males and females
Gender constancy	The understanding that gender remains the same throughout life, despite superficial changes in appearance or attitude
Gender identity	A person's awareness of being a male or female
Gender role	The behaviors and attitudes deemed appropriate for a given gender
Gender schema	A mental structure that organizes gender-related information
Gender stability	The understanding that gender generally does not change over time; however, superficial changes in appearance might bring a change in gender
Gender typing	The process of acquiring gender roles

CONTEXTUAL EXPLANATIONS

A contextual approach to understanding gender development emphasizes social learning and the influence of the sociocultural context in which children are raised. According to this approach, gender typing occurs through socialization, through a child's interpretation of the world around him or her, influenced by parents, peers, teachers, and culture. Social learning theory contributes the importance of models in acquiring gender-typical behavior (Bandura & Bussey, 2004). Children observe models—typically the same-sex parent, but also peers, other adults, and even characters in stories and television programs. They use models as guides to their own behavior, resulting in gender-typed behavior. Feedback from others serves as reinforcement. Sometimes parents or other adults will directly teach a child about gender-appropriate behavior or provide positive reinforcement for behaving in sex-consistent ways: Boys get approval for building bridges and running fast, whereas girls get approval for preparing a make-believe meal or keeping a pretty dress neat.

Parents

Gender socialization begins in infancy. Boys and girls have different social experiences from birth (Martin & Ruble, 2010). Parents perceive sons and daughters differently and have different expectations for them. For example, parents often describe competition, achievement, and activity as important for sons and warmth, politeness, and closely supervised activities as important for daughters (Turner & Gervai, 1995). Many parents encourage their children to play with gender-appropriate toys. Boys tend to receive toys that emphasize action and competition, such as cars, trains, and sports equipment, and girls tend to receive toys that focus on cooperation, nurturance, and physical attractiveness, such as baby dolls, Easy-Bake Ovens, and play makeup (Hanish et al., 2013). In one study, 3- and 5-year-old children were asked to identify "girl toys" and "boy toys" and then asked to predict parents' reactions to their preferences about gender-specific toys

Girls are more often encouraged to engage in gender atypical play, such as with trucks, than boys

and behaviors (Freeman, 2007). Children predicted that parents would approve of their playing with gender-stereotyped toys and disapprove of choices to play with cross-gender toys.

Gender-consistent behavior is socially regulated through approval. Parents tend to encourage boys' independent play, demands for attention, and even attempts to take toys from other children, whereas parents tend to direct girls' play, provide assistance, refer to emotions, and encourage girls to participate in household tasks (Basow, 2008; Hines, 2015). Boys tend to be reinforced for independent behavior whereas girls are reinforced for behavior emphasizing closeness and dependency. Mothers even differ in how they discuss emotions with girls and boys. Mothers label emotions for girls, teaching them to identify others' feelings; with boys they tend to explain about emotions, emphasizing causes and consequences in order to help them understand the importance of controlling how emotions are expressed (Bussey, 2013). Children internalize expectations about gender-related behavior as they make gains in self-regulation, such that they feel good about themselves when their behavior is in accord with their internal standards and experience negative feelings when their behavior is not (C. Leaper, 2013). In early childhood, ages 3 to 4, children begin to self-regulate their gender-related behaviors (Bussey & Bandura, 1992).

Boys tend to be more strongly gender socialized than girls, as parents tend to give girls more freedom in choice of clothes, activities, and playmates (Miedzian, 1991). Parents, especially fathers, tend to show more discomfort with sex-atypical behavior in boys (e.g., playing with dolls) than girls (e.g., playing with trucks; Basow, 2008; Lytton & Romney, 1991). Fathers play an important role in influencing gender typing. A study of preschool children in England and Hungary revealed that children whose fathers did more housework and child care tended to demonstrate less awareness of gender stereotypes and less gender-typed play (Turner & Gervai, 1995). Dutch fathers with strong stereotypical gender role attitudes tended to use more physical control strategies with their 3-year-old boys than girls, whereas fathers with counter-stereotypical attitudes used more physical control with girls; this differential treatment predicted gender differences in aggression one year later (Endendijk et al., 2017).

Peers

The peer group also serves as a powerful influence on gender typing in young children. As early as age 3, peers reinforce gender-typed behavior with praise, imitation, or participation. They criticize cross-gender activities and show more disapproval of boys who engage in gender-inappropriate behavior than of girls who are tomboys (Hanish et al., 2013; Ruble, Martin, & Berenbaum, 2006). Among older children, gender-atypical behavior is associated with exclusion and peer victimization (Zosuls, Andrews, Martin, England, & Field, 2016).

Girls and boys show different play styles. Boys use more commands, threats, and force; girls use more gentle tactics, such as persuasion, acceptance, and verbal requests, which are effective with other girls but ignored by boys (Leaper, 2013; Leaper, Tenenbaum, & Shaffer, 1999). Girls, therefore, may find interacting with boys unpleasant as boys pay little attention to their attempts at interaction and are generally nonresponsive.

In one study, differences in play styles were observed in children of Yauri, Nigeria. Girls play a popular game called *sunana bojo ne* in which 10 to 16 girls hold hands, form a half circle, and move clockwise while singing and dancing (Salamone, 1979). One girl remains in the middle, serving as song leader, and unexpectedly falls backward into the circle while the other girls catch her. Girls take turns playing the song leader and trusting their peers to catch them. Boys play a more common game of ring toss in which they compete against each other to toss a rubber ring around a bottle or stick. The last boy to score is teased mercilessly. These games encourage girls and boys to practice skills associated with their gender and necessary for success in adulthood: cooperation for girls and competition for boys.

Differences in play styles influence boys' and girls' choices of play partners and contribute to sex segregation (Martin, Fabes, Hanish, Leonard, & Dinella, 2011). Peer and parental attitudes tend to be similar and reinforce each other as both are part of a larger sociocultural system of socialization agents (Bandura & Bussey, 2004; Bussey & Bandura, 1992).

Adventurer Dora the Explorer presents a less traditional role model for girls.

Media

Children's television and G-rated movies tend to depict the world as gender stereotyped, and these media depictions can promote gender-typed behavior in children. Typical children's media display more male than female characters, with male characters in action roles such as officers or soldiers in the military, and female characters as more likely to have domestic roles and be in romantic relationships (England, Descartes, & Collier-Meek, 2011; Smith, Pieper, Granados, & Choueiti, 2010). Television commercials advertising toys tend to illustrate only one gender or the other, depending on the toy (Kahlenberg & Hein, 2010). Several Canadian towns that gained access to television for the first time in the 1980s demonstrated television's influence on gender typing: Children tended to have unstereotyped attitudes prior to gaining access to television, but 2 years later they demonstrated marked increases in gender-stereotyped attitudes (Kimball, 1986).

One study of 4- and 5-year-old children found that nearly all had viewed media featuring Disney Princess heroines, and two-thirds of girls played with Disney Princess toys at least once a week, as compared with only 4% of the boys (and 90% of the boys rarely, if ever, played with such toys, according to their parents). Longitudinal results revealed that Disney Princess engagement was associated with more female gender-stereotypical behavior 1 year later, even after controlling for initial levels of gender-stereotypical behavior. Parental discussion of media content strengthened associations between princess engagement and adherence to female gender-stereotypical behavior for both girls and boys (Coyne, Linder, Rasmussen, Nelson, & Birkbeck, 2016), yet children themselves also expect gender stereotypes and expect gender-neutral or atypical versions of fairy tales to conform to the usual gender stereotype (Evans, 1998).

Children's books are another form of media that supports gender typing. Overall, there are more male than female characters in children's literature, and female characters often need help while male characters tend to provide it (Beal, 1994; Evans, 1998). Coloring books display similar patterns, with more male than female characters, and male characters are depicted as older, stronger, more powerful, and more active than female characters (e.g., as superheroes versus princesses; Fitzpatrick & McPherson, 2010). Even cereal boxes depict twice as many male as female characters (Black, Marola, Littman, Chrisler, & Neace, 2009).

Culture

In addition to media, the larger culture and its many aspects also influence gender typing in that most cultures emphasize gender differences. Some societies closely link

CULTURAL INFLUENCES ON DEVELOPMENT

• • Cultural Views of Gender

Many cultures emphasize traditional gender roles, with women responsible for caring for the home and family.

Gender stereotypes appear in all cultures, but they vary in intensity, prominence, and developmental trajectory (Guimond et al., 2013; Kapadia & Gala, 2015). For example, longitudinal research with African American youth found that young girls and boys show knowledge of gender stereotypes, but from ages 9 to 15 they show declines in traditional gender attitudes that level off through age 18 (Lam, Stanik, & McHale, 2017). Traditional attitudes in mothers, but not fathers, predict stereotyped attitudes in children. European American youth show a similar pattern. Yet the magnitude of change may vary with ethnicity. Research has suggested that African American men and women are equally likely to endorse typically masculine traits as compared with European Americans, in which males are more likely to describe themselves with masculine traits than are women (Harris, 1996).

In Mexican American families, the traditional role of the female is to care for the children and take care of the home and males were expected to provide for the family (Cauce & Domenech-Rodríguez, 2002). These differences are related to the concept of *machismo*, which incorporates many traditional expectations of the male gender role, such as being unemotional, strong, authoritative, and aggressive. Yet gender differences in Mexican American males and females

may be declining as women are increasingly providing for the family by working outside the home as well as sharing in decision making in the family. As families become more acculturated to the United States, Mexican American mothers and fathers tend to endorse more gender-egalitarian attitudes, reporting attitudes favoring similar treatment of boys and girls (Campbell Leaper & Valin, 1996).

One longitudinal study examined the role of acculturation in Mexican American adolescents' views of gender roles. Mexican American adolescents born in Mexico and the United States were followed from ages 13 to 20 (Updegraff et al., 2014). Among the adolescents born in Mexico, girls showed declines in traditional attitudes from early to late adolescence, but males' attitudes were stable over time. U.S.-born males and females did not differ in their traditional gender attitude trajectories, with both declining over time. Mexico-born adolescents' likely greater exposure to Mexican culture, wherein attitudes about men's and women's roles are generally quite traditional, may influence their views of gender roles (Cauce & Domenech-Rodríguez, 2002). Yet in this study, only Mexico-born males maintained their traditional gender role attitudes during adolescence (Updegraff et al., 2014). In addition, the differences in Mexico-born males' versus females' trajectories suggested that males may be less influenced by acculturation processes, which are expected to lead to less traditional gender role attitudes. One possibility is that traditional gender role values in Mexican American families are advantageous for males, as Latino culture traditionally awards status and privilege (e.g., freedom to spend time outside the home) and fewer responsibilities (e.g., less involvement in housework) for adolescent and young adult males (Raffaelli & Ontai, 2004).

What Do You Think?

What gender-related values are evident within your culture or context, such as race, ethnicity, religion, or even neighborhood or part of the world? What are the accepted roles for men and women? Are gender roles changing over time in your context?

activities and dress with gender; girls and boys may attend sex-segregated schools, wear contrasting types of school uniforms, and never interact (Beal, 1994). Societies vary in the types of behavior that are considered appropriate for men and women. For example, farming is a task for women in many parts of the world, but in North America it is men who are traditionally in charge of farming tasks. The exact behaviors may vary across societies, but all societies have values regarding gender-appropriate behavior for males and females and all societies transmit these values to young children. In the Cultural Influences on Development feature, we take a closer look at the views of gender in particular cultures.

Theories of gender role development are summarized in Table 13.2.

TABLE 13.2 • Theories of Gender Role Development

THEORETICAL EXPLANATION	
Biological	Describes gender role development in evolutionary and biological terms. Males adapted to become more aggressive and competitive and females more nurturing as it ensured that their genes were passed to the next generation. Gender differences may also be explained by subtle differences in brain structure as well as differences in hormones.
Cognitive-developmental	The emergence of gender identity leads children to classify the world around them according to gender labels, and they begin to show more interest in gender-appropriate toys. After acquiring gender stability, children show an increase in stereotype knowledge, evaluate their own gender more positively, and demonstrate rigidity of gender-related beliefs. Gender constancy furthers gender typing as children attend more to norms of their sex. According to gender schema theory, once children can label their sex, their gender schema forms and becomes an organizing principle. Children notice differences between males and females in preferred clothes, toys, and activities, as well as how their culture classifies males and females as different and encompassing different roles. Children then use their gender schemas as guides for their behavior and attitudes, and gender typing occurs.
Contextual	Contextual explanations rely on social learning and the influence of the sociocultural context in which children are raised. Males and females have different social experiences from birth. Gender typing occurs through socialization, through a child's interpretation of the world around him or her, and modeling and reinforcement from parents, peers, and teachers.

 Thinking in Context 13.2

Consider gender role development from a bioecological perspective.

1. How might biological, cognitive, and socioemotional changes in a child influence the child's developing gender role?

2. How might mesosystem, exosystem, and microsystem factors, such as parents, peers, school, media, and neighborhood, influence gender development?

EMERGING SEXUALITY

LO 13.3 Discuss the development of sexuality and sexual orientation.

Sexuality takes many forms and is present early in life. With puberty, sexuality takes on new meaning. Sexuality is an important dimension of self. It is not simply about behavior, and it begins earlier than most people realize.

CHILDHOOD SEXUALITY

Childhood sexuality is not well understood, but developmental scientists generally agree that it is normal for children to have sexual feelings; nevertheless, such feelings are experienced and understood very differently than adult sexuality (Diamond 2015). Like gender and other aspects of development, children's sexuality is constructed through their everyday experiences. Sexual desire does not just switch on at puberty, but undergoes a gradual development during childhood and adolescence that reflects a progressive integration of biological, social, and psychological transitions and experiences within changing social contexts (Herdt & McClintock, 2000; McClintock & Herdt, 1996). Childhood self-stimulation is common, with studies suggesting that 40% to 60% of children show the behavior as early as 2 years old (Friedrich, 2003). Genital touching accompanied by flushing and quick breathing has been observed in 2-month-old infants (Leung & Robson, 1993). We do not know how children perceive self-stimulation, but such stimulation is unquestionably different from sexual expression in adults.

It is thought that **adrenarche**, the maturation of the adrenal glands, marks a transition in children's sexual desire between ages 6 and 10 (Herdt & McClintock, 2000). When the adrenal glands mature, they stimulate hormones that begin the changes we associate with puberty. Developmental increases in hormones are thought to trigger an increase in erotic interest and attractions. Many adults recall their first memorable sexual attractions to peers occurring at about age 10 (Diamond 2015). With puberty comes an increase in motivation and preoccupation in seeking sexual release that is partially attributable to sex hormones (Fortenberry, 2013).

ADOLESCENT SEXUALITY

It is commonly thought that the sex drive is particularly potent during adolescence due to the dramatic changes in hormone levels during puberty coupled with increased cultural emphasis on the emergent sexuality of youth (Diamond 2015). There is no definitive evidence that adolescents experience more intense sexual urges than adults, but brain research indicates that, compared with adults, adolescents have a stronger subcortical response combined with prefrontal development that is still incomplete. This imbalance is thought to contribute to adolescents' emotional and behavioral changes (Shulman et al., 2016). However, the increased importance of sexuality is not due only to puberty. Emerging cognitive abilities such as hypothetical thinking, perspective taking, self-consciousness, and decision making lead adolescents to be curious, reflective, and introspective about sexual feelings and behavior. The social recognition of sexuality as a task for adolescence also influences their experience. Adolescents become concerned with developing a sense of sexual identity.

Sexual identity is one's sense of self regarding sexuality, including one's awareness and comfort regarding one's sexual attitudes, interests, and behaviors. It develops in a process similar to other aspects of identity development, entailing a period of exploration and commitment (McClelland & Tolman, 2014). Sexuality influences and is influenced by adolescents' comfort with their bodies—their shape, size, and perceived attractiveness. It encompasses the sense of arousal, their understanding of its nature, and acceptance that it is normal and appropriate. Sexuality comprises decisions about sexual behavior, the degree and nature of exploration, degree of comfort in sexual activity, and decision whether or not to engage in sexual activity. Other aspects of sexuality concern the targets of sexual interest and, ultimately, adolescents' sexual orientation.

adrenarche Refers to the maturation of adrenal glands.

sexual identity An individual's sense of self regarding sexuality, including the awareness and comfort regarding personal sexual attitudes, interests, and behaviors, which develops through a period of exploration and commitment.

sexual orientation A term that refers to whether someone is sexually attracted to others of the same sex, opposite sex, or both.

SEXUAL ORIENTATION

Adolescents are driven to understand the sexual feelings they experience that determine their **sexual orientation**, which becomes an important contributor to their sense of self. Sexual orientation is an enduring pattern of emotional, romantic, and sexual attraction to opposite-sex partners (heterosexual), same-sex partners (gay or lesbian) or partners of both sexes (bisexual; Greenberg, 2017). Many youth enter a period of questioning in which they are uncertain of their sexuality and attempt to determine their true orientation (Saewyc, 2011). Similar to other aspects of identity, they explore and consider alternatives. For example, many preadolescents and young adolescents engage in sex play with members of the same sex, yet ultimately develop a heterosexual orientation. It is estimated that 2% to 4% of high school students in the United States identify themselves as gay, lesbian, or bisexual (Savin-Williams & Ream, 2007), similar to the

RosaIreneBetancourt 3/Alamy

Gay-straight alliances foster a culture of acceptance, help sexual minority peers connect with peers, and foster well-being in students.

finding that 2% and 1% of a sample of more than 34,000 adults labeled themselves as gay/lesbian and bisexual, respectively (Ward, Dahlhamer, Galinsky, & Joestl, 2014). Yet estimating the prevalence of sexual orientation is complicated because many sexual minority youth do not identify themselves as such until early adulthood or later, and reporting of same-sex attraction and behavior among adolescents and emerging adults is not stable (Savin-Williams & Ream, 2007). For example, longitudinal data with more than 10,000 seventh- to twelfth-grade students over a 6-year period revealed some migration over time in both directions—from opposite-sex attraction and behavior to same-sex attraction and behavior and vice versa (Saewyc, 2011). However, stability develops over time. More than 12,000 emerging adults (ages 18–24) surveyed over a 6-year period revealed that stability of sexual orientation was more common than change, especially among emerging adults who identified strongly as heterosexual or homosexual (as compared with bisexual, which was the most unstable category; Savin-Williams, Joyner, & Rieger, 2012).

Seventy years ago, the pioneer sex researcher Alfred Kinsey proposed that sexual orientation is a continuum with exclusive interest in the opposite sex on one pole and exclusive interest in the same sex on the other (Kinsey, Pomeroy, & Martin, 1948). Many researchers today view sexual orientation as a dynamic spectrum, ranging from exclusive opposite-sex attraction and relations to exclusive same-sex attraction and relations, with multiple sexual orientations in between (Bailey et al., 2016; Savin-Williams, 2016). Many people attracted to both sexes and attractions varying over time (see Figure 13.3). Large-scale surveys conducted in a variety of countries have revealed that the majority

FIGURE 13.3: **Average Prevalence for Each of Five Categories of Sexual Orientation in Recent Western Population Surveys**

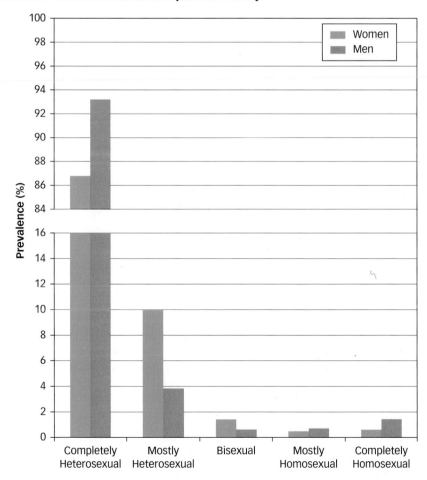

from Bailey et al. (2016). Sexual Orientation, Controversy, and Science

of individuals with same-sex attraction do not openly identify as lesbian, gay, or bisexual despite their same-sex attractions and/or behaviors (Chandra et al., 2013; Hayes et al., 2012). This is likely because many people experience attraction to both sexes and view their sexuality as ranging from primarily straight or gay, mostly straight or gay, to bisexual (Savin-Williams & Vrangalova, 2013). For example, one longitudinal study followed nearly 14,000 youth from ages 12 to 33 and found three general patterns of sexual attraction: heterosexual (88%), mostly heterosexual (10%), and LGB (2%; Calzo, Masyn, Austin, Jun, & Corliss, 2017). Sexual attraction does not always match behavior; many people experience attractions that they do not act on. In addition, a small minority of people report an asexual orientation, feeling no sexual attraction whatsoever (Greaves et al., 2017; Van Houdenhove, Gijs, T'Sjoen, & Enzlin, 2015)

Sexuality may be largely present at birth, perhaps influenced by biological factors such as genetics and exposure to sex hormones in the womb (Hines, 2011; LeVay, 2017). Research with about 4,000 Swedish identical twins found that genetics accounts for about 20% to 35% of the differences in sexual orientation in men and women (Långström, Rahman, Carlström, & Lichtenstein, 2010). Concordance studies suggest that a gay or lesbian orientation is more likely among identical twins than fraternal twins or nontwin siblings (Bailey et al., 2016). However, no specific genes have been associated with sexual orientation, and any such genes likely do not act alone but in conjunction with contextual factors that have yet to be identified (Greenberg, 2017; LeVay, 1993).

Cultures vary in attitudes about same-sex relations, but same-sex behavior is found in virtually all societies regardless of whether it is accepted or condemned (Ford & Beach, 1951; Whitam, 1983). In one striking exception, no same-sex behavior was found among the Aka foragers of the Central African Republic (Hewlett, Hewlett, & Hewlett, 2010). The anthropologists who studied the Aka reported that it was difficult to explain what they meant, as the Aka were not aware of same-sex behavior and had no name for it. Attitudes about same-sex behavior vary considerably across European nations (Lottes & Alkula, 2011). For example, people in Denmark, the Netherlands, and Sweden report the most positive attitudes toward gay, lesbian, and bisexual orientations. Positive attitudes are also found in a large group of countries including Austria, Belgium, France, Germany, Great Britain, Greece, Italy, and Spain. Attitudes are more negative in Bulgaria, Estonia, and Russia; and the countries with the most negative attitudes include Croatia, Lithuania, Poland, Portugal, Romania, and Ukraine (Hyde & DeLamater, 2017; Lottes & Alkula, 2011). In many places, lesbian, gay, bisexual, and transgender (LGBT) adults are met with structural stigma—policies that restrict their lifestyle (such as marriage), access to resources and rights (such as a spouse's health insurance coverage or adoption), and in some countries incarceration and even death (Hatzenbuehler, 2014). These systemic stressors can be damaging to LGBT individuals.

Many sexual minority individuals report feeling different from their peers at an early age. Gender nonconformity in early childhood (i.e., showing interest in toys, activities, and characteristics of the opposite sex) is associated with same-sex attraction, although the relation is far from 100% (Savin-Williams & Cohen, 2015). For example, in one study, by age 8, two-thirds of young people who later identified as LGB were considered gender atypical by others, especially parents (D'augelli, Grossman, & Starks, 2008). One study of more than 2,400 girls and nearly 2,200 boys found that the levels of gender-typed behavior (e.g., playing house or rough-and-tumble play) at ages 3.5 and 4.75 years, and to a lesser extent at age 2.5 years, predicted adolescents' sexual orientation at age 15 years (Li, Kung, & Hines, 2017).

In North America and many other developed countries, young people are disclosing their sexual orientation—"coming out" as gay or lesbian—at earlier ages than in prior generations, likely due to an increasingly inviting, positive cultural context for LGB young people (Calzo, Antonucci, Mays, & Cochran, 2011; Floyd & Bakeman, 2006; Lucassen et al., 2015). Research suggests that some sexual minority youth may disclose their sexuality starting at around age 14 or 15, yet many wait until late adolescence or emerging adulthood (Calzo et al., 2017; Maguen, Floyd, Bakeman, & Armistead, 2002; Savin-Williams & Ream, 2003). Young people most commonly disclose first to a best friend; parents are often last, as many young people report that they want to be absolutely certain of their sexuality before they initiate this significant disclosure (Cohen & Savin-Williams, 1996). Adolescents who anticipate negative responses from parents are less likely to disclose their sexual orientation; to avoid disclosure LGBT youth may become emotionally distant from their parents and friends (Ueno, 2005). Despite stereotypes, adolescents who come out to a parent are rarely met with ongoing condemnation, severe negative response, or expulsion (Savin-Williams, Dubé, & Dube, 1998). Many receive responses that range from neutral to positive (Samarova, Shilo, & Diamond, 2014).

Constructing an identity as a young person who is lesbian, gay, bisexual, or transgender can be complicated by the prejudice and discrimination that many LGBT youth experience in their schools and communities. LGBT adolescents experience more harassment and victimization by peers and report a more hostile peer environment than their heterosexual peers (Robinson & Espelage, 2013). Perceived discrimination and victimization by peers contributes to LGBT adolescents' increased risk for psychological and behavioral problems, such as depression, self-harm, suicide, running away, poor academic performance, substance use, and risky sexual practices (Almeida, Johnson, Corliss, Molnar, & Azrael, 2009; Collier, van Beusekom, Bos, & Sandfort, 2013; Haas et al., 2011; Mark L Hatzenbuehler, 2009; Plöderl et al., 2013).

More accepting reactions from others can buffer the psychological and behavioral risks that accompany perceived discrimination (Rosario, Schrimshaw, & Hunter, 2009). Family support has been found to buffer the effects of sexual orientation–based victimization (D'Augelli & Hershberger, 1993) and contribute to greater identity integration (Rosario, Schrimshaw, & Hunter, 2008). In this way, developmental psychologists have come to conclude that disclosing a sexual minority identity can be a positive event that facilitates the development of identity, self-esteem, and psychological health and can often reduce distress, anxiety, and depression (Juster, Smith, Ouellet, Sindi, & Lupien, 2013; Ueno, 2005; Vincke & van Heeringen, 2002). It can also be a means for obtaining social support and interpersonal closeness (Kosciw, Palmer, & Kull, 2015; Legate, Ryan, & Weinstein, 2012; Savin-Williams & Cohen, 2015).

Support from parents and peers can buffer the negative effects of stigmatization and victimization for LGBT individuals (Birkett, Newcomb, & Mustanski, 2015). For example, one study of a national sample of more than 7,800 LGBT secondary school students revealed that adolescents who had come "out" were more likely to experience peer victimization, but also reported higher self-esteem and fewer depressive symptoms than their "closeted" peers (Kosciw et al., 2015). Thus, being out may reflect, as well as promote, resilience within this population.

 Thinking in Context 13.3

1. For some, the concept of childhood sexuality is controversial. Why do you think this is so? What do you think?

2. How might contextual factors influence young people's exploration and expression of sexual orientation?

SEXUALITY AND SEXUAL ACTIVITY

LO 13.4 Identify the forms that sexuality and sexual activity take from adolescence through late adulthood, as well as associated health issues.

Sexual activity and relationships often emerge in adolescence, and sexuality continues to be important throughout the life course.

SEXUAL ACTIVITY IN ADOLESCENCE

Although researchers believe that sexual behaviors tend to progress from hand-holding to kissing, to touching through clothes and under clothes, to oral sex and then to genital intercourse, research on adolescent sexuality tends to focus on intercourse, leaving gaps in our knowledge about the range of sexual activity milestones young people experience (Diamond & Savin-Williams, 2009). Adolescents and emerging adults are about as likely to engage in oral sex as vaginal intercourse (Casey Copen, Chandra, & Martinez, 2012; Lefkowitz, Vasilenko, & Leavitt, 2016). Male and female high school students show similar rates of receiving oral sex (49% and 45% of males and females, respectively; Child Trends Data Bank, 2014). Oral sex does not seem to be a substitute for vaginal sex, as the majority of one sample of more than 12,000 adolescents initiated oral sex after experiencing first vaginal intercourse, and about one half initiated oral sex a year or more after the onset of vaginal sex (Haydon, Herring, Prinstein, & Halpern, 2012).

Many adults are surprised to learn that the overall rate of sexual intercourse among U.S. high school students has declined from 54% in 1991 to 47% in 2013 (Kaiser Family Foundation, 2014). Overall rates of sexual activity are similar internationally, with comparable declines in recent years (Guttmacher Institute, 2014). About 30% of 16-year-olds have had sexual intercourse, and most young people have sexual intercourse for the first time at about age 17 (Finer & Philbin, 2013; Guttmacher Institute, 2014). Figure 13.4 depicts rates of sexual activity by age. About one-third of high school students reported being sexually active, defined as within the previous 3 months. As shown in Figure 13.4, African American high school students are more likely to have had intercourse (60%) compared to white (44%) and Hispanic students (49%; Kaiser Family Foundation, 2014).

Ethnic differences in sexual activity are thought to be influenced by socioeconomic and contextual factors. For example, low socioeconomic status and belonging to a racial or ethnic minority increase the likelihood of growing up in a single-parent home, potentially with less parental monitoring, and in poor neighborhoods with fewer community resources—all of which are associated with early sexual activity (Browning, Leventhal, & Brooks-Gunn, 2004; Carlson, McNulty, Bellair, & Watts, 2014; Santelli, Lowry, Brener, & Robin, 2000). In addition, ethnic differences in rates of pubertal maturation, with African American girls experiencing puberty earlier than other girls, influence sexual activity, as early maturation is a risk factor for early sexual activity (Carlson et al., 2014; Moore, Harden, & Mendle, 2014).

Although sexual activity is normative in late adolescence, early sexual activity, prior to age 15, is associated with problem behaviors, including alcohol and substance use, poor academic achievement, and delinquent activity, as well as having a larger number of sex partners relative to peers (Armour & Haynie, 2007; McLeod & Knight, 2010; Sandfort, Orr, Hirsch, & Santelli, 2008). Yet a recent study suggests that the effects of early sexual initiation may apply only to girls. The researchers found that sexual initiation was associated with internalizing symptoms for girls who initiated sexual activity prior to age 15, but not with boys, nor with teens who initiated sexual activity later. Moreover, one year later there was no difference in internalizing symptoms between early and on-time sexually initiating girls, suggesting that early

FIGURE 13.4: Sexual Initiation During Adolescence

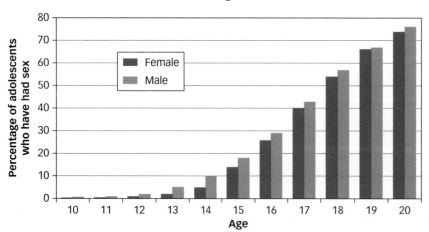

Source: Guttmacher Institute (2014).

sexual initiation may not produce lasting detriments to girls' mental health (Wesche, Kreager, Lefkowitz, & Siennick, 2017).

In recent years parents and health professionals have become increasingly concerned about adolescents' use of technology as tools for sexual exploration and expression. **Sexting**, the exchange of explicit sexual messages or images via mobile phone, is increasingly common among adolescents. Females and older youth are more likely to share sexual photos than males and younger youth. Several studies have found that sexting is associated with sexual activity, and especially risky sexual activity, in adolescents as young as 13 (Rice et al., 2012; Romo et al., 2017; Ybarra & Mitchell, 2014). A sample of 1,100 Czech adolescents aged 10–18

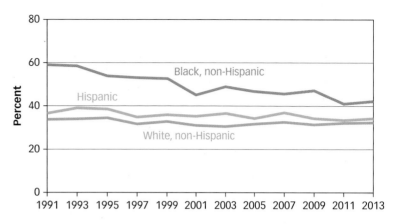

FIGURE 13.5: Percentage of High School Students Who Report They Are Sexually Active, 1991–2013

Source: Kaiser Family Foundation (2014).

suggested that sexting may be a precursor to offline sexual activity (Ševčíková, Blinka, & Daneback, 2017). One study of more than 17,000 adolescents aged 11–16 from 25 European countries revealed that sexting was associated with emotional problems and alcohol use in girls and boys of all ages (Ševčíková, 2016). Other research supports the link between sexting and adolescent problems such as substance use, depression, and low self-esteem as compared with peers (Van Ouytsel, Van Gool, Ponnet, & Walrave, 2014).

Another important contextual influence on adolescent sexual activity is the peer group. Adolescents with sexually active peers and who perceive positive attitudes about sex among schoolmates are more likely to initiate sexual activity and more frequently and with a greater number of sexual partners (Coley et al., 2014; Moore et al., 2014; White & Warner, 2015). In addition, adolescents' perceptions of the sexual norms in their neighborhood, as well as siblings' sexual activity, are associated with age of initiation, incidence of casual sex, and number of sexual partners, even after controlling for neighborhood demographic risk factors (Almy et al., 2015; Warner, Giordano, Manning, & Longmore, 2011).

What role do parents play in adolescent sexual activity? When parents and children communicate about sexuality—specifically, when they have open conversations characterized by warmth, support, and humor— adolescents tend to show a later onset of sexual activity and engage in less sexual risk taking than their peers (Lefkowitz & Stoppa, 2006; Lohman & Billings, 2008; Trejos-Castillo & Vazsonyi, 2009; Widman, Choukas-Bradley, Noar, Nesi, & Garrett, 2016). Authoritative parenting, regularly shared family activities (e.g., outings, game nights, or shared dinners), parental monitoring, and parental knowledge are associated with lower rates of sexual activity (Dittus et al., 2015; Huang, Murphy, & Hser, 2011; McElwain & Booth-LaForce, 2006).

Sexually Transmitted Infection

With sexual activity comes the risk of transmitting or acquiring **sexually transmitted infections (STIs)**, which are infections passed from one individual to another through sexual contact; STIs may be caused by viruses, bacteria, or parasites. In 2015, STIs—specifically, cases of chlamydia, gonorrhea, and syphilis—reached an all-time high in the United States (Centers for Disease Control and Prevention [CDC], 2016b). Although they represent only 25% of the sexually active population, 15- to 24-year-olds account for one-half to two-thirds of all STI diagnoses, depending on illness, each year. Untreated STIs can result in sterility and serious, even life-threatening, illnesses such as cancer. Despite the high risk for acquiring STIs among youth, only one-third of adolescent girls and less than half (45%) of young women ages 19 to 25 report that they have discussed STIs with their health care providers (Kaiser Family Foundation, 2014).

sexting The exchange of explicit sexual messages or images via mobile phone.

sexually transmitted infections (STIs) Infections passed from one individual to another through sexual contact.

Human papillomavirus (HPV) is the most common STI diagnosed in people of all ages, occurring in up to one half of adults ages 18 to 69. There are several types of HPV, with varying manifestations (McQuillan, Kruszon-Moran, Markowitz, Unger, & Paulose-Ram, 2017). Some HPV types can cause genital warts and are considered low risk, with a small chance for causing cancer. Other types are considered high risk; if untreated, they can cause cancer in different areas of the body—most commonly cervical cancer in women. HPV vaccines are available, and the CDC recommends HPV vaccinations for males and females starting at age 11. In 2015, 63% of females aged 13–17 had received one or more doses of the vaccine against HPV, and 42% had completed the recommended regimen of three doses as compared with 50% and 28% for males, respectively (Reagan-Steiner et al., 2016). Health care experts believe that HPV vaccination rates are low, compared to other vaccinations, because of vaccine cost, the belief that giving the vaccine might condone sexual activity, and for boys, the perceived lack of benefits (Brewer & Fazekas, 2007; Holman et al., 2014).

The most serious sexually transmitted infection is **human immunodeficiency virus (HIV)**, which causes **acquired immune deficiency syndrome (AIDS)**. Since 2005, rates of HIV infection have dropped 19% due to advances in prevention efforts which help people understand the causes of HIV and adopt safe-sex practices (CDC, 2015a). Young people aged 13 to 24 represented 1 in 5 of new HIV/AIDS diagnoses in 2015. Symptoms of AIDS, specifically a weakening of the immune system, occur about 8 to 10 years after infection with HIV. Among men, HIV is most often spread through same-sex activity, specifically anal intercourse (48%), injection drug use (25%), heterosexual contact (18%), and other sources, including multiple risk factors and contaminated blood transfusions (CDC, 2015b). The leading sources of HIV exposure for women are heterosexual contact (84%) and injection drug use (16%). Worldwide, heterosexual contact is the most common source of HIV infection.

Although most adolescents (about 85% of high school students) receive education and demonstrate basic knowledge about HIV/AIDS (Kann et al., 2014), most underestimate their own risks, know little about other STIs, and are not knowledgeable about how to protect themselves from STIs (Boyce, Doherty, Fortin, & MacKinnon, 2003). For example, in 2013 only 13% of high school students reported that they had ever been tested for HIV (Kann et al., 2014). The three ways to avoid STIs are to abstain from sex; to be in a long-term, mutually monogamous relationship with a partner who has been tested and does not have any STIs; or to use condoms consistently and correctly. Making and carrying out decisions to abstain from sex or to engage in safe sex is challenging for adolescents and emerging adults, but also for adults, as most middle-aged and older adults report engaging in unprotected sex (Pilowsky & Wu, 2015).

human immunodeficiency virus (HIV) The most serious sexually transmitted infection, which causes acquired immune deficiency syndrome (AIDS).

acquired immune deficiency syndrome (AIDS) A condition caused by the human immunodeficiency virus (HIV), the most serious sexually transmitted illness.

Adolescent mothers and their children face many risks to development, but educational, economic, and social supports can improve outcomes.

Adolescent Pregnancy

In 2014, the birth rate among 15- to 19-year-old girls in the United States was 24.2 per 1,000 girls, down from a high of 117 per 1,000 in 1990 (CDC, 2016c). The decline in adolescent birth rates can be attributed to an increase in contraceptive use (Lindberg, Santelli, & Desai, 2016). About three-quarters of sexually active 15- to 19-year-olds report using contraception during first intercourse (Kaiser Family Foundation, 2014; Martinez, Copen, & Abma, 2011). However, many adolescents use contraceptives only sporadically and not consistently (Pazol et al., 2015). Despite overall declines during the past two decades, the United States continues to have one of the highest teen birth rates in the developed world (see Table 13.3 and Figure 13.5; Sedgh, Finer, Bankole, Eilers, & Singh, 2015).

Adolescent mothers are less likely than their peers to achieve many of the typical markers of adulthood, such as completing high school, entering a stable marriage, and becoming financially and residentially independent (Casares, Lahiff, Eskenazi, & Halpern-Felsher, 2010; Taylor, 2009). Lack of resources such as child care, housing, and financial support are associated with poor educational outcomes; adolescents with child care and financial resources tend to show higher educational attainment (Casares et al., 2010; Mollborn, 2007). Although adolescent pregnancy is associated with negative outcomes, the risk factors for adolescent pregnancy are also those that place youth at risk for negative adult outcomes in general, such as extreme poverty, family instability, and few educational and community supports (Oxford et al., 2005). It is therefore difficult to determine the degree to which outcomes are caused by adolescent pregnancy itself or the contextual conditions that are associated with it.

It must be noted, however, that there is a great deal of variability in short- and long-term outcomes of teen pregnancy (Furstenberg, 2003; Miller, Forehand, & Kotchick, 1999). A longitudinal study of adolescent mothers showed more positive outcomes than are often reported: 17 years after giving birth as adolescents, more than 70% graduated from high school, 30% received a postsecondary degree, and half achieved income security (Furstenberg, 2003; Miller, Forehand, & Kotchick, 1999). In another longitudinal study of adolescent mothers, 85% showed positive adjustment including achievement of markers of adulthood such as financial independence, though about half of these young women experienced mental health issues such as anxiety or depression (Oxford, et al., 2005). Only about 15% of adolescent mothers experienced the most negative outcomes 17 years later, such as financial dependence, low education, unemployment, unstable housing, casual sexual activity, victimization by crime, criminal activity, and illicit drug use (Oxford, et al., 2005). These dire outcomes in early adulthood were predicted by drug and alcohol use, criminal activity, clinical depression, anxiety, and experience with violence during adolescence.

Infants born to adolescent mothers are at risk for preterm birth and low birth weight (Jeha, Usta, Ghulmiyyah, & Nassar, 2015; Xi-Kuan et al., 2007). Children of adolescent mothers tend to be at risk for a variety of negative developmental outcomes such as conduct and emotional problems, developmental delays, and poor academic achievement (Rafferty, Griffin, & Lodise, 2011; Tang, Davis-Kean, Chen, & Sexton, 2014). These outcomes are influenced by the characteristics of adolescents who are likely to become mothers, as well as the consequences of having a child at a young age (e.g., low level of maternal education, low socioeconomic status, frequent caretaker and residence changes, poor parenting; Carothers, Borkowski, & Whitman, 2006; De Genna, Larkby, & Cornelius, 2011; Rafferty et al., 2011). However, there is variability in outcomes. Many children of adolescent mothers demonstrate resilience and adjustment in spite of these risks (Levine, Emery, & Pollack, 2007; Rhule, McMahon, Spieker, & Munson, 2006). Positive adjustment is predicted by secure attachment, low maternal depressive symptoms, and positive parenting on the part of the mother, characterized by warmth, discussion, and stimulation.

Adolescent parents can be effective if provided with supports—economic, educational, and social. Effective supports for adolescent parents include access to health care and affordable child care; encouragement to stay in school; and training in vocational skills,

TABLE 13.2 • International Adolescent Birth Rates in 2012 (per 1,000 women)

COUNTRY	RATE
Australia	12
Austria	4
Brazil	71
Canada	14
China	9
Dominican Republic	100
France	6
Germany	4
Ireland	8
Japan	5
Netherlands	6
Russian Federation	26
Switzerland	2
United Kingdom	26
United States	31

Source: Adapted from World Bank (2014).

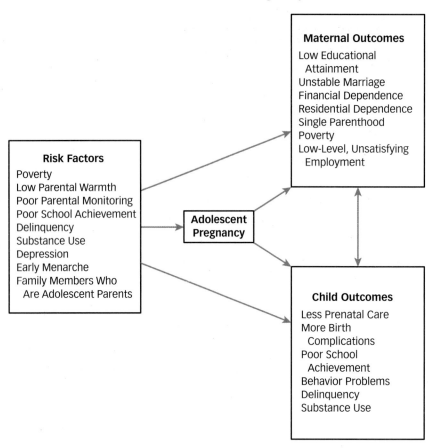

Risk factors for adolescent pregnancy also influence how adolescents adjust to parenthood, their long-term outcomes, and their children's outcomes. Protective factors—such as warm relationships with parents and other caring adults, parental monitoring, coping skills, and access to health care—promote positive adjustment in the face of risk and influence the outcomes of adolescent pregnancy for mothers and children.

parenting skills, and coping skills (Easterbrooks, Chaudhuri, Bartlett, & Copeman, 2011; Mollborn, 2007). Social support predicts increased parenting self-efficacy and parental satisfaction (Angley, Divney, Magriples, & Kershaw, 2015; Umaña-Taylor, Guimond, Updegraff, & Jahromi, 2013). Relationships with adults who are close, supportive, and provide guidance predict completing high school (Klaw, Rhodes, & Fitzgerald, 2003). Adolescent parents who share caregiving with their mothers or other adults learn as apprentices and become increasingly competent at parenting over time (Oberlander, Black, & Starr, 2007). Adolescent parents also benefit from relationships with adults who are sensitive not only to their needs as parents, but also to their own developmental needs for autonomy and support.

SEXUAL ACTIVITY IN EMERGING ADULTHOOD

As with other aspects of development, emerging adults show different patterns of sexual activity than those younger and older than they. Emerging adulthood is a time in which most young people are unmarried and free to engage in identity exploration, including defining a sense of sexual identity. The social script of emerging adulthood as a "time to experiment" is conducive to **casual sex**, which is sexual activity outside of romantic relationships. Particularly in the context of college, this experimentation is seen in sexual activity as well as other areas, such as intoxication (Kuperberg & Padgett, 2016).

Casual Sexual Activity

Casual sex has existed for decades (Claxton & van Dulmen, 2013), but has recently received media attention as young people, particularly college students, have increasingly referred to it as *hooking up* (Garcia, Reiber, Massey, & Merriwether, 2012)—a term that, like casual sex itself, also is not new (Glenn & Marquardt, 2001). Hooking up is not consistently defined by emerging adults, but it generally refers to a brief sexual encounter that can range from kissing to intercourse, without the expectation of forming a long-term relationship or attachment (Olmstead, Conrad, & Anders, 2017).

An estimated 60% to 80% of college students report at least one hookup (Garcia et al., 2012). For example, in one study of 24,000 students at 22 colleges in the United States surveyed between 2005 and 2011, about 68% of both men and women reported having engaged in hookups (Kuperberg & Padgett, 2016). Of the roughly 12,000 hookup encounters reported by students, 69% included sexual intercourse.

casual sex Sexual activity outside of romantic relationships.

Hookups often occur within the context of college parties and most frequently involve alcohol use (Bersamin, Paschall, Saltz, & Zamboanga, 2012; Patrick, Maggs, & Lefkowitz, 2015). Although some students report enthusiasm about their experiences, others report distress, particularly when it occurs in the context of drinking (Owen & Fincham, 2011). In one study of more than 800 college students, about one third of those who have hooked up while drinking reported that they would not have done so if they had been sober, with women most likely to regret the encounter (Labrie, Hummer, Ghaidarov, Lac, & Kenney, 2014). Negative emotional consequences are more common and more pronounced for women than men (Townsend & Wasserman, 2011; Claxton & van Dulmen, 2013). Yet research with nearly 4,000 students at 30 colleges across the United States revealed that both men and women who reported casual sex within the previous month scored lower than their peers on measures of psychological well-being (self-esteem, life satisfaction, psychological well-being, and happiness) and higher on measures of distress (anxiety, depression; Bersamin et al., 2014; Napper, Montes, Kenney, & LaBrie, 2016). Overall, men tend to report more pleasure and less guilt and regret after hookups compared with women, and in general experience more social and physical gratification benefits of engaging in hookups (Heldman & Wade, 2010). Men may even experience greater psychological distress than their peers if they do not engage in hookups (Claxton & van Dulmen, 2013). A double standard exists regarding the social acceptability of sex outside of romantic relationships, in which women receive negative social sanctions while men receive social rewards. This double standard regarding sexuality for men and women makes hooking up potentially more damaging for women (Kuperberg & Padgett, 2016; Napper et al., 2016).

Despite possible negative consequences, many young people perceive benefits to hooking up. The benefits, according to college students, include the idea that such encounters are easier and less time consuming than traditional romantic relationships, and that they have less potential to be "emotionally damaging" than a bad romantic relationship (Armstrong, Hamilton, & England, 2010; Claxton & van Dulmen, 2013). Some have suggested that the positive and negative outcomes of hookups depend on the individual's motivations. Generally, positive experiences are associated with positive motives for hooking up such as pleasure and self-exploration, whereas a sense of pressure, whether internal or external, is associated with negative experiences, especially in women (Snapp, Ryu, & Kerr, 2015). Similarly, a sample of more than 500 college students surveyed at the beginning and end of the school year found that non-autonomous reasons for hooking up (e.g., external pressure, coercion, or hooking up unintentionally) were linked to lower self-esteem, higher depression and anxiety, and more physical symptoms of distress than were autonomous reasons for hooking up (e.g., a desire for fun, exploration, or learning about one's sexuality; Vrangalova, 2015). Autonomous hookup motivation, was not associated with positive or negative outcomes. The context of sexual encounters and individuals' motivations for them may influence the outcomes they experience.

Sexual Coercion

Healthy sexual activity is consensual sexual activity. It is estimated that about 20% of women experience nonconsensual sexual activity; that is, they experience sexual assault or rape (Breiding et al., 2014). **Rape** refers to nonconsensual sexual penetration of the body by the body part of another person or object (Federal Bureau of Investigation, 2015), while **sexual assault** is a broader term referring to a wide variety of nonconsensual sexual contact or behavior. *Nonconsensual* is the key to identifying sexual assault: It includes instances in which the victim is coerced by fear tactics, such as threats or use of physical harm; or is incapable of giving consent due to the influence of drugs or alcohol or because of age. Most victims are young, with nearly 80% experiencing sexual assault prior to age 25; 40% of victims are under the age of 18 (Breiding et al., 2014). Although adolescence seems to be a period of high risk, college is also a vulnerable time. In a large,

rape Refers to nonconsensual sexual penetration of the body by the body part of another person or object.

sexual assault A broader term than rape, refers to a wide variety of nonconsensual sexual contact or behavior.

cross-sectional survey of campus sexual assault, 20% of undergraduate women indicated that they had been a victim of sexual assault since beginning college (Basile et al., 2016; Krebs, Lindquist, Warner, Fisher, & Martin, 2009).

Only a small minority of rapes (i.e., 13%) are committed by strangers. Instead, nearly half of all rapes are committed by acquaintances (Breiding, Chen, & Black, 2014). Among college students, 78% of rapes are committed by someone the victim knows (Sinozich, Sofi & Langton, 2014). The commonly used term *date rape* for nonconsensual sexual activity with an acquaintance downplays the severity of sexual assault. Acquaintance rape is the most commonly underreported type of crime. Many cases of date rape are premeditated and involve slipping powerful sedatives such as rohypnol (roofie) into a woman's drink. The drug makes the victim drowsy, unconscious, or unable to move, and often causes her to not recall the event the next day. When alcohol is involved, victims may blame themselves for drinking (Hock, 2015). Many victims wrongly assume that they sent "mixed signals" or that things "got out of hand."

Underreporting of rape is high. The actual number of incidents is hard to determine, but one study found that only about 20% of rapes had been reported to the police (Sinozich, Sofi & Langton, 2014). Sometimes victims believe that their attacker will deny the rape (as many acquaintance rapists even feel they have committed no sexual assault at all), making the case a "she said, he said" situation. They may want to avoid being judged negatively by friends, peers, or future potential dating partners. Many victims choose not to report rape out of a perhaps justifiable fear of being victimized again (Hock, 2015). In addition, many victims do not acknowledge rape or sexual assault, but instead use more benign labels such as "bad sex" or "miscommunication." One meta-analysis of 28 studies (with almost 6,000 participants) found that two thirds of women rape survivors, particularly those who experienced acquaintance rape, did not acknowledge that they had been raped (Wilson & Miller, 2016).

Survivors of sexual assault have a higher than average risk of developing post-traumatic stress disorder (PTSD) and depression, and of abusing alcohol and other substances (Ullman, Relyea, Peter-Hagene, & Vasquez, 2013; Zinzow et al., 2010). People with PTSD may have flashbacks to the traumatic experience, disturbing dreams, emotional numbing, and nervousness that can persist for years. Women's attributions for the assault influence their adjustment. Those who blame themselves tend to experience more adjustment difficulties, including a higher risk for depression (Vickerman & Margolin, 2009), whereas support from family and friends influences positive adjustment (Orchowski, Untied, & Gidycz, 2013).

What about men? Male rape is increasingly recognized and most states have revised their rape laws to be sex-neutral (Hock, 2015). Men may feel a greater sense of shame and stigma than women and are even less likely than women to report being sexually assaulted. An estimated 2% of men in the United States (i.e., about 2 million) have experienced sexual assault, with the majority committed by acquaintances (Breiding et al., 2014).

Contextual influences, such as the prevalence of rape myths, can affect the prevalence of sexual assault. College men are more accepting of rape myths than are women, and are more likely to cling to them following date rape education classes (Maxwell & Scott, 2014; Stewart, 2014). Gender-role stereotyping may contribute to the prevalence of sexual assault, as cultural stereotypes of men and women's roles, encouraging dominance, aggression, and competition in males and passivity in females, may support attitudes that are accepting of sexual violence. Research with college students has shown that students who are highly gender stereotyped and believe in strict gender roles are more likely than their peers to blame sexual assault survivors, express attitudes condoning nonconsensual sex, and be aroused by depictions of rape (Lambert & Raichle, 2000; Malamuth, Addison, & Koss, 2000). Men who engage in sexual assault tend to interpret women's behavior inaccurately, often perceiving warmth and friendliness as indicating sexual interest (Perilloux, Easton, & Buss, 2012). They buy into rape myths, such as the belief that a victim "asked for it" by dressing attractively or behaving flirtatiously; that nonconsensual sex with a romantic partner, friend, or acquaintance

LIVES IN CONTEXT

• • Adolescent Dating Violence

Many adolescents find themselves in abusive relationships, but dating violence is less likely to be reported than adult domestic violence.

As adolescents begin to date, some find themselves in tumultuous relationships characterized by physical violence. It is estimated that between 20% and 40% of adolescents report experiencing physical aggression in a dating relationship (Herrman, 2009; Raiford, Wingood, & DiClemente, 2007). The most serious dating violence, resulting in serious wounds or violent sexual assault, is less frequent, with less than 2% of adolescents reporting these forms of dating violence (Wolitzky-Taylor et al., 2008).

The majority of victims of dating violence are first victimized prior to age 15 (Leadbeater, Banister, Ellis, & Yeung, 2008). Dating violence often emerges within the context of mutual partner aggression in which both partners perpetrate and sustain aggression (Sears, Sandra Byers, & Lisa Price, 2007; T. S. Williams, Connolly, Pepler, Laporte, & Craig, 2008). Girls are more likely to inflict psychological abuse and minor physical abuse (slapping, throwing objects, pinching); whereas boys are more likely to inflict physical abuse, including severe types such as punching, as well as sexual abuse, making girls more likely to suffer physical wounds than boys. Physical violence tends to occur alongside other problematic relationship dynamics and behaviors such as verbal conflict, jealousy, and accusations of "cheating" (Giordano, Soto, Manning, & Longmore, 2010).

Who is most at risk for victimization? Risky activities, such as substance use and vandalism, as well as having friends and siblings who engage in risky activities, are associated with increased risk of victimization (East & Hokoda, 2015; Van Ouytsel, Ponnet, & Walrave, 2017). Many of the risk factors for experiencing dating victimization are also outcomes of dating violence, such as depression, anxiety, negative interactions with family and friends, low self-esteem, substance use, and adolescent pregnancy (Exner-Cortens, Eckenrode, & Rothman, 2013; Niolon et al., 2015). Adolescents who experience dating violence are at higher risk of victimization by intimate partner violence as adults (Exner-Cortens, Eckenrode, Bunge, & Rothman, 2017).

Although research has shown a correlation between men's rigid traditional views of gender and risk for committing dating violence (McCauley et al., 2013), the relationship is not causal. Instead, it is when rigid gender views are accompanied by favorable attitudes toward the use of force in relationships that men are at increased risk for committing dating violence (Reyes, Foshee, Niolon, Reidy, & Hall, 2016). As such, significant risk factors for engaging in dating violence include inadequate anger management, poor interpersonal skills, early involvement with antisocial peers, a history of problematic relationships with parents and peers, exposure to family violence and community violence, and a history of maltreatment in childhood (Foshee et al., 2014, 2015; Vagi et al., 2013).

Adolescent dating violence is less likely to be reported than adult domestic violence: Only about 1 in 11 cases is reported to adults or authorities (Herrman, 2009). Common reasons for not reporting dating violence include fear of retaliation, ongoing emotional ties, denial, self-blame, hope that it will get better, and helplessness. In addition, only about one third of adolescents report that they would intervene if they became aware of a peer's involvement in dating violence, typically expressing the belief that dating violence is the couple's own private business (Weisz & Black, 2008).

Encouraging close relationships with parents is an important way of preventing dating violence because adolescents learn about romantic relationships by observing and reflecting on the behaviors of others. Adolescent girls who are close with their parents are more likely than their peers to recognize unhealthy relationships, are less likely to be victimized by dating violence, and are more likely to seek help if a relationship begins to turn violent (Leadbeater et al., 2008).

What Do You Think?

1. From your perspective, how prevalent is dating violence in adolescence? Why do you think it occurs?

2. How might views about gender influence how members of a couple interact? Does gender influence risk for violence? What other factors, if any, matter?

---

cannot be considered rape; or that men are driven to commit rape by uncontrollable sexual impulses. Men who express such attitudes are more likely than other men to show suspicion of women, meaning that they generally doubt women's honesty in responding to sexual advances, particularly when a woman communicates clearly and assertively that she is rejecting an advance (Malamuth et al., 2000). Related to sexual assault is abuse or dating violence, a subject examined in Lives in Context.

SEXUAL ACTIVITY IN ADULTHOOD

Generally speaking, sexual activity is highest among people in young adulthood, from their mid-20s to mid-30s, and declines gradually for people in their 40s and again in their 50s, but the amount of decline is modest (King & Regan, 2014). It is estimated that young adults engage in sexual activity only about one to two times a month more than do their middle-aged counterparts (Debby Herbenick et al., 2010). Not surprisingly, sex predicts positive affect the next day (Debrot, Meuwly, Muise, Impett, & Schoebi, 2017), but there are also long-term associations. Research suggests that the frequency of sexual intercourse is associated with emotional, sexual, and relationship satisfaction, as well as overall happiness, in adults (Costa & Brody, 2012; McNulty, Wenner, & Fisher, 2016). The relationship between sexual well-being and happiness is seen in middle-aged and older adults in 29 countries (Laumann et al., 2006). For adults in relationships, however, the sexual frequency–happiness link peaks at once a week (Muise, Schimmack, & Impett, 2016).

For midlife adults, the major predictors of sexual activity are health and having a partner (King & Regan, 2014). By midlife there are more women than men in the general population, and women are much more likely to lack a partner. For example, in one study of about 1,300 midlife women, those who were married or cohabiting were 8 times more likely than their single peers to be sexually active (Thomas, Hess, & Thurston, 2015).

Physical changes that accompany biological aging can influence sexual activity. For example, the reduction in estrogen that accompanies menopause is associated with a reduction in vaginal lubrication. This can make sexual intercourse uncomfortable or even painful, but it is not an indicator of a lack of desire. Vaginal lubricants can relieve this symptom (Debra Herbenick et al., 2011). Many women show no change in sexual interest after menopause and some show an increased interest as contraception is no longer needed (DeLamater, 2012).

With age, men are more likely to experience difficulties establishing or maintaining erections (Araujo, Mohr, & McKinlay, 2004). Prevalence of *erectile dysfunction (ED)* ranges from 2% to 9% in men between the ages of 40 and 49 years. It then increases to 20–40% in men aged 60–69 years. In men older than 70 years, prevalence of erectile dysfunction ranges from 50% to 100% (Shamloul & Ghanem, 2013). ED is not inevitable, however, and it has a strong connection with health. Vascular disease is the most common cause of ED (Moore et al., 2014). A study of a sample of 651 men (ages 51–60 years) from the Vietnam Era Twin Study of Aging found that men with ED are at a 65% increased relative risk of developing coronary heart disease and a 43% increased risk of stroke within 10 years (Moore et al., 2014). ED has also been associated with poor cognitive performance, particularly on attention–executive–psychomotor speed tasks. There have long been stigmatizing misconceptions about ED, but it is now known that up to 80% of ED cases are due to physiological causes, with vascular disease being the most common etiology (Jackson et al., 2006). Not only is ED frequently due to vasculopathic processes, it has been well established that ED is a strong predictor of future cardiovascular diagnoses (Fang, Rosen, Vita, Ganz, & Kupelian, 2015).

SEXUALITY AND SEXUAL ACTIVITY IN LATE ADULTHOOD

Media images of sexuality have traditionally portrayed only attractive young people, shaping and reinforcing societal misconceptions that sexuality disappears in older people (Bauer, McAuliffe, & Nay, 2007). Even researchers who study sexuality often overlook the views and experiences of elders by focusing on those under the age of 60 (Gott, 2005; Smith, Rissel, Richters, Grulich, & de Visser, 2003). Many assume that sexuality is irrelevant to older people, reflecting the stereotype that aging is a feared negative event marked by rapid physical and cognitive decline. As the population of older adults increases and healthy aging becomes more common, widespread advertising of medications for sexual performance (e.g., to treat erectile dysfunction) may shift assumptions toward the view that older adults desire, but are physically unable to have, sex. In fact, however, adults remain interested and capable of sexual activity well into older adulthood.

Just as in middle age, good sex in the past predicts good sex in the future. For example, five decades of research has consistently shown that older people generally maintain sexual interest and remain sexually capable well into their 80s and often 90s (DeLamater & Koepsel, 2015; Gott & Hinchliff, 2003). Research conducted in Europe, the United States, Australia, and Asia confirms that many older people continue to view sexual interest and activity as important (Bauer, Haesler, & Fetherstonhaugh, 2016; Bauer et al., 2007; Hyde et al., 2010; Minichiello, Plummer, & Loxton, 2004; Palacios-Ceña et al., 2012). One study of older adults who have a sex partner found that all rated sex as "important" and more than one-third as "very important" in their lives (Gott & Hinchliff, 2003).

The nature of sexual expression often changes in older adulthood, but most older adults remain interested in, and satisfied by, sexual activity.

REUTERS/Lucy Nicholson

The frequency of sexual activity declines with age, but sexual satisfaction often remains unchanged (Minichiello et al., 2004; Thompson et al., 2011). In one study, 54% of men and 21% of women ages 70 to 80 reported having sexual intercourse within the past year, and nearly one quarter of those men and women had intercourse more than once a week (Nicolosi et al., 2006). One third of a sample of 75- to 85-year-old men reported having at least one sexual encounter within the past year (Hyde, et al., 2010). Likewise, in a 30-year longitudinal study of nearly 2,800 Australian men, 40% of those aged 75 to 79, but only 11% of those aged 90 to 95, reported having had sex in the past year (Doskoch, 2011). Reasons for lack of sexual activity include physical problems, lack of interest, partner's lack of interest, partner's physical problems, and the loss of a partner (Palacios-Ceña et al., 2012).

The nature of sexual expression shifts with age, encompassing an array of behaviors (e.g., self-stimulation, noncoital activity with partners) as well as sexual activity in both long-term and new relationships (Hodson & Skeen, 1994; McAuliffe, Bauer, & Nay, 2007). Because of the hormonal changes that accompany menopause, women may experience lack of vaginal lubrication and therefore find intercourse uncomfortable (DeLamater & Koepsel, 2015). With increasing age, males' erections tend to take longer to achieve, are less frequent, and more difficult to sustain than was the case when they were younger; however these normative changes should not be mistaken for erectile dysfunction (Araujo et al., 2004; Tan, 2011). Many factors may diminish sexual response and satisfaction: cigarette smoking, heavy drinking, obesity, poor health, and attitudes toward sexuality and aging, among others (DeLamater, 2012). Many illnesses encountered in advancing age (e.g., arthritis, heart disease, diabetes, Parkinson's disease, stroke, cancer, and depression) can have a negative impact on an individual's interest or participation in sexual activity (Syme, Klonoff, Macera, & Brodine, 2013; Taylor & Gosney, 2011). Likewise, prescription drugs, over-the-counter medications, and herbal supplements may have side effects that can alter or impair sexual function.

Sexual activity is a correlate of health, as those who report good health are more likely to be sexually active (DeLamater & Koepsel, 2015; Holden, Collins, Handelsman, Jolley, & Pitts, 2014). However, just as during other phases of life, there is a bidirectional relationship: Sexual activity is likely to enhance health by reducing stress and improving well-being (Brody, 2010).

LIFESPAN BRAIN DEVELOPMENT

• • Are There Sex Differences in the Brain?

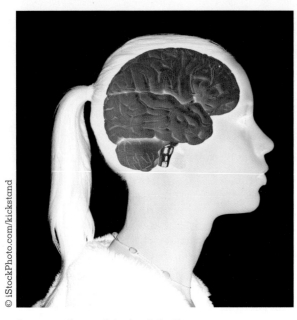

Are men and women's brains distinct?

We have seen that boys and girls experience different patterns and trajectories of biological change with puberty. Do these differences extend to brain development? Are there sex differences in brain development?

Across all periods in life, the brains of males and females are more alike than different. The most commonly reported sex difference is a 10% larger total brain size in males, even during early adolescence when girls, because of their earlier growth spurt, are on an average slightly taller than boys of the same age (Giedd et al., 2012; Lenroot et al., 2007). Boys and girls show similar developmental changes in grey and white brain matter but on different timetables, with girls reaching peaks in volume and cortical thickness earlier than boys (about 10.5 years and 14.5 years, respectively; Ball, Adamson, Beare, & Seal, 2017; Mills, Goddings et al., 2014). Some research suggests that there is more variability in neurological development among boys than girls; that is, boys show more individual differences in brain development than do girls (Wierenga, Sexton, Laake, Giedd, & Tamnes, 2017).

Puberty, specifically the increase in the sex hormones testosterone and estrogen, triggers a burst in brain development, synaptogenesis, and synaptic pruning (Ahmed et al., 2008; Sato, Schulz, Sisk, & Wood, 2008). Androgens and estrogens affect the brain in different ways that are related to differences in hormone receptor distribution

across brain regions (Bramen et al., 2012; Goddings et al., 2014). The amygdala, which plays a role in emotion, is rich in testosterone receptors, and the hippocampus, which influences aspects of memory and emotion, has more estrogen receptors (Bramen et al., 2012; Giedd et al., 2012; Neufang et al., 2009). The volumes of the amygdala and hippocampus increase during puberty in both males and females, but in different ratios related to the effects of testosterone and estrogen (Goddings et al., 2014). Sex differences emerge such that the amygdala shows greater thickening, as compared with the hippocampus, in boys and in girls, the hippocampus thickens proportionally more than the amygdala (Bramen et al., 2012; Neufang et al., 2009).

A recent study suggested that the sex differences in amygdala and hippocampus volumes correspond to pubertal development (Goddings et al., 2014). In this study of individuals aged 7 to 20, girls who were more pubertally mature than other girls showed a larger amygdala and hippocampus volume in late childhood and early adolescence, an earlier peak volume, and a smaller volume at the end of puberty than their less-mature peers. On the other hand, boys showed a linear increase in volume; boys who were more pubertally advanced than other boys showed larger volumes throughout the age range studied (Goddings et al., 2014). The peak in volume represents the burst of synaptogenesis that accompanies the introduction of pubertal hormones, appearing earlier in girls than boys. In turn, the reductions in volume reflect the maturational process of pruning. Girls who were more physically mature showed more thinning, whereas boys, who tend to lag in maturity, lag in pruning. Sex differences in the volume of the amygdala and hippocampus tend to be greater in the later stages of puberty, suggesting that boys and girls might begin and end the pruning process on a different timetable relative to puberty (Bramen et al., 2012).

Although sex differences in amygdala and hippocampal volumes are marked in adolescence, males and females may catch up to each other. Recent studies, including meta analyses of more than 100 studies, suggest that there are no sex differences in the amygdala and hippocampal volumes of adults (Marwha, Halari, & Eliot, 2017; Tan, Ma, Vira, Marwha, & Eliot, 2016).

What Do You Think?

1. **How might sex differences in brain development manifest in behavior?**

2. **Do boys and girls behave differently *because* of neurological differences? Why or why not?**

Thinking in Context 13.4

1. There are many commonly held, but inaccurate, beliefs about the nature of sexuality and associated health issues in adolescence and emerging adulthood. Identify two common beliefs and explain why they are inaccurate.

2. College students are at heightened risk of sexual assault. What is it about emerging adulthood and the college environment that contributes to the prevalence of sexual assault?

3. Recall from Chapter 1 that development reflects continuities and discontinuities. Do you think that the changes in sexuality during the adult years exemplify continuity or discontinuity in development (or both)? Explain your response.

 Apply Your Knowledge

Four-year-old Tony is an active, curious preschooler. His mother, Geneva, says he "plays hard." Tony says he wants to be the best, to climb the highest, and run the fastest. He feels that his father, Eric, is the best father in the whole wide world because Daddy is big and strong. Tony wants to be just like Daddy when he grows up.

Tony and Eric do all kinds of "boy things," as Geneva calls it. Tony says he thinks Daddy is smart and fun. Tony especially likes it when he and Eric wrestle on the floor each night when they watch sports on TV together. They like to watch contact sports, such as hockey, and they cheer together if the players start a fight. Tony also watches TV most afternoons while he waits for Eric to come home from work. Tony's favorite shows are crime-fighting cartoons, but he also likes to watch wrestling.

Geneva often scolds Tony for playing too roughly with other children. She used to put Tony in time out for 5 minutes when he misbehaved, but that did not decrease Tony's roughhousing and misbehaving. One time, when he hurt his cousin with his roughhousing, Geneva gave him a spanking to show him what it feels like and to stop his behavior. She had been so overcome with frustration over not being able to stop Tony's roughhousing that she didn't know what else to do. Geneva bought Tony a special doll for boys, named My Buddy, but this upset Eric, who said that dolls are for girls. Eric insisted that Geneva give away the My Buddy doll to charity.

Tony's preschool teacher has called his parents a few times to report Tony's aggressive behavior with other children—mostly boys, as he tends to be more gentle and agreeable with girls, as long as they don't defy him. Geneva has apologized for his aggressiveness and has taken time off from her job to observe Tony's class at preschool and encourage Tony to learn better social skills. Eric, however, says that rough play simply is what boys do, and expresses satisfaction at Tony's dominant behavior. He tells Tony to "be a man" and defend himself if other children try to push him around.

1. Describe the gender norms followed by Tony's mother and father. What messages is Tony receiving from each parent, from the media, and from the larger society?

2. According to the various theoretical perspectives presented in this chapter, how would you explain Tony's tendency to behave aggressively?

3. Considering what you have learned about gender roles and sexuality through the lifespan, what predictions would you make for Tony's sexual activity as he goes through puberty, the teenage and emerging adult years, and beyond?

Give your students the SAGE edge!

SAGE edge offers a robust online environment featuring an impressive array of free tools and resources for review, study, and further exploration, keeping both instructors and students on the cutting edge of teaching and learning. Learn more at **edge.sagepub.com/kuthertopical.**

CHAPTER 13 IN REVIEW

13.1 Describe the progression of gender development from infancy through late adulthood, including common stereotypes and sex differences.

KEY TERMS

transgender
gender stability
gender constancy

gender schema
gender schema theory
gender identity

SUMMARY

Gender stereotypes reflect generalizations about the behaviors and traits characteristic of men and women; however there are few sex differences in cognitive or social abilities. Gender role norms appear in most cultures. Gender typing begins in infancy. Young children have rigid beliefs about gender that influence their preferences and behavior. Gender rigidity tends to peak and decline in middle to late childhood. Early adolescents may experience gender intensification, but become more flexible through late adolescence. Adults' views of gender and the roles they adopt tend to shift over the lifespan, often becoming more traditional after the birth of a child and more fluid in midlife and older adulthood.

KEY TERMS

sex
gender
gender stereotypes
gender role norms

gender typing
gender identity
androgyny

REVIEW QUESTIONS

1. What are two examples of gender role norms?

2. What sex differences exist between males and females?

3. How do gender role knowledge and preferences develop from infancy through adolescence?

4. How do views of gender typically change in adulthood?

13.2 Compare and contrast biological, cognitive, and contextual accounts of gender role development.

SUMMARY

Children are immersed from birth in a gender-oriented world and they quickly learn about gender roles and gender stereotypes. Biological influences on gender role development include genes and hormones. Cognitive-developmental perspectives emphasize children's awareness and knowledge of gender as influences on their behavior. Some aspects of gender typing are influenced by modeling, reinforcement, and shaping by parents and peers. Contextual approaches to gender examine social learning and the influence of the sociocultural context in which children are raised. Children also learn about gender roles from various forms of media. Finally, societies generally emphasize different behaviors as appropriate for males and females—and cultures vary dramatically in how strictly gender stereotypes are applied.

REVIEW QUESTIONS

1. What are common biological explanations for gender role development?

2. How do advances in cognition contribute to gender role development?

3. Identify contextual influences on gender role development.

13.3 Discuss the development of sexuality and sexual orientation.

SUMMARY

Sexuality emerges in childhood and becomes meaningful in adolescence as young people develop a sense of sexual identity. One aspect of sexual identity is sexual orientation. Cultures vary in attitudes about same-sex relations, but same-sex behavior is found in virtually all societies. Young people today are disclosing their sexual orientation at earlier ages than prior generations, from mid-adolescence through emerging adulthood. Constructing an identity as a lesbian, gay, bisexual, or transgender young person can be complicated by the prejudice and discrimination that many LGBT youth experience in their schools and communities. If accompanied by support and acceptance, disclosing a sexual minority identity can facilitate the development of identity, self-esteem, and psychological health and can often reduce distress.

KEY TERMS

sexual identity
sexual orientation

adrenarche

REVIEW QUESTIONS

1. When does sexual development begin?

2. How do individuals begin to determine their sexual orientation?

3. How might contextual factors influence young people's exploration and expression of sexual orientation?

13.4 Identify the forms that sexuality and sexual activity take from adolescence through late adulthood, as well as associated health issues.

SUMMARY

Sexual activity is normative in late adolescence, but early sexual activity is associated with problem behaviors. Influences on sexual activity include the peer group, especially perceived peer behavior and sexual norms, and relationships with parents. Adolescents are disproportionally at risk for STI diagnoses. The birth rate in adolescent girls has declined consistently since 1990 but remains a pressing problem as adolescent motherhood is associated with risks to adolescent mothers and their children. Emerging adulthood is often a time of sexual experimentation that is accompanied by an increased likelihood of sexual assault. Sexual activity continues in middle and late adulthood and adults often maintain interest and ability well into late older adulthood.

KEY TERMS

sexting
sexually transmitted infections (STIs)
human immunodeficiency virus (HIV)
acquired immune deficiency syndrome (AIDS)
rape
sexual assault
casual sex

REVIEW QUESTIONS

1. What is normative sexual activity for adolescents and emerging adults?

2. What are three risks associated with sexual activity in adolescence and emerging adulthood?

3. How does sexual activity change over the adult years?

Test your understanding of the content.
Review the flashcards and quizzes at
edge.sagepub.com/kuthertopical

Contexts of Development

Throughout our lifespan, we are immersed in a system of contexts with which we interact, and those interactions influence our development and who we become.

The home context is central to development. Children are raised in many different kinds of families. Family stability is a better predictor of child outcomes than any particular type of family. Good relationships between parents and children tend to endure into adulthood.

All throughout life people choose friends who share similar interests and values. During adolescence, peer groups become tight-knit. The pressure to be accepted rises and then declines. Friendships tend to improve throughout adulthood and the social circle narrows in older adulthood as individuals cultivate fewer, but emotionally closer and more meaningful, relationships.

Children spend much of their time at school. The transitions to middle school and high school are often challenging and sometimes accompanied by declines in academic motivation and achievement. But most students rebound. Many people attend college, at least for a time, and the college context promotes cognitive and socioemotional development.

As they enter the work context, many young adults must realign their expectations with their experience. Job satisfaction tends to increase with age and a corresponding preference for intrinsic rewards. The work context is central for most adults, making retirement from work is a major life transition. Most adults adjust well and report increased life satisfaction, especially those who have planned for the financial and lifestyle changes that accompany retirement.

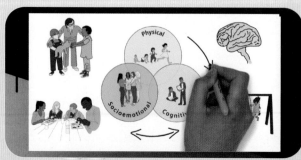

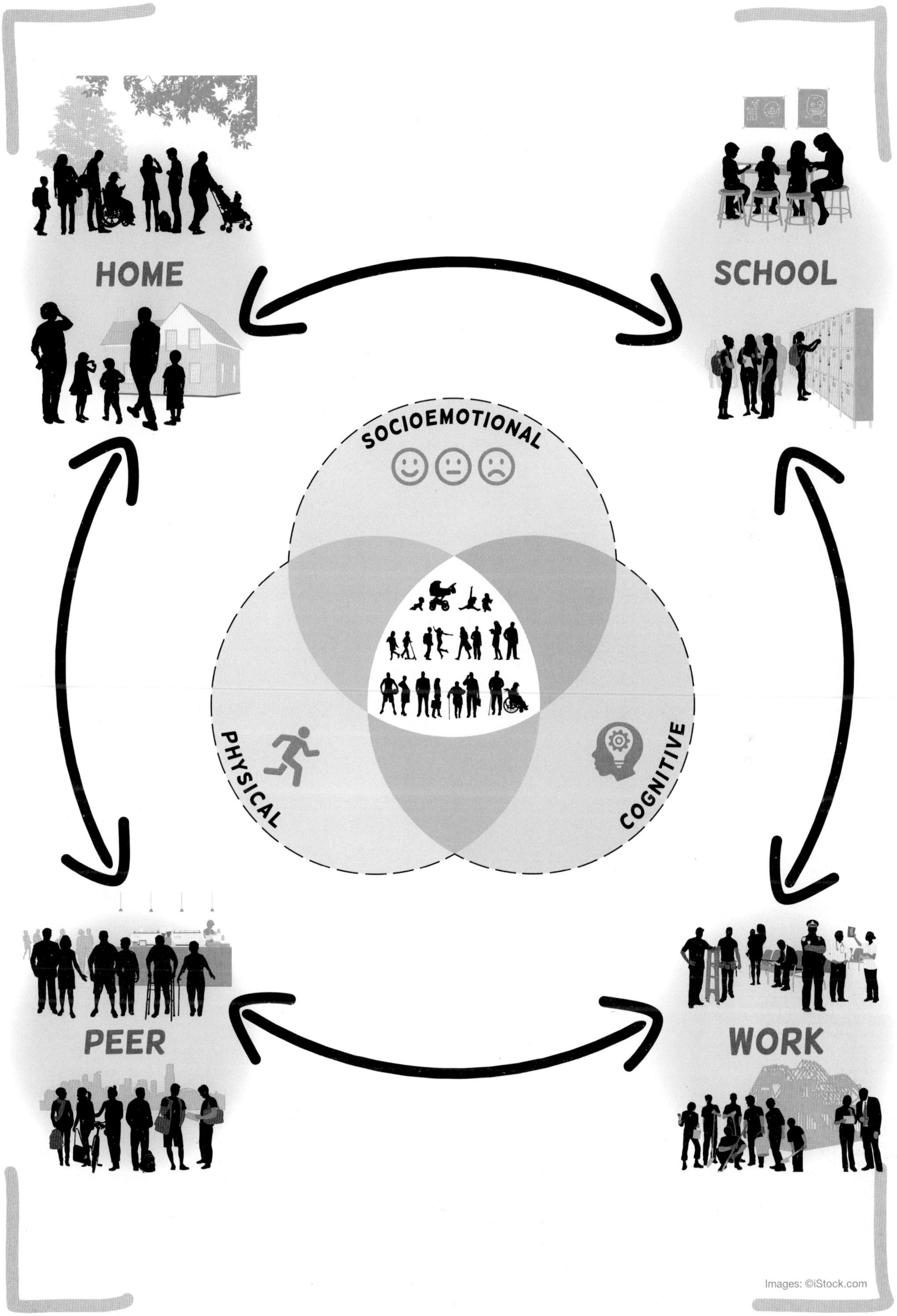

HOME

SCHOOL

SOCIOEMOTIONAL

PHYSICAL

COGNITIVE

PEER

WORK

Images: ©iStock.com

Social Relationships: Family and Peers

Learning Objectives

14.1 Discuss the influence of living arrangements and decisions about family formation on adult development.

14.2 Compare and contrast child outcomes associated with various family constellations.

14.3 Explain the effects of various parenting methods on children and adolescents.

14.4 Describe the changes that take place within family relationships after individuals reach adulthood.

14.5 Discuss how peer relationships develop and change throughout the lifespan.

Digital Resources

📄 Relationship Churning
🖥 Why Marry?

▶ Blended Families
📄 Poverty Among Grandmother-Headed Families

🔊 Tiger Parenting
▶ Parental Monitoring Online

🖥 Sandwich Generation on Steroids

▶ Technology and Social Media
🔊 Child's Play and the Brain

⑤SAGE edge™   Master these learning objectives with multimedia resources available at **edge.sagepub.com/kuthertopical** and *Lives in Context* video cases available in the interactive eBook.

"I'd like you all to meet my friend Ruth," Elaine announced to the members of her neighborhood book discussion group. "She's visiting from California. Ruth and I have been friends since kindergarten." "Wow!" responded Theresa. "How many years is that—more than 50?" Ruth and Elaine nodded. "We've lived on opposite coasts since we were in our 30s," said Ruth, "but we've stuck together through high school and college, marriages and divorces, raising kids, and all the ups and downs of our careers." What factors contribute to lasting friendships, and what benefits do peer relationships convey to individuals? This chapter examines the various ways in which we form relationships as we progress through the lifespan.

SOCIAL TRANSITIONS AND FAMILY FORMATION

LO 14.1 Discuss the influence of living arrangements and decisions about family formation on adult development.

Although most young people marry in early adulthood, trends such as late marriage, divorce, and cohabitation mean that many adults in the United States will spend a large part of their adult lives as unmarried. In addition, an increasing number of adults choose not to marry. While this is still a small minority, today it is more common than in the past for U.S. adults to remain single throughout their lives.

FIGURE 14.1: Reasons That People Are Not Married, by Age, 2014

% of never-married adults who say the main reason they are not currently married is . . .

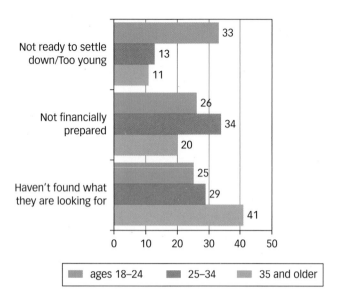

Not ready to settle down/Too young: 33, 13, 11

Not financially prepared: 26, 34, 20

Haven't found what they are looking for: 25, 29, 41

■ ages 18–24 ■ 25–34 ■ 35 and older

Note: Based on those who have never been married and want to get married are not sure (n=369). Volunteered responses of "Other" and "Don't know/Refused" not shown.

Source: Survey of U.S. adults conducted May 22–25 and May 29–June 1, 2014. Pew Research Center.

Most young adults in North America and Europe cohabitate, or live together, in committed relationships.

SINGLEHOOD

Singlehood, not living with a romantic partner, is common among U.S. young adults. About one third of 25- to 39-year-olds have never married, including 18% of 35- to 39-year-olds (U.S. Bureau of the Census, 2015). About half of single adults say they would like to get married in the future (Wang & Parker, 2014). Younger adults, under the age of 30, are more likely to say they would like to get married (66% as compared with 33% of adults 30 and older). In contrast with men, women tend to select mates who are the same age or older, are equally or better educated, and who are professionally successful. Because of these tendencies, highly educated professional women who are financially independent, and therefore lack an economic incentive to marry, may find few potential mates whom they consider suitable (Sharp & Ganong, 2007). Some women attribute singlehood to focusing more on career goals than marriage and others point to disappointing romantic relationships or to never meeting the right person (Baumbusch, 2004). Overall, women are more likely than men to remain single for many years or for their entire lives.

Adults who are likely to describe themselves as single by choice are those who are self-supporting, feel a sense of control over their romantic lives, and have not encountered anyone they wish to marry (Sharp & Ganong, 2007). Such young adults tend to report enjoying singlehood and the freedom to take risks and experiment with lifestyle changes (Austrom & Hanel, 1985). They also tend to tend to associate singlehood with independence, self-fulfillment, and autonomy throughout their life course, including in old age (Timonen & Doyle, 2013). Being single increases the social connections of both women and men. Compared to their married peers, single adults are more likely to stay in frequent touch with parents, friends, and neighbors, and to give and receive help from them, suggesting some important social benefits of singlehood (Sarkisian & Gerstel, 2016).

COHABITATION

The trend for increasing education and delayed career entry that is characteristic of emerging adulthood has led to a rise in **cohabitation**, the practice of unmarried couples sharing a home. Today, more than half of young adults in their 20s have lived with a romantic partner and about two-thirds of U.S. couples live together before marriage (Manning, 2013; Sassler & Miller, 2011). Cohabitation is even more common in Europe: More than 75% of couples in Northern and Central Europe and the UK cohabit, and about 90% do so in Sweden and Denmark (Hsueh, Morrison, & Doss, 2009; Manning, 2013; Popenoe, 2009).

Some young adults move in with their partners early in the relationship because of changes in employment or housing situations, for the sake of convenience, or in response to pregnancy (Sassler & Miller, 2011). Young adults commonly cite assessing romantic compatibility, convenience, and potential improvement in finances as reasons for cohabiting (Copen, Daniels, & Mosher, 2013; King & Scott, 2005). In the United States, young adults of low socioeconomic status, as well as of African American and Puerto Rican heritage, are more likely to cohabit as an alternative to marriage (Cherlin, 2010; Seltzer, 2004), whereas European American young adults are more likely to marry after a period of cohabitation (Lesthaeghe, López-Colás, & Neidert, 2016).

Sacramento Bee/Tribune/Getty

FIGURE 14.2: Percentage of Cohabiting Households in Selected Countries, Couples Ages 20 Years and Older

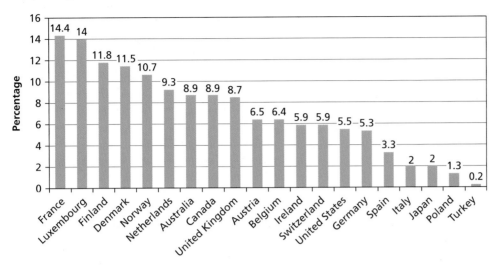

Source: Data from Organisation for Economic Co-operation and Development, 2009 (http://www.oecd.org/els/family/SF3_3_Cohabitation_rate_and_prevalence_of_other_forms_of_partnership_Jan2013.pdf).

Cultures differ in the acceptability of cohabitation and have different laws and policies pertaining to it. In many European countries, cohabitation is viewed not as a precursor but rather as an alternative to marriage. Cohabiting couples in those countries often hold legal rights similar to those of married couples and show similar levels of devotion as married couples (Hiekel, Liefbroer, & Poortman, 2014; Perelli-Harris & Gassen, 2012). Cohabiting couples in Canada are afforded the same rights as married couples after living together for a period of 1 to 3 years, depending on the province in which they reside (Le Bourdais & Lapierre-Adamcyk, 2004). In contrast, cohabitation is nearly unheard-of in some countries, such as Ireland, Italy, Japan, and the Philippines, where fewer than 10% of adults have ever lived with an unmarried partner (Batalova & Cohen, 2002; Williams, Kabamalan, & Ogena, 2007).

The stability of cohabiting unions also varies from one country to another. Overall, cohabiting couples in the United States tend to be less satisfied, show higher rates of intimate violence, and have less stable relationships than married couples; one third of cohabiting couples in the United States dissolve in 3 years (Jose, Daniel O'Leary, & Moyer, 2010; Kenney & McLanahan, 2006). Much of the research with U.S. samples suggests that cohabiting couples who go on to marry tend to have unhappier marriages with a greater likelihood of divorce than couples who did not live together before marriage (Copen et al., 2013; Jose et al., 2010; Kulik & Havusha-Morgenstern, 2011). In contrast, in Europe the rates of dissolution for cohabiting couples are similar to those of married couples (Hiekel et al., 2014; Perelli-Harris & Gassen, 2012). Among 15,000 British couples who dissolved their union, cohabiting unions were much shorter in duration—about 4 years, on average, as compared with 14 years for married couples (Gravningen et al., 2017). Cohabiting and married couples list similar reasons for break ups: most commonly, growing apart, followed by arguments.

According to some research, as cohabitation becomes more common, its association with marital instability is weakening (Manning & Cohen, 2012; Reinhold, 2010). Clearly, more research is needed as the association of cohabitation and marital stability among U.S. couples is complicated and is influenced by other relationship factors. For example, couples who enter cohabitation with marriage plans, such as while engaged, tend to experience marriages with levels of marital quality, stability, and distress similar to those of married respondents who had not cohabited (Rhoades, Stanley, & Markman, 2009; Stanley, Rhoades, Amato, Markman, & Johnson, 2010). In addition, the correlates of cohabitation vary with the couple's age group.

singlehood Refers to not living with a romantic partner.

cohabitation An arrangement in which a committed, unmarried, couple lives together in the same home.

Benjamin King/Shutterstock.com

The social clock marks normative age-graded events, such as graduations, marriage, and parenthood.

Rates of cohabitation among adults over age 50 have more than doubled since 2000 to 2.75 million adults, or 8% of persons over age 50 (S. L. Brown & Wright, 2016; U.S. Bureau of the Census, 2012). Compared with younger couples, older adults who cohabit tend to be in relationships of longer duration, and often view the relationship as an alternative to marriage (S. L. Brown, Bulanda, & Lee, 2012; King & Scott, 2005). Cohabiters over the age of 50 tend to report higher quality relationships than younger cohabiters: They perceive more fairness, more time spent alone with their partner, and fewer disagreements or arguments. They are also less likely to report thinking their relationship might be in trouble or that they will eventually separate (King & Scott, 2005). Cohabitation also shows similar health benefits to marriage, as older adult cohabiters do not differ from married couples in their reports of emotional satisfaction, pleasure, openness, time spent together, and criticism (Brown & Kawamura, 2010). This finding holds true in a variety of cultures. Research with British, Italian, and Danish middle-aged and older adult samples suggests that cohabitation brings mental health benefits, as well as physical health benefits such as reduced rates of disability and mortality (Juul Nilsson, Lund, & Avlund, 2008; Perelli-Harris & Styrc, 2016; Scafato et al., 2008).

MARRIAGE

Over the past half-century, marriage rates have declined to record lows—yet nearly all adults in the United States will marry. In 2014, more than 80% of adults had married by age 45, 90% by age 60, and more than 95% by age 80 (U.S. Bureau of the Census, 2015). The median age of first marriage in the United States is 27 and 29, for women and men respectively, an increase of more than 6 years since 1975 (U.S. Bureau of the Census, 2015a; see Figure 14.3). Similar age increases have occurred in Canada, with the average age at first marriage being 31 for males and 30 for females—up more than 6 years since 1975 (Milan, 2013) —as well as in some European countries. For example, in 2011 in Sweden, the median age was as high as 36 for men and 33 for women, up 7 years since 1980 (United Nations Economic Commission for Europe, 2015).

Despite this trend, there remains variability in the age of first marriage. Young people of low socioeconomic status tend to marry at younger ages than do those of higher

FIGURE 14.3: U.S. Median Age at First Marriage, 1890 to 2014

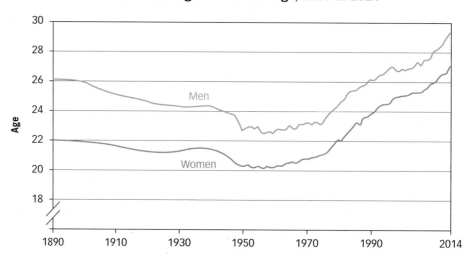

Source: U.S. Bureau of the Census (2015a).

socioeconomic status (Meier & Allen, 2008). In the United States, African Americans are the least likely to marry, and when they marry, they do so later and spend less time married than European Americans (Dixon, 2009). Factors that contribute to marriage rates of African American adults include the prevalence of more females than males, greater employment instability among African American males, and higher rates of cohabitation as compared with other ethnic groups (Lundberg & Pollak, 2016; Raley, Sweeney, & Wondra, 2015).

Generally speaking, there are economic, physical, and psychological benefits to marriage. Married people around the world tend to live longer, and are happier, physically healthier, wealthier, and in better mental health than non-married people (Grover & Helliwell, 2014; Koball, Moiduddin, Henderson, Goesling, & Besculides, 2010; Vanassche, Swicegood, & Matthijs, 2012). Nevertheless, the transition to marriage is often challenging, as newlyweds experience multiple changes during their first years of marriage, such as coordinating and making decisions about living arrangements, housework, eating habits, and sexual activity (Wallerstein, 1994). Many newlyweds struggle with rising debt, which is associated with higher levels of conflict (Dew, 2008). Most couples report a decline in relationship satisfaction during the first year of marriage (Kurdek, 2005). However, couples who are successful at managing the transition to married life express warmth, empathy, and respect in their relationship (Gadassi et al., 2015; Phillips, Bischoff, Abbott, & Xia, 2009). They are able to address differences and resolve conflicts constructively by expressing feelings calmly, listening, accepting responsibility, and compromising (Hanzal & Segrin, 2009). Partners in successful marriages are able to maintain positive emotions for their spouse even in the midst of conflict (Gottman & Gottman, 2017). In contrast, during arguments, unhappy couples easily sink into negative emotions that are overwhelming and, like quicksand, difficult to escape.

One of the best predictors of marital satisfaction and a long-lasting marriage is the partners' chronological maturity, or age. Generally speaking, the younger the bride and groom, the less likely they are to have a lifelong marriage (Amato & Irving, 2006; Cherlin, 2010). Forging an intimate relationship relies on a secure sense of identity, which many emerging adults are still developing. Marital success is also predicted by the degree of similarity between both members of the couple. Similarity in socioeconomic status, education, religion, and age all contribute to predicting a happy marriage (Gonzaga, Campos, & Bradbury, 2007). In addition, spouses reciprocally influence each other and tend, over a lifetime of marriage, to become more similar to each other in terms of personality (Caspi, Herbener, & Ozer, 1992) and markers of aging (Ko, Berg, Butner, Uchino, & Smith, 2007). They also become more similar in their general well-being, as measured by rates of depression, physical activity, and health, including chronic diseases such as high blood pressure (Bookwala & Jacobs, 2004; Pettee et al., 2006).

Men generally report being happier with their marriages than women, though the difference is small (Jackson, Miller, Oka, & Henry, 2014). Satisfaction, particularly in women, tends to be highest in egalitarian relationships in which home and family duties are shared and couples view themselves as equal contributors (Helms, Walls, Crouter, & McHale, 2010; Ogolsky, Dennison, & Monk, 2014). Marital satisfaction tends to wax and wane over the decades. Childrearing is associated with marital conflict, declines in marital satisfaction and intimacy, but increases in commitment (Bradbury, Fincham, & Beach, 2000; Lawrence, Rothman, Cobb, Rothman, & Bradbury, 2008). With children come financial pressures, increased responsibilities, and disagreements over child rearing and discipline techniques. In middle adulthood, marital satisfaction tends to increase as child rearing tasks and stress decline, family incomes rise, and spouses get better at understanding each other and have more time to spend together (Fincham, Beach, & Davila, 2007). The advances in emotion regulation that typically come with age may also improve the quality of marital interactions and predict satisfaction (Bloch, Haase, & Levenson, 2014).

Marriages in older adulthood are characterized by greater satisfaction, less negativity, and more positive interactions than in other developmental periods (Story et al., 2007). Older adults describe their relationships as having less conflict and higher levels of pleasure

REUTERS/Marcus Donner

The June 2015 Supreme Court ruling mandated the recognition of same-sex marriage nationwide.

and report greater positive affect in marital interaction than do younger adults (Carstensen, Fung, & Charles, 2003). Compared with middle-aged adults, older adults perceive more positive characteristics and fewer negative characteristics in their partners (Henry, Berg, Smith, & Florsheim, 2007). They also show greater positive sentiment override; that is, they appraise their spouse's behavior as more positive than do outside observers (Story et al., 2007). In other words, older married adults tend to view their spouses through rose-colored glasses.

SAME-SEX MARRIAGE

Like all people, gay and lesbian adults seek love, partnership, and close intimate relationships. Intimate relationships and marriage appear to have similar meanings for gay and lesbian couples as compared with heterosexual couples (Cherlin, 2013). Until recently, it was very difficult to study same-sex unions. With the 2015 Supreme Court decision in *Obergefell v. Hodges,* the United States joined more than a dozen countries that have national laws allowing gays and lesbians to marry, including Canada, Finland, Spain, the Netherlands, Argentina, and New Zealand (Pew Research Center, 2015a). Since gay and lesbian couples have increasingly begun forming legal unions through marriage (Riggle, Wickham, Rostosky, Rothblum, & Balsam, 2017), the literature comparing sexual minority and majority couples to date is sparse but growing.

Studies that have compared gay, lesbian, and heterosexual couples have found no significant differences in love, satisfaction, or the partners' evaluations of the strengths and weaknesses of their relationships (Frost, Meyer, & Hammack, 2015; Lavner, Waterman, & Peplau, 2014). Serious problems such as intimate partner violence, for example, exist in both types of relationships (Edwards, Sylaska, & Neal, 2015). Moreover, the breakup rate for same-sex couples is comparable to that for heterosexual couples (Rosenfeld, 2014). The available research suggests that gay and lesbian persons experience the same

FIGURE 14.4: Support of Same-Sex Marriage

% of U.S. adults who favor same-sex marriage, by generation (2001–2017)

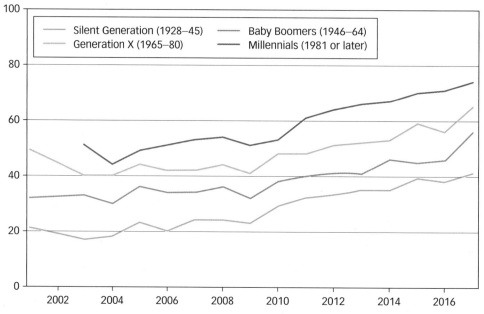

Source: Pew Research Center (2017).

psychological benefits from legal marriage, civil unions, and registered domestic partnerships as heterosexual couples (Riggle, Rostosky, & Horne, 2010; Wight, LeBlanc, de Vries, & Detels, 2012). A study of more than 36,000 people in the California Health Interview Survey found that lesbian, gay, and bisexual persons in a legal same-sex marriage were significantly less distressed than their LGB counterparts who were not in a same-sex legal relationship—and the same was true in comparing them with unmarried heterosexual persons. These findings suggest a mental health benefit to legal marriage (Wight, Leblanc, & Lee Badgett, 2013).

The stressors that gay men and lesbian women face, such as the experience of stigma and prejudice, might play a role in how same-sex marriage manifests in health and psychological well-being (Frost et al., 2015; Hatzenbuehler, 2014). Legal marriage may have the potential to offset the mental health impact of these stressors at the individual level and might offset the larger macro-level effects of sanctioned discrimination (Wight et al., 2013). This is supported by research conducted prior to the national legalization of marriage, suggesting that same-sex couples living in states with legally sanctioned marriage reported higher levels of self-assessed health, greater self-acceptance, and less isolation than those living in states that barred same sex marriage (Kail, Acosta, & Wright, 2015; Riggle et al., 2017). Likewise, legally married same-sex older adult couples reported better quality of life and more economic and social resources than unmarried partnered couples (Goldsen et al., 2017). Again, these adults were surveyed prior to the legalization of same-sex marriage in the United States. In this way, laws represent an important contextual influence on well-being. Moreover, recent surveys of U.S. adults have shown that nearly two-thirds (62%) say they supported same-sex marriage, compared with 32% who opposed it (Pew Research Center, 2017). As shown in Figure 14.4, there are large cohort differences such that younger generations express higher levels of support for same-sex marriage, but in recent decades older generations also have become more supportive of it. In general, research with heterosexual couples has shown that marital satisfaction is associated with physical and mental health, a longer life, and life satisfaction and well-being (Fincham & Beach, 2010; Liu & Waite, 2014). Same-sex marriages show similar benefits, although little research has been conducted to date (Cherlin, 2013; Wight et al., 2013).

DIVORCE

In the first few decades following the 1960s, divorce rates tripled in many Western industrialized countries, but have since stabilized and even declined (United Nations Statistics Division, 2014). In the United States, for example, the divorce rate increased during the 1970s, peaking at 5.2 divorces per 1,000 people in 1980, and then declined to 2.8 divorces per 1,000 people in 2014 (National Center for Health Statistics, 2015; United Nations Statistics Division, 2017). Despite global changes in divorce rates, there remain large international differences. The highest divorce rate is in the Russian Federation (4.5 per 1,000 persons) and the lowest in Ireland (.6), suggesting that social contextual factors unique to each culture play an influential role.

Despite the overall decline in divorces, the United States has one of the highest divorce rates in the world. Most U.S. marriages that end in divorce do so within the first 10 years (Copen, Daniels, Jonathan Vespa, & Mosher, 2012). By 45 years of age, more than one-third of men and women have been divorced (Kreider & Ellis, 2011).

We have seen that couples who are older and who share similarities in demographics, interests, personality, attitudes, and values are more likely to have successful marriages (Gonzaga et al., 2007; Hohmann-Marriott, 2006). Poor education, economic disadvantage, not attending religious services, and experiencing multiple life stressors and role overload increases the risk of divorce (Brock & Lawrence, 2008; Härkönen, 2014). Parental divorce influences children's adjustment and views of marriage. The number and quality of family transitions experienced in youth predicts attitudes toward marriage, relationship skills, and divorce (Paul R. Amato, 2010).

A critical predictor of divorce is the couple's communication and problem-solving style. Negative interaction patterns and difficulty regulating discussions predict later divorce even in newlyweds reporting high marital satisfaction, and these patterns are often evident even before marriage (Gottman & Gottman, 2017; Lavner & Bradbury, 2012). During conflict, troubled couples often experience negative emotions that are overwhelming and interfere with their connection to their partner. Unable to effectively resolve differences, when one member of the couple raises a concern, the other may retreat, reacting with anger, resentment, and defensiveness, creating a negative cycle (Ramos Salazar, 2015). Disagreements over finances are particularly strong predictors of divorce (Dew, Britt, & Huston, 2012).

The process of divorce entails a series of stressful experiences, such as conflict, physical separation, moving, distributing property, and, for some, child-custody negotiations. Regardless of who initiates a divorce, all family members feel stress and a confusing array of emotions, such as anger, despair, embarrassment, shame, failure—and, sometimes, relief (Clarke-Stewart & Brentano, 2006; Härkönen, 2014). Divorce is associated with decreased life satisfaction, heightened risk for a range of illnesses, and even a 20% to 30% increase in early mortality (Björkenstam, Hallqvist, Dalman, & Ljung, 2013; Holt-Lunstad, Smith, & Layton, 2010; Sbarra, Law, & Portley, 2011). Divorce is thought to be more harmful to women's health than to that of men, because it tends to represent a greater economic loss for women, often including a loss of health insurance (Lavelle & Smock, 2012).

Although some adults show poor health outcomes of divorce (Mancini, Bonanno, & Clark, 2011b; Sbarra, 2015), most people are resilient and fare well after divorce,

TABLE 14.1 • Correlates and Influences on Marriage and Divorce

Correlates of Marriage

- Good physical health
- Good mental health
- Positive sense of well-being

Ingredients in Marital Success

- Intimacy and commitment, expressed as warmth, attentiveness, empathy, acceptance, and respect
- Good communication skills including the ability to express concerns calmly and clarify the other's expressed wishes and needs
- Good conflict management skills including the ability to compromise, accept responsibility, and avoid defensiveness and criticism
- Effective conflict management and resolution
- Degree of similarity in education, religion, age, and socioeconomic status
- Perception of equity between partners

Risk Factors for Divorce

- Young age
- Multiple life stressors
- Dissimilarities in age, ethnicity, religion, attitudes, and values
- Poor education
- Economic disadvantage
- Poor coping, communication, and conflict resolution skills

Correlates of Divorce

- Loss of income and financial instability
- Risky behaviors such as drug and alcohol use and promiscuous sexual activity
- Poor self-care, including poor eating, sleeping, and working habits
- Negative emotions, such as anger, despair, and shame
- Poor physical and mental health
- Reduced social network and support
- Reduced life satisfaction

especially after the initial adjustment (Amato, 2010; Sbarra & Coan, 2017; Sbarra et al., 2015). For example, in one study of more than 600 German divorcees, nearly three-quarters experienced little change in life satisfaction during a 9-year period that included the divorce (Mancini et al., 2011). Women who successfully make the transition through a divorce tend to show positive long-term outcomes. They tend to become more tolerant, self-reliant, and nonconforming; all characteristics that are associated with the increased autonomy and self-reliance demands that come with divorce.

Overall, 40% of new marriages involve remarriage of one or both partners (Livingston, 2014). Women are more likely to not want to marry again (54%) as compared with men (30%). Men tend to remarry more quickly after divorce than do women; less is known about men's long-term adjustment to divorce. As with other life challenges, divorce represents an opportunity for growth and development, and adaptive outcomes following divorce appear to be the norm, not the exception (Perrig-Chiello, Hutchison, & Morselli, 2014). Table 14.1 summarizes correlates and influences on marriage and divorce.

CHILDBEARING

Until recent generations, having children was considered an inevitable part of adult life. Since the 1960s, effective methods of birth control and changing cultural views on parenthood and childlessness have made having children a choice (Mills, Rindfuss, McDonald, & te Velde, 2011). Consequently, childbearing rates have declined in most industrialized nations. For example, in the 1950s, the average number of children born to a woman in the United States was 3.8; today it is 2.1 (Central Intelligence Agency, 2013). The average number of children is even lower for many industrialized nations including Australia (1.8), Germany (1.4), and Japan (1.4), as compared with developing nations such as Niger (7.0), Somalia, (6.2), and Afghanistan (5.5; Central Intelligence Agency, 2013).

The rate of childbearing has implications not only for individuals and families, but also for societies and nations. The Cultural Influences on Development feature examines the one-child policy that was implemented in China in 1979.

FIGURE 14.5: Maternal Age at First Birth in the United States, 1970–2014

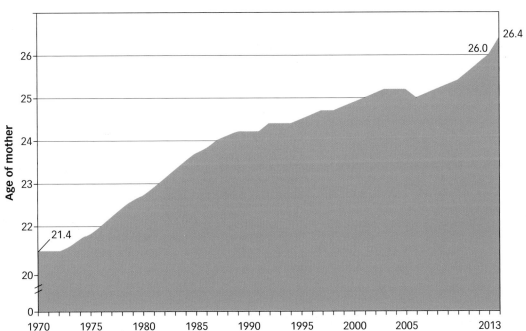

CULTURAL INFLUENCES ON DEVELOPMENT

• • China's One-Child Policy

David Pollack/Corbis

Posters such as this promoted the one-child policy as the key to greater resources and opportunities for families.

In 1979, the People's Republic of China implemented a policy designed to curb the nation's rapidly growing population that posed social, economic, and environmental problems. Known as the one-child policy, it restricted the number of children married couples could have to one. The one-child policy was most strictly implemented in urban areas (McLoughlin, 2005). Couples in rural areas, especially those who needed assistance to manage farms, were sometimes granted permission for two children if the first child was a girl and the couple waited 4 to 5 years between births (Yang, 2007). Members of some ethnic minorities were also permitted to have a second child.

The core of the one-child policy was a set of incentives, including health and education resources, but it was also enforced by means of penalties, such as out-of-plan birth fines (often two to three times that of a typical family's annual income), child-rearing, health care, and education penalties, and possibly other penalties such as a job

demotion or even job loss (McLoughlin, 2005). The official slogan of the one-child-policy was *you sheng you yu* ("give birth to fewer children, but give them better care and education"; Yang, 2007). In exchange for limiting parents' childbearing, the Chinese government provided greater opportunities and resources at the national, community, and household levels for only children who would thus be better off in physical and intellectual development than children with multiple siblings.

Limiting couples to one child led to greater involvement by parents in child care because children of all ages were viewed as more valued (Short, Fengying, Siyuan, & Mingliang, 2001; Yang, 2007). The one-child policy had an unintended effect of creating a child-centered culture with a strong belief and shared interest among the urban community in educating the only child regardless of the child's sex (F. Liu, 2006). This is a striking contrast with the Chinese tradition in which parents' academic expectations and investments were limited to their sons (Yang, 2007). Given Chinese culture's tradition of valuing of boys, the one-child policy is implicated in high rates of female infanticide and sex-selective abortions, leading to a significant gender imbalance (Mosher, 2006). A population survey of more than 4.5 million Chinese children and teens found that the male:female ratio was 126:100 overall, with several provinces showing ratios of more than 130:100 (Zhu, Lu, & Hesketh, 2009). Among second births, the ratio was as high as 149:100, with ratios of more than 160:100 in 9 provinces (Zhu et al., 2009). Sex-selective abortion accounts for almost all the excess male children in China (Mosher, 2006).

The one-child policy was intended to impart advantages to only children over those with siblings, specifically more attention and resources. Early research in the 1980s suggested that Chinese only children scored higher on measures of mathematics and verbal achievement, but displayed more egocentrism, uncooperativeness, difficulty managing emotions and impulses, and were less prosocial and respectful of elders than school-age children with siblings (Falbo, Poston, Triscari, & Zhang, 1997; McLoughlin, 2005). Research conducted in the 21st century, however, suggested no difference on psychosocial measures such as dependence, helping behaviors, independence, aggression, friendliness, curiosity, self-confidence, and social competence (X. Chen, Rubin, & Li, 1994; Guo, Yang, Liu, & Song, 2005; D. Wang et al., 2000).

A rapidly aging population in China, coupled with a much smaller workforce, has led to the end of the one-child policy. In 2014 the policy was relaxed in several cities to permit couples to have two children if one of the parents has no siblings (Burkitt, 2014). Couples must register and apply to have a second child. Beginning in 2016, all couples are permitted to have two children (Holliday, 2014). Despite the new relaxed guidelines, fewer couples are applying for a second child than expected. This may be because the one-child policy has changed perceived norms on family size.

What Do You Think?

1. **What reasons can you think of to justify a country having a one-child policy? What reasons against it can you think of?**

2. **Why do you think fewer Chinese couples are applying to have a second child than predicted?**

Although families are growing smaller, most married adults still become parents, but later in life than ever before. The average age at which U.S. women give birth has increased over the past three decades, from 21.4 in 1970 to 26.4 in 2014 (see Figure 14.5; Matthews & Hamilton, 2002, 2016). However, women who postpone childbearing to their early 30s are at increased risk for experiencing fertility difficulties (Schmidt, Sobotka, Bentzen, & Nyboe Andersen, 2012). The Lives in Context feature explores the phenomenon of postponing parenting until midlife.

Regardless of when parenthood happens, the transition is challenging. New parents experience the exciting yet overwhelming task of getting to know their infant while meeting his or her needs for constant attention, affection, and care. New parents are greeted with a host of new responsibilities and changes: caregiving responsibilities, added housework, financial demands, loss of sleep, and diminished leisure time. Such pressures are associated with a reduced sense of well-being and self-esteem after birth (Bleidorn et al., 2016; Nelson, Kushlev, & Lyubomirsky, 2014). Many new parents report not feeling prepared for the roller coaster of emotions ranging from joy to frustration and exhaustion that accompany parenthood (Galatzer-Levy, Mazursky, Mancini, & Bonanno, 2011; Stanca, 2012). Some research suggests that, even years after becoming parents, many people are unable to regain the happiness and life satisfaction that they enjoyed before having a child (Clark, Diener, Georgellis, & Lucas, 2008). Some theorize that parents' perceptions of the joys of parenthood, that "it's all worth it," may be a way of balancing the challenges, frustrations, and drops in happiness that accompany parenthood (Eibach & Mock, 2011).

The transition to parenthood places stress on even the best of marriages. Parenthood is associated with sudden declines in marital satisfaction for both parents as conflict tends to rise in response to increased financial, household, and parental demands and decreased leisure time (Don & Mickelson, 2014; Trillingsgaard, Baucom, & Heyman, 2014). During the transition to parenthood, most American and European couples, even those in relatively egalitarian marriages, shift toward traditional marital roles and division of labor (Dribe & Stanfors, 2009; Katz-Wise, Priess, & Hyde, 2010; Koivunen, Rothaupt, & Wolfgram, 2009). Mothers tend to report more stress and a higher workload with the advent of parenthood than do fathers (Widarsson et al., 2013), and this shift influences women's relationship satisfaction (Le, McDaniel, Leavitt, & Feinberg, 2016). In addition, most women experience a decline in physical activity and its accompanying health effects with motherhood (McIntyre & Rhodes, 2007; Perales, del Pozo-Cruz, & del Pozo-Cruz, 2015). In dual-earner couples, the greater the degree of shared parenting responsibilities, the greater the happiness of the couple, and especially of the mother (Chong & Mickelson, 2013).

As parents, gay and lesbian couples tend to coparent more equally and compatibly than heterosexual partners; however, their relationship dynamics often shift in similar ways as heterosexual parents (Biblarz & Savci, 2010). For example, lesbian couples with children may move from shared employment, decision making, and household work in exchange for differentiation between partners in child care and paid employment, similar

LIVES IN CONTEXT

• • First-Time Parenting in Midlife

Many adults become parents in middle adulthood.

A growing number of adults are postponing parenthood into midlife: Today it is not uncommon for adults in their 40s and early 50s to raise young children. We have discussed the biological changes in reproductive capacity that occur throughout young adulthood and middle adulthood. Whether through assisted reproduction, adoption, or chance, a growing number of new parents in industrialized nations are middle aged.

The transition to parenthood entails many changes for all parents. Midlife parents, however, may find the social side of their new role challenging as their daily experiences may not match those of their peers. Midlife parents of infants, for example, have different concerns and needs than their friends. A new mother may find that find that her social clock is discordant with her same-age peers who may be sending their children to college or planning for weddings and grandchildren. At the same time, a midlife mother may find herself much older than many of the other parents of infants she meets at child care, play groups, and parks. For these reasons, midlife parents may find the social side of parenting a challenge.

When asked, middle-aged parents cite benefits to being an older parent. Many midlife adults have established careers with financial security, enabling flexibility in how they spend their time. Midlife parents also feel that they are better prepared for parenthood than they would have been at a younger age. They feel mature, competent, and generative, and tend to be less stressed than younger parents (MacDougall, Beyene, & Nachtigall, 2012). Middle-aged parents also tend to experience greater increases in life satisfaction with the birth of their children and are less prone to depressive symptoms (Luhmann, Hofmann, Eid, & Lucas, 2012). They tend to take a more youthful perspective, seeing middle age as extending longer and old age as starting later than do those who have children early in life (Toothman & Barrett, 2011). The most common complaints of older parents include having less energy for parenting and feeling stigmatized as older parents (MacDougall et al., 2012).

Children also benefit from being raised by midlife parents. The cognitive and emotional changes that take place from young to middle adulthood contribute to midlife adults' readiness to parent. In some studies, mothers who were older when their first child was born tended to demonstrate more positive parenting behaviors such as hugs, kisses and praise; and fewer negative ones such as threats or slaps (Barnes, Gardiner, Sutcliffe, & Melhuish, 2013; Camberis, McMahon, Gibson, & Boivin, 2016). Finally, children raised by older mothers tend to be healthier, having fewer visits to the hospital, a greater likelihood of receiving all of their immunizations by 9 months of age, and higher scores on measures of cognitive, language, and social development through age 5 (Sutcliffe, Barnes, Belsky, Gardiner, & Melhuish, 2012; Tearne, 2015).

What Do You Think?

1. What are some of the challenges of becoming a parent in midlife? How might first-time parents address these challenges?

2. How might a child be influenced by parental age? How might having a parent who is older than the parents of one's peers influence children? Why?

to heterosexual couples (Goldberg & Perry-Jenkins, 2007). Less is known about gay men, but they seem to not show a domestic hierarchy that values paid work over homemaking. Instead, paid work may be seen as a compromise that takes the working partner away from spending time with their children (Kurdek, 2007).

CHILDLESSNESS

Although most adults have children, some remain childless. In 2014, 15% of all U.S. women ages 40 to 44 had not given birth to any children (Livingston, 2015). It is difficult for researchers to determine the rate of childlessness in men. Frequently childlessness is involuntary, the result of infertility or of postponing parenthood rather than choosing to be childless (te Velde, Habbema, Leridon, & Eijkemans, 2012). About 15% of women age

30 to 44 experience *impaired fecundity*, the inability to become pregnant or carry a fetus to term (U.S. Department of Health and Human Services, 2013). As shown in Figure 14.6, women who have never given birth experience impaired fecundity rates up to three times higher than women who have given birth at least once.

Childlessness appears to interfere with psychosocial development and personal adjustment only when it is involuntary and a result of circumstances beyond an individual's control (Roy, Schumm, & Britt., 2014). In both men and women, involuntary childlessness is associated with life dissatisfaction varying from ambivalence to deep disappointment, especially when it is accompanied by self-blame, rumination, and catastrophizing (Hadley & Hanley, 2011; Nichols & Pace-Nichols, 2000; Peterson, Gold, & Feingold, 2007). The social context also matters, as the extent to which childlessness is associated with lower psychological well-being appears to be associated with the degree to which a country and culture's norms are tolerant toward childlessness (Huijts, Kraaykamp, & Subramanian, 2011).

Some adults are childless by choice—or *childfree*, the term preferred by some. Common reasons for voluntary childlessness include the desire for flexibility and freedom from child care responsibility, pursuit of career aspirations, economic security, environmental reasons (e.g., not wanting to contribute to global overpopulation), and desires to preserve marital satisfaction. It is unclear how many women are childless by circumstance or by choice. One study of Italian women found that one third of those who were childless were so by choice (Koropeckyj-Cox & Pendell, 2007). Others were childless as a result of decisions to delay childbearing or the result of adverse external circumstances such as relationship dissolution.

Consistent predictors of childlessness include education and career status. High levels of education predict childlessness in women from Australia, the Netherlands, Finland, Germany, the UK, and the United States (Koropeckyj-Cox & Call, 2007; Waren & Pals, 2013). Women and men who are voluntarily childless tend to be less religious and more assertive, independent, and self-reliant than their peers, attributes which likely influence their adjustment throughout life (Avison & Furnham, 2015). Overall, adults who are childless by choice tend to be just as content with their lives as those who are parents. Positive attitudes toward childlessness are more common among adults who are college educated, childless, and female, while negative attitudes toward childlessness are more common among adults who are male, less educated, and have conservative religious beliefs (Koropeckyj-Cox & Pendell, 2007; Koropeckyj-Cox, Romano, & Moras, 2007).

FIGURE 14.6: Impaired Fecundity Among Females Aged 15-44 Years, by Age and Parity, 2006–2010

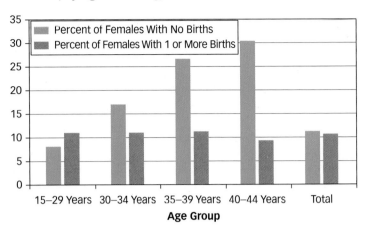

⚙ Thinking in Context 14.1

1. How might extended singlehood and cohabitation influence individuals' progression on developmental tasks such as Erikson's psychosocial stages in early adulthood (intimacy vs. isolation) and middle adulthood (generativity)?

2. What advice would you give to newlyweds? Given what is known about love, marriage, and divorce, what can they do to promote a happy marriage and reduce the likelihood of divorce? Alternatively, what can someone who is facing divorce do to aid their transition?

3. What personality, developmental, and life experience factors influence whether an adult will become a parent? How might contextual factors play a role in determining whether one becomes a parent and the timing of parenthood?

FAMILY CONSTELLATIONS

LO 14.2 Compare and contrast child outcomes associated with various family constellations.

Children are embedded in families that play an important role in their development. Children's relationships with parents and siblings are dynamic and reciprocal. Children influence and are influenced by every member of their family, and family members, in turn, interact. In earlier generations, it was assumed that most families conformed to a traditional model composed of a husband, wife, and one or more children born to them. Since the turn of the 21st century, however, this traditional family has become less common in the United States and other Western industrialized nations. Families today may take many forms, as we now explore.

SINGLE-PARENT FAMILIES

Over the past 60 years, the number of U.S. children reared in a two-parent home has declined by more than 20%, from 88% in 1958 to 65% in 2015 (see Figure 14.7; Child Trends Databank, 2015). Today, more than one-quarter of U.S. children under age 18 live with a single parent, most commonly with their mother (Child Trends Databank, 2015). African American children are disproportionally likely to live in a single-parent home; 49% of African American children live with their mother, as compared with 26% of Hispanic, 15% of non-Hispanic white, and 11% of Asian American children (see Figure 14.8). A great deal of research over multiple decades has compared the effects of family structure by studying children raised in single-parent families, stepfamilies (also called blended families, discussed later in this section), and two-parent families.

Generally, children in single-parent families, whether created through divorce, death, or having never married, tend to show more physical and mental health problems, poorer academic achievement, less social competence, and more behavior problems than do children in intact two-parent families (Taylor & Conger, 2017; Waldfogel, Craigie, & Brooks-Gunn, 2010). However, it is important to recognize that these effects tend to be small; the vast majority of children raised in one-parent homes are well-adjusted (Lamb, 2012). Moreover, there are more differences among children in single-parent homes than between children of single-parent homes and two-parent homes. Many of the differences associated with family structure are reduced or disappear when researchers take socioeconomic status into account, suggesting that differences in child well-being across family types are largely, though not entirely, influenced by family income, access to resources, and the stresses that accompany economic difficulties (Ryan, Claessens, & Markowitz, 2014).

About one-third of children raised in single-mother homes live in poverty, as compared with 16% of children in single-father homes and less than 6% of children in homes headed by a married couple (DeNavas-Walt & Proctor, 2014). Children in single-mother homes, regardless of ethnicity, are disproportionately likely to live in poverty (Damaske, Bratter, & Frech, 2017). Low socioeconomic status poses risks for academic, social, and behavioral problems. Economic disadvantage affects children in a myriad of ways, from having less money for books, clothes, and extracurricular activities to living in poorer school districts and neighborhoods. In addition, families headed by single mothers often experience multiple transitions, as single mothers tend to change jobs and homes more frequently than other mothers. Each transition poses challenges to children's adjustment

Vyacheslav Prokofyev /TASS/Getty Images

Over one-quarter of children are raised by a single parent, most often their mother. In what ways might single fathers differ in their parenting as compared with single mothers?

FIGURE 14.7: Living Arrangements of Children Under 18, 1970–2015

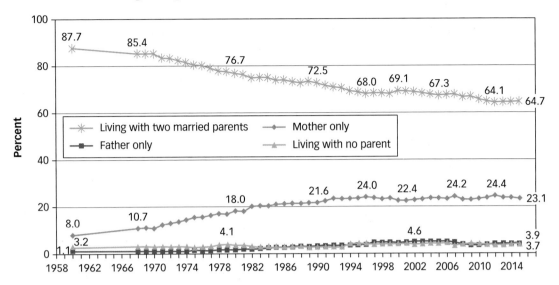

Source: Child Trends Databank (2015).

(Evans, Li, & Whipple, 2013). Single mothers report more depression and psychological problems than married mothers and, when depressed, undoubtedly function less well as parents (Reising et al., 2013; Waldfogel et al., 2010).

The single-parent household offers stability, continuity, and opportunities for child development, but access to economic and social resources influences the effects of single parenthood on children (Taylor & Conger, 2017). The level of social support afforded single mothers influences their abilities to provide emotional support for their children and implement effective parenting strategies (Wood & Woody, 2007). In African American communities, for example, single mothers are often integrated within their community, providing their children with opportunities to interact with many caring adult family members and friends of the family; thus, children are raised as members of a larger African American community (Jayakody & Kalil, 2002). Often an adult male, such as an uncle or grandfather, takes on a fathering role, helping a child build competence and develop a relationship with a caring adult male (Hill, Bush, & Roosa, 2003). In such families, grandmothers often are highly involved, warm, and helpful, taking on important

FIGURE 14.8: Living Arrangement of Children, by Race and Hispanic Origin, 2015

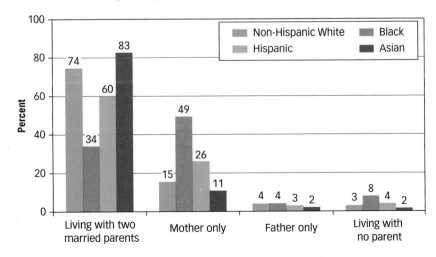

Source: Child Trends Databank (2015).

FIGURE 14.9: Median Income of Families in the United States, by Family Type, 1950–2010

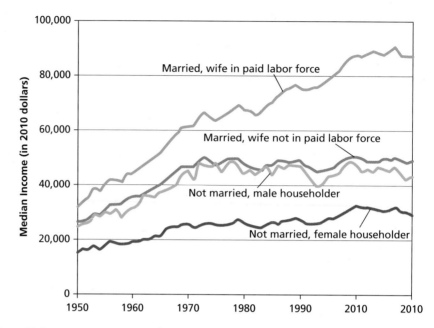

Source: U.S. Census Bureau, Current Population Survey, 2011 (http://familyfacts.org/charts/340/married-couple-families-have-higher-incomes).

support roles. In one study of UK single-parent homes, grandmothers served parental roles and aided their children much as would partners (Harper & Ruicheva, 2010). When children are close to highly involved extended family members, they develop family bonds and a sense of family honor that guides them and encourages them to succeed; this tends to hold true of all children, regardless of their family structure (Jaeger, 2012).

COHABITING FAMILIES

There are many kinds of families and not all are formed through marriage. Just as cohabitation is on the rise, so are cohabiting families (Child Trends Databank, 2015), as shown in

FIGURE 14.10: Number of Opposite-Sex Cohabiting Couples

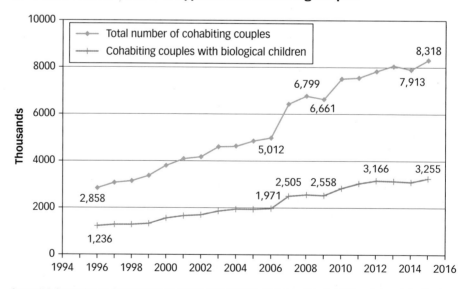

Source: U.S. Census Bureau, Current Population Survey, 2011 (http://familyfacts.org/charts/340/married-couple-families-have-higher-incomes).

Figure 14.10. An estimated 40% children will spend some time in a cohabiting-parent family before they reach age 12 (Manning, 2015). Children of unmarried cohabiting parents who have close caring relationships with them and whose union is stable develop as well as their counterparts whose parents' marriage is stable (Rose-Greenland & Smock, 2012).

A challenge to cohabitation is that relationships of unmarried cohabiting couples tend to be less stable than those of married couples (Manning, 2015). For example, about one third of cohabiting couples break up within 3 years (Copen et al., 2013). In contrast, about two thirds of first marriages remain intact after 10 years (Goodwin, Mosher, & Chandra, 2010). Children living in cohabiting households are much more likely to experience their parents' separation, more conflict in the home, and more transitions in family life than are children of married parents, all of which influence adjustment (Osborne, Manning, & Smock, 2007; Rose-Greenland & Smock, 2012).

Differences in socioeconomic status contribute to the varying outcomes in children's adjustment. On average, children raised in cohabiting-parent families experience economic situations that are better than those of children in single-parent families (e.g., higher parental education and family earnings), but more economically stressful than those reared by married parents (e.g., greater poverty and food insecurity; Manning, 2015; Manning & Brown, 2006). About 20% of children living in cohabiting families are poor, as compared with about 10% of children from two-parent married households and nearly 40% of children in single-parent households (Kennedy & Fitch, 2012).

The effect of cohabitation on children varies with contextual norms. Consensual unions and childbearing within cohabiting unions are more common among minority families (Kennedy & Bumpass, 2008). Black and Hispanic children spend more time in cohabiting parent unions than do white children—and the difference in economic advantage between marriage and cohabitation is smaller for cohabiting black and Hispanic families than for white families, perhaps partially accounting for minority children's more positive outcomes (Manning & Brown, 2006; Osborne et al., 2007).

SAME-SEX-PARENTED FAMILIES

In the early 1990s, a children's book titled *Heather Has Two Mommies* was a source of great controversy, as politicians and organizations opposed to lesbian, gay, bisexual, or transgender (LGBT) rights sought to ban it from libraries and schools. Today, children like the fictional Heather are not so unusual. An estimated 37% of LGBT-identified adults have a child at some time in their lives (Gates, 2013).

More than three decades of research conducted in the United States, the United Kingdom, Belgium, and the Netherlands has failed to reveal important differences in the adjustment or development of children and adolescents reared by same-sex couples compared to those reared by other-sex couples (Fedewa, Black, & Ahn, 2014; Patterson, 2009; Perrin & Siegel, 2013). Specifically, children and adolescents raised by lesbian mothers or gay fathers do not differ from other children on measures of emotional development, such as empathy and emotional regulation (Bos, Knox, van Rijn-van Gelderen, & Gartrell, 2016; Farr, 2017; Patterson, 2017). Instead, some studies have suggested that children raised by gay and lesbian parents may score higher in some aspects of social and academic competence, and show fewer social and behavioral problems and lower levels of aggression, than other children (Golombok et al., 2014, 2017; Miller, Kors, & Macfie, 2017). Moreover, children raised by lesbian mothers and gay fathers show similar patterns

REUTERS/Lucy Nicholson

Gay men and lesbian women experience a similar transition to parenthood and adoption of family roles as compared with heterosexual parents.

of gender identity and gender role development as children raised by heterosexual parents—they are not more likely to display a gay orientation in adulthood (Fedewa et al., 2014; Tasker & Patterson, 2007).

DIVORCED AND DIVORCING FAMILIES

Earlier in this chapter we discussed divorce from the perspective of the adults involved; now we turn to the effects of divorce on the family, particularly children. For many decades it was assumed that divorce caused significant and irreparable harm to children. Most researchers today take a neutral stance, viewing divorce as a common transition that many children experience and that poses some challenges to adjustment. Research has suggested that divorce has some negative effects on children's adjustment, such as internalizing and externalizing problems, but the effects are small, vary by particular outcome, are often transient, and do not apply to all boys and girls uniformly (Amato & Anthony, 2014; Weaver & Schofield, 2014).

Boys often respond to parental divorce with increases in behavior problems and delinquent activity (Malone et al., 2004). Girls tend to respond to divorce with anxiety and depression—and this response increases with age (Amato & Sobolewski, 2001; Størksen, Røysamb, Moum, & Tambs, 2005). Variations in child, parent, and family characteristics and contexts influence children's adjustment to parental divorce, but most children show improved adjustment within two years after the divorce, suggesting that the majority of children of divorce are resilient (Lamb, 2012).

Ultimately, divorce is not a discrete event in a family's experience. It is a transition that influences living arrangements, housing, income, and family roles. The transition begins well before the divorce is announced, because parental divorce tends to be preceded by a period of uncertainty and tension, often characterized by increases in conflict between parents (Amato, 2010). Harmful family processes, such as parental conflict, poor parent–child interactions, and ineffective parenting strategies, take a toll on children's emotional and psychological health and can precede parental divorce by as much as 8 to 12 years (Lansford, 2009; Potter, 2010). Exposure to high levels of parental conflict before and during divorce impairs children's emotional, psychological, and behavioral adaptation, which, in turn, predicts poor long-term outcomes and adjustment difficulties (Drapeau, Gagne, Saint-Jacques, Lepine, & Ivers, 2009; Harold, Aitken, & Shelton, 2007). Chronic exposure to parental conflict poses challenges to children's adjustment and is associated with increased physiological arousal and an elevated stress response (Davidson, O'Hara, & Beck, 2014; Davies & Martin, 2014).

Divorce triggers a reconfiguration of family roles, and parenting responsibilities shift disproportionately onto the resident parent. Over time, children tend to have decreasing contact with noncustodial fathers (Amato & Sobolewski, 2004). After divorce, children are typically raised by their mothers and experience a drop in income that influences their access to resources and opportunities, such as after-school programs and activities (Bratberg & Tjøtta, 2008; L White & Rogers, 2000). Mother-headed households often must move to more affordable housing, causing additional changes in children's school, community, and circle of friends and often reducing children's access to social support and opportunities to play with friends. Mothers who have not been in the workforce often must seek employment, and many working mothers must increase the hours they work, leading to less contact with their children. These changes contribute to inconsistencies in family routines, activities, and parental monitoring prior to, during, and after the divorce.

Parenting styles and parent–child interactions often shift as families adjust to divorce. As parents struggle with their own adaptation they may feel less effective in monitoring and disciplining their children and experience more conflict and less cohesion in their relationships with their children than prior to divorce (Wallerstein & Lewis, 2004; Amato, Kane, & James, 2011). High-quality family relationships, including positive interactions with the noncustodial parent and low levels of parent–parent conflict, can buffer children against these stressors (Bastaits & Mortelmans, 2016; Weaver & Schofield, 2014). When researchers take into account the quality of parenting and children's exposure to conflict, the link between parental divorce and children's adjustment lessens, suggesting that parenting strategies and relationships are more important influences on children's adjustment than divorce (Bing, Nelson, & Wesolowski, 2009; Whiteside & Becker, 2000).

Blended families include biological and nonbiological-step parents and often biological and nonbiological-step siblings, and pose challenges for adaptation.

BLENDED FAMILIES

About 15% of U.S. children live in a **blended family**: a family composed of a biological parent and a non-related adult, most commonly a mother and stepfather (Pew Research Center, 2015b). Blended families, also sometimes referred to as *stepfamilies* or *reconstituted families,* present children with new challenges and adjustments, as the multiple transitions entailed by divorce and remarriage are stressful. It is often difficult for blended families to integrate and balance the many relationships among custodial, noncustodial, and stepparents, in addition to grandparents and extended family members (Dupuis, 2010). For example, holidays may entail visiting three or four sets of relatives. Many children and adults look back on their parents' *remarriage* as more stressful than the divorce itself (Ahrons, 2007; Dunn, 2002).

Age influences adaptation to a blended family. School-age children and adolescents tend to display more difficulties in adjusting to remarriage than do younger children (Hennon, Hildenbrand, & Schedle, 2008; Ram & Hou, 2003). Both boys and girls tend to experience psychological distress in adjusting to remarriage; however, they may direct their distress in different ways. Living with a stepparent is associated with physical aggression, destructive behaviors, and other behavior problems among boys, and indirect, passive, and not easily noticeable aggression among girls that often appears as anxiety or depression (Hennon et al., 2008; Ram & Hou, 2003). Adjusting to being part of a blended family may pose challenges, but most children reared in stepfamilies do not differ from those raised in single-parent families in a variety of developmental outcomes including cognitive skills, hyperactivity, and aggression (Ahrons, 2007). Sometimes, moving to a stepfamily is even associated with improved adjustment, especially if it results in an increase in family income (Ryan et al., 2014).

Overall, blended families adapt more easily and children show better adjustment when stepparents build a warm friendship with the child and adopt their new roles slowly rather than rushing or forcing relationships (Doodson & Morley, 2006). However, stepmothers often find their role is challenging and ill defined, especially if a nonresident biological mother retains close and frequent contact with the children (Greeff & Du Toit, 2009). Stepmothers tend to report more depressive symptoms, parenting stress, and enjoy the parenting role less than do biological mothers (Shapiro & Stewart, 2011; Shapiro, 2014). Stepmothers may be expected to take on maternal roles and develop relationships quickly. However, in reality, stepparent–stepchild bonds take a great deal of time to develop. Thus, stepmothers may experience unrealistic guilt for not feeling maternal and for preferring life without stepchildren (Church, 2004; Felker, Fromme, Arnaut, & Stoll, 2002).

How well adults adjust to the role of stepparent is influenced by the support of the biological parent as well as the children's perception of their relationship with the stepparent and willingness to accept the adult into the family (Jensen & Howard, 2015). When stepmothers seek support and clarification of their role from their spouse and approach children with honesty and acceptance, they are more likely to find success in the stepmother role (Whiting, Smith, Barnett, & Grafsky, 2007). When stepparents are warm and involved

blended family A family composed of a biological parent and a non-related adult, most commonly a mother and stepfather.

Lives in Context Video 14.1
Blended Families

and do not exert authority too soon, children usually adjust quickly. After a challenging transition, many couples adjust to their roles as spouses and parents, and interactions with stepchildren improve (Jensen & Howard, 2015). The difficulties that stepparenting entails—especially child–parent conflicts—are among the reasons that the divorce rate is higher in couples with stepchildren (DeLongis & Zwicker, 2017; Teachman, 2008).

 Thinking in Context 14.2

1. Considering Bronfenbrenner's bioecological framework (see Chapter 1), what factors contribute to positive outcomes in children, regardless of family constellation?

2. Identify strengths at each bioecological level that are unique to single parent, cohabiting, same-sex, or divorced and blended families.

3. What characteristics of these family formations might foster children's healthy development?

PARENTING

LO 14.3 Explain the effects of various parenting methods on children and adolescents.

Parents have a tremendous influence on their children's development, not simply by meeting children's physical needs, but also through the relationships that develop between parents and children.

PARENTING STYLES

Parenting style, the emotional climate of the parent–child relationship, influences parents' efficacy, their relationship with their children, and their children's development. Parenting styles are displayed as enduring sets of parenting behaviors, combinations of warmth and acceptance, and boundaries and discipline, that occur across situations to form childrearing climates. In a classic series of studies, Diana Baumrind (1971) examined 103 preschoolers and their families through interviews, home observations, and other measures. She identified several parenting styles and the typical behavior and functioning of children that accompanies each style (see Table 14.2).

Authoritarian Parenting

In Baumrind's classification, parents who use an **authoritarian parenting style** emphasize behavioral control and obedience over warmth. They expect children to conform to parental standards without input or question, simply "because I say so." Violations are

parenting style Enduring sets of child-rearing behaviors a parent uses across situations to form a child-rearing climate.

authoritarian parenting style An approach to child-rearing that emphasizes high behavioral control and low levels of warmth and autonomy granting.

TABLE 14.2 • Parenting Styles

PARENTING STYLE	WARMTH	CONTROL
Authoritative	High	Firm, consistent, coupled with discussion
Authoritarian	Low	High, emphasizing control and punishment without discussion or explanation
Permissive	High	Low
Indifferent	Low	Low

accompanied by forceful and often arbitrary punishment, such as yelling, threatening, or spanking. Parents with an authoritarian style are less supportive and warm, and more detached, perhaps even appearing cold, compared with parents who practice other styles.

Children raised by authoritarian parents tend to be withdrawn, mistrustful, and anxious yet angry. They show more behavioral problems than other children, both as preschoolers and ten years later, as adolescents (Baumrind, Larzelere, & Owens, 2010). Children reared in authoritarian homes tend to be disruptive in their interactions with peers and tend to react with hostility when they experience frustrating interactions with peers (Gagnon et al., 2013). A recent meta-analysis of more than 1,400 studies concluded that harsh parenting and psychological control show the strongest associations with behavior problems in childhood and adolescence (Pinquart & Martin, 2017). Psychological control can inhibit development of autonomy, a critical task of adolescence, and is linked with low self-esteem, depression, low academic competence, and antisocial behavior in adolescence through early adulthood in young people around the world; these effects have been observed in adolescents from Africa, Asia, Europe, the Middle East, and the Americas (Ang, 2006; Barber, Stolz, & Olsen, 2005; Griffith & Grolnick, 2013; Lansford, Laird, Pettit, Bates, & Dodge, 2014; Uji, Sakamoto, Adachi, & Kitamura, 2013). Moreover, the behavior of parents and children interacts bidirectionally, influencing each other; as parenting becomes more harsh, children display more behavior problems, which, in turn, exacerbate negative parental behavior.

Permissive Parenting

Parents with a **permissive parenting style** are warm and accepting, even indulgent. They emphasize self-expression and have few rules and expectations for their children. Autonomy is not granted gradually and in developmentally appropriate ways in permissive households. Instead, children are permitted to monitor their own behavior and make their own decisions at an early age, often before they are able. For example, children may decide their own bedtime or monitor their own screen time. When rules are necessary, permissive parents may explain the reasons and consult children, but ultimately do not enforce the rules. Researchers have found that preschoolers raised by permissive parents tend to be more socioemotionally immature and show little self-control and self-regulatory capacity as compared with their peers (Piotrowski, Lapierre, & Linebarger, 2013). They often tend to be impulsive, rebellious, and bossy, and show less task persistence, low levels of school achievement, and more behavior problems (Jewell, Krohn, Scott, Carlton, & Meinz, 2008). A permissive parenting style interferes with the development of self-regulatory skills that are needed to develop academic and behavioral competence in childhood and adolescence (Fletcher, Darling, Steinberg, & Dornbusch, 1995; Maccoby, 2000). Adolescents reared in permissive homes are more likely to show immaturity and conformity to peers, as well as having difficulty with self-control (Hoeve, Dubas, Gerris, van der Laan, & Smeenk, 2011; Milevsky, Schlechter, Netter, & Keehn, 2007).

permissive parenting style A child-rearing approach characterized by high levels of warmth and low levels of control or discipline.

uninvolved parenting style A child-rearing style characterized by low levels of warmth and acceptance coupled with little control or discipline.

Uninvolved Parenting Style

Parents with an **uninvolved parenting style** focus on their own needs rather than those of the child (Maccoby & Martin, 1983). Parents who are under stress, emotionally detached, or who are depressed often lack time or energy to devote to their children, putting them at risk for an uninvolved parenting style (Maccoby & Martin, 1983). Uninvolved parents provide little support or warmth, exert little control over

Parenting style is an important influence on development. Authoritarian parenting emphasizes rigid strictness over warmth.

No-nonsense parenting is characterized by vigilant, strict control as well as warmth. African American children often report viewing this style as indicative of parental concern about their welfare and, unlike authoritarian parenting, this style is associated with positive outcomes—especially within challenging community contexts.

the child, and fail to recognize the child's need for affection and direction. At the extreme, uninvolved parenting is neglectful and a form of child maltreatment. Uninvolved parenting can have negative consequences for all forms of children's development—cognitive, emotional, social, and even physical. For example, young children reared in neglectful homes show less knowledge about emotions than do children raised with other parenting styles (Sullivan, Carmody, & Lewis, 2010).

Authoritative Parenting

The most positive developmental outcomes are associated with what Baumrind termed the **authoritative parenting style**. Authoritative parents are warm and sensitive to children's needs, but also are firm in their expectations that children conform to appropriate standards of behavior. While exerting firm, reasonable control, they engage the child in discussions about standards and grant children developmentally appropriate levels of autonomy, permitting decision making that is appropriate to children's abilities (Hart, Newell, & Olson, 2002). When a rule is violated, authoritative parents explain what the child did wrong and impose limited, developmentally appropriate punishments that are closely connected to the misdeed. Authoritative parents value and foster children's individuality. They encourage their children to have their own interests, opinions, and decisions, but, ultimately, they control the child's behavior. Children of authoritative parents display confidence, self-esteem, social skills, curiosity, high academic achievement, and score higher on measures of executive functioning; these positive effects persist throughout childhood into adolescence (Baumrind et al., 2010; Fay-Stammbach, Hawes, & Meredith, 2014; Milevsky et al., 2007). Parents in a given household often share a common parenting style, but when they do not, the presence of authoritative parenting in at least one parent buffers the negative outcomes associated with the other style and predicts positive adjustment (Hoeve et al., 2011; McKinney & Renk, 2011; Simons & Conger, 2007).

CULTURE, CONTEXT, AND PARENTING

Parenting and parent–child relationships are embedded in context and the effects of parenting styles vary with cultural and contextual factors. Although many studies have shown that authoritarian parenting is associated with negative outcomes in teens reared in Western cultures, studies with adolescents reared in non-Western and collectivist cultures have shown few negative outcomes of authoritarian parenting (Dwairy & Menshar, 2006; G. W. Peterson & Bush, 2013). Non-Western cultures tend to be more collectivist, particularly in comparison to Northern European and Anglo cultures, placing less emphasis on autonomy and identity and more on dependence and connection to family—characteristics that are consistent with authoritarian parenting. For example, research with Chinese, Turkish, and Arab adolescents reared in collectivist cultures has found that authoritarian parenting does not predict negative outcomes, likely because authoritarian parenting is well matched to collectivist cultures' valuing of interconnections over independence (Dwairy & Menshar, 2006). Research with Indonesian adolescents revealed that, as expected, authoritative parenting was associated with the most positive outcomes, but authoritarian parenting was not associated with either negative or positive outcomes (Abubakar, Van de Vijver, Suryani, Handayani, & Pandia, 2014). Indeed, some argue that it is inconsistency between the authoritarian parenting style and the culture that produces negative outcomes in Western cultures (Dwairy & Menshar, 2006).

A recent meta-analysis of 240 studies of families of various ethnic groups in Western countries and among different regions of the globe, and by level of collectivism/individualism in each of the countries, found more similarities than differences in

authoritative parenting style
An approach to child-rearing in which parents are warm and sensitive to children's needs, grant appropriate autonomy, and exert firm control.

associations between parenting styles and child outcomes (Pinquart & Kauser, 2017), yet there remain cultural variations in parenting. It is conceivable that the effectiveness of parenting style and disciplinary techniques may show subtle differences by cultural context (Cauce, 2008). For example, authoritarian parenting is associated with fewer negative outcomes among Latino American children as compared with non-Hispanic white families (Pinquart & Kauser, 2017). Likewise, the no-nonsense parenting style (see Chapter 12), common in African American families and Hispanic families, is adaptive and associated with positive outcomes in challenging school and neighborhood environments as compared with more supportive contexts (Simons, Simons, & Su, 2013).

Uninvolved parenting can make children feel invisible. Extreme forms of uninvolved parenting consitute neglect.

PARENT-CHILD RELATIONSHIPS, CONFLICT, AND MONITORING

Popular views of adolescence characterize it as a time of conflict for families. Julio's mother orders, "Clean your room," but Julio snaps back, "It's my room. I can have it my way!" Conflict between parents and adolescents tends to rise in early adolescence as adolescents begin to seek autonomy. Conflict peaks in middle adolescence and declines from middle to late adolescence as young people become more independent and begin to better understand their parents as people (Hadiwijaya, Klimstra, Vermunt, Branje, & Meeus, 2017).

Although conflict rises during early adolescence, the majority of adolescents and parents continue to have warm, close, communicative relationships. Most adolescents report respecting their parents and feeling close to and loved by them (Steinberg, 2001). Parent–adolescent conflict is generally innocuous bickering over mundane matters: small arguments over the details of life, such as household responsibilities, privileges, relationships, curfews, cleaning of the adolescent's bedroom, choices of media, or music volume (Van Doorn, Branje, & Meeus, 2011). Conflicts over religious, political, or social issues occur less frequently, as do conflicts concerning other potentially sensitive topics (e.g., substance use, dating, sexual relationships; Renk, Liljequist, Simpson, & Phares, 2005; Riesch et al., 2000). Adolescents report having three or four conflicts or disagreements with parents over the course of a typical day, but they also report having one or two conflicts with friends (Adams & Laursen, 2007).

Severe parent–adolescent conflict occurs in some families. Like many aspects of development, there tends to be continuity in parenting and parent–child relationships (Huey, Hiatt, Laursen, Burk, & Rubin, 2017). Patterns of harsh verbal discipline (yelling, threatening, punishment, shaming) and insensitive parenting established in early childhood tend to persist and worsen in middle childhood and adolescence (Bradley & Corwyn, 2008; Lansford, Staples, Bates, Pettit, & Dodge, 2013). It is associated with internalizing problems such as depression, externalizing problems such as aggression and delinquency, and social problems, such as social withdrawal and poor conflict resolution with peers, poor school achievement and, among girls, early sexual activity (Hofer et al., 2013; Keijsers, Loeber, Branje, & Meeus, 2011; Skinner & McHale, 2016; Weymouth, Buehler, Zhou, & Henson, 2016). Fortunately, intense conflict is not the norm; one study found it in less than 10% of families surveyed (Collins & Laursen, 2004). Healthy parent–adolescent relationships are characterized by warmth and emotional attachments with parents in which adolescents seek and receive guidance from parents, and parents provide developmentally appropriate freedom and decision-making ability (Steinberg, 2001). Conflict exists in these relationships, but conflict is coupled with acceptance, respect, and autonomy support.

From middle childhood into adolescence, parents must adapt their parenting strategies to children's increased ability to reason and their desire for independence. Adolescents strive for autonomy—the ability to make and carry out their own decisions—and they decreasingly rely on parents (Steinberg & Silverberg, 1986). The parenting challenge of adolescence is to offer increasing opportunities for adolescents to develop and practice autonomy while providing protection from danger and the consequences of poor decisions (Kobak, Abbott, Zisk, & Bounoua, 2017). Parents tend to use less direct management and instead begin to share power, for example by guiding and monitoring children's behavior from a distance, communicating expectations, and allowing children to be in charge of moment-to-moment decision making (Collins, Madsen, & Susman-Stillman, 2002).

One way in which parents balance autonomy granting with protection is through **parental monitoring**, being aware of their teens' whereabouts and companions. Parental monitoring is associated with overall well-being in adolescents, including academic achievement, delayed sexual initiation, and low levels of substance use and delinquent activity in youth of all ethnicities (Ethier, Harper, Hoo, & Dittus, 2016; Huang, Murphy, & Hser, 2011; Lopez-Tamayo, LaVome Robinson, Lambert, Jason, & Ialongo, 2016; Malczyk & Lawson, 2017). Effective parental monitoring is accompanied by warmth and is balanced with respect for adolescents' autonomy and privacy (Stattin & Kerr, 2000). When parents monitor too closely, such that adolescents feel they are intrusive, adolescents are likely to conceal their activities from their parents and continue to do so at least one year later (Rote & Smetana, 2015). What is considered effective parental monitoring changes as adolescents grow older. From middle to late adolescence, parental knowledge declines as adolescents establish a private sphere and disclose less as parents exert less control (Masche, 2010; Wang, Dishion, Stormshak, & Willett, 2011).

 Thinking in Context 14.3

1. What factors might influence whether a parent adopts an authoritative style of parenting? How might contextual factors, including family, work, community, culture, and society, along with prior experience, influence parenting style?

2. What challenges do parents face in modifying their parenting styles as children age?

FAMILY RELATIONSHIPS IN ADULTHOOD

LO 14.4 Describe the changes that take place within family relationships after individuals reach adulthood.

The family remains important to individuals as they reach middle adulthood, but family relationships undergo developmental changes. Parents and their children typically make the transition to living apart as children reach early adulthood, and parents come to terms with their hopes and expectations for their children's educational and career achievements. In middle adulthood, a person's status as a parent often changes to include that of a grandparent. And many adults find themselves caring for their own aging parents.

PARENT–ADULT CHILD RELATIONSHIPS

Sometime in middle adulthood, most parents launch their young adult children into the world. Many parents view their children's graduation from high school in a positive light while also experiencing some regrets, especially a sense of lost time with their children that cannot be regained (DeVries, Kerrick, & Oetinger, 2007). A son's or daughter's moving out of the family home is an important experience for parents and children as

parental monitoring Parents' awareness of their children's activities, whereabouts, and companions.

it marks the child's entry to adulthood and independent living. Mothers report the move as more stressful than fathers (Seiffge-Krenke, 2010), but most parents adjust well to their children's transition to independent living and the resulting empty nest (Mitchell & Lovegreen, 2009). Parents experience less distress over the transition when communication and affection continue after the child leaves the nest, but they report poor life satisfaction when parent–child communication declines (Lynn. White, 1994). Sometimes, however, parents hold higher expectations for autonomy for their emerging adult children than their children are willing and able to fulfill, with negative consequences for parents' adjustment (Kenyon &

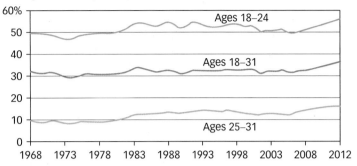

FIGURE 14.11: Cohort Differences in Living at Home

% living at home of parent(s)

Source: PEW Research Center (2017).

Koerner, 2009). Frequently the adult child's transition to independent living is gradual and nonlinear, involving intermittent moves back home (Mitchell, 2016).

Especially after the economic recession that affected much of the world in 2007–2008, it has become increasingly common for adult children to return home at some point in their 20s. More than one-third of U.S. young adults ages 18 to 31 live with their parents (Fry, 2016). Some research suggests that having at least one post-college-age child living at home is associated with lower psychological well-being among mothers (Pudrovska, 2009). More recent research suggests that contextual factors, specifically, the increasingly normative nature of so-called boomerang adult children, is associated with parental adjustment. Middle-aged parents surveyed in 2008 reported relatively low parental quality if an adult child was living in the home, but not when they were surveyed in 2013—adult children in the home became increasingly common in the intervening years, accounting for the change, as shown in Figure 14.11 (Davis, Kim, & Fingerman, 2016). Relations between U.S. parents and adult children may worsen when they continue to live together, perhaps because of the adult children's dependence on parents, financial or otherwise (Ward & Spitze, 2007). Negative interactions with adult children are consistently associated with parent reports of negative affect and predict daily patterns of the stress hormone cortisol (Birditt, Manalel, Kim, Zarit, & Fingerman, 2017).

Children's success in life influences their midlife parents' sense of well-being. Both mothers and fathers show negative emotional responses to their adult children's unmet career and relationships goals (Cichy, Lefkowitz, Davis, & Fingerman, 2013). Adult children's problems are associated with low parental well-being, including more negative than positive affect, low levels of self-esteem and poor parent–child relationships (Greenfield & Marks, 2006; Greenfield, Marks, Hay, Fingerman, & Lefkowitz, 2008). In one study of middle-aged adults, having an adult child with problems predicted poor parental well-being, regardless of the presence of another successful child, and the more problems in the family, the worse parental well-being (Fingerman, Cheng, Birditt, & Zarit, 2012). Parents who perceive their grown children as needing too much support report lower life satisfaction (Fingerman, Cheng, Wesselmann, et al., 2012).

In all nations, families who live apart continue to provide various forms of emotional and physical support to one another, including advice, babysitting, loans, car repair, and more (Farkas & Hogan, 1995; Haberkern & Szydlik, 2010). How much support family members provide each other depends on many factors, such as attachment, relationship quality, cultural norms, and resources. Familism, as mentioned in Chapter 11, is a value that mandates that the family comes before all else and that family members have a duty to care for one another, regardless of the problem or situation, whether personal, financial, or legal (Carlo, Koller, Raffaelli, & De Guzman, 2007); it is common in Hispanic cultures, among others. Financial resources also influence the level and types of support that family members provide. Poverty often leads family members to provide financial and physical assistance to each other, including living together. For example, in most nations, low-income families, such as single parents, immigrants, and members of minority groups, are more likely to live together in three-generation households (parents, children, and grandchildren; Burr & Mutchler, 1999). Generally speaking, early midlife parents continue to give children more assistance than they receive, especially when children are unmarried or facing challenging life transitions such as unemployment and career change or divorce (Zarit & Eggebeen, 2002).

Generally speaking, there is continuity in parent–child relationships throughout the lifespan. In one longitudinal study of New Zealand families, parental warmth and support in childhood and adolescence predicted contact and closeness with children in early adulthood (Belsky, Jaffee, Hsieh, & Silva, 2001). Most midlife parents are happy in their roles, but their satisfaction varies with parental age, health, ethnic background, parent–child relationship quality, and perception of how their children "turn out," which influence their subjective levels of happiness (Mitchell, 2010). Most older adults and their adult children keep in touch even when they are separated by great distances. Overall, adult daughters tend to be closer and more involved with parents than sons, communicating and visiting more often. In contrast with emotional support, few older adults receive instrumental assistance from adult children. Instead, many older adults, especially high socioeconomic elders, continue to assist their adult children, primarily financially (Grundy & Henretta, 2006).

GRANDPARENTHOOD

Most U.S. adults are grandparents by the time they reach their late 40s and early 50s (with an average age of 49 for women and 52 for men; Leopold & Skopek, 2015). In both the United States and Canada, grandparenthood is coming significantly later, yet adults are spending more years as grandparents than ever before (Margolis, 2016). Just as parenthood arrives later with each generation, so does the median age of grandparenthood. Similar to patterns of marriage and childbirth, grandparenthood occurs up to 3 years earlier in Eastern European countries (e.g., Poland, Ukraine, and Bulgaria) and up to 8 years later in Western European countries (e.g., the Netherlands, Switzerland, and Austria) and as compared with the United States (Leopold & Skopek, 2015). The role of grandparent is an important one for adults because, with increasing life spans, many will spend one third of their lives as grandparents (see Figure 14.12).

FIGURE 14.12: Age of Becoming a Grandparent, 2001–2015

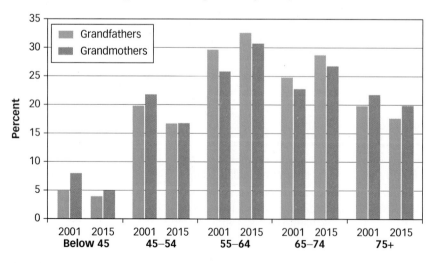

Source: The Long (Long) Wait to Be a Grandparent by Anne Tergesen, *The Wall Street Journal*, March 30, 2014. Reprinted with permission.

Grandparent involvement is associated with child well-being and adolescent adjustment (Griggs, Tan, Buchanan, Attar-Schwartz, & Flouri, 2010). For example, close nurturing relationships with grandparents are associated with positive adjustment and relatively few problem behaviors in adolescents in divorced and single-parent homes (Attar-Schwartz, Tan, Buchanan, Flouri, & Griggs, 2009; Henderson, Hayslip, Sanders, & Louden, 2009). In low-income families, grandparents often take on important financial and caregiving roles. Grandparent involvement is high in many minority households, such as Chinese, Korean, Mexican American, Native American, and Canadian aboriginal—this is especially the case

LIVES IN CONTEXT

• • Grandparents Raising Grandchildren

Raising grandchildren poses challenges as well as emotional rewards for adults.

Raising a child is both challenging and rewarding. Although child rearing is generally regarded as a one-time phase in the lifespan—reflected in such phrases as "starting a family" or "taking time off to raise a family"—some adults find themselves raising multiple cohorts of children as they take over the parenting of their children's children.

Overall, about 10% of U.S. children under the age of 18 are raised by grandparents, with African Americans most likely to be reared by a grandparent, followed by Hispanic children, and then European American children. Large proportions of Native American children are raised by grandparents; some Indian tribes estimate that up to 60% of their children are living in this type of situation (Goyer, 2006). The majority of custody arrangements are informal with no involvement from child welfare agencies. Grandparents often obtain custody of their grandchildren in response to parental absence or incapacitation from substance abuse, HIV/AIDS, incarceration, abandonment, mental or physical difficulties, or death (Dolbin-MacNab & Keiley, 2006).

The transition to parenting grandchildren is not easy, partly because the reasons for parental absence, such as incarceration or illness, are stressful to both the grandparent and grandchildren. Grandchildren often enter grandparent custodial arrangements with preexisting problems due to poor parenting and harsh contextual conditions (Smith & Hancock, 2010). Many children experience internalizing and externalizing difficulties, such as anxiety, depression, aggression, academic difficulties, behavior problems, anger, and guilt (Billing, Ehrle, & Kortenkamp, 2002; Guzell-Roe, Gerard, & Landry-Meyer, 2005). In addition, contextual factors make custodial grandparenting more difficult. Grandparent caregiver arrangements are especially common in low-income

communities, as kin offer a safety net for families in crisis and nearly 20% of custodial grandparents live in poverty (Bachman & Chase-Lansdale, 2005; Goyer, 2006).

As grandparent caregiving is not part of typical midlife development, it can be particularly difficult and stressful for adults. Perhaps because of the stress, financial difficulties, feelings of grief and anger toward the parent, and feelings of social isolation, grandparent caregivers tend to suffer more mental and physical health problems than those who do not care for their grandchildren (Edwards & Benson, 2010; Letiecq, Bailey, & Kurtz, 2008). Grandparents who care for grandchildren with emotional and behavioral problems tend to experience higher rates of anxiety, stress, and depression, and tend to report less life satisfaction (Doley, Bell, Watt, & Simpson, 2015). Research has shown that grandparents who are members of minority groups tend to experience greater risk of health problems because they are more likely to live in poverty and in disadvantaged neighborhoods; however, social support can buffer some negative outcomes (Chen, Mair, Bao, & Yang, 2014; Letiecq et al., 2008; Moore & Miller, 2007).

Despite these challenges, many grandparent caregivers adjust and report positive aspects of caregiving. Many frequently mention a sense of satisfaction in parenting, along with other positive feelings such as joy, pride in influencing their grandchildren, and love (Dolbin-MacNab, 2006). Several studies suggest that grandparent well-being is enhanced by raising grandchildren. Some grandparents report feeling fortunate to parent again and to have the opportunity to do a better job and to enjoy the love and companionship of grandchildren (Moore & Miller, 2007). Some grandparents report that raising their grandchildren is easier than parenting their own children because of greater wisdom and experience, feeling more relaxed, and having more time and attention to give to grandchildren (Dolbin-MacNab, 2006). Social support is an important influence on grandparent caregivers' sense of well-being and adjustment. Grandparents who feel that they have a social support network to turn to for emotional and physical assistance tend to show better adjustment and fewer problems (Williams, 2011).

What Do You Think?

1. In what ways do you think parenting a grandchild is different from raising one's own child?

2. What challenges might grandparents face in raising their grandchildren?

3. In what ways might raising a grandchild be *easier* than raising one's own child?

for grandmothers, who take on caregiver, mentor, and disciplinarian roles (Kamo, 1998; Werner, 1991; Williams & Torrez, 1998). Grandparent involvement is predated by regular contact, close relationships with grandchildren, and parental encouragement to visit with grandchildren. Grandparents who are engaged and spend time with their grandchildren tend to report high levels of life satisfaction (Moore & Rosenthal, 2015). Research with 14 European countries suggests that this is especially true for those who live in countries with high grandparent obligations, such as Italy and Greece (Neuberger & Haberkern, 2013). In some cases, grandparents step in as primary caretakers for their grandchildren, as discussed in the Lives in Context feature.

Relationships between grandparents and grandchildren are influenced by several factors, including grandparent and grandchild gender, geographic proximity, socioeconomic status, and culture. In most cultures, grandparents and grandchildren of the same sex tend to be closer than those of the opposite sex, especially grandmothers and granddaughters. Generally, grandmothers tend to have more contact with their grandchildren than do grandfathers and they tend to report higher satisfaction with the grandparent role (Silverstein & Marenco, 2001). Grandparents who live closer to their children tend to have closer relationships with their grandchildren than do those who have contact only on special occasions like holidays and birthdays. In Western nations, most grandparents are able to visit their grandchildren regularly, and those who live far away often remain involved in their grandchildren's lives despite the distance (American Association of Retired Persons, 2002). The farther away grandchildren and grandparents live from one another, the fewer face-to face contacts, landline phone contacts, and mobile contacts such as text messaging (Hurme, Westerback, & Quadrello, 2010). Because parents tend to regulate grandparent–grandchildren contact, grandparents' relationships with their own children influence their contact and relationships with their grandchildren.

About half of older adults in Western nations have an adult grandchild (American Association of Retired Persons, 2002). Similar to parent–child relationships, grandparent–grandchild relationships show continuity over time. Close grandparent–grandchild relationships in childhood predict close relations in adulthood (Geurts, Van Tilburg, & Poortman, 2012). Grandparents and adult grandchildren tend to agree that their relationships are close and enduring (Hayslip & Blumenthal, 2016; Villar, Celdrán, & Triadó, 2012). Over time, contact with grandchildren tends to decline as young and middle-aged grandchildren take on time-consuming family and work roles, but affection between grandchildren and grandparents remains strong (Silverstein & Marenco, 2001; Thiele & Whelan, 2008).

sandwich generation A popular image of midlife adults in which they scramble to meet the needs of both dependent children and frail elderly parents and thus sandwiched between the two.

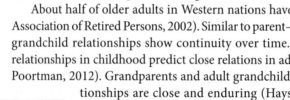

BSIP/Universal Images Group/Getty Images

Middle-aged adults often provide emotional support to their parents.

CARING FOR AGING PARENTS

Despite the popular image of the "**sandwich generation**"—midlife adults scrambling to meet the needs of both dependent children and frail elderly parents and thus sandwiched between the two (Riley & Bowen, 2005)—some experts argue that it is not very accurate (Grundy & Henretta, 2006). In 2012, only 15% of U.S. midlife adults reported providing financial support to a parent age 65 or older while raising a minor child or supporting a grown child (Parker & Patten, 2013). Rather than raising young children, most midlife parents have adult children. Midlife adults with adult children and parents over the age of 65 are more than twice as likely to provide financial support for their children than their parents, but provide similar levels of emotional support to both generations (Birditt et al., 2017; Parker & Patten, 2013).

Adults report a range of motivations for providing emotional and financial care to their aging parents, including obligation, reciprocity, and the quality of the relationship (Stuifbergen, Dykstra, Lanting, & van Delden, 2010). Young adults tend to adopt an idealistic perspective, perceiving strong obligations and ability to care for their parents, regardless of the level of care needed. In contrast, midlife adults adopt a more realistic perspective as they anticipate the need to provide care and appreciate the responsibilities and sacrifices given the specific level and nature of care needed by a parent (Gans & Silverstein, 2006).

The care that adult children provide aging parents is influenced by the parent–child relationship as well as family circumstances and ethnicity. In one large sample of middle-aged adults in the Netherlands, having few siblings, a widowed parent without a new partner, and a short geographical distance between the parent's and child's homes was positively associated with adult children's provision of care and support to parents (Stuifbergen, Van Delden, & Dykstra, 2008). African American and Hispanic adults at all income levels are more likely than European American non-Hispanic adults to provide aging parents with financial and caregiving assistance; this may reflect the cultural value of familism, mentioned earlier (Shuey & Hardy, 2003). Similarly, Chinese, Japanese, and Korean women tend to provide care for their husband's aging parents, who tend to live with them (Montgomery, Rowe, & Kosloski, 2007; Zhan, 2004). In Thai families, intergenerational relations between older-age parents and their children remain close throughout life, with more than 70% of older persons living with or next to a child (Knodel & Chayovan, 2009).

Generally speaking, parents and adult children who have a lifetime of close and positive relations tend to remain close, with adult children providing more assistance than do those whose family relations are less positive (Whitbeck & Hoyt, 1994). In middle age, many people look back and gain more appreciation for their parents' assistance and sacrifices over the years. Relationships between mothers and daughters, usually closer than other parent–child relationships, tend to become more intimate and complex as daughters enter middle age (Fingerman, 2000, 2001; Lefkowitz & Fingerman, 2003). Although parent–child ties influence caregiving, adults with weak parent–child relationships often provide care to parents out of a sense of duty (Silverstein, Conroy, Wang, Giarrusso, & Bengtson, 2002). Daughters, especially those who live in close proximity, are most likely to be parental caregivers (Pillemer & Suitor, 2014).

As adults' caregiving responsibilities increase, such as when an elderly parent develops dementia, they are more likely to experience conflicts among their many roles. Caregivers can feel overwhelmed by their obligations to parents, children, spouses, employers, and friends, and this role overload is associated with anxiety, exhaustion, and depression (Killian, Turner, & Cain, 2005; Savia, Almeida, Davey, & Zant, 2008). One study found that relationship quality declined over a 5-year period as older adults' disability increased and their children provided more assistance with self-care tasks (Kim et al., 2016). Adults of ethnic and cultural groups that emphasize familism and the duty to care for elders may to experience more anxiety and depression with caregiving than adults from other ethnicities (Dilworth-Anderson, Goodwin, & Williams, 2004).

There are also career and economic costs associated with caregiving. For example, men and women who participated in the Survey of Health, Ageing, and Retirement in Europe showed that giving informal care to one's elderly parents was associated with significant costs in terms of employment opportunities and participation (Bolin, Lindgren, & Lundborg, 2008). Among a U.S. sample of caregivers who reduced their work hours or left the workforce to care for a parent, about half reported losing income (Aumann, Galinsky, Sakai, Brown, & Bond, 2010). As women are more likely than men to be expected to provide care, caregiving can interfere with women's employment, causing losses in hours and earnings. According to one estimate, women who become caregivers to their parents may lose more than $300,000, on average, in income and benefits over their lifetime (MetLife Mature Market Institute, National Alliance for Caregiving, & Center for Long Term Care Research and Policy, 2011). Caregiving responsibilities for parents may place female caregivers at risk of living in poverty and requiring public assistance later in life (Lee, Tang, Kim, & Albert, 2015). Caregivers who face multiple career and child-rearing demands are at risk for role strain, depressive symptoms, a reduced sense of personal mastery and self-efficacy, and to engage in fewer outside activities (Mausbach et al., 2012; Wang, Shyu, Chen, & Yang, 2011).

Thinking in Context 14.4

1. Imagine that you are studying a family with midlife parents and a young adult child. What factors might influence the parents' relationship with their emerging adult child?

2. Suppose their son or daughter decided to move back home. What are some of the rewards and challenges that they might face as a couple and family?

3. When might they expect to become grandparents? Based on what you know about becoming a grandparent and the grandparent–grandchild relationship, what advice do you give these parents on what to expect?

PEER RELATIONSHIPS

LO 14.5 Discuss how peer relationships develop and change throughout the lifespan.

In addition to families, we have important social relationships with our peers throughout our lives. We form these relationships with our classmates, neighbors, work colleagues, and other kinds of acquaintances. Some of them become our lifelong friends, while others come and go quickly in our social orbit. In this section we explore how these peer relationships develop and how they change during the different phases of the lifespan.

PEER RELATIONSHIPS IN CHILDHOOD

Children tend to make friends quickly. In Western societies, children have many opportunities to form friendships with their same-age peers because their activities are often age segregated, beginning with infant play dates and continuing through the school years. Associating with children one's own age provides opportunities for mutual support through developmental milestones and for social comparison, both positive and negative.

Play and Development

Young children's early interactions with peers center on play, with important implications for their development. As discussed in Chapter 11, **rough-and-tumble play** involves running, climbing, chasing, jumping, and play fighting (Pellegrini & Smith, 1998). Rough-and-tumble play exercises children's gross motor skills and helps them to develop muscle strength and control. Both boys and girls engage in rough-and-tumble play, but boys do so at much higher rates. In one observation of preschool children, about 80% of the instances of rough-and-tumble play occurred in boys (Tannock, 2011).

Young children also engage in **sociodramatic play**, taking on roles and acting out stories and themes (Dunn & Hughes, 2001; see Chapter 10). By pretending to be mothers, astronauts, cartoon characters, and other personae, children learn how to explain their ideas and emotions; practice regulating emotions as they pretend to be sad, angry, or afraid; and develop a sense of self-concept as they differentiate themselves from the roles they play (Coplan & Arbeau, 2009; Ginsburg, 2007). Sociodramatic play begins in toddlerhood, when a 2-year-old may feed or punish a stuffed animal, and becomes more complex during childhood (Frahsek, Mack, Mack, Pfalz-Blezinger, & Knopf, 2010). Boys' sociodramatic play tends to involve activity and themes of danger and conflict, whereas girls' more often involves themes of cooperation and fostering orderly social relationships, such as pretending to enact household and school roles (e.g., parent, teacher; Nourot, 1998). As children progress through preschool, sociodramatic play becomes more complex, often entailing innovative and sophisticated story lines. Sociodramatic play helps children explore social rules and conventions, promotes language skills, and is associated with social competence (Gioia & Tobin, 2010; Newton & Jenvey, 2011).

rough-and-tumble play Social interaction involving chasing and play fighting with no intent to harm.
sociodramatic play Make-believe play in which children act out roles and themes.

Although children around the world play, peer activities take different forms by culture. Children in collectivist societies tend to play games that emphasize cooperation. For example, children in India tend to engage in sociodramatic play that involves activities practiced in unison coupled by close physical contact; a game called *bajtto*. Bajtto entails enacting a script about going to the market, pretending to cut and share a vegetable, and touching each other's elbows and hands as their imaginations carry out this script (Roopnarine, Hossain, Gill, & Brophy, 1994). In contrast, children from Western cultures that tend to emphasize the rights of the individual tend to play competitive games such as dodge ball, follow the leader, and hide and seek. Peer interactions and play, like other aspects of development, is shaped by the context in which it occurs.

Childhood Friendships

Children tend to choose friends who are like them in interests, play preferences, and demographics, such as race and ethnicity (Aboud, Mendelson, & Purdy, 2003, 2007). For example, in one study of 6- to 12-year-old U.S. children of Cambodian, Dominican, and Portuguese heritage, children become more proud of their heritage as they grew older, and in turn showed a greater preference to form friendships within their ethnic group (Marks, Szalacha, Lamarre, Boyd, & Coll, 2007). However, contextual characteristics, such as the ethnic diversity of a neighborhood or school, also influence children's choices of friends. In racially integrated schools, children are more likely to report having at least one close friend of another race (DuBois & Hirsch, 1990; McGlothlin & Killen, 2006). School-age girls may be more likely to have ethnically diverse social networks and cross-race friendships than boys (Lee, Howes, & Chamberlain, 2007). Once established, cross-race friendships are similar to same-race friendships with regard to intimacy, companionship, and security (Aboud et al., 2007; McDonald et al., 2013; McGlothlin, Killen, & Edmonds, 2005). Compared to children who do not have friends of other races, children in cross-race friendships tend to show a lower tolerance for excluding others (Killen, Kelly, Richardson, Crystal, & Ruck, 2010) and are less prone to peer victimization (Kawabata & Crick, 2011).

In middle to late childhood, friends are expected to be loyal and stick up for each other. Violations of trust, such as divulging secrets, breaking promises, and not helping a friend in need, can break up a friendship (Rubin, Coplan, Chen, Buskirk, & Wojslawowicz, 2005). With age, children differentiate among best friends, good friends, and casual friends, depending on how much time they spend together and how much they share with one another (Hartup & Stevens, 1999). By age 10 most children report having a best friend (Buhrmester, 1998; Erwin, 1998).

Friendships tend to remain stable from middle childhood into adolescence, especially among children whose friendships are high in relationship quality, characterized by sharing, mutual perspective taking, and compromise (Berndt, 2004; Poulin & Chan, 2010). However, because friendship is based largely on similar characteristics, proximity, and opportunities for interaction, friendships may come and go as children develop new interests, competencies, and values. They may also end as children progress into new contexts, such as a change of school or a family move to a different neighborhood (Cairns, Leung, Buchanan, & Cairns, 1995; Troutman & Fletcher, 2010). Older children become more upset at losing a friend, and find making friends more challenging than do young children (Erwin, 1998; Hartup, 2006; Laursen & Hartup, 2002).

Friendship dissolution may have serious consequences for children who are unable to replace the friendship (Bowker, Rubin, Burgess, Booth-Laforce, & Rose-Krasnor, 2006). Some children who experience

Children who live in diverse communites and attend schools that are racially integrated are more likely to report having close friends of another race.

disruption and loss of close friendships experience problems with depression, lone-liness, guilt, anger, anxiety, and acting-out behaviors; yet children with psychoso-cial problems are also at risk to experience friendship loss, and, in turn, show poor adjustment (Hektner et al., 2000; Ladd & Troop-Gordon, 2003; Rubin, Copian, Chen, Bowker, & McDonald, 2011). Many children replace "lost" friendships with "new" friendships. In one study of fifth graders, losing a friend was associated with adjust-ment difficulties only when the lost friendship was not replaced by a new friendship. For these children, the lost and new friendships were largely interchangeable (Bowker et al., 2006). For many children, the importance of stable best friendships during mid-dle childhood may have less to do with the relationship's length, and more to do with simply having a "buddy" by one's side who can provide companionship, recreation, validation, caring, help, and guidance.

Can a child be happy without friends, or without a best friend? An estimated 15% of children are chronically friendless or consistently without a mutual best friend (Rubin et al., 2005). Lacking a best friend itself is not necessarily harmful or indicative of prob-lems or loneliness (Klima & Repetti, 2008; Ladd, 1999). Some children simply prefer solitude; their preference for alone time is not driven by anxiety or fear (Coplan, Ooi, & Nocita, 2015). Although lacking close friends is not associated with maladjustment, social acceptance by the peer group does have an influence on children's adjustment (Klima & Repetti, 2008).

Peer Acceptance, Popularity, and Rejection

In childhood, peer evaluations become important sources of self-validation, self-esteem, and confidence (Ladd, 1999; LaFontana & Cillessen, 2010). Peer acceptance, the degree to which a child is viewed as a worthy social partner by his or her peers, becomes increasingly important in middle childhood. Some children stand out from their peers as exceptionally well liked or exceptionally disliked.

Children who are valued by their peers are said to be popular. **Popular children** tend to have a variety of positive characteristics, including helpfulness, trustworthiness, asser-tiveness, and prosocial habits (Kornbluh & Neal, 2016; Robertson et al., 2010). Popular children are skilled in emotional regulation and social information processing. That is, they are good at reading social situations, problem solving, self-disclosure, and conflict resolution (Blandon, Calkins, Grimm, Keane, & O'Brien, 2010; Rubin et al., 2011). For example, theory of mind predicts popularity throughout childhood (Slaughter, Imuta, Peterson, & Henry, 2015). Positive social competencies and prosocial behaviors are cyclical; children who excel at social interaction continue to do so, their peers tend to reciprocate, and positive effects on peer relationships increase (Laible, McGinley, Carlo, Augustine, & Murphy, 2014).

Children who experience **peer rejection** tend to be disliked and shunned by their peers. Children who have poor communication, language, emotional control, and social information processing skills are at risk for peer rejection (Bierman, Kalvin, & Heinrichs, 2015; Menting, van Lier, & Koot, 2011). For example, kindergarteners who had difficulty controlling their emotions were more likely than their more skilled peers to experience peer rejection through seventh grade (Bierman, Kalvin, & Heinrichs, 2014). Boys and girls with behavior problems are at risk for peer rejection—and peer rejection, in turn, is associated with increases in behavior problems throughout ele-mentary school as well as rule breaking in adolescence (Ettekal & Ladd, 2014; Sturaro, van Lier, Cuijpers, & Koot, 2011). Rejected children show two patterns of behavior, characterized by either aggression or withdrawal.

Aggressive-rejected children are confrontational, hostile toward other children, impul-sive, and hyperactive. They enter peer groups in destructive ways that disrupt the group's interaction or activity and direct attention to themselves (Lansford, Malone, Dodge, Pettit, & Bates, 2010; Wilson, 2006). Aggressive-rejected children tend to have difficulty taking

popular child A child who receives many positive ratings from peers indicating that he or she is accepted and valued by peers.

peer rejection An ongoing interaction in which a child is deliberately excluded by peers.

the perspective of others, and they tend to react aggressively to slights by peers, quickly assuming hostile intentions (Fite, Hendrickson, Rubens, Gabrielli, & Evans, 2013).

Other rejected children are socially withdrawn, passive, timid, anxious, and socially awkward. Withdrawn-rejected children tend to isolate themselves from peers, rarely initiate contact with peers, and speak less frequently than their peers (Rubin, Coplan, & Bowker, 2009). They tend to spend most of their time playing alone and on the periphery of the social scene, often because of shyness or social anxiety. In turn, socially withdrawn children are more likely to experience peer rejection and be disliked by their peers than other children, becoming more withdrawn over time (Coplan et al., 2013; Oh et al., 2008). Despite this, socially withdrawn children are just as likely to have a best friend as other children (Rubin, Wojslawowicz, Rose-Krasnor, Booth-LaForce, & Burgess, 2006).

Both aggressive-rejected and withdrawn-rejected children are similar in that they misinterpret other children's behaviors and motives, have trouble understanding and regulating their emotions, are poor listeners, and are less socially competent than other children (Ladd & Burgess, 2003). Peer rejection further hinders social development by depriving children of opportunities to learn and practice social skills such as interacting with other children, resolving conflict, and regulating emotions (Werner & Crick, 2004). Peer rejection is associated with short- and long-term problems, such as loneliness, anxiety, depression, low self-esteem, low academic achievement, and in adolescence, delinquency and school dropout (Fite et al., 2013; Menting, Koot, & van Lier, 2014; Schwartz, Lansford, Dodge, Pettit, & Bates, 2014; Zwierzynska, Wolke, & Lereya, 2013). The distress that accompanies chronic peer rejection is associated with high levels of activity in regions of the brain linked with detecting and experiencing the emotional distress caused by social

TABLE 14.3 • Characteristics of Popular and Rejected Children

	CHARACTERISTIC	OUTCOMES
Popular children	• Helpful, trustworthy, assertive • Cognitively skilled and achievement oriented • Socially skilled, able to self-disclose and provide emotional support • Good social problem-solving skills and conflict resolution skills • Prosocial orientation • Assume others have good intentions • A minority are also antisocial and aggressive. They interact with others in a hostile way, using physical or relational aggression, and are likely to bully other children.	• Positive characteristics are strengthened though experience and peer approval. • Positive peer evaluations are sources of self-validation, self-esteem, confidence, and attention from peers, and they influence adjustment. • Without intervention, the minority of popular adolescents who are aggressive are likely to continue patterns of physical or relational aggression in response to peer approval and acceptance.
Withdrawn-rejected children	• Passive, timid, and socially awkward • Social withdrawn, isolate themselves from others • Anxious • Poor social skills • Fear being disliked by peers • Misinterpret other children's behaviors and motives	• Similar outcomes for both types of rejected children • Negative characteristics are strengthened. • Few opportunities to learn and practice social skills, conflict resolution, and emotional regulation • Anxiety, depression, and low self-esteem • Behavior problems • Poor academic achievement • Increased physical and relational aggression over time • Withdrawal and loneliness
Aggressive-rejected children	• Confrontational, hostile toward other children • Impulsive and hyperactive • Difficulty with emotional regulation • Difficulty taking others' perspectives • Assume that their peers are out to get them • Poor social skills • Misinterpret other children's behaviors and motives	

exclusion. Moreover, the experience of chronic rejection is associated with heightened neural responses to exclusion, even when the child is not being excluded (Will, van Lier, Crone, & Güroğlu, 2016). Table 14.3 summarizes characteristics associated with popular children and those who are rejected.

PEER RELATIONSHIPS IN ADOLESCENCE

The most easily recognizable influence on adolescents, and that which gets the most attention from adults and the media, is the peer group. Each week, adolescents spend up to one third of their waking, nonschool hours with friends (Hartup & Stevens, 1997).

Adolescent Friendships

The typical adolescent has four to six close friends (Hartup & Stevens, 1999). Adolescent friendships are characterized by intimacy, self-disclosure, trust, and loyalty (Bauminger, Finzi-Dottan, Chason, & Har-Even, 2008). Adolescents also expect their friends to be there for them, stand up for them, and not share their secrets or harm them. Adolescent friendships tend to include cooperation, sharing, intimacy, and affirmation, which reflect their emerging capacities for perspective taking, social sensitivity, empathy, and social skills (Poulin & Chan, 2010).

Adolescent boys get together for activities, usually sports and competitive games, and tend to be more social and vocal in groups as compared with one-on-one situations. Boys tend to excel at being fun companions, coping with a friend who violates an expectation, and sustaining friendships within the context of having other friends (Rose & Asher, 2017). In contrast, most girls tend to prefer one-on-one interactions and often spend their time together talking, sharing thoughts and feelings, and supporting each other (Benenson & Heath, 2006). Overall, girls' friendships tend to be shorter in duration, but characterized by more closeness, than are those of boys (Benenson & Christakos, 2003). High-quality friendships characterized by sharing, intimacy, and open communication tend to endure over time (Hiatt, Laursen, Mooney, & Rubin, 2015). Among early adolescents it is estimated that one third to one half of friendships are unstable, with young people regularly losing friends and making new friendships (Poulin & Chan, 2010). After early adolescence friendships become more stable, with young people retaining the majority of their friendships over the course of a school year (Poulin & Chan, 2010).

As in childhood, similarity characterizes adolescent friendships. Friends tend to be similar in demographics, such as age, ethnicity, and socioeconomic status; they also tend to share psychological and developmental characteristics (Berndt & Murphy, 2002). Close friends and best friends tend to be similar in orientation toward risky activity, such as willingness to try drugs and engage in delinquency and dangerous behaviors such as unprotected sex (de Water, Burk, Cillessen, & Scheres, 2016; Henry, Schoeny, Deptula, & Slavick, 2007; Osgood et al., 2013; Scalco, Trucco, Coffman, & Colder, 2015). Adolescent friends tend to share interests, such as tastes in music; they are also similar in academic achievement, educational aspirations, and political beliefs; and they show similar trends in psychosocial development, such as identity status (Selfhout, Branje, ter Bogt, & Meeus, 2009; Shin & Ryan, 2014). Friends tend to select friends who are similar to themselves, but over time and through interaction, friends tend to become more similar to each other (Berndt & Murphy, 2002; Nurmi, 2004; Scalco et al., 2015). An important predictor of friendship stability in adolescence is similarity. In one study, adolescent

Adolescent friends share similar interests, attitudes, and behaviors and, over time, become more similar to each other.

LIFESPAN BRAIN DEVELOPMENT

• • Peer Interaction and the Brain

Social media interactions may be neurologically rewarding for teens.

Adolescents spend much of their time with friends. The peer group is especially salient during adolescence because interactions with friends become highly rewarding and motivating. Adolescents' strong desire to spend time with and earn the approval of peers is accompanied by distinct patterns of neurological activity (Steinberg, 2008). In one study, adolescents completed a risky driving task alone or in the presence of peers (Chein, Albert, O'Brien, Uckert, & Steinberg, 2011). The presence of peers was associated with increases in both risk taking and activity in the nucleus accumbens (NAcc), a subcortical structure that is part of the limbic system, a collection of brain structures that is implicated in emotion. The NAcc contains the brain's reward circuitry, playing a critical role in the experience of reward and pleasure, including social rewards and positive feedback, and in motivating goal-directed behavior (Fareri & Delgado, 2014). The NAcc shows greater responsivity to reward during the second decade of life, peaking in mid to late adolescence (Braams, van Duijvenvoorde, Peper, & Crone, 2015).

A great deal of adolescents' peer interaction occurs online via social media designed for mobile devices, such as Instagram and Snapchat (Lenhart, Purcell, Smith, & Zickuhr, 2010). Social and emotional processes typical of adolescence, such as peer influence, are also enacted on social media. For example, Smith, Chein, and Steinberg (2014) demonstrated increased NAcc activation and risky activity in a gambling task when adolescents believed that they were interacting with and being observed by an anonymous peer, suggesting that peer influence and its neurological correlates may also occur online. In addition, the level of NAcc response to positive social feedback has been linked to intensity of social media use (Meshi, Morawetz, & Heekeren, 2013), suggesting that social media interactions may also be neurologically rewarding.

A recent study examined whether peer influence processes occur online and whether the effects of peer processes can be observed in the brain (Sherman, Payton, Hernandez, Greenfield, & Dapretto, 2016). Adolescents were recruited to participate in an "internal social network" that simulated Instagram, a popular photo-sharing tool. Participants submitted their own Instagram photos and viewed both their own and other photos that they believed belonged to other members of the social network. The researchers manipulated how many "likes" accompanied each photo. Adolescents were more likely to "like" photographs they believed to be popular (those that were assigned many "likes"), and neural responses differed as a function of photograph popularity. When adolescents' own photographs received many "likes" (vs. few), they showed significantly greater activation of the NAcc, suggesting that "likes" may be experienced as rewarding and may motivate online behavior and continued use of social media. These findings are supported by prior research linking NAcc response to social evaluation and the role of the NAcc in reward and reinforcement (Meshi et al., 2013).

A follow-up study compared high school and college students on the Instagram-like social network task to determine whether peer influence and its neurological correlates are particularly high in adolescence as compared with emerging adulthood (Sherman, Greenfield, Hernandez, & Dapretto, 2017). Both high school and college students were more likely to "like" popular photographs than unpopular photographs, and they showed greater NAcc activation in response to popular photographs, especially when viewing their own images. Among high school students, the NAcc response when viewing their own photos with many "likes" rather than few increased with age, but no age differences emerged among college students. Prior research suggests that both peer influence and NAcc sensitivity to rewarding stimuli increase in adolescence and peak at around age 16–17 (Braams et al., 2015; Steinberg & Monahan, 2007). However, high school and college students did not differ in overall NAcc activation. Peer influence remains important in college, with similar neural correlates, suggesting a gradual path for social and neurological development from adolescence through emerging adulthood.

What Do You Think?

1. Why might adolescents find engaging in social media rewarding? What are the potential rewards? How might the rewards influence adolescents' behavior?

2. How might individuals' experience of social media and its effects change as they progress to and through adulthood?

friend dyads who differed in peer acceptance, physical aggression, and school competence in seventh grade were more likely to dissolve their friendship during high school than were dyads who were more similar (Hartl, Laursen, & Cillessen, 2015).

Sometimes, however, middle and older adolescents choose friends who are different from them, which encourages them to consider new perspectives. Cross-ethnic friendships, for example, are less common than same-ethnic friendships, but are associated with unique benefits. Adolescent members of cross-ethnic friendships show decreases in racial prejudice over time (Titzmann, Brenick, & Silbereisen, 2015). Ethnic minority adolescents with cross-ethnic friends perceive less discrimination, vulnerability, and relational victimization, and show higher rates of self-esteem and well-being over time than those without cross-ethnic friends (Bagci, Rutland, Kumashiro, Smith, & Blumberg, 2014; Graham, Munniksma, & Juvonen, 2014; Kawabata & Crick, 2011).

Close and stable friendships aid adolescents in their social adjustment (Bukowski, 2001; Kingery, Erdley, & Marshall, 2011), helping them explore and learn about themselves. By communicating with others and forming mutually self-disclosing supportive relationships, adolescents develop perspective taking, empathy, self-concept, and a sense of identity. Friends who are supportive and empathetic encourage prosocial behavior, promote psychological health, reduce the risk of delinquency, and help adolescents manage stress, such as the challenges of school transitions (Hiatt et al., 2015; Waldrip, Malcolm, & Jensen-Campbell, 2008; Wentzel, 2014).

Conformity, Cliques, and Crowds

Most adolescents experience pressure to conform to peer norms. Such pressure peaks at about age 14 and declines after age 18 (see Figure 14.9; Berndt & Murphy, 2002; Steinberg & Monahan, 2007). Peers tend to exert pressure to conform to day-to-day activities and personal choices such as appearance (clothing, hairstyle, makeup) and music (Brown, Lohr, & McClenahan, 1986; Steinberg, 2001). Adults tend to view peer pressure as a negative influence on adolescents, influencing them to behave in socially undesirable and even harmful ways. Adolescents' reporting of risky behavior such as smoking and unsafe sexual activity correlates with their peers' behaviors (Choukas-Bradley, Giletta, Widman, Cohen, & Prinstein, 2014; Henry et al., 2007; van de Bongardt, Reitz, Sandfort, & Deković, 2014). It is not simply peer behavior that influences adolescent behavior, but it is adolescents' perceptions of peer behavior, and beliefs about peers' activity, that predict engaging in risky activities such as smoking, alcohol use, and marijuana use (Duan, Chou, Andreeva, & Pentz, 2009). Young people vary in how they perceive and respond to peer pressure based on factors such as age, personal characteristics, and context, such as the presence of norms (Van Hoorn, Crone, & Van Leijenhorst, 2017). Adolescents are especially vulnerable to the negative effects of peer pressure during transitions such as entering a new school and undergoing puberty (Brechwald & Prinstein, 2011; Bukowski, Sippola, Hoza, & Newcomb, 2000).

Yet peer pressure is not always negative. Youths also report pressure from their friends to engage in prosocial and positive behaviors such as getting good grades, performing well athletically, getting along with parents, and avoiding smoking (Berndt & Murphy, 2002; Brown et al., 1986; Brown et al., 2008; Wentzel, 2014). For example, research with youths from Singapore demonstrates that peers exerted pressure on one another to conform to family and academic responsibilities—values that are particularly prized in Singapore culture (Sim & Koh, 2003). In laboratory experiments, adolescents were likely to show prosocial behavior after believing that anonymous peers approved of their prosocial actions, such as sharing coins with others (van Hoorn, van Dijk, Meuwese, Rieffe, & Crone, 2016).

During adolescence, one-on-one friendships tend to expand into tightly knit peer groups of anywhere from three to about nine, but most commonly around five members who are close friends. These close-knit, friendship-based groups are known as **cliques**. Like most close friends, members of cliques tend to share similarities such as

clique A tightly knit peer group of about three to eight close friends who share similarities such as demographics and attitudes.

demographics and attitudes (Lansford et al., 2009). The norms of expected behavior and values that govern cliques derive from interactions among the group members. Belonging to a peer group provides adolescents with a sense of inclusion, worth, support, and companionship (Lansford et al., 2009). In early adolescence, cliques tend to be sex segregated, with some composed of boys and others composed of girls. Girls' groups tend to be smaller than boys' groups but both are similarly tight knit (Gest, Davidson, Rulison, Moody, & Welsh, 2007). By mid-adolescence, cliques become mixed and form the basis for dating. A mixed-sex group of friends provides opportunities for adolescents to learn how to interact with others of the opposite sex in a safe, nonromantic context (Connolly, Craig, Goldberg, & Pepler, 2004). By late adolescence, especially after high school graduation, mixed-sex cliques tend to split up as adolescents enter college, the workforce, and other post-high-school activities (Connolly & Craig, 1999).

In contrast with cliques, which are an expansion of intimate friendships, **crowds** are larger and looser groups based on shared characteristics, interests, and reputation. Rather than voluntarily "joining," adolescents are sorted into crowds by their peers. Common categories of peer groups found in Western nations include Populars/Elites (high in social status), Athletes/Jocks (athletically oriented), Academics/Brains (academically oriented), and Partiers (highly social; care little about academics). Other types of crowds include Nonconformists (unconventional in dress and music), Deviants (defiant; engage in delinquent activity) and Normals (not clearly distinct on any particular trait; Delsing, ter Bogt, Engels, & Meeus, 2007; Kinney, 1999; Stone & Brown, 1999; Sussman, Pokhrel, Ashmore, & Brown, 2007; Verkooijen, de Vries, & Nielsen, 2007).

Crowd membership is based on an adolescent's image or reputation among peers (Brown, Bank, & Steinberg, 2008; Cross & Fletcher, 2009). Members of a crowd may or may not interact with one another; however, because of similarities in appearance, activities, and perceived attitudes, their peers consider them members of the same group (Verkooijen et al., 2007). Crowds differentiate young people on the basis of behaviors such as sexual activity, academic achievement, psychiatric symptoms, and health risks such as alcohol and substance use. In middle adolescence, as their cognitive and classification capacities increase, adolescents begin to classify their peers in more complex ways and hybrid crowds emerge, such as *popular-jocks*, and *partier-jocks*. As with cliques, crowds decline in late adolescence, especially after young people leave high school. However, recent research suggests that college students self-identify into crowds along four dimensions: social, scholastic, athletic, and counterculture, with social and counterculture affiliation predicting drug use (Hopmeyer & Medovoy, 2017). The extended transition to adulthood characterized by emerging adulthood changes norms.

crowd A large, loose group of individuals based on perceived characteristics, interests, stereotypes, and reputation.

dating Establishing romantic relationships, a type of romantic courtship.

Dating in Adolescence

Establishing romantic relationships, or **dating**, is part of the adolescent experience. Most young people in the United States have been involved in at least one romantic relationship by middle adolescence, and by age 18, more than 80% of young people have some dating experience (Carver, Joyner, & Udry, 2003). By late adolescence, the majority of adolescents are in an ongoing romantic relationship with one person (Collins & Steinberg, 2006; O'Sullivan, Cheng, Harris, & Brooks-Gunn, 2007). Dating typically begins through the intermingling of mixed-sex peer groups, progresses to group dating, and then one-on-one dating and romantic relationships (Connolly et al., 2004; Connolly, Nguyen, Pepler, Craig, & Jiang, 2013; Furman, 2002). Adolescents with larger social networks and greater

Dating is common in adolescence.

MJTH/Shutterstock.com

access to opposite-sex peers date more than those who are less social (Connolly & Furman, 2000). However, some research suggests that adolescents date outside of their friendship networks, and that preexisting friendships are not likely to transform into romantic relationships (Kreager, Molloy, Moody, & Feinberg, 2015).

Dating varies by culture. Youths in Western societies date earlier than those in Asian cultures. Similarly, Asian American adolescents begin dating later than African American, European American, and Latino adolescents in the United States (Regan, Durvasula, Howell, Ureño, & Rea, 2004). In the United States, early adolescents date for fun and for popularity with peers. Often the purpose of dating is simply to have a relationship (Furman, 2002). As teens grow older, the reasons reported for dating change. In late adolescence, dating fulfills needs for intimacy, support, and affection in both boys and girls (Furman, 2002; Giordano, Longmore, & Manning, 2006). However, adolescents' capacity for romantic intimacy develops slowly and is influenced by the quality of their experiences with intimacy in friendships and their attachments to parents (Connolly & Furman, 2000; Furman, 2002; Scharf & Mayseless, 2008; van de Bongardt, Yu, Deković, & Meeus, 2015). Adolescents interact with their romantic partners in ways that are similar to their interactions with parents and peers (Collins, Welsh, & Furman, 2009; Furman & Shomaker, 2008). Through close friendships and dating, adolescents learn to share of themselves, be sensitive to others' needs, and develop the capacity for intimacy.

In middle and late adolescence, dating is associated with positive self-concept, expectations for success in relationships, fewer feelings of alienation, and good health (Ciairano, Bonino, Kliewer, Miceli, & Jackson, 2006). Close romantic relationships provide opportunities to develop and practice sensitivity, cooperation, empathy, and social support, as well as to aid in identity development (Ciairano et al., 2006; Furman & Shaffer, 2003). Adolescents' behavior, such as academic achievement, tends to be very similar to that of their romantic partners (Giordano, Phelps, Manning, & Longmore, 2008). Early dating relative to peers is associated with increases in alcohol and substance use, smoking delinquency, and low academic competence during the adolescent years, as well as long-term depression, especially in early maturing girls (Connolly et al., 2013; Fidler, West, Jarvis, & Wardle, 2006; Furman & Collibee, 2014; Martin et al., 2007). Overall, romantic experiences in adolescence are continuous with romantic experiences in adulthood, suggesting that building romantic relationships is an important developmental task for adolescents (Collins et al., 2009). Adolescents who date fewer partners and experience better quality dating relationships in middle adolescence tend to demonstrate smoother partner interactions and relationship processes in young adulthood (e.g., negotiating conflict, appropriate caregiving) as compared with their peers who are more indiscriminate in their choice of dates (Madsen & Collins, 2011).

PEER RELATIONSHIPS IN ADULTHOOD

Relationships with peers continue to be important throughout adulthood, though they sometimes fulfill different functions than they do in childhood and adolescence. For example, peers may provide important career contacts; opportunities for collaboration in voluntary organizations, informal neighborhood groups, and social media exchanges; and social support systems beyond the extended family.

Adult Friendships

Like friendships in childhood and adolescence, adult friendships are based on similarity—shared demographics, such as age, sex, and socioeconomic status, interests, attitudes, and values (Hartup & Stevens, 1999; Wrzus, Zimmermann, Mund, & Neyer, 2016).

Friendships improve with age and are a powerful buffer against stress.

Leila Cutler/Alamy

Women tend to have more intimate and long-lasting friendships and rely more on friends to meet social and emotional needs than do men (Carbery & Buhrmester, 1998; Radmacher & Azmitia, 2006; Sherman & de Vries, 2000). Men's friendships tend to center around sharing information and activities, such as playing sports, rather than intimate disclosure (David-Barrett et al., 2015; Radmacher & Azmitia, 2006).

Throughout the lifespan, close friendships are based in reciprocity, emotional give and take, that entails intimacy, companionship, and support; and behaviors such as sharing, exchanging favors, and giving advice (Hartup & Stevens, 1999; Wrzus et al., 2016). Close friends attempt to improve each other's well-being by providing emotional and social support, and helping each other manage daily life, stressful transitions, and crises. Friendships offer powerful protection against stress for both men and women. Daily hassles, such as a challenging commute and juggling the demands of career and family; and major crises, such as illness or death, are stressors that tax individuals' coping resources and contribute to illness, aging-related physical changes, and even early death (Aldwin, 2007). Friendship quality is associated with psychological adjustment and well-being in emerging and young adults (Buote et al., 2007; Demir, Özen, Doğan, Bilyk, & Tyrell, 2011). Satisfaction with one's friendships is a better predictor of life satisfaction than is the number of friends (Gillespie, Lever, Frederick, & Royce, 2015).

Friendship changes over the course of adulthood. Young adults who are single tend to rely more heavily on friendships to fulfill needs for social support and acceptance than do married young adults (Carbery & Buhrmester, 1998). As adults establish careers they often have less time to spend with friends, yet friendship remains an important source of social support and is associated with well-being, positive affect, and self-esteem influence on well-being throughout life (Huxhold, Miche, & Schüz, 2014; Ueno & Adams, 2006). In older adulthood, individuals generally have more time to devote to leisure activities. Their friendships become more centered on activities, such as playing golf or card games, and they report having more fun with their friends than do younger adults (Larson, Mannell, & Zuzanek, 1986).

Friendships tend to improve with age. Whereas young adults tend to report having many friends and feel ambivalent or troubled about some, middle-aged and older adults tend to report fewer friends, but almost all are described as close and few to none are ambivalent or troubled (Fingerman, Hay, & Birditt, 2004). Older adults tend to have fewer friends, but more meaningful relationships than younger adults (Fingerman & Charles, 2010). Older adults describe close friendships as entailing mutual interests, a sense of belonging, and opportunities to share feelings (Field, 1999). Although friends become fewer in number, older adults form new friendships throughout their lives (Robles, Menkin, Robles, & Menkin, 2015). Similar to earlier in life, elders tend to choose friends who share similarities in age, race, ethnicity, and values. With increasing age and the death of friends, elders are more likely to report having friends of different generations (Johnson & Troll, 1994). Giving and receiving support from friends is an important influence on older adults' well-being and is associated with a relatively low risk of depression (Bishop, 2008; Thomas, 2010). Friendships are also crucial in helping to manage age-related losses in health as well as bereavement at the death of a loved one.

Aging and the Social World

Social support is important for well-being. However, social interaction tends to decline in older adulthood as social networks become smaller (Antonucci, Akiyama, & Takahashi, 2004; Shaw, Krause, Liang, & Bennett, 2007). Several perspectives account for changes in social interaction and elders' psychological functioning.

Disengagement, activity, and continuity theories. Why do older adults have fewer friends? An early perspective, **disengagement theory**, proposed that older adults disengage from society as they anticipate death. At the same time, society disengages from them (Cumming & Henry, 1961). Older adults withdraw and relinquish valued social roles, reduce their social interaction, and turn inward, spending more time thinking and reflecting. Society pulls away, reducing employment obligations and social responsibilities as they are transferred to younger people. According to disengagement theory,

disengagement theory A perspective that declines in social interaction in older age are due to mutual withdrawal between older adults and society as they anticipate death.

elders' withdrawal and society's simultaneous disengagement serve to allow older adults to advance into very old age and minimize the disruptive nature of their deaths to society. In this way they benefit both the older person and society.

In the years since disengagement theory was proposed, however, it has become apparent that its central tenet is not true: Rather than disengage, most older individuals prefer to remain active and engaged with others and they benefit from social engagement (Bengtson & DeLiema, 2016; Johnson & Mutchler, 2014). Any amount of social activity is more beneficial than a lack of involvement (Glass, Mendes De Leon, Bassuk, & Berkman, 2006; Hinterlong, Morrow-Howell, & Rozario, 2007). Many people continue rewarding aspects of their work after retirement or adopt new roles in their communities. Most older adults retain the same leisure activities from worker to retiree and many develop new hobbies (Scherger, Nazroo, & Higgs, 2011). Some have argued that disengagement does not reflect healthy development but rather a lack of opportunities for social engagement (Lang, Featherman, & Nesselroade, 1997).

In contrast to disengagement theory, **activity theory** posits that declines in social interaction are not a result of elders' desires, but are instead a function of social barriers to engagement. When they lose roles due to retirement or disability, they attempt to replace lost roles in an effort to stay active and busy. Volunteer work, for example, can replace career roles and protect against decline in health and psychological well-being (Hao, 2008; Morrow-Howell, Hinterlong, Rozario, & Tang, 2003). A 13-year longitudinal study following more than 2,700 elders aged 65 and older found that civic engagement in social and productive activities reduced mortality as much as did physical fitness (Glass et al., 2006). Yet it is not simply the quantity of activity and social relationships that influences health and well-being, but the quality, and individuals differ in their needs and desires (Bengtson & DeLiema, 2016; Pushkar et al., 2010). The more active elders are in roles they value—such as spouse, parent, friend, and volunteer—the more likely they are to report high levels of well-being and life satisfaction and to live longer, healthier lives (Adams, Leibbrandt, & Moon, 2011; Cherry et al., 2013; Litwin, 2003).

From the perspective of **continuity theory**, successful aging entails not simply remaining active but maintaining a sense of consistency in self from the past into the future. Despite changing roles, people are motivated to maintain their habits, personalities, and lifestyles, adapting as needed to maintain a sense of continuity, that they are the same person they have always been (Atchley, 1999). This entails acknowledging and minimizing losses, integrating them with their sense of self, and optimizing their strengths to construct a life path that maintains their sense of remaining the same person over time despite physical, cognitive, emotional, and social changes (Bengtson & DeLiema, 2016). Older adults tend to seek routine: familiar people, familiar activities, and familiar settings. Most of older adults' friends are old friends. Engaging in familiar activities with familiar people preserves a sense of self and offers comfort, social support, self-esteem, mastery, and identity (Pushkar et al., 2010).

Socioemotional selectivity theory. Older adults' narrowing social circles may rest on the uniquely human ability to monitor time. With advancing age, people become increasingly aware of their shrinking time horizon; that they have little time left to live. This awareness causes them to shift their goals and priorities and accounts for continuity and change in social relationships. According to **socioemotional selectivity theory**, older adults become increasingly motivated to derive emotional meaning from life and thereby cultivate emotionally close relationships and disengage from more peripheral social ties (Carstensen et al., 2011; English & Carstensen, 2016).

As perceived time left diminishes, people tend to discard peripheral relationships and focus on important ones, such as those with close family members and friends (English & Carstensen, 2014). In support of this, aging is related to steep declines in social relationships. A recent meta-analysis confirmed that during young adulthood, people continue to accumulate friends; hence their friendship networks increase (Wrzus, Hänel, Wagner, & Neyer, 2013). Older adults have fewer relationships in comparison with young adults, but their relationships are particularly close, supportive, and reciprocal (Huxhold, Fiori, & Windsor, 2013; Li, Fok, & Fung, 2011). Older adults place more emphasis on the

activity theory The view that older adults want to remain active and that declines in social interaction are not a result of elders' desires but are a function of social barriers to engagement.

continuity theory The perspective that older adults strive to maintain continuity and consistency in self across the past and into the future; successful elders retain a sense that they are the same person they have always been despite physical, cognitive, emotional, and social changes.

socioemotional selectivity theory The perspective that as the emotional regulation function of social interaction becomes increasingly important to older adults, they prefer to interact with familiar social partners, accounting for the narrowing of the social network with age.

emotional quality of their social relationships and interactions. As compared with young adults, older adults tend to perceive their social network as eliciting less negative emotion and more positive emotion (English & Carstensen, 2014). Despite an overall decline in the number of relationships, this process of strengthening and pruning relationships is associated with positive well-being; it allows older adults to focus their limited time and energy on relationships that are most beneficial while avoiding those that are inconsequential or detrimental, thereby maximizing their emotional well-being. In this sense, social selectivity is an emotional regulation strategy (Sims, Hogan, & Carstensen, 2015).

According to socioemotional selectivity theory, the functions of social interactions change with age and psychological and cognitive development (English & Carstensen, 2016). Specifically, the information-sharing function of friendship becomes less salient. For example, young adults often turn to friends for information, but older adults often have accumulated decades of knowledge. Therefore, it is the emotion-regulating function of social relationships that become more important during older adulthood (Carstensen & Mikels, 2005).

Generally, at all ages we look to friends to affirm our sense of identity and uniqueness, we choose friends who make us feel good, and we avoid those who evoke negative feelings. According to socioemotional selectivity theory, the emotional correlates of friendship—feeling good and avoiding feeling bad—become more important over the lifespan. As we age, older adults tend to narrow their circle of friends. They are less likely to approach new people for friendship, and thus they reduce the likelihood of rejection and negative feelings. As physical frailty and psychological changes pose more challenges for adaptation, older adults tend to place emphasis on having positive interactions with others, reducing negative interactions, and avoiding stress. Interacting with a handful of carefully chosen relatives and close friends increases the chances that older adults will have positive interactions. Therefore, smaller social networks are associated with greater life satisfaction in older adults than younger adults (Lang & Fingerman, 2004).

 Thinking in Context 14.5

1. Researchers who study peer relationships in adolescence might argue that cliques get a bad rap because they are commonly characterized as negative and harmful to adolescents. Compare the research on cliques with common views about cliques.

2. Considering Bronfenbrenner's bioecological theory, which perspective on adults' changing social world—disengagement, activity, continuous, or socioemotional selectivity theory—best incorporates a contextual perspective? Why?

3. In what ways are various aspects of social relationships (e.g., friendships, family relationships with siblings and children) continuous over the lifespan? In what ways do these relationships change?

Lives in Context Video 14.2
Technology and Social Media

© iStockphoto.com/diego_cervo

Apply Your Knowledge

Thirteen-year-old Farah stepped off the school bus and nervously adjusted her new sweater, anticipating comments from her friends, who would probably be hanging around the lockers at the north end of the quad as they did every morning. As she approached the group, Jamal looked up and called out, "Hey, Farah's wearing purple! Like that purple dinosaur!" Farah rolled her eyes—Jamal was always such a clown. "Where'd you get that? Did you pocket it when you were at the mall last night?" mocked Brittany. Brittany had challenged Farah to a shoplifting contest last month, but it made Farah uncomfortable and she didn't want to try it again. Farah tried to ignore Brittany's question as Margie offered her a cigarette. "I like the V-neck," said Margie, "it's a flattering style for you." "Thanks," said Farah, accepting the cigarette. "I'll pay you back later." A moment later Gary walked up, having just been dropped off at school by his older sister. He smiled and announced, "Party at my house this weekend. My parents are away. My sister says we can all go swimming if we clean up after ourselves—and her friends." Amid a chorus of groans, the group of half a dozen classmates agreed and began discussing what to bring to the party.

1. Describe the peer influences in Farah's life. Would you consider her group of friends a clique, a crowd, or something else?

2. Compare Farah's and her friends' interactions with the research literature on peer relations. What similarities and differences do you notice?

3. Considering what you have learned about social relationships over the lifespan, what predictions would you make for Farah as she develops through the teen years, into emerging adulthood, and beyond?

Give your students the SAGE edge!

SAGE edge offers a robust online environment featuring an impressive array of free tools and resources for review, study, and further exploration, keeping both instructors and students on the cutting edge of teaching and learning. Learn more at **edge.sagepub.com/kuthertopical.**

CHAPTER 14 IN REVIEW

14.1 Discuss the influence of living arrangements and decisions about family formation on adult development.

SUMMARY

Singlehood, not living with a romantic partner, is common among U.S. young adults. When young adults perceive themselves as single by choice, they tend to report enjoying singlehood and the social benefits that accompany it. Cohabitation is increasingly popular but, among young adults, is associated with less stable relationships as compared with marriage. There are economic, physical, and psychological benefits to marriage in both heterosexual and LGBT couples and age is one of the best predictors of marital satisfaction. Generally, older adult marriages tend to be characterized by greater satisfaction, less negativity, and more positive interactions as compared with younger adults. Divorce is accompanied by distress, but most adults are resilient. The transition to parenthood is challenging to most adults and their marriages. Childlessness appears to interfere with psychosocial development and personal adjustment only when it is involuntary.

KEY TERMS

singlehood   cohabitation

REVIEW QUESTIONS

1. What are some common living situations for adults today?

2. In what ways are singlehood, cohabitation, and marriage associated with well-being?

3. What are predictors and effects of experiencing divorce?

4. What are recent trends in childbearing?

14.2 Compare and contrast child outcomes associated with various family constellations.

SUMMARY

Children in single-parent and cohabiting homes tend to show more academic and behavior problems than children in two-parent married families, but these effects tend to be small. Many of the differences associated with family structure differences are reduced or disappear when researchers take socioeconomic status and family stability into account. Decades of research has shown no differences in the adjustment or development of children and adolescents reared by same-sex couples compared to those reared by other-sex couples. Parental conflict, however is associated with distress. Divorce has some negative effects on children's adjustment, such as internalizing and externalizing problems, but these effects are small, vary by particular

outcome, and are often transient. Most children show improved adjustment within two years after the divorce. Blended families present children with challenges for adjustment. Age influences adaptation as well as the relationship with the stepparent.

KEY TERM

blended family

REVIEW QUESTIONS

1. Compare child outcomes associated with single-parent and cohabiting parent families.

2. What does the research suggest about the efficacy of same-sex parents?

3. What are influences on adjustment for children in divorcing or remarrying homes?

14.3 Explain the effects of various parenting methods on children and adolescents.

SUMMARY

Parenting style, the emotional climate of the parent–child relationship, influences parents' efficacy, their relationship with their children, and their children's development. Authoritative parenting combines parental acceptance and limits, and is associated with positive social, academic, and emotional outcomes. Parenting and the effects of parenting style are influenced by culture, as children evaluate parental behavior in light of their culture and the emotional tone of the relationship. The majority of adolescents and their parents have warm, positive relationships. Severe parent-adolescent conflict is associated with internalizing and externalizing problems. One way in which parents balance autonomy with protection is through parental monitoring, which is associated with overall well-being.

KEY TERMS

parenting style   uninvolved parenting style
authoritarian parenting style   authoritative parenting style
permissive parenting style   parental monitoring

REVIEW QUESTIONS

1. What are Baumrind's four parenting styles? What are outcomes associated with each style?

2. What are contextual or cultural influences on parenting style?

3. How does parent-child conflict change over adolescence?

14.4 Describe the changes that take place within family relationships after individuals reach adulthood.

14.5 Discuss how peer relationships develop and change throughout the lifespan.

SUMMARY

Generally speaking, there is continuity in parent-child relationships throughout the lifespan. Most parents adjust well to the empty nest. Most older adults and their adult children keep in touch even when they are separated by great distance. In all nations, families who live apart continue to provide various forms of emotional and physical support to one another. The more grandparents are engaged with their grandchildren and spend time with them, the more they tend to report high levels of life satisfaction. Generally speaking, parents and adult children who have a lifetime of close and positive relations tend to remain close, and adult children tend to provide more assistance than do those whose family relations are less positive. As adults' caregiving responsibilities increase, such as when elderly parents require specialized care (e.g., in cases of dementia), they are likely to experience role overload.

KEY TERMS

sandwich generation

REVIEW QUESTIONS

1. What are common patterns of change in parent-adult child relationships?

2. What factors contribute to the quality of parent adult-child relationships?

SUMMARY

Young children's early interactions with peers center on play. Throughout life, friendships are characterized by similarity. In middle childhood through adolescence, trust and loyalty become important. Peer acceptance becomes increasingly important in middle childhood. Some children stand out from their peers as exceptionally well liked or exceptionally disliked; popular or rejected. During adolescence, peer groups become organized into cliques and crowds. The pressure to conform to peers rises in early adolescence, peaks at about age 14, and then declines. Peer pressure can center on negative behaviors but also on positive and prosocial behaviors. Friendships tend to improve during the adult years, yet in older adulthood the social circle narrows. Some point to disengagement, activity, or continuity theory as explanations for adults' reduced social activity. According to socioemotional selectivity theory, older adults become increasingly motivated to derive emotional meaning from life and thereby cultivate emotionally close relationships and disengage from more peripheral social ties.

KEY TERMS

rough-and-tumble play	dating
sociodramatic play	disengagement theory
popular children	activity theory
peer rejection	continuity theory
cliques	socioemotional selectivity theory
crowds	

REVIEW QUESTIONS

1. What is the nature of friendship in childhood?

2. How does friendship change in adolescence and adulthood?

3. Define the words *clique* and *crowd* and discuss peer conformity in adolescence.

4. Give an example illustrating socioemotional selectivity theory.

Test your understanding of the content.
Review the flashcards and quizzes at
edge.sagepub.com/kuthertopical

School, Achievement, and Work

Learning Objectives

15.1 Describe what children learn during early childhood and in elementary school.

15.2 Discuss the influences of secondary and postsecondary education on adjustment.

15.3 Explain the role of contextual factors in achievement attributions and motivation.

15.4 Compare the transition to work with the transition to retirement in terms of influence on satisfaction and adjustment.

Digital Resources

▶ Head Start Success Story

▣ Transition to School

▶ Emerging Adulthood: Choosing a Major

▣ Dropout Prevention

▣ The Myth of Meritocracy

▶ Retirement: Planning and Adjustment

◀)) The Glass Ceiling

$SAGE edge™ Master these learning objectives with multimedia resources available at **edge.sagepub.com/kuthertopical** and *Lives in Context* video cases available in the interactive eBook.

Throughout this book, we have seen that our development is influenced by interaction among the many contexts in which we are immersed. In this chapter, we examine two contexts that fulfill important roles in our development: school and work. North American children spend about 7 hours in school each day, with a typical school year consisting of 180 days in the United States and 194 in Canada. Most North American adults work year round and are granted an average of 10 to 14 vacation days each year.

EARLY CHILDHOOD AND ELEMENTARY EDUCATION

LO 15.1 Describe what children learn during early childhood and in elementary school.

All children enter first grade at about age 6. Many children attend kindergarten prior to entering elementary school, but only 15 states require children to complete kindergarten (Education Commission of the States, 2014). Early education is important for children's cognitive, social, and emotional development. Preschool programs provide educational experiences for children ages 2 to 5.

CHILD-CENTERED AND ACADEMICALLY CENTERED PROGRAMS

There are two general approaches to early childhood education. **Academically centered programs** emphasize providing children with structured learning environments

In this Montessori classroom, children explore and play together.

AP Photo/Lori Wolfe

in which teachers deliver direct instruction on letters, numbers, shapes, and academic skills. **Child-centered programs** take a contructivist approach that encourages children to actively build their own understanding of the world through observing, interacting with objects and people, and engaging in a variety of activities that allow them to manipulate materials and interact with teachers and peers (Kostelnik, Soderman, Whiren, & Rupiper, 2015). Children learn by doing, through play, and learn to problem solve, get along with others, communicate, and self-regulate.

Montessori schools, first created in the early 1900s by the Italian physician and educator Maria Montessori (1870–1952), exemplify the child–centered approach, in which children are viewed as active constructors of their own development and given freedom in choosing their activities. Teachers act as facilitators, providing a range of activities and materials, demonstrating ways of exploring them, and providing help when the child asks. The Montessori approach is credited with fostering independence, self-regulation, and cognitive and problem-solving skills.

In contrast, problems have been documented with teacher-directed rigid academic programs. Children immersed such programs sometimes show signs of stress such as rocking, may have less confidence in their skills, and may avoid challenging tasks as compared with children who are immersed in more active forms of play-based learning (Stipek, Feiler, Daniels, & Milburn, 1995). Such programs are also negatively associated with reading skills in first grade (Lerkkanen et al., 2016).

Instead of a purely academic approach, many practitioners advocate for developmentally appropriate practice, which tailors instruction to the age of the child, recognizing individual differences and the need for hands-on active teaching methods (Kostelnik et al., 2015). Teachers provide educational support in the form of learning goals, instructional support, and feedback, but they also emphasize emotional support and help children learn to manage their own behavior (Anderson & Phillips, 2017; Hamre, 2014). Responsive child–centered teaching is associated with higher reading and math scores during first grade (Lerkkanen et al., 2016).

Effective early childhood educational practice is influenced by cultural values (Gordon & Browne, 2016). In the United States, a society that emphasizes individuality, a child–centered approach in which children are given freedom of choice is associated with the most positive outcomes (Marcon, 1999). Yet in Japan, the most effective preschools tend to foster collectivist values and are society centered with an emphasis on social and classroom routines, skills, and promoting group harmony (Holloway, 1999; Nagayama & Gilliard, 2005). Japanese preschools prepare children for their roles in society and provide formal instruction in academic areas as well as art, swordsmanship, gymnastics, tea ceremonies, and Japanese dance. Much instruction is teacher-directed and children are instructed to sit, observe, and listen. Teachers are warm, but address the group as a whole rather than individuals. This structured approach is associated with positive outcomes in Japanese children (Holloway, 1999; Nagayama & Gilliard, 2005), illustrating the role of culture in influencing outcomes of early childhood education. Even within a given country such as the United States, there exist many ethnicities and corresponding cultures, such those of Native Americans and Mexican Americans. In each case, instruction that is informed by an understanding of children's home and community culture fosters a sense of academic belongingness that ultimately influences academic achievement (Gilliard & Moore, 2007; Gordon & Browne, 2016).

In Western countries children spend most of their day at school and, aside from household chores such as picking up their toys or cleaning their dinner plates, work is

academically centered programs An approach to early childhood education that emphasizes providing children with structured learning environments in which teachers deliver direct instruction on letters, numbers, shapes, and academic skills.

child-centered programs A constructivist approach to early childhood education that encourages children to actively build their own understanding of the world through observing, interacting with objects and people, and engaging in a variety of activities that allow them to manipulate materials and interact with teachers and peers.

CULTURAL INFLUENCES ON DEVELOPMENT

• • Efe Children's Work

REUTERS/James Akena

This child is learning by participating in activities that support his community.

The Efe people are members of a small, tightly knit hunter-gatherer community in the forests of the Democratic Republic of Congo. Unlike children in most industrialized societies, Efe children do not attend school (Morelli, Rogoff, & Angelillo, 2003). Instead, they are free to wander the village, enter most huts, and sleep with their parents or in the huts of other relatives. They spend their days accompanying adults as they gather food, collect firewood or water, or work in

their vegetable gardens. From the moment they can walk, Efe children are integrated into adult work. Although children spend their days accompanying adults as they hunt, forage, and maintain the household, they are not tutored in work activities. There is little adult–child interaction. Instead, adults expect children to learn from watching and participating.

Efe children learn through activity, and their play emulates and practices adult work. For example, Efe children pretend to make flat bread out of dirt, shoot animals with a bow and arrow, and nurture their dolls. Most striking, in comparison with Western children, are they ways in which Efe children contribute to their community at a very young age. By 3 years of age young Efe children are responsible for household and community activities such as kindling the fire, preparing and cooking food, and minding younger children.

What Do You Think?

1. How do the principles of social learning theory and Vygtosky's sociocultural theory (see Chapter 1) apply to the example of Efe children?

2. Should parents in Western industrialized societies encourage young children to be responsible for household and community tasks? Why or why not?

not a part of the typical Western child's day. Most children are segregated from adult work and know little about their parents' workplace. In contrast, children in many cultures around the world have the opportunity to learn through observing and participating in their community's work. The Cultural Influences on Development feature examines one of these cultures.

EARLY CHILDHOOD EDUCATION INTERVENTIONS

Recognizing that young children's developmental needs extend beyond education, one of the most successful early childhood education and intervention programs in the United States, Project Head Start (see Chapter 8), was created by the federal government in order to provide economically disadvantaged children with nutritional, health, and educational services during their early childhood years, prior to kindergarten (Ramey & Ramey, 1998). Parents of Head Start children also receive assistance, such as education about child development, vocational services, and programs addressing their emotional and social needs (Zigler & Styfco, 2004).

Over the past four decades, a great deal of research has been conducted on the effectiveness of Head Start. The most common finding is that Head Start improves cognitive performance, with gains in IQ and achievement scores in elementary school (Zhai, Brooks-Gunn, & Waldfogel, 2011). Compared with children who do not partici-pate in Head Start, those who do so have greater parental involvement in school, show higher math achievement scores in middle school, are less likely to be held back a grade or have problems with chronic absenteeism in middle school, and are more likely to graduate from high school (Duncan, Ludwig, & Magnuson, 2007; Joo, 2010; Phillips,

Gormley, & Anderson, 2016). Head Start is associated with other long-lasting social and physical effects, such as gains in social competence and health-related outcomes including immunizations (Huston, 2008). Yet some research has suggested that the cognitive effects of Head Start may fade over time such that, by late childhood, Head Start participants perform similarly to control group low SES children who have not participated in Head Start (U.S. Department of Health and Human Services & Administration for Children and Families, 2010). Early intervention may not compensate for the pervasive and long-lasting effects of poverty-stricken neighborhoods and inadequate public schools (Schnur & Belanger, 2000; Welshman, 2010). At the same time, long term advantageous effects of attending Head Start include higher graduation rates and lower rates of adolescent pregnancy and criminality for low income children who attend Head Start as compared with their control group peers (Duncan & Magnuson, 2013).

Additional evidence for the effectiveness of early childhood education interventions comes from the Carolina Abecedarian Project and the Perry Preschool Project, carried out in the 1960s and 1970s. Both of these programs enrolled children from families with incomes below the poverty line, and emphasized the provision of stimulating preschool experiences to promote motor, language, and social skills as well as cognitive skills including literacy and math. Special emphasis was placed on rich, responsive adult–child verbal communication as well as nutrition and health services. Children in these programs achieved higher reading and math scores in elementary school than their nonenrolled peers (Campbell & Ramey, 1994). As adolescents, they showed higher rates of high school graduation and college enrollment and lower rates of substance abuse and pregnancy (Campbell, Ramey, Pungello, Sparling, & Miller-Johnson, 2002; Muennig et al., 2011). At ages 30 and 40, early intervention participants showed higher levels of education and income (Campbell et al., 2012; Schweinhart et al., 2005).

The success of early education intervention programs has influenced a movement in the United States toward comprehensive prekindergarten (pre-K). Young children who participate in high-quality pre-K programs enter school with greater readiness to learn and score higher on reading and math tests than their peers (Gormley Jr, Phillips, Adelstein, & Shaw, 2010). About one half of states offer some form of state-funded pre-K without income restrictions (Barnett, Carolan, Squires, & Clarke Brown, K., Horowitz, 2015). A few states, including Oklahoma, Georgia, and Florida, provide universal pre-K to all children and many more states are moving in this direction (Williams, 2015). Beginning in the fall of 2017, New York City initiated a city-funded "3-K for all" program of free full-day preschool for all 3-year-olds (Taylor, 2017). Although some research suggests that half-day and more intense full-day programs do not differ in academic and social outcomes, full-day preschool incorporates the benefit of free child care to working parents that is likely of higher quality than they might have otherwise been able to afford (Leow & Wen, 2017). Funding public preschool programs is daunting, but the potential rewards are tremendous.

TRANSITION TO FIRST GRADE

As mentioned previously, most children go to kindergarten before entering first grade, and many go to preschool before kindergarten. Despite some experience with the educational system, children usually feel a mixture of excitement and anxiety upon entering first grade. For most children and parents, first grade holds symbolic value as the threshold to elementary school and older childhood.

Easing children's transition to first grade is important because adjustment and behavior during the first year of elementary school influences teacher perceptions as well as children's views of themselves, their academic performance, and class involvement (Zafiropoulou, Sotiriou, & Mitsiouli, 2007). Teachers play an important role in aiding children's adjustment to first grade. They provide both instructional and emotional support: For example, they attend to students' interests, promote initiative, provide appropriately challenging learning opportunities, and encourage positive social relationships. These forms of support help children develop academic skills, such as reading and mathematics, as well as social skills, such as self-control and the ability to follow directions (Lerkkanen et al., 2016; Perry, Donohue, & Weinstein, 2007).

High-quality, sensitive, responsive, and positive interactions with teachers are associated with greater student motivation and academic achievement and fewer problems with anxiety and poor behavior throughout elementary school (Cadima, Leal, & Burchinal, 2010; Maldonado-Carreño & Votruba-Drzal; Van Craeyevelt, Verschueren, Vancraeyveldt, Wouters, & Colpin, 2017). Conversely, teacher–child conflict is associated with aggression, poor social competence, and underachievement throughout elementary school (Runions et al., 2014; Spilt, Hughes, Wu, & Kwok; White, 2013).

The emotional support and social interaction provided by teachers influences children's adjustment to school.

First grade serves as a foundation for a child's educational career because the school curriculum of each grade builds on prior grades. Starting in first grade, reading and math skills build step by step each year, so that doing well in one year helps children perform well the next year (Entwisle, Alexander, & Steffel Olson, 2005). Early school failure is harmful to students' academic functioning and intellectual development because early academic deficiencies often persist through the school years and children may fall further behind with each successive year in school (Alexander, Entwisle, & Kabbani, 2001; Ferguson, Jimerson, & Dalton, 2001; Hong & Yu, 2007). In addition, children's performance in each grade is documented into a cumulative file that follows them from year to year, influencing teachers' perceptions and expectations of them, which, in turn, influences their educational success.

GRADE RETENTION AND SOCIAL PROMOTION

What should educators do when children fail to meet academic standards for promotion to the next grade level? In the 1970s, **social promotion**, the practice of promoting children to the next grade even when they have not met the academic standards, became a common educational practice because grade retention, or "getting left back," became viewed as damaging to children's self-esteem (Bowman, 2005; Kelly, 1999). As social promotion rose in popularity during the 1980s, schoolchildren's standardized test scores declined and school officials were criticized for promoting failing students to the next grade level (Shepard & Smith, 1990). By the 1990s, legislators and the general public called for an end to social promotion and many states banned social promotion in favor of grade retention as a way to remediate poor academic performance (Frey, 2005; Jimerson, 2001; Thomas, 2000).

About 10% of U.S. youth are retained in a grade one or more times by age 19; however, retention rates vary by state and in some cases are as high as 30% (National Center for Education Statistics, 2014a; Warren & Saliba, 2012; West, 2009). Students are retained for a variety of reasons: failure to meet criteria for promotion, frequent unexcused absences, social and cognitive immaturity, and the belief that an extra year of schooling will produce successful academic outcomes. African American and Hispanic students as well as those from poor households are disproportionately likely to be retained as compared with European American students and those from middle and high socioeconomic status homes (Frey, 2005; National Association of School Psychologists, 2003).

Does grade retention work? The cumulative evidence published to date shows that students who are retained in school, even in the first two years of elementary school, do not fare as well as promoted students. They later show poor performance in reading,

social promotion The practice of promoting children to the next grade even though they did not meet academic standards out of the belief that it will foster self-esteem.

mathematics, and language; poor school attendance; and more emotional and social difficulties as well as reporting greater dislike for school than do their peers who were promoted (Ehmke, Drechsel, & Carstensen, 2010; Hughes, Chen, Thoemmes, & Kwok, 2010; Wu, West, & Hughes, 2010).

In some cases, retention can be a wake-up call to children and parents, but more often it is the first step on a remedial track that leads to lowered expectations, poor performance, and ultimately dropping out of school. In the United States and Canada, retained children are 2 to 11 times more likely to drop out of school than their promoted peers (Guèvremont, Roos, & Brownell, 2007; Stearns, Moller, Potochnick, & Blau, 2007). In addition, retained students are less likely to enroll in postsecondary education and are more likely to work low-wage, low-status jobs as compared with low-achieving, promoted students (National Association of School Psychologists, 2003).

As shown in Table 15.1, the National Association of School Psychologists (2003) recommends providing students and families with a variety of academic and support resources to promote student achievement and address school failure. Promoting students to the next grade, paired with interventions that target a student's specific needs in class and at home, can help students achieve at grade level and beyond (Jimerson & Renshaw, 2012).

READING AND MATHEMATICS

Between ages 5 and 11, children become increasingly able to attend to stimuli, create and use strategies to manipulate information, store and retrieve information, and accumulate and apply knowledge. School children's growing ability to think logically underlies advances in problem-solving ability, but their understanding of logic is concrete, oriented toward the tangible. It may not be surprising, then, that effective instruction for older children is straightforward and concrete in nature (Simon, 2001). When children receive instruction that helps them see connections between new material and prior knowledge, builds on what they already know, and keeps pace with their growing abilities, they are better able to grasp and recall complex concepts and learn to read and write.

TABLE 15.1 • National Association of School Psychologists' Recommendations to Enhance Academic Achievement and Reduce Retention and Social Promotion

TARGET	ACTION
Parental Involvement	Encourage frequent contact with teachers and supervision of students' homework.
Instruction	Adopt age-appropriate and culturally sensitive instructional strategies.
	Systematically and continuously assess instructional strategies and effectiveness and modify instructional efforts in response.
	Implement effective early reading programs.
	Offer extended year, extended day, and summer school programs to develop and promote academic skills.
Student Academic Support	Use student support teams to identify students with specific learning or behavior problems, design interventions to address those problems, and evaluate the effectiveness of those interventions.
	Provide appropriate education services for children with educational disabilities, including collaboration between regular, remedial, and special education professionals.
Student Psychosocial Support	Create and implement school-based mental health programs that identify students in need of assistance and devise ways of aiding students.
	Use effective behavior management and cognitive behavior-modification strategies to reduce classroom behavior problems.
	Establish full-service schools to organize educational, social, and health services to meet the diverse needs of at-risk students.

An important task of middle childhood is developing skills in reading and writing. From a societal perspective, the abilities to read and to understand mathematics are fundamental to advancement in science and technology, which improve economic opportunities for both individuals and societies at large. In the early school grades, math achievement and reading comprehension are supported by children's cognitive development, specifically executive functioning skills and working memory (Cormier, McGrew, Bulut, & Funamoto, 2016; Mazzocco & Kover, 2007; Passolunghi, Mammarella, & Altoè, 2008).

Schooling plays a key role in enabling children to master reading and math. In past generations, most children were taught to read using the **phonics** method, based on memorizing rules and the sounds of each letter to sound out words. Phonics instruction usually involved rigorous drills and lessons to help children identify patterns of sound combinations in words (Brady, 2011; Rayner, Foorman, Perfetti, Pesetsky, & Seidenberg, 2001). In the late 1980s, the **whole-language approach** to reading instruction was introduced. In this approach, literacy is viewed as an extension of language, and children learn to read and write through trial-and-error discovery that is similar to how they learn to speak—without drills or learning phonics. The emphasis on children as active constructors of knowledge is appealing and in line with cognitive-developmental theory. As the whole-language approach is in widespread use in schools, many teachers today are not trained in phonics instruction. However, the research comparing the two approaches has offered little support for whole-language claims and overwhelming support for the efficacy of phonics training in improving children's reading skills (Brady, 2011; Cunningham, 2013; Jeynes, 2008; National Institute of Child Health and Human Development, 2000).

Unfortunately, a substantial number of U.S. children are poor readers and thereby at risk for poor academic achievement. In 2013, 32% of fourth-grade students were unable to meet basic standards for reading at their grade level (National Center for Education Statistics, 2014a). Early reading deficits influence all areas of academic competence (math, writing, science, etc.) and children who experience early difficulties in reading often remain behind (Hong & Yu, 2007; Juel, 1988). Although some research has found an overall tendency for children's attitudes, interests, and motivation in reading and writing to decline over the school years, the drop occurs more rapidly in worse readers (McKenna, Kear, & Ellsworth, 1995). Deficits in reading skill are associated with social adjustment problems, and this association increases over time (Benner, Beaudoin, Kinder, & Mooney, 2005). For example, children with poor reading skills also tend to have poor vocabularies, which may make it more difficult for them to successfully interact with peers (Benner, Nelson, & Epstein, 2002). Poor reading achievement in preschool and third grade predicts behavioral problems in first grade and fifth grade (Guo, Sun, Breit-Smith, Morrison, & Connor, 2015). Children with a limited knowledge of vocabulary tend to demonstrate larger academic and social deficits with time, relative to peers with a rich knowledge of vocabulary (Baker, Simmons, & Kame'enui, 1997).

Similar to reading, in past generations math was taught through rote learning activities such as drills, memorization of number facts (e.g., multiplication tables), and completion of workbooks. Many children found these methods boring or restrictive; they learned to dislike math and did not perform well. In response, new methods, rooted in Vygotsky's ideas (see Chapter 6), were developed to enhance students' interest and motivation in learning mathematics (Ginsburg, 1998). In 1989, the National Council of Teachers of Mathematics modified the national mathematics curriculum to emphasize mathematical concepts and problem solving, estimating, and probability; teachers were to encourage student interaction and social involvement in solving math problems. The emphasis changed from product—getting correct answers quickly—to process—learning how to understand and execute the steps in getting an answer. Teachers often use strategies that involve *manipulatives*, opportunities for students to interact physically with objects to learn target information, rather than relying solely on abstraction. Such strategies have been shown to be effective in enhancing problem solving and retention (Carbonneau, Marley, & Selig, 2013).

phonics An approach to reading instruction that emphasizes teaching children to sound out words and connect sounds to written symbols.

whole-language approach An approach to reading instruction that emphasizes meaning, not phonics. Children are exposed to reading materials without instruction and emphasis is on meaning-making.

In contrast with research findings about the whole-language approach to reading, changes in the mathematics curriculum are supported by student achievement, as fourth-grade students' mathematical skills have improved over the last two decades. Between 1990 and 2013, the proportion of fourth-grade students performing at or above the proficient level increased from 13% to 42% and the proportion that could not do math at their grade level fell from 50% in 1990 to 17% in 2013 (National Center for Education Statistics, 2014b). Although these represent important gains, the 17% statistic means that nearly one in five U.S. school children is still deficient in math skills, suggesting that there is more work to be done. The past decade has seen new educational initiatives with the intent to leave no children academically behind and to provide a core set of educational objectives and assessments that ensure that progress is made and children do not fall through the cracks.

 Thinking in Context 15.1

1. What were your earliest educational experiences? Did you go to preschool? Kindergarten? Would you characterize your early childhood educational setting as child centered or academically centered?

2. What do you remember of your experiences in first grade—your teacher, your classmates, how you spent your days? In your view, what is the purpose of first grade? What kinds of learning experiences are most important for children to have when they start school?

SECONDARY AND POSTSECONDARY EDUCATION

LO 15.2 Discuss the influences of secondary and postsecondary education on adjustment.

Schools remain important settings for development throughout adolescence and, for many, emerging adulthood or afterward. More young people than ever are enrolling in college, making it an increasingly common transition between secondary school and the workplace. Adolescents' experiences in secondary school hold implications for their post-secondary education and career.

TRANSITION TO JUNIOR HIGH OR MIDDLE SCHOOL AND HIGH SCHOOL

Apart from the home context, school is the most relevant and immediate context in which adolescents live. The structure of schools in the United States has changed dramatically since the mid-20th century. In past generations, students made only one school transition: from elementary school (kindergarten–Grade 8) to high school (Grades 9–12). Today, students make more school changes, or transitions, than ever before. Junior high schools, comprising seventh-, eighth-, and ninth-grade students, were created in the 1960s and were modeled after high schools, serving as mini-high schools. In the late 1970s and 1980s, educators began to recognize that young adolescents have different educational needs than middle and older adolescents, and junior high schools began to be converted and organized into middle schools of Grades 5 or 6 through 8 or 9 (Byrnes & Ruby, 2007). Middle schools are designed to provide more flexibility and autonomy than elementary schools while encouraging strong ties to adults, such as teachers and parents, as well as offering active learning that takes advantage of and stimulates young adolescents' emerging capacities for abstract reasoning (National Middle School Association, 2003).

Change, though often exciting, can pose stress to individuals of all ages. Most students find the transition to a new school challenging, such that academic motivation and achievement often suffer (Booth & Gerard, 2014; Madjar & Cohen-Malayev, 2016). As grades tend to decline with each school transition, students who experience more school transitions tend to perform more poorly than peers who have changed schools less often (Rudolph, Lambert, Clark, & Kurlakowsky, 2001; Seidman, Lambert, Allen, & Aber, 2003). Thus, early adolescents enrolled in K–8 schools tend to score higher in academic achievement, specifically math and reading, than do those in middle school, who have changed schools from elementary to middle school (Byrnes & Ruby, 2007). Larger cumulative declines in academic achievement are seen when students make two school transitions before high school (elementary to middle school and middle to high school) as compared with one (K–8 elementary school to high school; Crockett, Petersen, Graber, Schulenberg, & Ebata, 1989), although some research disputes the size of this difference (Weiss & Bearman, 2007). For most students, these adjustment difficulties are temporary and their achievement recovers within 1 to 2 years as they adapt to their new schools. However, students who perceive the school transition as more stressful than do their peers tend to show greater drops in motivation and academic achievement and less connectedness to school that persists well beyond the school transition (Goldstein, Boxer, & Rudolph, 2015).

CONTEXTUAL INFLUENCES ON ADJUSTMENT AT SCHOOL

The very nature of school transitions entails a complete shift in contexts, including environments, teachers, standards, support, and, often, peers. As adolescents enter middle school and then high school they are confronted with more stringent academic standards, yet many feel that their new environment provides less support. Middle schools were intended to be tailored to the needs of early adolescents, yet research suggests that many students view their middle school experiences less positively than their elementary school experiences (Byrnes & Ruby, 2007; Roeser, Eccles, & Sameroff, 2000; Wigfield & Eccles, 1994). Students commonly report feeling less connected to middle school teachers than to elementary school teachers, viewing the former as less friendly, supportive, and fair (Anderman & Midgley, 2004; Way, Reddy, & Rhodes, 2007). High school students often report that they receive less personal attention from teachers, more class lectures, fewer hands-on demonstration activities, and fewer opportunities to participate in class discussions and group decision making than they did in middle school (Gentle-Genitty, 2009; Seidman, Aber, & French, 2004).

Although it is tempting to blame adolescents' views about school on poor perspective taking or an immature prefrontal cortex, research suggests that many teachers' views corroborate them. For example, middle and junior high school teachers hold different beliefs about students than do elementary school teachers, even when they teach students of the same chronological age (Midgley, Anderman, & Hicks, 1995). They are less likely to report trusting their students and are more likely to emphasize discipline than their peers who teach elementary school. Middle school classrooms tend to be characterized by a greater emphasis on teacher control, offer fewer opportunities for student decision making and autonomy, and involve more frequent and formal evaluations than those in elementary school (Eccles et al., 1992; Eccles & Roeser, 2011).

According to researcher Jacqueline Eccles (2004), negative effects of school transitions can be explained by a poor **stage-environment fit**. Teachers become more stringent, less personal, and more directive at the same time as young people begin to place a high value on independence. Young adolescents need more guidance and assistance with academic, social, and mental health issues then they did when they were younger, just at the time when teachers report feeling less responsibility for students' problems (Eccles & Roeser, 2011). The mismatch of adolescents' changing developmental needs relative to school resources and emphases contributes to decline in academic performance, motivation, and overall functioning (Booth & Gerard, 2014).

stage-environment fit Refers to the match between the characteristics and supports of the school environment and the developing person's needs and capacities. Influences well-being.

•• Adolescent Employment

At least one-half of adolescents work and most are from middle-SES families and seek part-time employment as a source of spending money.

Working at a part-time job during high school is commonplace in the United States and Canada, with more than half of high school students reporting working at some point during the school year (Bachman, Johnston, & O'Malley, 2014). Labor force surveys report fewer employed adolescents (about 30%), but many of the jobs held by teens are "off the books"

and unrecorded (U.S. Bureau of Labor, 2015a). Regardless, adolescent employment today is at its lowest level since World War II (see Figure 15.1; Greene & Staff, 2012).

Most U.S. adolescents who work come from middle-SES families and seek part-time employment as a source of spending money (Bachman, Staff, O'Malley, & Freedman-Doan, 2013). Minority adolescents are less likely to work than white adolescents, largely because few jobs are available in the economically depressed areas where minority teens are likely to live.

About half of employed adolescents work 15 or fewer hours per week (Bachman et al., 2014). Working few hours (15 or less) appears to have little positive or negative effect on adolescents' academic or psychosocial functioning (Monahan, Lee, & Steinberg, 2011). On the other hand, working more than 20 hours each week, common to about one third of employed adolescents (Bachman et al., 2014), is associated with many poor outcomes. Although both adults and adolescents tend to view working as an opportunity to develop a sense of responsibility, research does not support this view (Monahan et al., 2011). For example, one area of responsibility that working is believed to affect is money management (i.e., a job may provide opportunities to learn how to budget, save, and spend wisely), yet most teens spend their earnings on personal expenses, such as clothes, and experience premature affluence—they get used to a luxurious

FIGURE 15.1: Employment of Adolescents and Adults in the United States, 1948–2014

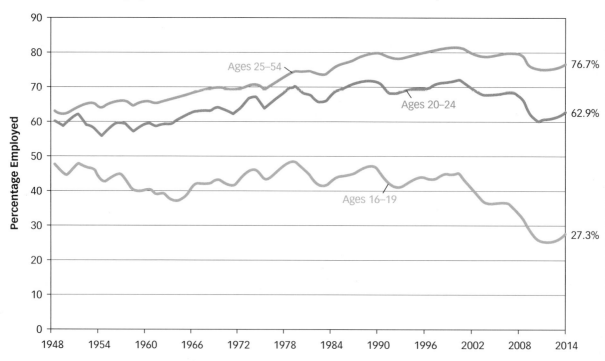

Source: Congressional Research Service (CRS), based on data from U.S Department of Labor, Bureau of Labor Statistics Current Population Survey.

standard of living before they have financial responsibilities (Bachman et al., 2013). Young adults who experienced premature affluence in their teen years may be less satisfied with their financial situation than are their peers did not work during high school.

More importantly, working more than 20 hours each week during adolescence is associated with parent-teen conflict at home; poor school attendance, performance, and motivation; risk of school dropout; and problem behaviors such as smoking, alcohol and substance use, early sexual activity, and delinquency (Bachman et al., 2013; Dumont, Leclerc, & McKinnon, 2009; Monahan et al., 2011; Staff, Vaneseltine, Woolnough, Silver, & Burrington, 2012). Some research suggests that the negative effects of long hours of employment are most evident for white middle-class adolescents and are associated with fewer disadvantages for Hispanic and African American adolescents from low-income families (Bachman et al., 2013). Yet other research suggests that intense adolescent employment is associated with detrimental developmental outcomes for youth regardless of neighborhood context (Kingston & Rose, 2015).

However, adolescent work can be a positive experience if it entails limited hours, and if it includes educational and vocational training opportunities and contact with adults (Greene & Staff, 2012; Mortimer & Johnson, 1998). The most common jobs available to adolescents often entail repetitive simple tasks, such as microwaving meals at a fast food restaurant (Steinberg, Fegley, & Dornbusch, 1993). Adolescent workers often have little contact with adults—their coworkers tend to be teens; supervisors tend to be not much older than they are; and customers, if the job is in food service or retail, tend to be adolescents (Greenberger & Steinberg, 1986). Work settings that emphasize vocational skills, such as answering phones as a receptionist, and in which adolescents interact with, and work alongside, adults, tend to promote positive attitudes toward work as well as academic motivation and achievement, and low levels of delinquency and drug and alcohol use (Staff & Uggen, 2003).

What Do You Think?

1. **Did you hold a job during adolescence? How do your experiences compare with these findings?**

2. **Are you in favor of setting limits on adolescent employment, such as the number of hours teens are permitted to work? Why or why not? What limits, if any, do you suggest?**

Vulnerable students, such as those from low-income families or who require special education services, tend to show especially large declines in academic achievement with each transition (Akos, Rose, & Orthner, 2014). Changes in school demographics, particularly a mismatch between the ethnic composition of elementary and middle school, or middle school and high school, can pose challenges to adolescents' adjustment (Douglass, Yip, & Shelton, 2014). One study of more than 900 entering high school students found that students who experienced more ethnic incongruence from middle to high school reported declining feelings of connectedness to school over time and increasing worries about their academic success (Benner & Graham, 2009). Students who moved to high schools with fewer students who were ethnically similar to themselves were most likely to experience a disconnect, as were African American male students. This is of particular concern because African American adolescents tend to experience more risk factors to academic achievement, more difficulties in school transitions, and more likelihood of falling behind during school transitions than adolescents of other ethnicities (Burchinal, Roberts, Zeisel, Hennon, & Hooper, 2006). Similarly, Latino students tend to be more sensitive to changes in the school climate and experience school transitions as more challenging than do white students (Espinoza & Juvonen, 2011).

Adolescents' success in navigating school transitions is also influenced by their experiences outside of school. Adolescents are most vulnerable to the negative effects of school transitions when they lack the social and emotional resources to cope with multiple stressors. Young people tend to experience school transitions with few problems if they feel supported by their families, have many friends, and cope well with day-to-day stressors (Kingery, Erdley, & Marshall, 2011; Rueger, Chen, Jenkins, & Choe, 2014; Seidman et al., 2003). One influence on academic achievement is part-time employment (see Lives in Context: Adolescent Employment). Finally, similar to other aspects of development, expectations matter. Adolescents who approached the transition to secondary school with positive expectations are likely to report a positive experience (Waters, Lester, & Cross, 2014).

Young people who drop out of school may take the GED as an alternative to earning a high school diploma.

SCHOOL DROPOUT

More than 80% of students who enter public high school as freshmen graduate on time (National Center for Education Statistics, 2014a). Although others eventually graduate, about 7% of high school students drop out, meaning that they do not finish high school. Who is likely to drop out of high school? It is the students who already face significant contextual risks to their development who are most likely to leave high school without a diploma. Students from low socioeconomic status are at highest risk of school dropout, and minority students are particularly vulnerable. Dropout rates have reached historic lows, however, with dramatic decreases for African American adolescents and especially Hispanic adolescents (see Figure 15.2).

Students with behavior problems are the ones most likely to drop out of high school, but many who drop out simply have academic problems, skip classes with increasing frequency, and finally completely disengage from school (Janosz, Archambault, Morizot, & Pagani, 2008; Wang & Fredricks). Research has found that dropping out of high school is not a solitary event, but rather the outcome of a long, gradual process of disengaging from school (Bowers & Sprott, 2012; Christenson & Thurlow, 2004; Henry, Knight, & Thornberry, 2012). Young people at risk for high school dropout show risk factors such as withdrawal (poor class participation or poor attendance) and unsuccessful school experiences (academic or behavioral problems) as early as first grade. Risks documented in first grade account for dropout almost as well as those documented in high school (Alexander et al., 2001; Entwisle et al., 2005). Lack of parental involvement in children's education places students at risk for school dropout—and when parents respond to poor grades with anger and punishment, this can further reduce adolescents' academic motivation and feelings of connectedness to school (Alivernini & Lucidi, 2011).

Students who are engaged and attached to school and who participate in many school-related activities are less likely to drop out than their less engaged peers (Janosz et al., 2008; Mahoney, 2014). Conversely, feelings of anonymity at school increase the

FIGURE 15.2: School Dropout Rates Among Youth Ages 16 to 24 in the United States, 1967–2014

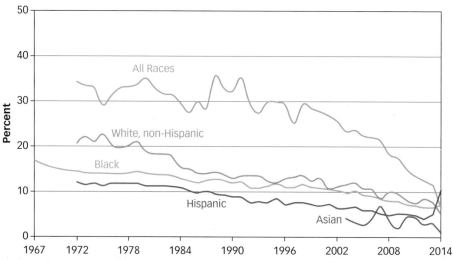

Source: Child Trends (2014).

risk of dropping out. Many of the unfavorable characteristics that students report of their high schools predict dropout: large schools, unsupportive teachers, and few opportunities to form personal relationships or to speak out in class (Battin-Pearson & Newcomb, 2000; Christenson & Thurlow, 2004; Croninger & Lee, 2001; Freeman & Simonsen, 2014); poor connections with teachers and poor support for meeting academic expectations (Jia, Konold, & Cornell, 2016); bullying and poor relationships with peers (Cornell, Gregory, Huang, & Fan, 2013; Frostad, Pijl, & Mjaavatn, 2014). Students who experience academic difficulties may be more vulnerable than their peers to the structural changes that are common during school transitions. Although dropout is often the result of extended difficulties, there is heterogeneity in paths; many students show few problems until a particularly disruptive event or situation, such as severe peer victimization, health problems, family instability, or long work hours, impairs their coping skills (Dupere et al., 2015). For example, in a study that examined three groups of Canadian high school students—recent dropouts, matched at-risk students who remain in school, and average students—results indicated that in comparison with the two other groups, dropouts were more than three times more likely to have experienced recent acute stressors, suggesting that it may be these acute stressors that place students at increased risk for dropout, over and above existing contextual risks (Dupéré et al., 2017).

Dropping out of high school is a serious event with lifelong consequences. Adults who did not finish high school demonstrate low levels of literacy relative to high school graduates, and this has dire consequences for their employment prospects. In 2013, 30% of high school dropouts aged 16–24 were unemployed (U.S. Bureau of Labor, 2014). Today's jobs require the ability to take in and manipulate information. Because young people without high school degrees lack the reading and information management skills that employers value, it is not surprising that high school dropouts in the United States and Canada experience more short- and long-term unemployment than graduates. When they are employed, they are more likely to hold low-paying jobs.

Young people who have dropped out of school have the option of taking a high school equivalency test, the **General Educational Development exam (GED)**, which was developed in the late 1940s as a way to certify that returning World War II veterans who had left high school to serve in the military were ready for college or the labor market. Although passing the GED exam can signify that a young person has accumulated the knowledge entailed in earning a high school diploma, GED holders do not fare as well as regular high school graduates in the labor market, and they tend to get much less postsecondary education (Tyler & Lofstrom, 2009).

DEVELOPMENTAL IMPACT OF ATTENDING COLLEGE

Attending college, at least for a time, has become a normative experience for emerging adults. In 2015, 69% of high school graduates in the United States enrolled in 2- or 4-year colleges (National Center for Education Statistics, 2017). Students enroll in college to learn about a specific field of study (i.e., a major) and to prepare for careers, but attending college is also associated with many positive developmental outcomes.

Adults of all ages often view their college years as highly influential in shaping their thoughts, values, and worldview (Patton, Renn, Guido-DiBrito, & Quaye, 2016). In addition to academic learning, college presents young people with various perspectives and encourages experimentation with alternative behavior, beliefs, and values. College students encounter a wealth of new experiences and opportunities for autonomy, ideas, and social demands. College courses often require students to construct arguments and solve complex problems, fostering the development of post-formal reasoning (Perry, 1970; Sinnott, 2003). Attending college is associated with advanced moral reasoning and the ability to synthesize the considerations of autonomy and individual rights with promotion of human welfare (Kohlberg & Ryncarz, 1990). In addition to intellectual growth, college students show advances in social development

General Educational Development exam (GED) A high school equivalency test that young people who drop out have the option of taking.

(Hassan, 2008). The expanded worldview that accompanies college attendance is displayed in young people's tolerance of diversity and their interest in subjects such as art, literature, and philosophy.

The positive impact of attending college is not simply a matter of the type of college one attends; research indicates that all institutions, public and private, selective and open enrollment, advance cognitive and psychological development (Mayhew et al., 2016; Montgomery & Côté, 2003). In addition, students at 2-year community colleges show similar cognitive gains to those of their peers at 4-year institutions (Pascarella, Bohr, & Nora, 1995). Rather than the type of institution attended, developmental outcomes are most influenced by student involvement in campus life and peer interaction in academic and social contexts. Students who live in residence halls have more opportunities to interact with peers and become involved in the academic and social aspects of campus life—and show the greatest cognitive gains in the college years (Reason, Terenzini, & Domingo, 2007; Terenzini, Pascarella, & Blimling, 1999). Education that challenges students and encourages them to consider perspectives other than their own, solve ambiguous, messy problems, and apply course work to real-world problems and activities with the guidance of supportive faculty promotes cognitive-affective complexity, which underlies adaptive functioning in college as well as all the contexts in which young adults are embedded (Patton et al., 2016; Reason et al., 2007).

Despite these benefits, however, many students do not complete college. Only about two-thirds of students who enroll in 4-year institutions graduate within 6 years, and one-third of students enrolled at 2-year institutions graduate within 3 years (National Center for Education Statistics, 2014a). Generally, student attrition is highest in colleges with open enrollment and those with relatively low admission requirements. How a student handles the transition to college itself predicts the likelihood of dropping out. While most students find the transition to college challenging, some fail to realize or act upon the fact that they are expected to take the initiative in requesting help as they face new demands. Such demands are not only academic (e.g., more difficult coursework) but also social (e.g., changes in living situation, whether a move to a dorm room or off-campus housing) and personal: new psychological demands for autonomy, motivation, study skills, and self-management (Cleary, Walter, & Jackson, 2011).

Students who are the first in their families to attend college (known as **first-generation college students**), as well as those who are from minority or low socioeconomic homes (who also are often first-generation students), tend to experience the most difficulty transitioning to college and are at highest risk of dropping out or attending discontinuously (Aronson, 2008; Fischer, 2007; Ishitani, 2006). In 2014, about 15% of all college students enrolled in the United States were African American and 17% were Hispanic (as compared with 68% white; National Center for Education Statistics [NCES], 2016). With few family and peer models of how to succeed in college, first-generation and minority students may feel isolated and find it difficult to understand and adjust to the college student role and expectations (Collier & Morgan, 2008; Orbe, 2008). Compared with white students and those whose parents attended college, they may be assigned to more remedial coursework; trail in the number of credits they earn in the first year of college; have difficulty deciding on a major; and be less active in campus, academic, and social activities—all of which are risk factors for college dropout (Aronson, 2008; Walpole, 2008).

Students' transition to college and success in college are also influenced by the college environment (Fischer, 2007). Institutions that are responsive to the academic, social, and cultural needs of students help them adjust to college and, ultimately, succeed (Mayhew et al., 2016). Reaching out to at-risk students during the first weeks of college can help them to feel connected to the institution. Social connection, communication skills, motivation, and study skills are associated with retention (Robbins, Allen, Casillas, Peterson, & Le, 2006). Students who live on campus, see faculty as concerned with their development, establish relationships with faculty and other students, and become involved in campus life are more likely to succeed and graduate from college (Mayhew et al., 2016; Pike & Kuh, 2005).

first-generation college students Students who are the first in their families to attend college.

Lives in Context Video 15.1
Emerging Adulthood: Choosing a Major

College and universities can provide opportunities for faculty and students to interact and form connections, help students develop study skills, and assist students in getting involved on campus. When students feel that they are part of a campus community they are more likely to persist and graduate.

NONTRADITIONAL COLLEGE STUDENTS

Virtually all research on the effects of college tends to focus on what most people think of as the typical college student, aged 18 through 22. However, 27% of college students are between ages 25 and 39 (National Center for Education Statistics, 2015). Why do students return to college, or attend for the first time in their mid-20s or beyond? **Nontraditional college students**—those older than the typical-age student—tend to report career reasons for returning to college (Kasworm, 2003). Some seek a college degree to be eligible for higher paying and more satisfying careers. Others enroll in college to change career paths. Employers sometimes encourage students to enroll in college to learn new skills.

Nontraditional students are more likely than traditional students to attend college part time, work full time, be financially independent, and have dependents, all of which pose significant challenges to success in college (Choy, 2002). They are more likely than other college students to juggle multiple life roles, such as worker, spouse, parent, and caregiver (Fairchild, 2003). Sometimes the demands of school, family, and work conflict. For example, work-related travel is often disruptive to child care as well as academic demands, resulting in class absences and missed assignments.

Many nontraditional students may find the practical details of college difficult to navigate, as most colleges are oriented toward traditional students (Fairchild, 2003). For example, classes that meet two or three days each week often conflict with work schedules. Evening classes often meet once per week, providing convenience at the expense of continuity and frequent contact with professors. Some students may find that required courses are offered only during the day. They may have difficulty accessing advisors and student support services. Nontraditional students are less likely than traditional students to earn a degree within 5 years (Choy, 2002).

However, nontraditional students bring several strengths. They tend to show a readiness to learn and a problem-centered orientation toward learning that emphasizes acquiring the knowledge and skills needed for career advancement (Ross-Gordon, 2011). Older students tend to have a more complex knowledge base from which to draw, and emphasize seeking meaning and applying what they learn to their lives (Fairchild, 2003). Their experience and multiple roles can help nontraditional learners make meaning of theoretical concepts that may be purely abstract to younger learners (Ross-Gordon, 2011).

Nontraditional undergraduate students typically seek colleges that are readily accessible, offer training relevant to their current life needs, and are cost effective, flexible in course scheduling, and supportive of adult lifestyle commitments (Kasworm, 2003). Many colleges and universities increasingly support the needs of nontraditional students by extending student services beyond business hours, providing adequate and close parking for those students who rush from work to school, and offering affordable on-campus child care for full- and part-time students, including evening students (Hadfield, 2003). Some also offer orientation programs for adult learners to provide information about support resources as well as help nontraditional students connect with one another and begin to build a social support network of peers.

Tom Uhlman/Alamy

Adults return to college for many reasons, including to change career paths, obtain higher paying and more satisfying careers, learn new skills, and fulfill personal goals.

nontraditional college student Refers to college students who are older than the typical-age student.

THE FORGOTTEN THIRD

It can be said that attending college is part of the American dream and has become expected of many youth. Yet in 2015, only 36% of adults held college degrees by age 29 (National Center for Education Statistics, 2016). Each year about one-third of high school graduates in the United States transition from high school to work without attending college. While some academically well-prepared students report forgoing college because of a desire to work or a lack of interest in academics, many cite economic barriers, such as the high cost of college or the need to support their family, as reasons for nonattendance (Bozick & DeLuca, 2011). The population of non-college-bound youth has been referred to in the literature as "forgotten" by educators, scholars, and policy makers, because relatively few resources are directed toward learning about them or assisting them, as compared with college-bound young adults.

Young adults who enter the workforce immediately after high school have fewer work opportunities than those of prior generations. In 2015, the rate of unemployment for high school graduates was twice that of bachelor's degree holders (U.S. Bureau of Labor, 2015a). In addition, many young people with high school degrees spend their first working years in jobs that are similar to those they held in high school: unskilled, with low pay and little security (Rosenbaum & Person, 2003). As illustrated in Figure 15.3, at all ages high school graduates earn less, and are more likely to be unemployed, than peers with college degrees.

The curricula of most secondary schools tend to be oriented toward college-bound students, and counseling tends to focus on helping students gain admission to college (Krei & Rosenbaum, 2000). Over the past three decades, secondary education has shifted toward emphasizing academics and reducing vocational training, leaving young adults who do not attend college ill prepared for the job market (Symonds, Schwartz, & Ferguson., 2011a). A solution proposed in the Pathways to Prosperity report from Harvard Graduate School of Education is for the U.S. educational system to support multiple pathways in the transition to adulthood (R. F. Ferguson & Lamback, 2014; Symonds, Schwartz, & Ferguson, 2011b). Opportunities for vocational training and to obtain relevant work experience will help young people try out careers and get relevant training for specific jobs. In addition, training programs should relay specific expectations for youth with regard to their responsibility in career training and decision making as well as the educational and vocational support they can expect in return (Symonds et al., 2011b). One way of providing such training is through apprenticeships, discussed in the Lives in Context feature.

FIGURE 15.3: Median Weekly Earnings by Education in 2016 (age 25 and older)

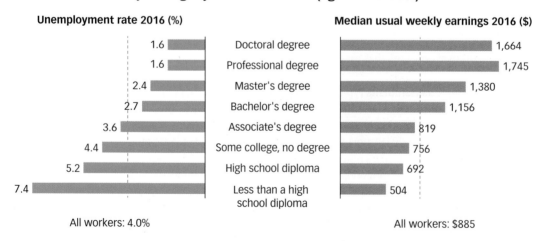

Source: U.S. Bureau of Labor Statistics (2015b).

LIVES IN CONTEXT

• • Apprenticeships

Through on-the-job training coupled with classroom instruction, apprenticeships help young people prepare for careers in a variety of vocational settings.

Most European countries place a much greater emphasis on vocational education than the United States. For example, non-college-bound youth in European nations such as Austria, Denmark, Switzerland, and Germany have the opportunity to participate in apprenticeship programs that combine on-the-job training and classroom instruction that often is tailored to each student. Germany is particularly known for offering apprenticeships coupled with vocational schooling in hundreds of blue- and white-collar occupations (Behrens, Pilz, & Greuling, 2008). Young people who

successfully complete training often are hired by their host company.

High school graduates in nations that employ apprenticeships enter the workforce with general and job-specific skills and a job, whereas North American employers tend to view high school graduates as poorly prepared for the world of work. To a certain extent this is true, as these workers often lack vocational training and experience outside of the high school curriculum. In response, the U.S. Department of Labor as well as many states have established a series of registered apprenticeships that combine on-the-job training with theoretical and practical classroom instruction to prepare young people to work in a variety of settings.

About 150,000 companies and organizations serve as program sponsors in the Apprenticeship USA registered program, training about 410,000 young people in more than 1,000 occupations in industries such as construction, manufacturing, health care, information technology, energy, telecommunications, and more (U.S. Department of Labor, 2015). Apprentices receive on-the-job training and instruction by employers, and earn wages during training. The programs must meet national standards for registration with the U.S. Department of Labor and training results in an industry-recognized credential. Apprentices who complete the program are often hired by their placement employers—a win–win solution for the program alumni as well as for the employers, which benefit by hiring employees who have acquired the specific skills they need.

What Do You Think?

1. Were you aware of apprenticeship opportunities as a high school student or as a college student? Why or why not?

2. In your view, what are the benefits of completing an apprenticeship? Are there any disadvantages to choosing an apprenticeship?

 Thinking in Context 15.2

1.   Discuss the ways in which the fit between a young person's needs—personal and developmental—and the opportunities and supports provided to her within the school system influences her academic adjustment during school transitions and likelihood of completing high school. What contributions to academic adjustment come from factors outside of school, such as in the home or within the peer network, community, and society?

2.   What are some of the reasons why a young adult might not attend college or might drop out? What can schools, colleges, parents, or policy makers do to help young adults attend and complete college?

ACHIEVEMENT MOTIVATION

LO 15.3 Explain the role of contextual factors in achievement attributions and motivation.

Performance at school and in the workplace is influenced by competence, but it also varies with individuals' level of **achievement motivation**, which is the willingness to persist at challenging tasks and meet high standards of accomplishment. The roots of achievement motivation lie in infants' earliest activities.

MASTERY MOTIVATION

From birth, infants are driven to interact with the world. Sumiko vigorously kicks her legs, watching as the mobile above her jiggles. Infants delight in seeing that they can influence their world. Recall that Piaget emphasized the cognitive results of these interactions, but they also reflect socioemotional development. Infants' drive to control their environment by rolling balls, opening and closing cabinets, and making the adults around them smile, is influenced by their growing sense of **mastery motivation**, the drive to explore, understand, and "master" one's environment (Jennings & Dietz, 2003).

All infants seek to learn about and control objects around them, but there are individual differences in mastery motivation and its display. One particular task or goal might be more appealing to one baby over another: for example, Jackson might pay attention to and spend time batting a toy that Corbin does not find interesting (Kenward, Folke, Holmberg, Johansson, & Gredebäck, 2009). Some infants show a higher level of mastery motivation than others. Mastery motivation is fostered by engaging and nurturing environments in which infants have the opportunity to exert control over stimuli and interactions. Toddlers delight in realizing that they can affect the objects and people around them, but when their attempts at mastery are met with indifference or negativity, their motivation drops (Joussemet, Landry, & Koestner, 2008). Toddlers' sense of mastery motivation influences their emerging self-concept, how they approach challenging tasks, and how they respond to success and failure.

How does mastery motivation change over time? In a classic study, 1- to 5-year-old children were presented with activities with clear achievement goals, such as hammering pegs into pegboards or knocking down pins with a play bowling ball (Stipek, Recchia, McClintic, & Lewis, 1992). The tasks were structured so that children either could or could not succeed. Young children's reactions proceeded through three phases. Infants under the age of 2 showed positive emotions when they succeeded. They did not seem to be concerned with others' reactions and evaluations and they did not appear to evaluate their own performance. They tended to be upset when they failed, but they either tried again or shifted their goals, such as playing differently (e.g., knocking pins together) or playing with another toy.

Two-year-old children, in contrast, paid more attention to adults. Their responses to success and failure were oriented toward adults' evaluations, seeking approval when they succeeded and turning away from adults when they failed. Three-year-old children were different still: They began to evaluate their own performance and were not as dependent on adults to recognize success as the 2-year-olds. They showed more intense reactions to winning and losing than did younger children and experienced pride in their achievements and shame in their failures, as compared with younger children's simple pleasure or disappointment. Researchers have observed that some preschoolers react very negatively to failure, feeling a great deal of shame that inhibits their desire to persist and try again. Low levels of mastery motivation may accompany overly harsh and controlling parenting that includes excessive personal criticism of children when they do not do well (Dweck & Master, 2009; Dweck 2002). Parent–child interactions influence how children understand and explain, or attribute, their performance.

achievement motivation The willingness to persist at challenging tasks and meet high standards of accomplishment.

mastery motivation The drive to explore, understand, and master one's environment.

ACHIEVEMENT ATTRIBUTIONS AND OUTCOMES

Young children tend to have a very positive sense of self, as described in Chapter 11. They are optimistic about their skills; often overly so, rating their own ability as very high and underestimating challenges and the difficulty of tasks. Upon failing, they typically believe that they will succeed on their next try (Boseovski, 2010). All children experience failure at least some of the time.

As children grow older, they receive more evaluative feedback from more sources; their cognitive skills permit them to understand, interpret, and integrate feedback; and they engage in more social comparison with peers. As a result, most children develop more realistic, if more negative, views of their abilities (Jacobs, Lanza, Osgood, Eccles, & Wigfield, 2002). With each increasing school grade, academic evaluation becomes more heavily emphasized, frequent, salient, and competitive—and children's self-assessments decline as they receive more negative evaluations of their competence (Wigfield, Muenks, & Rosenzweig, 2015). How children explain their own successes and failures is important for sustaining motivation and ultimately influencing their own achievement.

Some children gravitate toward internal attributions, emphasizing their own role in the outcome. Exam performance, for example, might be attributed to their ability or choice of study techniques, two factors that are within the child's control. Other children rely on external, uncontrollable attributions, such as luck, to explain their performance.

In addition to attributing success or failure to internal or external causes, children also vary in their mindset, or the degree to which they believe that their abilities and characteristics are modifiable. Some show a *growth mindset*, viewing their skills and characteristics as malleable or changeable. In contrast, others show a *fixed mindset*, believing that their characteristics are enduring and unchangeable.

Children who adopt internal explanations and a growth mindset tend to have a strong **mastery orientation**, a belief that success stems from trying hard and that failures are influenced by factors that can be controlled, like effort (Heyman & Dweck, 1998). When faced with challenges, children who are mastery oriented focus on changing or adapting their behavior. They show resilience and take steps, such as learning study strategies to improve their exam scores, to improve their performance (Dweck, 2017; Yeager & Dweck, 2012).

Other children respond to success and failure in maladaptive ways, by attributing success to external factors such as luck and attributing failure to internal factors such as ability. Some children adopt a **learned helplessness orientation**, characterized by a fixed mindset and the attribution of poor performance to internal factors. Children who show learned helplessness are overwhelmed by challenges, overly self-critical, feel incompetent, and avoid challenging tasks (Dweck & Master, 2009; Dweck, Walton, & Cohen, 2011; Dweck, 2017). A learned helplessness orientation can perpetuate poor performance. For example, students in fourth through sixth grades who were self-critical viewed their abilities as fixed, rated their own competence as lower, knew less about study strategies, avoided challenges, and performed more poorly at school than their non-self-critical peers (Pomerantz & Saxon, 2001). Poor performance, in turn, can confirm children's negative views of their ability and their sense of helplessness.

A mastery orientation has been shown to predict subsequent classroom engagement and higher grades among high school students (Ciarrochi, Heaven, & Davies, 2007; Glasgow, Dornbusch, Troyer, Steinberg, & Ritter, 1997; Heaven & Ciarrochi, 2008). The relation of attributions and achievement is bidirectional. For example, one longitudinal study of Australian adolescents that examined students through middle school and high school confirmed that a learned helplessness orientation was associated with poor school performance, and poor performance was, in turn, associated with subsequent attributions of helplessness (Chan & Moore, 2006). In another study, African American adolescents' attributions and school performance were assessed in Grades 8 and 11 (Swinton, Kurtz-Costes, Rowley, & Okeke-Adeyanju, 2011). Attributions for math successes and failures became more negative in the high school years, and early negative attributions about

mastery orientation A belief that success stems from trying hard and that failures are influenced by factors that can be controlled, like effort.

learned helplessness orientation An orientation characterized by a fixed mindset and the attribution of poor performance to internal factors.

Children look to their teachers for guidance in understanding themselves.

math predicted lower math engagement 3 years later. Research with college students has supported relations between attributions and achievement outcomes (Hsieh & Schallert, 2008). For example, students' causal attributions at college entry predict later grade point averages in college (Perry, Stupnisky, Daniels, & Haynes, 2008).

CONTEXTUAL INFLUENCES ON ACHIEVEMENT ATTRIBUTIONS AND MOTIVATION

Our views about our abilities and our explanations for our successes and failures are influenced by our interactions with the people around us. The contexts in which we are immersed, including factors such as parents and teachers, socioeconomic status and culture, also play a role in shaping our views of our abilities.

Parents

Parents influence children's achievement through their own beliefs and attitudes about ability. Children raised by parents with a fixed view of abilities tend to view their own ability as fixed and are more likely to show a learned helplessness orientation (Pomerantz & Dong, 2006). When parents believe that ability is unchangeable, they may provide few opportunities for children to improve and may ignore positive changes that children show. Warm and supportive parenting can help children to recognize their worth and appreciate their own competence. Authoritative parents who promote their children's autonomy, encourage their children to explore their environment, and permit them to take an active role in solving their own problems foster a mastery orientation (Raftery, Grolnick, & Flamm, 2012). In contrast, excessive control and harsh criticism can damage children's motivation. Not providing opportunities to problem solve or intervening when a child tries a challenging task may inhibit children's desire to succeed and foster helplessness (Moorman & Pomerantz, 2008; Orkin, May, & Wolf, 2017).

Parents also influence children through the home context they provide. Socioeconomic status influences children's motivation through the availability of opportunities and resources and through parents' behavior. Research has shown that children who grow up in high-SES families are more likely than their middle- or low-SES peers to show a greater mastery orientation and higher levels of achievement motivation, as well as better academic performance and greater involvement in organized activities after school (Mahoney, Vandell, Simpkins, & Zarrett, 2009; Wigfield, Eccles, et al., 2015). Children require not only opportunities to try new things, but also parents who are aware of and able to take advantage of opportunities (Archer et al., 2012; Simpkins, Delgado, Price, Quach, & Starbuck, 2013). Parents in low-SES families often work jobs that involve long hours, rotating and nonstandard shifts, and high physical demands. As a result, many low-SES parents lack the energy and time to devote to children, and they may be unaware of opportunities or unable to take advantage of them (Parra-Cardona, Cordova, Holtrop, Villarruel, & Wieling, 2008).

Teachers

Like parents, teachers support a mastery orientation in students if they are warm, helpful, and attribute children's failure to effort (Wentzel, 2002). Students who believe that their teachers provide a positive learning environment tend to work harder in class and show higher achievement than students who lack this belief, (Skinner, Zimmer-Gembeck, & Connell, 1998). When students view their teachers as unsupportive, they are more likely to attribute their performance to external factors such as luck or the teacher, and in turn tend to withdraw from class participation. As students' achievement declines, they tend to further doubt their abilities, creating a vicious cycle between helpless attributions and poor achievement. Teachers play an important role in fostering a mastery orientation. Teachers who relate failure back to their students' effort, are supportive of their students, and stress learning goals over performance goals are more likely to have mastery-oriented students (Meece, Anderman, & Anderman, 2006).

Peers

The peer group influences achievement motivation through adolescents' beliefs about their friends' behavior and attitudes as well as their perception of implicit norms of the group (Ryan & Patrick, 2001). Adolescents tend to affiliate with students who share their academic competence and orientation and become more similar over time through their interactions (Gremmen, Dijkstra, Steglich, & Veenstra, 2017; Rambaran et al., 2017). Peer orientation predicts adolescents' achievement motivation. Adolescents who have best friends who value academics are likely to have high achievement motivation and adolescents who view their friends as resistant to classroom norms are likely to have poor achievement motivation (Nelson & DeBacker, 2008). Perceived acceptance by peers is positively associated with achievement motivation. Middle and high school students who feel valued and respected by peers and who have high quality friendships are likely to have high achievement motivation (Nelson & DeBacker, 2008).

Cultural Influences

Culture has an important bearing on children's achievement attributions and motivation through its influence on parenting and family processes. For example, among Latino families, familism is protective of academic outcomes. Latino American college students who report higher levels of familism tend to demonstrate higher levels of intrinsic motivation and earn higher grades than their peers who lack a strong sense of familism (Próspero, Russell, & Vohra-Gupta, 2012). Similarly, a study of Mexican American male college students found that a strong sense of familism was accompanied by parental encouragement concerning college, and was positively related to persistence in college over time (Ojeda, Navarro, & Morales, 2011).

Children and adolescents of many cultures point to family as an important influence on achievement. One study of more than 5,300 New Zealand students in Grades 10 and 11 found ethnic differences in students' attributions of the role of family in their academic performance (McClure et al., 2011). Students from the Pacific islands (e.g., Samoa and Tonga) rated family as a particularly important influence on their best grades and rated family, teacher, luck, and friends as more important for their best marks than did European, Asian, or Maori (indigenous) students. Moreover, Maori and other Pacific Islander students were less likely to adopt internal attributions (e.g., ability, effort) for their best and worst marks compared with European and Asian students. Prior research has suggested that internal attributions are most common in Westerners (Reyna, 2008) and may be less common among people of other cultural backgrounds.

Parents in many Asian countries tend to hold a growth mindset and to view the application of effort as a moral responsibility (Mok, Kennedy, & Moore, 2011; Pomerantz, Ng, & Wang, 2008). Parents in many Asian cultures tend to focus more on children's failure in order to encourage them to make corrections. North American parents, on the other hand, tend to pay attention to children's success and its relevance for self-esteem. For example, when U.S. and Chinese mothers watched their fourth- and fifth-grade students solve a puzzle, the U.S. mothers offered more praise after the child succeeded, but the

Chinese mothers tended to point out poor performance and offer task-oriented statements to make the child try harder (e.g., "You only got 7 of 10"). After the mothers left the room, the children continued to play, and the Chinese children showed greater improvements in performance than the U.S. children (Ng, Pomerantz, & Lam, 2007).

Cultures also vary in the use and perception of criticism and praise. Students from some cultures may feel uncomfortable with praise because it singles them out from the group and, by implication, elevates them above their peers (Markus & Kitayama, 1991). Some students may be more motivated by critical feedback because their goal is to meet the expectations of their teachers and/or family (Pomerantz et al., 2008). One study found that Japanese college students were more responsive to negative feedback than were Canadian students, and were more self-critical, reluctant to conclude that they had performed better than their peers (Heine et al., 2001). The Canadian students, on the other hand, were reluctant to conclude that they did worse than other students. The culture and contexts in which we are immersed influence the ways in which we attribute—and the degree to which we acknowledge—success and failure.

 Thinking in Context 15.3

Consider the bioecological perspective in answering the following questions.

1.   What factors might influence the development of mastery motivation in infants and young children? Consider the microsystem, mesosystem, exosystem, and microsystem.

2.   How might each bioecological context influence whether children adopt a mastery orientation or a learned helplessness orientation?

3.   In what ways do these influences stay the same or change during childhood, adolescence, and adulthood?

CAREER DEVELOPMENT, WORK, AND RETIREMENT

LO 15.4 Compare the transition to work with the transition to retirement in terms of influence on satisfaction and adjustment.

Employment and the role of worker is a central part of most people's experience. Upon meeting a new person, one of the most common ice-breaker questions or topics of small talk concerns one's career: "What do you do?" In the following sections we consider career development, how people choose their careers, the experience of work, and how we transition away from the world of work.

CAREER DEVELOPMENT

Children often fantasize about careers as astronauts, actors, and rock stars—careers that bear little resemblance to the choices they ultimately make when they grow up. How do people select occupations in real life?

Occupational Stages

We develop occupational goals slowly over time. Developmental theorist Donald Super proposed that the development of occupational goals progresses through several stages during adolescence and early adulthood (Super & Hall, 1978; Super, 1990). The earliest stage of occupational development, known as *crystallization*, begins in adolescence. Adolescents from ages 14 through 18 begin to think about careers in increasingly complex ways, considering their own interests, personality, abilities, and values as well as the requirements of each career. Similar to the exploration entailed in identity development, career exploration is at first tentative. Adolescents seek information about careers by talking with family, friends, and teachers as well as through Internet searches. They compare what they learn with their own interests.

As individuals transition into young adulthood, around ages 18 to 21, they enter the *specification* stage in which they identify specific occupational goals and pursue the education needed to achieve them. As a first-year college student, Imani knew that she wanted to do something related to business, but had not yet selected among several possible majors. Once a young person has selected a general vocational area, he or she may experiment with possibilities before choosing an occupation. Imani considered several business-related majors including accounting, management, and entrepreneurship, and completed an internship at an investment firm before deciding to major in finance.

During *implementation*, typically from ages 21 to 24, young adults complete training, enter the job market, and make the transition to become employees. The developmental task of the implementation stage is to reconcile expectations about employment and career goals with available jobs. Young people may take temporary jobs or change jobs as they learn about work roles and attempt to match their goals with available positions. For example, Yolanda majored in education, but she found no teaching positions available at schools near her home. She accepted a temporary position running an after-school program while she applied for jobs in other cities and states. Even young adults who attain their "dream jobs" often find that they must tailor and adapt their expectations and goals in light of their career setting.

In the *stabilization* stage, young adults from ages 25 to 35 become established in a career; they settle into specific jobs, gain experience, and adapt to changes in their workplace and in their field of work. Toward the end of early adulthood, from age 35 and up, individuals progress through the final stage, *consolidation*. They accumulate experience and advance up the career ladder, moving into supervisory positions and becoming responsible for the next generation of workers.

According to Super's model, vocational maturity reflects the degree to which an individual's occupational behaviors and status match the age-appropriate occupational stage. Although a task- and stage-oriented approach to understanding career development remains useful, it is important to recognize that career development does not follow a universal pattern. Not everyone progresses through the stages in the prescribed order and at the same pace. For many adults, career development does not progress in a linear fashion; in fact, most adults do not hold the same occupation throughout adulthood. For example, adults in their 50s today have had an average of 9 occupations between the ages of 18 and 40 (U.S. Bureau of Labor, 2015b). Likewise, today's young adults in their 20s are likely to have held 6 different jobs between ages 18 and 26 (U.S. Bureau of Labor Statistics, 2014). Young adults can expect to change career paths one or more times throughout their lives. Nevertheless, in considering an adult's perspective on careers it is useful to conceptualize career development as entailing the four processes outlined by Super: crystallization, specification, implementation, and consolidation.

Influences on Vocational Choice

Many factors influence how young people perceive and evaluate occupational choices, but perhaps the most important factor in selecting a career is the match between young people's personality traits and abilities and their occupational interests. We are most satisfied when we select occupations that match our personalities and other individual traits, such as intelligence and skills. John Holland (1997) proposed that occupational choices can be categorized by six personality types, as shown in Table 15.2. Holland explained that each personality type is best suited to a particular type of vocation.

Although it is useful to consider careers in terms of Holland's six personality types, most people have traits that correspond to more than one personality type and are able to successfully pursue several career paths (Holland, 1997; Spokane & Cruza-Guet, 2005).

TABLE 15.2 • Holland Personality Types and Vocational Choice

PERSONALITY TYPE	VOCATIONAL INDICATIONS
Investigative	Enjoys working with ideas; likely to select a scientific career (e.g., biologist, physicist)
Social	Enjoys interacting with people; likely to select a human services career (e.g., teaching, nursing, counseling)
Realistic	Enjoys working with objects and real-world problems; likely to select a mechanical career (carpenter, mechanic, plumber)
Artistic	Enjoys individual expression; likely to select a career in the arts, including writing and performing arts
Conventional	Prefers well-structured tasks; values social status; likely to select a career in business (e.g., accounting, banking)
Enterprising	Enjoys leading and persuading others; values adventure; likely to select a career in sales or politics

Furthermore, many careers entail a variety of skills and talents that cross the boundaries of the six-factor typology.

Personality is an important influence on vocational choice; however, contextual influences such as family and educational opportunities also influence our choice of career. Parents influence their children's career development in a variety of ways. Parents tend to share personality characteristics and abilities with their children and influence educational attainment, which in turn influences career choice (Ellis & Bonin, 2003; Ingrid Schoon & Parsons, 2002). Parents also act as role models. SES and parents' occupational fields influence career choice (Schoon & Polek, 2011). Young people in high-SES households are more likely to receive career information from parents. In one study, African American mothers with at least some exposure to college were more likely than other mothers to use a variety of strategies to aid their daughters' progress on academic and career goals, such as gathering information about career options, colleges, and professionals from whom to seek advice (Kerpelman, Shoffner, & Ross-Griffin, 2002). Regardless of socioeconomic status, parents can provide support and motivation. Among low-SES first-generation college students, a sense of ethnic identity and maternal support predicted career expectations, and in turn, school engagement—the behavior needed to achieve vocational goals (Kantamneni, McCain, Shada, Hellwege, & Tate, 2016). Other research with college students in the Philippines showed that parent and teacher support predicted career optimism (Garcia, Restubog, Bordia, Bordia, & Roxas, 2015). Parental expectations and encouragement for academic success and pursuit of high-status occupations also predict vocational choice and success (Maier, 2005).

WORK

Throughout adult life, work is usually the mainstay that structures people's days, contributes to a sense of identity and self-esteem, and provides a number of benefits aside from income. Through work, people have opportunities to interact with others; to display generativity by creating products, items, and ideas, advising and mentoring others; and to contribute to the support of their families and communities.

Transition to Work

Many young people find themselves employed in careers that are not their first choice, often explaining that they simply "fell into it," without exerting much effort or a choice

(Arnett, 2004). Young people's jobs frequently do not match their interests and education. These mismatches are common during the early years of employment as young adults are learning about their competencies and preferences and comparing them with the reality they encounter in the workplace (Wilk, Desmarais, & Sackett, 1995). For example, one study of 1,200 Australian young adults found that 7 years after completing their schooling, only 20% were working in a field that represented their greatest interest (Athanasou, 2002). The day-to-day tasks entailed by a given occupation also often differ from young people's expectations, as young people are typically faced with more clerical and other paperwork, longer work hours, less supportive and instructive supervisors, and lower pay than expected (Hatcher & Crook, 1988). The reality that vocational expectations are not always achieved can be a shock and can influence self-concept and occupational development as young adults revise their expectations.

Young people begin work with expectations about what certain jobs will be like and how they will advance, but real-world experience often prompts them to change their occupational expectations. One longitudinal study that examined young people's occupational expectations annually during the first 7 years after high school found a great deal of instability in occupational expectations during the late teens and early 20s (Rindfuss, Cooksey, & Sutterlin, 1999). At age 30 less than half of the participants had careers that matched their expectations – even expectations measured at age 25. Among those who did not achieve their occupational expectations at age 30, men were more likely to move into managerial positions while women were more likely to move down or leave the work force. Falling short of one's occupational goals is associated with low job satisfaction and, in some men, depressive symptoms (Hardie, 2014). Finding a career that is a good fit to an adult's interests and abilities, whether by changing careers or revising expectations in light of experience, can aid an adult's well-being.

Managing expectations in light of reality often leads young adults to resign and seek alternative jobs and careers. It is not uncommon for an individual to undergo as many as seven job changes by age 28 (U.S. Bureau of Labor Statistics, 2014). By another estimate, young adults hold, on average, four jobs between the ages of 18 and 21, three between 22 and 24, and three between 25 and 28 (U.S. Bureau of Labor Statistics, 2016a). The median length of job tenure (i.e., time spent in a particular position) is about 4 years, on average, but varies with age. The median tenure of older workers ages 55 to 64 is 10 years, as compared with 3 years for young adults ages 25 to 34 (U.S. Bureau of Labor Statistics, 2016c).

Career development follows a myriad of paths. In Western industrialized societies, men most often are employed continuously after completing their formal education and until retirement, whereas women display more varied and discontinuous career trajectories, often interrupting or deferring their career in favor of childrearing and family caretaking (Hite & McDonald, 2003). In this sense, women may experience multiple transitions to and from work, with potential implications for their adjustment and satisfaction.

Job Satisfaction

A job is a source of income, but job satisfaction is influenced by more than high pay, as evidenced by research on gender differences in the workplace. Regardless of work experience, women tend to earn less than men (i.e., women earn, on average, $.80 for every dollar men earn; AAUW, 2017). The gender pay gap also grows with age. In 2015, among full-time workers ages 20–24, women were paid 90% of what men were paid on a weekly basis. By the time workers reach 55–64 years old, women are paid only 74% of what their male peers are paid. Paradoxically,

Demanding jobs whose responsiblities exceed workers' coping skills can lead to burnout, which is assocated with impairments in attention and concentration abilities, depression, illnesses, poor job performance, and workplace injuries.

however, women tend to show higher job satisfaction than men, or in some cases, similar levels of satisfaction to men (Donohue & Heywood, 2013; Zou, 2015). Research with European samples suggests that the gender–job satisfaction paradox is more apparent in countries where the job market is more challenging for women and nonexistent in countries that offer equal opportunities for women (Kaiser, 2007). Some research suggests that the gender difference lies in work orientations and preferences for extrinsic versus intrinsic rewards. Job satisfaction is more closely associated with intrinsic rewards (e.g., the pleasures of surmounting challenges, engaging in creative pursuits, and being productive) than with extrinsic rewards (e.g., high salaries and benefits). For women, job satisfaction is positively linked to both extrinsic and intrinsic rewards, but for men, job satisfaction tends to be positively linked primarily to extrinsic rewards (Linz & Semykina, 2013).

Samples of adults from the United States, Europe, China, Turkey, and Japan show that age is generally associated with increases in job satisfaction (Barnes-Farrell & Matthews, 2007). Age-related increases in satisfaction are related to shifts in reward preferences. Young adults tend to gravitate toward jobs that emphasize extrinsic rewards, whereas middle-aged employees tend to place greater importance on intrinsic rewards of work, including friendships with coworkers, self-esteem, and feeling that they are making a difference (Sterns & Huyck, 2001). Age-related increases in job satisfaction are greater professionals than blue-collar workers (Hochwarter, Ferris, Perrewé, Witt, & Kiewitz, 2001; Ng & Feldman, 2010). Blue-collar workers tend to have more highly structured jobs with fewer opportunities to control their activities than do white-collar workers, which may contribute to their relatively lower level of job satisfaction (Avolio & Sosik, 1999; Hu, Kaplan, & Dalal, 2010). Males in physically demanding occupations, such as laborers and construction workers, may find that the physical changes that occur over the course of middle adulthood make them less able to perform the tasks their jobs require (Gilbert & Constantine, 2005).

Some adults experience **job burnout**, a sense of mental exhaustion that accompanies long-term job stress, excessive workloads, and reduced feelings of control. Burnout is relatively frequent in professions that are interpersonally demanding and whose demands may exceed workers' coping skills, such as in the helping professions of health care, human services, and teaching (Malinen & Savolainen, 2016; Shanafelt et al., 2015). Employee burnout is a serious problem in the workplace, not simply through its association with poor job satisfaction. Burnout is linked with impairments in attention and concentration abilities, depression, illnesses, poor job performance, workplace injuries, and high levels of employee absenteeism and turnover (Deligkaris, Panagopoulou, Montgomery, & Masoura, 2014; Shirom & Melamed, 2005). When workers receive social support, assistance in managing workloads and reducing stress, and opportunities to participate in creating an attractive workplace environment, they are less likely to experience job burnout (Warr, 2007).

Diversity in the Workplace

In recent decades, the workplace in Western industrialized countries has become increasingly diverse as women and ethnic minorities have penetrated nearly all careers. Throughout Europe and North America, about half of the labor force is female (Eurostat, 2016; The World Bank, 2016). Fifty-seven percent of women in the United States work as compared with 47% of women in Canada (Statistics Canada, 2017; U.S. Bureau of Labor Statistics, 2015). Likewise, ethnic diversity is increasing in every occupation and every nation. Despite this, women and ethnic minorities face many obstacles to career success, often collectively known as the **glass ceiling**, the invisible barrier that prevents women and ethnic minorities from advancing to the highest levels of the career ladder.

Women and ethnic minorities tend to fill lower-level positions, and their numbers decline with each higher rung on the career ladder. Women in the United States hold about three-quarters of office and administrative support positions, but only 39% of

job burnout A sense of mental exhaustion that accompanies long-term job stress, excessive workloads, and reduced feelings of control.

glass ceiling An invisible barrier that prevents women and ethnic minorities from advancing to the highest levels of the career ladder.

FIGURE 15.4A: Employed People by Occupation, Race, and Ethnicity, 2015

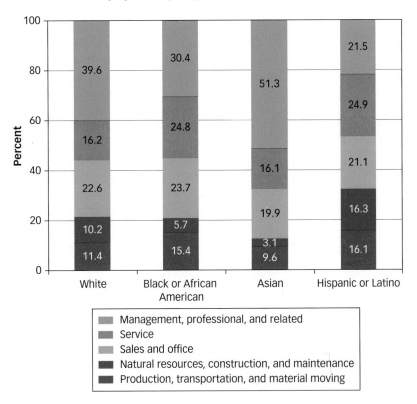

Source: Bureau of Labor Statistics.

management positions (U.S. Department of Labor, 2017). The effect is even more striking for ethnic minorities. As shown by Figure 15.4a, half of Asian American and 40% of white Americans hold managerial and professional positions, as compared with less than one-third of African Americans and less than one-quarter of Hispanic or Latino Americans (U.S. Bureau of Labor Statistics, 2016b).

As shown in Figure 15.4b, women, and especially ethnic minority women, are less likely than white men to hold senior executive jobs, the top level of management, in public and private sector organizations.

Although laws guarantee equal opportunity, racial bias remains an influence, even prior to a job interview. In one study, white male participants were asked to examine résumés that varied in quality (some indicated high qualifications and others low) and by the writer's race (African American, Hispanic, Asian, and white). The participants rated résumés from hypothetical Asian job seekers as highly qualified for high-status jobs, regardless of the actual résumé quality. When they were shown résumés indicating high qualifications, they rated them higher for white and Hispanic job seekers than for African Americans. In fact, they gave African American job seekers negative evaluations regardless of résumé quality. This result indicates how racial discrimination may make it difficult for even highly qualified African American candidates to obtain jobs (King, Madera, Hebl, Knight, & Mendoza, 2006). In another study, college students judged recommendation letters for hypothetical job candidates of various ethnicities; the results were similarly biased against African Americans (Morgan, Elder, & King, 2013).

In the workplace, discrimination is often subtle, such as an employer complimenting an African American employee's eloquence (and not her similarly articulate white colleague) or suggesting that an older worker (but not his young adult colleagues) leave work early to rest after a big meeting. Frequently, subtle discrimination is unintentional; however, it is just as damaging as overt discrimination (Jones, Peddie, Gilrane, King,

FIGURE 15.4B: U.S. Private Sector Executives, by Gender and Race/Ethnicity, 2014

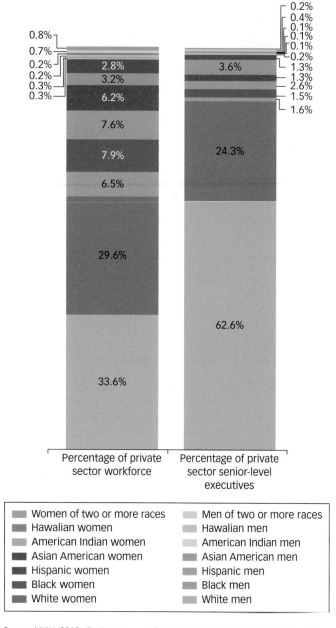

Women of two or more races	Men of two or more races
Hawalian women	Hawalian men
American Indian women	American Indian men
Asian American women	Asian American men
Hispanic women	Hispanic men
Black women	Black men
White women	White men

Source: AAUW (2016). Barriers and bias: The status of women in leadership. https://www.aauw.org/resource/barriers-and-bias/ Copyright © 2016 AAUW.

work–life balance The challenge of finding time and energy for both a career and and personal pursuits, such as family.

& Gray, 2016). Workers' perceptions of being discriminated against are related to poor physical health, including measures of stress, chronic illness, and acute illness, and mental health, such as depressive and anxiety symptoms (Mouzon, Taylor, Woodward, & Chatters, 2017; Triana, Jayasinghe, & Pieper, 2015).

Minority women are faced with multiple obstacles to their career success, often experiencing both gender and racial discrimination. Minority women who reach career success tend to display high *self-efficacy*, or feelings of personal control, and engage in active problem solving, confronting problems rather than avoiding them (Byars & Hackett, 1998). African American women who become leaders in their professions tend to report close supportive relationships with successful women, such as mentors, colleagues, and similarly successful friends, who help them set high expectations and provide support in achieving them. Mentoring is important for career development of all young adults (Combs & Milosevic, 2016). Women of color report strong desires to be mentored by women of their own ethnicity. However, the ethnic and gender obstacles to career success mean that women of color may find it difficult to establish a mentoring relationship with a mentor of their choice (Gonzáles-Figueroa & Young, 2005).

Work and Family

Work–life balance, the challenge of finding time and energy for both a career and personal pursuits such as family, is a concern to most families today, and especially to mothers. As shown in Figure 15.5, the proportion of working mothers has increased dramatically over the past four decades. In 2016 the majority of U.S. mothers of children under the age of 18, both married and unmarried, were working (68% vs. 76% for married mothers and unmarried mothers, respectively). Mothers with very young children are only slightly less likely to work than those with older children: More than 66% of mothers with a child under 6 years of age and 57% of mothers with an infant under a year old are in the labor force (U.S. Bureau of Labor Statistics, 2017).

Nearly all married fathers work and most share child care and household responsibilities with their wives, making work–life balance a task for both spouses. Most parents find it difficult to meet the competing demands of family and career, especially as the boundaries between today's workplace and home are often blurred because many adults are expected to bring work home or be available during nonwork hours via mobile devices.

Both men and women report feeling conflict between work and family obligations (Ammons & Kelly, 2008; Winslow, 2005). Control over work time predicts satisfaction with work–life balance and lower levels of work–life conflict (Carlson et al., 2011). A perceived loss of control accompanies a sense of role overload. More common among women, role overload refers to high levels of stress that result from attempting to balance the demands of multiple roles: employee, mother, and spouse (Cinamon & Rich, 2002; Gilbert & Kearney, 2006; Higgins, Duxbury, & Lyons, 2010). Role overload is associated with poor health, depressive symptoms, ineffective parenting, and marital conflict (Bryson, Warner-Smith, Brown, & Fray, 2007; Perry-Jenkins, Goldberg, Pierce, & Sayer, 2007). Successfully managing multiple roles entails setting priorities, such as de-emphasizing household chores and expectations of an immaculate home in favor of spending more time with children (Hewitt, Baxter, & Western, 2006). In addition, research suggests that women who best manage role overload are those who seek physical and emotional support from others (Higgins et al., 2010).

Work–life balance is a concern to adults in most Western countries. For example, research comparing employees across several European countries found that poor work–life balance was associated with perceived health, health complaints, and poor well-being in both men and women (Lunau, Bambra, Eikemo, van der Wel, & Dragano, 2014). Variations in the reported experience of work–life balance varied by country alongside differences in national regulations regarding work hours, sug-

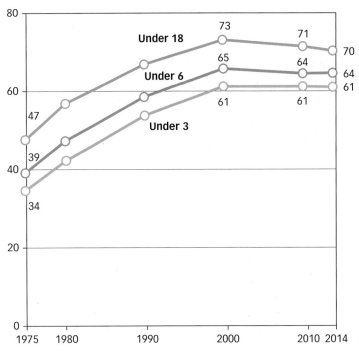

FIGURE 15.5: Labor Force Participation Among Mothers, 1975–2014

% of mothers who are in the labor force with children . . .

Source: Pew Research Center (2017).

gesting that workplace policies (often regulated by government) influence employees' sense of work–life balance and overall well-being. Workplace policies influence employee morale and productivity. Flexible policies that permit employees to balance home and work responsibilities (e.g., flexible starting and stopping times, opportunities to work from home, and time off to care for sick children) are positively associated with attendance, commitment to the organization, and work performance, and negatively associated with distress symptoms (Halpern, 2005). Workplaces with onsite child care show lower rates of employee absenteeism and higher productivity as compared with those without child care (Brandon & Temple, 2007). When adults are able to balance work and family, they are more productive and happy workers, more satisfied spouses, better parents, and experience greater well-being at home and work (Herrenkohl, Hong, Klika, Herrenkohl, & Russo, 2013; Lunau et al., 2014; Russo, Shteigman, & Carmeli, 2015).

RETIREMENT

At the beginning of the 20th century, nearly 70% of men over the age of 65 were in the workforce; in 2014, more than 100 years later, only about 18% of people over the age of 65 are in the workforce, with older men more likely to remain in the workforce than women (U.S. Bureau of Labor, 2015a). Adults in most developed countries, including the United States and Canada, are eligible for government-sponsored retirement funds. In the United States, Social Security permits people to receive retirement benefits as early as age 62 (Chappell, Gee, McDonald, & Stones, 2003; Schultz & Shoven, 2008). Social Security is discussed in the Lives in Context feature. An average worker today can look forward to approximately 15 years of retirement (Social Security Administration, 2015a). Many senior citizens may be retired for 20 or more years, or nearly one-quarter of their lives.

Being a grandparent provides opportunities to enjoy spending time and playing with children without the responsibility of parenthood.

Steve Mason/Photodisc/Thinkstock

Retirement Planning

Retirement is a process that begins long before the last day of employment. Typically it begins with imagining the possibility of retirement and what it might be like. Adults then assess their abilities and their resources to determine when is the best time to let go of the work role (Feldman & Beehr, 2011). Although most U.S. adults will spend many years in retirement, most are not financially prepared for it. About 4 in 10 adults report thinking about financial planning for retirement only sometimes, if at all (U.S. Federal Reserve, 2014). It is estimated that workers should plan for retirement income of at least 70% to 80% of their current pre-retirement income, yet about one third of middle-class households have no savings, including nearly 20% of adults ages 55 to 61 (Wells Fargo, 2014). In 2013, the median retirement account savings balance among all households ages 56 to 61 was only about $17,000 (Morrissey, 2016). People with a college degree are more likely to have retirement savings (76%) than those with a high school degree (43%) or no high school degree (11%). There are also large racial disparities in retirement savings, with white non-Hispanic adults having saved more than three times as much as those who are black or Hispanic (a median of $73,000 and $22,000, respectively; Morrissey, 2016). Income disparities associated with low levels of education and ethnic minority status contribute to differences in retirement savings. Retirement planning is also influenced by psychological factors. For example, adults with more positive beliefs about their ability to control aspects of aging are more likely to financially plan for retirement as compared with those with an intermittent, rather than constant, awareness of the aging process (Heraty & McCarthy, 2015).

The decision of when to retire is typically influenced by job conditions, health, finances, and personal preferences. Workers tend to retire early from jobs that are stressful or hazardous and tend to delay retirement from jobs that are highly stimulating, take place in pleasant environments, and are a source of identity and self-esteem (American Association of Retired Persons, 2008). Workers in professional occupations and those who are self-employed tend to stay in their jobs longer as compared with those in blue-collar or clerical positions. Women tend to retire earlier than men, often to care for an aging relative or spouse (Kim & Moen, 2001). Women in poverty, however, especially African American women, tend to work well into old age because they lack the financial resources to make retirement possible (Lee & Shaw, 2008; Verma, 2003).

Financial resources often are the determining factor with regard to whether and when an older adult retires. Changing economics influence older adults' abilities to retire, as personal retirement investments such as IRAs and 401(k) plans may lose value unexpectedly. The creation of Social Security was designed to aid elders in affording retirement (see the Lives in Context feature). Yet in 2012, about 4 in 10 of all U.S. adults expressed concern over whether they would have enough income and assets in retirement (Morin & Fry, 2012).

Most adults are aware that retirement planning entails preparing for changes in income, but planning for retirement should also include recognition of impending lifestyle changes and changes in the amount of free time available and how it will be used. Retirement represents a major life transition and adults who plan ahead for the financial

• • Social Security

President Franklin D. Roosevelt signing the Social Security Act

The Great Depression of the 1930s triggered a crisis in the economic life of the United States. It was against this backdrop that the Social Security Act emerged, signed by President Franklin D. Roosevelt in 1935. The Act created a social insurance program designed to pay retired workers age 65 or older a continuing income. The original Act provided only retirement benefits, and only to the worker. In 1939, amendments were enacted to add two new categories of benefits: payments to the spouse and minor children of a retired worker (dependent benefits) and payments to the family in the event of the premature death of a worker (survivor benefits; Social Security Administration, 2007). Amendments in the 1950s and 1960s allowed disabled workers and their dependents to qualify for benefits, and included the passage of Medicare, health coverage for Social Security beneficiaries. In 1977, responsibility for Medicare moved to the newly created Health Care Financing Administration. Because of these additional categories of benefits, about 1 in 3 Social Security beneficiaries is not a retiree (Shelton, 2007; Social Security Administration, 2008).

Social Security, also known as Old Age and Survivors Insurance and Disability Insurance (OASIDI), is funded by taxes paid by workers; the funds are invested in interest-bearing U.S. securities. Social Security provides older Americans with a dependable monthly income, with automatic increases tied to increases in the cost of living. Social Security has reduced poverty rates for older Americans by more than two thirds, from 35% in 1959 to less than 9% in 2012 (Dattalo, 2007; Shelton, 2013). More than 90% of U.S. retirees receive monthly Social Security benefit payments (Social Security Administration, 2014a).

Social Security was never intended as a sole form of income; instead, it was conceived as a supplement to income from a retirement plan, pension, and savings. However, today most employers do not offer a pension plan, and many workers cannot afford to contribute to a retirement plan (e.g., a 401k or a SEP-IRA) or to set aside savings on a regular basis. In 2014, one half of married couples and three quarters of single adults were getting at least half of their income from Social Security; and for one quarter and one half, respectively, Social Security was virtually their only income (Social Security Administration, 2014b). Moreover, Social Security provides critical income to older women and minorities, who are more likely than married and nonminority elders to rely on Social Security for 90% or more of their income (Social Security Administration, 2015b, 2015c).

Social Security is a pay-as-you-go retirement system. The Social Security taxes paid by today's workers and their employers are used to pay the benefits for today's retirees and other beneficiaries. There is considerable debate over whether Social Security trust funds can remain solvent over the long term. The main reason for Social Security's long-range financing problem is demographics. We are living longer and healthier lives than ever before. In addition, more than 80 million Baby Boomers started retiring in 2008. By 2050, when the surviving Baby Boomers will be over the age of 85, the population of older adults aged 65 and over is projected to be 83.7 million, about twice as many older Americans as there were in 2012 (Ortman, Velkoff, & Hogan, 2014). At the same time, the number of workers paying into Social Security per beneficiary will drop from 2.8 in 2014 to about 2.1 in 2034 (Social Security Administration, 2008). These demographic changes will strain Social Security financing.

Proposed strategies to make Social Security solvent over the long term include increasing payroll taxes, decreasing benefits, and privatizing Social Security. One option that began to be phased in in the early 2000s is to increase the retirement age for full Social Security benefits. Under current law, an increase will be phased in over 23 years, reaching age 67 in 2022. Another option is to raise Social Security taxes so that all future benefits could be paid. For example, some advocate raising the income cap above which high-income earners are exempt from Social Security payroll contributions. Critics argue that payroll taxes are already very high, having been raised 20 times since the program began, and that eventually Social Security taxes would have to be raised by about 50% to pay for all benefits owed. In short, there are no easy answers.

What Do You Think?

1. Do you agree or disagree with the phasing in of higher eligibility ages for receiving Social Security retirement benefits? Give reasons for your answer.

2. What information should researchers and policy makers gather to determine a fair and sustainable plan to make Social Security solvent? Consider each bioecological level. For example, what factors at the macrosystem level might be useful to policy makers? Exosystem factors? What microsystem or mesosystem factors might help policy makers in planning Social Security changes?

LIFESPAN BRAIN DEVELOPMENT

• • Poverty and Academic Achievement

Structural changes in the brain may account for the poor cognitive and behavioral outcomes associated with exposure to poverty.

In 2013, the American Academy of Pediatrics added child poverty to its *Agenda for Children* in recognition of poverty's broad and enduring effects on child health and development (American Academy of Pediatrics, 2017). In the United States, 43% of all children under 18 years of age live in low-income families (income less than $48,000 per year for a family of four), and 21% live in poor families (income less than $24,000; Jiang, Granja, & Koball, 2017). Children who live in poverty tend to perform poorly in school, with lower standardized test scores and lower educational attainment than their more advantaged peers (Hair, Hanson, Wolfe, Pollak, & Knight, 2015). The deficits accumulate, such that the longer children live in poverty the worse their academic performance (Hair et al., 2015). These patterns of poor achievement persist into adulthood, contributing to reduced occupational attainment, which contributes to low wages and income and an increased likelihood of residing and raising a family in poverty (Duncan, Magnuson, Kalil, & Ziol-Guest, 2012). The experience of poverty is thought to influence children's academic achievement through its negative effect on brain development (Hanson et al., 2013; Johnson, Riis, & Noble, 2016).

In a longitudinal analysis of 77 children between the early postnatal period and age 4, those in low-income or poor families had less total gray matter volume, especially in the frontal and parietal regions associated with executive function abilities (Hanson et al., 2013).

Another longitudinal study examining MRI scans of 389 children and adolescents linked exposure to poverty and structural differences in several areas of the brain associated with school readiness skills (Hair et al., 2015). Children below the poverty level had as much as 10% less gray matter than the norm for their age. The low-income children experienced maturational lags in the frontal and temporal lobes that accounted for some of the gap in their standardized test scores, as compared with higher-income peers (Hair et al., 2015). These findings suggest that poverty influences children's learning and achievement through its effect on brain development.

Poverty is thought to influence brain development by depriving the brain of key stimuli and increasing its exposure to negative input (Sheridan & McLaughlin, 2014). Poor cognitive stimulation may contribute to alterations in the brain areas responsible for executive function. Relative to their higher-SES peers, children from low-SES families are often exposed to fewer words and conversations and less complex and more directive speech (Fernald, Marchman, & Weisleder, 2013; Sheridan, Sarsour, Jutte, D'Esposito, & Boyce, 2012; Weisleder & Fernald, 2013). Children growing up in poverty have less access to toys, books, computers, and educational opportunities, important influences on cognitive and brain development.

Maternal deprivation and stress also play a role in the link between poverty and brain development (Johnson et al., 2016). When compared with their more-advantaged peers, children living in poverty experience less parental nurturance while confronting elevated levels of life stress including family conflict, separation, household crowding, and neighborhood disorder (Evans & Kim, 2013). Poor parenting and stress are associated with smaller gray- and white-matter volume and surface area in the prefrontal cortex and smaller hippocampal volume in childhood, adolescence, and adulthood (Hanson et al., 2013; Lawson, Duda, Avants, Wu, & Farah, 2013; Noble et al., 2015). Structural changes in the brain that accompany exposure to poverty help to explain the relationship between poverty, chronic stress, and poor cognitive and behavioral outcomes.

What Do You Think?

How might the detrimental effects of poverty be lessened? What can communities, schools, teachers, and parents do to reduce the negative effects of poverty on brain development?

and lifestyle changes that accompany retirement tend to show better adjustment and greater life satisfaction than those who do not plan (Hershey, Jacobs-Lawson, McArdle, & Hamagami, 2007; Jacobs-Lawson, Hershey, & Neukam, 2004).

Retirement and Adjustment

Work activities encompass much of adults' days, beginning in early adulthood. With retirement, most adults find that they need to determine how they will spend their time, often for the first time in their lives. With virtually unlimited possibilities, some adults may feel overwhelmed, at least temporarily; others are glad to devote themselves to endeavors they have "always wanted" to pursue, or to seek out entirely new activities and areas of interest. Some "give back" to the community or to their preretirement careers by volunteering. Others may learn a new language, accomplish home renovations, or spend more time with family members. Planning an active life contributes to postretirement adjustment and happiness (Noone, Stephens, & Alpass, 2009).

Research on retirement adjustment suggests that the majority of adults show an increase in life satisfaction and adjust well to their post-retirement life, but some show poor adjustment (Howe, Matthews, & Heard, 2010; Pinquart & Schindler, 2007). One study of Australian retirees found several patterns of adjustment. Some retirees maintained high life satisfaction across the retirement transition (40%), others experienced declining levels of life satisfaction from a high level prior to retirement (28%), some experienced low levels of life satisfaction that declined further (18%) and some reported increasing life satisfaction from a low level prior to retirement (14%). Overall, retirees who experienced significant declines in life satisfaction tended to have worse health and lower access to a range of social and economic resources prior to retirement, suggesting that preretirement experiences influence adjustment (Heybroek et al., 2015).

Adjustment to retirement is influenced by a complex web of influences, including characteristics of the individual, his or her social relationships, and the job (Wang, Henkens, & van Solinge, 2011). Some positive predictors of successful adjustment include physical health, finances, leisure, voluntary retirement, social integration, psychological health, and personality-related attributes (Barbosa, Monteiro, & Murta, 2016). Positive adjustment to retirement is also associated with engagement in satisfying relationships and leisure activities (Grotz et al., 2016; Siguaw, Sheng, & Simpson, 2017). Workers in high-stress, demanding jobs, or those that provide little satisfaction, tend to show positive adaptation to retirement (Adams, Prescher, Beehr, & Lepisto, 2002; Fehr, 2012). For them, retirement often comes as a relief. Those who are in highly satisfying, low-stress, pleasant jobs tend to experience more challenges in adaptation. Generally speaking, the greater the intrinsic value of the older worker's job, the lower the levels of retirement satisfaction (van Solinge & Henkens, 2008).

The characteristics of the retirement transition also matter. Increasingly, adults are taking the route of a gradual retirement, slowly decreasing their involvement and working part time, rather than an abrupt retirement (Calvo, Haverstick, & Sass, 2009). Workers often view the idea of gradual retirement as a more attractive alternative than a "cold turkey" or abrupt retirement. One study of Australian retirees found that those who had retired abruptly were more likely to rate their health as having deteriorated, whereas those who had retired gradually tended to report better adjustment to retirement life (De Vaus, Wells, Kendig, & Quine, 2007). However, the length of the transition, whether abrupt or gradual, matters less in determining happiness after retirement than the worker's sense of control over the transition—whether the retirement is chosen or forced (Calvo et al., 2009; De Vaus et al., 2007; Quine, Wells, de Vaus, & Kendig, 2007). Having a sense of control over the decision to retire, as well as the timing and manner of leaving work, has an important positive impact on psychological and social well-being that lasts throughout the retirement transition (Siguaw et al., 2017).

Lives in Context Video 15.2
Retirement: Planning and Adjustment

Thinking in Context 15.4

1. How does career choice illustrate the interplay between an individual's characteristics, development, and capacities on the one hand, and contextual factors, such as opportunities, choices, and socioeconomic status on the other hand? Provide examples.

2. How might we aid young adults as they transition into the work environment? What factors might improve their competence and satisfaction in their new role?

3. What can employers do to address diversity issues in the workplace and ensure fair treatment of all employees, regardless of race, ethnicity, or gender?

4. Identify individual and contextual influences on the decision to retire and adjustment to retirement. In what ways might the characteristics of jobs, individuals' education and experience, and other micro-, macro-, and exosystem factors influence retirement decisions and subsequent adjustment?

 # Apply Your Knowledge

Latisha dropped her bags on the floor of her dorm room and introduced herself to her new roommate, Denise. They got along easily, and after talking for some time Denise left to go to the library. Latisha marveled at their very different lives. Whereas Denise's parents are doctors, Latisha's mother works two jobs to pay the bills. Latisha considers herself very lucky to have won a scholarship to college. She worries about leaving her mother alone with her younger siblings—there's so much work to do and the little ones need a lot of supervision if they are to stay out of trouble in the neighborhood. Latisha worries that her little brothers will grow up too quickly and make dangerous decisions like joining one of the many neighborhood gangs. She realizes that she is very fortunate to be able to leave her poor community but worries that her absence will harm her family. At the same time, Latisha is delighted to have the opportunity to learn new things, to study with bright students and professors, and to prepare for a career as a doctor. As a pre-med major, Latisha has a very busy semester ahead and she hopes that she won't disappoint those who have given her such grand opportunities.

*   Consider Latisha's achievement motivation. Given what you know, what type of mindset and achievement orientation would you expect of Latisha? Why?

*   In what ways can Latisha expect to grow during the college years? What contributes to these changes?

*   How likely is Latisha to earn a college degree? What role does attending college play in career outcomes, employment, and salary in early adulthood?

*   What challenges do first-generation students, like Latisha, face in transitioning to and succeeding in college? What contextual factors influence these risks, and what might serve as protective factors and aid development?

Give your students the SAGE edge!

SAGE edge offers a robust online environment featuring an impressive array of free tools and resources for review, study, and further exploration, keeping both instructors and students on the cutting edge of teaching and learning. Learn more at **edge.sagepub.com/kuthertopical.**

CHAPTER 15 IN REVIEW

15.1 Describe what children learn during early childhood and in elementary school.

SUMMARY

First grade serves as a foundation for a child's educational career, and early school failure is harmful because early academic deficiencies often persist and worsen through the school years. In both reading and math instruction there has been movement from rote learning, such as phonics and mathematics drills, to instruction that emphasizes active learning, such as the whole-language approach and mathematics problem solving

KEY TERMS

academically centered programs
child-centered programs
phonics

whole-language approach
social promotion

REVIEW QUESTIONS

1. What are two approaches to early childhood education?
2. What are characteristics of effective early childhood education intervention programs?
3. What academic skills do children learn in preschool and elementary school?

15.2 Discuss the influences of secondary and postsecondary education on adjustment.

SUMMARY

School transitions are challenging and are often accompanied by declines in academic motivation and achievement. Negative effects of school transitions can be explained by a poor stage-environment fit. Adolescents are most vulnerable to the negative effects of school transitions when they lack the social and emotional resources to cope with multiple stressors.

Students from low socioeconomic status are at highest risk of school dropout and minority students are particularly vulnerable. School dropout is associated with unemployment in adulthood. Attending college advances cognitive and psychological development. First-generation students, as well as those from low-SES homes or who are from ethnic or racial minority backgrounds, often experience difficulty transitioning to college and are at high risk of dropout. The college environment also influences adjustment.

Nontraditional students tend to report career reasons for returning to college and are more likely than traditional students to attend college part-time, work full-time, be financially independent, and juggle multiple life roles, such as worker, spouse, parent, and caregiver, all of which pose challenges.

KEY TERMS

General Educational Development exam (GED)
first-generation college students

nontraditional college students
stage–environment fit

REVIEW QUESTIONS

1. What are common adolescent reactions to school transitions?
2. How might stage–environment fit influence adjustment?
3. What are risks for school dropout and long-term outcomes associated with dropout?
4. What are some of the developmental effects of college?

15.3 Explain the role of contextual factors in achievement attributions and motivation.

SUMMARY

Infants have a sense of mastery motivation in how they approach challenging tasks and how they respond to success and failure. Young children overestimate their own ability. As children grow older, they receive evaluative feedback from multiple sources and develop more realistic and more negative views about their ability. Individuals differ in mindset as well as with regard to whether they attribute their performance to internal or external causes. A mastery orientation is associated with academic success. A learned helplessness orientation is associated with poor performance. Parents and teachers who are warm and supporting promote a mastery orientation. Both SES and culture may influence achievement attributions.

KEY TERMS

achievement motivation
learned helplessness orientation

mastery motivation
mastery orientation

REVIEW QUESTIONS

1. What are mastery motivation and achievement motivation?
2. Compare mastery orientation with learned helplessness orientation.
3. How do contextual influences like parents, teachers, peers, and culture influence achievement motivation?

15.4 Compare the transition to work with the transition to retirement in terms of influence on satisfaction and adjustment.

to retirement is influenced by a complex web of influences, including characteristics of the individual, his or her social relationships, and the job that is being left behind.

SUMMARY

As adults enter the work world, many must realign their expectations in light of reality and change jobs multiple times. Job satisfaction is closely associated with intrinsic rewards, and age-related increases in job satisfaction are related to shifts in reward preferences. Workers' perceptions of discrimination, burnout, and role overload are related to poor physical and mental health, poor coping, and poor job performance. Retirement represents a major life transition and adults who plan ahead for the financial and lifestyle changes tend to show better adjustment and greater life satisfaction than those who do not plan. The decision of when to retire is influenced by job conditions, health, finances, and personal preferences. The majority of adults show an increase in life satisfaction and adjust well to retirement. Adjustment

KEY TERMS

glass ceiling
work–life balance
job burnout

REVIEW QUESTIONS

1. What common challenges are associated with the transition to work?
2. What predicts job satisfaction across adulthood?
3. What challenges does retirement pose for adults?
4. What predicts adjustment to retirement?

Test your understanding of the content.
Review the flashcards and quizzes at
edge.sagepub.com/kuthertopical

PRACTICE AND APPLY WHAT YOU'VE LEARNED

▶ **edge.sagepub.com/kuthertopical**

HEAD TO THE STUDY SITE WHERE YOU'LL FIND

- **eFlashcards to strengthen your understanding of key terms**
- **Practice quizzes to test your comprehension of key concepts**
- **Videos and multimedia content to enhance your exploration of key topics**

PART VI

Endings

CHAPTER 16
DEATH AND DYING

Death is a complex concept and our understanding of it shifts over our lifespan. Children's views of death change with cognitive development, from viewing it as a temporary and reversible state to a final biological inevitability. Conceptions of death continue to change in subtle ways over the course of the lifespan.

Reactions to death change with development. Children may fear abandonment whereas adolescents seek to develop their own understanding of mortality. Older adults tend to show less anxiety about death as compared with people of other ages. Losing a loved one poses challenges to adjustment at all times in life. The nature of grief varies with the relationship of the bereaved to the deceased as well as with the individuals' understanding of death and capacities for emotional regulation.

Cultural beliefs about the nature of death vary. For example, some cultures view life and death as phases of a cycle, and others view death as a continuation of life. In some cultures, parents shield children from death; in others, they encourage children to participate in mourning rituals. Cultures mourn the dead in different ways, such as by ceasing all activity or, alternatively, engaging in jovial celebrations of life.

There are many ways of understanding death, and many ways of grieving—all of which are influenced by our context.

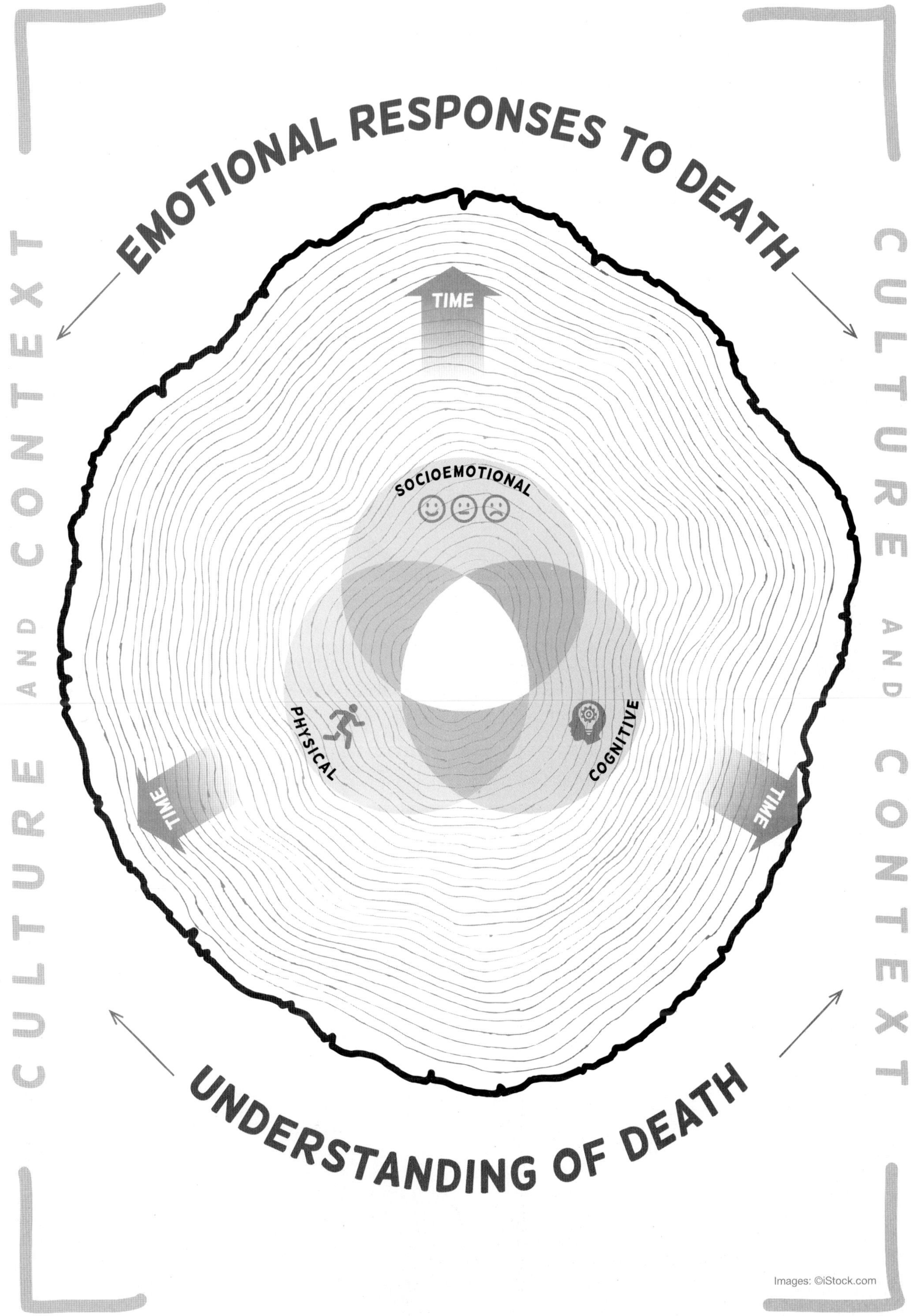

EMOTIONAL RESPONSES TO DEATH
TIME
SOCIOEMOTIONAL
PHYSICAL
COGNITIVE
TIME
TIME
UNDERSTANDING OF DEATH
CULTURE AND CONTEXT
CULTURE AND CONTEXT

Images: ©iStock.com

Death and Dying

Learning Objectives

16.1 Discuss the ways in which death has been defined and end-of-life issues that may arise.

16.2 Contrast child, adolescent, and adult understandings of death.

16.3 Describe the physical and emotional process of death as it is experienced over the lifespan.

16.4 Discuss typical grief reactions to the loss of loved ones and the influence of development on bereavement.

Digital Resources

🔊 The Case Against Assisted Suicide

▶ Hospice Misconceptions

▶ Developmental Tasks of Dying

📄 Children's Understanding of Death

📄 Lessons From Kubler-Ross

▶ Dealing With a Parent's Death

📄 The Dual-Process Model in Real Life

 **SAGE edge™** Master these learning objectives with multimedia resources available at **edge.sagepub.com/kuthertopical** and *Lives in Context* video cases available in the interactive eBook.

At its simplest, death is the absence of life. It is unavoidable, comes hand-in-hand with life, and is the final state of the lifespan. In this chapter, we examine death and death-related issues across the lifespan, including evolving definitions of death and how people of varying ages understand and experience death as well as bereavement processes. The circumstances that surround death and its timing in the lifespan have changed radically over the last century, alongside advances in life expectancy.

PATTERNS OF MORTALITY AND DEFINING DEATH

LO 16.1 Discuss the ways in which death has been defined and end-of-life issues that may arise.

Most babies born in 1900 did not live past age 50, but infants born in the United States today can be expected to live to about age 80—in some countries, such as Japan, people can expect to live even longer (85 years; Central Intelligence Agency, 2013). The rapid decline in mortality rates over the past 100 years can be attributed to advances in medicine and sanitation (CDC, 1999). Many once-fatal conditions and diseases are now treatable. In 1900, the top causes of death were infectious diseases, specifically pneumonia and flu, tuberculosis, and gastrointestinal infections (National Institute of Aging, 2011). Today each of these illnesses can be prevented and treated.

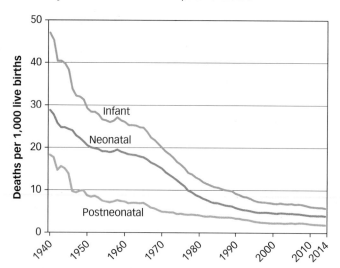

FIGURE 16.1: Infant, Neonatal, and Postneonatal Mortality Rates: United States, 1940–2014

MORTALITY

In the United States, overall mortality across all ages declined 60% between 1935 and 2010 (Hoyert, 2012). People of all ages demonstrate a reduced mortality rate, but the risk of dying has especially plummeted for infants and young children, with a 94% reduction in death rates among children aged 1 to 4, as compared with a 38% decline for adults aged 85 or more since 1960 (Hoyert, 2012). Similar changes have also occurred in the UK and other Western countries (Mathers, Stevens, Boerma, White, & Tobias, 2014; Office for National Statistics, 2014). Today women are less likely to die in childbirth, infants are more likely to survive their first year, children and adolescents are more likely to grow to adulthood, and adults are likely to overcome conditions that were once fatal.

As shown in Table 16.1, the leading causes of death vary by age. Infants under a year of age are most likely to die from genetic, prenatal, and birth complications, with sudden infant death syndrome the third most common cause of death (see the Applying Developmental Science feature). Childhood deaths are most often due to accidents. Illnesses and, alarmingly, homicide (which is most often the result of child maltreatment) are also common sources of mortality.

Adolescents and emerging adults are most likely to die from accidents, such as car accidents, drowning, and, starting in middle adolescence, unintentional poisoning, typically drug overdoses. Illnesses and homicide remain top sources of mortality, but it is in adolescence that suicide emerges as a common cause of death. This pattern of causes of mortality continues into early adulthood. During middle adulthood, cancer, heart disease, and injury become the top three causes, respectively. Suicide, the number five killer of adults aged 45–54, becomes less common in the later middle adulthood years, dropping

FIGURE 16.2: Death Rates, by Age and Sex: United States, 1955–2014

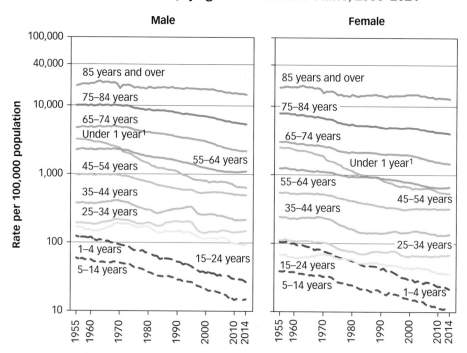

TABLE 16.1 • Top Five Causes of Death by Age Group, U.S. 2015

RANK	<1	1-4	5-9	10-14	15-24	25-34	35-44	45-54	55-64	65+	TOTAL
1	Congenital Anomalies 4,825	Unintentional Injury 1,235	Unintentional Injury 755	Unintentional Injury 763	Unintentional Injury 12,514	Unintentional Injury 19,795	Unintentional Injury 17,818	Malignant Neoplasms 43,054	Malignant Neoplasms 116,122	Heart Disease 507,138	Heart Disease 633,842
2	Short Gestation 4,084	Congenital Anomalies 435	Malignant Neoplasms 437	Malignant Neoplasms 428	Suicide 5,491	Suicide 6,947	Malignant Neoplasms 10,909	Heart Disease 34,248	Heart Disease 76,872	Malignant Neoplasms 419,389	Malignant Neoplasms 595,930
3	SIDS 1,568	Homicide 369	Congenital Anomalies 181	Suicide 409	Homicide 4,733	Homicide 4,863	Heart Disease 10,387	Unintentional Injury 21,499	Unintentional Injury 19,488	Chronic Low. Respiratory Disease 131,804	Chronic Low. Respiratory Disease 155,041
4	Maternal Pregnancy Comp. 1,522	Malignant Neoplasms 354	Homicide 140	Homicide 158	Malignant Neoplasms 1,469	Malignant Neoplasms 3,704	Suicide 6,936	Liver Disease 8,874	Chronic Low. Respiratory Disease 17,457	Cerebro-vascular 120,156	Unintentional Injury 146,571
5	Unintentional Injury 1,291	Heart Disease 147	Heart Disease 85	Congenital Anomalies 156	Heart Disease 997	Heart Disease 3,522	Homicide 2,895	Suicide 8,751	Diabetes Mellitus 14,166	Alzheimer's Disease 109,495	Cerebro-vascular 140,323
6	Placenta Cord. Membranes 910	Influenza & Pneumonia 88	Chronic Low. Respiratory Disease 80	Heart Disease 125	Congenital Anomalies 386	Liver Disease 844	Liver Disease 2,861	Diabetes Mellitus 6,212	Liver Disease 13,278	Diabetes Mellitus 56,142	Alzheimer's Disease 110,561
7	Bacterial Sepsis 599	Septicemia 54	Influenza & Pneumonia 44	Chronic Low Respiratory Disease 93	Chronic Low Respiratory Disease 202	Diabetes Mellitus 798	Diabetes Mellitus 1,986	Cerebro-vascular 5,307	Cerebro-vascular 12,116	Unintentional Injury 51,395	Diabetes Mellitus 79,535
8	Respiratory Distress 462	Perinatal Period 50	Cerebro-vascular 42	Cerebro-vascular 42	Diabetes Mellitus 196	Cerebro-vascular 567	Cerebro-vascular 1,788	Chronic Low. Respiratory Disease 4,345	Suicide 7,739	Influenza & Pneumonia 48,774	Influenza & Pneumonia 57,062
9	Circulatory System Disease 428	Cerebro-vascular 42	Benign Neoplasms 39	Influenza & Pneumonia 39	Influenza & Pneumonia 184	HIV 529	HIV 1,055	Septicemia 2,542	Septicemia 5,774	Nephritis 41,258	Nephritis 49,959
10	Neonatal Hemorrhage 406	Chronic Low Respiratory Disease 40	Septicemia 31	Two Tied: Benign Neo./ Septicemia 33	Cerebro-vascular 166	Congenital Anomalies 443	Septicemia 829	Nephritis 2,124	Nephritis 5,452	Septicemia 30,817	Suicide 44,193

[A table of 5 top causes of death by age will be created using data from the charts found here: https://www.cdc.gov/injury/wisqars/LeadingCauses.html]
Note: Heart disease in childhood is considered congenital rather than caused by lifestyle factors, as in adulthood.

Produced by: National Center for Injury Prevention and Control, CDC using WISQARS™.

• • Sudden Infant Death Syndrome

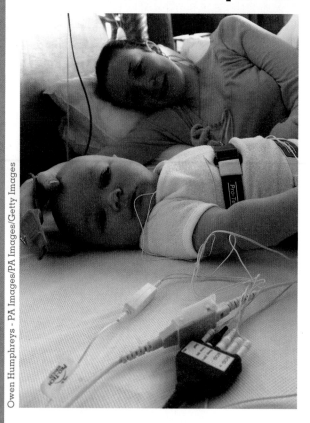

This baby boy is participating in a sleep study that examines the sleep patterns of mothers and babies when bed sharing, which researchers hope will help combat SIDS.

Today the leading cause of death of infants under the age of 1 is sudden infant death syndrome (SIDS; Bajanowski & Vennemann, 2017). SIDS is the diagnostic term used to describe the sudden unexpected death of an infant less than 1 year of age that occurs seemingly during sleep and remains unexplained after a thorough investigation, including an autopsy and review of the circumstances of death and the infant's clinical history (Task Force on Sudden Infant Death Syndrome, 2016).

What causes SIDS? It is believed to be the result of an interaction of factors, including an infant's biological vulnerability to SIDS coupled with exposure to a trigger or stressor that occurs during a critical period of development (Filiano & Kinney, 1994; Moon & Task Force on Sudden Infant Death Syndrome, 2016; Spinelli, Collins-Praino, Van Den Heuvel, & Byard, 2017). The first factor is unknown biological vulnerabilities, such as genetic abnormalities and mutations and prematurity, that may place infants at risk for SIDS. For example, a recent 10-year review of hundreds of SIDS cases in Australia confirmed that, although the underlying cause of SIDS remains unknown, mutations and genetic variants likely play a role (Evans, Bagnall, Duflou, & Semsarian,

2013). Second, environmental stressors or events that might trigger SIDS include risks as such as having the infant sleep on his or her stomach or side, use of soft bedding or other inappropriate sleep surfaces (including sofas), bed sharing, and exposure to tobacco smoke (Carlin et al., 2017). One review of several hundred cases in the UK found that more than a third of SIDS deaths infants were co-sleeping with adults at the time of death (Blair, Sidebotham, Berry, Evans, & Fleming, 2006). Finally, there are developmental periods in which infants are most vulnerable to SIDS. Most cases of SIDS occur between the 2nd and 5th month of life (Bajanowski & Vennemann, 2017). Therefore, it is thought that SIDS is most likely to occur when the triple risks—biological vulnerability, triggering events, and critical period of development—converge (Filiano & Kinney, 1994; Spinelli et al., 2017).

Ethnic differences appear in the prevalence of SIDS, with Native Americans and blacks showing the highest rates of SIDS in the United States, followed by non-Hispanic whites; Asian American and Hispanic infants show lower rates of SIDS than white infants (Parks, Erck Lambert, & Shapiro-Mendoza, 2017). Ethnic differences in SIDS are likely due to differences in socioeconomic and lifestyle factors associated with SIDS, such as lack of prenatal care, low rates of breast-feeding, maternal smoking, and low maternal age. Cultural practices, such as adult–infant bed-sharing, providing infants with soft bedding, and placing the sleeping baby in a separate room from caregivers increase SIDS risk (Colson et al., 2013; Mitchell, 2009; Parks et al., 2017; Shapiro-Mendoza et al., 2014). However, ethnic differences in SIDS are complex and influenced by context. For example, in one study in Chicago, infants of Mexican American U.S.-born mothers had a 50% greater rate of SIDS than infants of Mexican foreign-born mothers after controlling for factors associated with SIDS, including birth weight, maternal age, education, marital status, prenatal care, and socioeconomic status (Collins, Papacek, Schulte, & Drolet, 2001). Differences in acculturation and associated child care practices likely play a role in influencing SIDS risk, but they are not well understood (Parks et al., 2017).

In the 1990s, SIDS declined dramatically after the American Academy of Pediatrics, based on data from Europe, Australia, and the United States, recommended that infants be placed for sleep in a nonprone position (i.e., a supine position: on their backs) as a strategy to reduce the risk of SIDS (American Academy of Pediatrics Task Force on Infant Positioning and SIDS, 1992). Initiated in 1992, the "Back to Sleep" campaign publicized the importance of nonprone sleeping. Between 1992 and 2001, the SIDS rate declined dramatically in the United States and other countries that implemented nonprone/supine sleeping campaigns (Bajanowski & Vennemann, 2017; Bergman, 2015; Hauck & Tanabe, 2008; Moon & Task Force on Sudden Infant Death Syndrome, 2016), consistent with the steady increase in the prevalence of supine sleeping. In addition to placing infants

to eighth place. Chronic illnesses such as diabetes and diseases of the liver and respiratory system emerge as sources of mortality in midlife, particularly late midlife. Older adults over the age of 65 are most likely to die of chronic illnesses, with heart disease as the number one killer. In older adulthood, cerebrovascular accident (stroke) and Alzheimer's disease emerge as leading causes of death.

As shown in Table 16.1, although unintentional injuries are among the leading causes of death throughout the lifespan, the types of accidents that are most common vary with age. For example, although traffic accidents are common sources of death at all ages, pedestrian and bicycle accident deaths are most common in childhood and fire deaths in infancy and childhood. Unintended poisoning, usually substance abuse–related accidents (e.g., overdoses) emerge as leading causes of death in adolescence and persist through midlife. In older adulthood, falls become the most common cause of death.

DEFINING DEATH

At its simplest, death is the absence of life. In practice, defining death is much more complex. The actual moment of death is not easy to determine. In prior centuries, death was defined as the cessation of cardiopulmonary function. A person was dead once the heart stopped beating, now referred to as **clinical death**. When the heart stops beating, blood, and thereby oxygen, no longer circulates throughout the body and permanent brain damage can occur after 3 minutes of oxygen deprivation (Dennis, 2008). However, today's medical practices, including the widespread dissemination of cardiopulmonary resuscitation (CPR) techniques, have permitted many people to regain a heartbeat and be "revived" from clinical death. A heartbeat is no longer a clear marker of life, or in its absence, death.

Advances in technology have led to new ways of defining death. As mechanical ventilators became commonplace in operating rooms and intensive care settings, it became possible to artificially maintain patients who had irreversible injuries, to keep patients alive on ventilators. It is possible for the heart to continue to beat even though the person cannot eat, think, or breathe on his or her own. Therefore, more precise definitions of death are needed. In 1968 a physician-led committee out of Harvard Medical School concluded that patients who meet criteria for specific severe neurological injuries may be pronounced dead before cardiopulmonary cessation occurs (Harvard Medical School ad hoc Committee, 1968). That is, **whole brain death**, the irreversible loss of functioning in the entire brain, may occur prior to clinical death (Burkle, Sharp, & Wijdicks, 2014). Whole brain death is the death of the higher and lower brain regions, the cortex and brainstem, without possibility of resuscitation (McMahan, 2001). Death is declared if all criteria are met and other conditions that may mimic death, such as a drug overdose or deep coma, are ruled out. Patients who are brain dead may be temporarily sustained artificially for the purpose of organ donation.

clinical death Defines death as the moment the heart stops beating; blood, and thereby oxygen, no longer circulate throughout the body.

whole brain death Refers to the irreversible loss of functioning in the entire brain that may occur prior to clinical death.

The President's Commission for the Ethical Study of Problems in Medicine, Biomedical, and Behavioral Research (1981) established the criteria used to diagnose whole brain death:

1. No spontaneous movement in response to stimuli

2. No spontaneous respiration for at least one hour

3. Total lack of responsiveness to even the most painful stimuli

4. No eye movements, blinking, or pupil responses

5. No postural activity, swallowing, yawning, or vocalizing

6. No motor reflexes

7. A flat electroencephalogram (EEG) for at least 10 minutes

8. No change in any of these criteria when they are tested again 24 hours later

The report of the President's Council on Bioethics (2008) reaffirmed the whole brain definition of death. Under the Uniform Determination of Death Act, all 50 U.S. states and the District of Columbia apply the whole brain standard in defining death, thereby permitting a person to be declared legally dead and removed from life support.

The most controversial definition of death looks beyond the whole brain standard. In the late 19th century, several researchers and physicians noted instances in which brain damage caused a cease in cortical functioning while the heart continued to beat. The cortex is the part of the brain most vulnerable to conditions of *anoxia*, the loss of oxygen. Inadequate blood supply to the brain after heart attack, stroke, drowning, or traumatic brain injury, can irreparably damage the cortex while leaving the brainstem intact and functional. The neurons of the brainstem often survive stressors that kill cortex neurons (Brisson, Hsieh, Kim, Jin, & Andrew, 2014), resulting in cortical death, or a **persistent vegetative state (PVS)**, in which the person appears awake but is not aware, due to the permanent loss of all activity in the cortex (Zeman, 1997). Despite cortical death, PVS patients retain an intact brainstem which permits heart rate, respiration, and gastrointestinal activity to continue.

The PVS patient is neither clinically dead nor meets the criteria for whole brain death. He or she remains biologically alive despite lacking the capacity to regain awareness and cognitive capacities. The patient may open his or her eyelids and show sleep-wake cycles but does not show cognitive function, as indicated by measures of brain activity, such as MRI, EEG, and PET scans (Bender, Jox, Grill, Straube, & Lulé, 2015). Loved ones may be misled by spontaneous reflexive movements of the arms and legs and random facial expressions to believe that the patient is capable of cognitive functions and experiences emotions (Cranford, 2004). However, reflexes are controlled by the spinal cord and lower regions of the brain that are not involved in conscious awareness. When the condition first appears it is referred to as a vegetative state, but after 4 weeks the patient is diagnosed with persistent vegetative state (The Multi-Society Task Force on PVS, 1994). Approximately 30,000 U.S. patients are held captive in this condition (Brisson et al., 2014).

Although the medical community typically defines a PVS patient as dead given the irrevocable lack of awareness and loss of cortical function, PVS is does not meet the criteria for whole brain death (and, therefore, death)

persistent vegetative state (PVS) Cortical death when the person appears awake but is not aware, due to permanent loss of all activity in the cortex.

Nieves Melendez tends to her son, former professional boxer Prichard Colon, while he lies in a vegetative state after suffering a traumatic brain injury during his bout against Terrel Williams.

and is not recognized as death by U.S. legal statute (McMahan, 2001). Canada and several other countries, however, acknowledge cortical death (Teitelbaum & Shemie, 2016). Supporters of the cortical definition of death argue that the cortex is responsible for what makes us human—thought, emotion, and personality. From this view, when higher cortical functions have ceased, these capacities are lost. Courts require authoritative medical opinion that recovery is not possible before terminating life-prolonging activities (Cranford, 2004). Several lengthy and dramatic court cases have caused many people to consider and communicate their own wishes regarding how they want to die.

END-OF-LIFE ISSUES

People of all ages desire a sense of control in what happens to them, whether it is a simple as an infant's choice of play toy or as complex as an older adult's choice of living situation. This is especially true when it comes to the many decisions that surround death. **Dying with dignity** refers to ending life in a way that is true to one's preferences, controlling one's end-of-life care (Guo & Jacelon, 2014; Kastenbaum, 2012).

Advance Directives

Planning and communication are key to helping an individual die with dignity. The individual's wishes must be known ahead of time because dying patients are usually unable to express their wishes. Without prior communication dying patients often cannot participate in decisions about their own end-of-life care, such as pain management, life prolonging treatment, and memorial services. All of the persons who surround the patient—spouse, children, family members, friends, and health care workers—are likely to have different views regarding end-of-life care and postmortem decisions. The Patient Self-Determination Act (PSA) of 1990 guaranteed the right of all competent adults to have a say in decisions about their health care by putting their wishes regarding end of life and life sustaining treatment in writing. Advance directives, including a living will and a durable power of attorney, are an important way of ensuring that people's preferences regarding end-of-life care are known and respected.

A **living will** is a legal document that permits a person to make his or her wishes known regarding medical care in the event that the person is incapacitated by an illness or accident and is unable to speak for himself or herself. The individual can identify what, if any, medical intervention should be used to prolong his or her life if he or she is unable to express a preference. For example, should artificial respiration or a feeding tube be used? In a living will, a person can explicitly designate the medical treatment he or she does not want. A **durable power of attorney** for health care is a document in which individuals designate a trusted relative or friend (called a *health care proxy*) as legally authorized to make health care decisions on their behalf in the event that they are unable to do so. It is important to have both a living will and a durable power of attorney, as they each fulfill different functions.

Determining and communicating one's final wishes in order to construct advance directives can ease the process for the dying person and his or her family. Advance directives permit patients to take control over their health care, their deaths, and what happens to their bodies and possessions after death. They facilitate communication about health care needs and preferences and can reduce anxiety on the part of patients (Nelson & Nelson, 2014). Advance directives foster patients' autonomy and help them to retain a sense of dignity as they die. Caregivers benefit from advance directives as an understanding of the patient's wishes can help in decision making, reducing stress, emotional stain, and, potentially, guilt (Radwany et al., 2009).

Despite the many benefits of advance directives, they are underused. Overall, about one quarter of U.S. adults have written some form of advance directive (Rao, Anderson, Lin, & Laux, 2014). Older adults are most likely to have completed advance directives

dying with dignity Ending one's life in a way that is true to one's preferences and controlling end-of-life care.

living will A legal document that permits a person to make his or her wishes known regarding medical care in the event that the person is incapacitated by an illness or accident and is unable to speak for him- or herself.

(about 50%) and they are typically the ones to initiate conversations with family members about end-of-life issues (Pew Research Center, 2009). About one-third of 50- to 64-year-old adults and only about one-fifth of 30- to 49-year-old adults report having written down their wishes for end of life treatment. Yet advance directives are not just for the old or the ill. Many argue that it is the healthy—especially the young and healthy—who benefit most from living wills and health care proxies (Khan, 2014). Young people and their families are often unprepared for the decisions that may accompany the sudden loss of decision-making capacities and consciousness, such as from an accident or serious illness. Advance directives can spare spouses and families the anguish, guilt, and potential conflict among family members of making decisions for a loved one without knowing his or her wishes.

Euthanasia

Through a living will one might articulate when life prolonging care may be withdrawn and under what conditions euthanasia is acceptable. **Euthanasia** ("easy death") refers to the practice of assisting terminally ill people in dying more quickly (Jecker, 2006; van der Maas, 1991). It is controversial, but the courts have permitted euthanasia in many hopeless cases, such as that of a patient named Nancy Cruzan. On January 11, 1983, then-25-year-old Nancy Cruzan lost control of her car, was thrown from the vehicle, and landed face down in a water-filled ditch. She was resuscitated by paramedics after about 15 minutes without breathing. After 3 weeks in a coma, Nancy was diagnosed as being in a persistent vegetative state. She remained alive as a PVS patient until 1987, when Nancy's parents asked that her feeding tube be removed. Although a county judge authorized the request, the state of Missouri contested it. The resulting Supreme Court decision in Cruzan v. Director, Missouri Department of Health, held that treatment can be refused in extraordinary circumstances, but clear and convincing evidence of Nancy's own wishes would be needed. The court accepted testimony from friends and family that Nancy had told them she would not want to live in a disabled condition. Nancy Cruzan died 2 weeks after her feeding tube was removed, in December, 1990. The Cruzan case was pivotal in supporting the right-to-die movement.

Distinctions are commonly made between passive and active euthanasia (Jecker, 2006). **Passive euthanasia** occurs when life-sustaining treatment, such a ventilator, is withheld or withdrawn, allowing a person to die naturally, as happened in the case of Nancy Cruzan. In **active euthanasia**, death is deliberately induced, such as by administering a fatal dose of pain medication. More than two-thirds of U.S. adults and 95% of physicians support passive euthanasia (Curlin, Nwodim, Vance, Chin, & Lantos, 2008; Pew Research Center, 2013). A majority of adults say there are at least some situations in which they, personally, would want to halt medical treatment and be allowed to die. For example, 57% say they would tell their doctors to stop treatment if they had a disease with no hope of improvement and were suffering a great deal of pain. And about half (52%) say they would ask their doctors to stop treatment if they had an incurable disease and were totally dependent on someone else for their care. Yet, about a third of adults (35%) say they would tell their doctors to do everything possible to keep them alive—even in dire circumstances, such as having a disease with no hope of improvement and experiencing a great deal of pain (Pew Research Center, 2013). These are difficult questions and there is no clear consensus on solutions.

Physician-Assisted Suicide

Physician-assisted suicide is a type of voluntary active euthanasia in which terminally ill patients make the conscious decision that they want their life to end before dying becomes a protracted process. Patients receive from physicians the medical tools needed to end their lives. The patient self-administers the medication. Physician-assisted suicide is

euthanasia Refers to the practice of assisting terminally ill people in dying more quickly.

passive euthanasia Occurs when life-sustaining treatment, such as a ventilator, is withheld or withdrawn, allowing a person to die naturally.

active euthanasia Occurs when death is deliberately induced, such as by administering a fatal dose of pain medication.

physician assisted suicide A type of voluntary active euthanasia in which terminally ill patients make the conscious decision that they want their life to end before dying becomes a protracted process.

legal in the Netherlands, Luxembourg, and Switzerland (Grosse & Grosse, 2015) and is often tacitly accepted in other countries. Until recently, assisting a suicide was illegal throughout North America; however, Canada adopted physician-assisted suicide starting in 2016, and physician-assisted suicide is legal in several U.S. states (Fine, 2015; Ollove, 2015).

The most widely publicized cases of physician-assisted suicide involved Dr. Jack Kevorkian, a Michigan physician who helped more than 100 terminally ill patients end their lives. In 1989 Kevorkian created a "suicide machine" that allowed a patient to press a button to self-administer anesthesia and medication that stops the heart. In 1998 Kevorkian was arrested after a segment televised on the program *60 Minutes* aired in which he assisted in the death of a 52-year-old man who suffered from a terminal neurological disease. Although it was flagrantly displayed on television, the procedure was illegal and led to Kevorkian's arrest, trial, and conviction on second-degree murder charges. He was released from prison in 2007 after serving 8 years of a 10- to 25-year sentence. He died in 2011 after being diagnosed with liver cancer.

Dr. Jack Kevorkian (1928–2011) helped over 100 terminally ill patients end their lives, prompting a continuing debate over physician-assisted suicide.

As of 2017, the practice of physician-assisted suicide is legal in the U.S. states of Oregon, Montana, Washington, Vermont, and California (Ollove, 2015). Oregon was the first U.S. state to legalize assisted suicide. Under Oregon's Death with Dignity Act, enacted in 1997, terminally ill Oregonians may end their lives through the voluntary self-administration of lethal medications, expressly prescribed by a physician for that purpose. Under the Oregon law, an adult Oregon resident who has been diagnosed by a physician with a terminal illness that will kill the patient within 6 months may request in writing a prescription for a lethal dose of medication for the purpose of ending the patient's life. The patient must initiate the request and must be free of any mental condition that might impair judgment. The request must be confirmed by two witnesses, and at least one of them (1) must not be related to the patient; (2) must not be entitled to any portion of the patient's estate; (3) must not be the patient's physician, and (4) must not be employed by a health care facility caring for the patient. After the request is made, a second physician must examine the patient's medical records and confirm the diagnosis. If the request is authorized, the patient must wait an additional 15 days to make a second oral request before the prescription can be written.

Since the Oregon law was enacted in 1997, a total of 1,545 people have had prescriptions written and 991 patients have died from ingesting medication prescribed under the act (Oregon Public Health Division, 2016). More than two-thirds of the 991 patients

FIGURE 16.3: Public Opinion on Euthanasia in the United States, 2016

When a person has a disease that cannot be cured and is living in severe pain, do you think doctors should or should not be allowed by law to assist the patient to commit suicide if the patient requests it?

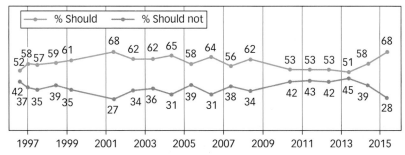

Source: Dugan (2015).

Hospice services permit dying patients to remain in their home, comfortable, and feel a sense of control in the death process. Counseling services help families assist the dying person, cope with their own needs, and strengthen connections with the dying person. Hospice services permit death with dignity that honors a loved one's wishes.

who died were over the age of 65 and the median age at time of death was 71. More than three-quarters had been diagnosed with cancer. The top three concerns reported by patients as influences on their decisions were being less able to engage in activities to enjoy life, loss of autonomy, and loss of dignity (Oregon Public Health Division, 2016). The Oregon Death with Dignity Act has permitted many suffering adults to end their lives on their own timetable; however, physician-assisted suicide remains controversial in the United States. As shown in Figure 16.1, most U.S. adults in 2016 (69%) agreed that euthanasia should be legal, that doctors should be allowed to end a patient's life by painless means. Moreover, 51% said they would consider ending their lives if faced with terminal illness (Swift, 2016). Yet debates regarding physician-assisted suicide are unlikely to be resolved at any time soon.

Hospice

The desire to die with dignity, minimal pain, and on one's own terms has advanced the hospice movement. **Hospice** is an approach to end-of-life care that emphasizes dying patients' needs for pain management, psychological, spiritual, and social support, and death with dignity (Ganzini et al., 2001; Russo, 2008). The philosophy of the hospice approach does not emphasize prolonging life but rather prolonging quality of life. Death occurs most often in hospitals (Weitzen, Teno, Fennell, & Mor, 2003), yet most dying people express the desire to die at home with family and friends. Dying persons have needs that set them apart from other hospital patients and hospital settings are often not equipped to meet these needs. Rather than medical treatment, dying patients require **palliative care**, focusing on controlling pain and related symptoms. Hospice services are enlisted after the physician and patient believe that the illness is terminal and no treatment or cure is possible.

Hospice services may be provided on an inpatient basis, at a formal hospice site that provides all care to patients, but they are frequently provided on an outpatient basis in a patient's home. Outpatient hospice service is becoming more common because it is cost effective and enables the patient to remain in the familiar surroundings of his or her home. Home hospice care is associated with increased satisfaction by patients and families (Candy, Holman, Leurent, Davis, & Jones, 2011). Whether hospice care is given on an inpatient or outpatient basis, the patient care team typically includes physicians, nurses, social workers, and counselors who act as spiritual and bereavement counselors who support the patient in facing his or her impending death and help the patient's loved ones cope with the loss.

 Thinking in Context 16.1

1. Evaluate the right-to-die concept. In your view, what is the value of this concept? How well is it embodied in advance directives, euthanasia, physician-assisted suicide, and hospice? Which of these approaches do you endorse, if any?

2. What advantages and disadvantages do you see to choosing hospice instead of standard medical care? Should some patients be required to transition to hospice? Why or why not?

3. From a bioecological perspective, discuss contextual factors that contribute to the declining mortality rate. Provide examples of influences at each bioecological level with particular attention to exosystem and macrosystem influences.

hospice An approach to end-of-life care that emphasizes a dying patient's need for pain management, psychological, spiritual, and social support as well as death with dignity.

palliative care An alternative to medical treatment in which dying patients receive medications to control pain and related symptoms.

CONCEPTIONS OF DEATH ACROSS THE LIFESPAN

LO 16.2 Contrast child, adolescent, and adult understandings of death.

There are many ways of conceptualizing death, and cultural beliefs about the nature of death vary. For example, many cultures in the South Pacific do not differentiate death as a separate category of functioning. Melanesians use the term *mate* to refer to the very old, the very sick, and the dead; all other living people are referred to as *toa* (Counts & Counts, 1985). Other South Pacific cultures explain that the life force leaves the body during sleep and illness; therefore, people experience forms of death over the course of their lifetime before experiencing a final death (Counts & Counts, 1985). The Kwanga of Papua New Guinea believe that most deaths are the result of magic and witchcraft (Brison, 1995). The Hopi Indians of North America view life and death as phases of a cycle (Oswalt, 1986), with death representing an altered state.

Many children and adults in various cultures express beliefs in noncorporeal continuation, the view that some form of life and personal continuity exists after the physical body had died (Kenyon, 2001). For example, a spirit may endure, life may persist in heaven, or a soul may be reincarnated into another body. These beliefs are consistent with the doctrine of many religions and can coexist with mature understandings of death as the irreversible and inevitable ceasing of biological functioning (Corr & Corr, 2013). Researchers generally agree that, in Western cultures, a person has a mature understanding of death when the following four components are understood (Barrett & Behne, 2005; Brent & Speece, 1993; Kenyon, 2001; Panagiotaki, Nobes, Ashraf, & Aubby, 2015; Slaughter & Griffiths, 2007):

1. *Nonfunctionality:* the understanding that death entails the complete and final end of all life-defining abilities or functional capacities, internal and external, that are typically attributed to a living body

2. *Irreversibility:* the understanding that the processes involved in the transition from being alive to being dead and the resulting state of being dead cannot be undone. Once a thing dies its physical body cannot be made alive again

3. *Inevitability:* the understanding that death is universal and that all living things will someday die

4. *Biological causality:* the understanding that death is caused by events or conditions that trigger natural processes within the organism and that it is not caused by bad behavior or wishes

CHILDREN'S UNDERSTANDING OF DEATH

Children do not understand loss and death in the same way as adults, but they often have a more mature understanding of these events than many adults expect (Gaab, Owens, & Macleod, 2013). Even infants can sense that something unusual is happening when the adults around them grieve. They notice changes in the emotional tone of their families, changes in caregivers, and the degree to which their emotional needs are met or interrupted (Leming & Dickinson, 2016). Young children, similarly, perceive events around them before they have developed the ability to understand or explain them.

Children encounter death in many ways. Grandparents, parents, other important adults, siblings, and friends may die. Pets are often children's first experience with unconditional love and most children will experience the death of a pet as a significant experience (Leming & Dickinson, 2016). Children have more exposure to death and death themes than many adults realize. They overhear adults talking about the deaths of elderly relatives or public figures. Television reports describe car crashes, homicides, disasters, and war. Death is a common topic in television programs. Considering such

The Cremation Ceremony held in Bali, Indonesia, is a ritual performed to send the deceased to the next life. The body is placed in a wood coffin inside a temple-like structure made of paper and wood. The structure and body are burned to release the deceased's spirit and enable reincarnation.

exposure to the subject of death, it is not surprising that children's play is riddled with death-related themes (Bettelheim, 1977; Opie & Opie, 1969). We have seen that play is the work of childhood, and as such it is a way that children make sense of the world, including death (Corr, 2010b). Children often act out crashes with their cars or killing with toy soldiers. Death themes appear in children's rhymes, songs, and fairy tales (Lamers, 1995): the song *Rock-a-Bye, Baby* culminates with a falling cradle (Achté, Fagerström, Pentikäinen, & Farberow, 1989), and the child's prayer "Now I lay me down to sleep" asks for safekeeping against danger and death. The wicked stepmother demands Snow White's heart as proof of her death, and the Big Bad Wolf in "The Three Little Pigs" falls down the chimney of the third pig's house into a pot of boiling water. Death themes in rhymes and play may help children work through fears related to loss in safe ways.

Young children between the ages of 3 and 5 tend to view death as temporary and reversible. They believe dead things can become alive spontaneously and as the result of medical intervention, after eating or drinking, and by magic, wishful thinking, or prayer (Corr, 2010b; Slaughter, 2005). They may imagine that the person who has died is actually still living, but under alternative circumstances (Barrett & Behne, 2005; Slaughter & Griffiths, 2007). They may describe death as sleep, with the corresponding ability to wake up, or a trip from which a person can return (Brent & Speece, 1993). They may personify death as a figure, a spirit that comes and "gets" you (Leming & Dickinson, 2016). They may believe that only people who want to die or who are bad die. Before they understand nonfunctionality, children view dead things as possessing reduced or diminished capacities, but retaining some functions such as the ability to feel hunger pangs, wishes, beliefs, and love (Bering & Bjorklund, 2004). Before they understand the inevitability of death, young children think that there are actions they could take to avoid death, such as being clever enough to outsmart it or being lucky (Speece & Brent, 1984). A mature understanding of biological death gradually emerges alongside cognitive development (Corr, 2010b).

The understanding that death is final, irreversible, and inevitable typically emerges between 5 and 7 years of age, corresponding to the transition from preoperational reasoning to concrete operational reasoning in Piaget's theory. Biological causality is the most complex element of the death concept and the final element to be acquired, emerging as early as 6 or 7, but more typically in late childhood (Bonoti, Leondari, & Mastora, 2013; Slaughter & Griffiths, 2007). Advances in executive function are closely related with the emergence of a biological theory of death as these cognitive capacities permit the abstract thinking needed for mature conceptions of death (Zaitchik, Iqbal, & Carey, 2014). Typically an understanding of the biological nature of death is mastered by about age 10 (Bonoti et al., 2013; Renaud, Engarhos, Schleifer, & Talwar, 2015). Research comparing white British, Muslim British, and Muslim Pakistani children suggests that this pattern of change in biological explanations for death occurs cross-culturally (Panagiotaki et al., 2015). Such findings are consistent with those from children in Australia (Slaughter & Griffiths, 2007), the United States (Lazar & Torney-Purta, 1991), and Israel (Schonfeld & Smilansky, 1989).

Despite cross-cultural similarities in biological conceptions of death, there are contextual differences in children's exposure to death and these differences influence children's conceptions of death. Some children receive more exposure to death through media depictions of war, accidents, and devastating living conditions. Others experience death firsthand. Many children in all parts of the world, including North America, are exposed directly to violence within their families and communities and may witness or be aware of traumatic events and deaths at home and in their neighborhoods. Children who reside in war-torn and poverty-stricken nations often experience multiple losses (Masten, Narayan, Silverman, & Osofsky, 2015). How children make sense of these events and how they

Children visit a relative's grave during the día de los muertos celebration.

understand death changes with age and experience. Children who have direct, personal experience of death tend to show a more advanced and realistic understanding of death than their peers (Bonoti et al., 2013; Hunter & Smith, 2008).

How parents talk to children about death, and whether they talk about death, influences children's understanding. Parents of young children, ages 3 to 6, tend to believe that their children hold misconceptions about death. They tend to avoid talking about death, believing that children are not capable of grasping or coping with it (Miller & Rosengren, 2014; Nguyen & Rosengren, 2004). U.S. parents often report shielding their young children from death by not taking them to funerals or memorial services; controlling their access to death in television and movies; and talking with them about death minimally, indirectly, or not at all (Miller & Rosengren, 2014). Parents are most likely to report having discussed death when the child has experienced a death of some kind, regardless of age; more conversations took place as the child's age increased (Renaud et al., 2015).

Culture is a powerful influence on conceptions of death. In contrast with the practice of shielding children from death, common among European American parents, Mexican and Mexican American parents report beliefs that children should become familiar with death and include them as active participants in rituals related to death, including wakes and funerals (Gutiérrez, Rosengren, & Miller, 2014b). These attitudes are supported by traditional Mexican practices, such as the Día de los Muertos (Day of the Dead) celebration, a national holiday held annually from October 31 to November 2, in which it is believed that dead relatives return to their homes to eat, drink, and visit with the living. The celebration includes images of death such as skeletons in festive outfits depicted engaging in everyday activities: dancing, playing instruments, getting married, and so forth. Children participate with community members in celebrations and vigils held in cemeteries (Gutierrez, 2009). The Día de los Muertos holiday is intended to welcome the deceased and to celebrate death as the continuation of life. It is not surprising that Mexican American young children are more likely than their European American peers to attribute biological and psychological properties to the dead (Gutiérrez et al., 2014b).

Culture and spirituality collaboratively influence individuals' views of death. In addition to biological explanations for death, children often develop spiritual or religious explanations. For example, Harris and Gimenez (2005) found that beliefs in the afterlife amongst Spanish children increased between the ages of 7 and 11, along with religious explanations for death. However, children were most likely to rely on religious explanations for death in response to vignettes highlighting religious themes as compared with vignettes highlighting

LIVES IN CONTEXT

• • Adolescent Suicide

Adolescents who attempt suicide feel isolated and alone and often lose interest in activities they once found fun.

Suicide is among the top three causes of death for adolescents and emerging adults in many Western countries, including the United States, Canada, UK, and Australia (Australian Institute of Health and Welfare, 2016; CDC, 2017; Office for National Statistics, 2015; Statistics Canada, 2015). Large gender differences exist in suicide. Although females display higher rates of depression and make

more suicide attempts, males are four times more likely to succeed in committing suicide (Xu, Kochanek, Murphy, & Arias, 2014). Girls tend to choose suicide methods that are slow and passive, and that they are likely to be revived from, such as overdoses of pills. Boys tend to choose methods that are quick and irreversible, such as firearms. The methods correspond to gender roles that expect males to be active, decisive, aggressive, and less open to discussing emotions than females (Canetto & Sakinofsky, 1998; Hepper, Dornan, & Lynch, 2012).

Adolescents who commit suicide are more likely to have experienced multiple stressful events such as parental divorce, abuse and neglect, conflict with parents, family members with emotional, psychological, or antisocial problems, and economic disadvantage, as well as final triggering events such as failure, loss of a friendship, or intense family arguments (Beautrais, 2003; Miranda & Shaffer, 2013). LGBT youth, especially male and bisexual youth, experience exceptionally high risk for suicide, with three to four times as many attempts as other youths (Grossman, Park, & Russell, 2016; Miranda-Mendizábal et al., 2017; Pompili et al., 2014). LGBT adolescents who attempt suicide often list family conflict, peer rejection, and inner conflict about their sexuality as influences on their attempts (Liu & Mustanski, 2012; Mustanski & Liu, 2013; Russell & Fish, 2016). Adolescents are more likely to attempt suicide following a friend's attempt (Nanayakkara,

TABLE 16.2 • Suicide Warning Signs

Any of the following behaviors can serve as a warning sign of increased suicide risk.
• change in eating and sleeping habits
• withdrawal from friends, family, and regular activities
• violent actions, rebellious behavior, or running away
• drug and alcohol use, especially changes in use
• unusual neglect of personal appearance
• marked personality change
• persistent boredom, difficulty concentrating, or a decline in the quality of schoolwork
• frequent complaints about physical symptoms, such as stomachaches, headaches, and fatigue
• loss of interest in pleasurable activities
• complaints of being a bad person or feeling rotten inside
• verbal hints, with statements such as, "I won't be a problem for you much longer," "Nothing matters," "It's no use," and "I won't see you again"
• putting one's affairs in order, for example, giving away favorite possessions, throwing away important belongings
• becoming suddenly cheerful after a period of depression
• have signs of psychosis (hallucinations or bizarre thoughts)
Most important: Stating "I want to kill myself" or "I'm going to commit suicide."

Source: Adapted from American Academy of Child and Adolescent Psychiatry (2008).

Misch, Chang, & Henry, 2013). Some adolescents who commit suicide first express their depression and frustration through antisocial activity such as bullying, fighting, stealing, substance abuse, and risk-taking (Fergusson, Woodward, & Horwood, 2000). Peer victimization is a risk factor for suicide attempts (Bauman, Toomey, & Walker, 2013); another risk factor is a high level of anxiety (Hill, Castellanos, & Pettit, 2011).

After a suicide, family, friends and schoolmates of the adolescent require immediate support and assistance in working through their grief and anger. The availability of support and counseling to all adolescents within the school and community after a suicide is important because adolescent suicides tend to occur in clusters, increasing the risk of suicide among adolescents in the community (Gould, Jamieson, & Romer, 2003; Haw, Hawton, Niedzwiedz, & Platt, 2013). School-based suicide prevention programs tend to increase awareness and knowledge about suicide, and are associated with lower rates of suicide (Zalsman et al., 2016).

Counseling and peer support groups can be provided by schools and community centers (Corrieri et al., 2014).

Although 20/20 hindsight can be quite clear, it is challenging to determine if a teen needs help before he or she attempts self-harm. Frequently, however, adolescents who attempt suicide show warning signs beforehand, as listed in Table 16.2. The availability and advertisement of telephone hotlines, such as the National Suicide Prevention Lifeline at (800) 273-8255 (and available at http://www.suicidepreventionlifeline.org/), can help adolescents who are in immediate danger of suicide.

What Do You Think?

Why does risk for suicide rise in adolescence? Identify factors that might contribute to the increased risk as well as factors that might protect adolescents from risk. Consider adolescent development—physical, cognitive, and socioemotional domains—and the contexts in which adolescents are immersed: peer, family, school, and neighborhood.

medical themes. Children who grow up in cultures that endorse both religious and biological views of death may hold explanations about death that appear incompatible, such as biological irreversibility and religious or spiritual contiuity (Gutiérrez, Rosengren, & Miller, 2014a; Legare, Evans, Rosengren, & Harris, 2012; Panagiotaki et al., 2015). It is not until later in development, particularly adolescence, that children gain the cognitive competence to integrate these ideas and understand death in religious or spiritual terms alongside biological models. Still, the extent to which children use religious and biological terms may vary by culture (Harris & Gimenez, 2005; Nguyen & Rosengren, 2004).

ADOLESCENTS' UNDERSTANDING OF DEATH

Adolescents often describe death as an enduring abstract state of nothingness that accompanies the inevitable and irreversible end of biological processes (Brent, Lin, Speece, Dong, & Yang, 1996). Adolescents' understanding of death reflects the intersection of biological, cognitive, and socioemotional development (Noppe & Noppe, 1991, 2004). As adolescents experience the rapid biological changes of puberty, this process may heighten their awareness of the inevitability of the biological changes of life. Although adolescents are cognitively aware that death is universal and can happen to anyone, at any time, this awareness often is not reflected in their risk-taking behavior. Instead, adolescents are prone to the personal fable (see Chapter 6), viewing themselves as unique and invulnerable to the negative consequences of risky behaviors, including death (Alberts, Elkind, & Ginsberg, 2007; Elkind, 1985). The risk-taking behavior characteristic of adolescence is a form of cheating death, an event that is perceived as a distant, but unlikely, possibility. However, some adolescents seek to harm themselves; adolescent suicide is examined in the Lives in Context feature.

Adolescents' advances in abstract reasoning are reflected in their interest in considering the meaning of death as well as whether some psychological functions, such as knowing and feeling, persist in a dying person after biological processes have ceased (Corr & Corr, 2013; Noppe & Noppe, 1991, 2004). Adolescents and adults across cultures often share a belief in an afterlife, whether religious or supernatural in origin (Bering & Bjorklund, 2004). This belief often arises in childhood, but it is in adolescence that we are first able to simultaneously hold a mature biological understanding of death as the end of all body functions alongside with cultural and religious beliefs about an afterlife. The two conceptions coexist and can be called upon as needed depending on the situation and what adolescents are trying to explain (Legare et al., 2012). For example, the Vezo people in rural Madagascar believe that dead ancestors are present among the living, watching and guiding (Astuti & Harris, 2008). Vezo children tend to emphasize biological explanations for death, but adolescents and adults hold both biological and spiritual explanations, reflecting their cognitive abilities to hold two differing perspectives at once.

ADULTS' UNDERSTANDING OF DEATH

Conceptions of death change in subtle ways over the course of adulthood. Young adults begin to apply their mature understanding of death to themselves. The personal fable declines and, as they take on adult roles, young adults begin to acknowledge their vulnerability. Risky activity declines and young adults' behavior begins to better align with their understanding of the inevitability of death.

An awareness of death increases as individuals progress through middle adulthood, when they are likely to gain experience through the deaths of parents, friends, siblings and colleagues. As midlife adults watch their children take on adult roles and as they become aware of their own aging bodies and minds, they develop a more personalized sense of their own mortality and the inevitability of the life cycle (Doka, 2015). The awareness of death can cause midlife adults to reevaluate their priorities, often leading them to pursue a sense of generativity, the need to give back and leave a lasting legacy (Freund & Ritter, 2009; McAdams, 2014). Midlife adults who look beyond their own losses to consider the profound meaning of their absence to significant others, such as spouses and children, may be deeply saddened by the thought of their own death.

Older adults are likely to have exposure to death many times over. With the deaths of many friends and family members, older adults may become socialized to the nature and inevitability of death (Cicirelli, 2002). They often talk about aging and death, perhaps helping them to prepare for the inevitability of their own death (Hallberg, 2013). They also spend more time thinking about the process and circumstances of dying than the state of death, as compared with midlife adults (Corr & Corr, 2013).

Lives in Context Video 16.1
Developmental Tasks of Dying

Cross-sectional and longitudinal studies suggest that death anxiety declines over the lifespan; older adults tend to report lower levels of death anxiety than young and middle-aged adults (Chopik, 2017; Krause, Pargament, & Ironson, 2016; Russac, Gatliff, Reece, & Spottswood, 2007; Thorson & Powell, 2000). Advances in psychosocial development, such an increasing ability to manage negative emotions, influence how older adults approach death and may account for their reduced anxiety compared to younger adults. In addition, religion, specifically a religious sense of hope (e.g., the conviction that their religious beliefs will bring opportunities or make things turn out well), reduces death anxiety among older adults (Krause et al., 2016). The psychosocial task of older adulthood is to consider the meaning of life and death. Engaging in life review and establishing a sense of ego integrity help older adults reduce regrets and construct a sense that their lives have been well lived (Erikson, 1982).

⚙️ Thinking in Context 16.2

1. How do children's and adolescents' understanding of death reflect their cognitive development? Explain how cognitive advances from Piagetian and information processing perspectives may underlie children's and adolescents' conceptions of death.

2. Recall Erikson's psychosocial stages of development (Chapter 1). How are the developmental tasks of adolescence and adulthood reflected in how people understand death? Provide specific examples of how tasks, such as identity development and the search for intimacy and generativity, might influence people's views of death.

DYING AND THE EXPERIENCE OF DEATH

LO 16.3 Describe the physical and emotional process of death as it is experienced over the lifespan.

When does dying begin? How does it occur? How is it experienced? These are questions that are challenging to answer. In the following sections we consider the biological changes that occur with death as well as the cognitive and socioemotional experience of death, how people experience their own deaths.

THE DYING PROCESS

There is great variability in the **dying trajectory**, or the rate of decline that people show prior to death (Cohen-Mansfield, Skornick-Bouchbinder, & Brill, 2017; Glaser & Strauss, 1968; Lunney, Lynn, Foley, Lipson, & Guralnik, 2003). Dying trajectories vary by duration and descent and can be categorized into four patterns. The first trajectory is the *abrupt-surprise death*, which is sudden, unexpected, and instantaneous, such as an accident, a shooting, or a heart attack. As shown in Figure 16.2, the person shows normal functioning until a steep, catastrophic decline occurs, bringing a sudden death without warning. The dying person and his or her family have no time to prepare or adjust beforehand. A second trajectory, the *short-term expected death* is a steady predictable decline due to a terminal illness such as cancer. (Teno, Weitzen, Fennell, & Mor, 2001) A third dying trajectory is referred to as an *expected lingering death* because it is anticipated but prolonged, such as in the case of frailty and old age. The fourth trajectory is referred to as

FIGURE 16.4: The Dying Trajectory

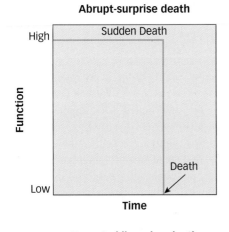

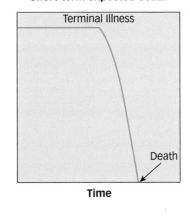

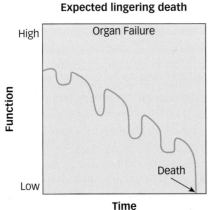

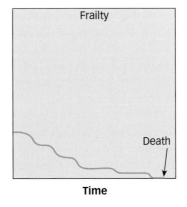

dying trajectory Refers to the variability in the rate of decline that people show prior to death.

entry-reentry deaths, because slow declines are punctuated by a series of crises and partial recoveries; the dying person may have repeated hospital stays, returning home between stays. The dying trajectory influences adaptation on the part of the dying person and his or her family. Typically the short-term expected death is most predictable and most likely to be experienced in hospice care as the lifespan is clearly identified as limited. Lingering and entry-reentry deaths are prolonged. They can tax caregivers' coping skills as such individuals are often not afforded hospice care until death is imminent.

There are predictable changes and symptoms that occur in the dying person hours and days before death; however, people vary in the number and severity of symptoms (Gavrin & Chapman, 1995). Toward the end of life many people lose their appetite, which is often distressing to family as the patient may show dramatic weight loss. People suffering from lengthy illnesses, such as cancer, AIDS, and neurodegenerative disorders, often show extreme weight loss and the loss of muscle mass, known as *cachexia* (Evans et al., 2008). As death is imminent, the person sleeps most of the time, may be disoriented and less able to see, and may experience visual and auditory hallucinations. Many terminally ill patients experience declines in cognitive function in the weeks prior to death.

The dying person may experience pain, shortness of breath, irregular breathing, nausea, disrupted bladder and bowel function, and lethargy (Gavrin & Chapman, 1995). As the person is closer to death he or she will lose interest and the ability to eat, drink, and talk, as well as show reduced mobility and drowsiness (Lichter & Hunt, 1990). Breathing will be difficult and the person may experience dry mouth and difficulty swallowing. Breathing becomes noisy, a gurgling or crackling sound with each breath that is referred to as the *death rattle.* The average time from the onset of the death rattle to death is about 16 hours (Peskin, 2017). Fluids may accumulate in the abdomen and extremities, leading to bloating. Psychological symptoms such as anxiety, depression, confusion, the inability to recognize family members, and delirium are common (Enck, 2003).

EMOTIONAL REACTIONS TO DYING

People tend to show a range of emotional reactions to the knowledge that they are dying. After conducting more than 200 interviews with terminally ill people, psychiatrist Elisabeth Kübler-Ross categorized people's reactions into five types or ways in which people deal with death: denial, anger, bargaining, depression and acceptance (Kübler-Ross, 1969). Although Kübler-Ross described these reactions as a series of stages, not everyone experiences all of them or proceeds through them at the same pace or in the same order (Corr, Nabe, & Corr, 2009; Kübler-Ross, 1974).

Upon learning that one has a terminal illness the first reaction is likely shock. For most people, denial ("It's not possible!") is the first stage of processing death, reflecting the initial reaction to the news. The person may not believe the diagnosis, deny that it is true, and might seek a second or third opinion. Once the dying person realizes that he or she truly is terminally ill, anger may set in. Dying people might ask themselves, "Why me?" Feeling cheated and robbed out of life, the person may harbor resentment and envy towards family, friends and caregivers, as it may seem unfair that others live while they must die. Anger is a very difficult stage, but with time and effort most dying people are able to manage and resolve their hostilities. The bargaining stage, like the other stages of dying, is common but not universal. The dying person bargains in order to find a way out. Perhaps a deal can be struck with God or fate: The dying person might promise to be a better person and help others if only he or she may survive. A parent might attempt to bargain a timetable, such as, "just let me live to see my daughter give birth." Eventually, when the person realizes that death cannot be escaped, prolonged, or bargained with, depression is common—especially as the illness becomes more evident because of pain, surgery, or a loss of functioning. Knowing it is the end brings profound sadness. During this stage the dying person feels great loss and sorrow with the knowledge that, for example, he or she will never return to work or home, that all relationships will end, and that the future is lost. The person may feel guilt over the illness and its consequences for his or her loved ones. Many dying people will tend to withdraw from emotional attachments to all but the few people with whom they have the most meaningful relationships. Sharing their feelings with others can help dying people come to an acceptance of death, the final stage. In this stage the dying person no longer fights death. He or she accepts that death is inevitable, seems at peace, and begins to detach him- or herself from the world.

Although it is useful to think of these reactions to impending death as stages, a stage view ignores the relevance of context—including relationships, illness, family, and situation (Kastenbaum 2009, 2012). Dying is an individual experience. The dying person has a myriad of emotions and must be allowed to experience and express them in order to come to terms with his or her own grief, complete unfinished business with loved ones, and to, ultimately, accept death (Corr & Corr, 2013). It is difficult to predict the psychological state and needs of a dying person as they vary greatly according to factors like age, experience, and the situation (Gavrin & Chapman, 1995).

THE EXPERIENCE OF ONE'S DEATH

Children, adolescents, and adults have very different sets of abilities and experiences that lead them to view the world in ways that are unique to their age group. We have seen that conceptions of death grow in complexity over time. How do children, adolescents, and adults experience their own deaths?

The Dying Child

Physicians and parents often find it difficult to talk to children about their prognosis and death (Bates & Kearney, 2015). As a result, children are less likely to develop a clear understanding of their condition and imminent death. Dying children who have been ill for a long time have been observed to show a maturity beyond their years (Leming & Dickinson, 2016). In a hospital setting it is natural for children to acquire information about their disease during the progression of the illness, though parents and doctors are often unaware that they are doing so (Corr, 2010a). Children's experiences are an important determinant of concepts of sickness, more so than age or intellectual ability (Corr, 2010b). A 3- or 4-year-old child who is dying might understand more about his or her illness and impending death than an older child who is well. Likewise, it is experience with the disease and its treatment that advances children's awareness of dying (Bluebond-Langner, 1989a; Cotton & Range, 2010; Hunter & Smith, 2008).

Children with life-threatening diseases tend to show a greater awareness of death than their healthy or chronically ill peers (Jay, Green, Johnson, Caldwell, & Nitschke, 1987a; O'Halloran & Altmaier, 1996). Anthropologist Myra Bluebond-Langner (1989) observed terminally ill 3- to 9-year-old children and noted that all became aware of the fact that they were dying before death was imminent. They also knew that death was a final and irreversible process, suggesting a mature concept of death. The children she studied showed awareness that they were dying by noting that they were never going back to school or that they would not be around for a birthday or holiday; some frankly said, "I am going to die." Stevens (2010) observed that not only did children know that they were dying before death was imminent, many kept that knowledge a secret. Just as parents try to protect children, children sometimes keep their knowledge that they are dying from their parents—in an attempt to protect them from distress.

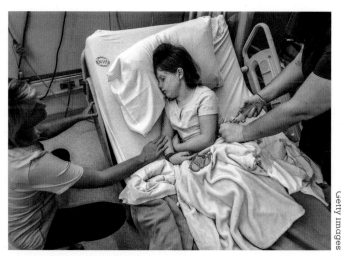

Physicians and parents often find it difficult to talk to children about their prognosis and death but many dying children express desire for the opportunity to seek closure and say goodbye to loved ones.

Pediatricians, social workers, and parents should arrive at a shared understanding of how to approach a terminally ill child's questions and what type of information is appropriate for the child. Because dying children tend to want to know about their illness and treatment (Bates & Kearney, 2015), experts advise that discussions about death should use concrete terms. Open-ended questions can gauge children's knowledge, and children's questions should be answered honestly and directly, in language suited to the child's developmental level (Slaughter & Griffiths, 2007). Part of the process of discussing the child's illness is simply being present for him or her. Children who are dying tend to express sadness and fears of loneliness, separation, and abandonment (Judd, 2014; Theunissen et al., 2007). Parents and loved ones are advised to stay with a dying child, reading, singing, holding, and sleeping with him or her.

The Dying Adolescent

Adolescents' abilities for abstract reasoning translate into more mature conceptions of death, its finality and permanence (Greydanus & Pratt, 2016). However, adolescents' responses to a terminal illness influence and are influenced by the normative developmental tasks they face. Adolescents tend to feel they have a right to know about their illness and prognosis, consistent with their emerging sense of autonomy (Pousset et al., 2009). The sense of invulnerability that is typical of adolescents can lead some to deny their illness or the need for treatment (Balk, 2009). The side effects of treatment, such as hair loss and weight loss or weight gain, can have devastating consequences for adolescents' body image, often causing much distress (Bates & Kearney, 2015) or even leading them to shun treatment.

Like patients in other age groups, adolescents who are terminally ill often spend a great deal of time in hospitals or other treatment facilities. Given than peer relationships are critical influences on adolescents' development and wellbeing, these lengthy absences from home and the normal social milieu can distance adolescents from their friends and make them feel increasingly different from their peers. Adolescents tend to focus on the social implications of their illness, such as their ability to attract a boyfriend or girlfriend, be rejected by peers, or lack independence from parents (Stevens & Dunsmore, 1996). Because of their illness, they may have few opportunities to exercise autonomy or experience independence, leading them to feel anger over what they are missing and their need to be dependent on parents and doctors.

As they begin to become aware of the future and develop a future orientation, dying adolescents may mourn the loss of the future. Many adolescents feel angry and cheated, that life is unjust (Corr & Corr, 2013). Given adolescents' drive for autonomy, it is important that they be kept informed and involved in planning treatment and decision making (Decker, Phillips, & Haase, 2004; Dunsmore & Quine, 1996; Jacobs et al., 2015). Dying adolescents especially need to live in the present, have the freedom to try out different ways of coping with illness-related challenges, and find meaning and purpose in both their lives and their deaths (Greydanus & Pratt, 2016; Stevens & Dunsmore, 1996).

The Dying Adult

Similar to adolescents, dying young adults often feel angry and that the world is unfair; they have many developmental tasks that will be unfulfilled. The primary psychosocial task of young adulthood consists of developing relationships, specifically, a sense of intimacy (Erikson, 1959). A terminal illness can pose challenges to satisfying intimacy needs as it is difficult to form close and secure relationships when one is ill and has limited time left to live. Isolation and abandonment are often principal fears of young adults who are dying (Corr & Corr, 2013). Young adults also lose the sense of an unlimited future. Goals, plans, and aspirations are threatened.

Whereas young adults miss out on the future, midlife adults mourn losing the present. They often worry about abandoning family and not having completed their journey. The normative process of taking stock in midlife transitions from planning for the future to putting affairs in order. Midlife adults who are dying have a need to find ways to continue to meet their responsibilities to others, such as children, after they die.

Older adults have a life to look back on. Their developmental task is to come to a sense of integrity after a successful life review (Erikson, 1982). Terminal illness may speed the process, adding stress, so that the elder may find it difficult to do the work involved in life review. Older adults are more likely than their younger counterparts to accept death, feel that it is appropriate, and be free of any sense of unfinished business. Older adults who are dying have a desire to close ties, to make peace with family, and engage in legacy work, leaving something behind (Leming & Dickinson, 2016).

 Thinking in Context 16.3

1. Do you think emotional responses to dying follow a stage pattern? Why or why not?

2. Provide examples of how children, adolescent, and adults' developmental competencies and tasks influence how they experience death.

BEREAVEMENT AND GRIEF

LO 16.4 Discuss typical grief reactions to the loss of loved ones and the influence of development on bereavement.

The death of a loved one brings on **bereavement**, a state of loss. It triggers an emotional response known as **grief**, which is an array of emotions such as hurt, anger, guilt, and confusion. **Mourning** refers to culturally patterned ritualistic ways of displaying and expressing bereavement, including special clothing, food, prayers, and gatherings. One of the first steps in mourning is to organize a funeral or other ritual to mark the occasion of the loved one's death; such customs are different in various cultures around the world, as described in the Cultural Influences on Development feature. Mourning rituals such as the Jewish custom of sitting *shiva*, ceasing usual activity and instead mourning and receiving visitors at home for a week, provides a sense of structure to help the bereaved manage the first days and weeks of bereavement. The process of coping with the loss of a loved one, however, is personal, complicated, and lengthy.

GRIEF PROCESS

There are no rules to grieving. People vary in the intensity of their reactions to loss and in the timing of their reactions (Wortman & Silver, 2001). People grieve differently, and the same person may react differently to different losses. Some might feel intense but short-lived grief, whereas others may feel grief linger for many months, or seem to resolve only to resurface periodically and unexpectedly. Grief is experienced and expressed in many ways, in both emotions, physical sensations, and behaviors (Kowalski & Bondmass, 2008; Mallon, 2008). Physical responses such as tightness in the chest, feeling out of breath, stomach pains, and weakness are common manifestations of grief. A range of emotions, from anger, anxiety, loneliness, guilt, helplessness, and even relief occur. Grieving persons may be preoccupied with the deceased or the dying event and confusion and disbelief. Behaviors such as looking for the person in crowds and familiar places, absentmindedness, sleep problems, avoiding reminders of the deceased, and loss of interest are common.

Grief is an active coping process in which the grieving person must confront the loss and come to terms with its effects on his or her physical world, interpersonal interactions, and sense of self (Buglass, 2010; Worden, 1991). The person in grief must acknowledge his or her emotions, make sense of them, and learn to manage them. Most important, and most difficult, the grieving person must adjust to life without the deceased without losing

bereavement The process of coping with the sense of loss that follows death.

grief The affective response to bereavement that includes distress and an intense array of emotions such as hurt, anger, and guilt.

mourning The ceremonies and rituals a culture prescribes for expressing bereavement.

• • Cultural Rituals Surrounding Death

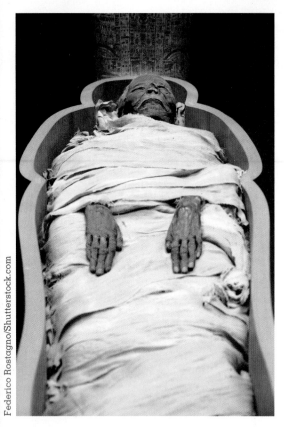

The ancient Egyptians preserved corpses as mummies and surrounded them with objects intended to assist them in the afterlife.

There is great variability in cultural views of the meaning of death and the rituals or other behaviors that express grief (Rosenblatt, 2008). Perhaps the most well-known death rituals were practiced by the ancient Egyptians. They believed that the body must be preserved through mummification in order to permanently house the spirit of the deceased in his or her new eternal life. The mummies were surrounded by valued objects and possessions and buried in elaborate tombs. Family members would regularly visit, bringing food and necessities to sustain them in the afterlife. Egyptian mummies are the most well-known, but mummies have been found in other parts of the world, such as the Andes mountains of Peru (Whitbourne, 2007).

The Bornu of Nigeria require family members to wash the deceased, wrap the body in a white cloth, and carry it to the burial ground (Cohen, 1967). In the French West Indies, the deceased's neighbors wash the body with rum, pour a liter or more of rum down the throat, and place the body on a bed (Horowitz, 1967).

In South Korea today, a small minority of people still choose to employ the services of a *mudang* (Korean "shaman") to conduct a lengthy ritual known as *Ogu Kut*, in which the *mudang* summons the deceased's spirit into the ritual space, expresses the latter's feelings of unhappiness through song, dance, and the spoken word, and encourages the bereaved to express their own grievances within symbolic psychodrama. Once the emotional ties between the bereaved and the deceased have been loosened, prayers for protection are offered to various deities, and the *mudang* guides the spirit towards the Buddhist paradise. Finally, the deceased's earthly possessions are cremated and the bereaved are left better able to move on in their lives (Mills, 2012).

Death rituals vary among religions. Among Hindus, a good death is a holy death, one that is welcomed by the dying person, who rests on the ground and is surrounded by family and friends chanting prayers (Dennis, 2008). Buddhists believe that the dying person's task is to gain insight. Death is not an end, as the individual will be reincarnated in the hopes of reaching nirvana, an ultimate, perfect state of enlightenment. Among Jews, the dying person remains part of the community and is never left alone before or immediately after death. Christians generally believe that death is the entry to an eternity in heaven or hell, and thereby is an event to be welcomed (generally) or feared (rarely). In Islam, death is united with life, because it is believed that the achievements and concerns of this life are fleeting and everyone should be mindful and ready for death. Muslim death rituals, such as saying prayers and washing the body, aid in the dying person's transition to the afterlife.

What Do You Think?

1. In your view, what purpose do death rituals fulfill?

2. Given the ethnic and religious diversity in the United States, many people have opportunities to learn about different cultural and religious approaches to coping with death. What customs, if any, have you observed?

the attachment to him or her (Stroebe, Schut, & Boerner, 2010). He or she must adapt to the loss by establishing new patterns of behavior and redefining relationships with family and friends in light of the loss (Attig, 1996; Leming & Dickinson, 2016). The grieving person must construct a new sense of self that takes into account the loss of the deceased and how that loss has changed everyday life.

It was once believed that effective grieving required loosening emotional ties to the deceased, permitting the grieving person to "work through" the death (Buglass, 2010;

Federico Rostagno/Shutterstock.com

Wright & Hogan, 2008). During a period of mourning the survivor would sever attachments to the deceased and become ready for new relationships and attachments. Instead, in recent decades theorists have come to view the bereaved person's continued attachment to the deceased as normative and potentially adaptive in providing a sense of continuity despite loss (Stroebe et al., 2010). Attachment is illustrated in several behaviors common among the bereaved, such as feeling that the deceased is watching over them, keeping the deceased's possessions, and talking about the deceased to keep his or her memory alive. Successful adaptation entails moving toward abstract manifestations of attachment, such as thoughts and memories, and away from concrete manifestations such as possessions (Field, Gal-Oz, & Bonanno, 2003). The deceased remains in mind, however. Grieving appears to involve learning to live with loss, rather than getting over loss.

MODELS OF GRIEVING

Although people vary in how they experience loss, some theorists posit phases or stages in grieving that are similar to the stages of emotional adjustment to death posited by Kübler-Ross (1969). People may traverse through several phases of mourning from shock, to intense grieving, to establishing a sense of balance, accommodating the loss into one's sense of being (Buglass, 2010; Wright & Hogan, 2008). For example, the initial reaction to loss is most often shock, a feeling of being dazed, detached, or stunned by the loss. As the person realizes the magnitude of loss, intense feelings of despair arise. The bereaved person may question their sense of self in light of the loss. With persistence the person begins to find a way of living without the loved one. Life will never be the same, but a "new normal" is created. Phases of mourning are useful in describing common reactions to loss; however, they represent a generalization and perhaps oversimplification of the process (Stroebe, Schut, & Boerner, 2017). The progression through grief is not linear; steps do not always occur in sequence and there is no universal timeframe for processing grief (Maciejewski, Zhang, Block, & Prigerson, 2007).

Other theorists view mourning as a set of tasks to accomplish. The bereaved person must accept the reality of the loss, experience the pain of grief, adjust to a life without the deceased and develop a new life while maintaining an enduring connection to the deceased (Howarth, 2011; Moos, 1994; Stroebe et al., 2010). Completing the first task, overcoming the initial sense of denial of the reality of the loss, may be especially difficult if the death was sudden or if the deceased lived far away. As the individual accepts the reality, the pain of grief can become overwhelming. Successfully managing this task requires finding ways of experiencing the pain that are not paralyzing, realizing that grief is to be expected. Adjusting to life without the deceased means that the individual must manage the practical details of life, identify the roles that the deceased filled in the relationship and household, and come to terms with the fact that he or she will no longer fill those roles. For example, children require care even after a parent has died; the surviving spouse must adjust to this reality and determine how to fulfill the roles of the deceased partner. Fulfilling these roles can help many bereaved adapt productively by developing new skills and growing (Jozefowski, 1999). The final task of mourning is to establish a new life that recognizes the enduring connection to the deceased, who will not be forgotten. This is often experienced as particularly challenging because the bereaved may not want to "move on," and may even feel it is disloyal to do so, but successful grieving entails learning how to live life without the physical presence of the deceased (Leming & Dickinson, 2016).

An alternative view of adaptation to loss emphasizes the stresses that accompany grief. According to the **dual-process model**, bereavement is accompanied by two types of stressors (Stroebe & Schut, 2010). The first is loss oriented and comprises the emotional aspects of grief that accompany the loss of an attachment figure, such managing emotions and breaking ties to the deceased (Stroebe, Schut, & Stroebe, 2005). Restoration-oriented

dual-process model A model of the brain consisting of two systems, one emotional and the other rational, that develop on different timeframes, accounting for typical adolescent behavior.

LIFESPAN BRAIN DEVELOPMENT

● ● Grief and the Brain

© iStockPhoto.com/KatarzynaBialasiewicz

The experience of grief might be described as stifling; it's a metaphorical weight dulling one's senses and thought. Grief is associated with a variety of cognitive changes, such as reductions in attention, memory, processing speed, and verbal fluency (Rosnick, Small, & Burton, 2010; Ward, Mathias, & Hitchings, 2007). In one study, individuals experiencing symptoms of grief were less able than nonbereaved individuals to regulate their attention in response to reminders of the deceased, and they showed attentional biases toward words that were associated with the deceased, as compared with other words (Freed, Yanagihara, Hirsch, & Mann, 2009). The strength of the attentional bias was associated with increased amygdala activity. Mourners showed reduced connectivity between regions of the brain that regulate attention and the amygdala, suggesting less control over their cognitive responses to emotional stimuli.

More serious and enduring grief is known as *complicated grief*, which includes persistent intense longing for and disruptive preoccupation with thoughts of the deceased (Shear, Frank, Houck, & Reynolds, 2005). These symptoms are prominent and elevated at 6 months and more after the loss. In one study, compared with either normal-grief or no-grief groups, participants with complicated grief performed worse in domains of executive function and information processing speed and had a lower total brain volume, as measured by structural brain imaging (Saavedra Pérez et al., 2015).

The stress that accompanies grief may influence cognitive and brain function. Adult neurogenesis has been shown to occur primarily in the hippocampus, an area responsible for learning and memory (Mirescu & Gould, 2006; Schoenfeld & Gould, 2013). The hippocampus is richly endowed with receptors sensitive to glucocorticoids, which are hormones that are released in response to stress; glucocorticoids play a role in regulating neurogenesis in adults (Egeland, Zunszain, & Pariante, 2015). In addition to its effects on the hippocampus, stress is thought to influence many neural processes, such as the maintenance of dendrites, neurotransmission, and overall plasticity (Mirescu & Gould, 2006; Schoenfeld & Gould, 2013). The stress that accompanies bereavement influences the emotional experience of grief and has neurological consequences with the potential to impair cognition.

What Do You Think?

How might the experience of grief illustrate the lifespan principle that domains of development interact? What might be some implications of this principle for helping bereaved individuals?

stressors represent secondary losses; these are the life changes that accompany the death, such as moving to a different residence, social isolation, establishing new roles, and managing practical details, such as paperwork. At any given time the grieving person may focus on the loss-oriented stressors or the life changes that comprise the restoration-oriented stressors. Healthy adjustment is promoted by alternating focus between the two types. When the person is able, he or she confronts the losses, yet at other times the person may set that task aside to instead consider restoration (Stroebe & Schut, 2010). In this way the grieving person adaptively copes as he or she is able, gradually moving forward. However, some bereaved individuals experience *overload*, the feeling that he or she has too much to deal with—whether too many losses, too many stimuli, too many stressors—and this can interfere with the grieving process (Stroebe & Schut, 2016).

CONTEXTUAL INFLUENCES ON THE GRIEF PROCESS

No two deaths are experienced in the same way. Deaths are interpreted and grieved differently based on a variety of factors, such as the age of the deceased, the nature of the death, and age of the bereaved. The death of a child or young adult is grieved more intensely and is viewed as more catastrophic than that of an older adult (Jecker, 2011). Younger and older adults judge a 19-year-old victim of a fatal car accident as a more tragic and unjust death than that of a 79-year-old victim (Chasteen & Madey, 2003). The young are grieved more intensely as they are viewed as robbed of the chance to experience significant life events such as falling in love or becoming a parent. They are not able to set and fulfill dreams. Generally, off time deaths, especially those that occur much before our expectations are particularly difficult (Moos, 1994).

The nature of the death influences how it is experienced and the grief process. Sudden, unexpected deaths are particularly challenging. Mourners are unprepared, with no support group in place. Many feel intense guilt and the need to assign blame and responsibility for accidental deaths. There often is no chance to say goodbye or mend relationships. Anger is a common reaction, especially if the deceased contributed to his or her demise through poor decisions. Traumatic deaths, such as from natural or man-made disasters, can leave losses that are difficult to make sense of. Feeling that a death is traumatic is associated with increase grief, depression, and loneliness (Tang & Chow, 2017).

When death is the result of a prolonged illness, it is no surprise, yet it is still a source of grief. Some theorists have posited the existence of anticipatory grief, feelings of loss that begin before a death occurs but are not fully realized (Fulton, Madden, & Minichiello, 1996; Fulton & Gottesman, 1980; Rando, 1988). People grieve losses as they happen. For example, a spouse of a terminally ill patient might grieve the parenting help or physical intimacy that they have already lost and anticipate losing the relationship itself. Each loss generates its own grief reaction and mourning process. Knowing that death is to come permits the dying to make decisions, tie loose ends, and strengthen relationships. Although many people believe that having the time and opportunity to prepare for loss will find it less distressing, research suggests that this is not true (Siegel & Weinstein, 2008; Sweeting & Gilhooly, 1990). All deaths are stressful, just in different ways.

ADJUSTING TO THE DEATH OF A LOVED ONE

Grieving is influenced by the relationship between the person and the deceased. Much of the literature on bereavement stems from comes from studying those who have lost a spouse.

Losing a Spouse

The term **widowhood** refers to the status of a person who has lost a spouse through death and has not remarried. About one third of U.S. older adults over the age of 65 are widowed. Women who have lost a spouse (widows) live longer than men (widowers) and are less likely to remarry. Thirty-five percent of women over the age of 65 are widowed, as compared with 11% of men (Administration on Aging, 2014). Losing a spouse begins one of the most stressful transitions in life. Widows have lost the person closest to them, a source of companionship, support, status, and income. Widowhood poses a challenge of renegotiating a sense of identity in light of the loss of the role of spouse, often the most long-lasting intimate role held in life (Lund & Caserta, 2001; Lund, Caserta, Dimond, & Gray, 1986). The identity development task posed by the loss of a spouse is to construct a sense of self that is separate from the spouse (Cheek, 2010; Naef, Ward, Mahrer-Imhof, & Grande, 2013). As in earlier periods of life, women who have myriad roles apart from spouse tend to fare better in adjusting to the death of a spouse than do women who have few roles, predominantly centered on their husbands. After becoming a widow, most older adults live alone, often in the same home. Those who relocate often do so for financial reasons and they tend to move closer to children and grandchildren, yet retain a separate residence.

Perhaps the greatest challenge to adjustment widows and widowers face is loneliness (Kowalski & Bondmass, 2008; Pinquart, 2003). Although widowhood marks the loss of a confidant, older adults often maintain and even increase their social participation following spousal loss (Donnelly & Hinterlong, 2010; Isherwood, King, & Luszcz, 2012).

widowhood Refers to the status of a person who has lost a spouse through death and has not remarried.

The greatest challenge to widowhood, more common among women, is loneliness, followed by financial concerns.

In one study in the Netherlands, older adults experienced increased contact and support, especially from their children and siblings, during the first 2 years of widowhood, but the amount of contact and support began to decrease about 2.5 years after the spouse's death (Guiaux, van Tilburg, & van Groenou, 2007). Other research showed stability in the level of social support received over the 2 years after the loss of a spouse (Powers, Bisconti, & Bergeman, 2014). A prospective study followed widowed adults over an 18-month period and found that close social relationships tended to remain stable, but widowhood brought both losses and gains in social support, which influenced adaptation (Ha, 2010). Specifically, the quality and continuity of support provided by children influences adaptation to spousal loss. Adults who perceived positive support (such as feeling loved, cared for, and heard) from their children 6 months after the death of their spouse showed few depressive symptoms 18 months later. In contrast, negative support (e.g., feeling that children are too demanding or critical) that remains steady, increases, or is accompanied by declines in positive support over time is associated with anger and symptoms of depression and anxiety (Ha, 2010). Maintaining close relationships with family and friends gives widows a sense of continuity which aids in adjusting to their loss.

Compared with their functioning prior to the loss of a spouse, bereaved adults show increased levels of depression, anxiety, stress, as well as poorer performance on cognitive tests measuring attention, processing speed, and memory (Rosnick, Small, & Burton, 2010; Ward, Mathias, & Hitchings, 2007). The prevalence of anxiety and depression is especially elevated in the first year after the loss of a spouse, with about 22% of newly widowed individuals meeting the diagnostic criteria for major depression (Onrust & Cuijpers, 2006). Social interaction, and especially helping others, aids in reducing depressive symptoms. Specifically, widowed adults who help others by providing instrumental support show an associated decline in depressive symptoms for 6 months to 18 months following spousal loss (Brown, Brown, House, & Smith, 2008). Depression declines with time (Powers et al., 2014), and men and women typically return to pre-widowhood mood levels within 24 months of being widowed (Sasson & Umberson, 2014).

Widowhood also poses risks to physical health. The increased likelihood for a recently widowed person to die, often called the **widowhood effect**, is one of the best documented examples of the relationship between social relations and health (Elwert & Christakis, 2008). The widowhood effect has been found among men and women of all ages throughout the world. Widowhood increases survivors' risk of dying from almost all causes (Subramanian, Elwert, & Christakis, 2008). One study of Norwegian adults found that the rate of mortality was highest for adults in late midlife (55–64); generally the risk for death declined over time after the spousal loss, but it remained high 7 years later (Brenn & Ytterstad, 2016).

Recent analyses put the excess mortality of widowhood (compared with marriage) among the elderly between 40% and 50% in the first 6 months (Moon, Kondo, Glymour, & Subramanian, 2011). However, the cause of spousal death matters. The mortality rate for widowed adults following spouses' death from Alzheimer's disease or Parkinson's disease is lower, suggesting that anticipatory grief may provide a buffer from the widowhood effect (Elwert & Christakis, 2008). This suggests that it may be the predictability of the death rather than the duration of the spouse's terminal illness that shields the survivor from some of the adverse consequences of bereavement.

Losing a spouse poses risks to mental and physical health for both men and women, but men tend to show more health problems, including an increased risk for dementia, and higher rates of mortality (Bennett, Hughes, & Smith, 2005; Gerritsen et al., 2017; Pinquart, 2003). Men tend to sustain a high level of depression 6 to 10 years after losing a spouse (Jadhav & Weir, 2017). In addition, widowers of all ages are at higher risk of suicide than their married counterparts (Erlangsen, Jeune, Bille-Brahe, & Vaupel, 2004;

widowhood effect Refers to the increased likelihood for a windowed person to die, illustrating the relationship between social relations and health.

Luoma & Pearson, 2002). Men often rely on their spouses for maintaining relationships with friends and family, managing household tasks, and assistance in coping with stress and managing emotions—and when the wife is no longer present to fulfill these roles, men tend to have difficulty asking for assistance (Lund & Caserta, 2001). Widowers are more likely to remarry than are widows, partly because there are far more single elderly women than men, but also because men have fewer social outlets and sources of support than women (Carr, 2004b).

The degree to which a spouse adapts to widowhood is influenced by a variety of factors, such as the circumstances surrounding the spouse's death and his or her age (McNamara & Rosenwax, 2010). Death of a spouse following a long illness such as cancer or Alzheimer's disease can evoke complex emotional responses because such illnesses involve drastic physical and mental deterioration and intense demands for caregiving (Rossi Ferrario, Cardillo, Vicario, Balzarini, & Zotti, 2004). In such cases, in addition to loss, the spouse may feel relief from watching a partner slip away and from the pressures of caregiving (Bonanno, Wortman, & Nesse, 2004). The complex intermingling of sorrow and relief may be confusing and the widowed spouse may feel guilty. Losing a spouse in young or middle adulthood is likely experienced very differently than in old age; however, there is little research on off-time widowhood. Unfulfilled roles, unfinished business, and an unlived life can make adjusting to an early widowhood especially difficult. Younger widowed adults likely have been married fewer years than older widowed adults, and they probably have greater responsibilities for dependent children and jobs. These responsibilities can be stressful, but on the positive side, children and coworkers may provide comfort and emotional support to young widowed adults.

Adults vary in the degree to which they show resilience in the face of a partner's death. Personal characteristics influence how people manage the transition to widowhood. Those who are outgoing, have high self-esteem, and a high sense of perceived self-efficacy in managing tasks of daily living tend to fare best (Carr, 2004a; McCrae & Costa, 1988; Moore & Stratton, 2002). One study of Australian adults who experienced spousal loss found that although about two-thirds showed increased life satisfaction over time, only 19% and 26% of individuals showed resilience with regard to negative affect (e.g., feeling down, worn out, tired, or unable to be cheered) and positive affect (feeling full of life, energetic, peaceful, or happy), respectively (Infurna & Luthar, 2017b). About one-third appeared to be resilient in terms of self-reported health and physical functioning. Very few adults showed resilience across all domains and about 20% were not resilient in any domain, suggesting that losing a spouse may pose lifelong challenges to physical and emotional health (Infurna & Luthar, 2017b).

Losing a Child

The most difficult of deaths to grieve is the loss of a child. It violates the perceived order of natural life and compromises the continuity of the family life cycle. Parenthood is a developmental achievement that provides a sense of purpose and engenders a sense of identity in people (Salmela-Aro, Nurmi, Saisto, & Halmesmäki, 2000; Smith, 2007). For parents, the loss of a child entails the loss of self and the loss of hopes and dreams for the child and the future (Wijngaards-de Meij et al., 2008). Parents grieve what could have been and what did not occur, the life their child did not have. In this way they lack a sense of closure (Woodgate, 2006).

Research suggests that the age of the child has little effect on the severity of the grief. Parents, especially mothers, often experience severe grief after miscarriages, still births, or the loss of a young infant (Adolfsson, 2011; Lang et al., 2011; Robinson, 2014). Parents of neonates and young infants grieve for the infant and the lost attachment, but also the lack of memories and being robbed of the opportunity to become a parent (Avelin, Rådestad, Säflund, Wredling, & Erlandsson, 2013; Cacciatore, 2010). Parents of children of all ages mourn unfulfilled dreams, unfinished tasks, and the resulting void in the family.

Guilt is a common response to losing a child (Leming & Dickinson, 2016). Parents may question their adequacy in providing care. This is especially true if the death resulted from a preventable accident, or when the causes of death are not understood, as in cases of Sudden Infant Death Syndrome (Corr & Corr, 2013). Loss of a child is associated with short- and long-term problems in physical health, mental health, and even mortality (Rogers, Floyd, Seltzer, Greenberg, & Hong, 2008; Song, Floyd, Seltzer, Greenberg, & Hong, 2010).

Bereaved parents tend to experience grief over a longer period than other bereaved people, with grief symptoms often lasting throughout the remainder of the parent's life (Keesee, Currier, & Neimeyer, 2008; Rogers et al., 2008). Parents often have difficulty finding meaning in their loss as the loss of a child is often perceived as "senseless" (Keesee et al., 2008; Wheeler, 2001). Transforming their identity as parent represents a crisis as adults must reshape their sense of purpose, identity, and legacy (De Vries, Lana, & Falck, 1994). Parents typically struggle with this task for years, if not a lifetime. One study of 156 bereaved parents (on average, about 6 years after the child's death) found that only about half found a sense of meaning in the death (Lichtenthal, Currier, Neimeyer, & Keesee, 2010). While about half of bereaved parents might show a reduction in negative affect over time, less than half report high levels of life satisfaction, about one third report good health, and a fifth or less report positive affect and physical functioning (Infurna & Luthar, 2017a). Mourning a child appears to be a lifelong event for most parents (Keesee et al., 2008).

Losing a Parent

Most adults expect their parents to precede them in death, yet even the expected death of a parent is difficult (Marks, Jun, & Song, 2007; Moss, Resch, & Moss, 1997). It is the loss of a lifelong relationship, attachment, and shared experiences. Adult children who acted as caregivers for their parents have devoted much time and energy to care for their parent, often reorganizing their lives in order to provide care (Weitzner, Haley, & Chen, 2000). The loss of parent may cause further household upheaval and the adult child may be unprepared to redirect his or her attention, efforts, and time (Hebert, Dang, & Schulz, 2006). Feelings of guilt and fear that one has not provided adequate care may be combined and heightened if the adult child felt overburdened by the level of care. Adult children may mourn lost opportunities to improve relationships and make amends for unfinished business.

Lives in Context Video 16.2
Dealing With a Parent's Death

The loss of a parent influences adults' sense of self. It often enhances adults' feelings of mortality as the loss of parents marks adult children as the oldest generation (Douglas, 1991). The parents are no longer the buffer or generational protection against old age and death. The death of a parent often sparks a shift in development, causing adult children to alter their sense of selves and realize their responsibilities to others. In this way, it can impart a sense of generativity to the next generation (Umberson, 2003; Umberson & Chen, 1994). Some adults experience tension between grieving their parents' death and facing one's own death and their own grief over perceived lost opportunities.

Death of a parent influences sibling relationships. They must reevaluate the meaning of family and their roles without the grounding role of their parents. The pattern of sibling relationships over the lifespan tends to intensify, such that good relationships often get better and, without the parent, poor relationships may worsen or disrupt. A parents' death changes the fabric of family relations.

BEREAVEMENT IN CHILDHOOD AND ADOLESCENCE

Losing a loved one in childhood or adolescence brings special challenges to the process of mourning. Cognitive and socioemotional development influence how children and adolescents understand, make sense of, and adjust to loss.

Bereavement in Childhood

Like adults, children's experience grief is influenced by the deceased's role in their life. Children's grief is uniquely affected by their developmental level, including cognitive and socioemotional development, as well as their understanding of the nature of death (Baker, Sedney, & Gross, 1992; Corr, 2010b; Jay, Green, Johnson, Caldwell, & Nitschke, 1987b). Children's first experience with death is often that of a grandparent. How this affects the child depends on their proximity and contact with the grandparent. Children with close relationships to grandparents, who experience their grandparents as caregivers and sources of unconditional love, are more likely to find death traumatic than are children whose grandparents live far away and with whom they have less contact. Many children find seeing parents and other adults upset distressing, perhaps increasing their sense of loss. However, there are no rules for children's grief (Leming & Dickinson, 2016).

Bereaved children often experience guilt. Many wonder if they caused the death to happen or if the loved one "went away" because of them. The degree to which children feel and express the fear that the death is somehow their fault varies with development (Wolfelt, 2013). This fear is most commonly and openly expressed by young children who are least able to understand the nature of death, but even older children worry. This is especially true in the case of sudden and accidental deaths. Children also worry about who will take care of them. If they conceptualize death as magic, they may fear that they are in danger. In cases of natural disasters and terror attacks children may feel worry about threats to themselves and their family. The replay of such disasters on television and in the media may intensify children's anxiety.

Bereaved children may experience grief for their parent for a longer period of time than do adults as they must grow up with the loss; their developmental milestones are affected and the death robs them of emotional support from caregivers (Baker et al., 1992; Wolfelt, 2013). Many children strive to maintain a connection to the deceased parent by talking to him or her, feeling that the parent is watching them, dreaming of the parent, and holding on to symbolic objects—particular dolls, pictures, or the parent's possessions.

Bereaved children need support, nurturance, and continuity in their lives. They need accurate information about the death and to have their fears addressed. Children want to know that they will be cared for. Adults should reassure children that they are not to blame, as well as provide support and listen (Corr & Corr, 2013). Children, especially younger children, will often require help in understanding and managing their conflicting emotions. Engaging in routine activities can help children gain a sense of normalcy despite all of the changes (Stokes, 2009). Adults should attempt to model healthy mourning by sharing their own grief and providing an example of how to experience grief in constructive ways (Saldinger, Porterfield, & Cain, 2014).

Bereavement in Adolescence

Adolescents' advancing cognitive abilities and their emerging sense of self influence how they grieve (Christ, Siegel, & Christ, 2002). Adolescents who lose their parents tend to feel intense loss, isolation, and the sense that the parent is irreplaceable and that loss cannot be overcome (Tyson-Rawson, 1996). Adolescents may be plagued by a strong sense that life is unfair. They are at risk to suffer social and interpersonal difficulties in adjustment, including internalizing symptoms such as

Adolescents tend to have mature conceptions about death, but their experience of grief is often influenced by their ability to understand and manage their own emotions.

anxiety and depression (Stikkelbroek, Bodden, Reitz, Vollebergh, & van Baar, 2016), yet often show a strong desire for others to include them and take interest in them (Meshot & Leitner, 1992). Many feel a strong presence of the deceased in dreams and in daily life, which can offer a sense of comfort and support (Meshot & Leitner, 1992).

Adolescents tend to have mature conceptions about death, but their experience of grief is often influenced by their ability to understand and manage their emotions as well as their experience of egocentric thought. The existence of the personal fable may lead them to view their grief as unique and incomprehensible—that others could not understand and certainly do not feel the way they do. Mourning adolescents commonly display intense emotional outbursts that are brief, but cyclical, punctuated by periods during which they resume normal activity (Christ et al., 2002; Noppe & Noppe, 1991). Alternatively, some adolescents may suppress their emotions altogether, out of fear of a loss of control (Robin & Omar, 2014). Adolescents may retreat into themselves, reading and listening to music, or they may act out, engaging in risky behaviors. With each developmental shift, adolescents must reinterpret the death in light of their new cognitive and emotional understanding (Brent, Melhem, Masten, Porta, & Payne, 2012; Noppe & Noppe, 2004).

The tasks of grieving intertwine and potentially interfere with the normative developmental tasks of adolescence, such as developing a sense of emotional autonomy as well as intimate relationships with friends (Brent et al., 2012; Robin & Omar, 2014). Adolescents who were concerned with establishing a sense of emotional autonomy prior to the parent's death may feel intense guilt. The grieving adolescent may find it challenging to develop a sense of autonomy while maintaining connection to the deceased parent, resulting in distress and often guilt. Grieving adolescents may feel that they are different from peers, and this "different" perception may impair their feelings of peer acceptance. They may also worry about how to act while grieving (Brent et al., 2012; Noppe & Noppe, 2004). Young adolescents who are concerned with peer acceptance may be reluctant to share their grief with friends, whereas middle and older adolescents who have formed intimate relationships with peers may find that support from friends can help them work through their pain (Dopp & Cain, 2012). However, if their friends do not understand their pain or are rejecting, the adolescent may be devastated and grieve not only the loss of the parent but of his or her friends too (Gray, 1989).

Bereaved adolescents need adults who are open to discussing whatever they would like to explore and who are careful listeners. Grieving adolescents commonly worry that will forget the person they have lost (Noppe & Noppe, 2004; Robin & Omar, 2014). Adults should attend to the feelings that underlie what the adolescent is saying and help the adolescent to understand that their feelings are important, real, and normal. Adults can help them to find ways to remember the deceased and make meaningful connections that retain their attachment with the deceased loved one.

 Thinking in Context 16.4

1. Identify factors within the person and context that may influence the degree and duration of grief. Explain these influences.

2. From your perspective, is the process of adjusting to the death of a loved one a continuous or discontinuous one? (Review these terms in Chapter 1.)

3. Much of what we know about bereavement comes from studying people who have lost a spouse. From your perspective, what are some of the challenges extending conclusions regarding widowhood to other forms of loss?

Death and loss are not easy topics to consider. We have seen that, regardless of age, both dying and grieving people have some common needs. All need to move past denial and accept the death, whether upcoming or having passed. Both the dying and grieving require help managing their emotional reactions to loss, including common physical reactions, such as stomach aches, headaches, and lethargy. People of all ages have a need to express their reactions to the loss and may need help identifying and articulating their reactions that may feel very strange and unfamiliar to them. Finally, the dying and the bereaved need to make some sense of the loss. The dying must connect to their loved ones and accept the loss. The bereaved, in turn, must find a way to maintain the connection to the deceased while moving on in their life, recognizing that in some ways they will never be the same.

 ## Apply Your Knowledge

Lying in bed, 88-year-old Margaret wakes and takes in her surroundings. Her daughter and granddaughter are in the room, one reading a magazine and the other reading her phone. Margaret is fortunate to have a private room in her nursing home, where she has been living since she suffered a stroke. Life here is better than she expected. The nurses are responsive, especially the kind night nurse who tells Margaret's daughter that she will check in often and does. The only thing Margaret doesn't like is that the nurses pressure her to socialize in the lounge each day. She'd rather sleep than be pushed out in her wheelchair to play games and watch television with the other elders. Her daughter urges her to eat, but she finds that she isn't very hungry anymore. Margaret feels lucky to have family who live nearby and visit very often. Margaret's children notice a change in their mother. She seems less sharp and each day seems a little bit more confused. She's often too tired to talk and drifts in and out of sleep.

With time, Margaret sleeps nearly all of the time. In addition to her stroke-related impairments, she has congestive heart failure, which is not responding to treatment. A few days before her 89th birthday, the doctors tell Margaret's daughter that the time is near.

Margaret's children and grandchildren gather in her room, waiting. They talk about old times and everyday life. Margaret is largely unconscious but now and then she calls out, moans, or talks to herself, reaching her arms out in front of her. As time goes on, her breathing becomes more labored and heavy, with occasional gasps. Margaret's children watch carefully and wait, attempting to talk with one another and retain a sense of normalcy. Finally, the room is quiet. Margaret's children know that she is gone. After 88 years and surrounded by family, Margaret has died.

1. What type of death trajectory does Margaret show? Explain your reasoning.

2. How might Margaret's 6-year-old grandchild understand her death? What might a child's grieving look like?

3. What would you expect from a 16-year-old grandchild?

4. How might children and adolescents' responses differ when considering a parent's death?

5. How might the adult child grieve for a parent?

CHAPTER 16 IN REVIEW

16.1 Discuss the ways in which death has been defined and end-of-life issues that may arise.

SUMMARY

Clinical death occurs when the heart stops beating. Advances in medicine have led to a definition of death as entailing whole brain death. Cortical death, but survival of the brainstem, is known as a persistent vegetative state. Advance directives, including a living will and durable power of attorney, permit individuals to make their wishes regarding end-of-life care known. Euthanasia refers to the practice of assisting terminally ill people in dying naturally. Physician-assisted suicide occurs when the terminally ill patient makes the conscious decision that they want their life to end and seeks assistance from a physician.

KEY TERMS

persistent vegetative state (PVS)
dying with dignity
living will
durable power of attorney
euthanasia
passive euthanasia

active euthanasia
physician-assisted suicide
hospice
clinical death
palliative care
whole brain death

REVIEW QUESTIONS

1. What are three ways of defining death?
2. What is a persistent vegetative state?
3. What is dying with dignity? What are ways of controlling one's end-of-life care?

16.2 Contrast child, adolescent, and adult understandings of death.

SUMMARY

Young children tend to view death as temporary and reversible. Children's understanding of death gradually emerges alongside cognitive development. The understanding that death is final, irreversible, and inevitable typically emerge between 5 and 7 years of age. Biological causality is the most complex element of the death concept and emerges as early as 6 or 7, but more typically in late childhood and is mastered by about age 10. Children who have direct, personal experience of death tend to show a more advanced understanding of death than their peers. Most adolescents evidence a mature conception of death, as the inevitable and irreversible end

of biological processes yet they often have difficulty appreciating it as an inevitability for themselves. Adolescents and adults across cultures often share a belief in an afterlife, whether religious or supernatural in origin. Conceptions of death change in subtle ways over the course of adulthood. Young adults begin to apply their mature understanding of death to themselves, acknowledging their own vulnerability. The awareness of death can cause midlife adults to reevaluate their priorities, often leading them to pursue a sense of generativity. Older adults experience less anxiety about death than younger adults.

REVIEW QUESTIONS

1. How do children and adolescents' understanding of death reflect their cognitive development?
2. What is a mature concept of death?
3. How do conceptions of death change over adulthood?

16.3 Describe the physical and emotional process of death as it is experienced over the lifespan.

KEY TERM

dying trajectory

SUMMARY

There are predictable changes and symptoms that occur in the dying person hours and days before death, but people vary in the number and severity of symptoms. People tend to show a range of emotional reactions to the knowledge that they are dying, including denial, anger, bargaining, depression, and acceptance. Although described as stages, not everyone experiences all of them or proceeds through them at the same pace or in the same order.

Children who are dying tend to express fears of loneliness, separation, and abandonment. Adolescents' sense of invulnerability can lead some to deny their illness or the need for treatment. Dying adolescents mourn the future, and have a need live in the present and to be involved in planning treatment and decision making. Young adults often feel angry and that the world is unfair. Midlife adults tend to mourn losing the present, abandoning family. Dying midlife adults have a need to find ways to continue to meet their responsibilities to others after death. Older adults talk more about death, think about it more, have more experience with it, and are more likely to accept death and feel that it is the appropriate.

REVIEW QUESTIONS

1. What is the dying trajectory?

2. What are physiological and emotional processes associated with dying?

3. How do the concerns and needs of dying individuals differ with development? 1. What is the dying trajectory?

 16.4 Discuss typical grief reactions to the loss of loved ones and the influence of development on bereavement.

SUMMARY

Some theorists posit phases or stages in grieving that are similar to the stages of emotional adjustment to death. Other theorists view mourning as a set of tasks to accomplish. According to the dual-process model, bereavement is accompanied by loss-oriented stressors and restoration-oriented stressors. Healthy adjustment is promoted by alternating focus between the two types of stressors. Bereavement is associated with increased levels of depression, anxiety, stress, and poor performance on cognitive tests and poor health. Bereaved parents often experience grief symptoms

throughout their lives and often have difficulty finding meaning in their loss. Children's grief is uniquely affected by their cognitive and socioemotional development, as well as their understanding of the nature of death. Adolescents tend to have mature conceptions about death, but their experience of grief is often influenced by their ability to understand and manage their emotions, their experience of egocentric thought, and their emerging sense of self.

KEY TERMS

bereavement
mourning
widowhood effect

dual-process model
grief
widowhood

REVIEW QUESTIONS

1. Define bereavement, grief, and mourning.

2. What is the dual process model of bereavement?

3. How does the relationship of the person to the deceased influence the grief process?

4. What developmental factors influence children and adolescents' grief process?

Test your understanding of the content.
Review the flashcards and quizzes at
edge.sagepub.com/kuthertopical

Aalsma, M. C., Lapsley, D. K., & Flannery, D. J. (2006). Personal fables, narcissism, and adolescent adjustment. *Psychology in the Schools*, 43(4), 481–491.

AAP Committee on Psychosocial Aspects of Child and Family Health. (1998). Guidance for effective discipline. *Pediatrics*, 101, 723–728.

AAP Council on Communications and Media. (2016). Virtual violence. *Pediatrics*, 138(2). doi:10.1542/peds.2016-1298

AAP Task Force on Circumcision. (2012). Circumcision policy statement. *Pediatrics*, 130(3), 585–586. http://doi.org/10.1542/peds.2012-1989

Aarnoudse-Moens, C. S. H., Weisglas-Kuperus, N., van Goudoever, J. B., & Oosterlaan, J. (2009). Meta-analysis of neurobehavioral outcomes in very preterm and/or very low birth weight children. *Pediatrics*, 124(2), 717–728. http://doi.org/10.1542/peds.2008-2816

Aarsland, D., Sardahaee, F. S., Anderssen, S., & Ballard, C. (2010). Is physical activity a potential preventive factor for vascular dementia? A systematic review. *Aging & Mental Health*, 14(4), 386–395. http://doi.org/10.1080/13607860903586136

AAUW. (2017). *The simple truth about the gender pay gap*. Retrieved from http://www.aauw.org/research/the-simple-truth-about-the-gender-pay-gap/

Abajobir, A. A., Kisely, S., Maravilla, J. C., Williams, G., & Najman, J. M. (2017). Gender differences in the association between childhood sexual abuse and risky sexual behaviours: A systematic review and meta-analysis. *Child Abuse & Neglect*, 63, 249–260. http://doi.org/10.1016/j.chiabu.2016.11.023

Abbott-Shim, M., Lambert, R., & McCarty, F. (2003). A comparison of school readiness outcomes for children randomly assigned to a Head Start program and the program's wait list. *Journal of Education for Students Placed at Risk*, 8(2), 191–214.

Abdelhadi, R. A., Bouma, S., Bairdain, S., Wolff, J., Legro, A., Plogsted, S., . . . ASPEN Malnutrition Committee. (2016). Characteristics of hospitalized children with a diagnosis of malnutrition: United States, 2010. *Journal of Parenteral and Enteral Nutrition*, 40(5), 623–635. http://doi.org/10.1177/0148607116633800

Ablewhite, J., Peel, I., McDaid, L., Hawkins, A., Goodenough, T., Deave, T., . . . Kessel, A. (2015). Parental perceptions of barriers and facilitators to preventing child unintentional injuries within the home: A qualitative study. *BMC Public Health*, 15(1), 280. http://doi.org/10.1186/s12889-015-1547-2

Aboud, F. E., Mendelson, M. J., & Purdy, K. T. (2003). Cross-race peer relations and friendship quality. *International Journal of Behavioral Development*, 27(2), 165.

Aboud, F. E., Mendelson, M. J., & Purdy, K. T. (2007). Ethnic heterogeneity of social networks and cross-ethnic friendships of elementary school boys and girls. *Merrill-Palmer Quarterly*, 53(3), 325–346.

Abraham, L. M., Crais, E., & Vernon-Feagans, L. (2013). Early maternal language use during book sharing in families from low-income environments. *American Journal of Speech-Language Pathology/American Speech-Language-Hearing Association*, 22(1), 71–83. http://doi.org/10.1044/1058-0360(2012/11-0153)

Abrams, A. P. (2014). Physiology of aging of older adults: Systemic and oral health considerations. *Dental Clinics of North America*, 58(4), 729–738. http://doi.org/10.1016/j.cden.2014.06.002

Abubakar, A., Van de Vijver, F. J. R., Suryani, A. O., Handayani, P., & Pandia, W. S. (2014). Perceptions of parenting styles and their associations with mental health and life satisfaction among urban Indonesian adolescents. *Journal of Child and Family Studies*. http://doi.org/10.1007/s10826-014-0070-x

Abu-Raiya, H., Pargament, K. I., Krause, N., & Ironson, G. (2015). Robust links between religious/spiritual struggles, psychological distress, and well-being in a national sample of American adults. *American Journal of Orthopsychiatry*, 85(6), 565–575. http://doi.org/10.1037/ort0000084

Acar, E., Dursun, O. B., Esin, İ. S., Öğütlü, H., Özcan, H., & Mutlu, M. (2015). Unintentional injuries in preschool-age children: Is there a correlation with parenting style and parental attention deficit and hyperactivity symptoms? *Medicine*, 94(32), e1378. http://doi.org/10.1097/MD.0000000000001378

Accornero, V. H., Anthony, J. C., Morrow, C. E., Xue, L., Mansoor, E., Johnson, A. L., . . . Bandstra, E. S. (2011). Estimated effect of prenatal cocaine exposure on examiner-rated behavior at age 7 years. *Neurotoxicology and Teratology*, 33(3), 370–378. http://doi.org/10.1016/j.ntt.2011.02.014

Achté, K., Fagerström, R., Pentikäinen, J., & Farberow, N. L. (1989). Themes of death and violence in lullabies of different countries. *OMEGA Journal of Death and Dying*, 20(3), 193–204. http://doi.org/10.2190/A7YP-TJ3C-M9C1-JY45

Ackard, D. M., Fulkerson, J. A., & Neumark-Sztainer, D. (2011). Stability of eating disorder diagnostic classifications in adolescents: Five-year longitudinal findings from a population-based study. *Eating Disorders*, 19(4), 308–322. http://doi.org/10.1080/10640266.2011.584804

Ackerman, P. L., & Beier, M. E. (2006). Determinants of domain knowledge and independent study learning in an adult sample. *Journal of Educational Psychology*, 98(2), 366–381.

Ackerman, S., Zuroff, D. C., & Moskowitz, D. S. (2000). Generativity in midlife and young adults: Links to agency, communion, and subjective well-being. *International Journal of Aging & Human Development*, 50(1), 17–41. http://dx.doi.org/10.2190/9F51-LR6T-JHRJ-2QW6

Ackil, J. K., & Zaragoza, M. (1995). Developmental differences in eyewitness suggestibility and memory for source. *Journal of Experimental Child Psychology*, 60, 57–83.

Acredolo, L. P., & Goodwyn, S. W. (1985). Symbolic gesturing in language development. *Human Development*, 28(1), 40–49. http://doi.org/10.1159/10.1159/000272934

Acredolo, L. P., & Goodwyn, S. (1988). Symbolic gesturing in normal infants. *Child Development*, 59(2), 450–466.

Acredolo, L. P., Goodwyn, S., & Abrams, D. (2009). *Baby signs: How to talk with your baby before your baby can talk* (3rd ed.).

Adam, E. K., Snell, E. K., & Pendry, P. (2007). Sleep timing and quantity in ecological and family context: A nationally representative time-diary study. *Journal of Family Psychology*, 21(1), 4–19. http://doi.org/10.1037/0893-3200.21.1.4

Adams, G. A., Prescher, J., Beehr, T. A., & Lepisto, L. (2002). Applying work-role attachment theory to retirement decision making. *International Journal of Aging & Human Development*, 54(2), 125–137. http://doi.org/10.2190/JRUQ-XQ2N-UP0A-M432

Adams, K. B., Leibbrandt, S., & Moon, H. (2011). A critical review of the literature on social and leisure activity and well-being in later life. *Ageing & Society*, 31(4), 683–712. http://doi.org/10.1017/s0144686x10001091

Adams, R. E., & Laursen, B. (2007). The correlates of conflict: Disagreement is not necessarily detrimental. *Journal of Family Psychology*, 21(3), 445–458.

Adams-Chapman, I., Hansen, N. I., Shankaran, S., Bell, E. F., Boghossian, N. S., Murray, J. C., . . . Stoll, B. (2013). Ten-year review of major birth defects in VLBW infants. *Pediatrics*, 132(1), 49–61. http://doi.org/10.1542/peds.2012-3111

Adelabu, D. H. (2008). Future time perspective, hope, and ethnic identity among African American adolescents. *Urban Education*, 43(3), 347–360.

Adminstration on Aging. (2014). *A profile of older Americans: 2014*. Retrieved from http://www.aoa.acl.gov/Aging_Statistics/Profile/index.aspx

Adolfsson, A. (2011). Meta-analysis to obtain a scale of psychological reaction after perinatal loss: Focus on miscarriage. *Psychology Research and Behavior Management*, 4, 29–39. http://doi.org/10.2147/PRBM.S17330

Adolph, K. E., & Berger, S. E. (2005). Physical and motor development. In M. H. Bornstein & M. E. Lamb (Eds.), *Developmental science: An advanced textbook* (5th ed., pp. 223–281). Mahwah, NJ: Lawrence Erlbaum.

Adolph, K. E., Cole, W. G., Komati, M., Garciaguirre, J. S., Badaly, D., Lingeman, J. M., . . . Sotsky, R. B. (2012). How do you learn to walk? Thousands of steps and dozens of falls per day. *Psychological Science*, 23(11), 1387–94. http://doi.org/10.1177/0956797612446346

Adolph, K. E., & Franchak, J. M. (2017). The development of motor behavior. *Wiley Interdisciplinary Reviews: Cognitive Science*, 8(1–2), e1430. http://doi.org/10.1002/wcs.1430

Adolph, K. E., Kretch, K. S., & LoBue, V. (2014). Fear of heights in infants? *Current Directions in Psychological Science*, 23(1), 60–66. http://doi.org/10.1177/0963721413498895

Adolph, K. E., & Tamis-LeMonda, C. S. (2014). The costs and benefits of development: The transition from crawling to walking. *Child Development Perspectives*, 8(4), 187–192. http://doi.org/10.1111/cdep.12085

Adrián, J. E., Clemente, R. A., & Villanueva, L. (2007). Mothers' use of cognitive state verbs in picture-book reading and the development of children's understanding of mind: A longitudinal study. *Child Development*, 78(4), 1052–1067.

Afifi, T. O., & MacMillan, H. L. (2011). Resilience following child maltreatment: A review of protective factors. *La Résilience Aprés La Maltraitance Clans L'enfance: Une Revue Des Facteurs Protecteurs*, 56(5), 266–272.

Afifi, T. O., Mota, N., MacMillan, H. L., & Sareen, J. (2013). Harsh physical punishment in childhood and adult physical health. *Pediatrics*, 132(2).

Agerup, T., Lydersen, S., Wallander, J., & Sund, A. M. (2015). Associations between parental attachment and course of depression between adolescence and young adulthood. *Child Psychiatry & Human Development*, 46(4), 632–642. http://doi.org/10.1007/s10578-014-0506-y

Agrigoroaei, S., Lee-Attardo, A., & Lachman, M. E. (2016). Stress and subjective age: Those with greater financial stress look older. *Research on Aging*. http://doi.org/10.1177/0164027516658502

Agronin, M. E. (2014). *Alzheimer's disease and other dementias: A practical guide*. New York, NY: Routledge.

Agustines, L. A., Lin, Y. G., Rumney, P. J., Lu, M. C., Bonebrake, R., Asrat, T., & Nageotte, M. (2000). Outcomes of extremely low-birth-weight infants between 500 and 750 g. *American Journal of Obstetrics and Gynecology*, 182, 1114–1116.

Agyei, S. B., van der Weel, F. R. R., & van der Meer, A. L. H. (2016). Development of visual motion perception for prospective control: Brain and behavioral studies in infants. *Frontiers in Psychology*, 7, 100. http://doi.org/10.3389/fpsyg.2016.00100

Ahmed, A., & Ruffman, T. (1998). Why do infants make A not B errors in a search task, yet show memory for location of hidden objects in a non-search task? *Developmental Psychology*, 34, 441–453.

Ahmed, E. I., Zehr, J. L., Schulz, K. M., Lorenz, B. H., Don Carlos, L. L., & Sisk, C. L. (2008). Pubertal hormones modulate the addition of new cells to sexually dimorphic brain regions. *Nature Neuroscience, 11*(9), 995–997. https://doi.org/10.1038/nn.2178

Ahnert, L., Pinquart, M., & Lamb, M. E. (2006). Security of children's relationships with nonparental care providers: A meta-analysis. *Child Development, 77*(3), 664–679. http://doi.org/10.1111/j.1467-8624.2006.00896.x

Ahrons, C. R. (2007). Family ties after divorce: Long-term implications for children. *Family Process, 46*(1), 53–65. http://doi.org/10.1111/j.1545-5300.2006.00191.x

Aiello, L. C., & Dunbar, R. I. M. (1993). Neocortex size, group size, and the evolution of language. *Current Anthropology, 34*(2), 184–193. http://doi.org/10.1086/204160

Aigner, T., Haag, J., Martin, J., & Buckwalter, J. (2007). Osteoarthritis: Aging of matrix and cells—going for a remedy. *Current Drug Targets, 8*(2), 325–331. http://doi.org/10.2174/138945007779940070

Ainsworth, M. D. S. (1974). Citation for the G. Stanley Hall Award to John Bowlby. *American Psychological Association Newsletter, 3,* 55–64.

Ainsworth, M. D. S., Blehar, M. C., Waters, E., & Wall, S. (1978). *Patterns of attachment.* Hillsdale, NJ: Lawrence Erlbaum.

Ajdacic-Gross, V., Horvath, S., Canjuga, M., Gamma, A., Angst, J., Rössler, W., & Eich, D. (2006). How ubiquitous are physical and psychological complaints in young and middle adulthood? *Social Psychiatry & Psychiatric Epidemiology, 41*(11), 881–888.

Akhtar, N., Jipson, J., & Callanan, M. A. (2001). Learning words through overhearing. *Child Development, 72,* 416–430.

Akolekar, R., Beta, J., Picciarelli, G., Ogilvie, C., & D'Antonio, F. (2015). Procedure-related risk of miscarriage following amniocentesis and chorionic villus sampling: A systematic review and meta-analysis. *Ultrasound in Obstetrics & Gynecology, 45*(1), 16–26. http://doi.org/10.1002/uog.14636

Akos, P., Rose, R. A., & Orthner, D. (2014). Sociodemographic moderators of middle school transition effects on academic achievement. *The Journal of Early Adolescence, 35*(2), 170–198. http://doi.org/10.1177/0272431614529367

Alaimo, K., Olson, C. M., & Frongillo Jr., E. A. (2001). Food insufficiency and American school-aged children's cognitive, academic, and psychosocial development. *Pediatrics, 108,* 44–53.

Alanis, M. C., & Lucidi, R. S. (2004). Neonatal circumcision: A review of the world's oldest and most controversial operation. *Obstetrical and Gynecological Survey, 59*(5), 379–395.

Alarcón-Rubio, D., Sánchez-Medina, J. A., & Prieto-García, J. R. (2014). Executive function and verbal self-regulation in childhood: Developmental linkages between partially internalized private speech and cognitive flexibility. *Early Childhood Research Quarterly, 29*(2), 95–105. http://doi.org/10.1016/j.ecresq.2013.11.002

Alati, R., Davey Smith, G., Lewis, S. J., Sayal, K., Draper, E. S., Golding, J., . . . Gray, R. (2013). Effect of prenatal alcohol exposure on childhood academic outcomes: Contrasting maternal and paternal associations in the ALSPAC study. *PloS One, 8*(10), e74844. http://doi.org/10.1371/journal.pone.0074844

Albers, E. M., Riksen-Walraven, J. M., & de Weerth, C. (2010). Developmental stimulation in child care centers contributes to young infants' cognitive development. *Infant Behavior & Development,* 33(4), 401–408. http://doi.org/10.1016/j.infbeh.2010.04.004

Albers, L. H., Johnson, D. E., Hostetter, M. K., Iverson, S., & Miller, L. C. (1997). Health of children adopted from the former Soviet Union and Eastern Europe: Comparison with preadoptive medical records. *Journal of American Medical Association, 278,* 922–924.

Albert, D., Chein, J., & Steinberg, L. (2013). The teenage brain: Peer influences on adolescent decision making. *Current Directions in Psychological Science.* http://doi.org/10.1177/0963721412471347

Alberts, A., Elkind, D., & Ginsberg, S. (2007). The personal fable and risk-taking in early adolescence. *Journal of Youth & Adolescence, 36*(1), 71–76.

Aldwin, C. M. (2007). *Stress, coping, and development: An integrative perspective* (2nd ed.). New York, NY: Guilford Press.

Aldwin, C. M., & Levenson, M. R. (2001). Stress, coping, and health at midlife: A developmental perspective. In M. E. Lachman (Ed.), *Handbook of midlife development* (pp. 188–214). Hoboken, NJ: John Wiley & Sons.

Aldwin, C. M., Spiro, A. I., & Park, C. (2006). Health, behavior, and optimal aging: A life span developmental perspective. In J. E. Birren & K. W. Schaire (Eds.), *Handbook of the psychology of aging* (6th ed., pp. 85–104). Amsterdam, NL: Elsevier.

Alexander, G. M., & Wilcox, T. (2012). Sex differences in early infancy. *Child Development Perspectives, 6*(4), 400–406.

Alexander, G. M., Wilcox, T., & Woods, R. (2009). Sex differences in infants' visual interest in toys. *Archives of Sexual Behavior, 38*(3), 427–433. http://doi.org/10.1007/s10508-008-9430-1

Alexander, G. R., & Slay, M. (2002). Prematurity at birth: Trends, racial disparities, and epidemiology. *Mental Retardation and Developmental Disabilities, 8,* 215–220.

Alexander, K. L., Entwisle, D. R., & Kabbani, N. S. (2001). The dropout process in life course perspective: Early risk factors at home and school. *Teachers College Record, 103,* 760–822.

Alferink, L. A., & Farmer-Dougan, V. (2010). Brain-(not) based education: Dangers of misunderstanding and misapplication of neuroscience research. *Exceptionality, 18*(1), 42–52. http://doi.org/10.1080/09362830903462573

Alfieri, T., Ruble, D. N., & Higgins, E. T. (1996). Gender stereotypes during adolescence: Developmental changes and the transition to junior high school. *Developmental Psychology, 32*(6), 1129–1137. http://doi.org/10.1037/0012-1649.32.6.1129

Ali, A., Ambler, G., Strydom, A., Rai, D., Cooper, C., McManus, S., . . . Stewart-Brown, S. (2013). The relationship between happiness and intelligent quotient: The contribution of socio-economic and clinical factors. *Psychological Medicine, 43*(6), 1303–1312. http://doi.org/10.1017/S0033291712002139

Alisat, S., & Pratt, M. W. (2012). Characteristics of young adults' personal religious narratives and their relation with the identity status model: A longitudinal, mixed methods study. *Identity, 12*(1), 29–52. http://doi.org/10.1080/15283488.2012.632392

Alivernini, F., & Lucidi, F. (2011). Relationship between social context, self-efficacy, motivation, academic achievement, and intention to drop out of high school: A longitudinal study. *The Journal of Educational Research, 104*(4), 241–252. http://doi.org/10.1080/00220671003728062

Allen, J. P., & Antonishak, J. (2008). Adolescent peer influences: Beyond the dark side. In M. J. Prinstein & K. A. Dodge (Eds.), *Understanding peer influence in children and adolescents* (pp. 141–160). New York, NY: Guilford Press.

Allen, J. P., Hauser, S. T., & Borman-Spurrell, E. (1996). Attachment theory as a framework for understanding sequelae of severe adolescent psychopathology: An 11-year follow-up study. *Journal of Consulting and Clinical Psychology, 64*(2), 254–263. http://doi.org/10.1037/0022-006X.64.2.254

Allen, J. P., & Miga, E. M. (2010). Attachment in adolescence: A move to the level of emotion regulation. *Journal of Social and Personal Relationships, 27*(2), 181–190. http://doi.org/10.1177/0265407509360898

Allen, S. E. M., & Crago, M. B. (1996). Early passive acquisition in Inukitut. *Journal of Child Language, 23,* 129–156.

Allen, S. F. (2003). Working parents with young children: Cross-national comparisons of policies and programmes in three countries. *International Journal of Social Welfare, 12*(4), 261. http://doi.org/10.1111/1467-9671.00281

Allison, A. C. (2004). Two lessons from the interface of genetics and medicine. *Genetics, 166*(4), 1591–1599.

Alloway, T. P., & Alloway, R. G. (2010). Investigating the predictive roles of working memory and IQ in academic attainment. *Journal of Experimental Child Psychology, 106*(1), 20–29. http://doi.org/10.1016/j.jecp.2009.11.003

Alma, M. A., van der Mei, S. F., Melis-Dankers, B. J. M., van Tilburg, T. G., Groothoff, J. W., & Suurmeijer, T. P. B. M. (2011). Participation of the elderly after vision loss. *Disability and Rehabilitation, 33*(1), 63–72. http://doi.org/10.3109/09638288.2010.488711

Almeida, D. M., Neupert, S. D., Banks, S. R., & Serido, J. (2005). Do daily stress processes account for socioeconomic health disparities? *Journals of Gerontology Series B: Psychological Sciences & Social Sciences, 60*(B), 34–39.

Almeida, J., Johnson, R. M., Corliss, H. L., Molnar, B. E., & Azrael, D. (2009). Emotional distress among LGBT youth: The influence of perceived discrimination based on sexual orientation. *Journal of Youth & Adolescence, 38*(7), 1001–1014. http://doi.org/10.1007/s10964-009-9397-9

Almeida, S., Rato, L., Sousa, M., Alves, M. G., & Oliveira, P. F. (2017). Fertility and sperm quality in the aging male. *Current Pharmaceutical Design.* http://doi.org/10.2174/1381612823666170503150313

Almy, B., Long, K., Lobato, D., Plante, W., Kao, B., & Houck, C. (2015). Perceptions of siblings' sexual activity predict sexual attitudes among at-risk adolescents. *Journal of Developmental and Behavioral Pediatrics, 36*(4), 258–266.

Al-Namlah, A. S., Meins, E., & Fernyhough, C. (2012). Self-regulatory private speech relates to children's recall and organization of autobiographical memories. *Early Childhood Research Quarterly, 27*(3), 441–446. http://doi.org/10.1016/j.ecresq.2012.02.005

Al-Owidha, A., Green, K. E., & Kroger, J. (2009). On the question of an identity status category order: Rasch model step and scale statistics used to identify category order. *International Journal of Behavioral Development, 33*(1), 88–96. http://doi.org/10.1177/0165025408100110

Al-Sahab, B., Ardern, C. I., Hamadeh, M. J., & Tamim, H. (2010). Age at menarche in Canada: results from the National Longitudinal Survey of Children & Youth. *BMC Public Health, 10*(1), 736. http://doi.org/10.1186/1471-2458-10-736

Alviola, P. A., Nayga, R. M., Thomsen, M. R., Danforth, D., & Smartt, J. (2014). The effect of fast-food restaurants on childhood obesity: A school level analysis. *Economics & Human Biology, 12,* 110–119. http://doi.org/10.1016/j.ehb.2013.05.001

REFERENCES

Alvord, M. K., & Grados, J. J. (2005). Enhancing resilience in children: A proactive approach. *Professional Psychology: Research and Practice*, 36(3), 238–245.

Alzheimer's Association. (2015). *2015 Alzheimer's disease facts and figures*. Retrieved from http://www.alz.org/facts/downloads/facts_figures_2015.pdf

Alzheimer's Association. (2017). 2017 Alzheimer's disease facts and figures. *Alzheimer's & Dementia*, 13(4), 325–373.

Alzheimer's Disease International. (2015). *World Alzheimer report 2014: Dementia and risk reduction*. Retrieved from http://www.alz.co.uk/research/world-report-2014

Amato, P. R. (1987). Family processes in one-parent, stepparent, and intact families: The child's point of view. *Journal of Marriage and the Family, 49*, 327–337.

Amato, P. R. (2010). Research on divorce: Continuing trends and new developments. *Journal of Marriage & Family, 72*(3), 650–666. http://doi.org/10.1111/j.1741-3737.2010.00723.x

Amato, P. R., & Anthony, C. J. (2014). Estimating the effects of parental divorce and death with fixed effects models. *Journal of Marriage and Family, 76*(2), 370–386. http://doi.org/10.1111/jomf.12100

Amato, P. R., & Irving, S. (2006). Historical trends in divorce in the United States. In M. A. Fine & J. H. Harvey (Eds.), *Handbook of divorce and relationship dissolution* (pp. 41–57). Mahwah, NJ: Lawrence Erlbaum.

Amato, P. R., Kane, J. B., & James, S. (2011). Reconsidering the "good divorce." *Family Relations, 60*(5), 511–524. http://doi.org/10.1111/j.1741-3729.2011.00666.x

Amato, P. R., & Sobolewski, J. M. (2001). The effects of divorce and marital discord on adult children's psychological well-being. *American Sociological Review, 66*, 900–921.

Amato, P. R., & Sobolewski, J. M. (2004). The effects of divorce on fathers and children: Nonresidential fathers and stepfathers. In M. E. Lamb (Ed.), *The role of the father in child development* (4th ed., pp. 341–367). Hoboken, NJ: John Wiley & Sons.

Ambwani, S., Thomas, K. M., Hopwood, C. J., Moss, S. A., & Grilo, C. M. (2014). Obesity stigmatization as the status quo: Structural considerations and prevalence among young adults in the U.S. *Eating Behaviors, 15*(3), 366–370. http://doi.org/10.1016/j.eatbeh.2014.04.005

Ameel, E., Verschueren, N., & Schaeken, W. (2007). The relevance of selecting what's relevant: A dual process approach to transitive reasoning with spatial relations. *Thinking & Reasoning, 13*(2), 164–167.

American Academy of Child and Adolescent Psychiatry. (2008). *Teen suicide. Facts for families*. Retrieved from http://www.aacap.org/galleries/FactsForFamilies/10_teen_suicide.pdf

American Academy of Ophthalmology. (2011). *Eye health statistics at a glance*. Retrieved from http://www.aao.org/newsroom/upload/Eye-Health-Statistics-April-2011.pdf

American Academy of Pediatrics. (2005). The changing concept of Sudden Infant Death Syndrome: Diagnostic coding shifts, controversies regarding the sleeping environment, and new variables to consider in reducing risk. *Pediatrics, 116*, 1245–1255.

American Academy of Pediatrics. (2013). Children, adolescents, and the media. *Pediatrics, 132*(5), 958–961. http://doi.org/10.1542/peds.2013-2656

American Academy of Pediatrics. (2017). *AAP agenda for children*. Retrieved from https://www.aap.org/en-us/about-the-aap/aap-facts/

AAP-Agenda-for-Children-Strategic-Plan/Pages/AAP-Agenda-for-Children-Strategic-Plan.aspx

American Academy of Pediatrics Committee on Infectious Diseases. (2015). Recommended childhood and adolescent immunization schedule: United States, 2015. *Pediatrics, 135*(2), 396–397. http://doi.org/10.1542/peds.2014-3955

American Academy of Pediatrics Council on Communications and Media. (2016). Media and young minds. *Pediatrics, 138*(5). Retrieved from http://pediatrics.aappublications.org/content/138/5/e20162591

American Academy of Pediatrics Task Force on Circumcision Policy. (1999). Circumcision policy statement. *Pediatrics, 103*, 686–693.

American Academy of Pediatrics Task Force on Infant Positioning and SIDS. (1992). Positioning and SIDS. *Pediatrics, 89*(6 Pt 1), 1120–1126. Retrieved from http://www.ncbi.nlm.nih.gov/pubmed/1503575

American Association of Retired Persons. (2002). *The Grandparent Study:2002 report*. Washington, DC: Author.

American Association of Retired Persons. (2008). *Update on the aged 55+ worker: 2007*. Washington, DC: Author.

American Association on Intellectual and Developmental Disabilities. (2009). *FAQ on intellectual disability*. Retrieved from http://www.aamr.org/content_104.cfm?navID=22

American Association on Intellectual and Developmental Disabilities. (2010). *Intellectual disability: Definition, classification, and systems of supports*. Washington, DC: Author.

American Diabetes Association. (2014). Standards of medical care in diabetes: 2014. *Diabetes Care, 37*(Suppl 1), S11-S66. http://doi.org/10.2337/dc13-S011

American Medical Association. (1999). *Neonatal circumcision*. Chicago: Author.

American Psychiatric Association. (2013). *Diagnostic and statistical manual of mental disorders* (5th ed.). Washington, DC: Author.

American Psychological Association. (2010). *Ethical principles of psychologists and code of conduct*. Washington, DC: Author. Retrieved from http://www.apa.org/ethics/code/principles.pdf

American Psychological Association. (2012). *Miller v. Alabama and Jackson v. Hobbs*. Retrieved from http://www.apa.org/about/offices/ogc/amicus/miller-hobbs.aspx

American Society of Plastic Surgeons. (2016). *2015 plastic surgery statistics report*. Retrieved from https://d2wirczt3b6wjm.cloudfront.net/News/Statistics/2015/plastic-surgery-statistics-full-report-2015.pdf

Amitay, E. L., Dubnov Raz, G., & Keinan-Boker, L. (2016). Breastfeeding, other early life exposures and childhood leukemia and lymphoma. *Nutrition and Cancer, 68*(6), 968–977. http://doi.org/10.1080/01635581.2016.1190020

Ammerman, S., Ryan, S., Adelman, W. P., The Committee on Substance Abuse, & The Committee on Adolescence. (2015). The impact of marijuana policies on youth: Clinical, research, and legal update. *Pediatrics, 135*(3), e769-85. http://doi.org/10.1542/peds.2014-4147

Ammons, S. K., & Kelly, E. L. (2008). Social class and the experience of work-family conflict during the transition to adulthood. *New Directions for Child & Adolescent Development, 2008*(119), 71–84. http://doi.org/10.1002/cd.210

Ampaabeng, S. K., & Tan, C. M. (2013). The long-term cognitive consequences of early childhood malnutrition: The case of famine in Ghana. *Journal*

of Health Economics, 32(6), 1013–1027. http://doi.org/10.1016/j.jhealeco.2013.08.001

An, J. S., & Cooney, T. M. (2006). Psychological well-being in mid to late life: The role of generativity development and parent-child relationships across the lifespan. *International Journal of Behavioral Development, 30*(5), 410–421.

Analitis, F., Velderman, M. K., Ravens-Sieberer, U., Detmar, S., Erhart, M., Herdman, M., . . . Rajmil, L. (2009). Being bullied: Associated factors in children and adolescents 8 to 18 years old in 11 European countries. *Pediatrics, 123*(2), 569–577. http://doi.org/10.1542/peds.2008-0323

Anastasi, A. (1958). Heredity, environment, and the question "how?". *Psychological Review, 65*, 197–208.

Andel, R., Crowe, M., Hahn, E. A., Mortimer, J. A., Pedersen, N. L., Fratiglioni, L., . . . Gatz, M. (2012). Work-related stress may increase the risk of vascular dementia. *Journal of the American Geriatrics Society, 60*(1), 60–67. http://doi.org/10.1111/j.1532-5415.2011.03777.x

Anderman, E. M., & Midgley, C. (2004). Changes in self-reported academic cheating across the transition from middle school to high school. *Contemporary Educational Psychology, 29*(4), 499–517.

Andersen, K., Lolk, A., Martinussen, T., & Kragh-Sørensen, P. (2010). Very mild to severe dementia and mortality: A 14-year follow-up—The Odense Study. *Dementia & Geriatric Cognitive Disorders, 29*(1), 61–67. http://doi.org/10.1159/000265553

Andersen, S. J. (2007). Osteoporosis in the older woman. *Clinical Obstetrics & Gynecology, 50*(3), 752–766.

Andersen, T. S. (2015). Race, ethnicity, and structural variations in youth risk of arrest: Evidence from a national longitudinal sample. *Criminal Justice and Behavior*. http://doi.org/10.1177/0093854815570963

Anderson, C. A., Shibuya, A., Ihori, N., Swing, E. L., Bushman, B. J., Sakamoto, A., . . . Saleem, M. (2010). Violent video game effects on aggression, empathy, and prosocial behavior in Eastern and Western countries: A meta-analytic review. *Psychological Bulletin, 136*(2), 151–173. http://doi.org/10.1037/a0018251

Anderson, D. R., & Pempek, T. A. (2005). Television and very young children. *American Behavioral Scientist, 48*(5), 505–522. http://doi.org/10.1177/0002764204271506

Anderson, J. R., & Gallup, G. G. (2015). Mirror self-recognition: A review and critique of attempts to promote and engineer self-recognition in primates. *Primates, 56*(4), 317–326. http://doi.org/10.1007/s10329-015-0488-9

Anderson, S., & Phillips, D. (2017). Is pre-k classroom quality associated with kindergarten and middle-school academic skills? *Developmental Psychology*. http://doi.org/10.1037/dev0000312

Anderson, V., Jacobs, R., Spencer-Smith, M., Coleman, L., Anderson, P., Williams, J., . . . Leventer, R. (2010). Does early age at brain insult predict worse outcome? Neuropsychological implications. *Journal of Pediatric Psychology, 35*(7), 716–727. http://doi.org/10.1093/jpepsy/jsp100

Anderson, V., Spencer-Smith, M. M., Coleman, L., Anderson, P. J., Greenham, M., Jacobs, R., . . . Leventer, R. J. (2014). Predicting neurocognitive and behavioural outcome after early brain insult. *Developmental Medicine and Child Neurology, 56*(4), 329–336. http://doi.org/10.1111/dmcn.12387

Anderson, V., Spencer-Smith, M., & Wood, A. (2011). Do children really recover better? Neurobehavioural plasticity after early brain insult. *Brain: A Journal of Neurology, 134*(Pt 8), 2197–2221. http://doi.org/10.1093/brain/awr103

Anderson, W. F., Rosenberg, P. S., Prat, A., Perou, C. M., & Sherman, M. E. (2014). How many etiological subtypes of breast cancer: Two, three, four, or more? *JNCI Journal of the National Cancer Institute, 106*(8). http://doi.org/10.1093/jnci/dju165

Andersson, B.-E. (1989). Effects of public day-care: A longitudinal study. *Child Development, 60*(4), 857. http://doi.org/10.1111/1467-8624.ep9676141

Andersson, G., Duvander, A.-Z., & Hank, K. (2004). Do child-care characteristics influence continued child bearing in Sweden? An investigation of the quantity, quality, and price dimension. *Journal of European Social Policy, 14*(4), 407–418. http://doi.org/10.1177/0958928704046881

Andersson, U. (2008). Working memory as a predictor of written arithmetical skills in children: The importance of central executive functions. *British Journal of Educational Psychology, 78*(2), 181–203.

Andreassen, C. S., Pallesen, S., & Griffiths, M. D. (2017). The relationship between addictive use of social media, narcissism, and self-esteem: Findings from a large national survey. *Addictive Behaviors, 64*, 287–293. http://doi.org/10.1016/j.addbeh.2016.03.006

Andrews, N. P., Fujii, H., Goronzy, J. J., & Weyand, C. M. (2010). Telomeres and immunological diseases of aging. *Gerontology, 56*(4), 390–403. http://doi.org/10.1159/000268620

Andruski, J. E., Casielles, E., & Nathan, G. (2013). Is bilingual babbling language-specific? Some evidence from a case study of Spanish–English dual acquisition. *Bilingualism: Language and Cognition, 17*(3), 660–672. http://doi.org/10.1017/S1366728913000655

Ang, R. P. (2006). Effects of parenting style on personal and social variables for Asian adolescents. *American Journal of Orthopsychiatry, 76*, 503–511.

Angley, M., Divney, A., Magriples, U., & Kershaw, T. (2015). Social support, family functioning and parenting competence in adolescent parents. *Maternal and Child Health Journal, 19*(1), 67–73. http://doi.org/10.1007/s10995-014-1496-x

Anglin, J. M. (1993). Vocabulary development: A morphological analysis. *Monographs of the Society for Research in Child Development, 59*(5) Serial No. 242.

Anjos, T., Altmäe, S., Emmett, P., Tiemeier, H., Closa-Monasterolo, R., Luque, V., . . . Campoy, C. (2013). Nutrition and neurodevelopment in children: Focus on NUTRIMENTHE project. *European Journal of Nutrition, 52*(8), 1825–1842. http://doi.org/10.1007/s00394-013-0560-4

Annett, M. (2002*). Handedness and brain asymmetry: The right shift theory.* Hove, UK: Psychology Press.

Anstey, K. J., Hofer, S. M., & Luszcz, M. A. (2003). A latent growth curve analysis of late-life sensory and cognitive function over 8 years: Evidence for specific and common factors underlying change. *Psychology and Aging, 18*(4), 714–726.

Anton, S., & Leeuwenburgh, C. (2013). Fasting or caloric restriction for healthy aging. *Experimental Gerontology, 48*(10), 1003–1005. http://doi.org/10.1016/j.exger.2013.04.011

Antonucci, T. C., Akiyama, H., & Takahashi, K. (2004). Attachment and close relationships across the lifespan. *Attachment & Human Development, 6*(4), 353–370. http://doi.org/10.1080/1461673042000303136

APA Task Force on Violent Media. (2015). *Technical report on the review of the violent video game literature.* Retrieved from http://www.apa.org/pi/families/violent-media.aspx

Apgar, V. (1953). A proposal for a new method of evaluation in the newborn infant. *Current Research in Anesthesia and Analgesia, 32*, 260–267.

Apperly, I. A., Samson, D., Humphreys, G. W., & Humphreys, G. W. (2009). Studies of adults can inform accounts of theory of mind development. *Developmental Psychology, 45*(1), 190–201.

Araujo, A. B., Mohr, B. A., & McKinlay, J. B. (2004). Changes in sexual function in middle-aged and older men: Longitudinal data from the Massachusetts Male Aging Study. *Journal of the American Geriatrics Society, 52*(9), 1502–1509. http://doi.org/10.1111/j.0002-8614.2004.52413.x

Araujo, A. B., O'Donnell, A. B., Brambilla, D. J., Simpson, W. B., Longcope, C., Matsumoto, A. M., & McKinlay, J. B. (2004). Prevalence and incidence of androgen deficiency in middle-aged and older men: Estimates from the Massachusetts Male Aging Study. *The Journal of Clinical Endocrinology and Metabolism, 89*(12), 5920–5926. http://doi.org/10.1210/jc.2003-031719

Archer, L., DeWitt, J., Osborne, J., Dillon, J., Willis, B., & Wong, B. (2012). Science aspirations, capital, and family habitus: How families shape children's engagement and identification with science. *American Educational Research Journal, 49*(5), 881–908. http://doi.org/10.3102/0002831211433290

Archer, S. L., & Waterman, A. S. (1990). Varieties of identity diffusions and foreclosures: An exploration of subcategories of the identity statuses. *Journal of Adolescent Research, 5*(1), 96–111.

Ardelt, M. (1998). Social crisis and individual growth: The long-term effects of the great depression. *Journal of Aging Studies, 12*(3), 291.

Ardelt, M. (2010). Are older adults wiser than college students? A comparison of two age cohorts. *Journal of Adult Development, 17*(4), 193–207. http://doi.org/10.1007/s10804-009-9088-5

Ardila, A. (2013). Development of metacognitive and emotional executive functions in children. *Applied Neuropsychology Child, 2*(2), 82–87. http://doi.org/10.1080/21622965.2013.748388

Ardila, A., Rosselli, M., Matute, E., & Inozemtseva, O. (2011). Gender differences in cognitive development. *Developmental Psychology, 47*(4), 984–990. http://doi.org/10.1037/a002381910.1037/a0023819.supp

Argue, A., Johnson, D. R., & White, L. K. (1999). Age and religiosity: Evidence from a three-wave panel analysis. *Journal for the Scientific Study of Religion, 38*(3), 423.

Arias, D. F., & Hernández, A. M. (2007). Emerging adulthood in Mexican and Spanish youth: Theories and realities. *Journal of Adolescent Research, 22*(5), 476–503.

Arija, V., Esparó, G., Fernández-Ballart, J., Murphy, M. M., Biarnés, E., & Canals, J. (2006). Nutritional status and performance in test of verbal and nonverbal intelligence in 6-year-old children. *Intelligence, 34*(2), 141–149.

Arim, R. G., Tramonte, L., Shapka, J. D., Dahinten, V. S., & Willms, J. D. (2011). The family antecedents and the subsequent outcomes of early puberty. *Journal of Youth and Adolescence, 40*(11), 1423–1435. http://doi.org/10.1007/s10964-011-9638-6

Armour, S., & Haynie, D. (2007). Adolescent sexual debut and later delinquency. *Journal of Youth & Adolescence, 36*(2), 141–152. http://doi.org/10.1007/s10964-006-9128-4

Armstrong, E. A., Hamilton, L., & England, P. (2010). Is hooking up bad for young women? *Contexts, 9*(3), 22–27. http://doi.org/10.1525/ctx.2010.9.3.22

Arnett, J. J. (1997). Young people's conceptions of the transition to adulthood. *Youth & Society, 29*(1), 3.

Arnett, J. J. (1999). Adolescent storm and stress, reconsidered. *The American Psychologist, 54*(5), 317–326. Retrieved from http://www.ncbi.nlm.nih.gov/pubmed/10354802

Arnett, J. J. (2000). Emerging adulthood: A theory of development from the late teens through the twenties. *American Psychologist, 55*(5), 469–480. http://doi.org/10.1037/0003-066X.55.5.469

Arnett, J. J. (2003). Conceptions of the transition to adulthood among emerging adults in American ethnic groups. *New Directions for Child & Adolescent Development, 2003*(100), 63–76.

Arnett, J. J. (2004). *Emerging adulthood: The winding road from the late teens through the twenties.* New York, NY: Oxford University Press.

Aronson, P. (2008). Breaking barriers or locked out? Class-based perceptions and experiences of postsecondary education. *New Directions for Child & Adolescent Development, 2008*(119), 41–54. http://doi.org/10.1002/cd.208

Arria, A. M., Caldeira, K. M., Allen, H. K., Vincent, K. B., Bugbee, B. A., & O'Grady, K. E. (2016). Drinking like an adult? Trajectories of alcohol use patterns before and after college graduation. *Alcoholism: Clinical and Experimental Research, 40*(3), 583–590. http://doi.org/10.1111/acer.12973

Arria, A. M., Derauf, C., LaGasse, L. L., Grant, P., Shah, R., Smith, L., . . . Lester, B. (2006). Methamphetamine and other substance use during pregnancy: Preliminary estimates from the Infant Development, Environment, and Lifestyle (IDEAL) Study. *Maternal & Child Health Journal, 10*(3), 293–302.

Arriaga, P., Montiero, M. B., & Esteves, F. (2011). Effects of playing violent computer games on emotional desensitization and aggressive behavior. *Journal of Applied Social Psychology, 41*(8), 1900–1925. http://doi.org/10.1111/j.1559-1816.2011.00791.x

Arsenis, N. C., You, T., Ogawa, E. F., Tinsley, G. M., & Zuo, L. (2015). Physical activity and telomere length: Impact of aging and potential mechanisms of action. *Oncotarget.* http://doi.org/10.18632/oncotarget.16726

Årseth, A. K., Kroger, J., Martinussen, M., & Marcia, J. E. (2009). Meta-analytic studies of identity status and the relational issues of attachment and intimacy. *Identity, 9*(1), 1–32. http://doi.org/10.1080/15283480802579532

Arthur, A. E., Bigler, R. S., & Ruble, D. N. (2009). An experimental test of the effects of gender constancy on sex typing. *Journal of Experimental Child Psychology, 104*(4), 427–446. http://doi.org/10.1016/j.jecp.2009.08.002

Artistico, D., Orom, H., Cervone, D., Krauss, S., & Houston, E. (2010). Everyday challenges in context: The influence of contextual factors on everyday problem solving among young, middle-aged, and older adults. *Experimental Aging Research, 36*(2), 230–247. http://doi.org/10.1080/03610731003613938

Artman, L., & Cahan, S. (1993). Schooling and the development of transitive inference. *Developmental Psychology, 29*(4), 753–759.

Asarnow, J. R. (2011). Promoting stress resistance in war-exposed children. *Journal of the American Academy of Child & Adolescent Psychiatry, 50*(4), 320–322. http://doi.org/10.1016/j.jaac.2011.01.010

Asato, M. R., Terwilliger, R., Woo, J., & Luna, B. (2010). White matter development in adolescence: A DTI study. *Cerebral Cortex, 20*(9), 2122–2131. http://doi.org/10.1093/cercor/bhp282

Ashley-Koch, A., Yang, Q., & Olney, R. (2000). Sickle hemoglobin (HbS_allele) and sickle cell disease: A huge review. *American Journal of Epidemiology, 151*, 839–845.

Ashman, S. B., & Dawson, G. (2002). Maternal depression, infant psychobiological development, and risk for depression. In S. H. Goodman & I. H. Gotlib (Eds.), *Children of depressed parents: Mechanisms of risk and implications for treatment* (pp. 37–58). Washington: American Psychological Association. http://doi.org/10.1037/10449-002

Aslan, A., & Bäuml, K.-H. T. (2010). Retrieval-induced forgetting in young children. *Psychonomic Bulletin & Review, 17*(5), 704–709. http://doi.org/10.3758/pbr.17.5.704

Aslan, U. B., Cavlak, U., Yagci, N., Akdag, B., Stewart, A. L., Miller, C. J., & Bloch, D. A. (2008). Balance performance, aging and falling: A comparative study based on a Turkish sample. *Archives of Gerontology and Geriatrics, 46*(3), 283–292. http://doi.org/10.1016/j.archger.2007.05.003

Aslin, R. N., Clayards, M. A., & Bardhan, N. P. (2008). Mechanisms of auditory reorganization during development: From sounds to words. In C. A. Nelson & M. Luciana (Eds.), *Handbook of developmental cognitive neuroscience* (2nd ed., pp. 97–116). Cambridge, MA: MIT Press.

Astington, J. W. (1993). *The child's discovery of the mind*. Cambridge, MA: Harvard University Press.

Aston, K. I., Peterson, C. M., & Carrell, D. T. (2008). Monozygotic twinning associated with assisted reproductive technologies: A review. *Reproduction, 136*, 377–386.

Astuti, R., & Harris, P. (2008). Understanding mortality and the life of the ancestors in rural Madagascar. *Cognitive Science: A Multidisciplinary Journal, 32*(4), 713–740. http://doi.org/10.1080/03640210802066907

Atance, C. M., & Jackson, L. K. (2009). The development and coherence of future-oriented behaviors during the preschool years. *Journal of Experimental Child Psychology, 102*(4), 379–391. http://doi.org/10.1016/j.jecp.2009.01.001

Atchley, R. C. (1999). *Continuity and adaptation in aging: Creating positive experiences*. Baltimore, MD: Johns Hopkins University Press.

Athanasou, J. A. (2002). Vocational pathways in the early part of a career: An Australian study. *Career Development Quarterly, 51*(1), 78–86.

Atran, S., & Medin, D. (2008). *The native mind and the cultural construction of nature*. Cambridge, MA: MIT Press.

Attar-Schwartz, S., Tan, J.-P., Buchanan, A., Flouri, E., & Griggs, J. (2009). Grandparenting and adolescent adjustment in two-parent biological, lone-parent, and step-families. *Journal of Family Psychology, 23*(1), 67–75. http://doi.org/10.1037/a0014383

Attems, J., Walker, L., & Jellinger, K. A. (2015). Olfaction and aging: A mini-review. *Gerontology, 61*(6), 485–490. http://doi.org/10.1159/000381619

Attig, T. (1996). *How we grieve: Relearning the world*. New York, NY: Oxford University Press.

Au, J., Sheehan, E., Tsai, N., Duncan, G. J., Buschkuehl, M., & Jaeggi, S. M. (2015). Improving fluid intelligence with training on working memory: A meta-analysis. *Psychonomic Bulletin & Review, 22*(2), 366–377. http://doi.org/10.3758/s13423-014-0699-x

Auer, R., Vittinghoff, E., Yaffe, K., Künzi, A., Kertesz, S. G., Levine, D. A., . . . Pletcher, M. J. (2016). Association between lifetime marijuana use and cognitive function in middle age. *JAMA Internal Medicine, 176*(3), 352. http://doi.org/10.1001/jamainternmed.2015.7841

Aumann, K., Galinsky, E., Sakai, K., Brown, M., & Bond, J. T. (2010). *The elder care study: Everyday realities and wishes for change*. New York, NY: Families and Work Institute.

Australian Institute of Health and Welfare. (2016). *Leading causes of death*. Retrieved from http://www.aihw.gov.au/deaths/leading-causes-of-death/

Austrom, D., & Hanel, K. (1985). Psychological issues of single life in Canada: An exploratory study. *International Journal of Women's Studies, 8*(1), 12–23.

Auyeung, B., Baron-Cohen, S., Ashwin, E., Knickmeyer, R., Taylor, K., Hackett, G., & Hines, M. (2009). Fetal testosterone predicts sexually differentiated childhood behavior in girls and in boys. *Psychological Science, 20*(2), 144–148. http://doi.org/10.1111/j.1467-9280.2009.02279.x

Avelin, P., Rådestad, I., Säflund, K., Wredling, R., & Erlandsson, K. (2013). Parental grief and relationships after the loss of a stillborn baby. *Midwifery, 29*(6), 668–673. http://doi.org/10.1016/j.midw.2012.06.007

Avis, N. E., Brockwell, S., & Colvin, A. (2005). A universal menopausal syndrome? *American Journal of Medicine, 118*(12), 1406. http://doi.org/10.1016/j.amjmed.2005.10.010

Avis, N. E., & Crawford, S. (2006). Menopause: Recent research findings. In S. K. Whitbourne & S. L. Willis (Eds.), *The baby boomers grow up: Contemporary perspectives on midlife* (pp. 75–109). Mahwah, NJ: Lawrence Erlbaum.

Avis, N. E., Crawford, S. L., Greendale, G., Bromberger, J. T., Everson-Rose, S. A., Gold, E. B., . . . Thurston, R. C. (2015). Duration of menopausal vasomotor symptoms over the menopause transition. *JAMA Internal Medicine, 175*(4), 531–539. http://doi.org/10.1001/jamainternmed.2014.8063

Avis, N. E., Stellato, R., Crawford, S., Bromberger, J., Ganz, P., Cain, V., & Kagawa-Singer, M. (2001). Is there a menopausal syndrome? Menopausal status and symptoms across racial/ethnic groups. *Social Science & Medicine, 52*(3), 345.

Avison, M., & Furnham, A. (2015). Personality and voluntary childlessness. *Journal of Population Research, 32*(1), 45–67. http://doi.org/10.1007/s12546-014-9140-6

Avolio, B. J., & Sosik, J. J. (1999). A life-span framework for assessing the impact of work on white-collar workers. In S. L. Willis & J. D. Reid (Eds.), *Life in the middle: Psychological and social development in middle age* (pp. 249–274). San Diego, CA: Academic Press.

Axe, J. B. (2007). Child care and child development: Results from the NICHD Study of Early Child Care and Youth Development. *Education & Treatment of Children, 30*(3), 129–136.

Axia, G., & Baroni, R. (1985). Linguistic politeness at different age levels. *Child Development, 56*, 918–927.

Axia, V. D., & Weisner, T. S. (2002). Infant stress reactivity and home cultural ecology of Italian infants and families. *Infant Behavior & Development, 25*(3), 255.

Ayers, B., Forshaw, M., & Hunter, M. S. (2010). The impact of attitudes towards the menopause on women's symptom experience: A systematic review. *Maturitas, 65*(1), 28–36. http://doi.org/10.1016/j.maturitas.2009.10.016

Aylward, G. P. (2005). Neurodevelopmental outcomes of infants born prematurely. *Developmental & Behavioral Pediatrics, 26*(6), 427–440.

Azmitia, M., & Perlmutter, M. (1989). Social influences on children's cognition: State of the art and future directions. *Advances in Child Development and Behavior, 22*, 89–144. http://doi.org/10.1016/S0065-2407(08)60413-9

Azofeifa, A., Mattson, M. E., Schauer, G., McAfee, T., Grant, A., & Lyerla, R. (2016). National estimates of marijuana use and related indicators? National Survey on Drug Use and Health, United States, 2002–2014. *MMWR. Surveillance Summaries, 65*(11), 1–28. http://doi.org/10.15585/mmwr.ss6511a1

Baams, L., Dubas, J. S., Overbeek, G., & van Aken, M. A. G. (2015). Transitions in body and behavior: A meta-analytic study on the relationship between pubertal development and adolescent sexual behavior. *The Journal of Adolescent Health: Official Publication of the Society for Adolescent Medicine*. http://doi.org/10.1016/j.jadohealth.2014.11.019

Bachman, H. J., & Chase-Lansdale, P. L. (2005). Custodial grandmothers' physical, mental, and economic well-being: Comparisons of primary caregivers from low-income neighborhoods. *Family Relations, 54*(4), 475–487.

Bachman, J. G., Johnston, L. D., & O'Malley, P. M. (2014). *Monitoring the future: Questionnaire responses from the nation's high school seniors, 2012*. Retrieved from http://monitoringthefuture.org/datavolumes/2012/2012dv.pdf

Bachman, J. G., O'Malley, P. M., Freedman-Doan, P., Trzesniewski, K. H., & Donnellan, M. B. (2011). Adolescent self-esteem: Differences by race/ethnicity, gender, and age. *Self and Identity: The Journal of the International Society for Self and Identity, 10*(4), 445–473. http://doi.org/10.1080/15298861003794538

Bachman, J. G., Staff, J., O'Malley, P. M., & Freedman-Doan, P. (2013). Adolescent work intensity, school performance, and substance use: Links vary by race/ethnicity and socioeconomic status. *Developmental Psychology, 49*(11), 2125–2134. http://doi.org/10.1037/a0031464

Backé, E.-M., Seidler, A., Latza, U., Rossnagel, K., & Schumann, B. (2012). The role of psychosocial stress at work for the development of cardiovascular diseases: A systematic review. *International Archives of Occupational and Environmental Health, 85*(1), 67–79. http://doi.org/10.1007/s00420-011-0643-6

Bäckman, L. (2008). Memory and cognition in preclinical dementia: What we know and what we do not know. *Canadian Journal of Psychiatry, 53*(6), 354–360.

Backschneider, A. G., Shatz, M., & Gelman, S. A. (1993). Preschoolers' ability to distinguish living kinds as a function of regrowth. *Child Development, 64*, 1242–1257.

Baddeley, A. (1986). *Working memory*. London: Oxford University Press.

Baddeley, A. (1996). Exploring the central executive. *The Quarterly Journal of Experimental Psychology, 49*(a), 5–28.

Baddeley, A. (2012). Working memory: Theories, models, and controversies. *Annual Review of Psychology, 63*, 1–29. http://doi.org/10.1146/annurev-psych-120710-100422

Bagci, S. C., Rutland, A., Kumashiro, M., Smith, P. K., & Blumberg, H. (2014). Are minority status children's cross-ethnic friendships beneficial in a multiethnic context? *The British Journal of Developmental Psychology, 32*(1), 107–115. http://doi.org/10.1111/bjdp.12028

Baglivio, M. T., Jackowski, K., Greenwald, M. A., & Howell, J. C. (2014). Serious, violent, and chronic juvenile offenders. *Criminology & Public Policy, 13*(1), 83–116. http://doi.org/10.1111/1745-9133.12064

Bahrick, L. E. (2002). Generalization of learning in three-and-a-half-month-old infants on the basis of amodal relations. *Child Development, 73*(3), 667–681.

Bailey, J. M., Vasey, P. L., Diamond, L. M., Breedlove, S. M., Vilain, E., & Epprecht, M. (2016). Sexual orientation, controversy, and science. *Psychological Science in the Public Interest, 17*(2), 45–101. http://doi.org/10.1177/1529100616637616

Baillargeon, R. (1987). Object permanence in 31/2- and 41/2-month-old-infants. *Developmental Psychology, 23*(5), 655–664.

REFERENCES

Baillargeon, R. (1994). How do infants learn about the physical world? *Current Directions in Psychological Science, 3*, 133–140.

Baillargeon, R., Li, J., Gertner, Y., & Wu, D. (2011). How do infants reason about physical events? In U. Goswami (Ed.), *The Wiley-Blackwell handbook of childhood cognitive development* (2nd ed., pp. 11–48). New York, NY: Wiley-Blackwell.

Baillieux, H., de Smet, H. J., Paquier, P. F., De Deyn, P. P., & Mariën, P. (2008). Cerebellar neurocognition: Insights into the bottom of the brain. *Clinical Neurology & Neurosurgery, 110*(8), 763–773. http://doi.org/10.1016/j.clineuro.2008.05.013

Bainbridge, D. (2003). *Making babies: The science of pregnancy*. Cambridge, MA: Harvard University Press.

Baines, H. L., Turnbull, D. M., & Greaves, L. C. (2014). Human stem cell aging: Do mitochondrial DNA mutations have a causal role? *Aging Cell, 13*(2), 201–205. http://doi.org/10.1111/acel.12199

Baird, D. T., Collins, J., Egozcue, J., Evers, L. H., Gianaroli, L., & Leridon, H. (2005). Fertility and ageing. *Human Reproduction Update, 11*, 261–276.

Bajanowski, T., & Vennemann, M. (2017). Sudden infant death syndrome (SIDS). In M. M. Houck (Ed.), *Forensic Pathology* (p. 259–266). Cambridge, MA: Elsevier.

Baker, D. P., Eslinger, P. J., Benavides, M., Peters, E., Dieckmann, N. F., & Leon, J. (2015). The cognitive impact of the education revolution: A possible cause of the Flynn Effect on population IQ. *Intelligence, 49*, 144–158. http://doi.org/10.1016/j.intell.2015.01.003

Baker, E. R., Tisak, M. S., & Tisak, J. (2016). What can boys and girls do? Preschoolers' perspectives regarding gender roles across domains of behavior. *Social Psychology of Education, 19*(1), 23–39. http://doi.org/10.1007/s11218-015-9320-z

Baker, H. (2007). Nutrition in the elderly: An overview. *Geriatrics, 62*(7), 28–31.

Baker, J. E., Sedney, M. A., & Gross, E. (1992). Psychological tasks for bereaved children. *The American Journal of Orthopsychiatry, 62*(1), 105–116. Retrieved from http://www.ncbi.nlm.nih.gov/pubmed/1546749

Baker, S. K., Simmons, D. C., & Kame'enui, E. J. (1997). Vocabulary acquisition: Research bases. In D. C. Simmons & E. J. Kame'enui (Eds.), *What reading research tells us about children with diverse learning needs: Bases and basics* (pp. 183–217). Mahwah, NJ: Lawrence Erlbaum.

Bakermans-Kranenburg, M. J., & van IJzendoorn, M. H. (2009). The first 10,000 adult attachment interviews: Distributions of adult attachment representations in clinical and non-clinical groups. *Attachment & Human Development, 11*(3), 223–263. http://doi.org/10.1080/14616730902814762

Bakermans-Kranenburg, M. J., & van IJzendoorn, M. H. (2015). The hidden efficacy of interventions: Gene × environment experiments from a differential susceptibility perspective. *Annual Review of Psychology, 66*(1), 381–409. http://doi.org/10.1146/annurev-psych-010814-015407

Baker-Ward, L., Gordon, B. N., Ornstein, P. A., Larus, D. M., & Clubb, P. A. (1993). Young children's long-term retention of a pediatric examination. *Child Development, 64*, 1519–1533.

Balan, R., Dobrean, A., Roman, G. D., & Balazsi, R. (2017). Indirect effects of parenting practices on internalizing problems among adolescents: The role of expressive suppression. *Journal of Child and Family Studies, 26*(1), 40–47. http://doi.org/10.1007/s10826-016-0532-4

Baldwin, C. L., & Ash, I. K. (2010). Impact of sensory acuity on auditory working memory span in young and older adults. *Psychology and Aging.* http://doi.org/10.1037/a0020360

Baldwin, D. A., Markman, E. M., Bill, B., Desjardins, R. N., Irwin, J. M., & Tidball, G. (1996). Infants' reliance on social criteria for establishing word-object relations. *Child Development, 67*, 3135–3153.

Bale, T. L. (2015). Epigenetic and transgenerational reprogramming of brain development. *Nature Reviews Neuroscience, 16*(6), 332–344. http://doi.org/10.1038/nrn3818

Balk, E. M. (2009). Adolescent development: The backstory to adolescent encounters with death and bereavement. In E. M. Balk & C. Corr (Eds.), *Adolescent encounters with death, bereavement, and coping* (pp. 3–20). New York, NY: Springer.

Ball, C. L., Smetana, J. G., & Sturge-Apple, M. L. (2016). Following my head and my heart: Integrating preschoolers' empathy, theory of mind, and moral judgments. *Child Development.* http://doi.org/10.1111/cdev.12605

Ball, G., Adamson, C., Beare, R., & Seal, M. L. (2017). *Modelling neuroanatomical variation due to age and sex during childhood and adolescence.* Retrieved from http://www.biorxiv.org/content/early/2017/04/11/126441

Ball, H. L., Hooker, E., & Kelly, P. J. (1999). Where will the baby sleep? Attitudes and practices of new and experienced parents regarding co-sleeping with their new-born infants. *American Anthropologist, 101*, 1–9.

Ball, H. L., Hooker, E., & Kelly, P. J. (2000). Parent-infant co-sleeping: Fathers' roles and perspectives. *Infant and Child Development, 9*, 67–74.

Balter, L., & Tamis-LeMonda, C. S. (2006). *Child psychology: A handbook of contemporary issues* (2nd ed.). New York, NY: Psychology Press.

Baltes, M. M., & Carstensen, L. L. (2003). The process of successful aging: Selection, optimization and compensation. In U. M. Staudinger & U. Lindenberger (Eds.), *Understanding human development: Dialogues with lifespan psychology* (pp. 81–104). Dordrecht, NL: Kluwer Academic.

Baltes, P. B. (1987). Theoretical propositions of life-span developmental psychology: On the dynamics between growth and decline. *Developmental Psychology, 23*, 611–626.

Baltes, P. B. (1997). On the incomplete architecture of human ontogeny: Selection, optimization, and compensation as foundation of developmental theory. *American Psychologist, 52*, 366–380.

Baltes, P. B., & Baltes, M. M. (1990). Psychological perspectives on successful aging: The model of selective optimization with compensation. In P. B. Baltes & M. M. Baltes (Eds.), *Successful aging: Perspectives from the behavioral sciences* (pp. 1–34). New York, NY: Cambridge University Press.

Baltes, P. B., & Kunzmann, U. (2003). Wisdom. *The Psychologist, 16*(3), 131–133.

Baltes, P. B., Lindenberger, U., & Staudinger, U. M. (1998). Life-span theory in developmental psychology. In R. M. Lerner (Ed.), *Handbook of child psychology: Vol. 1. Theoretical models of human development* (5th ed., pp. 1029–1143). New York: Wiley.

Baltes, P. B., & Staudinger, U. M. (2000). Wisdom: A metaheuristic (pragmatic) to orchestrate mind and virtue toward excellence. *American Psychologist, 55*(1), 122–136. http://doi.org/10.1037/0003-066X.55.1.122

Balzer, B. W. R., Duke, S.-A., Hawke, C. I., & Steinbeck, K. S. (2015). The effects of estradiol on mood and behavior in human female adolescents: A systematic review. *European Journal of Pediatrics.* http://doi.org/10.1007/s00431-014-2475-3

Bámaca, M. Y., Umaña-Taylor, A. J., Shin, N., & Alfaro, E. C. (2005). Latino adolescents' perception of parenting behaviors and self-esteem: Examining the role of neighborhood risk. *Family Relations, 54*(5), 621–632.

Bandettini, P. A. (2012). Twenty years of functional MRI: The science and the stories. *NeuroImage, 62*(2), 575–588. http://doi.org/10.1016/j.neuroimage.2012.04.026

Bandstra, E. S., Morrow, C. E., Mansoor, E., & Accornero, V. H. (2010). Prenatal drug exposure: Infant and toddler outcomes. *Journal of Addictive Diseases, 29*(2), 245–258. http://doi.org/10.1080/10550881003684871

Bandura, A. (1965). Influence of models' reinforcement contingencies on the acquisition of imitative responses. *Journal of Personality and Social Psychology, 1*(6), 589–595. http://doi.org/10.1037/h0022070

Bandura, A. (1977). *Social learning theory.* Englewood Cliffs, NJ: Prentice Hall.

Bandura, A. (1986). *Social foundations of thought and action: A social cognitive theory.* Englewood Cliffs, NJ: Prentice Hall.

Bandura, A. (2001). Social cognitive theory: An agentic. *Annual Reviews of Psychology, 52*, 1–26.

Bandura, A. (2011). But what about that gigantic elephant in the room? In R. M. Arkin (Ed.), *Most underappreciated: 50 prominent social psychologists describe their most unloved work* (pp. 51–59). New York: Oxford University Press.

Bandura, A. (2012). Social cognitive theory. In P. Van Lange (Ed.), *Handbook of theories of social psychology* (Vol. 1, pp. 349–373). Thousand Oaks, CA: SAGE.

Bandura, A., & Bussey, K. (2004). On broadening the cognitive, motivational, and sociostructural scope of theorizing about gender development and functioning: Comment on Martin, Ruble, and Szkrybalo (2002). *Psychological Bulletin, 130*(5), 691–701.

Bandura, A., Ross, D., & Ross, S. A. (1961). Transmission of aggression through imitation of aggressive models. *The Journal of Abnormal and Social Psychology, 63*(3), 575–582. http://doi.org/10.1037/h0045925

Bandura, A., Ross, D., & Ross, S. A. (1963). Vicarious reinforcement and imitative learning. *Journal of Abnormal and Social Psychology, 67*, 601–607.

Banich, M. T. (1998). Integration of information between the cerebral hemispheres. *Current Directions in Psychological Science, 7*, 32–37.

Banich, M. T., & Heller, W. (1998). Evolving perspectives on lateralization of function. *Current Directions in Psychological Science, 7*, 1–2.

Bannon, S. M., Salis, K. L., & O'Leary, K. D. (2015). Structural brain abnormalities in aggression and violent behavior. *Aggression and Violent Behavior, 25*, 323–331. http://doi.org/10.1016/j.avb.2015.09.016

Bansal, N., & Parle, M. (2014). Dementia: An overview. *Management, 1*(1), 281–297.

Banse, R., Gawronski, B., Rebetez, C., Gutt, H., & Morton, J. B. (2010). The development of spontaneous gender stereotyping in childhood: Relations to stereotype knowledge and stereotype flexibility. *Developmental Science, 13*(2), 298–306. http://doi.org/10.1111/j.1467-7687.2009.00880.x

Barac, R., & Bialystok, E. (2012). Bilingual effects on cognitive and linguistic development: Role of language, cultural background, and education. *Child Development, 83*(2), 413–422. http://doi.org/10.1111/j.1467-8624.2011.01707.x

Barac, R., Bialystok, E., Castro, D. C., & Sanchez, M. (2014). The cognitive development of young dual language learners: A critical review. *Early Childhood Research Quarterly, 29*(4), 699–714. http://doi.org/10.1016/j.ecresq.2014.02.003

Barak, B. (2009). Age identity: A cross-cultural global approach. *International Journal of Behavioral Development, 33*(1), 2–11. http://doi.org/10.1177/0165025408099485

Barber, B. K. (2002). *Intrusive parenting: How psychological control affects children and adolescents.* Washington, DC: American Psychological Association. http://doi.org/10.1037/10422-000

Barber, B. K., Stolz, H. E., & Olsen, J. A. (2005). Parental support, psychological control, and behavioral control: Assessing relevance across time, culture, and method. *Monographs of the Society for Research in Child Development, 70*(4), 1–137.

Barbosa, L. M., Monteiro, B., & Murta, S. G. (2016). Retirement adjustment predictors—A systematic review. *Work, Aging and Retirement, 2*(2), 262–280.

Bard, K. A., Todd, B. K., Bernier, C., Love, J., & Leavens, D. A. (2006). Self-awareness in human and chimpanzee infants: What is measured and what is meant by the mark and mirror test? *Infancy, 9*(2), 191–219. http://doi.org/10.1207/s15327078in0902_6

Bardsley, M. Z., Kowal, K., Levy, C., Gosek, A., Ayari, N., Tartaglia, N., . . . Ross, J. L. (2013). 47,XYY Syndrome: Clinical phenotype and timing of ascertainment. *The Journal of Pediatrics, 163*(4), 1085–1094. http://doi.org/10.1016/j.jpeds.2013.05.037

Bargh, J. A. (2013). Our unconscious mind. *Scientific American, 310*(1), 30–37. http://doi.org/10.1038/scientificamerican0114-30

Barglow, P., Vaughn, B. E., & Molitor, N. (1987). Effects of maternal absence due to employment on the quality of infant-mother attachment in a low-risk sample. *Child Development, 58*(4), 945–954.

Barker, E. D., Larsson, H., Viding, E., Maughan, B., Rijsdijk, F., Fontaine, N., & Plomin, R. (2009). Common genetic but specific environmental influences for aggressive and deceitful behaviors in preadolescent males. *Journal of Psychopathology & Behavioral Assessment, 31*(4), 299–308. http://doi.org/10.1007/s10862-009-9132-6

Barlow-Stewart, K. (2012). *Genes an chromosomes: The genome.* Sydney, Australia: Centre for Genetics Education. Retrieved from http://www.genetics.edu.au/Information/Genetics-Fact-Sheets/Genes-and-Chromosomes-FS1

Barlow-Stewart, K., & Saleh, M. (2012). *Prenatal testing overview.* Centre for genetics education. Retrieved from http://www.genetics.edu.au/Information/Genetics-Fact-Sheets/Prenatal-Testing-Overview-FS17

Barnea-Goraly, N., Menon, V., Eckert, M., Tamm, L., Bammer, R., Karchemskiy, A., . . . Reiss, A. L. (2005). White matter development during childhood and adolescence: A cross-sectional diffusion tensor imaging study. *Cerebral Cortex, 15*.

Barnes, A. B., Colton, T., Gundersen, J., Noller, K. L., Tilley, B. C., Strama, T., . . . O'Brien, P. C. (1980). Fertility and outcome of pregnancy in women exposed in utero to diethylstilbestrol. *The New England Journal of Medicine, 302*(11), 609–613. http://doi.org/10.1056/NEJM198003133021105

Barnes, G. M., Welte, J. W., Hoffman, J. H., & Tidwell, M.-C. O. (2010). Comparisons of gambling and alcohol use among college students and noncollege young people in the United States. *Journal of American College Health, 58*(5), 443–452.

Barnes, J., Gardiner, J., Sutcliffe, A., & Melhuish, E. (2013). The parenting of preschool children by older mothers in the United Kingdom. *European Journal of Developmental Psychology, 11*(4), 397–419. http://doi.org/10.1080/17405629.2013.863728

Barnes-Farrell, J. L., & Matthews, R. A. (2007). Age and work attitudes. In K. S. Shultz & G. A. Adams (Eds.), *Aging and work in the 21st century* (pp. 139–162). Mahwah, NJ: Lawrence Erlbaum.

Barnett, S. M., Ceci, S. J., & Williams, W. M. (2006). Is the ability to make a bacon sandwich a mark of intelligence? and other issues: Some reflections on Gardner's theory of multiple intelligences. In J. A. Schaler (Ed.), *Howard Gardner under fire: The rebel psychologist faces his critics* (pp. 95–114). Chicago, IL: Open Court.

Barnett, W. S., Carolan, M. E., Squires, J. H., & Clarke Brown, K., Horowitz, M. (2015). *The state of preschool 2014: State preschool yearbook.* New Brunswick, NJ: NIEER.

Barr, R. (2013). Memory constraints on infant learning from picture books, television, and touchscreens. *Child Development Perspectives, 7*(4), 205–210. http://doi.org/10.1111/cdep.12041

Barr, R., Dowden, A., & Hayne, H. (1996). Developmental changes in deferred imitation by 6- to 24-month-old infants. *Infant Behavior and Development, 19*, 159–170.

Barr, R. G., & Gunnar, M. (2000). Colic: The "transient responsivity" hypothesis. In R. G. Barr, B. Hopkins, & J. A. Green (Eds.), *Crying as a sign, a sympton, & a signal: Clinical emotional and developmental aspects of infant and toddler crying* (pp. 41–66). New York, NY: Cambridge University Press.

Barr, R. G., Konner, M., Bakeman, R., & Adamson, L. (1991). Crying in pKung San infants: A test of the cultural specificity hypothesis. *Developmental Medicine & Child Neurology, 33*(7), 601–610.

Barr, R., Marrott, H., & Rovee-Collier, C. (2003). The role of sensory preconditioning in memory retrieval by preverbal infants. *Learning & Behavior, 31*(2), 111–123.

Barrett, A. E., & Montepare, J. M. (2015). "It's about time": Applying life span and life course perspectives to the study of subjective age. *Annual Review of Gerontology and Geriatrics, 35*(1), 55–77. http://doi.org/10.1891/0198-8794.35.55

Barrett, A. E., & Robbins, C. (2008). The multiple sources of women's aging anxiety and their relationship with psychological distress. *Journal of Aging and Health, 20*(1), 32–65. http://doi.org/10.1177/0898264307309932

Barrett, H. C., & Behne, T. (2005). Children's understanding of death as the cessation of agency: A test using sleep versus death. *Cognition, 96*(2), 93–108. http://doi.org/10.1016/j.cognition.2004.05.004

Barrington-Trimis, J. L., Berhane, K., Unger, J. B., Cruz, T. B., Urman, R., Chou, C. P., . . . McConnell, R. (2016). The e-cigarette social environment, e-cigarette use, and susceptibility to cigarette smoking. *Journal of Adolescent Health, 59*(1), 75–80. http://doi.org/10.1016/j.jadohealth.2016.03.019

Barros, M. C. M., Mitsuhiro, S., Chalem, E., Laranjeira, R. R., & Guinsburg, R. (2011). Neurobehavior of late preterm infants of adolescent mothers. *Neonatology (16617800), 99*(2), 133–139. http://doi.org/10.1159/000313590

Barrouillet, P., Gavens, N., Vergauwe, E., Gaillard, V., & Camos, V. (2009). Working memory span development: A time-based resource-sharing model account. *Developmental Psychology, 45*(2), 477–490. http://doi.org/10.1037/a0014615

Barry, C. T., & Lee-Rowland, L. M. (2015). Has there been a recent increase in adolescent narcissism? Evidence from a sample of at-risk adolescents (2005–2014). *Personality and Individual Differences, 87*, 153–157. http://doi.org/10.1016/j.paid.2015.07.038

Bartel, K. A., Gradisar, M., & Williamson, P. (2014). Protective and risk factors for adolescent sleep: A meta-analytic review. *Sleep Medicine Reviews.* http://doi.org/10.1016/j.smrv.2014.08.002

Barth, R. P., Scarborough, A., Lloyd, E. C., Losby, J., Casanueva, C., & Mann, T. (2007). *Developmental status and early intervention service needs of maltreated children.* Washington, DC: U.S. Department of Health and Human Services, Office of the Assistant Secretary for Planning and Evaluation.

Barthel, F. P., Wei, W., Tang, M., Martinez-Ledesma, E., Hu, X., Amin, S. B., . . . Verhaak, R. G. W. (2017). Systematic analysis of telomere length and somatic alterations in 31 cancer types. *Nature Genetics, 49*(3), 349–357. http://doi.org/10.1038/ng.3781

Bartholomew, J., Holroyd, S., & Heffernan, T. M. (2010). Does cannabis use affect prospective memory in young adults? *Journal of Psychopharmacology, 24*(2), 241–246. http://doi.org/10.1177/0269881109106909

Bartone, P. T. (2006). Resilience under military operational stress: Can leaders influence hardiness. *Military Psychology, 18*, S131–S148.

Bartone, P. T., Roland, R. R., & Picano, J. J. (2008). Psychological hardiness predicts success in U.S. Army Special Forces candidates. *International Journal of Selection and Assessment, 16*(1), 78–81.

Barulli, D., & Stern, Y. (2013). Efficiency, capacity, compensation, maintenance, plasticity: Emerging concepts in cognitive reserve. *Trends in Cognitive Sciences, 17*(10), 502–509. http://doi.org/10.1016/j.tics.2013.08.012

Basile, K. C., DeGue, S., Jones, K., Freire, K., Dills, J., Smith, S. G., & Raiford, J. L. (2016). *STOP SV: A technical package to prevent sexual violence.* Retrieved from https://www.cdc.gov/violenceprevention/pdf/SV-Prevention-Technical-Package.pdf

Basow, S. (2008). Gender socialization, or how long a way has baby come? In J. C. Chrisler, C. Golden, & P. D. Rozee (Eds.), *Lectures on the psychology of women* (4th ed., pp. 81–95). New York, NY: McGraw-Hill.

Bassano, D. (2000). Early development of nouns and verbs in French: Exploring the interface between lexicon and grammar. *Journal of Child Language, 27*, 521–559.

Bassuk, S. S., & Manson, J. E. (2005). Epidemiological evidence for the role of physical activity in reducing risk of type 2 diabetes and cardiovascular disease. *Journal of Applied Physiology, 99*(3), 1193–1204.

Bastaits, K., & Mortelmans, D. (2016). Parenting as mediator between post-divorce family structure and children's well-being. *Journal of Child and Family Studies, 25*(7), 2178–2188. http://doi.org/10.1007/s10826-016-0395-8

Basten, U., Hilger, K., & Fiebach, C. J. (2015). Where smart brains are different: A quantitative meta-analysis of functional and structural brain imaging studies on intelligence. *Intelligence, 51*, 10–27. http://doi.org/10.1016/j.intell.2015.04.009

Basten, U., Stelzel, C., & Fiebach, C. J. (2013). Intelligence is differentially related to neural effort in the task-positive and the task-negative brain network. *Intelligence, 41*(5), 517–528. http://doi.org/10.1016/j.intell.2013.07.006

Batalova, J. A., & Cohen, P. N. (2002). Premarital cohabitation and housework: Couples in cross-national perspective. *Journal of Marriage & Family, 64*(3), 743–755.

Bates, A. T., & Kearney, J. A. (2015). Understanding death with limited experience in life: Dying children's and adolescents' understanding of their own terminal illness and death. *Current Opinion in Supportive and Palliative Care, 9*(1), 40–45. http://doi.org/10.1097/SPC.0000000000000118

Bates, E. (1990). Language about me and you: Pronominal reference and the emerging concept of self. In D. Cicchetti & M. Beeghly (Eds.), *The self in transition: Infancy to childhood* (pp. 165–182). Chicago: University of Chicago Press.

Bates, E., Bretherton, I., & Snyder, L. (1988). *From first words to grammar*. Cambridge, UK: Cambridge University Press.

Bates, J., Pettit, G., Dodge, K., & Ridge, B. (1998). Interaction of temperamental resistance to control and restrictive parenting in the development of externalizing behavior. *Developmental Psychology, 34*, 982–995.

Battin-Pearson, S., & Newcomb, M. D. (2000). Predictors of early high school dropout: A test of five theories. *Journal of Educational Psychology, 92*(3), 15p.

Batty, G. D., Deary, I. J., & Macintyre, S. (2006). Childhood IQ and life course socioeconomic position in relation to alcohol induced hangovers in adulthood: The Aberdeen children of the 1950s study. *Journal of Epidemiology and Community Health, 60*(10), 872–874. http://doi.org/10.1136/jech.2005.045039

Bauer, K. W., Larson, N. I., Nelson, M. C., Story, M., & Neumark-Sztainer, D. (2009). Fast food intake among adolescents: Secular and longitudinal trends from 1999 to 2004. *Preventive Medicine, 48*(3), 284–287. http://doi.org/10.1016/j.ypmed.2008.12.021

Bauer, M., Haesler, E., & Fetherstonhaugh, D. (2016). Let's talk about sex: Older people's views on the recognition of sexuality and sexual health in the health-care setting. *Health Expectations, 19*(6), 1237–1250. http://doi.org/10.1111/hex.12418

Bauer, M., McAuliffe, L., & Nay, R. (2007). Sexuality, health care and the older person: An overview of the literature. *International Journal of Older People Nursing, 2*(1), 63–68. Retrieved from r.nay@latrobe.edu.au

Bauer, P. J. (1996). Development of memory in early childhood. In N. Cowan (Ed.), *The development of memory in childhood* (pp. 83–112). Hove, UK: Psychology Press.

Baum, C. L., & Ruhm, C. J. (2009). Age, socioeconomic status and obesity growth. *Journal of Health Economics, 28*(3), 635–648. http://doi.org/10.1016/j.jhealeco.2009.01.004

Bauman, S., Toomey, R. B., & Walker, J. L. (2013). Associations among bullying, cyberbullying, and suicide in high school students. *Journal of Adolescence, 36*(2), 341–50. http://doi.org/10.1016/j.adolescence.2012.12.001

Baumbusch, J. L. (2004). Unclaimed treasures: Older women's reflections on lifelong singlehood. *Journal of Women & Aging, 16*(1/2), 105–121.

Baumeister, R. F., Tice, D. M., & Hutton, D. G. (1989). Self-presentational motivations and personality differences in self-esteem. *Journal of Personality, 57*(3), 547–579. http://doi.org/10.1111/j.1467-6494.1989.tb02384.x

Bauminger, N., Finzi-Dottan, R., Chason, S., & Har-Even, D. (2008). Intimacy in adolescent friendship: The roles of attachment, coherence, and self-disclosure. *Journal of Social & Personal Relationships, 25*(3), 409–428. http://doi.org/10.1177/0265407508090866

Baumrind, D. (1971). Current patterns of parental authority. *Developmental Psychology, 4*(Monograph 1), 1–103.

Baumrind, D. (1996). A blanket injunction against disciplinary use of spanking is not warranted by the data. *Pediatrics, 88*, 828–831.

Baumrind, D., Larzelere, R. E., & Owens, E. B. (2010). Effects of preschool parents' power assertive patterns and practices on adolescent development. *Parenting: Science & Practice, 10*(3), 157–201. http://doi.org/10.1080/15295190903290790

Baus, C., Costa, A., & Carreiras, M. (2013). On the effects of second language immersion on first language production. *Acta Psychologica, 142*(3), 402–409. http://doi.org/10.1016/j.actpsy.2013.01.010

Bava, S., & Tapert, S. F. (2010). Adolescent brain development and the risk for alcohol and other drug problems. *Neuropsychology Review, 20*(4), 398–413. http://doi.org/10.1007/s11065-010-9146-6

Baxter Magolda, M. B. (2004). Evolution of a constructivist conceptualization of epistemological reflection. *Educational Psychologist, 39*(1), 31–42. http://doi.org/10.1207/s15326985ep3901_4

Bayley, N. (1949). Consistency and variability in the growth of intelligence from birth to eighteen years. *The Pedagogical Seminary and Journal of Genetic Psychology, 75*(2), 165–196. http://doi.org/10.1080/08856559.1949.10533516

Bayley, N. (1955). On the growth of intelligence. *American Psychologist, 10*(12), 805–818. http://doi.org/10.1037/h0043803

Bayley, N. (1969). *Manual for the Bayley Scales of Infant Development*. San Antonio, TX: Psychological Corporation.

Bayley, N. (2005). *Bayley scales of infant and toddler development* (3rd ed.). San Antonio, TX: Psychological Corporation.

Bazzano, A. N., Kirkwood, B., Tawiah-Agyemang, C., Owusu-Agyei, S., & Adongo, P. (2008). Social costs of skilled attendance at birth in rural Ghana. *International Journal of Gynecology & Obstetrics, 102*(1), 91–94. http://doi.org/10.1016/j.ijgo.2008.02.004

Beach, S. R. H., Brody, G. H., Gunter, T. D., Packer, H., Wernett, P., & Philibert, R. A. (2010). Child maltreatment moderates the association of MAOA with symptoms of depression and antisocial personality disorder. *Journal of Family Psychology, 24*(1), 12–20.

Beal, C. R. (1994). *Boys and girls: The development of gender roles*. New York, NY: McGraw-Hill.

Beatty, W. W. (1992). Gonadal hormones and sex differences in nonreproductive behaviors. In A. A. Gerall, H. Moltz, & I. L. Ward (Eds.), *Handbook of behavioral neurobiology: Vol. 11. Sexual differentiation* (pp. 85–128). New York: Plenum.

Beauchamp, G. K., & Mennella, J. A. (2011). Flavor perception in human infants: Development and functional significance. *Digestion, 83 Suppl 1*, 1–6. http://doi.org/10.1159/000323397

Beautrais, A. L. (2003). Suicide and serious suicide attempts in youth: A multiple-group comparison study. *American Journal of Psychiatry, 160*, 1093–1100.

Becht, A. I., Nelemans, S. A., Branje, S. J. T., Vollebergh, W. A. M., Koot, H. M., Denissen, J. J. A., & Meeus, W. H. J. (2016). The quest for identity in adolescence: Heterogeneity in daily identity formation and psychosocial adjustment across 5 years. *Developmental Psychology, 52*(12), 2010–2021. http://doi.org/10.1037/dev0000245

Becker, A. E., Keel, P., Anderson-Fye, E. P., & Thomas, J. J. (2004). Genes and/or jeans? Genetic and socio-cultural contributions to risk for eating disorders. *Journal of Addictive Diseases, 23*(3), 81–103. http://doi.org/10.1300/J069v23n03_07

Becker-Stoll, F., Fremmer-Bombik, E., Wartner, U., Zimmermann, P., & Grossmann, K. E. (2008). Is attachment at ages 1, 6 and 16 related to autonomy and relatedness behavior of adolescents in interaction towards their mothers? *International Journal of Behavioral Development, 32*(5), 372–380. http://doi.org/10.1177/0165025408093654

Beebe, B., Jaffe, J., Markese, S., Buck, K., Chen, H., Cohen, P., . . . Feldstein, S. (2010). The origins of 12-month attachment: A microanalysis of 4-month mother-infant interaction. *Attachment & Human Development, 12*(1/2), 3–141. http://doi.org/10.1080/14616730903338985

Behnke, M., & Smith, V. C. (2013). Prenatal substance abuse: Short- and long-term effects on the exposed fetus. *Pediatrics, 131*(3), e1009-24. http://doi.org/10.1542/peds.2012-3931

Behrend, D. A., Rosengren, K., & Perlmetter, M. (1989). A new look at children's private speech: The effects of age, task difficulty, and parent presence. *International Journal of Behavioral Development, 12*, 305–320.

Behrend, D. A., Scofield, J., & Kleinknecht, E. E. (2001). Beyond fast mapping: Young children's extensions of novel words and novel facts. *Developmental Psychology, 37*, 698–705.

Behrens, K. Y., Parker, A. C., & Haltigan, J. D. (2011). Maternal sensitivity assessed during the Strange Situation procedure predicts child's attachment quality and reunion behaviors. *Infant Behavior & Development, 34*(2), 378–381. http://doi.org/10.1016/j.infbeh.2011.02.007

Behrens, M., Pilz, M., & Greuling, O. (2008). Taking a straightforward detour: Learning and labour market participation in the German apprenticeship system. *Journal of Vocational Education & Training, 60*(1), 93–104. http://doi.org/10.1080/13636820701837730

Beier, M. E., & Ackerman, P. L. (2005). Age, ability, and the role of prior knowledge on the acquisition of new domain knowledge: Promising results in a real-world learning environment. *Psychology and Aging, 20*(2), 341–355.

Beilin, H., & Fireman, G. (2000). The foundation of Piaget's theories: Mental and physical action. In H. W. Reese (Ed.), *Advances in child development and behavior* (Vol. 27, pp. 221–246). San Diego, CA: Academic Press.

Belcher, B. R., Berrigan, D., Dodd, K. W., Emken, B. A., Chou, C.-P., & Spruijt-Metz, D. (2010). Physical activity in US youth: Effect of race/ethnicity, age, gender, and weight status. *Medicine and Science in Sports and Exercise, 42*(12), 2211–2221. http://doi.org/10.1249/MSS.0b013e3181e1fba9

Bello, V. M. E., & Schultz, R. R. (2011). Prevalence of treatable and reversible dementias: A study in a dementia outpatient clinic. *Dementia & Neuropsychologia, 5*(1), 44–47.

Bellou, V., Belbasis, L., Tzoulaki, I., Evangelou, E., & Ioannidis, J. P. A. (2016). Environmental risk factors and Parkinson's disease: An umbrella review of meta-analyses. *Parkinsonism & Related Disorders, 23*, 1–9. http://doi.org/10.1016/j.parkreldis.2015.12.008

Belsky, J. (2005). Attachment theory and research in ecological perspective: Insights from the Pennsylvania Infant and Family Development Project and the NICHD Study of Early Child Care. In K. E. Grossmann, K. Grossmann, & E. Waters (Eds.), *Attachment from infancy to adulthood: The major longitudinal studies* (pp. 71–97). New York, NY: Guilford Press.

Belsky, J., & Fearon, R. M. P. (2002). Infant-mother attachment security, contextual risk, and early development: A moderational analyses. *Development and Psychopathology, 14*, 293–310.

Belsky, J., & Hartman, S. (2014). Gene-environment interaction in evolutionary perspective: Differential susceptibility to environmental influences. *World Psychiatry, 13*(1), 87–89. http://doi.org/10.1002/wps.20092

Belsky, J., Jaffee, S., Hsieh, K.-H., & Silva, P. A. (2001). Child-rearing antecedents of intergenerational relations in young adulthood: A prospective study. *Developmental Psychology, 37*(6), 801–813.

Belson, K. (2013). *Explaining the N.F.L. settlement.* Retrieved from http://www.nytimes.com/2013/08/30/sports/football/nfl-settlement-leaves-many-questions-for-fans.html

Belza, B., Walwick, J., Shiu-Thornton, S., Schwartz, S., Taylor, M., & LoGerfo, J. (2004). Older adult perspectives on physical activity and exercise: Voices from multiple cultures. *Preventing Chronic Disease, 1*(4), A09.

Bem, S. L. (1974). The measurement of psychological androgyny. *Journal of Consulting and Clinical Psychology, 42*(2), 155–162. Retrieved from http://www.ncbi.nlm.nih.gov/pubmed/4823550

Bem, S. L. (1985). Androgyny and gender schema theory: A conceptual and empirical integration. In T. B. Sondregger (Ed.), *Nebraska Symposium on Motivation, 1984: Psychology and gender* (pp. 76–103). Lincoln: University of Nebraska Press.

Benasich, A. A., & Brooks-Gunn, J. (1996). Maternal attitudes and knowledge of child-rearing: Associations with family and child outcomes. *Child Development, 67,* 1186–1205.

Benatar, M., & Benatar, D. (2003). Between prophylaxis and child abuse: The ethics of neonatal male circumcision. *American Journal of Bioethics, 3*(2), 35–48.

Bender, A., Jox, R. J., Grill, E., Straube, A., & Lulé, D. (2015). Persistent vegetative state and minimally conscious state: A systematic review and meta-analysis of diagnostic procedures. *Deutsches Ärzteblatt International, 112*(14), 235–242. http://doi.org/10.3238/arztebl.2015.0235

Bender, A. R., Völkle, M. C., & Raz, N. (2016). Differential aging of cerebral white matter in middle-aged and older adults: A seven-year follow-up. *NeuroImage, 125,* 74–83. http://doi.org/10.1016/j.neuroimage.2015.10.030

Bendersky, M., & Lewis, M. (1999). Prenatal cocaine exposure and neonatal condition. *Infant Behavior and Development, 22,* 353–366.

Benenson, J. F., & Christakos, A. (2003). The greater fragility of females' versus males' closest same-sex friendships. *Child Development, 74,* 1123–1129.

Benenson, J. F., & Heath, A. (2006). Boys withdraw more in one-on-one interactions, whereas girls withdraw more in groups. *Developmental Psychology, 42,* 272–282.

Bengtson, V. L., & DeLiema, M. (2016). Theories of aging and social gerontology: Explaining how social factors influence well-being in later life. In M. H. Meyer & E. A. Daniele (Eds.), *Gerontology: Changes, challenges, and solutions* (pp. 25–56). New York, NY: ABC-CLIO.

Bengston, V. L., Gans, D., Pulney, N. M., & Silverstein, M. (2009). *Handbook of theories of aging* (2nd ed.). New York, NY: Springer.

Bengtson, V. L., Silverstein, M., Putney, N. M., & Harris, S. C. (2015). Does religiousness increase with age? Age changes and generational differences over 35 years. *Journal for the Scientific Study of Religion, 54*(2), 363–379. http://doi.org/10.1111/jssr.12183

Benner, A. D., & Graham, S. (2009). The transition to high school as a developmental process among multiethnic urban youth. *Child Development, 80*(2), 356–376. http://doi.org/10.1111/j.1467-8624.2009.01265.x

Benner, G. J., Beaudoin, K., Kinder, D., & Mooney, P. (2005). The relationship between the beginning reading skills and social adjustment of a general sample of elementary aged children. *Education & Treatment of Children, 28*(3), 250–264.

Benner, G. J., Nelson, J. R., & Epstein, M. H. (2002). The language skills of students with emotional and behavioral disorders: A literature review. *Journal of Emotional and Behavioral Disorders, 10,* 43–59.

Bennett, D. S., Bendersky, M., & Lewis, M. (2005). Does the organization of emotional expression change over time? Facial expressivity from 4 to 12 months. *Infancy, 8*(2), 167–187. http://doi.org/10.1207/s15327078in0802_4

Bennett, I. J., & Madden, D. J. (2014). Disconnected aging: Cerebral white matter integrity and age-related differences in cognition. *Neuroscience, 276,* 187–205. http://doi.org/10.1016/j.neuroscience.2013.11.026

Bennett, K. M., Hughes, G. M., & Smith, P. T. O. (2005). Psychological response to later life widowhood: Coping and the effects of gender. *Omega: Journal of Death & Dying, 51*(1), 33–52.

Benoit, A., Lacourse, E., & Claes, M. (2013). Pubertal timing and depressive symptoms in late adolescence: The moderating role of individual, peer, and parental factors. *Development and Psychopathology, 25*(2), 455–71. http://doi.org/10.1017/S0954579412001174

Benowitz-Fredericks, C. A., Garcia, K., Massey, M., Vasagar, B., & Borzekowski, D. L. G. (2012). Body image, eating disorders, and the relationship to adolescent media use. *Pediatric Clinics of North America, 59*(3), 693–704. http://doi.org/10.1016/j.pcl.2012.03.017

Benson, J. E., Sabbagh, M. A., Carlson, S. M., & Zelazo, P. D. (2013). Individual differences in executive functioning predict preschoolers' improvement from theory-of-mind training. *Developmental Psychology, 49*(9), 1615–1627. http://doi.org/10.1037/a0031056

Benz, C. C. (2008). Impact of aging on the biology of breast cancer. *Critical Reviews in Oncology/Hematology, 66*(1), 65–74. http://doi.org/10.1016/j.critrevonc.2007.09.001

Berenbaum, S. A., & Beltz, A. M. (2011). Sexual differentiation of human behavior: Effects of prenatal and pubertal organizational hormones. *Frontiers in Neuroendocrinology, 32*(2), 183–200. http://doi.org/10.1016/j.yfrne.2011.03.001

Berenbaum, S. A., Blakemore, J. E. O., & Beltz, A. M. (2011). A role for biology in gender-related behavior. *Sex Roles, 64*(11–12), 804–825. http://doi.org/10.1007/s11199-011-9990-8

Berg, K. M., Kunins, H. V, Jackson, J. L., Nahvi, S., Chaudhry, A., Harris, K. A., . . . Arnsten, J. H. (2008). Association between alcohol consumption and both osteoporotic fracture and bone density. *American Journal of Medicine, 121*(5), 406–418. http://doi.org/10.1016/j.amjmed.2007.12.012

Berge, J. M., MacLehose, R. F., Larson, N., Laska, M., & Neumark-Sztainer, D. (2016). Family food preparation and its effects on adolescent dietary quality and eating patterns. *Journal of Adolescent Health.* http://doi.org/10.1016/j.jadohealth.2016.06.007

Berge, J. M., Wall, M., Hsueh, T.-F., Fulkerson, J. A., Larson, N., & Neumark-Sztainer, D. (2015). The protective role of family meals for youth obesity: 10-year longitudinal associations. *The Journal of Pediatrics, 166*(2), 296–301. http://doi.org/10.1016/j.jpeds.2014.08.030

Bergelson, E., & Swingley, D. (2012). At 6–9 months, human infants know the meanings of many common nouns. *Proceedings of the National Academy of Sciences of the United States of America, 109*(9), 3253–3258. http://doi.org/10.1073/pnas.1113380109

Berger, S. E., Theuring, C., & Adolph, K. E. (2007). How and when infants learn to climb stairs. *Infant Behavior & Development, 30*(1), 36–49. http://doi.org/10.1016/j.infbeh.2006.11.002

Bergland, A., Nicolaisen, M., & Thorsen, K. (2014). Predictors of subjective age in people aged 40–79 years: A five-year follow-up study. The impact of

mastery, mental and physical health. *Aging & Mental Health, 18*(5), 653–661. http://doi.org/10.1080/13607863.2013.869545

Bergman, N. J. (2015). Proposal for mechanisms of protection of supine sleep against sudden infant death syndrome: An integrated mechanism review. *Pediatric Research, 77*(1–1), 10–19. http://doi.org/10.1038/pr.2014.140

Bering, J. M., & Bjorklund, D. F. (2004). The natural emergence of reasoning about the afterlife as a developmental regularity. *Developmental Psychology, 40*(2), 217–233. http://doi.org/10.1037/0012-1649.40.2.217

Berk, L. E. (1986a). Development of private speech among preschool children. *Early Child Development and Care, 24,* 113–136.

Berk, L. E. (1986b). Relationship of elementary school children's private speech to behavioral accompaniment to task, attention, and task performance. *Developmental Psychology, 22,* 671–680.

Berk, L. E. (1992). The extracurriculum. In P. W. Jackson (Ed.), *Handbook of research on curriculum* (pp. 1003–1043). New York, NY: Macmillan.

Berk, L. E., & Garvin, R. A. (1984). Development of private speech among low-income Appalachian children. *Developmental Psychology, 20,* 271–286.

Berk, L. E., & Spuhl, S. (1995). Maternal interaction, private speech, and task performance in preschool children. *Early Childhood Research Quarterly, 10,* 145–169.

Berkman, N. D., Lohr, K. N., & Bulik, C. M. (2007). Outcomes of eating disorders: A systematic review of the literature. *International Journal of Eating Disorders, 40*(4), 293–309.

Berman, S. L., Weems, C. F., Rodriguez, E. T., & Zamora, I. J. (2006). The relation between identity status and romantic attachment style in middle and late adolescence. *Journal of Adolescence, 29*(5), 737–748.

Bernard, S., & Deleau, M. (2007). Conversational perspective-taking and false belief attribution: A longitudinal study. *British Journal of Developmental Psychology, 25*(3), 443–460.

Berndt, T. J. (2004). Children's friendships: Shifts over a half-century in perspectives on their development and their effects. *Merrill-Palmer Quarterly, 50*(3), 138–155.

Berndt, T. J., & Murphy, L. M. (2002). Influences of friends and friendships: Myths, truths, and research recommendations. In R. V Kail (Ed.), *Advances in child development and behavior* (Vol. 30, pp. 275–310). San Diego, CA: Academic Press.

Bernier, A., Calkins, S. D., & Bell, M. A. (2016). Longitudinal associations between the quality of mother-infant interactions and brain development across infancy. *Child Development, 87*(4), 1159–1174. http://doi.org/10.1111/cdev.12518

Bernier, A., & Meins, E. (2008). A threshold approach to understanding the origins of attachment disorganization. *Developmental Psychology, 44*(4), 969–982. http://doi.org/10.1037/0012-1649.444.969

Bernstein, D. M., Atance, C., Meltzoff, A. N., & Loftus, G. R. (2007). Hindsight bias and developing theories of mind. *Child Development, 78*(4), 1374–1394.

Berntsen, D., & Rubin, D. C. (2002). Emotionally charged autobiographical memories across the life span: The recall of happy, sad, traumatic and involuntary memories. *Psychology and Aging, 17*(4), 636–652.

Berra, S., Sabulsky, J., Rajmil, L., Passamonte, R., Pronsato, J., & Butinof, M. (2003). Correlates of breastfeeding duration in an urban cohort from Argentina. *Acta Paediatrics, 92,* 952–957.

Berridge, K. C., & Kringelbach, M. L. (2008). Affective neuroscience of pleasure: Reward in humans and animals. *Psychopharmacology, 199*(3), 457–80. https://doi.org/10.1007/s00213-008-1099-6

Bersamin, M. M., Paschall, M. J., Saltz, R. F., & Zamboanga, B. L. (2012). Young adults and casual sex: The relevance of college drinking settings. *Journal of Sex Research, 49*(2–3), 274–281. http://doi.org/10.1080/00224499.2010.548012

Bersamin, M. M., Zamboanga, B. L., Schwartz, S. J., Donnellan, M. B., Hudson, M., Weisskirch, R. S., . . . Caraway, S. J. (2014). Risky business: Is there an association between casual sex and mental health among emerging adults? *The Journal of Sex Research, 51*(1), 43–51. http://doi.org/10.1080/00224499.2013.772088

Bertenthal, B. I., & Campos, J. J. (1990). A systems approach to the organizing effects of self-produced locomotion during infancy. In C. Rovee-Collier & L. P. Lipsitt (Eds.), *Advances in infancy research* (pp. 1–60). Norwood, NJ: Ablex.

Bertenthal, B. I., Campos, J. J., & Barrett, K. (1984). Self-produced locomotion: An organizer of emotional, cognitive, and social development in infancy. In R. Emde & R. Harmon (Eds.), *Continuities and discontinuities in development* (pp. 174–210). New York, NY: Plenum.

Bertenthal, B. I., Longo, M. R., & Kenny, S. (2007). Phenomenal permanence and the development of predictive tracking in infancy. *Child Development, 78*(1), 350–363. http://doi.org/10.1111/j.1467-8624.2007.01002.x

Bertrand, R., & Camos, V. (2015). The role of attention in preschoolers' working memory. *Cognitive Development, 33*, 14–27. http://doi.org/10.1016/j.cogdev.2014.10.002

Berzonsky, M. D., & Kuk, L. S. (2000). Identity status, identity processing style, and the transition to university. *Journal of Adolescent Research, 15*, 81–99.

Best, D. L., House, A. S., Barnard, A. E., & Spicker, B. S. (1994). Parent-child interactions in France, Germany, and Italy: The effects of gender and culture. *Journal of Cross-Cultural Psychology, 25*(2), 181–193. http://doi.org/10.1177/0022022194252002

Best, D. L., & Williams, J. E. (2001). Gender and Culture. In D. Matsumoto (Ed.), *The handbook of culture and psychology* (pp. 195–219). New York, NY: Oxford University Press.

Best, L. E., Hayward, M. D., & Hidajat, M. M. (2005). Life course pathways to adult-onset diabetes. *Social Biology, 52*(3/4), 94–111.

Best, R. M., Dockrell, J. E., & Braisby, N. R. (2006). Real-world word learning: Exploring children's developing semantic representations of a science term. *British Journal of Developmental Psychology, 24*(2), 265–282.

Bettelheim, B. (1977). *The uses of enchantment—The meaning and importance of fairy tales.* New York: Vintage Books.

Bettens, K., Sleegers, K., & Van Broeckhoven, C. (2013). Genetic insights in Alzheimer's disease. *The Lancet. Neurology, 12*(1), 92–104. http://doi.org/10.1016/S1474-4422(12)70259-4

Beutel, M. E., Glaesmer, H., Wiltink, J., Marian, H., & Brähler, E. (2010). Life satisfaction, anxiety, depression and resilience across the life span of men. *Journal of the International Society for the Study of the Aging Male, 13*(1), 32–39.

Beyene, Y. (1986). Cultural significance and physiological manifestations of menopause: A biocultural analysis. *Culture, Medicine and Psychiatry, 10*(1), 47–71. http://doi.org/10.1007/BF00053262

Beyene, Y., & Martin, M. C. (2001). Menopausal experiences and bone density of Mayan women in Yucatan, Mexico. *American Journal of Human Biology, 13*(4), 505–511.

Beyers, W., & Seiffge-Krenke, I. (2010). Does identity precede intimacy? Testing Erikson's theory on romantic development in emerging adults of the 21st century. *Journal of Adolescent Research, 25*(3), 387–415. http://doi.org/10.1177/0743558410361370

Bialystok, E. (2011). Coordination of executive functions in monolingual and bilingual children. *Journal of Experimental Child Psychology, 110*(3), 461–468. http://doi.org/10.1016/j.jecp.2011.05.005

Bialystok, E. (2015). Bilingualism and the development of executive function: The role of attention. *Child Development Perspectives, 9*(2), 117–121. http://doi.org/10.1111/cdep.12116

Bialystok, E., & Craik, F. I. M. (2010). Structure and process in life-span cognitive development. In W. F. Overton (Ed.), *The handbook of life-span development*. Hoboken, NJ: John Wiley & Sons. http://doi.org/10.1002/9780470880166.hlsd001007

Bialystok, E., Peets, K. F., & Moreno, S. (2014). Producing bilinguals through immersion education: Development of metalinguistic awareness. *Applied Psycholinguistics, 35*(1), 177–191. http://doi.org/10.1017/S0142716412000288

Bian, L., Leslie, S.-J., & Cimpian, A. (2017). Gender stereotypes about intellectual ability emerge early and influence children's interests. *Science, 355*(6323), 389–391. http://doi.org/10.1126/science.aah6524

Biblarz, T. J., & Savci, E. (2010). Lesbian, gay, bisexual, and transgender families. *Journal of Marriage and Family, 72*(3), 480–497. http://doi.org/10.1111/j.1741-3737.2010.00714.x

Bibok, M. B., Carpendale, J. I. M., & Müller, U. (2009). Parental scaffolding and the development of executive function. *New Directions for Child & Adolescent Development, 2009*(123), 17–34. http://doi.org/10.1002/cd.233

Biehl, M., Natsuaki, M., & Ge, X. (2007). The influence of pubertal timing on alcohol use and heavy drinking trajectories. *Journal of Youth & Adolescence, 36*(2), 153–167.

Bielak, A. A. M. (2010). How can we not "lose it" if we still don't understand how to "use it"? Unanswered questions about the influence of activity participation on cognitive performance in older age—A mini-review. *Gerontology, 56*(5), 507–519. http://doi.org/10.1159/000264918

Bierman, K. L., Kalvin, C. B., & Heinrichs, B. S. (2014). Early Childhood Precursors and Adolescent Sequelae of Grade School Peer Rejection and Victimization. *Journal of Clinical Child and Adolescent Psychology*. http://doi.org/10.1080/15374416.2013.873983

Bigelow, A. E. (2001). Discovering self through other: Infants' preference for social contingency. *Bulletin of the Menninger Clinic, 65*(3), 335.

Billing, A., Ehrle, J., & Kortenkamp, K. (2002). *children cared for by relatives: What do we know about their well-being?* Washington DC: The Urban Institute.

Bing, N. M., Nelson, W. M., & Wesolowski, K. L. (2009). Comparing the Effects of Amount of Conflict on Children's Adjustment Following Parental Divorce. *Journal of Divorce & Remarriage, 50*(3), 159–171. http://doi.org/10.1080/10502550902717699

Binner, S. L., Mastrobattista, J. M., Day, M.-C., Swaim, L. S., & Monga, M. (2003). Effect of parental education on decision-making about neonatal circumcision. *Southern Medical Journal, 95*(4), 457–461.

Birch, L. L., & Fisher, J. A. (1995). Appetite and eating behavior in children. *Pediatric Clinics of North America, 42*, 931–953.

Birch, S. A. J. (2005). When knowledge is a curse: Biases in mental state attribution. *Current Directions in Psychological Science, 14*, 25–29.

Bird, R. J., & Hurren, B. J. (2016). Anatomical and clinical aspects of Klinefelter's syndrome. *Clinical Anatomy, 29*(5), 606–619. http://doi.org/10.1002/ca.22695

Birditt, K. S., & Fingerman, K. L. (2003). Age and Gender Differences in Adults' Descriptions of Emotional Reactions to Interpersonal Problems. *The Journals of Gerontology Series B: Psychological Sciences and Social Sciences, 58*(4), P237–P245. http://doi.org/10.1093/geronb/58.4.P237

Birditt, K. S., & Fingerman, K. L. (2005). Do We Get Better at Picking Our Battles? Age Group Differences in Descriptions of Behavioral Reactions to Interpersonal Tensions. *The Journals of Gerontology Series B: Psychological Sciences and Social Sciences, 60*(3), P121–P128. http://doi.org/10.1093/geronb/60.3.P121

Birditt, K. S., Manalel, J. A., Kim, K., Zarit, S. H., & Fingerman, K. L. (2017). Daily Interactions With Aging Parents and Adult Children: Associations With Negative Affect and Diurnal Cortisol. *Journal of Family Psychology*. http://doi.org/10.1037/fam0000317

Birkeland, M. S., Breivik, K., & Wold, B. (2014). Peer acceptance protects global self-esteem from negative effects of low closeness to parents during adolescence and early adulthood. *Journal of Youth and Adolescence, 43*(1), 70–80. http://doi.org/10.1007/s10964-013-9929-1

Birkett, M., Newcomb, M. E., & Mustanski, B. (2015). Does It Get Better? A Longitudinal Analysis of Psychological Distress and Victimization in Lesbian, Gay, Bisexual, Transgender, and Questioning Youth. *Journal of Adolescent Health, 56*(3), 280–285. http://doi.org/10.1016/j.jadohealth.2014.10.275

Birney, D. P., & Sternberg, R. J. (2011). The development of cognitive abilities. Developmental science: An advanced textbook. In M. H. Bornstein & M. E. Lamb (Eds.), *Developmental science: An advanced textbook* (6th ed., pp. 353–388). New York: Psychology Press.

Biro, F. M., Khoury, P., & Morrison, J. A. (2006). Influence of obesity on timing of puberty. *International Journal of Andrology, 29*(1), 272–277.

Biro, S., Alink, L. R. A., van IJzendoorn, M. H., & Bakermans-Kranenburg, M. J. (2014). Infants' monitoring of social interactions: The effect of emotional cues. *Emotion, 14*(2), 263–271.

Bishop, B. J. (2008). Stress and Depression among Older Residents in Religious Monasteries: Do Friends and God Matter? *International Journal of Aging & Human Development, 67*(1), 1–23.

Bisiacchi, P. S., Borella, E., Bergamaschi, S., Carretti, B., & Mondini, S. (2008). Interplay between memory and executive functions in normal and pathological aging. *Journal of Clinical & Experimental Neuropsychology, 30*(6), 723–733. http://doi.org/10.1080/13803390701689587

Björkenstam, E., Hallqvist, J., Dalman, C., & Ljung, R. (2013). Risk of new psychiatric episodes in the year following divorce in midlife: cause or selection? A nationwide register-based study of 703,960 individuals. *The International Journal of Social Psychiatry, 59*(8), 801–4. http://doi.org/10.1177/0020764012461213

Bjorklund, D. F. (2013). *Children's Strategies: Contemporary Views of Cognitive Development.* Psychology Press.

Bjorklund, D. F., & Douglas, R. N. (1997). The development of memory strategies. In N. Cowan (Ed.), *The development of memory in childhood* (pp. 83–111). Hove, UK: Psychology Press.

Bjorklund, D. F., & Myers, A. (2015). The Development of Cognitive Abilities. In M. H. Bornstein & M. E. Lamb (Eds.), *Developmental science: An advanced textbook* (pp. 391–441). New York: Psychology Press.

Bjorklund, D. F., & Pellegrini, A. D. (2000). Child development and evolutionary psychology. *Child Development*, 71(6), 1687–1708.

Black, B. S., Brandt, J., Rabins, P. V., Samus, Q. M., Steele, C. D., Lyketsos, C. G., & Rosenblatt, A. (2008). Participation in dementia research: rates and correlates of capacity to give informed consent. *Journal of Medical Ethics*, 34(3), 167–170. http://doi.org/10.1136/jme.2006.019786

Black, I. E., Menzel, N. N., & Bungum, T. J. (2015). The relationship among playground areas and physical activity levels in children. *Journal of Pediatric Health Care*, 29(2), 156–168. http://doi.org/10.1016/j.pedhc.2014.10.001

Black, K., Marola, J., Littman, A., Chrisler, J., & Neace, W. (2009). Gender and Form of Cereal Box Characters: Different Medium, Same Disparity. *Sex Roles*, 60(11/12), 882–889. http://doi.org/10.1007/s11199-008-9579-z

Blackburn, E. H., Epel, E. S., Lin, J., Sfeir, A., Lange, T. de, Blackburn, E. H., . . . Blau, H. M. (2015). Human telomere biology: A contributory and interactive factor in aging, disease risks, and protection. *Science (New York, N.Y.)*, 350(6265), 1193–8. http://doi.org/10.1126/science.aab3389

Blair, P. S., Sidebotham, P., Berry, P. J., Evans, M., & Fleming, P. J. (2006). Major epidemiological changes in sudden infant death syndrome: a 20-year population-based study in the UK. *Lancet (London, England)*, 367(9507), 314–9. http://doi.org/10.1016/S0140-6736(06)67968-3

Blair, R. J. R. (2007). The amygdala and ventromedial prefrontal cortex in morality and psychopathy. *Trends in Cognitive Sciences*, 11(9), 387–392. https://doi.org/10.1016/j.tics.2007.07.003

Blair, S. L. (2010). The influence of risk-taking behaviors on the transition into marriage: An examination of the long-term consequences of adolescent behavior. *Marriage & Family Review*, 46(1/2), 126–146. http://doi.org/10.1080/01494921003685169

Blakemore, J. E. O. (2003). Children's Beliefs About Violating Gender Norms: Boys Shouldn't Look Like Girls, and Girls Shouldn't Act Like Boys. *Sex Roles*, 48(9/10), 411–419. http://doi.org/10.1023/A:1023574427720

Blakemore, J. E. O., Berenbaum, S. A., & Liben, L. S. (2009). *Gender development. Gender development.* New York, NY: Psychology Press.

Blakemore, S. J. (2012). Imaging brain development: the adolescent brain. *NeuroImage*, 61(2), 397–406. http://doi.org/10.1016/j.neuroimage.2011.11.080

Blakemore, S. J., & Choudhury, S. s. (2006). Development of the adolescent brain: implications for executive function and social cognition. *Journal of Child Psychology & Psychiatry*, 47(3/4), 296–312.

Blakemore, S. J., & Mills, K. L. (2014). Is adolescence a sensitive period for sociocultural processing? *Annual Review of Psychology*, 65, 187–207. http://doi.org/10.1146/annurev-psych-010213-115202

Blanchard-Fields, F. (2007). Everyday Problem Solving and Emotion: An Adult Developmental Perspective. *Current Directions in Psychological Science*, 16(1), 26–31. http://doi.org/10.1111/j.1467-8721.2007.00469.x

Blanchette, N., Smith, M., Fernandes-Penney, A., King, S., & Read, S. (2001). Cognitive and motor development in children with vertically transmitted HIV infection. *Brain and Cognition*, 46(1–2), 50–53.

Blandon, A. Y., Calkins, S. D., Grimm, K. J., Keane, S. P., & O'Brien, M. (2010). Testing a developmental cascade model of emotional and social competence and early peer acceptance. *Development and Psychopathology*, 22(4), 737–48. http://doi.org/10.1017/S0954579410000428

Blau, N. (2016). Genetics of phenylketonuria: Then and now. *Human Mutation*, 37(6), 508–515. http://doi.org/10.1002/humu.22980

Blau, N., Shen, N., & Carducci, C. (2014). Molecular genetics and diagnosis of phenylketonuria: State of the art. *Expert Review of Molecular Diagnostics*, 14(6), 655–671. http://doi.org/10.1586/14737159.2014.923760

Blau, N., van Spronsen, F. J., & Levy, H. L. (2010). Phenylketonuria. *Lancet*, 376(9750), 1417–1427.

Bleah, D. A., & Ellett, M. L. (2010). Infant crying among recent African immigrants. *Health Care for Women International*, 31(7), 652–663. http://doi.org/10.1080/07399331003628446

Bleich, S. N., Segal, J., Wu, Y., Wilson, R., & Wang, Y. (2013). Systematic review of community-based childhood obesity prevention studies. *Pediatrics*, 132(1), e201-10. http://doi.org/10.1542/peds.2013-0886

Bleicher, K., Cumming, R. G., Naganathan, V., Seibel, M. J., Sambrook, P. N., Blyth, F. M., . . . Waite, L. M. (2011). Lifestyle factors, medications, and disease influence bone mineral density in older men: Findings from the CHAMP study. *Osteoporosis International : A Journal Established as Result of Cooperation between the European Foundation for Osteoporosis and the National Osteoporosis Foundation of the USA*, 22(9), 2421–37. http://doi.org/10.1007/s00198-010-1478-9

Bleidorn, W. (2015). What Accounts for Personality Maturation in Early Adulthood? *Current Directions in Psychological Science*, 24(3), 245–252. http://doi.org/10.1177/0963721414568662

Bleidorn, W., Buyukcan-Tetik, A., Schwaba, T., van Scheppingen, M. A., Denissen, J. J. A., & Finkenauer, C. (2016). Stability and Change in Self-Esteem During the Transition to Parenthood. *Social Psychological and Personality Science*, 7(6), 560–569. http://doi.org/10.1177/1948550616646428

Bleidorn, W., Klimstra, T. A., Denissen, J. J. A., Rentfrow, P. J., Potter, J., & Gosling, S. D. (2013). Personality Maturation Around the World: A Cross-Cultural Examination of Social-Investment Theory. *Psychological Science*, 24(12), 2530–2540. http://doi.org/10.1177/0956797613498396

Blennow, K., Mattsson, N., Schöll, M., Hansson, O., & Zetterberg, H. (2015). Amyloid biomarkers in Alzheimer's disease. *Trends in Pharmacological Sciences*, 36(5), 297–309. http://doi.org/10.1016/j.tips.2015.03.002

Bloch, L., Haase, C. M., & Levenson, R. W. (2014). Emotion regulation predicts marital satisfaction: more than a wives' tale. *Emotion (Washington, D.C.)*, 14(1), 130–44. http://doi.org/10.1037/a0034272

Bloemendaal, M., Zandbelt, B., Wegman, J., van de Rest, O., Cools, R., & Aarts, E. (2016). Contrasting neural effects of aging on proactive and reactive response inhibition. *Neurobiology of Aging*, 46, 96–106. http://doi.org/10.1016/j.neurobiolaging.2016.06.007

Blondell, S. J., Hammersley-Mather, R., & Veerman, J. L. (2014). Does physical activity prevent cognitive decline and dementia?: A systematic review and meta-analysis of longitudinal studies. *BMC Public Health*, 14(1), 510. http://doi.org/10.1186/1471-2458-14-510

Bloom, L. (2000). Commentary: Breaking the language barrier: An emergentist coalition model for the origins of word learning. *Monographs of the Society for Research in Child Development*, 65(3, Serial No. 262), 124–135.

Bluck, S., & Gluck, J. (2004). Making things better and learning a lesson: Experience wisdom across the lifespan. *Journal of Personality*, 72(3), 543–572.

Bluebond-langner, M. (1989a). Worlds of dying children and their well siblings. *Death Studies*, 13(1), 1–16. http://doi.org/10.1080/07481188908252274

Blumenthal, H., Leen-Feldner, E. W., Trainor, C. D., Babson, K. A., & Bunaciu, L. (2009). Interactive roles of pubertal timing and peer relations in predicting social anxiety symptoms among youth. *Journal of Adolescent Health*, 44(4), 401–403. http://doi.org/10.1016/j.jadohealth.2008.08.023

Blurton-Jones, M., & LaFerla, F. M. (2006). Pathways by which Aβ facilitates tau pathology. *Current Alzheimer Research*, 3(5), 437–448. http://doi.org/10.2174/156720506779025242

Bo, X., & Goldman, H. (2008). Newborn circumcision in Victoria, Australia: Reasons and parental attitudes. *ANZ Journal of Surgery*, 78(11), 1019–1022. http://doi.org/10.1111/j.1445-2197.2008.04723.x

Boake, C. (2002). From the Binet/Simon to the Wechsler/Bellevue: Tracing the History of Intelligence Testing. *Journal of Clinical and Experimental Neuropsychology (Neuropsychology, Development and Cognition: Section A)*, 24(3), 383–405. http://doi.org/10.1076/jcen.24.3.383.981

Boazman, J., & Sayler, M. (2011). Personal Well-Being of Gifted Students Following Participation in an Early College-Entrance Program. *Roeper Review*, 33(2), 76–85. http://doi.org/10.1080/02783193.2011.554153

Boccia, M., & Campos, J. J. (1989). Maternal emotional signals, social referencing, and infants' reactions to strangers. *New Directions for Child Development*, 44, 25–49. Retrieved from

Bogaert, A. F. (2005). Age at puberty and father absence in a national probability sample. *Journal of Adolescence*, 28(4), 541–546.

Bogartz, R. S., Shinskey, J. L., & Schilling, T. H. (2000). Object Permanence in Five-and-a-Half-Month-Old Infants? *Infancy*, 1(4), 403–428. http://doi.org/10.1207/S15327078IN0104_3

Bogg, T., & Roberts, B. W. (2013). The case for conscientiousness: evidence and implications for a personality trait marker of health and longevity. *Annals of Behavioral Medicine : A Publication of the Society of Behavioral Medicine*, 45(3), 278–88. http://doi.org/10.1007/s12160-012-9454-6

Bogin, B. (2011). Puberty and adolescence: An evolutionary perspective. In *Encyclopedia of Adolescence* (pp. 275–286). Elsevier. http://doi.org/10.1016/B978-0-12-373951-3.00033-8

Bohannon, J. N., Padgett, R. J., Nelson, K. E., & Mark, M. (1996). Useful evidence on negative evidence. *Developmental Psychology*, 32, 551–555.

Bohannon, J. N., & Stanowicz, L. (1988). The issue of negative evidence: Adult responses to children's language errors. *Developmental Psychology*, 24, 684–689.

Bohlmeijer, E., Roemer, M., Cuijpers, P., & Smit, F. (2007). The effects of reminiscence on psychological well-being in older adults: A meta-analysis. *Aging & Mental Health*, 11(3), 291–300. http://doi.org/10.1080/13607860600963547

Boivin, M., Brendgen, M., Vitaro, F., Forget-Dubois, N., Feng, B., Tremblay, R. E., & Dionne, G. (2013). Evidence of gene–environment correlation for peer difficulties: Disruptive behaviors predict early peer relation difficulties in school through genetic effects. *Development and Psychopathology*, 25(1), 79–92. http://doi.org/10.1017/S0954579412000910

Boker, S. M. (2013). Selection, optimization, compensation, and equilibrium dynamics. *GeroPsych: The Journal of Gerontopsychology and Geriatric Psychiatry*, 26(1), 61–73. http://doi.org/10.1024/1662-9647/a000081

Boland, A. M., Haden, C. A., & Ornstein, P. A. (2003). Boosting children's memory by training mothers in the use of an elaborative conversational style as an event unfolds. *Journal of Cognition and Development*, 4(1), 39–65.

Boldt, L. J., Kochanska, G., Yoon, J. E., & Koenig Nordling, J. (2014). Children's attachment to both parents from toddler age to middle childhood: links to adaptive and maladaptive outcomes. *Attachment & Human Development*, 16(3), 211–29. http://doi.org/10.1080/14616734.2014.889181

Bolger, K. E., Patterson, C. J., & Kupersmidt, J. B. (1998). Peer relationships and self-esteem among children who have been maltreated. *Child Development*, 69, 1171–1197.

Bolin, K., Lindgren, B., & Lundborg, P. (2008). Your next of kin or your own career?: Caring and working among the 50+ of Europe. *Journal of Health Economics*, 27(3), 718–738. http://doi.org/10.1016/j.jhealeco.2007.10.004

Bonanno, G. A., Wortman, C. B., & Nesse, R. M. (2004). Prospective Patterns of Resilience and Maladjustment During Widowhood. *Psychology and Aging*, 19(2), 260–271. http://doi.org/10.1037/0882-7974.19.2.260

Bonnel, S., Mohand-Said, S., & Sahel, J.-A. (2003). The aging of the retina. *Experimental Gerontology*, 38(8), 825. http://doi.org/10.1016/S0531-5565(03)00093-7

Bonnie, R. J., & Scott, E. S. (2013). The Teenage Brain: Adolescent Brain Research and the Law. *Current Directions in Psychological Science*, 22(2), 158–161. http://doi.org/10.1177/0963721412471678

Bonoti, F., Leondari, A., & Mastora, A. (2013). Exploring Children's Understanding of Death: Through Drawings and the Death Concept Questionnaire. *Death Studies*, 37(1), 47–60. http://doi.org/10.1080/07481187.2011.623216

Bookwala, J., & Jacobs, J. (2004). Age, Marital Processes, and Depressed Affect. *Gerontologist*, 44(3), 328–338.

Boor-Klip, H. J., Cillessen, A. H. N., & van Hell, J. G. (2014). Social Understanding of High-Ability Children in Middle and Late Childhood. *Gifted Child Quarterly*, 58(4), 259–271. http://doi.org/10.1177/0016986214547634

Booth, M. Z., & Gerard, J. M. (2014). Adolescents' Stage-Environment Fit in Middle and High School: The Relationship Between Students' Perceptions of Their Schools and Themselves. *Youth & Society*, 46(6), 735–755. http://doi.org/10.1177/0044118X12451276

Boots, E. A., Schultz, S. A., Almeida, R. P., Oh, J. M., Koscik, R. L., Dowling, M. N., . . . Okonkwo, O. C. (2015). Occupational Complexity and Cognitive Reserve in a Middle-Aged Cohort at Risk for Alzheimer's Disease. *Archives of Clinical Neuropsychology*, 30(7), 634–642. http://doi.org/10.1093/arclin/acv041

Borella, E., Carretti, B., Riboldi, F., & De Beni, R. (2010). Working memory training in older adults: Evidence of transfer and maintenance effects. *Psychology and Aging*. http://doi.org/10.1037/a0020683

Bornstein, M. H., & Arterberry, M. E. (2010). The development of object categorization in young children: Hierarchical inclusiveness, age, perceptual

attribute, and group versus individual analyses. *Developmental Psychology*, 46(2), 350–365. http://doi.org/10.1037/a0018411

Bornstein, M. H., Arterberry, M. E., & Lamb, M. E. (2013). *Development in Infancy: A Contemporary Introduction*. Psychology Press.

Bornstein, M. H., Arterberry, M. E., & Mash, C. (2004). Long-term memory for an emotional interpersonal interaction occurring at 5 months of age. *Infancy*, 6(4), 407–416.

Bornstein, M. H., Cote, L. R., Maital, S., Painter, K., Park, S.-Y., Pascual, L., . . . Vyt, A. (2004). Cross-linguistic analysis of vocabulary in young children: Spanish, Dutch, French, Hebrew, Italian, Korean, and American English. *Child Development*, 75(4), 1115–1139.

Bornstein, M. H., & Lamb, M. E. (1992). *Development in infancy* (3rd ed.). New York: McGraw-Hill.

Bornstein, M. H., & Lamb, M. E. (2011). *Developmental Science: An Advanced Textbook, Sixth Edition*. Psychology Press.

Bornstein, M. H., Putnick, D. L., Gartstein, M. A., Hahn, C.-S., Auestad, N., & O'Connor, D. L. (2015). Infant Temperament: Stability by Age, Gender, Birth Order, Term Status, and Socioeconomic Status. *Child Development*, 86(3), 844–863. http://doi.org/10.1111/cdev.12367

Bornstein, M. H., Slater, A., Brown, E., Roberts, E., & Barrett, J. (1997). Stability of mental development from infancy to later childhood: Three "waves" of research. In G. Bremner, A. Slater, & G. Butterworth (Eds.), *Infant development: Recent advances* (pp. 191–215). New York, NY: Psychology Press.

Borst, G., Poirel, N., Pineau, A., Cassotti, M., & Houdé, O. (2013). Inhibitory control efficiency in a Piaget-like class-inclusion task in school-age children and adults: a developmental negative priming study. *Developmental Psychology*, 49(7), 1366–74. http://doi.org/10.1037/a0029622

Bos, H. M. W., Knox, J. R., van Rijn-van Gelderen, L., & Gartrell, N. K. (2016). Same-Sex and Different-Sex Parent Households and Child Health Outcomes. *Journal of Developmental & Behavioral Pediatrics*, 37(3), 179–187. http://doi.org/10.1097/DBP0000000000000288

Bosch, A. M., Hutter, I., & van Ginneken, J. K. (2008). Perceptions of adolescents and their mothers on reproductive and sexual development in Matlab, Bangladesh. *International Journal of Adolescent Medicine and Health*, 20(3), 329–342.

Bosch, L., & Ramon-Casas, M. (2014). First translation equivalents in bilingual toddlers' expressive vocabulary: Does form similarity matter? *International Journal of Behavioral Development*, 38(4), 317–322. http://doi.org/10.1177/0165025414532559

Boseovski, J. J. (2010). Evidence for "rose-colored glasses": An examination of the positivity bias in young children's personality judgments. *Child Development Perspectives*, 4(3), 212–218. http://doi.org/10.1111/j.1750-8606.2010.00149.x

Bosman, E. A. (1993). Age-related differences in the motoric aspects of transcription typing skill. *Psychology and Aging*, 8, 87–102.

Boswell, G. H., Kahana, E., & Dilworth-Anderson, P. (2006). Spirituality and Healthy Lifestyle Behaviors: Stress Counter-balancing Effects on the Well-being of Older Adults. *Journal of Religion and Health*, 45(4), 587–602. http://doi.org/10.1007/s10943-006-9060-7

Bouchard, T. J. (2014). Genes, evolution and intelligence. *Behavior Genetics*, 44(6), 549–577. http://doi.org/10.1007/s10519-014-9646-x

Bouchard, T. J., & McGue, M. (1981). Familial studies of intelligence: A review. *Science*, 1055–1059.

Bouchard, T. J. J., Segal, N. L., Tellegen, A., McGue, M., Keyes, M., & Krueger, R. (2004). Genetic influence on social attitudes: Another challenge to psychology from behavior genetics. In L. F. DiLalla (Ed.), *Behavior genetics principles: Perspectives in development, personality, and psychopathology*. (pp. 89–104). Washington, DC: American Psychological Association.

Boundy, E. O., Dastjerdi, R., Spiegelman, D., Fawzi, W. W., Missmer, S. A., Lieberman, E., . . . Guedes, Z. (2015). Kangaroo mother care and neonatal outcomes: A meta-analysis. *Pediatrics*, 365(9462), 891–900. http://doi.org/10.1542/peds.2015-2238

Bourgeron, T. (2015). From the genetic architecture to synaptic plasticity in autism spectrum disorder. *Nature Reviews Neuroscience*, 16(9), 551–563. http://doi.org/10.1038/nrn3992

Bower, B. (1993). A child's theory of mind. *Science News*, 144, 40–42.

Bowers, A. J., & Sprott, R. (2012). Examining the Multiple Trajectories Associated with Dropping Out of High School: A Growth Mixture Model Analysis. *The Journal of Educational Research*, 105(3), 176–195. http://doi.org/10.1080/00220671.2011.552075

Bowker, J. C. W., Rubin, K. H., Burgess, K. B., Booth-Laforce, C., & Rose-Krasnor, L. (2006). Behavioral characteristics associated with stable and fluid best friendship patterns in middle childhood. *Merrill-Palmer Quarterly*, 52(4), 671–693.

Bowlby, J. (1969). *Attachment and loss: Vol. 1. Attachment*. New York: Basic Books.

Bowlby, J. (1973). *Attachment and loss: Vol. 2. Separation: Anxiety and anger*. New York: Basic Books.

Bowles, R. P., & Salthouse, T. A. (2003). Assessing the age-related effects of proactive interference on working memory tasks using the Rasch model. *Psychology and Aging*, 18(3), 608–615.

Bowman, L. J. (2005). Grade retention: Is it a help or hindrance to student academic success? *Preventing School Failure*, 49(3), 42–46.

Bowman, M. A., Prelow, H. M., & Weaver, S. R. (2007). Parenting Behaviors, Association with Deviant Peers, and Delinquency in African American Adolescents: A Mediated-Moderation Model. *Journal of Youth & Adolescence*, 36, 517–527.

Bowman, S. A., Gortmaker, S. L., Ebbeling, C. B., Pereira, M. A., & Ludwig, D. S. (2004). Effects of Fast-Food Consumption on Energy Intake and Diet Quality Among Children in a National Household Survey. *Pediatrics*, 113(1), 112–118.

Boyatzis, C. J., & Janicki, D. (2003). Parent-Child Communication about Religion: Survey and Diary Data on Unilateral Transmission and Bi-Directional Reciprocity Styles. *Review of Religious Research*, 44(3), 252. http://doi.org/10.2307/3512386

Boyce, W., Doherty, M., Fortin, C., & MacKinnon, D. (2003). *Canadian Youth, Sexual Health, and HIV/AIDS Study*. Toronto, Ontario: Council of Ministers of Education, Canada. Retrieved from http://www.cmec.ca/publications/aids/

Boyer, K. A., Andriacchi, T. P., Beaupre, G. S., Riley, P. O., Lipsitz, L. A., Wilson, D. K., & al., et. (2012). The role of physical activity in changes in walking mechanics with age. *Gait & Posture*, 36(1), 149–53. http://doi.org/10.1016/j.gaitpost.2012.02.007

Boyes, M. C., & Chandler, M. (1992). Cognitive development, epistemic doubt, and identity formation in adolescence. *Journal of Youth and Adolescence*, 21(3), 277–304.

Boynton-Jarrett, R., Wright, R. J., Putnam, F. W., Lividoti Hibert, E., Michels, K. B., Forman, M. R., & Rich-Edwards, J. (2013). Childhood abuse and age at menarche. *The Journal of Adolescent Health : Official Publication of the Society for Adolescent Medicine*, 52(2), 241–7. http://doi.org/10.1016/j.jadohealth.2012.06.006

Boysson-Bardies, B. De, Sagart, L., Durand, C., Eimas, P. D., Siqueland, E. R., Jusczyk, P., . . . OLLER, D. K. (1984). Discernible differences in the babbling of infants according to target language. *Journal of Child Language*, 11(1), 1–15. http://doi .org/10.1017/S0305000900005559

Bozick, R., & DeLuca, S. (2011). Not making the transition to college: School, work, and opportunities in the lives of American youth. *Social Science Research*, 40(4), 1249–1262. http://doi .org/10.1016/j.ssresearch.2011.02.003

Braams, B. R., van Duijvenvoorde, A. C. K., Peper, J. S., & Crone, E. A. (2015). Longitudinal changes in adolescent risk-taking: A comprehensive study of neural responses to rewards, pubertal development, and risk-taking behavior. *Journal of Neuroscience*, 35(18).

Bradbury, T. N., Fincham, F. D., & Beach, S. R. H. (2000). Research on the nature and determinants of marital satisfaction: A decade in review. *Journal of Marriage & Family*, 62(4), 964–980.

Bradley, R. H., & Corwyn, R. F. (2008). Infant temperament, parenting, and externalizing behavior in first grade: a test of the differential susceptibility hypothesis. *Journal of Child Psychology & Psychiatry*, 49(2), 124–131. http://doi. org/10.1111/j.1469-7610.2007.01829.x

Bradley-Whitman, M. A., & Lovell, M. A. (2013). Epigenetic changes in the progression of Alzheimer's disease. *Mechanisms of Aging and Development*, 134(10), 486–495. http://doi.org/10.1016/j. mad.2013.08.005

Bradmetz, J., & Schneider, R. (1999). Is Little Red Riding Hood afraid of her grandmother? Cognitive vs. emotional response to a false belief. *British Journal of Developmental Psychology*, 17(4), 501–514. http://doi.org/10.1348/026151099165438

Brady, K. W., & Goodman, J. C. (2014). The type, but not the amount, of information available influences toddlers' fast mapping and retention of new words. *American Journal of Speech-Language Pathology/American Speech-Language-Hearing Association*, 23(2), 120–133. http://doi. org/10.1044/2013_AJSLP-13-0013

Brady, S. A. (2011). Efficacy of phonics teaching for reading outcomes: Indications from post-NRP research. In S. A. Brady, D. Braze, & C. A. Fowler (Eds.), *Explaining individual differences in reading: Theory and evidence*. New York, NY: Psychology Press.

Brainerd, C. J., Bijou, S. W., Brainerd, C. J., Brainerd, C. J., Kaszor, P., Ennis, R. H., . . . Piaget, J. (1978). The stage question in cognitive-developmental theory. *Behavioral and Brain Sciences*, 1(2), 173. http://doi.org/10.1017/ S0140525X00073842

Bramen, J. E., Hranilovich, J. A., Dahl, R. E., Chen, J., Rosso, C., Forbes, E. E., . . . Sowell, E. R. (2012). Sex matters during adolescence: Testosterone-related cortical thickness maturation differs between boys and girls. *PLoS ONE*, 7(3), 1–9. https://doi. org/10.1371/journal.pone.0033850

Brandl, J. L. (2016). The puzzle of mirror self-recognition. *Phenomenology and the Cognitive Sciences*, 1–26. http://doi.org/10.1007/ s11097-016-9486-7

Brandon, P. D., & Temple, J. B. (2007). Family Provisions at the Workplace and Their Relationship to Absenteeism, Retention, and Productivity of Workers: Timely Evidence from Prior Data. *Australian Journal of Social Issues*, 42(4), 447–460.

Brassard, A., Péloquin, K., Dupuy, E., Wright, J., & Shaver, P. R. (2012). Romantic Attachment Insecurity Predicts Sexual Dissatisfaction in Couples Seeking Marital Therapy. *Journal of Sex & Marital Therapy*, 38(3), 245–262. http://doi.org/10.1080/00926 23X.2011.606881

Bratberg, E., & Tjøtta, S. (2008). Income effects of divorce in families with dependent children. *Journal of Population Economics*, 21(2), 439–461. http:// doi.org/10.1007/s00148-005-0029-8

Braun, S. M. G., & Jessberger, S. (2014). Adult neurogenesis: Mechanisms and functional significance. *Development*, 141(10), 1983–1986. http://doi.org/10.1242/dev.104596

Braungart-Rieker, J. M., Hill-Soderlund, A. L., & Karrass, J. (2010). Fear and anger reactivity trajectories from 4 to 16 months: the roles of temperament, regulation, and maternal sensitivity. *Developmental Psychology*, 46(4), 791–804. http:// doi.org/10.1037/a0019673

Braver, T. S., & West, R. (2008). Working memory, executive control, and aging. In F. I. M. Craik & T. A. Salthouse (Eds.), *The handbook of aging and cognition* (3rd ed., pp. 311–372). New York, NY: Psychology Press.

Brazelton, T. B. (1977). Implications of infant development among the Mayan Indians of Mexico. In P. H. Liederman, S. R. Tulikn, & A. Rosenfeld (Eds.), *Culture and infancy* (pp. 336–352). New York: Academic Press.

Brechwald, W. A., & Prinstein, M. J. (2011). Beyond Homophily: A Decade of Advances in Understanding Peer Influence Processes. *Journal of Research on Adolescence : The Official Journal of the Society for Research on Adolescence*, 21(1), 166–179. http:// doi.org/10.1111/j.1532-7795.2010.00721.x

Brehmer, Y., Westerberg, H., & Bäckman, L. (2012). Working-memory training in younger and older adults: training gains, transfer, and maintenance. *Frontiers in Human Neuroscience*, 6, 63. http://doi. org/10.3389/fnhum.2012.00063

Breiding, M. J., Chen, J., & Black, M. C. (2014). *Intimate Partner Violence in the United States - 2010*. Retrieved from https://www.ncjrs.gov/App/ Publications/abstract.aspx?ID=267363

Breiding, M. J., Smith, S. G., Basile, K. C., Walters, M. L., Chen, J., & Merrick, M. T. (2014). Prevalence and Characteristics of Sexual Violence, Stalking, and Intimate Partner Violence Victimization — National Intimate Partner and Sexual Violence Survey, United States, 2011. *Morbidity and Mortality Weekly Report*, 63 (SS08), 1–18. Retrieved from https://www.cdc. gov/mmwr/preview/mmwrhtml/ss6308a1.htm

Bremner, J. G., Slater, A. M., & Johnson, S. P. (2015). Perception of Object Persistence: The Origins of Object Permanence in Infancy. *Child Development Perspectives*, 9(1), 7–13. http://doi.org/10.1111/ cdep.12098

Brenn, T., & Ytterstad, E. (2016). Increased risk of death immediately after losing a spouse: Cause-specific mortality following widowhood in Norway. *Preventive Medicine*, 89, 251–256. http://doi. org/10.1016/j.ypmed.2016.06.019

Brenner, R. A., Simons-Morton, B. G., Bhaskar, B., Revenis, M., Das, A., & Clemens, J. D. (2003). Infant-Parent bed sharing in an inner-city population. *Archives of Pediatrics and Adolescent Medicine*, 157, 33–39.

Brent, D. A., Melhem, N. M., Masten, A. S., Porta, G., & Payne, M. W. (2012). Longitudinal effects of parental bereavement on adolescent developmental competence. *Journal of Clinical Child and Adolescent Psychology : The Official Journal for the Society of Clinical Child and Adolescent Psychology, American Psychological Association, Division 53*, 41(6), 778–91. http://doi.org/10.1080/15374416.201 2.717871

Brent, S. B., Lin, C., Speece, M. W., Dong, Q., & Yang, C. (1996). The Development of the Concept of Death Among Chinese and U.S. Children 3-17 Years of Age: From Binary to "Fuzzy" Concepts? *OMEGA–Journal of Death and Dying*, 33(1), 67–83. http://doi. org/10.2190/27L7-G7Q1-DY5Q-J9F3

Brent, S. B., & Speece, M. W. (1993). "Adult" conceptualization of irreversibility: Implications for the development of the concept of death. *Death Studies*, 17(3), 203–224. http://doi. org/10.1080/07481189308252618

Bretherton, I. (1992). The origins of attachment theory: John Bowlby and Mary Ainsworth. *Developmental Psychology*, 28, 759–775.

Bretherton, I., Fritz, J., Zahn-Waxler, C., & Ridgeway, D. (1986). Learning to talk about emotions: A functionalist perspective. *Child Development*, 57, 529–548.

Brewer, N. T., & Fazekas, K. I. (2007). Predictors of HPV vaccine acceptability: A theory-informed, systematic review. *Preventive Medicine*, 45(2), 107–114. http://doi.org/10.1016/j. ypmed.2007.05.013

Brewster, A. B. (1982). Chronically ill hospitalized children's concepts of their illness. *Pediatrics*, 69, 355–362.

Brichta, L., Greengard, P., & Flajolet, M. (2013). Advances in the pharmacological treatment of Parkinson's disease: targeting neurotransmitter systems. *Trends in Neurosciences*, 36(9), 543–54. http://doi.org/10.1016/j.tins.2013.06.003

Bridgett, D. J., Gartstein, M. A., Putnam, S. P., McKay, T., Iddins, E., Robertson, C., . . . Rittmueller, A. (2009). Maternal and contextual influences and the effect of temperament development during infancy on parenting in toddlerhood. *Infant Behavior & Development*, 32(1), 103–116. http://doi. org/10.1016/j.infbeh.2008.10.007

Briley, D. A., & Tucker-Drob, E. M. (2013). Explaining the increasing heritability of cognitive ability across development: A meta-analysis of longitudinal twin and adoption studies. *Psychological Science*, 24(9), 1704–1713. http://doi. org/10.1177/0956797613478618

Brim, O. G., Ryff, C. D., & Kessler, R. C. (2004). *How healthy are we? A national study of well-being at midlife*. The John D. and Catherine T. MacArthur foundation series on mental health and development. Studies on successful midlife development. Chicago, IL: University of Chicago Press.

Brison, K. J. (1995). You will never forget: Narrative, bereavement, and worldview among Kwanga women. *Ethos*, 23(4), 474–488. http://doi.org/10.1525/ eth.1995.23.4.02a00060

Brisson, C. D., Hsieh, Y.-T., Kim, D., Jin, A. Y., & Andrew, R. D. (2014). Brainstem neurons survive the identical ischemic stress that kills higher neurons: insight to the persistent vegetative state. *PloS One*, 9(5), e96585. http://doi.org/10.1371/journal. pone.0096585

Britto, R., Araújo, L., Barbosa, I., Silva, L., Rocha, S., & Valente, A. P. (2011). Hormonal therapy with estradiol and testosterone implants: Bone protection? *Gynecological Endocrinology*, 27(2), 96–100. http:// doi.org/10.3109/09513590.2010.489131

Britton, P. C., & Fuendeling, J. M. (2005). The Relations Among Varieties of Adult Attachment and the Components of Empathy. *The Journal of Social Psychology*, 145(5), 519–530. http://doi. org/10.3200/SOCP.145.5.519-530

Broberg, A. G., Wessels, H., Lamb, M. E., & Hwang, C. P. (1997). Effects of day care on the development of cognitive abilities in 8-year-olds: A longitudinal study. *Developmental Psychology*, 33(1), 62–69. http://doi.org/10.1037/0012-1649.33.1.62

Brock, R. L., & Lawrence, E. (2008). A longitudinal investigation of stress spillover in marriage: Does spousal support adequacy buffer the effects? *Journal of Family Psychology*, 22(1), 11–20.

Brocki, K. C., & Bohlin, G. (2004). Executive Functions in Children Aged 6 to 13: A Dimensional and Developmental Study. *Developmental Neuropsychology*, 26(2), 571–593.

Brockington, I. (1996). *Motherhood and mental health*. Oxford, England: Oxford University Press.

Brodie, B. (1974). Views of healthy children towards illness. *American Journal of Public Health*, *64*, 1156–1159.

Brody, G. H., & Flor, D. L. (1998). Maternal resources, parenting practices, and child competence in rural, single-parent African American families. *Child Development*, *69*, 803–816.

Brody, N., & Nathan. (1997). Intelligence, schooling, and society. *American Psychologist*, *52*(10), 1046–1050. http://doi.org/10.1037/0003-066X.52.10.1046

Brody, S. (2010). The relative health benefits of different sexual activities. *The Journal of Sexual Medicine*, *7*(4 Pt 1), 1336–61. http://doi.org/10.1111/j.1743-6109.2009.01677.x

Broesch, T. L., & Bryant, G. A. (2015). Prosody in Infant-Directed Speech Is Similar Across Western and Traditional Cultures. *Journal of Cognition and Development*, *16*(1), 31–43. http://doi.org/10.1080/15248372.2013.833923

Bronfenbrenner, U. (1979). *The ecology of human development: Experiments by nature and design*. Cambridge, MA: Harvard University Press.

Bronfenbrenner, U. (2005). The bioecological theory of human development. In U. Bronfenbrenner (Ed.), *Making human beings human: Bioecological perspectives on human development* (pp. 3 – 15). Thousand Oaks, CA: SAGE.

Bronfenbrenner, U., & Ceci, S. J. (1994). Nature-nurture reconceptualized in developmental perspective: A bioecological model. *Psychological Review*, *101*(4), 568–586.

Bronfenbrenner, U., & Evans, G. W. (2000). Developmental Science in the 21st Century: Emerging Questions, Theoretical Models, Research Designs and Empirical Findings. *Social Development*, *9*(1), 115–125. http://doi.org/10.1111/1467-9507.00114

Bronfenbrenner, U., & Morris, P. A. (2006). The bioecological model of human development. In R. M. Lerner & W. Damon (Eds.), *Handbook of child psychology:* (Vol. 1, p. 793–828. Hoboken). Hoboken, NJ: Wiley.

Brooker, R. J., Buss, K. A., Lemery-Chalfant, K., Aksan, N., Davidson, R. J., & Goldsmith, H. H. (2013). The development of stranger fear in infancy and toddlerhood: normative development, individual differences, antecedents, and outcomes. *Developmental Science*, *16*(6), 864–78. http://doi.org/10.1111/desc.12058

Brooks, C., & Bolzendahl, C. (2004). The transformation of US gender role attitudes: cohort replacement, social-structural change, and ideological learning. *Social Science Research*, *33*(1), 106–133. http://doi.org/10.1016/S0049-089X(03)00041-3

Brooks, R., & Meltzoff, A. N. (2008). Infant gaze following and pointing predict accelerated vocabulary growth through two years of age: A longitudinal, growth curve modeling study. *Journal of Child Language*, *35*(1), 207–220. http://doi.org/10.1017/s030500090700829x

Brooks-Gunn, J., Klebanov, P. K., & Duncan, G. J. (1996). Ethnic differences in children's intelligence test scores: Role of economic deprivation, home environment, and maternal characteristics. *Child Development*, *67*, 396–408.

Brooks-Gunn, J., & Ruble, D. N. (2013). Developmental processes in the experience of menarche. In J. E. S. A. Baum (Ed.), *Issues in child health and adolescent health: Handbook of psychology and health* (pp. 117–148). New York, NY: Psychology Press.

Broude, G. J. (1995). *Growing up: A cross-cultural encyclopedia*. Santa Barbara, CA: ABC-CLIO.

Broughton, J. (1981). Piaget's structural developmental psychology: Knowledge without a self and without history. *Human Development*, *24*, 320–346.

Brown, A. E., Carpenter, M. J., & Sutfin, E. L. (2011). Occasional smoking in college: Who, what, when and why? *Addictive Behaviors*, *36*(12), 1199–1204. http://doi.org/10.1016/j.addbeh.2011.07.024

Brown, A. S. (1991). A review of the tip-of-the-tongue experience. *Psychological Bulletin*, *109*(2), 204–223. http://doi.org/10.1037/0033-2909.109.2.204

Brown, B., Bank, H., & Steinberg, L. (2008). Smoke in the Looking Glass: Effects of Discordance Between Self- and Peer Rated Crowd Affiliation on Adolescent Anxiety, Depression and Self-feelings. *Journal of Youth & Adolescence*, *37*(10), 1163–1177. http://doi.org/10.1007/s10964-007-9198-y

Brown, B. B., Lohr, M. J., & McClenahan, E. L. (1986). Early adolescents' perceptions of peer pressure. *Journal of Early Adolescence*, *6*(2), 139–154.

Brown, F. L., & Slaughter, V. (2011). Normal body, beautiful body: discrepant perceptions reveal a pervasive "thin ideal" from childhood to adulthood. *Body Image*, *8*(2), 119–25. http://doi.org/10.1016/j.bodyim.2011.02.002

Brown, G. L., Mangelsdorf, S. C., & Neff, C. (2012). Father involvement, paternal sensitivity, and father-child attachment security in the first 3 years. *Journal of Family Psychology : JFP : Journal of the Division of Family Psychology of the American Psychological Association (Division 43)*, *26*(3), 421–30. http://doi.org/10.1037/a0027836

Brown, R. T., Antonuccio, D. O., DuPaul, G. J., Fristad, M. A., King, C. A., Leslie, L. K., . . . Vitiello, B. (2008). Autism spectrum disorders and mental retardation. In R. T. Brown, D. O. Antonuccio, G. J. DuPaul, M. A. Fristad, C. A. King, & et al (Eds.), *Childhood mental health disorders: Evidence base and contextual factors for psychosocial, psychopharmacological, and combined interventions.* (pp. 105–112). Washington, DC: American Psychological Association

Brown, R., & McNeill, D. (1966). The "tip of the tongue" phenomenon. *Journal of Verbal Learning and Verbal Behavior*, *5*(4), 325–337. http://doi.org/10.1016/S0022-5371(66)80040-3

Brown, S. A., McGue, M., Maggs, J., Schulenberg, J., Hingson, R., Swartzwelder, S., . . . Murphy, S. (2008). A Developmental Perspective on Alcohol and Youths 16 to 20 Years of Age. *Pediatrics*, *121*, S290–S310. http://doi.org/10.1542/peds.2007-2243D

Brown, S. L., & Kawamura, S. (2010). Relationship quality among cohabitors and marrieds in older adulthood. *Social Science Research*, *39*(5), 777–786. http://doi.org/10.1016/j.ssresearch.2010.04.010

Brown, S. L., & Wright, M. R. (2016). Older Adults' Attitudes Toward Cohabitation: Two Decades of Change. *The Journals of Gerontology Series B: Psychological Sciences and Social Sciences*, *71*(4), 755–764. http://doi.org/10.1093/geronb/gbv053

Brown, S. L., Bulanda, J. R., & Lee, G. R. (2012). Transitions Into and Out of Cohabitation in Later Life. *Journal of Marriage and the Family*, *74*(4), 774–793. http://doi.org/10.1111/j.1741-3737.2012.00994.x

Brown, T. T., & Jernigan, T. L. (2012). Brain development during the preschool years. *Neuropsychology Review*, *22*(4), 313–33. http://doi.org/10.1007/s11065-012-9214-1

Brownell, C. A. (2016). Prosocial Behavior in Infancy: The Role of Socialization. *Child Development Perspectives*, *10*(4), 222–227. http://doi.org/10.1111/cdep.12189

Brownie, S. (2006). Why are elderly individuals at risk of nutritional deficiency? *International Journal of Nursing Practice*, *12*(2), 110–118. http://doi.org/10.1111/j.1440-172X.2006.00557.x

Browning, C. R., Leventhal, T., & Brooks-Gunn, J. (2004). Neighborhood Context and Racial Differences in Early Adolescent Sexual Activity. *Demography*, *41*(4), 697–720. http://doi.org/10.1353/dem.2004.0029

Brubacher, S. P., Glisic, U. N. A., Roberts, K. P., & Powell, M. (2011). Children's ability to recall unique aspects of one occurrence of a repeated event. *Applied Cognitive Psychology*, *25*(3), 351–358. http://doi.org/10.1002/acp.1696

Bruer, J. T. (2008). In search of . . . brain-based education. In M. H. Immordino-Yang (Ed.), *The Jossey-Bass reader on the brain and learning* (pp. 51–69). San Francisco, CA: Jossey-Bass.

Brugman, D. (2010). Moral reasoning competence and the moral judgment-action discrepancy in young adolescents. In W. Koops, D. Brugman, & T. J. Ferguson (Eds.), *The development and structure of conscience* (p. 119–133). New York, NY: Psychology Press.

Brumariu, L. E. (2015). Parent-Child Attachment and Emotion Regulation. *New Directions for Child and Adolescent Development*, *2015*(148), 31–45. http://doi.org/10.1002/cad.20098

Brumback, T., Worley, M., Nguyen-Louie, T. T., Squeglia, L. M., Jacobus, J., & Tapert, S. F. (2016). Neural predictors of alcohol use and psychopathology symptoms in adolescents. *Development and Psychopathology*, *28*(4pt1), 1209–1216. http://doi.org/10.1017/S0954579416000766

Bruner, J. S. (1973). *Beyond the information given: Studies in the psychology of knowing*. New York, NY: WW Norton & Co.

Bruner, J. S., Goodnow, J. J., & Austin, G. A. (1956). *A study of thinking*. New York: Wiley.

Bryant, B. R., Bryant, D. P., Porterfield, J., Dennis, M. S., Falcomata, T., Valentine, C., . . . Bell, K. (2016). The Effects of a Tier 3 Intervention on the Mathematics Performance of Second Grade Students With Severe Mathematics Difficulties. *Journal of Learning Disabilities*, *49*(2), 176–88. http://doi.org/10.1177/0022219414538516

Bryant, G. A., Lienard, P., & Barrett, H. C. (2012). Recognizing infant-directed speech across distant cultures: Evidence from Africa. *Journal of Evolutionary Psychology*, *10*(2). http://doi.org/10.1556/JEP.10.2012.2.1

Bryck, R. L., & Fisher, P. A. (2012). Training the brain: Practical applications of neural plasticity from the intersection of cognitive neuroscience, developmental psychology, and prevention science. *American Psychologist*, *67*(2), 87–100.

Bryson, L., Warner-Smith, P., Brown, P., & Fray, L. (2007). Managing the workâ€"life roller-coaster: Private stress or public health issue? *Social Science & Medicine*, *65*(6), 1142–1153. http://doi.org/10.1016/j.socscimed.2007.04.027

Bucchianeri, M. M., Arikian, A. J., Hannan, P. J., Eisenberg, M. E., & Neumark-Sztainer, D. (2013). Body dissatisfaction from adolescence to young adulthood: Findings from a 10-year longitudinal study. *Body Image*, *10*(1), 1–7. http://doi.org/10.1016/j.bodyim.2012.09.001

Buchanan, C. M., & Hughes, J. L. (2009). Construction of Social Reality During Early Adolescence: Can Expecting Storm and Stress Increase Real or Perceived Storm and Stress? *Journal of Research on Adolescence (Blackwell Publishing Limited)*, *19*(2), 261–285. http://doi.org/10.1111/j.1532-7795.2009.00596.x

Buchanan, C. M., Eccles, J. S., & Becker, J. B. (1992). Are adolescents the victims of raging hormones? Evidence for activational effects of hormones on moods and behavior at adolescence. *Psychological Bulletin*, *111*, 62–107.

Buchanan-Barrow, E., & Barrett, M. (1998). Children's rule discrimination within the context of the school. *British Journal of Developmental Psychology*, *16*, 539–551.

Buford, T. W., Anton, S. D., Judge, A. R., Marzetti, E., Wohlgemuth, S. E., Carter, C. S., . . . Manini, T. M. (2010). Models of accelerated sarcopenia: Critical pieces for solving the puzzle of age-related muscle atrophy. *Ageing Research Reviews*, *9*(4), 369–383. http://doi.org/10.1016/j.arr.2010.04.004

Bugental, D. B., & Happaney, K. (2004). Predicting infant maltreatment in low-income families: The interactive effects of maternal attributions and child status at birth. *Developmental Psychology*, *40*(2), 234–243. http://doi.org/10.1037/0012-1649.40.2.234

Bugg, J. M., Zook, N. A., DeLosh, E. L., Davalos, D. B., & Davis, H. P. (2006). Age differences in fluid intelligence: Contributions of general slowing and frontal decline. *Brain & Cognition*, *62*(1), 9–16. http://doi.org/10.1016/j.bandc.2006.02.006

Buglass, E. (2010). Grief and bereavement theories. *Nursing Standard*, *24*(41), 44–47.

Buhrmester, D. (1998). Need fulfillment, interpersonal competence, and the developmental contexts of early adolescent friendship. In W. M. Bukowski, A. F. Newcomb, & W. W. Hartup (Eds.), *The company they keep: Friendship in childhood and adolescence.* (pp. 158–185). New York, NY: Cambridge University Press.

Bukowski, W. M. (2001). Friendship and the Worlds of Childhood. *New Directions for Child & Adolescent Development*, *2001*, 93–106.

Bukowski, W. M., Sippola, L., Hoza, B., & Newcomb, A. F. (2000). Pages from a Sociometric Notebook: An Analysis of Nomination and Rating Scale Measures of Acceptance, Rejection, and Social Preference. *New Directions for Child & Adolescent Development*, *20000*(88), 11–26.

Bulik, C. M., Berkman, N. D., Brownley, K. A., Sedway, J. A., Lohr, K. N., & Shapiro, J. R. (2007). Anorexia nervosa treatment: A systematic review of randomized controlled trials. *International Journal of Eating Disorders*, *40*(4), 321–336.

Bulik, C. M., Kleiman, S. C., & Yilmaz, Z. (2016). Genetic epidemiology of eating disorders. *Current Opinion in Psychiatry*, *29*(6), 383–388. http://doi.org/10.1097/YCO.0000000000000275

Bullock, M. (1985). Animism in childhood thinking: A new look at an old question. *Developmental Psychology*, *21*, 217–225.

Bullock, M., & Lutkenhaus, P. (1990). Who am I? Self-understanding in toddlers. *Merrill-Palmer Quarterly*, *36*, 217–238.

Bullock, M., Sodian, B., & Koerber, S. (2009). Doing experiments and understanding science: Development of scientific reasoning from childhood to adulthood. In W. Schneider & M. Bullock (Eds.), *Human development from early childhood to early adulthood: Findings from a 20 year longitudinal study.* (pp. 173–197). New York, NY: Psychology Press.

Bundak, R., Darendeliler, F., Gunoz, H., Bas, F., Saka, N., & Neyzi, O. (2007). Analysis of puberty and pubertal growth in healthy boys. *European Journal of Pediatrics*, *166*(6), 595–600.

Buote, V. M., Pancer, S. M., Pratt, M. W., Adams, G., Birnie-Lefcovitch, S., Polivy, J., & Wintre, M. G. (2007). The Importance of Friends: Friendship and Adjustment Among 1st-Year University Students. *Journal of Adolescent Research*, *22*(6), 665–689.

Burchinal, M., Roberts, J. E., Zeisel, S. A., Hennon, E. A., & Hooper, S. (2006). Social Risk and Protective Child, Parenting, and Child Care Factors in Early Elementary School Years. *Parenting: Science & Practice*, *6*(1), 79–113.

Burger, H. G., Hale, G. E., Robertson, D. M., & Dennerstein, L. (2007). A review of hormonal changes during the menopausal transition: Focus on findings from the Melbourne Womens Midlife Health Project. *Human Reproduction Update*, *13*(6), 559.

Burkam, D. T., Ready, D. D., Lee, V. E., & LoGerfo, L. F. (2004). Social-Class Differences in Summer Learning Between Kindergarten and First Grade: Model Specification and Estimation. *Sociology of Education*, *77*(1), 1–31. http://doi.org/10.1177/003804070407700101

Burke, D. M., & Shafto, M. A. (2004). Aging and Language Production. *Current Directions in Psychological Science*, *13*(1), 21–24. http://doi.org/10.1111/j.0963-7214.2004.01301006.x

Burkitt, L. (2014, November 7). China's Changed One-Child Policy Doesn't Give Baby Boost. *Wall Street Journal.* Retrieved from http://www.wsj.com/articles/chinas-changed-one-child-policy-doesnt-give-baby-boost-1415359577

Burkle, C. M., Sharp, R. R., & Wijdicks, E. F. (2014). Why brain death is considered death and why there should be no confusion. *Neurology*, *83*(16), 1464–9. http://doi.org/10.1212/WNL.0000000000000883

Burlew, A. K., Johnson, C., Smith, S., Sanders, A., Hall, R., Lampkin, B., & Schwaderer, M. (2012). Parenting and problem behaviors in children of substance abusing parents. *Child and Adolescent Mental Health*, *18*(4). http://doi.org/10.1111/camh.12001

Burnham, D., Kitamura, C., & Vollmer-Conna, U. (2002). What's new pussycat? On talking to babies and animals. *Science*, *296*, 1435.

Burns, G. W., & Bottino, P. J. (1989). *The science of genetics* (6th ed.). New York, NY: MacMillan.

Burr, J. A., & Mutchler, J. E. (1999). Race and ethnic variation in norms of filial responsibility among older persons. *Journal of Marriage & the Family*, *61*(3), 674–687. http://doi.org/10.2307/353569

Burt, A. (2009). A mechanistic explanation of popularity: Genes, rule breaking, and evocative gene–environment correlations. *Journal of Personality and Social Psychology*, *96*(4), 783–794. http://doi.org/10.1037/a0013702

Burton, C. L., Strauss, E., Hultsch, D. F., & Hunter, M. A. (2006). Cognitive Functioning and Everyday Problem Solving in Older Adults. *Clinical Neuropsychologist*, *20*(3), 432–452.

Burwell, R. A., & Shirk, S. R. (2006). Self Processes in Adolescent Depression: The Role of Self-Worth Contingencies. *Journal of Research on Adolescence (Blackwell Publishing Limited)*, *16*(3), 479–490. http://doi.org/10.1111/j.1532-7795.2006.00503.x

Busch, H., & Hofer, J. (2012). Self-regulation and milestones of adult development: intimacy and generativity. *Developmental Psychology*, *48*(1), 282–93. http://doi.org/10.1037/a0025521

Bush, N. R., Allison, A. L., Miller, A. L., Deardorff, J., Adler, N. E., & Boyce, W. T. (2017). Socioeconomic disparities in childhood obesity risk: Association with an oxytocin receptor polymorphism. *JAMA Pediatrics*, *171*(1), 61. http://doi.org/10.1001/jamapediatrics.2016.2332

Bushnell, I. W. R., Sai, F. Z., & Mullin, J. (1989). Neonatal recognition of the mother's face. *British Journal of Developmental Psychology*, *7*, 3–15.

Buss, A. H., & Plomin, R. (1984). *Temperament: Early developing personality traits.* Hillsdale, NJ: Lawrence Erlbaum.

Bussey, K. (1992). Lying and truthfulness: Children's definitions, standards, and evaluative reactions. *Child Development*, *63*, 129–137.

Bussey, K. (2013). Gender Development. In M. K. Ryan & N. R. Branscombe (Eds.), *The SAGE Handbook of Gender and Psychology.*

Bussey, K., & Bandura, A. (1992). Self-regulatory mechanisms governing gender development. *Child Development*, *63*, 1236–1250.

Busso, D. S., & Pollack, C. (2014). No brain left behind: Consequences of neuroscience discourse for education. *Learning, Media and Technology*, 1–19. http://doi.org/10.1080/17439884.2014.908908

Bustreo, F., Okwo-Bele, J.-M., & Kamara, L. (2015). World Health Organization perspectives on the contribution of the Global Alliance for Vaccines and Immunization on reducing child mortality. *Archives of Disease in Childhood*, *100*(Suppl 1), S34–S37. http://doi.org/10.1136/archdischild-2013-305693

Butler, R. (1998). Age trends in the use of social and temporal comparison for self-evaluation: Examination of a novel developmental hypothesis. *Child Development*, *69*, 1054–1073.

Butler, R. N. (1963). The Life Review: An Interpretation of Reminiscence in the Aged. *Psychiatry: Interpersonal and Biological Processes*, *26*(1), 65–76.

Butler, R. N. (1974). Succesful aging and the role of the life review. *Journal of the American Geriatrics Society*, *22*(12), 529–35. Retrieved from http://www.ncbi.nlm.nih.gov/pubmed/4420325

Butler, S. S., & Eckart, D. (2007). Civic Engagement Among Older Adults in a Rural Community: A Case Study of the Senior Companion Program. *Journal of Community Practice*, *15*(3), 77. http://doi.org/10.1300/J125v15n03_05

Buttelmann, D., Over, H., Carpenter, M., & Tomasello, M. (2014). Eighteen-month-olds understand false beliefs in an unexpected-contents task. *Journal of Experimental Child Psychology*, *119*, 120–6. http://doi.org/10.1016/j.jecp.2013.10.002

Butterworth, B. (2010). Foundational numerical capacities and the origins of dyscalculia. *Trends in Cognitive Sciences*, *14*(12), 534–541. http://doi.org/10.1016/j.tics.2010.09.007

Butz, A. M., Pulsifer, M., Marano, N., Belcher, H., Lears, M. K., & Royall, R. (2001). Effectiveness of a home intervention for perceived child behavioral problems and parenting stress in children with in utero drug exposure. *Archives of Pediatrics and Adolescent Medicine*, *155*, 1029–1037.

Byars, A. M., & Hackett, G. (1998). Applications of social cognitive theory to the career development of women of color. *Applied & Preventive Psychology*, *7*(4), 255–267. http://doi.org/10.1016/S0962-1849(98)80029-2

Bybee, J. A., & Wells, Y. V. (2003). The development of possible selves during adulthood. In J. Demick & C. Andreoletti (Eds.), *Handbook of adult development.* (pp. 257–270). New York, NY: Kluwer Academic/Plenum.

Bygdell, M., Vandenput, L., Ohlsson, C., & Kindblom, J. M. (2014). A secular trend for pubertal timing in Swedish men born 1946-1991 – the best cohort : Puberty: From bench to bedside. In *ENDO Meetings.* Retrieved from http://press.endocrine.org/doi/abs/10.1210/endo-meetings.2014.PE.10.OR11-3

Byrd, A. L., & Manuck, S. B. (2014). MAOA, childhood maltreatment, and antisocial behavior: meta-analysis of a gene-environment interaction. *Biological Psychiatry*, *75*(1), 9–17. http://doi.org/10.1016/j.biopsych.2013.05.004

Byrd, A. L., & Manuck, S. B. (2014). MAOA, childhood maltreatment, and antisocial behavior: Meta-analysis of a gene-environment interaction. *Biological Psychiatry*, *75*(1), 9–17. http://doi.org/10.1016/j.biopsych.2013.05.004

Byrnes, J. P., & Takahira, S. (1993). Explaining gender differences on SAT-math items. *Developmental Psychology, 29*(5), 805–810. http://doi.org/10.1037/0012-1649.29.5.805

Byrnes, V., & Ruby, A. (2007). Comparing Achievement between K–8 and Middle Schools: A Large-Scale Empirical Study. *American Journal of Education, 114*(1), 101–135.

Cabbage, L. A., & Neal, J. L. (2011). Over-the-counter medications and pregnancy: an integrative review. *The Nurse Practitioner, 36*(6), 22-8-9. http://doi.org/10.1097/01.NPR.0000397910.59950.71

Cabeza, R., & Nyberg, L. (2000). Neural bases of learning and memory: functional neuroimaging evidence. Current Opinion in Neurology, 13(4), 415–21. Retrieved from http://www.ncbi.nlm.nih.gov/pubmed/10970058

Cabinian, A., Sinsimer, D., Tang, M., Zumba, O., Mehta, H., Toma, A., . . . Richardson, B. (2016). Transfer of Maternal Immune Cells by Breastfeeding: Maternal Cytotoxic T Lymphocytes Present in Breast Milk Localize in the Peyer's Patches of the Nursed Infant. *PLOS ONE, 11*(6), e0156762. http://doi.org/10.1371/journal.pone.0156762

Cacciatore, J. (2010). The unique experiences of women and their families after the death of a baby. *Social Work in Health Care, 49*(2), 134–48. http://doi.org/10.1080/00981380903158078

Cadima, J., Leal, T., & Burchinal, M. (2010). The quality of teacher–student interactions: Associations with first graders' academic and behavioral outcomes. *Journal of School Psychology, 48*(6), 457–482. http://doi.org/10.1016/j.jsp.2010.09.001

Cairns, R. B., Leung, M.-C., Buchanan, L., & Cairns, B. D. (1995). Friendships and social networks in chidhood and adolescence: Fluidity, reliability, and interrelations. *Child Development, 66*, 1330–1345.

Caldera, Y. M. (2004). Paternal Involvement and Infant-Father Attachment: A Q-Set Study. *Fathering: A Journal of Theory, Research, & Practice about Men as Fathers, 2*(2), 191–210.

Caldera, Y. M., Huston, A. C., & O'Brien, M. (1989). Social Interactions and Play Patterns of Parents and Toddlers with Feminine, Masculine, and Neutral Toys. *Child Development, 60*(1), 70. http://doi.org/10.2307/1131072

Calhoun, S., Conner, E., Miller, M., & Messina, N. (2015). Improving the outcomes of children affected by parental substance abuse: A review of randomized controlled trials. *Substance Abuse and Rehabilitation, 6*, 15–24. http://doi.org/10.2147/SAR.S46439

Calkins, S. D., & Johnson, M. C. (1998). Toddler regulation of distress to frustrating events: Temperamental and maternal correlates. *Infant Behavior & Development, 21*, 379–395.

Callaghan, T. C. (1999). Early understanding and production of graphic symbols. *Child Development, 70*, 1314–1324.

Callaghan, T., Rochat, P., Lillard, A., Claux, M. L., Odden, H., Itakura, S., . . . Singh, S. (2005). Synchrony in the Onset of Mental-State Reasoning. *Psychological Science, 16*(5), 378–384.

Calle, E. E., Rodriguez, C., Walker-Thurmond, K., & Thun, M. J. (2003). Overweight, obesity, and mortality from cancer in a prospectively studied cohort of U.S. adults. *New England Journal of Medicine, 348*(17), 1625–1638.

Calvo, E., Haverstick, K., & Sass, S. A. (2009). Gradual Retirement, Sense of Control, and Retirees' Happiness. *Research on Aging, 31*(1), 112–135.

Calzo, J. P., Antonucci, T. C., Mays, V. M., & Cochran, S. D. (2011). Retrospective recall of sexual orientation identity development among gay, lesbian, and bisexual adults. *Developmental Psychology, 47*(6), 1658–73. http://doi.org/10.1037/a0025508

Calzo, J. P., Masyn, K. E., Austin, S. B., Jun, H.-J., & Corliss, H. L. (2017). Developmental Latent Patterns of Identification as Mostly Heterosexual Versus Lesbian, Gay, or Bisexual. *Journal of Research on Adolescence, 27*(1), 246–253. http://doi.org/10.1111/jora.12266

Calzo, J. P., Sonneville, K. R., Haines, J., Blood, E. A., Field, A. E., & Austin, S. B. (2012). The Development of Associations Among Body Mass Index, Body Dissatisfaction, and Weight and Shape Concern in Adolescent Boys and Girls. *Journal of Adolescent Health, 51*(5), 517–523. http://doi.org/10.1016/j.jadohealth.2012.02.021

Camberis, A.-L., McMahon, C. A., Gibson, F. L., & Boivin, J. (2016). Maternal Age, Psychological Maturity, Parenting Cognitions, and Mother-Infant Interaction. *Infancy, 21*(4), 396–422. http://doi.org/10.1111/infa.12116

Cameron, C. A., McKay, S., Susman, E. J., Wynne-Edwards, K., Wright, J. M., & Weinberg, J. (2016). Cortisol Stress Response Variability in Early Adolescence: Attachment, Affect and Sex. *Journal of Youth and Adolescence, 1*–17. http://doi.org/10.1007/s10964-016-0548-5

Cameron, H. A., & Glover, L. R. (2015). Adult neurogenesis: Beyond learning and memory. *Annual Review of Psychology, 66*, 53–81. http://doi.org/10.1146/annurev-psych-010814-015006

Camerota, M., Willoughby, M. T., Cox, M., Greenberg, M. T., & Family Life Project Investigators. (2015). Executive function in low birth weight preschoolers: The moderating effect of parenting. *Journal of Abnormal Child Psychology, 43*(8), 1551–1562. http://doi.org/10.1007/s10802-015-0032-9

Camos, V., & Barrouillet, P. (2011). Developmental change in working memory strategies: From passive maintenance to active refreshing. *Developmental Psychology, 47*(3), 898–904. http://doi.org/10.1037/a0023193

Campbell, A., Shirley, L., & Candy, J. (2004). A longitudinal study of gender-related cognition and behaviour. *Developmental Science, 7*(1), 1–9. http://doi.org/10.1111/j.1467-7687.2004.00316.x

Campbell, A., Shirley, L., & Caygill, L. (2002). Sex-typed preferences in three domains: do two-year-olds need cognitive variables? *British Journal of Psychology (London, England : 1953), 93*(Pt 2), 203–17.

Campbell, F. A., & Ramey, C. T. (1994). Effects of Early Intervention on Intellectual and Academic Achievement: A Follow-up Study of Children from Low-Income Families. *Child Development, 65*(2), 684–698. http://doi.org/10.1111/j.1467-8624.1994.tb00777.x

Campbell, F. A., Pungello, E. P., Burchinal, M., Kainz, K., Pan, Y., Wasik, B. H., . . . Ramey, C. T. (2012). Adult outcomes as a function of an early childhood educational program: an Abecedarian Project follow-up. *Developmental Psychology, 48*(4), 1033–43. http://doi.org/10.1037/a0026644

Campbell, F. A., Ramey, C. T., Pungello, E., Sparling, J., & Miller-Johnson, S. (2002). Early Childhood Education: Young Adult Outcomes From the Abecedarian Project. *Applied Developmental Science, 6*(1), 42–57.

Campisi, J. (2013). Aging, cellular senescence, and cancer. *Annual Review of Physiology, 75*, 685–705. http://doi.org/10.1146/annurev-physiol-030212-183653

Campos, J. J., Anderson, D. I., Barbu-Roth, M. A., Hubbard, E. M., Hertenstein, J. J., & Witherington, D. (2000). Travel broadens the mind. *Infancy, 1*, 149–219.

Campos, J. J., Kermoian, R., & Zumbahlen, M. R. (1992). Socioemotional transformation in the family system following infant crawling onset. In N. Eisenberg & R. A. Fabes (Eds.), *New directions for child development* (Vol. No. 55, pp. 25–40). San Francisco: Jossey-Bass.

Campos, J. J., Langer, A., & Krowitz, A. (1970). Cardiac responses on the visual cliff in prelocomotor human infants. *Science, 170*, 196–197.

Camras, L. A., Oster, H., Campos, J. J., Miyake, K., & Bradshaw, D. (1992). Japanese and American infants' responses to arm restraint. *Developmental Psychology, 28*, 578–583.

Canderelli, R., Leccesse, L. A., & Miller, N. L. (2007). Benefits of hormone replacement therapy in postmenopausal women. *Journal of the American Academy of Nurse Practitioners, 19*(12), 635–641.

Candy, B., Holman, A., Leurent, B., Davis, S., & Jones, L. (2011). Hospice care delivered at home, in nursing homes and in dedicated hospice facilities: A systematic review of quantitative and qualitative evidence. *International Journal of Nursing Studies, 48*(1), 121–133. http://doi.org/10.1016/j.ijnurstu.2010.08.003

Canetto, S. S., & Sakinofsky, I. (1998). The gender paradox in suicide. *Suicide and Life-Threatening Behavior, 28*, 1–23.

Cannon, J. R., & Greenamyre, J. T. (2013). Gene-environment interactions in Parkinson's disease: specific evidence in humans and mammalian models. *Neurobiology of Disease, 57*, 38–46. http://doi.org/10.1016/j.nbd.2012.06.025

Cannon, S. M., Einstein, G. P., & Tulp, O. L. (2017). Analysis of telomere length in aging and age -related illness. *The FASEB Journal, 31*(1 Supplement), 935.2-935.2. Retrieved from http://www.fasebj.org/content/31/1_Supplement/935.2.short

Caprara, G. V., Schwartz, S., Capanna, C., Vecchione, M., & Barbaranelli, C. (2006). Personality and Politics: Values, Traits, and Political Choice. *Political Psychology, 27*(1), 1–28. http://doi.org/10.1111/j.1467-9221.2006.00447.x

Carbery, J., & Buhrmester, D. (1998). Friendship and need fulfillment during three phases of young adulthood. *Journal of Social & Personal Relationships, 15*(3), 393.

Carbia, C., Cadaveira, F., López-Caneda, E., Caamaño-Isorna, F., Rodríguez Holguín, S., & Corral, M. (2017). Working memory over a six-year period in young binge drinkers. *Alcohol, 61*, 17–23. http://doi.org/10.1016/j.alcohol.2017.01.013

Carbonneau, K. J., Marley, S. C., & Selig, J. P. (2013). A meta-analysis of the efficacy of teaching mathematics with concrete manipulatives. *Journal of Educational Psychology, 105*(2), 380–400. http://doi.org/10.1037/a0031084

Card, N. A., Stucky, B. D., Sawalani, G. M., & Little, T. D. (2008). Direct and Indirect Aggression During Childhood and Adolescence: A Meta-Analytic Review of Gender Differences, Intercorrelations, and Relations to Maladjustment. *Child Development, 79*(5), 1185–1229. http://doi.org/10.1111/j.1467-8624.2008.01184.x

Carlin, R. F., Moon, R. Y., C, P.-M., HW, H., EA, M., & A, K. (2017). Risk Factors, Protective Factors, and Current Recommendations to Reduce Sudden Infant Death Syndrome. *JAMA Pediatrics, 171*(2), 175. http://doi.org/10.1001/jamapediatrics.2016.3345

Carlo, G. (2013). The Development and Correlates of Prosocial Moral Behaviors. In Melanie Killen & Judith G. Smetana (Eds.), *Handbook of Moral Development*. New York, NY: Routledge. http://doi.org/10.4324/9780203581957.ch10

Carlo, G., & Eisenberg, N. (1996). A cross-national study on the relations among prosocial moral. *Developmental Psychology, 32*(2), 231–241.

Carlo, G., Koller, S., Raffaelli, M., & De Guzman, M. R. T. (2007). Culture-Related Strengths Among Latin American Families: A Case Study of Brazil. *Marriage & Family Review, 42*(3), 335–360.

REFERENCES

Carlo, G., Mestre, M. V., McGinley, M. M., Tur-Porcar, A., Samper, P., & Opal, D. (2014). The protective role of prosocial behaviors on antisocial behaviors: The mediating effects of deviant peer affiliation. *Journal of Adolescence*, 37(4), 359–366. http://doi.org/10.1016/j.adolescence.2014.02.009

Carlo, G., Mestre, M. V., Samper, P., Tur, A., & Armenta, B. E. (2011). The longitudinal relations among dimensions of parenting styles, sympathy, prosocial moral reasoning, and prosocial behaviors. *International Journal of Behavioral Development*, 35(2), 116–124. http://doi.org/10.1177/0165025410375921

Carlson, D. L., McNulty, T. L., Bellair, P. E., & Watts, S. (2014). Neighborhoods and racial/ethnic disparities in adolescent sexual risk behavior. *Journal of Youth and Adolescence*, 43(9), 1536–49. http://doi.org/10.1007/s10964-013-0052-0

Carlson, D. S., Grzywacz, J. G., Ferguson, M., Hunter, E. M., Clinch, C. R., & Arcury, T. A. (2011). Health and turnover of working mothers after childbirth via the work-family interface: an analysis across time. *The Journal of Applied Psychology*, 96(5), 1045–54. http://doi.org/10.1037/a0023964

Carlson, M., Oshri, A., & Kwon, J. (2015). Child maltreatment and risk behaviors: The roles of callous/unemotional traits and conscientiousness. *Child Abuse & Neglect*, 50, 234–43. http://doi.org/10.1016/j.chiabu.2015.07.003

Carlson, S. M., Moses, L. J., & Claxton, L. J. (2004). Individual differences in executive functioning and theory of mind: An investigation of inhibitory control and planning ability. *Journal of Experimental Child Psychology*, 87(4), 299. http://doi.org/10.1016/j.jecp.2004.01.002

Carlson, V. J., & Harwood, R. L. (2003). Attachment, culture, and the caregiving system: The cultural patterning of everyday experiences among Anglo and Puerto Rican mother-infant pairs. *Infant Mental Health Journal*, 24, 53–73.

Carlsson, J., Wängqvist, M., & Frisén, A. (2015). Identity Development in the Late Twenties : A Never Ending Story, 51(3), 334–345.

Carlsson, J., Wängqvist, M., & Frisén, A. (2016). Life on hold: Staying in identity diffusion in the late twenties. *Journal of Adolescence*, 47, 220–229. http://doi.org/10.1016/j.adolescence.2015.10.023

Carothers, S. S., Borkowski, J. G., & Whitman, T. L. (2006). Children of Adolescent Mothers: Exposure to Negative Life Events and the Role of Social Supports on Their Socioemotional Adjustment. *Journal of Youth & Adolescence*, 35(5), 822–832. http://doi.org/10.1007/s10964-006-9096-8

Carpenter, S. M., Peters, E., Västfjäll, D., & Isen, A. M. (2013). Positive feelings facilitate working memory and complex decision making among older adults. *Cognition & Emotion*, 27(1), 184–92. http://doi.org/10.1080/02699931.2012.698251

Carr, D. (2004a). Gender, Preloss Marital Dependence, and Older Adults' Adjustment to Widowhood. *Journal of Marriage & Family*, 66(1), 220–235.

Carr, D. (2004b). The desire to date and remarry among older widows and widowers. *Journal of Marriage and Family*, 66(4), 1051–1068. Retrieved from carrds@rci.rutgers.edu

Carr, D., & Friedman, M. A. (2005). Is obesity stigmatizing? Body weight, perceived discrimination, and psychological well-being in the United States. *Journal of Health & Social Behavior*, 46(3), 244–259.

Carrion-Castillo, A., Franke, B., & Fisher, S. E. (2013). Molecular genetics of dyslexia: an overview. *Dyslexia (Chichester, England)*, 19(4), 214–40. http://doi.org/10.1002/dys.1464

Carskadon, M. A. (2009). Adolescents and sleep: Why teens can't get enough of a good thing. *Brown University Child & Adolescent Behavior Letter*, 25(4), 1–6.

Carskadon, M. A., & Tarokh, L. (2014). Developmental changes in sleep biology and potential effects on adolescent behavior and caffeine use. *Nutrition Reviews*, 72(suppl 1), 60–64. http://doi.org/10.1111/nure.12147

Carskadon, M. A., Acebo, C., & Jenni, O. G. (2004). Regulation of adolescent sleep: implications for behavior. *Annals of the New York Academy of Sciences*, 1021, 276–291.

Carson, A. S., & Banuazizi, A. (2008). "That"s not fair': Similarities and differences in distributive justice reasoning between American and Filipino children. *Journal of Cross-Cultural Psychology*, 39(4), 493–514.

Carson, N. (2014). *Foundations of behavioral neuroscience*. (9th ed.). Harlow, England: Pearson.

Carson, V. B., Vanderhorst, K., & Koenig, H. G. (2015). *Care Giving for Alzheimer's Disease: A Compassionate Guide for Clinicians and Loved Ones*. Springer.

Carson, V., Ridgers, N. D., Howard, B. J., Winkler, E. A. H., Healy, G. N., Owen, N., . . . Zheng, Y. (2013). Light-intensity physical activity and cardiometabolic biomarkers in US adolescents. *PLoS ONE*, 8(8). http://doi.org/10.1371/journal.pone.0071417

Carstensen, L. L., Fung, H. H., & Charles, S. T. (2003). Socioemotional selectivity theory and the regulation of emotion in the second half of life. *Motivation and Emotion*, 27(2), 103–123. http://doi.org/10.1023/A:1024569803230

Carstensen, L. L., & Mikels, J. A. (2005). At the intersection of emotion and cognition. Aging and the positivity effect. *Current Directions in Psychological Science*, 14(3), 117–121. http://doi.org/10.1111/j.0963-7214.2005.00348.x

Carstensen, L. L., Pasupathi, M., Mayr, U., & Nesselroade, J. R. (2000). Emotional experience in everyday life across the adult life span. *Journal of Personality and Social Psychology*, 79(4), 644–655. http://doi.org/10.1037/0022-3514.79.4.644

Carstensen, L. L., Turan, B., Scheibe, S., Ram, N., Ersner-Hershfield, H., Samanez-Larkin, G. R., . . . Nesselroade, J. R. (2011). Emotional experience improves with age: Evidence based on over 10 years of experience sampling. *Psychology and Aging*, 26(1), 21–33. http://doi.org/10.1037/a0021285

Carter, A. C., Brandon, K. O., & Goldman, M. S. (2010). The college and noncollege experience: A review of the factors that influence drinking behavior in young adulthood. *Journal of Studies on Alcohol & Drugs*, 71(5), 742–750.

Carter, C. S. (2014). Oxytocin pathways and the evolution of human behavior. *Annual Review of Psychology*, 65(1), 17–39. http://doi.org/10.1146/annurev-psych-010213-115110

Carter, R., Jaccard, J., Silverman, W. K., & Pina, A. A. (2009). Pubertal timing and its link to behavioral and emotional problems among at-risk African American adolescent girls. *Journal of Adolescence*, 32(3), 467–481. http://doi.org/10.1016/j.adolescence.2008.07.005

Carver, K., Joyner, K., & Udry, J. R. (2003). *National estimates of adolescent romantic relationships*. Mahwah, NJ: Lawrence Erlbaum.

Casanueva, C., Goldman-Fraser, J., Ringeisen, H., Lederman, C., Katz, L., & Osofsky, J. (2010). Maternal perceptions of temperament among infants and toddlers investigated for maltreatment: Implications for services need and referral. *Journal of Family Violence*, 25(6), 557–574. http://doi.org/10.1007/s10896-010-9316-6

Casares, W. N., Lahiff, M., Eskenazi, B., & Halpern-Felsher, B. L. (2010). Unpredicted trajectories: The relationship between race/ethnicity, pregnancy during adolescence, and young women's outcomes. *Journal of Adolescent Health*, 47(2), 143–150. http://doi.org/10.1016/j.jadohealth.2010.01.013

Case, R. (1998). The development of conceptual structures. In D. Khun & R. S. Siegler (Eds.), *Handbook of child psychology: Vol. 2. Cognition, perception, and language* (5th ed., pp. 745–800). New York: Wiley.

Case, R. (1999). Cognitive development. In M. Bennett (Ed.), *Developmental psychology: Achievements and prospects* (pp. 36–54). Philadelphia, PA: Taylor & Francis.

Case, R., Kurland, D. M., & Goldberg, J. (1982). Operational efficiency and the growth of short term memory span. *Journal of Experimental Child Psychology*, 33, 386–404.

Casey Copen, E., Chandra, A., & Martinez, G. (2012). Prevalence and timing of oral sex with opposite-sex partners among females and males aged 15–24 years: United States, 2007–2010. *National Health Statistics Reports*, 56.

Casey, B. J. (2015). Beyond simple models of self-control to circuit-based accounts of adolescent behavior. *Annual Review of Psychology*, 66, 295–319. http://doi.org/10.1146/annurev-psych-010814-015156

Casey, B., & Caudle, K. (2013). The Teenage Brain: Self Control. *Current Directions in Psychological Science*, 22(2), 82–87. http://doi.org/10.1177/0963721413480170

Casey, B., Jones, R. M., & Somerville, L. H. (2011). Braking and accelerating of the adolescent brain. *Journal of Research on Adolescence*, 21(1), 21–33. http://doi.org/10.1111/j.1532-7795.2010.00712.x

Casey, P., Goolsby, S., Berkowitz, C., Frank, D., Cook, J., Cutts, D., . . . Meyers, A. (2004). Maternal depression, changing public assistance, food security, and child health status. *Pediatrics*, 113(2), 298–304.

Caspi, A. (1998). Personality development across the life course. In N. Eisenberg (Ed.), *Handbook of child psychology: Vol.3. Social, emotional, and personality development* (5th ed., pp. 311–388). New York: Wiley.

Caspi, A., Harrington, H., Milne, B., Amell, J. W., Theodore, R. F., & Moffitt, T. E. (2003). Children's behavioral styles at age 3 are linked to their adult personality traits at age 26. *Journal of Personality*, 71(4), 495–514. http://doi.org/10.1111/1467-6494.7104001

Caspi, A., Herbener, E. S., & Ozer, D. J. (1992). Shared experiences and the similarity of personalities: A longitudinal study of married couples. *Journal of Personality and Social Psychology*, 62(2), 281–291. http://doi.org/10.1037/0022-3514.62.2.281

Caspi, A., McClay, J., Moffitt, T. E., Mill, J., Martin, J., Craig, I. W., . . . Poulton, R. (2002). Role of genotype in the cycle of violence in maltreated children. *Science*, 297(5582), 851–854. http://doi.org/10.1126/science.1072290

Caspi, A., & Shiner, R. (2008). Temperament and personality. In M. Rutter, D. V. M. Bishop, D. S. Pine, S. Scott, J. Stevenson, E. Taylor, & A. Thapar (Eds.), *Rutter's child and adolescent psychiatry* (pp. 182–198). Oxford, UK: Blackwell. http://doi.org/10.1002/9781444300895.ch14

Cassano, M., Perry-Parrish, C., & Zeman, J. (2007). Influence of gender on parental socialization of children's sadness regulation. *Social Development*, 16(2), 210–231. http://doi.org/10.1111/j.1467-9507.2007.00381.x

Cassibba, R., Sette, G., Bakermans-Kranenburg, M., van IJzendoorn, M. H. (2013). Attachment the Italian way: In search of specific patterns of infant and adult attachments in Italian typical and atypical samples. *European Psychologist, 18*(1). http://doi.org/10.1027/1016-9040/a000128

Castelo-Branco, C., & Davila, J. (2015). Menopause and aging skin in the elderly. In *Skin, Mucosa and Menopause* (pp. 345–357). Berlin, Heidelberg: Springer. http://doi.org/10.1007/978-3-662-44080-3_25

Castro, D. C., Páez, M. M., Dickinson, D. K., & Frede, E. (2011). Promoting language and literacy in young dual language learners: Research, practice, and policy. *Child Development Perspectives, 5*(1), 15–21. http://doi.org/10.1111/j.1750-8606.2010.00142.x

Castro, V. L., Halberstadt, A. G., Lozada, F. T., & Craig, A. B. (2015). Parents' emotion-related beliefs, behaviors, and skills predict children's recognition of emotion. *Infant and Child Development, 24*(1), 1–22. http://doi.org/10.1002/icd.1868

Castro-Chavira, S. A., Fernandez, T., Nicolini, H., Diaz-Cintra, S., & Prado-Alcala, R. A. (2015). Genetic markers in biological fluids for aging-related major neurocognitive disorder. *Current Alzheimer Research, 12*(3), 200–209.

Catani, C., Gewirtz, A. H., Wieling, E., Schauer, E., Elbert, T., & Neuner, F. (2010). Tsunami, war, and cumulative risk in the lives of Sri Lankan schoolchildren. *Child Development, 81*(4), 1176–1191. http://doi.org/10.1111/j.1467-8624.2010.01461.x

Catindig, J.-A. S., Venketasubramanian, N., Ikram, M. K., & Chen, C. (2012). Epidemiology of dementia in Asia: Insights on prevalence, trends and novel risk factors. *Journal of the Neurological Sciences, 321*(1–2), 11–6. http://doi.org/10.1016/j.jns.2012.07.023

Cattell, R. B. (1963). Theory of fluid and crystallized intelligence: A critical experiment. *Journal of Educational Psychology, 54*(1), 1–22. http://doi.org/10.1037/h0046743

Cauce, A. M. (2008). Parenting, culture, and context: Reflections on excavating culture. *Applied Developmental Science, 12*(4), 227–229. http://doi.org/10.1080/10888690802388177

Cauce, A., & Domenech-Rodríguez, M. (2002). Latino families: Myths and realities. In J. Contreras, A. Neal-Barnett, & K. Kerns (Eds.), *Latino children and families in the United States* (pp. 2–25). Westport, CT: Praeger.

Cauffman, E., Shulman, E. P., Steinberg, L., Claus, E., Banich, M. T., Graham, S., & Woolard, J. (2010). Age differences in affective decision making as indexed by performance on the Iowa Gambling Task. *Developmental Psychology, 46*(1), 193–207. http://doi.org/10.1037/a0016128

Cauffman, E., & Steinberg, L. (2000). (Im)maturity of judgment in adolescence: Why adolescents may be less culpable than adults. *Behavioral Sciences & the Law, 18*(6), 741–760.

Cauffman, E., & Steinberg, L. (2012). Emerging findings from research on adolescent development and juvenile justice. *Victims & Offenders, 7*(4), 428–449. http://doi.org/10.1080/15564886.2012.713901

Cavanaugh, J. C., & Perlmutter, M. (1982). Metamemory: A critical examination. *Child Development, 53*(1), 11–28.

Ceci, S. J. (1991). How much does schooling influence general intelligence and its cognitive components? A reassessment of the evidence. *Developmental Psychology, 27*, 703–722.

Ceci, S. J. (1999). Schooling and intelligence. In S. J. Ceci & W. M. Williams (Eds.), *The nature-nurture debate: The essential readings* (pp. 168–175). Oxford, UK: Blackwell.

Ceci, S. J., & Bruck, M. (1998). The ontogeny and durability of true and false memories: A fuzzy trace account. *Journal of Experimental Child Psychology, 71*, 165–169.

Ceci, S. J., & Friedman, R. D. (2000). The suggestibility of children: Scientific research and legal implications. *Cornell Law Review, 86*, 34–108.

Ceci, S. J., Ginther, D. K., Kahn, S., & Williams, W. M. (2014). Women in Academic Science. *Psychological Science in the Public Interest, 15*(3), 75–141. http://doi.org/10.1177/1529100614541236

Ceci, S. J., Huffman, M. L., Smith, E., & Loftus, E. F. (1994). Repeatedly thinking about a non-event: Source misattributions among preschoolers. *Consciousness and Cognition, 3*, 388–407.

Cecil, C. A. M., Viding, E., Fearon, P., Glaser, D., & McCrory, E. J. (2017). Disentangling the mental health impact of childhood abuse and neglect. *Child Abuse & Neglect, 63*, 106–119. http://doi.org/10.1016/j.chiabu.2016.11.024

Centers for Disease Control and Prevention. (1994). Vaccines for children program, 1994. *Morbidity and Mortality Weekly Report, 43*(39), 705.

Centers for Disease Control and Prevention. (1999). Achievements in public health, 1900–1999: Control of infectious diseases. *Morbidity and Mortality Weekly Report, 48*(29), 621–629. Retrieved from http://www.cdc.gov/mmwr/preview/mmwrhtml/mm4829a1.htm

Centers for Disease Control and Prevention. (2005). *Intellectual disability*. Retrieved from http://www.cdc.gov/ncbddd/dd/mr3.htm

Centers for Disease Control and Prevention. (2014a). *Birth defects: Data and statistics*. Retrieved from http://www.cdc.gov/ncbddd/birthdefects/data.html

Centers for Disease Control and Prevention. (2014b). *National diabetes statistics report: Estimates of diabetes and its burden in the United States, 2014*. Atlanta, GA: Author.

Centers for Disease Control and Prevention. (2015a). *Diagnoses of HIV infection in the United States and dependent areas, 2015*. Retrieved from https://www.cdc.gov/hiv/pdf/library/reports/surveillance/cdc-hiv-surveillance-report-2015-vol-27.pdf

Centers for Disease Control and Prevention. (2015b). *HIV in the United States: At a glance*. Retrieved from http://stacks.cdc.gov/view/cdc/35661/cdc_35661_DS1.pdf

Centers for Disease Control and Prevention. (2016a). QuickStats: Percentage distribution of respondent-assessed health status among adults aged ≥ 25 years, by completed education—National Health Interview Survey, United States, 2015. *Morbidity & Mortality Weekly Report, 65*, 1383. Retrieved from https://www.cdc.gov/mmwr/volumes/65/wr/mm6548a8.htm

Centers for Disease Control and Prevention. (2016b). *Sexually transmitted disease surveillance 2015*. Retrieved from https://www.cdc.gov/std/stats15/default.htm

Centers for Disease Control and Prevention. (2016c). *Teen pregnancy in the United States*. Retrieved from https://www.cdc.gov/teenpregnancy/about/

Centers for Disease Control and Prevention. (2017a). *Microcephaly & other birth defects*. Retrieved from https://www.cdc.gov/zika/healtheffects/birth_defects.html

Centers for Disease Control and Prevention. (2017b). *10 leading causes of death, by age group, United States: 2015*. Retrieved from https://www.cdc.gov/injury/images/lc-charts/leading_causes_of_death_age_group_2015_1050w740h.gif

Centifanti, L. C. M., Modecki, K. L., MacLellan, S., & Gowling, H. (2014). Driving under the influence of risky peers: An experimental study of adolescent risk taking. *Journal of Research on Adolescence*. http://doi.org/10.1111/jora.12187

Central Intelligence Agency. (2013). *World Fact Book, 2013–14*. Washington, DC: Author. Retrieved from https://www.cia.gov/library/publications/the-world-factbook/index.html

Cesario, S. K., & Hughes, L. A. (2007). Precocious puberty: A comprehensive review of literature. *Journal of Obstetric, Gynecologic, & Neonatal Nursing: Clinical Scholarship for the Care of Women, Childbearing Families, & Newborns, 36*(3), 263–274.

Chabris, C. F., Lee, J. J., Cesarini, D., Benjamin, D. J., & Laibson, D. I. (2015). The fourth law of behavior genetics. *Current Directions in Psychological Science, 24*(4), 304–312. http://doi.org/10.1177/0963721415580430

Chaibal, S., Bennett, S., Rattanathanthong, K., & Siritaratiwat, W. (2016). Early developmental milestones and age of independent walking in orphans compared with typical home-raised infants. *Early Human Development, 101*, 23–26. http://doi.org/10.1016/j.earlhumdev.2016.06.008

Chakravarthy, U., Evans, J., & Rosenfeld, P. J. (2010). Age related macular degeneration. *BMJ: British Medical Journal, 340*(7745), 526–530. http://doi.org/10.1136/bmj.c981

Chakravarty, E. F., Hubert, H. B., Lingala, V. B., & Fries, J. F. (2008). Reduced disability and mortality among aging runners. *Archives of Internal Medicine, 168*(15), 1638–1646.

Champion, K. M., & Clay, D. L. (2007). Individual Differences in Responses to Provocation and Frequent Victimization by Peers. *Child Psychiatry & Human Development, 37*(3), 205–220. http://doi.org/10.1007/s10578-006-0030-9

Chan, G. K., & Duque, G. (2002). age-related bone loss: Old bone, new facts. *Gerontology, 48*(2), 62–71.

Chan, L. K. S., & Moore, P. J. (2006). Development of attributional beliefs and strategic knowledge in years 5–9: A longitudinal analysis. *Educational Psychology, 26*(2), 161–185. http://doi.org/10.1080/01443410500344209

Chan, W., Kwok, Y., Choy, K., Leung, T., & Wang, C. (2013). Single fetal cells for non-invasive prenatal genetic diagnosis: Old myths New Prospective. *Med J Obstet Gynecol, 1*(1), 1004.

Chandler, M. J., & Carpendale, J. I. (1998). Inching toward a mature theory of mind. In M. Ferrari & R. J. Sternberg (Eds.), *Self-awareness: Its nature and development* (pp. 148–190). New York: Guilford.

Chandra, A., Copen, C. E., & Mosher, W. D. (2013). Sexual Behavior, Sexual Attraction, and Sexual Identity in the United States: Data from the 2006–2010 National Survey of Family Growth (pp. 45–66). Springer Netherlands. http://doi.org/10.1007/978-94-007-5512-3_4

Chandra-Mouli, V., & Patel, S. V. (2017). Mapping the knowledge and understanding of menarche, menstrual hygiene and menstrual health among adolescent girls in low- and middle-income countries. *Reproductive Health, 14*(1), 30. http://doi.org/10.1186/s12978-017-0293-6

Chang, D. S., Lasley, F. D., Das, I. J., Mendonca, M. S., & Dynlacht, J. R. (2014). Radiation effects in the embryo and fetus. In *Basic Radiotherapy Physics and Biology* (pp. 313–316). Cham: Springer International Publishing. http://doi.org/10.1007/978-3-319-06841-1_32

Chang, S. M., Grantham-McGregor, S. M., Powell, C. A., Vera-Hernández, M., Lopez-Boo, F., Baker-Henningham, H., . . . Aboud, F. (2015). Integrating a parenting intervention With routine primary health care: A cluster randomized trial. *Pediatrics, 136*(2), 272–80. http://doi.org/10.1542/peds.2015-0119

Chao, R. K. (2001). Extending research on the consequences of parenting style for Chinese Americans and European Americans. *Child Development, 72*, 1832–1843.

Chaplin, T. M. (2015). Gender and Emotion Expression: A Developmental Contextual Perspective. *Emotion Review, 7*(1), 14–21. http://doi.org/10.1177/1754073914544408

Chaplin, T. M., & Aldao, A. (2013). Gender differences in emotion expression in children: a meta-analytic review. *Psychological Bulletin, 139*(4), 735–65. http://doi.org/10.1037/a0030737

Chapman, B., Duberstein, P., Tindle, H. A., Sink, K. M., Robbins, J., Tancredi, D. J., & Franks, P. (2012). Personality predicts cognitive function over 7 years in older persons. *The American Journal of Geriatric Psychiatry : Official Journal of the American Association for Geriatric Psychiatry, 20*(7), 612–21. http://doi.org/10.1097/JGP.0b013e31822cc9cb

Chappell, N., Gee, E., McDonald, L., & Stones, M. (2003). *Aging in contemporary Canada:* Toronto: Pearson education canada.

Charles, S. T., & Carstensen, L. L. (2010). Social and emotional aging. *Annual Review of Psychology, 61*, 383–409. http://doi.org/10.1146/annurev.psych.093008.100448

Charles, S. T., & Leger, K. A. (2016). Age and emotion. In H. S. Friedman (Ed.), *Encyclopedia of mental health*. London, UK: Elsevier.

Charles, S. T., Mather, M., & Carstensen, L. L. (2003). Aging and emotional memory: The forgettable nature of negative images for older adults. *Journal of Experimental Psychology: General, 132*(2), 310–324. http://doi.org/10.1037/0096-3445.132.2.310

Charles, S., Mogle, J., & Urban, E. (2016). Daily events are important for age differences in mean and duration for negative affect but not positive affect. *Psychology and*. Retrieved from http://psycnet.apa.org/journals/pag/31/7/661/

Charlton, K. E., Batterham, M. J., Bowden, S., Ghosh, A., Caldwell, K., Barone, L., . . . Milosavljevic, M. (2013). A high prevalence of malnutrition in acute geriatric patients predicts adverse clinical outcomes and mortality within 12 months. *E-SPEN Journal, 8*(3), e120–e125. http://doi.org/10.1016/j.clnme.2013.03.004

Charpak, N., Gabriel Ruiz, J., Zupan, J., Cattaneo, A., Figueroa, Z., Tessier, R., . . . Worku, B. (2005). Kangaroo mother care: 25 years after. *Acta Paediatrica, 94*(5), 514–522. http://doi.org/10.1111/j.1651-2227.2005.tb01930.x

Chasteen, A. L., & Madey, S. F. (2003). Belief in a Just World and the Perceived Injustice of Dying Young or Old. *OMEGA - Journal of Death and Dying, 47*(4), 313–326. http://doi.org/10.2190/W7H7-TE9E-1FWN-B8XD

Chavous, T. M., Bernat, D. H., Schmeelk-Cone, K., Caldwell, C. H., Kohn-Wood, L., & Zimmerman, M. A. (2003). Racial Identity and Academic Attainment Among African American Adolescents. *Child Development, 74*(4), 1076–1090.

Cheah, C. S. L., Leung, C. Y. Y., Tahseen, M., & Schultz, D. (2009). Authoritative parenting among immigrant Chinese mothers of preschoolers. *Journal of Family Psychology, 23*(3), 311–320. http://doi.org/10.1037/a0015076

Cheek, C. (2010). Passing Over: Identity Transition in Widows. *International Journal of Aging & Human Development, 70*(4), 345–364. http://doi.org/10.2190/AG.70.4.d

Chein, J., Albert, D., O'Brien, L., Uckert, K., & Steinberg, L. (2011). Peers increase adolescent risk taking by enhancing activity in the brain's reward circuitry. *Developmental Science, 14*(2). https://doi.org/10.1111/J.1467-7687.2010.01035.X

Chen, E., & Miller, G. E. (2013). Socioeconomic Status and Health: Mediating and Moderating Factors. *Annual Review of Clinical Psychology, 9*(1), 723–749. http://doi.org/10.1146/annurev-clinpsy-050212-185634

Chen, F., Mair, C. A., Bao, L., & Yang, Y. C. (2014). Race/Ethnic Differentials in the Health Consequences of Caring for Grandchildren for Grandparents. *The Journals of Gerontology. Series B, Psychological Sciences and Social Sciences*, gbu160-. http://doi.org/10.1093/geronb/gbu160

Chen, H., Pine, D. S., Ernst, M., Gorodetsky, E., Kasen, S., Gordon, K., . . . Cohen, P. (2013). The MAOA gene predicts happiness in women. *Progress in Neuro-Psychopharmacology & Biological Psychiatry, 40*, 122–125. http://doi.org/10.1016/j.pnpbp.2012.07.018

Chen, J.-H. (2012). Maternal alcohol use during pregnancy, birth weight and early behavioral outcomes. *Alcohol & Alcoholism, 47*(6).

Chen, L.-M., & Kent, R. D. (2010). Segmental production in Mandarin-learning infants. *Journal of Child Language, 37*(2), 341–371. http://doi.org/10.1017/s0305000909009581

Chen, P., & Jacobson, K. C. (2012). Developmental trajectories of substance use from early adolescence to young adulthood: gender and racial/ethnic differences. *The Journal of Adolescent Health : Official Publication of the Society for Adolescent Medicine, 50*(2), 154–63. http://doi.org/10.1016/j.jadohealth.2011.05.013

Chen, P., & Vazsonyi, A. T. (2011). Future orientation, impulsivity, and problem behaviors: A longitudinal moderation model. *Developmental Psychology, 47*(6), 1633–1645.

Chen, P., & Vazsonyi, A. T. (2013). Future orientation, school contexts, and problem behaviors: a multilevel study. *Journal of Youth and Adolescence, 42*(1), 67–81. http://doi.org/10.1007/s10964-012-9785-4

Chen, P., Voisin, D. R., & Jacobson, K. C. (2013). Community Violence Exposure and Adolescent Delinquency: Examining a Spectrum of Promotive Factors. *Youth & Society*, 0044118X13475827-. http://doi.org/10.1177/0044118X13475827

Chen, T., & Li, D. (2007). The Roles of Working Memory Updating and Processing Speed in Mediating Age-related Differences in Fluid Intelligence. *Aging, Neuropsychology & Cognition, 14*(6), 631–646.

Chen, X., Rubin, K. H., & Li, B. (1994). Only children and sibling children in urban China: A re-examination. *International Journal of Behavioral Development, 17*(3), 413–421.

Chen, X., Schmidt, L. A., Chen, X., & Schmidt, L. A. (2015). Temperament and personality. In R. Lerner (Ed.), *Handbook of child psychology and developmental science* (pp. 1–49). Hoboken, NJ: John Wiley & Sons. http://doi.org/10.1002/9781118963418.childpsy305

Cheng, W., Rolls, E. T., Gu, H., Zhang, J., & Feng, J. (2015a). Autism: reduced connectivity between cortical areas involved in face expression, theory of mind, and the sense of self. *Brain, 138*(5), 1382–1393. http://doi.org/10.1093/brain/awv051

Cheng, W., Rolls, E. T., Gu, H., Zhang, J., & Feng, J. (2015b). Autism: reduced connectivity between cortical areas involved in face expression, theory of mind, and the sense of self. *Brain : A Journal of Neurology, 138*(Pt 5), 1382–93. http://doi.org/10.1093/brain/awv051

Cheour, M., Ceponiene, R., Leppanen, P., Alho, K., Kujala, T., Renlund, M., . . . Naatanen, R. (2002). The auditory sensory memory trace decays rapidly in newborns. *Scandinavian Journal of Psychology, 43*(1), 33–39. http://doi.org/10.1111/1467-9450.00266

Cherlin, A. J. (2010). Demographic Trends in the United States: A Review of Research in the 2000s. *Journal of Marriage & Family, 72*(3), 403–419. http://doi.org/10.1111/j.1741-3737.2010.00710.x

Cherlin, A. J. (2013). Health, marriage, and same-sex partnerships. *Journal of Health and Social Behavior, 54*(1), 64–6. http://doi.org/10.1177/0022146512474430

Cherry, K. E., Walker, E. J., Brown, J. S., Volaufova, J., LaMotte, L. R., Welsh, D. A., . . . Frisard, M. I. (2013). Social engagement and health in younger, older, and oldest-old adults in the Louisiana Healthy Aging Study. *Journal of Applied Gerontology : The Official Journal of the Southern Gerontological Society, 32*(1), 51–75. http://doi.org/10.1177/0733464811409034

Chertkow, H. (2008). Diagnosis and treatment of dementia: Introduction. *CMAJ: Canadian Medical Association Journal, 316*–321. http://doi.org/10.1503/cmaj.070795

Chess, S., & Thomas, A. (1984). *Origins and evolution of behavior disorders*. New York: Brunner/Mazel.

Chess, S., & Thomas, A. (1991). Temperament and the concept of goodness of fit. In J. Strelau & A. Angleitner (Eds.), *Explorations in temperament: International perspectives on theory and measurement* (pp. 15–28). New York: Plenum.

Chevalier, N., Kurth, S., Doucette, M. R., Wiseheart, M., Deoni, S. C. L., Dean, D. C., . . . Greenstein, D. (2015). Myelination is associated with processing speed in early childhood: Preliminary insights. *PLOS ONE, 10*(10). http://doi.org/10.1371/journal.pone.0139897

Chi, S., Yu, J.-T., Tan, M.-S., & Tan, L. (2014). Depression in Alzheimer's disease: epidemiology, mechanisms, and management. *Journal of Alzheimer's Disease : JAD, 42*(3), 739–55. http://doi.org/10.3233/JAD-140324

Chiao, J. Y., & Immordino-Yang, M. H. (2013). Modularity and the Cultural Mind: Contributions of Cultural Neuroscience to Cognitive Theory. *Perspectives on Psychological Science : A Journal of the Association for Psychological Science, 8*(1), 56–61. http://doi.org/10.1177/1745691612469032

Child Care Aware of America. (2016). *PARENTS AND THE HiGH COST OF CHILD CARE - 2016 Report*. Retrieved from http://usa.childcareaware.org/wp-content/uploads/2016/12/CCA_High_Cost_Report.pdf

Child Trends Data Bank. (2014). Oral sex behaviors among teens. Retrieved from https://www.childtrends.org/?indicators=oral-sex-behaviors-among-teens

Child Trends Data Bank. (2014a). *Unintentional Injuries*. Retrieved from http://www.childtrends.org/?indicators=unintentional-injuries

Child Trends Data Bank. (2014b). *Unintentional Injuries*.

Child Trends Databank. (2015). Family structure. Retrieved from https://www.childtrends.org/?indicators=family-structure

Child Trends. (2013a). *Breastfeeding: Indicators on Children and Youth*. Bethesda, MD. Retrieved from http://www.childtrends.org/wp-content/uploads/2012/10/90_Breastfeeding.pdf

Child Trends. (2013b). *Infant, child, and teen mortality*. Bethesda, MD.

Child Trends. (2015). *Immunization. Child Trends Databank Indicator*. Retrieved from http://www.childtrends.org/indicators/immunization/

Child Welfare Information Gateway. (2013). *What is child abuse and neglect? Recognizing the signs and symptoms.* Washington DC. Retrieved from https://www.childwelfare.gov/pubpdfs/whatiscan.pdf

Chin, A. L., Negash, S., & Hamilton, R. (2011). Diversity and disparity in dementia: the impact of ethnoracial differences in Alzheimer disease. *Alzheimer Disease and Associated Disorders, 25*(3), 187–95. http://doi.org/10.1097/WAD.0b013e318211c6c9

Chiu, L.-H. H. (1992). Self-esteem in American and Chinese (Taiwanese) children. *Current Psychology: Research and Reviews, 11,* 309–313.

Choe, D. E., Olson, S. L., & Sameroff, A. J. (2013). The interplay of externalizing problems and physical and inductive discipline during childhood. *Developmental Psychology, 49*(11), 2029–39. http://doi.org/10.1037/a0032054

Choi, J., & Silverman, I. (2003). Processes underlying sex differences in route-learning strategies in children and adolescents. *Personality and Individual Differences, 34*(7), 1153–1166. http://doi.org/10.1016/S0191-8869(02)00105-8

Chomsky, C. S. (1969). *The acquisition of syntax in children from five to ten.* Cambridge, MA: MIT Press.

Chomsky, N. (1959). Review of B. F. Skinner's Verbal Behavior. *Language, 35,* 26–58.

Chomsky, N. (1965). *Aspects of the theory of syntax.* Cambridge, MA: MIT Press.

Chonchaiya, W., & Pruksananonda, C. (2008). Television viewing associates with delayed language development. *Acta Paediatrica, 97*(7), 977–982. http://doi.org/10.1111/j.1651-2227.2008.00831.x

Chong, A., & Mickelson, K. D. (2013). Perceived Fairness and Relationship Satisfaction During the Transition to Parenthood: The Mediating Role of Spousal Support. *Journal of Family Issues,* 0192513X13516764-. http://doi.org/10.1177/0192513X13516764

Chopik, W. J. (2017). Death across the lifespan: Age differences in death-related thoughts and anxiety. *Death Studies, 41*(1), 69–77. http://doi.org/10.1080/07481187.2016.1206997

Chopik, W. J., Edelstein, R. S., & Fraley, R. C. (2013). From the Cradle to the Grave: Age Differences in Attachment From Early Adulthood to Old Age. *Journal of Personality, 81*(2), 171–183. http://doi.org/10.1111/j.1467-6494.2012.00793.x

Chou, R., Dana, T., Bougatsos, C., Fleming, C., & Beil, T. (2011). Screening adults aged 50 years or older for hearing loss: a review of the evidence for the U.S. preventive services task force. *Annals of Internal Medicine, 154*(5), 347–55. http://doi.org/10.7326/0003-4819-154-5-201103010-00009

Choukas-Bradley, S., Giletta, M., Widman, L., Cohen, G. L., & Prinstein, M. J. (2014). Experimentally measured susceptibility to peer influence and adolescent sexual behavior trajectories: A preliminary study. *Developmental Psychology, 50*(9), 2221–7. http://doi.org/10.1037/a0037300

Choy, S. (2002). *Nontraditional Un- dergraduates, NCES 2002-012.* Washington, DC. Retrieved from https://nces.ed.gov/pubs2002/2002012.pdf

Chrisler, J. C. (2008). The menstrual cycle in a biopsychosocial context. In F. L. Denmark & M. A. Paludi (Eds.), *Psychology of women: A handbook of issues and theories* (2nd ed., pp. 400–439.). Westport, CT: Praeger.

Christ, G. H., Siegel, K., & Christ, A. E. (2002). Adolescent Grief. *JAMA, 288*(10), 1269. http://doi.org/10.1001/jama.288.10.1269

Christakis, D. A. (2009). The effects of infant media usage: what do we know and what should we learn? *Acta Paediatrica, 98*(1), 8–16. http://doi.org/10.1111/j.1651-2227.2008.01027.x

Christenson, S. L., & Thurlow, M. L. (2004). School dropouts: Prevention considerations, interventions, and challenges. *Current Directions in Psychological Science, 13*(1), 36–39. http://doi.org/10.1111/j.0963-7214.2004.01301010.x

Chung, A., Backholer, K., Wong, E., Palermo, C., Keating, C., & Peeters, A. (2016). Trends in child and adolescent obesity prevalence in economically advanced countries according to socioeconomic position: A Systematic review. *Obesity Reviews, 17*(3), 276–295. http://doi.org/10.1111/obr.12360

Chung, H. L., & Steinberg, L. (2006). Relations Between Neighborhood Factors, Parenting Behaviors, Peer Deviance, and Delinquency Among Serious Juvenile Offenders. *Developmental Psychology, 42*(2), 319–331

Church, E. (2004). *Understanding stepmothers: Women share their struggles, successes, and insights.* Toronto: Harper Collins.

Ciairano, S., Bonino, S., Kliewer, W., Miceli, R., & Jackson, S. (2006). Dating, Sexual Activity, and Well-Being in Italian Adolescents. *Journal of Clinical Child & Adolescent Psychology, 35*(2), 275–282.

Ciarrochi, J., Heaven, P. C. L., & Davies, F. (2007). The impact of hope, self-esteem, and attributional style on adolescents' school grades and emotional well-being: A longitudinal study. *Journal of Research in Personality, 41*(6), 1161–1178. http://doi.org/10.1016/j.jrp.2007.02.001

Cicchetti, D. (2010). Resilience under conditions of extreme stress: a multilevel perspective. *World Psychiatry, 9*(3), 145–154. http://doi.org/10.1002/j.2051-5545.2010.tb00297.x

Cicchetti, D., & Banny, A. (2014). A Developmental Psychopathology Perspective on Child Maltreatment. In M. Lewis & K. D. Rudolph (Eds.), *Handbook of Developmental Psychopathology* (pp. 723–741). Boston, MA: Springer US. http://doi.org/10.1007/978-1-4614-9608-3

Cicchetti, D., Rogosch, F. A., & Sturge-Apple, M. L. (2007). Interactions of child maltreatment and serotonin transporter and monoamine oxidase A polymorphisms: Depressive symptomatology among adolescents from low socioeconomic status backgrounds. *Development and Psychopathology, 19*(4), 1161–80. http://doi.org/10.1017/S0954579407000600

Cicchetti, D., Rogosch, F. A., Toth, S. L., & Spagnola, M. (1997). Affect, cognition, and the emergence of self-knowledge in the toddler offspring of. *Journal of Experimental Child Psychology, 67*(3), 338.

Cicchino, J. B., & McCartt, A. T. (2015). *Critical older driver errors in a sample of serious U.S. crashes.* Arlington, VA:, VA:

Cichy, K. E., Lefkowitz, E. S., Davis, E. M., & Fingerman, K. L. (2013). "You are such a disappointment!": negative emotions and parents' perceptions of adult children's lack of success. *The Journals of Gerontology. Series B, Psychological Sciences and Social Sciences, 68*(6), 893–901. http://doi.org/10.1093/geronb/gbt053

Cicirelli, V. G. (2002). *Older adults' views on death. Older adults' views on death.* New York, NY: Springer.

Cicirelli, V. G. (2010). Attachment relationships in old age. *Journal of Social and Personal Relationships, 27*(2), 191–199. http://doi.org/10.1177/0265407509360984

Cierniak, R. (2011). Some words about the history of computed tomography. In *X-ray computed tomography in biomedical engineering* (pp. 7–19). London: Springer London. Retrieved from http://doi.org/10.1007/978-0-85729-027-4_2

Cinamon, R. G., & Rich, Y. (2002). Gender Differences in the Importance of Work and Family Roles: Implications for Work-Family Conflict. *Sex Roles, 47*(11/12), 531–541

Clapp, W. C., Rubens, M. T., Sabharwal, J., & Gazzaley, A. (2011). Deficit in switching between functional brain networks underlies the impact of multitasking on working memory in older adults. *Proceedings of the National Academy of Sciences of the United States of America, 108*(17), 7212–7. http://doi.org/10.1073/pnas.1015297108

Clark, A. E., Diener, E., Georgellis, Y., & Lucas, R. E. (2008). Lags And Leads in Life Satisfaction: a Test of the Baseline Hypothesis*. *The Economic Journal, 118*(529), F222–F243. http://doi.org/10.1111/j.1468-0297.2008.02150.x

Clark, D. A., Durbin, C. E., Hicks, B. M., Iacono, W. G., & McGue, M. (2016). Personality in the age of industry: Structure, heritability, and correlates of personality in middle childhood from the perspective of parents, teachers, and children. *Journal of Research in Personality.* http://doi.org/10.1016/j.jrp.2016.06.013

Clark, K. A., Helland, T., Specht, K., Narr, K. L., Manis, F. R., Toga, A. W., & Hugdahl, K. (2014). Neuroanatomical precursors of dyslexia identified from pre-reading through to age 11. *Brain: A Journal of Neurology.* http://doi.org/10.1093/brain/awu229

Clark, T. C., Lucassen, M. F. G., Bullen, P., Denny, S. J., Fleming, T. M., Robinson, E. M., & Rossen, F. V. (2014). The Health and Well-Being of Transgender High School Students: Results From the New Zealand Adolescent Health Survey (Youth '12). *Journal of Adolescent Health, 55*(1), 93–99. http://doi.org/10.1016/j.jadohealth.2013.11.008

Clarke-Stewart, A., & Brentano, C. (2006). *Divorce: Causes and consequences.* New Haven, CT: Yale University Press.

Clauss, D., & Baxter, S. (1997). Post adoption survey of Russian and Eastern European children. *Roots and Wings Adoption Magazine, 6,* 6–9.

Claxton, S. E., & van Dulmen, M. H. M. (2013). Casual Sexual Relationships and Experiences in Emerging Adulthood. *Emerging Adulthood, 1*(2), 138–150. http://doi.org/10.1177/2167696813487181

Clearfield, M. W. (2011). Learning to walk changes infants' social interactions. *Infant Behavior & Development, 34*(1), 15–25. http://doi.org/10.1016/j.infbeh.2010.04.008

Clearfield, M. W. (2011). Learning to walk changes infants' social interactions. *Infant Behavior & Development, 34*(1), 15–25. http://doi.org/10.1016/j.infbeh.2010.04.008

Cleary, M., Walter, G., & Jackson, D. (2011). Not Always Smooth Sailing": Mental Health Issues Associated with the Transition from High School to College. *Issues in Mental Health Nursing, 32*(4), 250–254. http://doi.org/10.3109/01612840.2010.548906

Cleveland, M. J., Mallett, K. A., White, H. R., Turrisi, R., & Favero, S. (2013). Patterns of alcohol use and related consequences in non-college-attending emerging adults. *Journal of Studies on Alcohol and Drugs, 74*(1), 84–93.

Clifford, A., Franklin, A., Davies, I. R. L., & Holmes, A. (2009). Electrophysiological markers of categorical perception of color in 7-month old infants. *Brain & Cognition, 71*(2), 165–172. http://doi.org/10.1016/j.bandc.2009.05.002

Cliffordson, C., & Gustafsson, J.-E. (2008). Effects of age and schooling on intellectual performance: Estimates obtained from analysis of continuous variation in age and length of schooling. *Intelligence, 36*(2), 143–152. http://doi.org/10.1016/j.intell.2007.03.006

Clifton, R. K., Morrongiello, B. A., Kulig, J. W., & Dowd, J. M. (1981). Newborns' orientation towards sound: Possible implications for cortical development. *Child Development, 53,* 833–838.

Clifton, R. K., Rochat, P., Robin, D. J., & Berthier, N. E. (1994). Multimodal perception in the control of infant reaching. *Journal of Experimental Psychology: Human Perception and Performance*, 20, 876–886.

Clynes, T. (2015). The "rage to master": What it takes for those scary-smart kids to succeed. Retrieved December 12, 2016, from http://www.salon.com/2015/06/13/talent_practice_luck_all_of_the_above_what_it_takes_for_the_gifted_child_to_succeed/

Cochet, H. (2012). Development of hand preference for object-directed actions and pointing gestures: A longitudinal study between 15 and 25 months of age. *Developmental Psychobiology*, 54(1), 105–111. http://doi.org/10.1002/dev.20576

Cohane, G. H., & Pope, H. G. (2001). Body image in boys: a review of the literature. *The International Journal of Eating Disorders*, 29(4), 373–9. Retrieved from http://www.ncbi.nlm.nih.gov/pubmed/11285574

Cohen Kadosh, K., Johnson, M. H., Dick, F., Cohen Kadosh, R., & Blakemore, S.-J. (2013). Effects of age, task performance, and structural brain development on face processing. *Cerebral Cortex (New York, N.Y. : 1991)*, 23(7), 1630–1642. http://doi.org/10.1093/cercor/bhs150

Cohen, A. O., & Casey, B. J. (2014). Rewiring juvenile justice: the intersection of developmental neuroscience and legal policy. *Trends in Cognitive Sciences*, 18(2), 63–5. http://doi.org/10.1016/j.tics.2013.11.002

Cohen, K. M., & Savin-Williams, R. C. (1996). *Developmental perspectives on coming out to self and others*. Harcourt Brace College Publishers. Retrieved from http://psycnet.apa.org/psycinfo/1996-97027-005

Cohen, L. B., & Cashon, C. H. (2006). Infant cognition. In D. Kuhn, R. S. Siegler, W. Damon, & R. M. Lerner (Eds.), *Handbook of child psychology: Cognition, perception, and language* (6th ed., Vol. 2, pp. 214–251). Hoboken, NJ: John Wiley & Sons.

Cohen, P., Kasen, S., Chen, H., Hartmark, C., & Gordon, K. (2003). Variations in patterns of developmental transitions in the emerging adulthood period. *Developmental Psychology*, 39(4), 657. Retrieved from http://www.ncbi.nlm.nih.gov/pubmed/12859120

Cohen, R. (1967). *The Kanuri of Bornu*. New York: Holt, Rinehart and Winston.

Cohen-Mansfield, J., Skornick-Bouchbinder, M., & Brill, S. (2017). Trajectories of end of life: A systematic review. *The Journals of Gerontology: Series B*, 27, 998. http://doi.org/10.1093/geronb/gbx093

Coie, J. D., & Dodge, K. A. (1998). Aggression and antisocial behavior. In N. Eisenberg (Ed.), *Handbook of child psychology: Social, emotional, and personality development* (5th ed., Vol. 3, pp. 786–788). New York, NY: Wiley.

Colby, A., & Damon, W. (1992). *Some do care: Contemporary lives of moral commitment*. New York, NY: Free Press.

Colby, A., Kohlberg, L., Gibbs, J., & Lieberman, M. (1983). A longitudinal study of moral judgment. *Monographs of the Society for Research in Child Development*, 48(1).

Cole, P. M., Martin, S. E., & Dennis, T. A. (2004). Emotion regulation as a scientific construct: Methodological challenges and directions for child development research. *Child Development*, 75(2), 317–333.

Cole, P. M., Tamang, B. L., & Shrestha, S. (2006). Cultural Variations in the Socialization of Young Children's Anger and Shame. *Child Development*, 77(5), 1237–1251. http://doi.org/10.1111/j.1467-8624.2006.00931.x

Cole, T. J. (2003). The secular trend in human physical growth: A biological view. *Economics and Human Biology*, 1(2), 161–168.

Cole, W. G., Lingeman, J. M., & Adolph, K. E. (2012). Go naked: diapers affect infant walking. *Developmental Science*, 15(6), 783–90. http://doi.org/10.1111/j.1467-7687.2012.01169.x

Coleman, P. G., Ivani-Chalian, C., & Robinson, M. (2004). Religious attitudes among British older people: stability and change in a 20-year longitudinal study. *Ageing & Society*, 24(2), 167–188.

Coleman-Jensen, A., Rabbitt, M., Gregory, C., & Singh, A. (2016). Household Food Security in the United States in 2015. Retrieved from https://www.ers.usda.gov/publications/pub-details/?pubid=79760

Coles, C. D., Goldstein, F. C., Lynch, M. E., Chen, X., Kable, J. A., Johnson, K. C., & Hu, X. (2011). Memory and brain volume in adults prenatally exposed to alcohol. *Brain & Cognition*, 75(1), 67–77. http://doi.org/10.1016/j.bandc.2010.08.013

Coley, R. L., Kull, M. A., & Carrano, J. (2014). Parental endorsement of spanking and children's internalizing and externalizing problems in African American and Hispanic families. *Journal of Family Psychology : JFP : Journal of the Division of Family Psychology of the American Psychological Association (Division 43)*, 28(1), 22–31. http://doi.org/10.1037/a0035272

Coley, R. L., Kull, M. A., & Carrano, J. (2014). Parental endorsement of spanking and children's internalizing and externalizing problems in African American and Hispanic families. *Journal of Family Psychology : JFP : Journal of the Division of Family Psychology of the American Psychological Association (Division 43)*, 28(1), 22–31. http://doi.org/10.1037/a0035272

Collette, F., & Van der Linden, M. (2002). Brain imaging of the central executive component of working memory. *Neuroscience & Biobehavioral Reviews*, 26(2), 105–125.

Collette, F., & Van der Linden, M. (2002). Brain imaging of the central executive component of working memory. *Neuroscience & Biobehavioral Reviews*, 26(2), 105–125.

Colley, R. C., Garriguet, D., Janssen, I., Craig, C. L., Clarke, J., & Tremblay, M. S. (2011). Physical activity of Canadian adults: Accelerometer results from the 2007 to 2009 Canadian Health Measures Survey. *Statistics Canada*, 22(1).

Collier, K. L., van Beusekom, G., Bos, H. M. W., & Sandfort, T. G. M. (2013). Sexual orientation and gender identity/expression related peer victimization in adolescence: a systematic review of associated psychosocial and health outcomes. *Journal of Sex Research*, 50(3–4), 299–317. http://doi.org/10.1080/00224499.2012.750639

Collier, P., & Morgan, D. (2008). "Is that paper really due today?": differences in first-generation and traditional college students' understandings of faculty expectations. *Higher Education*, 55(4), 425–446. http://doi.org/10.1007/s10734-007-9065-5

Collins, J. W., Papacek, E., Schulte, N. F., & Drolet, A. (2001). Differing postneonatal mortality rates of Mexican-American infants with United-States-born and Mexico-born mothers in Chicago. *Ethnicity & Disease*, 11(4), 606–13. Retrieved from http://www.ncbi.nlm.nih.gov/pubmed/11763285

Collins, L. K., Villanti, A. C., Pearson, J. L., Glasser, A. M., Johnson, A. L., Niaura, R. S., & Abrams, D. B. (2017). Frequency of Youth E-Cigarette, Tobacco, and Poly-Use in the United States, 2015: Update to Villanti et al., ?Frequency of Youth E-Cigarette and Tobacco Use Patterns in the United States: Measurement Precision Is Critical to Inform Public Health? *Nicotine & Tobacco Research*, 59(6), 612–619. http://doi.org/10.1093/ntr/ntx073

Collins, T. F. X. (2006). History and evolution of reproductive and developmental toxicology guidelines. *Current Pharmaceutical Design*, 12(12), 1449–1465.

Collins, W. A., & Laursen, B. (2004). Changing Relationships, Changing Youth: Interpersonal Contexts of Adolescent Development. *Journal of Early Adolescence*, 24(1), 55–62.

Collins, W. A., & Steinberg, L. (2006). Adolescent Development in Interpersonal Context. In N. Eisenberg, W. Damon, & R. M. Lerner (Eds.), *Handbook of child psychology: Vol. 3, Social, emotional, and personality development* (6th ed., pp. 1003–1067). Hoboken, NJ: John Wiley & Sons.

Collins, W. A., Madsen, S. D., & Susman-Stillman, A. (2002). Parenting during middle childhood. In M. H. Bornstein (Ed.), *Handbook of parenting* (2nd ed., Vol. 1, pp. 73–101). Mahwah, NJ: Lawrence Erlbaum.

Collins, W. A., Welsh, D. P., & Furman, W. (2009). Adolescent romantic relationships. *Annual Review of Psychology*, 60, 631–652. http://doi.org/10.1146/annurev.psych.60.110707.163459

Collura, T. F. (1993). History and evolution of electroencephalographic instruments and techniques. *Journal of Clinical Neurophysiology*, 10(4), 476–504. Retrieved from http://www.ncbi.nlm.nih.gov/pubmed/8308144

Colom, R., Flores-Mendoza, C. E., & Abad, F. J. (2007). generational changes on the draw-a-man test: A comparison of brazilian urban and rural children tested in 1930, 2002 and 2004. *Journal of Biosocial Science*, 39(1), 79. http://doi.org/10.1017/S0021932005001173

Colombo, J., Brez, C. C., & Curtindale, L. M. (2015). Infant perception and cognition. In R. M. Lerner, M. A. Easterbrooks, & J. Mistry (Eds.), *Handbook of developmental psychology* (2nd ed., Vol. 6, pp. 61–90). Hoboken, NJ: Wiley.

Colombo, J., McCollam, K., Coldren, J. T., Mitchell, D. W., & Rash, S. J. (1990). Form categorization in 10-month-olds. *Journal of Experimental Child Psychology*, 49, 173–188.

Colrain, I. M., & Baker, F. C. (2011). Changes in sleep as a function of adolescent development. *Neuropsychology Review*, 21(1), 5–21. http://doi.org/10.1007/s11065-010-9155-5

Colson, E. R., Willinger, M., Rybin, D., Heeren, T., Smith, L. A., Lister, G., & Corwin, M. J. (2013). Trends and Factors Associated With Infant Bed Sharing, 1993-2010. *JAMA Pediatrics*, 167(11), 1032. http://doi.org/10.1001/jamapediatrics.2013.2560

Colston, H. L. (2002). Contrast and assimilation in verbal irony. *Journal of Pragmatics*, 34, 111–142.

Combs, G. M., & Milosevic, I. (2016). Workplace Discrimination and the Wellbeing of Minority Women: Overview, Prospects, and Implications. In Mary L. Connerley & Jiyun Wu (Eds.), *Handbook on Well-Being of Working Women* (pp. 17–31). Dordrecht: Springer Netherlands. http://doi.org/10.1007/978-94-017-9897-6_2

Combs-Orme, T., & Renkert, L. E. (2009). Fathers and Their Infants: Caregiving and Affection in the Modern Family. *Journal of Human Behavior in the Social Environment*, 19(4), 394–418. http://doi.org/10.1080/10911350902790753

Commons, M. L., & Richards, F. A. (2002). Four Postformal Stages. In J. Demick & C. Andreoletti (Eds.), *Handbook of Adult Development* (pp. 199–219). Boston, MA: Springer US. http://doi.org/10.1007/978-1-4615-0617-1_11

Comunian, A. L., & Gielen, U. P. (2000). Sociomoral Reflection and Prosocial and Antisocial Behavior: Two Italian Studies. *Psychological Reports*, 87(1), 161–176.

Conboy, B. T., & Thal, D. J. (2006). Ties Between the Lexicon and Grammar: Cross-Sectional and Longitudinal Studies of Bilingual Toddlers. *Child Development*, 77(3), 712–735. http://doi.org/10.1111/j.1467-8624.2006.00899.x

Conger, R. D., & Donnellan, M. B. (2007). An Interactionist Perspective on the Socioeconomic Context of Human Development. *Annual Review of Psychology*, 58(1), 175–199. http://doi.org/10.1146/annurev.psych.58.110405.085551

Connell, C. M., Scott Roberts, J., McLaughlin, S. J., & Akinleye, D. (2009). Racial Differences in Knowledge and Beliefs About Alzheimer Disease. *Alzheimer Disease & Associated Disorders*, 23(2), 110–116. http://doi.org/10.1097/WAD.0b013e318192e94d

Conner, D. B., Knight, D. K., & Cross, D. R. (1997). Mothers' and fathers' scaffolding of their 2-year-olds during problem-solving and literacy interactions. *British Journal of Developmental Psychology*, 15, 323–338.

Connolly, J., & Craig, W. (1999). Conceptions of Cross-Sex Friendships and Romantic Relationships in Early Adolescence. *Journal of Youth & Adolescence*, 481–509, 14p.

Connolly, J., & Furman, W. (2000). The Role of Peers in the Emergence of Heterosexual Romantic Relationships in Adolescence. *Child Development*, 71, 1395–1409.

Connolly, J., Craig, W., Goldberg, A., & Pepler, D. (2004). Mixed-Gender Groups, Dating, and Romantic Relationships in Early Adolescence. *Journal of Research on Adolescence*, 14, 185–207.

Connolly, J., Nguyen, H. N. T., Pepler, D., Craig, W., & Jiang, D. (2013). Developmental trajectories of romantic stages and associations with problem behaviours during adolescence. *Journal of Adolescence*, 36(6), 1013–1024. http://doi.org/10.1016/j.adolescence.2013.08.006

Conradt, E. (2017). Using principles of behavioral epigenetics to advance research on early-life stress. *Child Development Perspectives*, 11(2), 107–112. http://doi.org/10.1111/cdep.12219

Conron, K. J., Scott, G., Stowell, G. S., & Landers, S. J. (2012). Transgender Health in Massachusetts: Results From a Household Probability Sample of Adults. *American Journal of Public Health*, 102(1), 118–122. http://doi.org/10.2105/AJPH.2011.300315

Conroy, D. A., Kurth, M. E., Brower, K. J., Strong, D. R., & Stein, M. D. (2015). Impact of marijuana use on self-rated cognition in young adult men and women. *The American Journal on Addictions / American Academy of Psychiatrists in Alcoholism and Addictions*, 24(2), 160–165. http://doi.org/10.1111/j.1521-0391.2014.12157.x

Consedine, N. S., & Magai, C. (2006). Emotional Development in Adulthood: A Developmental Functionalist Review and Critique. In *Handbook of adult development and learning* (pp. 123–148). Oxford University Press.

Conway, J. M., Amel, E. L., & Gerwien, D. P. (2009). Teaching and Learning in the Social Context: A Meta-Analysis of Service Learning's Effects on Academic, Personal, Social, and Citizenship Outcomes. *Teaching of Psychology*, 36(4), 233–245. http://doi.org/10.1080/00986280903172969

Cook, C. R., Williams, K. R., Guerra, N. G., & Kim, T. (2010). Variability in the prevalence of bullying and victimization: A cross-national and methodological analysis. In R. Jimerson, S. Swearer, & D. L. Espelage (Eds.), *Handbook of bullying in schools: An international perspective* (pp. 347– 362). New York, NY: Routledge.

Cooper, C., Javaid, M. K., & Arden, N. (2014). Epidemiology of osteoarthritis. In N. Arden, F. Blanco, C. Cooper, A. Guermazi, D. Hayashi, D. Hunter, . . . J.-Y. Roemer, F.W., Reginster (Eds.), *Atlas of Osteoarthritis* (pp. 21–36).

Tarporley: Springer Healthcare Ltd. http://doi.org/10.1007/978-1-910315-16-3_2

Cooper, J. C., Kreps, T. A., Wiebe, T., Pirkl, T., & Knutson, B. (2010). When giving is good: Ventromedial prefrontal cortex activation for others' intentions. *Neuron*, 67(3), 511–521. https://doi.org/10.1016/j.neuron.2010.06.030

Cooper, H., Valentine, J. C., Nye, B., & Lindsay, J. J. (1999). Relationships between five after-school activities and academic achievement. *Journal of Educational Psychology*, 91(2), 369–378.

Copeland, W. E., Wolke, D., Angold, A., & Costello, E. J. (2013). Adult psychiatric outcomes of bullying and being bullied by peers in childhood and adolescence. *JAMA Psychiatry*, 70(4), 419–26. http://doi.org/10.1001/jamapsychiatry.2013.504

Copen, C. E., Daniels, K., & Mosher, W. D. (2013). First Premarital Cohabitation in the United States: 2006–2010 National Survey of Family Growth. *National Health Statistics Reports*, 64.

Copen, C. E., Kimberly Daniels, Jonathan Vespa, & William D. Mosher. (2012). First Marriages in the United States: Data From the 2006–2010 National Survey of Family Growth. *National Health Statistics Reports*, 49. Retrieved from http://www.cdc.gov/nchs/data/nhsr/nhsr049.pdf#x2013;2010 National Survey of Family Growth [PDF - 419 KB%3C/a%3E

Coplan, R. J., & Arbeau, K. A. (2009). Peer interactions and play in early childhood. In K. H. Rubin, W. M. Bukowski, & B. Laursen (Eds.), *Handbook of peer interactions, relationships, and groups* (pp. 143–161). New York, NY: Guilford Press.

Coplan, R. J., Ooi, L. L., & Nocita, G. (2015). When One Is Company and Two Is a Crowd: Why Some Children Prefer Solitude. *Child Development Perspectives*, 9(3), 133–137. http://doi.org/10.1111/cdep.12131

Coplan, R. J., Rose-Krasnor, L., Weeks, M., Kingsbury, A., Kingsbury, M., & Bullock, A. (2013). Alone is a crowd: Social motivations, social withdrawal, and socioemotional functioning in later childhood. *Developmental Psychology*, 49(5), 861–875.

Corbetta, D., & Snapp-Childs, W. (2009). Seeing and touching: The role of sensory-motor experience on the development of infant reaching. *Infant Behavior & Development*, 32(1), 44–58. http://doi.org/10.1016/j.infbeh.2008.10.004

Cordain, L., Lindeberg, S., Hurtado, M., Hill, K., Eaton, S. B., & Brand-Miller, J. (2002). Acne vulgaris: A disease of western civilization. *Archives of Dermatology*, 138, 1584–90.

Cordero, A., Mulinare, J., Berry, R. J., Boyle, C., Dietz, W., Johnston Jr, R., . . . Popovic, T. (2010). CDC grand rounds: Additional opportunities to prevent neural tube defects with folic acid fortification. *MMWR: Morbidity & Mortality Weekly Report*, 59(31), 980–984.

Cordes, S., & Brannon, E. M. (2009). Crossing the divide: Infants discriminate small from large numerosities. *Developmental Psychology*, 45(6), 1583–1594. http://doi.org/10.1037/a0015666

Cormier, D. C., McGrew, K. S., Bulut, O., & Funamoto, A. (2016). Revisiting the Relations Between the WJ-IV Measures of Cattell-Horn-Carroll (CHC) Cognitive Abilities and Reading Achievement During the School-Age Years. *Journal of Psychoeducational Assessment*. http://doi.org/10.1177/0734282916659208

Cornell, D., & Limber, S. P. (2015). Law and policy on the concept of bullying at school. *The American Psychologist*, 70(4), 333–43. http://doi.org/10.1037/a0038558

Cornell, D., Gregory, A., Huang, F., & Fan, X. (2013). Perceived prevalence of teasing and bullying predicts high school dropout rates. *Journal of Educational Psychology*, 105(1), 138–149.

Corning, A. F., & Gondoli, D. M. (2012). *Who is most likely to fat talk? A social comparison perspective. Body Image* (Vol. 9).

Corr, C. . (2010a). Children, development, and encounters with death, bereavement and coping. In E. Balk, D & C. A. Corr (Eds.), *Children's encounters with death, bereavement, and coping* (pp. 3–20). Springer.

Corr, C. A. (2010b). Children's emerging awareness and understanding of loss and death. In E. Balk, D & C. A. Corr (Eds.), *Children's encounters with death, bereavement, and coping* (pp. 21–38). Springer.

Corr, C. A., & Corr, D. M. (2013). *Death and dying, life and living* (7th ed.). New York, NY: Cengage.

Corrieri, S., Heider, D., Conrad, I., Blume, A., König, H.-H., & Riedel-Heller, S. G. (2014). School-based prevention programs for depression and anxiety in adolescence: a systematic review. *Health Promotion International*, 29(3), 427–441. http://doi.org/10.1093/heapro/dat001

Corriveau, R. A., Bosetti, F., Emr, M., Gladman, J. T., Koenig, J. I., Moy, C. S., . . . Koroshetz, W. (2016). The Science of Vascular Contributions to Cognitive Impairment and Dementia (VCID): A Framework for Advancing Research Priorities in the Cerebrovascular Biology of Cognitive Decline. *Cellular and Molecular Neurobiology*, 36(2), 281–288. http://doi.org/10.1007/s10571-016-0334-7

Corwin, J., Loury, M., & Gilbert, A. N. (1995). Workplace, Age, and Sex as Mediators of Olfactory Function: Data from the National Geographic Smell Survey. *The Journals of Gerontology Series B: Psychological Sciences and Social Sciences*, 50B(4), P179–P186. http://doi.org/10.1093/geronb/50B.4.P179

Cosman, F., de Beur, S. J., LeBoff, M. S., Lewiecki, E. M., Tanner, B., Randall, S., & Lindsay, R. (2014). Clinician's Guide to Prevention and Treatment of Osteoporosis. *Osteoporosis International*, 25(10), 2359–2381. http://doi.org/10.1007/s00198-014-2794-2

Costa, P. J., Terracciano, A., & McCrae, R. R. (2001). Gender differences in personality traits across cultures: Robust and surprising findings. *Journal of Personality and Social Psychology*, 81(2), 322–331. http://doi.org/10.1037/0022-3514.81.2.322

Costa, P. T. J., McCrae, R. R., Zonderman, A. B., Barbano, H. E., Lebowitz, B., & Larson, D. M. (1986). Cross-sectional studies of personality in a national sample: II. Stability in neuroticism, extraversion, and openness. *Psychology and Aging*, 1(2), 144–149.

Costa, R. M., & Brody, S. (2012). Sexual Satisfaction, Relationship Satisfaction, and Health Are Associated with Greater Frequency of Penile–Vaginal Intercourse. *Archives of Sexual Behavior*, 41(1), 9–10. http://doi.org/10.1007/s10508-011-9847-9

Costos, D., Ackerman, R., & Paradis, L. (2002). Recollections of menarche: Communication between mothers and daughters regarding menstruation. *Sex Roles*, 46(1–2), 49–59. http://doi.org/10.1023/A:1016037618567

Côté, J. E. (2006). Emerging Adulthood as an Institutionalized Moratorium: Risks and Benefits to Identity Formation. In J. J. Arnett & J. L. Tanner (Eds.), *Emerging adults in America: Coming of age in the 21st century* (pp. 85–116). Washington, DC: American Psychological Association.

Côté, J. E. (2014). The Dangerous Myth of Emerging Adulthood: An Evidence-Based Critique of a Flawed Developmental Theory. *Applied Developmental Science*, 18(4), 177–188. Retrieved from http://www.tandfonline.com/doi/abs/10.1080/10888691.2014.954451#.VT0Q7JMug8Q

Côté, S. M. (2009). A developmental perspective on sex differences in aggressive behaviours.

In R. E. Tremblay, M. A. G. van Aken, & W. Koops (Eds.), *Development and prevention of behaviour problems: From genes to social policy.* (pp. 143–163). New York, NY: Psychology Press.

Cotton, C. R., & Range, L. M. (2010). Children's Death Concepts: Relationship to Cognitive Functioning, Age, Experience With Death, Fear of Death, and Hopelessness. *Journal of Clinical Child Psychology*.

Coubart, A., Izard, V., Spelke, E. S., Marie, J., & Streri, A. (2014). Dissociation between small and large numerosities in newborn infants. *Developmental Science*, 17(1), 11–22. http://doi.org/10.1111/desc.12108

Coughlin, J. W., Heinberg, L. J., Marinilli, A., & Guarda, A. S. (2003). Body image dissatisfaction in children: Prevalence and parental influence. *Healthy Weight Journal*, 17, 56–59.

Coulton, C. J., Korbin, J. E., & Su, M. (1999). Neighborhoods and child maltreatment: A multi-level study. *Child Abuse and Neglect*, 23, 1019–1040.

Counts, D. A., & Counts, D. R. (1985). I'm not dead yet? Aging and death: Processes and experiences in Kalia. In D. A. Counts & D. R. Counts (Eds.), *Aging and its transformations* (pp. 131–156). langham, MD: University of America Press.

Courage, M. L., & Adams, R. J. (1990). Visual acuity assessment from birth to three years using the acuity card procedures: Cross-sectional and longitudinal samples. *Optometry and Vision Science*, 67, 713–718.

Courage, M. L., & Cowan, N. (2009). *The development of memory in infancy and childhood* (2nd ed.). New York, NY: Psychology Press.

Courage, M. L., & Howe, M. L. (2010). To watch or not to watch: Infants and toddlers in a brave new electronic world. *Developmental Review*, 30(2), 101–115. http://doi.org/10.1016/j.dr.2010.03.002

Courage, M. L., Edison, S. C., & Howe, M. L. (2004). Variability in the early development of visual self-recognition. *Infant Behavior & Development*, 27(4), 509–532. http://doi.org/10.1016/j.infbeh.2004.06.001

Courage, M. L., Reynolds, G. D., & Richards, J. E. (2006). Infants' Attention to Patterned Stimuli: Developmental Change From 3 to 12 Months of Age. *Child Development*, 77(3), 680–695. http://doi.org/10.1111/j.1467-8624.2006.00897.x

Cousminer, D. L., Stergiakouli, E., Berry, D. J., Ang, W., Groen-Blokhuis, M. M., Körner, A., . . . Widen, E. (2014). Genome-wide association study of sexual maturation in males and females highlights a role for body mass and menarche loci in male puberty. *Human Molecular Genetics*, 23(16), 4452–4464. http://doi.org/10.1093/hmg/ddu150

Coutelle, C., & Waddington, S. N. (2012). The concept of prenatal gene therapy. In C. Coutelle (Ed.), *Methods in molecular biology* (Vol. 891, pp. 1–7). http://doi.org/10.1007/978-1-61779-873-3_1

Cowan, N., Hismjatullina, A., AuBuchon, A. M., Saults, J. S., Horton, N., Leadbitter, K., & Towse, J. (2010). With development, list recall includes more chunks, not just larger ones. *Developmental Psychology*, 46(5), 1119–1131. http://doi.org/10.1037/a0020618

Cowan, N., Nugent, L. D., Elliott, E. M., Ponomarev, I., & Saults, J. S. (1999). The role of attention in the development of short-term memory: Age differences in the verbal span of apprehension. *Child Development*, 70, 1082–1097.

Cowan, N., Ricker, T. J., Clark, K. M., Hinrichs, G. A., & Glass, B. A. (2015). Knowledge cannot explain the developmental growth of working memory capacity. *Developmental Science*, 18(1), 132–45. http://doi.org/10.1111/desc.12197

Cox, K. S., Wilt, J., Olson, B., & McAdams, D. P. (2010). Generativity, the Big Five, and Psychosocial Adaptation in Midlife Adults. *Journal of Personality*, 78(4), 1185–1208. http://doi.org/10.1111/j.1467-6494.2010.00647.x

Cox, M. V. (1993). *Children's drawings of the human figure.* Hillsdale, NJ:Lawrence Erlbaum.

Cox, M. V. (1997). *Drawings of people by the under-5s.* London: Falmer Press.

Cox, M., & Littlejohn, K. (1995). Children's use of converging obliques in their perspective drawings. *Educational Psychology*, 15, 127–139.

Coyl, D. D., Newland, L. A., & Freeman, H. (2010). Predicting preschoolers' attachment security from parenting behaviours, parents' attachment relationships and their use of social support. *Early Child Development and Care*, 180(4), 499–512. http://doi.org/10.1080/03004430802090463

Coyle, J. T. (2013). Brain structural alterations induced by fetal exposure to cocaine persist into adolescence and affect behavior. *JAMA Psychiatry*, 70(10), 1113–4. http://doi.org/10.1001/jamapsychiatry.2013.1949

Coyle, T. R., Pillow, D. R., Snyder, A. C., & Kochunov, P. (2011). Processing speed mediates the development of general intelligence (g) in adolescence. *Psychological Science*, 22(10), 1265–9. http://doi.org/10.1177/0956797611418243

Coyne, S. M., Linder, J. R., Rasmussen, E. E., Nelson, D. A., & Birkbeck, V. (2016). Pretty as a Princess: Longitudinal Effects of Engagement With Disney Princesses on Gender Stereotypes, Body Esteem, and Prosocial Behavior in Children. *Child Development*, 87(6), 1909–1925. http://doi.org/10.1111/cdev.12569

Crain, W. C. (2011). *Theories of development* (6th ed.). Englewood Cliffs, NJ: Prentice Hall.

Cramer, P. (2017). Identity change between late adolescence and adulthood. *Personality and Individual Differences*, 104, 538–543. http://doi.org/10.1016/j.paid.2016.08.044

Crawford, J. (1997). *Best evidence: Research foundations of the bilingual education act.* Washington, DC: National Clearinghouse for Bilingual Education.

Crean, R. D., Crane, N. A., & Mason, B. J. (2011). An evidence-based review of acute and long-term effects of cannabis use on executive cognitive functions. *Journal of Addiction Medicine*, 5(1), 1–8. http://doi.org/10.1097/ADM.0b013e31820c23fa

Creusere, M. A. (2000). A developmental test of theoretical perspectives on the understanding of verbal irony: Children's recognition of allusion and pragmatic insincerity. *Metaphor and Symbol*, 15, 29–45.

Crews, D., Gillette, R., Miller-Crews, I., & Gore, A. C. (2014). Nature, nurture and epigenetics. *Molecular and Cellular Endocrinology*, 398(1), 42–52. http://doi.org/10.1016/j.mce.2014.07.013

Crews, F. (1996). The verdict on Freud. *Psychological Science*, 7(2), 63–68.

Crews, J. E., Chou, C.-F., Stevens, J. A., & Saaddine, J. B. (2016). Falls among persons aged ≥ 65 years with and without severe vision impairment—United States, 2014. *MMWR. Morbidity and Mortality Weekly Report*, 65(17), 433–437. http://doi.org/10.15585/mmwr.mm6517a2

Cristofalo, V. J., Tresini, M., & Francis, M. K. (1999). Biological theories of senescence. In V. L. Bengtson & K. W. Schaie (Eds.), *Handbook of theories of aging* (pp. 98–112). New York, NY: Springer.

Crocetti, E., Klimstra, T. A., Hale, W. W., Koot, H. M., & Meeus, W. H. J. (2013). Impact of early adolescent externalizing problem behaviors on identity development in middle to late adolescence: A prospective 7-year longitudinal study. *Journal of Youth and Adolescence*, 42(11), 1745–58. http://doi.org/10.1007/s10964-013-9924-6

Crocetti, E., Klimstra, T., Keijsers, L., Hale Iii, W. W., & Meeus, W. H. J. (2009). Anxiety trajectories and identity development in adolescence: A five-wave longitudinal Study. *Journal of Youth & Adolescence*, 38(6), 839–849. http://doi.org/10.1007/s10964-008-9302-y

Crockenberg, S. C., & Leerkes, E. M. (2004). Infant and maternal behaviors regulate infant reactivity to novelty at 6 months. *Developmental Psychology*, 40(6), 1123–1132.

Crockett, L. J., Carlo, G., Wolff, J. M., & Hope, M. O. (2013). The role of pubertal timing and temperamental vulnerability in adolescents' internalizing symptoms. *Development and Psychopathology*, 25(2), 377–89. http://doi.org/10.1017/S0954579412001125

Crockett, L. J., Petersen, A. C., Graber, J. A., Schulenberg, J. E., & Ebata, A. (1989). School transitions and adjustment during early adolescence. *The Journal of Early Adolescence*, 9(3), 181–210. http://doi.org/10.1177/0272431689093002

Croninger, R. G., & Lee, V. E. (2001). Social capital and dropping out of high school: benefits to at-risk students of teachers' support and guidance. *Teachers College Record*, 103(4), 548–582.

Cross, C. P., Copping, L. T., & Campbell, A. (2011). Sex differences in impulsivity: A meta-analysis. *Psychological Bulletin*, 137(1), 97–130. http://doi.org/10.1037/a0021591

Cross, J. R., & Fletcher, K. L. (2009). The challenge of adolescent crowd research: Defining the crowd. *Journal of Youth & Adolescence*, 38(6), 747–764. http://doi.org/10.1007/s10964-008-9307-6

Cross, S., & Markus, H. (1991). Possible selves across the life span. *Human Development*, 34(4), 230–255.

Crosse, S., Kaye, E., & Ratnofsky, A. (1993). *A report on the maltreatment of children with disabilities.* Washington, DC: National Clearinghouse on Child Abuse and Neglect Information.

Crowley, S. J., Acebo, C., & Carskadon, M. A. (2007). Sleep, circadian rhythms, and delayed phase in adolescence. *Sleep Medicine*, 8(6), 602–612. http://doi.org/10.1016/j.sleep.2006.12.002

Cruickshanks, K. J., Nondahl, D. M., Tweed, T. S., Wiley, T. L., Klein, B. E. K., Klein, R., . . . Nash, S. D. (2010). Education, occupation, noise exposure history and the 10-yr cumulative incidence of hearing impairment in older adults. *Hearing Research*, 264(1/2), 3–9. http://doi.org/10.1016/j.heares.2009.10.008

Cuellar, J., Jones, D. J., & Sterrett, E. (2013). Examining parenting in the neighborhood context: A Review. *Journal of Child and Family Studies*, 24(1), 195–219. http://doi.org/10.1007/s10826-013-9826-y

Cuevas, K., & Bell, M. A. (2010). Developmental progression of looking and reaching performance on the A-not-B task. *Developmental Psychology*, 46(5), 1363–1371. http://doi.org/10.1037/a0020185

Cuevas, K., & Bell, M. A. (2013). Infant attention and early childhood executive function. *Child Development*, 85(2), 397–404. http://doi.org/10.1111/cdev.12126

Cully, J. A., LaVoie, D., & Gfeller, J. D. (2001). Reminiscence, personality, and psychological functioning in older adults. *The Gerontologist*, 41(1), 89–95.

Cumming, E. M., & Henry, W. E. (1961). *Growing old: The process of disengagement.* New York: Basic Books.

Cummings, E. M., Goeke-Morey, M. C., Merrilees, C. E., Taylor, L. K., & Shirlow, P. (2014). A social-ecological, process-oriented perspective on political violence and child development. *Child Development Perspectives*, 8(2), 82–89. http://doi.org/10.1111/cdep.12067

Cunningham, P. M. (2013). *Phonics they use : Words for reading and writing*. Pearson.

Cunningham, S. A., Kramer, M. R., & Narayan, K. M. V. (2014). Incidence of childhood obesity in the United States. *New England Journal of Medicine*, *370*(5), 403–411. http://doi.org/10.1056/NEJMoa1309753

Curlin, F. A., Nwodim, C., Vance, J. L., Chin, M. H., & Lantos, J. D. (2008). To die, to sleep: US physicians' religious and other objections to physician-assisted suicide, terminal sedation, and withdrawal of life support. *The American Journal of Hospice & Palliative Care*, *25*(2), 112–20. http://doi.org/10.1177/1049909107310141

Curtin, S. C., Abma, J. C., & Kost, K. (2015). 2010 pregnancy rates among U.S. women. *NCHS Health E-Stat*. Retrieved from http://www.cdc.gov/nchs/data/hestat/pregnancy/2010_pregnancy_rates.htm

Curtis, R. G., Windsor, T. D., & Soubelet, A. (2015). The relationship between Big-5 personality traits and cognitive ability in older adults—a review. *Neuropsychology, Development, and Cognition. Section B, Aging, Neuropsychology and Cognition*, *22*(1), 42–71. http://doi.org/10.1080/13825585.2014.888392

Cvencek, D., Meltzoff, A. N., & Greenwald, A. G. (2011). Math-gender stereotypes in elementary school children. *Child Development*, *82*(3), 766–779. http://doi.org/10.1111/j.1467-8624.2010.01529.x

D'Augelli, A. R., & Hershberger, S. L. (1993). Lesbian, gay, and bisexual youth in community settings: Personal challenges and mental health problems. *American Journal of Community Psychology*, *21*(4), 421–448. http://doi.org/10.1007/BF00942151

D'augelli, A. R., Grossman, A. H., & Starks, M. T. (2008). Gender atypicality and sexual orientation development among lesbian, gay, and bisexual youth. *Journal of GLBT Family Studies*, *4*(1), 121–143. http://doi.org/10.1080/15504280802084506

D'Esposito, M., Detre, J. A., Alsop, D. C., Shin, R. K., Atlas, S., & Grossman, M. (1995). The neural basis of the central executive system of working memory. *Nature*, *378*, 279–281.

D'Souza, H., Cowie, D., Karmiloff-Smith, A., & Bremner, A. J. (2016). Specialization of the motor system in infancy: From broad tuning to selectively specialized purposeful actions. *Developmental Science*. http://doi.org/10.1111/desc.12409

Dacre Pool, L., & Qualter, P. (2012). Improving emotional intelligence and emotional self-efficacy through a teaching intervention for university students. *Learning and Individual Differences*, *22*(3), 306–312. http://doi.org/10.1016/j.lindif.2012.01.010

Daffner, K. R., Chong, H., & Riis, J. (2007). Cognitive status impacts age-related changes in attention to novel and target events in normal adults. *Neuropsychology*, *21*(3), 291–300.

Dahl, A. (2015). The developing social context of infant helping in two U.S. samples. *Child Development*, *86*(4), 1080–1093. http://doi.org/10.1111/cdev.12361

Dahl, A., Campos, J. J., Anderson, D. I., Uchiyama, I., Witherington, D. C., Ueno, M., & Barbu-roth, M. (2013). The epigenesis of wariness of heights. *Psychological Science*. http://doi.org/10.1177/0956797613476047

Dajani, D. R., & Uddin, L. Q. (2016). Local brain connectivity across development in autism spectrum disorder: A cross-sectional investigation. *Autism Research*, *9*(1), 43–54. http://doi.org/10.1002/aur.1494

Daley, C. E., & Onwuegbuzie, A. J. (2011). Race and intelligence. In R. J. Sternberg & S. B. Kaufman (Eds.), *The cambridge handbook of intelligence* (p. 293–308.). New York: Cambridge University Press.

Damaske, S., Bratter, J. L., & Frech, A. (2017). Single mother families and employment, race, and poverty in changing economic times. *Social Science Research*, *62*, 120–133. http://doi.org/10.1016/j.ssresearch.2016.08.008

Damman, M., Henkens, K., & Kalmijn, M. (2015). Missing work after retirement: The role of life histories in the retirement adjustment process. *The Gerontologist*, *55*(5), 802–813. http://doi.org/10.1093/geront/gnt169

Damon, W. (1977). *The social world of the child*. San Francisco: Jossey-Bass.

Damon, W. (1980). Patterns of change in children's social reasoning: A two-year longitudinal study. *Child Development*, *51*(4), 1010–1017.

Damon, W. (1988). *The moral child*. New York: Free Press.

Damon, W., & Hart, D. (1988). *Self-understanding in childhood and adolescence*. New York: Cambridge University Press.

Damon, W., Menon, J., & Cotton Bronk, K. (2003). The development of purpose during adolescence. *Applied Developmental Science*, *7*(3), 119–128. http://doi.org/10.1207/S1532480XADS0703_2

Daneman, M., & Carpenter, P. A. (1980). Individual differences in working memory and reading. *Journal of Verbal Learning and Verbal Behavior*, *19*, 450–466.

Daniels, P., Noe, G. F., & Mayberry, R. (2006). Barriers to prenatal care among black women of low socioeconomic status. *American Journal of Health Behavior*, *30*(2), 188–198.

Danis, A., Bernard, J.-M., & Leproux, C. (2000). Shared picture-book reading: A sequential analysis of adult-child verbal interactions. *British Journal of Developmental Psychology*, *18*, 369–388.

Danovitch, J., & Bloom, P. (2009). Children's extension of disgust to physical and moral events. *Emotion (Washington, D.C.)*, *9*(1), 107–12. http://doi.org/10.1037/a0014113

Danzer, E., & Johnson, M. P. (2014). Fetal surgery for neural tube defects. *Seminars in Fetal and Neonatal Medicine*, *19*(1), 2–8. http://doi.org/10.1016/j.siny.2013.09.004

Dapretto, M., & Bjork, E. L. (2000). The development of word retrieval abilities in the second year and its relation to early vocabulary growth. *Child Development*, *71*, 635–648.

Darchia, N., & Cervena, K. (2014). The journey through the world of adolescent sleep. *Reviews in the Neurosciences*, *25*(4). http://doi.org/10.1515/revneuro-2013-0065

Dare, J. S. (2011). Transitions in midlife women's lives: Contemporary experiences. *Health Care for Women International*, *32*(2), 111–33. http://doi.org/10.1080/07399332.2010.500753

Darling, N. (2007). Ecological systems theory: The person in the center of the circles. *Research in Human Development*, *4*(3–4), 203–217. http://doi.org/10.1080/15427600701663023

Darowski, E. S., Helder, E., Zacks, R. T., Hasher, L., & Hambrick, D. Z. (2008). Age-related differences in cognition: The role of distraction control. *Neuropsychology*, *22*(5), 638–644.

Das, J. K., Salam, R. A., Thornburg, K. L., Prentice, A. M., Campisi, S., Lassi, Z. S., . . . Bhutta, Z. A. (2017). Nutrition in adolescents: Physiology, metabolism, and nutritional needs. *Annals of the New York Academy of Sciences*, *1393*(1), 21–33. http://doi.org/10.1111/nyas.13330

Daselaar, S., & Cabeza, R. (2005). Age-related changes in hemispheric organization. In R. Cabeza, L. Nyberg, & D. C. Park (Eds.), *Cognitive neuroscience of aging: Linking cognitive and cerebral aging* (pp. 325–353). New York, NY: Oxford University Press.

Dasen, P. R. (1994). Culture and cognitive development from a Piagetian perspective. In W. J. Lonner & R. Malpass (Eds.), *Psychology and culture*. Boston: Allyn & Bacon.

Dasgupta, D., & Ray, S. (2016). Is menopausal status related to women's attitudes toward menopause and aging? *Women & Health*, 1–18. http://doi.org/10.1080/03630242.2016.1160965

Dasgupta, N., & Stout, J. G. (2014). Girls and women in science, technology, engineering, and mathematics. *Policy Insights from the Behavioral and Brain Sciences*, *1*(1), 21–29. http://doi.org/10.1177/2372732214549471

Dattalo, P. (2007). Borrowing to save: A critique of recent proposals to partially privatize social security. *Social Work*, *52*(3), 233–242.

Davenport, S. W., Bergman, S. M., Bergman, J. Z., & Fearrington, M. E. (2014). Twitter versus Facebook: Exploring the role of narcissism in the motives and usage of different social media platforms. *Computers in Human Behavior*, *32*, 212–220. http://doi.org/10.1016/j.chb.2013.12.011

Davey, A., Elias, M. F., Siegler, I. C., Lele, U., Martin, P., Johnson, M. A., . . . Poon, L. W. (2010). Cognitive function, physical performance, health, and disease: Norms from the Georgia centenarian study. *Experimental Aging Research*, *36*(4), 394–425. http://doi.org/10.1080/0361073x.2010.509010

David, C. B., Nancy, M. H., & Ying-Bo, S. (2010). Oxidative damage and the prevention of age-related cataracts. *Ophthalmic Research*, *44*(3), 155–165.

David-Barrett, T., Rotkirch, A., Carney, J., Behncke Izquierdo, I., Krems, J. A., Townley, D., . . . Dunbar, R. I. M. (2015). Women favour dyadic relationships, but men prefer clubs: Cross-cultural evidence from social networking. *PLOS ONE*, *10*(3), e0118329. http://doi.org/10.1371/journal.pone.0118329

Davidson, R. D., O'Hara, K. L., & Beck, C. J. A. (2014). Psychological and biological processes in children associated with high conflict parental divorce. *Juvenile and Family Court Journal*, *65*(1), 29–44. http://doi.org/10.1111/jfcj.12015

Davies, C. G., & Thorn, B. L. (2002). Psychopharmacology with older adults in residential care. In R. D. Hill, B. L. Thorn, J. Bowling, & A. Morrison (Eds.), *Geriatric residential care* (pp. 161–181). Mahwah, NJ: Lawrence Erlbaum.

Davies, P., & Martin, M. (2014). Children's coping and adjustment in high-conflict homes: The reformulation of emotional security theory. *Child Development Perspectives*, *8*(4), 242–249. http://doi.org/10.1111/cdep.12094

Daviglus, M. L., Bell, C. C., Berrettini, W., Bowen, P. E., Connolly, E. S., Cox, N. J., . . . Trevisan, M. (2010). National Institutes of Health State-of-the-Science Conference statement: Preventing Alzheimer disease and cognitive decline. *Annals of Internal Medicine*. http://doi.org/10.1059/0003-4819-153-3-201008030-00260

Davis, A. S., & Escobar, L. F. (2013). Early childhood cognitive disorders: Down syndrome. In A. S. Davis (Ed.), *Psychopathology of childhood and adolescence: A neuropsychological approach* (pp. 569–580). New York, NY: Springer.

Davis, B., & Carpenter, C. (2009). Proximity of fast-food restaurants to schools and adolescent obesity. *American Journal of Public Health*, *99*(3), 505–510. http://doi.org/10.2105/ajph.2008.137638

Davis, E. M., Kim, K., & Fingerman, K. L. (2016). Is an empty nest best?: Coresidence with adult children and parental marital quality before and after the Great Recession. *The Journals of Gerontology Series B: Psychological Sciences and Social Sciences*, *55*, gbw022. http://doi.org/10.1093/geronb/gbw022

Davis, E. P., Glynn, L. M., Waffarn, F., & Sandman, C. A. (2011). Prenatal maternal stress programs infant stress regulation. *Journal of Child Psychology and Psychiatry, and Allied Disciplines, 52*(2), 119–29. http://doi.org/10.1111/j.1469-7610.2010.02314.x

Davis, J. M., Mendelson, B., Berkes, J. J., Suleta, K., Corsi, K. F., Booth, R. E., . . . Moos, R. (2016). Public health effects of medical marijuana legalization in Colorado. *American Journal of Preventive Medicine, 50*(3), 373–379. http://doi.org/10.1016/j.amepre.2015.06.034

Davis, N. L., & Degges-White, S. (2008). Catalysts for developing productive life reviews: A multiple case study. *Adultspan: Theory Research & Practice, 7*(2), 69–79

Davis, S. K., & Humphrey, N. (2012). Emotional intelligence predicts adolescent mental health beyond personality and cognitive ability. *Personality and Individual Differences, 52*(2), 144–149. http://doi.org/10.1016/j.paid.2011.09.016

Davis-Kean, P. E., Jager, J., & Andrew Collins, W. (2009). The self in action: An emerging link between self-beliefs and behaviors in middle childhood. *Child Development Perspectives, 3*(3), 184–188. http://doi.org/10.1111/j.1750-8606.2009.00104.x

Dawson, A. E., Allen, J. P., Marston, E. G., Hafen, C. A., & Schad, M. M. (2014). Adolescent insecure attachment as a predictor of maladaptive coping and externalizing behaviors in emerging adulthood. *Attachment & Human Development, 16*(5), 462–78. http://doi.org/10.1080/14616734.2014.934848

Dawson, T. L. (2002). New tools, new insights: Kohlberg's moral judgement stages revisited. *International Journal of Behavioral Development, 26*(2), 154–166.

Day, F. R., Thompson, D. J., Helgason, H., Chasman, D. I., Finucane, H., Sulem, P., . . . Perry, J. R. B. (2017). Genomic analyses identify hundreds of variants associated with age at menarche and support a role for puberty timing in cancer risk. *Nature Genetics, 49*(6), 834–841. http://doi.org/10.1038/ng.3841

Day, N., & Richardson, G. (2004). An analysis of the effects of prenatal alcohol exposure on growth: A teratologic model. *American Journal of Medical Genetics Part C: Seminars in Medical Genetics, 127*(1), 28–34.

Day, N., Leech, S., Richardson, G., Cornelius, M., Robles, N., & Larkby, C. (2002). Prenatal alcohol exposure predicts continued deficits in offspring size at 14 years of age. *Alcoholism: Clinical and Experimental Research, 26*, 1584–1591.

de Bellis, M. D., Hooper, S. R., Spratt, E. G., & Woolley, D. P. (2009). Neuropsychological findings in childhood neglect and their relationships to pediatric PTSD. *Journal of the International Neuropsychological Society, 15*(6), 868–878. http://doi.org/10.1017/s1355617709990464

Decety, J., Michalska, K. J., & Kinzler, K. D. (2012). The contribution of emotion and cognition to moral sensitivity: A neurodevelopmental study. *Cerebral Cortex, 22*(1), 209–220. https://doi.org/10.1093/cercor/bhr111

De Genna, N., Larkby, C., & Cornelius, M. (2011). Pubertal timing and early sexual intercourse in the offspring of teenage mothers. *Journal of Youth & Adolescence, 40*(10), 1315–1328. http://doi.org/10.1007/s10964-010-9609-3

de Graaf, C., Polet, P., & van Staveren, W. A. (1994). Sensory perception and pleasantness of food flavors in elderly Subjects. *Journal of Gerontology, 49*(3), P93–P99. http://doi.org/10.1093/geronj/49.3.P93

de Houwer, A., & Gillis, S. (1998). The Acquisition of Dutch. Amsterdam: Benjamins.

de la Torre, J. C. (2016). Masquerading as dementia. In *Alzheimer's Turning Point* (pp. 25–29). Cham: Springer International Publishing. http://doi.org/10.1007/978-3-319-34057-9_3

De Neys, W., & Glumicic, T. (2008). Conflict monitoring in dual process theories of thinking. *Cognition, 106*(3), 1248–1299. https://doi.org/10.1016/j.cognition.2007.06.002

de Onis, M., Blössner, M., & Borghi, E. (2010). WHO | Global prevalence and trends of overweight and obesity among preschool children. *The American Journal of Clinical Nutrition, 92*(5), 1257–64. http://doi.org/10.3945/ajcn.2010.29786

de Onis, M., Blössner, M., & Borghi, E. (2012). Prevalence and trends of stunting among preschool children, 1990-2020. *Public Health Nutrition, 15*(1), 142–8. http://doi.org/10.1017/S1368980011001315

De Rosnay, M., Fink, E., Begeer, S., Slaughter, V., Peterson, C., Astington, J. W., . . . Liu, D. (2014). Talking theory of mind talk: Young school-aged children's everyday conversation and understanding of mind and emotion. *Journal of Child Language, 41*(5), 1179–1193. http://doi.org/10.1017/S0305000913000433

de Sousa Freire, N. B., Santos Garcia, J. B., & Carvalho Lamy, Z. (2008). Evaluation of analgesic effect of skin-to-skin contact compared to oral glucose in preterm neonates. *Pain (03043959), 139*(1), 28–33. http://doi.org/10.1016/j.pain.2008.02.031

De Vaus, D., Wells, Y., Kendig, H., & Quine, S. (2007). Does gradual retirement have better outcomes than abrupt retirement? Results from an Australian panel study. *Ageing & Society, 27*(5), 667–682.

de Villiers, J. G., & de Villiers, P. A. (2014). The role of language in theory of mind development. *Topics in Language Disorders, 34*(4), 313–328. http://doi.org/10.1097/TLD.0000000000000037

de Vries, B., Lana, R. D., & Falck, V. T. (1994). Parental bereavement over the life course: A theoretical intersection and empirical review. *OMEGA-Journal of Death and Dying, 29*(1), 47–69. http://doi.org/10.2190/XG2G-G77D-27FL-BC0T

de Vries, S. L. A., Hoeve, M., Stams, G. J. J. M., & Asscher, J. J. (2016). Adolescent-parent attachment and externalizing behavior: The mediating role of individual and social factors. *Journal of Abnormal Child Psychology, 44*(2), 283–294. http://doi.org/10.1007/s10802-015-9999-5

de Waal, F. B. M. (1993). Sex differences in chimpanzee (and human) behavior: A matter of social values? In M. Hechter, L. Nadel, & R. E. Michod (Eds.), *The origin of values* (pp. 285–303). New York: Aldine de Gruyter.

de Water, E., Burk, W. J., Cillessen, A. H. N., & Scheres, A. (2016). Substance use and decision-making in adolescent best friendship dyads: The role of popularity. *Social Development*. http://doi.org/10.1111/sode.12227

de Wilde, A., Koot, H. M., & van Lier, P. A. C. (2016). Developmental links between children's working memory and their social relations with teachers and peers in the early school years. *Journal of Abnormal Child Psychology, 44*(1), 19–30. http://doi.org/10.1007/s10802-015-0053-4

de Wit, J. B. F., Stok, F. M., Smolenski, D. J., de Ridder, D. D. T., de Vet, E., Gaspar, T., . . . Luszczynska, A. (2015). Food culture in the home environment: Family meal practices and values can support healthy eating and self-regulation in young people in four European countries. *Applied Psychology. Health and Well-Being, 7*(1), 22–40. http://doi.org/10.1111/aphw.12034

Deák, G. O. (2006). Do children really confuse appearance and reality? *Trends in Cognitive Sciences, 10*(12), 546–550.

Deardorff, J., Abrams, B., Ekwaru, J. P., & Rehkopf, D. H. (2014). Socioeconomic status and age at menarche: An examination of multiple indicators in an ethnically diverse cohort. *Annals of Epidemiology, 24*(10), 727–33. http://doi.org/10.1016/j.annepidem.2014.07.002

Deardorff, J., Ekwaru, J. P., Kushi, L. H., Ellis, B. J., Greenspan, L. C., Mirabedi, A., . . . Hiatt, R. A. (2011). Father absence, body mass index, and pubertal timing in girls: Differential effects by family income and ethnicity. *The Journal of Adolescent Health : Official Publication of the Society for Adolescent Medicine, 48*(5), 441–7. http://doi.org/10.1016/j.jadohealth.2010.07.032

Deary, I. J. (2014). The stability of intelligence from childhood to old age. *Current Directions in Psychological Science, 23*(4), 239–245. http://doi.org/10.1177/0963721414536905

Deary, I. J., Batty, G. D., Pattie, A., & Gale, C. R. (2008). More intelligent, more dependable children live longer: A 55-year longitudinal study of a representative sample of the Scottish nation. *Psychological Science, 19*(9), 874–80. http://doi.org/10.1111/j.1467-9280.2008.02171.x

Deary, I. J., Pattie, A., & Starr, J. M. (2013). The stability of intelligence from age 11 to age 90 years : The Lothian Birth Cohort of 1921, 1–8. http://doi.org/10.1177/0956797613486487

Deary, I. J., Penke, L., & Johnson, W. (2010). The neuroscience of human intelligence differences. *Nature Reviews Neuroscience, 11*(3), 201. http://doi.org/10.1038/nrn2793

Deater-Deckard, K. (2001). Nonshared environmental processes in social emotional development: An observational study of identical twin differences in the preschool period. *Developmental Science, 4*(2), 1–7.

Deater-Deckard, K., & O'Connor, T. (2000). Parent-child mutuality in early childhood: Two behavioral genetic studies. *Developmental Psychology, 36*(5), 561–571.

Debrot, A., Meuwly, N., Muise, A., Impett, E. A., & Schoebi, D. (2017). More than just sex. *Personality and Social Psychology Bulletin, 43*(3), 287–299. http://doi.org/10.1177/0146167216684124

DeCamp, W., & Ferguson, C. J. (2017). The impact of degree of exposure to violent video games, family background, and other factors on youth violence. *Journal of Youth and Adolescence, 46*(2), 388–400. http://doi.org/10.1007/s10964-016-0561-8

Decker, C., Phillips, C. R., & Haase, J. E. (2004). Information needs of adolescents with cancer. *Journal of Pediatric Oncology Nursing, 21*(6), 327–334. Retrieved from http://jpo.sagepub.com/content/21/6/327.short

Defoe, I. N., Dubas, J. S., Figner, B., & Aken, M. a G. Van. (2012). A meta-analysis on age differences in risky decision making: Adolescents versus children and adults, *141*(1), 29. http://doi.org/10.1037/a0038088

DeFries, J. C., Gervais, M. C., & Thomas, E. A. (1978). Response to 30 generations of selection for open-field activity in laboratory mice. *Behavior Genetics, 8*(1), 3–13. http://doi.org/10.1007/bf01067700

DeFronzo, R. A., & Abdul-Ghani, M. (2011). Assessment and treatment of cardiovascular risk in prediabetes: Impaired glucose tolerance and impaired fasting glucose. *The American Journal of Cardiology, 108*(3), 3B–24B. http://doi.org/10.1016/j.amjcard.2011.03.013

Dehaan, L. (2006). Child care and development: Results from the NICHD study of early child care and youth development. The NICHD Early Child Care Research Network. *Journal of Marriage & Family, 68*(1), 252–253. http://doi.org/10.1111/j.1741-3737.2006.00245.x

Dehaene-Lambertz, G. (2017). The human infant brain: A neural architecture able to learn language. *Psychonomic Bulletin & Review, 24*(1), 48–55. http://doi.org/10.3758/s13423-016-1156-9

Dehaene-Lambertz, G., & Spelke, E. S. (2015). The infancy of the human brain. *Neuron, 88*(1), 93–109. http://doi.org/10.1016/j.neuron.2015.09.026

Dehaene-Lambertz, G., Hertz-Pannier, L., Dubois, J., Broca, P., Geschwind, N., Levitsky, W., . . . al., et. (2006). Nature and nurture in language acquisition: Anatomical and functional brain-imaging studies in infants. *Trends in Neurosciences, 29*(7), 367–73. http://doi.org/10.1016/j.tins.2006.05.011

DeLamater, J. (2012). Sexual Expression in Later Life: A Review and Synthesis. *Journal of Sex Research, 49*(2/3), 125–141. http://doi.org/10.1080/00224499.2011.603168

DeLamater, J., & Koepsel, E. (2015). Relationships and sexual expression in later life: A biopsychosocial perspective. *Sexual and Relationship Therapy, 30*(1), 37–59. http://doi.org/10.1080/14681994.2014.939506

Delanoë, D., Hajri, S., Bachelot, A., Mahfoudh Draoui, D., Hassoun, D., Marsicano, E., & Ringa, V. (2012). Class, gender and culture in the experience of menopause. A comparative survey in Tunisia and France. *Social Science & Medicine (1982), 75*(2), 401–9. http://doi.org/10.1016/j.socscimed.2012.02.051

Deligkaris, P., Panagopoulou, E., Montgomery, A. J., & Masoura, E. (2014). Job burnout and cognitive functioning: A systematic review. Retrieved from http://www.tandfonline.com/doi/abs/10.1080/02678373.2014.909545

Dellenbach, M., & Zimprich, D. (2008). Typical intellectual engagement and cognition in old age. *Aging, Neuropsychology & Cognition, 15*(2), 208–231. http://doi.org/10.1080/13825580701338094

Dellinger, A., & Gilchrist, J. (2017). Leading causes of fatal and nonfatal unintentional injury for children and teens and the role of lifestyle clinicians. *American Journal of Lifestyle Medicine,* 155982761769629. http://doi.org/10.1177/1559827617696297

DeLoache, J. S. (2000). Dual representation and young children's use of scale models. *Child Development, 71,* 329–338.

DeLoache, J. S., Chiong, C., Sherman, K., Islam, N., Vanderborght, M., Troseth, G. L., . . . O'Doherty, K. (2010). Do babies learn from baby media? *Psychological Science, 21*(11), 1570–1574. http://doi.org/10.1177/0956797610384145

DeLongis, A., & Zwicker, A. (2017). Marital satisfaction and divorce in couples in stepfamilies. *Current Opinion in Psychology, 13,* 158–161. http://doi.org/10.1016/j.copsyc.2016.11.003

Delsing, M. J. M. H., ter Bogt, T. F. M., Engels, R. C. M. E., & Meeus, W. H. J. (2007). Adolescents' peer crowd identification in the Netherlands: Structure and associations with problem behaviors. *Journal of Research on Adolescence, 17*(2), 467–480. http://doi.org/10.1111/j.1532-7795.2007.00530.x

Demaray, M. K., Malecki, C. K., & DeLong, L. K. (2006). Support in the lives of aggressive students, their victims, and their peers. In S. R. Jimerson & M. Furlong (Eds.), *Handbook of school violence and school safety: From research to practice* (pp. 21–29). Mahwah, NJ: Lawrence Erlbaum.

Demetriou, A., Christou, C., Spanoudis, G., & Platsidou, M. (2002). The development of mental processing: Efficiency, working memory and thinking. *Monographs of the Society for Research in Child Development, 67*(1), 1–154.

Deming, L., Chang, L., Tianyong, C., & Guiyun, L. (2003). The roles of processing speed and working

Memory in cognitive aging. *Acta Psychologica Sinica, 35*(4), 471–475.

Demir, M., Özen, A., Doğan, A., Bilyk, N. A., & Tyrell, F. A. (2011). I matter to my friend, therefore I am happy: Friendship, mattering, and happiness. *Journal of Happiness Studies, 12*(6), 983–1005. http://doi.org/10.1007/s10902-010-9240-8

Demorest, A., Meyer, C., Phelps, E., Gardner, H., & Winner, E. (1984). Words speak louder than actions:Understanding deliberately false remarks. *Child Development, 55,* 1527–1534.

Dempster, F. N. (1985). Short-term memory development. In C. J. Brainerd & M. Pressley (Eds.), *Basic processes in memory development* (pp. 208–248). New York: Springer-Verlag.

DeNavas-Walt, C., & Proctor, B. D. (2014). *Income and Poverty in the United States: 2013.* Washington DC. Retrieved from http://www.census.gov/hhes/www/poverty/data/incpovhlth/2013/

Deneault, J., & Ricard, M. (2006). The assessment of children's understanding of inclusion relations: Transitivity, asymmetry, and quantification. *Journal of Cognition & Development, 7*(4), 551–570.

Deneault, J., & Ricard, M. (2013). Are emotion and mind understanding differently linked to young children's social adjustment? Relationships between behavioral consequences of emotions, false belief, and SCBE. *The Journal of Genetic Psychology, 174*(1), 88–116. http://doi.org/10.1080/00221325.2011.642028

Denham, S. A., Bassett, H. H., & Wyatt, T. (2007). The socialization of emotional competence. In J. E. Grusec & P. D. Hastings (Eds.), *Handbook of socialization: Theory and research* (p. 614–637)). Guilford Press.

Denham, S. A., Bassett, H. H., & Zinsser, K. (2012). Early childhood teachers as socializers of young children's emotional competence. *Early Childhood Education Journal, 40*(3), 137–143. http://doi.org/10.1007/s10643-012-0504-2

Denham, S., & Kochanoff, A. T. (2002). Parental contributions to preschoolers' understanding of emotion. *Marriage & Family Review, 34*(3–4), 311–343. http://doi.org/10.1300/J002v34n03_06

Denissen, J. J. A., van Aken, M. A. G., Penke, L., & Wood, D. (2013). Self-regulation underlies temperament and personality: An integrative developmental framework. *Child Development Perspectives, 7*(4), 255–260. http://doi.org/10.1111/cdep.12050

Denissen, J. J. A., Zarrett, N. R., & Eccles, J. S. (2007). I like to do it, I'm able, and I know I am: Longitudinal couplings between domain-specific achievement, self-concept, and interest. *Child Development, 78*(2), 430–447.

Denney, N. W., Pearce, K. A., & Palmer, A. M. (1982). A developmental study of adults' performance on traditional and practical problem-solving tasks. *Experimental Aging Research, 8*(2), 115–8. http://doi.org/10.1080/03610738208258407

Dennis, D. (2008). *Living, dying, grieving.* Sudbury, MA: Jones & Bartlett.

Dennis, T. A., Cole, P. M., Zahn-Waxler, C., & Mizuta, I. (2002). Self in context: Autonomy and relatedness in Japanese and U. S. mother-preschooler dyads. *Child Development, 73,* 1803–1817.

Dennis, W. (1960). Causes of retardation among institutional children: Iran. *Journal of Genetic Psychology, 96,* 47–59.

Dennis, W., & Dennis, M. G. (1991). The effect of cradling practices upon the onset of walking in Hopi children. *Journal of Genetic Psychology, 152*(4), 563–572.

Deoni, S. C. L., Mercure, E., Blasi, A., Gasston, D., Thomson, A., Johnson, M., . . . Murphy, D.

G. M. (2011). Mapping infant brain myelination with magnetic resonance imaging. *The Journal of Neuroscience, 31*(2), 784–791. http://doi.org/10.1523/JNEUROSCI.2106-10.2011

Department of Health and Human Services. (2014). *The health consequences of smoking—50 years of progress. A report of the Surgeon General.* Atlanta, GA: Author. Retrieved from http://www.surgeongeneral.gov/library/reports/50-years-of-progress/

Department of Health and Human Services. (2015). Leading health indicators: Injury and violence. Retrieved from https://www.healthypeople.gov/2020/leading-health-indicators/2020-lhi-topics/Injury-and-Violence/data

DeRose, L. M., & Brooks-Gunn, J. (2006). Transition into adolescence: The role of pubertal processes. In L. Balter & C. S. Tamis-LeMonda (Eds.), *Child psychology: A handbook of contemporary issues* (2nd ed., pp. 385–414). New York, NY: Psychology Press.

DeRosier, M. E., & Mercer, S. H. (2009). Perceived behavioral atypicality as a predictor of social rejection and peer victimization: Implications for emotional adjustment and academic achievement. *Psychology in the Schools, 46*(4), 375–387.

Deutsch, W., & Pechmann, T. (1982). Social interaction and the development of definite descriptions. *Cognition, 11,* 159–184.

DeVries, H. M., Kerrick, S., & Oetinger, M. (2007). Satisfactions and regrets of midlife parents: A qualitative analysis. *Journal of Adult Development, 14*(1), 6–15. Retrieved from helen.m.devries@wheaton.edu

DeVries, R. (1969). Constancy of generic identity in the years three to six. *Monographs of the Society for Research in Child Development, 34*(Serial No. 127).

DeVries, R., & Zan, B. (2003). When Children Make Rules. *Educational Leadership, 61*(1), 64–67.

Dew, J. (2008). Debt change and marital satisfaction change in recently married couples. *Family Relations, 57*(1), 60–71. http://doi.org/10.1111/j.1741-3729.2007.00483.x

Dew, J., Britt, S., & Huston, S. (2012). Examining the relationship between financial issues and divorce. *Family Relations, 61*(4), 615–628. http://doi.org/10.1111/j.1741-3729.2012.00715.x

DeWolff, M. S., & van Ijzendoorn, M. H. (1997). Sensitivity and attachment: A meta-analysis on parental antecedents of infant attachment. *Child Development, 68,* 571–591.

Dewsbury, D. A. (1992). Comparative psychology and ethology: A reassessment. *American Psychologist, 47,* 208–215.

Dezutter, J., Toussaint, L., & Leijssen, M. (2014). Forgiveness, ego-integrity, and depressive symptoms in community-dwelling and residential elderly adults. *The Journals of Gerontology. Series B, Psychological Sciences and Social Sciences,* gbu146-. http://doi.org/10.1093/geronb/gbu146

Dhital, A., Pey, T., & Stanford, M. R. (2010). Visual loss and falls: A review. *Eye, 24*(9), 1437–1446. http://doi.org/10.1038/eye.2010.60

Diamond, A. (1985). The development of the ability to use recall to guide action as indicated by infants' performance on A-B. *Child Development, 56,* 868–883.

Diamond, A. (1991). Neuropsychological insights into the meaning of object concept development. In S. Carey & R. Gelman (Eds.), *The epigenesis of mind: Essays on biology and cognition* (pp. 67–110). Hillsdale, NJ: Lawrence Erlbaum.

Diamond, A. (2000). Close interrelation of motor development and cognitive development and of the cerebellum and prefrontal cortex. *Child Development, 71*(1), 44.

Diamond, A. (2013). Executive functions. *Annual Review of Psychology*, *64*, 135–168. http://doi.org/10.1146/annurev-psych-113011-143750

Diamond, L. M., & Savin-Williams, R. C. (2009). Adolescent sexuality. In R. M. Lerner & L. Steinberg (Eds.), *Handbook of adolescent psychology* (p. 479). Hoboken, NJ, USA: John Wiley & Sons, Inc.

Diego, M. A., Field, T., Hernandez-Reif, M., Deeds, O., Ascencio, A., & Begert, G. (2007). Preterm infant massage elicits consistent increases in vagal activity and gastric motility that are associated with greater weight gain. *Acta Paediatrica*, *96*(11), 1588–1591. http://doi.org/10.1111/j.1651-2227.2007.00476.x

Diehl, M., Coyle, N., & Labouvie-Vief, G. (1996). Age and sex differences in strategies of coping and defense across the life span. *Psychology and Aging*, *11*(1), 127–139. http://doi.org/10.1037/0882-7974.11.1.127

Diehl, M., Youngblade, L. M., Hay, E. L., & Chui, H. (2011). The development of self-representations across the life span. In K. L. Fingerman, C. A. Berg, & J. Smith (Eds.), *Handbook of life-span development* (pp. 611–646). New York, NY: Springer.

Diekman, A. B., Brown, E. R., Johnston, A. M., & Clark, E. K. (2010). Seeking congruity between goals and roles. *Psychological Science*, *21*(8), 1051–1057. http://doi.org/10.1177/0956797610377342

Diener, M. (2000). Gift from the Gods: A Balinese guide to early child rearing. In J. DeLoache & A. Gotleib (Eds.), *A world of babies: Imagined childcare guiles for seven societies*. Cambridge, England: Cambridge University Press.

Dieter, J. N. I., Field, T., Hernandez-Reif, M., Emory, E. K., & Redzepi, M. (2003). Stable preterm infants gain more weight and sleep less after five days of massage therapy. *Journal of Pediatric Psychology*, *28*(6), 403–411.

Dill, E. J., Vernberg, E. M., Fonagy, P., Twemlow, S. W., & Gamm, B. K. (2004). Negative affect in victimized children: The roles of social withdrawal, peer rejection, and attitudes towards bullying. *Journal of Abnormal Child Psychology*, *32*(2), 159–173.

Dillaway, H. E. (2008). "Why can't you control this?" How women's interactions with intimate partners define menopause and family. *Journal of Women & Aging*, *20*(1/2), 47–64.

Dilworth-Anderson, P., Goodwin, P. Y., & Williams, S. W. (2004). Can culture help explain the physical health effects of caregiving over time among African American caregivers? *Journals of Gerontology Series B: Psychological Sciences & Social Sciences*, *59B*(3), S138–S145.

Dimler, L. M., & Natsuaki, M. N. (2015). The effects of pubertal timing on externalizing behaviors in adolescence and early adulthood: A meta-analytic review. *Journal of Adolescence*, *45*, 160–170. http://doi.org/10.1016/j.adolescence.2015.07.021

Dion, J., Hains, J., Vachon, P., Plouffe, J., Laberge, L., Perron, M., . . . Leone, M. (2016). Correlates of body dissatisfaction in children. *The Journal of Pediatrics*, *171*, 202–7. http://doi.org/10.1016/j.jpeds.2015.12.045

DiPietro, J. A. (2000). Baby and the brain: Advances in child development. *Annual Review of Public Health*, *21*, 455–471.

Dirix, C. E. H., Nijhuis, J. G., Jongsma, H. W., & Hornstra, G. (2009). Aspects of fetal learning and memory. *Child Development*, *80*(4), 1251–1258. http://doi.org/10.1111/j.1467-8624.2009.01329.x

Dirks, J. (1982). The effect of a commercial game on children's Block Design scores on the WISC-R test. *Intelligence*, *6*, 109–123.

Dishion, T. J., & Patterson, G. R. (2016). The development and ecology of antisocial behavior: Linking etiology, prevention, and treatment. In D. Cicchetti (Ed.), *Developmental psychopathology*

(pp. 1–32). Hoboken, NJ: John Wiley & Sons. http://doi.org/10.1002/9781119125556.devpsy315

Dittus, P. J., Michael, S. L., Becasen, J. S., Gloppen, K. M., McCarthy, K., & Guilamo-Ramos, V. (2015). Parental monitoring and its associations with adolescent sexual risk behavior: A meta-analysis. *Pediatrics*, *136*(6).

Dixon, P. (2009). Marriage among African Americans: What does the research reveal? *Journal of African American Studies*, *13*(1), 29–46. http://doi.org/10.1007/s12111-008-9062-5

Dixon, R. A., & Lerner, R. M. (1999). History and systems in developmental psychology. In M. H. Bornstein & M. E. Lamb (Eds.), *Developmental psychology: An advanced textbook* (4th ed., pp. 3–54). Mahwah, NJ: Lawrence Erlbaum.

Djoussé, L., Driver, J. A., Gaziano, J. M., Buring, J. E., & Lee, I. M. (2013). Association between modifiable lifestyle factors and residual lifetime risk of diabetes. *Nutrition, Metabolism and Cardiovascular Diseases*, *23*(1), 17–22. http://doi.org/10.1016/j.numecd.2011.08.002

Djukic, M., Wedekind, D., Franz, A., Gremke, M., & Nau, R. (2015). Frequency of dementia syndromes with a potentially treatable cause in geriatric in-patients: Analysis of a 1-year interval. *European Archives of Psychiatry and Clinical Neuroscience*, *265*(5), 429–438. http://doi.org/10.1007/s00406-015-0583-3

Do, K.-A., Treloar, S., Pandeya, N., Purdie, D., Green, A., Heath, A., & Martin, N. (2013). Predictive factors of age at menopause in a large Australian twin study. *Human Biology*. Retrieved from http://digitalcommons.wayne.edu/humbiol/vol70/iss6/8

Dodge, K. A., & Coleman, D. L. (2009). *Preventing child maltreatment: Community approaches*. New York, NY: Guilford Press.

Dodge, K. A., & Rutter, M. (2011). *Gene–environment Interactions in developmental psychopathology*. New York, NY: Guilford Press.

Doherty-Sneddon, G. (2008). The great baby signing debate: Academia meets public interest. British Psychological Society. Retrieved from https://dspace.stir.ac.uk/handle/1893/385

Dohnt, H. K., & Tiggemann, M. (2005). Peer influences on body dissatisfaction and dieting awareness in young girls. *British Journal of Developmental Psychology*, *23*, 103–116.

Doka, K. J. (2015). The awareness of mortality: Continuing Kastenbaum's developmental legacy. *Omega*, *70*(1), 67–78. http://doi.org/10.2190/OM.70.1.g

Dolbier, C. L., Smith, S. E., & Steinhardt, M. A. (2007). Relationships of protective factors to stress and symptoms of illness. *American Journal of Health Behavior*, *31*(4), 423–433.

Dolbin-MacNab, M. L. (2006). Just like raising your own? Grandmothers' perceptions of parenting a second time around. *Family Relations*, *55*(5), 564–575.

Dolbin-MacNab, M. L., & Keiley, M. K. (2006). A systemic examination of grandparents' emotional closeness with their custodial grandchildren. *Research in Human Development*, *3*(1), 59–71.

Doley, R., Bell, R., Watt, B., & Simpson, H. (2015). Grandparents raising grandchildren: investigating factors associated with distress among custodial grandparent. *Journal of Family Studies*, 1–19. http://doi.org/10.1080/13229400.2015.1015215

Dolgin, K. G., & Behrend, D. A. (1984). Children's knowledge about animates and inanimates. *Child Development*, *55*, 1646–1650.

Dolinoy, D. C. (2008). The agouti mouse model: An epigenetic biosensor for nutritional and environmental alterations on the fetal epigenome. *Nutrition Reviews*, *66 Suppl 1*, S7-11. http://doi.org/10.1111/j.1753-4887.2008.00056.x

Domhardt, M., Münzer, A., Fegert, J. M., & Goldbeck, L. (2014). Resilience in Survivors of Child Sexual Abuse: A Systematic Review of the Literature. *Trauma, Violence & Abuse*, 1524838014557288-. http://doi.org/10.1177/1524838014557288

Don, B. P., & Mickelson, K. D. (2014). Relationship Satisfaction Trajectories Across the Transition to Parenthood Among Low-Risk Parents. *Journal of Marriage and Family*, *76*(3), 677–692. http://doi.org/10.1111/jomf.12111

Donaldson, S. K., & Westerman, M. A. (1986). Development of children's understanding of ambivalence and causal theories of emotions. *Developmental Psychology*, *22*(5), 655–662. http://doi.org/10.1037/0012-1649.22.5.655

Donatelle, R. (2004). *Health: The basics*. San Francisco: Benjamin Cummings.

Dondi, M., Simion, F., & Caltran, G. (1999). Can newborns discriminate between their own cry and the cry of another newborn infant? *Developmental Psychology*, *35*, 418–426.

Donohue, S. M., & Heywood, J. S. (2013). Job satisfaction and gender: An expanded specification from the NLSY. *International Journal of Manpower*. Retrieved from http://www.emeraldinsight.com/doi/abs/10.1108/01437720410536007

Doodson, L., & Morley, D. (2006). Understanding the roles of non-residential stepmothers. *Journal of Divorce & Remarriage*, *45*(3/4), 109–130. http://doi.org/10.1300/J087v45n03-06

Dopp, A. R., & Cain, A. C. (2012). The role of peer relationships in parental bereavement during childhood and adolescence. *Death Studies*, *36*(1), 41–60. http://doi.org/10.1080/07481187.2011.573175

Dorn, L. D., & Biro, F. M. (2011). Puberty and its measurement: A decade in review. *Journal of Research on Adolescence*, *21*(1), 180–195. http://doi.org/10.1111/j.1532-7795.2010.00722.x

Dorn, L. D., Dahl, R. E., Woodward, H. R., & Biro, F. (2006). Defining the boundaries of early adolescence: A user's guide to assessing pubertal status and pubertal timing in research with adolescents. *Applied Developmental Science*, *10*(1), 30–56.

Doskoch, P. (2011). Many men 75 and older consider sex important and remain sexually active. *Perspectives on Sexual and Reproductive Health*, *43*(1), 67–68. http://doi.org/10.1363/4306711

Dotterer, A. M., McHale, S. M., & Crouter, A. C. (2009). Sociocultural factors and school engagement among African American youth: The roles of racial discrimination, racial socialization, and ethnic identity. *Applied Developmental Science*, *13*(2), 61–73. http://doi.org/10.1080/10888690902801442

Doty, R. L., Shaman, P., Applebaum, S. L., Giberson, R., Siksorski, L., & Rosenberg, L. (1984). Smell identification ability: Changes with age. *Science (New York, N.Y.)*, *226*(4681), 1441–3. http://doi.org/10.1126/science.6505700

Douaud, G., Refsum, H., de Jager, C. A., Jacoby, R., Nichols, T. E., Smith, S. M., & Smith, A. D. (2013). Preventing Alzheimer's disease-related gray matter atrophy by B-vitamin treatment. *Proceedings of the National Academy of Sciences of the United States of America*, *110*(23), 9523–8. http://doi.org/10.1073/pnas.1301816110

Douglass, S., & Umaña-Taylor, A. J. (2016). Time-varying effects of family ethnic socialization on ethnic-racial identity development among Latino adolescents. *Developmental Psychology*, *52*(11), 1904–1912. http://doi.org/10.1037/dev0000141

Douglass, S., Yip, T., & Shelton, J. N. (2014). Intragroup contact and anxiety among ethnic minority adolescents: Considering ethnic identity and school diversity transitions. *Journal of Youth and Adolescence*, 43(10), 1628–41. http://doi.org/10.1007/s10964-014-0144-5

Douketis, J. D., Macie, C., Thabane, L., & Williamson, D. F. (2005). Systematic review of long-term weight loss studies in obese adults: Clinical significance and applicability to clinical practice. *International Journal of Obesity*, 29(10), 1153–1167.

Downs, A. C., & Fuller, M. J. (1991). Recollections of spermarche: An exploratory investigation. *Current Psychology*, 10(1/2), 93-.

Doyle-Thomas, K. A. R., Lee, W., Foster, N. E. V., Tryfon, A., Ouimet, T., Hyde, K. L., . . . Anagnostou, E. (2015). Atypical functional brain connectivity during rest in autism spectrum disorders. *Annals of Neurology*, 77(5), 866–876. http://doi.org/10.1002/ana.24391

Drapeau, S., Gagne, M.-H., Saint-Jacques, M.-C., Lepine, R., & Ivers, H. (2009). Post-separation conflict trajectories: A longitudinal study. *Marriage & Family Review*, 45(4), 353–373. http://doi.org/10.1080/01494920902821529

Dreyfuss, M., Caudle, K., Drysdale, A. T., Johnston, N. E., Cohen, A. O., Somerville, L. H., . . . Casey, B. J. (2014). Teens impulsively react rather than retreat from threat. *Developmental Neuroscience*, 36(3–4), 220–7. http://doi.org/10.1159/000357755

Dribe, M., & Stanfors, M. (2009). Does parenthood strengthen a traditional household division of labor? Evidence from Sweden. *Journal of Marriage & Family*, 71(1), 33–45. http://doi.org/10.1111/j.1741-3737.2008.00578.x

Drong, A. W., Lindgren, C. M., & McCarthy, M. I. (2012). The genetic and epigenetic basis of type 2 diabetes and obesity. *Clinical Pharmacology and Therapeutics*, 92(6), 707–15. http://doi.org/10.1038/clpt.2012.149

Duan, L., Chou, C.-P., Andreeva, V., & Pentz, M. (2009). Trajectories of peer social influences as long-term predictors of drug use from early through late adolescence. *Journal of Youth & Adolescence*, 38(3), 454–465. http://doi.org/10.1007/s10964-008-9310-y

Duboc, V., Dufourcq, P., Blader, P., & Roussigné, M. (2015). Asymmetry of the brain: Development and implications. *Annual Review of Genetics*, 49(1), 647–672. http://doi.org/10.1146/annurev-genet-112414-055322

DuBois, D. L., & Hirsch, B. J. (1990). School and neighborhood friendship patterns of blacks and whites in early adolescence. *Child Development*, 61, 524–536.

Dubois, J., Dehaene-Lambertz, G., Kulikova, S., Poupon, C., Hüppi, P. S., & Hertz-Pannier, L. (2013). The early development of brain white matter: A review of imaging studies in fetuses, newborns and infants. *Neuroscience*. http://doi.org/10.1016/j.neuroscience.2013.12.044

Dubois, L., Ohm Kyvik, K., Girard, M., Tatone-Tokuda, F., Pérusse, D., Hjelmborg, J., . . . Martin, N. G. (2012). Genetic and environmental contributions to weight, height, and BMI from birth to 19 years of age: an international study of over 12,000 twin pairs. *PloS One*, 7(2), e30153. http://doi.org/10.1371/journal.pone.0030153

Duch, H., Fisher, E. M., Ensari, I., & Harrington, A. (2013). Screen time use in children under 3 years old: A systematic review of correlates. *The International Journal of Behavioral Nutrition and Physical Activity*, 10(1), 102. http://doi.org/10.1186/1479-5868-10-102

Duchin, O., Marin, C., Mora-Plazas, M., Mendes de Leon, C., Lee, J. M., Baylin, A., & Villamor, E. (2015). A prospective study of body image dissatisfaction and BMI change in school-age children. *Public Health Nutrition*, 18(2), 322–38. http://doi.org/10.1017/S1368980014000366

Duckworth, a., & Gross, J. J. (2014). Self-control and grit: Related but separable determinants of success. *Current Directions in Psychological Science*, 23(5), 319–325. http://doi.org/10.1177/0963721414541462

Dudovitz, R. N., Chung, P. J., & Wong, M. D. (2017). Teachers and coaches in adolescent social networks are associated with healthier self-concept and decreased substance use. *Journal of School Health*, 87(1), 12–20. http://doi.org/10.1111/josh.12462

Dujardin, A., Santens, T., Braet, C., De Raedt, R., Vos, P., Maes, B., & Bosmans, G. (2016). Middle childhood support-seeking behavior during stress: Links with self-reported attachment and future depressive symptoms. *Child Development*, 87(1), 326–340. http://doi.org/10.1111/cdev.12491

Duke, S. A., Balzer, B. W. R., & Steinbeck, K. S. (2014). Testosterone and its effects on human male adolescent mood and behavior: A systematic review. *The Journal of Adolescent Health : Official Publication of the Society for Adolescent Medicine*, 55(3), 315–22. http://doi.org/10.1016/j.jadohealth.2014.05.007

Dulin, P. (2015). Volunteering in older adults in retirement. In *Encyclopedia of geropsychology* (pp. 1–7). Singapore: Springer Singapore. http://doi.org/10.1007/978-981-287-080-3_43-1

Dumith, S. C., Gigante, D. P., Domingues, M. R., & Kohl, H. W. (2011). Physical activity change during adolescence: A systematic review and a pooled analysis. *International Journal of Epidemiology*, 40(3), 685–98. http://doi.org/10.1093/ije/dyq272

Dumont, M., Leclerc, D., & McKinnon, S. (2009). Consequences of part-time work on the academic and psychosocial adaptation of adolescents. *Canadian Journal of School Psychology*, 24(1), 58–75. http://doi.org/10.1177/0829573509333197

Dumontheil, I. (2016). Adolescent brain development. *Current Opinion in Behavioral Sciences*, 10, 39–44. http://doi.org/10.1016/j.cobeha.2016.04.012

Dunaev, J. L., Schulz, J. L., & Markey, C. N. (2016). Cosmetic surgery attitudes among midlife women: Appearance esteem, weight esteem, and fear of negative appearance evaluation. *Journal of Health Psychology*, 1359105316642249. http://doi.org/10.1177/1359105316642249

Duncan, G. J., Ludwig, J., & Magnuson, K. A. (2007). Reducing poverty through preschool interventions. *The Future of Children*, 17(2), 143–160.

Duncan, G. J., & Magnuson, K. (2013). Investing in preschool programs. *The Journal of Economic Perspectives*, 27(2), 109–132. http://doi.org/10.1257/jep.27.2.109

Duncan, G. J., Magnuson, K., Kalil, A., & Ziol-Guest, K. (2012). The importance of early childhood poverty. *Social Indicators Research*, 108(1), 87–98. https://doi.org/10.1007/s11205-011-9867-9

Duncan, R. M., & Pratt, M. W. (1997). Microgenetic change in the quantity and quality of preschoolers' private speech. *International Journal of Behavioral Development*, 20, 367–383.

Duncan, S. C., Duncan, T. E., Strycker, L. A., & Chaumeton, N. R. (2007). A cohort-sequential latent growth model of physical activity from ages 12 to 17 years. *Annals of Behavioral Medicine*, 33(1), 80–89.

Dunham, Y., Baron, A. S., & Banaji, M. R. (2016). The development of implicit gender attitudes. *Developmental Science*, 19(5), 781–789. http://doi.org/10.1111/desc.12321

Dunkel Schetter, C., & Tanner, L. (2012). Anxiety, depression and stress in pregnancy: Implications for mothers, children, research, and practice. *Current Opinion in Psychiatry*, 25(2), 141–8. http://doi.org/10.1097/YCO.0b013e3283503680

Dunlosky, J., Kubat-Silman, A. K., & Hertzog, C. (2003). Training monitoring skills improves older adults' self-paced associative learning. *Psychology and Aging*, 18(2), 340–345. http://doi.org/10.1037/0882-7974.18.2.340

Dunn, J. (2002). The adjustment of children in stepfamilies: Lessons from community studies. *Child & Adolescent Mental Health*, 7(4), 154–161.

Dunn, J., & Hughes, C. (2001). "I got some swords and you're dead": Violent fantasy, antisocial behavior, friendship, and moral sensibility in young children. *Child Development*, 72, 491–505.

Dunsmore, J., & Quine, S. (1996). Information, support, and decision-making needs and preferences of adolescents with cancer. *Journal of Psychosocial Oncology*, 13(4), 39–56. http://doi.org/10.1300/J077V13N04_03

Dunst, C. J., & Gorman, E. (2009). Development of infant and toddler mark making and scribbling. *CELLReviews*, 2(2), 1–16.

Dupéré, V., Dion, E., Leventhal, T., Archambault, I., Crosnoe, R., & Janosz, M. (2017). High school dropout in proximal context: The triggering role of stressful life events. *Child Development*. http://doi.org/10.1111/cdev.12792

Dupere, V., Leventhal, T., Dion, E., Crosnoe, R., Archambault, I., & Janosz, M. (2015). Stressors and turning points in high school and dropout: A stress process, life course framework. *Review of Educational Research*, 85(4), 591–629. http://doi.org/10.3102/0034654314559845

Dupuis, S. (2010). Examining the blended family: The application of systems theory toward an understanding of the blended family system. *Journal of Couple & Relationship Therapy*, 9(3), 239–251. http://doi.org/10.1080/15332691.2010.491784

Durik, A., Hyde, J., & Clark, R. (2000). Sequelae of cesarean and vaginal deliveries: Psychosocial outcomes for mothers and infants. *Developmental Psychology*, 36, 251–260.

Durwood, L., McLaughlin, K. A., & Olson, K. R. (2017). Mental health and self-worth in socially transitioned transgender youth. *Journal of the American Academy of Child and Adolescent Psychiatry*, 56(2), 116–123.e2. http://doi.org/10.1016/j.jaac.2016.10.016

Duschinsky, R. (2015). The emergence of the disorganized/disoriented (D) attachment classification, 1979–1982. *History of Psychology*, 18(1), 32–46. http://doi.org/10.1037/a0038524

Dusek, J. B., & McIntyre, J. G. (2003). Self-concept and self-esteem development. In G. R. Adams & M. D. Berzonsky (Eds.), *Blackwell handbooks of developmental psychology* (pp. 290–309). Malden, MA: Blackwell.

Dutton, E., van der Linden, D., & Lynn, R. (2016). The negative Flynn Effect: A systematic literature review. *Intelligence*, 59, 163–169. http://doi.org/10.1016/j.intell.2016.10.002

Duyme, M., Dumaret, A. C., & Tomkiewicz, S. (1999). How can we boost IQs of "dull children"?: A late adoption study. *Proceedings of the National Academy of Sciences of the United States of America*, 96(15), 8790–4. http://doi.org/10.1073/PNAS.96.15.8790

Dwairy, M., & Menshar, K. E. (2006). Parenting style, individuation, and mental health of Egyptian adolescents. *Journal of Adolescence*, 29(1), 103–117. http://doi.org/10.1016/j.adolescence.2005.03.002

Dweck, C. S. (2002). The development of ability conceptions. In A. Wigfield & J. S. Eccles (Eds.), *Development of Achievement Motivation* (pp. 57–88). Elsevier. http://doi.org/10.1016/B978-012750053-9/50005-X

Dweck, C. S. (2017). The journey to children's mindsets—and beyond. *Child Development Perspectives*, 11(2), 139–144. http://doi.org/10.1111/cdep.12225

Dweck, C. S., & Master, A. (2009). Self-theories and motivation. In K. R. Wentzel & D. B. Miele (Eds.), *Handbook of motivation at school,* (p. 123–140.).

Dweck, C., Walton, G. M., & Cohen, G. L. (2011). *Academic tenacity: Mindset and skills that promote long-term learning.* Seattle, WA. Retrieved from http://web.stanford.edu/~gwalton/home/Welcome_files/DweckWaltonCohen_2014.pdf

Dye, F. J. (2000). *Human life before birth.* Amsterdam: Harwood.

Dyson, M. W., Olino, T. M., Durbin, C. E., Goldsmith, H. H., Bufferd, S. J., Miller, A. R., & Klein, D. N. (2015). The structural and rank-order stability of temperament in young children based on a laboratory-observational measure. *Psychological Assessment, 27*(4), 1388–1401. http://doi.org/10.1037/pas0000104

Dziewolska, H., & Cautilli, J. (2006). The effects of a motor training package on minimally assisted standing behavior in a three-month-old infant. *The Behavior Analyst Today, 7*(1), 111–120.

East, P. L., & Hokoda, A. (2015). Risk and protective factors for sexual and dating violence victimization: A longitudinal, prospective study of Latino and African American Adolescents. *Journal of Youth and Adolescence, 44*(6), 1288–1300. http://doi.org/10.1007/s10964-015-0273-5

Easterbrooks, M. A., Bartlett, J. D., Beeghly, M., & Thompson, R. A. (2012). Social and emotional development in infancy. In I. B. Weiner, R. M. Lerner, M. A. Easterbrooks, & J. Mistry (Eds.), *Handbook of psychology, developmental psychology* (p. 752). John Wiley & Sons.

Easterbrooks, M. A., Chaudhuri, J. H., Bartlett, J. D., & Copeman, A. (2011). Resilience in parenting among young mothers: Family and ecological risks and opportunities. *Children and Youth Services Review, 33*(1), 42–50. http://doi.org/10.1016/j.childyouth.2010.08.010

Ebbeling, C. B., Sinclair, K. B., Pereira, M. A., Garcia-Lago, E., Feldman, H. A., & Ludwig, D. S. (2004). Compensation for energy intake from fast food among overweight and lean adolescents. *JAMA, 291*(23), 2828–2833.

Ebisch, S. J., Perrucci, M. G., Mercuri, P., Romanelli, R., Mantini, D., Romani, G. L., . . . Saggino, A. (2012). Common and unique neuro-functional basis of induction, visualization, and spatial relationships as cognitive components of fluid intelligence. *NeuroImage, 62*(1), 331–342. http://doi.org/10.1016/j.neuroimage.2012.04.053

Eccles, J. S., & Roeser, R. W. (2011). Schools as developmental contexts during adolescence. *Journal of Research on Adolescence, 21*(1), 225–241. http://doi.org/10.1111/j.1532-7795.2010.00725.x

Eccles, J. S., Wigfield, A., Midgley, C., Reuman, D., Iver, D. Mac, & Feldlaufer, H. (1992). Negative effects of traditional middle schools on students' motivation. *Elementary School Journal, 93*(5), 553–74.

Eckerman, C. O., Hsu, H. C., Molitor, A., Leung, E. H. L., & Goldstein, R. F. (1999). Infant arousal as an en-face exchange with a new partner: Effects of prematurity and perinatal biological risk. *Developmental Psychology, 35*, 282–293.

Ecob, R., Sutton, G., Rudnicka, A., Smith, P., Power, C., Strachan, D., & Davis, A. (2008). Is the relation of social class to change in hearing threshold levels from childhood to middle age explained by noise, smoking, and drinking behaviour? *International Journal of Audiology, 47*(3), 100–108. http://doi.org/10.1080/14992020701647942

Eder, R. A. (1989). The emergent personologist: The structure and content of 3 ½, 5 ½, and 7 ½- year-olds' concepts of themselves and other persons. *Child Development, 60*, 1218–1228.

Edmonds, G. W., Goldberg, L. R., Hampson, S. E., & Barckley, M. (2013). Personality Stability from childhood to midlife: Relating Teachers' assessments in elementary school to observer- and self-ratings 40 years later. *Journal of Research in Personality, 47*(5), 505–513. http://doi.org/10.1016/j.jrp.2013.05.003

Education Commission of the States. (2014). *Child Must Attend Kindergarten.* Retrieved from http://ecs.force.com/mbdata/mbquestRT?rep=Kq1403

Edwards, K. M., Sylaska, K. M., & Neal, A. M. (2015). Intimate partner violence among sexual minority populations: A critical review of the literature and agenda for future research. *Psychology of Violence, 5*(2), 112–121.

Edwards, O. W., & Benson, N. F. (2010). A four-factor social support model to mediate stressors experienced by children raised by grandparents. *Journal of Applied School Psychology, 26*(1), 54–69. http://doi.org/10.1080/15377900903368862

Edwards, R., Carter, K., Peace, J., & Blakely, T. (2013). An examination of smoking initiation rates by age: Results from a large longitudinal study in New Zealand. *Australian and New Zealand Journal of Public Health, 37*(6), 516–9. Retrieved from http://www.ncbi.nlm.nih.gov/pubmed/24892149

Efron, R. (1990). *The decline and fall of hemispheric specialization.* Hillsdale, NJ: Lawrence Erlbaum.

Egan, B. M., Zhao, Y., & Axon, R. N. (2010). US trends in prevalence, awareness, treatment, and control of hypertension, 1988-2008. *JAMA, 303*(20), 2043–50. http://doi.org/10.1001/jama.2010.650

Egeland, M., Zunszain, P. A., & Pariante, C. M. (2015). Molecular mechanisms in the regulation of adult neurogenesis during stress. *Nature Reviews Neuroscience, 16*(4), 189–200. https://doi.org/10.1038/nrn3855

Ehlert, U., & Fischbacher, S. (2013). Reproductive health. In M. D. Gellman & J. R. Turner (Eds.), *Encyclopedia of Behavioral Medicine* (pp. 1658–1665). New York, NY: Springer New York. http://doi.org/10.1007/978-1-4419-1005-9

Ehmke, T., Drechsel, B., & Carstensen, C. H. (2010). Effects of grade retention on achievement and self-concept in science and mathematics. *Studies in Educational Evaluation, 36*(1/2), 27–35. http://doi.org/10.1016/j.stueduc.2010.10.003

Eibach, R. P., & Mock, S. E. (2011). Idealizing parenthood to rationalize parental investments. *Psychological Science, 22*(2), 203–8. http://doi.org/10.1177/0956797610397057

Eichenwald, E. C., & Stark, A. R. (2009). Management and outcomes of very low birth weight. *http://dx.doi.org/10.1056/NEJMra0707601.*

Eisbach, A. O. (2004). Children's developing awareness of diversity in people's trains of thoughts. *Child Development, 75*(6), 1694–1707.

Eisenberg, N., & Fabes, R. A. (1998). Prosocial development. In N. Eisenberg (Ed.), *Handbook of child psychology: Social, emotional, and personality development* (5th ed., Vol. 3, pp. 701–778). New York: Wiley.

Eisenberg, N., Cumberland, A., & Spinrad, T. L. (1998). Parental socialization of emotion. *Psychological Inquiry, 9*(4), 241–273. Retrieved from http://www.ncbi.nlm.nih.gov/pubmed/16865170

Eisenberg, N., Cumberland, A., Guthrie, I. K., Murphy, B. C., & Shepard, S. A. (2005). Age changes in prosocial responding and moral reasoning in adolescence and early adulthood. *Journal of Research on Adolescence, 15*(3), 235–260. http://doi.org/10.1111/j.1532-7795.2005.00095.x

Eisenberg, N., Fabes, R. A., & Spinrad, T. L. (2006). Prosocial development. In N. Eisenberg, W. Damon, & R. M. Lerner (Eds.), *Handbook of child psychology: Social, emotional, and personality development* (6th ed., Vol. 3, pp. 646–718). Hoboken, NJ: John Wiley & Sons.

Eisenberg, N., Fabes, R. A., Shepard, S. A., Murphy, B. C., Jones, S., & Guthrie, I. K. (1998). Contemporaneous and longitudinal prediction of children's sympathy from dispositional regulation and emotionality. *Developmental Psychology, 34*, 910–924.

Eisenberg, N., Spinrad, T. L., & Knafo-Noam, A. (2015). Prosocial development. In *Handbook of child psychology and developmental science* (pp. 1–47). Hoboken, NJ, USA: John Wiley & Sons, Inc. http://doi.org/10.1002/9781118963418.childpsy315

Eisenberg, S. L., Guo, L.-Y., & Germezia, M. (2012). How grammatical are 3-year-olds? *Language, Speech, and Hearing Services in Schools, 43*(1), 36–52. http://doi.org/10.1044/0161-1461(2011/10-0093)

Eisner, E. (2004). Multiple intelligences: Its tensions and possibilities. *Teachers College Record, 106*(1), 31–39.

Eisner, M. P., Malti, T., Eisner, M. P., & Malti, T. (2015). Aggressive and violent behavior. In *Handbook of child psychology and developmental science* (pp. 1–48). Hoboken, NJ, USA: John Wiley & Sons, Inc. http://doi.org/10.1002/9781118963418.childpsy319

Ekström, I., Sjölund, S., Nordin, S., Nordin Adolfsson, A., Adolfsson, R., Nilsson, L.-G., . . . Olofsson, J. K. (2017). Smell loss predicts mortality risk regardless of dementia conversion. *Journal of the American Geriatrics Society.* http://doi.org/10.1111/jgs.14770

Elder, G. H. J. (1999). *Children of the Great Depression: Social change in life experience (25th anniversary ed.).* Boulder, CO: Westview Press.

Elder, G. H. J. (2000). Life course theory. In A. E. Kazdin (Ed.), *Encyclopedia of psychology,* (Vol. 5, pp. 50–52). Washington, DC: American Psychological Association. http://doi.org/10.1037/10520-000

Elder, J. S. (2007). Circumcision. *BJU International, 99*(6), 1553–1564. http://doi.org/10.1111/j.1464-410X.2007.06959.x

Elias, C. F. (2012). Leptin action in pubertal development: Recent advances and unanswered questions. *Trends in Endocrinology and Metabolism: TEM, 23*(1), 9–15. http://doi.org/10.1016/j.tem.2011.09.002

Elicker, J., Englund, M., & Sroufe, L. A. (1992). Predicting peer competence and peer relationships in childhood from early parent-child relationships. In R. D. Parke & G. W. Ladd (Eds.), *Family-peer relationships: Modes of linkage* (pp. 77–106). Hillsdale, NJ: Lawrence Erlbaum.

Elkind, D. (1985). Egocentrism redux. *Developmental Review, 5*(3), 218–226. http://doi.org/10.1016/0273-2297(85)90010-3

Elkind, D., & Bowen, R. (1979). Imaginary audience behavior in children and adolescents. *Developmental Psychology, 15*(1), 38–44.

Ellis, B. J. (2004). Timing of pubertal maturation in girls: An integrated life history approach. *Psychological Bulletin, 130*, 920–958.

Ellis, K. J., Abrams, S. A., & Wong, W. W. (1997). Body composition of a young, multiethnic female population. *American Journal of Clinical Nutrition, 65*, 724–731.

Ellis, L., & Bonin, S. L. (2003). Genetics and occupation-related preferences. Evidence from adoptive and non-adoptive families. *Personality & Individual Differences, 35*(4), 929.

Ellis, S. A., & Gauvain, M. (1992). Social and cultural influences on children's collaborative interactions. In J. Winegar & L. T. Valsiner (Ed.), *Children's development within social context* (pp. 155–180). New York, NY: Lawrence Erlbaum.

Ellison, J. W., Rosenfeld, J. A., & Shaffer, L. G. (2013). Genetic basis of intellectual disability. *Annual Review of Medicine, 64,* 441–50. http://doi.org/10.1146/annurev-med-042711-140053

Elsabbagh, M., Hohenberger, A., Campos, R., Van Herwegen, J., Serres, J., de Schonen, S., . . . Karmiloff-Smith, A. (2013). Narrowing perceptual sensitivity to the native language in infancy: Exogenous influences on developmental timing. *Behavioral Sciences, 3*(1), 120–132. http://doi.org/10.3390/bs3010120

Else-Quest, N. M., Higgins, A., Allison, C., & Morton, L. C. (2012). Gender differences in self-conscious emotional experience: A meta-analysis. *Psychological Bulletin, 138*(5), 947–981. http://doi.org/10.1037/a0027930

Else-Quest, N. M., Hyde, J. S., Goldsmith, H. H., & Van Hulle, C. A. (2006). Gender differences in temperament: A meta-analysis. *Psychological Bulletin, 132*(1), 33–72. http://doi.org/10.1037/0033-2909.132.1.33

Elwert, F., & Christakis, N. A. (2008). The effect of widowhood on mortality by the causes of death of Both Spouses. *American Journal of Public Health, 98*(11), 2092–2098.

Emanuel, M., Rawlins, M., Duff, G., & Breckenridge, A. (2012). Thalidomide and its sequelae. *Lancet, 380*(9844), 781–783. http://doi.org/10.1016/S0140-6736(12)60468-1

Emery, L., Hale, S., & Myerson, J. (2008). Age differences in proactive interference, working memory, and abstract reasoning. *Psychology and Aging, 23*(3), 634–645.

Emmons, R. A., & Paloutzian, R. F. (2003). The psychology of religion. *Annual Review of Psychology, 54*(1), 377–402. http://doi.org/10.1146/annurev.psych.54.101601.145024

Emre, M., Ford, P. J., Bilgiç, B., & Uç, E. Y. (2014). Cognitive impairment and dementia in Parkinson's disease: Practical issues and management. *Movement Disorders, 29*(5), 663–672. http://doi.org/10.1002/mds.25870

Enck, G. E. (2003). *The dying process (Vol. 1).* Thousand Oaks: Sage, CA.

Endendijk, J. J., Groeneveld, M. G., van der Pol, L. D., van Berkel, S. R., Hallers-Haalboom, E. T., Bakermans-Kranenburg, M. J., & Mesman, J. (2017). Gender differences in child aggression: Relations with gender-differentiated parenting and parents' gender-role stereotypes. *Child Development, 88*(1), 299–316. http://doi.org/10.1111/cdev.12589

England, D. E., Descartes, L., & Collier-Meek, M. A. (2011). Gender role portrayal and the Disney princesses. *Sex Roles, 64*(7–8), 555–567. http://doi.org/10.1007/s11199-011-9930-7

Engle, P. L., & Breaux, C. (1998). Fathers' involvement with children: Perspectives from developing countries. *Social Policy Report, 12*(1), 1–21.

English, T., & Carstensen, L. L. (2014). Selective narrowing of social networks across adulthood is associated with improved emotional experience in daily life. *International Journal of Behavioral Development, 38*(2), 195–202. http://doi.org/10.1177/0165025413515404

English, T., & Carstensen, L. L. (2016). *Socioemotional selectivity theory,* 1–6. http://doi.org/10.1007/978-981-287-080-3_110-1

Englund, K., & Behne, D. (2006). Changes in infant directed speech in the first six months. *Infant & Child Development, 15,* 139–160.

Englund, M. M., Siebenbruner, J., Oliva, E. M., Egeland, B., Chung, C.-T., & Long, J. D. (2013). The developmental significance of late adolescent substance use for early adult functioning. *Developmental Psychology, 49*(8), 1554–64. http://doi.org/10.1037/a0030229

Engmann, B. (2011). Mild cognitive impairment in the elderly: A review of the influence of depression, possible other core symptoms, and diagnostic findings. *GeroPsych: The Journal of Gerontopsychology and Geriatric Psychiatry, 24*(2), 71–76.

Ennouri, K., & Bloch, H. (1996). Visual control of hand approach movements in new-borns. *British Journal of Developmental Psychology, 14*(3), 327–338. http://doi.org/10.1111/j.2044-835X.1996.tb00709.x

Enns, G. M., Koch, R., Brumm, V., Blakely, E., Suter, R., & Jurecki, E. (2010). Suboptimal outcomes in patients with PKU treated early with diet alone: Revisiting the evidence. *Molecular Genetics & Metabolism, 101*(2/3), 99–109. http://doi.org/10.1016/j.ymgme.2010.05.017

Enright, R. D., Bjerstedt, Å., Enright, W. F., Levy Jr., V. M., Lapsley, D. K., Buss, R. R., . . . Zindler, M. (1984). Distributive justice development: Cross-cultural, contextual, and longitudinal evaluations. *Child Development, 55*(5), 1737. http://doi.org/10.1111/1467-8624.ep7304494

Entwisle, D. R., Alexander, K. L., & Steffel Olson, L. (2005). First Grade and Educational Attainment by Age 22: A New Story. *American Journal of Sociology, 110*(5), 1458–1502.

Epel, E. S. (2009). Telomeres in a life-span perspective: A new "psychobiomarker"? *Current Directions in Psychological Science, 18*(1), 6–10. http://doi.org/10.1111/j.1467-8721.2009.01596.x

Epstein, R. (1991). Skinner, creativity, and the problem of spontaneous behavior. *Psychological Science, 2*(6), 362–370.

Erel, O., Oberman, Y., & Yirmiya, N. (2000). Maternal versus nonmaternal care and seven domains of children's development. *Psychological Bulletin, 126*(5), 727–747. http://doi.org/10.1037/0033-2909.126.5.727

Erickson, K. I., Raji, C. A., Lopez, O. L., Becker, J. T., Rosano, C., Newman, A. B., . . . Kuller, L. H. (2010). Physical activity predicts gray matter volume in late adulthood: The Cardiovascular Health Study. *Neurology, 75*(16), 1415–1422. http://doi.org/10.1212/WNL.0b013e3181f88359

Erickson, K. I., Voss, M. W., Prakash, R. S., Basak, C., Szabo, A., Chaddock, L., . . . Kramer, A. F. (2011). Exercise training increases size of hippocampus and improves memory. *Proceedings of the National Academy of Sciences of the United States of America, 108*(7), 3017–3022. http://doi.org/10.1073/pnas.1015950108

Ericsson, K. A. (2014). Expertise. *Current Biology : CB, 24*(11), R508-10. http://doi.org/10.1016/j.cub.2014.04.013

Ericsson, K. A., & Moxley, J. H. (2013). Experts' superior memory: From accumulation of chunks to building memory skills that mediate improved performance and learning. In T. J. Perfect (Ed.), *The SAGE handbook of applied memory.* Thousand Oaks, CA: Sage.

Erikson, E. H. (1950). *Childhood and society* (2nd ed.). New York, NY: Norton.

Erikson, E. H. (1959). *Identity and the life cycle* (Vol. 1). New York, NY: Norton.

Erikson, E. H. (1982). *The life cycle completed.* New York, NY: Norton.

Erlangsen, A., Jeune, B., Bille-Brahe, U., & Vaupel, J. W. (2004). Loss of partner and suicide risks among oldest old: A population-based register study. *Age & Ageing, 33*(4), 378–383. http://doi.org/10.1093/ageing/afh128

Ernst, A., Alkass, K., Bernard, S., Salehpour, M., Perl, S., Tisdale, J., . . . Frisén, J. (2014). Neurogenesis in the striatum of the adult human brain. *Cell, 156*(5), 1072–1083. http://doi.org/10.1016/j.cell.2014.01.044

Erol, R. Y., & Orth, U. (2011). Self-esteem development from age 14 to 30 years: A longitudinal study. *Journal of Personality and Social Psychology, 101*(3), 607–619. http://doi.org/10.1037/a0024299

Erol, R. Y., & Orth, U. (2017). Self-esteem and the quality of romantic relationships. *European Psychologist, 21,* 274–283.

Erwin, P. (1998). *Friendship in childhood and adolescence.* London: Routledge.

Eryigit Madzwamuse, S., Baumann, N., Jaekel, J., Bartmann, P., & Wolke, D. (2015). Neuro-cognitive performance of very preterm or very low birth weight adults at 26 years. *Journal of Child Psychology and Psychiatry, 56*(8), 857–864. http://doi.org/10.1111/jcpp.12358

Espelage, D. L., Low, S. K., & Jimerson, S. R. (2014). Understanding school climate, aggression, peer victimization, and bully perpetration: Contemporary science, practice, and policy. *School Psychology Quarterly, Vol 29*(3), 233–237.

Espeland, M. A., Bryan, R. N., Goveas, J. S., Robinson, J. G., Siddiqui, M. S., Liu, S., . . . Resnick, S. M. (2013). Influence of type 2 diabetes on brain volumes and changes in brain volumes: Results from the Women's Health Initiative Magnetic Resonance Imaging studies. *Diabetes Care, 36*(1), 90–7. http://doi.org/10.2337/dc12-0555

Espinoza, G., & Juvonen, J. (2011). Perceptions of the school social context across the transition to middle school: Heightened sensitivity among Latino students? *Journal of Educational Psychology, 103*(3), 749–758. http://doi.org/10.1037/a0023811

Estes, K. G., & Hurley, K. (2013). Infant-directed prosody helps infants map sounds to meanings. *Infancy, 18*(5). http://doi.org/10.1111/infa.12006

Esteve-Gilbert, N., Prieto, P., Balog, H. L., Brentari, D., Davis, B. L., MacNeilage, P. F., . . . Liszkowski, U. (2013). Prosody signals the emergence of intentional communication in the first year of life: Evidence from Catalan-babbling infants. *Journal of Child Language, 40*(5), 919–944. http://doi.org/10.1017/S0305000912000359

Ethier, K. A., Harper, C. R., Hoo, E., & Dittus, P. J. (2016). The longitudinal impact of perceptions of parental monitoring on adolescent initiation of sexual activity. *Journal of Adolescent Health, 59*(5), 570–576. http://doi.org/10.1016/j.jadohealth.2016.06.011

Ettekal, I., & Ladd, G. W. (2014). Developmental pathways from childhood aggression-disruptiveness, chronic peer rejection, and deviant friendships to early-adolescent rule breaking. *Child Development.* http://doi.org/10.1111/cdev.12321

Eurostat. (2016). Employment statistics. Retrieved from http://ec.europa.eu/eurostat/statistics-explained/index.php/Employment_statistics

Evans, A., Bagnall, R. D., Duflou, J., & Semsarian, C. (2013). Postmortem review and genetic analysis in sudden infant death syndrome: An 11-year review. *Human Pathology, 44*(9), 1730–1736. http://doi.org/10.1016/j.humpath.2013.04.024

Evans, D. W., Milanak, M. E., Medeiros, B., & Ross, J. L. (2002). Magical beliefs and rituals in young children. *Child Psychiatry and Human Development, 33,* 43–58.

Evans, E. H., Tovée, M. J., Boothroyd, L. G., & Drewett, R. F. (2013). Body dissatisfaction and disordered eating attitudes in 7- to 11-year-old girls: Testing a sociocultural model. *Body Image, 10*(1), 8–15. http://doi.org/10.1016/j.bodyim.2012.10.001

Evans, G. W. (2006). Child development and the physical environment. *Annual Review of Psychology, 57*(1), 423–451. http://doi.org/10.1146/annurev.psych.57.102904.190057

Evans, G. W., & Kim, P. (2013). Childhood poverty, chronic stress, self-regulation, and coping. *Child Development Perspectives, 7*(1), 43–48. http://doi.org/10.1111/cdep.12013

Evans, G. W., Li, D., & Whipple, S. S. (2013). Cumulative risk and child development. *Psychological Bulletin, 139*(6), 1342–96. http://doi.org/10.1037/a0031808

Evans, J. (1998). "Princesses are not into war "n things, they always scream and run off": Exploring gender stereotypes in picture books." *Reading,* 5–11.

Evans, S. Z., Simons, L. G., & Simons, R. L. (2014). Factors that influence trajectories of delinquency throughout adolescence. *Journal of Youth and Adolescence.* http://doi.org/10.1007/s10964-014-0197-5

Evans, W. J., Morley, J. E., Argilés, J., Bales, C., Baracos, V., Guttridge, D., . . . Anker, S. D. (2008). Cachexia: a new definition. *Clinical Nutrition (Edinburgh, Scotland), 27*(6), 793–9. http://doi.org/10.1016/j.clnu.2008.06.013

Eveleth, P. B., & Tanner, J. M. (1991). *Worldwide variation in human growth* (2nd ed.). Cambridge, UK: Cambridge University Press.

Everitt, B. J., Cardinal, R. N., Parkinson, J. A., & Robbins, T. W. (2003). Appetitive behavior. *Annals of the New York Academy of Sciences, 985*(1), 233–250.

Everman, D. B., & Cassidy, S. B. (2000). Genetics of childhood disorders: VII. Genomic Imprinting: Breaking the Rules. *Journal of the American Academy of Child & Adolescent Psychiatry, 39*, 386–389.

Exelmans, L., Custers, K., & Van den Bulck, J. (2015). Violent video games and delinquent behavior in adolescents: A risk factor perspective. *Aggressive Behavior, 41*(3), 267–279. http://doi.org/10.1002/ab.21587

Exner-Cortens, D., Eckenrode, J., & Rothman, E. (2013). Longitudinal associations between teen dating violence victimization and adverse health outcomes. *Pediatrics, 131*(1), 71–8. http://doi.org/10.1542/peds.2012-1029

Exner-Cortens, D., Eckenrode, J., Bunge, J., & Rothman, E. (2017). Revictimization after adolescent dating violence in a matched, national sample of youth. *Journal of Adolescent Health, 60*(2), 176–183. http://doi.org/10.1016/j.jadohealth.2016.09.015

Fabes, R. A., Eisenberg, N., McCormick, S. E., & Wilson, M. S. (1988). Preschoolers' attributions of the situational determinants of others' naturally occurring emotions. *Developmental Psychology, 24*(3), 376–385.

Fabiano-Smith, L., & Goldstein, B. A. (2010). Phonological acquisition in bilingual Spanish–English speaking children. *Journal of Speech, Language, and Hearing Research, 53*(1), 160. http://doi.org/10.1044/1092-4388(2009/07-0064)

Facio, A., & Micocci, F. (2003). Emerging adulthood in Argentina. In J. J. Arnett & N. L. Galambos (Eds.), *New directions in child development: Exploring Cultural Conceptions ofthe Transition to Adulthood* (Vol. 100, pp. 21–31.). San Francisco: Jossey-Bass.

Fadjukoff, P., & Kroger, J. (2016). Identity development in adulthood: Introduction. *Identity, 16*(1), 1–7. http://doi.org/10.1080/15283488.2015.1121821

Fadjukoff, P., Kokko, K., & Pulkkinen, L. (2007). Implications of timing of entering adulthood for identity achievement. *Journal of Adolescent Research, 22*(5), 504–530.

Fagan, J. F. (1973). Infants' delayed recognition memory and forgetting. *Journal of Experimental Child Psychology, 16*, 424–450.

Fagan, J. F. (2011). Intelligence in infancy. In R. J. Sternberg & S. B. Kaufman (Eds.), *The Cambridge handbook of intelligence* (p. 130–142.). Cambridge University Press. Retrieved from http://books.google.com/books?hl=en&lr=&id=FtYeTcNwzQ4C&pgis=1

Fagard, J., Spelke, E., & von Hofsten, C. (2009). Reaching and grasping a moving object in 6-, 8-, and 10-month-old infants: Laterality and performance. *Infant Behavior & Development, 32*(2), 137–146. http://doi.org/10.1016/j.infbeh.2008.12.002

Fagot, B. I. (1997). Attachment, parenting, and peer interactions of toddler children. *Developmental Psychology, 33*, 489–499.

Fairchild, E. E. (2003). Multiple roles of adult learners. *New Directions for Student Services, 2003*(102), 11–16. http://doi.org/10.1002/ss.84

Fakhouri, T. H. I., Hughes, J. P., Brody, D. J., Kit, B. K., & Ogden, C. L. (2013). Physical activity and screen-time viewing among elementary school-aged children in the United States from 2009 to 2010. *JAMA Pediatrics, 167*(3), 223–229. http://doi.org/10.1001/2013.jamapediatrics.122

Falbo, T., Poston Jr., D. L., Triscari, R. S., & Zhang, X. (1997). Self-enhancing illusions among Chinese schoolchildren. *Journal of Cross-Cultural Psychology, 28*, 172–191.

Fallone, M. D., LaGasse, L. L., Lester, B. M., Shankaran, S., Bada, H. S., & Bauer, C. R. (2014). Reactivity and regulation of motor responses in cocaine-exposed infants. *Neurotoxicology and Teratology, 43*, 25–32. http://doi.org/10.1016/j.ntt.2014.02.005

Fan, H. C., Gu, W., Wang, J., Blumenfeld, Y. J., El-Sayed, Y. Y., & Quake, S. R. (2012). Non-invasive prenatal measurement of the fetal genome. *Nature, 487*(7407), 320–324. http://doi.org/10.1038/nature11251

Fan, M., & Jin, Y. (2014). Do neighborhood parks and playgrounds reduce childhood obesity? *American Journal of Agricultural Economics, 96*(1), 26–42. http://doi.org/10.1093/ajae/aat047

Fang, S. C., Rosen, R. C., Vita, J. A., Ganz, P., & Kupelian, V. (2015). Changes in erectile dysfunction over time in relation to Framingham cardiovascular risk in the Boston Area Community Health (BACH) survey. *The Journal of Sexual Medicine, 12*(1), 100–108. http://doi.org/10.1111/jsm.12715

Fanti, K. A., Kimonis, E. R., Hadjicharalambous, M.-Z., & Steinberg, L. (2016). Do neurocognitive deficits in decision making differentiate conduct disorder subtypes? *European Child & Adolescent Psychiatry, 25*(9), 989–996. http://doi.org/10.1007/s00787-016-0822-9

Fantz, R. L. (1961). The origin of form perception. *Scientific American, 204*, 66–72.

Farage, M. A., Miller, K. W., Elsner, P., & Maibach, H. I. (2013). Characteristics of the aging skin. *Advances in Wound Care, 2*(1), 5–10. http://doi.org/10.1089/wound.2011.0356

Farber, D. A., & Beteleva, T. G. (2011). Development of the brain's organization of working memory in young schoolchildren. *Human Physiology, 37*(1), 1–13. http://doi.org/10.1134/s0362119710061015

Fareri, D. S., & Delgado, M. R. (2014). Social rewards and social networks in the human brain. *The Neuroscientist, 20*(4), 387–402. https://doi.org/10.1177/1073858414521869

Farkas, J. I., & Hogan, D. P. (1995). The demography of changing intergenerational relationships. In V. L. Bengtson, K. W. Schaie, & L. M. Burton (Eds.), *Adult intergenerational relations: Effects of societal change* (pp. 1–29). New York, NY: Springer.

Farooq, M. A., Parkinson, K. N., Adamson, A. J., Pearce, M. S., Reilly, J. K., Hughes, A. R., . . . Reilly, J. J. (2017). Timing of the decline in physical activity in childhood and adolescence: Gateshead Millennium Cohort Study. *British Journal of Sports Medicine,* bjsports-2016-096933. http://doi.org/10.1136/bjsports-2016-096933

Farr, R. H. (2017). Does parental sexual orientation matter? A longitudinal follow-up of adoptive families with school-age children. *Developmental Psychology, 53*(2), 252–264. http://doi.org/10.1037/dev0000228

Farrington, D. P. (2004). Conduct disorder, aggression, and delinquency. In R. M. Lerner & L. Steinberg (Eds.), *Handbook of adolescent psychology* (2nd ed., pp. 627–664). Hoboken, NJ: John Wiley & Sons.

Farrington, D. P., & Loeber, R. (2000). Epidemiology of juvenile violence. *Juvenile Violence, 9*, 733–748.

Farroni, T., Menon, E., Rigato, S., & Johnson, M. H. (2007). The perception of facial expressions in newborns. *European Journal of Developmental Psychology, 4*(1), 2–13. http://doi.org/10.1080/17405620601046832

Farsalinos, K. E., & Polosa, R. (2014). Safety evaluation and risk assessment of electronic cigarettes as tobacco cigarette substitutes: A systematic review. *Therapeutic Advances in Drug Safety, 5*(2), 67–86. http://doi.org/10.1177/2042098614524430

Farver, J. A. M., Xu, Y., Eppe, S., Fernandez, A., & Schwartz, D. (2005). Community violence, family conflict, and preschoolers' socioemotional functioning. *Developmental Psychology, 41*, 160–170.

Farzaneh-Far, R., Lin, J., Epel, E. S., Harris, W. S., Blackburn, E. H., & Whooley, M. A. (2010). Association of marine omega-3 fatty acid levels with telomeric aging in patients with coronary heart disease. *Journal of the American Medical Association, 303*(3), 250–257.

Fasig, L. G. (2000). Toddlers' understanding of ownership: Implications for self-concept development. *Social Development, 9*(3), 370–382.

Faulkner, J. A., Larkin, L. M., Claflin, D. R., & Brooks, S. V. (2007). Age-related changes in the structure and function of skeletal muscles. *Clinical & Experimental Pharmacology & Physiology, 34*(11), 1091–1096. http://doi.org/10.1111/j.1440-1681.2007.04752.x

Fawcett, L. M., & Garton, A. F. (2005). The effect of peer collaboration on children's problem-solving ability. *British Journal of Educational Psychology, 75*(2), 157–169. http://doi.org/10.1348/000709904X234ll

Fay-Stammbach, T., Hawes, D. J., & Meredith, P. (2014). Parenting influences on executive function in early childhood: A review. *Child Development Perspectives, 8*(4), 258–264. http://doi.org/10.1111/cdep.12095

Fearon, R. M. P., & Belsky, J. (2004). Attachment and attention: Protection in relation to gender and cumulative social-contextual adversity. *Child Development, 75*(6), 1677–1693. http://doi.org/10.1111/j.1467-8624.2004.00809.x

Federal Bureau of Investigation. (2015). *Crime in the United States, 2015.* Washington DC. Retrieved from https://ucr.fbi.gov/crime-in-the-u.s/2015/preliminary-semiannual-uniform-crime-report-januaryjune-2015

Federal Bureau of Investigation. (2015). *Crime in the United States, 2015.* Washington, DC. Retrieved from https://ucr.fbi.gov/crime-in-the-u.s/2015/preliminary-semiannual-uniform-crime-report-januaryjune-2015

Federal Interagency Forum on Aging-Related Statistics. (2016). *Older Americans 2016 key indicators of well-being*. Washington, DC. Retrieved from https://agingstats.gov/docs/LatestReport/Older-Americans-2016-Key-Indicators-of-WellBeing.pdf

Federal Interagency Forum on Child and Family Statistics. (2014). *America's Children: Key National Indicators of Well-Being, 2013*. Washington DC. Retrieved from http://www.childstats.gov/americaschildren

Federman, D. D., & Walford, G. A. (2007). Is male menopause real? (Cover story). *Newsweek, 149*(3), 58–60.

Fedewa, A. L., Black, W. W., & Ahn, S. (2014). Children and adolescents with same-gender parents: A meta-analytic approach in assessing outcomes. *Journal of GLBT Family Studies, 11*(1), 1–34. http://doi.org/10.1080/1550428X.2013.869486

Fehr, R. (2012). Is retirement always stressful? The potential impact of creativity. *American Psychologist, 67*(1), 76–77. http://doi.org/10.1037/a0026574

Feldman, D. C., & Beehr, T. A. (2011). A three-phase model of retirement decision making. *The American Psychologist, 66*(3), 193–203. http://doi.org/10.1037/a0022153

Feldman, P. J., Dunkel-Schetter, C., Sandman, C. A., & Wadhwa, P. D. (2000). Maternal social support predicts birth weight and fetal growth in human pregnancy. *Psychosomatic Medicine, 62*, 715–725.

Feldman, R. (2003). Infant–mother and infant–father synchrony: The coregulation of positive arousal. *Infant Mental Health Journal, 24*(1), 1–23. http://doi.org/10.1002/imhj.10041

Feldman, R. (2015). The adaptive human parental brain: Implications for children's social development. *Trends in Neurosciences, 38*(6), 387–399. https://doi.org/10.1016/j.tins.2015.04.004

Feldman, R., Dollberg, D., & Nadam, R. (2011). The expression and regulation of anger in toddlers: Relations to maternal behavior and mental representations. *Infant Behavior & Development, 34*(2), 310–20. http://doi.org/10.1016/j.infbeh.2011.02.001

Feldman, R., Granat, A., Pariente, C., Kanety, H., Kuint, J., & Gilboa-Schechtman, E. (2009). Maternal depression and anxiety across the postpartum year and infant social engagement, fear regulation, and stress reactivity. *Journal of the American Academy of Child & Adolescent Psychiatry, 48*(9), 919–927. http://doi.org/10.1097/CHI.0b013e3181b21651

Feldstein Ewing, S. W., Sakhardande, A., & Blakemore, S.-J. (2014). The effect of alcohol consumption on the adolescent brain: A systematic review of MRI and fMRI studies of alcohol-using youth. *NeuroImage: Clinical, 5*, 420–437. http://doi.org/10.1016/j.nicl.2014.06.011

Felker, J. A., Fromme, D. K., Arnaut, G. L., & Stoll, B. M. (2002). A qualitative analysis of stepfamilies: The stepparent. *Journal of Divorce & Remarriage, 38*(1/2), 125.

Feng, X., Harwood, R. L., Leyendecker, B., & Miller, A. M. (2001). Changes across the first year of life in infants' daily activities and social contacts among middle-class Anglo and Puerto Rican families. *Infant Behavior & Development, 24*(3), 317–339. http://doi.org/10.1016/s0163-6383(01)00080-7

Feng, Y., Jankovic, J., & Wu, Y.-C. (2014). Epigenetic mechanisms in Parkinson's disease. *Journal of the Neurological Sciences, 349*(1), 3–9. http://doi.org/10.1016/j.jns.2014.12.017

Fenstermacher, S. K., Barr, R., Salerno, K., Garcia, A., Shwery, C. E., Calvert, S. L., & Linebarger, D. L. (2010). Infant-directed media: An analysis of product information and claims. *Infant & Child Development, 19*(6), 556–557. http://doi.org/10.1002/icd.718

Ferber, S. G., & Makhoul, I. R. (2008). Neurobehavioural assessment of skin-to-skin effects on reaction to pain in preterm infants: A randomized, controlled within-subject trial. *Acta Paediatrica, 97*(2), 171–176. http://doi.org/10.1111/j.1651-2227.2007.00607.x

Ferguson, C. J. (2007). The good, the bad and the ugly: A meta-analytic review of positive and negative effects of violent Video Games. *Psychiatric Quarterly, 78*(4), 309–316. http://doi.org/10.1007/s11126-007-9056-9

Ferguson, C. J. (2015). Do angry birds make for angry children? A meta-analysis of video game influences on children's and adolescents' aggression, mental health, prosocial behavior, and academic performance. *Perspectives on Psychological Science, 10*(5), 646–666. http://doi.org/10.1177/1745691615592234

Ferguson, C. J., & Donnellan, M. B. (2014). Is the association between children's baby video viewing and poor language development robust? A reanalysis of Zimmerman, Christakis, and Meltzoff (2007). *Developmental Psychology, 50*(1), 129–37. http://doi.org/10.1037/a0033628

Ferguson, G. M., Hafen, C. A., & Laursen, B. (2010). Adolescent psychological and academic adjustment as a function of discrepancies between actual and ideal self-perceptions. *Journal of Youth and Adolescence, 39*(12), 1485–97. http://doi.org/10.1007/s10964-009-9461-5

Ferguson, P., Jimerson, S., & Dalton, M. (2001). Sorting out successful failures: Exploratory analyses of factors associated with academic and behavioral outcomes of retained students. *Psychology in the Schools, 38*, 327–342.

Ferguson, R. F., & Lambeck, S. (2014). *Creating Pathways to Prosperity: A Blueprint for Action . Report issued by the Pathways to Prosperity Project at the Harvard Graduate School of Education and the Achievement Gap Initiative at Harvard University*. Retrieved from http://www.agi.harvard.edu/pathways/CreatingPathwaystoProsperityReport2014.pdf

Fergusson, D. M., & Boden, J. M. (2008). Cannabis use and later life outcomes. *Addiction, 103*(6), 969–976. http://doi.org/10.1111/j.1360-0443.2008.02221.x

Fergusson, D. M., & Horwood, L. J. (2002). Male and female offending trajectories. *Development and Psychopathology, 14*(1), 159–177.

Fergusson, D. M., Boden, J. M., & Horwood, L. J. (2013). Childhood self-control and adult outcomes: Results from a 30-year longitudinal study. *Journal of the American Academy of Child & Adolescent Psychiatry, 52*(7), 709–717.e1. http://doi.org/10.1016/j.jaac.2013.04.008

Fergusson, D. M., Boden, J. M., Horwood, L. J., Miller, A. L., & Kennedy, M. A. (2011). MAOA, abuse exposure and antisocial behaviour: 30-year longitudinal study. *The British Journal of Psychiatry : The Journal of Mental Science, 198*(6), 457–63. http://doi.org/10.1192/bjp.bp.110.086991

Fergusson, D. M., Woodward, L. J., & Horwood, L. J. (2000). Risk factors and life processes associated with the onset of suicidal behaviour during adolescence and early adulthood. *Psychological Medicine, 30*, 23–39.

Ferholt, B., & Lecusay, R. (2010). Adult and child development in the Zone of Proximal Development: Socratic dialogue in a playworld. *Mind, Culture & Activity, 17*(1), 59–83. http://doi.org/10.1080/10749030903342246

Fernald, A., & Marchman, V. A. (2012). Individual differences in lexical processing at 18 months predict vocabulary growth in typically developing and late-talking toddlers. *Child Development, 83*(1), 203–222. http://doi.org/10.1111/j.1467-8624.2011.01692.x

Fernald, A., Marchman, V. A., & Weisleder, A. (2013). SES differences in language processing skill and vocabulary are evident at 18 months. *Developmental Science, 16*(2), 234–248. https://doi.org/10.1111/desc.12019

Fernald, A., & McRoberts, G. (1996). Prosaic bootstrapping: A critical analysis of the argument and the evidence. In J. L. Morgan & K. Demuth (Eds.), *Signal to syntax*. Hillsdale, NJ: Lawrence Erlbaum.

Fernald, A., & Morikawa, H. (1993). Common themes and cultural variations in Japanese and American mothers' speech to infants. *Child Development, 64*, 657–674.

Fernald, A., Marchman, V. A., & Weisleder, A. (2013). SES differences in language processing skill and vocabulary are evident at 18 months. *Developmental Science, 16*(2), 234–48. http://doi.org/10.1111/desc.12019

Fernyhough, C. (2008). Getting Vygotskian about theory of mind: Mediation, dialogue, and the development of social understanding. *Developmental Review, 28*(2), 225–262. http://doi.org/10.1016/j.dr.2007.03.001

Festa, E. K., Ott, B. R., Manning, K. J., Davis, J. D., & Heindel, W. C. (2013). Effect of cognitive status on self-regulatory driving behavior in older adults: An assessment of naturalistic driving using in-car video recordings. *Journal of Geriatric Psychiatry and Neurology, 26*(1), 10–8. http://doi.org/10.1177/0891988712473801

Fetters, L., & Hsiang-han, H. (2007). Motor development and sleep, play, and feeding positions in very-low-birthweight infants with and without white matter disease. *Developmental Medicine & Child Neurology, 49*(11), 807–813. http://doi.org/10.1111/j.1469-8749.2007.00807.x

Fidler, J. A., West, R., Jarvis, M. J., & Wardle, J. (2006). Early dating predicts smoking during adolescence: A prospective study. *Addiction, 101*(12), 1805–1813. http://doi.org/10.1111/j.1360-0443.2006.01613.x

Field, D. (1999). Stability of older women's friendships: A commentary on Roberto. *International Journal of Aging & Human Development, 48*(1), 81.

Field, N. P., Gal-Oz, E., & Bonanno, G. A. (2003). Continuing bonds and adjustment at 5 years after the death of a spouse. *Journal of Consulting and Clinical Psychology, 71*(1), 110–117. http://doi.org/10.1037/0022-006x.71.1.110

Field, T. (2011). Prenatal depression effects on early development: A review. *Infant Behavior & Development, 34*(1), 1–14. http://doi.org/10.1016/j.infbeh.2010.09.008

Field, T. M., Cohen, D., Garcia, R., & Greenberg, R. (1984). Mother-stranger face discrimination by the newborn. *Infant Behavior & Development, 7*, 19–25.

Figner, B., Mackinlay, R. J., Wilkening, F., & Weber, E. U. (2009). Affective and deliberative processes in risky choice: Age differences in risk taking in the Columbia Card Task. *Journal of Experimental Psychology: Learning, Memory, and Cognition, 35*(3), 709–730. http://doi.org/10.1037/a0014983

Fildes, A., Llewellyn, C., Van Jaarsveld, C. H. M., Fisher, A., Cooke, L., & Wardle, J. (2014). Common genetic architecture underlying food fussiness in children, and preference for fruits and vegetables. *Appetite, 76*, 200. http://doi.org/10.1016/j.appet.2014.01.023

Filiano, J. J., & Kinney, H. C. (1994). A perspective on neuropathologic findings in victims of the sudden infant death syndrome: The triple-risk model. *Neonatology, 65*(3–4), 194–197. http://doi.org/10.1159/000244052

Filippova, E., & Astington, J. W. (2008). Further development in social reasoning revealed in discourse irony understanding. *Child Development*, 79(1), 126–138.

Fillmore, L. W. (1991). When learning a second language means losing the first. *Early Childhood Research Quarterly*, 6(3), 323–346. http://doi.org/10.1016/S0885-2006(05)80059-6

Fincham, F. D., & Beach, S. R. H. (2010). Marriage in the new millennium: A decade in review. *Journal of Marriage and Family*, 72(3), 630–649. http://doi.org/10.1111/j.1741-3737.2010.00722.x

Fincham, F. D., Beach, S. R. H., & Davila, J. (2007). Longitudinal relations between forgiveness and conflict resolution in marriage. *Journal of Family Psychology*, 21(3), 542–545.

Finder, V. H. (2011). Alzheimer's disease: A general introduction and pathomechanism. *Journal of Alzheimer's Disease*, 22, 5–19. http://doi.org/10.3233/jad-2010-100975

Findlay, L. C., & Bowker, A. (2009). The link between competitive sport participation and self-concept in early adolescence: A consideration of gender and sport orientation. *Journal of Youth & Adolescence*, 38(1), 29–40. http://doi.org/10.1007/s10964-007-9244-9

Fine, S. (2015, February 6). Supreme Court rules Canadians have right to doctor-assisted suicide. *The Globe and Mail*. Retrieved from http://www.theglobeandmail.com/news/national/supreme-court-rules-on-doctor-assisted-suicide/article22828437/

Finegold, D. M. (2013). Overview of Genetics. In *Merck Manual*. Retrieved from http://www.merckmanuals.com/professional/special-subjects/general-principles-of-medical-genetics/overview-of-genetics

Finer, L. B., & Philbin, J. M. (2013). Sexual initiation, contraceptive use, and pregnancy among young adolescents. *Pediatrics*, 131(5), 886–91. http://doi.org/10.1542/peds.2012-3495

Fingerman, K. L. (2000). `We had a nice little chat': Age and generational differences in Mothers and Daughters. *Journals of Gerontology Series B: Psychological Sciences & Social Sciences*, 55B(2), P95.

Fingerman, K. L. (2001). A distant closeness: Intimacy between parents and their children in later life. *Generations*, 25(2), 26.

Fingerman, K. L., & Charles, S. T. (2010). It takes two to tango: Why older people have the best relationships. *Current Directions in Psychological Science* 19(3), 172–176. http://doi.org/10.1177/0963721410370297

Fingerman, K. L., Cheng, Y.-P., Birditt, K., & Zarit, S. (2012). Only as happy as the least happy child: Multiple grown children's problems and successes and middle-aged parents' well-being. *The Journals of Gerontology. Series B, Psychological Sciences and Social Sciences*, 67(2), 184–93. http://doi.org/10.1093/geronb/gbr086

Fingerman, K. L., Cheng, Y.-P., Wesselmann, E. D., Zarit, S., Furstenberg, F., & Birditt, K. S. (2012). Helicopter parents and landing pad kids: Intense parental support of grown children. *Journal of Marriage and Family*, 74(4), 880–896. http://doi.org/10.1111/j.1741-3737.2012.00987.x

Fingerman, K. L., Hay, E. L., & Birditt, K. S. (2004). The best of ties, the worst of ties: Close, problematic, and ambivalent social relationships. *Journal of Marriage & Family*, 66(3), 792–808.

Fingerman, K. L., Turiano, N. A., Davis, E., & Charles, S. T. (2013). Social and emotional aging. In J. Wilmoth & K. Ferraro (Eds.), *Gerontology: Perspectives and Issues* (pp. 127–148). New York: Springer.

Finkel, D., Reynolds, C. A., McArdle, J. J., & Pedersen, N. L. (2007). Age changes in processing speed as a leading indicator of cognitive aging. *Psychology and Aging*, 22(3), 558–568.

Finkelhor, D., Ormrod, R. K., & Turner, H. A. (2009). The developmental epidemiology of childhood victimization. *Journal of Interpersonal Violence*, 24(5), 711–731.

Finkelhor, D., Shattuck, A., Turner, H. A., & Hamby, S. L. (2014). The lifetime prevalence of child sexual abuse and sexual assault assessed in late adolescence. *The Journal of Adolescent Health : Official Publication of the Society for Adolescent Medicine*, 55(3), 329–33. http://doi.org/10.1016/j.jadohealth.2013.12.026

Finkelstein, J. A., & Schiffman, S. S. (1999). Workshop on taste and smell in the elderly: An overview. *Physiology & Behavior*, 66(2), 173–176. http://doi.org/10.1016/S0031-9384(98)00261-3

Firkowska-Mankiewicz, A. (2011). Adult careers: Does childhood IQ predict later life outcome? *Journal of Policy and Practice in Intellectual Disabilities*, 8(1), 1–9. http://doi.org/10.1111/j.1741-1130.2011.00281.x

Firooz, A., Rajabi-Estarabadi, A., Zartab, H., Pazhohi, N., Fanian, F., & Janani, L. (2017). The influence of gender and age on the thickness and echo-density of skin. *Skin Research and Technology*, 23(1), 13–20. http://doi.org/10.1111/srt.12294

Fischer, A. H., & Manstead, A. S. R. (2000). The relation between gender and emotion in different cultures. In A. H. Fischer (Ed.), *Gender and emotion* (pp. 71–94). Cambridge: Cambridge University Press. http://doi.org/10.1017/CBO9780511628191.005

Fischer, M. J. (2007). Settling into campus life: Differences by race/ethnicity in college involvement and outcomes. *Journal of Higher Education*, 78, 125–161.

Fischhoff, B. (2008). Assessing adolescent decision-making competence. *Developmental Review*, 28(1), 12–28. http://doi.org/10.1016/j.dr.2007.08.001

Fisher, C. B., Higgins-D'Alessandro, A., Rau, J. M., Kuther, T. L., & Belanger, S. (1996). Referring and reporting research participants at risk: Views from urban adolescents. *Child Development*, 67(5), 2086–2100.

Fisher, C. B., Busch-Rossnagel, Nancy A. Jopp, D. S., & Brown, J. (2013). Applied developmental science: Contributions and challenges for the 21st century., 6, 517–546. Hoboken.

Fisher, J. E., Yury, C., & Buchanan, J. A. (2006). Dementia. In J. E. Fisher & W. T. O'Donohue (Eds.), *Practitioner's guide to evidence-based psychotherapy* (pp. 214–229). New York, NY: Springer Science + Business Media.

Fishkin, J., Keniston, K., & McKinnon, C. (1973). Moral reasoning and political ideology. *Journal of Personality and Social Psychology*, 27(1), 109–119. http://doi.org/10.1037/h0034434

Fisk, J. D., Beattie, B. L., Donnelly, M., Byszewski, A., & Molnar, F. J. (2007). Disclosure of the diagnosis of dementia. *Alzheimer's & Dementia*, 3(4), 404–410. Retrieved from John.Fisk@cdha.nshealth.ca

Fite, P. J., Hendrickson, M., Rubens, S. L., Gabrielli, J., & Evans, S. (2013). The role of peer rejection in the link between reactive aggression and academic performance. *Child & Youth Care Forum*, 42(3), 193–205. http://doi.org/10.1007/s10566-013-9199-9

Fitneva, S. A., & Matsui, T. (2015). The emergence and development of language across cultures. In L. Arnett Jensen (Ed.), *The Oxford handbook of human development and culture*. London, UK: Oxford University Press. http://doi.org/10.1093/oxfordhb/9780199948550.013.8

Fitzpatrick, M., & McPherson, B. (2010). Coloring within the lines: Gender stereotypes in contemporary coloring books. *Sex Roles*, 62(1/2), 127–137. http://doi.org/10.1007/s11199-009-9703-8

Fivush, R. (1993). Developmental perspectives on autobiographical recall. In G. S. Goodman & B. L. Bottoms (Eds.), *Child victims, child witnesses* (pp. 1–24). New York: Guilford Press.

Fivush, R. (2011). The development of autobiographical memory. *Annual Review of Psychology*, 62, 559–82. http://doi.org/10.1146/annurev.psych.121208.131702

Fivush, R., & Nelson, K. (2004). Culture and language in the emergence of autobiographical memory. *Psychological Science*, 15(9), 573–7. http://doi.org/10.1111/j.0956-7976.2004.00722.x

Fivush, R., Hudson, J., & Nelson, K. (1983). Children's long-term memory for a novel event: An exploratory study. *Merrill-Palmer Quarterly*, 30, 303–316.

Flak, A. L., Su, S., Bertrand, J., Denny, C. H., Kesmodel, U. S., & Cogswell, M. E. (2014). The association of mild, moderate, and binge prenatal alcohol exposure and child neuropsychological outcomes: A meta-analysis. *Alcoholism: Clinical and Experimental Research*, 38(1), 214–226. http://doi.org/10.1111/acer.12214

Flament, F., Bazin, R., & Piot, B. (2013). Effect of the sun on visible clinical signs of aging in Caucasian skin. *Clinical, Cosmetic and Investigational Dermatology*, 6, 221. http://doi.org/10.2147/CCID.S44686

Flanagan, C. A., Kim, T., Collura, J., & Kopish, M. A. (2015). Community service and adolescents' social capital. *Journal of Research on Adolescence*, 25(2), 295–309. http://doi.org/10.1111/jora.12137

Flanders, J. L., Leo, V., Paquette, D., Pihl, R. O., & Séguin, J. R. (2009). Rough-and-tumble play and the regulation of aggression: An observational study of father–child play dyads. *Aggressive Behavior*, 35(4), 285–295. http://doi.org/10.1002/ab.20309

Flannery, D. J., Hussey, D., & Jefferis, E. (2005). Adolescent delinquency and violent behavior. In T. P. Gullotta & G. R. Adams (Eds.), *Handbook of adolescent behavioral problems: Evidence-based approaches to prevention and treatment* (pp. 415–438). New York, NY: Springer Science + Business Media.

Flatt, T. (2005). The evolutionary genetics of canalization. *Quarterly Review of Biology*, 80(3), 287–316.

Flavell, J. H. (1992). Cognitive development: Past, present, and future. *Developmental Psychology*, 28(998–1005).

Flavell, J. H. (1993). The development of children's understanding of false belief and the appearance-reality distinction. *International Journal of Psychology*, 28, 595–604.

Flavell, J. H. (1999). Cognitive development: Children's knowledge about the mind. *Annual Review of Psychology*, 50, 21–45.

Flavell, J. H. (2004). Theory-of-mind development: Retrospect and prospect. *Merrill-Palmer Quarterly: Journal of Developmental Psychology*, 50(3), 274–290.

Flavell, J. H., Everett, B. H., Croft, K., & Flavell, E. R. (1981). Young children's knowledge about visual perception: Further evidence for the level 1-level 2 distinction. *Developmental Psychology*, 17, 99–103.

Flavell, J. H., Flavell, E. R., & Green, F. L. (1983). Development of the appearance-reality distinction. *Cognitive Psychology*, 15, 95–120.

Flavell, J. H., Flavell, E. R., & Green, F. L. (1987). Young children's knowledge about apparent-real and pretend-real distinctions. *Developmental Psychology*, 23, 816–822.

Flavell, J. H., Flavell, E. R., & Green, F. L. (2001). Development of children's understanding of connections between thinking and feeling. *Psychological Science*, *12*(5), 430–2. Retrieved from http://www.ncbi.nlm.nih.gov/pubmed/11554679

Flavell, J. H., Friedrich, A. G., & Hoyt, J. D. (1970). Developmental changes in memorization processes. *Cognitive Psychology*, *1*, 324–340.

Flavell, J. H., Green, F. L., & Flavell, E. R. (1986). Development of knowledge about the appearance-reality distinction. *Monographs of the Society for Research in Child Development*, *51*(1, Serial No. 212).

Flavell, J. H., Green, F. L., & Flavell, E. R. (1989). Young children's ability to differentiate appearance-reality and level 2 perspectives in the tactile modality. *Child Development*, *60*, 201–213.

Flavell, J. H., Green, F. L., & Flavell, E. R. (1995). Young children's knowledge about thinking. *Monographs of the Society for Research in Child Development*, *60*(1, Serial No. 243).

Fleming, C. B., Guttmannova, K., Cambron, C., Rhew, I. C., Oesterle, S., Miech, R. A., . . . al., et. (2016). Examination of the divergence in trends for adolescent marijuana use and marijuana-specific risk factors in Washington State. *Journal of Adolescent Health*, *59*(3), 269–275. http://doi.org/10.1016/j.jadohealth.2016.05.008

Fletcher, A. C., Darling, N. E., Steinberg, L., & Dornbusch, S. (1995). The company they keep: Relation of adolescents' adjustment and behavior to their friends' perceptions of authoritative parenting in the social network. *Developmental Psychology*, *31*, 300–310.

Fletcher, G. E., Zach, T., Pramanik, A. K., & Ford, S. P. (2012). Multiple births. Retrieved from http://emedicine.medscape.com/article/977234-overview#a0199

Fletcher, J. M. (2012). Classification and identification of learning disabilities. Learning about learning disabilities. In B. Wong & D. L. Butler (Eds.), *Learning About Learning Disabilities*. Academic Press.

Fletcher, L. C. B., Burke, K. E., Caine, P. L., Rinne, N. L., Braniff, C. A., Davis, H. R., . . . Packer, C. (2013). Diagnosing Alzheimer's disease: Are we any nearer to useful biomarker-based, non-invasive tests? *GMS Health Technology Assessment*, *9*, Doc01. http://doi.org/10.3205/hta000107

Flieller, A. (1999). Comparison of the development of formal thought in adolescent cohorts aged 10 to 15 (1967-1996. *Developmental Psychology*, *35*(4), 1048.

Flink, L. E., Sciacca, R. R., Bier, M. L., Rodriguez, J., & Giardina, E.-G. V. (2013). Women at risk for cardiovascular disease Lack Knowledge of Heart Attack Symptoms. *Clinical Cardiology*, *36*(3), 133–138. http://doi.org/10.1002/clc.22092

Floccia, C., Christophe, A., & Bertoncini, J. (1997). High-amplitude sucking and newborns: The quest for underlying mechanisms. *Journal of Experimental Child Psychology*, *64*, 175–198.

Floyd, F. J., & Bakeman, R. (2006). Coming-out across the life course: Implications of age and historical context. *Archives of Sexual Behavior*, *35*(3), 287–296. http://doi.org/10.1007/s10508-006-9022-x

Flynn, E. (2016). *What is the NFL's concussion protocol?* Retrieved from https://www.si.com/nfl/nfl-concussion-protocol-policy-history

Flynn, J. (2008). Still a question of black vs white? In *New Scientist* (Vol. 199, pp. 48–50). Reed Business Information Limited (New Scientist).

Flynn, J. R. (1984). The mean IQ of Americans: Massive gains 1932 to 1978. *Psychological Bulletin*, *95*(1), 29–51. http://doi.org/10.1037/0033-2909.95.1.29

Flynn, J. R. (2012). *Are we getting smarter?* Cambridge: Cambridge University Press. http://doi.org/10.1017/CBO9781139235679

Flynn, J. R., & Rossi-Casé, L. (2012). IQ gains in Argentina between 1964 and 1998. *Intelligence*, *40*(2), 145–150. http://doi.org/10.1016/j.intell.2012.01.006

Flynn, J. R., & Weiss, L. G. (2007). American IQ gains from 1932 to 2002: The WISC subtests and educational progress. *International Journal of Testing*, *7*(2), 209–224.

Fogel, A. (2007). *Infancy: Infant, family, and society* (7th ed.). Cornwall-on-Hudson, NY: Sloan Educational.

Fonagy, P., & Target, M. (2000). The place of psychodynamic theory in developmental psychopathology. *Development & Psychopathology*, *12*(3), 407–425.

Font, S. A., & Berger, L. M. (2014). Child maltreatment and children's developmental trajectories in early to middle childhood. *Child Development*, *86*(2), 536–556. http://doi.org/10.1111/cdev.12322

Food and Agriculture Organization of the United Nations. (2009). *Summary of world food and agricultural statistics*. Rome, Italy: Author.

Ford, C. S., & Beach, F. A. (1951). *Patterns of sexual behavior*. Retrieved from http://psycnet.apa.org/psycinfo/1951-07882-000

Ford, D. Y. (2008). Intelligence testing and cultural diversity: The need for alternative instruments, policies, and procedures. In J. L. VanTassel-Baska (Ed.), *Alternative assessments with gifted and talented students* (pp. 107–128). Waco, TX: Prufrock Press.

Forestell, C. A. (2016). The development of flavor perception and acceptance: The roles of nature and nurture. *Nestle Nutrition Institute Workshop Series*, *85*, 135–143. http://doi.org/10.1159/000439504

Fortenberry, J. D. (2013). Puberty and adolescent sexuality. *Hormones and Behavior*, *64*(2), 280–7. http://doi.org/10.1016/j.yhbeh.2013.03.007

Foshee, V. A., McNaughton Reyes, H. L., Vivolo-Kantor, A. M., Basile, K. C., Chang, L.-Y., Faris, R., & Ennett, S. T. (2014). Bullying as a longitudinal predictor of adolescent dating violence. *The Journal of Adolescent Health*, *55*(3), 439–444. http://doi.org/10.1016/j.jadohealth.2014.03.004

Foshee, V. A., McNaughton Reyes, L., Tharp, A. T., Chang, L.-Y., Ennett, S. T., Simon, T. R., . . . Suchindran, C. (2015). Shared longitudinal predictors of physical peer and dating violence. *The Journal of Adolescent Health*, *56*(1), 106–112. http://doi.org/10.1016/j.jadohealth.2014.08.003

Fouts, H. N. (2008). Father involvement with young children among the Aka and Bofi foragers. *Cross-Cultural Research: The Journal of Comparative Social Science*, *42*(3), 290–312. http://doi.org/10.1177/1069397108317484

Fowler, P. J., Tompsett, C. J., Braciszewski, J. M., Jacques-Tiura, A. J., & Baltes, B. B. (2009). Community violence: A meta-analysis on the effect of exposure and mental health outcomes of children and adolescents. *Development and Psychopathology*, *21*(1), 227–259. http://doi.org/10.1017/s0954579409000145

Fox, K. A., & Saade, G. (2012). Fetal blood sampling and intrauterine transfusion. *NeoReviews*, *13*(11), e661–e669. http://doi.org/10.1542/neo.13-11-e661

Fox, S. E., Levitt, P., & Nelson, C. A. (2010). How the timing and quality of early experiences influence the development of brain architecture. *Child Development*, *81*(1), 28–40. http://doi.org/10.1111/j.1467-8624.2009.01380.x

Fracasso, M. P., & Busch-Rossnagel, N. A. (1992). Children and parents of Hispanic origin. In M. P. Procidano & C. B. Fisher (Eds.), *Families: A handbook for school professionals* (pp. 83–98). New York, NY: Teachers College Press.

Fradkin, C., Wallander, J. L., Elliott, M. N., Tortolero, S., Cuccaro, P., & Schuster, M. A. (2015). Associations between socioeconomic status and obesity in diverse, young adolescents: Variation across race/ethnicity and gender. *Health Psychology*, *34*(1), 1–9. http://doi.org/10.1037/hea0000099

Frahsek, S., Mack, W., Mack, C., Pfalz-Blezinger, C., & Knopf, M. (2010). Assessing different aspects of pretend play within a play setting: Towards a standardized assessment of pretend play in young children. *British Journal of Developmental Psychology*, *28*(2), 331–345. http://doi.org/10.1348/026151009x413666

Fraley, R. C., Roisman, G. I., Booth-LaForce, C., Owen, M. T., & Holland, A. S. (2013). Interpersonal and genetic origins of adult attachment styles: A longitudinal study from infancy to early adulthood. *Journal of Personality and Social Psychology*, *104*(5), 817–838. http://doi.org/10.1037/a0031435

Franić, S., Dolan, C. V., Broxholme, J., Hu, H., Zemojtel, T., Davies, G. E., . . . Boomsma, D. I. (2015). Mendelian and polygenic inheritance of intelligence: A common set of causal genes? Using next-generation sequencing to examine the effects of 168 intellectual disability genes on normal-range intelligence. *Intelligence*, *49*, 10–22. http://doi.org/10.1016/j.intell.2014.12.001

Franić, S., Groen-Blokhuis, M. M., Dolan, C. V, Kattenberg, M. V, Pool, R., Xiao, X., . . . Boomsma, D. I. (2015). Intelligence: Shared genetic basis between Mendelian disorders and a polygenic trait. *European Journal of Human Genetics*, *23*(10), 1378–1383. http://doi.org/10.1038/ejhg.2015.3

Frank, D. A., Augustyn, M., Knight, W. G., Pell, T., & Zuckerman, B. (2001). Growth, development, and behavior in early childhood following prenatal cocaine exposure: A systematic review. *Journal of the American Medical Association*, *285*, 1613–1625.

Frank, M. C., Vul, E., & Johnson, S. P. (2009). Development of infants' attention to faces during the first year. *Cognition*, *110*(2), 160–170. http://doi.org/10.1016/j.cognition.2008.11.010

Frankel, L. L. (2002). "I've never thought about it": Contradictions and taboos surrounding American males' experiences of first ejaculation (semenarche). *Journal of Men's Studies*, *11*(1), 37–54.

Frankenhuis, W. E., Panchanathan, K., & Clark Barrett, H. (2013). Bridging developmental systems theory and evolutionary psychology using dynamic optimization. *Developmental Science*, *16*(4), 584–598. http://doi.org/10.1111/desc.12053

Franks, P. W., & Pare, G. (2016). Putting the genome in context: Gene-environment interactions in type 2 diabetes. *Current Diabetes Reports*, *16*(7), 57. http://doi.org/10.1007/s11892-016-0758-y

Frank-Wilson, A. W., Farthing, J. P., Chilibeck, P. D., Arnold, C. M., Davison, K. S., Olszynski, W. P., & Kontulainen, S. A. (2016). Lower leg muscle density is independently associated with fall status in community-dwelling older adults. *Osteoporosis International*, *27*(7), 2231–2240. http://doi.org/10.1007/s00198-016-3514-x

Frascarolo, F. (2004). Paternal involvement in child caregiving and infant sociability. *Infant Mental Health Journal*, *25*(6), 509–521. http://doi.org/10.1002/imhj.20023

Frawley, T. J. (2008). Gender schema and prejudicial recall: How children misremember, fabricate, and distort gendered picture book information. *Journal of Research in Childhood Education*, *22*(3), 291–303.

Frederick, C. B., Snellman, K., & Putnam, R. D. (2014). Increasing socioeconomic disparities in adolescent obesity. *Proceedings of the National Academy of Sciences, 111*(4), 1338–1342. http://doi.org/10.1073/pnas.1321355110

Frederickson, N., Petrides, K. V., & Simmonds, E. (2012). Trait emotional intelligence as a predictor of socioemotional outcomes in early adolescence. *Personality and Individual Differences, 52*(3), 323–328. http://doi.org/10.1016/j.paid.2011.10.034

Freed, P. J., Yanagihara, T. K., Hirsch, J., & Mann, J. J. (2009). Neural mechanisms of grief regulation. *Biological Psychiatry, 66*(1), 33–40. https://doi.org/10.1016/j.biopsych.2009.01.019

Freedman, A. L. (2016). The circumcision debate: Beyond benefits and risks. *Pediatrics, 137*(5). http://doi.org/10.1542/peds.2016-0594

Freeman, J., & Simonsen, B. (2014). Examining the impact of policy and practice interventions on high school dropout and school completion rates: A systematic review of the literature. *Review of Educational Research.* http://doi.org/10.3102/0034654314554431

Freeman, N. (2007). Preschoolers' perceptions of gender appropriate toys and their parents' beliefs about genderized behaviors: Miscommunication, mixed messages, or hidden truths? *Early Childhood Education Journal, 34*(5), 357–366. http://doi.org/10.1007/s10643-006-0123-x

Freier, L., Cooper, R. P., & Mareschal, D. (2015). Preschool children's control of action outcomes. *Developmental Science.* http://doi.org/10.1111/desc.12354

Freund, A. M., & Baltes, P. B. (2007). Toward a theory of successful aging: Selection, optimization, and compensation. In R. Fernández-Ballesteros (Ed.), *Geropsychology: European perspectives for an aging world* (pp. 239–254). Ashland, OH: Hogrefe & Huber.

Freund, A. M., & Ritter, J. O. (2009). Midlife crisis: A debate. *Gerontology, 55*(5), 582–591. http://doi.org/10.1159/000227322

Freund, A. M., & Smith, J. (1999). Methodological comment: Temporal stability of older person's spontaneous self-definition. *Experimental Aging Research, 25*(1), 95.

Frey, N. (2005). Retention, social promotion, and academic redshirting: What do we know and need to know? *Remedial and Special Education, 26*(6), 332–346.

Friederici, A. D. (2006). The neural basis of language development and its impairment. *Neuron, 52*(6), 941–952.

Friedlmeier, W., Çorapçi, F., & Benga, O. (2015). Early emotional development in cultural perspective. In L. Arnett Jensen (Ed.), *The Oxford handbook of human development and culture.* London, UK: Oxford University Press. http://doi.org/10.1093/oxfordhb/9780199948550.013.9

Friedlmeier, W., Corapci, F., & Cole, P. M. (2011). Emotion socialization in cross-cultural perspective. *Social and Personality Psychology Compass, 5*(7), 410–427. http://doi.org/10.1111/j.1751-9004.2011.00362.x

Friedman, H. S., & Kern, M. L. (2014). Personality, well-being, and health. *Annual Review of Psychology, 65*(1), 719–742. http://doi.org/10.1146/annurev-psych-010213-115123

Friedman, S. L., & Scholnick, E. K. (1987). Setting the stage: An integrative framework for understanding research on planning. In S. L. Friedman & E. K. Scholnick (Eds.), *The developmental psychology of planning: Why, how, and when do we plan?* (pp. 3–22). Mahwah, NJ: Lawrence Erlbaum.

Friedrich, W. N. (2003). Studies of sexuality of nonabused children. In J. Bancroft (Ed.),

Sexual development in childhood (p. 107–120). Bloomington: Indiana University Press.

Frisch, M., Aigrain, Y., Barauskas, V., Bjarnason, R., Boddy, S.-A., Czauderna, P., . . . Wijnen, R. (2013). Cultural bias in the AAP's *2012 Technical Report and Policy Statement on Male Circumcision. Pediatrics, 131*(4). Retrieved from http://pediatrics.aappublications.org/content/131/4/796.short

Frisch, M., & Earp, B. D. (2016). Circumcision of male infants and children as a public health measure in developed countries: A critical assessment of recent evidence. *Global Public Health,* 1–16. http://doi.org/10.1080/17441692.2016.1184292

Frodi, A. M., Lamb, M. E., Hwang, C.-P., & Frodi, M. (1983). Father-mother infant interaction in traditional and nontraditional Swedish families: A longitudinal study. *Alternative Lifestyles, 5*(3), 142–163. http://doi.org/10.1007/bf01091325

Frost, D. M., Meyer, I. H., & Hammack, P. L. (2015). Health and well-being in emerging adults' same-sex relationships: Critical questions and directions for research in developmental science. *Emerging Adulthood, 3*(1), 3–13. http://doi.org/10.1177/2167696814535915

Frostad, P., Pijl, S. J., & Mjaavatn, P. E. (2014). Losing all interest in school: Social participation as a predictor of the intention to leave upper secondary school early. *Scandinavian Journal of Educational Research, 59*(1), 110–122. http://doi.org/10.1080/00313831.2014.904420

Fry, A. F., & Hale, S. (1996). Processing speed, working memory, and fluid intelligence: Evidence for a developmental cascade. *Psychological Science, 7,* 237–241.

Fry, C. L. (1985). Culture, behavior, and aging in the comparative perspective. In J. E. Birren & K. W. Schaie (Eds.), *Handbook of the psychology of aging* (2nd ed., pp. 216–244). New York, NY: Van Nostrand Reinhold.

Fry, P. S. (1995). A conceptual model of socialization and agentic trait factors that mediate the development of reminiscence styles and their health outcomes. In B. K. Haight & J. D. Webster (Eds.), *The art and science of reminiscing: Theory, research, methods, and applications* (pp. 49–60). Philadelphia, PA: Taylor & Francis.

Fry, R. (2016). *For first time in modern era, living with parents edges out other living arrangements for 18- to 34-year-olds.* Retrieved from http://www.pewsocialtrends.org/2016/05/24/for-first-time-in-modern-era-living-with-parents-edges-out-other-living-arrangements-for-18-to-34-year-olds/

Fryar, C. D., Carroll, M. D., & Ogden, C. L. (2016). Prevalence of overweight, obesity, and extreme obesity among adults aged 20 and over: United States, 1960–1962 through 2013–2014. *Health EStats.* Retrieved from https://www.cdc.gov/nchs/data/hestat/obesity_adult_13_14/obesity_adult_13_14.pdf

Fuchs, A.-R., Romero, R., Keefe, D., Parra, M., Oyarzun, E., & Behnke, E. (1991). Oxytocin secretion and human parturition: Pulse frequency and duration increase during spontaneous labor in women. *American Journal of Obstetrics and Gynecology, 165*(4), 1515–1523. https://doi.org/10.1016/S0002-9378(12)90793-0

Fuchs, L. S., Malone, A. S., Schumacher, R. F., Namkung, J., & Wang, A. (2016). Fraction intervention for students with mathematics difficulties: Lessons learned from five randomized controlled trials. *Journal of Learning Disabilities.* http://doi.org/10.1177/0022219416677249

Fuglset, T. S., Landrø, N. I., Reas, D. L., & Rø, Ø. (2016). Functional brain alterations in anorexia nervosa: A scoping review. *Journal of Eating Disorders, 4,* 32. http://doi.org/10.1186/s40337-016-0118-y

Fuhrmann, D., Knoll, L. J., & Blakemore, S.-J. (2015). Adolescence as a sensitive period of brain development. *Trends in Cognitive Sciences, 19*(10), 558–566. http://doi.org/10.1016/j.tics.2015.07.008

Fuligni, A. J., Witkow, M., & Garcia, C. (2005). Ethnic identity and the academic adjustment of adolescents from Mexican, Chinese, and European backgrounds. *Developmental Psychology, 41*(5), 799–811. Retrieved from afuligni@ucla.edu

Fulton, G., Madden, C., & Minichiello, V. (1996). The social construction of anticipatory grief. *Social Science & Medicine, 43*(9), 1349–1358. http://doi.org/10.1016/0277-9536(95)00447-5

Fulton, R., & Gottesman, D. J. (1980). Anticipatory grief: A psychosocial concept reconsidered. *The British Journal of Psychiatry, 137*(1), 45–54. http://doi.org/10.1192/bjp.137.1.45

Furby, L., & Beyth-Marom, R. (1992). Risk taking in adolescence: A decision-making perspective. *Developmental Review, 12*(1), 1–44.

Furman, W. (2002). The emerging field of adolescent romantic relationships. *Current Directions in Psychological Science, 11*(5), 177–180.

Furman, W., & Collibee, C. (2014). A matter of timing: Developmental theories of romantic involvement and psychosocial adjustment. *Development and Psychopathology, 26*(4), 1149–1160. http://doi.org/10.1017/S0954579414000182

Furman, W., & Shaffer, L. (2003). The role of romantic relationships in adolescent development. In P. Florsheim (Ed.), *Adolescent romantic relations and sexual behavior: Theory, research, and practical implications* (pp. 3–22). Mahwah, NJ: Lawrence Erlbaum.

Furman, W., & Shomaker, L. B. (2008). Patterns of interaction in adolescent romantic relationships: Distinct features and links to other close relationships. *Journal of Adolescence, 31*(6), 771–788. http://doi.org/10.1016/j.adolescence.2007.10.007

Furstenberg, F. (2003). Teenage childbearing as a public issue and private concern. *Annual Review of Psychology, 29,* 23–39.

Furuya-Kanamori, L., & Doi, S. A. R. (2016). Angry birds, angry children, and angry meta-analysts. *Perspectives on Psychological Science, 11*(3), 408–414. http://doi.org/10.1177/1745691616635599

Fuss, J., Auer, M. K., & Briken, P. (2015). Gender dysphoria in children and adolescents. *Current Opinion in Psychiatry, 28*(6), 430–434. http://doi.org/10.1097/YCO.0000000000000203

Gaab, E. M., Owens, G. R., & Macleod, R. D. (2013). Caregivers' estimations of their children's perceptions of death as a biological concept. *Death Studies, 37*(8), 693–703. http://doi.org/10.1080/07481187.2012.692454

Gabbard, C. P. (2012). *Lifelong motor development* (6th ed.). New York, NY: Pearson.

Gabriel, M. A. M., Alonso, C. R. P., Bértolo, J. D. L. C., Carbonero, S. C., Maestro, M. L., Pumarega, M. M., . . . Pablos, D. L. (2009). Age of sitting unsupported and independent walking in very low birth weight preterm infants with normal motor development at 2 years. *Acta Paediatrica, 98*(11), 1815–1821. http://doi.org/10.1111/j.1651-2227.2009.01475.x

Gadassi, R., Bar-Nahum, L. E., Newhouse, S., Anderson, R., Heiman, J. R., Rafaeli, E., & Janssen, E. (2015). Perceived partner responsiveness mediates the association between sexual and marital satisfaction: A daily diary study in newlywed couples. *Archives of Sexual Behavior.* http://doi.org/10.1007/s10508-014-0448-2

Gaddis, A., & Brooks-Gunn, J. (1985). The male experience of pubertal change. *Journal of Youth and Adolescence, 14*(1), 61–69.

Gaesser, B., Sacchetti, D. C., Addis, D. R., & Schacter, D. L. (2010). Characterizing age-related changes in remembering the past and imagining the future. *Psychology and Aging.* http://doi.org/10.1037/a0021054

Gagne, J. R. (2017). Self-control in childhood: A synthesis of perspectives and focus on early development. *Child Development Perspectives.* http://doi.org/10.1111/cdep.12223

Gagne, J. R., Vendlinski, M. K., & Goldsmith, H. H. (2009). The genetics of childhood temperament. In Y.-K. Kim (Ed.), *Handbook of behavior genetics* (pp. 251–267). New York, NY: Springer Science + Business Media.

Gagnon, S. G., Huelsman, T. J., Reichard, A. E., Kidder-Ashley, P., Griggs, M. S., Struby, J., & Bollinger, J. (2013). Help me play! Parental behaviors, child temperament, and preschool peer play. *Journal of Child and Family Studies, 23*(5), 872–884. http://doi.org/10.1007/s10826-013-9743-0

Gaillard, V., Barrouillet, P., Jarrold, C., & Camos, V. (2011). Developmental differences in working memory: Where do they come from? *Journal of Experimental Child Psychology, 110*(3), 469–479. http://doi.org/10.1016/j.jecp.2011.05.004

Gajdos, Z. K. Z., Henderson, K. D., Hirschhorn, J. N., & Palmert, M. R. (2010). Genetic determinants of pubertal timing in the general population. *Molecular and Cellular Endocrinology, 324*(1–2), 21–29. http://doi.org/10.1016/j.mce.2010.01.038

Galambos, N. L., Almeida, D. M., & Petersen, A. C. (1990). Masculinity, femininity, and sex role attitudes in early adolescence: Exploring gender intensification. *Child Development, 61*(6), 1905–1914. http://doi.org/10.1111/j.1467-8624.1990.tb03574.x

Galambos, N. L., Berenbaum, S. A., & McHale, S. M. (2009). Gender development in adolescence. In R. M. Lerner & L. Steinberg (Eds.), *Handbook of adolescent psychology* (Vol. 1, pp. 305–357). Hoboken, NJ: John Wiley & Sons. http://doi.org/10.1002/9780470479193.adlpsy001011

Galatzer-Levy, I. R., Mazursky, H., Mancini, A. D., & Bonanno, G. A. (2011). What we don't expect when expecting: Evidence for heterogeneity in subjective well-being in response to parenthood. *Journal of Family Psychology, 25*(3), 384–392. http://doi.org/10.1037/a0023759

Galbally, M., Lewis, A. J., van IJzendoorn, M., & Permezel, M. (2011). The role of oxytocin in mother-infant relations: A systematic review of human studies. *Harvard Review of Psychiatry, 19*(1), 1–14. https://doi.org/10.3109/10673229.2011.549771

Galek, K., Flannelly, K. J., Ellison, C. G., Silton, N. R., & Jankowski, K. R. B. (2015). Religion, meaning and purpose, and mental health. *Psychology of Religion and Spirituality, 7*(1), 1–12. http://doi.org/10.1037/a0037887

Gallagher, A. (2008). *Developing thinking with four and five year old pupils: The impact of a cognitive acceleration programme through early science skill development.* Dublin, Ireland: Dublin City University.

Gallahue, D. L., & Ozmun, J. C. (2006). *Understanding motor development: Infants, children, adolescents, adults* (6th ed.). Boston: McGraw-Hill.

Gallaway, P., Miyake, H., Buchowski, M., Shimada, M., Yoshitake, Y., Kim, A., & Hongu, N. (2017). Physical activity: A viable way to reduce the risks of mild cognitive impairment, Alzheimer's disease, and vascular dementia in older adults. *Brain Sciences, 7*(2), 22. http://doi.org/10.3390/brainsci7020022

Galler, J. R., Bryce, C. P., Waber, D., Hock, R. S., Exner, N., Eaglesfield, D., . . . Harrison, R. (2010). Early childhood malnutrition predicts depressive symptoms at ages 11–17. Journal of Child Psychology & Psychiatry, 51(7), 789–798. https://doi.org/10.1111/j.1469-7610.2010.02208.x

Galliher, R. V, Jones, M. D., & Dahl, A. (2011). Concurrent and longitudinal effects of ethnic identity and experiences of discrimination on psychosocial adjustment of Navajo adolescents. *Developmental Psychology, 47*(2), 509–526. http://doi.org/10.1037/a0021061

Gallup, G. G. (1977). Self-recognition in primates: A comparative approach to the bidirectional properties of consciousness. *American Psychologist, 2*, 329–338.

Ganger, J., & Brent, M. R. (2004). Reexamining the vocabulary spurt. *Developmental Psychology, 40*(4), 621–632.

Gans, C., & Crews, D. (1992). *Hormones, brain, and behavior: Biology of the reptiles.* Chicago: University of Chicago Press.

Gans, D., & Silverstein, M. (2006). Norms of filial responsibility for aging parents across time and generations. *Journal of Marriage & Family, 68*(4), 961–976.

Ganzini, L., Nelson, H. D., Lee, M. A., Kraemer, D. F., Schmidt, T. A., & Delorit, M. A. (2001). Oregon physicians' attitudes about and experiences with end-of-life care since passage of the Oregon Death with Dignity Act. *Journal of the American Medical Association, 285*(18), 2363.

Garcia, J. R., Reiber, C., Massey, S. G., & Merriwether, A. M. (2012). Sexual hookup culture: A review. *Review of General Psychology, 16*(2), 161–176. http://doi.org/10.1037/a0027911

Garcia, P. R. J. M., Restubog, S. L. D., Bordia, P., Bordia, S., & Roxas, R. E. O. (2015). Career optimism: The roles of contextual support and career decision-making self-efficacy. *Journal of Vocational Behavior, 88*, 10–18. http://doi.org/10.1016/j.jvb.2015.02.004

Garcia Coll, C. T. (1990). Developmental outcome of minority infants: A process-oriented look into our beginnings. *Child Development, 61*(2), 270. http://doi.org/10.1111/1467-8624.ep5878982

Gardiner, H., & Kosmitzki, C. (2018). *Lives across cultures: Cross-cultural human development* (6th ed.). Boston: Pearson.

Gardner, H. (1993). *Frames of mind: The theory of multiple intelligences.* New York: Basic Books. (original work published 1983)

Gardner, H. (1995). Reflections on multiple intelligences: Myths and messages. *Phi Delta Kappan*, 200–209.

Gardner, H. (1999). *Intelligence reframed: Multiple intelligences for the 21st century.* New York: Basic Books.

Gardner, H. (2013). *The unschooled mind: How children think and how schools should teach.* New York: Basic Books. Retrieved from http://books.google.com/books?id=4YqtMUVSsEEC&pgis=1

Gardner, H., & Moran, S. (2006). The science of multiple intelligences theory: A response to Lynn Waterhouse. *Educational Psychologist, 41*(4), 227–232. http://doi.org/10.1207/s15326985ep4104_2

Garner, P. W. (2003). Child and family correlates of toddlers' emotional and behavioral responses to a mishap. *Infant Mental Health Journal, 24*(6), 580.

Garrison, E. G., & Kobor, P. C. (2002). Weathering a political storm: A contextual perspective on a psychological research controversy. *American Psychologist, 57*(3), 165–175.

Gartstein, M. A., & Iverson, S. (2014). Attachment security: The role of infant, maternal, and contextual factors. *International Journal of Psychology & Psychological Therapy, 14*(2), 261–276.

Gartstein, M. A., Putnam, S. P., Aron, E. N., & Rothbart, M. K. (2016). *Temperament and personality.* London, UK: Oxford University Press. http://doi.org/10.1093/oxfordhb/9780199739134.013.2

Gass, M., & Dawson-Hughes, B. (2006). Preventing osteoporosis-related fractures: An overview. *American Journal of Medicine, 119*, S3–S11.

Gates, G. A., & Mills, J. H. (2005). Presbycusis. *Lancet, 366*(9491), 1111–1120. http://doi.org/10.1016/S0140-6736(05)67423-5

Gates, G. J. (2011). *How many people are lesbian, gay, bisexual and transgender?* Retrieved from https://escholarship.org/uc/item/09h684x2

Gates, G. J. (2013). *LGBT parenting in the United States.* Los Angeles, CA, CA. Retrieved from http://williamsinstitute.law.ucla.edu/wp-content/uploads/LGBT-Parenting.pdf

Gathercole, S. E. (1998). The development of memory. *Journal of Child Psychology and Psychiatry and Allied Disciplines, 39*, 3–27.

Gathercole, S. E., & Hitch, G. J. (1993). Developmental changes in short-term memory: A revised working memory perspective. In A. Collins, S. E. Gathercole, M. A. Conway, & P. E. Morris (Eds.), *Theories of memory* (pp. 189–210). Hove, England: Erlbaum.

Gathercole, S. E., Adams, A.-M. M., & Hitch, G. (1994). Do young children rehearse? An individual-differences analysis. *Memory and Cognition, 22*, 201–207.

Gathercole, S. E., Pickering, S. J., Ambridge, B., & Wearing, H. (2004). A structural analysis of working memory from 4 to 15 years of age. *Developmental Psychology, 40*, 177–190.

Gattario, K. H., Frisén, A., & Anderson-Fye, E. (2014). Body image and child well-being. In *Handbook of Child Well-Being* (pp. 2409–2436). Netherlands: . Springer.

Gavrin, J., & Chapman, C. R. (1995). Clinical management of dying patients. *Western Journal of Medicine, 163*, 268–277.

Gaylord-Harden, N. K., Dickson, D., & Pierre, C. (2016). Profiles of community violence exposure among African American youth: An examination of desensitization to violence using latent class analysis. *Journal of Interpersonal Violence, 31*(11), 2077–2101. http://doi.org/10.1177/0886260515572474

Gazzaley, A., Sheridan, M. A., Cooney, J. W., & D'Esposito, M. (2007). Age-related deficits in component processes of working memory. *Neuropsychology, 21*(5), 532–539.

Geerligs, L., Maurits, N. M., Renken, R. J., & Lorist, M. M. (2014). Reduced specificity of functional connectivity in the aging brain during task performance. *Human Brain Mapping, 35*(1), 319–30. http://doi.org/10.1002/hbm.22175

Geier, C. F. (2013). Adolescent cognitive control and reward processing: Implications for risk taking and substance use. *Hormones and Behavior, 64*(2), 333–42. http://doi.org/10.1016/j.yhbeh.2013.02.008

Geier, C. F., Terwilliger, R., Teslovich, T., Velanova, K., & Luna, B. (2010). Immaturities in reward processing and its influence on inhibitory control in adolescence. *Cerebral Cortex, 20*(7), 1613–1629. http://doi.org/10.1093/cercor/bhp225

Geier, C. F., Terwilliger, R., Teslovich, T., Velanova, K., & Luna, B. (2010). Immaturities in reward processing and its influence on inhibitory control in adolescence. *Cerebral Cortex, 20*(7), 1613–1629. http://doi.org/10.1093/cercor/bhp225

Gelman, R. (1969). Conservation acquisition: A problem of learning to attend to relevant attributes. *Journal of Experimental Child Psychology, 7*, 167–187. Gelman, R. (1972). Logical capacity of very young children: Number invariance rules. *Child Development, 43*, 75–90.

Gelman, R., & Shatz, M. (1978). Appropriate speech adjustments: The operation of conversational constraints on talk to two-year-olds. In M. Lewis & L. A. Rosenblum (Eds.), *Interaction, conversation, and the development of language* (pp. 27–61). New York: Wiley.

Gelman, R., & Shatz, M. (1978). Appropriate speech adjustments: The operation of conversational constraints on talk to two-year-olds. In M. Lewis & L. A. Rosenblum (Eds.), *Interaction, conversation, and the development of language* (pp. 27–61). New York: Wiley.

Gelman, S. A., & Opfer, J. E. (2002). Development of the animate-inanimate distinction. In U. Goswami (Ed.), *Blackwell handbook of childhood cognitive development* (pp. 151–166). Malden, MA: Blackwell.

Gelman, S. H., & Gottfried, G. M. (1996). Children's causal explanations of animate and inanimate motion. *Child Development*, 67, 1970–1987.

Genesee, F. (2006). Bilingual first language acquisition in perspective. In P. McCardle & E. Hoff (Eds.), *Childhood bilingualism: Research on infancy through school age* (pp. 45–67). Clevedon, UK:

Genesee, F., & Nicoladis, E. (2007). Bilingual first language acquisition. In E. Hoff & M. Shatz (Eds.), *Blackwell Handbook of Language Development* (pp. 324–344). Oxford, U. K: Blackwell.

Gentile, B., Twenge, J. M., & Campbell, W. K. (2010). Birth cohort differences in self-esteem, 1988–2008: A cross-temporal meta-analysis. *Review of General Psychology*, 14(3), 261–268. http://doi.org/10.1037/a0019919

Gentile, D. A., Li, D., Khoo, A., Prot, S., & Anderson, C. A. (2014). Mediators and moderators of long-term effects of violent video games on aggressive behavior. *JAMA Pediatrics*, 168(5), 450. http://doi.org/10.1001/jamapediatrics.2014.63

Gentle-Genitty, C. (2009). Best practice program for low-income African American students transitioning from middle to high school. *Children & Schools*, 31(2), 109–117.

George, L. K., Ellison, C. G., & Larson, D. B. (2002). Explaining the relationships between religious involvement and health. *Psychological Inquiry*, 13(3), 190–200. http://doi.org/10.1207/S15327965PLI1303_04

Georgsdottir, I., Haraldsson, A., & Dagbjartsson, A. (2013). Behavior and well-being of extremely low birth weight teenagers in Iceland. *Early Human Development*, 89(12), 999–1003. http://doi.org/10.1016/j.earlhumdev.2013.08.018

Gerber, J. S., & Offit, P. A. (2009). Vaccines and autism: A tale of shifting hypotheses. *Clinical Infectious Diseases*, 48(4), 456–461. http://doi.org/10.1086/596476

Gerritsen, L., Wang, H.-X., Reynolds, C. A., Fratiglioni, L., Gatz, M., & Pedersen, N. L. (2017). Influence of negative life events and widowhood on risk for dementia. *The American Journal of Geriatric Psychiatry*, 25(7), 766–778. http://doi.org/10.1016/j.jagp.2017.02.009

Gershkoff-Stowe, L. (2002). Object naming, vocabulary growth, and the development of word retrieval abilities. *Journal of Memory & Language*, 46(4), 665.

Gershkoff-Stowe, L., & Hahn, E. R. (2007). Fast mapping skills in the developing lexicon. *Journal of Speech, Language & Hearing Research*, 50(3), 682–697.

Gerstorf, D., Ram, N., Hoppmann, C., Willis, S. L., & Schaie, K. W. (2011). Cohort differences in cognitive aging and terminal decline in the Seattle Longitudinal Study. *Developmental Psychology*, 47(4), 1026–41. http://doi.org/10.1037/a0023426

Gervain, J., & Mehler, J. (2010). Speech perception and language acquisition in the first year of life. *Annual Review of Psychology*, 61, 191–218. http://doi.org/10.1146/annurev.psych.093008.100408

Gervain, J., Macagno, F., Cogoi, S., Peña, M., & Mehler, J. (2008). The neonate brain detects speech structure. *Proceedings of the National Academy of Sciences of the United States of America*, 105(37), 14222–14227. http://doi.org/10.1073/pnas.0806530105

Gest, S. D., Davidson, A. J., Rulison, K. L., Moody, J., & Welsh, J. A. (2007). Features of groups and status hierarchies in girls' and boys' early adolescent peer networks. *New Directions for Child & Adolescent Development*, 2007(118), 43–60.

Gettler, L. T., & McKenna, J. J. (2011). Evolutionary perspectives on mother-infant sleep proximity and breastfeeding in a laboratory setting. *American Journal of Physical Anthropology*, 144(3), 454–462. http://doi.org/10.1002/ajpa.21426

Geurts, T., Van Tilburg, T. G., & Poortman, A.-R. (2012). The grandparent-grandchild relationship in childhood and adulthood: A matter of continuation? *Personal Relationships*, 19(2), 267–278. http://doi.org/10.1111/j.1475-6811.2011.01354.x

Ghassabian, A., Sundaram, R., Bell, E., Bello, S. C., Kus, C., & Yeung, E. (2016). Gross motor milestones and subsequent development. *PEDIATRICS*, 138(1), e20154372–e20154372. http://doi.org/10.1542/peds.2015-4372

Ghosh, J. K. C., Wilhelm, M. H., Dunkel-Schetter, C., Lombardi, C. A., & Ritz, B. R. (2010). Paternal support and preterm birth, and the moderation of effects of chronic stress: A study in Los Angeles County mothers. *Archives of Women's Mental Health*, 13(4), 327–338. http://doi.org/10.1007/s00737-009-0135-9

Gibbs, J. C. (2003). *Moral development and reality: Beyond the theories of Kohlberg and Hoffman.* Thousand Oaks, CA: Sage.

Gibbs, J. C., Basinger, K. S., Grime, R. L., & Snarey, J. R. (2007). Moral judgment development across cultures: Revisiting Kohlberg's universality claims. *Developmental Review*, 27(4), 443–500. http://doi.org/10.1016/j.dr.2007.04.001

Gibson, E. J., & Pick, A. D. (2000). *An ecological approach to perceptual learning and development.* New York: Oxford University Press.

Gibson, E. J., & Walk, R. D. (1960). The "visual cliff." *Scientific American*, 202, 64–71.

Gibson, J. (1979). *The ecological approach to visual perception.* New York: Houghton, Mifflin. Retrieved from http://psycnet.apa.org/psycinfo/2003-00063-000

Gibson, L. Y., Byrne, S. M., Blair, E., Davis, E. A., Jacoby, P., & Zubrick, S. R. (2008). Clustering of psychosocial symptoms in overweight children. *Australian & New Zealand Journal of Psychiatry*, 42(2), 118–125. http://doi.org/10.1080/00048670701787560

Giedd, J. N., Lalonde, F. M., Celano, M. J., White, S. L., Wallace, G. L., Lee, N. R., & Lenroot, R. K. (2009). Anatomical brain magnetic resonance imaging of typically developing children and adolescents. *Journal of the American Academy of Child & Adolescent Psychiatry*, 48(5), 465–470. http://doi.org/10.1097/CHI.0b013e31819f215

Giedd, J. N., Raznahan, A., Mills, K. L., Lenroot, R. K., Evans, A., Kim, S., . . . Herbert, M. (2012). Review: Magnetic resonance imaging of male/female differences in human adolescent brain anatomy. *Biology of Sex Differences*, 3(1), 19. https://doi.org/10.1186/2042-6410-3-19

Gila, A., Castro, J., Cesena, J., & Toro, J. (2005). Anorexia nervosa in male adolescents: Body image, eating attitudes and psychological traits. *Journal of Adolescent Health*, 36, 221–226.

Gilbert, L. A., & Kearney, L. K. (2006). Sex, gender, and dual-earner families: Implications and applications for career counseling for women.

In W. B. Walsh & M. J. Heppner (Eds.), *Handbook of career counseling for women* (2nd ed., pp. 193–217). Mahwah, NJ: Lawrence Erlbaum.

Gilbert, R., & Constantine, K. (2005). When strength can't last a lifetime: Vocational challenges of male workers in early and middle adulthood. *Men and Masculinities*, 7(4), 424–433. http://doi.org/10.1177/1097184X03257582

Gilbert, S. F. (2001). Ecological developmental biology: Developmental biology meets the real world. *Developmental Biology*, 233, 1–12.

Gilbert, S. F. (2001). Ecological developmental biology: Developmental biology meets the real world. *Developmental Biology*, 233, 1–12.

Gil-Cazorla, R., Shah, S., & Naroo, S. A. (2015). A review of the surgical options for the correction of presbyopia. *The British Journal of Ophthalmology*, bjophthalmol-2015-306663-. http://doi.org/10.1136/bjophthalmol-2015-306663

Gillespie, B. J., Lever, J., Frederick, D., & Royce, T. (2015). Close adult friendships, gender, and the life cycle. *Journal of Social and Personal Relationships*, 32(6), 709–736. http://doi.org/10.1177/0265407514546977

Gilliard, J. L., & Moore, R. A. (2007). An investigation of how culture shapes curriculum in early care and education programs on a Native American Indian reservation. *Early Childhood Education Journal*, 34(4), 251–258. http://doi.org/10.1007/s10643-006-0136-5

Gilligan, C. (1982). *In a different voice: Psychological theory and women's development.* Cambridge, MA: Harvard University Press.

Gilligan, C., & Attanucci, J. (1988). Two moral orientations: Gender differences and similarities. *Merrill-Palmer Quarterly*, 34(3), 223–237.

Gilmore, C. K., McCarthy, S. E., & Spelke, E. S. (2010). Non-symbolic arithmetic abilities and mathematics achievement in the first year of formal schooling. *Cognition*, 115(3), 394–406. http://doi.org/10.1016/j.cognition.2010.02.002

Gilmour, H. (2007). Physically active Canadians. *Health Reports*, 18(3), 45–65.

Gini, G., & Pozzoli, T. (2009). Association between bullying and psychosomatic problems: A meta-analysis. *Pediatrics*, 123(3), 1059–1065. http://doi.org/10.1542/peds.2008-1215

Ginsburg, H. P. (1998). Mathematics learning disabilities: A view from developmental psychology. In D. P. Rivera (Ed.), *Mathematics education for students with learning disabilities* (pp. 33–58). Austin, TX: Pro-Ed.

Ginsburg, H. P., Pappas, S., & Seo, K. H. (2001). Everyday mathematical knowledge: Asking young children what is developmentally appropriate. In S. L. Golbeck (Ed.), *Psychological perspectives on early childhood education: Reframing dilemmas in research and practice* (pp. 181–219). Mahwah, NJ: Lawrence Erlbaum.

Ginsburg, K. R. (2007). The importance of play in promoting healthy child development and maintaining strong parent-child bonds. *Pediatrics*, 119(1), 182–191.

Giofrè, D., Mammarella, I. C., & Cornoldi, C. (2013). The structure of working memory and how it relates to intelligence in children. *Intelligence*, 41(5), 396–406. http://doi.org/10.1016/j.intell.2013.06.006

Gioia, K. A., & Tobin, R. M. (2010). Role of sociodramatic play in promoting self-regulation. In C. E. Schaefer (Ed.), *Play therapy for preschool children* (pp. 181–198). Washington, DC: American Psychological Association. http://doi.org/10.1037/12060-009

Giordano, P. C., Longmore, M. A., & Manning, W. D. (2006). Gender and the meanings of adolescent romantic relationships: A focus on boys. *American Sociological Review*, 71(2), 260–287.

Giordano, P. C., Phelps, K. D., Manning, W. D., & Longmore, M. A. (2008). Adolescent academic achievement and romantic relationships. *Social Science Research*, 37(1), 37–54. http://doi.org/10.1016/j.ssresearch.2007.06.004

Giordano, P. C., Soto, D. A., Manning, W. D., & Longmore, M. A. (2010). The characteristics of romantic relationships associated with teen dating violence. *Social Science Research*, 39(6), 863–874. http://doi.org/10.1016/j.ssresearch.2010.03.009

Giskes, K., van Lenthe, F., Avendano-Pabon, M., & Brug, J. (2011). A systematic review of environmental factors and obesogenic dietary intakes among adults: Are we getting closer to understanding obesogenic environments? *Obesity Reviews*, 12, e95–e106. http://doi.org/10.1111/j.1467-789X.2010.00769.x

Gjersoe, N. L., Hall, E. L., & Hood, B. (2015). Children attribute mental lives to toys when they are emotionally attached to them. *Cognitive Development*, 34, 28–38. http://doi.org/10.1016/j.cogdev.2014.12.002

Glaser, B. G., & Strauss, A. L. (1968). *Time for dying.* Chicago, IL: Aldine Publishing Company.

Glasgow, K. L., Dornbusch, S. M., Troyer, L., Steinberg, L., & Ritter, P. L. (1997). Parenting styles, adolescents' attributions, and educational outcomes in nine heterogeneous high schools. *Child Development*, 68(3), 507. http://doi.org/10.2307/1131675

Glass, T. A., Mendes De Leon, C. F., Bassuk, S. S., & Berkman, L. F. (2006). Social engagement and depressive symptoms in late life. *Journal of Aging & Health*, 16(4), 604–628.

Glasson, E. J., Dye, D. E., & Bittles, A. H. (2014). The triple challenges associated with age-related comorbidities in Down syndrome. *Journal of Intellectual Disability Research*, 58(4), 393–398. http://doi.org/10.1111/jir.12026

Glenn, N. D., & Marquardt, E. (2001). *Hooking up, hanging out, and hoping for Mr. Right : College women on dating and mating today.* Institute for American Values. Retrieved from https://eric.ed.gov/?id=ED461344

Glennen, S. (2002). Language development and delay in internationally adopted infants and toddlers: A review. *American Journal of Speech-Language Pathology*, 11, 333–339.

Glennen, S. (2014). A longitudinal study of language and speech in children who were internationally adopted at different ages. *Language, Speech, and Hearing Services in Schools*, 45(3), 185–203. http://doi.org/10.1044/2014_LSHSS-13-0035

Glennen, S., & Masters, M. (2002). Typical and atypical language development in infants and toddlers adopted from Eastern Europe. *American Journal of Speech-Language Pathology*, 11, 417–433.

Gliga, T., Elsabbagh, M., Andravizou, A., & Johnson, M. (2009). Faces attract infants' attention in complex displays. *Infancy*, 14(5), 550–562. http://doi.org/10.1080/15250000903144199

Glisky, E. L. (2007). Changes in cognitive function in human aging. In D. R. Riddle (Ed.), *Brain aging: Models, methods, and mechanisms* (pp. 3–20). Boca Raton, FL: CRC Press.

Glover, V. (2011). Annual research review: Prenatal stress and the origins of psychopathology: An evolutionary perspective. *Journal of Child Psychology and Psychiatry*, 52(4), 356–367. http://doi.org/10.1111/j.1469-7610.2011.02371.x

Go, A. S., Mozaffarian, D., Roger, V. L., Benjamin, E. J., Berry, J. D., Borden, W. B., . . . Turner, M. B. (2013). Heart disease and stroke statistics–2013 update: A report from the American Heart Association. *Circulation*, 127(1), e6–e245. http://doi.org/10.1161/CIR.0b013e31828124ad

Goddings, A.-L. (2015). The role of puberty in human adolescent brain development. In J.-P. Bourguignon, J.-C. Carel, & Y. Christen (Eds.), *Brain Crosstalk in Puberty and Adolescence* (Vol. 13, pp. 75–83). Cham: Springer International Publishing. http://doi.org/10.1007/978-3-319-09168-6

Goddings, A.-L., Mills, K. L., Clasen, L. S., Giedd, J. N., Viner, R. M., & Blakemore, S.-J. (2014). The influence of puberty on subcortical brain development. *NeuroImage*, 88, 242–51. http://doi.org/10.1016/j.neuroimage.2013.09.073

Godfrey, J. R., & Lawrence, R. A. (2010). Toward optimal health: The maternal benefits of breastfeeding. *Journal of Women's Health (15409996)*, 19(9), 1597–1602. http://doi.org/10.1089/jwh.2010.2290

Godley, S. H., Passetti, L. L., & White, M. K. (2006). Employment and adolescent alcohol and drug treatment and recovery: An exploratory study. *American Journal on Addictions*, 15, 137–143.

Gogtay, N., & Thompson, P. M. (2010). Mapping gray matter development: Implications for typical development and vulnerability to psychopathology. *Brain and Cognition*, 72(1), 6–15. http://doi.org/10.1016/j.bandc.2009.08.009

Gold, E. B., Crawford, S. L., Avis, N. E., Crandall, C. J., Matthews, K. A., Waetjen, L. E., . . . Harlow, S. D. (2013). Factors related to age at natural menopause: Longitudinal analyses from SWAN. *American Journal of Epidemiology*, 178(1), 70–83. http://doi.org/10.1093/aje/kws421

Goldberg, A. E., & Perry-Jenkins, M. (2004). Division of labor and working-class women's well-being across the transition to parenthood. *Journal of Family Psychology : JFP : Journal of the Division of Family Psychology of the American Psychological Association (Division 43)*, 18(1), 225–36. http://doi.org/10.1037/0893-3200.18.1.225

Goldberg, A. E., & Perry-Jenkins, M. (2007). The division of labor and perceptions of parental roles: Lesbian couples across the transition to parenthood. *Journal of Social & Personal Relationships*, 24(2), 297–318. http://doi.org/10.1177/0265407507075415

Goldberg, W. A., & Keller, M. A. (2007). Parent-infant co-sleeping: Why the interest and concern? *Infant and Child Development*, 16(4), 331–339. http://doi.org/10.1002/icd.523

Golden, N. H., Katzman, D. K., Sawyer, S. M., Ornstein, R. M., Rome, E. S., Garber, A. K., . . . Kreipe, R. E. (2015). Update on the medical management of eating disorders in adolescents. *The Journal of Adolescent Health : Official Publication of the Society for Adolescent Medicine*. http://doi.org/10.1016/j.jadohealth.2014.11.020

Goldman, E., Stamler, J., Kleinman, K., Kerner, S., & Lewis, O. (2016). Child mental health: Recent developments with respect to risk, resilience, and interventions. In Maya Rom Korin (Ed.), *Health promotion for children and adolescents* (pp. 99–123). Boston, MA: Springer US. http://doi.org/10.1007/978-1-4899-7711-3_6

Goldman, M. S., Greenbaum, P. E., Darkes, J., Brandon, K. O., & Del Boca, F. K. (2011). How many versus how much: 52 weeks of alcohol consumption in emerging adults. *Psychology of Addictive Behaviors*, 25(1), 16–27. http://doi.org/10.1037/a0021744

Goldschmidt, L., Richardson, G. A., Willford, J. A., Severtson, S. G., & Day, N. L. (2012). School achievement in 14-year-old youths prenatally exposed to marijuana. *Neurotoxicology and Teratology*, 34(1), 161–7. http://doi.org/10.1016/j.ntt.2011.08.009

Goldsen, J., Bryan, A. E. B., Kim, H.-J., Muraco, A., Jen, S., & Fredriksen-Goldsen, K. I. (2017). Who says I do: The changing context of marriage and health and quality of life for LGBT older adults. *The Gerontologist*, 57(suppl 1), S50–S62. http://doi.org/10.1093/geront/gnw174

Goldsmith, H. H., Buss, A. H., Plomin, R., Rothbart, M. K., Thomas, A., Chess, S., . . . al. (1987). Roundtable: What is temperament? Four approaches. *Child Development*, 58, 505–529.

Goldstein, M. H., & Schwade, J. A. (2008). Social feedback to infants' babbling facilitates rapid phonological learning. *Psychological Science*, 19(5), 515–523. http://doi.org/10.1111/j.1467-9280.2008.02117.x

Goldstein, S. E., Boxer, P., & Rudolph, E. (2015). Middle school transition stress: Links with academic performance, motivation, and school experiences. *Contemporary School Psychology*, 19(1), 21–29. http://doi.org/10.1007/s40688-014-0044-4

Golinkoff, R. M., Jacquet, R. C., Hirsh-Pasek, K., & Nandakumar, R. (1996). Lexical principles may underlie the learning of verbs. *Child Development*, 67, 3101–3119.

Golomb, C., & Galasso, L. (1995). Make believe and reality: Explorations of the imaginary realm. *Developmental Psychology*, 31, 800–810.

Golombok, S., Blake, L., Slutsky, J., Raffanello, E., Roman, G. D., & Ehrhardt, A. (2017). Parenting and the adjustment of children born to gay fathers through surrogacy. *Child Development*. http://doi.org/10.1111/cdev.12728

Golombok, S., Mellish, L., Jennings, S., Casey, P., Tasker, F., & Lamb, M. E. (2014). Adoptive gay father families: Parent-child relationships and children's psychological adjustment. *Child Development*, 85(2), 456–68. http://doi.org/10.1111/cdev.12155

Golombok, S., Rust, J., Zervoulis, K., Croudace, T., Golding, J., & Hines, M. (2008). Developmental trajectories of sex-typed behavior in boys and girls: A longitudinal general population study of children aged 2.5–8 years. *Child Development*, 79(5), 1583–1593. http://doi.org/10.1111/j.1467-8624.2008.01207.x

Golub, S. (1992). *Periods: From menarche to menopause.* Newbury Park, CA: Sage.

Gombert, J. E. (1992). *Metalinguistic development.* University of Chicago Press. Retrieved from https://books.google.com/books?id=TMuhVO7LBdAC&dq=Gombert,+J.+E.+(1992).+Metalinguistic+development&lr=&source=gbs_navlinks_s

Gomes, M. J., Martinez, P. F., Pagan, L. U., Damatto, R. L., Cezar, M. D. M., Lima, A. R. R., . . . Okoshi, M. P. (2017). Skeletal muscle aging: Influence of oxidative stress and physical exercise. *Oncotarget*, 8(12), 20428–20440. http://doi.org/10.18632/oncotarget.14670

Gomez, G. B., Kamb, M. L., Newman, L. M., Mark, J., Broutet, N., & Hawkes, S. J. (2013). Untreated maternal syphilis and adverse outcomes of pregnancy: A systematic review and meta-analysis. *Bulletin of the World Health Organization*, 91(3), 217–26. http://doi.org/10.2471/BLT.12.107623

Gómez-Ortiz, O., Romera, E. M., & Ortega-Ruiz, R. (2016). Parenting styles and bullying. The mediating role of parental psychological aggression and physical punishment. *Child Abuse & Neglect*, 51, 132–143. http://doi.org/10.1016/j.chiabu.2015.10.025

Gómez-Pérez, E., & Ostrosky-Solís, F. (2006). Attention and memory evaluation across the life span: Heterogeneous effects of age and education. *Journal of Clinical and Experimental Neuropsychology*, 28(4), 477–494. http://doi.org/10.1080/13803390590949296

Gonçalves, J. T., Schafer, S. T., & Gage, F. H. (2016). Adult neurogenesis in the hippocampus: From stem cells to behavior. *Cell*, 167(4), 897–914. http://doi.org/10.1016/j.cell.2016.10.021

Göncü, A., & Gauvain, M. (2012). Sociocultural approaches to educational psychology: Theory, research, and application. In J. Harris, Karen R. Graham, Steve Urdan, Tim McCormick, Christine B. Sinatra, & Gale M. Sweller (Ed.), *APA educational psychology handbook, Vol 1: Theories, constructs, and critical issues.* (pp. 125–154). Washington, DC: American Psychological Association. http://doi.org/10.1037/13273-006

Gong, L., Parikh, S., Rosenthal, P. J., & Greenhouse, B. (2013). Biochemical and immunological mechanisms by which sickle cell trait protects against malaria. *Malaria Journal*, 12, 317. http://doi.org/10.1186/1475-2875-12-317

Goniewicz, M. L., Lingas, E. O., & Hajek, P. (2013). Patterns of electronic cigarette use and user beliefs about their safety and benefits: An internet survey. *Drug and Alcohol Review*, 32(2), 133–40. http://doi.org/10.1111/j.1465-3362.2012.00512.x

Gonzaga, G. C., Campos, B., & Bradbury, T. (2007). Similarity, convergence, and relationship satisfaction in dating and married couples. *Journal of Personality and Social Psychology*, 93(1), 34–48.

Gonzales-Backen, M. A., Bámaca-Colbert, M. Y., & Allen, K. (2016). Ethnic identity trajectories among Mexican-origin girls during early and middle adolescence: Predicting future psychosocial adjustment. *Developmental Psychology*, 52(5), 790–797. http://doi.org/10.1037/a0040193

Gonzáles-Figueroa, E., & Young, A. M. (2005). Ethnic identity and mentoring among Latinas in professional roles. *Cultural Diversity and Ethnic Minority Psychology*, 11(3), 213–226.

Good, M., & Willoughby, T. (2008). Adolescence as a sensitive period for spiritual development. *Child Development Perspectives*, 2(1), 32–37. http://doi.org/10.1111/j.1750-8606.2008.00038.x

Goodman, G. S., & Aman, C. J. (1990). Children's use of anatomically detailed dolls to recount an event. *Child Development*, 61, 1859–1871.

Goodman, G. S., Rudy, L., Bottoms, B. L., & Aman, C. (1990). Children's concerns and memory: Issues of ecological validity in the study of children's eyewitness testimony. In R. Fivush & J. A. Hudson (Eds.), *Knowing and remembering in young children* (pp. 249–284). New York: Cambridge University Press.

Goodnow, J. J., & Lawrence, J. A. (2015). Children and cultural context. In *Handbook of Child Psychology and Developmental Science* (pp. 1–41). Hoboken, NJ, USA: John Wiley & Sons, Inc. http://doi.org/10.1002/9781118963418.childpsy419

Goodvin, R., Meyer, S., Thompson, R. A., & Hayes, R. (2008). Self-understanding in early childhood: Associations with child attachment security and maternal negative affect. *Attachment & Human Development*, 10(4), 433–450. http://doi.org/10.1080/14616730802461466

Goodvin, R., Meyer, S., Thompson, R. A., & Hayes, R. (2008). Self-understanding in early childhood: Associations with child attachment security and maternal negative affect. *Attachment & Human Development*, 10(4), 433–450. http://doi.org/10.1080/14616730802461466

Goodvin, R., Thompson, R. A., & Winer, A. C. (2015). The individual child: Temperament, emotion, self, and personality. In M. Bornstein & M. Lamb (Eds.), *Developmental psychology: An advanced textbook* (pp. 377–409). Psychology Press.

Goodwin, G. P., & Johnson-Laird, P. N. (2008). Transitive and pseudo-transitive inferences. *Cognition*, 108(2), 320–352. http://doi.org/10.1016/j.cognition.2008.02.010

Goodwin, P., Mosher, W., & Chandra, A. (2010). Marriage and cohabitation In the United States: A statistical portrait based on Cycle 6 (2002) of the National Survey of Family Growth. *Vital and Health Statistics*, 23(28).

Goodwyn, S. W., & Acredolo, L. P. (1998). Encouraging symbolic gestures: A new perspective on the relationship between gesture and speech. *New Directions for Child and Adolescent Development*, 1998(79), 61–73. http://doi.org/10.1002/cd.23219987905

Goossens, L. (2001). Global versus domain-specific statuses in identity research: A comparison of two self-report measures. *Journal of Adolescence*, 24(6), 681–699. http://doi.org/10.1006/jado.2001.0438

Gopnik, A., & Choi, S. (1995). *Beyond names for things: Children's acquisition of verbs.* Hillsdale, NJ: Lawrence Erlbaum.

Gordon, A. M., & Browne, K. W. (2016). *Beginning essentials in early childhood education.* Cengage Learning: Boston, MA.

Gordon, B. N., Baker-Ward, L., & Ornstein, P. A. (2001). Children's testimony: A review of research on memory for past experiences. *Clinical Child and Family Psychology Review*, 4(2), 157–181.

Gordon-Salant, S. J. (2005). Hearing loss and aging: New research findings and clinical implications. *Journal of Rehabilitation Research & Development*, 42, 9–23. http://doi.org/101682/JRRD.2005.01.0006

Gormley Jr, W. T., Phillips, D., Adelstein, S., & Shaw, C. (2010). Head Start's comparative advantage: Myth or reality? *Policy Studies Journal*, 38(3), 397–418. http://doi.org/10.1111/j.1541-0072.2010.00367.x

Gorter, J. W., Stewart, D., Smith, M. W., King, G., Wright, M., Nguyen, T., . . . Swinton, M. (2014). Pathways toward positive psychosocial outcomes and mental health for youth with disabilities: A knowledge synthesis of developmental trajectories. *Canadian Journal of Community Mental Health*, 33(1), 45–61. http://doi.org/10.7870/cjcmh-2014-005

Gostin, L. O., MJ, P., JW, P., J, H., WG, van P., YT, Y., . . . SB, O. (2015). Law, ethics, and public health in the vaccination debates. *JAMA*, 313(11), 1099. http://doi.org/10.1001/jama.2015.1518

Gott, M. (2005). *Sexuality, sexual health and ageing.* Maidenhead, Berkshire.: Open University Press.

Gott, M., & Hinchliff, S. (2003). How important is sex in later life? The views of older people. *Social Science and Medicine*, 56, 1617–1628.

Gottesman, I. I., & Hanson, D. R. (2005). Human development: Biological and genetic processes. *Annual Review of Psychology*, 56, 263–286.

Gottfried, G. M., & Gelman, S. A. (2005). Developing domain-specific causal-explanatory frameworks: The role of insides and immanence. *Cognitive Development*, 20(1), 137–158.

Gottlieb, G. (2000). Environmental and behavioral influences on gene activity. *Current Directions in Psychological Science*, 9, 93–97.

Gottlieb, G. (2007). Probabilistic epigenesis. *Developmental Science*, 10(1), 1–11.

Gottlieb, G., Wahlsten, D., & Lickliter, R. (1998). The significance of biology for human development: A developmental psychobiological systems view. In R. M. Lerner (Ed.), *Handbook of child psychology: Vol.1 Theoretical models of human development* (5th ed., pp. 233–273). New York: Wiley.

Gottman, J., & Gottman, J. (2017). The natural principles of love. *Journal of Family Theory & Review*, 9(1), 7–26. http://doi.org/10.1111/jftr.12182

Goubet, N., & Clifton, R. K. (1998). Object and event representation in 6½-month-old infants. *Developmental Psychology*, 34, 63–76.

Goubet, N., Rattaz, C., Pierrat, V., Allémann, E., Bullinger, A., & Lequien, P. (2002). Olfactory familiarization and discrimination in preterm and full-term newborns. *Infancy*, 3(1), 53–75.

Goubet, N., Strasbaugh, K., & Chesney, J. (2007). Familiarity breeds content? Soothing effect of a familiar odor on full-term newborns. *Journal of Developmental & Behavioral Pediatrics*, 28(3), 189–194. http://doi.org/10.1097/dbp.0b013e31802d0b8d

Gould, M., Jamieson, P., & Romer, D. (2003). Media contagion and suicide among the young. *American Behavioral Scientist*, 46(9), 1269.

Gow, A. J., Corley, J., Starr, J. M., & Deary, I. J. (2012). Reverse causation in activity-cognitive ability associations: the Lothian Birth Cohort 1936. *Psychology and Aging*, 27(1), 250–5. http://doi.org/10.1037/a0024144

Gower, A. L., Lingras, K. A., Mathieson, L. C., Kawabata, Y., & Crick, N. R. (2014). The role of preschool relational and physical aggression in the transition to kindergarten: Links with social-psychological adjustment. *Early Education and Development*, 25(5), 619–640. http://doi.org/10.1080/10409289.2014.844058

Goyer, A. (2006). *Intergenerational relationships: grandparents raising grandchildren.* Washington, DC: AARP.

Goymer, P. (2007). Genes know their left from their right. *Nature Reviews Genetics*, 8(9), 652. http://doi.org/10.1038/nrg2194

Graber, J. A., Nichols, T. R., & Brooks-Gunn, J. (2010). Putting pubertal timing in developmental context: implications for prevention. *Developmental Psychobiology*, 52(3), 254–62. http://doi.org/10.1002/dev.20438

Graber, J. A., Petersen, A. C., & Brooks-Gunn, J. (1996). Pubertal processes: Methods, measures, and models. In J. A. Graber, J. Brooks-Gunn, & A. C. Petersen (Eds.), *Transitions through adolescence: Interpersonal domains and context.* (pp. 23–53). Hoboken, NJ: Lawrence Erlbaum.

Gradin, M., Eriksson, M., Schollin, J., Holmqvist, G., & Holstein, A. (2002). Pain reduction at venipuncture in newborns: Oral glucose compared with local anesthetic cream. *Pediatrics*, 110(6), 1053–1057.

Gragnani, A., Cornick, S. Mac, Chominski, V., Ribeiro de Noronha, S. M., Alves Corrêa de Noronha, S. A., & Ferreira, L. M. (2014). Review of major theories of skin aging. *Advances in Aging Research*, 3(4), 265–284. http://doi.org/10.4236/aar.2014.34036

Graham, E. K., & Lachman, M. E. (2012). Personality stability is associated with better cognitive performance in adulthood: Are the stable more able? *The Journals of Gerontology. Series B, Psychological Sciences and Social Sciences*, 67(5), 545–54. http://doi.org/10.1093/geronb/gbr149

Graham, S., Munniksma, A., & Juvonen, J. (2014). Psychosocial benefits of cross-ethnic friendships in urban middle schools. *Child Development*, 85(2), 469–83. http://doi.org/10.1111/cdev.12159

Granacher, U., Muehlbauer, T., & Gruber, M. (2012). A qualitative review of balance and strength performance in healthy older adults: Impact for testing and training. *Journal of Aging Research*, 2012, 708905. http://doi.org/10.1155/2012/708905

Granic, I., & Patterson, G. R. (2006). Toward a comprehensive model of antisocial development: A dynamic systems approach. *Psychological Review*, 113(1), 101–131. http://doi.org/10.1037/0033-295X.113.1.101

Grant, A., Dennis, N. A., & Li, P. (2014). Cognitive control, cognitive reserve, and memory in the aging bilingual brain. *Frontiers in Psychology*, 5, 1401. http://doi.org/10.3389/fpsyg.2014.01401

Gratier, M., & Devouche, E. (2011). Imitation and repetition of prosodic contour in vocal interaction at 3 months. *Developmental Psychology, 47*, 67–76.

Gravningen, K., Mitchell, K. R., Wellings, K., Johnson, A. M., Geary, R., Jones, K. G., . . . Mercer, C. H. (2017). Reported reasons for breakdown of marriage and cohabitation in Britain: Findings from the third National Survey of Sexual Attitudes and Lifestyles (Natsal-3). *PLOS ONE, 12*(3), e0174129. http://doi.org/10.1371/journal.pone.0174129

Gray, K. A., Day, N. L., Leech, S., & Richardson, G. A. (2005). Prenatal marijuana exposure: Effect on child depressive symptoms at ten years of age. *Neurotoxicology & Teratology, 27*(3), 439–448.

Gray, R. E. (1989). Adolescents' perceptions of social support after the death of a parent. *Journal of Psychosocial Oncology, 7*(3), 127–144. http://doi.org/10.1300/J077v07n03_09

Greaves, L. M., Barlow, F. K., Lee, C. H. J., Matika, C. M., Wang, W., Lindsay, C.-J., . . . Sibley, C. G. (2017). The diversity and prevalence of sexual orientation self-labels in a New Zealand national sample. *Archives of Sexual Behavior, 46*(5), 1325–1336. http://doi.org/10.1007/s10508-016-0857-5

Greeff, A. P., & Du Toit, C. (2009). Resilience in remarried families. *American Journal of Family Therapy, 37*(2), 114–126. http://doi.org/10.1080/01926180802151919

Green, J. R., Nip, I. S. B., Wilson, E. M., Mefferd, A. S., & Yunusova, Y. (2010). Lip movement exaggerations during infant-directed speech. *Journal of Speech, Language & Hearing Research, 53*(6), 1529–1542. http://doi.org/10.1044/1092-4388(2010/09-0005)

Green, M., & Elliott, M. (2010). Religion, health, and psychological well-being. *Journal of Religion and Health, 49*(2), 149–163. http://doi.org/10.1007/s10943-009-9242-1

Green, M., & Piel, J. A. (2010). *Theories of human development: A comparative approach.* New York, NY: Routledge.

Greenberg, D. J., Hillman, D., & Grice, D. (1973). Infant and stranger variables related to stranger anxiety in the first year of life. *Developmental Psychology, 9*(2), 207–212. http://doi.org/10.1037/h0035084

Greenberg, J. S. (2017). *Exploring the dimensions of human sexuality.* Burlington, MA: Jones & Bartlett.

Greenberger, E., & Steinberg, L. (1986). *When teenagers work: The psychological and social costs of adolescent employment.* New York, NY: Basic Books.

Greene, J., & Haidt, J. (2002). How (and where) does moral judgment work? *Trends in Cognitive Sciences, 6*(12), 517–523. https://doi.org/10.1016/S1364-6613(02)02011-9

Greene, K. M., & Staff, J. (2012). Teenage employment and career readiness. *New Directions for Youth Development, 2012*(134), 23–31, 7–8. http://doi.org/10.1002/yd.20012

Greene, K., & Krcmar, M. (2000). Targeting adolescent risk-taking behaviors: The contributions of egocentrism and sensation-seeking. *Journal of Adolescence, 23*, 439–462.

Greenfield, E. A., & Marks, N. F. (2006). Linked lives: Adult children' problems and their parents' psychological and relational well-being. *Journal of Marriage & Family, 68*(2), 442–454.

Greenfield, E. A., Marks, N. F., Hay, E. L., Fingerman, K. L., & Lefkowitz, E. S. (2008). The worries adult children and their parents experience for one another. *International Journal of Aging & Human Development, 67*(2), 101–127.

Greenfield, P. M., Maynard, A. E., & Childs, C. P. (2003). Historical change, cultural learning, and cognitive representation in Zinacantec Maya children. *Cognitive Development, 18*(4), 455.

Greenhouse, L. (2005). Supreme Court, 5-4, Forbids execution in juvenile Crime. (Cover story). *New York Times*, pp. A1–A14.

Greenough, W. T., & Black, J. E. (1992). Induction of brain structure by experience: Substrates for cognitive development. In M. R. Gunnar & C. A. Nelson (Eds.), *Minnesota symposia on child psychology* (pp. 155–200). Hillsdale, NJ: Lawrence Erlbaum.

Gregg, A. R., Gross, S. J., Best, R. G., Monaghan, K. G., Bajaj, K., Skotko, B. G., . . . Watson, M. S. (2013). ACMG statement on noninvasive prenatal screening for fetal aneuploidy. *Genetics in Medicine, 15*(5), 395–398. http://doi.org/10.1038/gim.2013.29

Gregg, V., Gibbs, J. C., & Basinger, K. S. (1994). Patterns of developmental delay in moral judgment by male and female delinquents. *Merrill-Palmer Quarterly, 40*(4), 538–553.

Gregory, A. M., Light-Häusermann, J. H., Rijsdijk, F., & Eley, T. C. (2009). Behavioral genetic analyses of prosocial behavior in adolescents. *Developmental Science, 12*(1), 165–174. http://doi.org/10.1111/j.1467-7687.2008.00739.x

Gremmen, M. C., Dijkstra, J. K., Steglich, C., & Veenstra, R. (2017). First selection, then influence: Developmental differences in friendship dynamics regarding academic achievement. *Developmental Psychology, 53*(7), 1356–1370. http://doi.org/10.1037/dev0000314

Gresham, F. M., & MacMillan, D. L. (1997). Social competence and affective characteristics of students with mild disabilities. *Review of Educational Research, 67*, 377–415.

Grether, J. K., Anderson, M. C., Croen, L. A., Smith, D., & Windham, G. C. (2009). Risk of autism and increasing maternal and paternal age in a large North American population. *American Journal of Epidemiology, 170*(9), 1118–1126. http://doi.org/10.1093/aje/kwp247

Greydanus, D. E., & Pratt, H. D. (2016). Caring for the dying adolescent. *Int J Child Adolesc Health, 9*(3), 281–289.

Griffin, K. W., Bang, H., & Botvin, G. J. (2010). Age of alcohol and marijuana use onset predicts weekly substance use and related psychosocial problems during young adulthood. *Journal of Substance Use, 15*(3), 174–183. http://doi.org/10.3109/14659890903013109

Griffith, S. F., & Grolnick, W. S. (2013). Parenting in Caribbean families: A look at parental control, structure, and autonomy support. *Journal of Black Psychology, 40*(2), 166–190. http://doi.org/10.1177/0095798412475085

Griggs, J., Tan, J.-P., Buchanan, A., Attar-Schwartz, S., & Flouri, E. (2010). "They"ve always been there for me': Grandparental involvement and child well-being. *Children & Society, 24*(3), 200–214. http://doi.org/10.1111/j.1099-0860.2009.00215.x

Grigorenko, E. L., & Sternberg, R. J. (2003). The nature-nurture issue. In A. Slater & G. Bremner (Eds.), *An introduction to developmental psychology* (pp. 64–91). Malden, MA: Blackwell.

Grindler, N. M., Allsworth, J. E., Macones, G. A., Kannan, K., Roehl, K. A., & Cooper, A. R. (2015). Persistent organic pollutants and early menopause in U.S. Women. *PloS One, 10*(1), e0116057. http://doi.org/10.1371/journal.pone.0116057

Groh, A. M., Fearon, R. M. P., van IJzendoorn, M. H., Bakermans-Kranenburg, M. J., & Roisman, G. I. (2016). Attachment in the early life course: Meta-analytic evidence for Its role in socioemotional development. *Child Development Perspectives.* http://doi.org/10.1111/cdep.12213

Groh, A. M., Roisman, G. I., van Ijzendoorn, M. H., Bakermans-Kranenburg, M. J., & Fearon, R. P. (2012). The significance of insecure and disorganized attachment for children's internalizing symptoms: a meta-analytic study. *Child Development, 83*(2), 591–610. http://doi.org/10.1111/j.1467-8624.2011.01711.x

Grolnick, W. S., Bridges, L. J., & Connell, J. P. (1996). Emotion regulation in two-year-olds: Strategies and emotional expression in four contexts. *Child Development, 67*, 928–941.

Groot, C., Hooghiemstra, A. M., Raijmakers, P. G. H. M., van Berckel, B. N. M., Scheltens, P., Scherder, E. J. A., . . . Ossenkoppele, R. (2016). The effect of physical activity on cognitive function in patients with dementia: A meta-analysis of randomized control trials. *Ageing Research Reviews, 25*, 13–23. http://doi.org/10.1016/j.arr.2015.11.005

Grosjean, F. (2010). *Bilingual : Life and reality.* Cambridge, MA: Harvard University Press.

Gross, A. L., & Ballif, B. (1991). Children's understanding of emotion from facial expressions and situations: A review. *Developmental Review, 11*, 368–398.

Grosse, C., & Grosse, A. (2015). Assisted suicide: Models of legal regulation in selected European countries and the case law of the European Court of Human Rights. *Medicine, Science, and the Law, 55*(4), 246–58. http://doi.org/10.1177/0025802414540636

Grossman, A. H., Park, J. Y., & Russell, S. T. (2016). Transgender youth and suicidal behaviors: Applying the interpersonal psychological theory of suicide. *Journal of Gay & Lesbian Mental Health, 20*(4), 329–349. http://doi.org/10.1080/19359705.2016.1207581

Grossman, A. W., Churchill, J. D., McKinney, B. C., Kodish, I. M., & Otte, S. L. (2003). Experience effects on brain development: Possible contributions to psychopathology. *Journal of Child Psychology & Psychiatry & Allied Disciplines, 44*(1), 33–63.

Grossman, H., Bergmann, C., & Parker, S. (2006). Dementia: A brief review. *Mount Sinai Journal of Medicine, 73*(7), 985–992

Grossmann, K. E., & Waters, E. (2005). *Attachment from infancy to adulthood: The major longitudinal studies.* New York: Guilford Press.

Grossmann, K. E., Spangler, G., Suess, G., & Unzner, L. (1985). Maternal sensitivity and newborns' orientation responses as related to quality of attachment in Northern Germany. In I. Bretherton & E. Waters (Eds.), Growing points of attachment theory and research. *Monographs of the Society for Research in Child Development, 50*(1–2, Serial No. 209), 233–256.

Grossmann, K., Grossman, K. E., Fremmer-Bombik, E., Kindler, H., Scheuerer-Englisch, H., & Zimmermann, P. (2002). The Uniqueness of the child–father attachment relationship: Fathers' sensitive and challenging play as a pivotal variable in a 16-year longitudinal study. *Social Development, 11*(3), 301–337.

Grote, H. E., & Hannan, A. J. (2007). Regulators of adult neurogenesis in The healthy and diseased brain. *Clinical & Experimental Pharmacology & Physiology, 34*(5/6), 533–545.

Grotegut, C. A., Chisholm, C. A., Johnson, L. N. C., Brown, H. L., Heine, R. P., & James, A. H. (2014). Medical and obstetric complications among pregnant women aged 45 and older. *PloS One, 9*(4), e96237. http://doi.org/10.1371/journal.pone.0096237

Grotevant, H. D., Thorbecke, W., & Meyer, M. L. (1982). An extension of Marcia's Identity Status Interview into the interpersonal domain. *Journal of Youth and Adolescence, 11*(1), 33–47. http://doi.org/10.1007/BF01537815

Grotz, C., Matharan, F., Amieva, H., Pérès, K., Laberon, S., Vonthron, A.-M., . . . Letenneur, L. (2016). Psychological transition and adjustment processes related to retirement: Influence on cognitive functioning. *Aging & Mental Health*, 1–7. http://doi.org/10.1080/13607863.2016.1220920

Grover, S., & Helliwell, J. F. (2014). *How's Life at Home? New evidence on marriage and the set point for happiness*. Retrieved from http://www.nber.org/papers/w20794

Gruber, N., Mosimann, U. P., Müri, R. M., & Nef, T. (2013). Vision and night driving abilities of elderly drivers. *Traffic Injury Prevention*, 14(5), 477–85. http://doi.org/10.1080/15389588.2012.727510

Gruber, S. A., Sagar, K. A., Dahlgren, M. K., Racine, M., & Lukas, S. E. (2011). Age of onset of marijuana use and executive function. *Psychology of Addictive Behaviors*. http://doi.org/10.1037/a0026269

Gruenenfelder-Steiger, A. E., Harris, M. A., & Fend, H. A. (2016). Subjective and objective peer approval evaluations and self-esteem development: A test of reciprocal, prospective, and long-term effects. *Developmental Psychology*, 52(10), 1563–1577. http://doi.org/10.1037/dev0000147

Grühn, D., Rebucal, K., Diehl, M., Lumley, M., & Labouvie-Vief, G. (2008). Empathy across the adult lifespan: Longitudinal and experience-sampling findings. *Emotion (Washington, D.C.)*, 8(6), 753–65. http://doi.org/10.1037/a0014123

Grundy, E., & Henretta, J. C. (2006). Between elderly parents and adult children: A new look at the intergenerational care provided by the "sandwich generation." *Ageing & Society*, 26(5), 707–722.

Grusec, J. E. (1992). Social learning theory and developmental psychology: The legacies of Robert Sears and Albert Bandura. *Developmental Psychology*, 28(5), 776–786.

Grusec, J. E., & Goodnow, J. J. (1994). Impact of parental discipline methods on the child's internalization of values: A reconceptualization of current points of view. *Developmental Psychology*, 30, 4–19.

Guarch, J., Marcos, T., Salamero, M., Gastó, C., & Blesa, R. (2008). Mild cognitive impairment: A risk indicator of later dementia, or a preclinical phase of the disease? *International Journal of Geriatric Psychiatry*, 23(3), 257–265. http://doi.org/10.1002/gps.1871

Guèvremont, A., Roos, N. P., & Brownell, M. (2007). Predictors and consequences of grade retention: Examining data from Manitoba, Canada. *Canadian Journal of School Psychology*, 22(1), 50–67.

Guiaux, M., van Tilburg, T., & van Groenou, M. B. (2007). Changes in contact and support exchange in personal networks after widowhood. *Personal Relationships*, 14(3), 457–473.

Guignard, J.-H., & Lubart, T. (2006). Is it reasonable to be creative? In J. C. Kaufman & J. Baer (Eds.), *Creativity and reason in cognitive development* (pp. 269–281). Cambridge: Cambridge University Press. http://doi.org/10.1017/CBO9780511606915.016

Guimond, S., Chatard, A., & Lorenzi-Cioldi, F. (2013). The social psychology of gender across cultures. In *The SAGE Handbook of Gender and Psychology* (pp. 216–233). SAGE Publications, Ltd. http://doi.org/10.4135/9781446269930.n14

Guo, J. Y., Isohanni, M., Miettunen, J., Jääskeläinen, E., Kiviniemi, V., Nikkinen, J., . . . Murray, G. K. (2016). Brain structural changes in women and men during midlife. *Neuroscience Letters*, 615, 107–112. http://doi.org/10.1016/j.neulet.2016.01.007

Guo, L., Yang, L., Liu, Z., & Song, T. (2005). An experimental research on the formation of primary school pupils' self-confidence. *Psychological Science (China)*, 28(5), 1068–1071.

Guo, Q., & Jacelon, C. S. (2014). An integrative review of dignity in end-of-life care. *Palliative Medicine*, 28(7), 931–940. http://doi.org/10.1177/0269216314528399

Guo, Y., Sun, S., Breit-Smith, A., Morrison, F. J., & Connor, C. M. (2015). Behavioral engagement and reading achievement in elementary-school-age children: A longitudinal cross-lagged analysis. *Journal of Educational Psychology*, 107(2), 332–347. http://doi.org/10.1037/a0037638

Gupta, P., Sturdee, D. W., & Hunter, M. S. (2006). Mid-age health in women from the Indian subcontinent (MAHWIS): General health and the experience of menopause in women. *Climacteric*, 9(1), 13–22.

Gupta, R., Chari, D., & Ali, R. (2015). Reversible dementia in elderly: Really uncommon? *Journal of Geriatric Mental Health*, 2(1), 30. http://doi.org/10.4103/2348-9995.161378

Guralnick, M. J. (2017). Early intervention for children with intellectual disabilities: An update. *Journal of Applied Research in Intellectual Disabilities*, 30(2), 211–229. http://doi.org/10.1111/jar.12233

Gurland, B. J., Wilder, D. E., Lantigua, R., Stern, Y., Chen, J., Killeffer, E. H., & Mayeux, R. (1999). Rates of dementia in three ethnoracial groups. *International Journal of Geriatric Psychiatry*, 14(6), 481–93.

Gust, D. A., Strine, T. W., Maurice, E., Smith, P., Yusuf, H., Wilkinson, M., . . . et al. (2004). Underimmunization among children: Effects of vaccine safety concerns on immunization status. *Pediatrics*, 114(1), e16–e22.

Gustafson-Larson, A., & Terry, R. D. (1992). Weight-related behaviors and concerns of fourth-grade children. *Journal of the American Dietetic Association*, 92, 818–822.

Gutchess, A. H., & Boduroglu, A. (2015). Cognition in adulthood across cultures. In L. A. Jensen (Ed.), *The Oxford handbook of human development and culture* (pp. 621–636). New York: Oxford University Press. http://doi.org/10.1093/oxfordhb/9780199948550.013.38

Gutierrez, I. T. (2009). Understanding death in cultural context: A study of Mexican children and their families, *dissertation*. Retrieved from https://www.ideals.illinois.edu/handle/2142/72102

Gutiérrez, I. T., Rosengren, K. S., & Miller, P. J. (2014a). Children's understanding of death: Toward a contextualized and integrated account: VI. Mexican American immigrants in the Centerville region: Teachers, children, and parents. *Monographs of the Society for Research in Child Development*, 79(1), 97–112. http://doi.org/10.1111/mono.12081

Gutiérrez, I. T., Rosengren, K. S., & Miller, P. J. (2014b). VI. Mexican American immigrants in the Centerville Region: Teachers, Children, And Parents. *Monographs of the Society for Research in Child Development*, 79(1), 97–112. http://doi.org/10.1111/mono.12081

Gutmann, D. L. (1985). The parental imperative revisited: Towards a developmental psychology of adulthood and later life. In *Contributions to Human Development* (pp. 31–60). S Karger AG. http://doi.org/10.1159/000411472

Guttmacher Institute. (2014). *American teens' sexual and reproductive health*. Washington, DC: Guttmacher Institute. Retrieved from http://www.guttmacher.org/pubs/fb_ATSRH.html

Guzell-Roe, J. R., Gerard, J. M., & Landry-Meyer, L. (2005). Custodial grandparents' perceived control over caregiving outcomes: Raising children the second time around. *Journal of Intergenerational Relationships*, 3(2), 43–61. http://doi.org/10.1300/J194v03n02_04

Guzman, M. R. de, Do, K.-A., & Kok, C. (2014). The cultural contexts of children's prosocial behaviors. *Faculty Publications, Department of Child, Youth, and Family Studies*. Retrieved from http://digitalcommons.unl.edu/famconfacpub/103

Gwiazda, J., & Birch, E. (2001). Perceptual development: Vision. In E. B. Goldstein (Ed.), *Blackwell's Handbook of Perception*. Oxford: Blackwell.

Ha, J.-H. (2010). The effects of positive and negative support from children on widowed older adults' psychological adjustment: A longitudinal analysis. *Gerontologist*, 50(4), 471–481.

Haas, A. P., Eliason, M., Mays, V. M., Mathy, R. M., Cochran, S. D., D'Augelli, A. R., . . . Clayton, P. J. (2011). Suicide and suicide risk in lesbian, gay, bisexual, and transgender populations: Review and recommendations. *Journal of Homosexuality*, 58(1), 10–51. http://doi.org/10.1080/00918369.2011.534038

Haberkern, K., & Szydlik, M. (2010). State care provision, societal opinion and children's care of older parents in 11 European countries. *Ageing & Society*, 30(2), 299–323.

Haden, C. A., & Fivush, F. (1996). Contextual variation in maternal conversational styles. *Merrill-Palmer Quarterly*, 42, 200–227.

Hadfield, J. (2003). Recruiting and retaining adult students. *New Directions for Student Services*, 2003(102), 17–26. http://doi.org/10.1002/ss.85

Hadiwijaya, H., Klimstra, T. A., Vermunt, J. K., Branje, S. J. T., & Meeus, W. H. J. (2017). On the development of harmony, turbulence, and independence in parent–adolescent relationships: A five-wave longitudinal study. *Journal of Youth and Adolescence*, 1–17. http://doi.org/10.1007/s10964-016-0627-7

Hadley, P. A., Rispoli, M., Fitzgerald, C., & Bahnsen, A. (2011). Predictors of morphosyntactic growth in typically developing toddlers: Contributions of parent input and child sex. *Journal of Speech Language and Hearing Research*, 54(2), 549. http://doi.org/10.1044/1092-4388(2010/09-0216)

Hadley, R., & Hanley, T. (2011). Involuntarily childless men and the desire for fatherhood. *Journal of Reproductive and Infant Psychology*, 29(1), 56–68. http://doi.org/10.1080/02646838.2010.544294

Hafstad, G. S., Abebe, D. S., Torgersen, L., & von Soest, T. (2013). Picky eating in preschool children: The predictive role of the child's temperament and mother's negative affectivity. *Eating Behaviors*, 14(3), 274–7. http://doi.org/10.1016/j.eatbeh.2013.04.001

Hagerman, R. J. (2011). Fragile X syndrome and fragile X-associated disorders. In *Handbook of neurodevelopmental and genetic disorders in children* (2nd ed., pp. 261–275). New York, NY: Guilford Press.

Hagman, J., Gardner, R. M., Brown, D. L., Gralla, J., Fier, J. M., & Frank, G. K. W. (2015). Body size overestimation and its association with body mass index, body dissatisfaction, and drive for thinness in anorexia nervosa. *Eating and Weight Disorders: Studies on Anorexia, Bulimia and Obesity*, 20(4), 449–455. http://doi.org/10.1007/s40519-015-0193-0

Hahamy, A., Behrmann, M., & Malach, R. (2015). The idiosyncratic brain: Distortion of spontaneous connectivity patterns in autism spectrum disorder. *Nature Neuroscience*, 18(2), 302–309. http://doi.org/10.1038/nn.3919

Haidt, J. (2008). Morality. *Perspectives on Psychological Science*, 3(1), 65–72. http://doi.org/10.1111/j.1745-6916.2008.00063.x

Haidt, J. (2013). Moral psychology for the twenty-first century. *Journal of Moral Education*, 42(3), 281–297. http://doi.org/10.1080/03057240.2013.817327

Haier, R. J., Siegel, B. V., Nuechterlein, K. H., Hazlett, E., Wu, J. C., Paek, J., . . . Buchsbaum, M. S. (1988). Cortical glucose metabolic rate correlates of abstract reasoning and attention studied with positron emission tomography. *Intelligence*, 12(2), 199–217. http://doi.org/10.1016/0160-2896(88)90016-5

Haines, E. L., Deaux, K., & Lofaro, N. (2016). The times they are a-changing . . . or are they not? A comparison of gender stereotypes, 1983–2014. *Psychology of Women Quarterly, 40*(3), 353–363. http://doi.org/10.1177/0361684316634081

Hair, N. L., Hanson, J. L., Wolfe, B. L., Pollak, S. D., & Knight, R. T. (2015). Association of child poverty, brain development, and academic achievement. *JAMA Pediatrics, 169*(9), 822. https://doi.org/10.1001/jamapediatrics.2015.1475

Haith, M. M. (1993). Preparing for the 21st century: Some goals and challenges for studies of infant sensory and perceptual development. *Developmental Review, 13*, 354–371.

Hakuta, K., Bialystok, E., & Wiley, E. (2003). Critical evidence: A test of the critical-period hypothesis for second-language acquisitions. *Psychological Science, 14*, 31–38.

Halberstadt, A. G., Denham, S. A., & Dunsmore, J. C. (2001). Affective social competence. *Social Development, 10*(1), 79–119. http://doi.org/10.1111/1467-9507.00150

Haley, D. W., & Stansbury, K. (2003). Infant stress and parent responsiveness: Regulation of physiology and behavior during still-face and reunion. *Child Development, 74*(5), 1534–1546. http://doi.org/10.1111/1467-8624.00621

Halford, G. S. (1989). Reflections on 25 years of piagetian cognitive developmental psychology, 1963–1988. *Human Development, 32*(6), 325–357. http://doi.org/10.1159/000276484

Halford, G. S., & Andrews, G. (2011). Information-processing models of cognitive development. *The Wiley-Blackwell Handbook of Childhood Cognitive Development (2nd Ed.)*. Goswami, 697–721. Wiley-Blackwell.

Halim, M. L. D., Ruble, D. N., Tamis-LeMonda, C. S., Shrout, P. E., & Amodio, D. M. (2017). Gender Attitudes in early childhood: Behavioral consequences and cognitive antecedents. *Child Development*. http://doi.org/10.1111/cdev.12642

Halim, M. L., Ruble, D. N., Tamis-LeMonda, C. S., Zosuls, K. M., Lurye, L. E., & Greulich, F. K. (2014). Pink frilly dresses and the avoidance of all things "girly": Children's appearance rigidity and cognitive theories of gender development. *Developmental Psychology, 50*(4), 1091–101. http://doi.org/10.1037/a0034906

Halim, M. L., Ruble, D., Tamis-LeMonda, C., & Shrout, P. E. (2013). Rigidity in gender-typed behaviors in early childhood: A longitudinal study of ethnic minority children. *Child Development, 84*(4), 1269–84. http://doi.org/10.1111/cdev.12057

Hall, G. S. (1904). *Adolescence*. New York: Appleton.

Hall, S. P., & Brassard, M. R. (2008). Relational support as a predictor of identity status in an ethnically diverse early adolescent sample. *Journal of Early Adolescence, 28*(1), 92–114. http://doi.org/10.1177/0272431607308668

Hall, T. W., Edwards, E., & Wang, D. C. (2016). The spiritual development of emerging adults over the college years: A 4-year longitudinal investigation. *Psychology of Religion and Spirituality, 8*(3), 206–217. http://doi.org/10.1037/rel0000051

Hall, W. (2014). What has research over the past two decades revealed about the adverse health effects of recreational cannabis use? *Addiction, 110*(1). http://doi.org/10.1111/add.12703

Hall, W., & Lynskey, M. (2016). Evaluating the public health impacts of legalizing recreational cannabis use in the United States. *Addiction, 111*(10), 1764–1773. http://doi.org/10.1111/add.13428

Hallal, P. C., Andersen, L. B., Bull, F. C., Guthold, R., Haskell, W., & Ekelund, U. (2012). Global physical activity levels: Surveillance progress, pitfalls, and prospects. *Lancet, 380*(9838), 247–57. http://doi.org/10.1016/S0140-6736(12)60646-1

Hallberg, I. R. (2013). Death and dying from old people's point of view. A literature review. *Aging Clinical and Experimental Research, 16*(2), 87–103. http://doi.org/10.1007/BF03324537

Halpern, D. F. (2005). An anniversary celebration for multiple intelligences. *PsycCritiques: Contemporary Psychology - APA Review of Books, 20*(12), Article 9.

Halpern, D. F. (2005). How time-flexible work policies can reduce stress, improve health, and save money. *Stress & Health: Journal of the International Society for the Investigation of Stress, 21*(3), 157–168. http://doi.org/10.1002/smi.1049

Halpern, D. F., & LaMay, M. L. (2000). The Smarter Sex: A Critical Review of Sex Differences in Intelligence. *Educational Psychology Review, 12*(2), 229–246. http://doi.org/10.1023/A:1009027516424

Halpern, D., Valenzuela, S., & Katz, J. E. (2016). "Selfie-ists" or "Narci-selfiers"?: A cross-lagged panel analysis of selfie taking and narcissism. *Personality and Individual Differences, 97*, 98–101. http://doi.org/10.1016/j.paid.2016.03.019

Halpern-Felsher, B. L., & Cauffman, E. (2001). Costs and benefits of a decision. Decision-making competence in adolescents and adults. *Journal of Applied Developmental Psychology, 22*(3), 257–273.

Hamblin, J. (2013). Pecan, Caramel, Crawfish: Food Dialect Maps. Retrieved from https://www.theatlantic.com/health/archive/2013/06/pecan-caramel-crawfish-food-dialect-maps/276603/

Hamilton, B. E., Martin, J. A., Osterman, M., Curtin, S. C., & Mathews, T. J. (2015). Births: Final Data for 2014. *National Vital Statistics Reports Statistics Reports, 64*(12).

Hamilton, B. E., Martin, J. A., Osterman, M., Curtin, S. C., & Mathews, T. J. (2015). Births: Final Data for 2014. *National Vital Statistics Reports Statistics Reports, 64*(12).

Hamilton, C. E. (2000). Continuity and discontinuity of attachment from infancy through adolescence. *Child Development, 71*, 690–694.

Hamlin, J. K. (2013). Moral Judgment and Action in Preverbal Infants and Toddlers: Evidence for an Innate Moral Core. *Current Directions in Psychological Science, 22*(3), 186–193. http://doi.org/10.1177/0963721412470687

Hamlin, J. K. (2014). The Origins of Human Morality: Complex Socio-moral Evaluations by Preverbal Infants (pp. 165–188). Springer International Publishing. http://doi.org/10.1007/978-3-319-02904-7_10

Hammond, S. I., & Carpendale, J. I. M. (2015). Helping Children Help: The Relation between Maternal Scaffolding and Children's Early Help. *Social Development, 24*(2), 367–383. http://doi.org/10.1111/sode.12104

Hampson, S. E., Edmonds, G. W., Barckley, M., Goldberg, L. R., Dubanoski, J. P., & Hillier, T. A. (2016). A Big Five approach to self-regulation: personality traits and health trajectories in the Hawaii longitudinal study of personality and health. *Psychology, Health & Medicine, 21*(2), 152–162. http://doi.org/10.1080/13548506.2015.1061676

Hampson, S. E., & Goldberg, L. R. (2006). A First Large Cohort Study of Personality Trait Stability Over the 40 Years Between Elementary School and Midlife. *Journal of Personality and Social Psychology, 91*(4), 763–779.

Hampton, T. (2007). Food insecurity harms health, well-being of millions in the United States. *Journal of the American Medical Association, 298*, 1851–1853.

Hamre, B. K. (2014). Teachers' Daily interactions with children: An essential ingredient in effective early childhood programs. *Child Development Perspectives, 8*(4), 223–230. http://doi.org/10.1111/cdep.12090

Han, S., Northoff, G., Vogeley, K., Wexler, B. E., Kitayama, S., & Varnum, M. E. W. (2013). A cultural neuroscience approach to the biosocial nature of the human brain. *Annual Review of Psychology, 64*(1), 335–359. http://doi.org/10.1146/annurev-psych-071112-054629

Han, T. S., Hart, C. L., Haig, C., Logue, J., Upton, M. N., Watt, G. C. M., & Lean, M. E. J. (2015). Contributions of maternal and paternal adiposity and smoking to adult offspring adiposity and cardiovascular risk: The Midspan Family Study. *BMJ Open, 5*(11), e007682. http://doi.org/10.1136/bmjopen-2015-007682

Hanania, R., & Smith, L. B. (2010). Selective attention and attention switching: Towards a unified developmental approach. *Developmental Science, 13*(4), 622–635. http://doi.org/10.1111/j.1467-7687.2009.00921.x

Hancock, J. T., Dunham, P. J., & Purdy, K. (2000). Children's comprehension of critical and complimentary forms of verbal irony. *Journal of Cognition and Development, 1*, 227–248.

Handler, A., Rosenberg, D., Raube, K., & Lyons, S. (2003). Satisfaction and use of prenatal care: Their relationship among African-American women in a large managed care organization. *Birth: Issues in Perinatal Care, 30*(1), 23–30.

Hanish, L. D., Fabes, R. A., Leaper, C., Bigler, R., Hayes, A. R., Hamilton, V., & Beltz, A. M. (2013). Gender: Early socialization. In E. T. Gershoff, R. S. Mistry, & D. Crosby (Eds.), *Societal contexts of child development: Pathways of influence and implications for practice and policy*. London, UK: Oxford University Press.

Hanley, J. R., Cortis, C., Budd, M.-J., & Nozari, N. (2016). Did I say dog or cat? A study of semantic error detection and correction in children. *Journal of Experimental Child Psychology, 142*, 36–47. http://doi.org/10.1016/j.jecp.2015.09.008

Han-Na, K., Eun-Ju, L., Sung-Chul, J., Jong-Young, L., Hye Won, C., & Hyung-Lae, K. (2010). Genetic variants that affect length/height in infancy/early childhood in Vietnamese-Korean families. *Journal of Human Genetics, 55*(10), 681–690. http://doi.org/10.1038/jhg.2010.88

Hannan, M. T., Broe, K. E., Cupples, L. A., Dufour, A. B., Rockwell, M., & Kiel, D. P. (2012). Height loss predicts subsequent hip fracture in men and women of the Framingham Study. *Journal of Bone and Mineral Research : The Official Journal of the American Society for Bone and Mineral Research, 27*(1), 146–52. http://doi.org/10.1002/jbmr.557

Hannon, K. (2010). Dealing With the hormone dilemma. *U.S. News & World Report, 147*(2), 51–52.

Hans, S. L. (2002). Studies of prenatal exposure to drugs: Focusing on parental care of children. *Neurotoxicology & Teratology, 24*(3), 329–337.

Hansen, M. B., & Markman, E. M. (2005). Appearance questions can be misleading: A discourse-based account of the appearance-reality problem. *Cognitive Psychology, 50*(3), 233–263. http://doi.org/10.1016/j.cogpsych.2004.09.001

Hansen, M. B., & Markman, E. M. (2009). Children's use of mutual exclusivity to learn labels for parts of objects. *Developmental Psychology, 45*(2), 592–596. http://doi.org/10.1037/a0014838

Hanson, J. L., Hair, N., Shen, D. G., Shi, F., Gilmore, J. H., Wolfe, B. L., . . . Hickie, I. (2013). Family poverty affects the rate of human infant brain growth. *PLoS ONE, 8*(12), e80954. http://doi.org/10.1371/journal.pone.0080954

Hanzal, A., & Segrin, C. (2009). The role of conflict resolution styles in mediating the relationship between enduring vulnerabilities and marital quality. *Journal of Family Communication, 9*(3), 150–169. http://doi.org/10.1080/15267430902945612

Hao, Y. (2008). Productive activities and psychological well-being among older adults. *Journals of Gerontology: Series B: Psychological Sciences and Social Sciences, (2)*, S64-s72.

Happ, C., Melzer, A., & Steffgen, G. (2013). Superman vs. BAD Man? The effects of empathy and game character in violent video games. *Cyberpsychology, Behavior, and Social Networking, 16*(10), 774–778. http://doi.org/10.1089/cyber.2012.0695

Hardie, J. H. (2014). The consequences of unrealized occupational goals in the transition to adulthood. *Social Science Research, 48*, 196–211. http://doi.org/10.1016/j.ssresearch.2014.06.006

Hardin, D. S., Kemp, S. F., & Allen, D. B. (2007). Twenty Years of recombinant human growth hormone in children: Relevance to pediatric care providers. *Clinical Pediatrics, 46*(4), 279–286.

Hardy, S. A., Pratt, M. W., Pancer, S. M., Olsen, J. A., & Lawford, H. L. (2011). Community and religious involvement as contexts of identity change across late adolescence and emerging adulthood. *International Journal of Behavioral Development, 35*(2), 125–135. http://doi.org/10.1177/0165025410375920

Hardy, S. A., Walker, L. J., Rackham, D. D., & Olsen, J. A. (2012). Religiosity and adolescent empathy and aggression: The mediating role of moral identity. *Psychology of Religion and Spirituality, 4*(3), 237–248. http://doi.org/10.1037/a0027566

Hare, T. A., Tottenham, N., Galvan, A., Voss, H. U., Glover, G. H., & Casey, B. J. (2008). Biological substrates of emotional reactivity and regulation in adolescence during an emotional go-nogo task. *Biological Psychiatry, 63*(10), 927–934. http://doi.org/10.1016/j.biopsych.2008.03.015

Harenski, C. L., & Hamann, S. (2006). Neural correlates of regulating negative emotions related to moral violations. *NeuroImage, 30*(1), 313–324. https://doi.org/10.1016/j.neuroimage.2005.09.034

Haring, R., Ittermann, T., Völzke, H., Krebs, A., Zygmunt, M., Felix, S. B., . . . Wallaschofski, H. (2010). Prevalence, incidence and risk factors of testosterone deficiency in a population-based cohort of men: Results from the study of health in Pomerania. *The Aging Male : The Official Journal of the International Society for the Study of the Aging Male, 13*(4), 247–57. http://doi.org/10.3109/13685538.2010.487553

Härkönen, J. (2014). Divorce. In J. Treas, J. Scott, & M. Richards (Eds.) *The Wiley Blackwell companion to the sociology of families,* (pp. 303–322.).

Harley, B., & Jean, G. (1999). Vocabulary skills of French immersion students in their second language. *Zeitschrift Für Interkulturellen Fremdsprachenunterricht.* Retrieved from http://www.ualberta.ca

Harlow, H. F., & Zimmerman, R. (1959). Affectional responses in the infant monkey. *Science, 130*, 421–432.

Harman, D. (2006). Free radical theory of aging: an update: Increasing the functional life span. *Annals of the New York Academy of Sciences, 1067*, 10–21.

Harold, G. T., Aitken, J. J., & Shelton, K. H. (2007). Inter-parental conflict and children's academic attainment: A longitudinal analysis. *Journal of Child Psychology & Psychiatry & Allied Disciplines, 48*, 1223–1232.

Harper, S., & Ruicheva, I. (2010). Grandmothers as replacement parents and partners: The role of grandmotherhood in single parent families. *Journal of Intergenerational Relationships, 8*(3), 219–233. http://doi.org/10.1080/15350770.2010.498779

Harriman, A. E., & Lukosius, P. A. (1982). On why Wayne Dennis found Hopi infants retarded in age at onset of walking. *Perceptual & Motor Skills, 55*(1), 79–86.

Harris, A. C. (1996). African American and Anglo-American gender identities: An empirical study. *Journal of Black Psychology, 22*(2), 182–194. http://doi.org/10.1177/00957984960222004

Harris, C., Kelly, C., Valentine, J. C., & Muhlenbruck, L. (2000). Abstract. *Monographs of the Society for Research in Child Development, 65*(1), v–v. http://doi.org/10.1111/1540-5834.00058

Harris, J., Golinkoff, R. M., & Hirsh-Pasek, K. (2011). Lessons from the crib for the classroom: How children really learn vocabulary. In S. B. Neuman & D. K. Dickinson (Eds.), *Handbook of early literacy research, Vol 3* (p. 49–65.). New York: Guilford Press.

Harris, M. A., Gruenenfelder-Steiger, A. E., Ferrer, E., Donnellan, M. B., Allemand, M., Fend, H., . . . Trzesniewski, K. H. (2015). Do parents foster self-esteem? Testing the prospective impact of parent closeness on adolescent self-esteem. *Child Development.* http://doi.org/10.1111/cdev.12356

Harris, M., & Pexman, P. M. (2003). Children's perceptions of the social functions of verbal irony. *Discourse Processes, 36*, 147–165.

Harris, P. L., Johnson, C. N., Hutton, D., Andrews, G., & Cooke, T. (1989). Young children's theory of mind and emotion. *Cognition & Emotion, 3*(4), 379–400. http://doi.org/10.1080/02699938908412713

Harris, P., & Gimenez, M. (2005). Children's acceptance of conflicting testimony: The case of death. *Journal of Cognition and Culture, 5*(1), 143–164. http://doi.org/10.1163/1568537054068606

Harris, W. S., Miller, M., Tighe, A. P., Davidson, M. H., Schaefer, E. J., & Dimsdale, J. E. (2008). Psychological stress and cardiovascular disease. *Journal of the American College of Cardiology, 51*(13), 1237–1246. http://doi.org/10.1016/j.jacc.2007.12.024

Harris-McKoy, D., & Cui, M. (2012). Parental control, adolescent delinquency, and young adult criminal behavior. *Journal of Child and Family Studies, 22*(6), 836–843. http://doi.org/10.1007/s10826-012-9641-x

Harrison, L. J., & Ungerer, J. A. (2002). Maternal employment and infant-mother attachment security at 12 months postpartum. *Developmental Psychology, 38*(5), 758–73. Retrieved from http://www.ncbi.nlm.nih.gov/pubmed/12220053

Harrist, A. W., Swindle, T. M., Hubbs-Tait, L., Topham, G. L., Shriver, L. H., & Page, M. C. (2016). The social and emotional lives of overweight, obese, and severely obese children. *Child Development.* http://doi.org/10.1111/cdev.12548

Hart, B., & Risley, T. R. (1995). *Meaningful differences in the everyday experience of young American children.* Baltimore: Paul H. Brookes.

Hart, C. H., Newell, L. D., & Olson, S. F. (2002). Parenting skills and social/communicative competence in childhood. In J. O. Greene & B. R. Burleson (Eds.), *Handbook of communication and social interaction skill.* Hillsdale, NJ: Lawrence Erlbaum.

Hart, D., Atkins, R., & Tursi, N. (2006). Origins and developmental influences on self-esteem. In M. H. Kernis (Ed.), *Self-esteem issues and answers: A sourcebook of current perspectives* (pp. 157–162). New York, NY: Psychology Press.

Hart, D., Donnelly, T. M., Youniss, J., & Atkins, R. (2007). High school community service as a predictor of adult voting and volunteering. *American Educational Research Journal, 44*(1), 197–219. http://doi.org/10.3102/0002831206298173

Harter, S. (1990). Issues in the assessment of the self-concept of children and adolescents. In A. LaGreca (Ed.), *Through the eyes of a child* (pp. 292–325). Boston: Allyn and Bacon.

Harter, S. (1998). The development of self-representations. In N. Eisenberg (Ed.), *Handbook of child psychology: Vol. 3. Social, emotional, and personality development* (5th ed., pp. 553–618). New York: Wiley.

Harter, S. (1999). *The construction of the self: A developmental perspective.* New York: Guilford Press.

Harter, S. (2006a). Developmental and individual difference perspectives on self-esteem. In D. K. Mroczek & T. D. Little (Eds.), *Handbook of personality development* (pp. 311–334). Mahwah, NJ: Lawrence Erlbaum.

Harter, S. (2006b). The development of self-esteem. In M. H. Kernis (Ed.), *Self-esteem issues and answers: A sourcebook of current perspectives* (pp. 144–150). New York: Psychology Press.

Harter, S. (2006c). The self. In N. Eisenberg, W. Damon, & R. M. Lerner (Eds.), *Handbook of child psychology: Social, emotional, and personality development* (6th ed., Vol. 3, pp. 505–570). Hoboken, NJ: John Wiley & Sons.

Harter, S. (2012). Emerging self-processes during childhood and adolescence. In M. R. Leary & J. P. Tangney (Eds.), *Handbook of self and identity* (p. 680–715.). New York: Guilford Press.

Harter, S. (2012a). *The construction of the self, second edition: Developmental and sociocultural foundations.* New York: Guilford Press.

Harter, S. (2012b). *The construction of the self developmental and sociocultural foundations.* New York: Guilford Press.

Hartge, P. (2009). Genetics of reproductive lifespan. *Nature Genetics, 41*(6), 637–638. http://doi.org/10.1038/ng0609-637

Hartl, A. C., Laursen, B., & Cillessen, A. H. N. (2015). A survival analysis of adolescent friendships. *Psychological Science, 26*(8), 1304–1315. http://doi.org/10.1177/0956797615588751

Hartup, W. W. (2006). Relationships in early and middle childhood. In A. L. Vangelisti & D. Perlman (Eds.), *The Cambridge handbook of personal relationships* (pp. 177–190). New York, NY: Cambridge University Press.

Hartup, W. W., & Stevens, N. (1997). Friendships and adaptation in the life course. *Psychological Bulletin, 121*, 355–370.

Hartup, W. W., & Stevens, N. (1999). Friendships and adaptation across the life span. *Current Directions in Psychological Science, 8*, 76–79.

Harvard Medical School ad Hoc Committee. (1968). A definition of irreversible coma. *JAMA, 205*(6), 337. http://doi.org/10.1001/jama.1968.03140320031009

Harwood, R. L., Scholmerich, A., Schulze, P. A., & Gonzalez, Z. (1999). Cultural differences in maternal beliefs and behaviors: A study of middle class Anglo and Puerto Rican mother-infant pairs in four everyday situations. *Child Development, 70*, 1005–1016.

Harwood, R., Feng, X., & Yu, S. (2013). Preadoption adversities and postadoption mediators of mental health and school outcomes among international, foster, and private adoptees in the United States. *Journal of Family Psychology : JFP : Journal of the Division of Family Psychology of the American Psychological Association (Division 43), 27*(3), 409–20. http://doi.org/10.1037/a0032908

Hasan, Y., Bègue, L., Scharkow, M., & Bushman, B. J. (2013). The more you play, the more aggressive you become: A long-term experimental study of cumulative violent video game effects on hostile expectations and aggressive behavior. *Journal of Experimental Social Psychology* (Vol. 49).

Hasin, D. S., Wall, M., Keyes, K. M., Cerdá, M., Schulenberg, J., O'Malley, P. M., . . . Hall, W. (2015). Medical marijuana laws and adolescent marijuana use in the USA from 1991 to 2014: Results from annual, repeated cross-sectional surveys. *The Lancet Psychiatry, 2*(7), 601–608. http://doi.org/10.1016/S2215-0366(15)00217-5

Hassan, K. El. (2008). Identifying indicators of student developement in college. *College Student Journal*, 42(2), 517–530.

Hatcher, L., & Crook, J. C. (1988). First-job surprises for college graduates: An exploratory investigation. *Journal of College Student Development*, 29(5), 441–448.

Hatzenbuehler, M. L. (2009). How does sexual minority stigma "get under the skin"? A psychological mediation framework. *Psychological Bulletin*, 135(5), 707–30. http://doi.org/10.1037/a0016441

Hatzenbuehler, M. L. (2014). Structural stigma and the health of lesbian, gay, and bisexual populations. *Current Directions in Psychological Science*, 23(2), 127–132. http://doi.org/10.1177/0963721414523775

Hauck, F. R., & Tanabe, K. O. (2008). International trends in sudden infant death syndrome: Stabilization of rates requires further action. *Pediatrics*, 122(3).

Hauck, Y. L., Fenwick, J., Dhaliwal, S. S., & Butt, J. (2011). A western Australian survey of breastfeeding initiation, prevalence and early cessation patterns. *Maternal & Child Health Journal*, 15(2), 260–268. http://doi.org/10.1007/s10995-009-0554-2

Hauser, M. D., Yang, C., Berwick, R. C., Tattersall, I., Ryan, M. J., Watumull, J., . . . Lewontin, R. C. (2014). The mystery of language evolution. *Frontiers in Psychology*, 5, 401. http://doi.org/10.3389/fpsyg.2014.00401

Hauser, S. I., Economos, C. D., Nelson, M. E., Goldberg, J. P., Hyatt, R. R., Naumova, E. N., . . . Must, A. (2014). Household and family factors related to weight status in first through third graders: a cross-sectional study in Eastern Massachusetts. *BMC Pediatrics*, 14(1), 167. http://doi.org/10.1186/1471-2431-14-167

Haw, C., Hawton, K., Niedzwiedz, C., & Platt, S. (2013). Suicide clusters: A review of risk factors and mechanisms. *Suicide & Life-Threatening Behavior*, 43(1), 97–108. http://doi.org/10.1111/j.1943-278X.2012.00130.x

Hawkes, C. (2006). Olfaction in neurodegenerative disorder. In *Taste and Smell* (Vol. 63, pp. 133–151). Basel: KARGER. http://doi.org/10.1159/000093759

Hawkins, J. N. (1994). Issues of motivation in Asian education. In H. F. O'Neil Jr. & M. Drillings (Eds.), *Motivation: Theory and research* (pp. 101–115). Hillsdale, NJ: Lawrence Erlbaum.

Hay, C., Fortson, E. N., Hollist, D. R., Altheimer, I., & Schaible, L. M. (2007). Compounded risk: The implications for delinquency of coming from a poor family that lives in a poor community. *Journal of Youth & Adolescence*, 36, 593–605.

Hay, D. F. (2016). The early development of human aggression. *Child Development Perspectives*. http://doi.org/10.1111/cdep.12220

Hay, D. F., Hurst, S.-L., Waters, C. S., & Chadwick, A. (2011). Infants' use of force to defend toys: The origins of instrumental aggression. *Infancy*, 16(5), 471–489. http://doi.org/10.1111/j.1532-7078.2011.00069.x

Hay, E. L., & Diehl, M. (2010). Reactivity to daily stressors in adulthood: The importance of stressor type in characterizing risk factors. *Psychology and Aging*, 25(1), 118–131. http://doi.org/10.1037/a0018747

Hay, P. J., & Bacaltchuk, J. (2007). Bulimia nervosa. *American Family Physician*, 75, 1699–1702.

Haydon, A. A., Herring, A. H., Prinstein, M. J., & Halpern, C. T. (2012). Beyond age at first sex: Patterns of emerging sexual behavior in adolescence and young adulthood. *The Journal of Adolescent Health : Official Publication of the Society for Adolescent Medicine*, 50(5), 456–63. http://doi.org/10.1016/j.jadohealth.2011.09.006

Hayes, J., Chakraborty, A. T., McManus, S., Bebbington, P., Brugha, T., Nicholson, S., & King, M. (2012). Prevalence of same-sex behavior and orientation in England: Results from a national survey. *Archives of Sexual Behavior*, 41(3), 631–639. http://doi.org/10.1007/s10508-011-9856-8

Hayflick, L. (1996). *How and why we age*. New York, NY: Ballantine Books.

Hayne, H. (2004). Infant memory development: Implications for childhood amnesia. *Developmental Review*, 24, 33–73.

Hayne, H., Boniface, J., & Barr, R. (2000). The development of declarative memory in human infants: Age-related changes in deffered imitation. *Behavioral Neuroscience*, 114(1), 77–83. http://doi.org/10.1037/0735-7044.114.1.77

Hayslip Jr, B., & Blumenthal, H. (2016). Grandparenthood: A developmental perspective. In M. H. Meyer & E. Daniele (Eds.), *ChallengGerontology: Changes, Challenges, and Solutiones* (pp. 271–298). Praeger.

Hayslip, B. J., Panek, P. E., & Patrick, J. H. (2007). *Adult development and aging* (4th ed.). Malabar, FL: Krieger.

Hayward, R. D., & Krause, N. (2013). Changes in church-based social support relationships during older adulthood. *The Journals of Gerontology. Series B, Psychological Sciences and Social Sciences*, 68(1), 85–96. http://doi.org/10.1093/geronb/gbs100

Haywood, K. M., & Getchell, N. (2005). *Lifespan motor development* (4th ed.). Champaign, IL: Human Kinetics.

Hazan, C., & Shaver, P. (1987). Romantic love conceptualized as an attachment process. *Journal of Personality and Social Psychology*, 52(3), 511–524. http://doi.org/10.1037/0022-3514.52.3.511

Hazlett, H. C., Hammer, J., Hooper, S. R., & Kamphaus, R. W. (2011). Down syndrome. In S. Goldstein & C. R. Reynolds (Eds.), *Handbook of neurodevelopmental and genetic disorders in children* (2nd ed., pp. 362–381). New York, NY: Guilford Press.

He, M., Walle, E. A., & Campos, J. J. (2015). A cross-national investigation of the relationship between infant walking and language development. *Infancy*, 20(3), 283–305. http://doi.org/10.1111/infa.12071

Heaman, M. I., Sword, W., Elliott, L., Moffatt, M., Helewa, M. E., Morris, H., . . . Brown, J. (2015). Barriers and facilitators related to use of prenatal care by inner-city women: Perceptions of health care providers. *BMC Pregnancy and Childbirth*, 15(1), 2. http://doi.org/10.1186/s12884-015-0431-5

Heath, S. B. (1989). Oral and literate tradition among black Americans living in poverty. *American Psychologist*, 44, 367–373.

Heaven, P. C. L., & Ciarrochi, J. (2008). Parental styles, conscientiousness, and academic performance in high school: A three-wave longitudinal study. *Personality and Social Psychology Bulletin*, 34(4), 451–461. http://doi.org/10.1177/0146167207311909

Hebert, R. S., Dang, Q., & Schulz, R. (2006). Preparedness for the death of a loved one and mental health in bereaved caregivers of patients with dementia: Findings from the REACH study. *Journal of Palliative Medicine*, 9(3), 683–693. http://doi.org/10.1089/jpm.2006.9.683

Hecht, E. E., Mahovetz, L. M., Preuss, T. M., & Hopkins, W. D. (2016). A neuroanatomical predictor of mirror self-recognition in chimpanzees. *Social Cognitive and Affective Neuroscience*, nsw159. http://doi.org/10.1093/scan/nsw159

Heckhausen, J., & Brim, O. G. (1997). Perceived problems for self and others: Self-protection by social downgrading throughout adulthood. *Psychology and Aging*, 12(4), 610–619.

Heidenreich, P. A., Trogdon, J. G., Khavjou, O. A., Butler, J., Dracup, K., Ezekowitz, M. D., . . . Woo, Y. J. (2011). Forecasting the future of cardiovascular disease in the United States: A policy statement from the American Heart Association. *Circulation*, 123(8), 933–944. http://doi.org/10.1161/CIR.0b013e31820a55f5

Heikura, U., Taanila, A., Hartikainen, A.-L., Olsen, P., Linna, S.-L., von Wendt, L., & Järvelin, M.-R. (2008). Variations in prenatal sociodemographic factors associated with intellectual disability: A study of the 20-year interval between two birth cohorts in northern Finland. *American Journal of Epidemiology*, 167(2), 169–177. http://doi.org/10.1093/aje/kwm291

Heimann, M., & Meltzoff, A. N. (1996). Deferred imitation in 9- and 14-month-old infants: A longitudinal study of a Swedish sample. *British Journal of Developmental Psychology*, 14(1), 55–64. http://doi.org/10.1111/j.2044-835X.1996.tb00693.x

Heine, S. J., & Lehman, D. R. (1995). Cultural variation in unrealistic optimism: Does the West feel more invulnerable than the East? *Journal of Personality and Social Psychology*, 68, 595–607.

Heine, S. J., Kitayama, S., Lehman, D. R., Takata, T., Ide, E., Leung, C., & Matsumoto, H. (2001). Divergent consequences of success and failure in Japan and North America: An investigation of self-improving motivations and malleable selves. *Journal of Personality and Social Psychology*, 81(4), 599–615. http://doi.org/10.1037/0022-3514.81.4.599

Heinonen, I., Helajärvi, H., Pahkala, K., Heinonen, O. J., Hirvensalo, M., Pälve, K., . . . Raitakari, O. T. (2013). Sedentary behaviours and obesity in adults: The Cardiovascular Risk in Young Finns Study. *BMJ Open*, 3(6), e002901-. http://doi.org/10.1136/bmjopen-2013-002901

Hektner, J. M., August, G. J., & Realmuto, G. M. (2000). Patterns and Temporal Changes in Peer Affiliation Among Aggressive and Nonaggressive Children Participating in a Summer School Program. Preview By: Hektner, Joel M.; August, Gerald J.; Realmuto, George M.. Journal of Clinical Child Psychology, Dec2000, Vo. *Journal of Clinical Child Psychology*, 29, 603–614.

Heldman, C., & Wade, L. (2010). Hook-up culture: Setting a new research agenda. *Sexuality Research and Social Policy*, 7(4), 323–333. http://doi.org/10.1007/s13178-010-0024-z

Helming, K. A., Strickland, B., & Jacob, P. (2014). Making sense of early false-belief understanding. *Trends in Cognitive Sciences*, 18(4), 167–70. http://doi.org/10.1016/j.tics.2014.01.005

Helms, H. M., Walls, J. K., Crouter, A. C., & McHale, S. M. (2010). Provider role attitudes, marital satisfaction, role overload, and housework: A dyadic approach. *Journal of Family Psychology : JFP : Journal of the Division of Family Psychology of the American Psychological Association (Division 43)*, 24(5), 568–77. http://doi.org/10.1037/a0020637

Helms, J. E. (1992). Why is there no study of cultural equivalence in standardized cognitive ability testing? *American Psychologist*, 47, 1083–1101.

Helwig, C. C., & Prencipe, A. (1999). Children's judgments of flags and flag-burning. *Child Development*, 70, 132–143.

Helwig, C. C., Arnold, M. L., Tan, D., & Boyd, D. (2007). Mainland Chinese and Canadian adolescents' judgments and reasoning about the fairness of democratic and other forms of government. *Cognitive Development*, 22(1), 96–109.

Helzner, E. P., Cauley, J. A., Pratt, S. R., Wisniewski, S. R., Zmuda, J. M., Talbott, E. O., . . . al, et. (2005). Race and sex differences in age-related hearing loss: The health, aging and body composition study. *Journal of the American Geriatrics Society, 53*(12), 2119–2127.

Henderson, C. E., Hayslip, J. B., Sanders, L. M., & Louden, L. (2009). Grandmother–grandchild relationship quality predicts psychological adjustment among youth from divorced families. *Journal of Family Issues, 30*(9), 1245–1264.

Hendler, M., & Weisberg, P. (1992). Conservation acquisition, maintenance, and generalization of mentally retarded children using quality-rule training. *Journal of Experimental Child Psychology, 53*, 258–276.

Hendry, L. B., & Kloep, M. (2010). How universal is emerging adulthood? An empirical example. *Journal of Youth Studies, 13*(2), 169–179. http://doi.org/10.1080/13676260903295067

Hennon, C. B., Hildenbrand, B., & Schedle, A. (2008). Stepfamilies and children. In T. P. Gullotta & G. M. Blau (Eds.), *Family influences on childhood behavior and development: Evidence-based prevention and treatment approaches* (pp. 161–185). New York, NY: Routledge/Taylor & Francis Group.

Henry, D. B., Schoeny, M. E., Deptula, D. P., & Slavick, J. T. (2007). Peer selection and socialization effects on adolescent intercourse without a condom and attitudes about the costs of sex. *Child Development, 78*, 825–838.

Henry, K. L., Knight, K. E., & Thornberry, T. P. (2012). School disengagement as a predictor of dropout, delinquency, and problem substance use during adolescence and early adulthood. *Journal of Youth and Adolescence, 41*(2), 156–66. http://doi.org/10.1007/s10964-011-9665-3

Henry, N. J. M., Berg, C. A., Smith, T. W., & Florsheim, P. (2007). Positive and negative characteristics of marital interaction and their association with marital satisfaction in middle-aged and older couples. *Psychology and Aging, 22*(3), 428–441.

Hepach, R., Vaish, A., & Tomasello, M. (2012). Young children are intrinsically motivated to see others helped. *Psychological Science, 23*(9), 967–972. http://doi.org/10.1177/0956797612440571

Hepper, P. (2013). The developmental origins of laterality: Fetal handedness. *Developmental Psychobiology, 55*(6), 588–595. http://doi.org/10.1002/dev.21119

Hepper, P. (2015). Behavior during the prenatal period: Adaptive for development and survival. *Child Development Perspectives, 9*(1), 38–43. http://doi.org/10.1111/cdep.12104

Hepper, P. G., Dornan, J. C., & Lynch, C. (2012). Sex differences in fetal habituation. *Developmental Science, 15*(3), 373–83. http://doi.org/10.1111/j.1467-7687.2011.01132.x

Heraty, N., & McCarthy, J. (2015). Unearthing psychological predictors of financial planning for retirement among late career older workers: Do self-perceptions of aging matter? *Work, Aging and Retirement*, wav008. http://doi.org/10.1093/workar/wav008

Herbenick, D., Reece, M., Hensel, D., Sanders, S., Jozkowski, K., & Fortenberry, J. D. (2011). Association of lubricant use with women's sexual pleasure, sexual satisfaction, and genital symptoms: A prospective daily diary study. *The Journal of Sexual Medicine, 8*(1), 202–212. http://doi.org/10.1111/j.1743-6109.2010.02067.x

Herbenick, D., Reece, M., Schick, V., Sanders, S. A., Dodge, B., & Fortenberry, J. D. (2010). Sexual behavior in the United States: Results from a national probability sample of men and women ages 14–94. *The Journal of Sexual Medicine, 7*(s5), 255–265. http://doi.org/10.1111/J.1743-6109.2010.02012.X

Herbert, J., & Hayne, H. (2000). Memory retrieval by 18–30 month olds: Age related changes in representational flexibility. *Developmental Psychology, 36*, 473–484.

Herbert, J., & Lucassen, P. J. (2016). Depression as a risk factor for Alzheimer's disease: Genes, steroids, cytokines and neurogenesis – What do we need to know? *Frontiers in Neuroendocrinology, 41*, 153–171. http://doi.org/10.1016/j.yfrne.2015.12.001

Herdt, G., & McClintock, M. (2000). The magical age of 10. *Archives of Sexual Behavior, 29*(6), 587–606. http://doi.org/10.1023/A:1002006521067

Herlihy, A. S., & McLachlan, R. I. (2015). Screening for Klinefelter syndrome. *Current Opinion in Endocrinology & Diabetes and Obesity, 22*(3), 224–229. http://doi.org/10.1097/MED.0000000000000154

Herman, Gabor T. (2009). *Fundamentals of computerized tomography: Image reconstruction from projections.* London: Springer. Retrieved from http://dl.acm.org/citation.cfm?id=SERIES11874.1667091

Herman-Giddens, M. E. (2006). Recent data on pubertal milestones in United States children: The secular trend toward earlier development. *International Journal of Andrology, 29*(1), 241–246.

Herman-Giddens, M. E., Kaplowitz, P. B., & Wasserman, R. (2004). Navigating the recent articles on girls' puberty in pediatrics: What do we know and where do we go from here? *Pediatrics, 113*(4), 911–917.

Herman-Giddens, M. E., Steffes, J., Harris, D., Slora, E., Hussey, M., Dowshen, S. A., . . . Reiter, E. O. (2012). Secondary sexual characteristics in boys: Data from the Pediatric Research in Office Settings Network. *Pediatrics, 130*(5), e1058-68. http://doi.org/10.1542/peds.2011-3291

Hermans, E. A., Dubbelman, M., van der Heijde, G. L., & Heethaar, R. M. (2008). Change in the accommodative force on the lens of the human eye with age. *Vision Research, 48*(1), 119–126. http://doi.org/10.1016/j.visres.2007.10.017

Hermanto, N., Moreno, S., & Bialystok, E. (2012). Linguistic and metalinguistic outcomes of intense immersion education: How bilingual? *International Journal of Bilingual Education and Bilingualism, 15*(2), 131–145. http://doi.org/10.1080/13670050.2011.652591

Hernandez-Pavon, J. C., Sosa, M., Lutter, W. J., Maier, M., & Wakai, R. T. (2008). Auditory evoked responses in neonates by MEG. *AIP Conference Proceedings, 1032*(1), 114–117. http://doi.org/10.1063/1.2979244

Hernandez-Reif, M., Diego, M., & Field, T. (2007). Preterm infants show reduced stress behaviors and activity after 5 days of massage therapy. *Infant Behavior & Development, 30*(4), 557–561. http://doi.org/10.1016/j.infbeh.2007.04.002

Herrenkohl, T. I., Hong, S., Klika, J. B., Herrenkohl, R. C., & Russo, M. J. (2013). Developmental impacts of child abuse and neglect related to adult mental Health, substance use, and physical health. *Journal of Family Violence, 28*(2). http://doi.org/10.1007/s10896-012-9474-9

Herrera, B. M., Keildson, S., & Lindgren, C. M. (2011). Genetics and epigenetics of obesity. *Maturitas, 69*(1), 41–9. http://doi.org/10.1016/j.maturitas.2011.02.018

Herrman, J. W. (2009). There's a fine line . . . adolescent dating violence and prevention. *Pediatric Nursing, 35*(3), 164–170.

Hersh, A. L., Stefanick, M. L., & Stafford, R. S. (2004). National use of postmenopausal hormone therapy: Annual trends and response to recent evidence. *JAMA: Journal of the American Medical Association, 291*, 47–53.

Hershey, D. A., Jacobs-Lawson, J. M., McArdle, J. J., & Hamagami, F. (2007). Psychological foundations of financial planning for retirement. *Journal of Adult Development, 14*(1/2), 26–36. http://doi.org/10.1007/s10804-007-9028-1

Herzmann, G., & Curran, T. (2011). Experts' memory: An ERP study of perceptual expertise effects on encoding and recognition. *Memory & Cognition, 39*(3), 412–32. http://doi.org/10.3758/s13421-010-0036-1

Hess, T. M., Leclerc, C. M., Swaim, E., & Weatherbee, S. R. (2009). Aging and everyday judgments: The impact of motivational and processing resource factors. *Psychology and Aging, 24*(3), 735–740. http://doi.org/10.1037/a0016340

Hewitt, B., Baxter, J., & Western, M. (2006). Family, work and health: The impact of marriage, parenthood and employment on self-reported health of Australian men and women. *Journal of Sociology, 42*(1), 61–78.

Hewlett, B. S. (2008). Fathers and infants among Aka pygmies. In R. A. LeVine & R. S. New (Eds.), *Anthropology and child development: A cross-cultural reader.* (pp. 84–99). Malden: Blackwell Publishing.

Hewlett, B. S., Hewlett, B. S., & Hewlett, B. L. (2010). Sex and searching for children among Aka foragers and Ngandu farmers of central Africa. *African Study Monographs*, 107–125.

Hewlett, B. S., Lamb, M. E., Shannon, D., Leyendecker, B., & Scholmerich, A. (1998). Culture and early infancy among central African foragers and farmers. *Developmental Psychology, 34*, 653–661.

Heybroek, L., Haynes, M., Baxter, J., D, S., E, F. G., D, M., & V, K. S. (2015). Life satisfaction and retirement in australia: A longitudinal approach. *Work, Aging and Retirement, 1*(2), 166–180. http://doi.org/10.1093/workar/wav006

Heyes, C. (2014). False belief in infancy: A fresh look. *Developmental Science.* http://doi.org/10.1111/desc.12148

Heyman, G. D., & Dweck, C. S. (1998). Children's thinking about traits: Implications for judgments of the self and others. *Child Development, 69*(2), 391–403. http://doi.org/10.1111/j.1467-8624.1998.tb06197.x

Heyman, G. D., & Gelman, S. A. (2000). Beliefs about the origins of human psychological traits. *Developmental Psychology, 36*, 663–678.

Heyman, G. D., & Legare, C. H. (2004). Children's beliefs about gender differences in the academic and social domains. *Sex Roles, 50*(3/4), 227–239. http://doi.org/10.1023/B:SERS.0000015554.12336.30

Hiatt, C., Laursen, B., Mooney, K. S., & Rubin, K. H. (2015). Forms of friendship: A person-centered assessment of the quality, stability, and outcomes of different types of adolescent friends. *Personality and Individual Differences, 77*, 149–155. http://doi.org/10.1016/j.paid.2014.12.051

Hickey, M., Elliott, J., & Davison, S. L. (2012). Hormone replacement therapy. *BMJ (Clinical Research Ed.), 344*(feb16_2), e763. http://doi.org/10.1136/bmj.e763

Hicks-Pass, S. (2009). Corporal punishment in America today: Spare the rod, spoil the child? A systematic review of the literature. *Best Practice in Mental Health: An International Journal, 5*(2), 71–88.

Hiekel, N., Liefbroer, A. C., & Poortman, A.-R. (2014). Understanding diversity in the meaning of cohabitation across Europe. *European Journal of Population, 30*(4), 391–410. http://doi.org/10.1007/s10680-014-9321-1

Higgins, C. A., Duxbury, L. E., & Lyons, S. T. (2010). Coping with overload and stress: Men and women in dual-earner families. *Journal of Marriage and Family, 72*(4), 847–859. http://doi.org/10.1111/j.1741-3737.2010.00734.x

Higley, E., & Dozier, M. (2009). Nighttime maternal responsiveness and infant attachment at one year. *Attachment & Human Development, 11*(4), 347–363. http://doi.org/10.1080/14616730903016979

Hilarski, C. (2008). Child and adolescent sexual abuse. In C. Hilarski, J. S. Wodarski, & M. D. Feit (Eds.), *Handbook of social work in child and adolescent sexual abuse* (pp. 29–50). New York, NY: Haworth Press/Taylor & Francis Group.

Hill, H. A., Elam-Evans, L. D., Yankey, D., Singleton, J. A., & Kolasa, M. (2015). National, state, and selected local area vaccination coverage among children aged 19–35 months: United States, 2014. *Morbidity and Mortality Weekly Report, 64*(33), 889–896.

Hill, N. E., Bush, K. R., & Roosa, M. W. (2003). Parenting and socialization strategies and children's mental health: Low-income Mexican-American and Euro-American mothers and children. *Child Development, 74,* 189–204.

Hill, P. L., Turiano, N. A., Mroczek, D. K., & Roberts, B. W. (2012). Examining concurrent and longitudinal relations between personality traits and social well-being in adulthood. *Social Psychological and Personality Science, 3*(6), 698–705. http://doi.org/10.1177/1948550611433888

Hill, R. M., Castellanos, D., & Pettit, J. W. (2011). Suicide-related behaviors and anxiety in children and adolescents: A review. *Clinical Psychology Review, 31*(7), 1133–1144. http://doi.org/10.1016/j.cpr.2011.07.008

Hillerer, K. M., Jacobs, V. R., Fischer, T., & Aigner, L. (2014). The maternal brain: An organ with peripartal plasticity. *Neural Plasticity, 2014,* 574159. http://doi.org/10.1155/2014/574159

Himes, J. H. (2006). Examining the evidence for recent secular changes in the timing of puberty in US children in light of increases in the prevalence of obesity. *Molecular & Cellular Endocrinology, 254–255,* 13–21.

Hindin, S. B., & Zelinski, E. M. (2012). Extended practice and aerobic exercise interventions benefit untrained cognitive outcomes in older adults: A meta-analysis. *Journal of the American Geriatrics Society, 60*(1), 136–41. http://doi.org/10.1111/j.1532-5415.2011.03761.x

Hindman, A. H., & Wasik, B. A. (2015). Building vocabulary in two languages: An examination of Spanish-speaking Dual Language Learners in Head Start. *Early Childhood Research Quarterly, 31,* 19–33. http://doi.org/10.1016/j.ecresq.2014.12.006

Hinduja, S., & Patchin, J. (2015). *State Cyberbullying Laws: A Brief Review of State Cyberbullying Laws and Policies.* Retrieved from http://www.cyberbullying.us/Bullying-and-Cyberbullying-Laws.pdf

Hines, M. (2011). Gender development and the human brain. *Annual Review of Neuroscience, 34*(1), 69–88. http://doi.org/10.1146/annurev-neuro-061010-113654

Hines, M. (2015). Gendered development. In *Handbook of Child Psychology and Developmental Science* (pp. 1–46). Hoboken, NJ, USA: John Wiley & Sons, Inc. http://doi.org/10.1002/9781118963418.childpsy320

Hines, M. (2013). Sex and sex differences. In *The Oxford handbook of developmental psychology, Vol. 1: Body and mind.* New York: Oxford University Press. http://doi.org/10.1093/oxfordhb/9780199958450.013.0007

Hines, M., Pasterski, V., Spencer, D., Neufeld, S., Patalay, P., Hindmarsh, P. C., . . . Acerini, C. L. (2016). Prenatal androgen exposure alters girls' responses to information indicating gender-appropriate behaviour. *Philosophical Transactions of the Royal Society of London B: Biological Sciences, 371*(1688). Retrieved from http://rstb.royalsocietypublishing.org/content/371/1688/20150125

Hinkelman, L., & Bruno, M. (2008). Identification and reporting of child sexual abuse: The role of elementary school professionals. *Elementary School Journal, 108*(5), 376–391.

Hinterlong, J. E., Morrow-Howell, N., & Rozario, P. A. (2007). Productive engagement and late life physical and mental health: Findings from a nationally representative panel study. *Research on Aging, 29*(4), 348–370. http://doi.org/10.1177/0164027507300806

Hipson, W. E., & Séguin, D. G. (2016). Is good fit related to good behaviour? Goodness of fit between daycare teacher–child relationships, temperament, and prosocial behaviour. *Early Child Development and Care, 186*(5), 785–798. http://doi.org/10.1080/03004430.2015.1061518

Hitch, G. J., Towse, J. N., & Hutton, U. (2001). What limits children's working memory span? Theoretical accounts and applications for scholastic development. *Journal of Experimental Psychology: General, 130*(2), 184–198.

Hite, L. M., & McDonald, K. S. (2003). Career aspirations of non-managerial women: Adjustment and adaptation. *Journal of Career Development, 29*(4), 221–235.

Hithersay, R., Hamburg, S., Knight, B., & Strydom, A. (2017). Cognitive decline and dementia in Down syndrome. *Current Opinion in Psychiatry, 30*(2), 102–107. http://doi.org/10.1097/YCO.0000000000000307

Hjelmborg, J. vB., Iachine, I., Skytthe, A., Vaupel, J. W., McGue, M., Koskenvuo, M., . . . Christensen, K. (2006). Genetic influence on human lifespan and longevity. *Human Genetics, 119*(3), 312–321.

Hochwarter, W. A., Ferris, G. R., Perrewé, P. L., Witt, L. A., & Kiewitz, C. (2001). A note on the nonlinearity of the age-job-satisfaction relationship. *Journal of Applied Social Psychology, 31*(6), 1223–1237.

Hock, R. (2015). *Human sexuality.* Pearson.

Hodges-Simeon, C. R., Gurven, M., Cárdenas, R. A., & Gaulin, S. J. C. (2013). Voice change as a new measure of male pubertal timing: A study among Bolivian adolescents. *Annals of Human Biology, 40*(3), 209–19. http://doi.org/10.3109/03014460.2012.759622

Hodson, D. S., & Skeen, P. (1994). Sexuality and aging: The hammerlock of myths. *Journal of Applied Gerontology, 13*(3), 219–235. http://doi.org/10.1177/073346489401300301

Hoekzema, E., Barba-Müller, E., Pozzobon, C., Picado, M., Lucco, F., García-García, D., . . . Vilarroya, O. (2017). Pregnancy leads to long-lasting changes in human brain structure. *Nature Neuroscience, 20*(2), 287–296. http://doi.org/10.1038/nn.4458

Hoenig, M. C., Bischof, G. N., Hammes, J., Faber, J., Fliessbach, K., van Eimeren, T., & Drzezga, A. (2017). Tau pathology and cognitive reserve in Alzheimer's disease. *Neurobiology of Aging, 57,* 1–7. http://doi.org/10.1016/j.neurobiolaging.2017.05.004

Hoeve, M., Dubas, J. S., Gerris, J. R. M., van der Laan, P. H., & Smeenk, W. (2011). Maternal and paternal parenting styles: Unique and combined links to adolescent and early adult delinquency. *Journal of Adolescence, 34*(5), 813–27. http://doi.org/10.1016/j.adolescence.2011.02.004

Hoeve, M., Stams, G. J. J. M., van der Put, C. E., Dubas, J. S., van der Laan, P. H., & Gerris, J. R. M. (2012). A meta-analysis of attachment to parents and delinquency. *Journal of Abnormal Child Psychology, 40*(5), 771–785. http://doi.org/10.1007/s10802-011-9608-1

Hofer, C., Eisenberg, N., Spinrad, T. L., Morris, A. S., Gershoff, E., Valiente, C., . . . Eggum, N. D. (2013). Mother-adolescent conflict: Stability, change, and relations with externalizing and internalizing behavior

problems. *Social Development, 22*(2), 259–279. http://doi.org/10.1111/sode.12012

Hoff, E. (2003). Causes and consequences of SES-related differences in parent-to-child speech. In M. H. Bornstein & R. H. Bradley (Eds.), *Socioeconomic status, parenting, and child development. Monographs in parenting series* (pp. 147–160). Mahwah, NJ: Lawrence Erlbaum.

Hoff, E. (2003). The specificity of environmental influence: Socioeconomic status affects early vocabulary development via maternal speech. *Child Development, 74*(5), 1368–1378. http://doi.org/10.1111/1467-8624.00612

Hoff, E. (2014). *Language development.* Cengage Learning.

Hoff, E. (2015). Language development. In *Developmental science: An advanced textbook* (7th ed., pp. 443–488). New York: Taylor & Francis.

Hoff, E., & Core, C. (2015). What clinicians need to know about bilingual development. *Seminars in Speech and Language, 36*(2), 089–099. http://doi.org/10.1055/s-0035-1549104

Hoff, E., Core, C., Place, S., & Rumiche, R. (2012). Dual language exposure and early bilingual development. *Journal of Child Language, 39*(1), 1–27. http://doi.org/10.1017/S0305000910000759

Hoff, E., & Naigles, L. (2002). How children use input to acquire a lexicon. *Child Development, 73*(2), 418–433.

Hoff, E., Rumiche, R., Burridge, A., Ribot, K. M., & Welsh, S. N. (2014). Expressive vocabulary development in children from bilingual and monolingual homes: A longitudinal study from two to four years. *Early Childhood Research Quarterly, 29*(4), 433–444. http://doi.org/10.1016/j.ecresq.2014.04.012

Hoffman, L. W. (1974). Effects of maternal employment on the child: A review of the research. *Developmental Psychology, 10*(2), 204–228. Retrieved from http://www.childstats.gov/americaschildren13/index.asp

Hoffman, M. L. (1970). Moral development. In P. H. Mussen (Ed.), *Carmichael's manual of child psychology* (pp. 457—557). New York: Wiley.

Hoffman, M. L. (2000). *Empathy and moral development : implications for caring and justice.* Cambridge University Press.

Hoffman, M. L. (2007). The origins of empathic morality in toddlerhood. In C. A. Brownell & C. B. Kopp (Eds.), *Socioemotional development in the toddler years: Transitions and transformations* (pp. 132–145). New York, NY: Guilford Press.

Hoffmann, J., & Russ, S. (2012). Pretend play, creativity, and emotion regulation in children. *Psychology of Aesthetics, Creativity, and the Arts, 6*(2). http://doi.org/10.1037a0026299

Hofstede, G. (2001). *Culture's consequences: Comparing values, behaviors, institutions, and organizations across nations.* Thousand Oaks, CA: Sage.

Hogan, C. L., Mata, J., & Carstensen, L. L. (2013). Exercise holds immediate benefits for affect and cognition in younger and older adults. *Psychology and Aging, 28*(2), 587–594. http://doi.org/10.1037/a0032634

Hoggatt, K. J., Flores, M., Solorio, R., Wilhelm, M., & Ritz, B. (2012). The "Latina epidemiologic paradox" revisited: The role of birthplace and acculturation in predicting infant low birth weight for Latinas in Los Angeles, CA. *Journal of Immigrant and Minority Health, 14*(5), 875–884. http://doi.org/10.1007/s10903-011-9556-4

Hohmann-Marriott, B. E. (2006). Shared beliefs and the union stability of married and cohabiting couples. *Journal of Marriage & Family, 68*(4), 1015–1028.

Holden, C. A., Collins, V. R., Handelsman, D. J., Jolley, D., & Pitts, M. (2014). Healthy aging in a cross-sectional study of Australian men: What has sex got to do with it? *The Aging Male: The Official Journal of the International Society for the Study of the Aging Male, 17*(1), 25–29. http://doi.org/10.3109/13685538.2013.843167

Holland, J. L. (1997). *Making vocational choices: A theory of vocational personalities and work environments* (3rd ed.). Odessa, FL: Psychological Assessment Resources.

Hollenstein, T., & Lougheed, J. P. (2013). Beyond storm and stress: Typicality, transactions, timing, and temperament to account for adolescent change. *The American Psychologist, 68*(6), 444–454. http://doi.org/10.1037/a0033586

Holliday, K. (2014, October 21). China to ease 1-child rule further, but do people care? *CNBC News.* Retrieved from http://www.cnbc.com/id/102104640#

Holliday, R. (2006a). Epigenetics: A historical overview. *Epigenetics, 1*(2), 76–80. Retrieved from http://www.ncbi.nlm.nih.gov/pubmed/17998809

Holliday, R. (2006b). Epigenetics: a historical overview. *Epigenetics, 1*(2), 76–80.

Holliday, R. (2007). *Aging: The paradox of life.* New York: Springer.

Holloway, S. D. (1999). Divergent cultural models of child rearing and pedagogy in Japanese preschools. *New Directions for Child and Adolescent Development, 83*, 61–75.

Holman, D. M., Benard, V., Roland, K. B., Watson, M., Liddon, N., & Stokley, S. (2014). Barriers to human papillomavirus vaccination among US adolescents. *JAMA Pediatrics, 168*(1), 76. http://doi.org/10.1001/jamapediatrics.2013.2752

Holmes, C. J., Kim-Spoon, J., & Deater-Deckard, K. (2016). Linking executive function and peer problems from early childhood through middle adolescence. *Journal of Abnormal Child Psychology, 44*(1), 31–42. http://doi.org/10.1007/s10802-015-0044-5

Holt, J., Warren, L., & Wallace, R. (2006). What behavioral interventions are safe and effective for treating obesity? *Journal of Family Practice, 55*(6), 536–538.

Holt, M. K., Kaufman Kantor, G., & Finkelhor, D. (2009). Parent/child concordance about bullying involvement and family characteristics related to bullying and peer victimization. *Journal of School Violence, 8*(1), 42–63. http://doi.org/10.1080/15388220802067813

Holt, R. I. G., Phillips, D. I. W., Jameson, K. A., Cooper, C., Dennison, E. M., & Peveler, R. C. (2013). The relationship between depression, anxiety and cardiovascular disease: Findings from the Hertfordshire Cohort Study. *Journal of Affective Disorders, 150*(1), 84–90. http://doi.org/10.1016/j.jad.2013.02.026

Holt-Lunstad, J., Smith, T. B., & Layton, J. B. (2010). Social relationships and mortality risk: A meta-analytic review. *PLoS Medicine, 7*(7), e1000316. http://doi.org/10.1371/journal.pmed.1000316

Holtzer, R., Epstein, N., Mahoney, J. R., Izzetoglu, M., & Blumen, H. M. (2014). Neuroimaging of mobility in aging: A targeted review. *The Journals of Gerontology. Series A, Biological Sciences and Medical Sciences, 69*(11), 1375–88. http://doi.org/10.1093/gerona/glu052

Homan, K. J., & Boyatzis, C. J. (2010). Religiosity, sense of meaning, and health behavior in older adults. *International Journal for the Psychology of Religion, 20*(3), 173–186. http://doi.org/10.1080/10508619.2010.481225

Hong, G., & Yu, B. (2007). Early-grade retention and children's reading and math learning in elementary years. *Educational Evaluation and Policy Analysis, 29*(4), 239–261.

Honigman, R., & Castle, D. J. (2006). Aging and cosmetic enhancement. *Clinical Interventions in Aging, 1*(2), 115–9.

Honomichl, R. D., & Zhe, C. (2011). Relations as rules: The Role of attention in the dimensional change card sort task. *Developmental Psychology, 47*(1), 50–60. http://doi.org/10.1037/a0021025

Honzik, M. P. (1983). Measuring mental abilities in infancy: The value and limitations. . In M. Lewis (Ed.), *Origins of Intelligence* (2nd ed). New York: Plenum.

Honzik, M. P., Macfarlane, J. W., & Allen, L. (1948). The stability of mental test performance between two and eighteen years. *The Journal of Experimental Education, 17*(2), 309–324. http://doi.org/10.1080/00220973.1948.11010388

Hopkins, B. (1991). Facilitating early motor development: An intercultural study of West Indian mothers and their infants living in Britain. In J. K. Nugent, B. M. Lester, & T. B. Brazelton (Eds.), *The cultural context of infancy: Vol. 2. Multicultural and interdisciplinary approaches to parent-infant relations.* Norwood, NJ: Ablex.

Hopkins, B., & Westra, T. (1989). Maternal expectations of their infants' development: Some cultural differences. *Developmental Medicine & Child Neurology, 31*(3), 384–390.

Hopkins, B., & Westra, T. (1990). Motor development, maternal expectations, and the role of handling. *Infant Behavior & Development, 13*(1), 117–122.

Hopmeyer, A., & Medovoy, T. (2017). Emerging adults' self-identified peer crowd affiliations, risk behavior, and social–emotional adjustment in college. *Emerging Adulthood, 5*(2), 143–148. http://doi.org/10.1177/2167696816665055

Hoppmann, C. A., & Blanchard-Fields, F. (2010). Goals and everyday problem solving: Manipulating goal preferences in young and older adults. *Developmental Psychology, 46*(6), 1433–1443. http://doi.org/10.1037/a0020676

Horgan, D. (1978). The development of the full passive. *Journal of Child Language, 5*, 65–80.

Horn, J. L., & Cattell, R. B. (1966). Refinement and test of the theory of fluid and crystallized general intelligences. *Journal of Educational Psychology, 57*(5), 253–270.

Horn, J. L., & Cattell, R. B. (1967). Age differences in fluid and crystallized intelligence. *Acta Psychologica, 26*(2), 107–129. http://doi.org/10.1016/0001-6918(67)90011-X

Horn, J. L., & Donaldson, G. (1976). On the myth of intellectual decline in adulthood. *American Psychologist, 31*(10), 701–719.

Horn, J. L., & Masunaga, H. (2000). New directions for research into aging and intelligence: The development of expertise. In T. J. Perfect & E. A. Maylor (Eds.), *Models of cognitive aging* (pp. 125–159). New York, NY: Oxford University Press.

Horn, J. L., & Noll, J. (1997). Human cognitive capabilities: Gf-Gc theory. In D. P. Flanagan, J. L. Genshaft, & P. L. Harrison (Eds.), *Contemporary intellectual assessment: Theories, tests, and issues* (pp. 53–91). New York, NY: Guilford Press.

Horn, P. L., West, N. P., Pyne, D. B., Koerbin, G., Lehtinen, S. J., Fricker, P. A., & Cripps, A. W. (2015). Routine exercise alters measures of immunity and the acute phase reaction. *European Journal of Applied Physiology, 115*(2), 407–415. http://doi.org/10.1007/s00421-014-3028-1

Horne, Z., Powell, D., Kant, I., Hume, D., Kohlberg, L., Eskine, K., . . . Kant, I. (2016). How large is the role of emotion in judgments of moral dilemmas? *PLOS ONE, 11*(7). https://doi.org/10.1371/journal.pone.0154780

Horowitz, F. D., & O'Brien, M. (1986). Gifted and talented children: State of knowledge and directions for research. *American Psychologist, 41*(10), 1147–1152. http://doi.org/10.1037/0003-066X.41.10.1147

Horowitz, M. M. (1967). *Morne- Paysan: Peasant village in Martinique.* New York: Holt, Rinehart and Winston.

Hort, J., Bartos, A., Pirttilä, T., & Scheltens, P. (2010). Use of cerebrospinal fluid biomarkers in diagnosis of dementia across Europe. *European Journal of Neurology, 17*(1), 90–96. http://doi.org/10.1111/j.1468-1331.2009.02753.x

Hort, J., O'Brien, J. T., Gainotti, G., Pirttila, T., Popescu, B. O., Rektorova, I., . . . Scheltens, P. (2010). EFNS guidelines for the diagnosis and management of Alzheimer's disease. *European Journal of Neurology, 17*(10), 1236–1248. http://doi.org/10.1111/j.1468-1331.2010.03040.x

Hossain, Z., Field, T., Pickens, J., Malphurs, J., & Del Valle, C. (1997). Fathers' caregiving in low-income African-American and Hispanic-American families. *Early Development & Parenting, 6*(2), 73–82.

Hossain, Z., Roopnarine, J. L., Ismail, R., Hashmi, S. I., & Sombuling, A. (2007). Fathers' and mothers' reports of involvement in caring for infants in Kadazan families in Sabah, Malaysia. *Fathering: A Journal of Theory, Research, & Practice about Men as Fathers, 5*(1), 58–72. http://doi.org/10.3149/fth.0501.58

Hosseini, H., & Hosseini, N. (2008). Epidemiology and prevention of fall injuries among the elderly. *Hospital Topics, 86*(3), 15–20.

Hötting, K., & Röder, B. (2013). Beneficial effects of physical exercise on neuroplasticity and cognition. *Neuroscience & Biobehavioral Reviews, 37*(9), 2243–2257. http://doi.org/10.1016/j.neubiorev.2013.04.005

Hou, N., Hong, S., Wang, W., Olopade, O. I., Dignam, J. J., & Huo, D. (2013). Hormone replacement therapy and breast cancer: Heterogeneous risks by race, weight, and breast density. *Journal of the National Cancer Institute, 105*(18), 1365–1372. http://doi.org/10.1093/jnci/djt207

Houdé, O., Pineau, A., Leroux, G., Poirel, N., Perchey, G., Lanoë, C., . . . Mazoyer, B. (2011). Functional magnetic resonance imaging study of Piaget's conservation-of-number task in preschool and school-age children: A neo-Piagetian approach. *Journal of Experimental Child Psychology, 110*(3), 332–346. http://doi.org/10.1016/j.jecp.2011.04.008

Howard, B. V, Van Horn, L., Hsia, J., Manson, J. E., Stefanick, M. L., Wassertheil-Smoller, S., . . . Robbins, J. (2006). Low-fat diet and weight change in postmenopausal women. *JAMA: Journal of the American Medical Association 296*(4), 394-395 doi:10:100N jamd.296y.39A!

Howard-Jones, P. A. (2014). Neuroscience and education: Myths and messages. *Nature Reviews Neuroscience, 15*(12), 817–824. http://doi.org/10.1038/nrn3817

Howarth, R. (2011). Concepts and controversies in grief and loss. *Journal of Mental Health Counseling, 33*(1), 4–10. http://doi.org/10.17744/mehc.33.1.900m56162888u737

Howe, C., Matthews, L. R., & Heard, R. (2010). Work to retirement: A snapshot of psychological health in a multicultural Australia population. *Work: Journal of Prevention, Assessment & Rehabilitation, 36*(2), 119–127.

Howe, M. L., & Courage, M. L. (1993). On resolving the enigma of infantile amnesia. *Psychological Bulletin, 113*(2), 305–26. Retrieved from http://www.ncbi.nlm.nih.gov/pubmed/8451337

Howe, T.-H., Sheu, C.-F., Wang, T.-N., & Hsu, Y.-W. (2014). Parenting stress in families with very low birth weight preterm infants in early infancy. *Research in Developmental Disabilities, 35*(7), 1748–1756. http://doi.org/10.1016/j.ridd.2014.02.015

Howell, L. C., & Beth, A. (2002). Midlife myths and realities: Women reflect on their experiences. *Journal of Women & Aging, 14*(3/4), 189.

Hoyert, D. L. (2012). *75 years of mortality in the United States, 1935–2010.* Hyattsville, MD.

Hoyte, K. J., Brownell, H., & Wingfield, A. (2009). Components of speech prosody and their use in detection of syntactic structure by older adults. *Experimental Aging Research, 35*(1), 129–151. http://doi.org/10.1080/03610730802565091

Hsieh, P.-H. P., & Schallert, D. L. (2008). Implications from self-efficacy and attribution theories for an understanding of undergraduates' motivation in a foreign language course. *Contemporary Educational Psychology, 33*(4), 513–532. http://doi.org/10.1016/j.cedpsych.2008.01.003

Hsueh, A. C., Morrison, K. R., & Doss, B. D. (2009). Qualitative reports of problems in cohabiting relationships: Comparisons to married and dating relationships. *Journal of Family Psychology, 23*(2), 236–246. http://doi.org/10.1037/a0015364

Hu, X., Kaplan, S., & Dalal, R. S. (2010). An examination of blue- versus white-collar workers' conceptualizations of job satisfaction facets. *Journal of Vocational Behavior, 76*(2), 317–325. http://doi.org/10.1016/j.jvb.2009.10.014

Huang, D. Y. C., Murphy, D. A., & Hser, Y.-I. (2011). Parental monitoring during early adolescence deters adolescent sexual Initiation: Discrete-time survival mixture Analysis. *Journal of Child and Family Studies, 20*(4), 511–520. http://doi.org/10.1007/s10826-010-9418-z

Huang, G. G. (1995). Self-reported biliteracy and self-esteem: A study of Mexican American 8th graders. *Applied Psycholinguistics, 16,* 271–291.

Huang, K.-E., Xu, L., I, N. N., & Jaisamrarn, U. (2010). The Asian Menopause Survey: Knowledge, perceptions, hormone treatment and sexual function. *Maturitas, 65*(3), 276–283. http://doi.org/10.1016/j.maturitas.2009.11.015

Huang, M.-H. (2009). Race of the interviewer and the black–white test score gap. *Social Science Research, 38*(1), 29–38. http://doi.org/10.1016/j.ssresearch.2008.07.004

Huang, Z. J., Lewin, A., Mitchell, S. J., & Zhang, J. (2012). Variations in the relationship between maternal depression, maternal sensitivity, and child attachment by race/ethnicity and nativity: Findings from a nationally representative cohort study. *Maternal and Child Health Journal, 16*(1), 40–50. http://doi.org/10.1007/s10995-010-0716-2

Huddleston, T. (2016). Colorado's legal marijuana industry is worth $1 billion. *Fortune, February 1.* Retrieved from http://fortune.com/2016/02/11/marijuana-billion-dollars-colorado/

Hudon, T. M., Fennell, C. T., & Hoftyzer, M. (2013). Quality not quantity of television viewing is associated with bilingual toddlers' vocabulary scores. *Infant Behavior & Development, 36*(2), 245–54. http://doi.org/10.1016/j.infbeh.2013.01.010

Hudson, J. A., Fivush, R., & Kuebli, J. (1992). Scripts and episodes: The development of event memory. *Applied Cognitive Psychology, 6,* 483–505.

Huelke, D. F. (1998). An overview of anatomical considerations of infants and children in the adult world of automobile safety design. *Annual Proceedings / Association for the Advancement of Automotive Medicine.* Association for the Advancement of Automotive Medicine.

Huerta, T. R., Walker, D. M., Mullen, D., Johnson, T. J., & Ford, E. W. (2017). Trends in E-cigarette awareness and perceived harmfulness in the U.S. *American Journal of Preventive Medicine, 52*(3), 339–346. http://doi.org/10.1016/j.amepre.2016.10.017

Huesmann, L. R., Dubow, E. F., Boxer, P., Landau, S. F., Gvirsman, S. D., Shikaki, K., . . . Sapolsky, R. M. (2016). Children's exposure to violent political conflict stimulates aggression at peers by increasing emotional distress, aggressive script rehearsal, and normative beliefs favoring aggression. *Development and Psychopathology, 36*(7), 1–12. http://doi.org/10.1017/S0954579416001115

Huey, M., Hiatt, C., Laursen, B., Burk, W. J., & Rubin, K. (2017). Mother–adolescent conflict types and adolescent adjustment: A person-oriented analysis. *Journal of Family Psychology.* http://doi.org/10.1037/fam0000294

Hughes, C. H., & Dunn, J. (1998). Understanding mind and emotion: Longitudinal associations with mental-state talk between young friends. *Developmental Psychology, 34,* 1026–1037.

Hughes, C. H., & Ensor, R. (2007). Executive function and theory of mind: Predictive relations from ages 2 to 4. *Developmental Psychology, 43*(6), 1447–1459. http://doi.org/10.1037/0012-I 649.43.6.1447

Hughes, C. H., & Ensor, R. A. (2009). How do families help or hinder the emergence of early executive function? *New Directions for Child & Adolescent Development, 2009*(123), 35–50. http://doi.org/10.1002/cd.234

Hughes, C., & Devine, R. T. (2015). Individual differences in theory of mind from preschool to adolescence: Achievements and directions. *Child Development Perspectives, 9*(3). http://doi.org/10.1111/cdep.12124

Hughes, D., Hagelskamp, C., Way, N., & Foust, M. D. (2009). The role of mothers' and adolescents' perceptions of ethnic-racial socialization in shaping ethnic-racial identity among early adolescent boys and girls. *Journal of Youth & Adolescence, 38*(5), 605–626. http://doi.org/10.1007/s10964-009-9399-7

Hughes, J. N., Chen, Q., Thoemmes, F., & Kwok, O. (2010). An investigation of the relationship between retention in first grade and performance on high stakes tests in third grade. *Educational Evaluation and Policy Analysis, 32*(2), 166–182. http://doi.org/10.3102/0162373710367682

Hughes, M. (1975). Egocentrism in preschool children. *Unpublished doctoral dissertation.* Edinburgh, Scotland: Edinburgh University.

Hughes, M. C. B., Williams, G. M., Baker, P., & Green, A. C. (2013). Sunscreen and prevention of skin aging: A randomized trial. *Annals of Internal Medicine, 158*(11), 781–90. http://doi.org/10.7326/0003-4819-158-11-201306040-00002

Hughes, M. L., Geraci, L., & De Forrest, R. L. (2013). Aging 5 years in 5 minutes: The effect of taking a memory test on older adults' subjective age. *Psychological Science, 24*(12), 2481–8. http://doi.org/10.1177/0956797613494853

Huijbregts, S. C. J., Gassió, R., & Campistol, J. (2013). Executive functioning in context: Relevance for treatment and monitoring of phenylketonuria. *Molecular Genetics and Metabolism, 110,* S25–S30. http://doi.org/10.1016/j.ymgme.2013.10.001

Huijts, T., Kraaykamp, G., & Subramanian, S. V. (2011). Childlessness and psychological well-being in context: A multilevel study on 24 European countries. *European Sociological Review, 29*(1), 32–47. http://doi.org/10.1093/esr/jcr037

Huizink, A. C. (2013). Prenatal cannabis exposure and infant outcomes: Overview of studies. *Progress in Neuro-Psychopharmacology & Biological Psychiatry.* http://doi.org/10.1016/j.pnpbp.2013.09.014

Huizink, A., & Mulder, E. J. H. Ã. (2006). Maternal smoking, drinking or cannabis use during pregnancy and neurobehavioral and cognitive functioning in human offspring. *Neuroscience & Biobehavioral Reviews, 30*(1), 24–41.

Hunnius, S., & Geuze, R. H. (2004). Developmental changes in visual scanning of dynamic faces and abstract stimuli in infants: A longitudinal study. *Infancy, 6*(2), 231–255.

Hunter, S. B., & Smith, D. E. (2008). Predictors of children's understandings of death: Age, cognitive ability, death experience and maternal communicative competence. *OMEGA–Journal of Death and Dying, 57*(2), 143–162. http://doi.org/10.2190/OM.57.2.b

Huntsinger, C. S., Jose, P. E., & Larson, S. L. (1998). Do parent practices to encourage academic competence influence the social adjustment of young European American and Chinese American children? *Developmental Psychology, 34,* 747–756.

Hurd, Y., Wang, X., Anderson, V., Beck, O., Minkoff, H., & Dow-Edwards, D. (2005). Marijuana impairs growth in mid-gestation fetuses. *Neurotoxicology and Teratology, 27*(2), 221–229.

Hurme, H., Westerback, S., & Quadrello, T. (2010). Traditional and new forms of contact between grandparents and grandchildren. *Journal of Intergenerational Relationships, 8*(3), 264–280. http://doi.org/10.1080/15350770.2010.498739

Hurtado, N., Marchman, V. A., & Fernald, A. (2008). Does input influence uptake? Links between maternal talk, processing speed and vocabulary size in Spanish-learning children. *Developmental Science, 11*(6), F31–F39. http://doi.org/10.1111/j.1467-7687.2008.00768.x

Huston, A. C. (2008). From research to policy and back. *Child Development, 79*(1), 1–12. http://doi.org/10.1111/j.1467-8624.2007.01107.x

Hutchinson, E. A., De Luca, C. R., Doyle, L. W., Roberts, G., & Anderson, P. J. (2013). School-age outcomes of extremely preterm or extremely low birth weight children. *Pediatrics, 131*(4). http://doi.org/10.1542/peds.2012-2311

Hutteman, R., Hennecke, M., Orth, U., Reitz, A. K., & Specht, J. (2014). Developmental tasks as a framework to study personality development in adulthood and old age. *European Journal of Personality, 28*(3), 267–278.

Huttenlocher, J., Levine, S., & Vevea, J. (1998). Environmental input and cognitive growth: A study using time-period comparisons. *Child Development, 69,* 1012–1029.

Huttenlocher, J., Vasilyeva, M., Cymerman, E., & Levine, S. (2002). Language input and child syntax. *Cognitive Psychology, 45*(3), 337.

Huttenlocher, J., Waterfall, H., Vasilyeva, M., Vevea, J., & Hedges, L. V. (2010). Sources of variability in children's language growth. *Cognitive Psychology, 61*(4), 343–365. http://doi.org/10.1016/j.cogpsych.2010.08.002

Huxhold, O., Fiori, K. L., & Windsor, T. D. (2013). The dynamic interplay of social network characteristics, subjective well-being, and health: The costs and benefits of socio-emotional selectivity. *Psychology and Aging, 28*(1), 3–16. http://doi.org/10.1037/a0030170

Huxhold, O., Miche, M., & Schüz, B. (2014). Benefits of having friends in older ages: Differential effects of informal social activities on well-being in middle-aged and older adults. *The Journals of Gerontology. Series B, Psychological Sciences and Social Sciences, 69*(3), 366–75. http://doi.org/10.1093/geronb/gbt029

Huyck, M. H. (1996). Continuities and discontinuities in gender identity. In V. L. Bengtson (Ed.), *Adulthood and aging: Research on continuities and discontinuities* (pp. 98–121). New York, NY: Springer.

Huynh, H. T., Demeter, N. E., Burke, R. V., & Upperman, J. S. (2017). The role of adult perceptions and supervision behavior in preventing child injury. *Journal of Community Health*, 1–7. http://doi.org/10.1007/s10900-016-0300-9

Hvas, L., & Dorte Effersøe, G. (2008). Discourses on menopause Part II: How do women talk about menopause? *Health*, 12(2), 177–192. http://doi.org/10.1177/1363459307086842

Hwang, J.-H., Li, C.-W., Wu, C.-W., Chen, J.-H., & Liu, T.-C. (2007). Aging effects on the activation of the auditory cortex during binaural speech listening in white noise: An fMRI study. *Audiology & Neuro-Otology*, 12(5), 285–294.

Hyde, D. C., Flom, R., & Porter, C. L. (2016). Behavioral and neural foundations of multisensory face-voice perception in infancy. *Developmental Neuropsychology*, 41(5–8), 273–292. http://doi.org/10.1080/87565641.2016.1255744

Hyde, J. S. (2014). Gender similarities and differences. *Annual Review of Psychology*, 65, 373–98. http://doi.org/10.1146/annurev-psych-010213-115057

Hyde, J. S. (2016). Sex and cognition:Gender and cognitive functions. *Current Opinion in Neurobiology*, 38, 53–56. http://doi.org/10.1016/j.conb.2016.02.007

Hyde, J. S., & DeLamater, J. D. (2017). *Understanding human sexuality*. New York: McGraw = Hill.

Hyde, Z., Flicker, L., Hankey, G. J., Almeida, O. P., McCaul, K. A., Chubb, S. A. P., & Yeap, B. B. (2010). Prevalence of sexual activity and associated factors in men aged 75 to 95 years. *Annals of Internal Medicine*, 153(11), 693–702.

Iadecola, C. (2013). The pathobiology of vascular dementia. *Neuron*, 80(4), 844–866. http://doi.org/10.1016/j.neuron.2013.10.008

Idring, S., Magnusson, C., Lundberg, M., Ek, M., Rai, D., Svensson, A. C., . . . Lee, B. K. (2014). Parental age and the risk of autism spectrum disorders: Findings from a Swedish population-based cohort. *International Journal of Epidemiology*, 43(1), 107–115.

Iliffe, S., Robinson, L., Brayne, C., Goodman, C., Rait, G., Manthorpe, J., & Ashley, P. (2009). Primary care and dementia: Diagnosis, screening and disclosure. *International Journal of Geriatric Psychiatry*, 24(9), 895–901. http://doi.org/10.1002/gps.2204

Imbo, I., & Vandierendonck, A. (2007). The development of strategy use in elementary school children: Working memory and individual differences. *Journal of Experimental Child Psychology*, 96(4), 284–309.

Imdad, A., Yakoob, M. Y., & Bhutta, Z. A. (2011). Effect of breastfeeding promotion interventions on breastfeeding rates, with special focus on developing countries. *BMC Public Health*, 11(Suppl 3), 1–8. http://doi.org/10.1186/1471-2458-11-s3-s24

Imoscopi, A., Inelmen, E. M., Sergi, G., Miotto, F., & Manzato, E. (2012). Taste loss in the elderly: Epidemiology, causes and consequences. *Aging Clinical and Experimental Research*, 24(6), 570–579. http://doi.org/10.3275/8520

Imuta, K., Henry, J. D., Slaughter, V., Selcuk, B., & Ruffman, T. (2016). Theory of mind and prosocial behavior in childhood: A meta-analytic review. *Developmental Psychology*, 52(8), 1192–1205. http://doi.org/10.1037/dev0000140

Infurna, F. J., & Luthar, S. S. (2017a). Parents' adjustment following the death of their child: Resilience is multidimensional and differs across outcomes examined. *Journal of Research in Personality*, 68, 38–53. http://doi.org/10.1016/j.jrp.2017.04.004

Infurna, F. J., & Luthar, S. S. (2017b). The multidimensional nature of resilience to spousal loss. *Journal of Personality and Social Psychology*, 112(6), 926–947. http://doi.org/10.1037/pspp0000095

Inhelder, B., & Piaget, J. (1958). *The growth of logical thinking: From childhood to adolescence*. New York, NY: Basic Books.

Inhelder, B., & Piaget, J. (1964). *The early growth of logic in the child: Classification and seriation*. New York: Harper and Row.

Insurance Institute for Highway Safety. (2015). *Older drivers*. Retrieved from http://www.iihs.org/iihs/topics/t/older-drivers/qanda

Isbell, E., Fukuda, K., Neville, H. J., & Vogel, E. K. (2015). Visual working memory continues to develop through adolescence. *Frontiers in Psychology*, 6, 696. http://doi.org/10.3389/fpsyg.2015.00696

Ishitani, T. T. (2006). Studying attrition and degree completion behavior among first-generation college students in the United States. *Journal of Higher Education*, 77, 861–885.

Islami, F., Liu, Y., Jemal, A., Zhou, J., Weiderpass, E., Colditz, G., . . . Weiss, M. (2015). Breastfeeding and breast cancer risk by receptor status—a systematic review and meta-analysis. *Annals of Oncology*, 26(12). http://doi.org/10.1093/annonc/mdv379

Islander, U., Jochems, C., Lagerquist, M. K., Forsblad-d'Elia, H., & Carlsten, H. (2011). Estrogens in rheumatoid arthritis; The immune system and bone. *Molecular & Cellular Endocrinology*, 335(1), 14–29. http://doi.org/10.1016/j.mce.2010.05.018

Isomaa, R., Isomaa, A.-L., Marttunen, M., Kaltiala-Heino, R., & Björkqvist, K. (2009). The prevalence, incidence and development of eating disorders in Finnish adolescents—a two-step 3-year follow-up Study. *European Eating Disorders Review*, 17(3), 199–207. http://doi.org/10.1002/erv.919

Iverson, J. M., & Goldin-Meadow, S. (2005). Gesture paves the way for language development. *Psychological Science*, 16(5), 367–371. http://doi.org/10.1111/j.0956-7976.2005.01542.x

Izard, C. E. (2007). Basic emotions, natural kinds, emotion schemas, and a new paradigm. *Perspectives on Psychological Science*, 2(3), 260–280. http://doi.org/10.1111/j.1745-6916.2007.00044.x

Izard, C. E., Fantauzzo, C. A., Castle, J. M., Haynes, O. M., Rayias, M. F., & Putnam, P. H. (1995). The ontogeny and significance of infants' facial expressions in the first 9 months of life. *Developmental Psychology*, 31, 997–1013.

Jackson, G. R., & Owsley, C. (2003). Visual dysfunction, neurodegenerative diseases, and aging. *Neurologic Clinics*, 21(3), 709–728.

Jackson, G., Rosen, R. C., Kloner, R. A., Kostis, J. B., Martella, R., D'Andrea, F., . . . Shabsigh, R. (2006). The second princeton consensus on sexual dysfunction and cardiac risk: New guidelines for sexual medicine. *The Journal of Sexual Medicine*, 3(1), 28–36. http://doi.org/10.1111/j.1743-6109.2005.00196.x

Jackson, J. B., Miller, R. B., Oka, M., & Henry, R. G. (2014). Gender differences in marital satisfaction: A meta-analysis. *Journal of Marriage and Family*, 76(1), 105–129. http://doi.org/10.1111/jomf.12077

Jackson, K. M., Sher, K. J., & Park, A. (2005). Drinking among college students: Consumption and consequences. In M. Galanter (Ed.), *Recent developments in alcoholism: Vol. 17. Alcohol problems in adolescents and young adults* (pp. 85–117). New York: Springer.

Jacobs, E., Miller, L. C., & Tirella, L. G. (2010). Developmental and behavioral performance of internationally adopted preschoolers: A pilot study. *Child Psychiatry & Human Development*, 41(1), 15–29. http://doi.org/10.1007/s10578-009-0149-6

Jacobs, J. E., Lanza, S., Osgood, D. W., Eccles, J. S., & Wigfield, A. (2002). Changes in children's self-competence and values: Gender and domain differences across grades one through twelve. *Child Development*, 73, 509–527.

Jacobs, S., Perez, J., Cheng, Y. I., Sill, A., Wang, J., & Lyon, M. E. (2015). Adolescent end of life preferences and congruence with their parents' preferences: Results of a survey of adolescents with cancer. *Pediatric Blood & Cancer*, 62(4), 710–714. http://doi.org/10.1002/pbc.25358

Jacobs-Lawson, J. M., Hershey, D. A., & Neukam, K. A. (2004). Gender differences in factors that influence time spent planning for retirement. *Journal of Women & Aging*, 16(3/4), 55–69.

Jacobson, J. L., & Jacobson, S. W. (1996). Methodological considerations in behavioral toxicology in infants and children. *Developmental Psychology*, 32, 390–403.

Jacoby, L. L., Wahlheim, C. N., Rhodes, M. G., Daniels, K. A., & Rogers, C. S. (2010). Learning to diminish the effects of proactive interference: Reducing false memory for young and older adults. *Memory & Cognition*, 38(6), 820–829. http://doi.org/10.3758/mc.38.6.820

Jadav, S. D. (2004). Occupational female reproductive hazards. *Journal of Health Management*, 6(2), 201–210. http://doi.org/10.1177/097206340400600210

Jadhav, A., & Weir, D. (2017). Widowhood and depression in a cross-national perspective: Evidence from the United States, Europe, Korea, and China. *The Journals of Gerontology: Series B*, 1, 316–326. http://doi.org/10.1093/geronb/gbx021

Jadva, V., Hines, M., & Golombok, S. (2010). Infants' preferences for toys, colors, and shapes: sex differences and similarities. *Archives of Sexual Behavior*, 39(6), 1261–73. http://doi.org/10.1007/s10508-010-9618-z

Jaeger, M. M. (2012). The extended family and children's educational success. *American Sociological Review*, 77(6), 903–922. http://doi.org/10.1177/0003122412464040

Jaekel, J., Pluess, M., Belsky, J., & Wolke, D. (2015). Effects of maternal sensitivity on low birth weight children's academic achievement: A test of differential susceptibility versus diathesis stress. *Journal of Child Psychology and Psychiatry*, 56(6), 693–701. http://doi.org/10.1111/jcpp.12331

Jaffari-Bimmel, N., Juffer, F., van Ijzendoorn, M. H., Bakermans-Kranenburg, M. J., & Mooijaart, A. (2006). Social development from infancy to adolescence: Longitudinal and concurrent factors in an adoption sample. *Developmental Psychology*, 42(6), 1143–1153. http://doi.org/10.1037/0012-1649.42.6.1143

Jaffee, S., & Hyde, J. S. (2000). Gender differences in moral orientation: A meta-analysis. *Psychological Bulletin*, 126(5), 703.

Jager, R. D., Mieler, W. F., & Miller, J. W. (2008). Age-related macular degeneration. *New England Journal of Medicine*, 358(24), 2606–2617. http://doi.org/10.1056/NEJMra0801537

Jagers, R. J., Bingham, K., & Hans, S. L. (1996). Socialization and social judgments among inner-city African-American kindergartners. *Child Development*, 67, 140–150.

Jahns, L., Siega-Riz, A. M., & Popkin, B. M. (2001). The increasing prevalence of snacking among US children from 1977 to 1996. *Journal of Pediatrics*, 138, 493–498.

Jahromi, L. B., & Stifter, C. A. (2007). Individual differences in the contribution of maternal soothing to infant distress reduction. *Infancy*, 11(3), 255–269. http://doi.org/10.1080/15250000701310371

Jain, S., & Cohen, A. K. (2013). Behavioral adaptation among youth exposed to community violence: A longitudinal multidisciplinary study of family, peer and neighborhood-level protective factors. *Prevention Science*, 14(6), 606–617. http://doi.org/10.1007/s11121-012-0344-8

Jakulj, F., Zernicke, K., Bacon, S. L., van Wielingen, L. E., Key, B. L., West, S. G., & Campbell, T. S. (2007). A high-fat meal increases cardiovascular reactivity to psychological stress in healthy young adults. *Journal of Nutrition*, 137(4), 935–939.

Jambon, M., & Smetana, J. G. (2014). Moral complexity in middle childhood: Children's evaluations of necessary harm. *Developmental Psychology*, 50(1), 22–33.

James, J. B., & Lewkowicz, C. (1995). Rethinking the gender identity crossover hypothesis: A test of a new model. *Sex Roles*, 32(3), 185–207.

Jannasch, F., Kroger, J., & Schulze, M. B. (2017). Dietary patterns and type 2 diabetes: A systematic literature review and meta-analysis of prospective studies. *The Journal of Nutrition*, 147(6), 1174–1182. http://doi.org/10.3945/jn.116.242552

Janosz, M., Archambault, I., Morizot, J., & Pagani, L. S. (2008). School engagement trajectories and their differential predictive relations to dropout. *Journal of Social Issues*, 64(1), 21–40. http://doi.org/10.1111/j.1540-4560.2008.00546.x

Janse, E. (2009). Processing of fast speech by elderly listeners. *The Journal of the Acoustical Society of America*, 125(4), 2361–2373. http://doi.org/10.1121/1.3082117

Jansen, I. (2006). Decision making in childbirth: The influence of traditional structures in a Ghanaian village. *International Nursing Review*, 53(1), 41–46.

Jansen, P. W., de Barse, L. M., Jaddoe, V. W. V., Verhulst, F. C., Franco, O. H., & Tiemeier, H. (2017). Bi-directional associations between child fussy eating and parents' pressure to eat: Who influences whom? *Physiology & Behavior*, 176, 101–106. http://doi.org/10.1016/j.physbeh.2017.02.015

Janssen, I., Katzmarzyk, P. T., Boyce, W. F., Vereecken, C., Mulvihill, C., Roberts, C., . . . et al. (2005). Comparison of overweight and obesity prevalence in school-aged youth from 34 countries and their relationships with physical activity and dietary patterns. *Obesity Reviews*, 6, 123–132.

Janssen, I., LeBlanc, A. G., Janssen, I., Twisk, J., Tolfrey, K., Jones, A., . . . Janssen, I. (2010). Systematic review of the health benefits of physical activity and fitness in school-aged children and youth. *International Journal of Behavioral Nutrition and Physical Activity*, 7(1), 40. http://doi.org/10.1186/1479-5868-7-40

Janssens, J. M. A. M., & Dekovic, M. (1997). Child rearing, prosocial moral reasoning, and prosocial behaviour. *International Journal of Behavioral Development*, 20, 509–527.

Jaswal, V. K. (2010). Believing what you're told: Young children's trust in unexpected testimony about the physical world. *Cognitive Psychology*, 61(3), 248–272. http://doi.org/10.1016/j.cogpsych.2010.06.002

Javadi, A. H., Schmidt, D. H. K., & Smolka, M. N. (2014). Differential representation of feedback and decision in adolescents and adults. *Neuropsychologia*, 56, 280–288. http://doi.org/10.1016/j.neuropsychologia.2014.01.021

Jay, S. M., Green, V., Johnson, S., Caldwell, S., & Nitschke, R. (1987). Differences in death concepts between children wither cancer and physically healthy children. *Journal of Clinical Child Psychology*, 16(4), 301–306. http://doi.org/10.1207/s15374424jccp1604_2

Jayakody, R., & Kalil, A. (2002). Social fathering in low-income, African American families with preschool children. *Journal of Marriage and Family*, 64, 504–516.

Jean, A. D. L., & Stack, D. M. (2012). Full-term and very-low-birth-weight preterm infants' self-regulating behaviors during a still-face interaction: Influences of maternal touch. *Infant Behavior and Development*, 35(4), 779–791. http://doi.org/10.1016/j.infbeh.2012.07.023

Jecker, N. S. (2006). Euthanasia. In R. Schulz (Ed.), *The encyclopedia of aging* (4th ed., pp. 392–394). New York: Springer.

Jecker, N. S. (2011). Medical futility and the death of a child. *Journal of Bioethical Inquiry*, 8(2), 133–139. http://doi.org/10.1007/s11673-011-9288-0

Jefferies, A. L. (2012). Kangaroo care for the preterm infant and family. *Paediatrics & Child Health*, 17(3), 141–146.

Jeffreys, M., Lawlor, D. A., Galobardes, B., McCarron, P., Kinra, S., Ebrahim, S., & Smith, G. D. (2006). Lifecourse weight patterns and adult-onset diabetes: The Glasgow Alumni and British Women's Heart and Health studies. *International Journal of Obesity*, 30(3), 507–512.

Jeha, D., Usta, I., Ghulmiyyah, L., & Nassar, A. (2015). A review of the risks and consequences of adolescent pregnancy. *Journal of Neonatal-Perinatal Medicine*, 8(1), 1–8. http://doi.org/10.3233/NPM-15814038

Jemal, A., Thun, M. J., Ward, E. E., Henley, S. J., Cokkinides, V. E., & Murray, T. E. (2008). Mortality from leading causes by education and race in the United States, 2001. *American Journal of Preventive Medicine*, 34(1), 1–8.

Jenkins, J. M., & Astington, J. W. (1996). Cognitive factors and family structure associated with theory of mind development in young children. *Developmental Psychology*, 32, 70–78.

Jenkins, L. J., Yang, Y.-J., Goh, J., Hong, Y.-Y., & Park, D. C. (2010). Cultural differences in the lateral occipital complex while viewing incongruent scenes. *Social Cognitive and Affective Neuroscience*, 5(2–3), 236–241. http://doi.org/10.1093/scan/nsp056

Jenkins, L. N., Demaray, M. K., & Tennant, J. (2017). Social, emotional, and cognitive factors associated with bullying. *School Psychology Review*, 46(1), 42–64. http://doi.org/10.17105/SPR46-1.42-64

Jennings, K., & Dietz, L. (2003). Mastery motivation and goal persistence in young children. In M. H. Bornstein & L. Davidson (Eds.), *Well-being: Positive development across the life course* (pp. 295–309). Mahwah, NJ: Wiley.

Jensen, T. M., & Howard, M. O. (2015). Perceived stepparent–child relationship quality: A systematic review of stepchildren's perspectives. *Marriage & Family Review*, 1–55. http://doi.org/10.1080/01494929.2015.1006717

Jerome, G. J., Ko, S., Kauffman, D., Studenski, S. A., Ferrucci, L., & Simonsick, E. M. (2015). Gait characteristics associated with walking speed decline in older adults: Results from the Baltimore Longitudinal Study of Aging. *Archives of Gerontology and Geriatrics*, 60(2), 239–243. http://doi.org/10.1016/j.archger.2015.01.007

Jessen, K. R. (2004). Glial cells. *International Journal of Biochemistry & Cell Biology*, 36(10), 1861–1867.

Jewell, J. D., Krohn, E. J., Scott, V. G., Carlton, M., & Meinz, E. (2008). the differential impact of mothers' and fathers' discipline on preschool children's home and classroom behavior. *North American Journal of Psychology*, 10(1), 173–188.

Jeynes, W. H. (2008). A meta-analysis of the relationship between phonics instruction and minority elementary school student academic achievement. *Education & Urban Society*, 40(2), 151–166.

Jha, A. K., Baliga, S., Kumar, H. H., Rangnekar, A., & Baliga, B. S. (2015). Is there a preventive role for vernix caseosa? An invitro study. *Journal of Clinical and Diagnostic Research*, 9(11), SC13–16. http://doi.org/10.7860/JCDR/2015/14740.6784

Jhoo, J. H., Kim, K. W., Huh, Y., Lee, S. B., Park, J. H., Lee, J. J., . . . Woo, J. I. (2008). Prevalence of dementia and its subtypes in an elderly urban Korean population: Results from the Korean Longitudinal Study on Health and Aging (KLoSHA). *Dementia & Geriatric Cognitive Disorders*, 26(3), 270–276. http://doi.org/10.1159/000160960

Jia, G., & Aaronson, D. (2003). A longitudinal study of Chinese children and adolescents learning English in the United States. *Applied Psycholinguistics*, 24(1), 131–161. http://doi.org/10.1017/S0142716403000079

Jia, Y., Konold, T. R., & Cornell, D. (2016). Authoritative school climate and high school dropout rates. *School Psychology Quarterly*, 31(2), 289–303. http://doi.org/10.1037/spq0000139

Jiang, Y., Ekono, M., & Skinner, C. (2015). *Basic facts about low-income children: Children under 6 Years, 2013.* Retrieved from http://www.nccp.org/publications/pub_1097.html

Jiang, Y., Granja, M. R., & Koball, H. (2017). *Basic facts about low-income children.* Retrieved from http://www.nccp.org/publications/pub_1170.html

Jimerson, S. R. (2001). Meta-analysis of grade retention research: Implications for practice in the 21st century. *School Psychology Review*, 30(3), 420–437.

Jimerson, S. R., & Renshaw, T. L. (2012). Retention and social promotion. *Principal Leadership*, 13(1), 12–16.

Jin, M. K., Jacobvitz, D., Hazen, N., & Jung, S. H. (2012). Maternal sensitivity and infant attachment security in Korea: Cross-cultural validation of the Strange Situation. *Attachment & Human Development*, 14(1), 33–44. http://doi.org/10.1080/14616734.2012.636656

Jipson, J. L., Gülgöz, S., & Gelman, S. A. (2016). Parent–child conversations regarding the ontological status of a robotic dog. *Cognitive Development*, 39, 21–35. http://doi.org/10.1016/j.cogdev.2016.03.001

Jirikowic, T., Gelo, J., & Astley, S. (2010). Children and youth with fetal alcohol spectrum disorders: Summary of intervention recommendations after clinical diagnosis. *Intellectual and Developmental Disabilities*, 48(5), 330–344. http://doi.org/10.1352/1934-9556-48.5.330

Jiwa, N. S., Garrard, P., & Hainsworth, A. H. (2010). Experimental models of vascular dementia and vascular cognitive impairment: A systematic review. *Journal of Neurochemistry*, 115(4), 814–828. http://doi.org/10.1111/j.1471-4159.2010.06958.x

Johansson, J., Nordstrom, A., Gustafson, Y., Westling, G., & Nordstrom, P. (2017). Increased postural sway during quiet stance as a risk factor for prospective falls in community-dwelling elderly individuals. *Age and Ageing*, 10(Suppl 4), 1–6. http://doi.org/10.1093/ageing/afx083

Johnson, C. L., & Troll, L. E. (1994). Constraints and facilitators to friendships in late late life. *The Gerontologist*, 34(1), 79–87.

Johnson, C. V., & Hayes, J. A. (2003). Troubled spirits: Prevalence and predictors of religious and spiritual concerns among university students and counseling center clients. *Journal of Counseling Psychology*, 50(4), 409–419. http://doi.org/10.1037/0022-0167.50.4.409

Johnson, D. E. (2000). Medical and developmental sequelae of early childhood institutionalization in Eastern European adoptees. *31st Minnesota Symposium on Child Psychology*, 113–162.

Johnson, K. J., & Mutchler, J. E. (2014). The emergence of a positive gerontology: From disengagement to social involvement. *The Gerontologist*, *54*(1), 93–100. http://doi.org/10.1093/geront/gnt099

Johnson, S. B., Riis, J. L., & Noble, K. G. (2016). State of the art review: Poverty and the developing brain. *Pediatrics*. Retrieved from http://pediatrics.aappublications.org/content/early/2016/03/03/peds.2015-3075

Johnson, S. C., Dweck, C. S., & Chen, F. S. (2007). Evidence for infants' internal working models of attachment. *Psychological Science*, *18*(6), 501–502. http://doi.org/10.1111/j.1467-9280.2007.01929.x

Johnson, S. H., & Rybash, J. M. (1993). A cognitive neuroscience perspective on age-related slowing: Developmental changes in the functional architecture. In J. Cerella, J. M. Rybash, W. Hoyer, & M. L. Commons (Eds.), *Adult information processing: Limits on loss* (pp. 143–173). San Diego, CA: Academic Press.

Johnson, S. L., Dunleavy, J., Gemmell, N. J., & Nakagawa, S. (2015). Consistent age-dependent declines in human semen quality: A systematic review and meta-analysis. *Ageing Research Reviews*, *19C*, 22–33. http://doi.org/10.1016/j.arr.2014.10.007

Johnson, V. A., Kemp, A. H., Heard, R., Lennings, C. J., & Hickie, I. B. (2015). Childhood- versus adolescent-onset antisocial youth with conduct disorder: Psychiatric illness, neuropsychological and psychosocial function. *PLoS ONE*, *10*(4), e0121627. http://doi.org/10.1371/journal.pone.0121627

Johnston, J. C. (2005). Teaching gestural signs to infants to advance child development: A review of the evidence. *First Language*, *25*(2), 235–251. http://doi.org/10.1177/0142723705050340

Johnston, M. V, Ishida, A., Ishida, W. N., Matsushita, H. B., Nishimura, A., & Tsuji, M. (2009). Plasticity and injury in the developing brain. *Brain & Development*, *31*(1), 1–10. http://doi.org/10.1016/j.braindev.2008.03.014

Jolles, D. D., van Buchem, M. A., Crone, E. A., & Rombouts, S. A. R. B. (2011). A comprehensive study of whole-brain functional connectivity in children and young adults. *Cerebral Cortex*, *21*(2), 385–391. http://doi.org/10.1093/cercor/bhq104

Jonas, W., Atkinson, L., Steiner, M., Meaney, M. J., Wazana, A., & Fleming, A. S. (2015). Breastfeeding and maternal sensitivity predict early infant temperament. *Acta Paediatrica*, *104*(7), 678–686. http://doi.org/10.1111/apa.12987

Jones, A. P., Laurens, K. R., Herba, C. M., Barker, G. J., & Viding, E. (2009). Amygdala hypoactivity to fearful faces in boys with conduct problems and callous-unemotional traits. *American Journal of Psychiatry*, *166*(1), 95–102. http://doi.org/10.1176/appi.ajp.2008.07071050

Jones, C. J., Peskin, H., & Livson, N. (2011). Men's and women's change and individual differences in change in femininity from age 33 to 85: Results from the intergenerational studies. *Journal of Adult Development*, *18*(4), 155–163. http://doi.org/10.1007/s10804-010-9108-5

Jones, D. C., Abbey, B. B., & Cumberland, A. (1998). The development of display rule knowledge: Linkages with family expressiveness and social competence. *Child Development*, *69*(4), 1209–1222. http://doi.org/10.1111/j.1467-8624.1998.tb06168.x

Jones, D. J., Lewis, T., Litrownik, A., Thompson, R., Proctor, L. J., Isbell, P., . . . Runyan, D. (2013). Linking childhood sexual abuse and early adolescent risk behavior: The intervening role of internalizing and externalizing problems. *Journal of Abnormal Child Psychology*, *41*(1), 139–150. http://doi.org/10.1007/s10802-012-9656-1

Jones, E. J. H., & Herbert, J. S. (2006). Exploring memory in infancy: Deferred imitation and the development of declarative memory. *Infant & Child Development*, *15*, 195–205.

Jones, H. E. (2006). Drug addiction during pregnancy. *Current Directions in Psychological Science*, *15*(3), 126–130.

Jones, J. D., Cassidy, J., & Shaver, P. R. (2015). Parents' self-reported attachment styles: A review of links with parenting behaviors, emotions, and cognitions. *Personality and Social Psychology Review*, *19*(1), 44–76. http://doi.org/10.1177/1088868314541858

Jones, K. P., Peddie, C. I., Gilrane, V. L., King, E. B., & Gray, A. L. (2016). Not so subtle: A meta-analytic investigation of the correlates of subtle and overt discrimination. *Journal of Management*, *42*(6), 1588–1613. http://doi.org/10.1177/0149206313506466

Jones, L., Rowe, J., & Becker, T. (2009). Appraisal, coping, and social support as predictors of psychological distress and parenting efficacy in parents of premature infants. *Children's Health Care*, *38*(4), 245–262. http://doi.org/10.1080/02739610903235976

Jones, M. D., & Galliher, R. V. (2007). Ethnic identity and psychosocial functioning in Navajo adolescents. *Journal of Research on Adolescence*, *17*(4), 683–696. http://doi.org/10.1111/j.1532-7795.2007.00541.x

Jones, R. M., Akers, J. F., & White, J. M. (1994). Revised classification criteria for the Extended Objective Measure of Ego Identity Status (EOMEIS). *Journal of Adolescence*, *17*(6), 533–549.

Jones, W., & Klin, A. (2013). Attention to eyes is present but in decline in 2–6-month-old infants later diagnosed with autism. *Nature*, *504*(7480), 427–431. http://doi.org/10.1038/nature12715

Jonsson, B., Wiklund-Hörnqvist, C., Nyroos, M., & Börjesson, A. (2014). Self-reported memory strategies and their relationship to immediate and delayed text recall and working memory capacity. *Education Inquiry*, *5*. http://doi.org/10.3402/edui.v5.22850

Joo, M. (2010). Long-term effects of Head Start on academic and school outcomes of children in persistent poverty: Girls vs. boys. *Children & Youth Services Review*, *32*(6), 807–814. http://doi.org/10.1016/j.childyouth.2010.01.018

Jose, A., Daniel O'Leary, K., & Moyer, A. (2010). Does premarital cohabitation predict subsequent marital stability and marital quality? A meta-analysis. *Journal of Marriage & Family*, *72*(1), 105–116. http://doi.org/10.1111/j.1741-3737.2009.00686.x

Joseph, D. L., Jin, J., Newman, D. A., & O'Boyle, E. H. (2015). Why does self-reported emotional intelligence predict job performance? A meta-analytic investigation of mixed EI. *Journal of Applied Psychology*, *100*(2), 298–342. http://doi.org/10.1037/a0037681

Josephs, M., & Rakoczy, H. (2016). Young children think you can opt out of social-conventional but not moral practices. *Cognitive Development*, *39*, 197–204. http://doi.org/10.1016/j.cogdev.2016.07.002

Joussemet, M., Landry, R., & Koestner, R. (2008). A self-determination theory perspective on parenting. *Canadian Psychology*, *49*(3), 194–200. http://doi.org/10.1037/a0012754

Jozefowski, J. T. (1999). *The Phoenix phenomenon: Rising from the ashes of grief*. Northvale, NJ: Jason Aronso.

Juárez, S. P., & Merlo, J. (2013). Revisiting the effect of maternal smoking during pregnancy on offspring birthweight: A quasi-experimental sibling analysis in Sweden. *PloS One*, *8*(4), e61734. http://doi.org/10.1371/journal.pone.0061734

Judd, D. (2014). *Give sorrow words: Working with a dying child*. London: Karmac.

Juel, C. (1988). Learning to read and write: A longitudinal study of 54 children from first through fourth grades. *Journal of Educational Psychology*, *80*, 417–447.

Junaid, K. A., & Fellowes, S. (2006). Gender differences in the attainment of motor skills on the movement assessment battery for children. *Physical & Occupational Therapy in Pediatrics*, *26*(1/2), 5–11.

Jung, W. H., Prehn, K., Fang, Z., Korczykowski, M., Kable, J. W., Rao, H., & Robertson, D. C. (2016). Moral competence and brain connectivity: A resting-state fMRI study. *NeuroImage*, *141*, 408–415. https://doi.org/10.1016/j.neuroimage.2016.07.045

Just, M. A., & Carpenter, P. A. (1992). A capacity theory of comprehension: Individual differences in working memory. *Psychological Review*, *99*, 122–149.

Juster, R.-P., Smith, N. G., Ouellet, É., Sindi, S., & Lupien, S. J. (2013). Sexual orientation and disclosure in relation to psychiatric symptoms, diurnal cortisol, and allostatic load. *Psychosomatic Medicine*, *75*(2), 103–116. http://doi.org/10.1097/PSY.0b013e3182826881

Justice, E. M. (1986). Developmental changes in judgments of relative strategy effectiveness. *British Journal of Developmental Psychology*, *4*, 75–81.

Justice, E. M., Baker-Ward, L., Gupta, S., & Jannings, L. R. (1997). Means to the goal of remembering: Developmental changes in awareness of strategy use-performance relations. *Journal of Experimental Child Psychology*, *65*, 293–314.

Juul Nilsson, C., Lund, R., & Avlund, K. (2008). Cohabitation status and onset of disability among older Danes. *Journal of Aging & Health*, *20*(2), 235–253.

Juvonen, J., & Graham, S. (2014). Bullying in schools: The power of bullies and the plight of victims. *Annual Review of Psychology*, *65*, 159–185. http://doi.org/10.1146/annurev-psych-010213-115030

Kagan, J. (1983). Stress and coping in early development. In N. Garmezy & M. Rutter (Eds.), *Stress, coping, and development in children* (pp. 191–216). Baltimore, MD: Johns Hopkins University Press.

Kagan, J. (2008). In defense of qualitative changes in development. *Child Development*, *79*(6), 1606–1624. http://doi.org/10.1111/j.1467-8624.2008.01211.x

Kagan, J., Arcus, D., Snidman, N., Feng, W., Handler, J., & Greene, S. (1994). Reactivity in infants: A cross-national comparison. *Developmental Psychology*, *30*, 342–345.

Kahlenberg, S. G., & Hein, M. M. (2010). Progression on Nickelodeon? Gender-role stereotypes in toy commercials. *Sex Roles*, *62*(11–12), 830–847. http://doi.org/10.1007/s11199-009-9653-1

Kail, B. L., Acosta, K. L., & Wright, E. R. (2015). State-level marriage equality and the health of same-sex couples. *American Journal of Public Health*, *105*(6), 1101–1105. http://doi.org/10.2105/AJPH.2015.302589

Kail, R. (2000). Speed of information processing: Developmental change and links to intelligence. *Journal of School Psychology*, *38*, 51–61.

Kail, R. V, & Reese, H. W. (2002). *Advances in child development and behavior* (Vol. 29). San Diego, CA: Academic Press.

Kail, R. V. (2003). Information processing and memory. In M. H. Bornstein & L. Davidson (Eds.), *Well-being: Positive development across the life course* (pp. 269–279). Mahwah, NJ: Erlbaum.

Kail, R. V. (2008). Speed of processing in childhood and adolescence: Nature, consequences, and implications for understanding atypical development. In J. DeLuca & J. H. Kalmar (Eds.), *Information processing speed in clinical populations* (pp. 101–123). Philadelphia, PA: Taylor & Francis.

Kail, R., & Park, Y. (1992). Global developmental change in processing time. *Merrill-Palmer Quarterly, 38*, 525–541.

Kail, R., & Park, Y. (1994). Processing time, articulation time, and memory span. *Journal of Experimental Child Psychology, 57*, 281–291.

Kaiser Family Foundation. (2014). *Sexual health of adolescents and young adults in the United States.* Retrieved from http://kff.org/womens-health-policy/fact-sheet/sexual-health-of-adolescents-and-young-adults-in-the-united-states/

Kaiser, L. C. (2007). Gender-job satisfaction differences across Europe. *International Journal of Manpower, 28*(1), 75–94. http://doi.org/10.1108/01437720710733483

Kaiser, L., Allen, L., & American Dietetic Association. (2008). Position of the American Dietetic Association: Nutrition and lifestyle for a healthy pregnancy outcome. *Journal of the American Dietetic Association, 108*(3), 553–561. http://doi.org/10.1016/j.jada.2008.01.030

Kaiser, M. J., Bauer, J. M., Rämsch, C., Uter, W., Guigoz, Y., Cederholm, T., . . . Sieber, G. C. (2010). Frequency of malnutrition in older adults: A multinational perspective using the Mini Nutritional Assessment. *Journal of the American Geriatrics Society, 58*(9), 1734–1738. http://doi.org/10.1111/j.1532-5415.2010.03016.x

Kalaria, R. N. (2016). Neuropathological diagnosis of vascular cognitive impairment and vascular dementia with implications for Alzheimer's disease. *Acta Neuropathologica, 131*(5), 659–685. http://doi.org/10.1007/s00401-016-1571-z

Kalaria, R. N., Maestre, G. E., Arizaga, R., Friedland, R. P., Galasko, D., Hall, K., . . . Antuono, P. (2008). Alzheimer's disease and vascular dementia in developing countries: Prevalence, management, and risk factors. *Lancet Neurology, 7*(9), 812–826. http://doi.org/10.1016/S1474-4422(08)70169-8

Kalkwarf, H. J. (2007). Childhood and adolescent milk intake and adult bone health. *International Congress Series, 1297*, 39–49.

Kalsner, L., & Chamberlain, S. J. (2015). Prader-Willi, Angelman, and 15q11-q13 Duplication syndromes. *Pediatric Clinics of North America, 62*(3), 587–606. http://doi.org/10.1016/j.pcl.2015.03.004

Kalvapallé, R. (2017). *Weed around the world: What legal marijuana looks like in other countries.* Retrieved from http://globalnews.ca/news/3378603/marijuana-laws-around-the-world/

Kammeyer, A., & Luiten, R. M. (2015). Oxidation events and skin aging. *Ageing Research Reviews, 21*, 16–29. http://doi.org/10.1016/j.arr.2015.01.001

Kamo, Y. (1998). Asian grandparents. In M. E. Szinovacz (Ed.), *Handbook on grandparenthood* (pp. 97–112). Westport, CT: Greenwood Press.

Kan, P. F., & Kohnert, K. (2008). Fast mapping by bilingual preschool children. *Journal of Child Language, 35*(3), 495–514. http://doi.org/10.1017/S0305000907008604

Kan, P. F., & Kohnert, K. (2011). A growth curve analysis of novel word learning by sequential bilingual preschool children. *Bilingualism: Language and Cognition, 15*(3), 452–469. http://doi.org/10.1017/S1366728911000356

Kana, R. K., Maximo, J. O., Williams, D. L., Keller, T. A., Schipul, S. E., Cherkassky, V. L., . . . Müller, R. (2015). Aberrant functioning of the theory-of-mind network in children and adolescents with autism. *Molecular Autism, 6*(1), 59. http://doi.org/10.1186/s13229-015-0052-x

Kandler, C., Bleidorn, W., Riemann, R., Spinath, F. M., Thiel, W., & Angleitner, A. (2010). Sources of cumulative continuity in personality: A longitudinal multiple-rater twin study. *Journal of Personality and Social Psychology, 98*(6), 995–1008. http://doi.org/10.1037/a0019558

Kandler, C., Kornadt, A. E., Hagemeyer, B., & Neyer, F. J. (2015). Patterns and sources of personality development in old age. *Journal of Personality and Social Psychology, 109*(1), 175–191. http://doi.org/10.1037/pspp0000028

Kang, J.-H., Korecka, M., Figurski, M. J., Toledo, J. B., Blennow, K., Zetterberg, H., . . . Shaw, L. M. (2015). The Alzheimer's Disease Neuroimaging Initiative 2 Biomarker Core: A review of progress and plans. *Alzheimer's & Dementia, 11*(7), 772–791. http://doi.org/10.1016/j.jalz.2015.05.003

Kaniewski, M., Stevens, J. A., Parker, E. M., & Lee, R. (2015). An introduction to the Centers for Disease Control and Prevention's efforts to prevent older adult falls. *Frontiers in Public Health, 2*, e119. http://doi.org/10.3389/fpubh.2014.00119

Kann, L., Kinchen, S., Shanklin, S. L., Flint, K. H., Kawkins, J., Harris, W. A., . . . Zaza, S. (2014). Youth risk behavior surveillance: United States, 2013. *Morbidity and Mortality Weekly Report, 63*(Suppl 4), 1–168. Retrieved from http://www.ncbi.nlm.nih.gov/pubmed/24918634

Kanny, D., Liu, Y., Brewer, R. D., & Lu, H. (2013). Binge drinking—United States, 2011. *Morbidity and Mortality Weekly Report, 62*(3), 77–80.

Kantamneni, N., McCain, M. R. C., Shada, N., Hellwege, M. A., & Tate, J. (2016). Contextual factors in the career development of prospective first-generation college students. *Journal of Career Assessment.* http://doi.org/10.1177/1069072716680048

Kantomaa, M. T., Tammelin, T. H., Näyhä, S., & Taanila, A. M. (2007). Adolescents' physical activity in relation to family income and parents' education. *Preventive Medicine, 44*(5), 410–415.

Kapadia, S., & Gala, J. (2015). Gender across cultures. In L. A. Jensen (Ed.), *The Oxford handbook of human development and culture.* London, UK: Oxford University Press. http://doi.org/10.1093/oxfordhb/9780199948550.013.19

Kaplan, H., & Dove, H. (1987). Infant development among the Ache of eastern Paraguay. *Developmental Psychology, 23*(2), 190–198.

Kapoor, A., Lubach, G. R., Ziegler, T. E., & Coe, C. L. (2016). Hormone levels in neonatal hair reflect prior maternal stress exposure during pregnancy. *Psychoneuroendocrinology, 66*, 111–117. http://doi.org/10.1016/j.psyneuen.2016.01.010

Kaprio, J., Rimpela, A., Rimpelä, A., Winter, T., Viken, R. J., Rimpelä, M., & Rose, R. J. (1995). Common genetic influences on BMI and age at menarche. *Human Biology, 67*(5), 739. Retrieved from http://www.ncbi.nlm.nih.gov/pubmed/8543288

Karafantis, D. M., & Levy, S. R. (2004). The role of children's lay theories about the malleability of human attributes in beliefs about and volunteering for disadvantaged groups. *Child Development, 75*(1), 236–250. http://doi.org/10.1111/j.1467-8624.2004.00666.x

Karasik, D., Demissie, S., Cupples, L. A., & Kiel, D. P. (2005). Disentangling the genetic determinants of human aging: Biological age as an alternative to the use of survival measures. *Journals of Gerontology Series A: Biological Sciences & Medical Sciences, 60A*(5), 574–587.

Karasik, L. B., Tamis-LeMonda, C. S., & Adolph, K. E. (2011). Transition from crawling to walking and infants' actions with objects and people. *Child Development, 82*(4), 1199–1209. http://doi.org/10.1111/j.1467-8624

Karbach, J., & Verhaeghen, P. (2014). Making working memory work: A meta-analysis of executive-control and working memory training in older adults. *Psychological Science, 25*(11), 2027–2037. http://doi.org/10.1177/0956797614548725

Karelitz, T. M., Jarvin, L., Sternberg, R. J., Karelitz, T. M., Jarvin, L., & Sternberg, R. J. (2010). The meaning of wisdom and its development throughout life. In W. F. Overton (Ed.), *The handbook of life-span development.* Hoboken, NJ: John Wiley & Sons. http://doi.org/10.1002/9780470880166.hlsd001023

Karmiloff-Smith, A. (2009). Preaching to the converted? From constructivism to neuroconstructivism. *Child Development Perspectives, 3*(2), 99–102. http://doi.org/10.1111/j.1750-8606.2009.00086.x

Kärnä, A., Voeten, M., Poskiparta, E., & Salmivalli, C. (2010). Vulnerable children in varying classroom contexts: Bystanders' behaviors moderate the effects of risk factors on victimization. *Merrill-Palmer Quarterly: Journal of Developmental Psychology, 56*(3), 261–282.

Kastenbaum, R. J. (2012). *Death, society, and human experience.* New York, NY: Routledge.

Kasworm, C. E. (2003). Setting the stage: Adults in higher education. *New Directions for Student Services, 2003*(102), 3–10. http://doi.org/10.1002/ss.83

Katzman, D. K. (2005). Medical complications in adolescents with anorexia nervosa: A review of the literature. *International Journal of Eating Disorders, 37*, 52–59.

Katz-Wise, S. L., Priess, H. A., & Hyde, J. S. (2010). Gender-role attitudes and behavior across the transition to parenthood. *Developmental Psychology, 46*(1), 18–28. http://doi.org/10.1037/a0017820

Kaufman, A. S. (2001). WAIS-III IQs, Horn's theory, and generational changes from young adulthood to old age. *Intelligence, 29*(2), 131.

Kaufman, A. S., Flanagan, D. P., Alfonso, V. C., & Mascolo, J. T. (2006). Review of Wechsler Intelligence Scale for Children, Fourth Edition (WISC-IV). *Journal of Psychoeducational Assessment, 24*(3), 278–295.

Kaufman, J. C., Kaufman, S. B., & Plucker., J. A. (2013). Contemporary theories of intelligence. In J. Reisberg (Ed.), *Oxford handbook of cognitive psychology* (pp. 811–822). New York, NY: Oxford University Press.

Kaufman, J. C., Plucker, J. A., & Russell, C. M. (2012). Identifying and assessing creativity as a component of giftedness. *Journal of Psychoeducational Assessment, 30*(1), 60–73. http://doi.org/10.1177/0734282911428196

Kaufmann, L., Mazzocco, M. M., Dowker, A., von Aster, M., Göbel, S. M., Grabner, R. H., . . . Nuerk, H.-C. (2013). Dyscalculia from a developmental and differential perspective. *Frontiers in Psychology, 4*, 516. http://doi.org/10.3389/fpsyg.2013.00516

Kavé, G., Eyal, N., Shorek, A., & Cohen-Mansfield, J. (2008). Multilingualism and cognitive state in the oldest old. *Psychology and Aging, 23*(1), 70–78.

Kavšek, M. (2004). Predicting later IQ from infant visual habituation and dishabituation: A meta-analysis. *Journal of Applied Developmental Psychology, 25*(3), 369–393. http://doi.org/10.1016/j.appdev.2004.04.006

Kavšek, M. (2013). The comparator model of infant visual habituation and dishabituation: recent insights. *Developmental Psychobiology, 55*(8), 793–808. http://doi.org/10.1002/dev.21081

Kawabata, Y., & Crick, N. R. (2011). The significance of cross-racial/ethnic friendships: Associations with peer victimization, peer support, sociometric status, and classroom diversity. *Developmental Psychology, 47*(6), 1763–1775. http://doi.org/10.1037/a0025399

Kawabata, Y., Crick, N. R., & Hamaguchi, Y. (2010). The role of culture in relational aggression: Associations with social-psychological adjustment problems in Japanese and US school-aged children. *International Journal of Behavioral Development, 34*(4), 354–362. http://doi.org/10.1177/0165025409339151

Kawakami, K., Takai-Kawakami, K., Kawakami, F., Tomonaga, M., Suzuki, M., & Shimizu, Y. (2008). Roots of smile: A preterm neonates' study. *Infant Behavior & Development, 31*(3), 518–522. http://doi.org/10.1016/j.infbeh.2008.03.002

Kaye, W. H., Wierenga, C. E., Bailer, U. F., Simmons, A. N., & Bischoff-Grethe, A. (2013). Nothing tastes as good as skinny feels: The neurobiology of anorexia nervosa. *Trends in Neurosciences, 36*(2), 110–120. http://doi.org/10.1016/j.tins.2013.01.003

Kayed, N. S., Farstad, H., & van der Meer, A. L. H. (2008). Preterm infants' timing strategies to optical collisions. *Early Human Development, 84*(6), 381–388. http://doi.org/10.1016/j.earlhumdev.2007.10.006

Keating, D. P. (2004). Cognitive and brain development. In R. M. Lerner & L. Steinberg (Eds.), *Handbook of adolescent psychology* (2nd ed., pp. 45–84). Hoboken, NJ: John Wiley & Sons.

Keating, S. T., Plutzky, J., & El-Osta, A. (2016). Epigenetic changes in diabetes and cardiovascular risk. *Circulation Research, 118*(11), 1706–1722. http://doi.org/10.1161/CIRCRESAHA.116.306819

Keel, P. K. (2014). Bulimia nervosa. In R. L. Cautin & S. O. Lilienfeld (Eds.), *The encyclopedia of clinical psychology*. Hoboken, NJ: John Wiley & Sons.

Keesee, N. J., Currier, J. M., & Neimeyer, R. A. (2008). Predictors of grief following the death of one's child: The contribution of finding meaning. *Journal of Clinical Psychology, 64*(10), 1145–63. http://doi.org/10.1002/jclp.20502

Keightley, J., & Mitchell, A. (2004). What factors influence mental health professionals when deciding whether or not to share a diagnosis of dementia with the person? *Aging & Mental Health, 8*(1), 13–20.

Keijsers, L., Loeber, R., Branje, S., & Meeus, W. H. J. (2011). Bidirectional links and concurrent development of parent-child relationships and boys' offending behavior. *Journal of Abnormal Psychology.* http://doi.org/10.1037/a0024588

Kell, H. J., Lubinski, D., Benbow, C. P., & Steiger, J. H. (2013). Creativity and technical innovation: Spatial ability's unique role. *Psychological Science, 24*(9), 1831–1836. http://doi.org/10.1177/0956797613478615

Keller, H. (2003). Socialization for competence: Cultural models of infancy. *Human Development, 46*(5), 288–311.

Keller, K., & Engelhardt, M. (2013). Strength and muscle mass loss with aging process: Age and strength loss. *Muscles, Ligaments and Tendons Journal, 3*(4), 346–350.

Kellogg, R. (1970). Understanding children's art. In P. Cramer (Ed.), *Readings in developmental psychology today*. Delmar, CA: CRM.

Kelly, A., Winer, K. K., Kalkwarf, H., Oberfield, S. E., Lappe, J., Gilsanz, V., & Zemel, B. S. (2014). Age-based reference ranges for annual height velocity in US children. *The Journal of Clinical Endocrinology and Metabolism, 99*(6), 2104–2112. http://doi.org/10.1210/jc.2013-4455

Kelly, K. (1999). Retention vs. promotion: Schools search for alternatives. *Harvard Education Letter*

Research Online. Retrieved from http://www.edletter.org/past/issues/1999-jf/retention.shtml

Kelly, S. T., & Spencer, H. G. (2017). Population-genetic models of sex-limited genomic imprinting. *Theoretical Population Biology, 115*, 35–44. http://doi.org/10.1016/j.tpb.2017.03.004

Kendrick, D., Barlow, J., Hampshire, A., Stewart-Brown, S., & Polnay, L. (2008). Parenting interventions and the prevention of unintentional injuries in childhood: Systematic review and meta-analysis. *Child: Care, Health and Development, 34*(5), 682–695. http://doi.org/10.1111/j.1365-2214.2008.00849.x

Kennedy, Q., Taylor, J. L., Reade, G., & Yesavage, J. A. (2010). Age and expertise effects in aviation decision making and flight control in a flight simulator. *Aviation, Space, and Environmental Medicine, 81*(5), 489–497. Retrieved from http://www.pubmedcentral.nih.gov/articlerender.fcgi?artid=2905035&tool=pmcentrez&rendertype=abstract

Kennedy, S., & Bumpass, L. (2008). Cohabitation and children's living arrangements: New estimates from the United States. *Demographic Research, 19*, 1663–1692.

Kennedy, S., & Fitch, C. A. (2012). Measuring cohabitation and family structure in the United States: Assessing the impact of new data from the current population survey. *Demography, 49*(4), 1479–1498. http://doi.org/10.1007/s13524-012-0126-8

Kennedy, T. M., & Ceballo, R. (2014). Who, what, when, and where? Toward a dimensional conceptualization of community violence exposure. *Review of General Psychology, 18*(2), 69–81. http://doi.org/10.1037/gpr0000005

Kenney, C. T., & McLanahan, S. S. (2006). Why are cohabiting relationships more violent than marriages? *Demography, 43*(1), 127–140.

Kenny, L. C., Lavender, T., McNamee, R., O'Neill, S. M., Mills, T., & Khashan, A. S. (2013). Advanced maternal age and adverse pregnancy outcome: Evidence from a large contemporary cohort. *PloS One, 8*(2), e56583. http://doi.org/10.1371/journal.pone.0056583

Kenny, M. C., Capri, V., Thakkar-Kolar, R. R., Ryan, E. E., & Runyon, M. K. (2008). Child sexual abuse: From prevention to self-protection. *Child Abuse Review, 17*(1), 36–54.

Kenny, M. C., & McEachern, A. (2009). Children's self-concept: A multicultural comparison. *Professional School Counseling, 12*(3), 207–212.

Kenward, B., Folke, S., Holmberg, J., Johansson, A., & Gredebäck, G. (2009). Goal directedness and decision making in infants. *Developmental Psychology, 45*(3), 809–819. http://doi.org/10.1037/a0014076

Kenyon, B. L. (2001). Current research in children's conceptions of death: A critical review. *OMEGA—Journal of Death and Dying, 43*(1), 63–91. http://doi.org/10.2190/0X2B-B1N9-A579-DVK1

Kenyon, D. B., & Koerner, S. S. (2009). Examining emerging-adults' and parents' expectations about autonomy during the transition to college. *Journal of Adolescent Research, 24*(3), 293–320.

Kerns, K. A., & Brumariu, L. E. (2014). Is insecure parent-child attachment a risk factor for the development of anxiety in childhood or adolescence? *Child Development Perspectives, 8*(1), 12–17. http://doi.org/10.1111/cdep.12054

Kerpelman, J. L., Eryigit, S., & Stephens, C. J. (2008). African American adolescents' future education orientation: Associations with self-efficacy, ethnic identity, and perceived parental support. *Journal of Youth & Adolescence, 37*(8), 997–1008. http://doi.org/10.1007/s10964-007-9201-7

Kerpelman, J. L., Shoffner, M. F., & Ross-Griffin, S. (2002). African American mothers' and daughters' beliefs about possible selves and their strategies for reaching the adolescents' future academic and career goals. *Journal of Youth & Adolescence, 31*(4), 289.

Keski-Rahkonen, A., Bulik, C. M., Pietiläinen, K. H., Rose, R. J., Kaprio, J., & Rissanen, A. (2007). Eating styles, overweight and obesity in young adult twins. *European Journal of Clinical Nutrition, 61*(7), 822–829. http://doi.org/10.1038/sj.ejcn.1602601

Keski-Rahkonen, A., & Mustelin, L. (2016). Epidemiology of eating disorders in Europe. *Current Opinion in Psychiatry, 29*(6), 340–345. http://doi.org/10.1097/YCO.0000000000000278

Kessels, R. P. C., Meulenbroek, O., Fernandez, G., & Olde Rikkert, M. G. M. (2010). Spatial working memory in aging and mild cognitive impairment: Effects of task load and contextual cueing. *Aging, Neuropsychology & Cognition, 17*(5), 556–574. http://doi.org/10.1080/13825585.2010.481354

Kessler, R. C., Berglund, P. A., Chiu, W. T., Deitz, A. C., Hudson, J. I., Shahly, V., . . . Xavier, M. (2013). The prevalence and correlates of binge eating disorder in the World Health Organization World Mental Health Surveys. *Biological Psychiatry, 73*(9), 904–914. http://doi.org/10.1016/j.biopsych.2012.11.020

Keyes, C. L. M., & Reitzes, D. C. (2007). The role of religious identity in the mental health of older working and retired adults. *Aging & Mental Health, 11*(4), 434–443. http://doi.org/10.1080/13607860601086371

Keyes, C. L. M., & Westerhof, G. J. (2012). Chronological and subjective age differences in flourishing mental health and major depressive episode. *Aging & Mental Health, 16*(1), 67–74. http://doi.org/10.1080/13607863.2011.596811

Khalil, A., Syngelaki, A., Maiz, N., Zinevich, Y., & Nicolaides, K. H. (2013). Maternal age and adverse pregnancy outcome: A cohort study. *Ultrasound in Obstetrics & Gynecology, 42*(6), 634–643. http://doi.org/10.1002/uog.12494

Khan, A. (2014). For young and old, it's wise to have a living will to state health-care wishes. *U.S. News & World Report.* Retrieved from http://health.usnews.com/health-news/health-wellness/articles/2014/12/19/why-you-need-a-living-will-even-at-age-18

Khan, N., Afaq, F., & Mukhtar, H. (2010). Lifestyle as risk factor for cancer: Evidence from human studies. *Cancer Letters, 293*(2), 133–143. http://doi.org/10.1016/j.canlet.2009.12.013

Khan, S. D. (2017). Aging and male reproduction. In K. Gunasekaran & N. Pandiyan (Eds.), *Male infertility* (pp. 197–206). New Delhi: Springer India. http://doi.org/10.1007/978-81-322-3604-7_13

Kharitonova, M., Winter, W., & Sheridan, M. A. (2015). As working memory grows: A developmental account of neural bases of working memory capacity in 5- to 8-year old children and adults. *Journal of Cognitive Neuroscience, 27*(9), 1775–1788. http://doi.org/10.1162/jocn_a_00824

Khundrakpam, B. S., Lewis, J. D., Reid, A., Karama, S., Zhao, L., Chouinard-Decorte, F., & Evans, A. C. (2016). Imaging structural covariance in the development of intelligence. *NeuroImage.* http://doi.org/10.1016/j.neuroimage.2016.08.041

Kiang, L., Gonzales-Backen, M., Yip, T., Witkow, M., & Fuligni, A. J. (2006). Ethnic identity and the daily psychological well-being of adolescents from Mexican and Chinese backgrounds. *Child Development, 77*(5), 1338–1350.

Kiang, L., Moreno, A. J., & Robinson, J. L. (2004). Maternal preconceptions about parenting predict child temperament, maternal sensitivity, and children's empathy. *Developmental Psychology, 40*(6), 1081–1092. http://doi.org/10.1037/0012-1649.40.6.1081

Kiechl-Kohlendorfer, U., Ralser, E., Pupp Peglow, U., Reiter, G., Griesmaier, E., & Trawöger, R. (2010). Smoking in pregnancy: A risk factor for adverse neurodevelopmental outcome in preterm infants? *Acta Paediatrica, 99*(7), 1016–1019. http://doi.org/10.1111/j.1651-2227.2010.01749.x

Kilbride, H., Castor, C., Hoffman, E., & Fuger, K. L. (2000). Thirty-six-month outcome of prenatal cocaine exposure for term or near-term infants: Impact of early case management. *Journal of Developmental and Behavioral Pediatrics, 21,* 19–26.

Killen, M., Kelly, M., Richardson, C., Crystal, D., & Ruck, M. (2010). European-American children's and adolescents' evaluations of interracial exclusion. *Group Processes & Intergroup Relations, 13*(3), 283–300. http://doi.org/10.1177/1368430209346700

Killen, M., McGlothlin, H., & Lee-Kim, J. (2002). Between individuals and culture: Individuals' evaluations of exclusion from social groups. In H. Keller, Y. Poortinga, & A. Schoelmerich (Eds.), *Between biology and culture: Perspectives on ontogenetic development.* Cambridge, UK: Cambridge University Press.

Killen, M., & Nucci, L. P. (1995). Morality, autonomy, and social conflict. In M. Killen & D. Hart (Eds.), *Morality in everyday life: Developmental perspectives* (pp. 52–86). Cambridge, UK: Cambridge University Press.

Killen, M., & Smetana, J. G. (2015). Origins and development of morality. In *Handbook of Child Psychology and Developmental Science* (pp. 1–49). Hoboken, NJ: John Wiley & Sons. http://doi.org/10.1002/9781118963418.childpsy317 Killian, T., Turner, J., & Cain, R. (2005). Depressive symptoms of caregiving women in midlife: The role of physical health. *Journal of Women & Aging, 17*(1/2), 115–127. http://doi.org/10.1300/J074v17n01_09

Kilmann, P. R., Vendemia, J. M. C., Parnell, M. M., & Urbaniak, G. C. (2009). Parent characteristics linked with daughters' attachment styles. *Adolescence, 44*(175), 557–568. Retrieved from http://www.ncbi.nlm.nih.gov/pubmed/19950869

Kim, B.-R., & Teti, D. M. (2014). Maternal emotional availability during infant bedtime: An ecological framework. *Journal of Family Psychology, 28*(1), 1–11. http://doi.org/10.1037/a0035157

Kim, D. K., Bridges, C. B., & Harriman, K. H. (2016). Advisory Committee on Immunization Practices recommended immunization schedule for adults aged 19 years or older: United States, 2016. *American Journal of Transplantation, 16*(6), 1930–1932. http://doi.org/10.1111/ajt.13877

Kim, G., Walden, T. A., & Knieps, L. J. (2010). Impact and characteristics of positive and fearful emotional messages during infant social referencing. *Infant Behavior & Development, 33*(2), 189–195. http://doi.org/10.1016/j.infbeh.2009.12.009

Kim, H., Wildeman, C., Jonson-Reid, M., & Drake, B. (2017). Lifetime prevalence of investigating child maltreatment among US children. *American Journal of Public Health, 107*(2), 274–280. http://doi.org/10.2105/AJPH.2016.303545

Kim, J. E., & Moen, P. (2001). Is retirement good or bad for subjective well-being? *Current Directions in Psychological Science, 10*(3), 83–86. http://doi.org/10.1111/1467-8721.00121

Kim, K., Bangerter, L. R., Liu, Y., Polenick, C. A., Zarit, S. H., & Fingerman, K. L. (2016). Middle-aged offspring's support to aging parents with emerging disability. *The Gerontologist, 20.* http://doi.org/10.1093/geront/gnv686

Kim, M. (2016). A meta-analysis of the effects of enrichment programs on gifted students. *Gifted Child Quarterly, 60*(2), 102–116. http://doi.org/10.1177/0016986216630607

Kim, P., Feldman, R., Mayes, L. C., Eicher, V., Thompson, N., Leckman, J. F., & Swain, J. E. (2011). Breastfeeding, brain activation to own infant cry, and maternal sensitivity. *Journal of Child Psychology and Psychiatry, and Allied Disciplines, 52*(8), 907–915. https://doi.org/10.1111/j.1469-7610.2011.02406.x

Kim, S. H., Hus, V., & Lord, C. (2013). Autism diagnostic interview-revised. In *Encyclopedia of autism spectrum disorders* (pp. 345–349). New York, NY: Springer New York. http://doi.org/10.1007/978-1-4419-1698-3_894

Kimball, M. M. (1986). Television and sex-role attitudes. In T. M. Williams (Ed.), *The impact of television: A natural experiment in three communities* (pp. 265–301). Orlando, FL: Academic Press.

Kim-Cohen, J. (2007). Resilience and developmental psychopathology. *Child and Adolescent Psychiatric Clinics of North America, 16*(2), 271–283.

Kimmons, J. E., Gillespie, C., Seymour, J., Serdula, M., & Blanck, H. M. (2008). Fruit and vegetable intake among adolescents and adults in the United States: Percentage meeting individualized recommendations. *Medscape Journal of Medicine, 11*(1). Retrieved from http://www.pubmedcentral.nih.gov/articlerender.fcgi?artid=2654704

King, B. M., & Regan, P. C. (2014). *Human sexuality today.* New York, NY: Pearson.

King, E. B., Madera, J. M., Hebl, M. R., Knight, J. L., & Mendoza, S. A. (2006). What's in a name? A multiracial investigation of the role of occupational stereotypes in selection decisions. *Journal of Applied Social Psychology, 36*(5), 1145–1159.

King, P. E., & Boyatzis, C. J. (2015). Religious and spiritual development. In *Handbook of child psychology and developmental science* (pp. 1–48). Hoboken, NJ: John Wiley & Sons. http://doi.org/10.1002/9781118963418.childpsy323

King, P. E., Ramos, J. S., & Clardy, C. E. (2013). Searching for the sacred: Religion, spirituality, and adolescent development. In K. I. Pargament, J. J. Exline, & J. W. Jones (Eds.), *APA handbook of psychology, religion, and spirituality (Vol 1): Context, theory, and research.* (pp. 513–528). Washington, DC: American Psychological Association. http://doi.org/10.1037/14045-028

King, P. E., & Roeser, R. W. (2009). Religion and spirituality in adolescent development. In *Handbook of adolescent psychology.* Hoboken, NJ: John Wiley & Sons. http://doi.org/10.1002/9780470479193.adlpsy001014

King, P. M., & Kitchener, K. S. (1994). *Developing reflective judgment: Understanding and promoting intellectural growth and critical thinking in adolescents and adults.* San Francisco: Jossey-Bass.

King, P. M., & Kitchener, K. S. (2002). The reflective judgment model: Twenty years of research on epistemic cognition. In B. K. Hofer & P. R. Pintrich (Eds.), *Personal epistemology: The psychological beliefs about knoweldge and knowing* (pp. 37–61). Mahwah, NJ: Erlbaum.

King, P. M., & Kitchener, K. S. (2004). Reflective judgment: Theory and research on the development of epistemic assumptions through adulthood. *Educational Psychologist, 39,* 5–18.

King, V., & Scott, M. E. (2005). A comparison of cohabiting relationships among older and younger adults. *Journal of Marriage & Family, 67*(2), 271–285.

Kingery, J. N., Erdley, C. A., & Marshall, K. C. (2011). Peer acceptance and friendship as predictors of early adolescents' adjustment across the middle school transition. *Merrill-Palmer Quarterly, 57*(3), 215–243. http://doi.org/10.1353/mpq.2011.0012

Kingston, D., Tough, S., & Whitfield, H. (2012). Prenatal and postpartum maternal psychological distress and infant development: A systematic review. *Child Psychiatry and Human Development, 43*(5), 683–714. http://doi.org/10.1007/s10578-012-0291-4

Kingston, S., & Rose, A. (2015). Do the effects of adolescent employment differ by employment intensity and neighborhood context? *American Journal of Community Psychology, 55*(1–2), 37–47. http://doi.org/10.1007/s10464-014-9690-y

Kinney, D. A. (1999). From "headbangers" to "hippies": Delineating adolescents' active attempts to form an alternative peer culture. *New Directions for Child & Adolescent Development, 1999,* 21–35.

Kinsey, A. C., Pomeroy, W. B., & Martin, C. E. (1948). *Sexual behavior in the human male.* Philadelphia, PA: Saunders.

Kinsley, C. H., & Amory-Meyer, E. (2011). Why the maternal brain? *Journal of Neuroendocrinology, 23*(11), 974–983. http://doi.org/10.1111/j.1365-2826.2011.02194.x

Kirbach, S. E., & Mintzer, J. (2008). Alzheimer's disease burdens African-Americans: A review of epidemiological risk factors and implications for prevention and treatment. *Current Psychiatry Reviews, 4*(1), 58–62. Retrieved from kirbach@musc.edu

Kirk, E., Howlett, N., Pine, K. J., & Fletcher, B. C. (2013). To sign or not to sign? The impact of encouraging infants to gesture on infant language and maternal mind-mindedness. *Child Development, 84*(2), 574–90. http://doi.org/10.1111/j.1467-8624.2012.01874.x

Kish, J. K., Yu, M., Percy-Laurry, A., & Altekruse, S. F. (2014). Racial and ethnic disparities in cancer survival by neighborhood socioeconomic status in Surveillance, Epidemiology, and End Results (SEER) Registries. *Journal of the National Cancer Institute. Monographs, 2014*(49), 236–43. http://doi.org/10.1093/jncimonographs/lgu020

Kisilevsky, B. S., Hains, S. M. J., Brown, C. A., Lee, C. T., Cowperthwaite, B., Stutzman, S. S., . . . Wang, Z. (2009). Fetal sensitivity to properties of maternal speech and language. *Infant Behavior and Development, 32*(1), 59–71. http://doi.org/10.1016/j.infbeh.2008.10.002

Kister, M. C., & Patterson, C. J. (1980). Children's conceptions of the causes of illness. Understanding contagion and the use of immanent justice. *Child Development, 51,* 839–846.

Kit, B. K., Akinbami, L. J., Isfahani, N. S., & Ulrich, D. A. (2017). Gross motor development in children aged 3–5 years, United States 2012. *Maternal and Child Health Journal,* 1–8. http://doi.org/10.1007/s10995-017-2289-9

Kitamura, C., & Burnham, D. (2003). Pitch and communicative intent in mother's speech: Adjustments for age and sex in the first year. *Infancy, 4*(1), 85–110.

Kitayama, S., & Uskul, A. K. (2011). Culture, mind, and the brain: Current evidence and future directions. *Annual Review of Psychology, 62*(1), 419–449. http://doi.org/10.1146/annurev-psych-120709-145357

Kjeldsen, A., Janson, H., Stoolmiller, M., Torgersen, L., & Mathiesen, K. S. (2014). Externalising behaviour from infancy to mid-adolescence: Latent profiles and early predictors. *Journal of Applied Developmental Psychology, 35*(1), 25–34. http://doi.org/10.1016/j.appdev.2013.11.003

Klahr, A. M., Thomas, K. M., Hopwood, C. J., Klump, K. L., & Burt, S. A. (2013). Evocative gene–environment correlation in the mother–child relationship: A twin study of interpersonal processes. *Development and Psychopathology, 25*(1), 105–118. http://doi.org/10.1017/S0954579412000934

Klahr, D. (1985). Solving problems with ambiguous subgoal ordering: Preschoolers' performance. *Child Development, 56,* 940–952.

Klahr, D. (1992). Information-processing approaches. In R. Vasta (Ed.), *Six theories of child development:*

Revised formulations and current issues (pp. 133–185). London: Jessica Kingsley.

Klämbt, C. (2009). Modes and regulation of glial migration in vertebrates and invertebrates. *Nature Reviews Neuroscience, 10*(11), 769–779. http://doi.org/10.1038/nrn2720

Klaw, E. L., Rhodes, J. E., & Fitzgerald, L. F. (2003). Natural mentors in the lives of African American adolescent mothers: Tracking relationships over time. *Journal of Youth & Adolescence, 32*(3), 223.

Kleanthous, K., Dermitzaki, E., Papadimitriou, D. T., Papaevangelou, V., & Papadimitriou, A. (2017). Secular changes in the final height of Greek girls are levelling off. *Acta Paediatrica, 106*(2), 341–343. http://doi.org/10.1111/apa.13677

Klebanov, P. K., Brooks-Gunn, J., McCarton, C., & McCormick, M. C. (1998). The contribution of neighborhood and family income to developmental test scores over the first three years of life. *Child Development, 69*(5), 1420–1436.

Klein, M., & Stern, L. (1971). Low birth weight and the battered child syndrome. *Archives of Pediatrics & Adolescent Medicine, 122*(1), 15. http://doi.org/10.1001/archpedi.1971.02110010051005

Klein, P. J., & Meltzoff, A. N. (1999). Long-term memory, forgetting, and deferred imitation in 12-month-old infants. *Developmental Science, 2*, 102–113.

Kleinspehn-Ammerlahn, A., Kotter-Gruhn, D., & Smith, J. (2008). Self-perceptions of aging: Do subjective age and satisfaction with aging change during old age? *The Journals of Gerontology Series B: Psychological Sciences and Social Sciences, 63*(6), P377–P385. http://doi.org/10.1093/geronb/63.6.P377

Klima, T., & Repetti, R. L. (2008). Children's peer relations and their psychological adjustment: Differences between close friendships and the larger peer group. *Merrill-Palmer Quarterly, 54*(2), 151–178.

Klimstra, T. A., Kuppens, P., Luyckx, K., Branje, S., Hale, W. W., Oosterwegel, A., . . . Meeus, W. H. J. (2016). Daily dynamics of adolescent mood and identity. *Journal of Research on Adolescence, 26*(3), 459–473. http://doi.org/10.1111/jora.12205

Kline, D. W., & Li, W. (2005). Cataracts and the aging driver. *Ageing International, 30*(2), 105–121.

Klingner, J. K., Vaughn, S., Hughes, M. T., Schumm, J. S., & Elbaum, B. (1998). Outcomes for students with and without learning disabilities in inclusive classrooms. *Learning Disabilities Research and Practice, 13*, 153–161.

Klomek, A. B., Sourander, A., Kumpulainen, K., Piha, J., Tamminen, T., Moilanen, I., . . . Gould, M. S. (2008). Childhood bullying as a risk for later depression and suicidal ideation among Finnish males. *Journal of Affective Disorders, 109*(1/2), 47–55. http://doi.org/10.1016/j.jad.2007.12.226

Klöppel, S., Vongerichten, A., van Eimeren, T., Frackowiak, R. S. J., & Siebner, H. R. (2007). Can left-handedness be switched? Insights from an early switch of handwriting. *The Journal of Neuroscience, 27*(29), 7847–7853. http://doi.org/10.1523/jneurosci.1299-07.2007

Knafo, A., & Jaffee, S. R. (2013). Gene–environment correlation in developmental psychopathology. *Development and Psychopathology, 25*(1), 1–6. http://doi.org/10.1017/S0954579412000855

Knafo, A., Zahn-Waxler, C., Van Hulle, C., Robinson, J. L., & Rhee, S. H. (2008). The developmental origins of a disposition toward empathy: Genetic and environmental contributions. *Emotion, 8*(6), 737–752. http://doi.org/10.1037/a0014179

Knafo-Noam, A., Uzefovsky, F., Israel, S., Davidov, M., & Zahn-Waxler, C. (2015). The prosocial personality and its facets: genetic and environmental architecture of mother-reported behavior of 7-year-old

twins. *Frontiers in Psychology, 6*, 112. http://doi.org/10.3389/fpsyg.2015.00112

Knodel, J., & Chayovan, N. (2009). Intergenerational relationships and family care and support for Thai elderly. *Ageing International, 33*(1–4), 15–27. http://doi.org/10.1007/s12126-009-9026-7

Knopik, V. S., Maccani, M. A., Francazio, S., & McGeary, J. E. (2012). The epigenetics of maternal cigarette smoking during pregnancy and effects on child development. *Development and Psychopathology, 24*(4), 1377–1390. http://doi.org/10.1017/S0954579412000776

Knopman, D. S., & Roberts, R. (2010). Vascular risk factors: Imaging and neuropathologic correlates. *Journal of Alzheimer's Disease, 20*(3), 699–709. http://doi.org/10.3233/jad-2010-091555

Knopman, J. M., Krey, L. C., Oh, C., Lee, J., McCaffrey, C., & Noyes, N. (2014). What makes them split? Identifying risk factors that lead to monozygotic twins after in vitro fertilization. *Fertility and Sterility, 102*(1), 82–89. http://doi.org/10.1016/j.fertnstert.2014.03.039

Knox, P. L., Fagley, N. S., & Miller, P. M. (2004). Care and justice moral orientation among African American college students. *Journal of Adult Development, 11*(1), 41–45.

Knutson, B., & Cooper, J. C. (2005). Functional magnetic resonance imaging of reward prediction. *Current Opinion in Neurology, 18*(18). https://doi.org/00019052-200508000-00010

Ko, J. Y., Farr, S. L., Dietz, P. M., & Robbins, C. L. (2012). Depression and treatment among U.S. pregnant and nonpregnant women of reproductive age, 2005-2009. *Journal of Women's Health (2002), 21*(8), 830–836. http://doi.org/10.1089/jwh.2011.3466

Ko, K. J., Berg, C. A., Butner, J., Uchino, B. N., & Smith, T. W. (2007). Profiles of successful aging in middle-aged and older adult married couples. *Psychology and Aging, 22*(4), 705–718.

Kobak, R., Abbott, C., Zisk, A., & Bounoua, N. (2017). Adapting to the changing needs of adolescents: Parenting practices and challenges to sensitive attunement. *Current Opinion in Psychology, 15*, 137–142. http://doi.org/10.1016/j.copsyc.2017.02.018

Koball, H. L., Moiduddin, E., Henderson, J., Goesling, B., & Besculides, M. (2010). What do we know about the link between marriage and health? *Journal of Family Issues, 31*(8), 1019–1040. http://doi.org/10.1177/0192513X10365834

Kochanska, G., Casey, R. J., & Fukumoto, A. (1995). Toddlers' sensitivity to standard violations. *Child Development, 66*, 643–656.

Kochanska, G., & Kim, S. (2013). Early attachment organization with both parents and future behavior problems: From infancy to middle childhood. *Child Development, 84*(1), 283–96. http://doi.org/10.1111/j.1467-8624.2012.01852.x

Kochanska, G., & Knaack, A. (2003). Effortful control as a personality characteristic of young children: Antecedents, correlates, and consequences. *Journal of Personality, 71*(6), 1087. http://doi.org/10.1111/1467-6494.7106008

Koenen, K. C., Amstadter, A. B., & Nugent, N. (2012). Genetic methods in psychology. In H. Cooper, P. M. Camic, D. L. Long, A. T. Panter, D. Rindskopf, & K. J. Sher (Eds.), *APA handbook of research methods in psychology: Research designs: Quantitative, qualitative, neuropsychological, and biological.* (Vol. 2, pp. 663–680). Washington, DC: American Psychological Association. http://doi.org/10.1037/13620-000

Kogan, L. R., & Vacha-Haase, T. (2002). Supporting adaptation to new family roles in middle age. In C. L. Juntunen & D. R. Atkinson (Eds.), *Counseling across the lifespan: Prevention and treatment* (pp. 299–327). Thousand Oaks, CA: SAGE.

Koh, K. K., Han, S. H., Oh, P. C., Shin, E. K., & Quon, M. J. (2010). Combination therapy for treatment or prevention of atherosclerosis: Focus on the lipid-RAAS interaction. *Atherosclerosis, 209*(2), 307–313. http://doi.org/10.1016/j.atherosclerosis.2009.09.007

Kohama, S. G., Rosene, D. L., & Sherman, L. S. (2012). Age-related changes in human and non-human primate white matter: From myelination disturbances to cognitive decline. *Age, 34*(5), 1093–110. http://doi.org/10.1007/s11357-011-9357-7

Kohl, E., Steinbauer, J., Landthaler, M., & Szeimies, R.-M. (2011). Skin ageing. *Journal of the European Academy of Dermatology and Venereology, 25*(8), 873–884. http://doi.org/10.1111/j.1468-3083.2010.03963.x

Kohlberg, L. (1966). A cognitive-developmental analysis of children's sex-role concepts and attitudes. In E. E. Maccoby (Ed.), *The development of sex differences* (pp. 82–173). Stanford, CA: Stanford University Press.

Kohlberg, L. (1969). Stage and sequence: The cognitive-developmental approach to socialization. In D. A. Goslin (Ed.), *Handbook of socialization* (pp. 347–480). Chicago: Rand McNally.

Kohlberg, L. (1976). Moral stages and moralization: The cognitive developmental approach. In T. Lickona (Ed.), *Moral development and moral behavior: Theory, research, and social issues* (pp. 31–53). New York: Holt, Rinehart & Winston.

Kohlberg, L. (1981). *Essays on moral development.* San Francisco: Harper & Row.

Kohlberg, L., & Kramer, R. (1969). Continuities and discontinuities in childhood and adult moral development. *Human Development, 12*(2), 3–120.

Kohlberg, L., Levine, C., & Hewer, A. (1983). *Moral stages: A current formulation and a response to critics.* Basel, CH: Karger.

Kohlberg, L., & Ryncarz, R. A. (1990). Beyond justice reasoning: Moral development and consideration of a seventh stage. In C. N. Alexander & E. J. Langer (Eds.), *Higher stages of human development: Perspectives on adult growth* (pp. 191–207). New York, NY: Oxford University Press.

Kohnert, K. J., & Bates, E. (2002). Balancing bilinguals II. *Journal of Speech Language and Hearing Research, 45*(2), 347–359. http://doi.org/10.1044/1092-4388(2002/027)

Koivunen, J. M., Rothaupt, J. W., & Wolfgram, S. M. (2009). Gender dynamics and role adjustment during the transition to parenthood: Current perspectives. *Family Journal, 17*(4), 323–328. http://doi.org/10.1177/1066480709347360

Kojima, H. (1986). Becoming nurturant in Japan: Past and present. In A. Fogel & G. F. Melson (Eds.), *Origins of nurturance: Developmental, biological, and cultural perspectives on caregiving* (pp. 359–376). Hillsdale, NJ: Lawrence Erlbaum.

Kolb, B. (2015). *Fundamentals of human neuropsychology.* Basingstoke, UK: Worth.

Kolb, B., Gibb, R., & Robinson, T. E. (2003). Brain plasticity and behavior. *Current Directions in Psychological Science, 12*(1), 1–5. http://doi.org/10.1111/1467-8721.01210

Kolb, B., Mychasiuk, R., & Gibb, R. (2014). Brain development, experience, and behavior. *Pediatric Blood & Cancer, 61*(10), 1720–1723. http://doi.org/10.1002/pbc.24908

Kolling, T., Goertz, C., Stefanie, F., & Knopf, M. (2010). Memory development throughout the second year: Overall developmental pattern, individual differences, and developmental trajectories. *Infant Behavior & Development, 33*(2), 159–167. http://doi.org/10.1016/j.infbeh.2009.12.007

Korczyn, A. D., Vakhapova, V., & Grinberg, L. T. (2012). Vascular dementia. *Journal of the Neurological Sciences*, 322(1–2), 2–10. http://doi.org/10.1016/j.jns.2012.03.027

Kormi-Nouri, R., Shojaei, R.-S., Moniri, S., Gholami, A.-R., Moradi, A.-R., Akbari-Zardkhaneh, S., & Nilsson, L.-G. (2008). The effect of childhood bilingualism on episodic and semantic memory tasks. *Scandinavian Journal of Psychology*, 49(2), 93–109. Retrieved from reza.kormi-nouri@bsr.oru.se

Kornadt, A. E., & Rothermund, K. (2012). Internalization of age stereotypes into the self-concept via future self-views: A general model and domain-specific differences. *Psychology and Aging*, 27(1), 164–172. http://doi.org/10.1037/a0025110

Kornbluh, M., & Neal, J. W. (2016). Examining the many dimensions of children's popularity. *Journal of Social and Personal Relationships*, 33(1), 62–80. http://doi.org/10.1177/0265407514562562

Korner, A. F. (1969). Neonatal startles, smiles, erections, and reflex sucks as related to state, sex and individuality. *Child Development*, 40(4), 1039.

Koropeckyj-Cox, T., & Call, V. R. A. (2007). Characteristics of older childless persons and parents. *Journal of Family Issues*, 28(10), 1362–1414.

Koropeckyj-Cox, T., & Pendell, G. (2007). Attitudes about childlessness in the United States. *Journal of Family Issues*, 28(8), 1054–1082.

Koropeckyj-Cox, T., Romano, V. R., & Moras, A. (2007). Through the lenses of gender, race, and class: Students' perceptions of childless/childfree individuals and couples. *Sex Roles*, 56(7/8), 415–428.

Korte, J., Drossaert, C. H. C., Westerhof, G. J., & Bohlmeijer, E. T. (2014). Life review in groups? An explorative analysis of social processes that facilitate or hinder the effectiveness of life review. *Aging & Mental Health*, 18(3), 376–384. http://doi.org/10.1080/13607863.2013.837140

Kosciw, J. G., Palmer, N. A., & Kull, R. M. (2015). Reflecting resiliency: Openness about sexual orientation and/or gender identity and its relationship to well-being and educational outcomes for LGBT students. *American Journal of Community Psychology*, 55(1–2), 167–178. http://doi.org/10.1007/s10464-014-9642-6

Kostelnik, M. J., Soderman, A. K., Whiren, A. P., & Rupiper, M. Q. (2015). *Developmentally appropriate curriculum: Best practices in early childhood education*. Toronto: Pearson.

Kosterman, R., Bailey, J. A., Guttmannova, K., Jones, T. M., Eisenberg, N., Hill, K. G., . . . Zeger, S. (2016). Marijuana legalization and parents' attitudes, use, and parenting in Washington state. *Journal of Adolescent Health*, 59(4), 450–456. http://doi.org/10.1016/j.jadohealth.2016.07.004

Kotre, J. N. (1999). *Make it count: How to generate a legacy that gives meaning to your life*. New York, NY: Free Press.

Kotsopoulos, J., Huzarski, T., Gronwald, J., Moller, P., Lynch, H. T., Neuhausen, S. L., . . . Narod, S. A. (2016). Hormone replacement therapy after menopause and risk of breast cancer in BRCA1 mutation carriers: A case–control study. *Breast Cancer Research and Treatment*, 155(2), 365–373. http://doi.org/10.1007/s10549-016-3685-3

Kotwica, K. A., Ferre, C. L., & Michel, G. F. (2008). Relation of stable hand-use preferences to the development of skill for managing multiple objects from 7 to 13 months of age. *Developmental Psychobiology*, 50(5), 519–529. http://doi.org/10.1002/dev.20311

Kövecses, Z. (2000). *American English: An introduction*. Peterborough, Ontario, Canada: Broadview Press.

Kowalski, S. D., & Bondmass, M. D. (2008). Physiological and psychological symptoms of grief in widows. *Research in Nursing & Health*, 31(1), 23–30. http://doi.org/10.1002/nur.20228

Kowaz, A. M., & Marcia, J. E. (1991). Development and validation of a measure of Eriksonian industry. *Journal of Personality and Social Psychology*, 60(3), 390–397. http://doi.org/10.1037/0022-3514.60.3.390

Kraft, J. M., & Werner, J. S. (1999). Aging and the saturation of colors: 1. Colorimetric purity discrimination. *Journal of the Optical Society of America, A, Optics, Image Science & Vision*, 16(2), 223–230.

Kramer, A. F., & Madden, D. J. (2008). Attention. In F. I. M. Craik & T. A. Salthouse (Eds.), *The handbook of aging and cognition* (3rd ed., pp. 189–249). New York, NY: Psychology Press.

Kramer, D. (2003). The ontogeny of wisdom in its variations. In J. Demick & C. Andreoletti (Eds.), *Handbook of adult development* (pp. 131–151). New York, NY: Kluwer Academic.

Kramer, L. (2014). Learning emotional understanding and emotion regulation through sibling interaction. *Early Education and Development*, 25(2), 160–184. http://doi.org/10.1080/10409289.2014.838824

Krassner, A. M., Gartstein, M. A., Park, C., Dragan, W. Ł., Lecannelier, F., & Putnam, S. P. (2016). East–west, collectivist-individualist: A cross-cultural examination of temperament in toddlers from Chile, Poland, South Korea, and the U.S. *European Journal of Developmental Psychology*, 1–16. http://doi.org/10.1080/17405629.2016.1236722

Krause, N. (2005). God-mediated control and psychological well-being in late life. *Research on Aging*, 27(2), 136–164. http://doi.org/10.1177/0164027504270475

Krause, N. (2007). Longitudinal study of social support and meaning in life. *Psychology and Aging*, 22(3), 456–469.

Krause, N., Pargament, K. I., & Ironson, G. (2016). In the shadow of death: Religious hope as a moderator of the effects of age on death anxiety. *The Journals of Gerontology Series B: Psychological Sciences and Social Sciences*, 22. http://doi.org/10.1093/geronb/gbw039

Krcmar, M. (2014). Can infants and toddlers learn words from repeat exposure to an infant-directed DVD? *Journal of Broadcasting & Electronic Media*, 58(2), 196–214. http://doi.org/10.1080/08838151.2014.906429

Kreager, D. A., Molloy, L. E., Moody, J., & Feinberg, M. E. (2015). Friends first? The peer network origins of adolescent dating. *Journal of Research on Adolescence*. http://doi.org/10.1111/jora.12189

Krebs, C. P., Lindquist, C. H., Warner, T. D., Fisher, B. S., & Martin, S. L. (2009). College women's experiences with physically forced, alcohol- or other drug-enabled, and drug-facilitated sexual assault before and since entering college. *Journal of American College Health*, 57(6), 639–649. http://doi.org/10.3200/JACH.57.6.639-649

Krebs, D. L. (2003). Fictions and facts about evolutionary approaches to human behavior: Comment on Lickliter and Honeycutt (2003). *Psychological Bulletin*, 129(6), 842–847.

Krei, M. S., & Rosenbaum, J. E. (2000). Career and college advice to the forgotten half: What do counselors and vocational teachers advise? *Teachers College Record*, 103(5), 823–842. Retrieved from http://eric.ed.gov/?id=EJ638357

Kreider, R. M., & Ellis, R. (2011). *Number, timing, and duration of marriages and divorces: 2009. Current population reports*. Retrieved from https://www.census.gov/prod/2011pubs/p70-125.pdf

Kressley-Mba, R. A., Lurg, S., & Knopf, M. (2005). Testing for deferred imitation of 2- and 3-step action sequences with 6-month-olds. *Infant Behavior & Development*, 28(1), 82–86.

Kretch, K. S., Franchak, J. M., & Adolph, K. E. (2014). Crawling and walking infants see the world differently. *Child Development*, 85(4), 1503–1518. http://doi.org/10.1111/cdev.12206

Kretschmer, T., Sentse, M., Meeus, W., Verhulst, F. C., Veenstra, R., & Oldehinkel, A. J. (2016). Configurations of adolescents' peer experiences: Associations with parent-child relationship quality and parental problem behavior. *Journal of Research on Adolescence*, 26(3), 474–491. http://doi.org/10.1111/jora.12206

Krevans, J., & Gibbs, J. C. (1996). Parents' use of inductive discipline: Relations to children's empathy and prosocial behavior. *Child Development*, 67(6), 3263–3277. http://doi.org/10.1111/j.1467-8624.1996.tb01913.x

Kroger, J. (2007a). *Identity development: Adolescence through adulthood* (2nd ed.). Thousand Oaks, CA: SAGE.

Kroger, J. (2007b). Why is identity achievement so elusive? *Identity*, 7(4), 331–348. http://doi.org/10.1080/15283480701600793

Kroger, J. (2015). Identity development through adulthood: The move toward "wholeness." In K. C. McLean & M. Syed (Eds.), *The Oxford handbook of identity development* (pp. 65–80). New York, NY: Oxford University Press.

Kroger, J., Martinussen, M., & Marcia, J. E. (2010). Identity status change during adolescence and young adulthood: A meta-analysis. *Journal of Adolescence*, 33(5), 683–98. http://doi.org/10.1016/j.adolescence.2009.11.002

Kromm, H., Färber, M., & Holodynski, M. (2015). Felt or false smiles? Volitional regulation of emotional expression in 4-, 6-, and 8-year-old children. *Child Development*, 86(2), 579–597. http://doi.org/10.1111/cdev.12315

Kron-Sperl, V., Schneider, W., & Hasselhorn, M. (2008). The development and effectiveness of memory strategies in kindergarten and elementary school: Findings from the Warzburg and Gattingen longitudinal memory studies. *Cognitive Development*, 23(1), 79–104.

Kruszka, P., Porras, A. R., Sobering, A. K., Ikolo, F. A., La Qua, S., Shotelersuk, V., . . . Muenke, M. (2017). Down syndrome in diverse populations. *American Journal of Medical Genetics Part A*, 173(1), 42–53. http://doi.org/10.1002/ajmg.a.38043

Kübler-Ross, E. (1969). *On death and dying*. New York, NY: Collier Books/Macmillan.

Kucian, K., & von Aster, M. (2015). Developmental dyscalculia. *European Journal of Pediatrics*, 174(1), 1–13. http://doi.org/10.1007/s00431-014-2455-7

Kucker, S. C., McMurray, B., & Samuelson, L. K. (2015). Slowing down fast mapping: Redefining the dynamics of word learning. *Child Development Perspectives*, 9(2), 74–78. http://doi.org/10.1111/cdep.12110

Kuczmarski, R. J., Ogden, C. L., Grummer-Strawn, L. M., Flegal, K. M., Guo, S. S., Wei, R., . . . Johnson, C. L. (2000). *CDC Growth Charts: United States*. Washington, DC: National Center for Health Statistics. Retrieved from http://www.cdc.gov/nchs/data/ad/ad314.pdf

Kuczynski, L., & Kochanska, G. (1995). Function and content of maternal demands: Developmental significance of early demands for competent action. *Child Development*, 66(3), 616–628. http://doi.org/10.1111/j.1467-8624.1995.tb00893.x

Kuhl, P. K., Andruski, J. E., Christovich, I. A., Christovich, L. A., Kozhevnikova, E. V, Ryskina, V. L., & al., et. (1997). Cross-language analysis of phonetic units in language addressed to infants. *Science*, 277, 684–686.

Kuhl, P. K., Stevens, E., Hayashi, A., Deguchi, T., Kiritani, S., & Iverson, P. (2006). Infants show a facilitation effect for native language phonetic perception between 6 and 12 months. *Developmental Science, 9*(2), F13–F21. http://doi.org/10.1111/j.1467-7687.2006.00468.x

Kuhl, P. K., Tsao, F.-M., & Liu, H.-M. (2003). Foreign-language experience in infancy: effects of short-term exposure and social interaction on phonetic learning. *Proceedings of the National Academy of Sciences of the United States of America, 100*(15), 9096–9101. http://doi.org/10.1073/pnas.1532872100

Kuhlmeier, V., Dunfield, K., & O'Neill, A. (2014). Selectivity in Early Prosocial Behavior. *Frontiers in Psychology, 5*(836). http://doi.org/10.3389/fpsyg.2014.00836

Kuhn, D. (2000). Metacognitive Development. *Current Directions in Psychological Science, 9*, 178–181.

Kuhn, D. (2000). Theory of mind, metacognition, and reasoning: A life-span perspective. In P. Mitchell & K. J. Riggs (Eds.), *Children's reasoning and the mind* (pp. 301–326). Hove, UK: Psychology Press.

Kuhn, D. (2008). Formal operations from a twenty-first century perspective. *Human Development, 51*(1), 48–55. http://doi.org/10.1159/000113155

Kuhn, D. (2012). The development of causal reasoning. *Wiley Interdisciplinary Reviews: Cognitive Science, 3*(3), 327–335. http://doi.org/10.1002/wcs.1160

Kuhn, D., & Franklin, S. (2006). The second decade: What develops (and how). In D. Kuhn, R. S. Siegler, W. Damon, & R. M. Lerner (Eds.), *Handbook of child psychology: Vol 2, Cognition, perception, and language* (6th ed.; pp. 953–993). Hoboken, NJ: John Wiley & Sons.

Kuhn, D., Iordanou, K., Pease, M., & Wirkala, C. (2008). Beyond control of variables: What needs to develop to achieve skilled scientific thinking? *Cognitive Development, 23*(4), 435–451. http://doi.org/10.1016/j.cogdev.2008.09.006

Kuhn, D., Langer, J., Kohlberg, L., & Haan, N. S. (1977). The development of formal operations in logical and moral judgment. *Genetic Psychology Monographs, 95*(1), 97–188.

Kuhn, D., Pease, M., & Wirkala, C. (2009). Coordinating the effects of multiple variables: A skill fundamental to scientific thinking. *Journal of Experimental Child Psychology, 103*(3), 268–84. http://doi.org/10.1016/j.jecp.2009.01.009

Kulik, L., & Havusha-Morgenstern, H. (2011). Does cohabitation matter? Differences in initial marital adjustment among women who cohabited and those who did not. *Families in Society: The Journal of Contemporary Social Services, 92*(1), 120–127.

Kumar, S., & Kelly, A. S. (2017). Review of childhood obesity: From epidemiology, etiology, and comorbidities to clinical assessment and treatment. *Mayo Clinic Proceedings, 92*(2), 251–265. http://doi.org/10.1016/j.mayocp.2016.09.017

Kumpulainen, K., & Räsänen, E. (2000). Children involved in bullying at elementary school age: Their psychiatric symptoms and deviance in adolescence: An epidemiological sample. *Child Abuse & Neglect, 24*(12), 1567–1577.

Kunzmann, U., Little, T. D., & Smith, J. (2000). Is age-related stability of subjective well-being a paradox? Cross-sectional and longitudinal evidence from the Berlin Aging Study. *Psychology and Aging, 15*(3), 511–26. Retrieved from http://www.ncbi.nlm.nih.gov/pubmed/11014714

Kuo, Y.-L., Liao, H.-F., Chen, P.-C., Hsieh, W.-S., & Hwang, A.-W. (2008). The influence of wakeful prone positioning on motor development during the early life. *Journal of Developmental and Behavioral Pediatrics, 29*(5), 367–376. http://doi.org/10.1097/DBP.0b013e3181856d54

Kuperberg, A., & Padgett, J. E. (2016). The role of culture in explaining college students' selection into hookups, dates, and long-term romantic relationships. *Journal of Social and Personal Relationships, 33*(8), 1070–1096. http://doi.org/10.1177/0265407515616876

Kupfersmid, J. H., & Wonderly, D. M. (1980). Moral maturity and behavior: Failure to find a link. *Journal of Youth and Adolescence, 9*(3), 249–261.

Kurdek, L. A. (2005). Gender and marital satisfaction early in marriage: A growth curve approach. *Journal of Marriage and Family, 67*(1), 68–84.

Kurdek, L. A. (2007). The allocation of household labor by partners in gay and lesbian couples. *Journal of Family Issues, 28*(1), 132–148. http://doi.org/10.1177/0192513X06292019

Kurtz-Costes, B., Copping, K. E., Rowley, S. J., & Kinlaw, C. R. (2014). Gender and age differences in awareness and endorsement of gender stereotypes about academic abilities. *European Journal of Psychology of Education, 29*(4), 603–618. http://doi.org/10.1007/s10212-014-0216-7

Kuster, F., & Orth, U. (2013). The long-term stability of self-esteem: Its time-dependent decay and nonzero asymptote. *Personality and Social Psychology Bulletin, 39*(5), 677–690. http://doi.org/10.1177/0146167213480189

Kuster, F., Orth, U., & Meier, L. L. (2013). High self-esteem prospectively predicts better work conditions and outcomes. *Social Psychological and Personality Science, 4*(6), 668–675. http://doi.org/10.1177/1948550613479806

Kuther, T. L. (2003). Medical decision-making and minors: Issues of consent and assent. *Adolescence, 38*(150), 343–359.

Kuys, S. S., Peel, N. M., Klein, K., Slater, A., & Hubbard, R. E. (2014). Gait speed in ambulant older people in long term care: A systematic review and meta-analysis. *Journal of the American Medical Directors Association, 15*(3), 194–200. http://doi.org/10.1016/j.jamda.2013.10.015

La Rooy, D., Lamb, M. E., & Pipe, M. . (2011). Repeated interviewing: A critical evaluation of the risks and potential benefits. In *The evaluation of child sexual abuse allegations: A comprehensive guide to assessment and testimony.* (pp. 327–361). Chichester, UK: Wiley-Blackwell.

Laborde, S., Lautenbach, F., Allen, M. S., Herbert, C., & Achtzehn, S. (2014). The role of trait emotional intelligence in emotion regulation and performance under pressure. *Personality and Individual Differences, 57*, 43–47. http://doi.org/10.1016/j.paid.2013.09.013

Labouvie-Vief, G. (1980). Beyond formal operations: Uses and limits of pure logic in life-span development. *Human Development, 23*(3), 141–161.

Labouvie-Vief, G. (2003). Dynamic integration: Affect, cognition, and the self in adulthood. *Current Directions in Psychological Science, 12*(6), 201–206.

Labouvie-Vief, G. (2006). Emerging structures of adult thought. In J. J. Arnett & J. L. Tanner (Eds.), *Emerging adults in America: Coming of age in the 21st century* (pp. 59–84). Washington, DC: American Psychological Association.

Labouvie-Vief, G. (2015). *Integrating emotions and cognition throughout the lifespan.* New York: Springer.

Labouvie-Vief, G., & Diehl, M. (1999). Self and personality development. In J. C. Cavanaugh & S. K. Whitbourne (Eds.), *Gerontology: An interdisciplinary perspective* (pp. 238–268). New York, NY: Oxford University Press.

Labouvie-Vief, G., Grühn, D., & Studer, J. (2010). Dynamic integration of emotion and cognition: Equilibrium regulation in development and aging. In *The handbook of life-span development.* Hoboken, NJ, USA: John Wiley & Sons. http://doi.org/10.1002/9780470880166.hlsd002004

Labrie, J. W., Hummer, J. F., Ghaidarov, T. M., Lac, A., & Kenney, S. R. (2014). Hooking up in the college context: The event-level effects of alcohol use and partner familiarity on hookup behaviors and contentment. *Journal of Sex Research, 51*(1), 62–73. http://doi.org/10.1080/00224499.2012.714010

Lachman, M. E., Teshale, S., & Agrigoroaei, S. (2015). Midlife as a pivotal period in the life course: Balancing growth and decline at the crossroads of youth and old age. *International Journal of Behavioral Development, 39*(1), 20–31. http://doi.org/10.1177/0165025414533223

Lacourse, E., Nagin, D., & Tremblay, R. E. (2003). Developmental trajectories of boys' delinquent group membership and facilitation of violent behaviors during adolescence. *Development and Psychopathology, 15*(1), 183–197. Retrieved from eric.lacourse@umontreal.ca

Ladd, G. W. (1999). Peer relationships and social competence during early and middle childhood. *Annual Review of Psychology, 50*, 333–359. http://doi.org/10.1146/annurev.psych.50.1.333

Ladd, G. W., & Burgess, K. B. (2003). Charting the relationship trajectories of aggressive, withdrawn, and aggressive/withdrawn children during early grade school. In M. E. Hertzig & E. A. Farber (Eds.), *Annual progress in child psychiatry and child development: 2000–2001* (pp. 535–570). New York, NY: Brunner-Routledge.

Ladd, G. W., & Troop-Gordon, W. (2003). The role of chronic peer difficulties in the development of children's psychological adjustment problems. *Child Development, 74*(5), 1344–1367.

LaFontana, K. M., & Cillessen, A. H. N. (2010). Developmental changes in the priority of perceived status in childhood and adolescence. *Social Development, 19*(1), 130–147. http://doi.org/10.1111/j.1467-9507.2008.00522.x

LaFreniere, P., & MacDonald, K. (2013). A post-genomic view of behavioral development and adaptation to the environment. *Developmental Review, 33*(2), 89–109. http://doi.org/10.1016/j.dr.2013.01.002

Lagattuta, K. H., Kramer, H. J., Kennedy, K., Hjortsvang, K., Goldfarb, D., & Tashjian, S. (2015). Chapter six – beyond sally's missing marble: Further development in children's understanding of mind and emotion in middle childhood. In *Advances in Child Development and Behavior* (Vol. 48, pp. 185–217). http://doi.org/10.1016/bs.acdb.2014.11.005

Lagattuta, K. H., & Thompson, R. A. (2007). The development of self-conscious emotions: Cognitive processes and social influences. In J. L. Tracy, R. W. Robins, & J. P. Tangney (Eds.), *The self-conscious emotions: Theory and research* (pp. 91–113). New York, NY: Guilford Press.

Laghi, F., Baiocco, R., Lonigro, A., & Baumgartner, E. (2013). Exploring the relationship between identity status development and alcohol consumption among Italian adolescents. *The Journal of Psychology, 147*(3), 277–292. http://doi.org/10.1080/00223980.2012.688075

Lagouge, M., & Larsson, N.-G. (2013). The role of mitochondrial DNA mutations and free radicals in disease and ageing. *Journal of Internal Medicine, 273*(6), 529–43. http://doi.org/10.1111/joim.12055

Lahey, B., Hulle, C., D'Onofrio, B., Rodgers, J., & Waldman, I. (2008). Is parental knowledge of their adolescent offspring's whereabouts and peer associations spuriously associated with offspring delinquency? *Journal of Abnormal Child Psychology, 36*(6), 807–823. http://doi.org/10.1007/s10802-008-9214-z

Laible, D., McGinley, M., Carlo, G., Augustine, M., & Murphy, T. (2014). Does engaging in prosocial behavior make children see the world through rose-colored glasses? *Developmental Psychology, 50*(3), 872–880.

Lakshman, R., Elks, C. E., & Ong, K. K. (2012). Childhood obesity. *Circulation*, *126*(14), 1770–9. http://doi.org/10.1161/CIRCULATIONAHA.111.047738

Lam, C. B., Stanik, C., & McHale, S. M. (2017). The development and correlates of gender role attitudes in African American youth. *British Journal of Developmental Psychology*. http://doi.org/10.1111/bjdp.12182

Lamb, M. E. (1997). The development of father-infant relationships. In M. E. Lamb (Ed.), *The role of the father in child development*. New York: Wiley.

Lamb, M. E. (2012). Mothers, fathers, families, and circumstances: Factors affecting children's adjustment. *Applied Developmental Science*, *16*(2), 98–111. http://doi.org/10.1080/10888691.2012.667344

Lamb, M. E., & Lewis, C. (2015). The role of parent-child relationships in child development. In M. H. Bornstein & M. E. Lamb (Eds.), *Developmental science: An advanced textbook* (7th ed., pp. 469–517). New York, NY: Psychology Press.

Lambert, A. J., & Raichle, K. (2000). The role of political ideology in mediating judgments of blame in rape victims and their assailants: A test of the just world, personal responsibility, and legitimization hypotheses. *Personality and Social Psychology Bulletin*, *26*(7), 853–863. http://doi.org/10.1177/0146167200269010

Lambert, B. L., & Bauer, C. R. (2012). Developmental and behavioral consequences of prenatal cocaine exposure: A review. *Journal of Perinatology : Official Journal of the California Perinatal Association*, *32*(11), 819–28. http://doi.org/10.1038/jp.2012.90

Lambert, J.-C., Sleegers, K., González-Pérez, A., Ingelsson, M., Beecham, G. W., Hiltunen, M., . . . Tzourio, C. (2011). The CALHM1 P86L polymorphism is a genetic modifier of age at onset in Alzheimer's disease: A meta-analysis study. *Journal of Alzheimer's Disease*, *22*(1), 247–255. http://doi.org/10.3233/jad-2010-100933

Lamers, E. P. (1995). Children, death, and fairy tales. *OMEGA–Journal of Death and Dying*, *31*(2), 151–167. http://doi.org/10.2190/HXV5-WWE4-N1HH-4JEG

Lamotte, G., Skender, E., Rafferty, M. R., David, F. J., Sadowsky, S., & Corcos, D. M. (2015). Effects of progressive resistance exercise training on the motor and nonmotor features of Parkinson's disease: A review. *Kinesiology Review*, *4*, 11–27. http://doi.org/10.1123/kr.2014-0074

Lampl, M., Johnson, M. L., Frongillo Jr., E., & Frongillo, E. A. (2001). Mixed distribution analysis identifies saltation and stasis growth. *Annals of Human Biology*, *28*(4), 403–411.

Lampl, M., Veldhuis, J. D., & Johnson, M. L. (1992). Saltation and stasis: A model of human growth. *Science*, *258*, 801–803.

Lancy, D. (2008). The anthropology of childhood: Cherubs, chattel, changelings. *Utah State University Faculty Monographs*. Retrieved from http://digitalcommons.usu.edu/usufaculty_monographs/15

Lang, A., Fleiszer, A. R., Duhamel, F., Sword, W., Gilbert, K. R., & Corsini-Munt, S. (2011). Perinatal loss and parental grief: The challenge of ambiguity and disenfranchised grief. *OMEGA–Journal of Death and Dying*, *63*(2), 183–196. http://doi.org/10.2190/OM.63.2.e

Lang, F. R., & Fingerman, K. L. (2004). *Growing together: Personal relationships across the lifespan*. New York, NY: Cambridge University Press.

Lang, F. R., Featherman, D. L., & Nesselroade, J. R. (1997). Social self-efficacy and short-term variability in social relationships: The MacArthur Successful Aging Studies. *Psychology and Aging*, *12*(4), 657–666.

Lange, G., & Canoll, D. E. (2003). Mother-child conversation styles and children's laboratory memory for narrative and nonnarrative materials. *Journal of Cognition & Development*, *4*(4), 435–457.

Lange, H., Buse, J., Bender, S., Siegert, J., Knopf, H., & Roessner, V. (2016). Accident proneness in children and adolescents affected by ADHD and the impact of medication. *Journal of Attention Disorders*, *20*(6), 501–509. http://doi.org/10.1177/1087054713518237

Langfur, S. (2013). The You-I event: on the genesis of self-awareness. *Phenomenology and the Cognitive Sciences*, *12*(4), 769–790. http://doi.org/10.1007/s11097-012-9282-y

Långström, N., Rahman, Q., Carlström, E., & Lichtenstein, P. (2010). Genetic and environmental effects on same-sex sexual behavior: A population study of twins in Sweden. *Archives of Sexual Behavior*, *39*(1), 75–80. http://doi.org/10.1007/s10508-008-9386-1

Lansford, J. E. (2009). Parental divorce and children's adjustment. *Perspectives on Psychological Science*, *4*(2), 140–152. http://doi.org/10.1111/j.1745-6924.2009.01114.x

Lansford, J. E., Costanzo, P. R., Grimes, C., Putallaz, M., Miller, S., & Malone, P. S. (2009). Social network centrality and leadership status: Links with problem behaviors and tests of gender differences. *Merrill-Palmer Quarterly*, *55*(1), 1–25.

Lansford, J. E., Deater-Deckard, K., Dodge, K. A., Bates, J. E., & Pettit, G. S. (2004). Ethnic differences in the link between physical discipline and later adolescent externalizing behaviors. *Journal of Child Psychology & Psychiatry*, *45*(4), 801–812. http://doi.org/10.1111/j.1469-7610.2004.00273.x

Lansford, J. E., Laird, R. D., Pettit, G. S., Bates, J. E., & Dodge, K. A. (2014). Mothers' and fathers' autonomy-relevant parenting: Longitudinal links with adolescents' externalizing and internalizing behavior. *Journal of Youth and Adolescence*, *43*(11), 1877–1889. http://doi.org/10.1007/s10964-013-0079-2

Lansford, J. E., Malone, P. S., Dodge, K. A., Pettit, G. S., & Bates, J. E. (2010). Developmental cascades of peer rejection, social information processing biases, and aggression during middle childhood. *Development & Psychopathology*, *22*(3), 593–602. http://doi.org/10.1017/S0954579410000301

Lansford, J. E., Staples, A. D., Bates, J. E., Pettit, G. S., & Dodge, K. A. (2013). Trajectories of mothers' discipline strategies and interparental conflict: Interrelated change during middle childhood. *Journal of Family Communication*, *13*(3), 178–195. http://doi.org/10.1080/15267431.2013.796947

Lantz, P. M., House, J. S., Mero, R. P., & Williams, D. R. (2005). Stress, life events, and socioeconomic disparities in health: Results from the Americans' Changing Lives Study. *Journal of Health & Social Behavior*, *46*(3), 274–288.

Lanza, S. T., & Collins, L. M. (2006). A mixture model of discontinuous development in heavy drinking from ages 18 to 30: The role of college enrollment. *Journal of Studies on Alcohol*, *67*(4), 552–561.

Laplante-Lévesque, A., Hickson, L., & Worrall, L. (2010). Rehabilitation of older adults with hearing impairment: A critical review. *Journal of Aging & Health*, *22*(2), 143–153. http://doi.org/10.1177/0898264309352731

Lapp, L. K., & Spaniol, J. (2016). Aging and self-discrepancy: Evidence for adaptive change across the life span. *Experimental Aging Research*, *42*(2), 212–219. http://doi.org/10.1080/0361073X.2016.1132900

Lapsley, D. K., Jackson, S., Rice, K., & Shadid, G. E. (1988). Self-monitoring and the "new look" at the imaginary audience and personal fable: An ego-developmental analysis. *Journal of Adolescent Research*, *3*(1), 17–31.

Larsen, J. T., To, Y. M., & Fireman, G. (2007). Children's understanding and experience of mixed emotions. *Psychological Science*, *18*(2), 186–191. http://doi.org/10.1111/j.1467-9280.2007.01870.x

Larsen, W. J. (2001). *Human embryology*. New York: Churchill Livingstone.

Larson, R., & Csikszentmihalyi, M. (2014). The experience sampling method. In M. Csikszentmihalyi (Ed.), *Flow and the foundations of positive psychology* (pp. 21–34). Amsterdam: Springer Netherlands. Retrieved from http://link.springer.com/chapter/10.1007/978-94-017-9088-8_3

Larson, R., & Ham, M. (1993). Stress and "storm and stress" in early adolescence: The relationship of negative events with. *Developmental Psychology*, *29*(1), 130.

Larson, R., & Richards, M. (1998). Waiting for the weekend: Friday and Saturday night as the emotional climax of the week. *New Directions for Child & Adolescent Development*, *1998*(82), 37–51.

Larson, R., & Seepersad, S. (2003). Adolescents' leisure time in the United States: Partying, sports, and the American experiment. *New Directions for Child & Adolescent Development*, *2003*(99), 53–64.

Larson, R., Csikszentmihalyi, M., & Graef, R. (2014). Mood variability and the psycho-social adjustment of adolescents. In M. Csikszentmihalyi (Ed.), *Applications of Flow in Human Development and Education* (pp. 285–304). Amsterdam: Springer Netherlands. Retrieved from http://link.springer.com/chapter/10.1007/978-94-017-9094-9_15

Larson, R., Mannell, R., & Zuzanek, J. (1986). Daily well-being of older adults with friends and family. *Psychology and Aging*, *1*(2), 117–126. http://doi.org/10.1037/0882-7974.1.2.117

Larsson, M., Oberg-Blåvarg, C., & Jönsson, F. U. (2009). Bad odors stick better than good ones: Olfactory qualities and odor recognition. *Experimental Psychology*, *56*(6), 375–380. http://doi.org/10.1027/1618-3169.56.6.375

Lau, R., & Morse, C. A. (2003). Stress experiences of parents with premature infants in a special care nursery. *Stress and Health*, *19*, 69–78.

Laughton, B., Cornell, M., Boivin, M., & Van Rie, A. (2013). Neurodevelopment in perinatally HIV-infected children: A concern for adolescence. *Journal of the International AIDS Society*, *16*(1), 18603. http://doi.org/10.7448/IAS.16.1.18603

Laughton, D. S., Sheppard, A. L., & Davies, L. N. (2016). A longitudinal study of accommodative changes in biometry during incipient presbyopia. *Ophthalmic and Physiological Optics*, *36*(1), 33–42. http://doi.org/10.1111/opo.12242

Laumann, E. O., Paik, A., Glasser, D. B., Kang, J.-H., Wang, T., Levinson, B., . . . Gingell, C. (2006). A cross-national study of subjective sexual well-being among older women and men: Findings from the Global Study of Sexual Attitudes and Behaviors. *Archives of Sexual Behavior*, *35*(2), 143–159. http://doi.org/10.1007/s10508-005-9005-3

Laursen, B., & Hartup, W. W. (2002). The origins of reciprocity and social exchange in friendships. *New Directions for Child & Adolescent Development*, *2002*(95), 27–40.

Lavelle, B., & Smock, P. J. (2012). Divorce and women's risk of health insurance loss. *Journal of Health and Social Behavior*, *53*(4), 413–31. http://doi.org/10.1177/0022146512465758

Lavender, A. P., & Nosaka, K. (2007). Fluctuations of isometric force after eccentric exercise of the elbow flexors of young, middle-aged, and old men. *European Journal of Applied Physiology*, *100*(2), 161–167. http://doi.org/10.1007/s00421-007-0418-7

Lavner, J. A., & Bradbury, T. N. (2012). Why do even satisfied newlyweds eventually go on to divorce? *Journal of Family Psychology*, *26*(1), 1–10. http://doi.org/10.1037/a0025966

REFERENCES

Lavner, J. A., Waterman, J., & Peplau, L. A. (2014). Parent adjustment over time in gay, lesbian, and heterosexual parent families adopting from foster care. *The American Journal of Orthopsychiatry*, 84(1), 46–53. http://doi.org/10.1037/h0098853

Lawlor, D. A., Ebrahim, S., & Smith, G. D. (2003). The association of socio-economic position across the life course and age at menopause: The British Women's Heart and Health Study. *BJOG: An International Journal of Obstetrics & Gynaecology*, 110(12), 1078.

Lawrence, E., Rothman, A. D., Cobb, R. J., Rothman, M. T., & Bradbury, T. N. (2008). Marital satisfaction across the transition to parenthood. *Journal of Family Psychology*, 22(1), 41–50

Lawson, G. M., Duda, J. T., Avants, B. B., Wu, J., & Farah, M. J. (2013). Associations between children's socioeconomic status and prefrontal cortical thickness. *Developmental Science*, 16(5), 641–652. https://doi.org/10.1111/desc.12096

Lazar, A., & Torney-Purta, J. (1991). The development of the subconcepts of death in young children: A short-term longitudinal study. *Child Development*, 62(6), 1321–1333. http://doi.org/10.1111/j.1467-8624.1991.tb01608.x

Le Bourdais, C., & Lapierre-Adamcyk, É. (2004). Changes in conjugal life in Canada: Is cohabitation progressively replacing marriage? *Journal of Marriage & Family*, 66(4), 929–942

le Grange, D., & Schmidt, U. (2005). The treatment of adolescents with bulimia nervosa. *Journal of Mental Health*, 14(6), 587–597.

Le, Y., McDaniel, B. T., Leavitt, C. E., & Feinberg, M. E. (2016). Longitudinal associations between relationship quality and coparenting across the transition to parenthood: A dyadic perspective. *Journal of Family Psychology*, 30(8), 918–926. http://doi.org/10.1037/fam0000217

Leadbeater, B., Banister, E., Ellis, W., & Yeung, R. (2008). Victimization and relational aggression in adolescent romantic relationships: The influence of parental and peer behaviors, and individual adjustment. *Journal of Youth & Adolescence*, 37(3), 359–372. http://doi.org/10.1007/s10964-007-9269-0

Leahey, E., & Guo, G. (2001). Gender differences in mathematical trajectories. *Social Forces*, 80(2), 713–732. http://doi.org/10.1353/sof.2001.0102

Leaper, C. (2013). Gender development during childhood. In P. D. Zelaz (Ed.), *The Oxford handbook of developmental psychology, vol. 2: self and other*.

Leaper, C., Tenenbaum, H. R., & Shaffer, T. G. (1999). Communication patterns of African-American girls and boys from low-income, urban backgrounds. *Child Development*, 70, 1489–1503.

Leaper, C., & Valin, D. (1996). Predictors of Mexican American mothers' and fathers' attitudes toward gender equality. *Hispanic Journal of Behavioral Sciences*, 18(3), 343–355. http://doi.org/10.1177/07399863960183005

Learmonth, A. E., Lamberth, R., & Rovee-Collier, C. (2004). Generalizations of deferred imitation during the first year of life. *Journal of Experimental Child Psychology*, 88(4), 297–318.

Leather, C. V, & Henry, L. A. (1994). Working memory span and phonological awareness tasks as predictors of early reading ability. *Journal of Experimental Child Psychology*, 58, 88–111.

Lebel, C., Warner, T., Colby, J., Soderberg, L., Roussotte, F., Behnke, M., . . . Sowell, E. R. (2013). White matter microstructure abnormalities and executive function in adolescents with prenatal cocaine exposure. *Psychiatry Research*, 213(2), 161–168. http://doi.org/10.1016/j.pscychresns.2013.04.002

LeBlanc, E. S., O'Connor, E., Whitlock, E. P., Patnode, C. D., & Kapka, T. (2011). Effectiveness of primary care-relevant treatments for obesity in adults: A systematic evidence review for the U.S. Preventive Services Task Force. *Annals of Internal Medicine*, 155(7), 434–447.

Lecce, S., Demicheli, P., Zocchi, S., & Palladino, P. (2015). The origins of children's metamemory: The role of theory of mind. *Journal of Experimental Child Psychology*, 131, 56–72. http://doi.org/10.1016/j.jecp.2014.11.005

LeDoux, J. E., & Phelps, E. A. (2008). Emotional networks in the brain. In M. Lewis, J. M. Haviland-Jones, & L. F. Barrett (Eds.), *Handbook of emotions* (3rd ed., pp. 159–179). New York, NY: Guilford Press.

Lee, C., & Longo, V. (2016). Dietary restriction with and without caloric restriction for healthy aging. *F1000Research*, 5. http://doi.org/10.12688/f1000research.7136.1

Lee, C. M., Maggs, J. L., Neighbors, C., & Patrick, M. E. (2011). Positive and negative alcohol-related consequences: Associations with past drinking. *Journal of Adolescence*, 34(1), 87–94. http://doi.org/10.1016/j.adolescence.2010.01.009

Lee, C. M., Neighbors, C., & Woods, B. A. (2007). Marijuana motives: Young adults' reasons for using marijuana. *Addictive Behaviors*, 32(7), 1384–1394. http://doi.org/10.1016/j.addbeh.2006.09.010

Lee, E.-K. O. (2007). Religion and spirituality as predictors of well-being among Chinese American and Korean American older adults. *Journal of Religion, Spirituality & Aging*, 19(3), 77–100. http://doi.org/10.1300/J496v19n03_06

Lee, E.-K. O., & Sharpe, T. (2007a). Understanding religious/spiritual coping and support resources among African American oder adults: A Mixed-Method Approach. *Journal of Religion, Spirituality & Aging*, 19(3), 55–75.

Lee, H., & Galloway, J. C. (2012). Control in very young infants. *Physical Therapy*, 92(7), 935–947.

Lee, H.-C., Chang, C.-M., & Chi, C.-W. (2010). Somatic mutations of mitochondrial DNA in aging and cancer progression. *Ageing Research Reviews*, 9, S47–S58. http://doi.org/10.1016/j.arr.2010.08.009

Lee, H.-J., & Chou, L.-S. (2007). Balance control during stair negotiation in older adults. *Journal of Biomechanics*, 40(11), 2530–2536.

Lee, I. M., Hsieh, C. C., Paffenbarger, R. S., Paffenbarger, R. S., Hyde, R. T., Wing, A. L., . . . Colditz, G. A. (2002). Recommendations to increase physical activity in communities. *American Journal of Preventive Medicine*, 22(4), 67–72. http://doi.org/10.1016/S0749-3797(02)00433-6

Lee, J. M., Wasserman, R., Kaciroti, N., Gebremariam, A., Steffes, J., Dowshen, S., . . . Herman-Giddens, M. E. (2016). Timing of puberty in overweight versus obese boys. *Pediatrics*, 137(2). http://doi.org/10.1542/peds.2015-0164

Lee, L. J., & Lupo, P. J. (2013). Maternal smoking during pregnancy and the risk of congenital heart defects in offspring: A systematic review and metaanalysis. *Pediatric Cardiology*, 34(2), 398–407. http://doi.org/10.1007/s00246-012-0470-x

Lee, L., Howes, C., & Chamberlain, B. (2007). Ethnic heterogeneity of social networks and cross-ethnic friendships of elementary school boys and girls. *Merrill-Palmer Quarterly*, 53(3), 325–346.

Lee, M. R., Chassin, L., & Villalta, I. K. (2013). Maturing out of alcohol involvement: Transitions in latent drinking statuses from late adolescence to adulthood. *Development and Psychopathology*, 25(4), 1137–1153. http://doi.org/10.1017/S0954579413000424

Lee, S. J., Altschul, I., & Gershoff, E. T. (2013). Does warmth moderate longitudinal associations between maternal spanking and child aggression in early childhood? *Developmental Psychology*, 49(11), 2017–2028. http://doi.org/10.1037/a0031630

Lee, S. M., Daniels, M. H., & Kissinger, D. B. (2006). Parental influences on adolescent adjustment: Parenting styles versus parenting practices. *Family Journal*, 14, 253–259.

Lee, S., & Shaw, L. (2008). *From work to retirement: Tracking changes in women's poverty status*. Washington, DC: American Association of Retired Persons. Retrieved from http://www.aarp.org/research/assistance/lowincome/inb156_poverty.html

Lee, T., Kwong, W., Cheung, C., Ungar, M., & Cheung, M. (2010). Children's resilience-related beliefs as a predictor of positive child development in the face of adversities: Implications for interventions to enhance children's quality of life. *Social Indicators Research*, 95(3), 437–453. http://doi.org/10.1007/s11205-009-9530-x

Lee, Y., Tang, F., Kim, K. H., & Albert, S. M. (2015). The vicious cycle of parental caregiving and financial well-being: A longitudinal study of women. *The Journals of Gerontology Series B: Psychological Sciences and Social Sciences*, 70(3), 425–431. http://doi.org/10.1093/geronb/gbu001

Lee, Y.-A., & Goto, Y. (2015). Chronic stress effects on working memory: Association with prefrontal cortical tyrosine hydroxylase. *Behavioural Brain Research*, 286, 122–127. http://doi.org/10.1016/j.bbr.2015.03.007

Leenstra, T., Petersen, L. T., Kariuki, S. K., Oloo, A. J., Kager, P. A., & ter Kuile, F. O. (2005). Prevalence and severity of malnutrition and age at menarche; Cross-sectional studies in adolescent schoolgirls in western Kenya. *European Journal of Clinical Nutrition*, 59(1), 41–48. http://doi.org/10.1038/sj.ejcn.1602031

Lefkowitz, E. S., & Fingerman, K. L. (2003). Positive and negative emotional feelings and behaviors in mother-daughter ties in late life. *Journal of Family Psychology*, 17(4), 607–617.

Lefkowitz, E. S., & Stoppa, T. M. (2006). Positive sexual communication and socialization in the parent-adolescent context. *New Directions for Child & Adolescent Development*, 2006(112), 39–55.

Lefkowitz, E. S., Vasilenko, S. A., & Leavitt, C. E. (2016). Oral vs. vaginal sex experiences and consequences among first-year college students. *Archives of Sexual Behavior*, 45(2), 329–337. http://doi.org/10.1007/s10508-015-0654-6

Lefkowitz, E. S., & Zeldow, P. B. (2006). Masculinity and femininity predict optimal mental health: A belated test of the androgyny hypothesis. *Journal of Personality Assessment*, 87(1), 95–101.

Legare, C. H., Evans, E. M., Rosengren, K. S., & Harris, P. L. (2012). The coexistence of natural and supernatural explanations across cultures and development. *Child Development*, 83(3), 779–793. http://doi.org/10.1111/j.1467-8624.2012.01743.x

Legare, C. H., & Gelman, S. A. (2008). Bewitchment, biology, or both: The co-existence of natural and supernatural explanatory frameworks across development. *Cognitive Science*, 32(4), 607–642. http://doi.org/10.1080/03640210802066766

Legare, C. H., Wellman, H. M., & Gelman, S. A. (2009). Evidence for an explanation advantage in naive biological reasoning. *Cognitive Psychology*, 58(2), 177–194. http://doi.org/10.1016/j.cogpsych.2008.06.002

Legate, N., Ryan, R. M., & Weinstein, N. (2012). Is coming out always a "good thing"? Exploring the relations of autonomy support, outness, and wellness for lesbian, gay, and bisexual individuals. *Social Psychological and Personality Science*, 3(2), 145–152. http://doi.org/10.1177/1948550611411929

Leger, D. W., Thompson, R. A., Merritt, J. A., & Benz, J. J. (1996). Adult perception of emotion intensity in human infant cries: Effects of infant age and cry acoustics. *Child Development*, 67, 3238–3249.

Lehman, D. R., Lempert, R. O., & Nisbett, R. E. (1988). The effects of graduate training on reasoning: Formal discipline and thinking about everyday life events. *American Psychologist*, 43, 431–443. Retrieved from http://deepblue.lib.umich.edu/handle/2027.42/92173

Lehman, D. R., & Nisbett, R. E. (1990). A longitudinal study of the effects of undergraduate training on reasoning. *Developmental Psychology*, 26, 952–960.

Lehmann, M., & Hasselhorn, M. (2007). Variable memory strategy use in children's adaptive intratask learning behavior: Developmental changes and working memory influences in free recall. *Child Development*, 78(4), 1068–1082.

Leichsenring, F., & Rabung, S. (2008). Effectiveness of long-term psychodynamic psychotherapy. *Journal of the American Medical Association*, 300(13), 1551–1565.

Leichtman, M. D., & Ceci, S. J. (1995). The effects of stereotypes and suggestions on preschoolers' reports. *Developmental Psychology*, 31, 568–578.

Leigh-Paffenroth, E. D., & Elangovan, S. (2011). Temporal processing in low-frequency channels: Effects of age and hearing loss in middle-aged listeners. *Journal of the American Academy of Audiology*, 22(7), 393–404. http://doi.org/10.3766/jaaa.22.7.2

Lemere, C. (2013). Alzheimer's disease and Down syndrome. *Alzheimer's & Dementia*, 9(4), P513. http://doi.org/10.1016/j.jalz.2013.04.223

Lemerise, E. A., & Dodge, K. A. (2008). The development of anger and hostile interactions. In M. Lewis, J. M. Haviland-Jones, & L. F. Barrett (Eds.), *Handbook of emotions* (3rd ed., pp. 730–741). New York, NY: Guilford Press.

Lemery, K. S., Goldsmith, H. H., Klinnert, M. D., & Mrazel, D. A. (1999). Developmental models of infant and childhood temperament. *Developmental Psychology*, 35, 189–204.

Leming, M., & Dickinson, G. (2016). *Understanding dying, death, and bereavement*. New York, NY: Cengage Learning.

Lenhart, A., Kahne, J., Middaugh, E., MacGill, A., Evans, C., & Vitak, J. (2008). *Teens, video games and civics*. Retrieved from http://www.pewinternet.org/files/oldmedia//Files/Reports/2008/PIP_Teens_Games_and_Civics_Report_FINAL.pdf

Lenhart, A., Purcell, K., Smith, A., & Zickuhr, K. (2010). *Social media and young adults*. Retrieved from http://www.pewinternet.org/2010/02/03/social-media-and-young-adults/

Lenroot, R. K., Gogtay, N., Greenstein, D. K., Wells, E. M., Wallace, G. L., Clasen, L. S., . . . Giedd, J. N. (2007). Sexual dimorphism of brain developmental trajectories during childhood and adolescence. *NeuroImage*, 36(4), 1065–1073. https://doi.org/10.1016/j.neuroimage.2007.03.053

Leong, A., Porneala, B., Dupuis, J., Florez, J. C., & Meigs, J. B. (2016). Type 2 diabetes genetic predisposition, obesity, and all-cause mortality risk in the U.S.: A multiethnic analysis. *Diabetes Care*, 39(4).

Leopold, T., & Skopek, J. (2015). The demography of grandparenthood: An international profile. *Social Forces*, 94, 801–832. http://doi.org/10.1093/sf/sov066

Leow, C., & Wen, X. (2017). Is full day better than half day? A propensity score analysis of the association between Head Start program intensity and children's school performance in kindergarten. *Early Education and Development*, 28(2), 224–239. http://doi.org/10.1080/10409289.2016.1208600

Leppanen, J. M. (2011). Neural and developmental bases of the ability to recognize social signals of emotions. *Emotion Review*, 3(2), 179–188. http://doi.org/10.1177/1754073910387942

Lerkkanen, M.-K., Kiuru, N., Pakarinen, E., Poikkeus, A.-M., Rasku-Puttonen, H., Siekkinen, M., & Nurmi, J.-E. (2016). Child-centered versus teacher-directed teaching practices: Associations with the development of academic skills in the first grade at school. *Early Childhood Research Quarterly*, 36, 145–156. http://doi.org/10.1016/j.ecresq.2015.12.023

Lerner, R. M. (2010). Applied developmental science: Definitions and dimensions. In V. Maholmes & C. G. Lomonaco (Eds.), *Applied research in child and adolescent development: A practical guide* (pp. 37–58). New York: Taylor & Francis.

Lerner, R. M. (2012). Developmental science: Past, present, and future. *International Journal of Developmental Science*, 6(1–2), 29–36.

Lerner, R. M., Agans, J. P., DeSouza, L. M., & Gasca, S. (2013). Describing, explaining, and optimizing within-individual change across the life span: A relational developmental systems perspective. *Review of General Psychology*, 17(2), 179–183. http://doi.org/10.1037/a0032931

Lesinski, M., Hortobágyi, T., Muehlbauer, T., Gollhofer, A., & Granacher, U. (2015). Effects of balance training on balance performance in healthy older adults: A systematic review and meta-analysis. *Sports Medicine*, 45(12), 1721–1738. http://doi.org/10.1007/s40279-015-0375-y

Lester, B. M., Conradt, E., & Marsit, C. (2016). Introduction to the special section on epigenetics. *Child Development*, 87(1), 29–37. http://doi.org/10.1111/cdev.12489

Lesthaeghe, R. J., López-Colás, J., & Neidert, L. (2016). The social geography of unmarried cohabitation in the USA, 2007–2011. In A. Esteve & R. J. Lesthaeghe (Eds.), *Cohabitation and marriage in the Americas: Geo-historical legacies and new trends* (pp. 101–131). Geneva, CH: Springer International. http://doi.org/10.1007/978-3-319-31442-6_4

Leszko, M., Elleman, L. G., Bastarache, E. D., Graham, E. K., & Mroczek, D. K. (2016). Future directions in the study of personality in adulthood and older age. *Gerontology*, 62(2), 210–215. http://doi.org/10.1159/000434720

Letiecq, B. L., Bailey, S. J., & Kurtz, M. A. (2008). Depression among rural Native American and European American grandparents rearing their grandchildren. *Journal of Family Issues*, 29(3), 334–356.

Leung, A. K. C., & Robson, L. M. (1993). Childhood masturbation. *Clinical Pediatrics*, 32(4), 238–241. http://doi.org/10.1177/000992289303200410

Leung, C. B. (2008). Preschoolers' acquisition of scientific vocabulary through repeated read-aloud events, retellings, and hands-on science activities. *Reading Psychology*, 29(2), 165–193. http://doi.org/10.1080/02702710801964090

LeVay, S. (1993). *The sexual brain*. Cambridge, MA: The MIT Press.

LeVay, S. (2017). *Gay, straight, and the reason why : The science of sexual orientation*. London, UK: Oxford University Press. Retrieved from https://books.google.com/books?id=J6kDAAAQBAJ&lr=&source=gbs_navlinks_s

Leventon, J. S., & Bauer, P. J. (2013). The sustained effect of emotional signals on neural processing in 12-month-olds. *Developmental Science*, 16(4), 485–498. http://doi.org/10.1111/desc.12041

Leversen, J. S. R., Haga, M., Sigmundsson, H., Rebollo, I., & Colom, R. (2012). From children to adults: Motor performance across the life-span. *PLoS ONE*, 7(6), e38830. http://doi.org/10.1371/journal.pone.0038830

Levin, J. S., & Taylor, R. J. (1994). Race and gender differences in religiosity among older adults: Findings from four national surveys. *Journal of Gerontology*, 49(3), S137.

Levine, J. A., Emery, C. R., & Pollack, H. (2007). The well-being of children born to teen mothers. *Journal of Marriage and Family*, 69(1), 105–122. http://doi.org/10.1111/j.1741-3737.2006.00348.x

Levine, L. E. (1983). Mine: Self-definition in 2-year-old boys. *Developmental Psychology*, 19, 544–549.

Levine, L. J. (1995). Young children's understanding of the causes of anger and sadness. *Child Development*, 66(3), 697–709. http://doi.org/10.1111/j.1467-8624.1995.tb00899.x

Levine, L. J., Stein, N. L., & Liwag, M. D. (1999). Remembering children's emotions: Sources of concordance and discordance between parents and children. *Developmental Psychology*, 35, 790–801.

LeVine, R. A., Dixon, S., LeVine, S., Richman, A., Leiderman, P. H., Keeferk, C. H., . . . et al. (1994). *Child care and culture: Lessons from Africa*. New York: Cambridge University Press.

Levinson, D. J. (1978). *The seasons of a man's life*. New York: Knopf.

Levinson, D. J. (1996). *The seasons of a woman's life*. New York: Knopf.

Levitt, A. G., Aydelott Utman, J. G., Jakobson, R., Menn, L., Oller, D. K., & Stark, R. E. (1992). From babbling towards the sound systems of English and French: A longitudinal two-case study. *Journal of Child Language*, 19(1), 19. http://doi.org/10.1017/S0305000900013611

Levitt, T., Fugelsang, J., & Crossley, M. (2006). Processing speed, attentional capacity, and age-related memory change. *Experimental Aging Research*, 32(3), 263–295.

Levy, G. D. (1999). Gender-typed and non-gender-typed category awareness in toddlers. *Sex Roles*, 41(11/12), 851–873. http://doi.org/10.1023/A:1018832529622

Levy, G. D., & Carter, D. B. (1989). Gender schema, gender constancy, and gender-role knowledge: The roles of cognitive factors in preschoolers' gender-role stereotype attributions. *Developmental Psychology*, 25, 444–449.

Levy, G. D., & Haaf, R. A. (1994). Detection of gender-related categories by 10-month-old infants. *Infant Behavior & Development*, 17(4), 457–459. http://doi.org/10.1016/0163-6383(94)90037-x

Levy, G. D., Taylor, M. G., & Gelman, S. A. (1995). Traditional and evaluative aspects of flexibility in gender roles, social conventions, moral rules, and physical laws. *Child Development*, 66(2), 515–531. Retrieved from http://www.ncbi.nlm.nih.gov/pubmed/7750381

Lewis, B. A., Minnes, S., Short, E. J., Min, M. O., Wu, M., Lang, A., . . . Singer, L. T. (2013). Language outcomes at 12 years for children exposed prenatally to cocaine. *Journal of Speech, Language, and Hearing Research*, 56(5), 1662–1676. http://doi.org/10.1044/1092-4388(2013/12-0119)

Lewis, B. A., Minnes, S., Short, E. J., Weishampel, P., Satayathum, S., Min, M. O., . . . Singer, L. T. (2011). The effects of prenatal cocaine on language development at 10 years of age. *Neurotoxicology and Teratology*, 33(1), 17–24. http://doi.org/10.1016/j.ntt.2010.06.006

Lewis, C., & Lamb, M. E. (2003). Fathers' influences on children's development: The evidence from two-parent families. *European Journal of Psychology of Education*, 18(2), 212–228.

REFERENCES

Lewis, M. (2008). Self-conscious emotions: Embarrassment, pride, shame, and guilt. In M. Lewis, J. M. Haviland-Jones, & L. F. Barrett (Eds.), *Handbook of emotions* (3rd ed., pp. 742–756). New York, NY: Guilford Press.

Lewis, M. (2011). Inside and outside: The relation between emotional states and expressions. *Emotion Review*, *3*(2), 189–196. http://doi.org/10.1177/1754073910387947

Lewis, M., & Brooks-Gunn, J. (1979). *Social cognition and the acquisition of self*. New York: Plenum Press.

Lewis, M., & Carmody, D. P. (2008). Self-representation and brain development. *Developmental Psychology*, *44*(5), 1329–1334. http://doi.org/10.1037/a0012681

Lewis, M., Hitchcock, D. F. A., & Sullivan, M. W. (2004). Physiological and emotional reactivity to learning and frustration. *Infancy*, *6*(1), 121–143.

Lewis, M., Ramsay, D. S., & Kawakami, K. (1993). Differences between Japanese infants and Caucasian American infants in behavioral and cortisol response to inoculation. *Child Development*, *64*, 1722–1731.

Lewis, P. D. (2006). Novel human pathological mutations. *Human Genetics*, *119*(3), 359–364.

Lewkowicz, D. J. (2000). The development of intersensory temporal perception: An epigenetic systems/limitations view. *Psychological Bulletin*, *126*, 281–308.

Lewkowicz, D. J., & Lickliter, R. (1994). *The development of intersensory perception: Comparative perspectives*. Hillsdale, NJ: Lawrence Erlbaum.

Li, G., Kung, K. T. F., & Hines, M. (2017). Childhood gender-typed behavior and adolescent sexual orientation: A longitudinal population-based study. *Developmental Psychology*, *53*(4), 764–777. http://doi.org/10.1037/dev0000281

Li, J.-Q., Tan, L., Wang, H.-F., Tan, M.-S., Tan, L., Xu, W., . . . Yu, J.-T. (2016). Risk factors for predicting progression from mild cognitive impairment to Alzheimer's disease: A systematic review and meta-analysis of cohort studies. *Journal of Neurology, Neurosurgery & Psychiatry*, *87*(5), 476–484. http://doi.org/10.1136/jnnp-2014-310095

Li, R., Zhao, Z., Mokdad, A., & Barker, L. (2003). Prevalence of breastfeeding in the United States: The 2001 National Immunization Survey. *Pediatrics*, *111*(5), 1198–1201.

Li, T., Fok, H. K., & Fung, H. H. (2011). Is reciprocity always beneficial? Age differences in the association between support balance and life satisfaction. *Aging & Mental Health*, *15*(5), 541–547. http://doi.org/10.1080/13607863.2010.551340

Li, W.-F., Hou, S.-X., Yu, B., Li, M.-M., Férec, C., & Chen, J.-M. (2010). Genetics of osteoporosis: Accelerating pace in gene identification and validation. *Human Genetics*, *127*(3), 249–285. http://doi.org/10.1007/s00439-009-0773-z

Liben, L. S., Bigler, R. S., & Hilliard, L. J. (2013). Gender development. In E. T. Gershoff & R. S. Mistry (Eds.), *Societal contexts of child development: Pathways of influence and implications for practice and policy*. London, UK: Oxford University Press.

Libertus, K., Gibson, J., Hidayatallah, N. Z., Hirtle, J., Adcock, R. A., & Needham, A. (2013). Size matters: How age and reaching experiences shape infants' preferences for different sized objects. *Infant Behavior & Development*, *36*(2), 189–198. http://doi.org/10.1016/j.infbeh.2013.01.006

Libertus, K., Joh, A. S., & Needham, A. W. (2016). Motor training at 3 months affects object exploration 12 months later. *Developmental Science*, *19*(6), 1058–1066. http://doi.org/10.1111/desc.12370

Libertus, K., & Needham, A. (2010). Teach to reach: The effects of active vs. passive reaching experiences on action and perception. *Vision Research*, *50*(24), 2750–2757. http://doi.org/10.1016/j.visres.2010.09.001

Libertus, M. E., & Brannon, E. M. (2009). Behavioral and neural basis of number sense in infancy. *Current Directions in Psychological Science*, *18*(6), 346–351. http://doi.org/10.1111/j.1467-8721.2009.01665.x

Libertus, M. E., Starr, A., & Brannon, E. M. (2014). Number trumps area for 7-month-old infants. *Developmental Psychology*, *50*. http://doi.org/10.1037/a0032986

Lichtenthal, W. G., Currier, J. M., Neimeyer, R. A., & Keesee, N. J. (2010). Sense and significance: A mixed methods examination of meaning making after the loss of one's child. *Journal of Clinical Psychology*, *66*(7), 791–812. http://doi.org/10.1002/jclp.20700

Lichter, I., & Hunt, E. (1990). The last 48 hours of life. *Journal of Palliative Care*, *6*(4), 7–15. Retrieved from http://www.ncbi.nlm.nih.gov/pubmed/1704917

Lickliter, R., & Honeycutt, H. (2003). Developmental dynamics: Toward a biologically plausible evolutionary psychology. *Psychological Bulletin*, *129*(6), 819–835. http://doi.org/10.1037/0033-2909.129.6.866

Lickliter, R., & Honeycutt, H. (2013). A developmental evolutionary framework for psychology. *Review of General Psychology*, *17*(2). http://doi.org/10.1037/a0032932

Lieberman, A. F., & Van Horn, P. (2008). *Psychotherapy with infants and young children: Repairing the effects of stress and trauma on early attachment*. New York, NY: Guilford Press.

Lieven, E., & Stoll, S. (2010). Language. In M. H. Bornstein (Ed.), *Handbook of cultural developmental science* (pp. 143–160). New York: Psychology Press.

Lilgendahl, J. P., Helson, R., & John, O. P. (2013). Does ego development increase during midlife? The effects of openness and accommodative processing of difficult events. *Journal of Personality*, *81*(4), 403–416. http://doi.org/10.1111/jopy.12009

Lillard, A. (1998). Ethnopsychologies: Cultural variations in theories of mind. *Psychological Bulletin*, *123*, 3–32.

Lillevoll, K. R., Kroger, J., & Martinussen, M. (2013). Identity status and anxiety: A meta-analysis. *Identity*, *13*(3), 214–227. http://doi.org/10.1080/15283488.2013.799432

Limber, S. P., & Small, M. A. (2003). State laws and policies to address bullying in schools. *School Psychology Review*, *32*(3), 445–455.

Lin, A.-L., Parikh, I., Hoffman, J. D., & Ma, D. (2017). Neuroimaging biomarkers of caloric restriction on brain metabolic and vascular functions. *Current Nutrition Reports*, *6*(1), 41–48. http://doi.org/10.1007/s13668-017-0187-9

Lin, E. H. B. (2008). Depression and osteoarthritis. *American Journal of Medicine*, *121*(11), S16–S19. http://doi.org/10.1016/j.amjmed.2008.09.009

Lin, F. R., Thorpe, R., Gordon-Salant, S., & Ferrucci, L. (2011). Hearing loss prevalence and risk factors among older adults in the United States. *The Journals of Gerontology Series A: Biological Sciences and Medical Sciences*, *66A*(5), 582–590. http://doi.org/10.1093/gerona/glr002

Lin, J. B., Tsubota, K., & Apte, R. S. (2016). A glimpse at the aging eye. *NPJ Aging and Mechanisms of Disease*, *2*. http://doi.org/10.1038/npjamd.2016.3

Lin, J., Gan, C. M., Zhang, X., Jones, S., Sjöblom, T., Wood, L. D., . . . Velculescu, V. E. (2007). A multidimensional analysis of genes mutated in breast and colorectal cancers. *Genome Research*, *17*(9), 7.

Lin, L.-C., & Johnson, C. J. (2010). Phonological patterns in Mandarin–English bilingual children. *Clinical Linguistics & Phonetics*, *24*(4–5), 369–386. http://doi.org/10.3109/02699200903532482

Lindberg, L., Santelli, J., & Desai, S. (2016). Understanding the decline in adolescent fertility in the United States, 2007–2012. *Journal of Adolescent Health*, *59*(5), 577–583. http://doi.org/10.1016/j.jadohealth.2016.06.024

Lindberg, S. M., Hyde, J. S., Petersen, J. L., & Linn, M. C. (2010). New trends in gender and mathematics performance: A meta-analysis. *Psychological Bulletin*, *136*(6), 1123–1135. http://doi.org/10.1037/a0021276

Lindenberger, U., & Baltes, P. B. (1997). Intellectual functioning in old and very old age: Cross-sectional results from the Berlin Aging Study. *Psychology and Aging*, *12*(3), 410–432. http://doi.org/10.1037/0882-7974.12.3.410

Lindenberger, U., Scherer, H., & Baltes, P. B. (2001). The strong connection between sensory and cognitive performance in old age: Not due to sensory acuity reductions operating during cognitive assessment. *Psychology and Aging*, *16*(2), 196–205. http://doi.org/10.1037/0882-7974.16.2.196

Lindenburg, I. T. M., van Kamp, I. L., & Oepkes, D. (2014). Intrauterine blood transfusion: Current indications and associated risks. *Fetal Diagnosis and Therapy*, *36*(4), 263–271. http://doi.org/10.1159/000362812

Lindh-Åstrand, L., Hoffmann, M., Hammar, M., & Kjellgren, K. (2007). Women's conception of the menopausal transition: A qualitative study. *Journal of Clinical Nursing*, *16*(3), 509–517.

Lindsey, E. W., Colwell, M. J., Arsenio, W., Cooperman, S., Lover, A., Boulton, M., . . . Wechsler, D. (2013). Pretend and physical play: Links to preschoolers' affective social competence. *Merrill-Palmer Quarterly*, *59*(3), 330–360. http://doi.org/10.1353/mpq.2013.0015

Lindstrom, T. M., & Robinson, W. H. (2010). Rheumatoid arthritis: A role for immunosenescence? *Journal of the American Geriatrics Society*, *58*(8), 1565–1575. http://doi.org/10.1111/j.1532-5415.2010.02965.x

Linebarger, D. L., & Vaala, S. E. (2010). Screen media and language development in infants and toddlers: An ecological perspective. *Developmental Review*, *30*(2), 176–202. http://doi.org/10.1016/j.dr.2010.03.006

Linz, S., & Semykina, A. (2013). Job satisfaction, expectations, and gender: beyond the European Union. *International Journal of Manpower*, *34*(6), 584–615. http://doi.org/10.1108/IJM-06-2013-0149

Lioret, S., Maire, B., Volatier, J. L., & Charles, M. A. (2007). Child overweight in France and its relationship with physical activity, sedentary behaviour and socioeconomic status. *European Journal of Clinical Nutrition*, *61*(4), 509–516.

Lipka, O., & Siegel, L. S. (2007). The Development of reading skills in children with English as a second language. *Scientific Studies of Reading*, *11*(2), 105–131. http://doi.org/10.1080/10888430701343597

Lipowski, S. L., Merriman, W. E., & Dunlosky, J. (2013). Preschoolers can make highly accurate judgments of learning. *Developmental Psychology*, *49*(8), 1505–1516.

Lippman, L. H., & Keith, J. D. (2006). The demographics of spirituality among youth: International perspectives. In E. C. Roehlkepartain, P. E. King, L. Wagener, & P. L. Benson (Eds.), *The* handbook of spiritual development in childhood and adolescence (pp. 109–123). Thousand Oaks, CA: SAGE. http://doi.org/10.4135/9781412976657.n8

Lisdahl, K. M., Gilbart, E. R., Wright, N. E., & Shollenbarger, S. (2013). Dare to delay? The impacts of adolescent alcohol and marijuana use onset on cognition, brain structure, and function. Frontiers in Psychiatry, 4, 53. http://doi.org/10.3389/fpsyt.2013.00053

Litovsky, R. Y., & Ashmead, D. H. (1997). Development of binaural and spatial hearing in infants and children. In R. H. Gilkey & T. R. Anderson (Eds.), Binaural and special hearing in real and virtual environments (pp. 571–592). Mahwah, NJ: Lawrence Erlbaum.

Littleton, H. L., & Ollendick, T. (2003). Negative body image and disordered eating behavior in children and adolescents: What places youth at risk and how can these problems be prevented? Clinical Child and Family Psychology Review, 6(1), 51–66.

Littschwager, J. C., & Markman, E. M. (1994). Sixteen- and 24-month-olds' use of mutual exclusivity as a default assumption in second-label learning. Developmental Psychology, 30, 955–968.

Litwack, S. D., Aikins, J. W., & Cillessen, A. H. N. (2010). The distinct roles of sociometric and perceived popularity in friendship: Implications for adolescent depressive affect and self-esteem. The Journal of Early Adolescence, 32(2), 226–251. http://doi.org/10.1177/0272431610387142

Litwin, H. (2003). Social predictors of physical activity in later life: The contribution of social-network type. Journal of Aging and Physical Activity, 11(3), 389–406.

Liu, F. (2006). Boys as only children and girls as only children: Parental gendered expectations of the only child in the nuclear Chinese family in present-day China. Gender & Education, 18(5), 491–505.

Liu, H., Paige, N. M., Goldzweig, C. L., Wong, E., Zhou, A., Suttorp, M. J., . . . Shekelle, P. (2008). Screening for osteoporosis in men: A systematic review for an American College of Physicians guideline. Annals of Internal Medicine, 148(9), 685–701.

Liu, H., & Waite, L. (2014). Bad marriage, broken heart? Age and gender differences in the link between marital quality and cardiovascular risks among older adults. Journal of Health and Social Behavior, 55(4), 403–423. http://doi.org/10.1177/0022146514556893

Liu, J., & Eden, J. (2007). Experience and attitudes toward menopause in Chinese women living in Sydney: A cross sectional survey. Maturitas, 58(4), 359–365.

Liu, R. T., & Mustanski, B. (2012). Suicidal ideation and self-harm in lesbian, gay, bisexual, and transgender youth. American Journal of Preventive Medicine, 42(3), 221–228. http://doi.org/10.1016/j.amepre.2011.10.023

Liu, Y., Julkunen, V., Paajanen, T., Westman, E., Wahlund, L.-O., Aitken, A., . . . Soininen, H. (2012). Education increases reserve against Alzheimer's disease: Evidence from structural MRI analysis. Neuroradiology, 54(9), 929–938. http://doi.org/10.1007/s00234-012-1005-0

Livingston, G. (2014). Four in ten couples are saying "I do," again. Pew Research Center. Retrieved from http://www.pewsocialtrends.org/2014/11/14/four-in-ten-couples-are-saying-i-do-again/

Livingston, G. (2015). Childlessnesss. Retrieved from http://www.pewsocialtrends.org/2015/05/07/childlessness/

Lobo, M. A., & Galloway, J. C. (2012). Enhanced handling and positioning in early infancy advances development throughout the first year. Child Development, 83(4), 1290–1302. http://doi.org/10.1111/j.1467-8624.2012.01772.x

Lobstein, T., Jackson-Leach, R., Moodie, M. L., Hall, K. D., Gortmaker, S. L., Swinburn, B. A., . . . McPherson, K. (2015). Child and

adolescent obesity: Part of a bigger picture. Lancet, 385(9986), 2510–2520. http://doi.org/10.1016/S0140-6736(14)61746-3

LoBue, V., Nishida, T., Chiong, C., DeLoache, J. S., & Haidt, J. (2011). When getting something good is bad: Even three-year-olds react to inequality. Social Development, 20(1), 154–170. http://doi.org/10.1111/j.1467-9507.2009.00560.x

Lock, J. (2011). Evaluation of family treatment models for eating disorders. Current Opinion in Psychiatry, 24(4), 274–279. http://doi.org/10.1097/YCO.0b013e328346f71e

Lock, J., Le Grange, D., & Forsberg, S. (2007). Is family therapy effective in children with anorexia nervosa? Brown University Child & Adolescent Behavior Letter, 23(1), 3.

Lock, M., & Kaufert, P. (2001). Menopause, local biologies, and cultures of aging. American Journal of Human Biology, 13(4), 494–504.

Löckenhoff, C. E., & Carstensen, L. L. (2007). Aging, emotion, and health-related decision strategies: Motivational manipulations can reduce age differences. Psychology and Aging, 22(1), 134–146.

Löckenhoff, C. E., Chan, W., McCrae, R. R., De Fruyt, F., Jussim, L., De Bolle, M., . . . Terracciano, A. (2014). Gender stereotypes of personality: Universal and accurate? Journal of Cross-Cultural Psychology, 45(5), 675–694. http://doi.org/10.1177/0022022113520075

Löckenhoff, C. E., De Fruyt, F., Terracciano, A., McCrae, R. R., De Bolle, M., Costa Jr., P. T., . . . Yik, M. (2009). Perceptions of aging across 26 cultures and their culture-level associates. Psychology and Aging, 24(4), 941–954. http://doi.org/10.1037/a0016901

Lockl, K., & Schneider, W. (2007). Knowledge About the mind: Links between theory of mind and later metamemory. Child Development, 78(1), 148–167. http://doi.org/10.1111/j.1467-8624.2007.00990.x

Locurto, C. (1990). The malleability of IQ as judged from adoption studies. Intelligence, 14(3), 275–292. http://doi.org/10.1016/S0160-2896(10)80001-7

Lodi-Smith, J., & Roberts, B. W. (2010). Getting to know me: Social role experiences and age differences in self-concept carity during adulthood. Journal of Personality, 78(5), 1383–1410. http://doi.org/10.1111/j.1467-6494.2010.00655.x

Loef, M., & Walach, H. (2013). Midlife obesity and dementia: Meta-analysis and adjusted forecast of dementia prevalence in the united States and China. Obesity, 21(1), E51–E55. http://doi.org/10.1002/oby.20037

Loessl, B., Valerius, G., Kopasz, M., Hornyak, M., Riemann, D., & Voderholzer, U. (2008). Are adolescents chronically sleep-deprived? An investigation of sleep habits of adolescents in the Southwest of Germany. Child: Care, Health & Development, 34(5), 549–556. http://doi.org/10.1111/j.1365-2214.2008.00845.x

Logan, A. J., & Baker, J. (2007). Cross-sectional and longitudinal profiles of age related decline in golf performance. Journal of Sport & Exercise Psychology, 29, S15–S15.

Lohaus, A., Keller, H., Lamm, B., Teubert, M., Fassbender, I., Freitag, C., . . . Schwarzer, G. (2011). Infant development in two cultural contexts: Cameroonian Nso farmer and German middle-class infants. Journal of Reproductive and Infant Psychology, 29(2), 148–161. http://doi.org/10.1080/02646838.2011.558074

Lohman, B. J., & Billings, A. (2008). Protective and risk factors associated with adolescent boys' early sexual debut and risky sexual behaviors. Journal of Youth & Adolescence, 37(6), 723–735. http://doi.org/10.1007/s10964-008-9283-x

Lönnqvist, J. (2010). Cognition and mental ill-health. European Psychiatry, 25(5), 297–299. http://doi.org/10.1016/j.eurpsy.2010.01.006

Lopez-Larson, M. P., Rogowska, J., Bogorodzki, P., Bueler, C. E., McGlade, E. C., & Yurgelun-Todd, D. A. (2012). Cortico-cerebellar abnormalities in adolescents with heavy marijuana use. Psychiatry Research: Neuroimaging, 202(3), 224–232. http://doi.org/10.1016/j.pscychresns.2011.11.005

Lopez-Tamayo, R., LaVome Robinson, W., Lambert, S. F., Jason, L. A., & Ialongo, N. S. (2016). Parental monitoring, association with externalized behavior, and academic outcomes in urban African-American youth: A moderated mediation analysis. American Journal of Community Psychology, 57(3–4), 366–379. http://doi.org/10.1002/ajcp.12056

Lorente-Cebrián, S., Costa, A. G. V, Navas-Carretero, S., Zabala, M., Laiglesia, L. M., Martínez, J. A., & Moreno-Aliaga, M. J. (2015). An update on the role of omega-3 fatty acids on inflammatory and degenerative diseases. Journal of Physiology and Biochemistry, 71(2), 341–349. http://doi.org/10.1007/s13105-015-0395-y

Lorente-Cebrián, S., Costa, A. G. V, Navas-Carretero, S., Zabala, M., Martínez, J. A., & Moreno-Aliaga, M. J. (2013). Role of omega-3 fatty acids in obesity, metabolic syndrome, and cardiovascular diseases: A review of the evidence. Journal of Physiology and Biochemistry, 69(3), 633–651. http://doi.org/10.1007/s13105-013-0265-4

Lorenz, K. (1952). King Solomon's ring. New York: Crowell.

Lottes, I. L., & Alkula, T. (2011). An Investigation of sexuality-related attitudinal patterns and characteristics related to those patterns for 32 European countries. Sexuality Research and Social Policy, 8(2), 77–92. http://doi.org/10.1007/s13178-011-0038-1

Lozoff, B., Wolf, A. W., & Davis, N. S. (1984). Cosleeping in urban families with young children in the United States. Pediatrics, 74, 171–182.

Lu, H., Su, Y., & Wang., Q. (2008). Talking about others facilitates theory of mind in Chinese preschoolers. Developmental Psychology, 44(6), 1726–1736. http://doi.org/10.1037/a0013074

Lu, P. H., Lee, G. J., Tishler, T. A., Meghpara, M., Thompson, P. M., & Bartzokis, G. (2013). Myelin breakdown mediates age-related slowing in cognitive processing speed in healthy elderly men. Brain and Cognition, 81(1), 131–138. http://doi.org/10.1016/j.bandc.2012.09.006

Lu, S. (2005). What's wrong with just one drink? Prevention, 57(1), 121–122.

Lubinski, D., Benbow, C. P., Webb, R. M., & Bleske-Rechek, A. (2006). Tracking exceptional human capital over two decades. Psychological Science, 17(3), 194–199. http://doi.org/10.1111/j.1467-9280.2006.01685.x

Lubman, D. I., Cheetham, A., & Yücel, M. (2015). Cannabis and adolescent brain development. Pharmacology & Therapeutics, 148, 1–16. http://doi.org/10.1016/j.pharmthera.2014.11.009

Lucas, R. E., & Donnellan, M. B. (2011). Personality development across the life span: Longitudinal analyses with a national sample from Germany. Journal of Personality & Social Psychology, 101(4), 847–861. http://doi.org/10.1037/a0024298

Lucassen, M. F., Clark, T. C., Denny, S. J., Fleming, T. M., Rossen, F. V, Sheridan, J., . . . Robinson, E. M. (2015). What has changed from 2001 to 2012 for sexual minority youth in New Zealand? Journal of Paediatrics and Child Health, 51(4). http://doi.org/10.1111/jpc.12727

Lucassen, N., Tharner, A., Van Ijzendoorn, M. H., Bakermans-Kranenburg, M. J., Volling, B. L., Verhulst, F. C., . . . Tiemeier, H. (2011). The association between paternal sensitivity and infant-father attachment security: A meta-analysis of three decades of research. *Journal of Family Psychology, 25*(6), 986–992. http://doi.org/10.1037/a0025855

Luchetti, M., Terracciano, A., Stephan, Y., & Sutin, A. R. (2015). Personality and cognitive decline in older adults: Data from a longitudinal sample and meta-analysis. *The Journals of Gerontology. Series B, Psychological Sciences and Social Sciences.* http://doi.org/10.1093/geronb/gbu184

Luciana, M. (2003). Cognitive development in children born preterm: Implications for theories of brain plasticity following early injury. *Development and Psychopathology, 15*(4), 1017–1047. http://doi.org/10.1017/s095457940300049x

Luders, E., Narr, K. L., Thompson, P. M., & Toga, A. W. (2009). Neuroanatomical correlates of intelligence. *Intelligence, 37*(2), 156–163. http://doi.org/10.1016/j.intell.2008.07.002

Luders, E., Thompson, P. M., & Toga, A. W. (2010). The development of the corpus callosum in the healthy human brain. *The Journal of Neuroscience, 30*(33), 10985–10990. http://doi.org/10.1523/JNEUROSCI.5122-09.2010

Luecke-Aleksa, D., Anderson, D. R., Collins, P. A., & Schmitt, K. L. (1995). Gender constancy and television viewing. *Developmental Psychology, 31*, 773–780.

Luengo Kanacri, B. P., Pastorelli, C., Eisenberg, N., Zuffianò, A., & Caprara, G. V. (2013). The development of prosociality from adolescence to early adulthood: The role of effortful control. *Journal of Personality, 81*(3), 302–312. http://doi.org/10.1111/jopy.12001

Luhmann, M., Hofmann, W., Eid, M., & Lucas, R. E. (2012). Subjective well-being and adaptation to life events: A meta-analysis. *Journal of Personality and Social Psychology, 102*(3), 592–615. http://doi.org/10.1037/a0025948

Luman, E. T., Barker, L. E., McCauley, M. M., & Drews-Botsch, C. (2005). Timeliness of childhood immunizations: A state-specific analysis. *American Journal of Public Health, 95*(8), 1367–1374.

Luna, B., Garver, K. E., Urban, T. A., Lazar, N. A., & Sweeney, J. A. (2004). Maturation of cognitive processes from late childhood to adulthood. *Child Development, 75*(5), 1357–1372. http://doi.org/10.1111/j.1467-8624.2004.00745.x

Luna, B., Paulsen, D. J., Padmanabhan, A., & Geier, C. (2013). The teenage brain: Cognitive control and motivation. *Current Directions in Psychological Science, 22*(2), 94–100. http://doi.org/10.1177/0963721413478416

Lunau, T., Bambra, C., Eikemo, T. A., van der Wel, K. A., & Dragano, N. (2014). A balancing act? Work-life balance, health and well-being in European welfare states. *European Journal of Public Health, 24*(3), 422–427. http://doi.org/10.1093/eurpub/cku010

Lund, D. A., & Caserta, M. S. (2001). When the unexpected happens: Husbands coping with the deaths of their wives. In D. A. Lund (Ed.), *Men coping with grief* (pp. 147–167). Amityville, NY: Baywood.

Lund, D. A., Caserta, M. S., Dimond, M. F., & Gray, R. M. (1986). Impact of bereavement on the self-conceptions of older surviving spouses. *Symbolic Interaction, 9*(2), 235–244. http://doi.org/10.1525/si.1986.9.2.235

Lundberg, S. J., & Pollak, R. A. (2016). The evolving role of marriage: 1950–2010. *The Future of Children, 25*(2), 29–50. Retrieved from http://dspace.uib.no/handle/1956/12486

Lundsberg, L. S., Illuzzi, J. L., Belanger, K., Triche, E. W., & Bracken, M. B. (2015). Low-to-moderate prenatal alcohol consumption and the risk of selected birth outcomes: A prospective cohort study. *Annals of Epidemiology, 25*(1), 46–54. http://doi.org/10.1016/j.annepidem.2014.10.011

Lunney, J. R., Lynn, J., Foley, D. J., Lipson, S., & Guralnik, J. M. (2003). Patterns of functional decline at the end of life. *JAMA, 289*(18), 2387. http://doi.org/10.1001/jama.289.18.2387

Luo, Q., Nakic, M., Wheatley, T., Richell, R., Martin, A., & Blair, R. J. R. (2006). The neural basis of implicit moral attitude: An IAT study using event-related fMRI. *NeuroImage, 30*(4), 1449–1457. https://doi.org/10.1016/j.neuroimage.2005.11.005

Luoma, J. B., & Pearson, J. L. (2002). Suicide and marital status in the United States, 1991–1996: Is widowhood a risk factor? *American Journal of Public Health, 92*(9), 1518–1522. http://doi.org/10.2105/AJPH.92.9.1518

Lustig, C., Hasher, L., & Tonev, S. T. (2006). Distraction as a determinant of processing speed. *Psychonomic Bulletin & Review, 13*(4), 619–625.

Lustig, C., Shah, P., Seidler, R., & Reuter-Lorenz, P. A. (2009). Aging, training, and the brain: A review and future directions. *Neuropsychology Review, 19*(4), 504–522. https://doi.org/10.1007/s11065-009-9119-9

Luthar, S. S. (2006). Resilience in development: A synthesis of research across five decades. In D. Cicchetti & D. J. Cohen (Eds.), *Developmental psychopathology: Risk, disorder, and adaptation* (2nd ed., Vol. 3, pp. 739–795). Hoboken, NJ: John Wiley & Sons.

Luthar, S. S., Crossman, E. J., & Small, P. J. (2015). Resilience and adversity. In M. E. Lamb (Ed.), *Handbook of child psychology and developmental science* (pp. 1–40). Hoboken, NJ: John Wiley & Sons. http://doi.org/10.1002/9781118963418.childpsy307

Luttikhuizen dos Santos, E. S., de Kieviet, J. F., Königs, M., van Elburg, R. M., & Oosterlaan, J. (2013). Predictive value of the Bayley scales of infant development on development of very preterm/very low birth weight children: A meta-analysis. *Early Human Development, 89*(7), 487–496. http://doi.org/10.1016/j.earlhumdev.2013.03.008

Lutz, D. J., & Sternberg, R. J. (1999). Cognitive development. In M. H. Bornstein & M. E. Lamb (Eds.), *Developmental psychology: An advanced textbook* (4th ed., pp. 275–311). Mahwah, NJ: Lawrence Erlbaum.

Lux, V. (2013). With Gottlieb beyond Gottlieb: The role of epigenetics in psychobiological development. *International Journal of Developmental Science, 7*(2), 69–78. http://doi.org/10.3233/DEV-1300073

Luyckx, K., Schwartz, S. J., Berzonsky, M. D., Soenens, B., Vansteenkiste, M., Smits, I., & Goossens, L. (2008). Capturing ruminative exploration: Extending the four-dimensional model of identity formation in late adolescence. *Journal of Research in Personality, 42*(1), 58–82. http://doi.org/10.1016/j.jrp.2007.04.004

Lynch, A., Lee, H. M., Bhat, A., & Galloway, J. C. (2008). No stable arm preference during the pre-reaching period: A comparison of right and left hand kinematics with and without a toy present. *Developmental Psychobiology, 50*(4), 390–398. http://doi.org/10.1002/dev.20297

Lynn, R. (2009). What has caused the Flynn effect? Secular increases in the Development Quotients of infants. *Intelligence, 37*(1), 16–24. http://doi.org/10.1016/j.intell.2008.07.008

Lynn, R. (2013). Who discovered the Flynn effect? A review of early studies of the secular increase of intelligence. *Intelligence, 41*(6), 765–769. http://doi.org/10.1016/j.intell.2013.03.008

Lynn, R., Meisenberg, G., Mikk, J., & Williams, A. (2007). National IQs predict differences in scholastic achievement in 67 countries. *Journal of Biosocial Science, 39*(6), 861–874. http://doi.org/10.1017/S0021932007001964

Lynn, R., & Vanhanen, T. (2012). National IQs: A review of their educational, cognitive, economic, political, demographic, sociological, epidemiological, geographic and climatic correlates. *Intelligence, 40*(2), 226–234. http://doi.org/10.1016/j.intell.2011.11.004

Lyon, T. D., & Flavell, J. H. (1993). Young children's understanding of forgetting over time. *Child Development, 64*(3), 789–800. http://doi.org/10.1111/j.1467-8624.1993.tb02943.x

Lyons, R. A., Delahunty, A. M., Heaven, M., McCabe, M., Allen, H., & Nash, P. (2000). Incidence of childhood fractures in affluent and deprived areas: Population-based study. *British Medical Journal, 320*(7228), 149. Retrieved from http://www.ncbi.nlm.nih.gov/pubmed/10634734

Lyons-Ruth, K., Bronfman, E., & Parsons, E. (1999). Maternal frightened, frightening, or atypical behavior and disorganized infant attachment patterns. *Monographs of the Society for Research in Child Development, 64*(3), 67–96.

Lytton, H., & Romney, D. M. (1991). Parents' differential socialization of boys and girls: A meta-analysis. *Psychological Bulletin, 109*(2), 267–296.

Ma, L., & Ganea, P. A. (2010). Dealing with conflicting information: Young children's reliance on what they see versus what they are told. *Developmental Science, 13*(1), 151–160. http://doi.org/10.1111/j.1467-7687.2009.00878.x

Maakaron, J. E., & Taher, A. (2017). *Sickle cell anemia.* Retrieved from http://emedicine.medscape.com/article/205926-overview#a0156

Mabbott, D. J., Noseworthy, M., Bouffet, E., Laughlin, S., & Rockel, C. (2006). White matter growth as a mechanism of cognitive development in children. *NeuroImage, 33*(3), 936–946.

Macdonald, K., & Feifel, D. (2013). Helping oxytocin deliver: Considerations in the development of oxytocin-based therapeutics for brain disorders. *Frontiers in Neuroscience, 7*, 35. https://doi.org/10.3389/fnins.2013.00035

MacDougall, K., Beyene, Y., & Nachtigall, R. D. (2012). "Inconvenient biology:" Advantages and disadvantages of first-time parenting after age 40 using in vitro fertilization. *Human Reproduction, 27*(4), 1058–1065. http://doi.org/10.1093/humrep/des007

Maccoby, E. E. (2000). Parenting and its effects on children: On reading and misreading behavior genetics. *Annual Review of Psychology, 51*, 1–27.

Maccoby, E. E., & Jacklin, C. (1974). *The psychology of sex differences.* Stanford, CA: Stanford University Press.

Maccoby, E. E., & Jacklin, C. N. (1987). Gender segregation in childhood. *Advances in Child Development & Behavior, 20*, 239–287. http://doi.org/10.1016/S0065-2407(08)60404-8

Maccoby, E. E., & Martin, J. A. (1983). Socialization in the context of the family: Parent-child interaction. In E. M. Hetherington (Ed.), *Handbook of child psychology: Vol. 4. Socialization, personality, and social development* (4th ed., pp. 1–101). New York: Wiley.

MacConnell, A., & Daehler, M. W. (2004). The development of representational insight: Beyond the model/room paradigm. *Cognitive Development, 19*(3), 345–362.

Macek, P., Bejček, J., & Vaníčková, J. (2007). Contemporary Czech emerging adults: Generation growing up in the period of social changes. *Journal of Adolescent Research, 22*(5), 444–475.

Macfarlane, A. J. (1975). Olfaction in the development of social preferences in the human neonate. *Ciba Foundation Symposia, 33*, 103–117.

Maciejewski, P. K., Zhang, B., Block, S. D., & Prigerson, H. G. (2007). An empirical examination of the stage theory of grief. *JAMA, 297*(7), 716–723. http://doi.org/10.1001/jama.297.7.716

MacKay, D. F., Smith, G. C. S., Dobbie, R., & Pell, J. P. (2010). Gestational age at delivery and special educational need: Retrospective cohort study of 407,503 schoolchildren. *PLoS Medicine, 7*(6). http://doi.org/10.1371/journal.pmed.1000289

Mackenbach, J. P., Stirbu, I., Roskam, A.-J. R., Schaap, M. M., Menvielle, G., Leinsalu, M., & Kunst, A. E. (2008). Socioeconomic inequalities in health in 22 European countries. *New England Journal of Medicine, 358*(23), 2468–2481. http://doi.org/10.1056/NEJMsa0707519

Mackintosh, N. (2011). *IQ and human intelligence*. London, UK: Oxford University Press.

MacLean, P. S., Wing, R. R., Davidson, T., Epstein, L., Goodpaster, B., Hall, K. D., . . . Ryan, D. (2015). NIH working group report: Innovative research to improve maintenance of weight loss. *Obesity, 23*(1), 7–15. http://doi.org/10.1002/oby.20967

MacMillan, H. L., Boyle, M. H., Wong, M. Y.-Y. Y., Duku, E. K., Fleming, J. E., & Walsh, C. A. (1999). Slapping and spanking in childhood and its association with lifetime prevalence of psychiatric disorders in a general population sample. *Canadian Medical Association Journal, 161*(7), 805–809.

MacWhinney, B. (2015). Language development. In *Handbook of child psychology and developmental science* (pp. 1–43). Hoboken, NJ: John Wiley & Sons. http://doi.org/10.1002/9781118963418.childpsy208

Maddi, S. R. (2007a). Relevance of hardiness assessment and training to the military context. *Military Psychology, 19*(1), 61–70. http://doi.org/10.1080/08995600701323301

Maddi, S. R. (2007b). The story of hardiness: Twenty years of theorizing, research, and practice. In A. Monat, R. S. Lazarus, & G. Reevy (Eds.), *The Praeger handbook on stress and coping* (Vol. 2; pp. 327–340). Westport, CT: Praeger.

Maddi, S. R. (2013a). *Hardiness: Turning stressful circumstances into resilient growth*. Dordrecht: Springer Netherlands. http://doi.org/10.1007/978-94-007-5222-1

Maddi, S. R. (2013b). Personal hardiness as the basis for resilience. In *Hardiness: Turning stressful circumstances into resilient growth* (pp. 7–17). Dordrecht: Springer Netherlands. http://doi.org/10.1007/978-94-007-5222-1

Maddi, S. R. (2016). Hardiness as a pathway to resilience under stress. In U. Kumar (Ed.), *The Routledge international handbook of psychosocial resilience* (p. 104). New York, NY: Routledge.

Maddux, W. W., & Yuki, M. (2006). The "ripple effect": Cultural differences in perceptions of the consequences of events. *Personality and Social Psychology Bulletin, 32*(5), 669–683. http://doi.org/10.1177/0146167205283840

Madigan, S., Atkinson, L., Laurin, K., & Benoit, D. (2013). Attachment and internalizing behavior in early childhood: A meta-analysis. *Developmental Psychology, 49*(4), 672–689. http://doi.org/10.1037/a0028793

Madjar, N., & Cohen-Malayev, M. (2016). Perceived school climate across the transition from elementary to middle school. *School Psychology Quarterly, 31*(2), 270–288. http://doi.org/10.1037/spq0000129

Madon, S., Guyll, M., Spoth, R., & Willard, J. (2004). Self-fulfilling prophecies: The synergistic accumulative effect of parents' beliefs on children's drinking behavior. *Psychological Science, 15*(12), 837–845. http://doi.org/10.1111/j.0956-7976.2004.00764.x

Madsen, R., & Birkelund, R. (2016). Women's experiences during myocardial infarction: Systematic review and meta-ethnography. *Journal of Clinical Nursing, 25*(5–6), 599–609. http://doi.org/10.1111/jocn.13096

Madsen, S. D., & Collins, W. A. (2011). The salience of adolescent romantic experiences for romantic relationship qualities in young adulthood. *Journal of Research on Adolescence, 21*(4), 789–801. http://doi.org/10.1111/j.1532-7795.2011.00737.x

Maetzler, W., Liepelt, I., & Berg, D. (2009). Progression of Parkinson's disease in the clinical phase: Potential markers. *The Lancet Neurology, 8*(12), 1158–1171. http://doi.org/10.1016/s1474-4422(09)70291-1

Maggs, J. L., Jager, J., Patrick, M. E., & Schulenberg, J. (2012). Social role patterning in early adulthood in the USA: Adolescent predictors and concurrent well-being across four distinct configurations. *Longitudinal and Life Course Studies, 3*(2), 190–210.

Magolda, M. B. B. (2002). Episetomological reflection: The evolution of epistemological assumptions from 10 to 30. In B. K. Hofer & P. R. Pintrich (Eds.), *Personal epistemology* (pp. 89–102). Mahwah, NJ: Lawrence Erlbaum.

Maguen, S., Floyd, F. J., Bakeman, R., & Armistead, L. (2002). Developmental milestones and disclosure of sexual orientation among gay, lesbian, and bisexual youths. *Journal of Applied Developmental Psychology, 23*(2), 219–233.

Maguire, E. A., Spiers, H. J., Good, C. D., Hartley, T., Frackowiak, R. S. J., & Burgess, N. (2003). Navigation expertise and the human hippocampus: A structural brain imaging analysis. *Hippocampus, 13*(2), 250–259. http://doi.org/10.1002/hipo.10087

Mahatmya, D., & Lohman, B. (2011). Predictors of late adolescent delinquency: The protective role of after-school activities in low-income families. *Children and Youth Services Review, 33*(7), 1309–1317. http://doi.org/10.1016/j.childyouth.2011.03.005

Mahoney, J. L. (2014). School extracurricular activity participation and early school dropout: A mixed-method study of the role of peer social networks. *Journal of Educational and Developmental Psychology, 4*(1), 143. http://doi.org/10.5539/jedp.v4n1p143

Mahoney, J. L., Vandell, D. L., Simpkins, S., & Zarrett, N. (2009). *Adolescent out-of-school activities*. Hoboken, NJ: John Wiley & Sons.

Maier, K. S. (2005). Transmitting educational values: Parent occupation and adolescent development. In B. Schneider & L. J. Waite (Eds.), *Being together, working apart: Dual-career families and the work-life balance* (pp. 396–418). New York, NY: Cambridge University Press.

Maital, S. L., Dromi, E., Sagi, A., & Bornstein, M. H. (2000). The Hebrew Communicative Development Inventory: Language specific properties and cross-linguistic generalizations. *Journal of Child Language, 27*, 43–67.

Makel, M. C., Kell, H. J., Lubinski, D., Putallaz, M., & Benbow, C. P. (2016). When lightning strikes twice: Profoundly gifted, profoundly accomplished. *Psychological Science, 27*(7), 1004–1018. http://doi.org/10.1177/0956797616644735

Malamuth, N. M., Addison, T., & Koss, M. (2000). Pornography and sexual aggression: Are there reliable effects and can we understand them? *Annual Review of Sex Research, 11*, 26–91. Retrieved from http://psycnet.apa.org/psycinfo/2001-17368-002

Malatesta, C. Z., Grigoryev, P., Lamb, C., Albin, M., & Culver, C. (1986). Emotion socialization and expressive development in preterm and full-term infants. *Child Development, 57*, 316–330.

Malatesta, C. Z., & Haviland, J. M. (1982). Learning display rules: The socialization of emotion expression in infancy. *Child Development, 53*(4), 991–1003.

Malczyk, B. R., & Lawson, H. A. (2017). Parental monitoring, the parent-child relationship and children's academic engagement in mother-headed single-parent families. *Children and Youth Services Review, 73*, 274–282. http://doi.org/10.1016/j.childyouth.2016.12.019

Maldonado-Carreño, C., & Votruba-Drzal, E. Teacher-child relationships and the development of academic and behavioral skills during elementary school: A within- and between-child analysis. *Child Development, 82*(2), 601–616. http://doi.org/10.1111/j.1467-8624.2010.01533.x

Malina, R. M., & Bouchard, C. (1991). *Growth, maturation, and physical activity*. Champaign, IL: Human Kinetics Books.

Malinen, O.-P., & Savolainen, H. (2016). The effect of perceived school climate and teacher efficacy in behavior management on job satisfaction and burnout: A longitudinal study. *Teaching and Teacher Education, 60*, 144–152. http://doi.org/10.1016/j.tate.2016.08.012

Mallett, K. A., Varvil-Weld, L., Borsari, B., Read, J. P., Neighbors, C., & White, H. R. (2013). An update of research examining college student alcohol-related consequences: New perspectives and implications for interventions. *Alcoholism, Clinical and Experimental Research, 37*(5), 709–716. http://doi.org/10.1111/acer.12031

Mallon, B. (2008). *Death, dying and grief: Working with adult bereavement*. Thousand Oaks, CA: SAGE.

Malone, P. S., Lansford, J. E., Castellino, D. R., Berlin, L. J., Dodge, K. A., Bates, J. E., & Pettit, G. S. (2004). Divorce and child behavior problems: Applying latent change score models to life event data. *Structural Equation Modeling: A Multidisciplinary Journal, 11*(3), 401–423. http://doi.org/10.1207/s15328007sem1103_6

Maloney, M. J., McGuire, J. B., Daniels, S. R., & Specker, B. (1989). Dieting behavior and eating attitudes in children. *Pediatrics, 84*, 482–489.

Malouff, J. M., Schutte, N. S., & Thorsteinsson, E. B. (2014). Trait emotional intelligence and romantic relationship satisfaction: A meta-analysis. *The American Journal of Family Therapy, 42*(1), 53–66. http://doi.org/10.1080/01926187.2012.748549

Malti, T., Keller, M., & Buchmann, M. (2013). Do moral choices make us feel good? The development of adolescents' emotions following moral decision making. *Journal of Research on Adolescence, 23*(2), 389–397. http://doi.org/10.1111/jora.12005

Malti, T., & Latzko, B. (2010). Children's moral emotions and moral cognition: Towards an integrative perspective. *New Directions for Child & Adolescent Development, 2010*(129), 1–10. http://doi.org/10.1002/cd.272

Mammarella, N., Borella, E., Carretti, B., Leonardi, G., & Fairfield, B. (2013). Examining an emotion enhancement effect in working memory: Evidence from age-related differences. *Neuropsychological Rehabilitation, 23*(3), 416–428. http://doi.org/10.1080/09602011.2013.775065

Mancini, A. D., Bonanno, G. A., & Clark, A. E. (2011). Stepping off the hedonic treadmill. *Journal of Individual Differences, 32*(3), 144–152. http://doi.org/10.1027/1614-0001/a000047

Mandel, D. R., Jusczyk, P. W., & Pisoni, D. B. (1995). Infants' recogntition of the sound patterns of their own names. *Psychological Science, 6*(5), 314–317.

Mandler, J. M. (2000). What global-before-basic trend? Comment on perceptually based approaches to early categorizations. *Infancy, 1*, 99–110.

Mandler, J. M. (2004). *The foundations of mind: Origins of conceptual thought*. New York, NY: Oxford University Press.

Mandler, J. M., Fivush, R., & Reznick, J. S. (1987). The development of contextual categories.

Cognitive Development, 2(4), 339–354. http://doi.org/10.1016/s0885-2014(87)80012-6

Mandler, J. M., & McDonough, L. (1993). Concept formation in infancy. Cognitive Development, 8, 291–318.

Mandler, J. M., & McDonough, L. (1998). On developing a knowledge base in infancy. Developmental Psychology, 34, 1274–1288.

Manfra, L., & Winsler, A. (2006). Preschool children's awareness of private speech. International Journal of Behavioral Development, 30(6), 537–549.

Mangelsdorf, S. C. (1992). Developmental changes in infant-stranger interaction. Infant Behavior & Development, 15(2), 191–208. http://doi.org/10.1016/0163-6383(92)80023-n

Mangelsdorf, S. C., Plunkett, J. W., Dedrick, C. F., Berlin, M., Meisels, S. J., McHale, J. L., & Dichtellmiller, M. (1996). Attachment security in very low birth weight infants. Developmental Psychology, 32, 914–920.

Mangelsdorf, S. C., Shapiro, J. R., & Marzolf, D. (1995). Developmental and temperamental differences in emotion regulation in infancy. Child Development, 66, 1817–1828.

Mani, T. M., Bedwell, J. S., & Miller, L. S. (2005). Age-related decrements in performance on a brief continuous performance task. Archives of Clinical Neuropsychology, 20(5), 575–586.

Maniglio, R. (2013). Child sexual abuse in the etiology of anxiety disorders: A systematic review of reviews. Trauma, Violence & Abuse, 14(2), 96–112. http://doi.org/10.1177/1524838012470032

Manly, J. J. (2006). Deconstructing race and ethnicity. Medical Care, 44(Suppl 3), S10–S16. http://doi.org/10.1097/01.mlr.0000245427.22788.be

Manning, W. D. (2013). Trends in cohabitation: Over twenty years of change, 1987–2010. Bowling Green, OH: National Center for Family & Marriage Research.

Manning, W. D. (2015). Cohabitation and child well-being. The Future of Children, 25(2), 51–66. Retrieved from http://www.ncbi.nlm.nih.gov/pubmed/26929590

Manning, W. D., & Brown, S. (2006). Children's economic well-being in married and cohabiting parent families. Journal of Marriage & Family, 68(2), 345–362.

Manning, W. D., & Cohen, J. A. (2012). Premarital cohabitation and marital dissolution: An examination of recent marriages. Journal of Marriage and the Family, 74(2), 377–387. http://doi.org/10.1111/j.1741-3737.2012.00960.x

Manoach, D. S., Schlaug, G., Siewert, B., Darby, D. G., Bly, B. M., Benfield, A., . . . et al. (1997). Prefrontal cortex fMRI signal changes are correlated with working memory load. NeuroReport, 8, 545–549.

Manuck, S. B., & McCaffery, J. M. (2014). Gene-environment interaction. Annual Review of Psychology, 65, 41–70. http://dx.doi.org/10.1146/annurev-Psych-010213-115100.

Maqsood, A. R., Trueman, J. A., Whatmore, A. J., Westwood, M., Price, D. A., Hall, C. M., & Clayton, P. E. (2007). The relationship between nocturnal urinary leptin and gonadotrophins as children progress towards puberty. Hormone Research, 68(5), 225–230.

Marceau, K., Ram, N., Houts, R. M., Grimm, K. J., & Susman, E. J. (2011). Individual differences in boys' and girls' timing and tempo of puberty: Modeling development with nonlinear growth models. Developmental Psychology, 47(5), 1389–1409. http://doi.org/10.1037/a0023838

Marcia, J. E. (1966). Development and validation of ego-identity status. Journal of Personality and Social Psychology, 3(5), 551–558.

Marcia, J. E. (2002). Identity and psychosocial development in adulthood. Identity, 2(1), 7–28. http://doi.org/10.1207/S1532706XID0201_02

Marcon, R. A. (1999). Positive relationships between parent-school involvement and public school inner-city preschoolers' development and academic performance. School Psychology Review, 28, 395–412.

Marcovitch, S., Clearfield, M. W., Swingler, M., Calkins, S. D., & Bell, M. A. (2016). Attentional predictors of 5-month-olds' performance on a looking A-not-B task. Infant and Child Development, 25(4), 233–246. http://doi.org/10.1002/icd.1931

Marcus, M. B. (2008). MRI could be key in Alzheimer's fight. USA Today.

Margaretten, M. E., Katz, P, Schmajuk, G., & Yelin, E. (2013). Missed opportunities for depression screening in patients with arthritis in the United States. Journal of General Internal Medicine, 28(12), 1637–1642. http://doi.org/10.1007/s11606-013-2541-y

Margolis, A., Bansal, R., Hao, X., Algermissen, M., Erickson, C., Klahr, K. W., . . . Peterson, B. S. (2013). Using IQ discrepancy scores to examine the neural correlates of specific cognitive abilities. Journal of Neuroscience, 33(35), 14135–14145. http://doi.org/10.1523/JNEUROSCI.0775-13.2013

Margolis, R. (2016). The changing demography of grandparenthood. Journal of Marriage and Family, 78(3), 610–622. http://doi.org/10.1111/jomf.12286

Margran, T. H., & Boulton, M. (2005). Sensory impairment. In M. L. Johnson (Ed.), The Cambridge handbook of age and aging. New York, NY: Cambridge University Press.

Margrett, J. A., Allaire, J. C., Johnson, T. L., Daugherty, K. E., & Weatherbee, S. R. (2010). Everyday problem solving. In J. C. Cavanaugh, C. K. Cavanaugh, J. Berry, & R. West (Eds.), Aging in America, Vol 1: Psychological aspects (pp. 80–101). Santa Barbara, CA: Praeger/ABC-CLIO.

Margrett, J., Martin, P., Woodard, J. L., Miller, L. S., MacDonald, M., Baenziger, J., . . . Poon, L. (2010). Depression among centenarians and the oldest old: Contributions of cognition and personality. Gerontology, 56(1), 93–99. http://doi.org/10.1159/000272018

Marinellie, S. A., & Kneile, L. A. (2012). Acquiring knowledge of derived nominals and derived adjectives in context. Language Speech and Hearing Services in Schools, 43(1), 53. http://doi.org/10.1044/0161-1461(2011/10-0053)

Mariscal, M., Palma, S., Llorca, J., Pérez-Iglesias, R., Pardo-Crespo, R., & Delgado-Rodríguez, M. (2006). Pattern of alcohol consumption during pregnancy and risk for low birth weight. Annals of Epidemiology, 16(6), 432–438.

Markant, J. C., & Thomas, K. M. (2013). Postnatal brain development. In P. D. Zelazo (Ed.), The Oxford handbook of developmental psychology (Vol. 1). London, UK: Oxford University Press. http://doi.org/10.1093/oxfordhb/9780199958450.013.0006

Markman, E. M. (1987). How children constrain the possible meaning of words. In U. Neisser (Ed.), Congress and conceptual development: Ecological and intellectual factors in categorization (pp. 255–287). Cambridge, UK: Cambridge University Press.

Markman, E. M. (1990). Constraints children place on word meanings. Cognitive Science, 14, 57–77.

Markman, E. M., & Wachtel, G. F. (1988). Children's use of mutual exclusivity to constrain the meaning of words. Cognitive Psychology, 20(2), 121–157. http://doi.org/10.1016/0010-0285(88)90017-5

Marks, A. K., Szalacha, L. A., Lamarre, M., Boyd, M. J., & Coll, C. G. (2007). Emerging ethnic identity and interethnic group social preferences in middle childhood: Findings from the Children of Immigrants Development in Context (CIDC) study. International Journal of Behavioral Development, 31(5), 501–513.

Marks, N. F., Bumpass, L. L., & Jun, H. (2004). Family roles and well-being during the middle life course. In O. G. Brim, C. D. Ryff, & R. C. Kessler (Eds.), How healthy are we? A national study of well-being at midlife (pp. 514–549). Chicago, IL: University of Chicago Press.

Marks, N. F., Jun, H., & Song, J. (2007). Death of parents and adult psychological and physical well-being: A prospective U.S. national study. Journal of Family Issues, 28(12), 1611–1638. http://doi.org/10.1177/0192513X07302728

Markstrom-Adams, C., & Adams, G. R. (1995). Gender, ethnic group, and grade differences in psychosocial functioning during middle adolescence. Journal of Youth and Adolescence, 24(4), 397–417.

Markus, H. R., & Kitayama, S. (1991). Culture and the self: Implications for cognition, emotion, and motivation. Psychological Review, 98(2), 224–253. http://doi.org/10.1037/0033-295X.98.2.224

Marlier, L., & Schaal, B. (2005). Human newborns prefer human milk: Conspecific milk odor is attractive without postnatal exposure. Child Development, 76(1), 155–168.

Marriott, C., Hamilton-Giachritsis, C., & Harrop, C. (2014). Factors promoting resilience following childhood sexual abuse: A structured, narrative review of the literature. Child Abuse Review, 23(1), 17–34. http://doi.org/10.1002/car.2258

Marsh, H. W., Craven, R., & Debus, R. (1998). Structure, stability, and development of young children's self-concepts: A multicohort-multioccasion study. Child Development, 69, 1030–1053.

Marsh, H. W., Nagengast, B., & Morin, A. J. S. (2012). Measurement invariance of Big-Five factors over the life span: ESEM tests of gender, age, plasticity, maturity, and La Dolce Vita effects. Developmental Psychology. http://doi.org/10.1037/a002691310.1037/a0026913.supp (Supplemental)

Marsh, H. W., Trautwein, U., Lüdtke, O., Gerlach, E., & Brettschneider, W.-D. (2007). Longitudinal study of preadolescent sport self-concept and performance: Reciprocal effects and causal ordering. Child Development, 78(6), 1640–1656. http://doi.org/10.1111/j.1467-8624.2007.01094.x

Marsh, H. W., Trautwein, U., Lüdtke, O., Köller, O., & Baumert, J. (2006). Integration of multidimensional self-concept and core personality constructs: Construct validation and relations to well-being and achievement. Journal of Personality, 74, 403–456.

Marshall, B. L. (2007). Climacteric redux? Men & Masculinities, 9(4), 509–529.

Marshall, E. J. (2014). Adolescent alcohol use: Risks and consequences. Alcohol and Alcoholism, 49(2), 160–164. http://doi.org/10.1093/alcalc/agt180

Marshall, S. L., Parker, P. D., Ciarrochi, J., & Heaven, P. C. L. (2014). Is self-esteem a cause or consequence of social support? A 4-year longitudinal study. Child Development, 85(3), 1275–1291. http://doi.org/10.1111/cdev.12176

Martin, A., Igarashi, Y., Jincho, N., & Mazuka, R. (2016). Utterances in infant-directed speech are shorter, not slower. Cognition, 156, 52–59. http://doi.org/10.1016/j.cognition.2016.07.015

Martin, C., Fabes, R., Hanish, L., Leonard, S., & Dinella, L. (2011). Experienced and expected similarity to same-gender peers: Moving toward a comprehensive model of gender segregation. Sex Roles, 65(5/6), 421–434. http://doi.org/10.1007/s11199-011-0029-y

Martin, C. A., Lommel, K., Cox, J., Kelly, T., Rayens, M. K., Woodring, J. H., & Omar, H. (2007). Kiss and tell: What do we know about pre- and early adolescent females who report dating? A pilot study. *Journal of Pediatric & Adolescent Gynecology, 20,* 45–49.

Martin, C. L., Eisenbud, L., & Rose, H. (1995). Children's gender-based reasoning about toys. *Child Development, 66,* 1453–1471.

Martin, C. L., Kornienko, O., Schaefer, D. R., Hanish, L. D., Fabes, R. A., & Goble, P. (2013). The role of sex of peers and gender-typed activities in young children's peer affiliative networks: A longitudinal analysis of selection and influence. *Child Development, 84*(3), 921–37. http://doi.org/10.1111/cdev.12032

Martin, C. L., & Ruble, D. N. (2010). Patterns of gender development. *Annual Review of Psychology, 61,* 353–381. http://doi.org/10.1146/annurev.psych.093008.100511

Martin, C. L., Ruble, D. N., & Szkrybalo, J. (2002). Cognitive theories of early gender development. *Psychological Bulletin, 128,* 903–933.

Martin, J. A., Hamilton, B. E., & Osterman, M. J. K. (2012). Three decades of twin births in the United States, 1980–2009. *NCHS Data Brief, 80.* Retrieved from http://www.cdc.gov/nchs/data/databriefs/db80.pdf

Martin, J. A., Hamilton, B. E., Osterman, M. J. K., Curtin, S. C., & Mathews, T. J. (2013). Births: Final data for 2012. *National Vital Statistics Reports, 62*(9). Retrieved from http://www.cdc.gov/nchs/data/nvsr/nvsr62/nvsr62_09.pdf#table21

Martin, R. M. (1975). Effects of familiar and complex stimuli on infant attention. *Developmental Psychology, 11,* 178–185.

Martin, S. C. (2016, April 20). A brief history of marijuana law in America. *Time.* Retrieved from http://time.com/4298038/marijuana-history-in-america/

Martinez, G., Copen, C. E., & Abma, J. C. (2011). Teenagers in the United States: Sexual activity, contraceptive use, and childbearing, 2006–2010 national survey of family growth. *Vital and Health Statistics. Series 23, Data from the National Survey of Family Growth, 31,* 1–35. Retrieved from http://www.ncbi.nlm.nih.gov/pubmed/22256688

Marwha, D., Halari, M., & Eliot, L. (2017). Meta-analysis reveals a lack of sexual dimorphism in human amygdala volume. *NeuroImage, 147,* 282–294. https://doi.org/10.1016/j.neuroimage.2016.12.021

Mascalzoni, E., Regolin, L., Vallortigara, G., & Simion, F. (2013). The cradle of causal reasoning: Newborns' preference for physical causality. *Developmental Science, 16*(3), 327–335. http://doi.org/10.1111/desc.12018

Masche, J. G. (2010). Explanation of normative declines in parents' knowledge about their adolescent children. *Journal of Adolescence, 33*(2), 271–284. http://doi.org/10.1016/j.adolescence.2009.08.002

Mascola, A. J., Bryson, S. W., & Agras, W. S. (2010). Picky eating during childhood: A longitudinal study to age 11 years. *Eating Behaviors, 11*(4), 253–257. http://doi.org/10.1016/j.eatbeh.2010.05.006

Mason, P., & Narad, C. (2005). International adoption: A health and developmental perspective. *Seminars in Speech and Language, 26*(1), 1–9.

Mason, W. A., Hanson, K., Fleming, C. B., Ringle, J. L., & Haggerty, K. P. (2015). Washington state recreational marijuana legalization: Parent and adolescent perceptions, knowledge, and discussions in a sample of low-income families. *Substance Use & Misuse, 50*(5), 541–545. http://doi.org/10.3109/10826084.2014.952447

Mason, W. A., & Spoth, R. L. (2011). Longitudinal associations of alcohol involvement with subjective well-being in adolescence and prediction to alcohol problems in early adulthood. *Journal of Youth and Adolescence, 40*(9), 1215–1224. http://doi.org/10.1007/s10964-011-9632-z

Masoro, E. J., & Austad, S. N. (2005). *Handbook of the biology of aging* (6th ed.). New York: Academic Press.

Massey, C., & Gelman, R. (1988). Preschoolers' ability to decide whether a photographed unfamiliar object can move itself. *Developmental Psychology, 24*(3), 307–317.

Masten, A. S. (2011). Resilience in children threatened by extreme adversity: Frameworks for research, practice, and translational synergy. *Development and Psychopathology, 23*(2), 493–506. http://doi.org/10.1017/s0954579411000198

Masten, A. S. (2014). Global perspectives on resilience in children and youth. *Child Development, 85*(1), 6–20. http://doi.org/10.1111/cdev.12205

Masten, A. S. (2016). Resilience in developing systems: The promise of integrated approaches. *European Journal of Developmental Psychology, 13*(3), 297–312. http://doi.org/10.1080/17405629.2016.1147344

Masten, A. S., Best, K., & Garmezy, N. (1990). Resilience and development: Contributions from the study of children who overcome adversity. *Development and Psychopathology, 2,* 425–444.

Masten, A. S., & Coatsworth, J. D. (1998). The development of competence in favorable and unfavorable environments: Lessons from research on successful children. *American Psychologist, 53,* 205–220.

Masten, A. S., & Monn, A. R. (2015). Child and family resilience: A call for integrated science, practice, and professional training. *Family Relations, 64*(1), 5–21. http://doi.org/10.1111/fare.12103

Masten, A. S., & Narayan, A. J. (2012). Child development in the context of disaster, war, and terrorism: Pathways of risk and resilience. *Annual Review of Psychology, 63,* 227–257. http://doi.org/10.1146/annurev-psych-120710-100356

Masten, A. S., Narayan, A. J., Silverman, W. K., & Osofsky, J. D. (2015). Children in war and disaster. In *Handbook of child psychology and developmental science* (pp. 1–42). Hoboken, NJ: John Wiley & Sons. http://doi.org/10.1002/9781118963418.childpsy418

Mastwyk, M., Ames, D., Ellis, K. A., Chiu, E., & Dow, B. (2014). Disclosing a dementia diagnosis: What do patients and family consider important? *International Psychogeriatrics, 26*(8), 1263–1272. http://doi.org/10.1017/S1041610214000751

Matheny, A. P., Wachs, T. D., Ludwig, J. L., & Phillips, K. (1995). Bringing order out of chaos: Psychometric characteristics of the confusion, hubbub, and order scale. *Journal of Applied Developmental Psychology, 16*(3), 429–444. http://doi.org/10.1016/0193-3973(95)90028-4

Mather, K. A., Jorm, A. F., Parslow, R. A., & Christensen, H. (2011). Is telomere length a biomarker of aging? A review. *The Journals of Gerontology. Series A, Biological Sciences and Medical Sciences, 66*(2), 202–213. http://doi.org/10.1093/gerona/glq180

Mather, M. (2012). The emotion paradox in the aging brain. *Annals of the New York Academy of Sciences, 1251,* 33–49. http://doi.org/10.1111/j.1749-6632.2012.06471.x

Mather, M., & Carstensen, L. L. (2005). Aging and motivated cognition: The positivity effect in attention and memory. *Trends in Cognitive Sciences, 9*(10), 496–502. http://doi.org/10.1016/j.tics.2005.08.005

Mathers, C. D., Stevens, G. A., Boerma, T., White, R. A., & Tobias, M. I. (2014). Causes of international increases in older age life expectancy. *The Lancet, 385*(9967), 540–548. http://doi.org/10.1016/S0140-6736(14)60569-9

Mathews, T. J., & MacDorman, M. F. (2013). Infant mortality statistics from the 2010 period linked birth/infant death data set. *National Vital Statistics Reports, 62*(8). Retrieved from http://www.cdc.gov/nchs/data/nvsr/nvsr62/nvsr62_08.pdf

Matlin, M. W., & Foley, H. J. (1997). *Sensation and perception* (4th ed.). Boston: Allyn & Bacon.

Matthews, T. J., & Hamilton, B. E. (2002). Mean age of mother, 1970–2000. *National Vital and Statistics Reports, 51*(1). Retrieved from https://www.cdc.gov/nchs/data/nvsr/nvsr51/nvsr51_01.pdf

Matthews, T. J., & Hamilton, B. E. (2016). Mean age of mothers is on the rise: United States, 2000–2014. Retrieved from https://www.cdc.gov/nchs/products/databriefs/db232.htm

Mattson, S. N., Crocker, N., & Nguyen, T. T. (2011). Fetal alcohol spectrum disorders: Neuropsychological and behavioral features. *Neuropsychology Review, 21*(2), 81–101. http://doi.org/10.1007/s11065-011-9167-9

Maupin, R., Lyman, R., Fatsis, J., Prystowiski, E., Nguyen, A., Wright, C., . . . Miller, J. (2004). Characteristics of women who deliver with no prenatal care. *Journal of Maternal-Fetal and Neonatal Medicine, 16,* 45–50.

Maurer, D. (2017). Critical periods re-examined: Evidence from children treated for dense cataracts. *Cognitive Development.* http://doi.org/10.1016/j.cogdev.2017.02.006

Maurer, D., & Lewis, T. L. (2013). Sensitive periods in visual development. In P. D. Zelazo (Ed.), *The Oxford handbook of developmental psychology* (Vol. 1). London, UK: Oxford University Press. http://doi.org/10.1093/oxfordhb/9780199958450.013.0008

Mausbach, B. T., Roepke, S. K., Chattillion, E. A., Harmell, A. L., Moore, R., Romero-Moreno, R., . . . Grant, I. (2012). Multiple mediators of the relations between caregiving stress and depressive symptoms. *Aging & Mental Health, 16*(1), 27–38. http://doi.org/10.1080/13607863.2011.615738

Mavros, Y., Kay, S., Anderberg, K. A., Baker, M. K., Wang, Y., Zhao, R., . . . Fiatarone Singh, M. A. (2013). Changes in insulin resistance and HbA1c are related to exercise-mediated changes in body composition in older adults with type 2 diabetes: Interim outcomes from the GREAT2DO trial. *Diabetes Care, 36*(8), 2372–2379. http://doi.org/10.2337/dc12-2196

Mavroveli, S., Petrides, K. V., Rieffe, C., & Bakker, F. (2007). Trait emotional intelligence, psychological well-being and peer-rated social competence in adolescence. *British Journal of Developmental Psychology, 25*(2), 263–275. http://doi.org/10.1348/026151006X118577

Mavroveli, S., & Sánchez-Ruiz, M. J. (2011). Trait emotional intelligence influences on academic achievement and school behaviour. *British Journal of Educational Psychology, 81*(1), 112–134. http://doi.org/10.1348/2044-8279.002009

Maxson, S. C. (2013). Behavioral genetics. In R. J. Nelson, S. J. Y. Mizumori, & I. B. Weiner (Eds.), *Handbook of psychology: Behavioral neuroscience* (2nd ed., Vol. 3, p. 1–25). New York, NY: John Wiley & Sons.

Maxwell, L. E., & Evans, G. W. (2000). The effects of noise on pre-school children's pre-reading skills. *Journal of Environmental Psychology, 20*(1), 91–97. http://doi.org/10.1006/jevp.1999.0144

Maxwell, L., & Scott, G. (2014). A review of the role of radical feminist theories in the understanding of rape myth acceptance. *Journal of Sexual Aggression, 20*(1), 40–54. http://doi.org/10.1080/13552600.2013.773384

May, P. A., Baete, A., Russo, J., Elliott, A. J., Blankenship, J., Kalberg, W. O., . . . Vagnarelli, F. (2014). Prevalence and characteristics of fetal alcohol spectrum disorders. *Pediatrics*, 134(5), 855–866. http://doi.org/10.1542/peds.2013-3319

Mayeda, E. R., Glymour, M. M., Quesenberry, C. P., & Whitmer, R. A. (2016). Inequalities in dementia incidence between six racial and ethnic groups over 14 years. *Alzheimer's & Dementia*, 12(3), 216–224. http://doi.org/10.1016/j.jalz.2015.12.007

Mayer, A., & Träuble, B. E. (2013). Synchrony in the onset of mental state understanding across cultures? A study among children in Samoa. *International Journal of Behavioral Development*, 37(1), 21–28. http://doi.org/10.1177/0165025412454030

Mayer, A., & Träuble, B. (2015). The weird world of cross-cultural false-belief research: A true- and false-belief study among Samoan children based on commands. *Journal of Cognition and Development*, 16(4), 650–665. http://doi.org/10.1080/15248372.2014.926273

Mayer, M., Schmitt, K., Kapelari, K., Frisch, H., Köstl, G., & Voigt, M. (2010). Spontaneous growth in growth hormone deficiency from birth until 7 years of age: Development of disease-specific growth curves. *Hormone Research in Paediatrics*, 74(2), 136–144. http://doi.org/10.1159/000281020

Mayhew, M. J., Rockenbach, A. N., Bowman, N. A., Seifert, T. A., Wolniak, G. C., Pascarella, E. T., & Terenzini, P. Y. (2016). *How college affects students (Vol. 3): 21st century evidence that higher education works*. New York, NY: John Wiley & Sons.

Maynard, A. E. (2002). Cultural teaching: The development of teaching skills in Maya sibling interactions. *Child Development*, 73, 969–982.

Maynard, A. E. (2004). Cultures of teaching in childhood: Formal schooling and Maya sibling teaching at home. *Cognitive Development*, 19(4), 517–535.

Mayseless, O., & Scharf, M. (2003). What does it mean to be an adult? The Israeli experience. *New Directions for Child & Adolescent Development*, 2003(100), 5–20.

Mazul, M. C., Salm Ward, T. C., & Ngui, E. M. (2016). Anatomy of good prenatal care: Perspectives of low income African-American women on barriers and facilitators to prenatal care. *Journal of Racial and Ethnic Health Disparities*, 1–8. http://doi.org/10.1007/s40615-015-0204-x

Mazzocco, M. M. M., & Kover, S. T. (2007). A longitudinal assessment of executive function skills and their association with math performance. *Child Neuropsychology*, 13(1), 18–45.

McAdams, D. P. (2014). The life narrative at midlife. *New Directions for Child and Adolescent Development*, 2014(145), 57–69. http://doi.org/10.1002/cad.20067

McAdams, D. P., & Logan, R. L. (2004). What is generativity? In E. de St. Aubin, D. P. McAdams, & T.-C. Kim (Eds.), *The generative society: Caring for future generations* (pp. 15–31). Washington, DC: American Psychological Association. http://doi.org/10.1037/10622-002

McAdams, D. P., & Olson, B. D. (2010). Personality development: Continuity and change over the life course. *Annual Review of Psychology*, 61, 517–542. http://doi.org/10.1146/annurev.psych.093008.100507

McAlister, A. R., & Peterson, C. C. (2013). Siblings, theory of mind, and executive functioning in children aged 3-6 years: New longitudinal evidence. *Child Development*, 84(4), 1442–58. http://doi.org/10.1111/cdev.12043

McAlister, A., & Peterson, C. (2007). A longitudinal study of child siblings and theory of mind development. *Cognitive Development*, 22(2), 258–270.

McArdle, J. J., Ferrer-Caja, E., Hamagami, F., & Woodcock, R. W. (2002). Comparative longitudinal structural analyses of the growth and decline of multiple intellectual abilities over the life span. *Developmental Psychology*, 38(1), 115–142.

McAuley, E., Wójcicki, T. R., Gothe, N. P., Mailey, E. L., Szabo, A. N., Fanning, J., . . . Mullen, S. P. (2013). Effects of a DVD-delivered exercise intervention on physical function in older adults. *Journals of Gerontology Series A: Biological Sciences & Medical Sciences*, 68(9), 1076–1082.

McAuliffe, L., Bauer, M., & Nay, R. (2007). Barriers to the expression of sexuality in the older person: The role of the health professional. *International Journal of Older People Nursing*, 2(1), 69–75. Retrieved from r.nay@latrobe.edu.au

McCabe, D. P., Roediger III, H. L., McDaniel, M. A., Balota, D. A., & Hambrick, D. Z. (2010). The relationship between working memory capacity and executive functioning: Evidence for a common executive attention construct. *Neuropsychology*, 24(2), 222–243. http://doi.org/10.1037/a0017619

McCabe, M. P., Riccardelli, L. A., & Finemore, J. (2002). The role of puberty, media and popularity with peers on strategies to increase weight, decrease weight and increase muscle tone among adolescent boys and girls. *Journal of Psychosomatic Research*, 52, 145–153.

McCabe, M. P., Ricciardelli, L. A., Stanford, J., Holt, K., Keegan, S., & Miller, L. (2007). Where is all the pressure coming from? Messages from mothers and teachers about preschool children's appearance, diet and exercise. *European Eating Disorders Review*, 15(3), 221–230.

McCabe, S. E., West, B. T., Veliz, P., & Boyd, C. J. (2017). E-cigarette use, cigarette smoking, dual use, and problem behaviors among U.S. adolescents: Results from a national survey. *Journal of Adolescent Health*. http://doi.org/10.1016/j.jadohealth.2017.02.004

McCain, J. L., & Campbell, W. K. (2017). Narcissism and social media use: A meta-analytic review. *Psychology of Popular Media Culture*. http://doi.org/10.1037/ppm0000137

McCall, R. B., Appelbaum, M. I., & Hogarty, P. S. (1973). Developmental changes in mental performance. *Monographs of the Society for Research in Child Development*, 38(3), 1. http://doi.org/10.2307/1165768

McCall, R. B., & Carriger, M. S. (1993). A meta-analysis of infant habituation and recognition memory performance as predictors of later IQ. *Child Development*, 64(1), 57. http://doi.org/10.2307/1131437

McCarty, C. A., Stoep, A. Vander, & McCauley, E. (2007). Cognitive features associated with depressive symptoms in adolescence: Directionality and specificity. *Journal of Clinical Child & Adolescent Psychology*, 36(2), 147–158. http://doi.org/10.1080/15374410701274926

McCauley, H. L., Tancredi, D. J., Silverman, J. G., Decker, M. R., Austin, S. B., McCormick, M. C., . . . Miller, E. (2013). Gender-equitable attitudes, bystander behavior, and recent abuse perpetration against heterosexual dating partners of male high school athletes. *American Journal of Public Health*, 103(10), 1882–1887. http://doi.org/10.2105/AJPH.2013.301443

McClain, M.-C., & Pfeiffer, S. (2012). Identification of gifted students in the United States today: A look at state definitions, policies, and practices. *Journal of Applied School Psychology*, 28(1), 59–88. http://doi.org/10.1080/15377903.2012.643757

McCleery, J. P., Akshoomoff, N., Dobkins, K. R., & Carver, L. J. (2009). Atypical face versus object processing and hemispheric asymmetries in 10-month-old infants at risk for autism. *Biological Psychiatry*, 66(10), 950–957. http://doi.org/10.1016/j.biopsych.2009.07.031

McClelland, M. M., & Cameron, C. E. (2011). Self-regulation and academic achievement in elementary school children. *New Directions for Child and Adolescent Development*, 2011(133), 29–44. http://doi.org/10.1002/cd.302

McClelland, M. M., John Geldhof, G., Cameron, C. E., & Wanless, S. B. (2015). Development and self-regulation. In *Handbook of child psychology and developmental science* (pp. 1–43). Hoboken, NJ: John Wiley & Sons. http://doi.org/10.1002/9781118963418.childpsy114

McClelland, S. I., & Tolman, D. L. (2014). Adolescent sexuality. In T. Tio (Ed.), *Encyclopedia of critical psychology* (pp. 40–47). New York, NY: Springer.

McClintock, M. K., & Herdt, G. (1996). Rethinking puberty. *Current Directions in Psychological Science*, 5(6), 178–183. http://doi.org/10.1111/1467-8721.ep11512422

McClure, J., Meyer, L. H., Garisch, J., Fischer, R., Weir, K. F., & Walkey, F. H. (2011). Students' attributions for their best and worst marks: Do they relate to achievement? *Contemporary Educational Psychology*, 36(2), 71–81. http://doi.org/10.1016/j.cedpsych.2010.11.001

McClure, R., Kegler, S., Davey, T., & Clay, F. (2015). Contextual determinants of childhood injury: A systematic review of studies with multilevel analytic methods. *American Journal of Public Health*, 105(12), e37–e43. http://doi.org/10.2105/AJPH.2015.302883

McConnell, R., Barrington-Trimis, J. L., Wang, K., Urman, R., Hong, H., Unger, J., . . . Berhane, K. (2017). Electronic cigarette use and respiratory symptoms in adolescents. *American Journal of Respiratory and Critical Care Medicine*, 195(8), 1043–1049. http://doi.org/10.1164/rccm.201604-0804OC

McCord, J. (1996). Unintended consequences of punishment. *Pediatrics*, 88, 832–834.

McCoy, M. L., & Keen, S. M. (2009). *Child abuse and neglect*. New York, NY: Psychology Press.

McCoy, R. C., Hunt, C. E., Lesko, S. M., Venzina, R., Corwin, M. J., Willinger, M., . . . Mitchell, A. A. (2004). Frequency of bed sharing and its relationship to breastfeeding. *Developmental and Behavioral Pediatrics*, 25(3), 141–149.

McCrae, R. R. (2002). The maturation of personality psychology: Adult personality development and psychological well-being. *Journal of Research in Personality*, 36(4), 307–317.

McCrae, R. R., & Costa, P. T. (1988). Psychological resilience among widowed men and women: A 10-year follow-up of a national sample. *Journal of Social Issues*, 44(3), 129–142.

McCrae, R. R., & Costa, P. T. (2006). Cross-cultural perspectives on adult personality trait development. In D. K. Mroczek & T. D. Little (Eds.), *Handbook of personality development* (pp. 129–145). Mahwah, NJ: Lawrence Erlbaum.

McCrae, R. R., & Costa, P. T. (2008). The five-factor theory of personality. In O. P. John, R. W. Robins, & L. A. Pervin (Eds.), *Handbook of personality psychology: Theory and research* (3rd ed., pp. 159–181). New York, NY: Guilford Press.

McCrae, R. R., Terracciano, A., & The Personality Profiles of Cultures Project. (2005). Universal features of personality traits from the observer's perspective: Data from 50 cultures. *Journal of Personality and Social Psychology*, 88, 547–561.

McDonald, K. L., Dashiell-Aje, E., Menzer, M. M., Rubin, K. H., Oh, W., & Bowker, J. C. (2013). Contributions of racial and sociobehavioral homophily to friendship stability and quality among same-race and cross-race friends. *The Journal of Early Adolescence, 33*(7), 897–919. http://doi.org/10.1177/0272431612472259

McDonald, M. (1998). Burying Freud and praising him. *U.S. News & World Report, 125*(15), 60.

McDonald, M. A., Sigman, M., Espinosa, M. P., & Neumann, C. G. (1994). Impact of a temporary food shortage on children and their mothers. *Child Development, 65*, 404–415.

McDougall, P., & Vaillancourt, T. (2015). Long-term adult outcomes of peer victimization in childhood and adolescence: Pathways to adjustment and maladjustment. *The American Psychologist, 70*(4), 300–310. http://doi.org/10.1037/a0039174

McDowell, D. J., Kim, M., O'Neil, R., & Parke, R. D. (2002). Children's emotional regulation and social competence in middle childhood. *Marriage & Family Review, 34*(3–4), 345–364. http://doi.org/10.1300/J002v34n03_07

McElwain, N. L., & Booth-LaForce, C. (2006). Maternal sensitivity to infant distress and nondistress as predictors of infant-mother attachment security. *Journal of Family Psychology, 20*(2), 247–255. http://doi.org/10.1037/0893-3200.20.2.247

McElwain, N. L., & Volling, B. (2004). Attachment security and parental sensitivity during infancy: Associations with friendship quality and false-belief understanding at age 4. *Journal of Social & Personal Relationships, 21*(5), 639–667.

McFarland, D. A., & Thomas, R. J. (2006). Bowling young: How youth voluntary associations influence adult political participation. *American Sociological Review, 71*(3), 401–425. http://doi.org/10.1177/000312240607100303

McGinley, M., Lipperman-Kreda, S., Byrnes, H. F., & Carlo, G. (2010). Parental, social and dispositional pathways to Israeli adolescents' volunteering. *Journal of Applied Developmental Psychology, 31*(5), 386–394. http://doi.org/10.1016/j.appdev.2010.06.001

McGlade, M. S., Saha, S., & Dahlstrom, M. E. (2004). The Latina paradox: An opportunity for restructuring prenatal care delivery. *American Journal of Public Health, 94*(12), 2062–2065.

McGlothlin, H., & Killen, M. (2006). Intergroup attitudes of European American children attending ethnically homogeneous schools. *Child Development, 77*(5), 1375–1386.

McGlothlin, H., Killen, M., & Edmonds, C. (2005). European-American children's intergroup attitudes about peer relationships. *British Journal of Developmental Psychology, 23*(2), 227–249. http://doi.org/10.1348/026151005x26101

McGonigle-Chalmers, M., Slater, H., & Smith, A. (2014). Rethinking private speech in preschoolers: The effects of social presence. *Developmental Psychology, 50*(3), 829–836. http://doi.org/10.1037/a0033909

McGowan, J. E., Alderdice, F. A., Holmes, V. A., & Johnston, L. (2011). Early childhood development of late-preterm infants: A systematic review. *Pediatrics, 127*(6), 1111–1124. http://doi.org/10.1542/peds.2010-2257

McIlvane, J. M. (2007). Disentangling the effects of race and SES on arthritis-related symptoms, coping, and well-being in African American and White women. *Aging & Mental Health, 11*(5), 556–569. http://doi.org/10.1080/13607860601086520

McIlvane, J. M., Baker, T. A., & Mingo, C. A. (2008). Racial differences in arthritis-related stress, chronic life stress, and depressive symptoms among women with arthritis: A contextual perspective. *Journals of Gerontology Series B: Psychological Sciences & Social Sciences, 63B*(5), S320–S327.

McIndoe, S. (2017). *How the NHL concussion lawsuit could threaten the future of the league.* Retrieved from https://www.theguardian.com/sport/2017/apr/05/nhl-concussion-lawsuit-could-threaten-future-of-league

McIntyre, C. A., & Rhodes, R. E. (2007). Transitions to motherhood and its effect on physical activity. *Journal of Sport & Exercise Psychology, 29,* S186–S187.

McIntyre, K. P., Korn, J. H., & Matsuo, H. (2008). Sweating the small stuff: How different types of hassles result in the experience of stress. *Stress & Health, 24*(5), 383–392. http://doi.org/10.1002/smi.1190

McKee, A. C., Stein, T. D., Nowinski, C. J., Stern, R. A., Daneshvar, D. H., Alvarez, V. E., . . . Cantu, R. C. (2013). The spectrum of disease in chronic traumatic encephalopathy. *Brain, 136*(1), 43–64. http://doi.org/10.1093/brain/aws307

McKeering, H., & Pakenham, K. I. (2000). Gender and generativity issues in parenting: Do fathers benefit more than mothers from involvement in child care activities? *Sex Roles, 43*(7), 459–480.

McKenna, J. J. (2001). Why we never ask "Is it safe for infants to sleep alone?" *Academy of Breast Feeding Medicine News and Views, 7*(4), 32, 38.

McKenna, J. J., & Mosko, S. (1993). Evolution and infant sleep: An experimental study of infant-parent co-sleeping and its implications for SIDS. *Acta Paediatrica Supplement, 389,* 31–36.

McKenna, J. J., & Volpe, L. E. (2007). Sleeping with baby: An Internet-based sampling of parental experiences, choices, perceptions, and interpretations in a Western industrialized context. *Infant and Child Development, 16*(4), 359–385. http://doi.org/10.1002/icd.525

McKenna, M. C., Kear, D. J., & Ellsworth, R. A. (1995). Children's attitudes toward reading: A national survey. *Reading Research Quarterly, 30,* 934–956.

McKey, R. H., Condelli, L., Ganson, H., Barrett, B. J., McConkey, C., & Plantz, M. C. (1985). *The impact of Head Start on children, families, and communities (Final report of the Head Start Evaluation Synthesis, and Utilization Project).* Washington, DC: U.S. Department of Health and Human Services, Administration on Children, Youth, and Families.

McKhann, G. M., Knopman, D. S., Chertkow, H., Hyman, B. T., Jack, C. R., Kawas, C. H., . . . Phelps, C. H. (2011). The diagnosis of dementia due to Alzheimer's disease: Recommendations from the National Institute on Aging-Alzheimer's Association workgroups on diagnostic guidelines for Alzheimer's disease. *Alzheimer's & Dementia, 7*(3), 263–269. http://doi.org/10.1016/j.jalz.2011.03.005

McKinney, C., & Renk, K. (2011). A multivariate model of parent-adolescent relationship variables in early adolescence. *Child Psychiatry and Human Development, 42*(4), 442–462. http://doi.org/10.1007/s10578-011-0228-3

McKnight-Eily, L. R., Eaton, D. K., Lowry, R., Croft, J. B., Presley-Cantrell, L., & Perry, G. S. (2011). Relationships between hours of sleep and health-risk behaviors in US adolescent students. *Preventive Medicine, 53*(4–5), 271–273. http://doi.org/10.1016/j.ypmed.2011.06.020

McKusick, V. A. (1998). *Mendelian inheritance in man: A catalog of human genes and genetic disorders* (12th ed.). Baltimore, MD: Johns Hopkins University Press.

McKusick, V. A. (2007). Mendelian inheritance in man and its online version, OMIM. *American Journal of Human Genetics, 80*(4), 588–604. http://doi.org/10.1086/514346

McKusick-Nathans Institute of Genetic Medicine. (2016). *OMIM: Online mendelian inheritance in man.* Retrieved from http://www.omim.org/about

McLachlan, K., Roesch, R., Viljoen, J. L., & Douglas, K. S. (2014). Evaluating the psychelegal abilities of young offenders with fetal alcohol spectrum disorder. *Law and Human Behavior, 38*(1), 10–22. http://doi.org/10.1037/lhb0000037

McLean, K. C. (2005). Late adolescent identity development: Narrative meaning making and memory telling. *Developmental Psychology, 41*(4), 683–691.

McLean, S. A., Paxton, S. J., & Wertheim, E. H. (2016). Does media literacy mitigate risk for reduced body satisfaction following exposure to thin-ideal media? *Journal of Youth and Adolescence, 45*(8), 1678–1695. http://doi.org/10.1007/s10964-016-0440-3

McLeod, J. D., & Knight, S. (2010). The association of socioemotional problems with early sexual initiation. *Perspectives on Sexual and Reproductive Health, 42*(2), 93–101. http://doi.org/10.1363/4209310

McLeod, P., Sommerville, P., & Reed, N. (2005). Are automated actions beyond conscious access? In J. Duncan, P. McLeod, & L. Phillips (Eds.), *Measuring the mind* (pp. 359–371). New York: Oxford University Press.

McLloyd, V. C. (1998). Children in poverty, development, public policy, and practice. In I. E. Siegel & K. A. Renninger (Eds.), *Handbook of child psychology* (4th ed.). New York: Wiley.

McLoughlin, C. S. (2005). The coming-of-age of China's single-child policy. *Psychology in the Schools, 42*(3), 305–313. http://doi.org/10.1002/pits.20081

McLoyd, V. C., & Smith, J. (2002). Physical discipline and behavior problems in African American, European American, and Hispanic children: Emotional support as a moderator. *Journal of Marriage and Family, 64,* 40–53.

McMahan, J. (2001). Brain death, cortical death and persistent vegetative state. In H. Kuhse & R. Singer (Eds.), *A Companion to bioethics* (pp. 250–260). New York: Blackwell.

McMahan True, M., Pisani, L., & Oumar, F. (2001). Infant-mother attachment among the Dogon of Mali. *Child Development, 72*(5), 1451.

McMahon, S. D., Todd, N. R., Martinez, A., Coker, C., Sheu, C.-F., Washburn, J., & Shah, S. (2013). Aggressive and prosocial behavior: Community violence, cognitive, and behavioral predictors among urban African American youth. *American Journal of Community Psychology, 51*(3–4), 407–21. http://doi.org/10.1007/s10464-012-9560-4

McNamara, B., & Rosenwax, L. (2010). Which carers of family members at the end of life need more support from health services and why? *Social Science & Medicine, 70*(7), 1035–1041. http://doi.org/10.1016/j.socscimed.2009.11.029

McNamara, M., Batur, P., & DeSapri, K. T. (2015). In the clinic. Perimenopause. *Annals of Internal Medicine, 162*(3), ITC1-15. http://doi.org/10.7326/AITC201502030

McNulty, J. K., Wenner, C. A., & Fisher, T. D. (2016). Longitudinal associations among relationship satisfaction, Sexual satisfaction, and frequency of sex in early marriage. *Archives of Sexual Behavior, 45*(1), 85–97. http://doi.org/10.1007/s10508-014-0444-6

McQuillan, G., Kruszon-Moran, D., Markowitz, L. E., Unger, E. R., & Paulose-Ram, R. (2017). Prevalence of HPV in adults aged 18–69: United States, 2011–2014. *NCHS Data Briefs, 280.* Retrieved from https://www.cdc.gov/nchs/data/databriefs/db280.pdf

McSweeney Cody, M., O'Sullivan, P., Elberson, K., Moser, D. K., & Garvin, B. J., J. C. (2003). Women's Early Warning Symptoms of Acute Myocardial Infarction. *Circulation, 108,* 2619–2623.

REFERENCES

McVey, G. L., Levine, M., Piran, N., & Ferguson, H. B. (2013). *Preventing Eating-Related and Weight-Related Disorders: Collaborative Research, Advocacy, and Policy Change: Collaborative Research, Advocacy, and Policy Change*. Toronto, ON: Wilfrid Laurier Univ. Press.

McVey, G. L., Tweed, S., & Blackmore, E. (2004). Dieting among preadolescent and young adolescent females. *Canadian Medical Association Journal*, *170*(10), 1559–1561.

Meaney, M. J. (2010). Epigenetics and the biological definition of gene · environment interactions. *Child Development*, *81*(1), 41–79.

Meece, J. L., Anderman, E. M., & Anderman, L. H. (2006). Classroom Goal Structure, Student Motivation, and Academic Achievement. *Annual Review of Psychology*, *57*(1), 487–503. http://doi.org/10.1146/annurev.psych.56.091103.070258

Meehan, C. L., & Hawks, S. (2013). Cooperative breeding and attachment among the Aka foragers. In Naomi Quinn & jeannette Marie Mageo (Eds.), *Attachment reconsidered* (pp. 85–113). New york: Palgrave Macmillan. http://doi.org/10.1057/9781137386724_4

Meeus, W. H. J. (1996). Studies on identity development in adolescence: An overview of research and some new data. *Journal of Youth & Adolescence*, *25*, 569–599.

Meeus, W. H. J. (2011). The study of adolescent identity formation 2000–2010: A review of longitudinal research. *Journal of Research on Adolescence*, *21*(1), 75–94. http://doi.org/10.1111/j.1532-7795.2010.00716.x

Meeus, W. H. J., & de Wied, M. (2007). Relationships with parents and identity in adolescence: A review of 25 years of research. In M. Watzlawik & A. Born (Eds.), *Capturing identity: Quantitative and qualitative methods* (pp. 131–147). Lanham, MD: University Press of America.

Meeus, W. H. J., Iedema, J., Maassen, G., & Engels, R. (2005). Separation-individuation revisited: On the interplay of parent-adolescent relations, identity and emotional adjustment in adolescence. *Journal of Adolescence*, *28*(1), 89–106.

Meeus, W. H. J., Oosterwegel, A., & Vollerbergh, W. (2002). Parental and peer attachment and identity development in adolescence. *Journal of Adolescence*, *25*, 93–107.

Mehta, K. M., & Yeo, G. W. (2017). Systematic review of dementia prevalence and incidence in United States race/ethnic populations. *Alzheimer's & Dementia*, *13*(1), 72–83. http://doi.org/10.1016/j.jalz.2016.06.2360

Meier, A., & Allen, G. (2008). Intimate relationship development during the transition to adulthood: Differences by social class. *New Directions for Child & Adolescent Development*, *2008*(119), 25–39.

Meier, L. L., Orth, U., Denissen, J. J. A., & Kühnel, A. (2011). Age differences in instability, contingency, and level of self-esteem across the life span. *Journal of Research in Personality*, *45*(6), 604–612. http://doi.org/10.1016/j.jrp.2011.08.008

Meijer, W. A., de Groot, R. H. M., van Gerven, P. W. M., van Boxtel, M. P. J., & Jolles, J. (2009). Level of processing and reaction time in young and middle-aged adults and the effect of education. *European Journal of Cognitive Psychology*, *21*(2/3), 216–234. http://doi.org/10.1080/09541440802091780

Meins, E., Fernyhough, C., Fradley, E., & Tuckey, M. (2001). Rethinking maternal sensitivity: Mothers' comments on infants' mental processes predict security of attachment at 12 months. *Journal of Child Psychology and Psychiatry*, *42*(5). http://doi.org/10.1017/S0021963001007302

Meisel, J. M. (1989). Early differentiation of languages in bilingual children. In K. Hyltenstam &

L. K. Obler (Eds.), *Bilingualism across the lifespan: Aspects of acquisition, maturity and loss* (pp. 13–40). London, UK: Cambridge University Press.

Melby-Lervåg, M., Redick, T. S., & Hulme, C. (2016). Working memory training does not improve performance on measures of intelligence or other measures of "Far Transfer": Evidence from a meta-analytic review. *Perspectives on Psychological Science : A Journal of the Association for Psychological Science*, *11*(4), 512–34. http://doi.org/10.1177/1745691616635612

Meléndez, L. (2005). Parental beliefs and practices around early self-regulation: The impact of culture and immigration. *Infants & Young Children*, *18*(2), 136–146.

Meletis, C. D., & Zabriskie., N. (2007). Common nutrient depletions caused by pharmaceuticals. *Alternative and Complementary Therapies*, *13*, 10–17.

Melinder, A., Endestad, T. O. R., & Magnussen, S. (2006). Relations between episodic memory, suggestibility, theory of mind, and cognitive inhibition in the preschool child. *Scandinavian Journal of Psychology*, *47*(6), 485–495.

Meltzoff, A. N. (1990). Towards a developmental cognitive science. *Annals of the New York Academy of Sciences*, *608*, 1–37.

Meltzoff, A. N. (2007). "Like me": a foundation for social cognition. *Developmental Science*, *10*(1), 126–134. http://doi.org/10.1111/j.1467-7687.2007.00574.x

Meltzoff, A. N., & Moore, M. K. (1994). Imitation, memory, and the representation of persons. *Infant Behavior & Development*, *17*(1), 83–99. http://doi.org/10.1016/0163-6383(94)90024-8

Mendez, M., Durtschi, J., Neppl, T. K., & Stith, S. M. (2016). Corporal punishment and externalizing behaviors in toddlers: The moderating role of positive and harsh parenting. *Journal of Family Psychology*, *30*(8), 887–895. http://doi.org/10.1037/fam0000187

Mendle, J. (2014). Beyond pubertal timing: New directions for studying individual differences in development. *Current Directions in Psychological Science*, *23*(3), 215–219. http://doi.org/10.1177/0963721414530144

Mendle, J., & Ferrero, J. (2012). Detrimental psychological outcomes associated with pubertal timing in adolescent boys. *Developmental Review*, *32*(1), 49–66. http://doi.org/10.1016/j.dr.2011.11.001

Mendle, J., Turkheimer, E., & Emery, R. E. (2007). Detrimental psychological outcomes associated with early pubertal timing in adolescent girls. *Developmental Review*, *27*(2), 151–171.

Mendle, J., Turkheimer, E., D'Onofrio, B. M., Lynch, S. K., Emery, R. E., Slutske, W. S., & Martin, N. G. (2006). Family structure and age at menarche: A children-of-twins approach. *Developmental Psychology*, *42*, 533–542.

Menesini, E., & Salmivalli, C. (2017). Bullying in schools: The state of knowledge and effective interventions. *Psychology, Health & Medicine*, 1–14. http://doi.org/10.1080/13548506.2017.1279740

Mennella, J. A., & Beauchamp, G. K. (2002). Flavor experiences during formula feeding are related to preferences during childhood. *Early Human Development*, *68*(2), 71–82.

Menon, V. (2016). Working memory in children's math learning and its disruption in dyscalculia. *Current Opinion in Behavioral Sciences*, *10*, 125–132. http://doi.org/10.1016/j.cobeha.2016.05.014

Menting, B., Koot, H., & van Lier, P. (2014). Peer acceptance and the development of emotional and behavioural problems: Results from a preventive intervention study. *International Journal of Behavioral Development*, 0165025414558853-. http://doi.org/10.1177/0165025414558853

Menting, B., van Lier, P. A. C., & Koot, H. M. (2011). Language skills, peer rejection, and the development of externalizing behavior from kindergarten to fourth grade. *Journal of Child Psychology & Psychiatry*, *52*(1), 72–79. http://doi.org/10.1111/j.1469-7610.2010.02279.x

Mercer, N. (2008). Talk and the development of reasoning and understanding. *Human Development*, *51*(1), 90–100. http://doi.org/10.1159/000113158

Mercuri, E., Baranello, G., Romeo, D. M. M., Cesarini, L., & Ricci, D. (2007). The development of vision. *Early Human Development*, *83*(12), 795–800. http://doi.org/10.1016/j.earlhumdev.2007.09.014

Meschke, L. L., Holl, J., & Messelt, S. (2013). Older not wiser: risk of prenatal alcohol use by maternal age. *Maternal and Child Health Journal*, *17*(1), 147–55. http://doi.org/10.1007/s10995-012-0953-7

Meshi, D., Morawetz, C., & Heekeren, H. R. (2013). Nucleus accumbens response to gains in reputation for the self, relative to gains for others predicts social media use. *Frontiers in Human Neuroscience, 7*, 439. https://doi.org/10.3389/fnhum.2013.00439

Meshot, C. M., & Leitner, L. M. (1992). Adolescent mourning and parental death. *OMEGA–Journal of Death and Dying*, *26*(4), 287–299. http://doi.org/10.2190/CHE4-F4ND-QY8C-J2Y5

Mesman, J., Stoel, R., Bakermans-Kranenburg, M. J., van IJzendoorn, M. H., Juffer, F., Koot, H. M., & Alink, L. R. A. (2009). Predicting growth curves of early childhood externalizing problems: Differential susceptibility of children with difficult temperament. *Journal of Abnormal Child Psychology*, *37*(5), 625–636. http://doi.org/10.1007/s10802-009-9298-0

Messinger, D., & Fogel, A. (2007). The interactive development of social smiling. In R. V Kail (Ed.), *Advances in child development and behavior* (Vol. 35; pp. 327–366). San Diego, CA: Elsevier Academic Press.

Metcalf, B. S., Hosking, J., Jeffery, A. N., Henley, W. E., & Wilkin, T. J. (2015). Exploring the adolescent fall in physical activity: A 10-yr cohort study (EarlyBird 41). *Medicine and Science in Sports and Exercise*, *47*(10), 2084–92. http://doi.org/10.1249/MSS.0000000000000644

MetLife Mature Market Institute, National Alliance for Caregiving, & Center for Long Term Care Research and Policy. (2011). *The MetLife study of caregiving costs to working caregivers: Double jeopardy for baby boomers caring for their parents*. New York, NY: MetLife.

Mez, J., Daneshvar, D. H., Kiernan, P. T., Abdolmohammadi, B., Alvarez, V. E., Huber, B. R., . . . McKee, A. C. (2017). Clinicopathological Evaluation of Chronic Traumatic Encephalopathy in Players of American Football. *JAMA, 318*(4), 360 -370. https://doi.org/10.1001/JAMA.2017.8334

Micalizzi, L., Wang, M., & Saudino, K. J. (2015). Difficult temperament and negative parenting in early childhood: A genetically informed cross-lagged analysis. *Developmental Science*. http://doi.org/10.1111/desc.12355

Mickelson, K. D., Kessler, R. C., & Shaver, P. R. (1997). Adult attachment in a nationally representative sample. *Journal of Personality and Social Psychology*, *73*(5), 1092–1106. http://doi.org/10.1037/0022-3514.73.5.1092

Midgley, C., Anderman, E., & Hicks, L. (1995). Differences between elementary and middle school teachers and students: A goal theory approach. *The Journal of Early Adolescence*, *15*(1), 90–113. http://doi.org/10.1177/0272431695015001006

Midobuche, E. (2001). More than empty footprints in the sand: Educating immigrant children. *Harvard Educational Review*, *71*, 529–535.

Miech, R. A., Johnston, L. D., O'Malley, P. M., Bachman, J. G., & Schulenberg, J. E. (2015). *Monitoring the Future national survey results on* drug use, 1975–2014: Volume I, Secondary school students. Retrieved from http://monitoringthefuture.org/pubs.html#monograp

Miech, R. A., Johnston, L. D., O'Malley, P. M., Bachman, J. G., Schulenberg, J. E., & Patrick, M. E. (2017). Monitoring the Future national survey results on drug use, 1975–2016: Volume I, Secondary school students. Retrieved from http://www.monitoringthefuture.org/pubs/monographs/mtf-vol1_2016.pdf

Miedzian, M. (1991). Boys will be boys: Breaking the link between masculinity and violence. New York: Doubleday.

Mielck, A., Vogelmann, M., Leidl, R., Mielck, A., Reitmeir, P., Vogelmann, M., . . . Williams, A. (2014). Health-related quality of life and socioeconomic status: Inequalities among adults with a chronic disease. Health and Quality of Life Outcomes, 12(1), 58. http://doi.org/10.1186/1477-7525-12-58

Mikels, J. A., Larkin, G. R., Reuter-Lorenz, P. A., & Cartensen, L. L. (2005). Divergent trajectories in the aging mind: Changes in working memory for affective versus visual information with age. Psychology and Aging, 20(4), 542–53. http://doi.org/10.1037/0882-7974.20.4.542

Mikels, J. A., Löckenhoff, C. E., Maglio, S. J., Goldstein, M. K., Garber, A., & Carstensen, L. L. (2010). Following your heart or your head: Focusing on emotions versus information differentially influences the decisions of younger and older adults. Journal of Experimental Psychology. Applied, 16(1), 87–95. http://doi.org/10.1037/a0018500

Mikulincer, M., & Shaver, P. R. (2008). Adult attachment and affect regulation. In J. Cassidy & P. R. Shaver (Eds.), Handbook of attachment: Theory, research, and clinical applications (2nd ed., pp. 503–531). New York: Guilford Press.

Mikulincer, M., & Shaver, P. R. (2012). Adult attachment orientations and relationship processes. Journal of Family Theory & Review, 4(4), 259–274. http://doi.org/10.1111/j.1756-2589.2012.00142.x

Mikulincer, M., & Shaver, P. R. (2013). Adult attachment and happiness: Individual differences in the experience and consequences of positive emotions. In I. Boniwell, S. A. David, & A. Conley Ayers (Eds.), Oxford handbook of happiness. London, UK: Oxford University Press. http://doi.org/10.1093/oxfordhb/9780199557257.013.0061

Mikulincer, M., & Shaver, P. R. (2015). The psychological effects of the contextual activation of security-enhancing mental representations in adulthood. Current Opinion in Psychology, 1, 18–21. http://doi.org/10.1016/j.copsyc.2015.01.008

Milevsky, A., Schlechter, M., Netter, S., & Keehn, D. (2007). Maternal and paternal parenting styles in adolescents: Associations with self-esteem, Depression and Life-Satisfaction. Journal of Child & Family Studies, 16(1), 39–47. http://doi.org/10.1007/s10826-006-9066-5

Milholland, B., Suh, Y., & Vijg, J. (2017). Mutation and catastrophe in the aging genome. Experimental Gerontology. http://doi.org/10.1016/j.exger.2017.02.073

Miller, B. G., Kors, S., & Macfie, J. (2017). No differences? Meta-analytic comparisons of psychological adjustment in children of gay fathers and heterosexual parents. Psychology of Sexual Orientation and Gender Diversity, 4(1), 14–22. http://doi.org/10.1037/sgd0000203

Miller, C. F., Trautner, H. M., & Ruble, D. N. (2006). The role of gender stereotypes in children's preferences and behavior. In L. Balter & C. S. Tamis-LeMonda (Eds.), Child psychology: A handbook of contemporary issues (2nd ed., pp. 293–323). New York, NY: Psychology Press.

Miller, D. B., & O'Callaghan, J. P. (2015). Biomarkers of Parkinson's disease: Present and future. Metabolism, 64(3), S40–S46. http://doi.org/10.1016/j.metabol.2014.10.030

Miller, D. I., & Halpern, D. F. (2014). The new science of cognitive sex differences. Trends in Cognitive Sciences, 18(1), 37–45. http://doi.org/10.1016/j.tics.2013.10.011

Miller, D. T., Weinstein, S. M., & Karniol, R. (1978). Effects of age and self-verbalization on children's ability to delay gratification. Developmental Psychology, 14(5), 569–570. http://doi.org/10.1037/0012-1649.14.5.569

Miller, J. E., Hammond, G. C., Strunk, T., Moore, H. C., Leonard, H., Carter, K. W., . . . Burgner, D. P. (2016). Association of gestational age and growth measures at birth with infection-related admissions to hospital throughout childhood: A population-based, data-linkage study from Western Australia. The Lancet Infectious Diseases. http://doi.org/10.1016/S1473-3099(16)00150-X

Miller, J. G. (1997). Culture and self: Uncovering the cultural grounding of psychological theory. In J. G. Snodgrass & R. L. Thompson (Eds.), The self across psychology: Self-recognition, self-awareness, and the self-concept (pp. 217–231). New York: New York Academy of Sciences.

Miller, J. G., & Bersoff, D. M. (1995). Development in the context of everyday family relationships: Culture, interpersonal morality, and adaptation. In M. Killen & D. Hart (Eds.), Morality in everyday life: Developmental perspectives (pp. 259–282). New York, NY: Cambridge University Press.

Miller, K. S., Forehand, R., & Kotchick, B. A. (1999). Adolescent sexual behavior in two ethnic minority samples: The role of family variables. Journal of Marriage & Family, 61, 85–98.

Miller, L. C. (2000). Initial assessment of growth, development, and the effects of institutionalization in internationally adopted children. Pediatrics Annals, 69, 1092–1106.

Miller, L. C., & Hendrie, N. W. (2000). Health of children adopted from China. Pediatrics, 105, 1–6.

Miller, L. S., Mitchell, M. B., Woodard, J. L., Davey, A., Martin, P., & Poon, L. W. (2010). Cognitive performance in centenarians and the oldest old: Norms from the Georgia Centenarian Study. Aging, Neuropsychology & Cognition, 17(5), 575–590. http://doi.org/10.1080/13825585.2010.481355

Miller, L., Tseng, B., Tirella, L., Chan, W., & Feig, E. (2008). Health of children adopted from Ethiopia. Maternal & Child Health Journal, 12(5), 599–605. http://doi.org/10.1007/s10995-007-0274-4

Miller, P. H. (2016). Theories of developmental psychology (6th ed.). New York: Worth.

Miller, P. H., & Seier, W. L. (1994). Strategy utilization deficiencies in children: When, where, and why. In H. W. Reese (Ed.), Advances in child development and behavior (Vol. 24, pp. 107–156). New York: Academic Press.

Miller, P. J., & Rosengren, K. S. (2014). Children's understanding of death: Toward a contextualized and integrated account. Monographs of the Society for Research in Child Development, 79(1), 113–124. http://doi.org/10.1111/mono.12082

Miller-Cotto, D., & Byrnes, J. P. (2016). Ethnic/racial identity and academic achievement: A meta-analytic review. Developmental Review, 41, 51–70. http://doi.org/10.1016/j.dr.2016.06.003

Milligan, K., Astington, J. W., & Dack, L. A. (2007). Language and theory of mind: Meta-analysis of the relation between language ability and false-belief understanding. Child Development, 78(2), 622–646.

Mills, K. L., Goddings, A.-L., Clasen, L. S., Giedd, J. N., & Blakemore, S.-J. (2014). The developmental mismatch in structural brain maturation during adolescence. Developmental Neuroscience, 36(3–4), 147–160. http://doi.org/10.1159/000362328

Mills, K. L., Lalonde, F., Clasen, L. S., Giedd, J. N., & Blakemore, S.-J. (2014). Developmental changes in the structure of the social brain in late childhood and adolescence. Social Cognitive and Affective Neuroscience, 9(1), 123–131. https://doi.org/10.1093/scan/nss113

Mills, M., Rindfuss, R. R., McDonald, P., & te Velde, E. (2011). Why do people postpone parenthood? Reasons and social policy incentives. Human Reproduction Update, 17(6), 848–860.

Mills, S. (2012). Sounds to soothe the soul: Music and bereavement in a traditional South Korean death ritual. Mortality, 17(2), 145–157. http://doi.org/10.1080/13576275.2012.675231

Mills-Koonce, W. R., Garrett-Peters, P., Barnett, M., Granger, D. A., Blair, C., & Cox, M. J. (2011). Father contributions to cortisol responses in infancy and toddlerhood. Developmental Psychology, 47(2), 388–395. http://doi.org/10.1037/a0021066

Millstein, S. G., & Halpern-Felsher, B. L. (2002). Perceptions of risk and vulnerability. Journal of Adolescent Health, 31, 10–27.

Min, M. O., Minnes, S., Yoon, S., Short, E. J., & Singer, L. T. (2014). Self-reported adolescent behavioral adjustment: Effects of prenatal cocaine exposure. The Journal of Adolescent Health : Official Publication of the Society for Adolescent Medicine. http://doi.org/10.1016/j.jadohealth.2013.12.032

Minagawa-Kawai, Y., van der Lely, H., Ramus, F., Sato, Y., Mazuka, R., & Dupoux, E. (2011). Optical brain imaging reveals general auditory and language-specific processing in early infant development. Cerebral Cortex, 21(2), 254–261. http://doi.org/10.1093/cercor/bhq082

Miner, J. L., & Clarke-Stewart, K. A. (2008). Trajectories of externalizing behavior from age 2 to age 9: Relations with gender, temperament, ethnicity, parenting, and rater. Developmental Psychology, 44(3), 771–786. http://doi.org/10.1037/0012-1649.44.3.771

Minichiello, V., Plummer, D., & Loxton, D. (2004). Factors predicting sexual relationships in older people: An Australian study. Australasian Journal on Ageing, 23, 125–130.

Minkoff, H., & Berkowitz, R. (2014). The case for universal prenatal genetic counseling. Obstetrics & Gynecology, 123(6), 1335–1338. http://doi.org/10.1097/AOG.0000000000000267

Miranda, R., & Shaffer, D. (2013). Understanding the suicidal moment in adolescence. Annals of the New York Academy of Sciences, 1304, 14–21. http://doi.org/10.1111/nyas.12291

Miranda-Mendizábal, A., Castellví, P., Parés-Badell, O., Almenara, J., Alonso, I., Blasco, M. J., . . . Alonso, J. (2017). Sexual orientation and suicidal behaviour in adolescents and young adults: Systematic review and meta-analysis. The British Journal of Psychiatry. Retrieved from http://bjp.rcpsych.org/content/early/2017/02/20/bjp.bp.116.196345

Mirelman, A., Herman, T., Brozgol, M., Dorfman, M., Sprecher, E., Schweiger, A., . . . Giladi, N. (2012). Executive function and falls in older adults: New findings from a five-year prospective study link fall risk to cognition. PLoS ONE, 7(6), e40297. http://doi.org/10.1371/journal.pone.0040297

Mirescu, C., & Gould, E. (2006). Stress and adult neurogenesis. Hippocampus, 16(3), 233–238. https://doi.org/10.1002/hipo.20155

Misailidi, P. (2006). Young children's display rule knowledge: Understanding the distinction between apparent and real emotions and the motives underlying the use of display rules. Social Behavior and Personality: An International Journal, 34(10), 1285–1296. http://doi.org/10.2224/sbp.2006.34.10.1285

Misca, G. (2014). The "quiet migration": Is intercountry adoption a successful intervention in the lives of vulnerable children? *Family Court Review, 52*(1), 60–68. http://doi.org/10.1111/fcre.12070

Misch, D. A. (2007). Natural recovery from alcohol abuse among college students. *Journal of American College Health, 55*(4), 215–218.

Mischel, H. N., & Mischel, W. (1983). The development of children's knowledge of self-control strategies. *Child Development, 54*(3), 603. http://doi.org/10.2307/1130047

Mischel, W., Ayduk, O., Berman, M. G., Casey, B. J., Gotlib, I. H., Jonides, J., . . . Shoda, Y. (2011). "Willpower" over the life span: Decomposing self-regulation. *Social Cognitive and Affective Neuroscience, 6*(2), 252–256. http://doi.org/10.1093/scan/nsq081

Mischel, W., & Baker, N. (1975). Cognitive appraisals and transformations in delay behavior. *Journal of Personality and Social Psychology, 31*(2), 254–261. Retrieved from https://insights.ovid.com/personality-social-psychology/jpspy/1975/02/000/cognitive-appraisals-transformations-delay/9/00005205

Mischel, W., & Ebbesen, E. B. (1970). Attention in delay of gratification. *Journal of Personality and Social Psychology, 16*(2), 329–337. http://doi.org/10.1037/h0029815

Mischel, W., Shoda, Y., & Rodriguez, M. I. (1989). Delay of gratification in children. *Science, 244*(4907), 933–938.

Mitchell, B. A. (2010). Happiness in midlife parental roles: A contextual mixed methods analysis. *Family Relations, 59*(3), 326–339.

Mitchell, B. A. (2016). Empty nest. In *Encyclopedia of family studies* (pp. 1–4). Hoboken, NJ: John Wiley & Sons. http://doi.org/10.1002/9781119085621.wbefs008

Mitchell, B. A., & Lovegreen, L. D. (2009). The empty nest syndrome in midlife families: A multimethod exploration of parental gender differences and cultural dynamics. *Journal of Family Issues, 30*(12), 1651–1670.

Mitchell, E. A. (2009). Risk factors for SIDS. *British Medical Journal, 339,* 873–874. http://doi.org/10.1136/bmj.b3466

Mitchell, J. A., Rodriguez, D., Schmitz, K. H., & Audrain-McGovern, J. (2013a). Greater screen time is associated with adolescent obesity: A longitudinal study of the BMI distribution from ages 14 to 18. *Obesity, 21*(3), 572–575. http://doi.org/10.1002/oby.20157

Mitchell, J. A., Rodriguez, D., Schmitz, K. H., & Audrain-McGovern, J. (2013b). Sleep duration and adolescent obesity. *Pediatrics, 131*(5), e1428-34. http://doi.org/10.1542/peds.2012-2368

Mitchell, P., & Kikuno, H. (2000). Belief as construction: Inference and processing bias. In P. Mitchell & K. J. Riggs (Eds.), *Children's reasoning and the mind* (pp. 281–299). Hove, England: Psychology Press.

Mitchell, W. K., Williams, J., Atherton, P., Larvin, M., Lund, J., & Narici, M. (2012). Sarcopenia, dynapenia, and the impact of advancing age on human skeletal muscle size and strength; A quantitative review. *Frontiers in Physiology, 3,* 260. http://doi.org/10.3389/fphys.2012.00260

Mitteldorf, J. (2016). An epigenetic clock controls aging. *Biogerontology, 17*(1), 257–265. http://doi.org/10.1007/s10522-015-9617-5

Miura, Y., & Endo, T. (2010). Survival responses to oxidative stress and aging. *Geriatrics & Gerontology International, 10,* S1–S9. https://doi.org/10.1111/j.1447-0594.2010.00597.x

Mix, K. S., Huttenlocher, J., & Levine, S. C. (2002). Multiple cues for quantification in infancy: Is number one of them? *Psychological Bulletin, 128*(2), 278–94. Retrieved from http://www.ncbi.nlm.nih.gov/pubmed/11931520

Miyamoto, K., Inoue, Y., Hsueh, K., Liang, Z., Yan, X., Yoshii, T., & Furue, M. (2011). Characterization of comprehensive appearances of skin ageing: An 11-year longitudinal study on facial skin ageing in Japanese females at Akita. *Journal of Dermatological Science, 64*(3), 229–236. http://doi.org/10.1016/j.jdermsci.2011.09.009

Mock, S. E., & Eibach, R. P. (2011). Aging attitudes moderate the effect of subjective age on psychological well-being: Evidence from a 10-year longitudinal study. *Psychology and Aging, 26*(4), 979–986. Retrieved from http://cat.inist.fr/?aModele=afficheN&cpsidt=25229491

Modecki, K. L. (2014). Maturity of judgment. In *Encyclopedia of adolescence* (pp. 1660–1665). New York: Springer.

Moffitt, T., Poulton, R., & Caspi, A. (2013). Lifelong impact of early self-control. *American Scientist, 101*(5), 352. http://doi.org/10.1511/2013.104.352

Mohammad, E. T., Shapiro, E. R., Wainwright, L. D., & Carter, A. S. (2015). Impacts of family and community violence exposure on child coping and mental health. *Journal of Abnormal Child Psychology, 43*(2), 203–215. http://doi.org/10.1007/s10802-014-9889-2

Mojon-Azzi, S. M., Sousa-Poza, & Mojon, D. S. (2008). Impact of low vision on well-being in 10 European countries. *Ophthalmologica, 222*(3), 205–212.

Mok, M. M. C., Kennedy, K. J., & Moore, P. J. (2011). Academic attribution of secondary students: Gender, year level and achievement level. *Educational Psychology, 31*(1), 87–104. http://doi.org/10.1080/01443410.2010.518596

Mok, R. M., Myers, N. E., Wallis, G., & Nobre, A. C. (2016). Behavioral and neural markers of flexible attention over working memory in aging. *Cerebral Cortex, 26*(4), 1831–1842. http://doi.org/10.1093/cercor/bhw011

Molfese, D. L. (1977). Infant cerebral asymmetry. In S. J. Segalowitz & F. A. Gruber (Eds.), *Language development and neurological theory*. Orlando, FL: Academic Press.

Molgat, M. (2007). Do transitions and social structures matter? How "emerging adults" define themselves as adults. *Journal of Youth Studies, 10*(5), 495–516. http://doi.org/10.1080/13676260701580769

Molina, E., del Rincon, I., Restrepo, J. F., Battafarano, D. F., & Escalante, A. (2015). Association of socioeconomic status with treatment delays, disease activity, joint damage, and disability in rheumatoid arthritis. *Arthritis Care & Research, 67*(7), 940–946. http://doi.org/10.1002/acr.22542

Molinari, V., McCullough, L. B., Coverdale, J. H., & Workman, R. (2006). Principles and practice of geriatric assent. *Aging & Mental Health, 10*(1), 48–54. http://doi.org/10.1080/13607860500307829

Moll, J., Zahn, R., de Oliveira-Souza, R., & Krueger, F. (2005). Opinion: The neural basis of human moral cognition. *National Review of Neuroscience, 6,* 799–809.

Mollborn, S. (2007). Making the best of a bad situation: Material resources and teenage parenthood. *Journal of Marriage & Family, 69*(1), 92–104. http://doi.org/10.1111/j.1741-3737.2006.00347.x

Molnar, B. E., Goerge, R. M., Gilsanz, P., Hill, A., Subramanian, S. V, Holton, J. K., . . . Beardslee, W. R. (2016). Neighborhood-level social processes and substantiated cases of child maltreatment. *Child Abuse & Neglect, 51,* 41–53. http://doi.org/10.1016/j.chiabu.2015.11.007

Monaghan, C., & Begley, A. (2004). Dementia diagnosis and disclosure: A dilemma in practice. *Journal of Clinical Nursing, 13,* 22–29. http://doi.org/10.1111/j.1365-2702.2004.00922.x

Monahan, K. C., Lee, J. M., & Steinberg, L. (2011). Revisiting the impact of part-time work on adolescent adjustment: Distinguishing between selection and socialization using propensity score matching. *Child Development, 82*(1), 96–112. http://doi.org/10.1111/j.1467-8624.2010.01543.x

Monahan, K. C., Steinberg, L., Cauffman, E., & Mulvey, E. P. (2013). Psychosocial (im)maturity from adolescence to early adulthood: Distinguishing between adolescence-limited and persisting antisocial behavior. *Development and Psychopathology, 25*(4 Pt 1), 1093–105. http://doi.org/10.1017/S0954579413000394

Monk, C. S., Webb, S. J., & Nelson, C. A. (2001). Prenatal neurobiological development: Molecular mechanisms and anatomical change. *Developmental Neuropsychology, 19*(2), 211–236.

Monte, A. A., Zane, R. D., & Heard, K. J. (2015). The implications of marijuana legalization in Colorado. *JAMA, 313*(3), 241–2. http://doi.org/10.1001/jama.2014.17057

Montecino-Rodriguez, E., Berent-Maoz, B., & Dorshkind, K. (2013). Causes, consequences, and reversal of immune system aging. *The Journal of Clinical Investigation, 123*(3), 958–965. http://doi.org/10.1172/JCI64096

Montesanto, A., Latorre, V., Giordano, M., Martino, C., Domma, F., & Passarino, G. (2011). The genetic component of human longevity: Analysis of the survival advantage of parents and siblings of Italian nonagenarians. *European Journal of Human Genetics, 19*(8), 882–886. http://doi.org/10.1038/ejhg.2011.40

Montgomery, M. J., & Côté, J. E. (2003). College as a transition to adulthood. In G. R. Adams & M. D. Berzonsky (Eds.), *Blackwell handbook of adolescence* (pp. 149–172). Malden, MA: Blackwell.

Montgomery, R. J. V, Rowe, J. M., & Kosloski, K. (2007). Family caregiving. In J. A. Blackburn & C. N. Dulmus (Eds.), *Handbook of gerontology: Evidence-based approaches to theory, practice, and policy* (pp. 426–454). Hoboken, NJ: John Wiley & Sons.

Moon, C., Cooper, R. P., & Fifer, W. P. (1993). Two-day-old infants prefer their native language. *Infant Behavior and Development, 16,* 495–500.

Moon, J. R., Kondo, N., Glymour, M. M., & Subramanian, S. V. (2011). Widowhood and mortality: a meta-analysis. *PloS One, 6*(8), e23465. http://doi.org/10.1371/journal.pone.0023465

Moon, R. Y., & Task Force on Sudden Infant Death Syndrome. (2016). SIDS and other sleep-related infant deaths: Evidence base for 2016 updated recommendations for a safe infant sleeping environment. *Pediatrics, 138*(5), e20162940–e20162940. http://doi.org/10.1542/peds.2016-2940

Moore, A. J., & Stratton, D. C. (2002). *Resilient widowers: Older men speak for themselves.* New York, NY: Springer.

Moore, C. S., Grant, M. D., Zink, T. A., Panizzon, M. S., Franz, C. E., Logue, M. W., . . . Lyons, M. J. (2014). Erectile dysfunction, vascular risk, and cognitive performance in late middle age. *Psychology and Aging, 29*(1), 163–172. http://doi.org/10.1037/a0035463

Moore, C., Angelopoulos, M., & Bennett, P. (1999). Word learning in the context of referential and salience cues. *Developmental Psychology, 35,* 60–68.

Moore, K. L., & Persaud, T. V. N. (2016). *Before we are born: Essentials of embryology and birth defects* (9th ed.). Philadelphia: Saunders.

Moore, S. M., & Rosenthal, D. A. (2015). Personal growth, grandmother engagement and satisfaction among non-custodial grandmothers. *Aging & Mental Health*, 19(2), 136–143. http://doi.org/10.1080/13607863.2014.920302

Moore, S. R., Harden, K. P., & Mendle, J. (2014). Pubertal timing and adolescent sexual behavior in girls. *Developmental Psychology*, 50(6), 1734–1745. http://doi.org/10.1037/a0036027

Moore, V. R., & Miller, S. D. (2007). Coping resources: Effects on the psychological well-being of African American grandparents raising grandchildren. *Journal of Health & Social Policy*, 22(3/4), 137–148.

Moorman, E. A., & Pomerantz, E. M. (2008). The role of mothers' control in children's mastery orientation: A time frame analysis. *Journal of Family Psychology*, 22(5), 734–741. http://doi.org/10.1037/0893-3200.22.5.734

Moos, N. L. (1994). An integrative model of grief. *Death Studies*, 19(4), 337–64.

Moran, R. J., Symmonds, M., Dolan, R. J., & Friston, K. J. (2014). The brain ages optimally to model its environment: Evidence from sensory learning over the adult lifespan. *PLoS Computational Biology*, 10(1), 1–8. http://doi.org/10.1371/journal.pcbi.1003422

Morawska, A., & Sanders, M. (2011). Parental use of time out revisited: A useful or harmful parenting strategy? *Journal of Child & Family Studies*, 20(1), 1–8. http://doi.org/10.1007/s10826-010-9371-x

Morelli, G., Rogoff, B., Oppenheim, D., & Goldsmith, D. (1992). Cultural variation in infants' sleeping arrangements: Questions of independence. *Developmental Psychology*, 28, 604–613.

Morf, C. C., & Rhodewalt, F. (2001). Unraveling the paradoxes of narcissism: A dynamic self-regulatory processing model. *Psychological Inquiry*, 12(4), 177–196. http://doi.org/10.1207/S15327965PLI1204_1

Morgan, C. D., Covington, J. W., Geisler, M. W., Polich, J., & Murphy, C. (1997). Olfactory event-related potentials: Older males demonstrate the greatest deficits. *Electroencephalography and Clinical Neurophysiology/Evoked Potentials Section*, 104(4), 351–358. http://doi.org/10.1016/S0168-5597(97)00020-8

Morgan, W. B., Elder, K. B., & King, E. B. (2013). The emergence and reduction of bias in letters of recommendation. *Journal of Applied Social Psychology*, 43(11), 2297–2306. http://doi.org/10.1111/jasp.12179

Morgos, D., Worden, J. W., & Gupta, L. (2007). Psychosocial effects of war experiences among displaced children in southern Darfur. *Omega: Journal of Death & Dying*, 56(3), 229–253. http://doi.org/10.2190/OM.56.3.b

Moriguchi, Y. (2014). The early development of executive function and its relation to social interaction: A brief review. *Frontiers in Psychology*, 5, 388. http://doi.org/10.3389/fpsyg.2014.00388

Moriguchi, Y., Kanda, T., Ishiguro, H., Shimada, Y., & Itakura, S. (2011). Can young children learn words from a robot? *Interaction Studies: Social Behaviour and Communication in Biological and Artificial Systems*, 12(1), 107–118.

Morin, R., & Fry, R. (2012). *More Americans Worry about Financing Retirement*. Retrieved from http://www.pewsocialtrends.org/2012/10/22/more-americans-worry-about-financing-retirement/

Morizot, J., & Le Blanc, M. (2003). Continuity and change in personality traits from adolescence to midlife: A 25-year longitudinal study comparing representative and adjudicated men. *Journal of Personality*, 71(5), 705.

Morra, S., Gobbo, C., Marini, Z., & Sheese, R. (2008). *Cognitive development: Neo-Piagetian perspectives*. New York, NY: Taylor & Francis Group.

Morris, A. S., Silk, J. S., Morris, M. D. S., Steinberg, L., Aucoin, K. J., & Keyes, A. W. (2011). The influence of mother–child emotion regulation strategies on children's expression of anger and sadness. *Developmental Psychology*, 47(1), 213–225. http://doi.org/10.1037/a0021021

Morris, B. J., Kennedy, S. E., Wodak, A. D., Mindel, A., Golovsky, D., Schrieber, L., . . . Ziegler, J. B. (2017). Early infant male circumcision: Systematic review, risk-benefit analysis, and progress in policy. *World Journal of Clinical Pediatrics*, 6(1), 89–102. http://doi.org/10.5409/wjcp.v6.i1.89

Morrissey, M. (2016). *The State of American Retirement. Retirement Inequality Chartbook*. Retrieved from http://www.epi.org/publication/retirement-in-america/#charts

Morrongiello, B. A., Corbett, M., McCourt, M., & Johnston, N. (2006). Understanding unintentional injury risk in young children II. The contribution of caregiver supervision, child attributes, and parent attributes. *Journal of Pediatric Psychology*, 31(6), 540–551. http://doi.org/10.1093/jpepsy/jsj073

Morrow, D. G., Menard, W. E., Ridolfo, H. E., Stine-Morrow, E. A. L., Teller, T., & Bryant, D. (2003). Expertise, cognitive ability, and age effects on pilot communication. *International Journal of Aviation Psychology*, 13(4), 345.

Morrow, D. G., & Schriver, A. (2007). External support for pilot communication: Implications for age-related design. *International Journal of Cognitive Technology*, 12(1), 21–30.

Morrow-Howell, N., Hinterlong, J., Rozario, P. A., & Tang., F. (2003). Effects of volunteering on the well-being of older adults. *Journals of Gerontology Series B: Psychological Sciences & Social Sciences*, 58B(3), S137.

Mortensen, L., Meyer, A. S., & Humphreys, G. W. (2006). Age-related effects on speech production: A review. *Language & Cognitive Processes*, 21(1–3), 238–290.

Mortimer, J. T., & Johnson, M. K. (1998). New perspectives on adolescent work and the transition to adulthood. In R. Jessor (Ed.), *New perspectives on adolescent risk behavior.* (pp. 425–496). New York, NY: Cambridge University Press.

Moses, L. J., Baldwin, D. A., Rosicky, J. G., & Tidball, G. (2001). Evidence for referential understanding in the emotions domain at twelve and eighteen months. *Child Development*, 72, 718–735.

Moses, L. J., Carlson, S. M., & Sabbagh, M. A. (2005). On the specificity of the relation between executive function and children's theories of mind. In W. Schneider, R. Schumann-Hengsteler, & B. Sodian (Eds.), *Young children's cognitive development: Interrelationships among executive functioning, working memory, verbal ability, and theory of mind* (pp. 131–145). Mahwah, NJ: Lawrence Erlbaum.

Moses, L. J., Coon, J. A., & Wusinich, N. (2000). Young children's understanding of desire information. *Developmental Psychology*, 36, 77–90.

Mosher, S. W. (2006). China's one-child policy: Twenty-five years later. *Human Life Review*, 32(1), 76–101.

Moshman, D. (2005). *Adolescent psychological development: Rationality, morality, and identity* (2nd ed). Mahwah, NJ: Lawrence Erlbaum.

Moskalev, A. A., Aliper, A. M., Smit-McBride, Z., Buzdin, A., & Zhavoronkov, A. (2014). Genetics and epigenetics of aging and longevity. *Cell Cycle*, 13(7), 1063–1077. http://doi.org/10.4161/cc.28433

Mosko, S., Richard, C., & McKenna, J. (1997). Maternal sleep and arousals during bedsharing with infants. *Sleep*, 201(2), 142–150.

Moss, E., & Lecompte, V. (2015). Attachment and socioemotional problems in middle childhood. *New Directions for Child and Adolescent Development*, 2015(148), 63–76. http://doi.org/10.1002/cad.20095

Moss, M. S., Resch, N., & Moss, S. Z. (1997). The role of gender in middle-age children's responses to parent death. *Omega: Journal of Death and Dying*, 35(1), 43–65.

Motta-Mena, N. V., & Scherf, K. S. (2017). Pubertal development shapes perception of complex facial expressions. *Developmental Science*, 20(4), e12451. http://doi.org/10.1111/desc.12451

Mouratidi, P-S., Bonoti, F., & Leondari, A. (2016). Childrens perceptions of illness and health: An analysis of drawings. *Health Education Journal*, 75(4), 434 447. http://doi.org/10.1177/0017896915599416

Mouzon, D. M., Taylor, R. J., Woodward, A. T., & Chatters, L. M. (2017). Everyday racial discrimination, everyday non-racial discrimination, and physical health among African-Americans. *Journal of Ethnic & Cultural Diversity in Social Work*, 26(1–2), 68–80. http://doi.org/10.1080/15313204.2016.1187103

Moxley, J. H., & Charness, N. (2013). Meta-analysis of age and skill effects on recalling chess positions and selecting the best move. *Psychonomic Bulletin & Review*, 20(5), 1017–1022. http://doi.org/10.3758/s13423-013-0420-5

Mpofu, E., & Vijver, F. J. R. van de. (2000). Taxonomic structure in early to middle childhood: A longitudinal study with Zimbabwean schoolchildren. *International Journal of Behavioral Development*, 24(2), 204–212.

Mrick, S. E., & Mrtorell, G. A. (2011). Sticks and stones may break my bones: Protective factors for the effects of perceived discrimination on social competence in adolescence. *Personal Relationships*, 18(3), 487–501. http://doi.org/10.1111/j.1475-6811.2010.01320.x

Mroczek, D. K., & Kolarz, C. M. (1998). The effect of age on positive and negative affect: A developmental perspective on happiness. *Journal of Personality and Social Psychology*, 75(5), 1333–1349. http://doi.org/10.1037/0022-3514.75.5.1333

Mroczek, D. K., & Spiro, A. (2007). Personality change influences mortality in older men. *Psychological Science*, 18(5), 371–376. http://doi.org/10.1111/j.1467-9280.2007.01907.x

Mroczek, D. K., Spiro, A. I. I. I., & Griffin, P. W. (2006). Personality and aging. In J. E. Birren & K. W. Schaire (Eds.), *Handbook of the psychology of aging* (6th ed., pp. 363–377). Amsterdam, NL: Elsevier.

Mrug, S., Elliott, M. N., Davies, S., Tortolero, S. R., Cuccaro, P., & Schuster, M. A. (2014). Early puberty, negative peer influence, and problem behaviors in adolescent girls. *Pediatrics*, 133(1), 7–14. http://doi.org/10.1542/peds.2013-0628

Mrug, S., Loosier, P. S., & Windle, M. (2008). Violence exposure across multiple contexts: Individual and joint effects on adjustment. *American Journal of Orthopsychiatry*, 78(1), 70–84. http://doi.org/10.1037/0002-9432.78.1.70

Mu, Y., & Gage, F. H. (2011). Adult hippocampal neurogenesis and its role in Alzheimer's disease. *Molecular Neurodegeneration*, 6, 85. http://doi.org/10.1186/1750-1326-6-85

Muangpaisan, W., Petcharat, C., & Srinonprasert, V. (2012). Prevalence of potentially reversible conditions in dementia and mild cognitive impairment in a geriatric clinic. *Geriatrics & Gerontology International*, 12(1), 59–64. http://doi.org/10.1111/j.1447-0594.2011.00728.x

Mueller, V., & Sepulveda, A. (2014). Parental perception of a baby sign workshop on stress and parent–child interaction. *Early Child Development and Care, 184*(3), 450–468. http://doi.org/10.1080/03004430.2013.797899

Muennig, P., Robertson, D., Johnson, G., Campbell, F., Pungello, E. P., & Neidell, M. (2011). The effect of an early education program on adult health: The Carolina Abecedarian Project randomized controlled trial. *American Journal of Public Health, 101*(3), 512–6. http://doi.org/10.2105/AJPH.2010.200063

Muenssinger, J., Matuz, T., Schleger, F., Kiefer-Schmidt, I., Goelz, R., Wacker-Gussmann, A., . . . Preissl, H. (2013). Auditory habituation in the fetus and neonate:An fMEG study. *Developmental Science, 16*(2), 287–95. http://doi.org/10.1111/desc.12025

Muir, D., & Clifton, R. (1985). Infants' orientation to the location of sound sources. In G. Gottlieb & N. Krasnegor (Eds.), *The measurement of audtion and vision during the first year of life: A methodological overview* (pp. 171–194). Norwood, NJ: Ablex.

Muise, A., Schimmack, U., & Impett, E. A. (2016). Sexual frequency predicts greater well-being, but more is not always better. *Social Psychological and Personality Science, 7*(4), 295–302. http://doi.org/10.1177/1948550615616462

Mulvaney, M. K., & Mebert, C. J. (2007). Parental corporal punishment predicts behavior problems in early childhood. *Journal of Family Psychology, 21*(3), 389–397. http://doi.org/10.1037/0893-3200.21.3.389

Mumme, D. L., Fernald, A., & Herrera, C. (1996). Infants' responses to facial and vocal emotional signals in a social referencing paradigm. *Child Development, 67*, 3219–3237.

Murachver, T., Pipe, M., Gordon, R., Owens, J. L., & Fivush, R. (1996). Do, show, and tell: Children's event memories acquired through direct experience, observation, and stories. *Child Development, 67*, 3029–3044.

Murphy, G. L. (2002). *The big book of concepts.* Cambridge, MA: MIT Press.

Murray-Close, D., Crick, N. R., & Galotti, K. M. (2006). Children's moral reasoning regarding physical and relational aggression. *Social Development, 15*(3), 345–372.

Murry, V. M., Brody, G. H., Simons, R. L., Cutrona, C. E., & Gibbons, F. X. (2008). Disentangling ethnicity and context as predictors of parenting within rural African American families. *Applied Developmental Science, 12*(4), 202–210. http://doi.org/10.1080/10888690802388144

Murthy, V. H. (2017). E-cigarette use among youth and young adults. *JAMA Pediatrics, 171*(3), 209. http://doi.org/10.1001/jamapediatrics.2016.4662

Murty, V. P., Calabro, F., & Luna, B. (2016). The role of experience in adolescent cognitive development: Integration of executive, memory, and mesolimbic systems. *Neuroscience & Biobehavioral Reviews, 70*, 46–58. http://doi.org/10.1016/j.neubiorev.2016.07.034

Muscari, A., Giannoni, C., Pierpaoli, L., Berzigotti, A., Maietta, P., Foschi, E., . . . Zoli, M. (2010). Chronic endurance exercise training prevents aging-related cognitive decline in healthy older adults: A randomized controlled trial. *International Journal of Geriatric Psychiatry, 25*(10), 1055–1064.

Muscat, T., Obst, P., Cockshaw, W., & Thorpe, K. (2014). Beliefs about infant regulation, early infant behaviors and maternal postnatal depressive symptoms. *Birth, 41*(2), 206–213. http://doi.org/10.1111/birt.12107

Mussen, P., & Eisenberg-Berg, N. (1977). *Roots of caring, sharing, and helping.* San Francisco: Freeman.

Mustanski, B., & Liu, R. T. (2013). A longitudinal study of predictors of suicide attempts among lesbian, gay, bisexual, and transgender youth. *Archives of Sexual Behavior, 42*(3), 437–48. http://doi.org/10.1007/s10508-012-0013-9

Myant, K. A., & Williams, J. M. (2005). Children's concepts of health and illness: Understanding of contagious illnesses, non-contagious illnesses and injuries. *Journal of Health Psychology, 10*(6), 805–819.

Myers, C. E., Klein, B. E. K., Gangnon, R., Sivakumaran, T. A., Iyengar, S. K., & Klein, R. (2014). Cigarette smoking and the natural history of age-related macular degeneration: the Beaver Dam Eye Study. *Ophthalmology, 121*(10), 1949–1955. http://doi.org/10.1016/j.ophtha.2014.04.040

Myers, N. A., & Perlmutter, M. (2014). Memory in the years from two to five. In P. A. Ornstein (Ed.), *Memory development in children* (p. 191–218.). Psychology Press.

Nachmias, M., Gunnar, M., Mangelsdorf, S., Parritz, R. H., & Buss, K. (1996). Behavioral inhibition and stress reactivity: The moderating role of attachment security. *Child Development, 67*(2), 508. http://doi.org/10.2307/1131829

Nachtigall, M. J., Nazem, T. G., Nachtigall, R. H., & Goldstein, S. R. (2013). Osteoporosis risk factors and early life-style modifications to decrease disease burden in women. *Clinical Obstetrics and Gynecology, 56*(4), 650–3. http://doi.org/10.1097/GRF.0b013e3182aa1daf

Nader, P. R., Bradley, R. H., Houts, R. M., McRitchie, S. L., & O'Brien, M. (2008). Moderate-to-vigorous physical activity from ages 9 to 15 years. *Journal of the American Medical Association, 300*(3), 295–305.

Nader, P. R., O'Brien, M., Houts, R., Bradley, R., Belsky, J., Crosnoe, R., . . . National Institute of Child Health and Human Development Early Child Care Research Network. (2006). Identifying risk for obesity in early childhood. *Pediatrics, 118*(3), e594–601. http://doi.org/10.1542/peds.2005-2801

Naef, R., Ward, R., Mahrer-Imhof, R., & Grande, G. (2013). Characteristics of the bereavement experience of older persons after spousal loss: An integrative review. *International Journal of Nursing Studies, 50*(8), 1108–1121. http://doi.org/10.1016/j.ijnurstu.2012.11.026

Nagayama, M., & Gilliard, J. L. (2005). An investigation of Japanese and American early care and education. *Early Childhood Education Journal, 33*(3), 137–143.

Nagy, G. R., Győrffy, B., Nagy, B., & Rigó, J. (2013). Lower risk for Down syndrome associated with longer oral contraceptive use: A case-control study of women of advanced maternal age presenting for prenatal diagnosis. *Contraception, 87*(4), 455–8. http://doi.org/10.1016/j.contraception.2012.08.040

Nagy, W. E., & Scott, J. A. (2000). Vocabulary processes. In M. L. Kamil & P. B. Mosenthal (Eds.), *Handbook of reading research* (Vol. 3, pp. 269–284). Mahwah, NJ: Erlbaum.

Nair, A. K., Sabbagh, M. N., Tucker, A. M., & Stern, Y. (2014). Cognitive reserve and the aging brain. In A. K. Nair & M. N. Sabbagh (Eds.), *Geriatric Neurology.* Chichester, UK: John Wiley & Sons, Ltd. http://doi.org/10.1002/9781118730676

Nalls, M. A., Pankratz, N., Lill, C. M., Do, C. B., Hernandez, D. G., Saad, M., . . . Singleton, A. B. (2014). Large-scale meta-analysis of genome-wide association data identifies six new risk loci for Parkinson's disease. *Nature Genetics, 46*(9), 989–993. http://doi.org/10.1038/ng.3043

Nanayakkara, S., Misch, D., Chang, L., & Henry, D. (2013). Depression and exposure to suicide predict suicide attempt. *Depression and Anxiety, 30*(10), 991–6. http://doi.org/10.1002/da.22143

Náñez Sr., J. E., & Yonas, A. (1994). Effects of luminance and texture motion on infant defensive reactions to optical collision. *Infant Behavior & Development, 17*, 165–174.

Nantel-Vivier, A., Kokko, K., Caprara, G. V., Pastorelli, C., Gerbino, M. G., Paciello, M., . . . Tremblay, R. E. (2009). Prosocial development from childhood to adolescence: A multi-informant perspective with Canadian and Italian longitudinal studies. *Journal of Child Psychology and Psychiatry, 50*(5), 590–598. http://doi.org/10.1111/j.1469-7610.2008.02039.x

Napper, L. E., Montes, K. S., Kenney, S. R., & LaBrie, J. W. (2016). Assessing the personal negative impacts of hooking up experienced by college students: Gender differences and mental health. *The Journal of Sex Research, 53*(7), 766–775. http://doi.org/10.1080/00224499.2015.1065951

Naseeb, M. A., & Volpe, S. L. (2017). Protein and exercise in the prevention of sarcopenia and aging. *Nutrition Research, 40*, 1–20. http://doi.org/10.1016/j.nutres.2017.01.001

National Academy of Sciences. (1995). *On being a scientist: Responsible conduct in research.* Washington, DC: National Academy Press.

National Association of School Psychologists. (2003). *Position statement on student grade retention and social promotion.* Retrieved from http://www.nasponline.org/about_nasp/pospaper_graderetent.aspx

National Center for Biotechnology Information. (2004). *What is a genome?* Retrieved from http://www.ncbi.nlm.nih.gov/About/primer/genetics_genome.html

National Center for Chronic Disease Prevention and Health Promotion. (2010). Prevalence of doctor-diagnosed arthritis and arthritis-attributable activity limitation: United States, 2007-2009. *Morbidity and Mortality Weekly Report, 59*(39), 1261–1265.

National Center for Education Statistics. (2014a). *The condition of education, 2014.* Retrieved from http://nces.ed.gov/pubsearch/pubsinfo.asp?pubid=2014083

National Center for Education Statistics. (2014b). *The Nation's Report Card, 2014.* Retrieved from http://www.nationsreportcard.gov/reading_math_2013/#/

National Center for Education Statistics. (2015). *Digest of Education Statistics, 2013.* Retrieved from https://nces.ed.gov/programs/digest/d13/index.asp

National Center for Education Statistics. (2016a). *Fall enrollment of U.S. residents in degree-granting postsecondary institutions, by race/ethnicity: Selected years, 1976 through 2025.* Retrieved from https://nces.ed.gov

National Center for Education Statistics. (2016b). *Table 322.10. Bachelor's degrees conferred by postsecondary institutions, by field of study: Selected years, 1970-71 through 2014-15.* Retrieved from https://nces.ed.gov/programs/digest/d16/tables/dt16_322.10.asp

National Center for Education Statistics. (2016c). *What are the trends in the educational level of the United States population?* Retrieved from https://nces.ed.gov/fastfacts/display.asp?id=27

National Center for Education Statistics. (2017). *Immediate College Enrollment Rate.* Retrieved from https://nces.ed.gov/programs/coe/indicator_cpa.asp

National Center for Health Statistics. (2015a). *Deaths: Final Data for 2013.* Retrieved from http://www.cdc.gov/nchs/data/nvsr/nvsr64/nvsr64_02.pdf

National Center for Health Statistics. (2015b). *Provisional number of divorces and annulments and rate: United States, 2000-2011.* Retrieved from http://www.cdc.gov/nchs/nvss/marriage_divorce_tables.htm

National Coalition for Women and Girls in Education. (2017). *Title IX and athletics leveling the playing field leads to long-term success.* Retrieved from http://www.ncwge.org/TitleIX45/Title IX and Athletics.pdf

National Conference of State Legislatures. (2017). *State medical marijuana laws.* Retrieved from http://www.ncsl.org/research/health/state-medical-marijuana-laws.aspx

National Council on Alcoholism and Drug Dependence. (2015). *Alcohol and crime.* Retrieved from https://ncadd.org/learn-about-alcohol/alcohol-and-crime

National Highway Traffic Safety Administration. (2016). *Traffic Safety Facts–2015.* Retrieved from https://crashstats.nhtsa.dot.gov

National Institute of Aging. (2011). *Global health and aging.* Retrieved from https://www.nia.nih.gov/research/publication/global-health-and-aging/preface

National Institute of Allergy and infectious Diseases. (2014). *NIH trial tests very early anti-HIV therapy in HIV-infected newborns.* Retrieved from http://www.niaid.nih.gov/news/newsreleases/2014/Pages/IMPAACTP1115.aspx

National Institute of Child Health and Human Development. (2000). *Teaching children to read: An evidence-based assessment of the scientific research literature on reading and its implications for reading instruction.* Washington, DC: Author.

National Institute on Drug Abuse. (2005). *Research Report Series: Marijuana Abuse.* Retrieved from http://www.drugabuse.gov/ResearchReports/Marijuana/default.html

National Institute on Drug Abuse. (2009). *Are there effective treatments for tobacco addiction?* Retrieved from http://www.nida.nih.gov/ResearchReports/Nicotine/treatment.html

National Library of Medicine. (2013). *Home reference handbook: Help me understand genetics.* Retrieved from http://ghr.nlm.nih.gov/handbook

National Middle School Association. (2003). *This we believe: Successful schools for young adolescents.* Westerville, OH: Author.

National Parkinson Foundation. (2008). *About Parkinson's Disease.* Retrieved from http://www.parkinson.org

National Survey of Children's Health. (2014). *Weight Status: Data query from the Child and Adolescent Health Measurement Initiative NSCH 2007 Resource Center for Child and Adolescent Health website.* Retrieved from http://www.childhealthdata.org/browse/survey/results?q=226

Natsuaki, M. N., Biehl, M. C., Ge., X., & Xiaojia, G. (2009). Trajectories of depressed mood from early adolescence to young adulthood: The effects of pubertal timing and adolescent dating. *Journal of Research on Adolescence, 19*(1), 47–74. http://doi.org/10.1111/j.1532-7795.2009.00581.x

Neberich, W., Penke, L., Lehnart, J., & Asendorpf, J. B. (2010). Family of origin, age at menarche, and reproductive strategies: A test of four evolutionary-developmental models. *European Journal of Developmental Psychology, 7*(2), 153–177. http://doi.org/10.1080/17405620801928029

Negriff, S., & Susman, E. J. (2011). Pubertal timing, depression, and externalizing problems: A framework, review, and examination of gender differences. *Journal of Research on Adolescence, 21*(3), 717–746. http://doi.org/10.1111/j.1532-7795.2010.00708.x

Neisser, U. (1993). *The perceived self: Ecological and interpersonal sources of self-knowledge.* New York, NY: Cambridge University Press.

Neisser, U. (1998). *The rising curve: Long-term gains in IQ and related measures.* Washington, DC: American Psychological Association. http://doi.org/10.1037/10270-000

Neisser, U., Boodoo, G., Bouchard Jr., T. J., Boykin, A. W., Brody, N., Ceci, S. J., . . . et al. (1996). Intelligence: Knowns and unknowns. *American Psychologist, 51*(2), 77–101.

Nelson, C. A. (2011). Neural development and lifelong plasticity. In D. P. Keating (Ed.), *Nature and nurture in early child development* (pp. 45–69). New York, NY: Cambridge University Press.

Nelson, C. A., & Bloom, F. E. (1997). Child development and neuroscience. *Child Development, 69,* 970–987.

Nelson, C. A., & Luciana, M. (2008). *Handbook of developmental cognitive neuroscience* (2nd ed.). Cambridge: MIT Press.

Nelson, C. A., Thomas, K. M., & de Haan, M. (2006). *Neuroscience of cognitive development: The role of experience and the developing brain.* Hoboken, NJ: Wiley.

Nelson, E. L., Campbell, J. M., & Michel, G. F. (2013). Unimanual to bimanual: Tracking the development of handedness from 6 to 24 months. *Infant Behavior & Development, 36*(2), 181–188. http://doi.org/10.1016/j.infbeh.2013.01.009

Nelson, E. L., Campbell, J. M., & Michel, G. F. (2015). Early handedness in infancy predicts language stability in toddlers. *Developmental Psychology, 50*(3), 809–814. http://doi.org/10.1037/a0033803.

Nelson, H. D. (2008). Menopause. *Lancet, 371*(9614), 760–770.

Nelson, H. D., Humphrey, L. L., LeBlanc, E., Miller, J., Takano, L., Chan, B. K. S., . . . Teutsch, S. M. (2002). *Postmenopausal hormone replacement therapy for primary prevention of chronic conditions: Summary of the evidence for the U.S. Preventive Services Task Force.* Rockville, MD: Agency for Healthcare Research and Quality.

Nelson, J. M., & Nelson, T. C. (2014). Advance directives: Empowering patients at the end of life. *The Nurse Practitioner, 39*(11), 34–40. http://doi.org/10.1097/01.NPR.0000454979.98327.89

Nelson, K. (1993). The psychological and social origins of autobiographical memory. *Psychological Science, 4,* 1–8.

Nelson, K., & Fivush, R. (2004). The emergence of autobiographical memory: A social cultural developmental theory. *Psychological Review, 111*(2), 486–511. http://doi.org/10.1037/0033-295X.111.2.486

Nelson, L. H., White, K. R., & Grewe, J. (2012). Evidence for website claims about the benefits of teaching sign language to infants and toddlers with normal hearing. *Infant and Child Development, 21*(5), 474–502. http://doi.org/10.1002/icd.1748

Nelson, L. J. (2009). An examination of emerging adulthood in Romanian college students. *International Journal of Behavioral Development, 33*(5), 402–411. http://doi.org/10.1177/0165025409340093

Nelson, L. J., & Barry, C. M. (2005). Distinguishing features of emerging adulthood: The role of self-classification as an adult. *Journal of Adolescent Research, 90,* 242–262.

Nelson, L. J., Badger, S., & Wu, B. (2004). The influence of culture in emerging adulthood: Perspectives of Chinese college students. *International Journal of Behavioral Development, 28,* 26–36.

Nelson, R. M., & DeBacker, T. K. (2008). Achievement motivation in adolescents: The role of peer climate and best friends. *The Journal of Experimental Education, 76*(2), 170–189. http://doi.org/10.3200/JEXE.76.2.170-190

Nelson, S. K., Kushlev, K., & Lyubomirsky, S. (2014). The pains and pleasures of parenting: When, why, and how is parenthood associated with more or less well-being? *Psychological Bulletin, 140*(3), 846–895. http://doi.org/10.1037/a0035444

Nelson, T. J., & Alkon, D. L. (2015). Molecular regulation of synaptogenesis during associative learning and memory. *Brain Research, 1621,* 239–251. http://doi.org/10.1016/j.brainres.2014.11.054

Nerini, A., Matera, C., & Stefanile, C. (2014). Psychosocial predictors in consideration of cosmetic surgery among women. *Aesthetic Plastic Surgery, 38*(2), 461–466. http://doi.org/10.1007/s00266-014-0294-6

Nese, R. N. T., Horner, R. H., Dickey, C. R., Stiller, B., & Tomlanovich, A. (2014). Decreasing bullying behaviors in middle school: Expect respect. *School Psychology Quarterly, 29*(3), 272–286.

Neubauer, A. C., & Fink, A. (2009). Intelligence and neural efficiency. *Neuroscience & Biobehavioral Reviews, 33*(7), 1004–1023. http://doi.org/10.1016/j.neubiorev.2009.04.001

Neubauer, A. C., Fink, A., & Schrausser, D. G. (2002). Intelligence and neural efficiency: The influence of task content and sex on the brain–IQ relationship. *Intelligence, 30*(6), 515–536. http://doi.org/10.1016/S0160-2896(02)00091-0

Neuberger, F. S., & Haberkern, K. (2013). Structured ambivalence in grandchild care and the quality of life among European grandparents. *European Journal of Ageing, 11*(2), 171–181. http://doi.org/10.1007/s10433-013-0294-4

Neufang, S., Specht, K., Hausmann, M., Gunturkun, O., Herpertz-Dahlmann, B., Fink, G. R., & Konrad, K. (2009). Sex differences and the impact of steroid hormones on the developing human brain. *Cerebral Cortex, 19*(2), 464–473. https://doi.org/10.1093/cercor/bhn100

Neuman, S. B., Kaefer, T., Pinkham, A., & Strouse, G. (2014). Can babies learn to read? A randomized trial of baby media. *Journal of Educational Psychology.*

Neumark-Sztainer, D., Sherwood, N. E., Coller, T., & Hannan, P. J. (2000). Primary prevention of disordered eating among preadolescent girls: Feasibility and short-term effect of a community-based intervention. *Journal of the American Dietetic Association, 100*(12), 1466–73. http://doi.org/10.1016/S0002-8223(00)00410-7

Neville, H. J., & Bavelier, D. (2001). Variability of developmental plasticity: Carnegie Mellon symposia on cognition. In J. L. McClelland & R. S. Siegler (Eds.), *Mechanisms of cognitive development: Behavioral and neural perspectives* (pp. 271–301). Mahwah, NJ: Erlbaum.

Newcombe, N., & Huttenlocher, J. (1992). Children's early ability to solve perspective-taking problems. *Developmental Psychology, 28,* 635–643.

Newell, F. N. (2004). Cross-modal object recognition. In G. A. Calvert, C. Spence, & B. E. Stein (Eds.), *The handbook of multisensory processes* (pp. 123–139). Cambridge, MA: MIT Press.

Newell, K. M., Vaillancourt, D. E., & Sosnoff, J. (2006). Aging, complexity, and motor performance. In J. E. Birren & K. W. Schaire (Eds.), *Handbook of the psychology of aging* (6th ed.). (pp. 163–182). Amsterdam, Netherlands: Elsevier.

Newport, F. (2006). *Religion most important to blacks, women, and older Americans: Gallup Poll.* Retrieved from http://www.gallup.com/poll/25585/Religion-Most-Important-Blacks-Women-Older-Americans.aspx

Newson, R. S., & Kemps, E. B. (2008). Relationship between fitness and cognitive performance in younger and older adults. *Psychology & Health, 23*(3), 369–386. http://doi.org/10.1080/08870440701421545

Newton, E. K., Laible, D., Carlo, G., Steele, J. S., & McGinley, M. (2014). Do sensitive parents foster kind children, or vice versa? Bidirectional influences between children's prosocial behavior and parental sensitivity. *Developmental Psychology, 50*(6), 1808–16. http://doi.org/10.1037/a0036495

Newton, E., & Jenvey, V. (2011). Play and theory of mind: Associations with social competence in young children. *Early Child Development & Care, 181*(6), 761–773. http://doi.org/10.1080/03004430.2010.486898

Newton, N., & Stewart, A. J. (2010). The middle ages: Change in women's personalities and social roles. *Psychology of Women Quarterly, 34*(1), 75–84. http://doi.org/10.1111/j.1471-6402.2009.01543.x

Ng, F. F.-Y., Pomerantz, E. M., & Lam, S. (2007). European American and Chinese parents' responses to children's success and failure: Implications for children's responses. *Developmental Psychology, 43*(5), 1239–1255. http://doi.org/10.1037/0012-1649.43.5.1239

Ng, T. W. H., & Feldman, D. C. (2010). The relationships of age with job attitudes: A meta-analysis. *Personnel Psychology, 63*(3), 677–718. http://doi.org/10.1111/j.1744-6570.2010.01184.x

Nguyen, S. P., & Rosengren, K. S. (2004). Parental reports of children's biological knowledge and misconceptions. *International Journal of Behavioral Development, 28*(5), 411–420. http://doi.org/10.1080/01650250444000108

NHL Public Relations. (2016). *NHL updates concussion protocol.* Retrieved from https://www.nhl.com/news/nhl-updates-concussion-protocol/c-282571624

NICHD Early Child Care Research Network. (2005). Early child care and children's development in the primary grades: Follow-up results from the NICHD Study of Early Child Care. *American Educational Research Journal, 42*(3), 537–570. http://doi.org/10.3102/00028312042003537

Nichols, W. C., & Pace-Nichols, M. A. (2000). Childless married couples. In W. C. Nichols, M. A. Pace-Nichols, D. S. Becvar, & A. Y. Napier (Eds.), *Handbook of family development and intervention* (pp. 171–188). Hoboken, NJ: John Wiley & Sons.

Nickels, S., Truong, T., Hein, R., Stevens, K., Buck, K., Behrens, S., . . . Chang-Claude, J. (2013). Evidence of gene-environment interactions between common breast cancer susceptibility loci and established environmental risk factors. *PLoS Genetics, 9*(3), e1003284. http://doi.org/10.1371/journal.pgen.1003284

Nicklas, J. M., Huskey, K. W., Davis, R. B., & Wee, C. C. (2012). Successful weight loss among obese U.S. adults. *American Journal of Preventive Medicine* (Vol. 42).

Nicklaus, S. (2009). Development of food variety in children. *Appetite, 52*(1), 253–255. http://doi.org/10.1016/j.appet.2008.09.018

Nicolosi, A., Buvat, J., Glasser, D. B., Hartmann, U., Laumann & E. W., & Gingell, C. (2006). Sexual behaviour, sexual dysfunctions and related help seeking patterns in middle-aged and elderly Europeans: The global study of sexual attitudes and behaviors. *World Journal of Urology, 24*, 423–428.

Niemann, C., Godde, B., & Voelcker-Rehage, C. (2014). Not only cardiovascular, but also coordinative exercise increases hippocampal volume in older adults. *Frontiers in Aging Neuroscience, 6*, 170. http://doi.org/10.3389/fnagi.2014.00170

NIH Osteoporosis and Related Bone Diseases National Resource Center. (2007). *Osteoporosis.* Retrieved from http://www.niams.nih.gov/Health_Info/Bone/Osteoporosis/default.asp

Nikulina, V., Widom, C. S., & Brzustowicz, L. M. (2012). Child abuse and neglect, MAOA, and mental

health outcomes: A prospective examination. *Biological Psychiatry, 71*(4), 350–357. http://doi.org/10.1016/j.biopsych.2011.09.008

Nilsson, J., Thomas, A. J., O'Brien, J. T., & Gallagher, P. (2014). White matter and cognitive decline in aging: A focus on processing speed and variability. *Journal of the International Neuropsychological Society, 20*(3), 262–267. http://doi.org/10.1017/S1355617713001458

Niolon, P. H., Vivolo-Kantor, A. M., Latzman, N. E., Valle, L. A., Kuoh, H., Burton, T., . . . Tharp, A. T. (2015). Prevalence of teen dating violence and co-occurring risk factors among middle school youth in high-risk urban communities. *Journal of Adolescent Health, 56*(2), S5–S13. http://doi.org/10.1016/j.jadohealth.2014.07.019

Nippold, M. A., Taylor, C. L., & Baker, J. M. (1996). Idiom understanding in Australian youth: A cross-cultural comparison. *Journal of Speech and Hearing Research, 39*, 442–447.

Nisan, M., & Kohlberg, L. (1982). Universality and variation in moral judgment: A longitudinal and cross-sectional study in Turkey. *Child Development, 53*(4), 865–877.

Nisbett, R. E., Aronson, J., Blair, C., Dickens, W., Flynn, J., Halpern, D. F., & Turkheimer, E. (2013). Intelligence: New findings and theoretical developments. *American Psychologist, 67*(2), 130–159. http://doi.org/10.1037/a0026699

Nisbett, R. E., & Miyamoto, Y. (2005). The influence of culture: Holistic versus analytic perception. *Trends in Cognitive Sciences, 9*(10), 467–473. http://doi.org/10.1016/j.tics.2005.08.004

Nisbett, R. E., Peng, K., Choi, I., & Norenzayan, A. (2001). Culture and systems of thought: Holistic versus analytic cognition. *Psychological Review, 108*(2), 291–310. http://doi.org/10.1037/0033-295X.108.2.291

Nishitani, S., Miyamura, T., Tagawa, M., Sumi, M., Takase, R., Doi, H., . . . Shinohara, K. (2009). The calming effect of a maternal breast milk odor on the human newborn infant. *Neuroscience Research, 63*(1), 66–71. http://doi.org/10.1016/j.neures.2008.10.007

Nishiyori, R., Bisconti, S., Meehan, S. K., & Ulrich, B. D. (2016). Developmental changes in motor cortex activity as infants develop functional motor skills. *Developmental Psychobiology, 58*(6), 773–783. http://doi.org/10.1002/dev.21418

Nithianantharajah, J., & Hannan, A. J. (2009). The neurobiology of brain and cognitive reserve: Mental and physical activity as modulators of brain disorders. *Progress in Neurobiology, 89*(4), 369–382. http://doi.org/10.1016/j.pneurobio.2009.10.001

Nobes, G., & Pawson, C. (2003). Children's understanding of social rules and social status. *Merrill-Palmer Quarterly, 49*, 77–99.

Noble, K. G., Houston, S. M., Brito, N. H., Bartsch, H., Kan, E., Kuperman, J. M., . . . Sowell, E. R. (2015). Family income, parental education and brain structure in children and adolescents. *Nature Neuroscience, 18*(5), 773–778. https://doi.org/10.1038/nn.3983

Noone, J. H., Stephens, C., & Alpass, F. M. (2009). Preretirement planning and well-being in later life: A prospective study. *Research on Aging, 31*(3), 295–317.

Noppe, I. C., & Noppe, L. D. (2004). Adolescent experiences with death: Letting go of immortality. *Journal of Mental Health Counseling, 26*(2), 146–167. http://doi.org/10.17744/mehc.26.2.py2tk0kmay1ukc3v

Noppe, L. D., & Noppe, I. C. (1991a). Dialectical themes in adolescent conceptions of death. *Journal of Adolescent Research, 6*(1), 28–42. http://doi.org/10.1177/074355489161003

Nordin, S. M., Harris, G., & Cumming, J. (2003). Disturbed eating in young, competitive gymnasts: Differences between three gymnastics disciplines. *European Journal of Sport Science, 3*(5), 1–14.

Nordstrom-Klee, B., Delaney-Black, V., Covington, C., Ager, J., & Sokol, R. (2002). Growth from birth onwards of children prenatally exposed to drugs: A literature review. *Neurotoxicology & Teratology, 24*(4), 481–488.

Norman, R. (2008). Reproductive changes in the female lifespan. In J. J. Robert-McComb, R. Norman, & M. Zumwalt (Eds.), *The active female: Health issues throughout the lifespan* (pp. 17–24). Totowa, NJ: Humana Press.

Northern, J. L., & Downs, M. (2014). *Hearing in children* (6th ed.). San Diego, CA: Plural.

Northoff, G., & Hayes, D. J. (2011). Is our self nothing but reward? *Biological Psychiatry, 69*(11), 1019–25. https://doi.org/10.1016/j.biopsych.2010.12.014

Nosek, M., Kennedy, H. P., & Gudmundsdottir, M. (2012). Distress during the menopause transition: A rich contextual analysis of midlife women's narratives. *SAGE Open, 2*(3). http://doi.org/10.1177/2158244012455178

Nourot, P. M. (1998). Sociodramatic play: Pretending together. In D. P. Fromberg & D. Bergen (Eds.), *Play from birth to twelve and beyond: Contexts, perspectives, and meanings* (pp. 378–391). New York, NY: Garland.

Nowakowski, R. S. (1987). Basic concepts of CNS development. *Child Development, 58*, 595–598.

Nowicka, P., & Flodmark, C.-E. (2007). Physical activity: Key issues in treatment of childhood obesity. *Acta Paediatrica, 96*, 39–45.

NPD Group. (2011). *Kids and gaming, 2011.* Port Washington, NY: Author.

Nucci, L. P. (1996). Morality and the personal sphere of action. In E. Reed, E. Turiel, & T. Brown (Eds.), *Values and knowledge* (pp. 41–60). Hillsdale, NJ: Lawrence Erlbaum.

Nucci, L. P. (2001). *Education in the moral domain.* Cambridge, UK: Cambridge University Press.

Nucci, L. P., & Turiel, E. (1978). Social interactions and the development of social concepts in preschool children. *Child Development, 49*(2), 400–407.

Nugent, B. M., & McCarthy, M. M. (2011). Epigenetic underpinnings of developmental sex differences in the brain. *Neuroendocrinology, 93*(3), 150–158. http://doi.org/10.1159/000325264

Nunnally, J. C. (1975). Psychometric theory: 25 years ago and now. *Educational Researcher, 4*(10), 7. http://doi.org/10.2307/1175619

Nurkkala, M., Kaikkonen, K., Vanhala, M. L., Karhunen, L., Keränen, A.-M., & Korpelainen, R. (2015). Lifestyle intervention has a beneficial effect on eating behavior and long-term weight loss in obese adults. *Eating Behaviors, 18*, 179–185. http://doi.org/10.1016/j.eatbeh.2015.05.009

Nurmi, J.-E. (1991). How do adolescents see their future? A review of the development of future orientation and planning. *Developmental Review, 11*(1), 1–59.

Nurmi, J.-E. (2004). Socialization and self-development: Channeling, selection, adjustment, and reflection. In R. M. Lerner & L. Steinberg (Eds.), *Handbook of adolescent psychology* (2nd ed., pp. 85–124). Hoboken, NJ: John Wiley & Sons.

Nussbaumer, D., Grabner, R. H., & Stern, E. (2015). Neural efficiency in working memory tasks: The impact of task demand. *Intelligence, 50*, 196–208. http://doi.org/10.1016/j.intell.2015.04.004

Nuttall, A. K., Valentino, K., Comas, M., McNeill, A. T., & Stey, P. C. (2014). Autobiographical memory specificity among preschool-aged children. *Developmental Psychology, 50*(7), 1963–1972.

Nyiti, R. M. (1982). The validity of "cultural differences explanations" for cross-cultural variation in the rate of Piagetian cognitive development. In H. W. Stevenson & D. A. Wagner (Eds.), *Cultural perspectives on child development* (pp. 146–166). San Francisco: W. H. Freeman.

O'Brennan, L. M., Bradshaw, C. P., & Sawyer, A. L. (2009). Examining developmental differences in the social-emotional problems among frequent bullies, victims, and bully/victims. *Psychology in the Schools, 46*(2), 100–115.

O'Brien, E., Konrath, S. H., Grühn, D., & Hagen, A. L. (2013). Empathic concern and perspective taking: linear and quadratic effects of age across the adult life span. *The Journals of Gerontology. Series B, Psychological Sciences and Social Sciences, 68*(2), 168–175. http://doi.org/10.1093/geronb/gbs055

O'Brien, J. T., & Thomas, A. (2015). Vascular dementia. *Lancet, 386*(10004), 1698–1706. http://doi.org/10.1016/S0140-6736(15)00463-8

O'Conner-Von, S., & Turner, H. N. (2013). American Society for Pain Management Nursing (ASPMN) position statement: Male infant circumcision pain management. *Pain Management Nursing, 14*(4), 379–382. http://doi.org/10.1016/j.pmn.2011.08.007

O'Doherty, K., Troseth, G. L., Shimpi, P. M., Goldenberg, E., Akhtar, N., & Saylor, M. M. (2011). Third-party social interaction and word learning from video. *Child Development, 82*(3), 902–915. http://doi.org/10.1111/j.1467-8624.2011.01579.x

O'Halloran, C. M., & Altmaier, E. M. (1996). Awareness of death among children: Does a life-threatening illness alter the process of discovery? *Journal of Counseling & Development, 74*(3), 259–262. http://doi.org/10.1002/j.1556-6676.1996.tb01862.x

O'Hara, M. W., & McCabe, J. E. (2013). Postpartum depression: Current status and future directions. *Annual Review of Clinical Psychology, 9*, 379–407. http://doi.org/10.1146/annurev-clinpsy-050212-185612

O'Leary, C. M., & Bower, C. (2012). Guidelines for pregnancy: What's an acceptable risk, and how is the evidence (finally) shaping up? *Drug and Alcohol Review, 31*(2), 170–183. http://doi.org/10.1111/j.1465-3362.2011.00331.x

O'Leary, C., Leonard, H., Bourke, J., D'Antoine, H., Bartu, A., & Bower, C. (2013). Intellectual disability: Population-based estimates of the proportion attributable to maternal alcohol use disorder during pregnancy. *Developmental Medicine & Child Neurology, 55*(3), 271–277. http://doi.org/10.1111/dmcn.12029

O'Rourke, N., Cappeliez, P., & Claxton, A. (2011). Functions of reminiscence and the psychological well-being of young-old and older adults over time. *Aging & Mental Health, 15*(2), 272–281. http://doi.org/10.1080/13607861003713281

O'Rourke, N., King, D. B., & Cappeliez, P. (2016). Reminiscence functions over time: Consistency of self functions and variation of prosocial functions. *Memory*, 1–9. http://doi.org/10.1080/09658211.2016.1179331

O'Sullivan, L. F., Cheng, M. M., Harris, K. M., & Brooks-Gunn, J. (2007). I wanna hold your hand: The progression of social, romantic and sexual events in adolescent relationships. *Perspectives on Sexual & Reproductive Health, 39*(2), 100–107. http://doi.org/10.1363/3910007

Oakes, L. M. (2010). Using habituation of looking time to assess mental processes in infancy. *Journal of Cognition & Development, 11*(3), 255–268. http://doi.org/10.1080/15248371003699977

Oakes, L. M., Coppage, D. J., & Dingel, A. (1997). By land or by sea: The role of perceptual similarity in infants' categorization of animals. *Developmental Psychology, 33*, 396–407.

Oakes, L. M., & Madole, K. L. (2003). Principles of developmental change in infants' category formation. In D. H. Rakison & L. M. Oakes (Eds.), *Early category and concept development: Making sense of the blooming, buzzing confusion* (pp. 132–158). New York, NY: Oxford University Press.

Obeidallah, D. A., Brennan, R. T., Brooks-Gunn, J., Kindlon, D., & Earls, F. (2000). Socioeconomic status, race, and girls' pubertal maturation: Results from the project on human development in Chicago neighborhoods. *Journal of Research on Adolescence, 10*(4), 443–464.

Obeidallah, D., Brennan, R. T., Brooks-Gunn, J., & Earls, F. (2004). Links between pubertal timing and neighborhood contexts: Implications for girls' violent behavior. *Journal of the American Academy of Child & Adolescent Psychiatry, 43*(12), 1460–1468.

Oberlander, S. E., Black, M. M., & Starr, J. R. H. (2007). African American adolescent mothers and grandmothers: A multigenerational approach to parenting. *American Journal of Community Psychology, 39*(1/2), 37–46. http://doi.org/10.1007/s10464-007-9087-2

Obernier, K., Tong, C. K., & Alvarez-Buylla, A. (2014). Restricted nature of adult neural stem cells: Re-evaluation of their potential for brain repair. *Frontiers in Neuroscience, 8*, 162. http://doi.org/10.3389/fnins.2014.00162

Ochs, E., & Izquierdo, C. (2009). Responsibility in childhood: Three developmental trajectories. *Ethos, 37*(4), 391–413. http://doi.org/10.1111/j.1548-1352.2009.01066.x

Ochs, E., & Schieffein, B. (1984). Language acquisition and socialization: Three developmental stories and their implications. In R. A. L. Shweder (Ed.), *Culture theory: Essays on mind, self, and emotion* (pp. 276–320). Cambridge, UK: Cambridge University Press.

Oddi, K. B., Murdock, K. W., Vadnais, S., Bridgett, D. J., & Gartstein, M. A. (2013). Maternal and infant temperament characteristics as contributors to parenting stress in the first year postpartum. *Infant and Child Development, 22*(6), 553–579. http://doi.org/10.1002/icd.1813

Odibo, A. O. (2015). Amniocentesis, chorionic villus sampling, and fetal blood sampling. In *Genetic disorders and the fetus* (pp. 68–97). Hoboken, NJ: John Wiley & Sons. http://doi.org/10.1002/9781118981559.ch2

Offer, D., Ostrov, E., Howard, K. I., & Atkinson, R. (1988). *The teenage world: Adolescents' self-image in ten countries* (Vol. 11). New York, NY: Springer Science & Business Media.

Office for National Statistics. (2014). *Death registrations summary tables, England and Wales, 2013*. Retrieved from http://www.ons.gov.uk/ons/rel/vsob1/death-reg-sum-tables/2013/sty-mortality-rates-by-age.html

Office for National Statistics. (2015). *What are the top causes of death by age and gender?* Retrieved from http://visual.ons.gov.uk/what-are-the-top-causes-of-death-by-age-and-gender/

Office of Juvenile Justice and Delinquency Prevention. (2014). *Statistical briefing book.* Retrieved from http://www.ojjdp.gov/ojstatbb/

Office of the Surgeon General. (2016). *A report of the Surgeon General: Executive summary.* Atlanta, GA: Author.

Ogolsky, B. G., Dennison, R. P., & Monk, J. K. (2014). The role of couple discrepancies in cognitive and behavioral egalitarianism in marital quality. *Sex Roles, 70*(7–8), 329–342. http://doi.org/10.1007/s11199-014-0365-9

Oh, J. S., & Fuligni, A. J. (2010). The role of heritage language development in the ethnic identity and family relationships of adolescents from immigrant backgrounds. *Social Development, 19*(1), 202–220. http://doi.org/10.1111/j.1467-9507.2008.00530.x

Oh, W., Rubin, K. H., Bowker, J. C., Booth-LaForce, C., Rose-Krasno, L., & Laursen, B. (2008). Trajectories of social withdrawal from middle childhood to early adolescence. *Journal of Abnormal Child Psychology, 36*(4), 553–566. http://doi.org/10.1007/s10802-007-9199-z

Ojalehto, B. L., & Medin, D. (2015a). Emerging trends in culture and concepts. In R. A. Scott & M. C. Buchmann (Ed.), *Emerging trends in the social and behavioral sciences* (pp. 1–15). Hoboken, NJ: John Wiley & Sons.

Ojalehto, B. L., & Medin, D. L. (2015b). Perspectives on culture and concepts. *Annual Review of Psychology, 66*(1), 249–275. http://doi.org/10.1146/annurev-psych-010814-015120

Ojeda, L., Navarro, R. L., & Morales, A. (2011). The role of la familia on Mexican American men's college persistence intentions. *Psychology of Men & Masculinity, 12*(3), 216–229. http://doi.org/10.1037/a0020091

Ojodu, J., Hulihan, M. M., Pope, S. N., & Grant, A. M. (2014). Incidence of sickle cell trait — United States, 2010. *Morbidity and Mortality Weekly Report, 63*(49), 1155–1158. Retrieved from https://www.cdc.gov/mmwr/preview/mmwrhtml/mm6349a3.htm

Okagaki, L., & Sternberg, R. J. (1993). Parental beliefs and children's school performance. *Child Development, 64*, 36–56.

Okonkwo, O. C., Cohen, R. A., Gunstad, J., Tremont, G., Alosco, M. L., & Poppas, A. (2010). Longitudinal trajectories of cognitive decline among older adults with cardiovascular disease. *Cerebrovascular Diseases, 30*(4), 362–373. http://doi.org/10.1159/000319564

Oldenburg, B., van Duijn, M., Sentse, M., Huitsing, G., van der Ploeg, R., Salmivalli, C., & Veenstra, R. (2014). Teacher characteristics and peer victimization in elementary schools: A classroom-level perspective. *Journal of Abnormal Child Psychology.* http://doi.org/10.1007/s10802-013-9847-4

Oller, D. K., Eilers, R. E., & Basinger, D. (2001). Intuitive identification of infant vocal sounds by parents. *Developmental Science, 4*(1), 49–60.

Ollove, M. (2015). *More states consider "death with dignity" laws.* Retrieved from http://www.pewtrusts.org/en/research-and-analysis/blogs/stateline/2015/3/09/more-states-consider-death-with-dignity-laws

Olmstead, S. B., Conrad, K. A., & Anders, K. M. (2017). First-semester college students' definitions of and expectations for engaging in hookups. *Journal of Adolescent Research.* http://doi.org/10.1177/0743558417698571

Olsen, R. K., Pangelinan, M. M., Bogulski, C., Chakravarty, M. M., Luk, G., Grady, C. L., & Bialystok, E. (2015). The effect of lifelong bilingualism on regional grey and white matter volume. *Brain Research, 1612*, 128–139. http://doi.org/10.1016/j.brainres.2015.02.034

Olson, K. R., Durwood, L., DeMeules, M., & McLaughlin, K. A. (2016). Mental health of transgender children who are supported in their identities. *Pediatrics, 137*(3), e20153223. http://doi.org/10.1542/peds.2015-3223

Olson, K. R., Key, A. C., & Eaton, N. R. (2015). Gender cognition in transgender children. *Psychological Science, 26*(4), 467–474. http://doi.org/10.1177/0956797614568156

Olsson, B., Lautner, R., Andreasson, Uhrfelt, A., Portelius, E., Bjerke, M., . . . Zetterberg, H. (2016).

CSF and blood biomarkers for the diagnosis of Alzheimer's disease: A systematic review and meta-analysis. *The Lancet Neurology, 15*(7), 673–684. http://doi.org/10.1016/S1474-4422(16)00070-3

Olweus, D. (1995). Bullying or peer abuse at school: Facts and intervention. *Current Directions in Psychological Science, 4*, 196–200.

Olweus, D., & Limber, S. P. (2010). Bullying in school: Evaluation and dissemination of the Olweus Bullying Prevention Program. *American Journal of Orthopsychiatry, 80*(1), 124–134. http://doi.org/10.1111/j.1939-0025.2010.01015.x

Omar, H., McElderry, D., & Zakharia, R. (2003). Educating adolescents about puberty: What are we missing? *International Journal Of Adolescent Medicine And Health, 15*, 79–83.

Ongley, S. F., Nola, M., & Malti, T. (2014). Children's giving: Moral reasoning and moral emotions in the development of donation behaviors. *Frontiers in Psychology, 5*, 458. http://doi.org/10.3389/fpsyg.2014.00458

Onishi, K. H., & Baillargeon, R. (2005). Do 15-month-old infants understand false beliefs? *Science, 308*(5719), 255–258. http://doi.org/10.1126/science.1107621

Onrust, S. A., & Cuijpers, P. (2006). Mood and anxiety disorders in widowhood: A systematic review. *Aging & Mental Health, 10*(4), 327–334. http://doi.org/10.1080/13607860600638529

Opie, I., & Opie, P. (1969). *Children's games in street and playground: Chasing, catching, seeking, hunting, racing, dueling, exerting, daring, guessing, acting, and pretending.* Oxford, UK: Oxford University Press.

Opresko, P. L., & Shay, J. W. (2017). Telomere-associated aging disorders. *Ageing Research Reviews, 33*, 52–66. http://doi.org/10.1016/j.arr.2016.05.009

Orbe, M. P. (2008). Theorizing multidimensional identity negotiation: Reflections on the lived experiences of first-generation college students. *New Directions for Child & Adolescent Development, 2008*(120), 81–95.

Orchowski, L. M., Untied, A. S., & Gidycz, C. A. (2013). Social reactions to disclosure of sexual victimization and adjustment among survivors of sexual assault. *Journal of Interpersonal Violence, 28*(10), 2005–2023. http://doi.org/10.1177/0886260512471085

Oregon Public Health Division. (2016). *Oregon Death With Dignity Act: 2015 data summary.* Retrieved from https://public.health.oregon.gov/ProviderPartnerResources/EvaluationResearch/DeathwithDignityAct/Documents/year18.pdf

Orkin, M., May, S., & Wolf, M. (2017). How parental support during homework contributes to helpless behaviors among struggling readers. *Reading Psychology, 38*(5), 506–541. http://doi.org/10.1080/02702711.2017.1299822

Ormerod, T. C. (2005). Planning and ill-defined problems. In R. Morris & G. Ward (Eds.), *The cognitive psychology of planning.* London: Psychology Press.

Ornstein, P. A., & Light, L. L. (2010). Memory development across the life span. In W. F. Overton (Ed.), *The handbook of life-span development.* Hoboken, NJ: John Wiley & Sons. http://doi.org/10.1002/9780470880166.hlsd001009

Orth, U., Maes, J., & Schmitt, M. (2015). Self-esteem development across the life span: A longitudinal study with a large sample from Germany. *Developmental Psychology, 51*(2), 248–259.

Orth, U., & Robins, R. W. (2014). The development of self-esteem. *Current Directions in Psychological Science, 23*(5), 381–387. http://doi.org/10.1177/0963721414547414

Orth, U., Robins, R. W., & Widaman, K. F. (2012). Life-span development of self-esteem and its effects on important life outcomes. *Journal of Personality and Social Psychology, 102*(6), 1271–1288. http://doi.org/10.1037/a0025558

Orth, U., Trzesniewski, K. H., & Robins, R. W. (2010). Self-esteem development from young adulthood to old age: A cohort-sequential longitudinal study. *Journal of Personality and Social Psychology, 98*(4), 645–658. http://doi.org/10.1037/a0018769

Ortman, J. M., Velkoff, V. A., & Hogan, H. (2014). An aging nation: The older population in the United States. *Current Population Reports.* Retrieved from https://www.census.gov/prod/2014pubs/p25-1140.pdf

Ortolano, S., Mahmud, Z., Iqbal Kabir, A., & Levinson, F. (2003). Effect of targeted food supplementation and services in the Bangladesh Integrated Nutrition Project on women and their pregnancy outcomes. *Journal of Health, Population, and Nutrition, 21*(2), 83–89.

Orzano, A. J., & Scott, J. G. (2004). Diagnosis and treatment of obesity in adults: An applied evidence-based review. *The Journal of the American Board of Family Practice, 17*(5), 359–369.

Osborne, C., Manning, W. D., & Smock, P. J. (2007). Married and cohabiting parents' relationship stability: A focus on race and ethnicity. *Journal of Marriage & Family, 69*(5), 1345–1366.

Osgood, D. W., Ragan, D. T., Wallace, L., Gest, S. D., Feinberg, M. E., & Moody, J. (2013). Peers and the emergence of alcohol use: Influence and selection processes in adolescent friendship networks. *Journal of Research on Adolescence, 23*(3). http://doi.org/10.1111/jora.12059

Osorio, A., Fay, S., Pouthas, V., & Ballesteros, S. (2010). Ageing affects brain activity in highly educated older adults: An ERP study using a word-stem priming task. *Cortex: A Journal Devoted to the Study of the Nervous System and Behavior, 46*(4), 522–534. http://doi.org/10.1016/j.cortex.2009.09.003

Ossher, L., Flegal, K. E., & Lustig, C. (2013). Everyday memory errors in older adults. *Neuropsychology and Cognition, 20*(2), 220–242. http://doi.org/10.1080/13825585.2012.690365

Ostrov, J. M., & Godleski, S. A. (2010). Toward an integrated gender-linked model of aggression subtypes in early and middle childhood. *Psychological Review, 117*(1), 233–242. http://doi.org/10.1037/a0018070

Otter, M., Schrander-Stumpel, C. T. R. M., & Curfs, L. M. G. (2009). Triple X syndrome: A review of the literature. *European Journal of Human Genetics, 18*(3), 265–271. http://doi.org/10.1038/ejhg.2009.109

Ottoni-Wilhelm, M., Estell, D. B., & Perdue, N. H. (2014). Role-modeling and conversations about giving in the socialization of adolescent charitable giving and volunteering. *Journal of Adolescence, 37*(1), 53–66. http://doi.org/10.1016/j.adolescence.2013.10.010

Oveisi, S., Eftekhare Ardabili, H., Majdzadeh R., Mohammadkhani, P., Alaqband Rad, J., & Loo, J. (2010). Mothers' attitudes toward corporal punishment of children in Qazvin-Iran. *Journal of Family Violence, 25*(2), 159–164. http://doi.org/10.1007/s10896-009-9279-7

Owen, J., & Fincham, F. D. (2011). Young adults' emotional reactions after hooking up encounters. *Archives of Sexual Behavior, 40*(2), 321–330. http://doi.org/10.1007/s10508-010-9652-x

Owens, J. A., Belon, K., & Moss, P. (2010). Impact of delaying school start time on adolescent sleep, mood, and behavior. *Archives of Pediatrics & Adolescent Medicine, 164*(7), 608–614. http://doi.org/10.1001/archpediatrics.2010.96

Owens, R. E. (2015). *Language development: An introduction.* Boston, MA: Pearson.

Owings, M., Uddin, S., & Williams, S. (2013). Trends in circumcision among male newborns born in U.S. hospitals: 1979–2010. *NCHS Health E-Stat.* Retrieved from http://www.cdc.gov/nchs/data/hestat/circumcision_2013/circumcision_2013.htm

Owsley, C. (2011). Aging and vision. *Vision Research, 51*(13), 1610–1622. http://doi.org/10.1016/j.visres.2010.10.020

Owsley, C. (2016). Vision and aging. *Annual Review of Vision Science, 2*(1), 255–271. http://doi.org/10.1146/annurev-vision-111815-114550

Owsley, C., McGwin, G., Jackson, G. R., Kallies, K., & Clark, M. (2007). Cone- and rod-mediated dark adaptation impairment in age-related maculopathy. *Ophthalmology, 114*(9), 1728–1735.

Oxford, M. L., Gilchrist, L. D., Lohr, M. J., Gillmore, M. R., Morrison, D. M., & Spieker, S. J. (2005). Life course heterogeneity in the transition from adolescence to adulthood among adolescent mothers. *Journal of Research on Adolescence, 15*(4), 479–504.

Pachucki, M. C., & Goodman, E. (2015). Social relationships and obesity: Benefits of incorporating a lifecourse perspective. *Current Obesity Reports.* http://doi.org/10.1007/s13679-015-0145-z

Pacula, R. L., Powell, D., Heaton, P., & Sevigny, E. L. (2015). Assessing the effects of medical marijuana laws on marijuana use: The devil is in the details. *Journal of Policy Analysis and Management, 34*(1), 7–31. Retrieved from http://www.ncbi.nlm.nih.gov/pubmed/25558490

Padmanabhan, A., & Luna, B. (2014). Developmental imaging genetics: Linking dopamine function to adolescent behavior. *Brain and Cognition, 89*, 27–38. http://doi.org/10.1016/j.bandc.2013.09.011

Paillard, T., Rolland, Y., de Souto Barreto, P., Kalil-Gaspar, P., Marcuzzo, S., & Achaval, M. (2015). Protective effects of physical exercise in Alzheimer's disease and Parkinson's disease: A narrative review. *Journal of Clinical Neurology, 11*(3), 212. http://doi.org/10.3988/jcn.2015.11.3.212

Paix, B. R., & Peterson, S. E. (2012). Circumcision of neonates and children without appropriate anaesthesia is unacceptable practice. *Anaesthesia & Intensive Care, 40*(3).

Palacios, J., Román, M., Moreno, C., León, E., & Peñarrubia, M.-G. (2014). Differential plasticity in the recovery of adopted children after early adversity. *Child Development Perspectives, 8*(3), 169–174. http://doi.org/10.1111/cdep.12083

Palacios-Ceña, D., Carrasco-Garrido, P., Hernández-Barrera, V., Alonso-Blanco, C., Jiménez-García, R., & Fernández-de-las-Peñas, C. (2012). Sexual behaviors among older adults in Spain: Results from a population-based national sexual health survey. *The Journal of Sexual Medicine, 9*(1), 121–129. http://doi.org/10.1111/j.1743-6109.2011.02511.x

Palamar, J. J., Griffin-Tomas, M., & Kamboukos, D. (2015). Reasons for recent marijuana use in relation to use of other illicit drugs among high school seniors in the United States. *The American Journal of Drug and Alcohol Abuse, 41*(4), 323–331. http://doi.org/10.3109/00952990.2015.1045977

Palmer, A. (2003). Growth failure is important factor in the survival rate of HIV-infected children. *HIV Clinician, 15*(2), 1–4.

Palta, P., Schneider, A. L. C., Biessels, G. J., Touradji, P., & Hill-Briggs, F. (2014). Magnitude of cognitive dysfunction in adults with type 2 diabetes: A meta-analysis of six cognitive domains and the most frequently reported neuropsychological tests within domains. *Journal of the International Neuropsychological Society, 20*(3), 278–291. http://doi.org/10.1017/S1355617713001483

Panagiotaki, G., Nobes, G., Ashraf, A., & Aubby, H. (2015). British and Pakistani children's understanding of death: Cultural and developmental influences. *British Journal of Developmental Psychology, 33*(1), 31–44. http://doi.org/10.1111/bjdp.12064

Panay, N., Hamoda, H., Arya, R., & Savvas, M. (2013). The 2013 British Menopause Society & Women's Health Concern recommendations on hormone replacement therapy. *Menopause International, 19*(2), 59–68. http://doi.org/10.1177/1754045313489645

Panula, J., Pihlajamäki, H., Mattila, V. M., Jaatinen, P., Vahlberg, T., Aarnio, P., & Kivelä, S. L. (2011). Mortality and cause of death in hip fracture patients aged 65 or older: A population-based study. *BMC Musculoskeletal Disorders, 12*(1).

Panza, F., Solfrizzi, V., & Capurso, A. (2004). *Diet and cognitive decline*. Hauppauge, NY: Nova Science.

Papadimitriou, A. (2016). Timing of puberty and secular trend in human maturation. In P. Kumanov & A. Agarwal (Eds.), *Puberty* (pp. 121–136). Geneva, CH: Springer International. http://doi.org/10.1007/978-3-319-32122-6_9

Papoušek, M., & Papoušek, H. (1990). Excessive infant crying and intuitive parental care: Buffering support and its failures in parent-infant interaction. *Early Child Development and Care, 65*, 117–126. http://doi.org/10.1080/0300443900650114

Paradise, R., & Rogoff, B. (2009). Side by side: Learning by observing and pitching in. *Ethos, 37*(1), 102–138. http://doi.org/10.1111/j.1548-1352.2009.01033.x

Paramei, G. V., & Oakley, B. (2014). Variation of color discrimination across the life span. *Journal of the Optical Society of America, 31*(4), 375-384. http://doi.org/10.1364/JOSAA.31.00A375

Park, C. J., Yelland, G. W., Taffe, J. R., & Gray, K. M. (2012). Brief report: The relationship between language skills, adaptive behavior, and emotional and behavior problems in pre-schoolers with autism. *Journal of Autism and Developmental Disorders, 42*(12), 2761–2766. http://doi.org/10.1007/s10803-012-1534-8

Park, M., Katon, W. J., & Wolf, F. M. (2013). Depression and risk of mortality in individuals with diabetes: A meta-analysis and systematic review. *General Hospital Psychiatry, 35*(3), 217–225. http://doi.org/10.1016/j.genhosppsych.2013.01.006

Parker, K., & Patten, E. (2013). *The sandwich generation: Rising financial burdens for middle-aged Americans*. Retrieved from http://www.pewsocialtrends.org/2013/01/30/the-sandwich-generation/

Parker, K., & Wang, W. (2013). *Modern parenthood: Roles of moms and dads converge as they balance work and family*. Retrieved from http://www.pewsocialtrends.org/2013/03/14/modern-parenthood-roles-of-moms-and-dads-converge-as-they-balance-work-and-family/

Parker, R. G. (1995). Reminiscence: A community theory framework. *The Gerontologist, 35*(4), 515–525.

Parker, S. E., Mai, C. T., Canfield, M. A., Rickard, R., Wang, Y., Meyer, R. E., . . . Correa, A. (2010). Updated national birth prevalence estimates for selected birth defects in the United States, 2004–2006. *Birth Defects Research, 88*(12), 1008–1016. http://doi.org/10.1002/bdra.20735

Parks, S. E., Erck Lambert, A. B., & Shapiro-Mendoza, C. K. (2017). Racial and ethnic trends in sudden unexpected infant deaths: United States, 1995–2013. *Pediatrics*. Retrieved from http://pediatrics.aappublications.org/content/early/2017/05/11/peds.2016-3844?utm_source=TrendMD&utm_medium=TrendMD&utm_campaign=Pediatrics_TrendMD_1

Parladé, M. V, & Iverson, J. M. (2011). The interplay between language, gesture, and affect during communicative transition: A dynamic systems approach. *Developmental Psychology*. http://doi.org/10.1037/a0021811

Parnetti, L., Cicognola, C., Eusebi, P., & Chiasserini, D. (2016). Value of cerebrospinal fluid α-synuclein species as biomarker in Parkinson's diagnosis and prognosis. *Biomarkers in Medicine, 10*(1), 35–49. http://doi.org/10.2217/bmm.15.107

Parra, M., Hoff, E., & Core, C. (2011). Relations among language exposure, phonological memory, and language development in Spanish–English bilingually developing 2-year-olds. *Journal of Experimental Child Psychology, 108*(1), 113–125. http://doi.org/10.1016/j.jecp.2010.07.011

Parra-Cardona, J. R., Cordova, D., Holtrop, K., Villarruel, F. A., & Wieling, E. (2008). Shared ancestry, evolving stories: Similar and contrasting life experiences described by foreign-born and U.S.-born Latino parents. *Family Process, 47*(2), 157–172. http://doi.org/10.1111/j.1545-5300.2008.00246.x

Partridge, S., Balayla, J., Holcroft, C., & Abenhaim, H. (2012). Inadequate prenatal care utilization and risks of infant mortality and poor birth outcome: A retrospective analysis of 28,729,765 U.S. deliveries over 8 years. *American Journal of Perinatology, 29*(10), 787–794. http://doi.org/10.1055/s-0032-1316439

Pascalis, O., Dechonen, S., Morton, J., Duruelle, C., & Grenet, F. (1995). Mother's face recognition in neonates: A replication and an extension. *Infant Behavior and Development, 18*, 79–85.

Pascarella, E., Bohr, L., & Nora, A. (1995). Cognitive effects of 2-year and 4-year colleges: New evidence. *Educational Evaluation and Policy Analysis, 17*(1), 83–96.

Pascoe, J. M., Wood, D. L., Duffee, J. H., & Kuo, A. (2016). Mediators and adverse effects of child poverty in the United States. *Pediatrics, 137*(4), e20160340–e20160340. http://doi.org/10.1542/peds.2016-0340

Pascual-Leone, L. (2000). Reflections on working memory: Are the two models complementary? *Journal of Experimental Child Psychology, 77*, 138–154.

Passey, M. E., Sanson-Fisher, R. W., D'Este, C. A., & Stirling, J. M. (2014). Tobacco, alcohol and cannabis use during pregnancy: Clustering of risks. *Drug and Alcohol Dependence, 134*, 44–50. http://doi.org/10.1016/j.drugalcdep.2013.09.008

Passolunghi, M. C., Mammarella, I. C., & Altoè, G. (2008). Cognitive abilities as precursors of the early acquisition of mathematical skills during first through second grades. *Developmental Neuropsychology, 33*(3), 229–250. http://doi.org/10.1080/87565640801982320

Passolunghi, M. C., Rueda Ferreira, T. I., & Tomasetto, C. (2014). Math–gender stereotypes and math-related beliefs in childhood and early adolescence. *Learning and Individual Differences, 34*, 70–76. http://doi.org/10.1016/j.lindif.2014.05.005

Pasupathi, M., & Mansour, E. (2006). Adult age differences in autobiographical reasoning in narratives. *Developmental Psychology, 42*(5), 798–808.

Patel, D. R., & Luckstead, E. F. (2000). Sport participation, risk taking, and health risk behaviors. *Adolescent Medicine, 11*, 141–155.

Patel, K. A., Oram, R. A., Flanagan, S. E., De Franco, E., Colclough, K., Shepherd, M., ... Hattersley, A. T. (2016). Type 1 diabetes genetic risk score: A novel tool to discriminate monogenic and type 1 diabetes. *Diabetes*. Retrieved from http://diabetes.diabetesjournals.org/content/early/2016/03/28/db15-1690

Patrick, E., & Abravanel, E. (2000). The self-regulatory nature of preschool children's private speech in a naturalistic setting. *Applied Psycholinguistics, 21*, 45–61.

Patrick, M. E., Bray, B. C., & Berglund, P. A. (2016). Reasons for marijuana use among young adults and long-term associations with marijuana use and problems. *Journal of Studies on Alcohol and Drugs, 77*(6), 881–888. http://doi.org/10.15288/jsad.2016.77.881

Patrick, M. E., Maggs, J. L., & Lefkowitz, E. S. (2015). Daily associations between drinking and sex among college students: A longitudinal measurement burst design. *Journal of Research on Adolescence, 25*(2), 377–386. http://doi.org/10.1111/jora.12135

Patterson, C. J. (2009). Children of lesbian and gay parents: Psychology, law, and policy. *American Psychologist, 64*(8), 727–736. http://doi.org/10.1037/0003-066x.64.8.727

Patterson, C. J. (2017). Parents' sexual orientation and children's development. *Child Development Perspectives, 11*(1), 45–49. http://doi.org/10.1111/cdep.12207

Patterson, M. L., & Werker, J. F. (2002). Infants' ability to match dynamic phonetic and gender information in the face and voice. *Journal of Experimental Child Psychology, 81*(1), 93–115. http://doi.org/10.1006/jecp.2001.2644

Patton, L. D., Renn, K. A., Guido-DiBrito, F., & Quaye, S. J. (2016). *Student development in college: Theory, research, and practice*. New York, NY: Wiley.

Paúl, C., Ribeiro, O., & Santos, P. (2010). Cognitive impairment in old people living in the community. *Archives of Gerontology & Geriatrics, 51*(2), 121–124. http://doi.org/10.1016/j.archger.2009.09.037

Paul, L. (2011). Diet, nutrition and telomere length. *The Journal of Nutritional Biochemistry, 22*(10), 895–901. http://doi.org/10.1016/j.jnutbio.2010.12.001

Paulsen, D. J., Hallquist, M. N., Geier, C. F., & Luna, B. (2014). Effects of incentives, age, and behavior on brain activation during inhibitory control: A longitudinal fMRI study. *Developmental Cognitive Neuroscience, 11*, 105–115. http://doi.org/10.dcn.2014.09.003

Paulus, M. (2014a). The early origins of human charity: Developmental changes in preschoolers' sharing with poor and wealthy individuals. *Frontiers in Psychology, 5*, 344. http://doi.org/10.3389/fpsyg.2014.00344

Paulus, M. (2014b). The emergence of prosocial behavior: Why do infants and toddlers help, comfort, and share? *Child Development Perspectives, 8*(2), 77–81. http://doi.org/10.1111/cdep.12066

Paulus, M., & Moore, C. (2014). The development of recipient-dependent sharing behavior and sharing expectations in preschool children. *Developmental Psychology, 50*(3), 914–921. http://doi.org/10.1037/a0034169

Paulussen-Hoogeboom, M. C., Stams, G. J. J. M., Hermanns, J. M. A., & Peetsma, T. T. D. (2007). Child negative emotionality and parenting from infancy to preschool: A meta-analytic review. *Developmental Psychology, 43*(2), 438–453. http://doi.org/10.1037/0012-1649.43.2.438

Pavarini, G., Hollanda Souza, D., & Hawk, C. K. (2012). Parental practices and theory of mind development. *Journal of Child and Family Studies, 22*(6), 844–853. http://doi.org/10.1007/s10826-012-9643-8

Pavone, V., Lionetti, E., Gargano, V., Evola, F. R., Costarella, L., & Sessa, G. (2011). Growing pains: A study of 30 cases and a review of the literature. *Journal of Pediatric Orthopedics, 31*(5), 606–609. http://doi.org/10.1097/BPO.0b013e318220ba5e

Payette, H. (2005). Nutrition as a determinant of functional autonomy and quality of life in aging: A research program. *Canadian Journal of Physiology & Pharmacology*, *83*(11), 1061–1070. http://doi.org/10.1139/Y05-086

Payne, V. G., & Isaacs, L. D. (2016). *Human motor development: A lifespan approach*. New York, NY: McGraw-Hill. Retrieved from http://dl.acm.org/citation.cfm?id=1214267

Pazol, K., Whiteman, M. K., Folger, S. G., Kourtis, A. P., Marchbanks, P. A., & Jamieson, D. J. (2015). Sporadic contraceptive use and nonuse: Age-specific prevalence and associated factors. *American Journal of Obstetrics and Gynecology*, *212*(3), 324.e1-8. http://doi.org/10.1016/j.ajog.2014.10.004

Peake, S. J., Dishion, T. J., Stormshak, E. A., Moore, W. E., & Pfeifer, J. H. (2013). Risk-taking and social exclusion in adolescence: Neural mechanisms underlying peer influences on decision making. *NeuroImage*, *82*, 23–34. http://doi.org/10.1016/j.neuroimage.2013.05.061

Pearson, A. L., Bentham, G., Day, P., Kingham, S., Flegal, K., Carroll, M., . . . Brug, J. (2014). Associations between neighbourhood environmental characteristics and obesity and related behaviours among adult New Zealanders. *BMC Public Health*, *14*(1), 553. http://doi.org/10.1186/1471-2458-14-553

Pearson, N., & Biddle, S. J. H. (2011). Sedentary behavior and dietary intake in children, adolescents, and adults: A systematic review. *American Journal of Preventive Medicine*, *41*(2), 178–188. http://doi.org/10.1016/j.amepre.2011.05.002

Pearson, R. M., Lightman, S. L., & Evans, J. (2009). Emotional sensitivity for motherhood: Late pregnancy is associated with enhanced accuracy to encode emotional faces. *Hormones and Behavior*, *56*(5), 557–563. http://doi.org/10.1016/j.yhbeh.2009.09.013

Pedditizi, E., Peters, R., & Beckett, N. (2016). The risk of overweight/obesity in mid-life and late life for the development of dementia: A systematic review and meta-analysis of longitudinal studies. *Age and Ageing*, *45*(1), 14–21. http://doi.org/10.1093/ageing/afv151

Pedlow, R., Sanson, A., Prior, M., & Oberklaid, F. (1993). Stability of maternally reported temperament from infancy to 8 years. *Developmental Psychology*, *29*, 998–1007.

Pelaez, M., Virues-Ortega, J., & Gewirtz, J. L. (2011). Reinforcement of vocalizations through contingent vocal imitation. *Journal of Applied Behavior Analysis*, *44*(1), 33–40. http://doi.org/10.1901/jaba.2011.44-33

Pellegrini, A. D., & Roseth, C. J. (2006). Relational aggression and relationships in preschoolers: A discussion of methods, gender differences, and function. *Journal of Applied Developmental Psychology*, *27*(3), 269–276.

Pellegrini, A. D., & Smith, P. K. (1998). Physical activity play: The nature and function of a neglected aspect of play. *Child Development*, *69*, 577–598.

Pemberton Roben, C. K., Bass, A. J., Moore, G. A., Murray-Kolb, L., Tan, P. Z., Gilmore, R. O., . . . Teti, L. O. (2012). Let me go: The influences of crawling experience and temperament on the development of anger expression. *Infancy*, *17*(5), 558–577. http://doi.org/10.1111/j.1532-7078.2011.00092.x

Pemment, J. (2013). The neurobiology of antisocial personality disorder: The quest for rehabilitation and treatment. *Aggression & Violent Behavior*, *18*(1), 79–82. http://doi.org/10.1016/j.avb.2012.10.004

Penke, L., Denissen, J. J. A., & Miller, G. F. (2007). The evolutionary genetics of personality. *European Journal of Personality*, *21*(5), 549–587. http://doi.org/10.1002/per.629

Penke, L., Maniega, S. M., Bastin, M. E., Valdés Hernández, M. C., Murray, C., Royle, N. A., . . . Deary, I. J. (2012). Brain white matter tract integrity as a neural foundation for general intelligence. *Molecular Psychiatry*, *17*(10), 1026–1030. http://doi.org/10.1038/mp.2012.66

Perales, F., del Pozo-Cruz, J., & del Pozo-Cruz, B. (2015). Long-term dynamics in physical activity behaviour across the transition to parenthood. *International Journal of Public Health*, *60*(3), 301–308. http://doi.org/10.1007/s00038-015-0653-3

Perelli-Harris, B., & Gassen, N. S. (2012). How similar are cohabitation and marriage? Legal approaches to cohabitation across Western Europe. *Population and Development Review*, *38*(3), 435–467. http://doi.org/10.1111/j.1728-4457.2012.00511.x

Perelli-Harris, B., & Styrc, M. (2016). *Re-evaluating the link between marriage and mental well-being: How do early life conditions attenuate differences between cohabitation and marriage?* Southampton: ESRC Centre for Population Change Working Papers, 75. Retrieved from https://eprints.soton.ac.uk/386841/

Perilloux, C., Easton, J. A., & Buss, D. M. (2012). The misperception of sexual interest. *Psychological Science*, *23*(2), 146–151. http://doi.org/10.1177/0956797611424162

Perl, D. P. (2010). Neuropathology of Alzheimer's disease. *Mount Sinai Journal of Medicine*, *77*(1), 32–42. http://doi.org/10.1002/msj.20157

Perlman, S. B., Huppert, T. J., & Luna, B. (2016). Functional near-infrared spectroscopy evidence for development of prefrontal engagement in working memory in early through middle childhood. *Cerebral Cortex*, *26*(6), 2790–2799. http://doi.org/10.1093/cercor/bhv139

Perlmutter, M. (1984). Continuities and discontinuities in early human memory: Paradigms, processes, and performances. In J. R. V. Kail & N. R. Spear (Eds.), *Comparative perspectives on the development of memory* (pp. 253–287). Hillsdale, NJ: Lawrence Erlbaum.

Perlmutter, M., Kaplan, M., & Nyquest, L. (1990). Development of adaptive competence in adulthood. *Human Development*, *33*, 185–197.

Perner, J. (2000). About + belief + counterfactual. In P. Mitchell & K. Riggs (Eds.), *Children's reasoning and the mind* (pp. 367–397). Hove, UK: Psychology Press.

Perren, S., Ettekal, I., & Ladd, G. (2013). The impact of peer victimization on later maladjustment: Mediating and moderating effects of hostile and self-blaming attributions. *Journal of Child Psychology and Psychiatry, and Allied Disciplines*, *54*(1), 46–55. http://doi.org/10.1111/j.1469-7610.2012.02618.x

Perrig-Chiello, P., Hutchison, S., & Morselli, D. (2014). Patterns of psychological adaptation to divorce after a long-term marriage. *Journal of Social and Personal Relationships*, *32*(3), 386–405. http://doi.org/10.1177/0265407514533769

Perrin, E. C., & Siegel, B. S. (2013). Promoting the well-being of children whose parents are gay or lesbian. *Pediatrics*, *131*(4), e1374-83. http://doi.org/10.1542/peds.2013-0377

Perry, K. E., Donohue, K. M., & Weinstein, R. S. (2007). Teaching practices and the promotion of achievement and adjustment in first grade. *Journal of School Psychology*, *45*(3), 269–292.

Perry, R. P., Stupnisky, R. H., Daniels, L. M., & Haynes, T. L. (2008). Attributional (explanatory) thinking about failure in new achievement settings. *European Journal of Psychology of Education*, *23*(4), 459–475. http://doi.org/10.1007/BF03172753

Perry, W. G. (1970). *Forms of intellectual and ethical development in the college years: A scheme*. San Franscisco, CA: Jossey-Bass.

Perry-Jenkins, M., Goldberg, A. E., Pierce, C. P., & Sayer, A. G. (2007). Shift work, role overload, and the transition to parenthood. *Journal of Marriage & Family*, *69*(1), 123–138.

Peskin, S. M. (2017, June 20). The symptoms of dying. *New York Times*. Retrieved from https://mobile.nytimes.com/2017/06/20/well/live/the-symptoms-of-dying.html

Pesu, L., Viljaranta, J., & Aunola, K. (2016). The role of parents' and teachers' beliefs in children's self-concept development. *Journal of Applied Developmental Psychology*, *44*(May-June), 63–71. http://doi.org/10.1016/j.appdev.2016.03.001

Peter, V., Kalashnikova, M., Santos, A., & Burnham, D. (2016). Mature neural responses to infant-directed speech but not adult-directed speech in pre-verbal infants. *Scientific Reports*, *6*. http://doi.org/10.1038/srep34273

Peters, A., & Kemper, T. (2012). A review of the structural alterations in the cerebral hemispheres of the aging rhesus monkey. *Neurobiology of Aging*, *33*(10), 2357–2372. http://doi.org/10.1016/j.neurobiolaging.2011.11.015

Peters, S. A. E., Huxley, R. R., & Woodward, M. (2014). Diabetes as a risk factor for stroke in women compared with men: A systematic review and meta-analysis of 64 cohorts, including 775,385 individuals and 12,539 strokes. *The Lancet*, *383*(9933), 1973–1980. http://doi.org/10.1016/S0140-6736(14)60040-4

Petersen, S. E., & Posner, M. I. (2012). The attention system of the human brain: 20 years after. *Annual Review of Neuroscience*, *35*, 73–89. http://doi.org/10.1146/annurev-neuro-062111-150525

Peterson, B. D., Gold, L., & Feingold, T. (2007). The experience and influence of infertility: Considerations for couple counselors. *Family Journal*, 251–257.

Peterson, G. W., & Bush, K. R. (2013). Conceptualizing cultural influences on socialization: Comparing parent–adolescent relationships in the United States and Mexico. In G. W. Peterson & K. R. Bush (Eds.), *Handbook of marriage and the family* (pp. 177–208). New York, NY: Springer.

Peterson, M. D., Rhea, M. R., Sen, A., & Gordon, P. M. (2010). Resistance exercise for muscular strength in older adults: A meta-analysis. *Ageing Research Reviews*, *9*(3), 226–237. http://doi.org/10.1016/j.arr.2010.03.004

Peterson, R. L., & Pennington, B. F. (2012). Developmental dyslexia. *Lancet*, *379*(9830), 1997–2007. http://doi.org/10.1016/S0140-6736(12)60198-6

Petitto, L. A., Berens, M. S., Kovelman, I., Dubins, M. H., Jasinska, K., & Shalinsky, M. (2012). The "perceptual wedge hypothesis" as the basis for bilingual babies' phonetic processing advantage: New insights from fNIRS brain imaging. *Brain and Language*, *121*(2), 130–143. http://doi.org/10.1016/j.bandl.2011.05.003

Petrides, K. V., Mikolajczak, M., Mavroveli, S., Sanchez-Ruiz, M.-J., Furnham, A., & Perez-Gonzalez, J.-C. (2016). Developments in trait emotional intelligence research. *Emotion Review*, *8*(4), 335–341. http://doi.org/10.1177/1754073916650493

Petrou, S., & Kupek, E. (2010). Poverty and childhood undernutrition in developing countries: A multi-national cohort study. *Social Science & Medicine*, *71*(7), 1366–1373. http://doi.org/10.1016/j.socscimed.2010.06.038

Pettee, K. K., Brach, J. S., Kriska, A. M., Boudreau, R., Richardson, C. R., Colbert, L. H., . . . Newman, A. B. (2006). Influence of marital status on physical activity levels among older adults. *Medicine & Science in Sports & Exercise*, *38*(3), 541–546.

Pettygrove, D. M., Hammond, S. I., Karahuta, E. L., Waugh, W. E., & Brownell, C. A. (2013). From cleaning up to helping out: Parental socialization and children's early prosocial behavior. *Infant Behavior and Development, 36*.

Pew Forum on Religious and Public Life. (2008). *U.S. religious landscape survey. Religious affiliation: Diverse and dynamic*. Washington, DC: Author.

Pew Research Center. (2009a). *End-of-life decisions: How Americans cope*. Retrieved from http://www.pewsocialtrends.org/2009/08/20/end-of-life-decisions-how-americans-cope/

Pew Research Center. (2009b). *Growing old in America: Expectations vs. Reality*. Retrieved from http://www.pewsocialtrends.org/2009/06/29/growing-old-in-america-expectations-vs-reality/

Pew Research Center. (2013). *Views on end-of-life medical treatments*. Retrieved from http://www.pewforum.org/2013/11/21/views-on-end-of-life-medical-treatments/

Pew Research Center. (2015a). *Gay marriage around the world*. Retrieved from http://www.pewforum.org/2013/12/19/gay-marriage-around-the-world-2013/

Pew Research Center. (2015b). *Parenting in America: The American family today*. Retrieved from http://www.pewsocialtrends.org/2015/12/17/1-the-american-family-today/

Pew Research Center. (2016). *The gender gap in religion around the world*. Retrieved from http://www.pewforum.org/2016/03/22/the-gender-gap-in-religion-around-the-world/

Pew Research Center. (2017). *Changing attitudes on gay marriage*. Retrieved from http://www.pewforum.org/fact-sheet/changing-attitudes-on-gay-marriage/

Pexman, P. M., Glenwright, M., Hala, S., Kowbel, S. L., & Jungen, S. (2006). Children's use of trait information in understanding verbal irony. *Metaphor & Symbol, 21*(1), 39–60.

Pfeifer, J. H., Kahn, L. E., Merchant, J. S., Peake, S. J., Veroude, K., Masten, C. L., . . . Dapretto, M. (2013). Longitudinal change in the neural bases of adolescent social self-evaluations: Effects of age and pubertal development. *The Journal of Neuroscience, 33*(17), 7415–7419. https://doi.org/10.1523/JNEUROSCI.4074-12.2013

Pfeifer, J. H., Lieberman, M. D., & Dapretto, M. (2007). "I know you are but what am I?": Neural bases of self- and social knowledge retrieval in children and adults. *Journal of Cognitive Neuroscience, 19*(8), 1323–1337. https://doi.org/10.1162/jocn.2007.19.8.1323

Pfeifer, J. H., & Peake, S. J. (2012). Self-development: Integrating cognitive, socioemotional, and neuroimaging perspectives. *Developmental Cognitive Neuroscience, 2*(1), 55–69. https://doi.org/10.1016/j.dcn.2011.07.012

Phani, S., Loike, J. D., & Przedborski, S. (2012). Neurodegeneration and inflammation in Parkinson's disease. *Parkinsonism & Related Disorders, 18*(1), S207–S209. http://doi.org/10.1016/S1353-8020(11)70064-5

Phelps, E. A., & LeDoux, J. E. (2005). Contributions of the amygdala to emotion processing: From animal models to human behavior. *Neuron, 48*(2), 175–187. http://doi.org/10.1016/j.neuron.2005.09.025

Phillips, D., Gormley, W., & Anderson, S. (2016). The effects of Tulsa's CAP Head Start program on middle-school academic outcomes and progress. *Developmental Psychology, 52*(8), 1247–1261. http://doi.org/10.1037/dev0000151

Phillips, E. E., Bischoff, R. J., Abbott, D. A., & Xia, Y. (2009). Connecting behaviors and

newlyweds' sense of shared-meaning and relationship satisfaction. *Journal of Couple & Relationship Therapy, 8*(3), 247–263. http://doi.org/10.1080/15332690903049257

Phillips, L. H., MacLean, R. D. J., & Allen, R. (2002). Age and the understanding of emotions: Neuropsychological and sociocognitive perspectives. *Psychological Sciences and Social Sciences, 57*(6), P526–P530. http://doi.org/10.1093/geronb/57.6.P526

Phillips, M., Crouse, J., & Ralph, J. (1998). Does the black–white test score gap widen after children enter school? In M. Jencks & C. Phillips (Ed.), *The black-white test score gap* (pp. 229–272). Washington, DC: Brookings Institution Press.

Phinney, J. S. (2000). Identity formation across cultures: The interaction of personal, societal, and historical change. *Human Development, 43*(1), 27–31.

Phinney, J. S., & Chavira, V. (1995). Parental ethnic socialization and adolescent coping with problems related to ethnicity. *Journal of Research on Adolescence, 5*(1), 31–53.

Phinney, J. S., & Ong, A. D. (2007). Conceptualization and measurement of ethnic identity: Current status and future directions. *Journal of Counseling Psychology, 54*(3), 271–281. http://doi.org/10.1037/0022-067.54.3.271

Phinney, J. S., Romero, I., Nava, M., & Huang, D. (2001). The role of language, parents, and peers in ethnic identity among adolescents in immigrant families. *Journal of Youth and Adolescence, 30*(2), 135–153.

Piaget, J. (1929). *The child's conception of the world*. London, UK: Routledge & Kegan Paul.

Piaget, J. (1932). *The moral judgment of the child*. New York, NY: Harcourt Brace.

Piaget, J. (1952). *The origins of intelligence in children*. New York, NY: International Universities Press. (Original work published in 1936)

Piaget, J. (1962). *Play, dreams, and imitation in childhood*. New York, NY: Norton.

Piaget, J. (1970). Piaget's theory. In P. H. Mussen (Ed.), *Carmichael's manual of child psychology* (Vol. 1). New York, NY: Wiley.

Piaget, J. (1972). Intellectual evolution from adolescence to adulthood. *Human Development, 51*(1), 40–47. http://doi.org/10.1159/000112531

Piaget, J., & Inhelder, B. (1967). *The child's conception of space*. New York, NY: Norton.

Pickens, J., Field, T., & Nawrocki, T. (2001). Frontal EEG asymmetry in response to emotional vignettes in preschool-age children. *International Journal of Behavioral Development, 25*, 105–112.

Piek, J. P., Dawson, L., Smith, L. M., & Gasson, N. (2008). The role of early fine and gross motor development on later motor and cognitive ability. *Human Movement Science, 27*(5), 668–681. http://doi.org/10.1016/j.humov.2007.11.002

Pierrehumbert, B., Nicole, A., Muller-Nix, C., Forcada-Guex, M., & Ansermet, F. (2003). Parental post-traumatic reactions after premature birth: Implications for sleeping and eating problems in the infant. *Archives of Disease in Childhood, 88*(5), 400F–404. http://doi.org/10.1136/fn.88.5.F400

Pieters, S., Burk, W. J., Van der Vorst, H., Dahl, R. E., Wiers, R. W., & Engels, R. C. M. E. (2015). Prospective relationships between sleep problems and substance use, internalizing and externalizing problems. *Journal of Youth and Adolescence, 44*(2), 379–388. http://doi.org/10.1007/s10964-014-0213-9

Pietschnig, J., Penke, L., Wicherts, J. M., Zeiler, M., & Voracek, M. (2015). Meta-analysis of associations between human brain volume and

intelligence differences: How strong are they and what do they mean? *Neuroscience & Biobehavioral Reviews, 57*, 411–432. http://doi.org/10.1016/j.neubiorev.2015.09.017

Pietschnig, J., & Voracek, M. (2015). One century of global IQ gains: A formal meta-analysis of the Flynn effect (1909–2013). *Perspectives on Psychological Science, 10*(3), 282–306. http://doi.org/10.1177/1745691615577701

Pike, G. R., & Kuh, G. D. (2005). First- and second-generation college students: A comparison of their engagement and intellectual development. *Journal of Higher Education, 76*(3), 276–300.

Pike, K. M., Hoek, H. W., & Dunne, P. E. (2014). Cultural trends and eating disorders. *Current Opinion in Psychiatry, 27*(6), 436–442. http://doi.org/10.1097/YCO.0000000000000100

Pilar Matud, M., Bethencourt, J. M., & Ibáñez, I. (2014). Relevance of gender roles in life satisfaction in adult people. *Personality and Individual Differences, 70*, 206–211. http://doi.org/10.1016/j.paid.2014.06.046

Pillemer, K., & Suitor, J. J. (2014). Who provides care? A prospective study of caregiving among adult siblings. *The Gerontologist, 54*(4), 589–598. http://doi.org/10.1093/geront/gnt066

Pillow, B. H. (2008). Development of children's understanding of cognitive activities. *Journal of Genetic Psychology, 169*(4), 297–321.

Pillow, B. H., & Henrichon, A. J. (1996). There's more to the picture than meets the eye: Young children's difficulty understanding biased interpretation. *Child Development, 67*, 803–819.

Pilowsky, D. J., & Wu, L.-T. (2015). Sexual risk behaviors and HIV risk among Americans aged 50 years or older: A review. *Substance Abuse and Rehabilitation, 6*, 51–60. http://doi.org/10.2147/SAR.S78808

Pineau, A., & Streri, A. (1990). Intermodal transfer of spatial arrangement of the component parts of an object in 4/5 month-old infants. *Perception, 19*, 795–804.

Pinker, S., & Bloom, P. (1990). Natural language and natural selection. *Behavioral and Brain Sciences, 13*(4), 707–727. http://doi.org/10.1017/S0140525X00081061

Pinker, S., Lebeaux, D. S., & Frost, L. A. (1987). Productivity and constraints in the acquisition of the passive. *Cognition, 26*, 195–267.

Pinquart, M. (2003). Loneliness in married, widowed, divorced, and never-married older adults. *Journal of Social & Personal Relationships, 20*(1), 31.

Pinquart, M., & Forstmeier, S. (2012). Effects of reminiscence interventions on psychosocial outcomes: A meta-analysis. *Aging & Mental Health, 16*(5), 541–558. http://doi.org/10.1080/13607863.2011.651434

Pinquart, M., & Kauser, R. (2017). Do the associations of parenting styles with behavior problems and academic achievement vary by culture? Results from a meta-analysis. *Cultural Diversity and Ethnic Minority Psychology*. http://doi.org/10.1037/cdp0000149

Pinquart, M., & Martin, M. (2017). Associations of parenting dimensions and styles with externalizing problems of children and adolescents: An updated meta-analysis. *Developmental Psychology, 53*(5), 873–932. http://doi.org/10.1037/dev0000295

Pinquart, M., & Schindler, I. (2007). Changes of life satisfaction in the transition to retirement: A latent-class approach. *Psychology & Aging, 22*(3), 442–455. http://doi.org/10.1037/0882-7974.22.3.442

Pinsker, J. E. (2012). Turner syndrome: Updating the paradigm of clinical care. *The Journal of Clinical*

Endocrinology & Metabolism, 97(6), E994–E1003. http://doi.org/10.1210/jc.2012-1245

Piolino, P., Coste, C., Martinelli, P., Macé, A.-L., Quinette, P., Guillery-Girard, B., & Belleville, S. (2010). Reduced specificity of autobiographical memory and aging: Do the executive and feature binding functions of working memory have a role? *Neuropsychologia, 48*(2), 429–440. http://doi.org/10.1016/j.neuropsychologia.2009.09.035

Piolino, P., Desgranges, B., Clarys, D., Guillery-Girard, B., Taconnat, L., Isingrini, M., & Eustache, F. (2006). Autobiographical memory, autonoetic consciousness, and self-perspective in aging. *Psychology and Aging, 21*(3), 510–525.

Piotrowski, J. T., Lapierre, M. A., & Linebarger, D. L. (2013). Investigating correlates of self-regulation in early childhood with a representative sample of English-speaking American families. *Journal of Child and Family Studies, 22*(3), 423–436. http://doi.org/10.1007/s10826-012-9595-z

Pipe, M. E., Lamb, M. E., Orbach, Y., & Esplin, E. (2004). Recent research on children's testimony about experienced and witnessed events. *Developmental Review, 24*, 440–468.

Piquero, A. R., & Moffitt, T. E. (2013). Moffitt's developmental taxonomy of antisocial behavior. In *Encyclopedia of criminology and criminal justice* (pp. 3121–3127).

Pittman, J. F., Keiley, M. K., Kerpelman, J. L., & Vaughn, B. E. (2011). Attachment, identity, and intimacy: Parallels between Bowlby's and Erikson's paradigms. *Journal of Family Theory & Review, 3*(1), 32–46. http://doi.org/10.1111/j.1756-2589.2010.00079.x

Plassman, B. L., Langa, K. M., Fisher, G. G., Heeringa, S. G., Weir, D. R., Ofstedal, M. B., . . . Wallace, R. B. (2007). Prevalence of dementia in the United States: The aging, demographics, and memory study. *Neuroepidemiology, 29*(1), 125–132.

Pliatsikas, C., Moschopoulou, E., & Saddy, J. D. (2015). The effects of bilingualism on the white matter structure of the brain. *Proceedings of the National Academy of Sciences, 112*(5), 1334–1337. http://doi.org/10.1073/pnas.1414183112

Plöderl, M., Wagenmakers, E.-J., Tremblay, P., Ramsay, R., Kralovec, K., Fartacek, C., & Fartacek, R. (2013). Suicide risk and sexual orientation: A critical review. *Archives of Sexual Behavior, 42*(5), 715–727. http://doi.org/10.1007/s10508-012-0056-y

Plomin, R., & Asbury, K. (2001). Nature and nurture in the family. *Marriage & Family Review, 33*(2/3), 273–283.

Plomin, R., & Daniels, D. (2011). Why are children in the same family so different from one another? *International Journal of Epidemiology, 40*(3), 563–582.

Plomin, R., & Deary, I. J. (2015). Genetics and intelligence differences: Five special findings. *Molecular Psychiatry, 20*(1), 98–108. http://doi.org/10.1038/mp.2014.105

Plomin, R., DeFries, J. C., Knopik, V. S., & Neiderhiser, J. M. (2013). *Behavioral genetics* (6th ed.). New York, NY: Worth.

Plomin, R., DeFries, J. C., Knopik, V. S., & Neiderhiser, J. M. (2016). Top 10 replicated findings from behavioral genetics. *Perspectives on Psychological Science, 11*(1), 3–23. http://doi.org/10.1177/1745691615617439

Plomin, R., DeFries, J. C., & Loehlin, J. C. (1977). Genotype-environment interaction and correlation in the analysis of human behavior. *Psychological Bulletin, 84*(2), 309–322. http://doi.org/10.1037/0033-2909.84.2.309

Plomin, R., & Spinath, F. M. (2004). Intelligence: Genetics, genes, and genomics. *Journal of*

Personality & Social Psychology, 86(1), 112–129. http://doi.org/10.1037/0022-3514.86.1.112

Pluess, M., & Belsky, J. (2009). Differential susceptibility to rearing experience: The case of childcare. *Journal of Child Psychology & Psychiatry, 50*(4), 396–404. http://doi.org/10.1111/j.1469-7610.2008.01992.x

Pluess, M., & Birkbeck, J. B. (2010). differential susceptibility to parenting and quality child care. *Developmental Psychology, 46*(2), 379–390.

Poehlmann, J., Schwichtenberg, A. J. M., Shlafer, R. J., Hahn, E., Bianchi, J.-P., & Warner, R. (2011). Emerging self-regulation in toddlers born preterm or low birth weight: Differential susceptibility to parenting? *Development & Psychopathology, 23*(1), 177–193. http://doi.org/10.1017/s0954579410000726

Poirel, N., Borst, G., Simon, G., Rossi, S., Cassotti, M., Pineau, A., & Houdé, O. (2012). Number conservation is related to children's prefrontal inhibitory control: An fMRI study of a Piagetian task. *PLoS ONE, 7*(7), e40802. Retrieved from https://hal.archives-ouvertes.fr/hal-00839858/

Pollack, A., & McNeil Jr., D. G. (2013, March 4). In medical first, a baby with H.I.V. is deemed cured. *New York Times.* Retrieved from http://www.who.int/hiv/pub/progress_report2011/en/

Pollack, S., & Bechner, A. (2000). *Wisconsin international adoption research project: A study of our children's development.* Madison: University of Wisconsin.

Pomerantz, E. M., & Dong, W. (2006). Effects of mothers' perceptions of children's competence: The moderating role of mothers' theories of competence. *Developmental Psychology, 42*(5), 950–961. http://doi.org/10.1037/0012-1649.42.5.950

Pomerantz, E. M., Ng, F. F.-Y., & Wang, Q. (2008). Culture, parenting, and motivation: The case of East Asia and the United States. In M. L. Maehr, S. A. Karabenick, & T. C. Urdan (Eds.), *Advances in motivation and achievement: Social psychological perspectives* (pp. 209–240.).

Pomerantz, E. M., & Saxon, J. L. (2001). Conceptions of ability as stable and self-evaluative processes: A longitudinal examination. *Child Development, 72*(1), 152–173. http://doi.org/10.1111/1467-8624.00271

Pompili, M., Lester, D., Forte, A., Seretti, M. E., Erbuto, D., Lamis, D. A., . . . Girardi, P. (2014). Bisexuality and suicide: A systematic review of the current literature. *The Journal of Sexual Medicine, 11*(8), 1903–1913. http://doi.org/10.1111/jsm.12581

Pons, F., Harris, P. L., & de Rosnay, M. (2004). Emotion comprehension between 3 and 11 years: Developmental periods and hierarchical organization. *European Journal of Developmental Psychology, 1*(2), 127–152. http://doi.org/10.1080/17405620344000022

Poole, D. A., & White, L. T. (1991). Effects of question repetition on the eyewitness testimony of children and adults. *Developmental Psychology, 27*, 975–986.

Poole, D. A., & White, L. T. (1993). Two years later: Effects of question repetition and retention interval on the eyewitness testimony of children and adults. *Developmental Psychology, 29*, 844–853.

Popenoe, D. (2009). Cohabitation, marriage, and child well-being: A cross-national perspective. *Society, 46*(5), 429–436. http://doi.org/10.1007/s12115-009-9242-5

Poppen, P. (1974). Sex differences in moral judgment. *Personality and Social Psychology Bulletin, 1*(1), 313–315. http://doi.org/10.1177/014616727401001106

Porter, C. L., & Hsu, H.-C. (2003). First-time mothers' perceptions of efficacy during the transition to

motherhood: Links to infant temperament. *Journal of Family Psychology, 17*(1), 54–64. http://doi.org/10.1037/0893-3200.17.1.54

Porter, R., Varendi, H., Christensson, K., Porter, R. H., & Winberg, J. (1998). Soothing effect of amniotic fluid smell in newborn infants. *Early Human Development, 51*, 47–55.

Portnow, L. H., Vaillancourt, D. E., & Okun, M. S. (2013). The history of cerebral PET scanning: From physiology to cutting-edge technology. *Neurology, 80*(10), 952–956. http://doi.org/10.1212/WNL.0b013e318285c135

Poskitt, E. M. E. (2009). Countries in transition: Underweight to obesity non-stop? *Annals of Tropical Paediatrics, 29*(1), 1–11.

Posner, M. I. (2001). The developing human brain. *Developmental Science, 4*(3), 253–387.

Posner, R. B. (2006). Early menarche: A review of research on trends in timing, racial differences, etiology and psychosocial consequences. *Sex Roles, 54*(5/6), 315–322.

Potegal, M., Robison, S., Anderson, F., Jordan, C., & Shapiro, E. (2007). Sequence and priming in 15-month-olds' reactions to brief arm restraint: Evidence for a hierarchy of anger responses. *Aggressive Behavior, 33*(6), 508–518. http://doi.org/10.1002/ab.20207

Potter, D. (2010). Psychosocial well-being and the relationship between divorce and children's academic achievement. *Journal of Marriage & Family, 72*(4), 933–946. http://doi.org/10.1111/j.1741-3737.2010.00740.x

Poudevigne, M. S., O'Connor, P. J., Laing, E. M., Wilson, A. M. R., Modlesky, C. M., & Lewis, R. D. (2003). Body images of 4- to 8-year-old girls at the outset of their first artistic gymnastics class. *International Journal of Eating Disorders, 34*, 244–250.

Poulin, F., & Chan, A. (2010). Friendship stability and change in childhood and adolescence. *Developmental Review, 30*(3), 257–272. http://doi.org/10.1016/j.dr.2009.01.001

Poulin-Dublis, D., & Héroux, G. (1994). Movement and children's attributions of life properties. *International Journal of Behavioral Development, 17*, 329–347.

Poulin-Dubois, D., Serbin, L. A., & Derbyshire, A. (1998). Toddlers' intermodal and verbal knowledge about gender. *Merrill-Palmer Quarterly.* Retrieved from http://psycnet.apa.org/psycinfo/1998-10856-004

Poulin-Dubois, D., Serbin, L. A., Eichstedt, J. A., Sen, M. G., & Beissel, C. F. (2002). Men don't put on make-up: Toddlers' knowledge of the gender stereotyping of household activities. *Social Development, 11*(2), 166–181. http://doi.org/10.1111/1467-9507.00193

Pousset, G., Bilsen, J., De Wilde, J., Benoit, Y., Verlooy, J., Bomans, A., . . . Mortier, F. (2009). Attitudes of adolescent cancer survivors toward end-of-life decisions for minors. *Pediatrics, 124*(6). Retrieved from http://pediatrics.aappublications.org/content/124/6/e1142

Powell, M. P., & Schulte, T. (2011). Turner syndrome. In S. Goldstein & C. R. Reynolds (Eds.), *Handbook of neurodevelopmental and genetic disorders in children* (2nd ed., pp. 261–275). New York, NY: Guilford Press.

Power, F. C., Higgins, A., & Kohlberg, L. (1989). *Lawrence Kohlberg's approach to moral education.* New York, NY: Columbia University Press.

Power, L., & McKinney, C. (2013). Emerging adult perceptions of parental religiosity and parenting practices: Relationships with emerging adult religiosity and psychological adjustment. *Psychology* of Religion and Spirituality, 5(2), 99–109. http://doi.org/10.1037/a0030046

Power, R., & Pluess, M. (2015). Heritability estimates of the Big Five personality traits based on common genetic variants. Translational Psychiatry, 5. http://doi.org/10.1038/tp.2015.96

Powers, S. M., Bisconti, T. L., & Bergeman, C. S. (2014). Trajectories of social support and well-being across the first two years of widowhood. Death Studies, 38(8), 499–509. http://doi.org/10.1080/07481187.2013.846436

Pozzoli, T., Gini, G., & Vieno, A. (2012). The role of individual correlates and class norms in defending and passive bystanding behavior in bullying: A multilevel analysis. Child Development, 83(6), 1917–1931. http://doi.org/10.1111/j.1467-8624.2012.01831.x

Prady, S. L., Kiernan, K., Fairley, L., Wilson, S., & Wright, J. (2014). Self-reported maternal parenting style and confidence and infant temperament in a multi-ethnic community: Results from the Born in Bradford cohort. Journal of Child Health Care, 18(1), 31–46. http://doi.org/10.1177/1367493512473855

Prakash, R. S., Voss, M. W., Erickson, K. I., & Kramer, A. F. (2015). Physical activity and cognitive vitality. Annual Review of Psychology, 66(1), 769–797. http://doi.org/10.1146/annurev-psych-010814-015249

Pratt, M. W., Hunsberger, B., Pancer, S. M., & Alisat, S. (2003). A longitudinal analysis of personal values socialization: Correlates of a moral self-ideal in late adolescence. Social Development, 12(4), 563–585. http://doi.org/10.1111/1467-9507.00249

Prebble, S. C., Addis, D. R., & Tippett, L. J. (2013). Autobiographical memory and sense of self. Psychological Bulletin, 139(4), 815–840. http://doi.org/10.1037/a0030146

Preckel, F., Niepel, C., Schneider, M., & Brunner, M. (2013). Self-concept in adolescence: A longitudinal study on reciprocal effects of self-perceptions in academic and social domains. Journal of Adolescence, 36(6), 1165–1175. http://doi.org/10.1016/j.adolescence.2013.09.001

Prehn, K., Jumpertz von Schwartzenberg, R., Mai, K., Zeitz, U., Witte, A. V., Hampel, D., . . . Flöel, A. (2016). Caloric restriction in older adults: Differential effects of weight loss and reduced weight on brain structure and function. Cerebral Cortex, 28(Supp. 1). http://doi.org/10.1093/cercor/bhw008

Prehn, K., Wartenburger, I., Mériau, K., Scheibe, C., Goodenough, O. R., Villringer, A., . . . Heekeren, H. R. (2008). Individual differences in moral judgment competence influence neural correlates of socio-normative judgments. Social Cognitive and Affective Neuroscience, 3(1), 33–46. https://doi.org/10.1093/scan/nsm037

Prentice, D. A., & Carranza, E. (2002). What women and men should be, shouldn't be, are allowed to be, and don't have to be: The contents of prescriptive gender stereotypes. Psychology of Women Quarterly, 26(4), 269–281. http://doi.org/10.1111/1471-6402.t01-1-00066

Previc, F. H. (1991). A general theory concerning the prenatal origins of cerebral lateralization in humans. Psychological Review, 98(3), 299–334. http://doi.org/10.1037/0033-295x.98.3.299

Price, D., Jarman, A. P., Mason, J. O., & Kind, P. C. (2011). Building brains: An introduction to neural development (Google eBook). New York, NY: John Wiley & Sons. Retrieved from http://books.google.com/books?id=0PBVlxmlmAQC&pgis=1

Priel, B., & deSchonen, S. (1986). Self-recognition: A study of a population without mirrors. Journal of Experimental Child Psychology, 41, 237–250.

Priess, H. A., & Lindberg, S. M. (2016). Gender intensification. In R. J. R. Levesque (Ed.), Encyclopedia of adolescence (pp. 1135–1142). New York, NY: Springer. http://doi.org/10.1007/978-1-4419-1695-2_391

Priess, H. A., Lindberg, S. M., & Hyde, J. S. (2009). Adolescent gender-role identity and mental health: Gender intensification revisited. Child Development, 80(5), 1531–1544. http://doi.org/10.1111/j.1467-8624.2009.01349.x

Prifitera, A., & Saklofske, D. H. (1998). WISC-III clinical use and interpretation: Scientist-practitoner perspectives. San Diego, CA: Elsevier Academic Press.

Principe, G. F., Ornstein, P. A., Baker-Ward, L., & Gordon, B. N. (2000). The effects of intervening experiences on children's memory for a physical examination. Applied Cognitive Psychology, 14, 59–80.

Pringsheim, T., Jette, N., Frolkis, A., & Steeves, T. D. L. (2014). The prevalence of Parkinson's disease: A systematic review and meta-analysis. Movement Disorders, 29(13), 1583–1590. http://doi.org/10.1002/mds.25945

Privado, J., de Urturi, C. S., Dávila, J., López, C., Burgaleta, M., Román, F. J., . . . Colom, R. (2014). White matter integrity predicts individual differences in (fluid) intelligence through working memory. Personality and Individual Differences, 60. http://doi.org/10.1016/j.paid.2013.07.347

Procianoy, R. S., Mendes, E. W., & Silveira, R. C. (2010). Massage therapy improves neurodevelopment outcome at two years corrected age for very low birth weight infants. Early Human Development, 86(1), 7–11. http://doi.org/10.1016/j.earlhumdev.2009.12.001

Próspero, M., Russell, A. C., & Vohra-Gupta, S. (2012). Effects of motivation on educational attainment. Journal of Hispanic Higher Education, 11(1), 100–119. http://doi.org/10.1177/1538192711435556

Provins, K. A. (1997). Handedness and speech: A critical reappraisal of the role of genetic and environmental factors in the cerebral lateralization of function. Psychological Review, 104(3), 554–571. http://doi.org/10.1037/0033-295x.104.3.554

Pudrovska, T. (2009). Parenthood, stress, and mental health in late midlife and early old age. The International Journal of Aging & Human Development, 68(2), 127–147. http://doi.org/10.2190/AG.68.2.b

Puhl, R. M., & Heuer, C. A. (2009). The stigma of obesity: A review and update. Obesity, 17(5), 941–964. http://doi.org/10.1038/oby.2008.636

Puhl, R. M., & Latner, J. D. (2007). Stigma, obesity, and the health of the nation's children. Psychological Bulletin, 133(4), 557–580.

Puhl, R. M., Wall, M. M., Chen, C., Bryn Austin, S., Eisenberg, M. E., & Neumark-Sztainer, D. (2017). Experiences of weight teasing in adolescence and weight-related outcomes in adulthood: A 15-year longitudinal study. Preventive Medicine, 100, 173–179. http://doi.org/10.1016/j.ypmed.2017.04.023

Pulgarón, E. R. (2013). Childhood obesity: A review of increased risk for physical and psychological comorbidities. Clinical Therapeutics, 35(1), A18–A32. http://doi.org/10.1016/j.clinthera.2012.12.014

Pulkkinen, L., Feldt, T., & Kokko, K. (2005). Personality in young adulthood and functioning in middle age. In S. L. Willis & M. Martin (Eds.), Middle adulthood: A lifespan perspective (pp. 99–141). Thousand Oaks, CA: SAGE.

Punamäki, R.-L., Palosaari, E., Diab, M., Peltonen, K., & Qouta, S. R. (2014). Trajectories of posttraumatic stress symptoms (PTSS) after major war among Palestinian children: Trauma, family- and child-related

predictors. Journal of Affective Disorders, 172C, 133–140. http://doi.org/10.1016/j.jad.2014.09.021

Purohit, N., & Kalairajah, Y. (2010). Are patients with fractured hips giving valid consent for surgery? International Journal of Risk & Safety in Medicine, 22(2), 71–76.

Pushkar, D., Chaikelson, J., Conway, M., Etezadi, J., Giannopoulus, C., Li, K., & Wrosch, C. (2010). Testing continuity and activity variables as predictors of positive and negative affect in retirement. The Journals of Gerontology: Series B: Psychological Sciences and Social Sciences, 65B(1), 42–49. http://doi.org/10.1093/geronb/gbp079

Putman, S. E. (2009). The monsters in my head: Posttraumatic stress disorder and the child survivor of sexual abuse. Journal of Counseling & Development, 87(1), 80–89.

Qiu, A., Mori, S., & Miller, M. I. (2015). Diffusion tensor imaging for understanding brain development in early life. Annual Review of Psychology, 66, 853–876. http://doi.org/10.1146/annurev-psych-010814-015340

Quan, T., & Fisher, G. J. (2015). Role of age-associated alterations of the dermal extracellular matrix microenvironment in human skin aging: A mini-review. Gerontology. http://doi.org/10.1159/000371708

Quane, J. M., & Rankin, B. H. (2006). Does it pay to participate? Neighborhood-based organizations and the social development of urban adolescents. Children & Youth Services Review, 28, 1229–1250.

Quaranta, N., Coppola, F., Casulli, M., Barulli, M. R., Panza, F., Tortelli, R., . . . Logroscino, G. (2015). Epidemiology of age related hearing loss: A review. Hearing, Balance and Communication, 1–5. http://doi.org/10.3109/21695717.2014.994869

Quek, Y.-H., Tam, W. W. S., Zhang, M. W. B., & Ho, R. C. M. (2017). Exploring the association between childhood and adolescent obesity and depression: A meta-analysis. Obesity Reviews. http://doi.org/10.1111/obr.12535

Quine, S., Wells, Y., de Vaus, D., & Kendig, H. (2007). When choice in retirement decisions is missing: Qualitative and quantitative findings of impact on well-being. Australasian Journal on Aging, 26(4), 173–179. Retrieved from y.wells@latrobe.edu.au

Quinn, P. C., Doran, M. M., Reiss, J. E., & Hoffman, J. E. (2010). Neural markers of subordinate-level categorization in 6- to 7-month-old infants. Developmental Science, 13(3), 499–507. http://doi.org/10.1111/j.1467-7687.2009.00903.x

Quinn, P. C., & Eimas, P. D. (1996). Perceptual organization and categorization in young infants. In C. Rovee-Collier & L. P. Lipsitt (Eds.), Advances in infancy research (Vol. 10, pp. 1–36). Norwood, NJ: Ablex.

Quinn, P. C., Eimas, P. D., & Rosenkrantz, S. L. (1993). Evidence for representations of perceptual similar natural categories by 3- and 4-month-old infants. Perception, 22, 463–475.

Quinn, P. C., & Liben, L. S. (2014). A sex difference in mental rotation in infants: Convergent evidence. Infancy, 19(1), 103–116. http://doi.org/10.1111/infa.12033

Quinn, P. C., Yahr, J., Kuhn, A., Slater, A. M., & Pascalis, O. (2002). Representation of the gender of human faces by infants: A preference for female. Perception, 31(9), 1109–1121. http://doi.org/10.1068/p3331

Quintana, S. M. (2007). Racial and ethnic identity: Developmental perspectives and research. Journal of Counseling Psychology, 54(3), 259–270.

Radak, Z., Chung, H. Y., Koltai, E., Taylor, A. W., & Goto, S. (2008). Exercise, oxidative stress and hormesis. Aging Research Reviews, 7(1), 34–42. http://doi.org/10.1016/j.arr.2007.04.004

Radmacher, K., & Azmitia, M. (2006). Are there gendered pathways to intimacy in early adolescents' and emerging adults' friendships? *Journal of Adolescent Research*, 21(4), 415–448.

Radvansky, G. A., Zacks, R. T., & Hasher, L. (2005). Age and inhibition: The retrieval of situation models. *Journals of Gerontology Series B: Psychological Sciences & Social Sciences*, 60B(5), P276–P278.

Radwany, S., Albanese, T., Clough, L., Sims, L., Mason, H., & Jahangiri, S. (2009). End-of-life decision making and emotional burden: Placing family meetings in context. *The American Journal of Hospice & Palliative Care*, 26(5), 376–383. http://doi.org/10.1177/1049909109338515

Raevuori, A., Keski-Rahkonen, A., & Hoek, H. W. (2014). A review of eating disorders in males. *Current Opinion in Psychiatry*, 27(6), 426–430. http://doi.org/10.1097/YCO.0000000000000113

Raffaelli, M., & Ontai, L. L. (2004). Gender socialization in Latino/a families: Results from two retrospective studies. *Sex Roles*, 50(5/6), 287–299. http://doi.org/10.1023/B:SERS.0000018886.58945.06

Rafferty, Y., Griffin, K. W., & Lodise, M. (2011). Adolescent motherhood and developmental outcomes of children in early Head Start: The influence of maternal parenting behaviors, well-being, and risk factors within the family setting. *American Journal of Orthopsychiatry*, 81(2), 228–245. http://doi.org/10.1111/j.1939-0025.2011.01092.x

Raftery, J. N., Grolnick, W. S., & Flamm, E. S. (2012). Families as facilitators of student engagement: Toward a home-school partnership model. In S. L. Christenson, A. L. Reschly, & C. Wylie (Eds.), *Handbook of research on student engagement* (pp. 343–364). Boston, MA: Springer. http://doi.org/10.1007/978-1-4614-2018-7_16

Rageliené, T. (2016). Links of adolescents identity development and relationship with peers: A systematic literature review. *Journal of the Canadian Academy of Child and Adolescent Psychiatry*, 25(2), 97–105.

Raiford, J. L., Wingood, G. M., & DiClemente, R. J. (2007). Prevalence, incidence, and predictors of dating violence: A longitudinal study of African American female adolescents. *Journal of Women's Health*, 16(6), 822–832. http://doi.org/10.1089/jwh.2006.0002

Raikes, H. A., & Thompson, R. A. (2008). Attachment security and parenting quality predict children's problem-solving, attributions, and loneliness with peers. *Attachment & Human Development*, 10(3), 319–344. http://doi.org/10.1080/14616730802113620

Rainwater-Lovett, K., Luzuriaga, K., & Persaud, D. (2015). Very early combination antiretroviral therapy in infants: Prospects for cure. *Current Opinion in HIV and AIDS*, 10(1), 4–11. http://doi.org/10.1097/COH.0000000000000127

Raj, T., Chibnik, L. B., McCabe, C., Wong, A., Replogle, J. M., Yu, L., . . . De Jager, P. L. (2017). Genetic architecture of age-related cognitive decline in African Americans. *Neurology Genetics*, 3(1), e125. http://doi.org/10.1212/NXG.0000000000000125

Rakison, D. H., & Butterworth, G. E. (1998). Infants' use of object parts in early categorization. *Developmental Psychology*, 34, 49–62.

Rakoczy, H., Warneken, F., & Tomasello, M. (2007). "This way!" "No! That way!" 3-year olds know that two people can have mutually incompatible desires. *Cognitive Development*, 22(1), 47–68.

Raley, R. K., Sweeney, M. M., & Wondra, D. (2015). The growing racial and ethnic divide in U.S. marriage patterns. *The Future of Children*, 25(2), 89–109. Retrieved from http://www.ncbi.nlm.nih.gov/pubmed/27134512

Ram, B., & Hou, F. (2003). Changes in family structure and child outcomes: Roles of economic and familial resources. *Policy Studies Journal*, 31(3), 309–330.

Ram, G., & Chinen, J. (2011). Infections and immunodeficiency in Down syndrome. *Clinical and Experimental Immunology*, 164(1), 9–16. http://doi.org/10.1111/j.1365-2249.2011.04335.x

Raman, L., & Gelman, S. A. (2005). Children's understanding of the transmission of genetic disorders and contagious illnesses. *Developmental Psychology*, 41(1), 171–182.

Raman, L., & Gelman, S. A. (2008). Do children endorse psychosocial factors in the transmission of illness and disgust? *Developmental Psychology*, 44(3), 801–813.

Raman, L., & Winer, G. A. (2002). Children's and adults' understanding of illness: Evidence in support of a coexistence model. *Genetic, Social, and General Psychology Monographs*, 128(4), 325–355.

Rambaran, J. A., Hopmeyer, A., Schwartz, D., Steglich, C., Badaly, D., & Veenstra, R. (2017). Academic functioning and peer influences: A short-term longitudinal study of network-behavior dynamics in middle adolescence. *Child Development*, 88(2), 523–543. http://doi.org/10.1111/cdev.12611

Ramey, C. T., & Ramey, S. L. (1998). Prevention of intellectual disabilities: Early interventions to improve cognitive development. *Preventive Medicine*, 27, 224–232.

Ramos Salazar, L. (2015). The negative reciprocity process in marital relationships: A literature review. *Aggression and Violent Behavior*, 24, 113–119. http://doi.org/10.1016/j.avb.2015.05.008

Ramsdell, H. L., Oller, D. K., Buder, E. H., Ethington, C. A., & Chorna, L. (2012). Identification of prelinguistic phonological categories. *Journal of Speech, Language, and Hearing Research*, 55(6), 1626–1639. http://doi.org/10.1044/1092-4388(2012/11-0250)

Ramus, F. (2014). Neuroimaging sheds new light on the phonological deficit in dyslexia. *Trends in Cognitive Sciences*, 18(6), 274–275. http://doi.org/10.1016/j.tics.2014.01.009

Rando, T. A. (1988). Anticipatory grief: The term is a misnomer but the phenomenon exists. *Journal of Palliative Care*, 4(1–2), 70–73. Retrieved from http://www.ncbi.nlm.nih.gov/pubmed/3171779

Rangel, A., Camerer, C., & Montague, P. R. (2008). A framework for studying the neurobiology of value-based decision making: Nature reviews. *Neuroscience*, 9(7), 545–556. https://doi.org/10.1038/nrn2357

Ranson, K. E., & Urichuk, L. J. (2008). The effect of parent-child attachment relationships on child biopsychosocial outcomes: A review. *Early Child Development and Care*, 178(2), 129–152. http://doi.org/10.1080/03004430600685282

Rao, J. K., Anderson, L. A., Lin, F.-C., & Laux, J. P. (2014). Completion of advance directives among U.S. consumers. *American Journal of Preventive Medicine*, 46(1), 65–70. http://doi.org/10.1016/j.amepre.2013.09.008

Rapin, I., Shalev, R. S., Manor, O., Kerem, B., al., et, Molko, N., . . . Honda, M. (2016). Dyscalculia and the calculating brain. *Pediatric Neurology*, 61, 11–20. http://doi.org/10.1016/j.pediatrneurol.2016.02.007

Rasheed, S., Frongillo, E. A., Devine, C. M., Alam, D. S., & Rasmussen, K. M. (2009). Maternal, infant, and household factors are associated with breast-feeding trajectories during infants' first 6 months of life in Matlab, Bangladesh. *Journal of Nutrition*, 139(8), 1582–1587. http://doi.org/10.3945/jn.108.102392

Rasmussen, A. R., Wohlfahrt-Veje, C., Tefre de Renzy-Martin, K., Hagen, C. P., Tinggaard, J., Mouritsen, A., . . . Group, N. C. S. (2015). Validity of self-assessment of pubertal maturation. *Pediatrics*, 135(1), 86–93. http://doi.org/10.1542/peds.2014-0793

Ratcliff, R., Thapar, A., & McKoon, G. (2006). Aging and individual differences in rapid two-choice decisions. *Psychonomic Bulletin & Review*, 13(4), 626–635.

Ratnarajah, N., Rifkin-Graboi, A., Fortier, M. V, Chong, Y. S., Kwek, K., Saw, S.-M., . . . Qiu, A. (2013). Structural connectivity asymmetry in the neonatal brain. *NeuroImage*, 75, 187–194. http://doi.org/10.1016/j.neuroimage.2013.02.052

Rattaz, C., Goubet, N., & Bullinger, A. (2005). The calming effect of a familiar odor on full-term newborns. *Journal of Developmental and Behavioral Pediatrics*, 26(2), 86–92.

Raviv, T., Kessenich, M., & Morrison, F. J. (2004). A mediational model of the association between socioeconomic status and 3-year-old language abilities: The role of parenting factors. *Early Childhood Research Quarterly*, 19(4), 528–547. http://doi.org/10.1016/j.ecresq.2004.10.007

Rayner, K., Foorman, B. R., Perfetti, C. A., Pesetsky, D., & Seidenberg, M. S. (2001). How psychological science informs the teaching of reading. *Psychological Science in the Public Interest*, 2, 31–74.

Raz, N., Rodrigue, K. M., Kennedy, K. M., & Acker, J. D. (2007). Vascular health and longitudinal changes in brain and cognition in middle-aged and older adults. *Neuropsychology*, 21(2), 149–157.

Razmus, I. S., Dalton, M. E., & Wilson, D. (2004). Pain management for newborn circumcision. *Pediatric Nursing*, 30(5), 414–427.

Ready, R. E., Carvalho, J. O., & Åkerstedt, A. M. (2012). Evaluative organization of the self-concept in younger, midlife, and older adults. *Research on Aging*, 34(1), 56–79. http://doi.org/10.1177/0164027511415244

Reagan-Steiner, S., Yankey, D., Jeyarajah, J., Elam-Evans, L. D., Curtis, C. R., MacNeil, J., . . . Singleton, J. A. (2016). National, regional, state, and selected local area vaccination coverage among adolescents aged 13–17 years: United States, 2015. *Morbidity and Mortality Weekly Report*, 65(33), 850–858. http://doi.org/10.15585/mmwr.mm6533a4

Reason, R. D., Terenzini, P. T., & Domingo, R. J. (2007). Developing social and personal competence in the first year of college. *Review of Higher Education*, 30(3), 271–299.

Reavis, R. D., Keane, S. P., & Calkins, S. D. (2010). Trajectories of peer victimization: The role of multiple relationships. *Merrill-Palmer Quarterly: Journal of Developmental Psychology*, 56(3), 303–332.

Rebar, A. L., Stanton, R., Geard, D., Short, C., Duncan, M. J., & Vandelanotte, C. (2015). A meta-meta-analysis of the effect of physical activity on depression and anxiety in non-clinical adult populations. *Health Psychology Review*, 9(3), 366–378. http://doi.org/10.1080/17437199.2015.1022901

Reckdenwald, A., Ford, J. A., & Murray, B. N. (2016). Alcohol use in emerging adulthood: Can Moffitt's developmental theory help us understand binge drinking among college students? *Journal of Child & Adolescent Substance Abuse*, 1–7. http://doi.org/10.1080/1067828X.2015.1103347

Redick, T. S., Unsworth, N., Kelly, A. J., & Engle, R. W. (2012). Faster, smarter? Working memory capacity and perceptual speed in relation to fluid intelligence. *Journal of Cognitive Psychology*, 24(7), 844–854. http://doi.org/10.1080/20445911.2012.704359

Reed, A. E., & Carstensen, L. L. (2012). The theory behind the age-related positivity effect. *Frontiers in Psychology*, 3, 339. http://doi.org/10.3389/fpsyg.2012.00339

REFERENCES

Reed, A. E., & Carstensen, L. L. (2015). Age-related positivity effect and its implications for social and health gerontology. In N. A. Pachana (Ed.), *Encyclopedia of geropsychology* (pp. 1–9). Singapore: Springer. http://doi.org/10.1007/978-981-287-080-3_50-1

Reed, A. E., Chan, L., & Mikels, J. A. (2014). Meta-analysis of the age-related positivity effect: Age differences in preferences for positive over negative information. *Psychology and Aging*, 29(1), 1–15. http://doi.org/10.1037/a0035194

Reed, T. D., & Neville, H. A. (2014). The influence of religiosity and spirituality on psychological well-being among black women. *Journal of Black Psychology*, 40(4), 384–401. http://doi.org/10.1177/0095798413490956

Reel, J. J. (2012). *Eating disorders: An encyclopedia of causes, treatment, and prevention.* Santa Barbara, CA: ABC-CLIO.

Reese, E., & Fivush, R. (1993). Parental styles for talking about the past. *Developmental Psychology*, 29, 596–606.

Reese, E., Haden, C. A., & Fivush, R. (1993). Mother-child conversations about the past: Relationships of style and memory over time. *Cognitive Development*, 8, 403–430.

Regan, P. C., Durvasula, R., Howell, L., Ureño, O., & Rea, M. (2004). Gender, ethnicity, and the developmental timing of first sexual and romantic experiences. *Social Behavior & Personality: An International Journal*, 32(7), 667–676.

Rehm, C. D., Drewnowski, A., & Monsivais, P. (2015). Potential population-level nutritional impact of replacing whole and reduced-fat milk with low-fat and skim milk among US children aged 2–19 years. Journal of Nutrition Education and Behavior, 47(1), 61 -68.e1. https://doi.org/10.1016/j.jneb.2014.11.001

Reich, R. R., Cummings, J. R., Greenbaum, P. E., Moltisanti, A. J., & Goldman, M. S. (2015). The temporal "pulse" of drinking: Tracking 5 years of binge drinking in emerging adults. *Journal of Abnormal Psychology*, 124(3), 635–647. http://doi.org/10.1037/abn0000061

Reilly, J. J. (2007). Childhood obesity: An overview. *Children & Society*, 21(5), 390–396.

Reinhold, S. (2010). Reassessing the link between premarital cohabitation and marital instability. *Demography*, 47(3), 719–733. http://doi.org/10.1353/dem.0.0122

Reis, O., & Youniss, J. (2004). Patterns in identity change and development in relationships with mothers and friends. *Journal of Adolescent Research*, 19(1), 31–44.

Reising, M. M., Watson, K. H., Hardcastle, E. J., Merchant, M. J., Roberts, L., Forehand, R., & Compas, B. E. (2013). Parental depression and economic disadvantage: The role of parenting in associations with internalizing and externalizing symptoms in children and adolescents. *Journal of Child and Family Studies*, 22(3). http://doi.org/10.1007/s10826-012-9582-4

Reiter, E. O., & Lee, P. A. (2001). Have the onset and tempo of puberty changed? *Archives of Pediatrics & Adolescent Medicine*, 155, 988-989.

Rektorova, I., Rusina, R., Hort, J., & Matej, R. (2009). The degenerative dementias. In R. P. Lisak, D. D. Truong, W. M. Carroll, & R. Bhidayasiri (Eds.), *International neurology: A clinical approach*. Hoboken, NJ: John Wiley & Sons.

Relji , G., Ferring, D., & Martin, R. (2014). A meta-analysis on the effectiveness of bilingual programs in europe. *Review of Educational Research*. http://doi.org/10.3102/0034654314548514

Rembeck, G., Möller, M., & Gunnarsson, R. (2006). Attitudes and feelings toward menstruation and womanhood in girls at menarche. *Acta Paediatrica*, 95(6), 707–714.

Renaud, S.-J., Engarhos, P., Schleifer, M., & Talwar, V. (2015). Children's earliest experiences with death: Circumstances, conversations, explanations, and parental satisfaction. *Infant and Child Development*, 24(2), 157–174. http://doi.org/10.1002/icd.1889

Renk, K., Liljequist, L., Simpson, J. E., & Phares, V. (2005). Gender and age differences in the topics of parent-adolescent conflict. *Family Journal*, 13(2), 139–149. http://doi.org/10.1177/1066480704271190

Reuter-Lorenz, P. A., & Cappell, K. A. (2008). Neurocognitive aging and the compensation hypothesis. *Current Directions in Psychological Science*, 17(3), 177–182. http://doi.org/10.1111/j.1467-8721.2008.00570.x

Reyes, H. L. M., Foshee, V. A., Niolon, P. H., Reidy, D. E., & Hall, J. E. (2016). Gender role attitudes and male adolescent dating violence perpetration: Normative beliefs as moderators. *Journal of Youth and Adolescence*, 45(2), 350–360. http://doi.org/10.1007/s10964-015-0278-0

Reyna, C. (2008). Ian is intelligent but Leshaun is lazy: Antecedents and consequences of attributional stereotypes in the classroom. *European Journal of Psychology of Education*, 23(4), 439–458. http://doi.org/10.1007/BF03172752

Reyna, V. F., & Farley, F. (2006). Risk and rationality in adolescent decision making: Implications for theory, practice, and public policy. *Psychological Science in the Public Interest*, 7(1), 1–44.

Reyna, V. F., & Rivers, S. E. (2008). Current theories of risk and rational decision making. *Developmental Review*, 28(1), 1–11. http://doi.org/10.1016/j.dr.2008.01.002

Reynolds, B. M., & Juvonen, J. (2011). The role of early maturation, perceived popularity, and rumors in the emergence of internalizing symptoms among adolescent girls. *Journal of Youth and Adolescence*, 40(11), 1407–1422. http://doi.org/10.1007/s10964-010-9619-1

Reynolds, G. D. (2015). Infant visual attention and object recognition. *Behavioural Brain Research*, 285, 34–43. http://doi.org/10.1016/j.bbr.2015.01.015

Reynolds, G. D., Zhang, D., & Guy, M. W. (2013). Infant attention to dynamic audiovisual stimuli: Look duration from 3 to 9 months of age. *Infancy*, 18(4), 554–577. http://doi.org/10.1111/j.1532-7078.2012.00134.x

Rhoades, G. K., Stanley, S. M., & Markman, H. J. (2009). The pre-engagement cohabitation effect: A replication and extension of previous findings. *Journal of Family Psychology*, 23(1), 107–111. http://doi.org/10.1037/a0014358

Rhone, M., & Basu, A. (2008). Phytochemicals and age-related eye diseases. *Nutrition Reviews*, 66(8), 465–472. http://doi.org/10.1111/j.1753-4887.2008.00078.x

Rhule, D. M., McMahon, R. J., Spieker, S. J., & Munson, J. A. (2006). Positive adjustment and associated protective factors in children of adolescent mothers. *Journal of Child & Family Studies*, 15(2), 224–244.

Rice, C., & Cunningham, D. A. (2002). Aging of the neuromuscular system: Influences of gender and physical activity. In R. J. Scephard (Ed.), *Gender, physical ativity, and aging* (pp. 121–150). Boca Raton, FL: CBC Press.

Rice, C., Koinis, D., Sullivan, K., Tager-Flusberg, H., & Winner, E. (1997). When 3-year-olds pass the appearance-reality test. *Developmental Psychology*, 33, 54–61.

Rice, C., & Pasupathi, M. (2010). Reflecting on self-relevant experiences: Adult age differences. *Developmental Psychology*, 46(2), 479–490. http://doi.org/10.1037/a0018098

Rice, E., Rhoades, H., Winetrobe, H., Sanchez, M., Montoya, J., Plant, A., & Kordic, T. (2012). Sexually explicit cell phone messaging associated with sexual risk among adolescents. *Pediatrics*, 130(4), 667–673. http://doi.org/10.1542/peds.2012-0021

Richards, J. E. (2010). The development of attention to simple and complex visual stimuli in infants: Behavioral and psychophysiological measures. *Developmental Review*, 30(2), 203–219. http://doi.org/10.1016/j.dr.2010.03.005

Richards, J. E. (2011). Infant attention, arousal, and the brain. In L. M. Oakes, C. H. Cashon, M. Casasola, & D. H. Rakison (Eds.), *Infant perception and cognition: Recent advances, emerging theories, and future directions* (pp. 27–49). New York, NY: Oxford University Press.

Richards, J. E., & Holley, F. B. (1999). Infant attention and the development of smooth pursuit tracking. *Developmental Psychology*, 35, 856–867.

Richards, M. H., & Larson, R. (1993). Pubertal development and the daily subjective states of young adolescents. *Journal of Research on Adolescence*, 3(2), 145–169.

Richards, T. L., Dager, S. R., Corina, D., Serafini, S., Heide, A. C., & Steury, K. (1999). Dyslexic children have abnormal brain lactate response to reading-related language tasks. *American Journal of Neuroradiology*, 20, 1393–1398.

Richardson, K., & Norgate, S. H. (2015). Does IQ really predict job performance? *Applied Developmental Science*, 19(3), 153–169. http://doi.org/10.1080/10888691.2014.983635

Richardson, S. M., Paxton, S. J., & Thomson, J. S. (2009). Is BodyThink an efficacious body image and self-esteem program? A controlled evaluation with adolescents. *Body Image*, 6(2), 75–82. http://doi.org/10.1016/j.bodyim.2008.11.001

Richmond, R. C., Simpkin, A. J., Woodward, G., Gaunt, T. R., Lyttleton, O., McArdle, W. L., . . . Relton, C. L. (2015). Prenatal exposure to maternal smoking and offspring DNA methylation across the lifecourse: Findings from the Avon Longitudinal Study of Parents and Children (ALSPAC). *Human Molecular Genetics*, 24(8), 2201–2217. http://doi.org/10.1093/hmg/ddu739

Richmond, S., Johnson, K. A., Seal, M. L., Allen, N. B., & Whittle, S. (2016). Development of brain networks and relevance of environmental and genetic factors: A systematic review. *Neuroscience & Biobehavioral Reviews*, 71, 215–239. http://doi.org/10.1016/j.neubiorev.2016.08.024

Rickard, I. J., Frankenhuis, W. E., & Nettle, D. (2014). Why are childhood family factors associated with timing of maturation? A role for internal prediction. *Perspectives on Psychological Science*, 9(1), 3–15. http://doi.org/10.1177/1745691613513467

Rideout, V. J. (2010). *Generation M2: Media in the lives of 8- to 18-year-olds.* Retrieved from http://kff.org/other/event/generation-m2-media-in-the-lives-of/

Rideout, V. J. (2013). *Zero to eight: Children's media use in America 2013.* Retrieved from https://www.commonsensemedia.org/research/zero-to-eight-childrens-media-use-in-america-2013

Riesch, S. K., Bush, L., Nelson, C. J., Ohm, B. J., Portz, P. A., Abell, B., . . . Jenkins, P (2000). Topics of conflict between parents and young adolescents. *Journal of the Society of Pediatric Nurses*, 5(1), 27.

Riggins, T. (2014). Longitudinal investigation of source memory reveals different developmental trajectories for item memory and binding. *Developmental Psychology*, 50(2), 449–459. http://doi.org/10.1037/a0033622

Riggle, E. D. B., Rostosky, S. S., & Horne, S. G. (2010). Psychological distress, well-being, and legal recognition in same-sex couple relationships. *Journal of Family Psychology*, 24(1), 82–86. http://doi.org/10.1037/a0017942

REFERENCES

Riggle, E. D. B., Wickham, R. E., Rostosky, S. S., Rothblum, E. D., & Balsam, K. F. (2017). Impact of civil marriage recognition for long-term same-sex couples. *Sexuality Research and Social Policy, 14*(2), 223–232. http://doi.org/10.1007/s13178-016-0243-z

Riley, E. P., Infante, M. A., & Warren, K. R. (2011). Fetal alcohol spectrum disorders: An overview. *Neuropsychology Review, 21*(2), 73–80. http://doi.org/10.1007/s11065-011-9166-x

Riley, L. D., & Bowen, C. (2005). The sandwich generation: Challenges and coping strategies of multigenerational families. *Family Journal, 13*(1), 52–58. http://doi.org/10.1177/1066480704270099

Rimoin, D. L., Connor, J. M., & Pyeritz, R. E. (1997). Nature and frequency of genetic disease. In D. L. Rimoin, J. M. Connor, & R. E. Pyeritz (Eds.), *Emery and Rimoin's principles and practices of medical genetics* (3rd ed., Vol. 1, pp. 31–34). New York, NY: Churchill Livingstone.

Rind, B., Tromovitch, P., & Bauserman, R. (1998). A meta-analytic examination of assumed properties of child sexual abuse using college samples. *Psychological Bulletin, 124*(1), 22–53.

Rindermann, H., & Thompson, J. (2013). Ability rise in NAEP and narrowing ethnic gaps? *Intelligence, 41*(6), 821–831. http://doi.org/10.1016/j.intell.2013.06.016

Rindfuss, R. R., Cooksey, E. C., & Sutterlin, R. L. (1999). Young adult occupational achievement. *Work & Occupations, 26*(2), 220–263.

Ringman, J. M., & Varpetian, A. (2009). Other dementias. In R. P. Lisak, D. D. Truong, W. M. Carroll, & R. Bhidayasiri (Eds.), *International neurology: A clinical approach* (pp. 137–143). Hoboken, NJ: John Wiley & Sons.

Ritchie, K., Bora, S., & Woodward, L. J. (2015). Social development of children born very preterm: A systematic review. *Developmental Medicine & Child Neurology, 57*(10), 899–918. http://doi.org/10.1111/dmcn.12783

Ritchie, S. J., Booth, T., Valdés Hernández, M. del C., Corley, J., Maniega, S. M., Gow, A. J., . . . Deary, I. J. (2015). Beyond a bigger brain: Multivariable structural brain imaging and intelligence. *Intelligence, 51*, 47–56. http://doi.org/10.1016/j.intell.2015.05.001

Riva Crugnola, C., Tambelli, R., Spinelli, M., Gazzotti, S., Caprin, C., & Albizzati, A. (2011). Attachment patterns and emotion regulation strategies in the second year. *Infant Behavior & Development, 34*(1), 136–151. http://doi.org/10.1016/j.infbeh.2010.11.002

Rivas-Drake, D., Seaton, E. K., Markstrom, C., Quintana, S., Syed, M., Lee, R. M., . . . Yip, T. (2014). Ethnic and racial identity in adolescence: Implications for psychosocial, academic, and health outcomes. *Child Development, 85*(1), 40–57. http://doi.org/10.1111/cdev.12200

Rivera, S. M., Wakely, A., & Langer, J. (1999). The drawbridge phenomenon: Representational reasoning or perceptual preference? *Developmental Psychology, 35*(2), 427–435.

Rivers, S. E., Reyna, V. F., & Mills, B. (2008). Risk taking under the influence: A fuzzy-trace theory of emotion in adolescence. *Developmental Review, 28*(1), 107–144. http://doi.org/10.1016/j.dr.2007.11.002

Rizzi, L., Rosset, I., & Roriz-Cruz, M. (2014). Global epidemiology of dementia: Alzheimer's and vascular types. *BioMed Research International, 2014*, 908915. http://doi.org/10.1155/2014/908915

Rizzo, G., Arcuti, S., Martino, D., Copetti, M., Fontana, A., & Logroscino, G. (2015). Accuracy of clinical diagnosis of Parkinson's disease: A systematic review and Bayesian meta-analysis. *Neurology, 84*(14), S36.001. Retrieved from http://www.neurology.org/content/84/14_Supplement/S36.001.short

Robbins, J. (2005). Contexts, collaboration, and cultural tools: A sociocultural perspective on researching children's thinking. *Contemporary Issues in Early Childhood, 6*(2), 140. http://doi.org/10.2304/ciec.2005.6.2.4

Robbins, S. B., Allen, J., Casillas, A., Peterson, C. H., & Le, H. (2006). Unraveling the differential effects of motivational and skills, social, and self-management measures from traditional predictors of college outcomes. *Journal of Educational Psychology, 98*(3), 598–616.

Roben, C. K. P., Moore, G. A., Cole, P. M., Molenaar, P., Leve, L. D., Shaw, D. S., . . . Neiderhiser, J. M. (2015). Transactional patterns of maternal depressive symptoms and mother-child mutual negativity in an adoption sample. *Infant and Child Development, 24*(3), 322–342. http://doi.org/10.1002/icd.1906

Roberts, B. W., & Caspi, A. (2003). The cumulative continuity model of personality development: Striking a balance between continuity and change in personality traits across the life course. In M. Ursula & U. Lindenberger (Eds.), *Understanding human development: Dialogues with lifespan psychology* (pp. 183–214). Dordrecht, NL: Kluwer Academic.

Roberts, B. W., & DelVecchio, W. F. (2000). The rank-order consistency of personality traits from childhood to old age: A quantitative review of longitudinal studies. *Psychological Bulletin, 126*(1), 3–25. http://doi.org/10.1037/0033-2909.126.1.3

Roberts, B. W., & Mroczek, D. (2008). Personality trait change in adulthood. *Current Directions in Psychological Science, 17*(1), 31–35. http://doi.org/10.1111/j.1467-8721.2008.00543.x

Roberts, B. W., Walton, K. E., & Viechtbauer, W. (2006). Patterns of mean-level change in personality traits across the life course: A meta-analysis of longitudinal studies. *Psychological Bulletin, 132*(1), 1–25.

Roberts, G., Quach, J., Mensah, F., Gathercole, S., Gold, L., Anderson, P., . . . Wake, M. (2015). Schooling duration rather than chronological age predicts working memory between 6 and 7 years. *Journal of Developmental & Behavioral Pediatrics, 36*(2), 68–74. http://doi.org/10.1097/DBP.0000000000000121

Roberts, J. E., & Bell, M. A. (2002). The effects of age and sex on mental rotation performance, verbal performance, and brain electrical activity. *Developmental Psychobiology, 40*(4), 391–407. http://doi.org/10.1002/dev.10039

Roberts, J. S., Connell, C. M., Cisewski, D., Hipps, Y. G., Demissie, S., & Green, R. C. (2003). Differences between African Americans and whites in their perceptions of Alzheimer disease. *Alzheimer Disease and Associated Disorders, 17*(1), 19–26. Retrieved from http://www.ncbi.nlm.nih.gov/pubmed/12621316

Roberts, R. O., Knopman, D. S., Przybelski, S. A., Mielke, M. M., Kantarci, K., Preboske, G. M., . . . Jack, C. R. (2014). Association of type 2 diabetes with brain atrophy and cognitive impairment. *Neurology, 82*(13), 1132–1141. http://doi.org/10.1212/WNL.0000000000000269

Roberts, S. B., & Rosenberg, I. (2006). Nutrition and aging: Changes in the regulation of energy metabolism with aging. *Physiological Reviews, 86*(2), 651–667. http://doi.org/10.1152/physrev.00019.2005

Robertson, D. L., Farmer, T. W., Fraser, M. W., Day, S. H., Duncan, T., Crowther, A., & Dadisman, K. A. (2010). Interpersonal competence configurations and peer relations in early elementary classrooms: Perceived popular and unpopular aggressive subtypes. *International Journal of Behavioral Development, 34*(1), 73–87. http://doi.org/10.1177/0165025409345074

Robin, L., & Omar, H. (2014). Adolescent bereavement. In J. Merrick, A. Tenenbaum, & H. A. Omar (Eds.), *School, adolescence, and health issues* (pp. 97–108). Hauppauge, NY: Nova Science. Retrieved from http://uknowledge.uky.edu/pediatrics_facpub/121

Robins, R. W., & Trzesniewski, K. H. (2005). Self-esteem development across the lifespan. *Current Directions in Psychological Science, 14*(3), 158–162. http://doi.org/10.1111/j.0963-7214.2005.00353.x

Robins, R. W., Trzesniewski, K. H., Tracy, J. L., Gosling, S. D., & Potter, J. (2002). Global self-esteem across the life span. *Psychology and Aging, 17*(3), 423–434. Retrieved from http://www.ncbi.nlm.nih.gov/pubmed/12243384

Robinson, G. E. (2014). Pregnancy loss. *Best Practice & Research. Clinical Obstetrics & Gynaecology, 28*(1), 169–178. http://doi.org/10.1016/j.bpobgyn.2013.08.012

Robinson, J. B., Burns, B. M., & Davis, D. W. (2009). Maternal scaffolding and attention regulation in children living in poverty. *Journal of Applied Developmental Psychology, 30*(2), 82–91. http://doi.org/10.1016/j.appdev.2008.10.013

Robinson, J. P., & Espelage, D. L. (2013). Peer victimization and sexual risk differences between lesbian, gay, bisexual, transgender, or questioning and nontransgender heterosexual youths in grades 7–12. *American Journal of Public Health, 103*(10), 1810–1819. http://doi.org/10.2105/AJPH.2013.301387

Robles, T. F., & Menkin, J. A. (2015). Social relationships and health in older adulthood. In R. A. Scott & M. C. Buchmann (Eds.), *Emerging trends in the social and behavioral sciences* (pp. 1–15). Hoboken, NJ: John Wiley & Sons. http://doi.org/10.1002/9781118900772.etrds0310

Rocha, E. M., Marche, T. A., & Briere, J. L. (2013). The effect of forced-choice questions on children's suggestibility: A comparison of multiple-choice and yes/no questions. *Canadian Journal of Behavioural Science, 45*(1), 1–11. http://dx.doi.org/10.1037/a0028507

Rochat, P. (1998). Self-perception and action in infancy. *Experimental Brain Research, 123*(1–2), 102–109. http://doi.org/10.1007/s002210050550

Rochat, P. (2010). Emerging self-concept. In J. G. Bremner & T. D. Wachs (Eds.), *The Wiley-Blackwell handbook of infant development* (pp. 320–344). Oxford, UK: Wiley-Blackwell. http://doi.org/10.1002/9781444327564.ch10

Rochat, P., & Striano, T. (1999). Social–cognitive development in the first year. In P. Rochat (Ed.), *Early social cognition: Understanding others in the first months of life* (pp. 3–34). Mahwah, NJ: Lawrence Erlbaum.

Rock, P. F., Cole, D. J., Houshyar, S., Lythcott, M., & Prinstein, M. J. (2011). Peer status in an ethnic context: Associations with African American adolescents' ethnic identity. *Journal of Applied Developmental Psychology, 32*(4), 163–169. http://doi.org/10.1016/j.appdev.2011.03.002

Rodkin, P. C., Espelage, D. L., & Hanish, L. D. (2015). A relational framework for understanding bullying: Developmental antecedents and outcomes. *The American Psychologist, 70*(4), 311–321. http://doi.org/10.1037/a0038658

Rodriguez, C. (2017). Marijuana legalization in Europe: Is France next? *Forbes.* Retrieved from https://www.forbes.com/sites/ceciliarodriguez/2017/01/06/marijuana-legalization-in-europe-is-france-next/#669531f6c96e

Rodriguez, E. T., & Tamis-LeMonda, C. S. (2011). Trajectories of the home learning environment across the first 5 years: Associations with children's vocabulary and literacy skills at prekindergarten. *Child Development*, 82(4), 1058–1075. http://doi.org/10.1111/j.1467-8624.2011.01614.x

Roebers, C. M., & Feurer, E. (2016). Linking executive functions and procedural metacognition. *Child Development Perspectives*, 10(1), 39–44. http://doi.org/10.1111/cdep.12159

Roediger, H. L., & Marsh, E. J. (2003). Episodic and autobiographical memory. In I. B. Weiner (Ed.), *Handbook of psychology: Complex learning and memory processes*. Hoboken, NJ: John Wiley & Sons.

Roelants, M., Hauspie, R., & Hoppenbrouwers, K. (2010). Breastfeeding, growth and growth standards: Performance of the WHO growth standards for monitoring growth of Belgian children. *Annals of Human Biology*, 37(1), 2–9. http://doi.org/10.3109/03014460903089500

Roeser, R. W., Eccles, J. S., & Sameroff, A. J. (2000). School as a context of early adolescents' academic and social-emotional development: A summary of research findings. *Elementary School Journal*, 100(5), 443–471.

Rogers, C. H., Floyd, F. J., Seltzer, M. M., Greenberg, J., & Hong, J. (2008). Long-term effects of the death of a child on parents' adjustment in midlife. *Journal of Family Psychology*, 22(2), 203–211. http://doi.org/10.1037/0893-3200.22.2.203

Rogler, L. H. (2002). Historical generations and psychology: The case of the Great Depression and World War II. *American Psychologist*, 57, 1013–1023.

Rogoff, B. (1990). *Apprenticeship in thinking: Cognitive development in social context*. New York, NY: Oxford University Press.

Rogoff, B. (1998). Cognition as a collaborative process. In D. Kuhn & R. S. Siegler (Eds.), *Handbook of child psychology: Vol. 2. Cognition, perception, and language* (5th ed., pp. 679–744). New York, NY: Wiley.

Rogoff, B. (2003). *The cultural nature of human development*. New York, NY: Oxford University Press.

Rogoff, B. (2016). Culture and participation: A paradigm shift. *Current Opinion in Psychology*, 8, 182–189. http://doi.org/10.1016/j.copsyc.2015.12.002

Rogoff, B., & Chavajay, P. (1995). What's become of research on the cultural basis of cognitive development? *American Psychologist*, 50, 859–877.

Rogoff, B.. & Morelli, G. (1989). Perspectives on children's development from cultural development. *American Psychology* 343–348.

Rogoff, B., Mosier, C., Mistry, J., & Göncü, A. (1993). Toddlers' guided participation with their caregivers in cultural activity. In E. A. Forman, N. Minick, & C. A. Stone (Eds.), *Contexts for learning* (pp. 230–253). New York, NY: Oxford University Press.

Rogoff, B., & Waddell, K. J. (1982). Memory for information organized in a scene by children from two cultures. *Child Development*, 53(5), 1224–1228. Retrieved from http://www.ncbi.nlm.nih.gov/pubmed/7140428

Roid, G. H. (2003). *Stanford-Binet intelligence scales examiner manual* (5th ed.). Itasca, IL: Riverside.

Rollins, B., Francis, L., & BeLue, R. (2007). Family meal frequency and weight status in young children. *Annals of Epidemiology*, 17(9), 745.

Rolstad, K. (2005). The big picture: A meta-analysis of program effectiveness research on English–language learners. *Educational Policy*, 19(4), 572–594. http://doi.org/10.1177/0895904805278067

Romani, C., Palermo, L., MacDonald, A., Limback, E., Hall, S. K., & Geberhiwot, T. (2017). The impact of phenylalanine levels on cognitive outcomes in adults with phenylketonuria: Effects across tasks and developmental stages. *Neuropsychology*, 31(3), 242–254. http://doi.org/10.1037/neu0000336

Romero, A. J., Edwards, L. M., Fryberg, S. A., & Orduña, M. (2014). Resilience to discrimination stress across ethnic identity stages of development. *Journal of Applied Social Psychology*, 44(1), 1–11. http://doi.org/10.1111/jasp.12192

Romero, A. J., & Roberts, R. E. (2003). The impact of multiple dimensions of ethnic identity on discrimination and adolescents' self-esteem. *Journal of Applied Social Psychology*, 33(11), 2288–2305.

Romo, D. L., Garnett, C., Younger, A. P., Stockwell, M. S., Soren, K., Catallozzi, M., & Neu, N. (2017). Social media use and its association with sexual risk and parental monitoring among a primarily Hispanic adolescent population. *Journal of Pediatric and Adolescent Gynecology*. http://doi.org/10.1016/j.jpag.2017.02.004

Ronneberg, C. R., Miller, E. A., Dugan, E., & Porell, F. (2014). The protective effects of religiosity on depression: A 2-year prospective study. *The Gerontologist*. http://doi.org/10.1093/geront/gnu073

Roopnarine, J. L., Hossain, Z., Gill, P., & Brophy, H. (1994). Play in the East Indian context. In J. L. Roopnarine, J. E. Johnson, & F. H. Hooper (Eds.), *Children's play in diverse cultures* (pp. 9–30). Albany: State University of New York Press.

Roopnarine, J. L., Talukder, E., Jain, D., Joshi, P., & Srivastav, P. (1992). Personal well-being, kinship tie, and mother-infant and father-infant interactions in single-wage and dual-wage families in New Delhi, India. *Journal of Marriage & Family*, 54(2), 293–301.

Roper, J. A., Kang, N., Ben, J., Cauraugh, J. H., Okun, M. S., & Hass, C. J. (2016). Deep brain stimulation improves gait velocity in Parkinson's disease: A systematic review and meta-analysis. *Journal of Neurology*, 263(6), 1195–1203. http://doi.org/10.1007/s00415-016-8129-9

Roring, R. W., & Charness, N. (2007). A multilevel model analysis of expertise in chess across the lifespan. *Psychology and Aging*, 22(2), 291–299.

Rosano, C., Guralnik, J., Pahor, M., Glynn, N. W., Newman, A. B., Ibrahim, T. S., . . . Aizenstein, H. J. (2017). Hippocampal response to a 24-month physical activity intervention in sedentary older adults. *The American Journal of Geriatric Psychiatry*, 25(3), 209–217. http://doi.org/10.1016/j.jagp.2016.11.007

Rosario, M., Schrimshaw, E. W., & Hunter, J. (2008). Predicting different patterns of sexual identity development over time among lesbian, gay, and bisexual youths: A cluster analytic approach. *American Journal of Community Psychology*, 42(3–4), 266–282. http://doi.org/10.1007/s10464-008-9207-7

Rosario, M., Schrimshaw, E. W., & Hunter, J. (2009). Disclosure of sexual orientation and subsequent substance use and abuse among lesbian, gay, and bisexual youths: Critical role of disclosure reactions. *Psychology of Addictive Behaviors*, 23(1), 175–184. http://doi.org/10.1037/a0014284

Rose, A. J., & Asher, S. R. (2017). The social tasks of friendship: Do boys and girls excel in different tasks? *Child Development Perspectives*, 11(1), 3–8. http://doi.org/10.1111/cdep.12214

Rose, S. A., & Feldman, J. F. (1995). Prediction of IQ and specific cognitive abilities from infancy measures. *Developmental Psychology*, 31, 685–696.

Rose, S. A., Feldman, J. F., & Jankowski, J. J. (2009). Information processing in toddlers: Continuity from infancy and persistence of preterm deficits. *Intelligence*, 37(3), 311–320. http://doi.org/10.1016/j.intell.2009.02.002

Rose, S. A., Feldman, J. F., & Jankowski, J. J. (2012). Implications of infant cognition for executive functions at age 11. *Psychological Science*, 23(11), 1345–1355. http://doi.org/10.1177/0956797612444902

Rose, S. A., Feldman, J. F., Jankowski, J. J., & Van Rossem, R. (2011). The structure of memory in infants and toddlers: An SEM study with full-terms and preterms. *Developmental Science*, 14(1), 83–91. http://doi.org/10.1111/j.1467-7687.2010.00959.x

Rose, S. A., Feldman, J. F., Jankowski, J. J., & Van Rossem, R. (2012). Information processing from infancy to 11 years: Continuities and prediction of IQ. *Intelligence*, 40(5), 445–457. http://doi.org/10.1016/j.intell.2012.05.007

Rose, S. A., Gottfried, A. W., & Bridger, W. H. (1981). Cross-modal and information processing by the sense of touch in infancy. *Developmental Psychology*, 17(1), 90–98.

Roseberry, S., Hirsh-Pasek, K., & Golinkoff, R. M. (2014). Skype me! Socially contingent interactions help toddlers learn language. *Child Development*, 85(3), 956–970. http://doi.org/10.1111/cdev.12166

Rose-Greenland, F., & Smock, P. J. (2012). Living together unmarried: What do we know about cohabiting families? In G. W. Peterson & K. R. Bush (Eds.), *Handbook of marriage and the family*. New York, NY: Springer.

Rosén, C., Hansson, O., Blennow, K., & Zetterberg, H. (2013). Fluid biomarkers in Alzheimer's disease: Current concepts. *Molecular Neurodegeneration*, 8, 20. http://doi.org/10.1186/1750-1326-8-20

Rosen, G. D. (2006). *The dyslexic brain: New pathways in neuroscience discovery*. Mahwah, NJ: Lawrence Erlbaum.

Rosen, W. D., Adamson, L. B., & Bakeman, R. (1992). An experimental investigation of infant social referencing: Mothers' messages and gender differences. *Developmental Psychology*, 28, 1172–1178.

Rosenbaum, J. E., & Person, A. E. (2003). Beyond college for all: Policies and practices to improve transitions into college and jobs. *Professional School Counseling*, 6(4), 252.

Rosenberg, M. (1965). *Society and the adolescent self-image*. Princeton, NJ: Princeton University Press.

Rosenberg, R. D., & Feigenson, L. (2013). Infants hierarchically organize memory representations. *Developmental Science*, 16(4), 610–621. http://doi.org/10.1111/desc.12055

Rosenberg, S. D., Rosenberg, H. J., & Farrell, M. P. (1999). The midlife crisis revisited. In S. L. Willis & J. D. Reid (Eds.), *Life in the middle: Psychological and social development in middle age* (pp. 47–73). San Diego, CA: Academic Press.

Rosenblatt, P. C. (2008). Grief across cultures: A review and research agenda. In M. S. Stroebe, R. O. Hansson, H. Schut, W. Stroebe, & E. Van den Blink (Eds.), *Handbook of bereavement research and practice: Advances in theory and intervention* (pp. 207–222). Washington, DC: American Psychological Association.

Rosenfeld, M. J. (2014). Couple longevity in the era of same-sex marriage in the United States. *Journal of Marriage and Family*, 76(5), 905–918. http://doi.org/10.1111/jomf.12141

Rosenkoetter, L. I. (1973). Resistance to temptation: Inhibitory and disinhibitory effects of models. *Developmental Psychology*, 8, 80–84.

Rosenzweig, M. R. (1984). Experience, memory, and the brain. *American Psychologist*, 39, 365–376.

Rosenzweig, M. R. (2002). Animal research on effects of experience on brain and behavior: Implications for rehabilitation. *Infants & Young*

Children: An Interdisciplinary Journal of Special Care Practices, 15(2), 1–10.

Roser, M. (2016). *Child mortality*. Retrieved from https://ourworldindata.org/child-mortality/

Rosnick, C. B., Small, B. J., & Burton, A. M. (2010). The effect of spousal bereavement on cognitive functioning in a sample of older adults. *Aging, Neuropsychology & Cognition, 17*(3), 257–269. http://doi.org/10.1080/13825580903042692

Ross, E. S. (2017). Flavor and taste development in the first years of life. *Nestle Nutrition Institute Workshop Series, 87*, 49–58. http://doi.org/10.1159/000448937

Ross-Gordon, J. M. (2011). Research on adult learners: Supporting the needs of a student population that is no longer nontraditional. *Peer Review, 3*(1), 26–29. Retrieved from http://www.aacu.org/publications-research/periodicals/research-adult-learners-supporting-needs-student-population-no

Rossi, A. S. (2004). The menopausal transition and aging processes. In O. G. Brim, C. D. Ryff, & R. C. Kessler (Eds.), *How healthy are we? A national study of well-being at midlife* (pp. 153–201). Chicago, IL: University of Chicago Press.

Rossi Ferrario, S., Cardillo, V., Vicario, F., Balzarini, E., & Zotti, A. M. (2004). Advanced cancer at home: Caregiving and bereavement. *Palliative Medicine, 18*(2), 129–136. http://doi.org/10.1191/0269216304pm870oa

Rossouw, J. E., Prentice, R. L., Manson, J. E., Wu, L., David Barad, M. D., Barnabei, V. M., . . . Stefanick, M. L. (2007). Postmenopausal hormone therapy and risk of cardiovascular disease by age and years since menopause. *Journal of the American Medical Association, 297*, 1465–1477.

Rote, W. M., & Smetana, J. G. (2015). Beliefs about parents' right to know: Domain differences and associations with change in concealment. *Journal of Research on Adolescence, 25*. http://doi.org/10.1111/jora.12194

Rotenberg, K. J., & Mayer, E. V. (1990). Delay of gratification in native and white children: A cross-cultural comparison. *International Journal of Behavioral Development, 13*(1), 23–30. http://doi.org/10.1177/016502549001300102

Roth, S. M. (2015). Physical activity may improve aging through impacts on telomere biology. *Kinesiology Review, 4*(1), 99–106. http://doi.org/10.1123/kr.2014-0083

Rothbart, M. K. (2011). *Becoming who we are: Temperament and personality in development*. New York, NY: Guilford Press. Retrieved from http://books.google.com/books?hl=en&lr=&id=StR9ernDY-kC&pgis=1

Rothbart, M. K., & Bates, J. E. (1998). Temperament. In N. Eisenberg (Ed.), *Handbook of child psychology: Vol. 3. Social, emotional, and personality development* (5th ed., pp. 105–176). New York, NY: Wiley.

Rothbart, M. K. (1986). Longitudinal observation of infant temperament. *Developmental Psychology, 22*(3), 356–365. http://doi.org/10.1037/0012-1649.22.3.356

Rothbaum, F., Pott, M., Azuma, H., Miyake, K., & Weisz, J. (2000). The development of close relationships in Japan and the United States: Paths of symbiotic harmony and generative tension. *Child Development, 71*, 1121–1142.

Rothbaum, F., Weisz, J., Pott, M., Miyake, K., & Morelli, G. (2000). Attachment and culture: Security in the United States and Japan. *American Psychologist, 55*, 1093–1104.

Roth-Cline, M., & Nelson, R. M. (2013). Parental permission and child assent in research on children. *The Yale Journal of Biology and Medicine, 86*(3), 291–301. Retrieved from http://www.ncbi.nlm.nih.gov/pubmed/24058304

Rothgänger, H. (2003). Analysis of the sounds of the child in the first year of age and a comparison to the language. *Early Human Development, 75*(1/2), 55–69.

Roussotte, F. F., Bramen, J. E., Nunez, S. C., Quandt, L. C., Smith, L., O'Connor, M. J., . . . Sowell, E. R. (2011). Abnormal brain activation during working memory in children with prenatal exposure to drugs of abuse: The effects of methamphetamine, alcohol, and polydrug exposure. *NeuroImage, 54*(4), 3067–3075.

Rovee-Collier, C. K. (1999). The development of infant memory. *Current Directions in Psychological Science, 8*, 80–85.

Rovee-Collier, C. K., & Bhatt, R. S. (1993). Evidence of long-term memory in infancy. *Annals of Child Development, 9*, 1–45.

Rovee-Collier, C., Hayne, H., & Colombo, J. (2002). *The development of implicit and explicit memory*. Amsterdam, NL: John Benjamins.

Rowe, G., Hasher, L., & Turcotte, J. (2010). Interference, aging, and visuospatial working memory: The role of similarity. *Neuropsychology, 24*(6), 804–807. http://doi.org/10.1037/a0020244

Rowe, M. L. (2012). A longitudinal investigation of the role of quantity and quality of child-directed speech in vocabulary development. *Child Development, 83*(5), 1762–1774. http://doi.org/10.1111/j.1467-8624.2012.01805.x

Roy, R. N., Schumm, W. R., & Britt, S. L. (2014). Voluntary versus involuntary childlessness. In *Transition to parenthood* (pp. 49–68). New York, NY: Springer.

Roy, T., & Lloyd, C. E. (2012). Epidemiology of depression and diabetes: A systematic review. *Journal of Affective Disorders, 142*, S8–S21. http://doi.org/10.1016/S0165-0327(12)70004-6

Rozas, A. X. P., Juncos-Rabadán, O., & González, M. S. R. (2008). Processing speed, inhibitory control, and working memory: Three important factors to account for age-related cognitive decline. *International Journal of Aging & Human Development, 66*(2), 115–130.

Rubin, D. C. (2000). Autobiographical memory and aging. In D. C. Park & N. Schwarz (Eds.), *Cognitive aging: A primer* (pp. 131–149). New York, NY: Psychology Press.

Rubin, D. C., & Berntsen, D. (2006). People over forty feel 20% younger than their age: Subjective age across the lifespan. *Psychonomic Bulletin & Review, 13*(5), 776–780. http://doi.org/10.3758/BF03193996

Rubin, K. H., Copian, R., Chen, X., Bowker, J., & McDonald, K. L. (2011). Peer relationships in childhood. In M. H. Bornstein & M. E. Lamb (Eds.), *Developmental science: An advanced textbook* (6th ed., pp. 519–570). New York, NY: Psychology Press.

Rubin, K. H., Coplan, R. J., & Bowker, J. C. (2009). Social withdrawal in childhood. *Annual Review of Psychology, 60*(1), 141–171. http://doi.org/10.1146/annurev.psych.60110707.163642

Rubin, K. H., Coplan, R., Chen, X., Buskirk, A. A., & Wojslawowicz, J. C. (2005). Peer relationships in childhood. In M. H. Bornstein & M. E. Lamb (Eds.), *Developmental science: An advanced textbook* (5th ed., pp. 469–512). Mahwah, NJ: Lawrence Erlbaum.

Rubin, K. H., Hastings, P., Chen, X., Stewart, S., & McNichol, K. (1998). Interpersonal and maternal correlates of aggression, conflict, and externalizing problems in toddlers. *Child Development, 69*, 1614–1629.

Rubin, K. H., Wojslawowicz, J. C., Rose-Krasnor, L., Booth-LaForce, C., & Burgess, K. B. (2006). The best friendships of shy/withdrawn children: Prevalence,

stability, and relationship quality. *Journal of Abnormal Child Psychology, 34*(2), 143–157. http://doi.org/10.1007/s10802-005-9017-4

Ruble, D. N., Grosovsky, E. H., Frey, K. S., & Cohen, R. (1992). Developmental changes in competence assessment. In A. K. Boggiano & T. S. Pittman (Eds.), *Achievement and motivation: A social developmental perspective* (pp. 138–164). New York, NY: Cambridge University Press.

Ruble, D. N., Martin, C. L., & Berenbaum, S. A. (2006). Gender development. In N. Eisenberg, W. Damon, & R. M. Lerner (Eds.), *Handbook of child psychology: Vol. 3, Social, emotional, and personality development* (6th ed., pp. 858–932). Hoboken, NJ: John Wiley & Sons.

Ruble, D. N., Taylor, L. J., Cyphers, L., Greulich, F. K., Lurye, L. E., & Shrout, P. E. (2007). The role of gender constancy in early gender development. *Child Development, 78*(4), 1121–1136.

Rudiger, J. A., & Winstead, B. A. (2013). Body talk and body-related co-rumination: Associations with body image, eating attitudes, and psychological adjustment. *Body Image, 10*(4), 462–471. http://doi.org/10.1016/j.bodyim.2013.07.010

Rudin, C. (2004). Die Prävention der vertikalen HIV-Ubertragung—eine Erfolgsgeschichte. *Therapeutische Umschau. Revue Thérapeutique, 61*, 599–602.

Rudman, L. A., & Glick, P. (2001). Prescriptive gender stereotypes and backlash toward agentic women. *Journal of Social Issues, 57*(4), 743–762. http://doi.org/10.1111/0022-4537.00239

Rudolph, K. D., Lambert, S. F., Clark, A. G., & Kurlakowsky, K. D. (2001). Negotiating the transition to middle school: The role of self-regulatory processes. *Child Development, 72*(3), 929–947.

Rudolph, K. D., Troop-Gordon, W., Lambert, S. F., & Natsuaki, M. N. (2014). Long-term consequences of pubertal timing for youth depression: Identifying personal and contextual pathways of risk. *Development and Psychopathology, 26*(4), 1423–1444.

Rueda, M. R. (2013). Development of attention. In *The Oxford handbook of cognitive neuroscience, Vol. 1: Core topics* (p. 656). Retrieved from http://books.google.com/books?hl=en&lr=&id=CtIBAgAAQBAJ&pgis=1

Rueger, S. Y., Chen, P., Jenkins, L. N., & Choe, H. J. (2014). Effects of perceived support from mothers, fathers, and teachers on depressive symptoms during the transition to middle school. *Journal of Youth and Adolescence, 43*(4), 655–670. http://doi.org/10.1007/s10964-013-0039-x

Ruff, H. A., & Kohler, C. J. (1978). Tactual-visual transfer in six-month-old infants. *Infant Behavior & Development, 1*, 259–264.

Ruff, H. A., & Rothbart, M. K. (1996). *Attention in early development*. New York, NY: Oxford University Press.

Ruffman, T., Perner, J., & Parkin, L. (1999). How parenting style affects false belief development. *Social Development, 8*, 395–411.

Ruffman, T., Slade, L., & Crowe, E. (2002). The relation between children's and mothers' mental state language and theory-of-mind understanding. *Child Development, 73*, 734–751.

Ruiz, J. M., Hamann, H. A., Mehl, M. R., & O'Connor, M.-F. (2016). The Hispanic health paradox: From epidemiological phenomenon to contribution opportunities for psychological science. *Group Processes & Intergroup Relations, 19*(4), 462–476. http://doi.org/10.1177/1368430216638540

Runco, M. A., & Acar, S. (2012). Divergent thinking as an indicator of creative potential. *Creativity Research Journal, 24*(1), 66–75. http://doi.org/10.1080/10400419.2012.652929

Runions, K. C., Vitaro, F., Cross, D., Shaw, T., Hall, M., & Boivin, M. (2014). Teacher–child relationship, parenting, and growth in likelihood and severity of physical aggression in the early school years. *Merrill-Palmer Quarterly, 60*(3), 274–301. Retrieved from http://muse.jhu.edu/journals/merrill-palmer_quarterly/v060/60.3.runions.html

Ruppar, T. M., & Schneider, J. K. (2007). Self-reported exercise behavior and interpretations of exercise in older adults. *Western Journal of Nursing Research, 29*(2), 140–157.

Rushton, J. P., & Bons, T. A. (2005). Mate choice and friendship in twins: Evidence for genetic similarity. *Psychological Science, 16*(7), 555–559. http://doi.org/10.1111/j.0956-7976.2005.01574.x

Russac, R. J., Gatliff, C., Reece, M., & Spottswood, D. (2007). Death anxiety across the adult years: An examination of age and gender effects. *Death Studies, 31*(6), 549–561. http://doi.org/10.1080/07481180701356936

Russell, M. J. (1976). Human olfactory communication. *Nature, 260*, 520–522.

Russell, S. T., & Fish, J. N. (2016). Mental health in lesbian, gay, bisexual, and transgender (LGBT) youth. *Annual Review of Clinical Psychology, 12*(1), 465–487. http://doi.org/10.1146/annurev-clinpsy-021815-093153

Russo, M., Shteigman, A., & Carmeli, A. (2015). Workplace and family support and work–life balance: Implications for individual psychological availability and energy at work. *The Journal of Positive Psychology*, 1–16. http://doi.org/10.1080/17439760.2015.1025424

Russo, R. (2008). *A healing touch: True stories of life, death, and hospice.* Camden, MI: Down East Books.

Rutherford, A. (2000). Radical behaviorism and psychology's public: B. F. Skinner in the popular press, 1934–1990. *History of Psychology, 3*(4), 371–395.

Rutter, M. (2010). Gene–environment interplay. *Depression & Anxiety, 27*, 1–4.

Rutter, M. (2012). Gene–environment interdependence. *European Journal of Developmental Psychology, 9*(4), 391–412.

Rutter, M., Giller, H., & Hagell, A. (1998). *Antisocial behavior by young people.* New York, NY: Cambridge University Press.

Rutter, M., Thapar, A., Pine, D. S., Leckman, J. F., Scott, S., Snowling, M. J., & Taylor, E. (2015). Resilience: Concepts, findings, and clinical implications. In A. Thapar, D. S. Pine, J. F. Leckman, S. Scott, M. J. Snowling, & E. Taylor (Eds.), *Rutter's child and adolescent psychiatry* (pp. 341–351). Chichester, UK: John Wiley & Sons. http://doi.org/10.1002/9781118381953.ch27

Ruzgis, P., & Grigorenko, E. L. (1994). Cultural meaning systems, intelligence, and personality. In R. J. Sternberg & P. Ruzgis (Eds.), *Personality and intelligence* (pp. 248–270). New York, NY: Cambridge University Press.

Ryalls, B. O. (2000). Dimensional adjectives: Factors affecting children's ability to compare objects using novel words. *Journal of Experimental Child Psychology, 76*(1), 26–49.

Ryan, A. M., & Patrick, H. (2001). The classroom social environment and changes in adolescents' motivation and engagement during middle school. *American Educational Research Journal, 38*(2), 437–460.

Ryan, C., Russell, S. T., Huebner, D., Diaz, R., & Sanchez, J. (2010). Family acceptance in adolescence and the health of LGBT young adults. *Journal of Child and Adolescent Psychiatric Nursing, 23*(4), 205–213. http://doi.org/10.1111/j.1744-6171.2010.00246.x

Ryan, R. M., Claessens, A., & Markowitz, A. J. (2014). Associations between family structure change and child behavior problems: The moderating effect of family income. *Child Development.* http://doi.org/10.1111/cdev.12283

Ryan, R. M., Fauth, R. C., & Brooks-Gunn, J. (2006). Childhood poverty. In B. Spodek & O. N. Saracho (Eds.), *Handbook of research on the education of young children* (p. 600). Lawrence Erlbaum.

Ryan, S. M., & Nolan, Y. M. (2016). Neuroinflammation negatively affects adult hippocampal neurogenesis and cognition: Can exercise compensate? *Neuroscience & Biobehavioral Reviews, 61*, 121–131. http://doi.org/10.1016/j.neubiorev.2015.12.004

Ryff, C. D. (1991). Possible selves in adulthood and old age: A tale of shifting horizons. *Psychology and Aging, 6*(2), 286–295.

Ryff, C. D. (1995). Psychological well-being in adult life. *Current Directions in Psychological Science, 4*(4), 99–104. http://doi.org/10.1111/1467-8721.ep10772395

Ryff, C. D. (2014). Psychological well-being revisited: Advances in the science and practice of eudaimonia. *Psychotherapy and Psychosomatics, 83*(1), 10–28. http://doi.org/10.1159/000353263

Saarni, C. (2000). Emotional competence: A developmental perspective. In R. Bar-On & J. D. A. Parker (Eds.), *The handbook of emotional intelligence: Theory, development, assessment, and application at home, school, and in the workplace* (pp. 68–69). New York, NY: Jossey-Bass.

Saarni, C., Mumme, D. L., & Campos, J. J. (1998). Emotional development: Action, communication, and understanding. In N. Eisenberg & W. Damon (Eds.), *Handbook of child psychology: Social, emotional, and personality development* (5th ed., Vol. 3, pp. 237–309). Hoboken, NJ: John Wiley & Sons.

Saavedra Pérez, H. C., Ikram, M. A., Direk, N., Prigerson, H. G., Freak-Poli, R., Verhaaren, B. F. J., . . . Tiemeier, H. (2015). Cognition, structural brain changes and complicated grief: A population-based study. *Psychological Medicine, 45*(7), 1389–1399. https://doi.org/10.1017/S0033291714002499

Sabbagh, M. A., Xu, F., Carlson, S. M., Moses, L. J., & Lee., K. (2006). The development of executive functioning and theory of mind. *Psychological Science, 17*(1), 74–81.

Sadler, T. L. (2015). *Langman's medical embryology* (13th ed.). New York, NY: Lippincott Williams & Wilkins.

Saewyc, E. M. (2011). Research on adolescent sexual orientation: Development, health disparities, stigma, and resilience. *Journal of Research on Adolescence, 21*(1), 256–272. http://doi.org/10.1111/j.1532-7795.2010.00727.x

Safdar, S., Friedlmeier, W., Matsumoto, D., Yoo, S. H., Kwantes, C. T., Kakai, H., & Shigemasu, E. (2009). Variations of emotional display rules within and across cultures: A comparison between Canada, USA, and Japan. *Canadian Journal of Behavioural Science/Revue Canadienne Des Sciences Du Comportement, 41*(1), 1–10. http://doi.org/10.1037/a0014387

Safe Kids Worldwide. (2015). *Overview of childhood injury morbidity and mortality in the U.S.* Fact sheet. Retrieved from https://www.safekids.org/sites/default/files/documents/skw_overview_fact_sheet_november_2014.pdf

Sagi, A., Lamb, M. E., Lewkowicz, K. S., Shoham, R., Dvir, R., & Estes, D. (1985). Security of infant-mother, -father, and -metapelet attachments among kibbutz-reared Israeli children. *Monographs of the Society for Research in Child Development, 50*(1/2), 257–275. http://doi.org/10.1111/1540-5834.ep11890146

Sagi, A., Van IJzendoorn, M. H., & Koren-Karie, N. (1991). Primary appraisal of the Strange Situation: A cross-cultural analysis of preseparation episodes. *Developmental Psychology, 27*(4), 587–596.

Sagi-Schwartz, A. (2008). The well being of children living in chronic war zones: The Palestinian-Israeli case. *International Journal of Behavioral Development, 32*(4), 322–336. http://doi.org/10.1177/0165025408090974

Sai, F. Z. (2005). The role of the mother's voice in developing mother's face preference: Evidence for intermodal perception at birth. *Infant & Child Development, 14*, 29–50.

Sailor, K. A., Schinder, A. F., & Lledo, P.-M. (2017). Adult neurogenesis beyond the niche: Its potential for driving brain plasticity. *Current Opinion in Neurobiology, 42*, 111–117. http://doi.org/10.1016/j.conb.2016.12.001

Sala, M. N., Pons, F., & Molina, P. (2014). Emotion regulation strategies in preschool children. *British Journal of Developmental Psychology, 32*(4), 440–453. http://doi.org/10.1111/bjdp.12055

Sala, P., Prefumo, F., Pastorino, D., Buffi, D., Gaggero, C. R., Foppiano, M., & De Biasio, P. (2014). Fetal surgery. *Obstetrical & Gynecological Survey, 69*(4), 218–228. http://doi.org/10.1097/OGX.0000000000000061

Salamone, F. A. (1979). Children's games as mechanisms for easing ethnic interaction in ethnically heterogeneous communities: A Nigerian case. *Anthropos, 5*, 202–210.

Saldinger, A., Porterfield, K., & Cain, A. C. (2014). Meeting the needs of parentally bereaved children: A framework for child-centered parenting. *Psychiatry, 67*, 331–352. Retrieved from http://www.tandfonline.com/doi/abs/10.1521/psyc.67.4.331.56562

Saleem, M., Anderson, C. A., & Gentile, D. A. (2012). Effects of prosocial, neutral, and violent video games on children's helpful and hurtful behaviors. *Aggressive Behavior, 38*(4), 281–287. http://doi.org/10.1002/ab.21428

Salekin, R. T., & Averett, C. A. (2008). Personality in childhood and adolescence. In M. Hersen & A. M. Gross (Eds.), *Handbook of clinical psychology, vol 2: Children and adolescents.* (pp. 351–385). Hoboken, NJ: John Wiley & Sons.

Salem Yaniv, S., Levy, A., Wiznitzer, A., Holcberg, G., Mazor, M., & Sheiner, E. (2011). A significant linear association exists between advanced maternal age and adverse perinatal outcome. *Archives of Gynecology and Obstetrics, 283*(4), 755–759. http://doi.org/10.1007/s00404-010-1459-4

Salihu, H. M., Shumpert, M. N., Slay, M., Kirby, R. S., & Alexander, G. R. (2003). Childbearing beyond maternal age 50 and fetal outcomes in the United States. *Obstetrics & Gynecology, 102*, 1006–1014.

Salmela-Aro, K., Nurmi, J.-E., Saisto, T., & Halmesmäki, E. (2000). Women's and men's personal goals during the transition to parenthood. *Journal of Family Psychology, 14*(2), 171–186.

Salmivalli, C. (2010). Bullying and the peer group: A review. *Aggression and Violent Behavior, 15*(2), 112–120. http://doi.org/10.1016/j.avb.2009.08.007

Salmivalli, C. (2014). Participant roles in bullying: How can peer bystanders be utilized in interventions? *Theory Into Practice, 53*(4), 286–292. http://doi.org/10.1080/00405841.2014.947222

Salmon, D. A., Moulton, L. H., Omer, S. B., deHart, M. P., Stokley, S., & Halsey, N. A. (2005). Factors associated with refusal of childhood vaccines among parents of school-aged children: A case-control study. *Archives of Pediatrics and Adolescent Medicine, 159*, 470–476.

Salmon, D. P., & Bondi, M. W. (2009). Neuropsychological assessment of dementia. *Annual Review Psychology*, *60*, 257–282.

Salovey, P., & Mayer, J. D. (1989). Emotional intelligence. *Imagination, Cognition and Personality*, *9*(3), 185–211. http://doi.org/10.2190/DUGG-P24E-52WK-6CDG

Salter, M. D. (1940). *An evaluation of adjustment based upon the concept of security*. Toronto, ON: University of Toronto Press.

Salthouse, T. A. (1984). Effects of age and skill in typing. *Journal of Experimental Psychology: General*, *113*, 345–371.

Salthouse, T. A. (1993). Speed mediation of adult age differences in cognition. *Developmental Psychology*, *29*(4), 722–738.

Salthouse, T. A. (1996). Constraints on theories of cognitive aging. *Psychonomic Bulletin & Review*, *3*(3), 287–299.

Salthouse, T. A. (2011). Neuroanatomical substrates of age-related cognitive decline. *Psychological Bulletin*, *137*(5), 753–84. http://doi.org/10.1037/a0023262

Salthouse, T. A. (2012). Consequences of age-related cognitive declines. *Annual Review of Psychology*, *63*, 201–26. http://doi.org/10.1146/annurev-psych-120710-100328

Salthouse, T. A. (2014). Why are there different age relations in cross-sectional and longitudinal comparisons of cognitive functioning? *Current Directions in Psychological Science*, *23*(4), 252–256. http://doi.org/10.1177/0963721414535212

Salthouse, T. A., & Madden, D. J. (2013). Information processing speed and aging. In J. DeLuca & J. H. Kalmar (Eds.), *Information processing speed in clinical populations* (pp. 221–239). New York, NY: Psychology Press.

Salthouse, T. A., & Pink, J. E. (2008). Why is working memory related to fluid intelligence? *Psychonomic Bulletin & Review*, *15*(2), 364–371.

Salvioli, S., Monti, D., Lanzarini, C., Conte, M., Pirazzini, C., Giulia Bacalini, M., . . . Franceschi, C. (2013). Immune system, cell senescence, aging and longevity: Inflamm-aging reappraised. *Current Pharmaceutical Design*, *19*(9), 1675–1679.

Samanez-Larkin, G. R., Robertson, E. R., Mikels, J. A., Carstensen, L. L., & Gotlib, I. H. (2009). Selective attention to emotion in the aging brain. *Psychology and Aging*, *24*(3), 519–529. http://doi.org/10.1037/a0016952

Samarova, V., Shilo, G., & Diamond, G. M. (2014). Changes in youths' perceived parental acceptance of their sexual minority status over time. *Journal of Research on Adolescence*, *24*(4), 681–688. http://doi.org/10.1111/jora.12071

Sameroff, A. (2010). A unified theory of development: A dialectic integration of nature and nurture. *Child Development*, *81*(1), 6–22. http://doi.org/10.1111/j.1467-8624.2009.01378.x

Sameroff, A. J., & Chandler, P. J. (1975). Reproductive risk and the continuum of caretaking causality. In F. D. Horowitz, M. Hetherington, S. Scarr-Salapatek, & G. Siegel (Eds.), *Review of child development research* (Vol. 4, pp. 187–244). Chicago, IL: University of Chicago Press.

Sameroff, A. J., Seifer, R., Baldwin, A., & Baldwin, C. (1993). Stability of intelligence from preschool to adolescence: The influence of social and family risk factors. *Child Development*, *64*(1), 80–97. http://doi.org/10.1111/j.1467-8624.1993.tb02896.x

Sampselle, C. M., Harris, V., Harlow, S. D., & Sowers, M. (2002). Midlife development and menopause in African American and Caucasian women. *Health Care for Women International*, *23*(4), 351–363.

Sánchez, P. J., & Wendel, G. D. (1997). Syphilis in pregnancy. *Clinics in Perinatology*, *24*(1), 71–90.

Sanchez-Garrido, M. A., & Tena-Sempere, M. (2013). Metabolic control of puberty: Roles of leptin and kisspeptins. *Hormones and Behavior*, *64*(2), 187–194. http://doi.org/10.1016/j.yhbeh.2013.01.014

Sanchez-Ruiz, M.-J., Mavroveli, S., & Poullis, J. (2013). Trait emotional intelligence and its links to university performance: An examination. *Personality and Individual Differences*, *54*(5), 658–662. http://doi.org/10.1016/j.paid.2012.11.013

Sanchez-Vaznaugh, E. V., Braveman, P. A., Egerter, S., Marchi, K. S., Heck, K., & Curtis, M. (2016). Latina birth outcomes in California: Not so paradoxical. *Maternal and Child Health Journal*, 1–12. http://doi.org/10.1007/s10995-016-1988-y

Sanchis-Gomar, F., Olaso-Gonzalez, G., Corella, D., Gomez-Cabrera, M. C., & Vina, J. (2011). Increased average longevity among the "Tour de France" cyclists. *International Journal of Sports Medicine*, *32*(8), 644–647. http://doi.org/10.1055/s-0031-1271711

Sandfort, T. G. M., Orr, M., Hirsch, J. S., & Santelli, J. (2008). Long-term health correlates of timing of sexual debut: Results from a national U.S. study. *American Journal of Public Health*, *98*(1), 155–161.

Sandlin, D., McGwin, G., & Owsley, C. (2014). Association between vision impairment and driving exposure in older adults aged 70 years and over: A population-based examination. *Acta Ophthalmologica*, *92*(3), e207-e212. http://doi.org/10.1111/aos.12050

Sandvik, A. M., Bartone, P. T., Hystad, S. W., Phillips, T. M., Thayer, J. F., & Johnsen, B. H. (2013). Psychological hardiness predicts neuroimmunological responses to stress. *Psychology, Health & Medicine*, *18*(6), 705–713. http://doi.org/10.1080/13548506.2013.772304

Sansavini, A., Bertoncini, J., & Giovanelli, G. (1997). Newborns discriminate the rhythm of multisyllabic stressed words. *Developmental Psychology*, *33*(1), 3–11.

Santelli, J. S., Lowry, R., Brener, N. D., & Robin, L. (2000). The association of sexual behaviors with socioeconomic status, family structure, and race/ethnicity among U.S. adolescents. *American Journal of Public Health*, *90*(10), 1582–1588.

Santis, M., Cavaliere, A. F., Straface, G., & Caruso, A. (2006). Rubella infection in pregnancy. *Reproductive Toxicology*, *21*(4), 390–398.

Santoro, N. (2016). Perimenopause: From research to practice. *Journal of Women's Health*, *25*(4), 332–339. http://doi.org/10.1089/jwh.2015.5556

Sapp, F., Lee, K., & Muir, D. (2000). Three-year-olds' difficulty with the appearance-reality distinction: Is it real or is it apparent? *Developmental Psychology*, *36*, 547–560.

Saraç, F., Öztekin, K., & Çelebi, G. (2011). Early menopause association with employment, smoking, divorced marital status and low leptin levels. *Gynecological Endocrinology*, *27*(4), 273–278. http://doi.org/10.3109/09513590.2010.491165

Saraiya, A., Garakani, A., & Billick, S. B. (2013). Mental health approaches to child victims of acts of terrorism. *The Psychiatric Quarterly*, *84*(1), 115–24. http://doi.org/10.1007/s11126-012-9232-4

Sarkadi, A., Kristiansson, R., Oberklaid, F., & Bremberg, S. (2008). Fathers' involvement and children's developmental outcomes: A systematic review of longitudinal studies. *Acta Paediatrica*, *97*(2), 153–158. http://doi.org/10.1111/j.1651-2227.2007.00572.x

Sarkisian, N., & Gerstel, N. (2016). Does singlehood isolate or integrate? Examining the link between marital status and ties to kin, friends, and neighbors. *Journal of Social and Personal Relationships*, *33*(3), 361–384. http://doi.org/10.1177/0265407515597564

Sarwer, D. B., & Crerand, C. E. (2004). Body image and cosmetic medical treatments. *Body Image*, *1*(1), 99–111. http://doi.org/10.1016/S1740-1445(03)00003-2

Sasaki, J. Y., & Kim, H. S. (2017). Nature, nurture, and their interplay. *Journal of Cross-Cultural Psychology*, *48*(1), 4–22. http://doi.org/10.1177/0022022116680481

Saßenroth, D., Meyer, A., Salewsky, B., Kroh, M., Norman, K., Steinhagen-Thiessen, E., . . . MacKenzie, C. (2015). Sports and exercise at different ages and leukocyte telomere length in later life: Data from the Berlin Aging Study II (BASE-II). *PloS One*, *10*(12), e0142131. http://doi.org/10.1371/journal.pone.0142131

Sassler, S., & Miller, A. J. (2011). Class differences in cohabitation processes. *Family Relations*, *60*(2), 163–177. http://doi.org/10.1111/j.1741-3729.2010.00640.x

Sasson, I., & Umberson, D. J. (2014). Widowhood and depression: New light on gender differences, selection, and psychological adjustment. *The Journals of Gerontology. Series B, Psychological Sciences and Social Sciences*, *69*(1), 135–145. http://doi.org/10.1093/geronb/gbt058

Sato, S. M., Schulz, K. M., Sisk, C. L., & Wood, R. I. (2008). Adolescents and androgens, receptors and rewards. *Hormones and Behavior*, *53*(5), 647–658. https://doi.org/10.1016/j.yhbeh.2008.01.010

Sattler, C., Toro, P., Schönknecht, P., & Schröder, J. (2012). Cognitive activity, education and socioeconomic status as preventive factors for mild cognitive impairment and Alzheimer's disease. *Psychiatry Research*, *196*(1), 90–95. http://doi.org/10.1016/j.psychres.2011.11.012

Saucier, M. G. (2004). Midlife and beyond: Issues for aging women. *Journal of Counseling & Development*, *82*(4), 420–425. http://doi.org/10.1002/j.1556-6678.2004.tb00329.x

Saudino, K. J., & Micalizzi, L. (2015). Emerging trends in behavioral genetic studies of child temperament. *Child Development Perspectives*, *9*(3), 144–148. http://doi.org/10.1111/cdep.12123

Savelsbergh, G., van der Kamp, J., & van Wermeskerken, M. (2013). The development of reaching actions. In P. D. Zelazo (Ed.), *The Oxford handbook of developmental psychology, Vol. 1*. London, UK: Oxford University Press. http://doi.org/10.1093/oxfordhb/9780199958450.013.0014

Savia, J., Almeida, D. M., Davey, A., & Zant, S. H. (2008). Routine assistance to parents: Effects on daily mood and other stressors. *Journals of Gerontology Series B: Psychological Sciences & Social Sciences*, *36B*(3), S154–S161.

Savin-Williams, R. C. (2016). Sexual orientation: Categories or continuum? Commentary on Bailey et al. (2016). *Psychological Science in the Public Interest*, *17*(2), 37–44. http://doi.org/10.1177/1529100616637618

Savin-Williams, R. C., & Cohen, K. M. (2015). Developmental trajectories and milestones of lesbian, gay, and bisexual young people. *International Review of Psychiatry*, *27*(5), 357–366. http://doi.org/10.3109/09540261.2015.1093465

Savin-Williams, R. C., & Ream, G. L. (2003). Sex variations in the disclosure to parents of same-sex attractions. *Journal of Family Psychology*, *17*(3), 429–438. http://doi.org/10.1037/0893-3200.17.3.429

Savin-Williams, R. C., & Ream, G. L. (2007). Prevalence and stability of sexual orientation components during adolescence and young adulthood. *Archives of Sexual Behavior, 36*(3), 385–394. http://doi.org/10.1007/s10508-006-9088-5

Savin-Williams, R. C., & Vrangalova, Z. (2013). Mostly heterosexual as a distinct sexual orientation group: A systematic review of the empirical evidence. *Developmental Review, 33*(1), 58–88. http://doi.org/10.1016/j.dr.2013.01.001

Savin-Williams, R. C., Dubé, E. M., & Dube, E. M. (1998). Parental reactions to their child's disclosure of a gay/lesbian identity. *Family Relations, 47*(1), 7. http://doi.org/10.2307/584845

Savin-Williams, R. C., Joyner, K., & Rieger, G. (2012). Prevalence and stability of self-reported sexual orientation identity during young adulthood. *Archives of Sexual Behavior, 41*(1), 103–110. http://doi.org/10.1007/s10508-012-9913-y

Sawyer, K. S., Denham, S., DeMulder, E., Blair, K., Auerbach-Major, S., & Levitas, J. (2002). The contribution of older siblings' reaction to emotions to preschoolers' emotional and social competence. *Marriage & Family Review, 34*(3/4), 183.

Saxton, M. (1997). The contrast theory of negative input. *Journal of Child Language, 24*, 139–161.

Sayfan, L., & Lagattuta, K. H. (2009). Scaring the monster away: What children know about managing fears of real and imaginary creatures. *Child Development, 80*(6), 1756–1774. http://doi.org/10.1111/j.1467-8624.2009.01366.x

Sbarra, D. A. (2015). Divorce and health: Current trends and future directions. *Psychosomatic Medicine, 77*(3), 227–236.

Sbarra, D. A., & Coan, J. A. (2017). Divorce and health: Good data in need of better theory. *Current Opinion in Psychology, 13*, 91–95. http://doi.org/10.1016/j.copsyc.2016.05.014

Sbarra, D. A., Hasselmo, K., & Bourassa, K. J. (2015). Divorce and health: Beyond individual differences. *Current Directions in Psychological Science, 24*(2), 109–113. http://doi.org/10.1177/0963721414559125

Sbarra, D. A., Law, R. W., & Portley, R. M. (2011). Divorce and death: A meta-analysis and research agenda for clinical, social, and health psychology. *Perspectives on Psychological Science, 6*(5), 454–474. http://doi.org/10.1177/1745691611414724

Scafato, E., Galluzzo, L., Gandin, C., Ghirini, S., Baldereschi, M., Capurso, A., . . . Farchi, G. (2008). Marital and cohabitation status as predictors of mortality: A 10-year follow-up of an Italian elderly cohort. *Social Science & Medicine, 67*(9), 1456–1464. http://doi.org/10.1016/j.socscimed.2008.06.026

Scalco, M. D., Trucco, E. M., Coffman, D. L., & Colder, C. R. (2015). Selection and socialization effects in early adolescent alcohol use: A propensity score analysis. *Journal of Abnormal Child Psychology*. http://doi.org/10.1007/s10802-014-9969-3

Scarmeas, N., & Stern, Y. (2003). Cognitive reserve and lifestyle. *Journal of Clinical and Experimental Neuropsychology, 25*(5), 625–633. http://doi.org/10.1076/jcen.25.5.625.14576

Scarr, S. (1992). Developmental theories for the 1990s: Development and individual differences. *Child Development, 63*(1), 1–19. http://doi.org/10.1111/1467-8624.ep9203091721

Scarr, S., & McCartney, K. (1983). How people make their own environments: A theory of genotype environment effects. *Child Development, 54*(2), 424. http://doi.org/10.1111/1467-8624.ep8877295

Scarr, S., & Weinberg, R. A. (1983). The Minnesota Adoption Studies: Genetic differences and malleability. *Child Development, 54*(2), 260. http://doi.org/10.2307/1129689

Schaal, B. (2017). Infants and children making sense of scents. In *Springer handbook of odor* (pp. 107–108). Cham: Springer International Publishing. http://doi.org/10.1007/978-3-319-26932-0_43

Schaal, B., Montagner, H., Hertling, E., Bolzoni, D., Moyse, R., & Quichon, R. (1980). Olfactory stimulations in mother-infant relationships. *Reproduction, Nutrition, Développement, 20*, 843–858.

Schachner, A., & Hannon, E. E. (2011). Infant-directed speech drives social preferences in 5-month-old infants. *Developmental Psychology, 47*(1), 19–25. http://doi.org/10.1037/a0020740

Schaefer, J. D., Caspi, A., Belsky, D. W., Harrington, H., Houts, R., Israel, S., . . . Moffitt, T. E. (2016). Early-life intelligence predicts midlife biological age. *The Journals of Gerontology. Series B, Psychological Sciences and Social Sciences, 71*(6), 968–977. http://doi.org/10.1093/geronb/gbv035

Schafer, M. H., & Shippee, T. P. (2010). Age identity, gender, and perceptions of decline: Does feeling older lead to pessimistic dispositions about cognitive aging? *Journals of Gerontology Series B: Psychological Sciences & Social Sciences, 65B*(1), 91–96.

Schaie, K. W. (1993). The Seattle Longitudinal Studies of adult intelligence. *Current Directions in Psychological Science, 2*(6), 171–175.

Schaie, K. W. (2013). *Developmental Influences on adult intelligence: The Seattle Longitudinal Study*. New York: Oxford University Press.

Schaie, K. W., & Willis, S. L. (1986). Can decline in adult intellectual functioning be reversed? *Developmental Psychology, 22*(2), 223–232. http://doi.org/10.1037/0012-1649.22.2.223

Schaie, K. W., & Zanjani, F. A. K. (2006). Intellectual development across adulthood. In C. Hoare (Ed.), *Handbook of adult development and learning.* (pp. 99–122). New York, NY, US: Oxford University Press.

Schalock, R. L. (2015). Intellectual disability. In *The Encyclopedia of Clinical Psychology* (pp. 1–7). Hoboken, NJ, USA: John Wiley & Sons, Inc. http://doi.org/10.1002/9781118625392.wbecp062

Scharf, M., & Mayseless, O. (2008). Late adolescent girls' relationships with parents and romantic partner: The distinct role of mothers and fathers. *Journal of Adolescence, 31*(6), 837–855. http://doi.org/10.1016/j.adolescence.2008.06.012

Schelleman-Offermans, K., Knibbe, R. A., & Kuntsche, E. (2013). Are the effects of early pubertal timing on the initiation of weekly alcohol use mediated by peers and/or parents? A longitudinal study. *Developmental Psychology, 49*(7), 1277–1285.

Schepis, T. S., Adinoff, B., & Rao, U. (2008). Neurobiological processes in adolescent addictive disorders. *American Journal on Addictions, 17*(1), 6–23. http://doi.org/10.1080/10550490701756146

Scherer, M. (1985). How many ways is a child intelligent? *Instructor*, 32–35.

Scherger, S., Nazroo, J., & Higgs, P. (2011). Leisure activities and retirement: Do structures of inequality change in old age? *Ageing & Society, 31*(1), 146–172. http://doi.org/10.1017/s0144686x10000577

Schiefman, S., Van Gundy, K., & Taylor, J. (2001). Status, role, and resource explanations for age patterns in psychological distress. *Journal of Health & Social Behavior, 42*(1), 80–96.

Schiffman, S. S. (2009). Effects of aging on the human taste system. *Annals of the New York Academy of Sciences, 1170*(1), 725–729. http://doi.org/10.1111/j.1749-6632.2009.03924.x

Schirda, B., Valentine, T. R., Aldao, A., & Prakash, R. S. (2016). Age-related differences in emotion regulation strategies: Examining the role of

contextual factors. *Developmental Psychology, 52*(9), 1370–1380. http://doi.org/10.1037/dev0000194

Schlam, T. R., Wilson, N. L., Shoda, Y., Mischel, W., & Ayduk, O. (2013). Preschoolers' delay of gratification predicts their body mass 30 years later. *The Journal of Pediatrics, 162*(1), 90–93. http://doi.org/10.1016/j.jpeds.2012.06.049

Schmidt, F. L., & Hunter, J. (2004). General mental ability in the world of work: Occupational attainment and job performance. *Journal of Personality and Social Psychology, 86*(1), 162–173. http://doi.org/10.1037/0022-3514.86.1.162

Schmidt, H., Freudenberger, P., Seiler, S., & Schmidt, R. (2012). Genetics of subcortical vascular dementia. *Experimental Gerontology, 47*(11), 873–7. http://doi.org/10.1016/j.exger.2012.06.003

Schmidt, L., Sobotka, T., Bentzen, J. G., & Nyboe Andersen, A. (2012). Demographic and medical consequences of the postponement of parenthood. *Human Reproduction Update, 18*(1), 29–43. http://doi.org/10.1093/humupd/dmr040

Schmitt, D. P., & Allik, J. (2005). Simultaneous administration of the Rosenberg self-esteem scale in 53 nations: Exploring the universal and culture-specific features of global self-esteem. *Journal of Personality and Social Psychology, 89*(4), 623–642. http://doi.org/10.1037/0022-3514.89.4.623

Schneider, W., & Bjorklund, D. F. (1992). Expertise, aptitude, and strategic remembering. *Child Development, 63*(2), 461–473. http://doi.org/10.1111/j.1467-8624.1992.tb01640.x

Schneider, W., & Pressley, M. (2013). *Memory development between 2 and 20*. New York: Springer-Verlag.

Schnur, E., & Belanger, S. (2000). What works in Head Start. In M. P. Kluger, G. Alexander, & P. A. Curtis (Eds.), *What works in child welfare* (pp. 277–284). Washington, DC: Child Welfare League of America.

Schnur, E., & Belanger, S. (2000). What works in Head Start. In M. P. Kluger, G. Alexander, & P. A. Curtis (Eds.), *What works in child welfare* (pp. 277–284). Washington, DC: Child Welfare League of America.

Schober, P. S. (2013). The parenthood effect on gender inequality: Explaining the change in paid and domestic work when British couples become parents. *European Sociological Review, 29*(1), 74–85. http://doi.org/10.1093/esr/jcr041

Schoenbaum, G., & Roesch, M. (2005). Orbitofrontal cortex, associative learning, and expectancies. *Neuron, 47*(5), 633–636. https://doi.org/10.1016/j.neuron.2005.07.018

Schoenfeld, T. J., & Gould, E. (2013). Differential effects of stress and glucocorticoids on adult neurogenesis. In C. Belzung & P. Wigmore (Eds.), *Neurogenesis and neural plasticity* (pp. 139–164). Berlin: Springer. https://doi.org/10.1007/7854_2012_233

Schoenmaker, C., Juffer, F., van IJzendoorn, M. H., Linting, M., van der Voort, A., & Bakermans-Kranenburg, M. J. (2015). From maternal sensitivity in infancy to adult attachment representations: A longitudinal adoption study with secure base scripts. *Attachment & Human Development, 17*(3), 241–256. http://doi.org/10.1080/14616734.2015.1037315

Schoenmaker, C., Juffer, F., van IJzendoorn, M. H., van den Dries, L., Linting, M., van der Voort, A., & Bakermans-Kranenburg, M. J. (2015). Cognitive and health-related outcomes after exposure to early malnutrition: The Leiden longitudinal study of international adoptees. *Children and Youth Services Review, 48*, 80–86. http://doi.org/10.1016/j.childyouth.2014.12.010

Schonert-Reichl, K. A. (1999). Relations of peer acceptance, friendship adjustment, and social behavior to moral reasoning during early adolescence. *Journal of Early Adolescence*, 19(2), 31p.

Schonfeld, D. J., & Smilansky, S. (1989). A cross-cultural comparison of Israeli and American children's death concepts. *Death Studies*, 13(6), 593–604. http://doi.org/10.1080/07481188908252335

Schoon, I., & Parsons, S. (2002). Competence in the face of adversity: The influence of early family environment and long-term consequences. *Children & Society*, 16(4), 260–272.

Schoon, I., & Polek, E. (2011). Teenage career aspirations and adult career attainment: The role of gender, social background and general cognitive ability. *International Journal of Behavioral Development*, 35(3), 210–217. http://doi.org/10.1177/0165025411398183

Schöttker, B., Brenner, H., Jansen, E. H., Gardiner, J., Peasey, A., Kubínová, R., . . . Tosukhowong, P. (2015). Evidence for the free radical/oxidative stress theory of ageing from the CHANCES consortium: A meta-analysis of individual participant data. *BMC Medicine*, 13(1), 300. http://doi.org/10.1186/s12916-015-0537-7

Schrager, S., & Potter, B. E. (2004). Diethylstilbestrol exposure. *American Family Physician*, 69(10), 2395–2400.

Schreiber, J. (1977). Birth, the family and the community: A southern Italian example. *Birth and the Family Journal*, 4, 153–157.

Schroots, J. J. F., van Dijkum, C., & Assink, M. H. J. (2004). Autobiographical memory from a life span perspective. *International Journal of Aging & Human Development*, 58(1), 69–85.

Schubert, C. R., Cruickshanks, K. J., Fischer, M. E., Huang, G.-H., Klein, B. E. K., Klein, R., . . . Nondahl, D. M. (2012). Olfactory impairment in an adult population: the Beaver Dam Offspring Study. *Chemical Senses*, 37(4), 325–34. http://doi.org/10.1093/chemse/bjr102

Schubert, C. R., Fischer, M. E., Pinto, A. A., Klein, B. E. K., Klein, R., Tweed, T. S., & Cruickshanks, K. J. (2016). Sensory impairments and risk of mortality in older adults. *The Journals of Gerontology Series A: Biological Sciences and Medical Sciences*, 84(5), glw036. http://doi.org/10.1093/gerona/glw036

Schuff, N., Tosun, D., Insel, P. S., Chiang, G. C., Truran, D., Aisen, P. S., . . . Weiner, M. W. (2012). Nonlinear time course of brain volume loss in cognitively normal and impaired elders. *Neurobiology of Aging*, 33(5), 845–55. http://doi.org/10.1016/j.neurobiolaging.2010.07.012

Schuh-Huerta, S. M., Johnson, N. A., Rosen, M. P., Sternfeld, B., Cedars, M. I., & Reijo Pera, R. A. (2012). Genetic variants and environmental factors associated with hormonal markers of ovarian reserve in Caucasian and African American women. *Human Reproduction (Oxford, England)*, 27(2), 594–608. http://doi.org/10.1093/humrep/der391

Schultz, G. P., & Shoven, J. B. (2008). *Putting our house in order: A guide to social security and health care reform*. W. W. Norton.

Schulz, R., & Curnow, C. (1988). Peak performance and age among superathletes: Track and field, swimming, baseball, tennis, and golf. *Journal of Gerontology*, 43, 113–120.

Schulze, P. A., & Carlisle, S. A. (2010). What research does and doesn't say about breastfeeding: A critical review. *Early Child Development & Care*, 180(6), 703–718. http://doi.org/10.1080/03004430802263870

Schurz, M., Radua, J., Aichhorn, M., Richlan, F., & Perner, J. (2014). Fractionating theory of mind: A meta-analysis of functional brain imaging studies. *Neuroscience & Biobehavioral Reviews*, 42, 9–34. http://doi.org/10.1016/j.neubiorev.2014.01.009

Schurz, M., Wimmer, H., Richlan, F., Ludersdorfer, P., Klackl, J., & Kronbichler, M. (2014). Resting-state and task-based functional brain connectivity in developmental dyslexia. *Cerebral Cortex*, bhu184-. http://doi.org/10.1093/cercor/bhu184

Schutte, N. S., Malouff, J. M., & Thorsteinsson, E. B. (2013). Increasing emotional intelligence through training: Current status and future directions the nature of emotional intelligence. *International Journal of Emotional Education*, 5(1), 56–72.

Schwartz, B. L., & Frazier, L. D. (2005). Tip-of-the-tongue states and aging: Contrasting psycholinguistic and metacognitive perspectives. *Journal of General Psychology*, 132(4), 377–391.

Schwartz, D., Lansford, J. E., Dodge, K. A., Pettit, G. S., & Bates, J. E. (2014). Peer victimization during middle childhood as a lead indicator of internalizing problems and diagnostic outcomes in late adolescence. *Journal of Clinical Child and Adolescent Psychology*. http://doi.org/10.1080/15374416.2014.881293

Schwartz, P. D., Maynard, A. M., & Uzelac, S. M. (2008). Adolescent egocentrism: A contemporary view. *Adolescence*, 43(171), 441–448.

Schwartz, S. J. (2004). Brief report: Construct validity of two identity status measures: The EIPQ and the EOM-EIS-II. *Journal of Adolescence*, 27, 477–483.

Schwartz, S. J., Luyckx, K., & Crocetti, E. (2015). What have we learned since Schwartz (2001)? In K. C. McLean & M. Syed (Eds.), *The Oxford handbook of identity development*. Oxford University Press. http://doi.org/10.1093/oxfordhb/9780199936564.013.028

Schwartz, S. J., Zamboanga, B. L., Luyckx, K., Meca, A., & Ritchie, R. A. (2013a). Identity in emerging adulthood: Reviewing the field and looking forward. *Emerging Adulthood*, 1(2), 96–113. http://doi.org/10.1177/2167696813479781

Schwebel, D. C., Rosen, C. S., & Singer, J. L. (1999). Preschoolers' pretend play and theory of mind: The role of jointly constructed pretence. *British Journal of Developmental Psychology*, 17(3), 333–348. http://doi.org/10.1348/026151099165320

Schweinhart, L. J., Montie, J., Iang, Z., Barnett, W. S., Belfield, C. R., & Nores, M. (2005). *Lifetime effects: The High/Scope Perry Preschool study through age 40*. Ypsilanti, MI: High/Scope Press.

Scott Adzick, N. (2013). Fetal surgery for spina bifida: Past, present, future. *Seminars in Pediatric Surgery*, 22(1), 10–17. http://doi.org/10.1053/j.sempedsurg.2012.10.003

Scott, E., & Panksepp, J. (2003). Rough-and-tumble play in human children. *Aggressive Behavior*, 29(6), 539–551. http://doi.org/10.1002/ab.10062

Scott, R. A., Langenberg, C., Sharp, S. J., Franks, P. W., Rolandsson, O., Drogan, D., . . . Wareham, N. J. (2013). The link between family history and risk of type 2 diabetes is not explained by anthropometric, lifestyle or genetic risk factors: The EPIC-InterAct study. *Diabetologia*, 56(1), 60–9. http://doi.org/10.1007/s00125-012-2715-x

Scutti, S. (2015). Puberty comes earlier and earlier for girls. Retrieved February 7, 2015, from http://www.newsweek.com/2015/02/06/puberty-comes-earlier-and-earlier-girls-301920.html

Sears, H. A., Sandra Byers, E., & Lisa Price, E. (2007). The co-occurrence of adolescent boys' and girls' use of psychologically, physically, and sexually abusive behaviours in their dating relationships. *Journal of Adolescence*, 30(3), 487–504. http://doi.org/10.1016/j.adolescence.2006.05.002

Sedgh, G., Finer, L. B., Bankole, A., Eilers, M. A., & Singh, S. (2015). Adolescent pregnancy, birth, and abortion rates across countries: levels and recent trends. *The Journal of Adolescent Health : Official Publication of the Society for Adolescent Medicine*, 56(2), 223–30. http://doi.org/10.1016/j.jadohealth.2014.09.007

Sedivy, J. M. (2007). Telomeres limit cancer growth by inducing senescence: Long-sought in vivo evidence obtained. *Cancer Cell*, 11(5), 389–391.

Segal, J., & Newman, R. S. (2015). Infant preferences for structural and prosodic properties of infant-directed speech in the second year of life. *Infancy*, 20(3), 339–351. http://doi.org/10.1111/infa.12077

Segel-Karpas, D., Ayalon, L., & Lachman, M. E. (2016). Loneliness and depressive symptoms: The moderating role of the transition into retirement. *Aging & Mental Health*, 1–6. http://doi.org/10.1080/13607863.2016.1226770

Seger, J. Y., & Thorstensson, A. (2000). Muscle strength and electromyogram in boys and girls followed through puberty. *European Journal of Applied Physiology*, 81(1–2), 54–61. http://doi.org/10.1007/PL00013797

Seidman, E., Aber, J. L., & French, S. E. (2004). The organization of schooling and adolescent development. In K. I. Maton, C. J. Schellenbach, B. J. Leadbeater, & A. L. Solarz (Eds.), *Investing in children, youth, families, and communities: Strengths-based research and policy*. (pp. 233–250). Washington, DC: American Psychological Association.

Seidman, E., Lambert, L. E., Allen, L., & Aber, J. L. (2003). Urban adolescents' transition to junior high school and protective family transactions. *Journal of Early Adolescence*, 23(2), 166–194.

Seidman, S. N., & Weiser, M. (2013). Testosterone and mood in aging men. *The Psychiatric Clinics of North America*, 36(1), 177–82. http://doi.org/10.1016/j.psc.2013.01.007

Seiffge-Krenke, I. (2010). Predicting the timing of leaving home and related developmental tasks: Parents' and children's perspectives. *Journal of Social & Personal Relationships*, 27(4), 495–518. http://doi.org/10.1177/0265407510363426

Selfhout, M. H. W., Branje, S. J. T., ter Bogt, T. F. M., & Meeus, W. H. J. (2009). The role of music preferences in early adolescents' friendship formation and stability. *Journal of Adolescence*, 32(1), 95–107. http://doi.org/10.1016/j.adolescence.2007.11.004

Seltzer, J. A. (2004). Cohabitation in the United States and Britain: Demography, kinship, and the future. *Journal of Marriage & Family*, 66(4), 921–928.

Senju, A. (2012). Spontaneous theory of mind and its absence in autism spectrum disorders. *The Neuroscientist : A Review Journal Bringing Neurobiology, Neurology and Psychiatry*, 18(2), 108–13. http://doi.org/10.1177/1073858410397208

Serbin, L. A., Powlishta, K. K., & Gulko, J. (1993). The development of sex typing in middle childhood. *Monographs of the Society for Research in Child Development*, 58(2), 1–99. Retrieved from http://www.ncbi.nlm.nih.gov/pubmed/8474512

Serpell, R. (1974). Aspects of intelligence in a developing country. *African Social Research*, 17, 578–596.

Serpell, R., & Jere-Folotiya, J. (2008). Developmental assessment, cultural context, gender, and schooling in Zambia. *International Journal of Psychology*, 43(2), 88–96.

Servey, J., & Chang, J. (2014). Over-the-counter medications in pregnancy. *American Family Physician*, 90(8), 548–55. Retrieved from http://www.ncbi.nlm.nih.gov/pubmed/25369643

Servin, A., Bohlin, G., & Berlin, L. (1999). Sex differences in 1-, 3-, and 5-year-olds' toy-choice in a structured play-session. *Scandinavian Journal of Psychology*, 40(1), 43–48. http://doi.org/10.1111/1467-9450.00096

Seshadri, S., & Wolf, P. A. (2007). Lifetime risk of stroke and dementia: Current concepts, and estimates from the Framingham Study. *Lancet Neurology*, pp. 1106–1114.

Sethna, V. F., Perry, E., Domoney, J., Iles, J., Psychogiou, L., Rowbotham, N. E. L., . . . Ramchandani, P. G. (2016). Father-child interactions at 3-months and 2 years: Contributions to children's cognitive development at 2 years.

Ševčíková, A. (2016). Girls' and boys' experience with teen sexting in early and late adolescence. *Journal of Adolescence*, 51, 156–162. http://doi.org/10.1016/j.adolescence.2016.06.007

Ševčíková, A., Blinka, L., & Daneback, K. (2017). Sexting as a predictor of sexual behavior in a sample of Czech adolescents. *European Journal of Developmental Psychology*, 1–12. http://doi.org/10.1080/17405629.2017.1295842

Shad, M. U., Bidesi, A. S., Chen, L.-A., Thomas, B. P., Ernst, M., & Rao, U. (2011). Neurobiology of decision-making in adolescents. *Behavioural Brain Research*, 217(1), 67–76. http://doi.org/10.1016/j.bbr.2010.09.033

Shahbazian, N., Barati, M., Arian, P., & Saadati, N. (2012). Comparison of complications of chorionic villus sampling and amniocentesis. *International Journal of Fertility & Sterility*, 5(4), 241–244.

Shalev, I., Entringer, S., Wadhwa, P. D., Wolkowitz, O. M., Puterman, E., Lin, J., & Epel, E. S. (2013). Stress and telomere biology: A lifespan perspective. *Psychoneuroendocrinology*, 38(9), 1835–42. http://doi.org/10.1016/j.psyneuen.2013.03.010

Shalitin, S., & Kiess, W. (2017). Putative effects of obesity on linear growth and puberty. *Hormone Research in Paediatrics*. http://doi.org/10.1159/000455968

Shamloul, R., & Ghanem, H. (2013). Erectile dysfunction. *The Lancet*, 381(9861), 153–165. http://doi.org/10.1016/S0140-6736(12)60520-0

Shanafelt, T. D., Hasan, O., Dyrbye, L. N., Sinsky, C., Satele, D., Sloan, J., & West, C. P. (2015). Changes in burnout and satisfaction with work-life balance in physicians and the general US working population between 2011 and 2014. *Mayo Clinic Proceedings*, 90(12), 1600–1613. http://doi.org/10.1016/j.mayocp.2015.08.023

Shanahan, M. J. (2000). Pathways to adulthood in changing socities: Variability and mechanisms in life course perspective. *Annual Review of Sociology*, 26(1), 667.

Shapiro, B., Fagen, J., Prigot, J., Carroll, M., & Shalan, J. (1998). Infants' emotional and regulatory behaviors in response to violations of expectancies. *Infant Behavior and Development*, 27, 299–313.

Shapiro, D. (2014). Stepparents and parenting stress: The roles of gender, marital quality, and views about gender roles. *Family Process*, 53(1), 97–108. http://doi.org/10.1111/famp.12062

Shapiro, D. N., & Stewart, A. J. (2011). Parenting stress, perceived child regard, and depressive symptoms among stepmothers and biological mothers. *Family Relations*, 60(5), 533–544. http://doi.org/10.1111/j.1741-3729.2011.00665.x

Shapiro-Mendoza, C. K., Colson, E. R., Willinger, M., Rybin, D. V., Camperlengo, L., & Corwin, M. J. (2014). Trends in infant bedding use: National infant sleep position study, 1993–2010. *Pediatrics*. Retrieved from http://pediatrics.aappublications.org/content/early/2014/11/25/peds.2014-1793

Sharon, T. (2015). Constructing adulthood: markers of adulthood and well-being among emerging adults. *Emerging Adulthood*, 2167696815579826. http://doi.org/10.1177/2167696815579826

Sharp, E. A., & Ganong, L. (2007). Living in the gray: Women's experiences of missing the marital transition. *Journal of Marriage and Family*, 69(3), 831–844. http://doi.org/10.1111/j.1741-3737.2007.00408.x

Sharp, G., Tiggemann, M., & Mattiske, J. (2014). The role of media and peer influences in Australian women's attitudes towards cosmetic surgery. *Body Image*, 11(4), 482–7. http://doi.org/10.1016/j.bodyim.2014.07.009

Sharp, S. I., Aarsland, D., Day, S., Sønnesyn, H., & Ballard, C. (2011). Hypertension is a potential risk factor for vascular dementia: Systematic review. *International Journal of Geriatric Psychiatry*, 26(7), 661–9. http://doi.org/10.1002/gps.2572

Sharpe, K. H., McClements, P., Clark, D. I., Collins, J., Springbett, A., & Brewster, D. H. (2010). Reduced risk of oestrogen receptor positive breast cancer among peri- and post-menopausal women in Scotland following a striking decrease in use of hormone replacement therapy. *European Journal of Cancer*, 46(5), 937–943. http://doi.org/10.1016/j.ejca.2010.01.003

Shatz, M., & Gelman, R. (1973). The development of communication skills: Modifications in the speech of young children as a function of listener. *Monographs of the Society for Research in Child Development*, 38(5, Serial No. 152).

Shaver, P. R., & Mikulincer, M. (2007). *Adult attachment strategies and the regulation of emotion*. (J. J. Gross, Ed.).New York: Guilford Press.

Shaver, P. R., & Mikulincer, M. (2014). Attachment bonds in romantic relationships. In *Mechanisms of social connection: From brain to group*. (pp. 273–290). Washington: American Psychological Association. http://doi.org/10.1037/14250-016

Shaw, B. A., Krause, N., Liang, J., & Bennett, J. (2007). Tracking changes in social relations throughout late life. *Journals of Gerontology Series B: Psychological Sciences & Social Sciences*, 62B(2), S90–S99.

Shaywitz, S. E., Shaywitz, B. A., Pugh, K. A., Fulbright, R. K., Constable, R. T., Mencl, W. E., . . . et al. (1998). Functional disruption of the organization of the brain for reading in dyslexia. *Proceedings of the National Academy of Sciences of the United States of America*, 95, 2636–2641.

Shea, S. E. (2012). Intellectual disability (mental retardation). *Pediatrics in Review*, 33(3), 110–121. doi:http://doi.org/10.1542/pir.33-3-110

Shear, K., Frank, E., Houck, P. R., & Reynolds, C. F. (2005). Treatment of complicated grief. *JAMA*, 293(21), 2601. https://doi.org/10.1001/jama.293.21.2601

Sheehy, A., Gasser, T., Molinari, R., & Largo, R. H. (2009). *An analysis of variance of the pubertal and midgrowth spurts for length and width*. Retrieved from http://informahealthcare.com/doi/abs/10.1080/030144699282642

Shelder, J., & Block, J. (1990). Adolescent drug use and psychological health: A longitudinal inquiry. *American Psychologist*, 45(5), 612–630.

Sheldon, P., & Bryant, K. (2016). Instagram: Motives for its use and relationship to narcissism and contextual age. *Computers in Human Behavior*, 58, 89–97. http://doi.org/10.1016/j.chb.2015.12.059

Shelton, A. (2007). *Social security: Basic data*. Washington, DC: American Association of Retired Persons.

Shelton, A. (2013). Social security: Still lifting many older americans out of poverty. Retrieved from http://blog.aarp.org/2013/07/01/social-security-still-lifting-many-older-americans-out-of-poverty/

Sheng, L., Bedore, L. M., Peña, E. D., & Fiestas, C. (2011). Semantic development in Spanish-English bilingual children: Effects of age and language experience. *Child Development*, 84(3), 1034–45. http://doi.org/10.1111/cdev.12015

Shenhav, A., & Greene, J. D. (2010). Moral judgments recruit domain-general valuation mechanisms to integrate representations of probability and magnitude. *Neuron*, 67(4), 667–677. https://doi.org/10.1016/j.neuron.2010.07.020

Shepard, L. S., & Smith, M. L. (1990). Synthesis of research on grade retention. *Educational Leadership*, 47(8), 84–88.

Sheppard, L. D. (2008). Intelligence and speed of information-processing: A review of 50 years of research. *Personality & Individual Differences*, 44(3), 533–549. http://doi.org/10.1016/j.paid.2007.09.015

Sheppard, P., & Sear, R. (2012). Father absence predicts age at sexual maturity and reproductive timing in British men. *Biology Letters*, 8(2), 237–40. http://doi.org/10.1098/rsbl.2011.0747

Sheridan, M. A., & McLaughlin, K. A. (2014). Dimensions of early experience and neural development: Deprivation and threat. *Trends in Cognitive Sciences*, 18(11), 580–585. https://doi.org/10.1016/j.tics.2014.09.001

Sheridan, M. A., Sarsour, K., Jutte, D., D'Esposito, M., & Boyce, W. T. (2012). The impact of social disparity on prefrontal function in childhood. *PLoS ONE*, 7(4), e35744. https://doi.org/10.1371/journal.pone.0035744

Sherman, A. M., & de Vries, B. (2000). Friendship in childhood and adulthood: Lessons across the lifespan. *International Journal of Aging & Human Development*, 51(1), 31.

Sherman, L. E., Greenfield, P. M., Hernandez, L. M., & Dapretto, M. (2017). Peer influence via Instagram: Effects on brain and behavior in adolescence and young adulthood. *Child Development*, 1(1), 1–11. https://doi.org/10.1111/cdev.12838

Sherman, L. E., Payton, A. A., Hernandez, L. M., Greenfield, P. M., & Dapretto, M. (2016). The power of the like in adolescence. *Psychological Science*, 27(7), 1027–1035. https://doi.org/10.1177/0956797616645673

Sherr, L., Mueller, J., & Varrall, R. (2009). A systematic review of cognitive development and child human immunodeficiency virus infection. *Psychology, Health & Medicine*, 14(4), 387–404. http://doi.org/10.1080/13548500903012897

Shetgiri, R., Lin, H., & Flores, G. (2013). Trends in risk and protective factors for child bullying perpetration in the United States. *Child Psychiatry and Human Development*, 44(1), 89–104. http://doi.org/10.1007/s10578-012-0312-3

Shim, S.-S., Malone, F., Canick, J., Ball, R., Nyberg, D., Comstock, C., . . . Abuhamad, A. (2014). Chorionic villus sampling. *Journal of Genetic Medicine*, 11(2), 43–48. http://doi.org/10.5734/JGM.2014.11.2.43

Shin, H., & Ryan, A. M. (2014). Early adolescent friendships and academic adjustment: Examining selection and influence processes with longitudinal social network analysis. *Developmental Psychology*, 50(11), 2462–72. http://doi.org/10.1037/a0037922

Shiner, R. L., & DeYoung, C. G. (2013). The Structure of temperament and personality traits. In P. D. Zelazo (Ed.), *The Oxford handbook of developmental psychology, Vol. 2: Self and other* (Vol. 1). Oxford University Press. http://doi.org/10.1093/oxfordhb/9780199958474.013.0006

Shiner, R. L., Masten, A. S., & Tellegen, A. (2002). A developmental perspective on personality in emerging adulthood: Childhood antecedents and concurrent adaptation. *Journal of Personality and Social Psychology, 83*(5), 1165–1177. http://doi.org/10.1037/0022-3514.83.5.1165

Shinskey, J. L. (2012). Disappearing décalage: Object search in light and dark at 6 months. *Infancy, 17*(3), 272–294. http://doi.org/10.1111/j.1532-7078.2011.00078.x

Shinskey, J. L., & Munakata, Y. (2003). Are infants in the dark about hidden objects? *Developmental Science, 6,* 273–282.

Shiota, M. N., & Levenson, R. W. (2007). Birds of a feather don't always fly farthest: Similarity in Big Five personality predicts more negative marital satisfaction trajectories in long-term marriages. *Psychology and Aging, 22*(4), 666–675.

Ship, J. A., & Weiffenbach, J. M. (1993). Age, gender, medical treatment, and medication effects on smell identification. *Journal of Gerontology, 48*(1), M26–M32. http://doi.org/10.1093/geronj/48.1.M26

Shipman, K. L., & Zeman, J. (2001). Socialization of children's emotion regulation in mother–child dyads: A developmental psychopathology perspective. *Development and Psychopathology, 13*(2), 317–336.

Shirom, A., & Melamed, S. (2005). Does burnout affect physical health? A review of the evidence. In A.-S. G. Antoniou & C. L. Cooper (Eds.), *Research companion to organizational health psychology.* (pp. 599–622). Northampton, MA US: Edward Elgar Publishing.

Shores, M. M. (2014). The implications of low testosterone on mortality in men. *Current Sexual Health Reports, 6*(4), 235–243. http://doi.org/10.1007/s11930-014-0030-x

Short, S. E., Fengying, Z., Siyuan, X., & Mingliang, Y. (2001). China's one-child policy and the care of children: An analysis of qualitative and quantitative data. *Social Forces, 79*(3), 913–943.

Shringarpure, R., & Davies, K. J. A. (2009). Free radicals and oxidative stress in aging. In V. L. Bengston, D. Gans, N. M. Pulney, & M. Silverstein (Eds.), *Handbook of theories of aging (2nd ed.).* (pp. 229–243). New York, NY US: Springer Publishing Co.

Shu, C.-H., Hummel, T., Lee, P.-L., Chiu, C.-H., Lin, S.-H., & Yuan, B.-C. (2009). The proportion of self-rated olfactory dysfunction does not change across the life span. *American Journal of Rhinology & Allergy, 23*(4), 413–6. http://doi.org/10.2500/ajra.2009.23.3343

Shuey, K., & Hardy, M. A. (2003). Assistance to aging parents and parents-in-law: Does lineage affect family allocation decisions? *Journal of Marriage and Family, 65*(2), 418–431. Retrieved from shuey@email.unc.edu

Shulman, E. P., & Cauffman, E. (2013). Reward-biased risk appraisal and its relation to juvenile versus adult crime. *Law and Human Behavior, 37*(6), 412–23. http://doi.org/10.1037/lhb0000033

Shulman, E. P., Smith, A. R., Silva, K., Icenogle, G., Duell, N., Chein, J., & Steinberg, L. (2016). The dual systems model: Review, reappraisal, and reaffirmation. *Developmental Cognitive Neuroscience, 17,* 103–117. http://doi.org/10.1016/j.dcn.2015.12.010

Shumway-Cook, A., Guralnik, J. M., Phillips, C. L., Coppin, A. K., Ciol, M. A., Bandinelli, S., & Ferrucci, L. (2007). Age-associated declines in complex walking task performance: The walking InCHIANTI toolkit. *Journal of the American Geriatrics Society, 55*(1), 58–65. http://doi.org/10.1111/j.1532-5415.2006.00962.x

Siegel, K., & Weinstein, L. (2008). Anticipatory grief reconsidered. *Journal of Psychosocial Oncology, 1*(2), 61–73. http://doi.org/10.1300/J077v01n02_04

Siegel, L. S. (1994). Working memory and reading: A life-span perspective. *International Journal of Behavioural Development, 17,* 109–124.

Siegel, R. L., Ma, J., Zou, Z., & Jemal, A. (2014). Cancer statistics, 2014. *CA: A Cancer Journal for Clinicians, 64*(1), 9–29. http://doi.org/10.3322/caac.21208

Siegel, R. L., Miller, K. D., & Jemal, A. (2016). Cancer statistics, 2016. *CA: A Cancer Journal for Clinicians, 66*(1), 7–30. http://doi.org/10.3322/caac.21332

Siegler, R. S. (1998). *Emerging minds: The process of change in children's thinking.* New York: Oxford University Press.

Siegler, R. S., & Richards, D. (1982). The development of intelligence. In R. Sternberg (Ed.), *Handbook of human intelligence.* London: Cambridge University Press.

Siekerman, K., Barbu-Roth, M., Anderson, D. I., Donnelly, A., Goffinet, F., & Teulier, C. (2015). Treadmill stimulation improves newborn stepping. *Developmental Psychobiology, 57*(2), 247–254. http://doi.org/10.1002/dev.21270

Sigelman, C. K., Carr, M. B., & Begley, N. L. (1986). Developmental changes in the influence of sex-role stereotypes on person perception. *Child Study Journal.* Retrieved from http://psycnet.apa.org/psycinfo/1987-10006-001

Sigman, M. (1995). Nutrition and child development: More food for thought. *Current Directions in Psychological Science, 4*(2), 52–55.

Signorella, M., & Liben, L. S. (1984). Recall and reconstruction of gender-related pictures: Effects of attitude, task difficulty, and age. *Child Development, 55,* 393–405.

Siguaw, J. A., Sheng, X., & Simpson, P. M. (2017). Biopsychosocial and retirement factors influencing satisfaction with life. International Journal of HUman Development, 85(4) *http://dx.doi.org/10.1177/0091415016685833.* http://doi.org/10.1177/0091415016685833

Silins, E., Horwood, L. J., Patton, G. C., Fergusson, D. M., Olsson, C. A., Hutchinson, D. M., . . . Mattick, R. P. (2014). Young adult sequelae of adolescent cannabis use: An integrative analysis. *The Lancet Psychiatry, 1*(4), 286–293. http://doi.org/10.1016/S2215-0366(14)70307-4

Sills, J., Rowse, G., & Emerson, L.-M. (2016). The role of collaboration in the cognitive development of young children: A systematic review. *Child: Care, Health and Development, 42*(3), 313–324. http://doi.org/10.1111/cch.12330

Silva, M., Strasser, K., & Cain, K. (2014). Early narrative skills in Chilean preschool: Questions scaffold the production of coherent narratives. *Early Childhood Research Quarterly, 29*(2), 205–213. http://doi.org/10.1016/j.ecresq.2014.02.002

Silveri, M. M., Dager, A. D., Cohen-Gilbert, J. E., & Sneider, J. T. (2016). Neurobiological signatures associated with alcohol and drug use in the human adolescent brain. *Neuroscience & Biobehavioral Reviews.* http://doi.org/10.1016/j.neubiorev.2016.06.042

Silveri, M. M., Tzilos, G. K., & Yurgelun-Todd, D. A. (2008). Relationship between white matter volume and cognitive performance during adolescence: Effects of age, sex and risk for drug use. *Addiction, 103*(9), 1509–1520. http://doi.org/10.1111/j.1360-0443.2008.02272.x

Silverstein, M., & Marenco, A. (2001). How Americans enact the grandparent role across the family life course. *Journal of Family Issues, 22*(4), 493–522.

Silverstein, M., Conroy, S. J., Wang, H., Giarrusso, R., & Bengtson, V. L. (2002). Reciprocity in parent-child relations over the adult life course. *Journals of Gerontology Series B: Psychological Sciences & Social Sciences, 57B*(1), 3.

Sim, T. N., & Koh, S. F. (2003). A domain conceptualization of adolescent susceptibility to peer pressure. *Journal of Research on Adolescence, 13,* 58–80.

Simkin, P., Whalley, J., & Keppler, A. (2001). *Pregnancy, childbirth, and the newborn.* New York: Simon & Schuster.

Simmonds, D., & Luna, B. (2015). Protracted development of brain systems underlying working memory in adolescence: A longitudinal study. Doctoral dissertation, University of Pittsburgh. Retrieved from d-scholarship.pitt.edu/25045.

Simon, H. A. (2001). Learning to research about learning. In S. M. Carver & D. Klahr (Eds.), *Cognition and instruction* (pp. 205–226). Mahwah, NJ: Lawrence Erlbaum.

Simon, J. B., Nail, P. R., Swindle, T., Bihm, E. M., & Joshi, K. (2016). Defensive egotism and self-esteem: A cross-cultural examination of the dynamics of bullying in middle school. *Self and Identity, 1–28.* http://doi.org/10.1080/15298868.2016.1232660

Simons, G. F., & Fennig, C. D. (2017). *Ethnologue: Languages of the world, twentieth edition.* Dallas, Texas: SIL International.

Simons, J. S., Wills, T. A., & Neal, D. J. (2014). The many faces of affect: A multilevel model of drinking frequency/quantity and alcohol dependence symptoms among young adults. *Journal of Abnormal Psychology, 123*(3), 676–94. http://doi.org/10.1037/a0036926

Simons, L. G., & Conger, R. D. (2007). Linking mother–father differences in parenting to a typology of family parenting styles and adolescent outcomes. *Journal of Family Issues, 28,* 212–241.

Simons, L. G., Simons, R. L., & Su, X. (2013). Consequences of corporal punishment among African Americans: The importance of context and outcome. *Journal of Youth and Adolescence, 42*(8), 1273–1285. http://doi.org/10.1007/s10964-012-9853-9

Simons, L., Schrager, S. M., Clark, L. F., Belzer, M., & Olson, J. (2013). Parental support and mental health among transgender adolescents. *Journal of Adolescent Health, 53*(6), 791–793. http://doi.org/10.1016/j.jadohealth.2013.07.019

Simons-Morton, B., Haynie, D., Liu, D., Chaurasia, A., Li, K., & Hingson, R. (2016). The effect of residence, school status, work status, and social influence on the prevalence of alcohol use among emerging adults. *Journal of Studies on Alcohol and Drugs, 77*(1), 121–32. http://doi.org/10.15288/JSAD.2016.77.121

Simonton, D. K., & Song, A. V. (2009). Eminence, IQ, physical and mental health, and achievement domain : Cox's 282 Geniuses revisited. *Psychological Science, 20*(4), 429–34. http://doi.org/10.1111/J.1467-9280.2009.02313.X

Simpkins, S. D., Delgado, M. Y., Price, C. D., Quach, A., & Starbuck, E. (2013). Socioeconomic status, ethnicity, culture, and immigration: Examining the potential mechanisms underlying Mexican-origin adolescents' organized activity participation. *Developmental Psychology, 49*(4), 706–721. http://doi.org/10.1037/a0028399

Simpson, D. B., Cloud, D. S., Newman, J. L., & Fuqua, D. R. (2008). Sex and gender differences in religiousness and spirituality. *Journal of Psychology & Theology, 36*(1), 42–52.

Sims, T., Hogan, C. L., & Carstensen, L. L. (2015). Selectivity as an emotion regulation strategy: Lessons from older adults. *Current Opinion in Psychology, 3,* 80–84. http://doi.org/10.1016/j.copsyc.2015.02.012

Sin, H. P. Y., Liu, D. T. L., & Lam, D. S. C. (2013). Lifestyle modification, nutritional and vitamins supplements for age-related macular degeneration. *Acta Ophthalmologica*, *91*(1), 6–11. http://doi.org/10.1111/j.1755-3768.2011.02357.x

Sinclair, K. D., & Watkins, A. J. (2013). Parental diet, pregnancy outcomes and offspring health: Metabolic determinants in developing oocytes and embryos. *Reproduction, Fertility, and Development*, *26*(1), 99–114. http://doi.org/10.1071/RD13290

Singer, J. L., & Singer, D. G. (1998). Barney & Friends as entertainment and education: Evaluating the quality and effectiveness of a television series for preschool children. In J. K. Asamen & G. L. Berry (Eds.), *Research paradigms, television, and social behavior* (pp. 305–367). Thousand Oaks, CA: Sage.

Singer, L. T., Minnes, S., Min, M. O., Lewis, B. A., & Short, E. J. (2015). Prenatal cocaine exposure and child outcomes: A conference report based on a prospective study from Cleveland. *Human Psychopharmacology: Clinical and Experimental*, *30*(4), 285–289. http://doi.org/10.1002/hup.2454

Singer, T., Lindenberger, U., & Baltes, P. B. (2003). Plasticity of memory for new learning in very old age: A story of major loss? *Psychology and Aging*, *18*(2), 306–317.

Singer, T., Verhaeghen, P., Ghisletta, P., Lindenberger, U., & Baltes, P. B. (2003). The fate of cognition in very old age: Six-year longitudinal findings in the Berlin Aging Study (BASE). *Psychology and Aging*, *18*(2), 318–331.

Singh, G. K., & Kogan, M. D. (2007). Widening socioeconomic disparities in US childhood mortality, 1969–2000. *American Journal of Public Health*, *97*(9), 1658–1665.

Singh, L., Nestor, S., Parikh, C., & Yull, A. (2009). Influences of infant-directed speech on early word recognition. *Infancy*, *14*(6), 654–666. http://doi.org/10.1080/15250000903263973

Singh, T., Arrazola, R. A., Corey, C. G., Husten, C. G., Neff, L. J., Homa, D. M., & King, B. A. (2016). Tobacco use among middle and high school students — United States, 2011–2015. *MMWR. Morbidity and Mortality Weekly Report*, *65*(14), 361–367. http://doi.org/10.15585/mmwr.mm6514a1

Sinha, J. W., Cnaan, R. A., & Gelles, R. J. (2007). Adolescent risk behaviors and religion: Findings from a national study. *Journal of Adolescence*, *30*(2), 231–249.

Sinnott, J. D. (1998). *The development of logic in adulthood: Postformal thought and its applications.* New York: Plenum.

Sinnott, J. D. (2003). Postformal thought and adult development: Living in balance. In J. Demick & C. Andreoletti (Eds.), *Handbook of adult development* (pp. 221–238). New York: Kluwer.

Sinozich, Sofi, & Langton, L. (2014). *Rape and sexual assault victimization among college-age females, 1995–2013.* Washington DC. Retrieved from https://assets.documentcloud.org/documents/1378364/rsavcaf9513.pdf

Siris, E. S., Adler, R., Bilezikian, J., Bolognese, M., Dawson-Hughes, B., Favus, M. J., . . . Watts, N. B. (2014). The clinical diagnosis of osteoporosis: A position statement from the National Bone Health Alliance Working Group. *Osteoporosis International*, *25*(5), 1439–1443. http://doi.org/10.1007/s00198-014-2655-z

Sirsch, U., Dreher, E., Mayr, E., & Willinger, U. (2009). What does it take to be an adult in Austria?: Views of adulthood in Austrian adolescents, Emerging Adults, and Adults. *Journal of Adolescent Research*, *24*(3), 275–292.

Sisson, S. B., & Katzmarzyk, P. T. (2008). International prevalence of physical activity in youth and adults. *Obesity Reviews*, *9*(6), 606–614. http://doi.org/10.1111/j.1467-789X.2008.00506.x

Skinner, B. F. (1957). *Verbal behavior.* New York: Appleton-Century-Crofts.

Skinner, E. A., Zimmer-Gembeck, M. J., & Connell, J. P. (1998). Individual differences and the development of perceived control. *Monographs of the Society for Research in Child Development*, *63*(2–3, Serial No. 254).

Skinner, O. D., & McHale, S. M. (2016). Parent–adolescent conflict in African American families. *Journal of Youth and Adolescence*, *45*(10), 2080–2093. http://doi.org/10.1007/s10964-016-0514-2

Skitka, L. J., Bauman, C. W., & Mullen, E. (2016). Morality and Justice. In Clara Sabbagh & Manfred Schmitt (Eds.), *Handbook of social justice theory and research* (pp. 407–423). New York, NY: Springer New York. http://doi.org/10.1007/978-1-4939-3216-0_22

Skoog, T., & Stattin, H. (2014). Why and under what contextual conditions do early-maturing girls develop problem behaviors? *Child Development Perspectives*, *8*(3), 158–162. http://doi.org/10.1111/cdep.12076

Skoog, T., Özdemir, S. B., & Stattin, H. (2016). Understanding the link between pubertal timing in girls and the development of depressive symptoms: The role of sexual harassment. *Journal of Youth and Adolescence*, *45*(2), 316–327. http://doi.org/10.1007/s10964-015-0292-2

Skosnik, P. D., Edwards, C. R., O'Donnell, B. F., Steffen, A., Steinmetz, J. E., & Hetrick, W. P. (2008). Cannabis use disrupts eyeblink conditioning: evidence for cannabinoid modulation of cerebellar-dependent learning. *Neuropsychopharmacology*, *33*(7), 1432–1440. http://doi.org/10.1038/sj.npp.1301506

Slack, M. K. (2006). Interpreting current physical activity guidelines and incorporating them into practice for health promotion and disease prevention. *American Journal of Health-System Pharmacy*, *63*(17), 1647–1653.

Slater, A., Quinn, P. C., Brown, E., & Hayes, R. (1999). Intermodal perception at birth: Intersensory redundancy guides newborn infants' learning of arbitrary auditory-visual pairings. *Developmental Science*, *2*(3), 333–338.

Slater, A., Rose, D., & Morison, V. (1984). New-born infants' perception of similarities and differences between two- and three-dimensional stimuli. *British Journal of Developmental Psychology*, *3*, 211–220.

Slaughter, V. (2005). Young children's understanding of death. *Australian Psychologist*, *40*(3), 179–186.

Slaughter, V., & Griffiths, M. (2007). Death understanding and fear of death in young children. *Clinical Child Psychology and Psychiatry*, *12*(4), 525–535. http://doi.org/10.1177/1359104507080980

Slaughter, V., & McConnell, D. (2003). Emergence of joint attention: Relationships between gaze following, social referencing, imitation, and naming in infancy. *Journal of Genetic Psychology*, *164*(1), 54.

Slaughter, V., Imuta, K., Peterson, C. C., & Henry, J. D. (2015). Meta-analysis of theory of mind and peer popularity in the preschool and early school years. *Child Development*, *86*(4), 1159–1174. http://doi.org/10.1111/cdev.12372

Slaughter, V., & Perez-Zapata, D. (2014). Cultural variations in the development of mind reading. *Child Development Perspectives*, *8*(4), 237–241. http://doi.org/10.1111/cdep.12091

Slaughter, V., Peterson, C. C., & Mackintosh, E. (2007). Mind what mother says: Narrative input and theory of mind in typical children and those on the autism spectrum. *Child Development*, *78*(3), 839–858.

Slee, P. T., & Mohyla, J. (2007). The PEACE Pack: An evaluation of interventions to reduce bullying in four Australian primary schools. *Educational Research*, *49*(2), 103–114.

Slevec, J., & Tiggemann, M. (2010). Attitudes toward cosmetic surgery in middle-aged women: Body image, aging anxiety, and the media. *Psychology of Women Quarterly*, *34*(1), 65–74. http://doi.org/10.1111/j.1471-6402.2009.01542.x

Sloan, R. P., Shapiro, P. A., DeMeersman, R. E., Bagiella, E., Brondolo, E. N., McKinley, P. S., . . . Myers, M. M. (2009). The effect of aerobic training and cardiac autonomie regulation in young adults. *American Journal of Public Health*, *99*(5), 921–928.

Slone, M., & Mann, S. (2016). Effects of war, terrorism and armed conflict on young children: A systematic review. *Child Psychiatry & Human Development*, *47*(6), 950–965. http://doi.org/10.1007/s10578-016-0626-7

Smach, M. A., Charfeddine, B., Ben Othman, L., Lammouchi, T., Dridi, H., Nafati, S., . . . Limem, K. (2009). Evaluation of cerebrospinal fluid tau/beta-amyloid(42) ratio as diagnostic markers for Alzheimer disease. *European Neurology*, *62*(6), 349–355. http://doi.org/10.1159/000241881

Smetana, J. G. (1995). Morality in context: Abstractions, ambiguities, and applications. In R. Vasta (Ed.), *Annals of Child Development* (Vol. 10, pp. 83–130). London: Jessica Kingsley.

Smetana, J. G., & Braeges, J. L. (1990). The development of toddler's moral and conventional judgments. *Merrill-Palmer Quarterly*, *36*, 329–346.

Smetana, J. G., Jambon, M., & Ball., C. (2013). The social domain approach to children's moral and social judgments. In M. Killen & J. G. Smetana (Eds.), *Handbook of moral development*. New York: Psychology Press.

Smetana, J. G., Tasopoulos-Chan, M., Gettman, D. C., Villalobos, M., Campione-Barr, N., & Metzger, A. (2009). Adolescents' and parents' evaluations of helping versus fulfilling personal desires in family situations. *Child Development*, *80*(1), 280–294. http://doi.org/10.1111/j.1467-8624.2008.01259.x

Smink, F. R. E., van Hoeken, D., & Hoek, H. W. (2013). Epidemiology, course, and outcome of eating disorders. *Current Opinion in Psychiatry*, *26*(6), 543–8. http://doi.org/10.1097/YCO.0b013e328365a24f

Smink, F. R. E., van Hoeken, D., Oldenhinkel, A. J., & Hoek, H. W. (2014). Prevalence and severity of DSM-5 eating disorders in a community cohort of adolescents. *The International Journal of Eating Disorders*, *47*(6), 610–9. http://doi.org/10.1002/eat.22316

Smith, A. M. A., Rissel, C. E., Richters, J., Grulich, A. E., & de Visser, R. O. (2003). Sex in Australia: Reflections and recommendations for future research. *Australian & New Zealand Journal of Public Health*, *27*, 251–256.

Smith, A. R., Chein, J., & Steinberg, L. (2013). Impact of socio-emotional context, brain development, and pubertal maturation on adolescent risk-taking. *Hormones and Behavior*, *64*(2), 323–332. http://doi.org/10.1016/j.yhbeh.2013.03.006

Smith, A. R., Chein, J., & Steinberg, L. (2014). Peers increase adolescent risk-taking even when the probabilities of negative outcomes are known. *Developmental Psychology*, *50*(5), 1564–1568. https://doi.org/10.1037/a0035696

Smith, A. R., Steinberg, L., Strang, N., & Chein, J. (2015). Age differences in the impact of peers on adolescents' and adults' neural response to reward. *Developmental Cognitive Neuroscience*, *11*, 75–82. http://doi.org/10.1016/j.dcn.2014.08.010

Smith, G. C., & Hancock, G. R. (2010). Custodial grandmother-grandfather dyads: Pathways among marital distress, grandparent dysphoria, parenting practice, and grandchild adjustment. *Family Relations*, *59*(1), 45–59. http://doi.org/10.1111/j.1741-3729.2009.00585.x

Smith, J. A. (2007). Identity development during the transition to motherhood: An interpretative phenomenological analysis. *Journal of Reproductive and Infant Psychology*, 17(3), 281–299. http://doi.org/10.1080/02646839908404595

Smith, J. D. L., Nagy, T. R., & Allison, D. B. (2010). Calorie restriction: What recent results suggest for the future of ageing research. *European Journal of Clinical Investigation*, 40(5), 440–450. http://doi.org/10.1111/j.1365-2362.2010.02276.x

Smith, J., & Freund, A. M. (2002). The dynamics of possible selves in old age. *Journals of Gerontology Series B: Psychological Sciences & Social Sciences*, 57B(6), P492.

Smith, S., Pieper, K., Granados, A., & Choueiti, M. (2010). Assessing gender-related portrayals in top-grossing g-rated films. *Sex Roles*, 62(11/12), 774–786. http://doi.org/10.1007/s11199-009-9736-z

Smith, T. E., & Leaper, C. (2006). Self-perceived gender typicality and the peer context during adolescence. *Journal of Research on Adolescence*, 16(1), 91–104. http://doi.org/10.1111/j.1532-7795.2006.00123.x

Smithers, L. G., Golley, R. K., Brazionis, L., & Lynch, J. W. (2011). Characterizing whole diets of young children from developed countries and the association between diet and health: A systematic review. *Nutrition Reviews*, 69(8), 449–467. http://doi.org/10.1111/j.1753-4887.2011.00407.x

Smokowski, P. R., Rose, R. A., & Bacallao, M. (2010). Influence of risk factors and cultural assets on Latino adolescents' trajectories of self-esteem and internalizing symptoms. *Child Psychiatry and Human Development*, 41(2), 133–155. http://doi.org/10.1007/s10578-009-0157-6

Smolak, L. (2011). Body image development in childhood. In T. F. Cash & L. Smolak (Eds.), *Body image: A handbook of science, practice, and prevention* (pp. 67–75). New York, NY: Guilford Press.

Snapp, S., Ryu, E., & Kerr, J. (2015). The Upside to Hooking Up: College Students' Positive Hookup Experiences. *International Journal of Sexual Health*, 27(1), 43–56. http://doi.org/10.1080/19317611.2014.939247

Snarey, J. R. (1985). Cross-cultural universality of social-moral development: a critical review of Kohlbergian research. *Psychological Bulletin*, 97(2), 202–232.

Snowling, M. J. (2013). Early identification and interventions for dyslexia: A contemporary view. *Journal of Research in Special Educational Needs*, 13(1), 7–14. http://doi.org/10.1111/j.1471-3802.2012.01262.x

Soares, J. M., Marques, P., Alves, V., & Sousa, N. (2013). A hitchhiker's guide to diffusion tensor imaging. *Frontiers in Neuroscience*, 7, 31. Retrieved from http://doi.org/10.3389/fnins.2013.00031

Soares, R. R. (2007). On the determinants of mortality reductions in the developing world. *Population and Development Review*, 33(2), 247–287. http://doi.org/10.1111/j.1728-4457.2007.00169.x

Sobanko, J. F., Taglienti, A. J., Wilson, A. J., Sarwer, D. B., Margolis, D. J., Dai, J., . . . Pusic, A. (2015). Motivations for seeking minimally invasive cosmetic procedures in an academic outpatient setting. *Aesthetic Surgery Journal / the American Society for Aesthetic Plastic Surgery*, 35(8), 1014–20. http://doi.org/10.1093/asj/sjv094

Social Security Administration. (2007). *Social security: A brief history*. Washington, DC: Social Security Administration. Retrieved from http://www.ssa.gov/history/pdf/2007historybooklet.pdf

Social Security Administration. (2008). *The future of social security*. Washington DC: Social Security Administration.

Social Security Administration. (2014a). Social security basic facts. Retrieved from http://www.ssa.gov/news/press/basicfact.html

Social Security Administration. (2014b). Social security basic facts.

Social Security Administration. (2015a). Life expectancy. Retrieved from http://www.ssa.gov/planners/lifeexpectancy.html

Social Security Administration. (2015b). Social security is important To African Americans. Retrieved from http://www.ssa.gov/news/press/factsheets/africanamer.htm

Social Security Administration. (2015c). Social security is important to women. Retrieved April 8, 2015, from http://www.ssa.gov/news/press/factsheets/women-alt.pdf

Society for Research in Child Development. (2007). *Ethical standards in research*. Washington, DC. Retrieved from http://www.srcd.org/about-us/ethical-standards-research

Sohn, K. (2016). Improvement in the biological standard of living in 20th century Korea: Evidence from age at menarche. *American Journal of Human Biology*, 29(1). http://doi.org/10.1002/ajhb.22882

Solomon, D. H., Ayanian, J. Z., Yelin, E., Shaykevich, T., Brookhart, M. A., & Katz, J. N. (2012). Use of disease-modifying medications for rheumatoid arthritis by race and ethnicity in the National Ambulatory Medical Care Survey. *Arthritis Care & Research*, 64(2), 184–9. http://doi.org/10.1002/acr.20674

Song, A. V, & Ling, P. M. (2011). Social smoking among young adults: Investigation of intentions and attempts to quit. *American Journal of Public Health*, 101(7), 1291–1296. http://doi.org/10.2105/ajph.2010.300012

Song, J., Floyd, F. J., Seltzer, M. M., Greenberg, J. S., & Hong, J. (2010). Long-term effects of child death on parents' health related quality of life: A dyadic analysis. *Family Relations*, 59(3), 269–282. http://doi.org/10.1111/j.1741-3729.2010.00601.x

Song, Y., Ma, J., Li, L.-B., Dong, B., Wang, Z., & Agardh, A. (2016). Secular trends for age at spermarche among Chinese boys from 11 ethnic minorities, 1995-2010: A multiple cross-sectional study. *BMJ Open*, 6(2), e010518. http://doi.org/10.1136/bmjopen-2015-010518

Sorkhabi, N. (2005). Applicability of Baumrind's parent typology to collective cultures: Analysis of cultural explanations of parent socialization effects. *International Journal of Behavioral Development*, 29(6), 552–563.

Sorond, F. A., Cruz-Almeida, Y., Clark, D. J., Viswanathan, A., Scherzer, C. R., De Jager, P., . . . Lipsitz, L. A. (2015). Aging, the central nervous system, and mobility in older adults: Neural mechanisms of mobility impairment. *The Journals of Gerontology Series A: Biological Sciences and Medical Sciences*, 70(12), 1526–1532. http://doi.org/10.1093/gerona/glv130

Soto, C. J. (2015). Is happiness good for your personality? Concurrent and prospective relations of the Big Five with subjective well-being. *Journal of Personality*, 83(1), 45–55. http://doi.org/10.1111/jopy.12081

Soto, C. J., & Tackett, J. L. (2015). Personality traits in childhood and adolescence: Structure, development, and outcomes. *Current Directions in Psychological Science*, 24(5), 358–362. http://doi.org/10.1177/0963721415589345

Soto, C. J., John, O. P., Gosling, S. D., & Potter, J. (2011). Age differences in personality traits from 10 to 65: Big Five domains and facets in a large cross-sectional sample. *Journal of Personality and Social Psychology*, 100(2), 330–348. http://doi.org/10.1037/a0021717

Soto, C. J., John, O. P., Gosling, S. D., & Potter, J. (2011). Age differences in personality traits from 10 to 65: Big Five domains and facets in a large cross-sectional sample. *Journal of Personality and Social Psychology*, 100(2), 330–348. http://doi.org/10.1037/a0021717

Soubry, A., Hoyo, C., Jirtle, R. L., & Murphy, S. K. (2014). A paternal environmental legacy: Evidence for epigenetic inheritance through the male germ line. *BioEssays : News and Reviews in Molecular, Cellular and Developmental Biology*, 36(4), 359–71. http://doi.org/10.1002/bies.201300113

Sousa, D. A. (2001). *How the brain learns: A classroom teacher's guide*. Thousand Oaks, CA: Corwin.

Spalding, K. L., Bergmann, O., Alkass, K., Bernard, S., Salehpour, M., Huttner, H. B., . . . Frisén, J. (2013). Dynamics of hippocampal neurogenesis in adult humans. *Cell*, 153(6), 1219–27. http://doi.org/10.1016/j.cell.2013.05.002

Spalletta, G., Caltagirone, C., Girardi, P., Gianni, W., Casini, A. R., & Palmer, K. (2012). The role of persistent and incident major depression on rate of cognitive deterioration in newly diagnosed Alzheimer's disease patients. *Psychiatry Research*, 198(2), 263–8. http://doi.org/10.1016/j.psychres.2011.11.018

Speakman, J. R., & Mitchell, S. E. (2011). Caloric restriction. *Molecular Aspects of Medicine*, 32(3), 159–221. http://doi.org/10.1016/j.mam.2011.07.001

Spear, L. P. (2011). Adolescent neurobehavioral characteristics, alcohol sensitivities, and intake: Setting the stage for alcohol use disorders? *Child Development Perspectives*, 5(4), 231–238. http://doi.org/10.1111/j.1750-8606.2011.00182.x

Spear, L. P. (2013). Adolescent neurodevelopment. *The Journal of Adolescent Health : Official Publication of the Society for Adolescent Medicine*, 52(2 Suppl 2), S7-13. http://doi.org/10.1016/j.jadohealth.2012.05.006

Spearman, C., & C. (1904). General intelligence objectively determined and measured. *The American Journal of Psychology*, 15(2), 201. http://doi.org/10.2307/1412107

Speece, M. W., & Brent, S. B. (1984). Children's understanding of death: A review of three components of a death concept. *Child Development*, 55(5), 1671. http://doi.org/10.1111/1467-8624.ep7304478

Spelke, E. S. (1976). Infants' intermodal perception of events. *Cognitive Psychology*, 8, 553–560.

Spelke, E. S. (2016). Core knowledge and conceptual change. In D. Barner & andrew scott Baron (Eds.), *Core knowledge and conceptual change*. (pp. 279–300). New York: Oxford University Press.

Spelke, E. S., & Kinzler, K. D. (2007). Core knowledge. *Developmental Science*, 10(1), 89–96. http://doi.org/10.1111/j.1467-7687.2007.00569.x

Spelke, E., Lee, S. A., & Izard, V. (2010). Beyond core knowledge: Natural geometry. *Cognitive Science: A Multidisciplinary Journal*, 34(5), 863–884. http://doi.org/10.1111/j.1551-6709.2010.01110.x

Spencer, J. P., Vereijken, B., Diedrich, F. J., & Thelen, E. (2000). Posture and the emergence of manual skills. *Developmental Science*, 3(2), 216–217.

Spencer, M. B., Swanson, D. P., & Harpalani, V. (2015). Development of the Self. In *Handbook of Child Psychology and Developmental Science* (pp. 1–44). Hoboken, NJ, USA: John Wiley & Sons, Inc. http://doi.org/10.1002/9781118963418.childpsy318

Spielberg, J. M., Olino, T. M., Forbes, E. E., & Dahl, R. E. (2014). Exciting fear in adolescence: Does pubertal development alter threat processing? *Developmental Cognitive Neuroscience, 8*, 86–95. http://doi.org/10.1016/j.dcn.2014.01.004

Spilt, J. L., Hughes, J. N., Wu, J.-Y., & Kwok, O.-M. Dynamics of teacher-student relationships: stability and change across elementary school and the influence on children's academic success. *Child Development, 83*(4), 1180–95. http://doi.org/10.1111/j.1467-8624.2012.01761.x

Spinelli, J., Collins-Praino, L., Van Den Heuvel, C., & Byard, R. W. (2017). Evolution and significance of the triple risk model in sudden infant death syndrome. *Journal of Paediatrics and Child Health, 53*(2), 112–115. http://doi.org/10.1111/jpc.13429

Spokane, A. R., & Cruza-Guet, M. C. (2005). Holland's Theory of Vocational Personalities in Work Environments. In S. D. Brown & R. W. Lent (Eds.), *Career development and counseling: Putting theory and research to work.* (pp. 24–41). Hoboken, NJ, US: John Wiley & Sons Inc.

Sprecher, S., Brooks, J. E., & Avogo, W. (2013). Self-Esteem Among Young Adults: Differences and Similarities Based on Gender, Race, and Cohort (1990–2012). *Sex Roles, 69*(5–6), 264–275. http://doi.org/10.1007/s11199-013-0295-y

Springer, S. P., & Deutsch, G. (1998). *Left brain, right brain: Perspectives from cognitive neuroscience* (5th ed.). New York: Freeman.

Squeglia, L. M., & Gray, K. M. (2016). Alcohol and Drug Use and the Developing Brain. *Current Psychiatry Reports, 18*(5), 46. http://doi.org/10.1007/s11920-016-0689-y

Squeglia, L. M., Tapert, S. F., Sullivan, E. V., Jacobus, J., Meloy, M. J., Rohlfing, T., & Pfefferbaum, A. (2015). Brain Development in Heavy-Drinking Adolescents. *American Journal of Psychiatry, 172*(6), 531–542. http://doi.org/10.1176/appi.ajp.2015.14101249

Srabstein, J., Joshi, P. T., Due, P., Wright, J., Leventhal, B., Merrick, J., . . . Riibner, K. (2008). Antibullying legislation: A public health perspective. *Journal of Adolescent Health, 42*(1), 11–20. http://doi.org/10.1016/j.jadohealth.2007.10.007

Sridhar, D., & Vaughn, S. (2001). Social functioning of students with learning disabilities. In D. P. Hallahan & B. K. Keogh (Eds.), *Research and global perspectives in learning disabilities* (pp. 65–91). Mahwah, NJ: Lawrence Erlbaum.

Srikanth, S., & Nagaraja, A. V. (2005). A prospective study of reversible dementias: Frequency, causes, clinical profile and results of treatment. *Neurology India, 53*(3), 291–294.

Srinivasan, V., Braidy, N., Chan, E. K. W., Xu, Y.-H., & Chan, D. K. Y. (2016). Genetic and environmental factors in vascular dementia: An update of blood brain barrier dysfunction. *Clinical and Experimental Pharmacology and Physiology, 43*(5), 515–521. http://doi.org/10.1111/1440-1681.12558

Srivastava, S., John, O. P., Gosling, S. D., & Potter, J. (2003). Development of personality in early and middle adulthood: Set like plaster or persistent change? *Journal of Personality and Social Psychology, 84*, 1041–1053.

Sroufe, L. A. (1977). Wariness of strangers and the study of infant development. *Child Development, 48*(3), 731–746.

Sroufe, L. A. (1997). Psychopathology as an outcome of development. *Development and Psychopathology, 7*, 323–336.

Sroufe, L. A., & Waters, E. (1976). The ontogenesis of smiling and laughter: A perspective on the organization of development in infancy. *Psychological Review, 83*(3), 173–189. http://doi.org/10.1037/0033-295x.83.3.173

Srour, M., & Shevell, M. (2014). Genetics and the investigation of developmental delay/intellectual disability. *Archives of Disease in Childhood, 99*(4), 386–9. http://doi.org/10.1136/archdischild-2013-304063

Stacks, A. M., Oshio, T., Gerard, J., & Roe, J. (2009). The moderating effect of parental warmth on the association between spanking and child aggression: A longitudinal approach. *Infant & Child Development, 18*(2), 178–194. http://doi.org/10.1002/icd.596

Staff, J., & Uggen, C. (2003). The fruits of good work: Early work experiences and adolescent deviance. *Journal of Research in Crime & Delinquency, 40*(3), 263–290.

Staff, J., Vaneseltine, M., Woolnough, A., Silver, E., & Burrington, L. (2012). Adolescent work experiences and family formation behavior. *Journal of Research on Adolescence : The Official Journal of the Society for Research on Adolescence, 22*(1), 150–164. http://doi.org/10.1111/j.1532-7795.2011.00755.x

Stanca, L. (2012). Suffer the little children: Measuring the effects of parenthood on well-being worldwide. *Journal of Economic Behavior & Organization, 81*(3), 742–750. http://doi.org/10.1016/j.jebo.2010.12.019

Stang, J. S., & Stotmeister, B. (2017). Nutrition in adolescence. In Norman J. Temple, Ted Wilson, & George A. Bray (Eds.), *Nutrition guide for physicians and related healthcare professionals* (pp. 29–39). Cham: Springer International Publishing. http://doi.org/10.1007/978-3-319-49929-1_4

Stanley, S. M., Rhoades, G. K., Amato, P. R., Markman, H. J., & Johnson, C. A. (2010). The timing of cohabitation and engagement: Impact on first and second marriages. *Journal of Marriage and the Family, 72*(4), 906–918. http://doi.org/10.1111/j.1741-3737.2010.00738.x

Stapel, J. C., van Wijk, I., Bekkering, H., & Hunnius, S. (2016). Eighteen-month-old infants show distinct electrophysiological responses to their own faces. *Developmental Science.* http://doi.org/10.1111/desc.12437

Stark, A. D., Bennet, G. C., Stone, D. H., & Chishti, P. (2002). Association between childhood fractures and poverty: Population based study. *BMJ (Clinical Research Ed.), 324*(7335), 457. Retrieved from http://www.ncbi.nlm.nih.gov/pubmed/11859047

Starkstein, S. E., Jorge, R., Mizrahi, R., & Robinson, R. G. (2005). The construct of minor and major depression in Alzheimer's disease. *The American Journal of Psychiatry, 162*(11), 2086–93. http://doi.org/10.1176/appi.ajp.162.11.2086

Starkstein, S. E., Mizrahi, R., & Power, B. D. (2008). Depression in Alzheimer's disease: Phenomenology, clinical correlates and treatment. *International Review of Psychiatry, 20*(4), 382–388. http://doi.org/10.1080/09540260802094480

Statistics Canada. (2015). *The 10 leading causes of death, 2011.* Retrieved from http://www.statcan.gc.ca/pub/82-625-x/2014001/article/11896-eng.htm

Statistics Canada. (2017). *Labour force characteristics by sex and age group.* Retrieved from http://www.statcan.gc.ca/tables-tableaux/sum-som/l01/cst01/labor05-eng.htm

Stattin, H., & Kerr, M. (2000). Parental monitoring: A reinterpretation. *Child Development, 71*, 1072–1086.

Staudinger, U. M., & Baltes, P. B. (1996). Interactive minds: A facilitative setting of wisdom-related performance? *Journal of Personality & Social Psychology, 71*(4), 746–762.

Staudinger, U. M., & Lindenberger, U. (2003). *Understanding human development: Dialogues with lifespan psychology.* Dordrecht, Netherlands: Kluwer Academic Publishers.

Staudinger, U. M., Dörner, J., & Mickler, C. (2005). Wisdom and personality. In R. J. Sternberg & J. Jordan (Eds.), *A handbook of wisdom: Psychological perspectives.* (pp. 191–219). New York: Cambridge University Press.

Staudinger, U. M., Kessler, E.-M., & Dörner, J. (2006). Wisdom in social context. In K. W. Schaie & L. L. Carstensen (Eds.), *Social structures, aging, and self-regulation in the elderly.* (pp. 33–67). New York, NY: Springer Publishing Co.

Stearns, E., Moller, S., Potochnick, S., & Blau, J. (2007). Staying back and dropping out: The relationship between grade retention and school dropout. *Sociology of Education, 80*(3), 210–240.

Steelandt, S., Thierry, B., Broihanne, M.-H., & Dufour, V. (2012). The ability of children to delay gratification in an exchange task. *Cognition, 122*(3), 416–425. http://doi.org/10.1016/j.cognition.2011.11.009

Steele, C. M. (1997). A threat in the air: How stereotypes shape intellectual identity and performance. *American Psychologist, 52*(6), 613–629. http://doi.org/10.1037/0003-066X.52.6.613

Steele, C. M., & Aronson, J. (1995). Stereotype threat and the intellectual test performance of African Americans. *Journal of Personality and Social Psychology, 69*(5), 797–811. http://doi.org/10.1037/0022-3514.69.5.797

Steele, H., Steele, M., & Croft, C. (2008). Early attachment predicts emotion recognition at 6 and 11 years old. *Attachment & Human Development, 10*(4), 379–393. http://doi.org/10.1080/14616730802461409

Steensma, T. D., & Cohen-Kettenis, P. T. (2011). Gender transitioning before puberty? *Archives of Sexual Behavior, 40*(4), 649–650. http://doi.org/10.1007/s10508-011-9752-2

Steensma, T. D., Kreukels, B. P. C., de Vries, A. L. C., & Cohen-Kettenis, P. T. (2013). Gender identity development in adolescence. *Hormones and Behavior, 64*(2), 288–297. http://doi.org/10.1016/j.yhbeh.2013.02.020

Stefanou, C., & McCabe, M. P. (2012). Adult attachment and sexual functioning: A review of past research. *The Journal of Sexual Medicine, 9*(10), 2499–2507. http://doi.org/10.1111/j.1743-6109.2012.02843.x

Steiger, A. E., Allemand, M., Robins, R. W., & Fend, H. A. (2014). Low and decreasing self-esteem during adolescence predict adult depression two decades later. *Journal of Personality and Social Psychology, 106*(2), 325–38. http://doi.org/10.1037/a0035133

Stein, C., Fisher, L., Berkey, C., & Colditz, G. (2007). Adolescent physical activity and perceived competence: Does change in activity level impact self-perception? *Journal of Adolescent Health, 40*(5), 462.e1-8.

Stein, J. H., & Reiser, L. W. (1994). A study of white middle-class adolescent boys' responses to "semenarche" (the first ejaculation). *Journal of Youth and Adolescence, 23*(3), 373–384. http://doi.org/10.1007/BF01536725

Stein, Z., & Kuhn, L. (2009). Breast feeding: A time to craft new policies. *Journal of Public Health Policy, 30*(3), 300–310. http://doi.org/10.1057/jphp.2009.23

Steinberg, L. (2001). We know some things: Parent-adolescent relationships in retrospect and prospect. *Journal of Research on Adolescence, 11*(1), 1–19.

Steinberg, L. (2008). A social neuroscience perspective on adolescent risk-taking. *Developmental Review, 28*(1), 78–106. http://doi.org/10.1016/j.dr.2007.08.002

Steinberg, L. (2013). Does recent research on adolescent brain development inform the mature minor doctrine? *Journal of Medicine and Philosophy, 38*, 256–267. http://doi.org/10.1093/jmp/jht017

Steinberg, L., & Monahan, K. C. (2007). Age differences in resistance to peer influence. *Developmental Psychology, 43*(6), 1531–1543. http://doi.org/10.1037/0012-1649.43.6.1531

Steinberg, L., & Scott, E. S. (2003). Less guilty by reason of adolescence: Developmental immaturity, diminished responsibility, and the juvenile death penalty. *American Psychologist, 58*(12), 1009–1018.

Steinberg, L., & Silverberg, S. B. (1986). The vicissitudes of autonomy in early adolescence. *Child Development, 57*(4), 841.

Steinberg, L., Fegley, S., & Dornbusch, S. M. (1993). Negative impact of part-time work on adolescent adjustment: Evidence from a longitudinal study. *Developmental Psychology, 29*(2), 171–180.

Steinberg, L., Graham, S., O'Brien, L., Woolard, J., Cauffman, E., & Banich, M. (2009). Age differences in future orientation and delay discounting. *Child Development, 80*(1), 28–44. http://doi.org/10.1111/j.1467-8624.2008.01244.x

Steinberg, L., Icenogle, G., Shulman, E. P., Breiner, K., Chein, J., Bacchini, D., . . . Takash, H. M. S. (2017). Around the world, adolescence is a time of heightened sensation seeking and immature self-regulation. *Developmental Science*, e12532. http://doi.org/10.1111/desc.12532

Steiner, J. E. (1979). Human facial expressions in response to taste and smell stimulations. In L. P. Lipsitt & H. W. Reese (Eds.), *Advances in child development: Vol 13* (pp. 257–295). New York: Academic Press.

Steinmetz, K. (2016). These states just legalized marijuana. *Time, Nov. 8, 20.* Retrieved from http://time.com/4559278/marijuana-election-results-2016/

Stepankova, H., Lukavsky, J., Buschkuehl, M., Kopecek, M., Ripova, D., & Jaeggi, S. M. (2014). The malleability of working memory and visuospatial skills: A randomized controlled study in older adults. *Developmental Psychology, 50*(4), 1049–1059. http://doi.org/10.1037/a0034913

Stephan, Y., Caudroit, J., Jaconelli, A., & Terracciano, A. (2014). Subjective age and cognitive functioning: A 10-year prospective study. *The American Journal of Geriatric Psychiatry : Official Journal of the American Association for Geriatric Psychiatry, 22*(11), 1180–7. http://doi.org/10.1016/j.jagp.2013.03.007

Stephan, Y., Sutin, A. R., Caudroit, J., & Terracciano, A. (2015). Subjective age and changes in memory in older adults. *The Journals of Gerontology. Series B, Psychological Sciences and Social Sciences,* gbv010-. http://doi.org/10.1093/geronb/gbv010

Stephens, P. J., Tarpey, P. S., Davies, H., Van Loo, P., Greenman, C., Wedge, D. C., . . . Stratton, M. R. (2012). The landscape of cancer genes and mutational processes in breast cancer. *Nature, 486*(7403), 400–4. http://doi.org/10.1038/nature11017

Stern, Y. (2012). Cognitive reserve in ageing and Alzheimer's disease. *The Lancet. Neurology, 11*(11), 1006–12. http://doi.org/10.1016/S1474-4422(12)70191-6

Sternberg, R. J. (1985). *Beyond IQ: A triarchic theory of human intelligence.* Cambridge, UK: Cambridge University Press.

Sternberg, R. J. (2005). The triarchic theory of successful intelligence. In D. P. Flanagan & P. L. Harrison (Eds.), *Contemporary intellectual assessment: Theories, tests, and issues.* (pp. 103–119). New York, NY US: Guilford Press.

Sternberg, R. J. (2007). Intelligence and culture. In S. Kitayama & D. Cohen (Eds.), *Handbook of cultural psychology.* (pp. 547–568). New York: Guilford Press.

Sternberg, R. J. (2011). The theory of successful intelligence. In R. J. Sternberg & S. B. Kaufman (Eds.), *The Cambridge handbook of intelligence* (pp. 504–527). New York: Cambridge University Press.

Sternberg, R. J. (2014a). Teaching about the nature of intelligence. *Intelligence, 42*, 176–179. http://doi.org/10.1016/j.intell.2013.08.010

Sternberg, R. J. (2014b). The development of adaptive competence: Why cultural psychology is necessary and not just nice. *Developmental Review, 34*(3), 208–224. http://doi.org/10.1016/j.dr.2014.05.004

Sternberg, R. J. (2015). Still searching for the zipperump-a-zoo: A reflection after 40 years. *Child Development Perspectives, 9*(2), 106–110. http://doi.org/10.1111/cdep.12113

Sternberg, R. J., & Grigorenko, E. L. (2008). Ability testing across cultures. In L. A. Suzuki & J. G. Ponterotto (Eds.), *Handbook of multicultural assessment: Clinical, psychological, and educational applications.* (pp. 449–470). San Francisco, CA: Jossey-Bass.

Sternberg, R. J., Grigorenko, E. L., & Bundy, D. A. (2001). The predictive value of IQ. *Merrill-Palmer Quarterly, 47*, 1–41.

Sterns, H. L., & Huyck, M. H. (2001). The role of work in midlife. In M. E. Lachman (Ed.), *Handbook of midlife development.* (pp. 447–486). Hoboken, NJ: John Wiley & Sons Inc.

Stessman, J., Hammerman-Rozenberg, R., Maaravi, Y., Azoulai, D., & Cohen, A. (2005). Strategies to enhance longevity and independent function: The Jerusalem Longitudinal Study. *Mechanisms of Ageing and Development, 126*(2), 327–331.

Stevens, E. N., Lovejoy, M. C., & Pittman, L. D. (2014). Understanding the relationship between actual:ideal discrepancies and depressive symptoms: A developmental examination. *Journal of Adolescence, 37*(5), 612–21. http://doi.org/10.1016/j.adolescence.2014.04.013

Stevens, M. M., & Dunsmore, J. C. (1996). Adolescents who are living with a life-threatening illness. In C. A. Corr & D. E. Balk (Eds.), *Handbook of adolescent death and bereavement* (pp. 107–135). New York: Springer.

Stevens, M. M., Rytmeister, R. J., Protor, M. T., & Bolster, P. (2010). children living with life-threatening or life-limiting illnesses: A dispatch from the front lines. In E. Balk, D & C. A. Corr (Eds.), *Children's encounters with death, bereavement, and coping* (pp. 147–166). New York: Springer.

Stevenson, H. W., Lee, S., & Mu, X. (2000). Successful achievement in mathematics: China and the United States. In C. F. M. van Lieshout & P. G. Heymans (Eds.), *Developing talent across the life span.* (pp. 167–183). New York: Psychology Press.

Stevenson, J. C., Hodis, H. N., Pickar, J. H., & Lobo, R. A. (2009). Coronary heart disease and menopause management: The swinging pondulum of HRT. *Atherosclerosis (00219150), 207*(2), 336–340. http://doi.org/10.1016/j.atherosclerosis.2009.05.033

Steves, C. J., Spector, T. D., & Jackson, S. H. D. (2012). Ageing, genes, environment and epigenetics: What twin studies tell us now, and in the future. *Age & Ageing, 41*(5), 581–586.

Stewart, A. L. (2014). The Men's Project: A sexual assault prevention program targeting college men. *Psychology of Men & Masculinity, 15*(4), 481–485. http://doi.org/10.1037/a0033947

Stewart, R., & Wingfield, A. (2009). Hearing loss and cognitive effort in older adults' report accuracy for verbal materials. *Journal of the American Academy of Audiology, 20*(2), 147–154. http://doi.org/10.3766/jaaa.20.2.7

Stickgold, R., & Walker, M. P. (2013). Sleep-dependent memory triage: Evolving generalization through selective processing. *Nature Neuroscience, 16*(2), 139–145. http://doi.org/10.1038/nn.3303

Stidham-Hall, K., Moreau, C., & Trussell, J. (2012). Patterns and correlates of parental and formal sexual and reproductive health communication for adolescent women in the United States, 2002-2008. *The Journal of Adolescent Health : Official Publication of the Society for Adolescent Medicine, 50*(4), 410–3. http://doi.org/10.1016/j.jadohealth.2011.06.007

Stikkelbroek, Y., Bodden, D. H. M., Reitz, E., Vollebergh, W. A. M., & van Baar, A. L. (2016). Mental health of adolescents before and after the death of a parent or sibling. *European Child & Adolescent Psychiatry, 25*(1), 49–59. http://doi.org/10.1007/s00787-015-0695-3

Stiles, J., & Jernigan, T. L. (2010). The basics of brain development. *Neuropsychology Review, 20*(4), 327–348. http://doi.org/10.1007/s11065-010-9148-4

Stillman, C. M., Weinstein, A. M., Marsland, A. L., Gianaros, P. J., & Erickson, K. I. (2017). Body-brain connections: The effects of obesity and behavioral interventions on neurocognitive aging. *Frontiers in Aging Neuroscience, 9*, 115. http://doi.org/10.3389/fnagi.2017.00115

Stine-Morrow, E. A. L., Soederberg Miller, L. M., Gagne, D. D., & Hertzog, C. (2008). Self-regulated reading in adulthood. *Psychology and Aging, 23*(1), 131–53. http://doi.org/10.1037/0882-7974.23.1.131

Stipek, D. (1995). *The development of pride and shame in toddlers.* (J. P. Tangney & K. W. Fischer, Eds.). New York: Guilford Press.

Stipek, D., Feiler, R., Daniels, D., & Milburn, S. (1995). Effects of different instructional approaches on young children's achievement and motivation. *Child Development, 66*, 209–223.

Stipek, D., Gralinski, J. H., & Kopp, C. B. (1990). Self-concept development in the toddler years. *Developmental Psychology, 26*(6), 972–977. http://doi.org/10.1037/0012-1649.26.6.972

Stipek, D., Recchia, S., McClintic, S., & Lewis, M. (1992). Self-evaluation in young children. *Monographs of the Society for Research in Child Development, 57*(1), i. http://doi.org/10.2307/1166190

St-Laurent, M., Abdi, H., Burianová, H., & Grady, C. L. (2011). Influence of aging on the neural correlates of autobiographical, episodic, and semantic memory retrieval. *Journal of Cognitive Neuroscience, 23*(12), 4150–63. http://doi.org/10.1162/jocn_a_00079

Stojković, I. (2013). Pubertal timing and self-esteem in adolescents: The mediating role of body-image and social relations. *European Journal of Developmental Psychology, 10*(3), 359–377. http://doi.org/10.1080/17405629.2012.682145

Stokes, J. (2009). Resilience and bereaved children. *Bereavement Care, 28*(1), 9–17. http://doi.org/10.1080/02682620902746078

Stolarski, M., Jasielska, D., & Zajenkowski, M. (2015). Are all smart nations happier? Country aggregate IQ predicts happiness, but the relationship is moderated by individualism–collectivism. *Intelligence, 50*, 153–158. http://doi.org/10.1016/j.intell.2015.04.003

Stoll, B. J., Hansen, N. I., Bell, E. F., & Shankaran, S. (2010). Neonatal outcomes of extremely preterm infants from the NICHD neonatal research network. *Pediatrics, 126*(3), 443–456. http://doi.org/10.1542/peds.2009-2959

Stone, M. M., Blumberg, F. C., Blair, C., & Cancelli, A. A. (2016). The "EF" in deficiency: Examining the linkages between executive function and the utilization deficiency observed in preschoolers. *Journal of Experimental Child Psychology* (Vol. 152).

Stone, M. R., & Brown, B. B. (1999). Identity claims and projections: Descriptions of self and crowds in secondary school. *New Directions for Child & Adolescent Development, 1999*(84), 7–20.

Storandt, M. (2008). Cognitive deficits in the early stages of Alzheimer's disease. *Current Directions in Psychological Science, 17*(3), 198–202. http://doi.org/10.1111/j.1467-8721.2008.00574.x

Storbeck, J., & Maswood, R. (2016). Happiness increases verbal and spatial working memory capacity where sadness does not: Emotion, working memory and executive control. *Cognition and Emotion, 30*(5), 925–938. http://doi.org/10.1080/02699931.2015.1034091

Størksen, I., Røysamb, E., Moum, T., & Tambs, K. (2005). Adolescents with a childhood experience of parental divorce: A longitudinal study of mental health and adjustment. *Journal of Adolescence, 28*(6), 725–39. http://doi.org/10.1016/j.adolescence.2005.01.001

Story, T. N., Berg, C. A., Smith, T. W., Beveridge, R., Henry, N. J. M., & Pearce, G. (2007). Age, marital satisfaction, and optimism as predictors of positive sentiment override in middle-aged and older married couples. *Psychology and Aging, 22*(4), 719–727.

Strachan, S. M., Brawley, L. R., Spink, K., & Glazebrook, K. (2010). Older adults' physically-active identity: Relationships between social cognitions, physical activity and satisfaction with life. *Psychology of Sport and Exercise, 11*(2), 114–121. http://doi.org/10.1016/j.psychsport.2009.09.002

Strang, N. M., Chein, J. M., & Steinberg, L. (2013). The value of the dual systems model of adolescent risk-taking. *Frontiers in Human Neuroscience, 7,* 223. http://doi.org/10.3389/fnhum.2013.00223

Strathearn, L., Fonagy, P., Amico, J., & Montague, P. R. (2009). Adult attachment predicts maternal brain and oxytocin response to infant cues. *Neuropsychopharmacology, 34*(13), 2655–2666. https://doi.org/10.1038/npp.2009.103

Strathearn, L., Jian, L., Fonagy, P., & Montague, P. R. (2008). What's in a smile? Maternal brain responses to infant facial cues. *Pediatrics, 122*(1), 40–51. http://doi.org/10.1542/peds.2007-1566

Strauss, J. R. (2011). Contextual infuences on women's health concerns and attitudes toward menopause. *Health & Social Work, 36*(2), 121–127. http://doi.org/10.1093/hsw/36.2.121

Strenk, S. A., Strenk, L. M., & Koretz, J. F. (2005). The mechanism of presbyopia. *Progress in Retinal & Eye Research, 24*(3), 379–393. http://doi.org/10.1016/j.preteyeres.2004.11.001

Strenziok, M., Parasuraman, R., Clarke, E., Cisler, D. S., Thompson, J. C., & Greenwood, P. M. (2014). Neurocognitive enhancement in older adults: Comparison of three cognitive training tasks to test a hypothesis of training transfer in brain connectivity. *NeuroImage, 85 Pt 3,* 1027–39. http://doi.org/10.1016/j.neuroimage.2013.07.069

Streri, A., Hevia, M., Izard, V., & Coubart, A. (2013). What do we know about neonatal cognition? *Behavioral Sciences, 3*(1), 154–169. http://doi.org/10.3390/bs3010154

Striano, T., & Rochat, P. (2000). Emergence of selective social referencing in infancy. *Infancy, 1,* 253–264.

Striano, T., Vaish, A., & Benigno, J. P. (2006). The meaning of infants' looks: Information seeking and comfort seeking? *British Journal of Developmental Psychology, 24*(3), 615–630. http://doi.org/10.1348/026151005x67566

Striepens, N., Kendrick, K. M., Maier, W., & Hurlemann, R. (2011). Prosocial effects of oxytocin and clinical evidence for its therapeutic potential. *Frontiers in Neuroendocrinology, 32*(4), 426–450. http://doi.org/10.1016/j.yfrne.2011.07.001

Strober, M., Freeman, R., Lampert, C., Diamond, J., & Kaye, W. (2014). Controlled family study of anorexia nervosa and bulimia nervosa: Evidence of shared liability and transmission of partial syndromes. *American Journal of Psychiatry.* Retrieved from http://ajp.psychiatryonline.org/doi/10.1176/appi.ajp.157.3.393

Stroebe, M., & Schut, H. (2010). The dual process model of coping with bereavement: A decade on. *Omega: Journal of Death and Dying, 61*(4), 273–289. http://doi.org/10.2190/OM.61.4.b

Stroebe, M., & Schut, H. (2016). Overload: A missing link in the dual process model? *OMEGA - Journal of Death and Dying, 74*(1), 96–109. http://doi.org/10.1177/0030222816666540

Stroebe, M., Schut, H., & Boerner, K. (2010). Continuing bonds in adaptation to bereavement: Toward theoretical integration. *Clinical Psychology Review, 30*(2), 259–268. http://doi.org/10.1016/j.cpr.2009.11.007

Stroebe, M., Schut, H., & Boerner, K. (2017). Cautioning health-care professionals. *OMEGA - Journal of Death and Dying, 74*(4), 455–473. http://doi.org/10.1177/0030222817691870

Stroebe, M., Schut, H., & Stroebe, W. (2005). Attachment in coping with bereavement: A theoretical integration. *Review of General Psychology, 9*(1), 48–66. http://doi.org/10.1037/1089-2680.9.1.48

Stroth, S., Hille, K., Spitzer, M., & Reinhardt, R. (2009). Aerobic endurance exercise benefits memory and affect in young adults. *Neuropsychological Rehabilitation, 19*(2), 223–243. http://doi.org/10.1080/09602010802091183

Strough, J., Patrick, J. H., & Swenson, L. M. (2003). Strategies for solving everyday problems faced by grandparents: The role of experience. In B. Hayslip Jr. & J. H. Patrick (Eds.), *Working with custodial grandparents.* (pp. 257–275). New York, NY US: Springer Publishing Co.

Stuart-Cassel, V., Bell, A., & Springer, J. F. (2011). *Analysis of state bullying laws and policies.* Retrieved from http://www2.ed.gov/rschstat/eval/bullying/state-bullying-laws/state-bullying-laws.pdf

Studenski, S. (2011). Gait speed and survival in older adults. *JAMA, 305*(1), 50. http://doi.org/10.1001/jama.2010.1923

Stuifbergen, M. C., Dykstra, P. A., Lanting, K. N., & van Delden, J. J. M. (2010). Autonomy in an ascribed relationship: The case of adult children and elderly parents. *Journal of Aging Studies, 24*(4), 257–265. http://doi.org/10.1016/j.jaging.2010.05.006

Stuifbergen, M. C., Van Delden, J. J. M., & Dykstra, P. A. (2008). The implications of today's family structures for support giving to older parents. *Ageing & Society, 28*(3), 413–434. http://doi.org/10.1017/S0144686X07006666

Sturaro, C., van Lier, P. A. C., Cuijpers, P., & Koot, H. M. (2011). The role of peer relationships in the development of early school-age externalizing problems. *Child Development, 82*(3), 758–765. http://doi.org/10.1111/j.1467-8624.2010.01532.x

Subotnik, R. F., Olszewski-Kubilius, P., & Worrell, F. C. (2011). Rethinking giftedness and gifted education: A proposed direction forward based on psychological science. *Psychological Science in the Public Interest : A Journal of the American Psychological Society, 12*(1), 3–54. http://doi.org/10.1177/1529100611418056

Subrahmanyam, K., & Greenfield, P. M. (1996). Effect of video game practice on spatial skills in girls and boys. In P. M. Greenfield & R. R. Cocking (Eds.), *Interacting with video* (pp. 95–114). Norwood, NJ: Ablex.

Subramanian, S. V, Elwert, F., & Christakis, N. (2008). Widowhood and mortality among the elderly: The modifying role of neighborhood concentration of widowed individuals. *Social Science & Medicine, 66*(4), 873–884. Retrieved from svsubram@hsph.harvard.edu

Substance Abuse and Mental Health Services Administration. (2014). *Results from the 2013 National Survey on Drug Use and Health: Summary of National Findings.* Rockville, MD: Retrieved from http://www.samhsa.gov/data/sites/default/files/NSDUHresultsPDFWHTML2013/Web/NSDUHresults2013.pdf

Suddendorf, T., & Butler, D. L. (2013). The nature of visual self-recognition. *Trends in Cognitive Sciences, 17*(3), 121–127. http://doi.org/10.1016/j.tics.2013.01.004

Sudfeld, C. R., Charles McCoy, D., Danaei, G., Fink, G., Ezzati, M., Andrews, K. G., & Fawzi, W. W. (2015). Linear growth and child development in low- and middle-income countries: A meta-analysis. *Pediatrics, 135*(5). Retrieved from http://pediatrics.aappublications.org/content/135/5/e1266.short

Sugarman, J., Roter, D., Cain, C., Wallace, R., Schmechel, D., & Welsh-Bohmer, K. A. (2007). Proxies and consent discussions for dementia research. *Journal of the American Geriatrics Society, 55*(4), 556–561. http://doi.org/10.1111/j.1532-5415.2007.01101.x

Sugita, Y. (2004). Experience in early infancy is indispensable for color perception. *American Journal of Ophthalmology, 138*(5), 902.

Sullivan, J. L. (2003). Prevention of mother-to-child transmission of HIV: What next? *Journal of Acquired Immune Deficiency Syndromes, 34*(Suppl. 1), S67–S72.

Sullivan, M. W., & Lewis, M. (2003). Contextual determinants of anger and other negative expressions in young infants. *Developmental Psychology, 39*(4), 693–705. http://doi.org/10.1037/0012-1649.39.4.693

Sullivan, M. W., & Lewis, M. (2012). Relations of early goal blockage response and gender to subsequent tantrum behavior. *Infancy : The Official Journal of the International Society on Infant Studies, 17*(2), 159–178. http://doi.org/10.1111/j.1532-7078.2011.00077.x

Sullivan, M. W., Carmody, D. P., & Lewis, M. (2010). How neglect and punitiveness influence emotion knowledge. *Child Psychiatry and Human Development, 41*(3), 285–298. http://doi.org/10.1007/s10578-009-0168-3

Sun, J.-H., Tan, L., Wang, H.-F., Tan, M.-S., Tan, L., Li, J.-Q., . . . Yu, J.-T. (2015). Genetics of vascular dementia: Systematic review and meta-analysis. *Journal of Alzheimer's Disease, 46*(3), 611–629. http://doi.org/10.3233/JAD-143102

Sun, Y., Mensah, F. K., Azzopardi, P., Patton, G. C., & Wake, M. (2017). Childhood Social disadvantage and pubertal timing: A national birth cohort from Australia. *Pediatrics.* Retrieved from http://pediatrics.aappublications.org/content/early/2017/05/19/peds.2016-4099

Sundberg, U. (1998). *Mother tongue-phonetic aspects of infant-directed speech. Doctoral Dissertation.* PERILUS, Stockholm.

Sundet, J. M., Barlaug, D. G., & Torjussen, T. M. (2004). The end of the Flynn effect? A study of secular trends in mean intelligence test scores of Norwegian conscripts during half a century. *Intelligence, 32,* 349–362.

Super, C. M., & Harkness, S. (1982). The infant's niche in rural Kenya and metropolitan America. In L. L. Adler (Ed.), *Cross-cultural research at issue* (pp. 247–255). New York: Academic Press.

Super, C. M., & Harkness, S. (2010). Culture and infancy. In J. Gavin Bremner & Theodore D. Wachs (Eds.), *The Wiley-Blackwell handbook of infant development* (pp. 623–649). Oxford, UK: Wiley-Blackwell. http://doi.org/10.1002/9781444327564.ch21

Super, C. M., & Harkness, S. (2015). Chartingn infant development. In L. A. Jensen (Ed.), *The Oxford handbook of human development and culture.* Oxford University Press. http://doi.org/10.1093/oxfordhb/9780199948550.013.6

Super, D. E. (1990). A life-span, life-space approach to career development. In D. Brown & L. Brooks (Eds.), *Career choice and development: Applying contemporary theories to practice (2nd ed.).* (pp. 197–261). San Francisco, CA, US: Jossey-Bass.

Super, D. E., & Hall, D. T. (1978). Career development: Exploration and planning. *Annual Review of Psychology, 29,* 333–72. http://doi.org/10.1146/annurev.ps.29.020178.002001

Sussman, M., Trocio, J., Best, C., Mirkin, S., Bushmakin, A. G., Yood, R., . . . Gallia, C. (2015). Prevalence of menopausal symptoms among mid-life women: Findings from electronic medical records. *BMC Women's Health, 15*(1), 58. http://doi.org/10.1186/s12905-015-0217-y

Sussman, S., Pokhrel, P., Ashmore, R. D., & Brown, B. B. (2007). Adolescent peer group identification and characteristics: A review of the literature. *Addictive Behaviors, 32,* 1602–1627.

Sutcliffe, A. G., Barnes, J., Belsky, J., Gardiner, J., & Melhuish, E. (2012). The health and development of children born to older mothers in the United Kingdom: Observational study using longitudinal cohort data. *BMJ (Clinical Research Ed.), 345*(aug21_1), e5116. http://doi.org/10.1136/bmj.e5116

Suzumori, N., & Sugiura-Ogasawara, M. (2010). Genetic factors as a cause of miscarriage. *Current Medicinal Chemistry, 17*(29), 3431–7. Retrieved from http://www.ncbi.nlm.nih.gov/pubmed/20712563

Svetlova, M., Nichols, S. R., & Brownell, C. A. (2010). Toddlers prosocial behavior: From instrumental to empathic to altruistic helping. *Child Development, 81*(6), 1814–1827. http://doi.org/10.1111/j.1467-8624.2010.01512.x

Swain, J. E., Kim, P., Spicer, J., Ho, S. S., Dayton, C. J., Elmadih, A., & Abel, K. M. (2014). Approaching the biology of human parental attachment: Brain imaging, oxytocin and coordinated assessments of mothers and fathers. *Brain Research, 1580,* 78–101. https://doi.org/10.1016/j.brainres.2014.03.007

Swain, J. E., Tasgin, E., Mayes, L. C., Feldman, R., Constable, R. T., & Leckman, J. F. (2008). Maternal brain response to own baby-cry is affected by cesarean section delivery. *Journal of Child Psychology and Psychiatry and Allied Disciplines, 49*(10), 1042–1052. https://doi.org/10.1111/j.1469-7610.2008.01963.x

Swearer, S. M., & Hymel, S. (2015). Understanding the psychology of bullying: Moving toward a social-ecological diathesis-stress model. *The American Psychologist, 70*(4), 344–53. http://doi.org/10.1037/a0038929

Sweeting, H. N., & Gilhooly, M. L. M. (1990). Anticipatory grief: A review. *Social Science & Medicine, 30*(10), 1073–1080. http://doi.org/10.1016/0277-9536(90)90293-2

Swenson, N. C. (2000). Comparing traditional and collaborative settings for language intervention. *Communication Disorders Quarterly, 22,* 12–18.

Swift, A. (2016). Euthanasia still acceptable to solid majority in U.S. Retrieved from http://www.gallup.com/poll/193082/euthanasia-acceptable-solid-majority.aspx

Swift, W., Coffey, C., Carlin, J. B., Degenhardt, L., & Patton, G. C. (2008). Adolescent cannabis users at 24 years: Trajectories to regular weekly use and dependence in young adulthood. *Addiction, 103*(8), 1361–1370. http://doi.org/10.1111/j.1360-0443.2008.02246.x

Swinton, A. D., Kurtz-Costes, B., Rowley, S. J., & Okeke-Adeyanju, N. (2011). A longitudinal examination of African American adolescents' attributions about achievement outcomes. *Child Development, 82*(5), 1486–500. http://doi.org/10.1111/j.1467-8624.2011.01623.x

Syed, M., Walker, L. H. M., Lee, R. M., Umaña-Taylor, A. J., Zamboanga, B. L., Schwartz, S. J., . . . Huynh, Q.-L. (2013). A two-factor model of ethnic identity exploration: Implications for identity coherence and well-being. *Cultural Diversity and Ethnic Minority Psychology, 19*(2), 143–154. http://doi.org/10.1037/a0030564

Sylvain-Roy, S., Lungu, O., & Belleville, S. (2014). Normal aging of the attentional control functions that underlie working memory. *The Journals of Gerontology. Series B, Psychological Sciences and Social Sciences,* gbt166-. http://doi.org/10.1093/geronb/gbt166

Syme, M. L., Klonoff, E. A., Macera, C. A., & Brodine, S. K. (2013). Predicting sexual decline and dissatisfaction among older adults: The role of partnered and individual physical and mental health factors. *The Journals of Gerontology. Series B, Psychological Sciences and Social Sciences, 68*(3), 323–32. http://doi.org/10.1093/geronb/gbs087

Symonds, W. C., Schwartz, R., & Ferguson., R. F. (2011a). *Pathways to prosperity: Meeting the challenge of preparing young Americans.* Cambridge, MA. Retrieved from http://www.sawdc.com/media/5959/pathways_to_prosperity_feb2011.pdf

Symonds, W. C., Schwartz, R., & Ferguson., R. F. (2011b). *Pathways to prosperity: Meeting the challenge of preparing young Americans.* Cambridge, MA.

Symons, D. (2004). Mental state discourse and theory of mind: Internalisation of self–other understanding within a social–cognitive framework. *Developmental Review, 24,* 159–188.

Szaflarski, J. P., Binder, J. R., Possing, E. T., McKiernan, K. A., Ward, B. D., & Hammeke, T. A. (2002). Language lateralization in left-handed and ambidextrous people: fMRI data. *Neurology, 59*(2), 238–244.

Szyf, M. (2015). Nongenetic inheritance and transgenerational epigenetics. *Trends in Molecular Medicine, 21*(2), 134–44. http://doi.org/10.1016/j.molmed.2014.12.004

Taber-Thomas, B., & Perez-Edgar, K. (2015). Emerging adulthood brain development. In J. J. Arnett (Ed.), *The Oxford handbook of emerging adulthood* (pp. 126–141). New York: Oxford University Press.

Tabor, A., & Alfirevic, Z. (2010). Update on procedure-related risks for prenatal diagnosis techniques. *Fetal Diagnosis & Therapy, 27*(1), 1–7. http://doi.org/10.1159/000271995

Tabrett, D. R., & Latham, K. (2010). Depression and vision loss. *Optician, 240*(6274), 22–29.

Tabrizi, S. H., Segovia-Siapco, G., Burkholder, N. M., & Sabaté, J. (2014). Comparison of food intake patterns of adolescents with USDA My Plate Dietary Guidelines (1024.15). The FASEB Journal, 28(1 Supplement), 1024-15.

Tackett, J. L. (2006). Evaluating models of the personality–psychopathology relationship in children and adolescents. *Clinical Psychology Review, 26*(5), 584–599. http://doi.org/10.1016/j.cpr.2006.04.003

Tackett, J. L., Kushner, S. C., Herzhoff, K., Smack, A. J., Reardon, K. W., Achenbach, T. M., . . . Wen, L. (2014). Viewing relational aggression through multiple lenses: Temperament, personality, and personality pathology. *Development and Psychopathology, 26*(3), 863–877. http://doi.org/10.1017/S0954579414000443

Tager-Flusberg, H. (2001). A re-examination of the theory of mind hypothesis of autism. In J. Burack, T. Charman, N. Yirmiya, & P. Zelazo (Eds.), *The development of autism: Perspectives from theory and research* (pp. 173–193). Mahwah, NJ: Lawrence Erlbaum.

Takagi, M., Youssef, G., & Lorenzetti, V. (2016). Neuroimaging of the human brain in adolescent substance users. In D. De Micheli, A. L. Monezi Andrade, E. A. da Silva, & M. L. O. de Souza Formigoni (Eds.), *Drug abuse in adolescence* (pp. 69–99). Geneva, CH: Springer. http://doi.org/10.1007/978-3-319-17795-3_6

Takahashi, K. (1990). Are the key assumptions of the "Strange Situation" procedure universal? A view from Japanese research. *Human Development, 33,* 23–30.

Takahashi, R. H., Nagao, T., & Gouras, G. K. (2017). Plaque formation and the intraneuronal accumulation of ?-amyloid in Alzheimer's disease. *Pathology International, 67*(4), 185–193. http://doi.org/10.1111/pin.12520

Tamis-LeMonda, C. S., Bornstein, M. H., & Baumwell, L. (2001). Maternal responsiveness and children's achievement of language milestones. *Child Development, 72*(3), 748–767. Retrieved from http://www.ncbi.nlm.nih.gov/pubmed/11405580

Tamis-LeMonda, C. S., Briggs, R. D., McClowry, S. G., & Snow, D. L. (2009). Maternal control and sensitivity, child gender, and maternal education in relation to children's behavioral outcomes in African American families. *Journal of Applied Developmental Psychology, 30*(3), 321–331. http://doi.org/10.1016/j.appdev.2008.12.018

Tamis-LeMonda, C. S., Kahana-Kalman, R., & Yoshikawa, H. (2009). Father involvement in immigrant and ethnically diverse families from the prenatal period to the second year: Prediction and mediating mechanisms. *Sex Roles, 60*(7), 496–509. http://doi.org/10.1007/s11199-009-9593-9

Tamis-LeMonda, C. S., Kuchirko, Y., & Song, L. (2014). Why is infant language learning facilitated by parental responsiveness? *Current Directions in Psychological Science, 23*(2), 121–126. http://doi.org/10.1177/0963721414522813

Tamis-LeMonda, C. S., Shannon, J. D., Cabrera, N. J., & Lamb, M. E. (2004). Fathers and mothers at play with their 2- and 3-year-olds: Contributions to language and cognitive development. *Child Development, 75*(6), 1806–20. http://doi.org/10.1111/j.1467-8624.2004.00818.x

Tamnes, C. K., Walhovd, K. B., Grydeland, H., Holland, D., Østby, Y., Dale, A. M., & Fjell, A. M. (2013). Longitudinal working memory development is related to structural maturation of frontal and parietal cortices. *Journal of Cognitive Neuroscience, 25*(10), 1611–1623. http://doi.org/10.1162/jocn_a_00434

Tan, A., Ma, W., Vira, A., Marwha, D., & Eliot, L. (2016). The human hippocampus is not sexually-dimorphic: Meta-analysis of structural MRI volumes. *NeuroImage, 124,* 350–366. https://doi.org/10.1016/j.neuroimage.2015.08.050

Tan, J. S. L., Wang, J. J., Younan, C., Cumming, R. G., Rochtchina, E., & Mitchell, P. (2008). Smoking and the long-term incidence of cataract: The Blue Mountains Eye Study. *Ophthalmic Epidemiology, 15*(3), 155–161. http://doi.org/10.1080/09286580701840362

Tan, R. S. (2011). *Aging men's health: A case-based approach.* New York: Thieme.

Tan, Z. S., Spartano, N. L., Beiser, A. S., DeCarli, C., Auerbach, S. H., Vasan, R. S., & Seshadri, S. (2016). Physical activity, brain volume, and dementia risk: The Framingham Study. *The Journals of Gerontology Series A: Biological Sciences and Medical Sciences, 31*(6). http://doi.org/10.1093/gerona/glw130

Tang, S., & Chow, A. Y. M. (2017). How do risk factors affect bereavement outcomes in later life? An exploration of the mediating role of dual process coping. *Psychiatry Research, 255*, 297–303. http://doi.org/10.1016/j.psychres.2017.06.001

Tang, S., Davis-Kean, P. E., Chen, M., & Sexton, H. R. (2014). Adolescent pregnancy's intergenerational effects: Does an adolescent mother's education have consequences for her children's achievement? *Journal of Research on Adolescence.* http://doi.org/10.1111/jora.12182

Tang., F. (2008). Socioeconomic disparities in voluntary organization involvement among older adults. *Nonprofit & Voluntary Sector Quarterly, 37*(1), 57–75.

Tanner, J. L. (2014). Emerging adulthood. In R. J. R. Levesque (Ed.), *Encyclopedia of adolescence* (pp. 818–825). New York, NY: Springer New York. http://doi.org/10.1007/978-1-4419-1695-2

Tanner, J. M. (1990). *Foetus into man: Physical growth from conception to maturity.* Cambridge, MA: Cambridge University Press.

Tannock, M. (2011). Observing young children's rough-and-tumble play. *Australasian Journal of Early Childhood, 36*(2), 13–20.

Tapia-Rojas, C., Aranguiz, F., Varela-Nallar, L., & Inestrosa, N. C. (2016). Voluntary running attenuates memory loss, decreases neuropathological changes and induces neurogenesis in a mouse model of Alzheimer's disease. *Brain Pathology, 26*(1), 62–74. http://doi.org/10.1111/bpa.12255

Tardif, T., Fletcher, P., Liang, W., Zhang, Z., Kaciroti, N., & Marchman, V. A. (2008). Baby's first 10 words. *Developmental Psychology, 44*(4), 929–938. http://doi.org/10.1037/0012-1649.44.4.929

Tardif, T., Shatz, M., & Naigles, L. (1997). Caregiver speech and children's use of nouns versus verbs: A comparison of English, Italian, and Mandarin. *Journal of Child Language, 24*, 535–565.

Tardon, A., Lee, W. J., Delgado-Rodriguez, M., Dosemeci, M., Albanes, D., Hoover, R., & Blair, A. (2005). Leisure-time physical activity and lung cancer: A meta-analysis. *Cancer Causes & Control: CCC, 16*(4), 389–397.

Tashkin, D. P. (2013). Effects of marijuana smoking on the lung. *Annals of the American Thoracic Society, 10*(3), 239–247. Retrieved from http://www.atsjournals.org/doi/abs/10.1513/annalsats.201212-127fr#.ValGhflojxE

Task Force on Sudden Infant Death Syndrome. (2016). SIDS and other sleep-related infant deaths: Updated 2016 recommendations for a safe infant sleeping environment. *Pediatrics, 138*(5), e20162938–e20162938. http://doi.org/10.1542/peds.2016-2938

Tasker, F., & Patterson, C. J. (2007). Research on gay and lesbian parenting: Retrospect and prospect. *Journal of GLBT Family Studies, 3*(2/3), 9–34.

Tatangelo, G., McCabe, M., Mellor, D., & Mealey, A. (2016). A systematic review of body dissatisfaction and sociocultural messages related to the body among preschool children. *Body Image, 18*, 86–95. http://doi.org/10.1016/j.bodyim.2016.06.003

Tatone, C. (2008). Oocyte senescence: A firm link to age-related female subfertility. *Gynecological Endocrinology, 24*(2), 59–63. http://doi.org/10.1080/09513590701733504

Taumoepeau, M. (2015). From talk to thought. *Journal of Cross-Cultural Psychology, 46*(9), 1169–1190. http://doi.org/10.1177/0022022115604393

Tawfik, H., Kline, J., Jacobson, J., Tehranifar, P., Protacio, A., Flom, J. D., . . . Terry, M. B. (2015). Life course exposure to smoke and early menopause and menopausal transition.

Menopause, 22(10), 1076–1083. http://doi.org/10.1097/GME.0000000000000444

Taylor, A., & Gosney, M. A. (2011). Sexuality in older age: Essential considerations for healthcare professionals. *Age and Ageing, 40*(5), 538–43. http://doi.org/10.1093/ageing/afr049

Taylor, H. G., Klein, N., Minich, N. M., & Hack, M. (2001). Long-term family outcomes for children with very low birth weights. *Archives of Pediatrics & Adolescent Medicine, 155.*

Taylor, J. H., & Walker, L. J. (1997). Moral climate and the development of moral reasoning: The effects of dyadic discussions between. *Journal of Moral Education, 26*(1), 21–45.

Taylor, J. L. (2009). Midlife impacts of adolescent parenthood. *Journal of Family Issues, 30*(4), 484–510.

Taylor, K. (2017, April 24). New York City will offer free preschool for all 3-year-olds. *New York Times.* Retrieved from https://www.nytimes.com/2017/04/24/nyregion/de-blasio-pre-k-expansion.html?_r=0

Taylor, L. E., Swerdfeger, A. L., & Eslick, G. D. (2014). Vaccines are not associated with autism: An evidence-based meta-analysis of case-control and cohort studies. *Vaccine, 32*(29), 3623–3629. http://doi.org/10.1016/j.vaccine.2014.04.085

Taylor, N., Donovan, W., & Leavitt, L. (2008). Consistency in infant sleeping arrangements and mother-infant interaction. *Infant Mental Health Journal, 29*(2), 77–94. http://doi.org/10.1002/imhj.20170

Taylor, Z. E., & Conger, R. D. (2017). Promoting strengths and resilience in single-mother families. *Child Development, 88*(2), 350–358. http://doi.org/10.1111/cdev.12741

Taylor, Z. E., Eisenberg, N., Spinrad, T. L., Eggum, N. D., & Sulik, M. J. (2013). The relations of ego-resiliency and emotion socialization to the development of empathy and prosocial behavior across early childhood. *Emotion, 13*(5). http://doi.org/10.1037/a0032894

Tchaconas, A., & Adesman, A. (2013). Autism spectrum disorders. *Current Opinion in Pediatrics, 25*(1), 130–144. http://doi.org/10.1097/MOP.0b013e32835c2b70

Tchernof, A., & Després, J.-P. (2013). Pathophysiology of human visceral obesity: An update. *Physiological Reviews, 93*(1), 359–404. http://doi.org/10.1152/physrev.00033.2011

te Nijenhuis, J. (2013). The Flynn effect, group differences, and g loadings. *Personality and Individual Differences, 55*(3), 224–228. http://doi.org/10.1016/j.paid.2011.12.023

te Velde, E., Habbema, D., Leridon, H., & Eijkemans, M. (2012). The effect of postponement of first motherhood on permanent involuntary childlessness and total fertility rate in six European countries since the 1970s. *Human Reproduction (Oxford, England), 27*(4), 1179–83. http://doi.org/10.1093/humrep/der455

Teachman, J. (2008). Complex life course patterns and the risk of divorce in second marriages. *Journal of Marriage & Family, 70*(2), 294–305. http://doi.org/10.1111/j.1741-3737.2008.00482.x

Tearne, J. E. (2015). Older maternal age and child behavioral and cognitive outcomes: A review of the literature. *Fertility and Sterility, 103*(6), 1381–1391. http://doi.org/10.1016/j.fertnstert.2015.04.027

Teasdale, T. W., & Owen, D. R. (2000). Forty-year secular trends in cognitive abilities. *Intelligence, 28*, 115–120.

Teitelbaum, J., & Shemie, S. (2016). Brain death. In *Oxford textbook of neurocritical care* (pp. 390–398).

Oxford University Press. http://doi.org/10.1093/med/9780198739555.003.0029

Teller, D. Y. (1997). First glances: The vision of infants. *Investigative Ophthalmology & Visual Science, 38*, 2183–2203.

Teller, D. Y. (1998). Spatial and temporal aspects of infant color vision. *Vision Research, 38*, 3275–3282.

Telzer, E. H., Fuligni, A. J., Lieberman, M. D., & Galván, A. (2013). The effects of poor quality sleep on brain function and risk taking in adolescence. *NeuroImage, 71*, 275–83. http://doi.org/10.1016/j.neuroimage.2013.01.025

Telzer, E. H., Tsai, K. M., Gonzales, N., & Fuligni, A. J. (2015). Mexican American adolescents' family obligation values and behaviors: Links to internalizing symptoms across time and context. *Developmental Psychology, 51*(1), 75–86. http://doi.org/10.1037/a0038434

ten Brinke, L. F., Bolandzadeh, N., Nagamatsu, L. S., Hsu, C. L., Davis, J. C., Miran-Khan, K., & Liu-Ambrose, T. (2015). Aerobic exercise increases hippocampal volume in older women with probable mild cognitive impairment: A 6-month randomised controlled trial. *British Journal of Sports Medicine, 49*(4), 248–254. http://doi.org/10.1136/bjsports-2013-093184

Teno, J. M., Weitzen, S., Fennell, M. L., & Mor, V. (2001). Dying trajectory in the last year of life: Does cancer trajectory fit other diseases? *Journal of Palliative Medicine, 4*(4), 457–464. http://doi.org/10.1089/109662101753381593

Terenzini, P. T., Pascarella, E. T., & Blimling, G. S. (1999). Students' out-of-class experiences and their influence on learning and cognitive development: A literature review. *Journal of College Student Development, 40*(5), 610–623.

Terman, L. M. (1917). *The Stanford revision and extension of the Binet-Simon scale for measuring intelligence.* Warwick & York, Incorporated.

Terry, K. j., & Talon, J. (2004). *Child sexual abuse: A review of the literature.* New York: John Jay College. Retrieved from www.usccb.org/nrb/johnjaystudy/litreview.pdf

Terwogt, M. M., & Stegge, H. (1995). Children's understanding of the strategic control of negative emotions. In James A. Russell, José-Miguel Fernández-Dols, Antony S. R. Manstead, & J. C. Wellenkamp (Eds.), *Everyday conceptions of emotion* (pp. 373–390). Dordrecht: Springer Netherlands. http://doi.org/10.1007/978-94-015-8484-5_21

Testa, M., Quigley, B. M., & Das Eiden, R. (2003). The effects of prenatal alcohol exposure on infant mental development: A meta-analytical review. *Alcohol & Alcoholism, 38*(4), 295–304

The World Bank. (2016). Labor force, female (% of total labor force). Retrieved from http://data.worldbank.org/indicator/SL.TLF.TOTL.FE.ZS

Thelen, E. (1995). Motor development: A new synthesis. *American Psychologist, 50*(2), 79–95. http://doi.org/10.1037/0003-066X.50.2.79

Thelen, E. (2000). Motor development as foundation and future of developmental psychology. *International Journal of Behavioral Development, 24*(4), 385–397.

Thelen, E., Fisher, D. M., & Ridley-Johnson, R. (2002). The relationship between physical growth and a newborn reflex. *Infant Behavior & Development, 25*(1), 72–85.

Theodora, M., Antsaklis, A., Antsaklis, P., Blanas, K., Daskalakis, G., Sindos, M., . . . Papantoniou, N. (2016). Fetal loss following second trimester amniocentesis. Who is at greater risk? How to counsel pregnant women? *The Journal of Maternal-Fetal & Neonatal Medicine, 29*(4), 590–595. http://doi.org/10.3109/14767058.2015.1012061

Theunissen, J. M. J., Hoogerbrugge, P. M., van Achterberg, T., Prins, J. B., Vernooij-Dassen, M. J. F. J., & van den Ende, C. H. M. (2007). Symptoms in the palliative phase of children with cancer. *Pediatric Blood & Cancer*, 49(2), 160–165. http://doi.org/10.1002/pbc.21042

Thiele, D. M., & Whelan, T. A. (2008). The relationship between grandparent satisfaction, meaning, and generativity. *International Journal of Aging & Human Development*, 66(1), 21–48.

Thiessen, E. D., Hill, E. A., & Saffran, J. R. (2005). Infant-directed speech facilitates word segmentation. *Infancy*, 7(1), 53–71.

Thomaes, S., Reijntjes, A., Orobio de Castro, B., Bushman, B. J., Poorthuis, A., & Telch, M. J. (2010). I Like Me If You Like Me: On the Interpersonal Modulation and Regulation of Preadolescents' State Self-Esteem. *Child Development*, 81(3), 811–825. http://doi.org/10.1111/j.1467-8624.2010.01435.x

Thoman, E. B., & Ingersoll, E. W. (1993). Learning in premature infants. *Developmental Psychology*, 28, 692–700.

Thomas, A., & Chess, S. (1977). *Temperament and development*. New York: Brunner/Mazel.

Thomas, A., Chess, S., & Birch, H. G. (1970). The origin of personality. *Scientific American*, 223, 102–109.

Thomas, H. N., Hess, R., & Thurston, R. C. (2015). Correlates of Sexual Activity and Satisfaction in Midlife and Older Women. *Annals of Family Medicine*, 13(4), 336–42. http://doi.org/10.1370/afm.1820

Thomas, J. D., Warren, K. R., & Hewitt, B. G. (2010). Fetal alcohol spectrum disorders. *Alcohol Research & Health*, 33(1/2), 118–126.

Thomas, J. J., Eddy, K. T., Ruscio, J., Ng, K. L., Casale, K. E., Becker, A. E., & Lee, S. (2015). Do recognizable lifetime eating disorder phenotypes naturally occur in a culturally Asian population? A combined latent profile and taxometric approach. *European Eating Disorders Review*, 23(3), 199–209. http://doi.org/10.1002/erv.2357

Thomas, L. A., De Bellis, M. D., Graham, R., & LaBar, K. S. (2007). Development of emotional facial recognition in late childhood and adolescence. *Developmental Science*, 10(5), 547–558. http://doi.org/10.1111/j.1467-7687.2007.00614.x

Thomas, P. A. (2010). Is it better to give or to receive? Social support and the well-being of older adults. *The Journals of Gerontology: Series B: Psychological Sciences and Social Sciences*, 65B(3), 351–357. http://doi.org/10.1093/geronb/gbp113

Thomas, R. M. (2004). *Comparing theories of child development* (6th ed.). Belmont, CA: Wadsworth.

Thomas, S., & Kunzmann, U. (2014). Age differences in wisdom-related knowledge: Does the age relevance of the task matter? *The Journals of Gerontology. Series B, Psychological Sciences and Social Sciences*, 69(6), 897–905. http://doi.org/10.1093/geronb/gbt076

Thomas, V. G. (2000). Ending social promotion: Help or hindrance? *Kappa Delta Pi Record*, 37(1), 30–32.

Thompson, A. E., & Voyer, D. (2014). Sex differences in the ability to recognise non-verbal displays of emotion: A meta-analysis. *Cognition and Emotion*, 28(7), 1164–1195. http://doi.org/10.1080/02699931.2013.875889

Thompson, R. A. (1990). Vulnerability in research: A developmental perspective on research risk. *Child Development*, 61, 1–16.

Thompson, R. A. (1994). Emotion regulation: A theme in search of definition. In N. Fox (Ed.), The development of emotion regulation and dysregulation: Biological and behavioral considerations. *Monographs of the Society for Research in Child Development*, 59(2–3, Serial No. 240), 25–52.

Thompson, R. A. (1998). Early sociopersonality development. In W. Damon, D. Kuhn, & R. S. Siegler (Eds.), *Handbook of child psychology: Social, emotional, and personality development*. New York: Wiley.

Thompson, R. A. (2000). The legacy of early attachments. *Child Development*, 71(1), 145–152.

Thompson, R. A. (2004). Development in the first years of life. In E. F. Zigler, D. G. Singer, & S. J. Bishop-Josef (Eds.), *Children's play: The roots of reading*. (pp. 15–31). Washington, DC: ZERO TO THREE/National Center for Infants, Toddlers and Families.

Thompson, R. A. (2011). Emotion and emotion regulation: Two sides of the developing coin. *Emotion Review*, 3(1), 53–61. http://doi.org/10.1177/1754073910380969

Thompson, R. A., & Goodvin, R. (2007). Taming the tempest in the teapot: Emotion regulation in toddlers. In C. A. Brownell & C. B. Kopp (Eds.), *Transitions in early socioemotional development: The toddler years* (pp. 320–341). New York: Guilford.

Thompson, R. A., & Limber, S. (1991). "Social anxiety" in infancy: Stranger wariness and separation distress. In H. Leitenberg (Ed.), *Handbook of social and evaluation anxiety* (pp. 85–137). New York: Plenum.

Thompson, R. A., & Limber, S. P. (1990). "Social anxiety" in infancy: Stranger and separation reactions. In H. Leitenberg (Ed.), *Handbook of social and evaluation anxiety*. (pp. 85–137). New York, NY: Plenum.

Thompson, R. A., & Newton, E. K. (2013). Baby altruists? Examining the complexity of prosocial motivation in young children. *Infancy*, 18(1), 120–133. http://doi.org/10.1111/j.1532-7078.2012.00139.x

Thompson, R. A., Winer, A. C., & Goodvin, R. (2013). The individual child: Temperament, emotion, self, and personality. In M. H. Bornstein & M. E. Lamb (Eds.), *Developmental science: An advanced textbook (5th ed.)*.

Thompson, R. F. (1993). *The brain: A neuroscience primer* (3rd ed.). New York: Worth.

Thompson, W. K., Charo, L., Vahia, I. V, Depp, C., Allison, M., & Jeste, D. V. (2011). Association between higher levels of sexual function, activity, and satisfaction and self-rated successful aging in older postmenopausal women. *Journal of the American Geriatrics Society*, 59(8), 1503–1508. http://doi.org/10.1111/j.1532-5415.2011.03495.x

Thornton, W. J. L., & Dumke, H. A. (2005). Age differences in everyday problem-solving and decision-making effectiveness: A meta-analytic review. *Psychology and Aging*, 20(1), 85–99.

Thorson, J. A., & Powell, F. C. (2000). Death anxiety in younger and older adults. In A. Tomer (Ed.), *Death attitudes and the older adult: Theories, concepts, and applications*. (pp. 123–136). New York, NY: Brunner-Routledge.

Thurstone, & L., L. (1938). *Primary mental abilities*. *Psychometric Monographs*, 1, ix-121.

Tick, B., Bolton, P., Happé, F., Rutter, M., & Rijsdijk, F. (2016). Heritability of autism spectrum disorders: A meta-analysis of twin studies. *Journal of Child Psychology and Psychiatry, and Allied Disciplines*, 57(5), 585–95. http://doi.org/10.1111/jcpp.12499

Tiemeier, H., Lenroot, R. K., Greenstein, D. K., Tran, L., Pierson, R., & Giedd, J. N. (2010). Cerebellum development during childhood and adolescence: A longitudinal morphometric MRI study. *Neuroimage*, 49(1), 63–70. http://doi.org/10.1016/j.neuroimage.2009.08.016

Tiggeman, M., & Wilson-Barrett, E. (1998). Children's figure ratings: Relationship to self-esteem and negative stereotyping. *International Journal of Eating Disorders*, 23, 83–88.

Timiras, P. S. (2003). *Physiological basis of aging and geriatics* (3rd ed.). Boca Raton, FL: CRC Press.

Timonen, V., & Doyle, M. (2013). Life-long singlehood:Intersections of the past and the present. *Ageing and Society*, 34(10), 1749–1770. http://doi.org/10.1017/S0144686X13000500

Tinggaard, J., Mieritz, M. G., Sørensen, K., Mouritsen, A., Hagen, C. P., Aksglaede, L., . . . Juul, A. (2012). The physiology and timing of male puberty. *Current Opinion in Endocrinology, Diabetes, and Obesity*, 19(3), 197–203. http://doi.org/10.1097/MED.0b013e3283535614

Tinker, S. C., Cogswell, M. E., Devine, O., & Berry, R. J. (2010). Folic acid intake among U.S. women aged 15–44 years, National Health and Nutrition Examination Survey, 2003–2006. *American Journal of Preventive Medicine*, 38(5), 534–542. http://doi.org/10.1016/j.amepre.2010.01.025

Tisak, M. S., Holub, S. C., & Tisak, J. (2007). What nice things do boys and girls do? Preschoolers' perspectives of peers' behaviors at school and at home. *Early Education and Development*, 18(2), 183–199.

Tither, J. M., & Ellis, B. J. (2008). Impact of fathers on daughters' age at menarche: A genetically and environmentally controlled sibling study. *Developmental Psychology*, 44(5), 1409–1420. http://doi.org/10.1037/a0013065

Titz, C., & Karbach, J. (2014). Working memory and executive functions: Effects of training on academic achievement. *Psychological Research*, 78(6), 852–868. http://doi.org/10.1007/s00426-013-0537-1

Titzmann, P. F., Brenick, A., & Silbereisen, R. K. (2015). Friendships fighting prejudice: A longitudinal perspective on adolescents' cross-group friendships with immigrants. *Journal of Youth and Adolescence*. http://doi.org/10.1007/s10964-015-0256-6

Tobin, D. J. (2017). Introduction to skin aging. *Journal of Tissue Viability*, 26(1), 37–46. http://doi.org/10.1016/j.jtv.2016.03.002

Tomasello, M. (2009). *Constructing a language: A usage-based theory of language acquisition*. Harvard University Press.

Tomasello, M. (2012). A usage-based approach to child language acquisition. *Proceedings of the Annual Meeting of the Berkeley Linguistics Society*, 26(1).

Tomova, A., Lalabonova, C., Robeva, R. N., & Kumanov, P. T. (2011). Timing of pubertal maturation according to the age at first conscious ejaculation. *Andrologia*, 43(3), 163–6. http://doi.org/10.1111/j.1439-0272.2009.01037.x

Toner, I. J., & Smith, R. A. (1977). Age and overt verbalization in delay-maintenance behavior in children. *Journal of Experimental Child Psychology*, 24(1), 123–128. http://doi.org/10.1016/0022-0965(77)90025-X

Tong, X., Deacon, S. H., & Cain, K. (2014). Morphological and syntactic awareness in poor comprehenders: Another piece of the puzzle. *Journal of Learning Disabilities*, 47(1), 22 33. http://doi.org/10.1177/0022219413509971

Tononi, G., & Cirelli, C. (2014). Sleep and the price of plasticity: From synaptic and cellular homeostasis to memory consolidation and integration. *Neuron*, 81(1), 12–34. http://doi.org/10.1016/j.neuron.2013.12.025

Toomela, A. (2003). Developmental stages in children's drawings of a cube and a doll. *TRAMES: A Journal of the Humanities & Social Sciences*, 7(3), 164–182.

Toomey, R. B., Card, N. A., & Casper, D. M. (2014). Peers' perceptions of gender nonconformity: Associations with overt and relational peer victimization and aggression in early adolescence. *The Journal of Early Adolescence*, 34(4), 463–485. http://doi.org/10.1177/0272431613495446

Toothman, E. L., & Barrett, A. E. (2011). Mapping midlife: An examination of social factors shaping conceptions of the timing of middle age. *Advances in Life Course Research, 16*(3), 99–111. http://doi.org/10.1016/j.alcr.2011.08.003

Torpey, K., Kabaso, M., Kasonde, P., Dirks, R., Bweupe, M., Thompson, C., & Mukadi, Y. D. (2010). Increasing the uptake of prevention of mother-to-child transmission of HIV services in a resource-limited setting. *BMC Health Services Research, 10*, 29–36. http://doi.org/10.1186/1472-6963-10-29

Torpey, K., Kasonde, P., Kabaso, M., Weaver, M. A., Bryan, G., Mukonka, V., . . . Colebunders, R. (2010). Reducing pediatric HIV infection:Estimating mother-to-child transmission rates in a program setting in Zambia. *Journal of Acquired Immune Deficiency Syndromes (1999), 54*(4), 415–422.

Torr, J., Strydom, A., Patti, P., & Jokinen, N. (2010). Down syndrome: Morbidity and mortality. *Journal of Policy & Practice In Intellectual Disabilities, 7*, 70–81. http://doi.org/10.1111

Torrey, B. B., & Haub, C. (2004). A comparison of US and Canadian mortality in 1998. *Population & Development Review, 30*(3), 519–530. R

Tosto, G., Bird, T. D., Bennett, D. A., Boeve, B. F., Brickman, A. M., Cruchaga, C., . . . Mayeux, R. (2016). The role of cardiovascular risk factors and stroke in familial Alzheimer disease. *JAMA Neurology, 73*(10), 1231. http://doi.org/10.1001/jamaneurol.2016.2539

Toulouse, A., & Sullivan, A. M. (2008). Progress in Parkinson's disease: Where do we stand? *Progress in Neurobiology, 85*(4), 376–392. http://doi.org/10.1016/j.pneurobio.2008.05.003

Tourlouki, E., Polychronopoulos, E., Zeimbekis, A., Tsakountakis, N., Bountziouka, V., Lioliou, E., . . . Panagiotakos, D. B. (2010). The "secrets" of the long livers in Mediterranean islands: The MEDIS study. *European Journal of Public Health, 20*(6), 659–664.

Toyama, M. (2001). Developmental changes in social comparison in pre-school and elementary school children: Perceptions, feelings, and behavior. *Japanese Journal of Educational Psychology, 49*, 500–507.

Trahan, L. H., Stuebing, K. K., Fletcher, J. M., & Hiscock, M. (2014). The Flynn effect: A meta-analysis. *Psychological Bulletin, 140*(5), 1332–60. http://doi.org/10.1037/a0037173

Trautner, H. M., Ruble, D. N., Cyphers, L., Kirsten, B., Behrendt, R., & Hartmann, P. (2005). Rigidity and flexibility of gender stereotypes in childhood: Developmental or differential? *Infant and Child Development, 14*(4), 365–381. http://doi.org/10.1002/icd.399

Trawick-Smith, J., & Dziurgot, T. (2011). "Good-fit" teacher–child play interactions and the subsequent autonomous play of preschool children. *Early Childhood Research Quarterly, 26*(1), 110–123. http://doi.org/10.1016/j.ecresq.2010.04.005

Trejos-Castillo, E., & Vazsonyi, A. T. (2009). Risky sexual behaviors in first and second generation Hispanic ilmmigrant youth. *Journal of Youth & Adolescence, 38*(5), 719–731. http://doi.org/10.1007/s10964-008-9369-5

Tremblay, K., & Ross, B. (2007). Auditory rehabilitation and the aging brain. *ASHA Leader, 12*(16), 12–13.

Tremblay, L., & Limbos, M. (2009). Body image disturbance and psychopathology in children: Research evidence and implications for prevention and treatment. *Current Psychiatry Reviews, 5*(1), 62–72. http://doi.org/10.2174/157340009787315307

Tremblay, L., Lovsin, T., Zecevic, C., & Larivière, M. (2011). Perceptions of self in 3–5-year-old children:

A preliminary investigation into the early emergence of body dissatisfaction. *Body Image, 8*(3), 287–92. http://doi.org/10.1016/j.bodyim.2011.04.004

Tremblay, M.-C., Pluye, P., Gore, G., Granikov, V., Filion, K. B., & Eisenberg, M. J. (2015). Regulation profiles of e-cigarettes in the United States: A critical review with qualitative synthesis. *BMC Medicine, 13*(1), 130. http://doi.org/10.1186/s12916-015-0370-z

Tremblay, R. E. (2009). The development of chronic physical aggression: Genes and environments matter from the beginning. In R. E. Tremblay, M. A. G. van Aken, & W. Koops (Eds.), *Development and prevention of behaviour problems: From genes to social policy.* (pp. 113–130). New York, NY: Psychology Press.

Tremblay, R. E. (2014). Early development of physical aggression and early risk factors for chronic physical aggression in humans. *Current Topics in Behavioral Neurosciences.* http://doi.org/10.1007/7854_2013_262

Tremblay, R. E., Nagin, D. S., Séguin, J. R., Zoccolillo, M., Zelazo, P. D., Boivin, M., . . . Japel, C. (2004). Physical aggression during early childhood: Trajectories and predictors. *Pediatrics, 114*(1), e43–e50.

Trettien, A. W. (1990). Creeping and walking. *American Journal of Psychology, 12*, 1–57.

Trevathan, W. R., & McKenna, J. J. (1994). Evolutionary environments of human birth and infancy: Insights to apply to contemporary life. *Children's Environments, 11*, 88–104.

Triana, M. del C., Jayasinghe, M., & Pieper, J. R. (2015). Perceived workplace racial discrimination and its correlates: A meta-analysis. *Journal of Organizational Behavior, 36*(4), 491–513. http://doi.org/10.1002/job.1988

Triandis, & H.C (2000). Cultural syndromes and subjective well-being. In E. Diener & E. M. Suh (Eds.), *Culture and subjective well-being* (pp. 13–36). Cambridge, MA: The MIT Press.

Trillingsgaard, T., Baucom, K. J. W., & Heyman, R. E. (2014). Predictors of change in relationship satisfaction during the transition to parenthood. *Family Relations, 63*(5), 667–679. http://doi.org/10.1111/fare.12089

Troncoso, J. C., Zonderman, A. B., Resnick, S. M., Crain, B., Pletnikova, O., & O'Brien, R. J. (2008). Effect of infarcts on dementia in the Baltimore Longitudinal Study of Aging. *Annals of Neurology, 64*(2), 168–176. Retrieved from robrien@jhmi.edu

Tronick, E. Z. (1989). Emotions and emotional communication in infants. *American Psychologist, 44*, 112–119.

Tronick, E. Z., & Cohn, J. F. (1989). Infant-mother face-to-face interaction: Age and gender differences in coordination and the occurrence of miscoordination. *Child Development, 60*, 85–92.

Tronick, E. Z., Als, H., Adamson, L., Wise, S., & Brazelton, B. (1978). The infants' response to entrapment between contradictory messages in face-to-face interaction. *American Academy of Child Psychiatry, 1*, 1–13.

Tronick, E. Z., Morelli, G. A., & Ivey, P. K. (1992). The Efe forager infant and toddler's pattern of social relationships: Multiple and simultaneous. *Developmental Psychology, 28*, 568–577.

Troutman, D. R., & Fletcher, A. C. (2010). Context and companionship in children's short-term versus long-term friendships. *Journal of Social & Personal Relationships, 27*(8), 1060–1074. http://doi.org/10.1177/0265407510381253

Truong, D. D., & Wolters, E. C. (2009). Recognition and management of Parkinson's disease during the premotor (prodromal) phase. *Expert Review of Neurotherapeutics, 9*(6), 847–857. http://doi.org/10.1586/ern.09.50

Truscott, R. J. (2009). Presbyopia. Emerging from a blur towards an understanding of the molecular basis for this most common eye condition. *Experimental Eye Research, 88*(2), 241–247. http://doi.org/10.1016/j.exer.2008.07.003

Trzesniewski, K. H., Donnellan, M. B., & Robins, R. W. (2008). Do today's young people really think they are so extraordinary? *Psychological Science, 19*(2), 181–188. http://doi.org/10.1111/j.1467-9280.2008.02065.x

Tseng, V. (2012). The uses of research in policy and practice. *Social Policy Report of the Society for Research in Child Development, 26*(2).

Tsujimoto, S., Kuwajima, M., & Sawaguchi, T. (2007). Developmental fractionation of working memory and response inhibition during childhood. *Experimental Psychology, 54*(1), 30–37.

Tu, W., Wagner, E. K., Eckert, G. J., Yu, Z., Hannon, T., Pratt, J. H., & He, C. (2015). Associations between menarche-related genetic variants and pubertal growth in male and female adolescents. *The Journal of Adolescent Health : Official Publication of the Society for Adolescent Medicine, 56*(1), 66–72. http://doi.org/10.1016/j.jadohealth.2014.07.020

Tucker, B., & Young, A. (2005). Growing up Mikea: Children's time allocation and tuber foraging in southwestern Madagascar. In B. S. Hewlett & M. E. Lamb. (Eds.), *Huntergatherer childhoods: Evolutionary, developmental and cultural perspectives* (pp. 147–174). New Brunswick,: NJ: Transaction.

Tucker, J., & McGuire, W. (2004). Epidemiology of preterm birth. *British Medical Journal, 329*, 675–678. Retrieved from http://bmj.bmjjournals.com/cgi/content/full/329/7467/675

Tulving, E. (2002). Episodic memory: From mind to brain. *Annual Review of Psychology, 53*, 1–25.

Tunau, K., Adamu, A., Hassan, M., Ahmed, Y., & Ekele, B. (2012). Age at menarche among school girls in Sokoto, Northern Nigeria. *Annals of African Medicine.* Usmanu Danfodiyo University Teaching Hospital. Retrieved from http://www.ajol.info/index.php/aam/article/view/75230

Turcotte Benedict, F., Vivier, P. M., & Gjelsvik, A. (2014). Mental health and bullying in the United States among children aged 6 to 17 years. *Journal of Interpersonal Violence*, 0886260514536279-. http://doi.org/10.1177/0886260514536279

Turfkruyer, M., & Verhasselt, V. (2015). Breast milk and its impact on maturation of the neonatal immune system. *Current Opinion in Infectious Diseases, 28*(3), 199–206. http://doi.org/10.1097/QCO.0000000000000165

Turiano, N. A., Chapman, B. P., Gruenewald, T. L., & Mroczek, D. K. (2015). Personality and the leading behavioral contributors of mortality. *Health Psychology : Official Journal of the Division of Health Psychology, American Psychological Association, 34*(1), 51–60. http://doi.org/10.1037/hea0000038

Turiel, E. (1998). The development of morality. In N. Eisenberg (Ed.), *Handbook of child psychology, Vol. 3: Social, emotional, and personality development* (5th ed., pp. 863–932). New York: Wiley.

Turiel, E. (2008). Thought about actions in social domains: Morality, social conventions, and social interactions. *Cognitive Development, 23*(1), 136–154. http://doi.org/10.1016/j.cogdev.2007.04.001

Turkheimer, E., Haley, A., Waldron, M., D'Onofrio, B., & Gottesman, I. I. (2003). Socioeconomic status modifies heritability of IQ in young children. *Psychological Science, 14*(6), 623–628.

Turnbull, K., & Justice, L. M. (2016). *Language development from theory to practice.* Pearson.

Turner, B. O., Marinsek, N., Ryhal, E., & Miller, M. B. (2015). Hemispheric lateralization in reasoning. *Annals of the New York Academy of Sciences, 1359*(1), 47–64. http://doi.org/10.1111/nyas.12940

Turner, G. R., & Spreng, R. N. (2012). Executive functions and neurocognitive aging: Dissociable patterns of brain activity. *Neurobiology of Aging, 33*(4), 826.e1-13. http://doi.org/10.1016/j.neurobiolaging.2011.06.005

Turner, P. J., & Gervai, J. (1995). A multidimensional study of gender typing in preschool children and their parents: Personality, attitudes, preferences, behavior, and cultural differences. *British Journal of Developmental Psychology, 11*, 323–342.

Twardosz, S., & Lutzker, J. R. (2009). Child maltreatment and the developing brain: A review of neuroscience perspectives. *Aggression and Violent Behavior, 15*(1), 59–68. http://doi.org/10.1016/j.avb.2009.08.003

Twenge, J. M. (1997). Attitudes toward women, 1970–1995. *Psychology of Women Quarterly, 21*(1), 35–51. http://doi.org/10.1111/j.1471-6402.1997.tb00099.x

Twenge, J. M., & Campbell, W. K. (2009). *The narcissism epidemic : Living in the age of entitlement.* New York Simon & Schuster.

Twenge, J. M., & Foster, J. D. (2010). Birth cohort increases in narcissistic personality traits among American college students, 1982–2009. *Social Psychological and Personality Science, 1*(1), 99–106. http://doi.org/10.1177/1948550609355719

Twenge, J. M., Konrath, S., Foster, J. D., Keith Campbell, W., & Bushman, B. J. (2008). Egos inflating over time: A cross-temporal meta-analysis of the narcissistic personality inventory. *Journal of Personality, 76*(4), 875–902. http://doi.org/10.1111/j.1467-6494.2008.00507.x

Tyler, J. H., & Lofstrom, M. (2009). Finishing high school: Alternative pathways and dropout recovery. *The Future of Children / Center for the Future of Children, the David and Lucile Packard Foundation, 19*(1), 77–103. Retrieved from http://europepmc.org/abstract/med/21141706

Tyrka, A. R., Graber, J. A., & Brooks-Gunn, J. (2000). The development of disordered eating: Correlates and predictors of eating problems in the context of adolescence. In A. J. Sameroff, M. Lewis, & S. M. Miller (Eds.), *Handbook of developmental psychopathology (2nd ed.).* (pp. 607–624). Dordrecht,Netherlands: Kluwer Academic Publishers.

Tyson-Rawson, K. J. (1996). Adolescent responses to the death of a parent. In C. Corr & E. M. Balk (Eds.), *Handbook of adolescent death and bereavement,* (pp. 155–172). Springer.

Tzeng, O., Jackson, J., & Karlson, H. (1991). *Theories of child abuse and neglect: Differential perspectives, summaries, and evaluations.* New York: Praeger Publishers.

U.S. Bureau of Labor Statistics. (2014). *America's young adults at 27: Labor market activity, education, and household composition: Results from a longitudinal survey summary.* Retrieved from http://www.bls.gov/news.release/nlsyth.nr0.htm

U.S. Bureau of Labor Statistics. (2016). *Employment characteristics of families—2015.* Retrieved from https://www.bls.gov/news.release/pdf/famee.pdf

U.S. Bureau of the Census. (2012). *Current Population Survey.* Washington, DC: U.S. Bureau of the Census. Retrieved from http://www.bls.gov/emp/ep_chart_001.htm

U.S. Bureau of the Census. (2015). Table A1. Marital Status Of People 15 Years And Over, By Age, Sex, Personal Earnings, Race, and Hispanic Origin: 2014. Retrieved from http://www.census.gov/hhes/families/data/cps2014A.html

U.S. Department of Health and Human Services. (2009). *Code of Federal Regulations TITLE 45 Department of Health and Human Services PART 46.* Washington DC. Retrieved from http://www.hhs.gov/ohrp/humansubjects/guidance/45cfr46.html

U.S. Department of Health and Human Services. (2011). The Surgeon General's Call to Action to Support Breastfeeding. . (O. of the S. General., Ed.). Washington, DC: U.S. Department of Health and Human Services.

U.S. Department of Health and Human Services. (2013a). *Child Health USA 2013.* Rockville, Maryland. Retrieved from http://mchb.hrsa.gov/chusa13/index.html

U.S. Department of Health and Human Services. (2013b). *Child Maltreatment 2012.* Washington, DC: U.S. Department of Health and Human Services. Retrieved from http://www.acf.hhs.gov/programs/cb/resource/child-maltreatment-2012

U.S. Department of Health and Human Services. (2014). *Child Health USA 2014.* Rockville, Maryland. Retrieved from http://www.mchb.hrsa.gov/chusa14/index.html

U.S. Department of Health and Human Services. (2016). *Child maltreatment, 2014.* Retrieved from http://www.acf.hhs.gov/sites/default/files/cb/cm2014.pdf

U.S. Department of State. (2014). *FY 2013 Annual Report on Intercountry Adoption.* Washington DC. Retrieved from http://adoption.state.gov/content/pdf/fy2013_annual_report.pdf

Ueno, K. (2005). Sexual orientation and psychological distress in adolescence: Examining interpersonal stressors and social support processes. *Social Psychology Quarterly, 68*(3), 258–277.

Ueno, K., & Adams, R. G. (2006). Adult friendship: A decade review. In P. Noller & J. A. Feeney (Eds.), *Close relationships: Functions, forms and processes.* (pp. 151–169). Hove England: Psychology Press/Taylor & Francis (UK).

Uhlmann, W. R., Schuette, J. L., & Yashar, B. (2009). *A guide to genetic counseling* (2nd ed.). Wiley-Blackwell.

Uji, M., Sakamoto, A., Adachi, K., & Kitamura, T. (2013). The impact of authoritative, authoritarian, and permissive parenting styles on children's later mental health in Japan: Focusing on parent and child gender. *Journal of Child and Family Studies, 23*(2), 293–302. http://doi.org/10.1007/s10826-013-9740-3

UK Department of Health. (2005). *Reduce the risk of cot death : An easy guide.* London: UK Department of Health.

Ullian, E. M., Sapperstein, S. K., Christopherson, K. S., & Barres, B. A. (2001). Control of synapse number by glia. *Science, 291*, 657–661.

Ullman, H., Almeida, R., & Klingberg, T. Structural maturation and brain activity predict future working memory capacity during childhood development. *Journal of Neuroscience.* doi: 10.1523/JNEUROSCI.0842-13.2014

Ullman, S. E., Relyea, M., Peter-Hagene, L., & Vasquez, A. L. (2013). Trauma histories, substance use coping, PTSD, and problem substance use among sexual assault victims. *Addictive Behaviors, 38*(6), 2219–2223. http://doi.org/10.1016/j.addbeh.2013.01.027

Ulrich, D. A., Lloyd, M. C., Tiernan, C. W., Looper, J. E., & Angulo-Barroso, R. M. (2008). Effects of intensity of treadmill training on developmental outcomes and stepping in infants with down syndrome: A randomized trial. *Physical Therapy, 88*(1), 114–122.

Umaña-Taylor, A. J. (2016). Ethnic-racial identity: Conceptualization, development, and youth adjustment. In L. Balter & C. S. Tamis-LeMonda (Eds.), *Child psychology: A handbook of contemporary issues* (p. 505). New York, NY: Routledge.

Umaña-Taylor, A. J., Alfaro, E. C., Bámaca, M. Y., & Guimond, A. B. (2009). The central role of familial ethnic socialization in Latino adolescents' cultural orientation. *Journal of Marriage & Family, 71*(1), 46–60. http://doi.org/10.1111/j.1741-3737.2008.00579.x

Umaña-Taylor, A. J., Bhanot, R., & Shin, N. (2006). Ethnic identity formation during adolescence: The critical role of families. *Journal of Family Issues, 27*(3), 390–414. http://doi.org/10.1177/0192513x05282960

Umaña-Taylor, A. J., Guimond, A. B., Updegraff, K. A., & Jahromi, L. (2013). A longitudinal examination of support, self-esteem, and Mexican-origin adolescent mothers' parenting efficacy. *Journal of Marriage and the Family, 75*(3). http://doi.org/10.1111/jomf.12019

Umaña-Taylor, A. J., Quintana, S. M., Lee, R. M., Cross, W. E., Rivas-Drake, D., Schwartz, S. J., . . . Seaton, E. (2014a). Ethnic and racial identity during adolescence and into young adulthood: An integrated conceptualization. *Child Development, 85*(1), 21–39. http://doi.org/10.1111/cdev.12196

Umaña-Taylor, A. J., Quintana, S. M., Lee, R. M., Cross, W. E., Rivas-Drake, D., Schwartz, S. J., . . . Seaton, E. (2014b). Ethnic and racial identity during adolescence and into young adulthood: An integrated conceptualization. *Child Development, 85*(1), 21–39. http://doi.org/10.1111/cdev.12196

Umberson, D. (2003). *Death of a parent: Transition to a new adult identity.* New York: Cambridge University Press.

Umberson, D., & Chen, M. D. (1994). Effects of a parent's death on adult children: Relationship salience and reaction to loss. *American Sociological Review, 59*(1), 152–168. http://doi.org/10.2307/2096138

UNICEF. (2009). *The state of the world's children special edition: Celebrating 20 years of the convention on the rights of the child.* UNICEF.

United Nations Children's Fund. (2013). *Towards an AIDS-free generation: Children and AIDS Sixth Stocktaking Report.* New York. Retrieved from http://www.childinfo.org/files/str6_full_report_29-11-2013.pdf

United Nations Economic Commission for Europe. (2015). Statistical Database. Retrieved May 5, 2015, from http://w3.unece.org/pxweb/QuickStatistics/IndicatorsList.asp?lang=1#17

United Nations Statistics Division. (2014). *Demographic Yearbook: 2013.* Retrieved from http://unstats.un.org/unsd/demographic/products/dyb/dyb2.htm

United Nations Statistics Division. (2017). Divorces and crude divorce rates by urban/rural residence: 2011–2015. Retrieved from https://unstats.un.org/Unsd/demographic/products/dyb/dyb2015/Table25.pdf

United States Department of Health and Human Services. (2014). *National Survey on Drug Use and Health, 2013.* Ann Arbor, MI. Retrieved from http://doi.org/10.3886/ICPSR35509.v1

Unsworth, N., Fukuda, K., Awh, E., & Vogel, E. K. (2014). Working memory and fluid intelligence: Capacity, attention control, and secondary memory retrieval. *Cognitive Psychology, 71*, 1–26. http://doi.org/10.1016/j.cogpsych.2014.01.003

Unsworth, S. J., Levin, W., Bang, M., Washinawatok, K., Waxman, S. R., & Medin, D. . (2012). cultural differences in children's ecological reasoning and psychological closeness to nature: Evidence from Menominee and European American children. *Journal of Cognition and Culture, 12*(1–2), 17–29. http://doi.org/10.1163/156853712X633901

Updegraff, K. A., McHale, S. M., Zeiders, K. H., Umaña-Taylor, A. J., Perez-Brena, N. J., Wheeler, L. A., & Rodríguez De Jesús, S. A. (2014). Mexican-American adolescents' gender role attitude development: The role of adolescents' gender and nativity and parents' gender role attitudes. *Journal of Youth and Adolescence, 43*(12), 2041–53. http://doi.org/10.1007/s10964-014-0128-5

Ursache, A., Blair, C., Stifter, C., & Voegtline, K. T. F. L. P. I. (2013). Emotional reactivity and regulation in infancy interact to predict executive functioning in early childhood. *Developmental Psychology, 40*(1), 760.

US Bureau of Labor Statistics. (2015). *Women in the laborforce: A databook. BLS Reports.* Retrieved from https://www.bls.gov/opub/reports/womens-databook/archive/women-in-the-labor-force-a-databook-2015.pdf

US Bureau of Labor Statistics. (2016a). *America's Young Adults at 29: Labor Market Activity, Education and Partner Status: Results from a Longitudinal Survey.* Retrieved from https://www.bls.gov/news.release/nlsyth.nr0.htm

US Bureau of Labor Statistics. (2016b). Labor force characteristics by race and ethnicity, 2015. *BLS Reports.*

US Bureau of Labor Statistics. (2016c). Median years of tenure with current employer for employed wage and salary workers by age and sex, selected years, 2006-16. Retrieved from https://www.bls.gov/news.release/tenure.t01.htm

US Bureau of Labor Statistics. (2017). Employment Characteristics of Families Summary. Retrieved from https://www.bls.gov/news.release/famee.nr0.htm

US Bureau of Labor. (2014). *College Enrollment and Work Activity of 2013 High School Graduates.* Washington DC. Retrieved from http://www.bls.gov/news.release/hsgec.nr0.htm

US Bureau of Labor. (2015a). *Labor force statistics from the current population survey: Employment status of the civilian noninstitutional population by age, sex, and race.* Washington DC. Retrieved from http://www.bls.gov/cps/cpsaat03.htm

US Bureau of Labor. (2015b). *Number of Jobs Held, Labor Market Activity, and Earnings Growth Among the Youngest Baby Boomers: Results from a Longitudinal Survey Summary.* Retrieved from http://www.bls.gov/news.release/nlsoy.nr0.htm

US Bureau of the Census. (2015). Census Bureau Reports at Least 350 Languages Spoken in U.S. Homes. Retrieved from https://www.census.gov/newsroom/press-releases/2015/cb15-185.html

US Bureau of the Census. (2015a). *Estimated Median Age at First Marriage, by Sex: 1890 to the Present; Current Population Survey.* Retrieved from http://www.census.gov/hhes/families/data/marital.html

US Bureau of the Census. (2015b). *Marital Status Of People 15 Years And Over, By Age, Sex, Personal Earnings, Race, And Hispanic Origin: 2014; Current Population Survey.* Retrieved from https://www.census.gov/hhes/families/data/cps2014A.html

US Department of Health and Human Services, & Administration for Children and Families. (2010). *Head Start Impact Study: Final Report.* Washington, DC.

US Department of Health and Human Services. (2008). *2008 physical activity guidelines for Americans.* Retrieved from http://www.health.gov/PAGuidelines.

US Department of Labor. (2015). *Registered Apprenticeship National Results Fiscal Year 2014.* Retrieved from http://doleta.gov/oa/data_statistics.cfm

US Department of Labor. (2017). HOUSEHOLD DATA ANNUAL AVERAGES 11. Employed persons by detailed occupation, sex, race, and Hispanic or Latino ethnicity. Retrieved from https://www.bls.gov/cps/cpsaat11.htm

US Federal Reserve. (2014). *Report on the Economic Well-Being of U.S. Households in 2013.* Retrieved from http://www.federalreserve.gov/econresdata/2013-report-economic-well-being-us-households-201407.pdf

US Food and Drug Administration. (2016). *Vaporizers, E-Cigarettes, and other Electronic Nicotine Delivery Systems (ENDS).* Retrieved from http://www.fda.gov/TobaccoProducts/Labeling/ProductsIngredientsComponents/ucm456610.htm#reporting

USDA. (2000). Pyramid Servings Intake by US Children and Adults: 1994-96, 1998. Retrieved from http://www.barc.usda.gov/bhnrc/cnrg.

Uylings, H. B. M. (2006). Development of the human cortex and the concept of "critical" or "sensitive" periods. *Language Learning, 56,* 59–90.

Vagelatos, N. T., & Eslick, G. D. (2013). Type 2 diabetes as a risk factor for Alzheimer's disease: The confounders, interactions, and neuropathology associated with this relationship. *Epidemiologic Reviews, 35,* 152–60. http://doi.org/10.1093/epirev/mxs012

Vagi, K. J., Rothman, E. F., Latzman, N. E., Tharp, A. T., Hall, D. M., & Breiding, M. J. (2013). Beyond correlates: A review of risk and protective factors for adolescent dating violence perpetration. *Journal of Youth and Adolescence, 42*(4), 633–649. http://doi.org/10.1007/s10964-013-9907-7

Vaillant, G. E. (1994). "Successful aging" and psychosocial well-being: Evidence from a 45-year study. In E. H. Thompson Jr. (Ed.), *Older men's lives.* (pp. 22–41). Thousand Oaks, CA Sage.

Vaillant, G. E. (2004). Positive Aging. In P. A. Linley & S. Joseph (Eds.), *Positive psychology in practice.* (pp. 561–578). Hoboken, NJ US: John Wiley & Sons Inc.

Vainionpää, K., & Topo, P. (2006). The construction of male menopause in Finnish popular magazines. *Critical Public Health, 16*(1), 19–34.

Vaish, A., Grossmann, T., & Woodward, A. (2008). Not all emotions are created equal: The negativity bias in social-emotional development. *Psychological Bulletin, 134*(3), 383–403. http://doi.org/10.1037/0033-2909.134.3.383

Valentine, J. C., DuBois, D. L., & Cooper, H. (2004). The Relation Between Self-Beliefs and Academic Achievement: A Meta-Analytic Review. *Educational Psychologist, 39,* 111–133.

Valko, M., Jomova, K., Rhodes, C. J., Kuča, K., & Musílek, K. (2016). Redox- and non-redox-metal-induced formation of free radicals and their role in human disease. *Archives of Toxicology, 90*(1), 1–37. http://doi.org/10.1007/s00204-015-1579-5

Vallortigara, G. (2012). Core knowledge of object, number, and geometry: a comparative and neural approach. *Cognitive Neuropsychology, 29*(1–2), 213–36. http://doi.org/10.1080/02643294.2012.654772

Vallotton, C., & Ayoub, C. (2011). Use your words: The role of language in the development of toddlers' self-regulation. *Early Childhood Research Quarterly, 26*(2), 169–181. Retrieved

van Aken, M. A. G. (2009). Personality in children and adolescents: Development and consequences. In R. E. Tremblay, M. A. G. van Aken, & W. Koops (Eds.), *Development and prevention of behaviour problems: From genes to social policy.* (pp. 131–142). New York, NY US: Psychology Press. Retrieved from

Van Assche, L., Luyten, P., Bruffaerts, R., Persoons, P., van de Ven, L., & Vandenbulcke, M. (2013). Attachment in old age: Theoretical assumptions, empirical findings and implications for clinical practice. *Clinical Psychology Review, 33*(1), 67–81. http://doi.org/10.1016/j.cpr.2012.10.003

van Bokhorst-de van der Schueren, M. A. E., Lonterman-Monasch, S., de Vries, O. J., Danner, S. A., Kramer, M. H. H., & Muller, M. (2013). Prevalence and determinants of malnutrition in geriatric outpatients. *Clinical Nutrition (Edinburgh, Scotland), 32*(6), 1007–11. http://doi.org/10.1016/j.clnu.2013.05.007

Van Craeyevelt, S., Verschueren, K., Vancraeyveldt, C., Wouters, S., & Colpin, H. (2017). The role of preschool teacher-child interactions in academic adjustment: An intervention study with Playing-2-gether. *British Journal of Educational Psychology.* http://doi.org/10.1111/bjep.12153

van de Bongardt, D., Reitz, E., Sandfort, T., & Deković, M. (2014). A Meta-Analysis of the Relations Between Three Types of Peer Norms and Adolescent Sexual Behavior. *Personality and Social Psychology Review : An Official Journal of the Society for Personality and Social Psychology, Inc,* 1088868314544223-. http://doi.org/10.1177/1088868314544223

van de Bongardt, D., Yu, R., Deković, M., & Meeus, W. H. J. (2015). Romantic relationships and sexuality in adolescence and young adulthood: The role of parents, peers, and partners. *European Journal of Developmental Psychology, 12*(5), 497–515. http://doi.org/10.1080/17405629.2015.1068689

Van de Vondervoort, J. W., & Hamlin, J. K. (2016). Evidence for intuitive morality: preverbal infants make sociomoral evaluations. *Child Development Perspectives, 10*(3), 143–148. http://doi.org/10.1111/cdep.12175

van de Vorst, I. E., Koek, H. L., Stein, C. E., Bots, M. L., & Vaartjes, I. (2016). Socioeconomic disparities and mortality after a diagnosis of dementia: Results from a nationwide registry linkage study. *American Journal of Epidemiology, 184*(3), 219–226. http://doi.org/10.1093/aje/kwv319

Van den Akker, A. L., Deković, M., Asscher, J., & Prinzie, P. (2014). Mean-level personality development across childhood and adolescence: A temporary defiance of the maturity principle and bidirectional associations with parenting. *Journal of Personality and Social Psychology, 107*(4), 736–50. http://doi.org/10.1037/a0037248

van den Boom, D. C. (1997). Sensitivity and attachment: Next steps for developmentalists. *Child Development, 68*(4), 592. http://doi.org/10.1111/1467-8624.ep9710021673

van den Bosch, G. E., El Marroun, H., Schmidt, M. N., Tibboel, D., Manoach, D. S., Calhoun, V. D., & White, T. J. H. (2014). Brain connectivity during verbal working memory in children and adolescents. *Human Brain Mapping, 35*(2), 698–711. http://doi.org/10.1002/hbm.22193

van den Dungen, P., van Kuijk, L., van Marwijk, H., van der Wouden, J., Moll van Charante, E., van der Horst, H., & van Hout, H. (2014). Preferences regarding disclosure of a diagnosis of dementia: A systematic review. *International Psychogeriatrics, 26*(10), 1603–1618. Retrieved from http://journals.cambridge.org/abstract_S1041610214000969

van der Maas, P. (1991). Euthanasia and other medical decisions concerning the end of life. *The Lancet, 338*(8768), 669–674. http://doi.org/10.1016/0140-6736(91)91241-L

Van der Mussele, S., Bekelaar, K., Le Bastard, N., Vermeiren, Y., Saerens, J., Somers, N., . . . Engelborghs, S. (2013). Prevalence and associated behavioral symptoms of depression in mild cognitive impairment and dementia due to Alzheimer's disease. *International Journal of Geriatric Psychiatry, 28*(9), 947–58. http://doi.org/10.1002/gps.3909

van der Niet, A. G., Smith, J., Scherder, E. J. A., Oosterlaan, J., Hartman, E., & Visscher, C. (2015). Associations between daily physical activity and executive functioning in primary school-aged children. *Journal of Science and Medicine in Sport*, *18*(6), 673–677. http://doi.org/10.1016/j.jsams.2014.09.006

van der Stel, M., & Veenman, M. V. J. (2013). Metacognitive skills and intellectual ability of young adolescents: A longitudinal study from a developmental perspective. *European Journal of Psychology of Education*, *29*(1), 117–137. http://doi.org/10.1007/s10212-013-0190-5

Van Dijk, K. R. A., Van Gerven, P. W. M., Van Boxtel, M. P. J., Van Der Elst, W., & Jolles, J. (2008). No protective effects of education during normal cognitive aging: Results from the 6-year follow-up of the Maastricht Aging Study. *Psychology & Aging*, *23*(1), 119–130. http://doi.org/10.1037/0882-7974.23.1.119

Van Dijk, M. P. A., Branje, S., Keijsers, L., Hawk, S. T., Hale, W. W., & Meeus, W. H. J. (2014). Self-concept clarity across adolescence: Longitudinal associations with open communication with parents and internalizing symptoms. *Journal of Youth and Adolescence*, *43*(11), 1861–76. http://doi.org/10.1007/s10964-013-0055-x

van Dijken, M. W., Stams, G. J. J. M., & de Winter, M. (2016). Can community-based interventions prevent child maltreatment? *Children and Youth Services Review*, *61*, 149–158. http://doi.org/10.1016/j.childyouth.2015.12.007

van Dooren, F. E. P., Nefs, G., Schram, M. T., Verhey, F. R. J., Denollet, J., & Pouwer, F. (2013). Depression and risk of mortality in people with diabetes mellitus: A systematic review and meta-analysis. *PloS One*, *8*(3), e57058. http://doi.org/10.1371/journal.pone.0057058

Van Doorn, M. D., Branje, S. J. T., & Meeus, W. H. J. (2011). Developmental changes in conflict resolution styles in parent-adolescent relationships: A four-wave longitudinal study. *Journal of Youth and Adolescence*, *40*(1), 97–107. http://doi.org/10.1007/s10964-010-9516-7

van Duijvenvoorde, A. C. K., Huizenga, H. M., Somerville, L. H., Delgado, M. R., Powers, A., Weeda, W. D., . . . Figner, B. (2015). Neural correlates of expected risks and returns in risky choice across development. *The Journal of Neuroscience*, *35*(4), 1549–1560. http://doi.org/10.1523/JNEUROSCI.1924-14.2015

van Duijvenvoorde, A. C. K., Jansen, B. R. J., Visser, I., & Huizenga, H. M. (2010). Affective and cognitive decision-making in adolescents. *Developmental Neuropsychology*, *35*(5), 539–554. http://doi.org/10.1080/87565641.2010.494749

van Gelder, M. M. H. J., Reefhuis, J., Caton, A. R., Werler, M. M., Druschel, C. M., & Roeleveld, N. (2010). Characteristics of pregnant illicit drug users and associations between cannabis use and perinatal outcome in a population-based study. *Drug & Alcohol Dependence*, *109*(1–3), 243–247. http://doi.org/10.1016/j.drugalcdep.2010.01.007

Van Gerven, P. W. M., Van Boxtel, M. P. J., Meijer, W. A., Willems, D., & Jolles, J. (2007). On the relative role of inhibition in age-related working memory decline. *Aging, Neuropsychology & Cognition*, *14*(1), 95–107.

van Goethem, A. A. J., van Hoof, A., van Aken, M. A. G., Orobio de Castro, B., & Raaijmakers, Q. A. W. (2014). Socialising adolescent volunteering: How important are parents and friends? Age dependent effects of parents and friends on adolescents' volunteering behaviours. *Journal of Applied Developmental Psychology*, *35*(2), 94–101. http://doi.org/10.1016/j.appdev.2013.12.003

Van Hoorn, J., Crone, E. A., & Van Leijenhorst, L. (2017). Hanging out with the right crowd: Peer influence on risk-taking behavior in adolescence. *Journal of Research on Adolescence*, *27*(1), 189–200. http://doi.org/10.1111/jora.12265

van Hoorn, J., van Dijk, E., Meuwese, R., Rieffe, C., & Crone, E. A. (2016). Peer influence on prosocial behavior in adolescence. *Journal of Research on Adolescence*, *26*(1), 90–100. http://doi.org/10.1111/jora.12173

Van Horn, D., & Kan, P. F. (2015). Fast mapping by bilingual children: Storybooks and cartoons. *Child Language Teaching and Therapy*. http://doi.org/10.1177/0265659015584975

van Houdenhove, E., Gijs, L., T'Sjoen, G., & Enzlin, P. (2015). Asexuality: A multidimensional approach. *The Journal of Sex Research*, *52*(6), 669–678. http://doi.org/10.1080/00224499.2014.898015

van IJzendoorn, M. H., & De Wolff, M. S. (1997). In search of the absent father—Meta-analyses of infant-father attachment: A rejoinder. *Child Development*, *68*(4), 604. http://doi.org/10.1111/1467-8624.ep9710021677

Van IJzendoorn, M. H., & Kroonenberg, P. M. (1988). Cross-cultural patterns of attachment: A meta-analysis of the Strange Situation. *Child Development*, *59*, 147–156.

Van Leijenhorst, L., Zanolie, K., Van Meel, C. S., Westenberg, P. M., Rombouts, S. A. R. B., & Crone, E. A. (2010). What motivates the adolescent? Brain regions mediating reward sensitivity across adolescence. *Cerebral Cortex*, *20*(1), 61–69. http://doi.org/10.1093/cercor/bhp078

van Nispen, R. M. A., Vreeken, H. L., Comijs, H. C., Deeg, D. J. H., & van Rens, G. H. M. B. (2016). Role of vision loss, functional limitations and the supporting network in depression in a general population. *Acta Ophthalmologica*, *94*(1), 76–82. http://doi.org/10.1111/aos.12896

Van Ouytsel, J., Ponnet, K., & Walrave, M. (2017). The associations of adolescents' dating violence victimization, well-being and engagement in risk behaviors. *Journal of Adolescence*, *55*, 66–71. Retrieved from http://www.sciencedirect.com/science/article/pii/S0140197116301749

Van Ouytsel, J., Van Gool, E., Ponnet, K., & Walrave, M. (2014). Brief report: The association between adolescents' characteristics and engagement in sexting. *Journal of Adolescence*, *37*(8), 1387–1391. http://doi.org/10.1016/j.adolescence.2014.10.004

van Solinge, H., & Henkens, K. (2008). Adjustment to and satisfaction with retirement: Two of a kind? *Psychology and Aging*, *23*(2), 422–434.

Vanassche, S., Swicegood, G., & Matthijs, K. (2012). Marriage and children as a key to happiness? Cross-national differences in the effects of marital status and children on well-being. *Journal of Happiness Studies*, *14*(2), 501–524. http://doi.org/10.1007/s10902-012-9340-8

Vandell, D. L., Belsky, J., Burchinal, M., Steinberg, L., & Vandergrift, N. (2010). Do effects of early child care extend to age 15 years? Results from the NICHD study of early child care and youth development. *Child Development*, *81*(3), 737–756. http://doi.org/10.1111/j.1467-8624.2010.01431.x

Vandell, D. L., Burchinal, M., & Pierce, K. M. (2016). Early child care and adolescent functioning at the end of high school: Results from the NICHD study of early child care and youth development. *Developmental Psychology*, *52*(10), 1634–1645. http://doi.org/10.1037/dev0000169

Vanderbilt-Adriance, E., & Shaw, D. (2008). Protective factors and the development of resilience in the context of neighborhood disadvantage. *Journal of Abnormal Child Psychology*, *36*(6), 887–901. http://doi.org/10.1007/s10802-008-9220-1

Vandermaas-Peeler, M., Massey, K., & Kendall, A. (2016). Parent guidance of young children's scientific and mathematical reasoning in a science museum. *Early Childhood Education Journal*, *44*(3), 217–224. http://doi.org/10.1007/s10643-015-0714-5

Vandewater, E., & Stewart, A. (2006). Paths to late midlife well-being for women and men: The importance of identity development and social role quality. *Journal of Adult Development*, *13*(2), 76–83.

Vanhalst, J., Luyckx, K., Scholte, R. H. J., Engels, R. C. M. E., & Goossens, L. (2013). Low self-esteem as a risk factor for loneliness in adolescence: Perceived—but not actual—social acceptance as an underlying mechanism. *Journal of Abnormal Child Psychology*, *41*(7), 1067–1081. http://doi.org/10.1007/s10802-013-9751-y

Vanhees, K., Vonhögen, I. G. C., van Schooten, F. J., & Godschalk, R. W. L. (2014). You are what you eat, and so are your children: The impact of micronutrients on the epigenetic programming of offspring. *Cellular and Molecular Life Sciences*, *71*(2), 271–285. http://doi.org/10.1007/s00018-013-1427-9

Vannasing, P., Florea, O., González-Frankenberger, B., Tremblay, J., Paquette, N., Safi, D., . . . Gallagher, A. (2016). Distinct hemispheric specializations for native and non-native languages in one-day-old newborns identified by fNIRS. *Neuropsychologia*, *84*, 63–69. http://doi.org/10.1016/j.neuropsychologia.2016.01.038

Vargesson, N. (2009). Thalidomide-induced limb defects: Resolving a 50-year-old puzzle. *BioEssays*, *31*(12), 1327–1336. http://doi.org/10.1002/bies.200900103

Vasto, S., Candore, G., Listì, F., Balistreri, C. R., Colonna-Romano, G., Malavolta, M., . . . Caruso, C. (2008). Inflammation, genes and zinc in Alzheimer's disease. *Brain Research Reviews*, *58*(1), 96–105. http://doi.org/10.1016/j.brainresrev.2007.12.001

Vaughn, B. E., Kopp, C. B., & Krakow, J. B. (1984). The emergence and consolidation of self-control from eighteen to thirty months of age: Normative trends and individual differences. *Child Development*, *55*(3), 990–1004. http://doi.org/10.1111/1467-8624.ep12427046

Vaughn, S., & Klingner, J. K. (1998). Students' perceptions of inclusion and resource room settings. *Journal of Special Education*, *32*, 79–88.

Vazsonyi, A. T., & Huang, L. (2010). Where self-control comes from: On the development of self-control and its relationship to deviance over time. *Developmental Psychology*, *46*(1), 245–257. http://doi.org/10.1037/a0016538

Veenhoven, R., & Choi, Y. (2012). Does intelligence boost happiness? Smartness of all pays more than being smarter than others. *International Journal of Happiness and Development*, *1*(1), 5. http://doi.org/10.1504/IJHD.2012.050808

Veenstra, R., Lindenberg, S., Oldehinkel, A. J., De Winter, A. F., Verhulst, F. C., & Ormel, J. (2005). Bullying and victimization in elementary schools: A comparison of bullies, victims, bully/victims, and uninvolved preadolescents. *Developmental Psychology*, *41*(4), 672–682. http://doi.org/10.1037/0012-1649.41.4.672

Venkatesh, K. K., Lurie, M. N., Triche, E. W., De Bruyn, G., Harwell, J. I., McGarvey, S. T., & Gray, G. E. (2010). Growth of infants born to HIV-infected women in South Africa according to maternal and infant characteristics. *Tropical Medicine & International Health*, *15*(11), 1364–1374. http://doi.org/10.1111/j.1365-3156.2010.02634.x

Verdelho, A., Madureira, S., Ferro, J. M., Baezner, H., Blahak, C., Poggesi, A., . . . Inzitari, D. (2012). Physical activity prevents progression for cognitive impairment and vascular dementia: Results from the LADIS (Leukoaraiosis and Disability) study. *Journal of Cerebral Circulation*, *43*(12), 3331–3335. http://doi.org/10.1161/STROKEAHA.112.661793

Vereijken, B., & Thelen, E. (1997). Training infant treadmill stepping: The role of individual pattern stability. *Developmental Psychobiology*, 30, 89–102.

Vergés, A., Jackson, K. M., Bucholz, K. K., Grant, J. D., Trull, T. J., Wood, P. K., & Sher, K. J. (2011). Deconstructing the age-prevalence curve of alcohol dependence: Why "maturing out" is only a small piece of the puzzle. *Journal of Abnormal Psychology*, 121(2), 511–523. http://doi.org/10.1037/a0026027

Verhaeghen, P., Steitz, D. W., Sliwinski, M. J., & Cerella, J. (2003). Aging and dual-task performance: A meta-analysis. *Psychology and Aging*, 18(3), 443–460. Retrieved from pverhaeg@psych.syr.edu

Verhage, M. L., Oosterman, M., & Schuengel, C. (2013). Parenting self-efficacy predicts perceptions of infant negative temperament characteristics, not vice versa. *Journal of Family Psychology*, 27(5), 844–849. http://doi.org/10.1037/a0034263

Verkaik, R., Nuyen, J., Schellevis, F., & Francke, A. (2007). The relationship between severity of Alzheimer's disease and prevalence of comorbid depressive symptoms and depression: A systematic review. *International Journal of Geriatric Psychiatry*, 22(11), 1063–1086.

Verkooijen, K. T., de Vries, N. K., & Nielsen, G. A. (2007). Youth crowds and substance use: The impact of perceived group norm and multiple group identification. *Psychology of Addictive Behaviors*, 21(1), 55–61. http://doi.org/10.1037/0893-164x.21.1.55

Verma, S. (2003). *Retirement coverage of women and minorities: Analysis from SIPP 1998 data.* Washington, DC: American Association of Retired Persons. Retrieved from http://www.aarp.org/research/financial/pensions/aresearch-import-350-DD92.html

Vernon-Feagans, L., Garrett-Peters, P., Willoughby, M., & Mills-Koonce, R. (2012). Chaos, poverty, and parenting: Predictors of early language development. *Early Childhood Research Quarterly*, 27(3), 339–351. http://doi.org/10.1016/j.ecresq.2011.11.001

Veroude, K., Zhang-James, Y., Fernàndez-Castillo, N., Bakker, M. J., Cormand, B., & Faraone, S. V. (2016). Genetics of aggressive behavior: An overview. *American Journal of Medical Genetics Part B: Neuropsychiatric Genetics*, 171(1), 3–43. http://doi.org/10.1002/ajmg.b.32364

Vestergren, P., & Nilsson, L.-G. (2011). Perceived causes of everyday memory problems in a population-based sample aged 39–99. *Applied Cognitive Psychology*, 25(4), 641–646. http://doi.org/10.1002/acp.1734

Vickerman, K. A., & Margolin, G. (2009). Rape treatment outcome research: Empirical findings and state of the literature. *Clinical Psychology Review*, 29(5), 431–448. http://doi.org/10.1016/j.cpr.2009.04.004

Victora, C. G. (2009). Nutrition in early life: A global priority. *Lancet*, 374(9696), 1123–1125.

Victora, C. G., Bahl, R., Barros, A. J. D., França, G. V. A., Horton, S., Krasevec, J., . . . Rollins, N. C. (2016). Breastfeeding in the 21st century: Epidemiology, mechanisms, and lifelong effect. *The Lancet*, 387(10017), 475–490. http://doi.org/10.1016/S0140-6736(15)01024-7

Vieweg, V. R., Johnston, C. H., Lanier, J. O., Fernandez, A., & Pandurangi, A. K. (2007). Correlation between high risk obesity groups and low socioeconomic status in school children. *Southern Medical Journal*, 100(1), 8–13.

Vigeh, M., Yokoyama, K., Matsukawa, T., Shinohara, A., & Ohtani, K. (2014). Low level prenatal blood lead adversely affects early childhood mental development. *Journal of Child Neurology*, 29(10), 1305–1311. http://doi.org/10.1177/0883073813516999

Vigil, P., Orellana, R. F., Cortés, M. E., Molina, C. T., Switzer, B. E., & Klaus, H. (2011). Endocrine modulation of the adolescent brain: A review. *Journal of Pediatric and Adolescent Gynecology*, 24(6), 330–337. http://doi.org/10.1016/j.jpag.2011.01.061

Vilasboas, T., Herbet, G., & Duffau, H. (2017). Challenging the myth of right nondominant hemisphere: Lessons from corticosubcortical stimulation mapping in awake surgery and surgical implications. *World Neurosurgery*, 103, 449–456. http://doi.org/10.1016/j.wneu.2017.04.021

Villamor, E., & Jansen, E. C. (2016). Nutritional determinants of the timing of puberty. *Annual Review of Public Health*, 37, 33–46. http://dx.doi.org/10.1146/annurev-Publhealth-031914-122606

Villar, F., Celdrán, M., & Triadó, C. (2012). Grandmothers offering regular auxiliary care for their grandchildren: An expression of generativity in later life? *Journal of Women & Aging*, 24(4), 292–312. http://doi.org/10.1080/08952841.2012.708576

Vincent, N. J. (2009). Exposure to community violence and the family: Disruptions in functioning and relationships. *Families in Society*, 90(2), 137–143.

Vincke, J., & van Heeringen, K. (2002). Confidant support and the mental wellbeing of lesbian and gay young adults: A longitudinal analysis. *Journal of Community & Applied Social Psychology*, 12(3), 181–193. http://doi.org/10.1002/casp.671

Vinden, P. (1996). Junín Quechua children's understanding of mind. *Child Development*, 67, 1707–1716.

Vinters, H. V. (2015). Emerging concepts in Alzheimer's disease. *Annual Review of Pathology: Mechanisms of Disease*, 10(1), 291–319. http://doi.org/10.1146/annurev-pathol-020712-163927

Visschedijk, J., Achterberg, W., van Balen, R., & Hertogh, C. (2010). Fear of falling after hip fracture: A systematic review of measurement instruments, prevalence, interventions, and related factors. *Journal of the American Geriatrics Society*, 58(9), 1739–1748. http://doi.org/10.1111/j.1532-5415.2010.03036.x

Visscher, M., & Narendran, V. (2014). Vernix caseosa: Formation and functions. *Newborn and Infant Nursing Reviews*, 14(4), 142–146. http://doi.org/10.1053/j.nainr.2014.10.005

Vissers, L. E. L. M., Gilissen, C., & Veltman, J. A. (2015). Genetic studies in intellectual disability and related disorders. *Nature Reviews Genetics*, 17(1), 9–18. http://doi.org/10.1038/nrg3999

Voelcker-Rehage, C., & Alberts, J. L. (2007). Effect of motor practice on dual-task performance in older adult. *Journals of Gerontology: Series B: Psychological Sciences and Social Sciences*, 3, P141–P148. Retrieved from albertj@ccf.org

Voelcker-Rehage, C., Stronge, A. J., & Alberts, J. L. (2006). Age-related differences in working memory and force control under dual-task conditions. *Aging, Neuropsychology, and Cognition*, 13(3), 366–384.

Voelker, D. K., Gould, D., & Reel, J. J. (2014). Prevalence and correlates of disordered eating in female figure skaters. *Psychology of Sport and Exercise*, 15(6), 696–704. http://doi.org/10.1016/j.psychsport.2013.12.002

Vogelstein, B., & Kinzler, K. W. (2004). Cancer genes and the pathways they control. *Nature Medicine*, 10(8), 789–799.

Vogt, D. S., Rizvi, S. L., & Shipherd, J. C. (2008). Longitudinal investigation of reciprocal relationship between stress reactions and hardiness. *Personality and Social Psychology Bulletin*, 34(1), 61–73.

Vo-Jutabha, E. D., Dinh, K. T., McHale, J. P., & Valsiner, J. (2009). A qualitative analysis of Vietnamese adolescent identity exploration within and outside an ethnic enclave. *Journal of Youth and Adolescence*, 38(5), 672–690. http://doi.org/10.1007/s10964-008-9365-9 Volterra, V., & Taeschner, T. (1978). The acquisition and development of language by bilingual children. *Journal of Child Language*, 5(2), 311–326. http://doi.org/10.1017/S0305000900007492

von Arnim, C. A. F., Gola, U., & Biesalski, H. K. (2010). More than the sum of its parts? Nutrition in Alzheimer's disease. *Nutrition*, 26(7/8), 694–700. http://doi.org/10.1016/j.nut.2009.11.009

von Hofsten, C., & Rönnqvist, L. (1993). The structuring of neonatal arm movements. *Child Development*, 64(4), 1046–57. Retrieved from http://www.ncbi.nlm.nih.gov/pubmed/8404256

von Hofsten, C., Kochukhova, O., & Rosander, K. (2007). Predictive tracking over occlusions by 4-month-old infants. *Developmental Science*, 10(5), 625–640. http://doi.org/10.1111/j.1467-7687.2006.00604.x

von Soest, T., Wichstrøm, L., & Kvalem, I. L. (2016). The development of global and domain-specific self-esteem from age 13 to 31. *Journal of Personality and Social Psychology*, 110(4), 592–608. http://doi.org/10.1037/pspp0000060

Vona-Davis, L., & Rose, D. P. (2009). The influence of socioeconomic disparities on breast cancer tumor biology and prognosis: A review. *Journal of Women's Health (15409996)*, 18(6), 883–893. http://doi.org/10.1089/jwh.2008.1127

Vondracek, S. F. (2010). Managing osteoporosis in postmenopausal women. *American Journal of Health-System Pharmacy*, 67, S9–S19. http://doi.org/10.2146/ajhp100076

Vorstman, J. A. S., & Ophoff, R. A. (2013). Genetic causes of developmental disorders. *Current Opinion in Neurology*, 26(2), 128–36. http://doi.org/10.1097/WC0.0b013e32835f1a30

Voss, M. W., Erickson, K. I., Prakash, R. S., Chaddock, L., Kim, J. S., Alves, H., . . . Kramer, A. F. (2013). Neurobiological markers of exercise-related brain plasticity in older adults. *Brain, Behavior, and Immunity*, 28, 90–99. http://doi.org/10.1016/j.bbi.2012.10.021

Votruba-Drzal, E., Miller, P., & Coley, R. L. (2016). Poverty, urbanicity, and children's development of early academic skills. *Child Development Perspectives*, 10(1), 3–9. http://doi.org/10.1111/cdep.12152

Vouloumanos, A., Hauser, M. D., Werker, J. F., & Martin, A. (2010). The tuning of human neonates' preference for speech. *Child Development*, 81(2), 517–527. http://doi.org/10.1111/j.1467-8624.2009.01412.x

Vrangalova, Z. (2015). Does casual sex harm college students' well-being? A longitudinal investigation of the role of motivation. *Archives of Sexual Behavior*, 44(4), 945–959. http://doi.org/10.1007/s10508-013-0255-1

Vygotsky, L. S. (1962). *Thought and language.* Cambridge, MA: MIT Press. (Original work published in 1934)

Vygotsky, L. S. (1978). *Mind in society: The development of higher psychological processes.* Cambridge, MA: Harvard University Press.

Vygotsky, L. S., & Minick, N. (1987). *Thinking and speech.* (T. N. Minick, Ed.). New York: Plenum Press.

Waasdorp, T. E., & Bradshaw, C. P. (2011). Examining student responses to frequent bullying: A latent class approach. *Journal of Educational Psychology*, 103(2), 336–352. http://doi.org/10.1037/a0022747

Waddington, C. H. (1971). Concepts of development. In E. Tobach, L. R. Aronson, & E. Shaw (Eds.), *The biopsychology of development* (pp. 17–23). San Diego, CA: Academic Press.

Wagner, J., Lüdtke, O., Jonkmann, K., & Trautwein, U. (2013). Cherish yourself: Longitudinal patterns and conditions of self-esteem change in the transition to young adulthood. *Journal of Personality and Social Psychology*, 104(1), 148–163. http://doi.org/10.1037/a0029680

Wagner, M. F., Milner, J. S., McCarthy, R. J., Crouch, J. L., McCanne, T. R., & Skowronski, J. J. (2015). Facial emotion recognition accuracy and child physical abuse: An experiment and a meta-analysis. *Psychology of Violence*, 5(2), 154–162. http://doi.org/10.1037/a0036014

Wagnsson, S., Lindwall, M., & Gustafsson, H. (2014). Participation in organized sport and self-esteem across adolescence: The mediating role of perceived sport competence. *Journal of Sport & Exercise Psychology*, 36(6), 584–94. http://doi.org/10.1123/jsep.2013-0137

Wakefield, W. D., & Hudley, C. (2007). Ethnic and racial identity and adolescent well-being. *Theory Into Practice*, 46(2), 147–154. http://doi.org/10.1080/00405840701233099

Waldeck, S. E. (2003). Social norm theory and male circumcision: Why parents circumcise. *American Journal of Bioethics*, 3(2), 56–57.

Waldfogel, J. (2006). Early childhood policy: A comparative perspective. In K. McCartney & D. Phillips (Eds.), *Blackwell handbook of early childhood development.* (pp. 576–594). Malden: Blackwell Publishing. Retrieved from h

Waldfogel, J., Craigie, T.-A., & Brooks-Gunn, J. (2010). Fragile families and child wellbeing. *The Future of Children*, 20(2), 87–112.

Waldman, I. D., Tackett, J. L., Van Hulle, C. A., Applegate, B., Pardini, D., Frick, P. J., & Lahey, B. B. (2011). Child and adolescent conduct disorder substantially shares genetic influences with three socioemotional dispositions. *Journal of Abnormal Psychology*, 120(1), 57–70. http://doi.org/10.1037/a0021351

Waldrip, A. M., Malcolm, K. T., & Jensen-Campbell, L. A. (2008). With a little help from your friends: The importance of high-quality friendships on early adolescent adjustment. *Social Development*, 17(4), 832–852. http://doi.org/10.1111/j.1467-9507.2008.00476.x

Waldron, N. L., & McLeskey, J. (1998). The effects of an inclusive school program on students with mild and severe learning disabilities. *Exceptional Children*, 64, 395–405.

Walk, R. D. (1968). Monocular compared to binocular depth perception in human infants. *Science*, 162, 473–475.

Walker, C. M., & Gopnik, A. (2013). Principles in causal learning, (November). http://doi.org/10.1177/0956797613502983

Walker, J. (2008). Osteoporosis: Pathogenesis, diagnosis and management. *Nursing Standard*, 22(17), 48–56.

Walker, L. J. (1989). A longitudinal study of moral reasoning. *Child Development*, 60(1), 157.

Walker, L. J. (2004). Progress and prospects in the psychology of moral development. *Merrill-Palmer Quarterly*, 50(4), 546–557.

Walker, L. J., & Taylor, J. H. (1991). Family interactions and the development of moral reasoning. *Child Development*, 62, 264–283.

Walker, S. (2005). Gender differences in the relationship between young children's peer-related social competence and individual differences in theory of mind. *Journal of Genetic Psychology*, 166(3), 297–312.

Wallerstein, J. S. (1994). The early psychological tasks of marriage: Part I. *American Journal of Orthopsychiatry*, 64(4), 640–650.

Wallerstein, J. S., & Lewis, J. M. (2004). The unexpected legacy of divorce: report of a 25-year study. *Psychoanalytic Psychology*, 21(3), 353–370.

Walpole, M. (2008). Emerging from the pipeline: African American students, socioeconomic status, and college experiences and outcomes. *Research in Higher Education*, 49(3), 237–255. http://doi.org/10.1007/s11162-007-9079-y

Walsh, B. A., & Blewitt, P. (2006). The effect of questioning style during storybook reading on novel vocabulary acquisition of preschoolers. *Early Childhood Education Journal*, 33(4), 273–278. http://doi.org/10.1007/s10643-005-0052-0

Walter, S., Atzmon, G., Demerath, E. W., Garcia, M. E., Kaplan, R. C., Kumari, M., . . . Evans, D. A. (2011). A genome-wide association study of aging. *Neurobiology of Aging*, 32(11), 2109.e15-2109.e28. http://doi.org/10.1016/j.neurobiolaging.2011.05.026

Waltes, R., Duketis, E., Knapp, M., Anney, R. J. L., Huguet, G., Schlitt, S., . . . Chiocchetti, A. G. (2014). Common variants in genes of the postsynaptic FMRP signalling pathway are risk factors for autism spectrum disorders. *Human Genetics*, 133(6), 781–92. http://doi.org/10.1007/s00439-013-1416-y

Walton, G. M., & Spencer, S. J. (2009). Latent ability: Grades and test scores systematically underestimate the intellectual ability of negatively stereotyped students. *Psychological Science*, 20(9), 1132–9. http://doi.org/10.1111/j.1467-9280.2009.02417.x

Walton, K., Kuczynski, L., Haycraft, E., Breen, A., & Haines, J. (2017). Time to re-think picky eating?: A relational approach to understanding picky eating. *The International Journal of Behavioral Nutrition and Physical Activity*, 14(1), 62. http://doi.org/10.1186/s12966-017-0520-0

Walvoord, E. C. (2010). The timing of puberty: is it changing? Does it matter? *The Journal of Adolescent Health : Official Publication of the Society for Adolescent Medicine*, 47(5), 433–9. http://doi.org/10.1016/j.jadohealth.2010.05.018

Wane, S., Van Uffelen, J. G. Z., & Brown, W. (2010). Determinants of weight gain in young women: A review of the literature. *Journal of Women's Health (15409996)*, 19(7), 1327–1340. http://doi.org/10.1089/jwh.2009.1738

Wang, C., Xia, Y., Li, W., Wilson, S. M., Bush, K., & Peterson, G. (2014). Parenting behaviors, adolescent depressive symptoms, and problem behavior: The role of self-esteem and school adjustment difficulties among chinese adolescents. *Journal of Family Issues*. http://doi.org/10.1177/0192513X14542433

Wang, D., Kato, N., Inaba, Y., Tango, T., Yoshida, Y., Kusaka, Y., . . . Zhang, Q. (2000). Physical and personality traits of preschool children in Fuzhou, China: Only child vs sibling. *Child: Care, Health & Development*, 26(1), 49–60.

Wang, F., Christ, S. L., Mills-Koonce, W. R., Garrett-Peters, P., & Cox, M. J. (2013). Association between Maternal sensitivity and Externalizing Behavior from Preschool to Preadolescence. *Journal of Applied Developmental Psychology*, 34(2), 89–100. http://doi.org/10.1016/j.appdev.2012.11.003

Wang, G. S., Le Lait, M.-C., Deakyne, S. J., Bronstein, A. C., Bajaj, L., & Roosevelt, G. (2016). Unintentional pediatric exposures to marijuana in Colorado, 2009-2015. *JAMA Pediatrics*, 170(9), e160971. http://doi.org/10.1001/jamapediatrics.2016.0971

Wang, H., Lin, S. L., Leung, G. M., & Schooling, C. M. (2016). Age at onset of puberty and adolescent depression: Children of 1997 birth cohort. *Pediatrics*, 137(6), e20153231–e20153231. http://doi.org/10.1542/peds.2015-3231

Wang, J., Sun, X., & Yang, Q. X. (2016). Early aging effect on the function of the human central olfactory system. *The Journals of Gerontology Series A: Biological Sciences and Medical Sciences*, 21(2), glw104. http://doi.org/10.1093/gerona/glw104

Wang, M., Henkens, K., & van Solinge, H. (2011). A review of theoretical and empirical advancements. *The American Psychologist*, 66(3), 204–213. http://doi.org/10.1037/a0022414

Wang, M.-T., & Dishion, T. J. (2012). The Trajectories of adolescents' perceptions of school climate, deviant peer affiliation, and behavioral problems during the middle school years. *Journal of Research on Adolescence*, 22(1), 40–53. http://doi.org/10.1111/j.1532-7795.2011.00763.x

Wang, M.-T., & Fredricks, J. A. The reciprocal links between school engagement, youth problem behaviors, and school dropout during adolescence. *Child Development*, 85(2), 722–37. http://doi.org/10.1111/cdev.12138

Wang, M.-T., & Kenny, S. (2014). Parental physical punishment and adolescent adjustment: Bidirectionality and the moderation effects of child ethnicity and parental warmth. *Journal of Abnormal Child Psychology*, 42(5), 717–730. http://doi.org/10.1007/s10802-013-9827-8

Wang, M.-T., & Sheikh-Khalil, S. Does parental involvement matter for student achievement and mental health in high school? *Child Development*, 85(2), 610–25. http://doi.org/10.1111/cdev.12153

Wang, M.-T., Dishion, T. J., Stormshak, E. A., & Willett, J. B. (2011). Trajectories of family management practices and early adolescent behavioral outcomes. *Developmental Psychology*, 47(5), 1324–41. http://doi.org/10.1037/a0024026

Wang, S., & Young, K. M. (2014). White matter plasticity in adulthood. *Neuroscience*, 276, 148–60. http://doi.org/10.1016/j.neuroscience.2013.10.018

Wang, S., Luo, X., Barnes, D., Sano, M., & Yaffe, K. (2014). Physical activity and risk of cognitive impairment among oldest-old women. *The American Journal of Geriatric Psychiatry : Official Journal of the American Association for Geriatric Psychiatry*, 22(11), 1149–57. http://doi.org/10.1016/j.jagp.2013.03.002

Wang, S., Zhang, Y., & Baillargeon, R. (2016). *Young infants view physically possible support events as unexpected: New evidence for rule learning. Cognition* (Vol. 157).

Wang, W., & Parker, K. (2014). *Record share of Americans have never married.* Retrieved from http://www.pewsocialtrends.org/2014/09/24/record-share-of-americans-have-never-married/

Wang, X., Bernas, R., & Eberhard, P. (2008). Responding to children's everyday transgressions in Chinese working-class families. *Journal of Moral Education*, 37(1), 55–79. http://doi.org/10.1080/03057240701803684

Wang, Y., & Lim, H. (2012). The global childhood obesity epidemic and the association between socio-economic status and childhood obesity. *International Review of Psychiatry (Abingdon, England)*, 24(3), 176–88. http://doi.org/10.3109/09540261.2012.688195

Wang, Y.-N., Shyu, Y.-I. L., Chen, M.-C., & Yang, P.-S. (2011). Reconciling work and family caregiving among adult-child family caregivers of older people with dementia: Effects on role strain and depressive symptoms. *Journal of Advanced Nursing*, 67(4), 829–40. http://doi.org/10.1111/j.1365-2648.2010.05505.x

Wängqvist, M., Carlsson, J., van der Lee, M., & Frisén, A. (2016). Identity development and romantic relationships in the late twenties. *Identity*, 16(1), 24–44. http://doi.org/10.1080/15283488.2015.1121819

Wängqvist, M., Lamb, M. E., Frisén, A., & Hwang, C. P. (2015). Child and adolescent predictors of personality in early adulthood. *Child Development*. http://doi.org/10.1111/cdev.12362

Wannamethee, S. G., Shaper, A. G., & Alberti, K. G. (2000). Physical activity, metabolic factors, and the incidence of coronary heart disease and type 2 diabetes. *Archives of Internal Medicine, 160*(14), 2108–2116.

Ward, B. W., Dahlhamer, J. M., Galinsky, A. M., & Joestl, S. S. (2014). Sexual orientation and health among U.S. adults: National health interview survey, 2013. *National Health Statistics Reports, 77,* 1–10. Retrieved from http://www.ncbi.nlm.nih.gov/pubmed/25025690

Ward, L., Mathias, J. L., & Hitchings, S. E. (2007). Relationships between bereavement and cognitive functioning in older adults. *Gerontology, 53*(6), 362–372. http://doi.org/10.1159/000104787

Ward, R. A., & Spitze, G. D. (2007). Nestleaving and coresidence by young adult children: The role of family relations. *Research on Aging, 29*(3), 257–277.

Ware, R. E., de Montalembert, M., Tshilolo, L., & Abboud, M. R. (2017). Sickle cell disease. *The Lancet.* http://doi.org/10.1016/S0140-6736(17)30193-9

Waren, W., & Pals, H. (2013). Comparing characteristics of voluntarily childless men and women. *Journal of Population Research, 30*(2), 151–170. http://doi.org/10.1007/s12546-012-9103-8

Wark, G. R., & Krebs, D. L. (1996). Gender and dilemma differences in real-life moral judgment. *Developmental Psychology, 32,* 220–231.

Warneken, F., Lohse, K., Melis, A. P., & Tomasello, M. (2011). Young children share the spoils after collaboration. *Psychological Science, 22*(2), 267–273. http://doi.org/10.1177/0956797610395392

Warneken, F., & Tomasello, M. (2006). Altruistic helping in human infants and young chimpanzees. *Science, 311*(5765), 1301–1303.

Warner, T. D., Giordano, P. C., Manning, W. D., & Longmore, M. A. (2011). Everybody's doin' it (right?): Neighborhood norms and sexual activity in adolescence. *Social Science Research, 40*(6), 1676–1690. http://doi.org/10.1016/j.ssresearch.2011.06.009

Warr, P. (2007). *Work, happiness, and unhappiness.* Mahwah, NJ: Lawrence Erlbaum.

Warren, A. R., & Lane, P. (1995). Effects of timing and type of questioning on eyewitness accuracy and suggestibility. In M. S. Zaragoza, J. R. Graham, G. C. N. Hall, R. Hirschman, & Y. S. Ben-Porath (Eds.), *Memory and testimony in the child witness* (pp. 44–60). Thousand Oaks, CA: SAGE.

Warren, J. R., & Saliba, J. (2012). First- through eighth-grade retention rates for all 50 states: A new method and initial results. *Educational Researcher, 41*(8), 320–329. http://doi.org/10.3102/0013189X12457813

Warren, K. R., Hewitt, B. G., & Thomas, J. D. (2011). Fetal alcohol spectrum disorders: Research challenges and opportunities. *Alcohol Research & Health, 34*(1), 4–14.

Warren, Z., McPheeters, M. L., Sathe, N., Foss-Feig, J. H., Glasser, A., & Veenstra-VanderWeele, J. (2011). A systematic review of early intensive intervention for autism spectrum disorders. *Pediatrics, 127*(5). doi:10.1542/peds.2011-0426

Wartella, E. A., & Lauricella, A. R. (2012). Should babies be watching television and DVDs? *Pediatric Clinics of North America, 59*(3), 613–621. http://doi.org/10.1016/j.pcl.2012.03.027

Wass, R., & Golding, C. (2014). Sharpening a tool for teaching: The zone of proximal development. *Teaching in Higher Education, 19*(6), 671–684. http://doi.org/10.1080/13562517.2014.901958

Watamura, S. E., Phillips, D. A., Morrissey, T. W., McCartney, K., & Bub, K. (2011). Double jeopardy: Poorer social-emotional outcomes for children in the NICHD SECCYD experiencing home and child-care environments that confer risk. *Child Development, 82*(1), 48–65. http://doi.org/10.1111/j.1467-8624.2010.01540.x

Watanabe, H., Forssman, L., Green, D., Bohlin, G., & von Hofsten, C. (2012). Attention demands influence 10- and 12-month-old infants' perseverative behavior. *Developmental Psychology, 48*(1), 46–55. http://doi.org/10.1037/a0025412

Waterhouse, L. (2006). Multiple intelligences, the Mozart effect, and emotional intelligence: A critical review. *Educational Psychologist, 41*(4), 207–225. http://doi.org/10.1207/s15326985ep4104_1

Waterland, R. A., & Jirtle, R. L. (2003). Transposable elements: Targets for early nutritional effects on epigenetic gene regulation. *Molecular and Cellular Biology, 23*(15), 5293–300.

Waters, E., Matas, L., & Sroufe, L. A. (1975). Infants' reactions to an approaching stranger: Description, validation, and functional significance of wariness. *Child Development, 46*(2), 348–356.

Waters, E., Merrick, S., Treboux, D., Crowell, J., & Albersheim, L. (2000). Attachment security in infancy and early adulthood: A twenty-year longitudinal study. *Child Development, 71,* 684–689.

Waters, S. F., West, T. V., & Mendes, W. B. (2014). Stress contagion: Physiological covariation between mothers and infants. *Psychological Science, 25*(4), 934–942. http://doi.org/10.1177/0956797613518352

Waters, S. K., Lester, L., & Cross, D. (2014). Transition to secondary school: Expectation versus experience. *Australian Journal of Education, 58*(2), 153–166. http://doi.org/10.1177/0004944114523371

Watkins, M. W., & Smith, L. G. (2013). Long-term stability of the *Wechsler Intelligence Scale for Children—Fourth Edition. Psychological Assessment, 25*(3), 477–483. http://doi.org/10.1037/a0031653

Watson, G. (2008). *Genetics and health.* Washington, DC: Genetics and Public Policy Center. Retrieved from http://www.dnapolicy.org/science.gh.php

Watson, J. (1925). *Behaviorism.* New York, NY: Norton.

Watson, N. F., Martin, J. L., Wise, M. S., Carden, K. A., Kirsch, D. B., Kristo, D. A., . . . American Academy of Sleep Medicine Board of Directors. (2017). Delaying middle school and high school start times promotes student health and performance: An American Academy of Sleep Medicine position statement. *Journal of Clinical Sleep Medicine, 13*(4), 623–625. http://doi.org/10.5664/jcsm.6558

Watson, S. M. R., & Gable, R. A. (2013). Unraveling the complex nature of mathematics learning disability: Implications for research and practice. *Learning Disability Quarterly, 36*(3), 178–187. http://doi.org/10.1177/0731948712461489

Watson, T. L., & Blanchard-Fields, F. (1998). Thinking with your head and your heart: Age differences in everyday problem-solving strategy preferences. *Aging, Neuropsychology, and Cognition, 5*(3), 225–240.

Waxman, S. R., & Hatch, T. (1992). Beyond the basics: Preschool children label objects flexibly at multiple hierarchical level. *Journal of Child Language, 19,* 153–166.

Waxman, S., Fu, X., Arunachalam, S., Leddon, E., Geraghty, K., & Song, H. (2013). Are nouns learned before verbs? Infants provide insight into a long-standing debate. *Child Development Perspectives, 7*(3), 155–159. http://doi.org/10.1111/cdep.12032

Way, N., Reddy, R., & Rhodes, J. (2007). Students' perceptions of school climate during the middle school years: Associations with trajectories of psychological and behavioral adjustment. *American Journal of Community Psychology, 40*(3–4), 194–213. http://doi.org/10.1007/s10464-007-9143-y

Way, N., Santos, C., Niwa, E. Y., & Kim-Gervey, C. (2008). To be or not to be: An exploration of ethnic identity development in context. *New Directions for Child & Adolescent Development, 2008*(120), 61–79.

Weaver, C. M., Gordon, C. M., Janz, K. F., Kalkwarf, H. J., Lappe, J. M., Lewis, R., . . . Zemel, B. S. (2016). The National Osteoporosis Foundation's position statement on peak bone mass development and lifestyle factors: A systematic review and implementation recommendations. *Osteoporosis International, 27*(4), 1281–386. http://doi.org/10.1007/s00198-015-3440-3

Weaver, J. M., & Schofield, T. J. (2014). Mediation and moderation of divorce effects on children's behavior problems. *Journal of Family Psychology.* Retrieved from http://dx.doi.org/10.1037/fam0000043

Weaver, J., Crespi, S., Tosetti, M., & Morrone, M. (2015). Map of visual activity in the infant brain sheds light on neural development. *PLOS Biology, 13*(9), e1002261. http://doi.org/10.1371/journal.pbio.1002261

Webster, J. D., Bohlmeijer, E. T., & Westerhof, G. J. (2010). Mapping the future of reminiscence: A conceptual guide for research and practice. *Research on Aging, 32*(4), 527–564. http://doi.org/10.1177/0164027510364122

Wechsler, D. (1944). *The measurement of adult intelligence* (3rd ed.). Baltimore, MD: Williams & Wilkins.

Wechsler, D. (2008). *Wechsler adult intelligence scale* (4th ed.). San Antonio, TX: Pearson.

Wechsler, D. (2012). *Wechsler preschool and primary scale of intelligence* (4th ed.). San Antonio, TX: Pearson.

Wechsler, D. (2014). *Wechsler intelligence scale for children* (5th ed.). San Antonio, TX: NCS Pearson.

Weerdesteyn, V., Nienhuis, B., Geurts, A. C. H., & Duysens, J. (2007). Age-related deficits in early response characteristics of obstacle avoidance under time pressure. *Journals of Gerontology Series A: Biological Sciences & Medical Sciences, 62A*(9), 1042–1047.

Wei, W., Lu, H., Zhao, H., Chen, C., Dong, Q., & Zhou, X. (2012). Gender differences in children's arithmetic performance are accounted for by gender differences in language abilities. *Psychological Science, 23*(3), 320–330. http://doi.org/10.1177/0956797611427168

Weil, L. G., Fleming, S. M., Dumontheil, I., Kilford, E. J., Weil, R. S., Rees, G., . . . Blakemore, S.-J. (2013). The development of metacognitive ability in adolescence. *Consciousness and Cognition, 22*(1), 264–271.

Weinberg, M. K., & Tronick, E. Z. (1994). Beyond the face: An empirical study of infant affective configurations of facial, vocal, gestural, and regulatory behaviors. *Child Development, 65,* 1503–1515.

Weinberg, M. K., & Tronick, E. Z. (1996). Infants' affective reactions to the resumption of maternal interaction after the still-face. *Child Development, 67,* 905–914.

Weinberg, M. K., Tronick, E. Z., Cohn, J. F., & Olson, K. L. (1999). Gender differences in emotional expressivity and self-regulation during early infancy. *Developmental Psychology, 35*(1), 175–188. http://doi.org/10.1037/0012-1649.35.1.175

Weinfield, N. S., Sroufe, L. A., & Egeland, B. (2000). Attachment from infancy to early adulthood in a high-risk sample: Continuity, discontinuity, and their correlates. *Child Development, 71,* 695–702.

REFERENCES

Weinfield, N. S., Sroufe, L. A., Egeland, B., & Carlson, E. (2008). Individual differences in infant-caregiver attachment: Conceptual and empirical aspects of security. In J. Cassidy & P. R. Shaver (Eds.), *Handbook of attachment: Theory, research, and clinical applications.* New York, NY: Guilford Press.

Weinhold, B. (2009). Environmental factors in birth defects. *Environmental Health Perspectives, 117*(10), A440–A447.

Weis, R. (2013). *Introduction to abnormal child and adolescent psychology* (2nd ed.). Thousand Oaks, CA: SAGE.

Weis, R., & Toolis, E. E. (2010). Parenting across cultural contexts in the USA: Assessing parenting behaviour in an ethnically and socioeconomically diverse sample. *Early Child Development & Care, 180*(7), 849–867. http://doi.org/10.1080/03004430802472083

Weisgram, E. S. (2016). The cognitive construction of gender stereotypes: Evidence for the dual pathways model of gender differentiation. *Sex Roles, 75*(7–8), 301–313. http://doi.org/10.1007/s11199-016-0624-z

Weisleder, A., & Fernald, A. (2013). Talking to children matters: Early language experience strengthens processing and builds vocabulary. *Psychological Science, 24*(11), 2143–2152. http://doi.org/10.1177/0956797613488145

Weiss, B., Dodge, K. A., Bates, J. E., & Pettit, G. S. (1992). Some consequences of early harsh discipline: Child aggression and a maladaptive social information processing style. *Child Development, 63,* 1321–1335.

Weiss, D., & Lang, F. R. (2012). "They" are old but "I" feel younger: Age-group dissociation as a self-protective strategy in old age. *Psychology and Aging, 27*(1), 153–163. http://doi.org/10.1037/a0024887

Weisz, A. N., & Black, B. M. (2002). Gender and moral reasoning: African American youth respond to dating dilemmas. *Journal of Human Behavior in the Social Environment, 5*(1), 35–52.

Weisz, A. N., & Black, B. M. (2008). Peer intervention in dating violence: Beliefs of African-American middle school adolescents. *Journal of Ethnic & Cultural Diversity in Social Work, 17*(2), 177–196. http://doi.org/10.1080/15313200801947223

Weitzen, S., Teno, J. M., Fennell, M., & Mor, V. (2003). Factors associated with site of death: A national study of where people die. *Medical Care, 41*(2), 323–335. http://doi.org/10.1097/01.MLR.0000044913.37084.27

Weitzner, M. A., Haley, W. E., & Chen, H. (2000). The family caregiver of the older cancer patient. *Hematology/Oncology Clinics of North America, 14*(1), 269–281. http://doi.org/10.1016/S0889-8588(05)70288-4

Wellman, H. M. (1977). Tip of the tongue and feeling of knowing experience: A developmental study of memory monitoring. *Child Development, 48*(1), 13–21.

Wellman, H. M., & Banerjee, M. (1991). Mind and emotion: Children's understanding of the emotional consequences of beliefs and desires. *British Journal of Developmental Psychology, 9,* 191–214.

Wellman, H. M., Cross, D., & Watson, J. (2001). Meta-analysis of theory-of-mind development: The truth about false belief. *Child Development, 72*(3), 655.

Wellman, H. M., Fang, F., & Peterson, C. C. (2011). Sequential progressions in a theory-of-mind scale: Longitudinal perspectives. *Child Development, 82*(3), 780–792. http://doi.org/10.1111/j.1467-8624.2011.01583.x

Wellman, H. M., & Liu, D. (2004). Scaling of theory-of-mind tasks. *Child Development, 75*(2), 523–541.

Wellman, H. M., Phillips, A. T., & Rodriguez, T. (2000). Young children's understanding of perception, desire, and emotion. *Child Development, 71,* 895–912.

Wellman, H. M., Somerville, S. C., & Haake, R. J. (1979). Development of search procedures in real-life spatial environments. *Developmental Psychology, 15,* 530–542.

Wells Fargo. (2014). *2014 Wells Fargo middle class retirement study.* Retrieved from https://www08.wellsfargomedia.com/downloads/pdf/com/retirement-employee-benefits/insights/2014-retirement-study.pdf

Welmer, A.-K., Rizzuto, D., Laukka, E. J., Johnell, K., & Fratiglioni, L. (2016). Cognitive and physical function in relation to the risk of injurious falls in older adults: A population-based study. *The Journals of Gerontology Series A: Biological Sciences and Medical Sciences, 68*(5). http://doi.org/10.1093/gerona/glw141

Welshman, J. (2010). From Head Start to Sure Start: Reflections on policy transfer. *Children & Society, 24*(2), 89–99. http://doi.org/10.1111/j.1099-0860.2008.00201.x

Welsman, J. R., Armstrong, N., Kirby, B. J., Winsley, R. J., Parsons, G., & Sharpe, P. (1997). Exercise performance and magnetic resonance imaging-determined thigh muscle volume in children. *European Journal of Applied Physiology and Occupational Physiology, 76*(1), 92–97. http://doi.org/10.1007/s004210050218

Wentzel, K. R. (2002). Are effective teachers like good parents? Teaching styles and student adjustment in early adolescence. *Child Development, 73*(1), 287–301.

Wentzel, K. R. (2014). Prosocial behavior and peer relations in adolescence. In G. C. Laura & M. Padilla-Walker (Ed.), *Prosocial development: A multidimensional approach* (pp. 178–200.). London, UK: Oxford University Press.

Werker, J. (2012). Perceptual foundations of bilingual acquisition in infancy. *Annals of the New York Academy of Sciences, 1251*(1), 50–61. http://doi.org/10.1111/j.1749-6632.2012.06484.x

Werker, J. F., Yeung, H. H., & Yoshida, K. A. (2012). How do infants become experts at native-speech perception? *Current Directions in Psychological Science, 21*(4), 221–226. http://doi.org/10.1177/0963721412449459

Werner, E. E. (1991). Grandparent-grandchild relationships amongst U.S. ethnic groups. In P. K. Smith (Ed.), *The psychology of grandparenthood: An international perspective* (pp. 68–82). Florence, KY: Taylor & Frances/Routledge.

Werner, E. E. (1995). Resilience in development. *Current Directions in Psychological Science, 4*(3), 81–85.

Werner, E. E. (2012). Children and war: Risk, resilience, and recovery. *Development and Psychopathology, 24*(2), 553–558. Retrieved from http://journals.cambridge.org/abstract_S0954579412000156

Werner, N. E., & Crick, N. R. (2004). Maladaptive peer relationships and the development of relational and physical aggression during middle childhood. *Social Development, 13*(4), 495–514.

Wertheimer, M. (1961). Psychomotor coordination of auditory and visual space at birth. *Science, 134,* 1692.

Wertlieb, D. (2003). Applied developmental science. In R. M. Lerner, M. A. Easterbrooks, & J. Mistry (Eds.), *Handbook of psychology: Developmental psychology* (Vol. 6, pp. 43–64). New York, NY: Wiley.

Wertsch, J. V. (1998). *Mind as action.* New York: Oxford University Press.

Wesche, R., Kreager, D. A., Lefkowitz, E. S., & Siennick, S. E. (2017). Early sexual initiation and mental health: A fleeting association or enduring change? *Journal of Research on Adolescence.* http://doi.org/10.1111/jora.12303

Wesley, M. J., Hanlon, C. A., & Porrino, L. J. (2011). Poor decision-making by chronic marijuana users is associated with decreased functional responsiveness to negative consequences. *Psychiatry Research: Neuroimaging Section, 191*(1), 51–59. http://doi.org/10.1016/j.pscychresns.2010.10.002

West, T. C. (2009). *Still a freshman: Examining the prevalence and characteristics of ninth-grade retention across six states.* Baltimore, MD: Johns Hopkins University Press.

Westen, D. (1998). The scientific legacy of Sigmund Freud: Toward a psychodynamically informed psychological science. *Psychological Bulletin, 124,* 333–371.

Westerhof, G. J. (2015). Life review and life-story work. In S. Krauss Whitbourne (Ed.), *The encyclopedia of adulthood and aging* (pp. 1–5). Hoboken, NJ: John Wiley & Sons. http://doi.org/10.1002/9781118521373.wbeaa209

Westerhof, G. J., & Bohlmeijer, E. T. (2014). Celebrating fifty years of research and applications in reminiscence and life review: State of the art and new directions. *Journal of Aging Studies, 29,* 107–114. http://doi.org/10.1016/j.jaging.2014.02.003

Westerhof, G. J., Bohlmeijer, E., & Webster, J. D. (2010). Reminiscence and mental health: A review of recent progress in theory, research and interventions. *Ageing & Society, 30*(4), 697–721.

Wethington, E. (2000). Expecting stress: Americans and the "midlife crisis." *Motivation and Emotion, 24*(2), 85–103.

Wethington, E., Kessler, R. C., & Pixley, J. E. (2004). Turning points in adulthood. In O. G. Brim, C. D. Ryff, & R. C. Kessler (Eds.), *How healthy are we? A national study of well-being at midlife* (pp. 586–613). Chicago, IL: University of Chicago Press.

Weymouth, B. B., Buehler, C., Zhou, N., & Henson, R. A. (2016). A meta-analysis of parent-adolescent conflict: Disagreement, hostility, and youth maladjustment. *Journal of Family Theory & Review, 8*(1), 95–112. http://doi.org/10.1111/jftr.12126

Wheeler, I. (2001). Parental bereavement: The crisis of meaning. *Death Studies, 25*(1), 51–66. http://doi.org/10.1080/074811801750058627

Wheeler, J. A., Kenney, K., & Temple, V. (2013). Fetal alcohol spectrum disorder: Exploratory investigation of services and interventions for adults. *Journal on Developmental Disabilities, 19*(3), 62–75.

Whelan, R., Watts, R., Orr, C. A., Althoff, R. R., Artiges, E., Banaschewski, T., . . . IMAGEN Consortium. (2014). Neuropsychosocial profiles of current and future adolescent alcohol misusers. *Nature, 512*(7513), 185–189. http://doi.org/10.1038/nature13402

Whitam, F. L. (1983). Culturally invariable properties of male homosexuality: Tentative conclusions from cross-cultural research. *Archives of Sexual Behavior, 12*(3), 207–226. http://doi.org/10.1007/BF01542072

Whitbeck, L., & Hoyt, D. R. (1994). Early family relationships, intergenerational solidarity, and support provided to parents by their adult children. *Journal of Gerontology, 49*(2), S85–S94.

Whitbourne, S. K. (2007). *Adult development and aging: Biopsychosocial perspectives.* New York, NY: Wiley.

White, C. N., & Warner, L. A. (2015). Influence of family and school-level factors on age of sexual initiation. *The Journal of Adolescent Health*, *56*(2), 231–237. http://doi.org/10.1016/j.jadohealth.2014.09.017

White, E. S., & Mistry, R. S. (2016). Parent civic beliefs, civic participation, socialization practices, and child civic engagement. *Applied Developmental Science*, *20*(1), 44–60. http://doi.org/10.1080/10888691.2015.1049346

White, H.-R., & Jackson, K. (2005). Social and psychological influences on emerging adult drinking behavior. *Alcohol Research & Health*, *28*(4), 182–190.

White, K. M. (2013). Associations between teacher–child relationships and children's writing in kindergarten and first grade. *Early Childhood Research Quarterly*, *28*(1), 166–176. http://doi.org/10.1016/j.ecresq.2012.05.004

White, L. (1994). Coresidence and leaving home: Young adults and their parents. *Annual Review of Sociology*, *20*(1), 81–102.

White, L., & Rogers, S. J. (2000). Economic circumstances and family outcomes: A review of the 1990s. *Journal of Marriage and the Family*, *62*, 1035–1051.

Whiteside, M. F., & Becker, B. J. (2000). Parental factors and the young child's postdivorce adjustment: A meta-analysis with implications for parenting arrangements. *Journal of Family Psychology*, *14*, 5–26.

Whiting, B., & Edwards, C. P. (1988). A cross-cultural analysis of sex differences in the behavior of children aged 3 through 11. In G. Handel (Ed.), *Childhood socialization* (pp. 281–297). New York, NY: Aldine de Gruyter.

Whiting, B., & Whiting, J. W. (1975). *Children of six cultures: A psycho-cultural analysis*. Cambridge, MA: Harvard University Press.

Whiting, J. B., Smith, D. R., Barnett, T., & Grafsky, E. L. (2007). Overcoming the Cinderella myth: A mixed methods study of successful stepmothers. *Journal of Divorce & Remarriage*, *47*(1/2), 95–109.

Whiting, P., & Bradley, L. J. (2007). Artful witnessing of the story: Loss in aging adults. *Adultspan: Theory Research & Practice*, *6*(2), 119–128.

Widaman, K. F. (2009). Phenylketonuria in children and mothers: Genes, environments, behavior. *Current Directions in Psychological Science*, *18*(1), 48–52. http://doi.org/10.1111/j.1467-8721.2009.01604.x

Widarsson, M., Engström, G., Rosenblad, A., Kerstis, B., Edlund, B., & Lundberg, P. (2013). Parental stress in early parenthood among mothers and fathers in Sweden. *Scandinavian Journal of Caring Sciences*, *27*(4), 839–847. http://doi.org/10.1111/j.1471-6712.2012.01088.x

Widman, L., Choukas-Bradley, S., Noar, S. M., Nesi, J., & Garrett, K. (2016). Parent-adolescent sexual communication and adolescent safer sex behavior: A meta-analysis. *JAMA Pediatrics*, *170*(1), 52–61. http://doi.org/10.1001/jamapediatrics.2015.2731

Widom, C. S. (2014). Longterm consequences of child maltreatment. In J. E. Korbin & R. D. Krugman (Eds.), *Handbook of child maltreatment* (Vol. 2, pp. 225–247). Dordrecht, NL: Springer. http://doi.org/10.1007/978-94-007-7208-3

Wiegand, C., Raschke, C., & Elsner, P. (2017). Skin aging: A brief summary of characteristic changes. In M. A. Farage, K. W. Miller, & H. I. Maibac (Eds.), *Textbook of aging skin* (pp. 55–65). Berlin, DE: Springer. http://doi.org/10.1007/978-3-662-47398-6_5

Wierenga, L. M., Sexton, J. A., Laake, P., Giedd, J. N., & Tamnes, C. K. (2017). A key characteristic of sex differences in the developing brain: Greater variability in brain structure of boys than girls. *Cerebral Cortex*, *17*(14), 1–11. https://doi.org/10.1093/cercor/bhx154

Wigfield, A., & Eccles, J. S. (1994). Children's competence beliefs, achievement values, and general self-esteem. *Journal of Early Adolescence*, *14*(2), 107–139.

Wigfield, A., Eccles, J. S., Fredricks, J. A., Simpkins, S., Roeser, R. W., Schiefele, U., . . . Schiefele, U. (2015). Development of achievement motivation and engagement. In *Handbook of child psychology and developmental science* (pp. 1–44). Hoboken, NJ: John Wiley & Sons. http://doi.org/10.1002/9781118963418.childpsy316

Wigfield, A., Muenks, K., & Rosenzweig, E. Q. (2015). Children's achievement motivation in school. In C. M. Rubie-Davies, J. M. Stephens, & P. Watson (Eds.), *Routledge international handbook of social psychology of the classroom* (pp. 9–20). London: Routledge.

Wight, R. G., Leblanc, A. J., & Lee Badgett, M. V. (2013). Same-sex legal marriage and psychological well-being: Findings from the California Health Interview Survey. *American Journal of Public Health*, *103*(2), 339–346. http://doi.org/10.2105/AJPH.2012.301113

Wight, R. G., LeBlanc, A. J., de Vries, B., & Detels, R. (2012). Stress and mental health among midlife and older gay-identified men. *American Journal of Public Health*, *102*(3), 503–10. http://doi.org/10.2105/AJPH.2011.300384

Wiik, K. L., & Gunnar, M. R. (2009). Development and social regulation of stress neurobiology in human development. In J. Quas & R. Fivush (Eds.), *Emotion in memory and development* (pp. 256–277). London, UK: Oxford University Press. http://doi.org/10.1093/acprof:oso/9780195326932.003.0010

Wiik, K. L., Loman, M. M., Van Ryzin, M. J., Armstrong, J. M., Essex, M. J., Pollak, S. D., & Gunnar, M. R. (2011). Behavioral and emotional symptoms of post-institutionalized children in middle childhood. *Journal of Child Psychology & Psychiatry*, *52*(1), 56–63. http://doi.org/10.1111/j.1469-7610.2010.02294.x

Wijngaards-de Meij, L., Stroebe, M., Schut, H., Stroebe, W., van den Bout, J., van der Heijden, P. G. M., & Dijkstra, I. (2008). Parents grieving the loss of their child: Interdependence in coping. *British Journal of Clinical Psychology*, *47*(1), 31–42. http://doi.org/10.1348/014466507x216152

Wilk, S. L., Desmarais, L. B., & Sackett, P. R. (1995). Gravitation to jobs commensurate with ability: Longitudinal and cross-sectional tests. *Journal of Applied Psychology*, *80*(1), 79–85.

Wilkinson, P. O., Trzaskowski, M., Haworth, C. M. A., & Eley, T. C. (2013). The role of gene–environment correlations and interactions in middle childhood depressive symptoms. *Development and Psychopathology*, *25*(1), 93–104. http://doi.org/10.1017/S0954579412000922

Will, G.-J., van Lier, P. A. C., Crone, E. A., & Güroğlu, B. (2016). Chronic childhood peer rejection is associated with heightened neural responses to social exclusion during adolescence. *Journal of Abnormal Child Psychology*, *44*(1), 43–55. http://doi.org/10.1007/s10802-015-9983-0

Williams, E. (2015). *Pre-kindergarten across states*. Retrieved from http://www.edcentral.org/prekstatefunding/

Williams, J. E., & Best, D. L. (1982). *Measuring sex stereotypes: A thirty-nation study*. Beverly Hills, CA: SAGE.

Williams, J. L., Aiyer, S. M., Durkee, M. I., & Tolan, P. H. (2014). The protective role of ethnic identity for urban adolescent males facing multiple stressors. *Journal of Youth and Adolescence*, *43*(10), 1728–1741. http://doi.org/10.1007/s10964-013-0071-x

Williams, J., Mai, C. T., Mulinare, J., Isenburg, J., Flood, T. J., Ethen, M., . . . Centers for Disease Control and Prevention. (2015). Updated estimates of neural tube defects prevented by mandatory folic acid fortification: United States, 1995–2011. *Morbidity and Mortality Weekly Report*, *64*(1), 1–5. Retrieved from http://www.ncbi.nlm.nih.gov/pubmed/25590678

Williams, L., Kabamalan, M., & Ogena, N. (2007). Cohabitation in the Philippines: Attitudes and behaviors among young women and men. *Journal of Marriage & Family*, *69*(5), 1244–1256.

Williams, M. N. (2011). The changing roles of grandparents raising grandchildren. *Journal of Human Behavior in the Social Environment*, *21*(8), 948–962. http://doi.org/10.1080/10911359.2011.588535

Williams, N., & Torrez, D. J. (1998). Grandparenthood among Hispanics. In M. E. Szinovacz (Ed.), *Handbook on grandparenthood* (pp. 87–96). Westport, CT: Greenwood Press.

Williams, R. (2007). The psychosocial consequences for children of mass violence, terrorism and disasters. *International Review of Psychiatry*, *19*(3), 263–277. http://doi.org/10.1080/09540260701349480

Williams, R. L. (2013). Overview of the Flynn effect. *Intelligence*, *41*(6), 753–764. http://doi.org/10.1016/j.intell.2013.04.010

Williams, T. S., Connolly, J., Pepler, D., Laporte, L., & Craig, W. (2008). Risk models of dating aggression across different adolescent relationships: A developmental psychopathology approach. *Journal of Consulting and Clinical Psychology*, *76*(4), 622–632. http://doi.org/10.1037/0022-006x.76.4.622

Willinger, M., Ko, C.-W., Hoffman, H. J., Kessler, R. C., & Corwin, M. J. (2003). Trends in infant bed sharing in the United States, 1993–2000. *Archives of Pediatrics and Adolescent Medicine*, *157*, 43–49.

Willis, J. (2007). Which brain research can educators trust? *Phi Delta Kappan*, *88*(9), 697–699.

Wilson, B. J. (2006). The entry behavior of aggressive/rejected children: The contributions of status and temperament. *Social Development*, *15*(3), 463–479.

Wilson, G. T., Grilo, C. M., & Vitousek, K. M. (2007). Psychological treatment of eating disorders. *American Psychologist*, *62*(3), 199–216.

Wilson, L. C., & Miller, K. E. (2016). Meta-analysis of the prevalence of unacknowledged rape. *Trauma, Violence, & Abuse*, *17*(2), 149–159. http://doi.org/10.1177/1524838015576391

Wilson, R. S., & Harpring, E. B. (1972). Mental and motor development in infant twins. *Developmental Psychology*, *7*(3), 277–287.

Wilson, S. L. (2003). Post-institutionalization: The effects of early deprivation on development of Romanian adoptees. *Child & Adolescent Social Work Journal*, *20*(6), 473–483.

Wilson, S. L., & Weaver, T. L. (2009). Follow-up of developmental attainment and behavioral adjustment for toddlers adopted internationally into the USA. *International Social Work*, *52*(5), 679–684. http://doi.org/10.1177/0020872809337684

Wilson, S., Schalet, B. D., Hicks, B. M., & Zucker, R. A. (2013). Identifying early childhood personality dimensions using the California Child Q-Set and prospective associations with behavioral and psychosocial development. *Journal of Research in Personality*, *47*(4), 339–350. http://doi.org/10.1016/j.jrp.2013.02.010

Wilt, J., Cox, K., & McAdams, D. P. (2010). The Eriksonian life story: Developmental scripts and psychosocial adaptation. *Journal of Adult Development*, *17*(3), 156–161. http://doi.org/10.1007/s10804-010-9093-8

Windle, G., Hughes, D., Linck, P., Russell, I., & Woods, B. (2010). Is exercise effective in promoting mental well-being in older age? A systematic review. *Aging & Mental Health*, *14*(6), 652–669. http://doi.org/10.1080/13607861003713232

Windle, M., Spear, L. P., Fuligni, A. J., Angold, A., Brown, J. D., Pine, D., . . . Dahl, R. E. (2008). Transitions into underage and problem drinking: Developmental processes and mechanisms between 10 and 15 years of age. *Pediatrics*, *121*, S273–S289. http://doi.org/10.1542/peds.2007-2243C

Windsor, T. D., Anstey, K. J., & Rodgers, B. (2008). Volunteering and psychological well-being among young-old adults: How much is too much? *Gerontologist*, *48*(1), 59–70.

Winegar, L., & Valsiner, J. (1992). *Children's development within the social context*. Hillsdale, NJ: Lawrence Erlbaum.

Wing, R. R., & Phelan, S. (2005). Long-term weight loss maintenance. *American Journal of Clinical Nutrition*, *82*(1), 222S–225. Retrieved from http://ajcn.nutrition.org/content/82/1/222S.long

Wingfield, A., Tun, P. A., & McCoy, S. L. (2005). Hearing loss in older adulthood. *Current Directions in Psychological Science*, *14*(3), 144–148. http://doi.org/10.1111/j.0963-7214.2005.00356.x

Wink, P., & Dillon, M. (2002). Spiritual development across the adult life course: Findings from a longitudinal study. *Journal of Adult Development*, *9*(1), 79–94. Retrieved from pwink@wellesley.edu

Wink, P., Dillon, M., & Prettyman, A. (2007). Religion as moderator of the sense of control-health connection: Gender differences. *Journal of Religion, Spirituality & Aging*, *19*(4), 21–41. Retrieved from pwink@wellesley.edu

Winner, E. (1986). Where pelicans kiss seals. *Psychology Today*, *20*(8), 25–35.

Winner, E. (1988). *The point of words: Children's understanding of metaphor and irony*. Cambridge, MA: Harvard University Press.

Winsler, A., Carlton, M. P., & Barry, M. J. (2000). Age-related changes in preschool children's systematic use of private speech in a natural setting. *Journal of Child Language*, *27*, 665–687.

Winsler, A., Diaz, R. M., & Montero, I. (1997). The role of private speech in the transition from collaborative to independent task performance in young children. *Early Childhood Research Quarterly*, *12*, 59–79.

Winsler, A., Fernyhough, C., & Montero, I. (2009). *Private speech, executive functioning, and the development of verbal self-regulation*. Cambridge, UK: Cambridge University Press.

Winslow, S. (2005). Work-family conflict, gender, and parenthood, 1977–1997. *Journal of Family Issues*, *26*(6), 727–755. http://doi.org/10.1177/0192513X05277522

Wintergerst, E. S., Maggini, S., & Hornig, D. H. (2007). Contribution of selected vitamins and trace elements to immune function. *Annals of Nutrition & Metabolism*, *51*(4), 301–323.

Wirdefeldt, K., Adami, H.-O., Cole, P., Trichopoulos, D., & Mandel, J. (2011). Epidemiology and etiology of Parkinson's disease: A review of the evidence. *European Journal of Epidemiology*, *26* (Supp. 1), S1-S58. http://doi.org/10.1007/s10654-011-9581-6

Wiseman, F. K., Al-Janabi, T., Hardy, J., Karmiloff-Smith, A., Nizetic, D., Tybulewicz, V. L. J., . . . Strydom, A. (2015). A genetic cause of

Alzheimer disease: Mechanistic insights from Down syndrome. *Neuroscience*, *16*(9), 564–574. http://doi.org/10.1038/nrn3983

Wissink, I. B., Dekovic, M., & Meijer, A. M. (2006). Parenting behavior, quality of the parent-adolescent relationship, and adolescent functioning in four ethnic groups. *Journal of Early Adolescence*, *26*(2), 133–159.

Witherington, D. C., Campos, J. J., Anderson, D. I., Lejeune, L., & Seah, E. (2005). Avoidance of heights on the visual cliff in newly walking infants. *Infancy*, *7*(3), 285–298. http://doi.org/10.1207/s15327078in0703_4

Withers, M., Moran, R., Nicassio, P., Weisman, M. H., & Karpouzas, G. A. (2015). Perspectives of vulnerable U.S. Hispanics with rheumatoid arthritis on depression: Awareness, barriers to disclosure, and treatment options. *Arthritis Care & Research*, *67*(4), 484–492. http://doi.org/10.1002/acr.22462

Wohlfahrt-Veje, C., Mouritsen, A., Hagen, C. P., Tinggaard, J., Mieritz, M. G., Boas, M., . . . Main, K. M. (2016). Pubertal onset in boys and girls is influenced by pubertal timing of both parents. *The Journal of Clinical Endocrinology & Metabolism*, *101*(7), 2667–2674. http://dx.doi.org/10.1210/jc.2016-1073

Wojcicki, J. M., Heyman, M. B., Elwan, D., Lin, J., Blackburn, E., & Epel, E. (2016). Early exclusive breastfeeding is associated with longer telomeres in Latino preschool children. *The American Journal of Clinical Nutrition*, *104*(2), 397–405. http://doi.org/10.3945/ajcn.115.115428

Wolfe, C. D., & Bell, M. A. (2007). The integration of cognition and emotion during infancy and early childhood: Regulatory processes associated with the development of working memory. *Brain and Cognition*, *65*(1), 3–13. http://doi.org/10.1016/j.bandc.2006.01.009

Wolfe, S. E., Reisig, M. D., & Holtfreter, K. (2016). Low self-control and crime in late adulthood. *Research on Aging*, *38*(7), 767–790. http://doi.org/10.1177/0164027515604722

Wolfelt, A. (2013). *Healing the bereaved child*. New York, NY: Routledge.

Wolfson, A. R., & Carskadon, M. A. (1998). Sleep schedules and daytime functioning in adolescents. *Child Development*, *4*, 875–888.

Wolfson, A. R., Spaulding, N. L., Dandrow, C., & Baroni, E. M. (2007). Middle school start times: The importance of a good night's sleep for young adolescents. *Behavioral Sleep Medicine*, *5*(3), 194–209. http://doi.org/10.1080/15402000701263809

Wolitzky-Taylor, K. B., Ruggiero, K. J., Danielson, C. K., Resnick, H. S., Hanson, R. F., Smith, D. W., . . . Kilpatrick, D. G. (2008). Prevalence and correlates of dating violence in a national sample of adolescents. *Journal of the American Academy of Child & Adolescent Psychiatry*, *47*(7), 755–762. http://doi.org/10.1097/CHI.0b013e318172ef5f

Wolke, D., Eryigit-Madzwamuse, S., & Gutbrod, T. (2014). Very preterm/very low birthweight infants' attachment: Infant and maternal characteristics. *Archives of Disease in Childhood: Fetal and Neonatal Edition*, *99*(1), F70–F75. http://doi.org/10.1136/archdischild-2013-303788

Wong, C. A., Eccles, J. S., & Sameroff, A. (2003). The influence of ethnic discrimination and ethnic identification on African American adolescents' school and socioemotional adjustment. *Journal of Personality*, *71*(6), 1197–1232.

Wong, M. M., Robertson, G. C., & Dyson, R. B. (2015). Prospective relationship between poor sleep and substance-related problems in a national sample of adolescents. *Alcoholism, Clinical and Experimental Research*. http://doi.org/10.1111/acer.12618

Wood, D., & Woody, D. J. (2007). The significance of social support on parenting among a group of single, low-income, African American mothers. *Journal of Human Behavior in the Social Environment*, *15*(2/3), 183–198.

Woodgate, R. L. (2006). Living in a world without closure: Reality for parents who have experienced the death of a child. *Journal of Palliative Care*, *22*(2), 75–82.

Woods, B., & Pratt, R. (2005). Awareness in dementia: Ethical and legal issues in relation to people with dementia. *Aging & Mental Health*, *9*(5), 423–429. Retrieved from b.woods@bangor.ac.uk

Woods, R. J., & Wilcox, T. (2013). Posture support improves object individuation in infants. *Developmental Psychology*, *49*(8), 1413–1424. http://doi.org/10.1037/a0030344

Woodward, A. L., Markman, E. M., & Fitzsimmons, C. M. (1994). Rapid word learning in 13- and 18-month-olds. *Developmental Psychology*, *30*, 553–556.

Woolley, J. D., & Ghossainy, M. (2013). Revisiting the fantasy-reality distinction: Children as naïve skeptics. *Child Development*, *84*(5), 1496–1510. http://doi.org/10.1111/cdev.12081

Worden, J. W. (1991). *Grief counseling and grief therapy: A handbook for the mental health practitioner* (2nd ed.). New York, NY: Springer.

World Health Organization. (2009). *BMI classification*. Retrieved from http://apps.who.int/bmi/index.jsp?introPage=intro_3.html

World Health Organization. (2010). *Guidelines on HIV and infant feeding 2010: Principles and recommendations for feeding in the context of HIV and a summary of evidence*. Geneva, CH: Author.

World Health Organization. (2011). *WHO progress report 2011: Global HIV/AIDS response*. Retrieved from http://www.who.int/hiv/pub/progress_report2011/en/

World Health Organization. (2012). *Dementia: A public health priority*. Retrieved from http://www.alzheimer.ca/en/sk/Get-involved/Raise-your-voice/~/media/WHO_ADI_dementia_report_final.ashx

World Health Organization. (2015). *World health statistics 2015*. Retrieved from http://www.who.int/gho/publications/world_health_statistics/2015/en/

Worobey, J. (2014). Physical activity in infancy: Developmental aspects, measurement, and importance. *American Journal of Clinical Nutrition*, *99*(3), 729S–733S. http://doi.org/10.3945/ajcn.113.072397

Wortman, C. B., & Silver, R. C. (2001). The myths of coping with loss revisited. In M. S. Stroebe, R. O. Hansson, W. Stroebe, & H. Schut (Eds.), *Handbook of bereavement research: Consequences, coping, and care*. Washington, DC: American Psychological Association.

Wortman, J., Lucas, R. E., & Donnellan, M. B. (2012). Stability and change in the Big Five personality domains: Evidence from a longitudinal study of Australians. *Psychology and Aging*, *27*(4), 867–874. http://doi.org/10.1037/a002932210.1037/a0029322.supp

Wouters, S., Doumen, S., Germeijs, V., Colpin, H., & Verschueren, K. (2013). Contingencies of self-worth in early adolescence: The antecedent role of perceived parenting. *Social Development*, *22*(2), 242–258. http://doi.org/10.1111/sode.12010

Wraw, C., Deary, I. J., Gale, C. R., & Der, G. (2015). Intelligence in youth and health at age 50. *Intelligence*, *53*, 23–32. http://doi.org/10.1016/j.intell.2015.08.001

Wray-Lake, L., & Syvertsen, A. K. (2011). The developmental roots of social responsibility in childhood and adolescence. *New Directions for Child* and Adolescent Development, 2011(134), 11–25. http://doi.org/10.1002/cd.308

Wray-Lake, L., Syvertsen, A. K., & Flanagan, C. A. (2016). Developmental change in social responsibility during adolescence: An ecological perspective. Developmental Psychology, 52(1), 130–142. http://doi.org/10.1037/dev0000067

Wright, A. W., Austin, M., Booth, C., & Kliewer, W. (2016). Exposure to community violence and physical health outcomes in youth: A systematic review. Journal of Pediatric Psychology. http://doi.org/10.1093/jpepsy/jsw088

Wright, B. C., & Smailes, J. (2015). Factors and processes in children's transitive deductions. Journal of Cognitive Psychology, 27(8), 967–978. http://doi.org/10.1080/20445911.2015.1063641

Wright, N. C., Looker, A. C., Saag, K. G., Curtis, J. R., Delzell, E. S., Randall, S., & Dawson-Hughes, B. (2014). The recent prevalence of osteoporosis and low bone mass in the United States based on bone mineral density at the femoral neck or lumbar spine. Journal of Bone and Mineral Research, 29(11), 2520–2526. http://doi.org/10.1002/jbmr.2269

Wright, P. M., & Hogan, N. S. (2008). Grief theories and models: Applications to hospice nursing practice. Journal of Hospice & Palliative Nursing, 10(6), 350–356.

Wrzus, C., Hänel, M., Wagner, J., & Neyer, F. J. (2013). Social network changes and life events across the life span: A meta-analysis. Psychological Bulletin, 139(1), 53–80. http://doi.org/10.1037/a0028601

Wrzus, C., Wagner, G. G., & Riediger, M. (2016). Personality-situation transactions from adolescence to old age. Journal of Personality and Social Psychology, 110(5), 782–799. http://doi.org/10.1037/pspp0000054

Wrzus, C., Zimmermann, J., Mund, M., & Neyer, F. J. (2016). Friendships in young and middle adulthood. In M. Hojjat & A. Moyer (Eds.), The psychology of friendship (pp. 21–38). London, UK: Oxford University Press. http://doi.org/10.1093/acprof:oso/9780190222024.003.0002

Wu, C.-S., Jew, C. P., & Lu, H.-C. (2011). Lasting impacts of prenatal cannabis exposure and the role of endogenous cannabinoids in the developing brain. Future Neurology, 6(4), 459–480. Retrieved from http://www.pubmedcentral.nih.gov/articlerender.fcgi?artid=3252200&tool=pmcentrez&rendertype=abstract

Wu, M., Kumar, A., & Yang, S. (2016). Development and aging of superficial white matter myelin from young adulthood to old age: Mapping by vertex-based surface statistics (VBSS). Human Brain Mapping, 37(5), 1759–1769. http://doi.org/10.1002/hbm.23134

Wu, T., Mendola, P., & Buck, G. M. (2002). Ethnic differences in the presence of secondary sex characteristics and menarche among U.S. girls: The Third National Health and Nutrition Examination Survey, 1988–1994. Pediatrics, 110(4), 752.

Wu, W., West, S. G., & Hughes, J. N. (2010). Effect of grade retention in first grade on psychosocial outcomes. Journal of Educational Psychology, 102(1), 135–152. http://doi.org/10.1037/a0016664

Wyatt, J. M., & Carlo, G. (2002). What will my parents think? Relations among adolescents' expected parental reactions, prosocial moral reasoning, and prosocial and antisocial behaviors. Journal of Adolescent Research, 17, 646–667.

Wysman, L., Scoboria, A., Gawrylowicz, J., & Memon, A. (2014). The cognitive interview buffers the effects of subsequent repeated questioning in the absence of negative feedback. Behavioral Sciences & the Law, 32(2), 207–219. http://doi.org/10.1002/bsl.2115

Xi, H., Li, C., Ren, F., Zhang, H., & Zhang, L. (2013). Telomere, aging and age-related diseases. Aging Clinical and Experimental Research, 25(2), 139–146. http://doi.org/10.1007/s40520-013-0021-1

Xiao-na, H., Hui-shan, W., Li-jin, Z., & Xi-cheng, L. (2010). Co-sleeping and children's sleep in China. Biological Rhythm Research, 41(3), 169–181. http://doi.org/10.1080/09291011003687940

Xie, L., Kang, H., Xu, Q., Chen, M. J., Liao, Y., Thiyagarajan, M., . . . Nedergaard, M. (2013). Sleep drives metabolic clearance from the adult brain. Science, 342(6156), 373–377. http://doi.org/10.1126/science.1241224

Xie, X., Ding, G., Cui, C., Chen, L., Gao, Y., Zhou, Y., . . . Tian, Y. (2013). The effects of low-level prenatal lead exposure on birth outcomes. Environmental Pollution, 175, 30–34. http://doi.org/10.1016/j.envpol.2012.12.013

Xi-Kuan, C., Shi Wu, W., Nathalie, F., Kitaw, D., George, G. R., & Mark, W. (2007). Teenage pregnancy and adverse birth outcomes: A large population based retrospective cohort study. International Journal of Epidemiology, 36, 368.

Xu, F., & Kushnir, T. (2013). Infants are rational constructivist learners. Current Directions in Psychological Science, 22(1). http://doi.org/10.1177/0963721412469396

Xu, J., Kochanek, K. D., Murphy, S. L., & Arias, E. (2014). Mortality in the United States, 2012. NCHS Data Brief, 168, 1–8. Retrieved from http://europepmc.org/abstract/med/25296181

Xu, J., Murphy, S. L., Kochanek, K. D., & Bastian, B. A. (2016). Deaths: Final data for 2013. National Vital and Statistics Reports, 64(2), 1–118.

Xu, W., Yu, J.-T., Tan, M.-S., & Tan, L. (2015). Cognitive reserve and Alzheimer's disease. Molecular Neurobiology, 51(1), 187–208. http://doi.org/10.1007/s12035-014-8720-y

Xu, Y., Farver, J. A. M., Zhang, Z., Zeng, Q., Yu, L., & Cai., B. (2005). Mainland Chinese parenting styles and parent-child interaction. International Journal of Behavioral Development, 29(6), 524–531.

Xu, Z., Duc, K. D., Holcman, D., & Teixeira, M. T. (2013). The length of the shortest telomere as the major determinant of the onset of replicative senescence. Genetics, 194(4), 847–857. http://doi.org/10.1534/genetics.113.152322

Yager, Z., Diedrichs, P. C., Ricciardelli, L. A., & Halliwell, E. (2013). What works in secondary schools? A systematic review of classroom-based body image programs. Body Image, 10(3), 271–281. http://doi.org/10.1016/j.bodyim.2013.04.001

Yamagata, K. (2007). Differential emergence of representational systems: Drawings, letters, and numerals. Cognitive Development, 22(2), 244–257.

Yamin, C. K., Bitton, A., & Bates, D. W. (2010). E-cigarettes: A rapidly growing Internet phenomenon. Annals of Internal Medicine, 153(9), 607–609. http://doi.org/10.7326/0003-4819-153-9-201011020-00011

Yang, J. (2007). The one-child policy and school attendance in China. Comparative Education Review, 51(4), 471–495.

Yang, S., & Sternberg, R. J. (1997). Conceptions of intelligence in ancient Chinese philosophy. Journal of Theoretical and Philosophical Psychology, 17(2), 101–119.

Yang, X., Askarova, S., & Lee, J. C. M. (2010). Membrane biophysics and mechanics in Alzheimer's disease. Molecular Neurobiology, 41(2–3), 138–148. http://doi.org/10.1007/s12035-010-8121-9

Yang, Y. T., Delamater, P. L., Leslie, T. F., & Mello, M. M. (2016). Sociodemographic predictors of vaccination exemptions on the basis of personal belief in California. American Journal of Public Health, 106(1), 172–177. http://doi.org/10.2105/AJPH.2015.302926

Yarrow, M. R., Scott, P. M., & Waxler, C. Z. (1973). Learning concern for others. Developmental Psychology, 8, 240–260.

Yates, M., & Youniss, J. (1996). Community service and political-moral identity in adolescents. Journal of Research on Adolescence. http://doi.org/10.1111/j.1467-9507.1996.tb00073.x

Yau, G., Schluchter, M., Taylor, H. G., Margevicius, S., Forrest, C. B., Andreias, L., . . . Hack, M. (2013). Bullying of extremely low birth weight children: Associated risk factors during adolescence. Early Human Development, 89(5), 333–338. http://doi.org/10.1016/j.earlhumdev.2012.11.004

Yau, J., & Smetana, J. G. (2003). Conceptions of moral, social-conventional, and personal events among Chinese preschoolers in Hong Kong. Child Development, 74(3), 647–658.

Yavorsky, J. E., Dush, C. M. K., & Schoppe-Sullivan, S. J. (2015). The production of inequality: The gender division of labor across the transition to parenthood. Journal of Marriage and the Family, 77(3), 662–679. http://doi.org/10.1111/jomf.12189

Ybarra, M. L., & Mitchell, K. J. (2014). "Sexting" and its relation to sexual activity and sexual risk behavior in a national survey of adolescents. Journal of Adolescent, 55(6), 757–764. http://doi.org/10.1016/j.jadohealth.2014.07.012

Yeager, D. S., & Dweck, C. S. (2012). Mindsets that promote resilience: When students believe that personal characteristics can be developed. Educational Psychologist, 47(4), 302–314. http://doi.org/10.1080/00461520.2012.722805

Yip, T. (2014). Ethnic identity in everyday life: The influence of identity development status. Child Development, 85(1), 205–219. http://doi.org/10.1111/cdev.12107

Yonker, J. E., Schnabelrauch, C. A., & DeHaan, L. G. (2012). The relationship between spirituality and religiosity on psychological outcomes in adolescents and emerging adults: A meta-analytic review. Journal of Adolescence, 35(2), 299–314. http://doi.org/10.1016/j.adolescence.2011.08.010

Yoon-Mi, H. (2009). Genetic and environmental contributions to childhood temperament in South Korean twins. Twin Research & Human Genetics, 12(6), 549–554. http://doi.org/10.1375/twin.12.6.549

Young, L., & Koenigs, M. (2008). Investigating emotion in moral cognition: A review of evidence from functional neuroimaging and neuropsychology. British Medical Bulletin, 84(1), 69–79. https://doi.org/10.1093/bmb/ldm031

Youngblade, L. M., & Dunn, J. (1995). Individual differences in young children's pretend play with mother and sibling: Links to relationships and understanding of other people's feelings and beliefs. Child Development, 66(5), 1472–1492. http://doi.org/10.1111/j.1467-8624.1995.tb00946.x

Ysseldyk, R., Haslam, S. A., & Haslam, C. (2013). Abide with me: Religious group identification among older adults promotes health and well-being by maintaining multiple group memberships. Aging & Mental Health, 17(7), 869–879. http://doi.org/10.1080/13607863.2013.799120

Yuill, N., & Perner, J. (1988). Intentionality and knowledge in children's judgments of actor's responsibility and recipient's emotional reaction. Developmental Psychology, 24, 358–365.

Yurgelun-Todd, D. (2007). Emotional and cognitive changes during adolescence. Current Opinion in Neurobiology, 17(2), 251–257.

Zafiropoulou, M., Sotiriou, A., & Mitsiouli, V. (2007). Relation of self-concept in kindergarten and first grade to school adjustment. *Perceptual & Motor Skills, 104*(3), 1313–1327. http://doi.org/10.2466/PMS.104.4.1313-1327

Zahn-Waxler, C., Friedman, R. J., Cole, P. M., Mizuta, I., & Hiruma, N. (1996). Japanese and United States preschool children's responses to conflict and distress. *Child Development, 67,* 2462–2477.

Zaitchik, D., Iqbal, Y., & Carey, S. (2014). The effect of executive function on biological reasoning in young children: An individual differences study. *Child Development, 85*(1), 160–175. http://doi.org/10.1111/cdev.12145

Zalsman, G., Hawton, K., Wasserman, D., van Heeringen, K., Arensman, E., Sarchiapone, M., . . . Zohar, J. (2016). Suicide prevention strategies revisited: 10-year systematic review. *The Lancet Psychiatry, 3*(7), 646–659. http://doi.org/10.1016/S2215-0366(16)30030-X

Zampieri, B. L., Biselli-Périco, J. M., de Souza, J. E. S., Bürger, M. C., Silva Júnior, W. A., Goloni-Bertollo, E. M., . . . Flavell, R. (2014). Altered expression of immune-related genes in children with Down syndrome. *PLoS ONE, 9*(9), e107218. http://doi.org/10.1371/journal.pone.0107218

Zarit, S. H., & Eggebeen, D. J. (2002). Parent-child relationships in adulthood and later years. In M. H. Bornstein (Ed.), *Handbook of parenting: Vol. 1: Children and parenting* (2nd ed., pp. 135–161). Mahwah, NJ: Lawrence Erlbaum.

Zeanah, C. H. (2009). The importance of early experiences: Clinical, research, and policy perspectives. *Journal of Loss & Trauma, 14*(4), 266–279. http://doi.org/10.1080/15325020903004426

Zeiders, K. H., Umaña-Taylor, A. J., & Derlan, C. L. (2013). Trajectories of depressive symptoms and self-esteem in Latino youths: Examining the role of gender and perceived discrimination. *Developmental Psychology, 49*(5), 951–963. http://doi.org/10.1037/a0028866

Zeidler, D. L., Sadler, T. D., Applebaum, S., & Callahan, B. E. (2009). Advancing reflective judgment through socioscientific issues. *Journal of Research in Science Teaching, 46*(1), 74–101. http://doi.org/10.1002/tea.20281

Zeidner, M., Matthews, G., & Roberts, R. D. (2012). The emotional intelligence, health, and well-being nexus: What have we learned and what have we missed? *Applied Psychology: Health and Well-Being, 4*(1), 1–30. http://doi.org/10.1111/j.1758-0854.2011.01062.x

Zelazo, N. A., Zelazo, P. R., Cohen, K. M., & Zelazo, P. D. (1993). Specificity of practice effects on elementary neuromotor patterns. *Developmental Psychology, 29,* 686–691.

Zelazo, P. D., & Carlson, S. M. (2012). Hot and cool executive function in childhood and adolescence: Development and plasticity. *Child Development Perspectives.* http://doi.org/10.1111/j.1750-8606.2012.00246.x

Zelazo, P. D., Reznick, J. S., & Spinazzola, J. (1998). Representational flexibility and response control in a multistep, multilocation search task. *Developmental Psychology, 34,* 203–214.

Zelazo, P. R. (1983). The development of walking: New findings on old assumptions. *Journal of Motor Behavior, 2,* 99–137.

Zeman, A. (1997). Persistent vegetative state. *Lancet, 350*(9080), 795–799. http://doi.org/10.1016/S0140-6736(97)06447-7

Zeman, J., & Garber, J. (1996). Display rules for anger, sadness, and pain: It depends on who is watching. *Child Development, 67*(3), 957–973. http://doi.org/10.1111/j.1467-8624.1996.tb01776.x

Zeman, J., Cassano, M., & Adrian, M. C. (2012). Socialization influences on children's and adolescents' emotional self-regulation processes. In K. Caplovitz Barrett, N. A. Fox, G. A. Morgan, & D. J. Fidler (Eds.), *Handbook of self-regulatory processes in development.* New York, NY: Routledge. http://doi.org/10.4324/9780203080719.ch5

Zhai, F., Brooks-Gunn, J., & Waldfogel, J. (2011). Head Start and urban children's school readiness: A birth cohort study in 18 cities. *Developmental Psychology, 47*(1), 134–152. http://doi.org/10.1037/a0020784

Zhai, Z. W., Pajtek, S., Luna, B., Geier, C. F., Ridenour, T. A., & Clark, D. B. (2014). Reward-modulated response inhibition, cognitive shifting, and the orbital frontal cortex in early adolescence. *Journal of Research on Adolescence.* http://doi.org/10.1111/jora.12168

Zhan, H. J. (2004). Willingness and expectations: Intergenerational differences in attitudes toward filial responsibility in China. *Marriage & Family Review, 36*(1/2), 175–200. http://doi.org/10.1300/J002v36n01_08

Zhang, C., Brook, J. S., Leukefeld, C. G., & Brook, D. W. (2016). Trajectories of marijuana use from adolescence to adulthood as predictors of unemployment status in the early forties. *The American Journal on Addictions, 25*(3), 203–209. http://doi.org/10.1111/ajad.12361

Zhang, L. (1999). A comparison of U.S. and Chinese university students' cognitive development: The cross-cultural applicability of Perry's theory. *Journal of Psychology, 133*(4), 425–440.

Zhang, L. (2004). The Perry scheme: Across cultures, across approaches to the study of human psychology. *Journal of Adult Development, 11*(2), 123–138.

Zhang, L., & Watkins, D. (2001). Cognitive development and student approaches to learning: An investigation of Perry's theory with Chinese and U.S. university students. *Higher Education, 41*(3), 239–261.

Zhang, Y., Niu, B., Yu, D., Cheng, X., Liu, B., & Deng, J. (2010). Radial glial cells and the lamination of the cerebellar cortex. *Brain Structure & Function, 215*(2), 115–122. http://doi.org/10.1007/s00429-010-0278-5

Zhao, G., Ford, E. S., Tsai, J., Li, C., Ahluwalia, I. B., Pearson, W. S., . . . Croft, J. B. (2012). Trends in health-related behavioral risk factors among pregnant women in the United States: 2001–2009. *Journal of Women's Health, 21*(3), 255–263. http://doi.org/10.1089/jwh.2011.2931

Zhou, D., Lebel, C., Treit, S., Evans, A., & Beaulieu, C. (2015). Accelerated longitudinal cortical thinning in adolescence. *NeuroImage, 104,* 138–145. http://doi.org/10.1016/j.neuroimage.2014.10.005

Zhu, L., & Liu, G. (2007). Preschool children's understanding of illness. *Acta Psychologica Sinica, 39*(1), 96–103.

Zhu, W. X., Lu, L., & Hesketh, T. (2009). China's excess males, sex selective abortion, and one child policy: Analysis of data from 2005 national intercensus survey. *British Medical Journal, 338*(7700), 920–923.

Ziegler-Graham, K., Brookmeyer, R., Johnson, E., & Arrighi, H. M. (2008). Worldwide variation in the doubling time of Alzheimer's disease incidence rates. *Alzheimer's & Dementia, 4*(5), 316–323.

Zigler, E., & Styfco, S. J. (1993). *Head Start and beyond.* New Haven, CT: Yale University Press.

Zigler, E., & Styfco, S. J. (2004). Moving Head Start to the states: One experiment too many. *Applied Developmental Science, 8*(1), 51–55.

Zimmer-Gembeck, M. J., & Petherick, J. (2006). Intimacy dating goals and relationship satisfaction during adolescence and emerging adulthood: Identity formation, age and sex as moderators. *International Journal of Behavioral Development, 30*(2), 167–177.

Zimmerman, F. J., Christakis, D. A., & Meltzoff, A. N. (2007). Associations between media viewing and language development in children under age 2 years. *Journal of Pediatrics, 151*(4), 364–368. http://doi.org/10.1016/j.jpeds.2007.04.071

Zimmermann, P., & Becker-Stoll, F. (2002). Stability attachment representations during adolescence: The influence of ego-identity status. *Journal of Adolescence, 25,* 107–135.

Zimmermann, P., & Iwanski, A. (2014). Emotion regulation from early adolescence to emerging adulthood and middle adulthood: Age differences, gender differences, and emotion-specific developmental variations. *International Journal of Behavioral Development, 38*(2), 182–194. http://doi.org/10.1177/0165025413515405

Zinzow, H. M., Resnick, H. S., McCauley, J. L., Amstadter, A. B., Ruggiero, K. J., & Kilpatrick, D. G. (2010). The role of rape tactics in risk for posttraumatic stress disorder and major depression: Results from a national sample of college women. *Depression and Anxiety, 27*(8). http://doi.org/10.1002/da.20719

Zipprich, J., Winter, K., Hacker, J., Xia, D., Watt, J., & Harriman, K. (2015). Measles outbreak California, December 2014–February 2015. *Morbidity and Mortality Weekly Report, 64*(6), 153–154. Retrieved from https://www.cdc.gov/mmwr/preview/mmwrhtml/mm6406a5.htm

Zosh, J. M., Brinster, M., & Halberda, J. (2013). Optimal contrast: Competition between two referents improves word learning. *Applied Developmental Science, 17*(1), 20–28. http://doi.org/10.1080/10888691.2013.748420

Zosuls, K. M., Andrews, N. C. Z., Martin, C. L., England, D. E., & Field, R. D. (2016). Developmental changes in the link between gender typicality and peer victimization and exclusion. *Sex Roles, 75*(5–6), 243–256. http://doi.org/10.1007/s11199-016-0608-z

Zosuls, K. M., Ruble, D. N., Tamis-LeMonda, C. S., Shrout, P. E., Bornstein, M. H., & Greulich, F. K. (2009). The acquisition of gender labels in infancy: Implications for gender-typed play. *Developmental Psychology, 45*(3), 688–701. http://doi.org/10.1037/a0014053

Zou, M. (2015). Gender, work orientations and job satisfaction. *Work, Employment & Society, 29*(1), 3–22. http://doi.org/10.1177/0950017014559267

Zucker, K. J., Wood, H., Singh, D., & Bradley, S. J. (2012). A developmental, biopsychosocial model for the treatment of children with gender identity disorder. *Journal of Homosexuality, 59*(3), 369–397. http://doi.org/10.1080/00918369.2012.653309

Zuckerman, G. (2007). Child-adult interaction that creates a zone of proximal development. *Journal of Russian & East European Psychology, 45*(3), 43–69. http://doi.org/10.2753/RPO1061-0405450302

Zwierzynska, K., Wolke, D., & Lereya, T. S. (2013). Peer victimization in childhood and internalizing problems in adolescence: A prospective longitudinal study. *Journal of Abnormal Child Psychology, 41*(2), 309–323. http://doi.org/10.1007/s10802-012-9678-8

REFERENCES

academically centered programs An approach to early childhood education that emphasizes providing children with structured learning environments in which teachers deliver direct instruction on letters, numbers, shapes, and academic skills.

accommodation In Piaget's theory, the process by which schemas are modified or created to include new experiences.

achievement motivation The willingness to persist at challenging tasks and meet high standards of accomplishment.

acquired immune deficiency syndrome (AIDS) A condition caused by the human immunodeficiency virus (HIV), the most serious sexually transmitted illness.

active euthanasia Occurs when death is deliberately induced, such as by administering a fatal dose of pain medication.

activity theory The view that older adults want to remain active and that declines in social interaction are not a result of elders' desires but are a function of social barriers to engagement.

adolescent egocentrism A characteristic of adolescents thinking in which adolescents show preoccupation with themselves and have difficulty separating others' perspectives from their own.

adolescent growth spurt The first outward sign of puberty, refers to a rapid gain in height and weight that generally begins in girls at about age 10 and in boys about age 12.

adrenarche Refers to the maturation of adrenal glands.

affordances Refers to the actional properties of objects — their nature, opportunities, and limits.

aggression Behavior that harms or violates the rights of others, whether overtly or covertly.

Alzheimer's disease A neurodegenerative disorder characterized by dementia, the deterioration of memory and personality, and marked by the presence of presence of amyloid plaques and neurofibrillary tangles in the cerebral cortex.

amygdala A brain structure that is part of the limbic system and plays a role in emotion, especially fear and anger.

amyloid plaque Found in the brains of patients with Alzheimer's disease, deposits of beta-amyloid accumulate along with clumps of dead neurons and glial cells.

androgyny The gender identity of those who score high on both masculine and feminine characteristics.

anencephaly A neural tube defect that results in the failure of all or part of the brain to develop, resulting in death prior to or shortly after birth.

animism The belief that inanimate objects are alive and have feelings and intentions.

anorexia nervosa An eating disorder characterized by compulsive starvation and extreme weight loss and accompanied by a distorted body image.

antisocial behavior Behavior that harms others, is disruptive or hostile, or that transgresses social norms.

Apgar scale A quick overall assessment of a baby's immediate health at birth, including appearance, pulse, grimace, activity, and respiration.

appearance–reality distinction The ability to distinguish between what something appears to be from what it really is.

applied developmental science A field that studies lifespan interactions between individuals and the contexts in which they live and applies research findings to real-world settings, such as to influence social policy and create interventions.

assimilation In Piaget's theory, the process by which new experiences are interpreted and integrated into preexisting schemas.

attachment A lasting emotional tie between two individuals who strive to maintain closeness and act to ensure that the relationship continues.

attention The ability to direct one's awareness.

authoritarian parenting style An approach to child-rearing that emphasizes high behavioral control and low levels of warmth and autonomy granting.

authoritative parenting style An approach to child-rearing in which parents are warm and sensitive to children's needs, grant appropriate autonomy, and exert firm control.

autism spectrum disorders (ASD) Refer to a family of disorders that range in severity and are marked by social and communication deficits, often accompanied by restrictive and repetitive behaviors.

autobiographical memory The recollection of a personal event that occurred at a specific time and place in one's past.

autonomous morality Piaget's second stage of morality in which children have a more flexible view of rules, believing that rules are self-chosen rather than simply imposed upon them.

babbling An infant's repetition of syllables such as "ba-ba-ba-ba" and "ma-ma-ma," which begins at about 6 months of age.

basic emotion Emotions that are universal in humans, appear early in life, and are thought to have a long evolutional history, such as happiness, interest, surprise, fear, anger, sadness, and disgust.

behavioral genetics The field of study that examines how genes and environment combine to influence the diversity of human traits, abilities, and behaviors.

behaviorism A theoretical approach that studies how observable behavior is controlled by the physical and social environment through conditioning.

bereavement The process of coping with the sense of loss that follows death.

biculturalism The practice of adopting values and practices from two cultures.

Big 5 personality traits Five clusters of personality traits that reflect an inborn predisposition that is stable throughout life. The five traits are: openness, conscientiousness, extroversion, agreeableness, and neuroticism.

binge drinking Heavy episodic drinking; consuming five or more alcoholic beverages in one sitting for men and four drinks in one sitting for women.

bioecological systems theory A theory introduced by Bronfenbrenner that emphasizes the role of context in development, positing that contexts are organized into a series of systems in which individuals are embedded and that interact with one another and the person to influence development.

blastocyst A thin-walled, fluid-filled sphere containing an inner mass of cells from which the embryo will develop; is implanted into the uterine wall during the germinal period.

blended family A family composed of a biological parent and a non-related adult, most commonly a mother and stepfather.

body mass index (BMI) A measure of body fat based on weight in kilograms divided by height in meters squared (k/m^2).

Broca's area The region in the brain that controls the ability to use language for expression; damage to the area inhibits fluent speech.

bulimia nervosa An eating disorder characterized by recurrent episodes of binge eating and subsequent purging usually by induced vomiting and the use of laxatives.

bully-victim A child who attacks or inflicts harm on others and who is also attacked or harmed by others; the child is both bully and victim.

canalization The tendency for a trait that is biologically programmed to be restricted to only a few outcomes.

canonical babbling A type of babbling with well-formed syllables that sounds like language.

cardiovascular disease (heart disease) A disease marked by high blood pressure, high blood cholesterol, plaque buildup in the arteries, irregular heartbeat, and possible heart attack.

care orientation Gilligan's feminine mode of moral reasoning, characterized by a desire to maintain relationships and a responsibility to avoid hurting others.

casual sex Sexual activity outside of romantic relationships.

cataract A clouding of the lens of the eye, resulting in blurred, foggy vision; can lead to blindness.

categorical self A classification of the self based on broad ways in which people differ, such as sex, age, and physical characteristics, which children use to guide their behavior.

categorization An adaptive mental process in which objects are grouped into conceptual categories, allowing for organized storage of information in memory, efficient retrieval of that information, and the capacity to respond with familiarity to new stimuli from a common class.

cell differentiation Begins roughly 72 hours after fertilization when the organism consists of about 16 to 32 cells.

central executive In information processing, the part of our mental system that directs the flow of information and regulates cognitive activities such as attention, action, and problem solving.

centration The tendency to focus on one part of a stimulus, situation, or idea and exclude all others; a characteristic of preoperational thought.

cephalocaudal development The principle that growth proceeds from the head downward; the head and upper regions of the body develop before the lower regions.

cesarean section Also known as a C-section; a surgical procedure that removes the fetus from the uterus through the abdomen.

child abuse Any intentional harm to a minor (under the age of 18), including actions that harm the child physically, emotionally, sexually, or through neglect.

child-centered programs A constructivist approach to early childhood education that encourages children to actively build their own understanding of the world through observing, interacting with objects and people, and engaging in a variety of activities that allow them to manipulate materials and interact with teachers and peers.

chromosome One of 46 rodlike molecules that contain 23 pairs of DNA found in every body cell and collectively contain all of the genes.

chronosystem In bioecological systems theory, refers to how the people and contexts change over time.

circular reaction In Piaget's theory, the repetition of an action and its response in which infants try to repeat a newly discovered event caused by their own motor activity.

classical conditioning A form of learning in which an environmental stimulus becomes associated with stimuli that elicit reflex responses.

classification The ability to organize things into groups based on similar characteristics.

clinical death Defines death as the moment the heart stops beating; blood, and thereby oxygen, no longer circulate throughout the body.

clique A tightly knit peer group of about three to eight close friends who share similarities such as demographics and attitudes.

cognitive development Maturation of mental processes and tools individuals use to obtain knowledge, think, and solve problems.

cognitive reserve The ability to make flexible and efficient use of available brain resources that permits cognitive efficiency, flexibility, and adaptability; it is cultivated throughout life from experience and environmental factors.

cognitive-affective complexity A form of mature thinking that involves emotional awareness, the ability to integrate and regulate intense emotions, and the recognition and appreciation of individual experience.

cognitive-developmental perspective A perspective posited by Piaget that views individuals as active explorers of their world, learning by interacting with the world around them and describes cognitive development as progressing through stages.

cohabitation An arrangement in which a committed, unmarried, couple lives together in the same home.

cohort A generation of people born at the same time, influenced by the same historical and cultural conditions.

concrete operational stage of reasoning Piaget's third stage of reasoning, from about 6 to 11, in which thought becomes logical and is applied to direct tangible experiences but not to abstract problems.

conduct disorder A psychiatric diagnosis that refers to a severe form of antisocial behavior, characterized by aggressive behaviors that involve the destruction of property, stealing, or robbing others, or causing pain to others.

conservation The principle that a physical quantity, such as number, mass, or volume, remains the same even when its appearance changes.

context Unique conditions in which a person develops, including aspects of the physical and social environment such as family, neighborhood, culture, and historical time period.

continuity theory The perspective that older adults strive to maintain continuity and consistency in self across the past and into the future; successful elders retain a sense that they are the same person they have always been despite physical, cognitive, emotional, and social changes.

continuous development The view that development consists of gradual cumulative changes in existing skills and capacities.

conventional moral reasoning The second level of Kohlberg's theory in which moral decisions are based on conforming to social rules.

cooing An infant's repetition of vowel sounds, such as "ahhhh," "ohhh," and "eeee" that begins between 2 and 3 months of age.

core knowledge perspective A framework explaining that infants are born with several innate knowledge systems or core domains of thought that enable early rapid learning and adaptation.

corpus callosum A thick band of nerve fibers that connects the left and right hemispheres of the brain, allowing communication.

correlational research A research design that measures relationships among participants' measured characteristics, behaviors, and development.

cross-sectional research A developmental research design that compares people of different ages at a single point in time to infer age differences.

crowd A large, loose group of individuals based on perceived characteristics, interests, stereotypes, and reputation.

crystallized intelligence Intellectual ability that reflects accumulated knowledge acquired through experience and learning.

culture A set of customs, knowledge, attitudes, and values shared by a group of people and learned through interactions with group members.

daily hassles Small stresses that quickly accumulate to influence adults' mood and ability to cope.

dating Establishing romantic relationships, a type of romantic courtship.

deferred imitation Imitating the behavior of an absent model.

delay of gratification A measure of self-control in which researchers administer tasks in which children have to wait a period of time to achieve a reward.

dementia A progressive deterioration in mental abilities due to changes in the brain that influence higher cortical functions such as thinking, memory, comprehension, and emotional control and are reflected in impaired thought and behavior, interfering with the adult's ability to engage in everyday activities.

dependent variable The behavior under study in an experiment; it is expected to be affected by changes in the independent variable.

developmental dyslexia The most commonly diagnosed learning disability in which children tend to be bright yet they have difficulty with reading, with reading achievement below that predicted by age or IQ.

diabetes A disease marked by high levels of blood glucose that occurs when the body is unable to regulate the amount of glucose in the bloodstream because there is not enough insulin produced (type 1 diabetes) or the body shows insulin resistance and becomes less sensitive to it, failing to respond to it (type 2 diabetes). Symptoms include fatigue, great thirst, blurred vision, frequent infections, and slow healing.

difficult temperament A temperament characterized by irregularity in biological rhythms, slow adaptation to change, and a tendency for intense negative reactions.

discipline The methods a parent uses to teach and socialize children.

discontinuous development The view that growth entails abrupt transformations in abilities and capacities in which new ways of interacting with the world emerge.

disengagement theory A perspective that declines in social interaction in older age are due to mutual withdrawal between older adults and society as they anticipate death.

dizygotic (DZ) twin Also known as a fraternal twin; occurs when two ova are released and each is fertilized by a different sperm; the resulting offspring share 50% of the genetic material.

DNA Deoxyribonucleic acid; the chemical structure, shaped like a twisted ladder, that contains all of the genes.

dominant–recessive inheritance A form of genetic inheritance in which the phenotype reflects only the dominant allele of a heterozygous pair.

Down syndrome Also known as trisomy 21; a condition in which a third, extra chromosome appears at the 21st site. Down syndrome is associated with distinctive physical characteristics accompanied by developmental disability.

dual language learning Also known as two-way immersion; an approach in which children are taught and develop skills in two languages.

dualistic thinking Polar reasoning in which knowledge and accounts of phenomena are viewed as absolute facts, either right or wrong with no in-between.

dual-process model A model of the brain consisting of two systems, one emotional and the other rational, that develop on different timeframes, accounting for typical adolescent behavior.

dying with dignity Ending one's life in a way that is true to one's preferences and controlling end-of-life care.

dying trajectory Refers to the variability in the rate of decline that people show prior to death.

dynamic systems A framework describing motor skills as resulting from ongoing interactions among physical, cognitive, and socioemotional influences and environmental supports in which previously mastered skills are combined to provide more complex and effective ways of exploring and controlling the environment.

dyscalculia Refers to a mathematics disability.

easy temperament A temperament characterized by regularity in biological rhythms, the tendency to adapt easily to new experiences, and a general cheerfulness.

egocentrism Piaget's term for children's inability to take another person's point of view or perspective and to assume that others share the same feelings, knowledge, and physical view of the world.

embryo Prenatal organism between about 2 and 8 weeks after conception; a period of major structural development.

embryonic period Occurs about 2 to 8 weeks after pregnancy, in which rapid structural development takes place.

emerging adulthood An extended transition to adulthood that takes place from ages 18 to 25, in which a young person is no longer an adolescent yet has not assumed the roles that comprise adulthood.

emotional competence The combination of processes we develop as we become capable of new and more complex emotions and relationships with others and develop a greater sense of self-understanding, social awareness, and self-management.

emotional display rule Unstated cultural guidelines for acceptable emotions and emotional expression that are communicated to children via parents' emotional behavior, expressions, and socialization.

emotional regulation The ability to adjust and control our emotional state to influence how and when emotions are expressed.

empathy The capacity to understand another person's emotions and concerns.

epigenetic framework A perspective stating that development results from reciprocal interactions between genetics and the environment such that the expression of genetic inheritance is influenced by environmental forces.

episodic memory Memory for every day experiences.

epistemic cognition The ways in which an individual understands how he or she arrived at ideas, beliefs, and conclusions.

estrogen The primary female sex hormone responsible for development and regulation of the female reproductive system and secondary sex characteristics.

ethnic identity A sense of membership to an ethnic group and viewing the attitudes and practicesassociated with that group as an enduring part of the self.

ethological theory A perspective that emphasizes the evolutionary basis of behavior and its adaptive value in ensuring survival of a species.

evolutionary developmental theory A perspective that applies principles of evolution and scientific knowledge about the interactive influence of genetic and environmental mechanisms to understand the adaptive value of developmental changes that are experienced with age.

euthanasia Refers to the practice of assisting terminally ill people in dying more quickly.

executive function The set of cognitive operations that support planning, decision-making, and goal setting abilities, such as the ability to control attention, coordinate information in working memory, and inhibit impulses.

exosystem In bioecological systems theory, social settings in which an individual does not participate but have an indirect influence on development.

expansion Adult response to children's speech that elaborate and enriches its complexity.

experience–dependent brain development Brain growth and development in response to specific learning experiences.

experience–expectant brain development Brain growth and development that is dependent on basic environmental experiences, such as visual and auditory stimulation, in order to develop normally.

experience sampling method A technique that gives researchers a window into people's days.

experimental design A research design that permits inferences about cause and effect by exerting control, systematically manipulating a variable, and studying the effects on measured variables.

expertise An elaborate and integrated knowledge base that underlies extraordinary proficiency in given area.

false-belief task A task that requires children to understand that someone does not share their knowledge.

familism The cultural belief that family members should support one another; that the family should take precedence over individuals and the community.

fast mapping A process by which children learn new words after only a brief encounter, connecting it with their own mental categories.

fetal alcohol spectrum disorders The continuum of physical, mental, and behavioral outcomes caused by prenatal exposure to alcohol.

fetal alcohol syndrome (FAS) The most severe form of fetal alcohol spectrum disorder accompanying heavy prenatal exposure to alcohol, including a distinct pattern of facial characteristics, growth deficiencies, and deficits in intellectual development.

fine motor development Development of the ability to control small movements of the fingers such as reaching and grasping.

first-generation college students Students who are the first in their families to attend college.

fluid intelligence Intellectual ability that reflects basic information processing skills, including working memory, processing speed, and the ability to detect relations among stimuli and draw inferences. Underlies learning, is not influenced by culture, and reflects brain functioning.

Flynn effect The rise in IQ scores that over generations in many nations.

formal operational reasoning Piaget's fourth stage of cognitive development, characterized by abstract, logical, and systematic thinking.

fragile X syndrome An example of a dominant–recessive disorder carried on the X chromosome.

free radical A highly reactive, corrosive substance that forms when a cell is exposed to oxygen. Through chemical reactions, free radicals destroy DNA, proteins, and other cellular materials.

gender Is determined by socialization and the roles that the individual adopts.

gender constancy A child's understanding of the biological permanence of gender and that it does not change regardless of appearance, activities, or attitudes.

gender identity One's image of oneself as masculine or feminine, embodying the roles and behaviors that society associates with males and females.

gender norms The activities, attitudes, skills, and characteristics that are considered appropriate for males or females.

gender schema A concept or a mental structure that organizes gender-related information and embodies their understanding of what it means to be a male or female.

gender schema theory An approach to gender typing that emphasizes information processing and environmental influences that influence the development of gender-related beliefs, which then guide children's behaviors and attitudes.

gender stability In Kohlberg's view, young children's recognition that gender does not change over time, though it is not yet understood as a biological construct but rather based on external traits and behaviors.

gender stereotypes Refer to broad generalized judgments of the activities, attitudes, skills, and characteristics deemed appropriate for males or females in a given culture.

gender typing The process in which young children acquire the characteristics and attitudes that are considered appropriate for males or females.

gene–environment correlation The idea that many of an individual's traits are supported by his or her genes and environment; there are three types of correlations: passive, reactive, and active.

gene–environment interactions Refer to the dynamic interplay between our genes and our environment in determining out characteristics, behavior, physical, cognitive, and social development as well as health.

generativity The seventh stage in Erikson's theory in which adults seek to move beyond a concern for their own personal goals and welfare in order to guide future generations and give back to society.

general educational development exam (GED) A high school equivalency test that young people who drop out have the option of taking.

genomic imprinting The instance when the expression of a gene is determined by whether it is inherited from the mother or father.

genotype An individual's collection of genes that contain instructions for all physical and psychological characteristics, including hair, eye color, personality, health, and behavior.

germinal period Also referred to as the period of the zygote, refers to the first two weeks after conception.

glass ceiling An invisible barrier that prevents women and ethnic minorities from advancing to the highest levels of the career ladder.

glial cell A type of brain cell that nourishes neurons and provides structure to the brain.

global self-esteem An overall evaluation of self-worth.

goodness of fit The compatibility between a child's temperament and his or her environment, especially the parent's temperament and child-rearing methods; the greater the degree of match, the more favorable the child's adjustment.

grammar The rules of language.

grief The affective response to bereavement that includes distress and an intense array of emotions such as hurt, anger, and guilt.

gross motor development Development of the ability to control large movements of the body, such as walking and jumping.

growth norm The expectation for typical gains and variations in height and weight for children based on their chronological age and ethnic background.

guided participation Also known as apprenticeship in thinking; the process by which people learn from others who guide them, providing a scaffold to help them accomplish more than the child could do alone.

hardiness Personal qualities, including a sense of control, orientation towards personal growth, and commitment to life choices, that influences adults' ability to adapt to changes and life circumstances.

hemispheric dominance A process in which one hemisphere becomes stronger and more adept than the other.

heritability A measure of the extent to which variation of a certain trait can be traced to genes.

heteronomous morality Piaget's first stage of morality when children become aware of rules and view them as sacred and unalterable.

heterozygous Refers to a chromosomal pair consisting of two different alleles.

holophrase A one-word expression used to convey a complete thought.

homozygous Refers to a chromosomal pair consisting of two identical alleles.

hormone A chemical that is produced and secreted into the bloodstream to affect and influence physiological functions.

hospice An approach to end-of-life care that emphasizes a dying patient's need for pain management, psychological, spiritual, and social support as well as death with dignity.

human immunodeficiency virus (HIV) The most serious sexually transmitted infection, which causes acquired immune deficiency syndrome (AIDS).

hypothalamus-pituitary-gonadal axis (HPG) The collective effects of the hypothalamus, pituitary gland, and gonads behaving in cooperation in regulating the hormones that drive puberty.

hypothesis A proposed explanation for a phenomenon that can be tested.

hypothetical–deductive reasoning The ability to consider propositions, probabilities, generate and systematically test hypotheses, and draw conclusions.

ideal self A sense of self that is characterized by traits that one values.

identity A coherent organized sense of self that includes values, attitudes, and goals to which one is committed.

identity achievement The identity state in which after undergoing a period of exploration a person commits to self-chosen values and goals.

identity diffusion The identity state in which an individual has not undergone exploration nor committed to self-chosen values and goals.

identity foreclosure The identity state in which an individual has not undergone exploration but has committed to values and goals chosen by an authority figure.

identity status The degree to which individuals have explored possible selves and whether they have committed to specific beliefs and goals, assessed by administering interview and survey measures, and categorized into four identity statuses.

imaginary audience A manifestation of adolescent egocentrism in which assume that they are the focus of others' attention.

immersion A strategy in which all instruction occurs in the majority language; children learn a second language, such as English, and course content simultaneously.

implantation The process by which the blastocyst becomes attached to the uterine wall, completed by about 10 days after fertilization.

inclusion The approach in which children with learning disabilities learn alongside other children in the regular classroom for all or part of the day, accompanied by additional educational support of a teacher or paraprofessional who is specially trained to meet their needs.

incomplete dominance A genetic inheritance pattern in which both genes are expressed in the phenotype.

independent variable The factor proposed to change the behavior under study in an experiment; it is systematically manipulated during an experiment.

indifferent gonad A gonad in an embryo that has not yet differentiated into testes or ovaries.

inductive discipline Strategy to control children's behavior that relies on reasoning and discussion.

infant-directed speech (motherese) Uses shorter words and sentences, higher and more varied pitch, repetitions, a slower rate, and longer pauses.

infantile amnesia A phenomenon in which most children and adults are unable to recall events that happened before age 3.

information processing theory A perspective that uses a computer analogy to describe how the mind receives information and manipulates, stores, recalls, and uses it to solve problems.

informed consent A participant's informed (knowledge of the scope of the research and potential harm and benefits of participating), rational, and voluntary agreement to participate in a study.

instrumental aggression Behavior that hurts someone else in order to achieve a goal such as gaining a possession.

intellectual disability Characterized by deficits in cognitive functioning and age-appropriate adaptive behavior, such as social, communication, and self-care skills that begin before 18 years of age; formerly known as mental retardation.

intelligence An individual's ability to adapt to the world.

intelligence test (IQ test) A test designed to measure the aptitude to learn at school, intellectual aptitude.

intermodal perception The process of combining information from more than one sensory system such as visual and auditory senses.

internal working model A set of expectations about one's worthiness of love and the availability of attachment figures during times of distress.

irreversibility A characteristic of preoperational thought in which a child does not understand that an action can be reversed and a thing restored to its original state.

job burnout A sense of mental exhaustion that accompanies long-term job stress, excessive workloads, and reduced feelings of control.

justice orientation A male mode of moral reasoning proposed by Gilligan that emphasizes the abstract principles of fairness and individualism.

kangaroo care An intervention for low-birthweight babies in which the infant is placed vertically against the parent's chest, under the shirt, providing skin-to-skin contact.

kwashiorkor A malnutritive disease in children caused by deprivation of protein and calories and characterized by lethargy and the bloating and swelling of the stomach.

language acquisition device (LAD) In Chomsky's theory, an innate facilitator of language that allows infants to quickly and efficiently analyze everyday speech and determine its rules, regardless of their native language.

lanugo A fine, down-like hair that covers the fetus's body.

lateralization The process by which the two hemispheres of the brain become specialized to carry out different functions.

learned helplessness orientation An orientation characterized by a fixed mindset and the attribution of poor performance to internal factors.

learning disability A diagnosis for a child who demonstrates great difficulty in aspects of learning such as reading or mathematics, and shows achievement behind that expected given the child's IQ.

life review The reflection on past experiences and one's life, permitting greater self-understanding and the assignment of meaning to their lives.

life structure In Levinson's theory, a person's overall organization of his or her life, particularly dreams, goals, and relationships with significant others as well as institutions, such as marriage, family, and vocation.

lifespan human development An approach to studying human development that examines ways in which individuals grow, change, and stay the same throughout their lives, from conception to death.

limbic system A collection of brain structures responsible for emotion.

living will A legal document that permits a person to make his or her wishes known regarding medical care in the event that the person is incapacitated by an illness or accident and is unable to speak for him- or herself.

logical extension A strategy children use to increase their vocabulary in which they extend a new word to other objects in the same category.

longitudinal research A developmental study in which one group of participants is studied repeatedly to infer age changes.

long-term memory The component of the information processing system that is an unlimited store that holds information indefinitely, until it is retrieved to manipulate working memory.

low birthweight Classifies infants who weigh less than 2,500 grams (5.5 pounds) at birth.

macrosystem In bioecological systems theory, the sociohistorical context—cultural values, laws, and cultural values—in which the microsystem, mesosystem, and exosystem are embedded, posing indirect influences on individuals.

macular degeneration A substantial loss of cells in the center area of the retina (the macula), causing blurring and eventual loss of central vision; its onset is influenced by heredity and environmental factors.

mainstreaming The approach in which children with disabilities are educated in the regular classroom with their nondisabled peers.

mandated reporter A professional who is legally obligated to report suspected child maltreatment to law enforcement.

marasmus A wasting disease in which the body's fat and muscle are depleted; growth stops, the body wastes away, taking on a hollow appearance.

mastery motivation The drive to explore, understand, and master one's environment.

mastery orientation A belief that success stems from trying hard and that failures are influenced by factors that can be controlled, like effort.

meiosis The process by which a gamete is formed, containing one-half of the cell's chromosomes producing creating ova and sperm with 23 single, unpaired chromosomes.

memory strategy Deliberate cognitive activities that make an individual more likely to remember information.

menarche A girl's first menstrual period.

metacognition The ability to think about thinking; knowledge of how the mind works.

menopause The end of menstruation and a woman's reproductive capacity.

mental representation An internal depiction of an object; thinking of an object using mental pictures.

mesosystem In bioecological systems theory, the relations and interactions among microsystems.

metamemory An aspect of metacognition that refers to the understanding of memory and how to use strategies to enhance memory.

microsystem In bioecological systems theory, the innermost level of context, which includes an individual's immediate physical and social environment.

midlife crisis A period of self-doubt and stress attributed to entering midlife once thought to contribute to a major reorganization of personality in midlife. Now thought to occur in a small minority of adults and to be related to history more than age.

monozygotic (MZ) twin Also known as an identical twin; occurs when the zygote splits apart early in development. The resulting offspring share 100% of their genetic material.

mitosis The process of cell duplication in which DNA is replicated and the resulting cell is genetically identical to the original.

morphology The understanding of the way that sounds combined to form words.

mourning The ceremonies and rituals a culture prescribes for expressing bereavement.

multiple intelligence theory Gardner's proposition that human intelligence is composed of a varied set of abilities.

mutation A sudden permanent change in the structure of genes.

mutual exclusivity assumption When learning new words, young children assume that objects have only one label or name.

myelination The process in which neurons are coated in a fatty substance, myelin, which contributes to faster neural communication.

naming explosion (vocabulary spurt) A vocabulary spurt; a period of rapid vocabulary learning that begins about 16 to 18 months of age.

naturalistic observation A research method in which a researcher views and records an individual's behavior in natural, real-world settings.

nature–nurture issue A debate within the field of human development regarding whether development is caused by nature (genetics or heredity) or nurture (the physical and social environment).

neural tube Forms during the third week after conception and will develop into the central nervous system (brain and spinal cord).

neurofibrillary tangle A twisted bundle of threads of a protein called tau that occur in the brain when neurons collapse; found in individuals with Alzheimer's disease.

neurogenesis The production of new neurons.

neuron A nerve cell that stores and transmits information; billions of neurons comprise the brain.

niche-picking An active gene–environment correlation in which individuals seek out experiences and environments that complement their genetic tendencies.

nontraditional college student Refers to college students who are older than the typical-age student. **s** –

object identity The understanding that certain characteristics of an object do not change despite superficial changes in the object's appearance.

object permanence The understanding that objects continue to exist outside of sight.

observational learning Learning that occurs by watching and imitating models, as posited by social learning theory.

open-ended interview A research method in which a researcher asks a participant questions using a flexible, conversational style and may vary the order of questions, probe, and ask follow-up questions based on the participant's responses.

operant conditioning A form of learning in which behavior increases or decreases based on environmental consequences.

osteoarthritis The most common type of arthritis; it affects joints that are injured by overuse, most commonly the hips, knees, lower back, and hands, in which the cartilage protecting the ends of the bones where they meet at the joints wears away, and joints become less flexible and swell.

osteoporosis A condition characterized by severe loss of bone mass, leading to increased risk of fractures.

overextension A vocabulary error in which the infant applies a word too broadly to a wider class of objects than appropriate.

overregularization errors Grammatical mistakes that children make because they apply grammatical rules too stringently to words that are exceptions.

ovum The female reproductive cell or egg cell.

palliative care An alternative to medical treatment in which dying patients receive medications to control pain and related symptoms.

parental monitoring Parents' awareness of their children's activities, whereabouts, and companions.

parenting style Enduring sets of child-rearing behaviors a parent uses across situations to form a child-rearing climate.

passive euthanasia Occurs when life-sustaining treatment, such as a ventilator, is withheld or withdrawn, allowing a person to die naturally.

Parkinson's disease A chronic progressive brain disorder caused by deterioration of neurons in the substantia nigra; characterized by muscle rigidity, tremors, and sometimes dementia.

peer rejection An ongoing interaction in which a child is deliberately excluded by peers.

peer victimization Also known as bullying; an ongoing interaction in which a child becomes a frequent target of physical, verbal, or social harm by another child or children.

permissive parenting style A child-rearing approach characterized by high levels of warmth and low levels of control or discipline.

persistent vegetative state (PVS) Cortical death when the person appears awake but is not aware, due to permanent loss of all activity in the cortex.

personal fable A manifestation of adolescent egocentrism in which adolescents believe their thoughts, feelings, and experiences are more special and unique than anyone else's, as well as the sense that they are invulnerable.

phenotype The observable physical or behavioral characteristics of a person, eye, hair color, or height.

phenylketonuria (PKU) A recessive disorder that prevents the body from producing an enzyme that breaks down phenylalanine (an amino acid) from proteins, that, without treatment, leads to buildup that damages the central nervous system.

phonics An approach to reading instruction that emphasizes teaching children to sound out words and connect sounds to written symbols.

phonology Refers to the knowledge of sounds used in a given language.

physical development Body maturation, including body size, proportion, appearance, health, and perceptual abilities.

physician assisted suicide A type of voluntary active euthanasia in which terminally ill patients make the conscious decision that they want their life to end before dying becomes a protracted process.

placenta The principal organ of exchange between the mother and the developing organism, enabling the exchange of nutrients, oxygen, and wastes via the umbilical cord.

plasticity A characteristic of development that refers to malleability, or openness to change in response to experience.

polygenic inheritance Occurs when a trait is a function of the interaction of many genes, such as with height, intelligence, and temperament.

popular child A child who receives many positive ratings from peers indicating that he or she is accepted and valued by peers.

possible self Future-oriented representations of self-concept into the future; who an individual might become, both hoped for and feared, that guides and motivates choices and behaviors.

post-conventional moral reasoning Kohlberg's third level of moral reasoning emphasizing autonomous decision-making based on principles such as valuing human dignity.

post-formal reasoning A stage of cognitive development proposed to follow Piaget's formal operational stage. Thinking and problem solving is restructured in adulthood to integrate abstract reasoning with practical considerations, recognizing that most problems have multiple causes and solutions, some solutions are better than others, and all problems involve uncertainty.

postpartum depression Moderate to severe depression occurring in a woman after giving birth, usually within the first 3 months after delivery.

pragmatic thought In Labouvie-Vief's theory, a type of thinking where logic is used as a tool to address everyday problems and contradictions are viewed as part of life.

pragmatics The practical application of language for everyday communication.

preconventional reasoning Kohlberg's first level of reasoning in which young children's behavior is governed by punishment and gaining rewards.

preoperational reasoning Piaget's second stage of cognitive development, between about age 2 and 6, characterized by advances in symbolic thought, but thought is not yet logical.

presbycusis Age-related hearing loss, first to the high frequency sounds, gradually spreading.

presbyopia An age-related condition in which the lens becomes less able to adjust its focus on objects at a close range.

preterm A birth that occurs 35 or fewer weeks after conception.

primary circular reaction In Piaget's theory, repeating an action that produced a chance event involving the infant's body.

primary mental abilities A concept proposed by L.L. Thurston, intelligence is comprised of several abilities that are independent of one another.

primary sex characteristics The reproductive organs; in females, this includes the ovaries, fallopian tubes, uterus, and vagina and in males, this includes the penis, testes, scrotum, seminal vesicles, and prostate gland.

private speech Self-directed speech that children use to guide their behavior.

proactive interference A phenomenon that occurs when information that has previously been remembered interferes with memory for new information.

Project Head Start Early childhood intervention program education program funded by the US federal government that provides low-income children with nutritional, health, and educational services, as well as helps parent become involved in their children's development.

prosocial behavior Actions that are oriented toward others for the pure sake of helping, without a reward.

protective factor Variable that is thought to reduce the poor outcomes associated with adverse circumstances.

proximodistal development The principle that growth and development proceed from the center of the body outward.

psychoanalytic theory A perspective introduced by Freud that development and behavior is stagelike and influenced by inner drives, memories, and conflicts of which an individual is unaware and cannot control.

psychosocial development Refers to changes in how we understand and interact with others, as well as changes in how we understand ourselves and our roles as members of society.

psychosocial moratorium In Erikson's theory, a period in which the individual is free to explore identity possibilities before committing to an identity.

puberty The biological transition to adulthood, in which hormones cause the body to physically mature and permit sexual reproduction.

punishment In operant conditioning, the process in which a behavior is followed by an aversive or unpleasant outcome that decreases the likelihood of a response.

questionnaire A research method in which researchers use a survey or set of questions to collect data from large samples of people.

random assignment A method of assigning participants that ensures each participant has an equal chance of being assigned to the experimental group or control group.

range of reaction The concept that a genetic trait may be expressed in a wide range of phenotypes dependent on environmental opportunities and constraints.

rape Refers to nonconsensual sexual penetration of the body by the body part of another person or object.

reactive aggression An impulsive, hostile response to provocation or a blocked goal.

real self Who an individual is, his or her personal characteristics. The match between the real self and aspirational, ideal self influences well-being.

recall memory Remembering a stimulus that is not present.

recast When an adult repeats a child's sentence back to him or her in a new grammatical form, helping the child to acquire grammatical rules more quickly.

reciprocal determinism A perspective positing that individuals and the environment interact and influence each other.

recognition memory The ability to identify a previously encountered stimulus.

reflective judgment Mature type of reasoning that synthesizes contradictions among perspectives.

reflex An involuntary and automatic response to stimuli.

reinforcement In operant conditioning, the process by which a behavior is followed by a desirable outcome increases the likelihood of a response.

relational aggression Harming someone through nonphysical acts aimed at harming a person's connections with others, such as by exclusion and rumor spreading.

relativistic thinking Type of reasoning in which knowledge is viewed as subjective and dependent on the situation.

religiosity Refers to religious involvement, sharing the attitudes and beliefs of a religion, and participating in its practices.

reminiscence The process of telling stories from one's past, to oneself or others.

resilience The ability to adapt to serious adversity.

reversibility The understanding that an object that has been physically altered can be returned to its original state or a process can be done and undone.

risk factors Individual or contextual challenges that tax an individual's coping capacities and can evoke psychological stress.

rough-and-tumble play Social interaction involving chasing and play fighting with no intent to harm.

sandwich generation A popular image of midlife adults in which they scramble to meet the needs of both dependent children and frail elderly parents and thus sandwiched between the two.

sarcopenia The age-related loss of muscle mass and strength.

scaffolding Temporary support that permits a child to bridge the gap between his or her current competence level and the task at hand.

schema A mental representation, such as concepts, ideas, and ways of interacting with the world.

scientific method The process of forming and answering questions using systematic observations and gathering information.

script Description of what occurs in a certain situation and used as a guide to understand and organize daily experiences.

secondary circular reaction In Piaget's theory, repeating an action that produced a chance event that triggers a response in the external environment.

secondary sex characteristics Physical traits that indicate sexual maturity but are not directly related to fertility, such as breast development and the growth of body hair.

secular trend The change from one generation to the next in an aspect of development, such as body size or in the timing of puberty.

secure attachment The attachment pattern in which an infant uses the caregiver as a secure base from which to explore, seeks contact during reunions, and is easily comforted by the caregiver.

secure base The use of a caregiver as a foundation from which to explore and return to for emotional support.

selective attention The ability to focus on relevant stimuli and ignore others.

selective optimization with compensation An approach by which people maintain high levels of functioning by narrowing their goals, selecting personally valued attributes to optimize, and compensating for losses.

self-concept The set of attributes, abilities, and characteristics that a person uses to describe and define him- or herself.

self-conscious emotion Emotions that requires cognitive development and an awareness of self, such as empathy, embarrassment, shame, and guilt.

self-esteem The general emotional evaluation of one's own worth.

self-harm Deliberate and voluntary physical personal injury that is not life-threatening and is without any conscious suicidal intent.

self-recognition The ability to identify the self, typically measured as mirror recognition.

self-regulation The ability to control one's impulses and appropriately direct behavior.

semantics Refers to the meaning or content of words and sentences.

senescence A pattern of gradual age-related declines in physical functioning.

sensory memory The first step in the information processing system in which stimuli are stored for a brief moment in its original form to enable it to be processed.

separation protest (separation anxiety) Occurs when infants respond to the departure of a caregiver with fear, distress, and crying.

sequential research design A developmental design in which multiple groups of participants of different ages are followed over time, combining cross-sectional and longitudinal research.

seriation A type of classification that involves ordering objects in a series according to a physical dimension such as height, weight, or color.

sex Is biological and determined by genetics.

sexting The exchange of explicit sexual messages or images via mobile phone.

sexual assault A broader term than rape, refers to a wide variety of nonconsensual sexual contact or behavior.

sexual identity An individual's sense of self regarding sexuality, including the awareness and comfort regarding personal sexual attitudes, interests, and behaviors, which develops through a period of exploration and commitment.

sexual orientation A term that refers to whether someone is sexually attracted to others of the same sex, opposite sex, or both.

sexually transmitted infections (STIs) Infections passed from one individual to another through sexual contact.

sickle cell trait A recessive trait, more often affecting African Americans than Caucasians or Asian Americans, that causes red blood cells to become crescent or sickle shaped, resulting in difficulty distributing oxygen throughout the circulatory system.

signaling behaviors Behaviors that infants use, including crying and smiling, to bring the caregiver into contact.

singlehood Refers to not living with a romantic partner.

slow-to-warm-up temperament A temperament characterized by mild irregularity in biological rhythms, slow adaptation to change, mildly negative mood.

small for date Describes an infant who is full term but who has significantly lower weight than expected for the gestational age.

social comparison The tendency to compare and judge one's abilities, achievements, and behaviors in relation to others.

social learning theory An approach that emphasizes the role of modeling and observational learning over people's behavior in addition to reinforcement and punishment.

social promotion The practice of promoting children to the next grade even though they did not meet academic standards out of the belief that it will foster self-esteem.

social referencing Seeking information from caregivers about how to interpret unfamiliar or ambiguous events by observing their emotional expressions and reactions.

social smile A smile that emerges between 6 and 10 weeks in response to seeing familiar people.

sociocultural theory Vygotsky's perspective that individuals acquire culturally relevant ways of thinking through social interactions with members of their culture.

sociodramatic play Make-believe play in which children act out roles and themes.

socioemotional development Maturation of social and emotional functioning, which includes changes in personality, emotions, personal perceptions, social skills, and interpersonal relationships.

socioemotional selectivity theory The perspective that as the emotional regulation function of social interaction becomes increasingly important to older adults, they prefer to interact with familiar social partners, accounting for the narrowing of the social network with age.

spina bifida A neural tube that results in spinal nerves growing outside of the vertebrae, often resulting in paralysis and developmental disability.

spirituality A more general term than religiosity and denotes a search for meaning beyond the self.

stage-environment fit Refers to the match between the characteristics and supports of the school environment and the developing person's needs and capacities. Influences well-being.

stem cell An undifferentiated master cell with the capacity to generate into any type of specialized cell in the body.

stereotype threat The fear that one will be judged to have the qualities associated with negative stereotypes about one's ethnic group.

Strange Situation A structured laboratory procedure that measures the security of attachment by observing infants' reactions to being separated from the caregiver in an unfamiliar environment.

stranger wariness Also known as stranger anxiety; an infant's expression of fear of unfamiliar people.

structured interview A research method in which each participant is asked the same set of questions in the same way.

structured observation An observational measure in which an individual's behavior is viewed and recorded in a controlled environment; a situation created by the experimenter.

synaptic pruning The process by which neural connections, that are seldom used, disappear.

syntax Refers to the knowledge of the structure of sentences; that is, the rules by which words are to be combined to form sentences.

telegraphic speech Two-word utterances produced by toddlers that communicate only the essential words.

telomere A type of DNA that caps both ends of chromosomes and shortens with each cell division. Eventually telomeres shorten past a critical length and cause the cell to stop duplicating.

temperament Characteristic differences among individuals in emotional reactivity, self-regulation, and activity that influences reactions to the environment and are stable, and appear early in life.

teratogen An environmental factor that causes damage to prenatal development.

tertiary circular reaction In Piaget's theory, repeating an action to explore and experiment in order to see the results and learn about the world.

testosterone The primary male sex hormone responsible for development and regulation of the male reproductive system and secondary sex characteristics.

theory An organized set of observations to describe, explain, and predict a phenomenon.

theory of mind Children's awareness of their own and other people's mental processes and realization that other people do not share their thoughts.

three mountains task A classic Piagetian task used to illustrate preoperational children's egocentrism.

time out A discipline technique in which a child is removed from a situation for a period of time.

transgender Refers to those who do not identify with their biological sex but instead adopt an opposite-sex identity.

transitive inference A classification skill in which a child can infer the relationship between two objects by understanding each object's relationship to a third object.

triarchic theory of intelligence Sternberg's theory positing three independent forms of intelligence: analytical, creative, and applied.

underextension A vocabulary error in which the infant applies a word too narrowly to a single object rather than the more appropriate, wider class of objects.

uninvolved parenting style A child-rearing style characterized by low levels of warmth and acceptance coupled with little control or discipline.

universal grammar In Chomsky's theory, rules that apply to all human languages.

vaccine A small dose of inactive virus that is injected into the body to stimulate the production of antibodies to guard against a disease.

vascular dementia Neurocognitive disorder in which sporadic and progressive losses occur, caused by small blockages of blood vessels in the brain.

vernix caseosa Greasy material that protects the fetal skin from abrasions, chapping, and hardening that can occur from exposure to amniotic fluid.

violation-of-expectation task A method in which infants are shown events that appear to violate physical laws. Increased attention to the unexpected event suggests that the infant is surprised and therefore has an understanding and expectations of the physical world.

Wernicke's area The region of the brain that is responsible for language comprehension; damage to this area impairs the ability to understand others' speech and sometimes the ability to speak coherently.

whole brain death Refers to the irreversible loss of functioning in the entire brain that may occur prior to clinical death.

whole-language approach An approach to reading instruction that emphasizes meaning, not phonics. Children are exposed to reading materials without instruction and emphasis is on meaning-making.

work-life balance The challenge of finding time and energy for both a career and and personal pursuits, such as family.

widowhood Refers to the status of a person who has lost a spouse through death and has not remarried.

widowhood effect Refers to the increased likelihood for a windowed person to die, illustrating the relationship between social relations and health.

wisdom Expertise in the conduct and meanings of life, characterized by emotional maturity and the ability to show insight and apply it to problems.

working memory The component of the information processing system that holds and processes information that is being manipulated, encoded, or retrieved and is responsible for maintaining and processing information used in cognitive tasks.

zone of proximal development Vygotsky's term for the tasks that children cannot do alone but can exercise with the aid of more skilled partners.

zygote A fertilized ovum.

INDEX